DEVELOPING PARALEGAL SKILLS

▶ Proofreading Legal Documents / 13
▶ Interviewing a Client / 16
▶ Working for a Public Defender / 29
▶ Confidentiality and Client Information / 66
▶ Creating a Trust Account / 73
▶ Organizing E-mail / 82
▶ Adequate Supervision / 98
▶ What if You Learn Your Client Is Planning to Commit a Crime? / 99
▶ Building an Ethical Wall / 107
▶ The Dangers of the Unauthorized Practice of Law / 116
▶ Requirements for Specific Performance / 135
▶ State versus Federal Regulation / 147
▶ Approval to Practice before the IRS / 149
▶ Choice of Courts: State or Federal? / 164
▶ Federal Court Jurisdiction / 173
▶ To Sue or Not to Sue / 177
▶ Defining the Issues to Be Researched / 196
▶ Reading Statutory Law / 226–227
▶ Internet-Based Research / 246
▶ Cite Checking on Westlaw / 255
▶ Medical Research on the Internet / 260
▶ Creating a User-Friendly Document / 273
▶ Effective Editing / 282
▶ Reviewing Attorney-Generated Documents / 290
▶ File Workup / 306

▶ A Checklist for Drafting a Complaint in a Federal Civil Case / 313
▶ Deposition Summaries / 332
▶ Electronic Discovery / 340
▶ Checking the Accident Scene / 369
▶ Accessing Government Information / 376
▶ Powerpoint Presentations / 388
▶ The Prosecutor's Office—Warrant Division / 436
▶ Discovery in the Criminal Case / 446
▶ Preparing Graphic Presentations / 448
▶ A Claim of False Imprisonment / 463
▶ Product Liability Paralegals / 483
▶ Discharged for Garnishment / 488
▶ Assessing Contractual Capacity / 503
▶ Contract Review / 508
▶ Reviewing the Closing Package / 537
▶ Medical Records / 549
▶ Preparing for Property-Settlement Negotiations / 567
▶ Drafting a Client's Will / 572
▶ Estate Planning / 574
▶ Reserving a Corporate Name / 593
▶ A Case of *Respondeat Superior* / 601
▶ Assisting with a Workers' Compensation Claim / 606
▶ Preparing a Proof of Claim / 629
▶ Monitoring the *Federal Register* / 637

D0161282

ETHICS WATCH

▶ Paralegal Expertise and Legal Advice / 5
▶ The Importance of Being Honest / 41
▶ Back Up Your Work / 77
▶ Social Events and Confidentiality / 101
▶ The Statute of Limitations and the Duty of Competence / 143
▶ Potential Arbitration Problems / 183
▶ Using Secondary Sources / 206
▶ Finding Ethics Opinions on the Web / 250
▶ Letters and the Unauthorized Practice of Law / 291
▶ Keeping Client Information Confidential / 325

▶ Interviewing Clients and The Unauthorized Practice of Law / 364
▶ Communicating with Jurors / 397
▶ The Importance of Accuracy / 447
▶ Confidentiality and Product Liability / 480
▶ Potential Conflicts of Interest / 505
▶ Accurate Paperwork and Real Estate Transactions / 534
▶ Wills and Paralegal Supervision / 570
▶ Dispensing Legal Advice / 604
▶ The Perils of Independent Practice / 628

TODAY'S PROFESSIONAL PARALEGAL

▶ A Winning Combination / 17

▶ A View from the Inside: Assisting a Civil Litigation Paralegal / 53

▶ A Paralegal Manager at Work / 83

▶ Working for the Attorney Discipline Board / 122

▶ Working for an Administrative Agency / 153

▶ Arbitrating Commercial Contracts / 185

▶ Mapping Out a Research Strategy / 231

▶ Locating Guardians and Wards / 266

▶ Preparing the Internal Memorandum / 295

▶ Witness Coordination / 342

▶ Interviewing a Client / 379

▶ Drafting *Voir Dire* Questions Like a Pro / 410

▶ Working for the District Court / 452

▶ Developing a Life-Care Plan / 489

▶ Confidentiality Agreements / 521

▶ Handling and Avoiding Malpractice Claims / 550–551

▶ Meeting with the Personal Representative / 577

▶ Developing a Policy on Sexual Harassment / 608

▶ Gathering Information for a Bankruptcy Petition / 642

FEATURED CONTRIBUTORS

▶ Sally B. Bisson: The Paralegal at Work / 6–7

▶ Linda J. Wolf, ACP: Plan and Pursue Your Desired Career / 38–39

▶ Wendy B. Edson: Ten Tips for Effective Communication / 80–81

▶ Lisa L. Newcity: Ten Tips for Ethics and the Paralegal / 112–113

▶ S. Whittington Brown: The Interrelationship of the Various Areas of Law / 144–145

▶ Fernaundra Ferguson: Mediation: Career Opportunities for Paralegals / 180–181

▶ E. J. Yera: Ten Tips for Effective Legal Research / 208–209

▶ Matt Cornick: Tips for Doing Online Legal Research / 240–241

▶ William Putman: Tips for Making Legal Writing Easier / 280–281

▶ Janet M. Powell: Litigation Paralegal / 307

▶ P. David Palmiere: Ten Tips for the Effective Use of Interrogatories / 358–359

▶ Dwayne E. Krager: Litigation Paralegal / 398–399

▶ Pamela Poole Weber: Paralegals and Criminal Litigation / 438–439

▶ Beth Walston-Dunham: Is There a Place for Paralegals in the Field of Medical Malpractice? / 476–477

▶ Deborah E. Bouchoux: Strategies for Protecting Intellectual Property: The Intellectual Property Audit / 518–519

▶ Daniel F. Hinkel: Protecting the Real Estate Purchaser: The Legal Due-Diligence Team / 540–541

▶ Nancy R. Gallo: Paralegals in Family Law Practice / 558

▶ Angela Schneeman: Going Corporate / 590–591

▶ Jo-Christy Brown: A Primer on Key Terms in the Chapter 7 Bankruptcy Process / 626–627

Paralegal
Today

5TH
EDITION

THE LEGAL TEAM AT WORK

Roger LeRoy Miller
Mary Meinzinger Urisko

DELMAR CENGAGE Learning

Options.

Over 300 products in every area of the law: textbooks, online courses, CD-ROMs, reference books, companion Web sites, and more – helping you succeed in the classroom and on the job.

Support.

We offer unparalleled, practical support: robust instructor and student supplements to ensure the best learning experience, custom publishing to meet your unique needs, and other benefits such as Delmar Cengage Learning's Student Achievement Award. And our sales representatives are always ready to provide you with dependable service.

Feedback.

As always, we want to hear from you! Your feedback is our best resource for improving the quality of our products. Contact your sales representative or write us at the address below if you have any comments about our materials or if you have a product proposal.

Accounting and Financials for the Law Office • Administrative Law • Alternative Dispute Resolution • Bankruptcy Business Organizations/Corporations • Careers and Employment • Civil Litigation and Procedure • CLA Exam Preparation • Computer Applications in the Law Office • Constitutional Law • Contract Law • Court Reporting Criminal Law and Procedure • Document Preparation • Elder Law • Employment Law • Environmental Law • Ethics Evidence Law • Family Law • Health Care Law • Immigration Law • Intellectual Property • Internships Interviewing and Investigation • Introduction to Law • Introduction to Paralegalism • Juvenile Law • Law Office Management • Law Office Procedures • Legal Nurse Consulting • Legal Research, Writing, and Analysis • Legal Terminology • Legal Transcription • Media and Entertainment Law • Medical Malpractice Law Product Liability • Real Estate Law • Reference Materials • Social Security • Sports Law • Torts and Personal Injury Law • Wills, Trusts, and Estate Administration • Workers' Compensation Law

DELMAR CENGAGE Learning
5 Maxwell Drive
Clifton Park, New York 12065-2919

For additional information, find us online at:
www.delmar.cengage.com

Paralegal *Today*

5TH EDITION

THE LEGAL TEAM AT WORK

Roger LeRoy Miller
Mary Meinzinger Urisko

DELMAR
CENGAGE Learning™

Australia • Brazil • Japan • Korea • Mexico • Singapore • Spain • United Kingdom • United States

DELMAR
CENGAGE Learning™

Paralegal Today:
The Legal Team at Work, Fifth Edition
Roger LeRoy Miller and
Mary Meinzinger Urisko

Vice President, Career and Professional
Editorial: Dave Garza

Director of Learning Solutions:
Sandy Clark

Senior Acquisitions Editor:
Shelley Esposito

Managing Editor: Larry Main

Senior Product Manager:
Melissa Riveglia

Editorial Assistant: Danielle Klahr

Vice President, Career and Professional
Marketing: Jennifer Baker

Marketing Director: Deborah Yarnell

Marketing Manager: Erin Brennan

Marketing Coordinator:
Jonathan Sheehan

Production Director: Wendy Troeger

Production Manager: Mark Bernard

Senior Content Project Manager:
Betty Dickson

Senior Art Director: Joy Kocsis

Senior Technology Product Manager:
Joe Pliss

For product information and technology assistance, contact us at
Cengage Learning Customer & Sales Support, 1-800-354-9706
For permission to use material from this text or product,
submit all requests online at **www.cengage.com/permissions**.
Further permissions questions can be e-mailed to
permissionrequest@cengage.com

Library of Congress Control Number: 2009925903
ISBN-13: 978-1-4390-5701-8
ISBN-10: 1-4390-5701-X

Delmar
5 Maxwell Drive
Clifton Park, NY 12065-2919
USA

Cengage Learning is a leading provider of customized learning solutions with office locations around the globe, including Singapore, the United Kingdom, Australia, Mexico, Brazil, and Japan. Locate your local office at: **international. cengage.com/region**

Cengage Learning products are represented in Canada by Nelson Education, Ltd.

To learn more about Delmar, visit **www.cengage.com/delmar**
Purchase any of our products at your local college store or at our preferred online store **www.ichapters.com**

Notice to the Reader
Publisher does not warrant or guarantee any of the products described herein or perform any independent analysis in connection with any of the product information contained herein. Publisher does not assume, and expressly disclaims, any obligation to obtain and include information other than that provided to it by the manufacturer. The reader is expressly warned to consider and adopt all safety precautions that might be indicated by the activities described herein and to avoid all potential hazards. By following the instructions contained herein, the reader willingly assumes all risks in connection with such instructions. The reader is notified that this text is an educational tool, not a practice book. Since the law is in constant change, no rule or statement of law in this book should be relied upon for any service to any client. The reader should always refer to standard legal sources for the current rule or law. If legal advice or other expert assistance is required, the services of the appropriate professional should be sought. The publisher makes no representations or warranties of any kind, including but not limited to, the warranties of fitness for particular purpose or merchantability, nor are any such representations implied with respect to the material set forth herein, and the publisher takes no responsibility with respect to such material. The publisher shall not be liable for any special, consequential, or exemplary damages resulting, in whole or part, from the readers' use of, or reliance upon, this material.

Printed in the United States of America
1 2 3 4 5 6 7 12 11 10 09

To Marcel Maier,

Thanks for your guiding
hand in all fiscal matters.
Working with you continues
to be a pleasure and so
does your friendship.

R.L.M.

To the paralegal students
at Madonna University.
You are my inspiration.
May this book be yours.

M.M.U.

CONTENTS IN BRIEF

Preface / xxv

Introduction to the Student / xli

1 THE PARALEGAL PROFESSION   1

CHAPTER 1   Today's Professional Paralegal / 2

CHAPTER 2   Career Opportunities / 22

CHAPTER 3   The Inner Workings of the Law Office / 59

CHAPTER 4   Ethics and Professional Responsibility / 89

CHAPTER 5   Sources of American Law / 128

CHAPTER 6   The Court System and Alternative Dispute Resolution / 160

2 LEGAL PROCEDURES AND PARALEGAL SKILLS   193

CHAPTER 7   Legal Research and Analysis / 194

CHAPTER 8   Contemporary Online Legal Research / 238

CHAPTER 9   Legal Writing: Form and Substance / 270

CHAPTER 10   Civil Litigation: Before the Trial / 300

CHAPTER 11   Conducting Interviews and Investigations / 349

CHAPTER 12   Trial Procedures / 386

CHAPTER 13   Criminal Law and Procedures / 416

3 KEY ELEMENTS OF THE LAW   459

CHAPTER 14 Tort Law, Product Liability, and Consumer Law / 460

CHAPTER 15 Contracts and Intellectual Property Law / 496

CHAPTER 16 Real Property and Insurance Law / 529

CHAPTER 17 Family Law and Estates / 556

CHAPTER 18 Business Organizations and Employment Law / 583

CHAPTER 19 Bankruptcy and Environmental Law / 615

APPENDICES

A NALA's Code of Ethics and Professional Responsibility / 647

B NALA's Model Standards and Guidelines for Utilization of Paralegals / 649

C NFPA's Model Code of Ethics and Professional Responsibility and Guidelines for Enforcement / 653

D NALS Code of Ethics and Professional Responsibility / 663

E Paralegal Ethics and Regulation: How to Find State-Specific Information / 665

F Paralegal Associations / 667

G Information on NALA's CLA/CP Program / 673

H Information on NFPA's PACE™ Examination / 683

I Information on NALS Certification / 687

J The Constitution of the United States / 691

K Spanish Equivalents for Important Legal Terms in English / 705

Glossary / 711

Index / 735

CONTENTS

Preface / xxv

Introduction to the Student / xli

1 THE PARALEGAL PROFESSION   1

CHAPTER 1   Today's Professional Paralegal / 2

Introduction / 3

What Is a Paralegal? / 3

What Do Paralegals Do? / 4

    A Sampling of Paralegal Tasks / 4

    Paralegals' Duties Vary / 5

    Paralegals and Technology / 6

Paralegal Education / 7

    Educational Options / 8

    Curriculum—A Blend of Substantive and Procedural Law / 8

    The Role of the AAfPE and ABA in Paralegal Education / 9

    Certification / 9

    Continuing Legal Education / 10

Paralegal Skills and Attributes / 10

    Analytical Skills / 11

    Communication Skills / 11

    Computer Skills / 13

    Organizational Skills / 14

    Interpersonal Skills / 14

    The Ability to Keep Confidences / 14

    Professionalism / 16

The Future of the Profession / 18

Ethics Watch: Paralegal Expertise and Legal Advice   5

Featured Contributor: Sally B. Bisson, "The Paralegal at Work"   6

In the Office: Use Time Wisely   11

Developing Paralegal Skills: Proofreading Legal Documents   13

Going Green: Flip It Over   14

Technology and Today's Paralegal: Online Resources for Paralegals   15

Developing Paralegal Skills: Interviewing a Client   16

Today's Professional Paralegal: A Winning Combination   17

In the Office: Stress Problems 24

Going Green: What's in That Office Lamp? 26

Developing Paralegal Skills: Working for a Public Defender 29

Technology and Today's Paralegal: More Career Opportunities for Tech-Savvy Paralegals 34

Featured Contributor: Linda J. Wolf, "Plan and Pursue Your Desired Career" 38

Ethics Watch: The Importance of Being Honest 41

Today's Professional Paralegal: A View from the Inside: Assisting a Civil Litigation Paralegal 53

CHAPTER 2   Career Opportunities / 22

Introduction / 23

Where Paralegals Work / 23

    Law Firms / 23

    Corporations and Other Business Organizations / 25

    Government / 25

    Legal Aid Offices / 26

    Freelance Paralegals / 27

Paralegal Specialties / 27

    Litigation / 27

    Corporate Law / 28

    Contract Law / 28

    Real Estate Law / 29

    Personal-Injury Law / 30

    Insurance Law / 30

    Employment and Labor Law / 30

    Estate Planning and Probate Administration / 31

    Bankruptcy Law / 31

    Intellectual Property Law / 31

    Environmental Law / 32

    Family Law / 32

    Criminal Law / 32

    Additional Specialty Areas / 33

Paralegal Compensation / 33

    Compensation Surveys / 33

    Job Benefits / 35

    Salaries versus Hourly Wages / 36

    Federal Law and Overtime Pay / 36

Planning Your Career / 37

    Defining Your Long-Term Goals / 37

    Short-Term Goals and Job Realities / 37

Locating Potential Employers / 39

    Networking / 40

    Finding Available Jobs / 40

    Identifying Possible Employers / 40

    Job-Placement Services / 42

Marketing Your Skills / 42

    The Application Process / 42

    The Interview / 47

    The Follow-Up/Thank-You Letter / 49

    Job-Hunting Files / 50

    Salary Negotiations / 50

Reevaluating Your Career / 52

    Career Paths / 54

    Creating Opportunities / 54

    Other Options / 54

CHAPTER 3   The Inner Workings of the Law Office / 59

Introduction / 60

The Organizational Structure of Law Firms / 60

    Sole Proprietorships / 60

    Partnerships / 61

    Professional Corporations / 61

Law Office Management and Personnel / 62

Employment Policies / 62

    Performance Evaluations / 63

    Employment Termination / 64

    Employment Discrimination / 65

Filing Procedures / 65

    Client Files / 66

    Work Product Files and Reference Materials / 68

    Forms Files / 68

Financial Procedures / 69

    Fee Arrangements / 69

    Client Trust Accounts / 71

    Billing and Timekeeping Procedures / 72

    Ethics and Client Billing Practices / 76

Communicating with Clients / 78

Law Office Culture and Politics / 82

CHAPTER 4   Ethics and Professional Responsibility / 89

Introduction / 90

The Regulation of Attorneys / 90

    Who Are the Regulators? / 90

    Licensing Requirements / 91

    Ethical Codes and Rules / 92

    Sanctions for Violations / 93

Attorney Ethics and Paralegal Practice / 94

    The Duty of Competence / 94

    Confidentiality of Information / 97

    Confidentiality and the Attorney-Client Privilege / 102

    Conflict of Interest / 103

The Indirect Regulation of Paralegals / 108

    Paralegal Ethical Codes / 108

    Guidelines for the Utilization of Paralegals / 109

    The Increasing Scope of Paralegal Responsibilities / 111

Developing Paralegal Skills: Confidentiality and Client Information 66

Going Green: Fewer CDs 67

Developing Paralegal Skills: Creating a Trust Account 73

Ethics Watch: Back Up Your Work 77

In the Office: Get Priorities Right 78

Technology and Today's Paralegal: Cyberspace Communications 79

Featured Contributor: Wendy B. Edson, "Ten Tips for Effective Communication" 80

Developing Paralegal Skills: Organizing E-Mail 82

Today's Professional Paralegal: A Paralegal Manager at Work 83

Going Green: Saving Juice 97

Developing Paralegal Skills: Adequate Supervision 98

Developing Paralegal Skills: What If You Learn Your Client Is Planning to Commit a Crime? 99

Ethics Watch: Social Events and Confidentiality 101

In the Office: Am I Clear? 102

Technology and Today's Paralegal: Electronic Communications and Confidentiality 104

Developing Paralegal Skills: Building an Ethical Wall 107

Featured Contributor: Lisa L. Newcity, "Ten Tips for Ethics and the Paralegal" 112

Developing Paralegal Skills: The Dangers of the Unauthorized Practice of Law 116

Today's Professional Paralegal:
Working for the Attorney
Discipline Board 122

In the Office: Daily Cleanup 131

**Technology and Today's
Paralegal:** Cases of First
Impression and the Internet 132

Going Green: Recycle Electronic
Junk 134

Developing Paralegal Skills:
Requirements for Specific
Performance 135

Ethics Watch: The Statute of
Limitations and the Duty of
Competence 143

Featured Contributor:
S. Whittington Brown, "The
Interrelationship of the Various
Areas of Law" 144

**Developing Paralegal
Skills:** State versus Federal
Regulation 147

Developing Paralegal Skills:
Approval to Practice Before the
IRS 149

Today's Professional Paralegal:
Working for an Administrative
Agency 153

The Unauthorized Practice of Law / 114
    State UPL Statutes / 114
    The Prohibition against Fee Splitting / 115
    Giving Legal Opinions and Advice / 115
    Representing Clients in Court / 117
    Disclosure of Paralegal Status / 117
    Paralegals Freelancing for Attorneys / 117
    Legal Technicians (Independent Paralegals) and UPL / 118

Should Paralegals Be Licensed? / 119
    General Licensing / 119
    Limited Licensing / 120
    Direct Regulation—The Pros and Cons / 120
    Other Considerations / 121

A Final Note / 122

CHAPTER 5 Sources of American Law / 128

Introduction / 129

The Framework of American Law / 129
    What Is the Law? / 129
    Primary Sources of American Law / 129

Case Law and the Common Law Tradition / 130
    The Doctrine of *Stare Decisis* / 130
    Remedies at Law versus Remedies in Equity / 131
    The Common Law Today / 135
    Statutory Law and the Common Law / 136
    The Terminology of Case Law / 136
    The Adversarial System of Justice / 138

Constitutional Law / 139
    The Federal Constitution / 139
    State Constitutions / 141

Statutory Law / 142
    Federal Statutes / 142
    State Statutes / 146
    Local Ordinances / 147
    Uniform Laws / 147

Administrative Law / 148
    Agency Creation / 148
    Rulemaking / 150
    Investigation and Enforcement / 150
    Adjudication / 150

National and International Law / 151
    National Law / 151
    International Law / 152

CHAPTER 6 The Court System and Alternative Dispute Resolution / 160

Introduction / 161

Basic Judicial Requirements / 161

Standing to Sue / 161

Types of Jurisdiction / 162

Jurisdiction of the Federal Courts / 163

Jurisdiction in Cyberspace / 165

Venue / 166

Judicial Procedures / 166

State Court Systems / 167

Trial Courts / 168

Appellate, or Reviewing, Courts / 169

The Federal Court System / 170

U.S. District Courts / 171

U.S. Courts of Appeals / 171

The United States Supreme Court / 172

Alternative Dispute Resolution / 173

Negotiation / 174

Mediation / 175

Arbitration / 178

Other ADR Forms / 182

Yet Another Approach—Collaborative Law / 183

Court-Referred ADR / 183

Providers of ADR Services / 184

Online Dispute Resolution / 184

2 LEGAL PROCEDURES AND PARALEGAL SKILLS 193

CHAPTER 7 Legal Research and Analysis / 194

Introduction / 195

Researching Case Law—The Preliminary Steps / 195

Defining the Issue / 195

Determining Your Research Goals / 197

Finding Relevant Cases / 199

Legal Encyclopedias / 199

Case Digests / 201

Annotations: *American Law Reports* / 203

Other Secondary Sources / 204

The Case Reporting System / 205

State Court Decisions / 206

Federal Court Decisions / 214

United States Supreme Court Decisions / 214

Developing Paralegal Skills: Choice of Courts: State or Federal? 164

In the Office: Watch Those Deadlines! 167

Going Green: How Do You Drink Your Coffee or Tea? 169

Developing Paralegal Skills: Federal Court Jurisdiction 173

Technology and Today's Paralegal: Courts in the Internet Age 174

Developing Paralegal Skills: To Sue or Not to Sue 177

Featured Contributor: Fernaundra Ferguson, "Mediation: Career Opportunities for Paralegals" 180

Ethics Watch: Potential Arbitration Problems 183

Today's Professional Paralegal: Arbitrating Commercial Contracts 185

Developing Paralegal Skills: Defining the Issues to Be Researched 196

In the Office: Efficiency in Research 198

Ethics Watch: Using Secondary Sources 206

Featured Contributor: E. J. Yera, "Ten Tips for Effective Legal Research" 208

Going Green: Save a Tree 220

Developing Paralegal Skills: Reading Statutory Law 226

Technology and Today's Paralegal: Looking Ahead 230

Today's Professional Paralegal: Mapping Out a Research Strategy 231

Analyzing Case Law / 215

The Components of a Case / 215

Analyzing Cases / 220

Summarizing and Briefing Cases / 221

IRAC: A Method for Briefing Cases / 222

Researching Constitutional and Statutory Law / 223

Finding Constitutional Law / 223

Finding Statutory Law / 223

Analyzing Statutory Law / 225

Rules of Construction / 226

The Plain Meaning Rule / 226

Previous Judicial Interpretation / 227

Legislative Intent / 228

Researching Administrative Law / 229

The *Code of Federal Regulations* / 229

Finding Tools for Administrative Law / 229

CHAPTER 8 Contemporary Online Legal Research / 238

Introduction / 239

Going Online—An Internet Primer / 239

Internet Tools / 240

Navigating the Internet / 242

A Threshold Question: Is the Internet the Right Research Tool for Your Project? / 244

Free Legal Resources on the Internet / 244

General Legal Resources / 245

Specific Legal Resources / 246

Government Sites / 249

Lexis and Westlaw / 249

Accessing Westlaw or Lexis / 250

Conducting a Search / 251

Checking Citations / 251

Shepard's Citations / 252

KeyCite / 254

Selecting a Database / 255

Searching a Database / 255

Searching within Results / 257

Is Westlaw or Lexis Better? / 257

Alternative Online Programs / 257

PACER / 257

Fastcase / 258

Loislaw / 258

Featured Contributor: Matt Cornick, "Tips for Doing Online Legal Research" 240

Going Green: Save by Snoozing 242

Developing Paralegal Skills: Internet-Based Research 246

In the Office: Clean Electronic Files 247

Technology and Today's Paralegal: Be Prepared for Disaster! 248

Ethics Watch: Finding Ethics Opinions on the Web 250

Developing Paralegal Skills: Cite Checking on Westlaw 255

Developing Paralegal Skills: Medical Research on the Internet 260

Today's Professional Paralegal: Locating Guardians and Wards 266

Casemaker / 258

VersusLaw / 259

Conducting Online Research / 259

Plan Ahead—Analyze the Facts and Identify the Issues / 259

Online Research Strategies / 259

Evaluating What You Find / 262

Updating Your Results / 263

Locating People and Investigating Companies / 264

CHAPTER 9 Legal Writing: Form and Substance / 270

Introduction / 271

Legal Writing—The Preliminaries / 271

Understanding the Assignment / 271

Time Constraints and Flexibility / 271

Writing Approaches / 272

The Importance of Good Writing Skills / 272

Organize and Outline Your Presentation / 273

Choice of Format / 274

Structural Devices / 274

Write to Your Audience / 274

Avoid Legalese: Use Everyday English / 275

Be Brief and to the Point / 275

Writing Basics: Sentences / 275

Writing Basics: Paragraphs and Transitions / 277

Avoid Pronoun Confusion / 278

Be Alert for Sexist Language / 278

Proofread and Revise Your Document / 279

Pleadings and Discovery / 279

General Legal Correspondence / 280

General Format for Legal Correspondence / 282

Types of Legal Letters / 285

The Legal Memorandum / 287

Heading / 288

Statement of the Facts / 289

Questions Presented / 290

Brief Conclusion / 291

Discussion and Analysis / 291

Conclusion / 293

Developing Paralegal Skills: Creating a User-Friendly Document 273

Technology and Today's Paralegal: Online "Plain English" Guidelines 276

Going Green: Don't Work So Often 279

Featured Contributor: William Putman, "Tips for Making Legal Writing Easier" 280

Developing Paralegal Skills: Effective Editing 282

In the Office: Time Management 284

Developing Paralegal Skills: Reviewing Attorney-Generated Documents 290

Ethics Watch: Letters and the Unauthorized Practice of Law 291

Today's Professional Paralegal: Preparing the Internal Memorandum 295

In the Office: Hacking Legal Files 304

Developing Paralegal Skills: File Workup 306

Featured Contributor: Janet M. Powell, "Litigation Paralegal" 307

Going Green: Toward the Paperless Office 312

Developing Paralegal Skills: A Checklist for Drafting a Complaint in a Federal Civil Case 313

Ethics Watch: Keeping Client Information Confidential 325

Developing Paralegal Skills: Deposition Summaries 332

Technology and Today's Paralegal: Who Bears the Costs of Electronic Discovery? 338

Developing Paralegal Skills: Electronic Discovery 340

Today's Professional Paralegal: Witness Coordination 342

CHAPTER 10 Civil Litigation: Before the Trial / 300

Introduction / 301

Civil Litigation—A Bird's-Eye View / 301
Pretrial Settlements / 301
Procedural Requirements / 301
A Hypothetical Lawsuit / 302

The Preliminaries / 303
The Initial Client Interview / 303
Preliminary Investigation / 303
Creating the Litigation File / 304

The Pleadings / 305
Drafting the Complaint / 306
Filing the Complaint / 312
Service of Process / 315
The Defendant's Response / 318
The Scheduling Conference / 321
Amending the Pleadings / 322

Pretrial Motions / 322
Motion for Judgment on the Pleadings / 322
Motion for Summary Judgment / 322

Traditional Discovery Tools / 324
Interrogatories / 324
Depositions / 328
Requests for Production and Physical Examination / 332
Requests for Admission / 333

The Duty to Disclose under FRCP 26 / 333
Initial Disclosures / 334
Failure to Disclose / 334
Discovery Plan / 335
Subsequent Disclosures / 336

Discovery of Electronic Evidence / 337
The Advantages of Electronic Evidence / 337
The Sources of Electronic Evidence / 338
The Special Requirements of Electronic Evidence / 340

Going Green: Getting to the Office 351

Featured Contributor: P. David Palmiere, "Ten Tips for the Effective Use of Interrogatories" 358

In the Office: Handling Client Documents 362

Technology and Today's Paralegal: Communicating through Graphics 363

CHAPTER 11 Conducting Interviews and Investigations / 349

Introduction / 350

Planning the Interview / 350
Know What Information You Want / 350
Standardized Interview Forms / 350
Recording the Interview / 351

Interviewing Skills / 353
Interpersonal Skills / 354

Questioning Skills / 354

Listening Skills / 356

Interviewing Clients / 357

The Initial Client Interview / 357

Subsequent Client Interviews / 360

The Informational Interview / 360

Summarizing the Interview / 360

Interviewing Witnesses / 362

Types of Witnesses / 362

Questioning Witnesses / 365

Checking a Witness's Qualifications / 366

Winding Up the Interview / 367

Witness Statements / 367

Planning and Conducting Investigations / 368

Where Do You Start? / 368

Creating an Investigation Plan / 370

Locating Witnesses / 373

Accessing Government Information / 374

Investigation and the Rules of Evidence / 374

Summarizing Your Results / 380

CHAPTER 12   Trial Procedures / 386

Introduction / 387

Preparing for Trial / 387

Contacting and Preparing Witnesses / 387

Exhibits and Displays / 391

The Trial Notebook / 391

Pretrial Conference / 393

Jury Selection / 394

Voir Dire / 395

Challenges during *Voir Dire* / 395

The Paralegal's Role during *Voir Dire* / 396

Alternate Jurors / 396

The Trial / 396

Opening Statements / 397

The Plaintiff's Case / 399

Motion for a Directed Verdict / 402

The Defendant's Case / 403

Closing Arguments / 404

Jury Instructions / 405

The Verdict / 406

Posttrial Motions and Procedures / 406

Posttrial Motions / 406

Ethics Watch: Interviewing Clients and the Unauthorized Practice of Law 364

Developing Paralegal Skills: Checking the Accident Scene 369

Developing Paralegal Skills: Accessing Government Information 376

Today's Professional Paralegal: Interviewing a Client 379

Developing Paralegal Skills: PowerPoint Presentations 388

Going Green: What Are You Wearing? 391

Technology and Today's Paralegal: Courtroom Technology 392

Ethics Watch: Communicating with Jurors 397

Featured Contributor: Dwayne E. Krager, "Litigation Paralegal" 398

In the Office: Protecting Confidential Information 404

Developing Paralegal Skills: Locating Assets 409

Today's Professional Paralegal: Drafting *Voir Dire* Questions Like a Pro 410

Going Green: Sharing Work Online   425

Developing Paralegal Skills: The Prosecutor's Office—Warrant Division   436

Featured Contributor: Pamela Poole Weber, "Paralegals and Criminal Litigation"   438

Developing Paralegal Skills: Discovery in the Criminal Case   446

Ethics Watch: The Importance of Accuracy   447

Developing Paralegal Skills: Preparing Graphic Presentations   448

Technology and Today's Paralegal: Evolving Technology, Security, and Evidence   450

In the Office: The Benefits of Good Record Keeping   451

Today's Professional Paralegal: Working for the District Court   452

Appealing the Verdict / 407

Enforcing the Judgment / 408

CHAPTER 13   Criminal Law and Procedures / 416

Introduction / 417

What Is a Crime? / 417
   Key Differences between Civil Law and Criminal Law / 418
   Civil Liability for Criminal Acts / 418
   Classifications of Crimes / 418
   Jurisdiction over Crimes / 420

Elements of Criminal Liability / 420
   The Criminal Act / 420
   State of Mind / 420
   Corporate Criminal Liability / 421
   Defenses to Criminal Liability / 421

Types of Crimes / 423
   Violent Crime / 423
   Property Crime / 423
   Public Order Crime / 424
   White-Collar Crime / 424
   Organized Crime / 426

Cyber Crimes / 427
   Cyber Theft / 427
   Cyberstalking / 427
   Hacking / 428
   Prosecuting Cyber Crimes / 428

Constitutional Safeguards / 429
   The Exclusionary Rule / 430
   The *Miranda* Rule / 430

Criminal Procedures prior to Prosecution / 431
   Arrest and Booking / 431
   Investigation after the Arrest / 434

The Prosecution Begins / 435
   Complaint and Initial Appearance / 436
   Preliminary Hearing / 440
   Grand Jury Review / 441
   Arraignment / 442
   Pretrial Motions / 442
   Discovery / 443

The Trial / 446

  The Presumption of Innocence / 447

  The Privilege against Self-Incrimination / 447

  The Right to a Speedy Trial / 447

  The Requirement for a Unanimous Verdict / 448

  Sentencing / 449

  Diversion / 451

  Appeal / 453

3 KEY ELEMENTS OF THE LAW 459

CHAPTER 14 Tort Law, Product Liability, and Consumer Law / 460

Introduction / 461

The Basis of Tort Law / 461

Intentional Torts / 461

  Intentional Torts against Persons / 461

  Intentional Torts against Property / 467

Negligence / 470

  The Duty of Care and Its Breach / 471

  The Injury Requirement and Damages / 472

  Causation / 472

  Defenses to Negligence / 473

  Special Negligence Doctrines and Statutes / 474

Cyber Torts: Defamation Online / 476

  Liability of Internet Service Providers / 477

  Piercing the Veil of Anonymity / 477

Strict Liability / 478

  Abnormally Dangerous Activities / 478

  Other Applications of Strict Liability / 478

Product Liability / 478

  Theories of Product Liability / 479

  Defenses to Product Liability / 481

Consumer Law / 482

  Deceptive Advertising / 482

  Labeling and Packaging Laws / 484

  Sales Transactions / 484

  Consumer Health and Safety / 484

  Consumer Credit Protection / 485

Developing Paralegal Skills: A Claim of False Imprisonment 463

In the Office: Online Privacy 466

Technology and Today's Paralegal: Identity Theft, Spam, and Related Legal Issues 468

Featured Contributor: Beth Walston-Dunham, "Is There a Place for Paralegals in the Field of Medical Malpractice?" 476

Going Green: Flip That Switch 479

Ethics Watch: Confidentiality and Product Liability 480

Developing Paralegal Skills: Product Liability Paralegals 483

Developing Paralegal Skills: Discharged for Garnishment 488

Today's Professional Paralegal: Developing a Life-Care Plan 489

Technology and Today's Paralegal: Contract Forms 499

Developing Paralegal Skills: Assessing Contractual Capacity 503

Ethics Watch: Potential Conflicts of Interest 505

Developing Paralegal Skills: Contract Review 508

In the Office: Listen Up 509

Going Green: Recycle In and Out 510

Featured Contributor: Deborah E. Bouchoux, "Strategies for Protecting Intellectual Property: The Intellectual Property Audit" 518

Today's Professional Paralegal: Confidentiality Agreements 521

Ethics Watch: Accurate Paperwork and Real Estate Transactions 534

Developing Paralegal Skills: Reviewing the Closing Package 537

Featured Contributor: Daniel F. Hinkel, "Protecting the Real Estate Purchaser: The Legal Due-Diligence Team" 540

Going Green: What Am I Breathing? 544

In the Office: Clarifying Instructions 545

Technology and Today's Paralegal: Online Resources Concerning Insurance Claims 547

Developing Paralegal Skills: Medical Records 549

Today's Professional Paralegal: Handling and Avoiding Malpractice Claims 550

CHAPTER 15 Contracts and Intellectual Property Law / 496

Introduction / 497

Requirements to Form a Valid Contract / 497

Agreement / 498

Consideration / 500

Contractual Capacity / 502

Legality / 502

Defenses to Contract Enforceability / 503

Genuineness of Assent / 503

Unconscionable Contracts or Clauses / 505

The Statute of Frauds / 505

Sales Contracts and Warranties / 506

The Scope of UCC Article 2 / 507

Warranties under the UCC / 507

Contract Performance and Remedies / 508

Contract Performance / 508

Contract Remedies / 509

Remedies for Breach of Sales Contracts / 511

Electronic Contracting and Electronic Signatures / 511

Online Offers and Acceptances / 511

E-Signatures / 512

State Laws Governing E-Signatures / 513

Federal Law on E-Signatures and E-Documents / 513

Intellectual Property Law / 514

Patents / 516

Copyrights / 516

Trademarks and Related Property / 517

Trade Secrets / 520

CHAPTER 16 Real Property and Insurance Law / 529

Introduction / 530

Real Property / 530

Ownership Rights in Property / 530

The Transfer and Sale of Real Property / 531

Leases / 536

Commercial Leases / 537

Insurance Law / 539

Classifications of Insurance / 539

Insurance Terminology / 539

Insurable Interest / 542

The Insurance Contract / 543

CHAPTER 17 Family Law and Estates / 556

Introduction / 557

Family Law / 557

Marriage Requirements / 557

Common Law Marriages / 559

Marital Duties / 559

Parental Rights and Obligations / 560

Adoption / 561

Marriage Termination / 562

Child Custody / 564

Child Support / 565

Spousal Support / 566

Property Division / 567

Prenuptial Agreements / 568

Wills, Trusts, and Estates / 569

Wills / 569

Trusts / 571

Other Estate-Planning Devices / 574

Estate Administration / 575

CHAPTER 18 Business Organizations and Employment Law / 583

Introduction / 584

Forms of Business Organization / 584

Sole Proprietorships / 584

Partnerships / 585

Corporations / 588

Limited Liability Organizations / 596

Agency Law / 598

Employees and Independent Contractors / 598

Agency Formation / 599

Fiduciary Duties / 599

Agency Relationships and Third Parties / 599

Employment Law / 601

Employment at Will / 602

Wrongful Discharge / 602

Labor Laws / 602

Family and Medical Leave / 603

State Workers' Compensation Laws / 604

Employment Discrimination / 605

Featured Contributor: Nancy R. Gallo, "Paralegals in Family Law Practice" 558

In the Office: Protecting Client Information and Client Interests 566

Developing Paralegal Skills: Preparing for Property-Settlement Negotiations 567

Ethics Watch: Wills and Paralegal Supervision 570

Going Green: Stay Home 571

Developing Paralegal Skills: Drafting a Client's Will 572

Developing Paralegal Skills: Estate Planning 574

Technology and Today's Paralegal: Online Help for Estate Planning 575

Today's Professional Paralegal: Meeting with the Personal Representative 577

Going Green: Out to Lunch? 584

Featured Contributor: Angela Schneeman, "Going Corporate" 590

Developing Paralegal Skills: Reserving a Corporate Name 593

Technology and Today's Paralegal: Online Incorporation 594

Developing Paralegal Skills: A Case of *Respondeat Superior* 601

In the Office: Productive Meetings 603

Ethics Watch: Dispensing Legal Advice 604

Developing Paralegal Skills: Assisting with a Workers' Compensation Claim 606

Today's Professional Paralegal: Developing a Policy on Sexual Harassment 608

Going Green: What Are You Sitting On? 620

In the Office: Dress for Success 621

Featured Contributor: Jo-Christy Brown, "A Primer on Key Terms in the Chapter 7 Bankruptcy Process" 626

Ethics Watch: The Perils of Independent Practice 628

Developing Paralegal Skills: Preparing a Proof of Claim 629

Technology and Today's Paralegal: Environmental Compliance 636

Developing Paralegal Skills: Monitoring the *Federal Register* 637

Today's Professional Paralegal: Gathering Information for a Bankruptcy Petition 642

CHAPTER 19   Bankruptcy and Environmental Law / 615

Introduction / 616

The Bankruptcy Code / 616

Goals of Bankruptcy Law / 616

Bankruptcy Courts / 616

Types of Bankruptcy Relief / 617

Liquidation Proceedings / 617

Voluntary Bankruptcy / 617

Involuntary Bankruptcy / 620

Automatic Stay / 621

Bankruptcy Estate / 621

Creditors' Meeting / 622

Creditors' Claims / 622

Exemptions / 622

The Homestead Exemption / 623

The Bankruptcy Trustee / 623

Distribution of Property / 624

Discharge / 625

Individual Repayment Plans / 628

Filing the Petition / 629

Filing the Plan / 629

Confirmation of the Plan / 630

Objections to the Plan / 630

Modification of the Plan / 630

Discharge / 630

Reorganizations / 631

Workouts / 631

Must Be in the Best Interests of the Creditors / 631

Debtor in Possession / 631

Creditors' Committees / 632

The Reorganization Plan / 632

Environmental Law / 634

Federal Regulation of the Environment / 634

Air Pollution / 635

Water Pollution / 637

Toxic Chemicals / 639

APPENDICES

A NALA's Code of Ethics and Professional Responsibility / 647

B NALA's Model Standards and Guidelines for Utilization of Paralegals / 649

C NFPA's Model Code of Ethics and Professional Responsibility and Guidelines for Enforcement / 653

D NALS Code of Ethics and Professional Responsibility / 663

E Paralegal Ethics and Regulation: How to Find State-Specific Information / 665

F Paralegal Associations / 667

G Information on NALA's CLA/CP Program / 673

H Information on NFPA's PACE™ Examination / 683

I Information on NALS Certification / 687

J The Constitution of the United States / 691

K Spanish Equivalents for Important Legal Terms in English / 705

Glossary / 711

Index / 735

PREFACE

The economic crisis that has dominated headlines and Americans' lives from 2008 to today heralds a new era in this country. One aspect of the new era involves an attempt to reduce costs. Americans, as producers and consumers, have figured out new ways to live without spending as much as they used to. It follows that when people must seek the help of attorneys, they expect those attorneys to proceed in the most cost-effective way. Consequently, paralegals, or legal assistants, are being asked to do more work than ever before. It is not surprising that the paralegal occupation has been rapidly growing. We have tried to impart the excitement that surrounds the paralegal profession throughout the pages of this textbook. This new edition is both accessible and motivational. The many features and striking design encourage learning.

Paralegal Today, Fifth Edition, is replete with pedagogical aids that guarantee that students will maintain their interest in this subject. We use real-world examples, plus numerous boxed features. Those of you who have used the text before already know that it has perhaps the most extensive supplements package ever offered.

All of the basic areas of paralegal studies are covered in *Paralegal Today,* including careers, ethics and professional responsibility, pretrial preparation, trial procedures, criminal law, legal interviewing and investigation, legal research and analysis, computer-assisted legal research, and legal writing. The book also provides in-depth coverage of substantive law, including bankruptcy, contracts, intellectual property, torts, product liability, real property, estates, business organizations, and family law. In addition, there are a number of key features, which we describe in this preface.

TWO NEW FEATURES

This edition of *Paralegal Today* breaks ground with two new features that you will find in every chapter.

- *Going Green*—We all know that everyone should do her or his part to help preserve our environment. To this end, we present "Going Green" tips throughout the book. These tips explain to students how, when they are working in a law office, they can conserve natural resources and act in other ways that are environmentally sound. As we all know, "Every little bit helps." This is certainly true for helping the environment and that is what this new feature emphasizes.

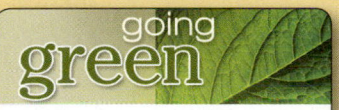

FLIP IT OVER

Drafts of documents and other work can be printed on the back of paper that has been used on one side. So long as the paper is not wrinkled, it can be used again for drafts. Of course, you must make sure that the discarded work is not sensitive legal material that should have been destroyed.

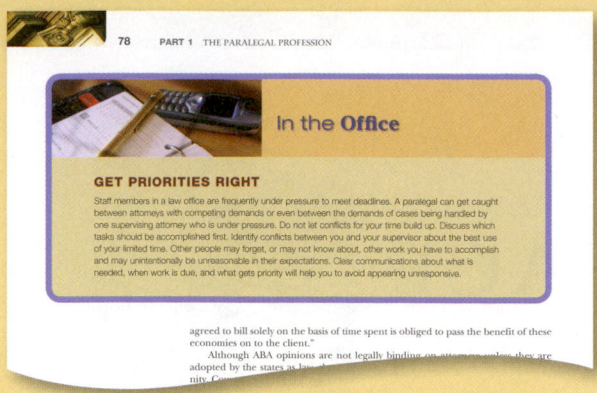

- *In the Office*—Paralegals work in offices, and paralegal students should gain skills that will help them make those offices run better—and, secondarily, that will impress their bosses. This new feature presents practical tips to help paralegals better organize their work, protect client confidentiality, and reduce stress in their day-to-day jobs.

A PRACTICAL, REALISTIC APPROACH

There sometimes exists an enormous gulf between classroom learning and on-the-job realities. We have tried to bridge this gulf in *Paralegal Today*, Fifth Edition, by offering a text full of practical advice and "hands-on" activities.

Exercises at the end of each chapter provide opportunities for your students to apply the concepts and skills discussed in the chapter. Many of the book's other key features, which you will read about shortly, were designed to give students a glimpse of the types of situations and demands they may encounter on the job as professional paralegals. A special introduction to the student, which appears before Chapter 1, contains practical advice and tips on how to master the legal concepts and procedures presented in this text—advice and tips that your students can also apply later, on the job.

Paralegal Today, Fifth Edition, also realistically portrays paralegal working environments and on-the-job challenges. Each chapter, for example, describes challenges to a paralegal's ethical obligations. These realistic situations give students a better understanding of how seemingly abstract ethical rules affect the tasks performed by attorneys and paralegals in the legal workplace.

TECHNOLOGY

We have attempted to make sure that *Paralegal Today*, Fifth Edition, is the most up-to-date text available in today's marketplace. To that end, we have included in this edition materials and features indicating how the latest developments in technology are affecting the law, the legal workplace, and paralegal tasks. These features and materials will help your students learn how to take advantage of technology to enhance their quality and productivity as paralegals.

A Chapter on Contemporary Online Legal Research

Chapter 8 is devoted to contemporary online legal research. It shows students how to do legal research and investigation using the legal databases provided by Westlaw® and Lexis®, as well as many other online information sources.

A Feature Focusing on Technology

The *Technology and Today's Paralegal* feature appears in each chapter. These updated features focus on how technology is affecting a specific aspect of paralegal work or on how paralegals can use technology to their benefit. For example, in Chapter 2 (Career Opportunities), the feature looks at the career opportunities available for tech-savvy paralegals. Titles of other *Technology and Today's Paralegal* features include the following:

- Be Prepared for Disaster! (Chapter 8).
- Who Bears the Costs of Electronic Discovery? (Chapter 10).
- Evolving Technology, Security, and Evidence (Chapter 13).
- Identity Theft, Spam, and Related Legal Issues (Chapter 14).
- Online Resources Concerning Insurance Claims (Chapter 16).
- Environmental Compliance (Chapter 19).

Margin Web Sites

Most chapters include several features titled *On the Web* in the margins. These features offer Web sites that students can access for further information on the topic being discussed in the text.

Chapter-Ending Internet Exercises

To help your students navigate the Web and find various types of information online, we have included at the end of each chapter one or more Internet exercises in a section titled *Using Internet Resources*. Each exercise directs the student to a specific Web site and asks a series of questions about the materials available at that site.

DELMAR CENGAGE LEARNING'S PARALEGAL ONLINE RESOURCE CENTER

The Delmar Cengage Learning Paralegal Web site, at **www.paralegal.delmar.cengage.com**, offers resources for paralegal professionals, instructors, and students. At this site, you and your students will find many links to legal and paralegal information sites. The site also hosts a page dedicated to *Paralegal Today*, Fifth Edition, where you and your students can find text updates, hot links, and other resources.

THE ORGANIZATION OF THIS TEXTBOOK

As paralegal instructors know, materials should be presented in such a way that students can build their skills and knowledge bases block by block. This is difficult because, no matter where you begin, you will need to refer to some information that has not yet been presented to the student. For example, if you try to explain what paralegals do on the first or second day of class, you will necessarily have to mention terms that may be unfamiliar to the students, such as *litigation* or *substantive law* or *procedural law*. In this text, the authors have attempted, when possible, to organize the topics covered in such a way that the student is not mystified by terms and concepts not yet discussed.

Content Presentation

No one way of organizing the coverage of topics in a paralegal text will be suitable for every instructor, but we have attempted to accommodate your needs as much as possible by organizing the text into three basic parts. Part 1 (Chapters 1–6) focuses primarily on the paralegal profession—its origins and development, the wide array of paralegal careers, the requirements and procedures that students can expect to encounter in the legal workplace, and the threshold ethical responsibilities of the profession. Part 1 also discusses the structure of the American legal system—the sources of law and the courts.

Part 2 (Chapters 7–13) looks in detail at legal procedures and paralegal skills. The student learns about the basic procedural requirements in civil and criminal litigation, as well as the skills involved in conducting interviews and investigations, legal research and analysis, and legal writing.

Part 3 (Chapters 14–19) focuses on substantive law. The areas of law treated in this part of the text include torts, product liability, consumer law, contracts, intellectual property, insurance, real property, estates, family law, business organizations, employment, bankruptcy, and environmental law. Additionally, the chapters covering substantive law include many numbered, highlighted examples to provide real-world illustrations of the legal concepts being discussed.

A Flexible Arrangement

It is our hope that this organization of the materials will allow the greatest flexibility for instructors. Although to a certain extent each chapter in the text builds on information contained in previous chapters, the chapters and parts can also be used independently. In other words, instructors who wish to alter the presentation of topics to fit their course outlines, or who wish to use selected chapters or parts only, will find it relatively easy to do so.

KEY FEATURES

In addition to the *Technology and Today's Paralegal* features and the new *Going Green* and *In the Office* features, which we have already discussed, every chapter in this text has the following features. Each feature is set apart and used both to instruct and to pique the interest of your paralegal students.

Developing Paralegal Skills

The *Developing Paralegal Skills* features present hypothetical examples of paralegals at work to help your students develop crucial paralegal skills. The features include checklists and practical tips. Some examples are the following:

- Working for a Public Defender (Chapter 2).
- Checking the Accident Scene (Chapter 11).

- PowerPoint Presentations (Chapter 12).
- Estate Planning (Chapter 17).
- Assisting with a Workers' Compensation Claim (Chapter 18).

Ethics Watch

Ethics Watch features typically take a student into a hypothetical situation that clearly presents an ethical problem. All are tied to specific ethical principles of the NALA, NFPA, or ABA. When possible, students are told what they should and should not do in the particular situations discussed. Some examples are the following:

- The Importance of Being Honest (Chapter 2).
- Using Secondary Sources (Chapter 7).
- Keeping Client Information Confidential (Chapter 10).
- Accurate Paperwork and Real Estate Transactions (Chapter 16).

Featured Contributor Articles

Each chapter features a contributed article written by an educator or an expert in the field. These articles offer your students practical tips on some aspect of paralegal work relating to the topic covered in the chapter. Some examples are the following:

- "The Interrelationship of the Various Areas of Law," by S. Whittington Brown, an attorney with the Arkansas Department of Human Services (Chapter 5).
- "Tips for Making Legal Writing Easier," by William Putman, an attorney who has specialized in paralegal education for many years and who has published a number of texts on legal analysis and writing (Chapter 9).
- "Is There a Place for Paralegals in the Field of Medical Malpractice?" by Beth Walston-Dunham, a paralegal educator and author of *Medical Malpractice Law and Litigation,* published by Delmar Cengage Learning (Chapter 14).
- "Protecting the Real Estate Purchaser: The Legal Due-Diligence Team," by Daniel F. Hinkel, vice president and corporate counsel for ING Investment Management, LLC, in Atlanta, Georgia (Chapter 16).

Today's Professional Paralegal

Near the end of every chapter we include a special feature entitled *Today's Professional Paralegal.* This important feature exposes your students to situations that they are likely to encounter on the job and offers guidance on how certain types of problems can be resolved. Some examples are the following:

- A View from the Inside: Assisting a Civil Litigation Paralegal (Chapter 2).
- Preparing the Internal Memorandum (Chapter 9).
- Confidentiality Agreements (Chapter 15).
- Handling and Avoiding Malpractice Claims (Chapter 16).
- Meeting with the Personal Representative (Chapter 17).

OTHER SPECIAL PEDAGOGICAL FEATURES

We have included in *Paralegal Today*, Fifth Edition, a number of additional pedagogical features, including those discussed below.

Chapter Outlines

On every chapter-opening page, a *Chapter Outline* lists the first-level headings within the chapter. These outlines allow you and your students to tell at a glance what topics are covered in the chapters.

Chapter Objectives

In every chapter, just following the *Chapter Outline*, we list five or six chapter objectives. Your students will know immediately what is expected of them as they read each chapter.

estate administration
The process in which a decedent's personal representative settles the affairs of the decedent's estate (collects assets, pays debts and taxes, and distributes the remaining assets to heirs); the process is usually overseen by a probate court.

joint tenancy
The joint ownership of property by two or more co-owners in which each co-owner owns an undivided portion of the property. On the death of one of the joint tenants, his or her ownership interest automatically passes to the surviving joint tenant or tenants.

Margin Web Sites

As already mentioned, *On the Web* features appear in the page margins throughout the text. These features direct students to specific Web sites for further information on the topics being discussed.

Vocabulary and Margin Definitions

Legal terminology is often a major challenge for beginning paralegal students. We use an important pedagogical device—margin definitions—to help your students understand legal terms. Whenever an important term is introduced, it appears in colored type and is defined. In addition, the term is listed and defined in the margin of the page, alongside the paragraph in which the term appears (see the examples on the left).

At the end of each chapter, all terms that have appeared in colored type within the chapter are listed in alphabetical order in a section called *Key Terms and Concepts*. Your students can examine this list to make sure that they understand all of the important terms introduced in the chapter. For easy reference and review, each term in the list is followed by the number of the page on which it was defined.

All terms in colored type are again listed and defined in the *Glossary* at the end of the text. Spanish equivalents to many important legal terms in English are provided in a separate glossary in Appendix K.

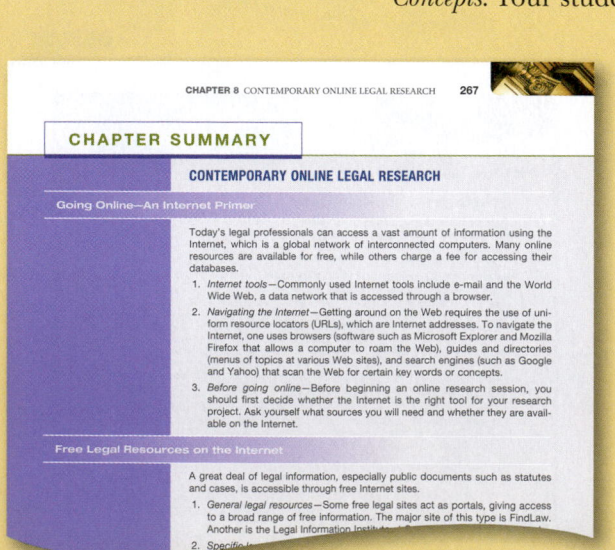

Chapter Summaries

We have included a graphic chapter summary at the conclusion of each chapter in the Fifth Edition. These summaries illustrate important concepts from the chapter and show how the concepts are related to one another. The major topics discussed in the chapter appear in the left-hand column of the summary, with a synopsis of the concepts discussed under each topic listed in the right-hand column. This visually appealing format facilitates the student's review of the chapter contents.

Exhibits and Forms

When appropriate, we present exhibits illustrating important forms or concepts relating to paralegal work. Many exhibits are filled in with hypothetical data. Exhibits and forms in *Paralegal Today*, Fifth Edition, include those listed below:

- A Sample Client Bill (Chapter 3).
- The Articles of the U.S. Constitution (Chapter 5).
- Examples of Boolean Searches (Chapter 8).
- A Typical Case Flowchart (Chapter 10).

CHAPTER-ENDING MATERIALS FOR REVIEW AND STUDY

Every chapter contains numerous chapter-ending pedagogical materials. These materials are designed to provide a wide variety of assignments for your students. The chapter-ending pedagogy begins with the *Key Terms and Concepts*, followed by the chapter summaries, which we have already mentioned. Then follow the materials described below.

Questions for Review

Every chapter includes a number of relatively straightforward questions for review. These questions are designed to test the student's knowledge of the basic concepts discussed in the chapter.

Ethical Questions

Because of the importance of ethical issues in paralegal training, we have also included one or more ethical questions at the end of each chapter. Each question presents a hypothetical situation, which is followed by one or two questions about what the paralegal should do to solve the dilemma.

Practice Questions and Assignments

The hands-on approach to learning paralegal skills is emphasized in the practice questions and assignments. There are several of these questions and assignments at the end of each chapter. A particular situation is presented, and the student is asked to actually carry out an assignment.

Questions for Critical Analysis

Every chapter has several questions for critical analysis. These questions are designed to elicit critical evaluation and discussion of issues relating to the topics covered in the chapter.

Projects

There are one or more projects at the end of every chapter. These are specific work tasks that your students can carry out. Often, these projects involve obtaining information from sources that paralegals may deal with on the job, such as a library, a court, a prosecutor's office, or a police department.

Using Internet Resources

As already mentioned, concluding the chapter-ending materials in each chapter is a section titled *Using Internet Resources.* The Internet exercises presented in these sections are designed to familiarize students with useful Web sites and with the extensive array of resources available online.

APPENDICES

To make this text a reference source for your students, we have included the appendices listed below.

A NALA's Code of Ethics and Professional Responsibility

B NALA's Model Standards and Guidelines for Utilization of Paralegals

C NFPA's Model Code of Ethics and Professional Responsibility and Guidelines for Enforcement

D NALS Code of Ethics and Professional Responsibility

E Paralegal Ethics and Regulation: How to Find State-Specific Information

F Paralegal Associations

G Information on NALA's CLA/CP Program

H Information on NFPA's PACE™ Examination

I Information on NALS Certification

J The Constitution of the United States

K Spanish Equivalents for Important Legal Terms in English

FOR USERS OF THE FOURTH EDITION

Those of you who have used the Fourth Edition of *Paralegal Today* will probably want to know some of the major changes that have been made for the Fifth Edition. Generally, all of the elements in the Fifth Edition—including the text, exhibits, features, and end-of-chapter pedagogy—have been rewritten, revised, or updated as necessary to reflect new laws, procedures, and technological developments. We think that we have improved the text greatly, thanks to many suggestions from users of previous editions as well as from other paralegal educators and legal professionals.

Organizational Changes

The sequence of chapters has been significantly changed based on recommendations of faculty using the text.

- Part 1, The Paralegal Profession, now has six chapters instead of four. The Inner Workings of the Law Office, formerly Chapter 4, now comes before Ethics and Professional Responsibility, formerly Chapter 3, because students should comprehend the structure of law practice before considering ethics issues. Chapter 5, Sources of American Law, and Chapter 6, The Court System and Alternative Dispute Resolution, have been moved up into Part 1, providing background for later discussions of procedures and research.

- Legal Procedures and Paralegal Skills has been moved forward to precede discussions of specific areas of the law; it is now Part 2. This part still contains seven chapters, but the ordering has been changed. Legal Research and Analysis has been moved to the front of the section and is now Chapter 7. It is followed, as before, by Contemporary Online Legal Research and Legal Writing: Form and Substance. Those chapters are followed by four chapters covering civil and criminal procedures and litigation, as well as interviews and investigations.

- Key Elements of the Law, formerly Part 2, is now Part 3. It contains six chapters that give students exposure to various law topics, including the major common law areas and such additional subjects as intellectual property, family law, and bankruptcy.

We believe instructors will find this ordering of chapters more suitable to the needs of most students.

New Features and Major Changes

In addition to the usual improvement and updating of the body of the text, some larger changes affect the text in positive ways.

- The previous edition had a Featured Guest and a paralegal profile. To eliminate redundancy, these have been changed to one feature per chapter, called *Featured Contributor,* that draws on the best of these features.

- The *Ethics Watch* features have been revised to link the contents to specific ethical rules of the NALA, NFPA, or ABA. This should help make it clear to students that the situations described are relevant to careers.

- Each chapter includes a new feature called *In the Office.* These features provide practical tips to help students develop skills that will make their offices run more smoothly. The purpose is to raise awareness of how to be a productive, effective professional.

- Environmental awareness has spread to offices, and each chapter has a brief *Going Green* feature providing a little tip on how paralegals can conserve resources while being productive.

- The chapters discussing substantive areas of law provide examples of the roles often played by paralegals who work in these areas. For example, the discussion of bankruptcy law is followed by a description of duties often performed by paralegals in that area, making the material more relevant.

- The chapter on legal research, now called Contemporary Online Legal Research, has been greatly restructured. Changes include more prominent discussions of Lexis and Westlaw and the expanded explanations of major tools such as Auto-Cite and KeyCite. The chapter now also offers coverage of newer competitors, such as Loislaw and VersusLaw, to make students aware of the growing number of alternative research services that are less costly than Lexis and Westlaw.

Significant Revisions to Chapters

In addition to the changes discussed above, all chapters have been revised. Of course, we constantly strive to enhance readability. To that end, we have deleted or summarized material not critical to the purpose of the text or the course. Here, we summarize some other major changes in each chapter.

- **Chapter 1** (Today's Professional Paralegal)—This chapter has been revised to include the most recent views of the major professional paralegal organizations about the role of paralegals in the practice of law today. The *Technology and Today's Paralegal* feature, Online Resources for Paralegals, is all new.

- **Chapter 2** (Career Opportunities)—This chapter has been updated with the newest data on salaries and job opportunities in the paralegal profession. Marketing Your Skills, an appendix in the Fourth Edition, has been integrated into the chapter because it is particularly important in a lean job market.

- **Chapter 3** (The Inner Workings of the Law Office)—This was previously Chapter 4, but following the recommendation of adopters, we have changed the chapter order so that office structure is covered before the subject of ethics. A discussion of IOLTA accounts has been added. A revised *Developing Paralegal Skills* feature, concerning protecting the confidentiality of client information, is included.

- **Chapter 4** (Ethics and Professional Responsibility)—This was Chapter 3 in the previous edition. The new placement allows for a progression of topics preferred by many users. There are two revised *Developing Paralegal Skills* features in the chapter. One is on the unauthorized practice of law. The other is on the ethical and legal issues involved if one learns that a client may be going to commit a crime.

- **Chapter 5** (Sources of American Law)—The *Technology and Today's Paralegal* feature on cases of first impression has been revised, along with other text matter. As requested by reviewers, the sequence of some material has been changed so that the common law is covered earlier in the chapter.

- **Chapter 6** (The Court System and Alternative Dispute Resolution)—New examples have been added for greater clarity in this last chapter of the introductory section of the textbook.

- **Chapter 7** (Legal Research and Analysis)—This chapter begins the second part of the text, Legal Procedures and Paralegal Skills, which has been moved up in the Fifth Edition. A new case has been developed to help students learn the structure of a court decision. A discussion of the IRAC method of briefing cases has also been added along with a completely revised *Developing Paralegal Skills* feature on reading statutory law.

- **Chapter 8** (Contemporary Online Legal Research)—This chapter has been completely revised and moved up in placement because of the continuing evolution of online research and its centrality in the role of the paralegal. Besides Lexis and Westlaw, other services, such as Loislaw and VersusLaw, are included. A new *Developing Paralegal Skills* feature on internet research has been added along with a new *Featured Contributor* article.

- **Chapter 9** (Legal Writing: Form and Substance)—This chapter, which was at the end of the previous edition, now is at the center of the text, as recommended by adopters. The chapter has been edited for relevance and includes new material on avoiding confusion through clear legal writing.

- **Chapter 10** (Civil Litigation: Before the Trial)—This chapter has been moved to immediately follow the chapter on legal research and writing. It includes a new section on electronic court filing. Changes in the *Developing Paralegal Skills* feature titled "A Checklist for Drafting a Complaint in a Federal Civil Case" keep the material timely.

- **Chapter 11** (Conducting Interviews and Investigations)—The *Technology and Today's Paralegal* feature, "Communicating through Graphics," is new. Together with a new sample e-mail to a client, these changes show how classic legal skills can incorporate new technology.

- **Chapter 12** (Trial Procedures)—Previously Chapter 15, this chapter has been moved up to bring the sequence of information in line with instructors' preferences. The chapter has been revised and includes a new *Featured Contributor* article.

- **Chapter 13** (Criminal Law and Procedures)—New material on cyber crimes, such as cyberstalking and cyberbullying, has been added to ensure relevance to modern criminal problems. The *Technology and Today's Paralegal* feature, "Evolving Technology, Security, and Evidence," is new to this edition.

- **Chapter 14** (Tort Law, Product Liability, and Consumer Law)—This is the first chapter in Part 3, Key Elements of the Law. The completely revised *Technology and Today's Paralegal* feature, which concerns Internet-based fraud, is part of our effort to ensure that material remains relevant.

- **Chapter 15** (Contracts and Intellectual Property Law)—This chapter has been revised and updated. More contract examples have been included, along with a discussion of the Economic Espionage Act.

- **Chapter 16** (Real Property and Insurance Law)—The material in this chapter has been restructured for greater relevance to areas of law that frequently involve paralegals. New material on easements and commercial property contracts has been included.

- **Chapter 17** (Family Law and Estates)—The structure of this chapter has been revised for greater readability, and the chapter includes new material on trusts and the interstate enforcement of child-support agreements.

- **Chapter 18** (Business Organizations and Employment Law)—This chapter, previously called Laws Affecting Business, has been tightened to focus on the areas of law most relevant to paralegals. Based on instructor feedback, coverage of negotiable instruments has been dropped. A substantially revised *Developing Paralegal Skills* feature on reserving corporate names and trademarks is included, and a section on professional corporations and a new *Featured Contributor* essay have been added.

- **Chapter 19** (Bankruptcy and Environmental Law)—Bankruptcy coverage has been updated to reflect the evolution of procedures since the implementation of the 2005 reforms, such as the income test to determine eligibility for Chapter 7 or Chapter 13. A new *Featured Contributor* article also discusses key terms in bankruptcy. The environmental section has been updated and remains a popular topic with students.

SUPPLEMENTAL TEACHING/LEARNING MATERIALS

Paralegal Today, Fifth Edition, is accompanied by what is likely the largest number of teaching and learning supplements available for any text of its kind. We understand that instructors face a difficult task in finding the time necessary to teach the materials that they wish to cover during each term. In conjunction with a number of our colleagues, we have developed supplementary teaching materials that we believe are the best obtainable today. Each component of the supplements package is described below.

Student StudyWARE™ CD-ROM

The new accompanying CD-ROM includes interactive StudyWARE™ software that provides additional material to help students master the important concepts in the course. Many helpful questions that previously appeared at the end of the text chapters have been moved to the CD. The CD-ROM includes:

- Multiple-choice and true/false quizzing.
- Case studies with multiple-choice follow-up questions.
- Flashcards.
- Video clips from *ABC News* with discussion questions.

Instructor's Manual

The Instructor's Manual has been greatly revised to incorporate changes in the text and to provide comprehensive teaching support. The Instructor's Manual contains the following:

- A sample course syllabus.
- Detailed lecture outlines.
- Teaching suggestions.

- Answers to end-of-chapter questions.
- Testbank and answer key.

INSTRUCTOR RESOURCES

Instructor Resources

Spend less time planning and more time teaching. With Delmar Cengage Learning's Instructor Resources to Accompany *Paralegal Today: The Legal Team at Work,* preparing for class and evaluating students has never been easier! This invaluable CD-ROM allows you anywhere, anytime access to instructor resources:

- The Instructor's Manual contains various resources for each chapter of the book.
- The Computerized Testbank in ExamView makes generating tests and quizzes a snap. With many questions and different styles to choose from, you can create customized assessments for your students with the click of a button. Add your own unique questions and print rationales for easy class preparation.
- Customizable PowerPoint® Presentations focus on key points for each chapter. (PowerPoint® is a registered trademark of the Microsoft Corporation.)

All of these instructor materials are also posted on our Web site, in the Online Resources section.

WebTUTOR™

The WebTUTOR™ supplement allows you, as the instructor, to take learning beyond the classroom. This online courseware is designed to complement the text and benefit students and instructors alike by helping to better manage your time, prepare for exams, organize your notes, and more. WebTUTOR™ allows you to extend your reach beyond the classroom.

Online Companion™

The Online Companion™ can be found at **www.paralegal.delmar.cengage.com** in the Online Companion™ section of the Web site.

- **Study Guide**—Students can use the Study Guide to review chapter overviews and chapter objectives to reinforce chapter learning goals. This resource also contains extensive outlines for each chapter that will help students organize information and show how the concepts in the text relate to each other. In addition, students will discover study tips and practical advice that will help ease the way through studying, test taking, writing essays, and more.
- **Online Quizzing**—Student interactive online quizzing is also available. This resource provides students with a chance to answer review questions directly relating to the text for each chapter. Each answer presents students with instant feedback and clarifies the rationale for correct and incorrect choices. This self-assessment tool can be accessed at school or at home, giving students more flexibility and opportunity to study.

Web Page

Come visit our Web site at **www.paralegal.delmar.cengage.com**, where you will find valuable information, such as hot links and sample materials to download, as well as other Delmar Cengage Learning products.

Supplements At-a-Glance

SUPPLEMENT:	WHAT IT IS:	WHAT'S IN IT:
Student CD-ROM	Software program (CD-ROM in the back of the book). StudyWARE™ is like the student's own interactive private tutor, reinforcing the material in the text in an exciting and fun environment!	StudyWARE™ software with multiple-choice and true/false quizzing, case studies with multiple-choice follow-up questions, flashcards, video clips from *ABC News* with discussion questions
Online Instructor's Manual	Resources for the instructor, posted online at **www.paralegal.delmar.cengage.com** in the Online Resources section	• Instructor's Manual with sample course syllabus; detailed lecture outlines; teaching suggestions; answers to end-of-chapter questions; test bank and answer key • PowerPoint® Presentations
Instructor Resources CD-ROM **INSTRUCTOR RESOURCES**	Resources for the instructor, available on CD-ROM	• Instructor's Manual with sample course syllabus; detailed lecture outlines; teaching suggestions; answers to end-of-chapter questions; test bank and answer key; • Computerized Testbank in ExamView with many questions and styles to choose from to create customized assessments for your students. • PowerPoint® Presentations
WebTUTOR™ WebTUTOR™	WebTUTOR™ supplemental courseware is the best way to use the Internet to turn everyone in your class into a front-row student. It complements Delmar, Cengage Learning paralegal textbooks by providing interactive reinforcement that helps students grasp complex concepts. WebTUTOR™ allows you to know quickly what concepts your students are or aren't grasping.	• Automatic and immediate feedback from quizzes and exams • Online exercises that reinforce learning • Flashcards that include audio support • Greater interaction and involvement through online discussion forums
Online Companion™ ONLINE COMPANION	Additional resources for the student, posted online at **www.paralegal.delmar.cengage.com** in the Online Companion™ section	• Study Guide with chapter overviews, objectives, and outlines • Online quizzing
Introduction to Paralegal Studies Online Course	Robust Online Course available on both Blackboard and WebCT. (Availability upon request for eCollege, Angel, Desire2Learn, and more.) The course can be used along with this textbook or any book for the introductory course. See a demo at **cengagesites.com/academic/?site=4074**	Includes 16 lessons with an Introduction; Objectives; Lecture Outline; Video Activities; Journal Activities; Group Activities; Internet Activities; Discussion Questions; Ethics Question; Glossary Terms; Weblinks; Study Notes; and Quizzing for the student. Instructor materials include PowerPoints® and Testbanks.

ACKNOWLEDGMENTS FOR PREVIOUS EDITIONS

Numerous careful and conscientious individuals have helped us in this undertaking from the beginning. We continue to be indebted to those whose contributions helped to make previous editions of *Paralegal Today* a valuable teaching/learning text. We particularly thank the following paralegal educators for their insightful criticisms and comments:

Laura Barnard
Lakeland Community College, OH

Lia Barone
Norwalk Community College, CT

Carol Brady
Milwaukee Area Technical College, WI

Rhonda Brashears
Certified Paralegal, TX

Debra Brown
Coastline Community College, CA

Chelsea Campbell
Lehman College, NY

Linda S. Cioffredi
Woodbury College, VT

Jeptha Clemens
Northwest Mississippi Community
College, MS

Arlene A. Cleveland
Pellissippi State Technical Community
College, TN

Lynne D. Dahlborg
Suffolk University, MA

Kevin R. Derr
Pennsylvania College of
Technology, PA

Bob Diotalevi
Florida Gulf Coast University, FL

Donna Hamblin Donathan
Marshall University Community
College, OH

Dora Dye
City College of San Francisco, CA

Wendy B. Edson
Hilbert College, NY

Leslie Sturdivant Ennis
Samford University, AL

Pamela Faller
College of the Sequoias, CA

Gary Glascom
Cedar Crest College, PA

Dolores Grissom
Samford University, AL

Paul D. Guymon
William Rainey Harper College, IL

Sharon Halford
Community College of Aurora, CO

Linda Wilke Heil
Central Community College, NE

Jean A. Hellman
Loyola University, Chicago, IL

Melinda Hess
College of Saint Mary, NE

Louise Hoover
Rockford Business College, IL

Marlene L. Hoover
El Camino College, CA

Susan J. Howery
Yavapai College, AZ

Jill Jasperson
Utah Valley State College, UT

Melissa M. Jones
Samford University, AL

Deborah Winfrey Keene
Lansing Community College, MI

Jennifer Allen Labosky
Davidson County Community
College, NC

Dora J. Lew
California State University,
Hayward, CA

Mary Hatfield Lowe
Westark Community College, AZ

Gerald A. Loy
Broome Community College, NY

Linda Mort
Kellogg Community College, MI

Constance Ford Mungle
Oklahoma City University, OK

H. Margaret Nickerson
William Woods College, MO

Martha G. Nielson
University of California, San Diego, CA

Elizabeth L. Nobis
Lansing Community College, MI

Joy D. O'Donnell
Pima Community College, AZ

Anthony Piazza
David N. Myers College, OH

Francis D. Polk
Ocean County College, NJ

Ruth-Ellen Post
Rivier College, NH

Elizabeth Raulerson
Indian River Community College, FL

Kathleen Mercer Reed
University of Toledo, OH

Lynn Retzak
Lakeshore Technical Institute, WI

Evelyn L. Riyhani
University of California, Irvine, CA

Melanie A. P. Rowand
California State University,
  Hayward, CA

Vitonio F. San Juan
University of La Verne, CA

Susan F. Schulz
Southern Career Institute, FL

John G. Thomas III
North Hampton County Community
  College, PA

Loretta Thornhill
Hagerstown Community College, MD

Julia Tryk
Cuyahoga Community College, OH

ACKNOWLEDGMENTS FOR THE FIFTH EDITION

During the preparation of the Fifth Edition of *Paralegal Today*, several professionals offered us penetrating criticisms, comments, and suggestions for improving the text. While we haven't been able to comply with every request, the reviewers listed below will see that many of their suggestions have been taken to heart.

Dora Dye
City College of San Francisco, CA

Jameka Ellison
Everest University—Lakeland, FL

Paul Guymon
William Rainey Harper College, IL

Vera Haus
McIntosh College, NH

Deborah Keene
Lansing Community College, MI

Paula Montlary
Florida Career College, FL

Sean Scott
St. Petersburg College, FL

Joanne Spillman
Westwood College Online, CO

Derek Thomson
Bryant and Stratton College, NY

Stonewall Van Wie III
Del Mar College, TX

Lorrie Watson
Orangeburg Calhoun Technical
  College, SC

We also are grateful to the following *Featured Contributors* to *Paralegal Today*, Fifth Edition, for enhancing the quality of our book with their tips and illuminating insights into paralegal practice:

Sally Bisson
College of St. Mary, Omaha, NE

Deborah E. Bouchoux
Georgetown University,
  Washington, DC

Jo-Christy Brown
Attorney, Austin, TX

S. Whittington Brown
Attorney, Arkansas Department of
  Human Services

Matthew Cornick
Clayton State University, GA

Wendy B. Edson
Hilbert College, NY

Fernaundra Ferguson
University of West Florida

Nancy R. Gallo
Sussex County Community College, NJ

Daniel F. Hinkel
Vice President and Corporate Counsel,
    ING Investment Management, LLC,
    Atlanta, GA

Dwayne E. Krager
Foley & Lardner, LLP, Milwaukee, WI

Lisa L. Newcity
Roger Williams University, RI

P. David Palmiere
Oakland University, MI

Janet Powell
Ogletree, Deakins, Nash, Smoak, &
    Stewart, Miami, FL

William Putman
Paralegal Educator/Author

Angela Schneeman
Paralegal and Author

Beth Walston-Dunham
Paralegal Educator/Author

Pamela Poole Weber
Seminole Community College, FL

Linda J. Wolf
Sidley Austin, LLP, Dallas, TX

E. J. Yera
U.S. Attorney's Office, Miami, FL

In preparing this text, we were also the beneficiaries of the expertise brought to the project by the editorial and production staff of Delmar Cengage Learning. Our editor, Shelley Esposito, successfully guided the project through each phase and put together a supplements package that is without parallel in the teaching and learning of paralegal skills. Melissa Riveglia, our senior product manager, was also incredibly helpful in putting together the teaching/learning package. We also wish to thank Betty Dickson, senior content project manager, for her assistance throughout the production process. Additionally, we wish to thank Erin Brennan, our marketing manager, and Joy Kocsis, our art director, for their valuable contributions to the project.

A number of other individuals contributed significantly to the quality of *Paralegalism Today,* Fifth Edition. We wish to thank Roger Meiners for his assistance in creating what we believe is the best introductory paralegal text on the market today. We also thank Suzanne Jasin for her special efforts on the project. We also were fortunate to have had the copyediting skills of Beverly Peavler, and we are grateful to Pat Lewis and Lorretta Palagi, whose proofreading skills will not go unnoticed. Finally, we are indebted to the staff at Parkwood Composition, our compositor, whose ability to generate the pages for this text quickly and accurately made it possible for us to meet our ambitious printing schedule.

We know that we are not perfect. If you or your students have suggestions on how we can improve this book, write to us. That way, we can make *Paralegal Today* an even better book in the future. We promise to answer every single letter that we receive.

Roger LeRoy Miller
Mary Meinzinger Urisko

INTRODUCTION TO THE STUDENT

The law can be a difficult subject because it uses a specialized vocabulary and requires substantial time and effort to learn. Those who work with and teach law believe that the subject matter is exciting and definitely worth your efforts. Everything in *Paralegal Today: The Legal Team at Work*, Fifth Edition, has been written for the purpose of helping you learn the most important aspects of law and legal procedures.

In today's workplace, learning is a lifelong process. Your learning of legal concepts and procedures will not end when you finish your paralegal studies. Rather, the end of your studies marks the beginning of your learning about law and legal procedures in practice. Just as valuable to you as the knowledge base you can acquire from mastering the legal concepts and terms in *Paralegal Today*, Fifth Edition, is a knowledge of *how to learn* those legal concepts and terms. The focus in this introduction, therefore, is on developing learning skills that you can apply to any subject matter and at any time throughout your career.

The suggestions and study tips offered in this introduction can help you "learn how to learn" law and procedures and maximize your chances of success as a paralegal student. They can also help you build lifelong learning habits that you can use in other classes and throughout your career as a paralegal.

MASTERING YOUR TEXT

A common mistake is assuming that the best way to understand the content of written material is to read and reread that material. True, if you have read through a chapter ten times, you have probably acquired a knowledge of its contents, but think of the time you have spent in the process. You want to strive to use your time *effectively*. We offer some suggestions here on how to study the chapters of *Paralegal Today* most effectively.

Read One Section at a Time

A piano student once said to her teacher, "This piece is so complicated. How can I possibly learn it?" The teacher responded, "It's simple: measure by measure." That advice can be applied to any challenging task. As a paralegal student, you are faced with the job of learning complicated legal concepts and procedures. By dividing your work up into manageable units, you will find that, before long, you have achieved your goal. Each chapter in *Paralegal Today*, Fifth Edition, is divided into several major sections. By concentrating on sections, rather than chapters, you will find it easier to master the chapter's contents.

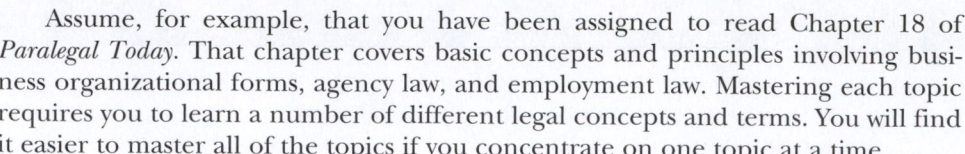

Assume, for example, that you have been assigned to read Chapter 18 of *Paralegal Today*. That chapter covers basic concepts and principles involving business organizational forms, agency law, and employment law. Mastering each topic requires you to learn a number of different legal concepts and terms. You will find it easier to master all of the topics if you concentrate on one topic at a time.

Once you have read through a section, do not stop there. Go back through the section again and organize the material in your mind. Outlining the section is one way to mentally organize what you have read.

Make an Outline

An outline is a method for organizing information. An outline can be helpful because it illustrates visually how concepts relate to each other and because writing it forces us to think about the material and explain it to ourselves. Outlining can be done as part of your reading of each section, but your outline will be more accurate (and more helpful later on) if you have already read through a section and have a general understanding of the topics covered in that section.

The Benefits of Outlining

Although you may not believe that you need to outline, experience shows that the act of *physically* creating an outline for a chapter helps most students to greatly improve their ability to retain and master the material being studied. Even if you make an outline that is no more than the headings in the text, you will be studying more efficiently than you otherwise would be.

Outlining is also a paralegal skill. As a paralegal, you will often present legal concepts and fact patterns in an outline format. For example, paralegals frequently create legal memoranda to summarize their research results. The legal memorandum is usually presented in an outline format, which indicates how the topics covered in the memo relate to one another logically or sequentially. There is no better time to master the skill of outlining than while you are a student. You can learn this skill by outlining sections and chapters of *Paralegal Today*.

Identify the Main Concepts in Each Section

In outlining a chapter, you can use the outline at the beginning of the chapter as a starting point. The chapter-opening outlines include the headings of the major sections in the chapter. Use these headings as a guide when creating a more detailed outline. Be careful, though. To make an effective outline, you have to be selective. Outlines that contain all the information in the text are not very useful. Your objective is to identify main concepts and to arrange more detailed concepts under those main concepts. Therefore, in outlining, your first goal is to *identify the main concepts in each section*. Often the headings in your textbook and in the chapter-opening outlines are sufficient as identifiers of the major concepts. You may decide, however, that you want to phrase an identifier in a way more meaningful to you.

Outline Format

Your outline should consist of several levels written in a standard outline format. The most important concepts are assigned uppercase Roman numerals; the second most important, capital letters; the third most important, numbers; the fourth most important, lowercase letters; and the fifth most important, lowercase roman numerals. The number of levels you use varies, of course, with the complexity of the subject matter. In some outlines, or portions of outlines, you may need to use only two levels. In others, you may need five or more levels.

As an example of how to use numerals and letters in an outline, we present below a partial outline of the contracts section in Chapter 15 of *Paralegal Today*, Fifth Edition.

FUNDAMENTAL LEGAL CONCEPTS: CONTRACTS

I. Definition of a contract: A contract is any agreement (based on a promise or an exchange of promises) that can be enforced in court. A promise is an assurance that one will or will not do something in the future.

II. Requirements to form a valid contract

    A. Agreement—Agreement is divided into two events: an offer and an acceptance. One party must offer to enter into a legal agreement, and another party must accept the terms of the offer.

        1. The offer—Three elements are necessary:

            a. The offeror (the party making the offer) must have the intent to be bound by the offer.

            b. The terms of the offer must be reasonably certain or definite (note that some terms may be left open in sales contracts).

            c. The offer must be communicated to the offeree (the party to whom the offer is made).

        2. Termination of the offer—The offeror can normally revoke (take back) an offer at any time prior to acceptance.

            a. Both a rejection of the offer and the making of a counteroffer (by the offeree) terminate the original offer.

        3. Acceptance—Acceptance by the offeree results in a legally binding contract (provided that all of the other requirements of a valid contract are met).

            a. The terms of the offer must be accepted exactly as stated by the offeror (the mirror image rule).

            b. Acceptance must be timely—within the time period designated by the offeror or within a reasonable time.

            c. Under the mailbox rule, acceptance becomes valid the moment it is deposited in the mail (even if it is never received by the offeror).

    B. Consideration . . .

Consider Marking Your Text

From kindergarten through high school, you typically did not own your own textbooks. They were made available by the school system. You may have been told not to mark in them. Now that you own your text, you can greatly improve your learning by marking it. There is a trade-off here. The more you mark up your textbook, the less you will receive from the bookstore if you sell it back at the end of the semester. The benefit is a better understanding of the subject matter. The cost is the reduction in the price you get at resale. Additionally, if you want a text that you can mark with your own notations, you will have to buy a new one or a used one that has no markings. Both carry a higher price tag than a used textbook with markings.

The Benefits of Marking

Marking is helpful because it makes you an *active* participant in the mastery of the material. Researchers have shown that the physical act of marking, like the act of outlining, helps us better retain material. The better the material is organized in our minds, the more we remember. There are two types of readers—passive and active. The active reader outlines and/or marks. Active readers typically do better on exams. Perhaps one of the reasons that active readers retain more is because the physical act of outlining and/or marking requires greater concentration. It is through greater concentration that more is remembered.

Different Ways of Marking

The most commonly used forms of marking are to underline important points or to use a highlighter or marker, in yellow or some other transparent color. Marking also includes circling, numbering, using arrows, making brief notes, and any other method that lets you locate things when you go back to skim the pages in your textbook prior to an exam or when creating your outline.

Points to Remember When Marking

Here are two important points to remember when marking your text:

1. *Read the entire section before you begin marking.* You cannot mark a section until you know what is important, and you cannot know what is important until you read the whole section.

2. *Do not mark too extensively.* You should mark your text selectively. If you fill up each page with arrows, asterisks, circles, and highlighting, marking will be of little use. When you go back to review the material, you will not be able to find what was important. The key is *selective* activity. Mark each page in a way that allows you to see the most important points at a glance.

Memory Devices

During the course of your study of *Paralegal Today*, Fifth Edition, you will read many legal terms that will be new to you. Your challenge is to remember these terms and incorporate them into your own "working" vocabulary. You also need to remember legal concepts and principles. We look here at some techniques for learning and retaining legal terms and concepts.

Flashcards

Using flashcards is a remarkably effective method of learning new terms or concepts. Through repetition, or drilling, flashcards force you to recall certain ideas and repeat them. Although published flashcards are available in many bookstores, you should try to create your own. Write the key term or concept on one side of an index card, for instance, and the definition, process, or description on the other side.

There are several advantages to creating your own flashcards. First, writing the information will help you insert the term into your permanent memory. Second, you do not need flashcards for terms that you already know or that you will not need to know for your particular course. Third, you can phrase the answer in a meaningful way, with unique cues that are designed just for your purposes. This personalizes the flashcard, making the information easier to remember. Finally, you can modify the definition, if need be, so that it matches more closely the definition preferred by your instructor.

It is helpful to create your flashcards consistently and routinely at a given point in the learning process. One good moment is when you are reading or outlining your text. Make a flashcard for each term defined in the margin, and write the margin definition on the flashcard.

Take your flashcards with you when you're on the go. Review them at lunch, while you wait in line, or when you ride the bus. When a flashcard contains a term that is difficult to pronounce, say the term aloud, if possible, as often as you can. When you have a term memorized, set that card aside but save it as an exam-review device for later in the term. Prepare new cards as you cover new terms or concepts in class.

Mnemonics

One method that students commonly employ to remember legal concepts and principles is the use of mnemonic (pronounced "nee-*mahn*-ick") devices. Mnemonic devices are merely aids to memory. A mnemonic device can be a word, a formula, or a rhyme. As an aid to remembering the elements of a cause of action in negligence (see Chapter 14), for example, you might use the mnemonic ABCD, in which the letters represent the following concepts:

A represents "A duty of care."

B represents "Breach of the duty of care."

C represents "Causation (the breach must cause an injury)."

D represents "Damage (injury or harm)."

Similarly, to remember the basic activities that paralegals may not legally undertake (see Chapter 4), you might use the mnemonic FACt, in which the letters represent the following concepts:

F represents "fees"—paralegals may not set legal fees.

A represents "advice"—paralegals may not give legal advice.

Ct represents "court"—paralegals, with some exceptions, may not represent clients in court.

Whenever you want to memorize various components of a legal doctrine or concept, consider devising a mnemonic. Mnemonics need not make sense in themselves. The point is, if they help you remember something, then use them. Any association you can make with a difficult term to help you pronounce it, spell it, or define it more easily is a useful learning tool.

Identify What You Do Not Understand

One of the most important things you can do before class is clarify in your mind which terms, concepts, or procedures you *do not* understand. You can do this when marking your text by placing check marks or question marks by material that is unclear to you. Similarly, you can include questions in your outline. For example, in the sample partial outline presented earlier in this introduction, you might add a query following the subsection on acceptance that reads, "What is considered a 'reasonable time'"?

Once you have outlined and marked your text, go back to any problem areas that you have encountered and *think about them*. It is exciting to figure out difficult material on your own. If you still do not understand a concept, make a note to follow up on this topic later in the classroom. Perhaps the instructor's lecture will clarify the issue. If not, make a point of asking for clarification. Most instructors appreciate questions—and so do other students. If you "don't get it," you can be sure others don't get it either.

As a paralegal, you may be frequently asked to undertake preliminary investigations of legal claims. Identifying what facts are *not known* is the starting point for any investigation and focuses investigatory efforts. As a student, you might think about class time as an opportunity to "investigate" further the subject matter of your course. Identifying before class what you do not know about a topic allows you to focus your "investigative" efforts, particularly your listening efforts, during class and to maximize classroom opportunities for learning.

LEARNING IN THE CLASSROOM

The classroom is the heart of your learning experience as a paralegal student. Each instructor has a plan for the course that includes many elements, which are brought together during class sessions. A major element in your instructor's course plan is, of course, the material presented in your textbook, *Paralegal Today*. As discussed in the preceding section, reading your textbook assignments before class is one way to enhance your chances of mastering the subject matter of the course. Equally important are listening carefully to your instructor and taking good notes.

Be an Active Listener

The ability to listen actively is a learned skill and one that will benefit you throughout your career as a paralegal. When your supervising attorney gives instructions, it is crucial that you understand those instructions clearly. If you do not, you will need to ask the attorney to clarify the instructions until you know exactly what your assignment is. Similarly, when you are interviewing clients or witnesses, you will need to constantly interact, mentally, with the information the client or witness is giving you so that you can follow up, immediately if necessary, with further questions or actions.

As a student, you can practice listening skills in the classroom that you will need to exercise later on the job. The more immediate benefit of listening actively is, of course, a better chance of obtaining an excellent course grade.

In a nutshell, active listening as a student requires you to do the following:

1. *Listen attentively.* For anything to be communicated verbally by one person to another, the listener has to pay attention. Otherwise, no communication takes place. If you find your attention wandering in the classroom, make a conscious effort to be alert and focus on what is being said.

2. *Mentally interact with what is being said.* Active listening involves mentally "acting" on the information conveyed by the speaker. For example, if your instructor is discussing the elements required for a cause of action in negligence, you do not want simply to write down, word for word, what the instructor is saying. Rather, first make sure that you *understand* the meaning of what is being said. This requires you to think about what is being said in the context of what else you know about the topic. Does the information make sense within that context? Does what you are hearing raise questions in your mind? If so, make a note of them.

3. *Ask for clarification.* If you do not understand what the instructor is saying or if something is confusing, ask for clarification. How you do this will depend to some extent on the size of your class and the degree of classroom formality. In some classes, you might feel comfortable raising your hand and questioning the instructor at that point during the lecture or discussion. In other classes, you might make a note to talk to the instructor about the topic after class or later, during the instructor's office hours.

Take Good Notes

The ability to take good notes is another skill that will help you excel both in your paralegal studies and on the job as a paralegal. Ideally, you will understand everything that is being said in the classroom, and note taking will simply consist of jotting down, in your own words, brief phrases and sentences to remind you of what was stated. Often, however, you may not understand fully what the instructor is talking about, or the class period may be half over before it becomes clear to you where your instructor is going with a certain idea or topic. In the meantime, should you take notes?

The best answer to this question is, of course, "Ask for clarification." But in some situations, interrupting a lecturer may be awkward. In such situations, the wiser choice might be to take notes. Write down, to the extent possible, what the instructor is saying, including brief summaries of any examples the instructor is presenting. Later, when you have more knowledge of the subject, what the instructor said during that period may fall into place. If not, ask for clarification.

Two other suggestions for taking good notes and making effective use of them are the following: (1) develop and use a shorthand system and (2) review and summarize your notes as soon as possible after class.

Develop and Use a Shorthand System

There may be times during a lecture when you want to take extensive notes. For example, your instructor may be discussing a hypothetical scenario to illustrate a legal concept. Because you know that hypothetical examples are useful in understanding (and later reviewing) legal concepts, you want to include a description of the example in your notes. Using abbreviations and symbols can help you include more information in less time.

In taking notes on a hypothetical example, consider using a single letter to represent each person or entity involved in the example. This eliminates the need to write and rewrite the names as they are used. For example, if the example involves three business firms, you could designate each firm by a letter: *A* could stand for Abel Electronics, *B* for Brentwood Manufacturing, and *C* for Crandall Industries.

Certain symbols and abbreviations, including those listed below, are fairly widely used as a kind of "shorthand" by legal professionals and others to designate certain concepts, parties, or procedures:

Δ or **D**	defendant
π or **P**	plaintiff
≈	similar to
≠	not equal to, not the same as
∴	therefore
a/k/a	also known as
atty	attorney
b/c or **b/cz**	because
b/p	burden of proof
cert	*certiorari*
dely	delivery
dep	deposition
disc	discovery
JML	judgment as a matter of law
JNOV	judgment *non obstante veredicto* (notwithstanding the verdict)
JOP	judgment on the pleadings
juris or **jx**	jurisdiction
K	contract
mtg	mortgage
n/a	not applicable
neg	negligence
PL	paralegal
Q	as a consequence, consequently
re	regarding
§ or **sec**	section
s/b	should be
S/F	Statute of Frauds
S/L	statute of limitations

You can expand on this list by creating and using other symbols or abbreviations. Once you develop a workable shorthand system, routinely use it in the classroom and then carry it over to your job. Most organizations you will work for will also use symbols and abbreviations, which you can add to your shorthand system. It may also be helpful to become familiar with proofing symbols, which are listed under "proofreading" in the dictionary.

Review and Revise Your Notes after Each Class

An excellent habit to form is reviewing and revising your class notes as soon as possible after the class period ends. Often, at the moment you write notes, you are not sure of how they fit in the overall design of the lecture. After class, however, you usually have a better perspective and know how the "pieces of the puzzle" fit together. Reviewing and summarizing your notes while the topic is still fresh in your mind—at the end of each day, for example—gives you the opportunity to reorganize them in a logical manner.

Consider typing up your notes. That way, when you want to review them, you will be able to read and revise them quickly. Using a basic outline format when typing your notes will be particularly helpful later. You can understand at a glance the logical relationships between the various statements made in class.

Although reviewing and summarizing your notes may seem overly time consuming, in the long run it pays off. First, as with outlining and marking a text, reviewing your notes after class allows you to learn actively—you can think about what was covered during the class period, place various concepts in perspective, and decide what you do or do not understand after you complete your review. Second, you have probably already learned that memory is fickle. Even though we think we will not forget something we learned, we often do. When preparing for an exam, for example, you will want to remember what the instructor said in class about a particular topic. But, if you are like most people, your memory of that day and that class period may be rather fuzzy several weeks later. If you have taken good notes and summarized them legibly and logically, you will be able to review the topic quickly and effectively.

Networking in the Classroom

Several times in *Paralegal Today,* the authors and the featured contributors mention the importance of networking. The best time to begin networking is now. Consciously make an effort to get to know your instructor. Let him or her come to know you and your interests. Later, when looking for a job, you may want to ask that instructor for a reference.

Similarly, make an effort to become acquainted with other students in your class. Compared with students who are taking other college courses, those in paralegal studies are more likely to be working in the same geographic area and may eventually belong to the same paralegal associations. Establishing connections with your classmates now may lead to networking possibilities later on the job. One good way to establish long-term relationships with other students is by forming a study group.

Forming and Organizing a Study Group

Many paralegal students join study groups to exchange ideas, to share the task of outlining subjects, to prepare for examinations, and to lend support to each other. If you want to start a study group, a good way to find potential members is to observe your classmates and decide which students participate actively and frequently in class. Approach these students with your idea of forming a study group. The number of participants in a study group can vary. Ordinarily, three to five members are enough for a good discussion. Including more than six members may defeat the goal of having each person participate effectively.

Some students form study groups that meet on an "as needed" basis. For example, any member can call a meeting when there is an upcoming exam or difficult subject matter to be learned. Other students establish ongoing study groups that meet throughout the year (and sometimes throughout the entire paralegal program). Study groups can even continue on to prepare for certification exams. The group works as a team and as such is an excellent preparatory device for working as part of a legal team in a law firm. The group also provides a great way to build relationships with other future paralegals with whom you can network later on the job.

Meeting Times and Places

It is helpful to set up a regular meeting time and hold that time sacred. The members must be committed to the meeting times and to completing their assignments, or the group will not serve its purpose. Study groups can meet anywhere. You might meet in a classroom, another school room, a member's home, a park, or a coffee shop. Many paralegal schools have multipurpose rooms or study areas available to students who wish to meet. Some rooms are equipped with easels or drawing boards, which facilitate discussions. Audiovisual equipment may also be available, such as a television with a DVD player for viewing recorded lectures. The group should select a meeting place that has limited distractions and sufficient space to accommodate each member's opened books, notes, and other materials.

Work Allocation

Teamwork is very important in the paralegal profession. Study groups can help you learn to function as a member of a team by distributing the workload among the group. Tasks (such as outlining chapters) should be allocated among the group members. It is important to define clearly who will be doing what work. It may be a good idea at the close of each meeting to have each member state out loud what tasks he or she will be responsible for completing prior to the next meeting. Whatever work one member does, he or she should make copies to distribute to the other members at the meeting.

Evaluating Your Group

You should realize from the outset that your study group will be of little help if you are doing most of the work. You need to make sure that everyone who joins the group is as committed to learning the material as you are and that you make this concern known to the others. The teamwork approach is only effective if everybody contributes. Teamwork involves trust and reliance. If you cannot trust one of the members to form an accurate outline of a topic, you will not be able to rely on that outline. You will end up doing the work yourself, just as a precaution. Therefore, be selective about whom you invite to join the group. If you join an already existing group, leave it if it turns out to be a waste of your time.

ORGANIZING YOUR WORK PRODUCT

The learning experience includes many elements: reading assignments, classroom lectures, special homework assignments, research projects, and possibly study-group meetings. For example, if you are studying pretrial litigation procedures, you will read Chapter 10 of *Paralegal Today*. Your instructor will also devote class time to a discussion of these procedures. Additionally, you may be asked to create a sample complaint or to check your state's rules governing the filing of complaints in state courts. You also might have notes on a study-group discussion of these procedures.

How can you best organize all the materials generated during the coverage of a given topic? Here are a few suggestions that you might find useful. If you follow these suggestions, you will find that reviewing the information before exams is relatively easy—most of the work will already have been done.

Consider Using a Three-Ring Binder

An excellent way to integrate what you have learned is by using a three-ring binder and divider sheets with tabs for the different topics you cover. As you begin studying *Paralegal Today,* for example, consider having a different section in your binder for each chapter. Within that section, you can place your chapter outline, notes taken in the classroom or during other reading assignments, samples of projects relating to topics in that chapter, and the like.

Integrate Your Notes into One Document, If Possible

If you have used a computer to key in your chapter outlines and class notes, consider incorporating everything you have learned about a topic into one document—a master, detailed outline of the topic. You can do this relatively easily by using the "cut and paste" feature of word-processing programs. The result will be a comprehensive outline of a topic that will make reviewing the topic before an exam (and perhaps later, on the job) a simple matter.

THE BENEFITS OF USING A COMPUTER

The text often mentions the importance of computer skills. If you do not already have a personal computer, see if you can arrange to use one on a routine basis. Perhaps your school has computers available for student use.

Using a computer has many benefits. First, you can practice your keyboarding and word-processing skills (essential for paralegals) as you take notes or work on research or other class projects. Second, you can type up and better organize your notes. Such time is well spent because it increases your knowledge of the topics and makes it easy to review prior to exams.

Finally, a key benefit of using a computer is the quality of the work product you submit to your instructor. The editing and formatting features of word-processing programs allow you to correct mistakes, reorganize your presentation, and revise your document with little effort. The spell-checker and grammar-checker features help you avoid glaring errors. The formatting features allow you to present your document in an attractive format. You can change margins and use different fonts (such as italics or boldface) to emphasize certain words or phrases, for example.

As a paralegal, you will be using a word-processing program to generate your work. The more you can learn about computers and word processing as a student, the easier it will be for you to perform your job.

GOING ONLINE

Another benefit of using a computer is the ability to go online and access the vast resources available on the Internet. Chapter 8 of *Paralegal Today,* Fifth Edition, discusses how the Internet is used by legal professionals to obtain information on many topics. Most colleges offer free Internet access to their students. If you do not have a personal computer, check with your school or library to see how you can get access to one.

You can get information online about most of the topics covered in this text. To help you learn how to find and evaluate online information, every chapter ends with Internet exercises in a section titled *Using Internet Resources.* We also provide Internet addresses for numerous Web sites in the margins of the pages. At these Web sites, you will find additional information about the topic being discussed in the text. In the *Technology and Today's Paralegal* features throughout this text, we provide other Web sites when appropriate, and Chapter 8 (Contemporary Online Legal Research) contains numerous references to Web sites that offer useful information for paralegals and other legal professionals.

Internet sites tend to come and go, so there is no guarantee that a site referred to in this text will be there by the time you look for it. We have tried, though, to

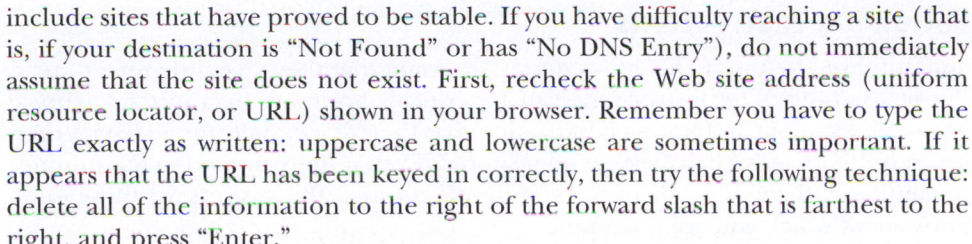

include sites that have proved to be stable. If you have difficulty reaching a site (that is, if your destination is "Not Found" or has "No DNS Entry"), do not immediately assume that the site does not exist. First, recheck the Web site address (uniform resource locator, or URL) shown in your browser. Remember you have to type the URL exactly as written: uppercase and lowercase are sometimes important. If it appears that the URL has been keyed in correctly, then try the following technique: delete all of the information to the right of the forward slash that is farthest to the right, and press "Enter."

PREPARING FOR EXAMS

Being prepared for exams is crucial to doing well as a paralegal student. If you have followed the study tips and suggestions given here, you will have little problem preparing for an exam. You will have at your fingertips detailed outlines of the topics covered, a marked textbook that allows you to review concepts quickly, and class notes. If you have integrated your outlines and class notes in one comprehensive, detailed outline, you will have an even easier task when it comes time to prepare for an examination.

In addition to mastering the material presented in *Paralegal Today* and in the classroom, to do well on an exam you should develop an exam-taking strategy. For example, before any exam, you should find answers to the following questions:

- What type of exam are you going to take—essay, objective, or both?
- What reading materials and lectures will be covered on the exam?
- What materials should you bring to the exam? Will you need paper to write on, or will paper be provided?
- Will you be allowed to refer to your text or notes during the exam (as in an open-book exam)?
- Will the exam be computerized? If so, you will probably need to bring several number 2 pencils to the exam.
- How much time will be allowed for the exam?

The more you can find out in advance about an exam, the better you can prepare for it. Suppose you learn there will be an essay question on the exam. One way to prepare is to practice writing timed essays. In other words, find out how much time you will have for each essay question—say, fifteen minutes—and then practice writing an answer to a sample essay question during a fifteen-minute time period. This is the only way you will develop the skills needed to pace yourself for an essay exam so you don't "run out of time." Because most essay exams are "closed book," do your timed essay practice without using the book.

Usually, you can anticipate certain essay exam questions. You do this by going over the major concept headings in your lecture notes and in your text. Search for the themes that tie the materials together, and then think about questions that your instructor might ask. You might even list possible essay questions and write a short outline for each of the questions most likely to be asked. Some instructors give their students a list of questions from which the essay questions on the exam will be drawn. This gives you an opportunity to prepare answers for each of the questions in advance. Even though you might not be able to use your sample essays when you take the test, you will have organized the material in your mind.

TAKING EXAMS

While taking exams, you can employ several strategies to improve your grade, including those discussed below.

Following Instructions

Students are often in such a hurry to start an exam that they take little time to read the instructions. The instructions can be critical, however. In a multiple-choice exam, for example, if there is no indication that there is a penalty for guessing, then you should never leave a question unanswered. Even if there are only a few minutes remaining at the end of the exam, you should guess at the answers for those questions about which you are uncertain.

You also need to make sure that you are following the specific procedures required for the exam. Some exams require that you use a number 2 lead pencil to fill in the dots on a machine-graded answer sheet. Other exams require underlining or circling. In short, read the instructions carefully.

Finally, check to make sure that you have all the pages of the examination and have put your name on it. If you are uncertain if all the pages are in your copy of the exam, ask the instructor or the exam proctor. Simply claiming later that you did not have all the pages will pose a problem for both you and your instructor. Do not take a chance. Double-check to make sure.

Use Exam Time Effectively

Examinations are often timed. In other words, you must answer a question or cluster of questions within a specified time period. If you must complete thirty multiple-choice questions in one hour, then you have two minutes to work on each question. If you finish fifteen of those questions in fifteen minutes, then you will have banked fifteen minutes that can be spent elsewhere on the examination or used to double-check your answers.

Consider the following example. Assume that you have ninety minutes for the entire exam—thirty minutes to answer the multiple-choice questions, fifteen minutes to answer the true-false questions, and forty-five minutes to answer a long essay question. If you can shave ten minutes off the time it takes to answer the multiple-choice section and five minutes off the time it takes to answer the true-false questions, you will have fifteen additional minutes to complete the long essay question.

Taking Objective Examinations

The most important point to discover initially with any objective test, such as a multiple-choice test, is whether there is a penalty for guessing. If there is none, you have nothing to lose by guessing. In contrast, if a point or portion of a point will be subtracted for each incorrect answer, then you probably should not answer any question purely through guesswork.

Students usually commit one of two errors when they read objective-exam questions: (1) they read things into the questions that do not exist, or (2) they skip over certain words or phrases.

Most test questions include key words such as:

- all
- always
- never
- only

If you miss these key words, you will be missing the "trick" part of the question. Also, you must look for questions that are only *partly* correct, particularly if you are answering true/false questions.

Never answer a multiple-choice question without reading all of the alternatives. More than one of them may appear at first glance to be correct. If several answers seem correct, make sure you select the one that seems the *most* correct.

Whenever the answer to an objective question is not obvious, start with the process of elimination. Throw out the answers that are clearly incorrect. Even when there is a penalty for guessing, if you can throw out several obviously incorrect answers, you may wish to guess by choosing among the remaining ones because your probability of choosing the correct answer is relatively high. Typically, the easiest way to eliminate incorrect answers is to look for those that are meaningless, illogical, or inconsistent. Often, test authors put in choices that make perfect sense and are indeed true but are not the answer to the question you are to answer.

Writing Essay Exams

As with objective exams, you need to read the directions for essay exams carefully. It is best to write out a brief outline *before* you start answering the question. This will give you the chance to organize your thoughts better. The outline should present your conclusion in one or two sentences, then your supporting argument. Take care not to include in your essay information that is irrelevant, even if you think it is interesting. It is important to stay on the subject. We can tell you from firsthand experience that no instructor likes to read answers to unasked questions.

Finally, write as legibly as possible. Instructors will find it easier to be favorably inclined toward your essay if they do not have to reread it several times to decipher the handwriting.

THE PARALEGAL PROFESSION

PART

1

CHAPTER 1

Today's Professional Paralegal

CHAPTER 2

Career Opportunities

CHAPTER 3

The Inner Workings of the Law Office

CHAPTER 4

Ethics and Professional Responsibility

CHAPTER 5

Sources of American Law

CHAPTER 6

The Court System and Alternative Dispute Resolution

TODAY'S PROFESSIONAL PARALEGAL

CHAPTER OUTLINE

Introduction

What Is a Paralegal?

What Do Paralegals Do?

Paralegal Education

Paralegal Skills and Attributes

The Future of the Profession

AFTER COMPLETING THIS CHAPTER, YOU WILL KNOW:

- ▶ What a paralegal is.
- ▶ What kinds of tasks paralegals perform.
- ▶ The names of some of the professional associations of paralegals.
- ▶ What kinds of education and training are available to paralegals.
- ▶ Whether paralegals must be certified or licensed.
- ▶ Some skills and attributes of the professional paralegal.

INTRODUCTION

If you are considering a career as a paralegal, be prepared to be part of an exciting and growing profession. Over time, law firms have been giving more and more responsibilities to paralegals. The opportunities for paralegals who want to work outside of law firms (in corporations or government agencies, for example) are also expanding. As the profession has grown, the average paralegal salary has increased. According to one survey, in 2009 paralegals earned average compensation of $54,859.[1]

How do you know if you want to become part of this dynamic profession? The first step in finding out is to become familiar with what a paralegal is, what kinds of work paralegals do, and what education and skills are needed. These are the topics covered in this chapter. In Chapter 2, you will learn about where paralegals work, how much they earn, and how they got their jobs. As you read through the chapters in this book, remember that this is only an introduction to the profession and the starting point of your education. You should supplement what you learn in the classroom by talking and networking with paralegals who work in various professional environments. After all, in today's competitive job market, whom you know can sometimes be as important as what you know in getting the job you desire.

WHAT IS A PARALEGAL?

The issue of how, exactly, the term *paralegal* should be defined has been debated for years. The word has been commonly used since the 1970s. This debate probably stems from the fact that paralegals perform such a wide variety of duties that it is difficult to come up with a "one-size-fits-all" definition. Adding to the problem is the use of two different labels—*paralegal* and *legal assistant*—to describe essentially the same job or person. These different labels often confuse the public and have fueled debates within the profession.

In this book, we use the terms *paralegal* and *legal assistant* interchangeably, as is often done in the legal community. Although some people or groups may prefer one label over the other, such disagreement does not mean that the labels describe different job duties. Indeed, some persons who are trained professional paralegals may be called something else entirely at their workplace, such as *legal technician* or *legal research specialist.*

After years of disagreement, two of the major organizations involved reached a consensus on the definition of paralegal. The **American Bar Association (ABA)**, which is a national association for attorneys, and the **National Association of Legal Assistants (NALA)**, which is the largest national organization of paralegals, now jointly agree to the following definition:

> A **legal assistant** or **paralegal** is a person qualified by education, training, or work experience who is employed or retained by a lawyer, law office, corporation, governmental agency or other entity who performs specifically delegated substantive legal work, for which a lawyer is responsible.

The **National Federation of Paralegal Associations (NFPA)**, which is the second largest paralegal association, prefers the term *paralegal* to *legal assistant.*[2] Members of NFPA were concerned by the fact that many attorneys refer to their secretaries as legal assistants and wanted to distinguish the role of paralegals as professionals. The NFPA gives the following definition for *paralegal:*

> A Paralegal is a person, qualified through education, training or work experience to perform substantive legal work that requires knowledge of legal concepts and is customarily, but not exclusively, performed by a lawyer. This person may be retained or employed by a lawyer, law office, governmental agency or other entity or may be authorized by administrative, statutory or court authority to perform this work. Substantive shall mean work requiring recognition, evaluation, organization, analysis, and communication of relevant facts and legal concepts.

American Bar Association (ABA)
A voluntary national association of attorneys. The ABA plays an active role in developing educational and ethical standards for attorneys and in pursuing improvements in the administration of justice.

National Association of Legal Assistants (NALA)
One of the two largest national paralegal associations in the United States; formed in 1975. NALA is actively involved in paralegal professional development.

paralegal or legal assistant
A person qualified by education, training, or work experience who is employed or retained by a lawyer, law office, corporation, governmental agency, or other entity and who performs specifically delegated substantive legal work, for which a lawyer is responsible.

National Federation of Paralegal Associations (NFPA)
One of the two largest national paralegal associations in the United States; formed in 1974. NFPA is actively involved in paralegal professional development.

American Association for Paralegal Education (AAfPE)
A national organization of paralegal educators; the AAfPE was established in 1981 to promote high standards for paralegal education.

Another major organization, the **American Association for Paralegal Education (AAfPE)**, provides the following definition:

> Paralegals perform substantive and procedural legal work as authorized by law, which work, in the absence of the paralegal, would be performed by an attorney. Paralegals have knowledge of the law gained through education, or education and work experience, which qualifies them to perform legal work. Paralegals adhere to recognized ethical standards and rules of professional responsibility.

Regardless of which term is used, paralegals or legal assistants today perform many functions that traditionally were performed by attorneys. The paralegal's work falls somewhere between that of an attorney and that of a legal secretary. As the definitions above indicate, paralegals perform substantive legal work that they are trained to perform through education, experience, or (usually) both.

WHAT DO PARALEGALS DO?

Paralegals assist attorneys in many different ways. The following list is a sampling of some of the tasks that legal assistants typically perform in a traditional setting—the law office. Keep in mind, though, that today's paralegals work in many nontraditional settings, including corporations, government agencies, courts, insurance companies, real estate firms, and almost any other entity that uses legal services. Throughout this book, you will read about the specific tasks that paralegals perform in different settings.

A Sampling of Paralegal Tasks

Typically, legal assistants perform the following tasks:

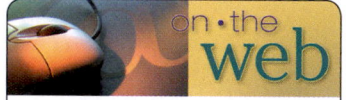

For more information on the definitions of *paralegal* and *legal assistant* given by the ABA, NALA, NFPA, and AAfPE, go to the following Web sites:

ABA: **www.abanet.org**
NALA: **www.nala.org**
NFPA: **www.paralegals.org**
AAfPE: **www.aafpe.org**

- *Conduct client interviews and maintain contact with clients*—provided that the client is aware of the status and function of the legal assistant and the legal assistant does not give legal advice (see the *Ethics Watch* feature).

- *Locate and interview witnesses*—to gather relevant facts and information about a lawsuit, for example.

- *Conduct legal investigations*—to obtain, organize, and evaluate information from a variety of sources, such as police reports, medical records, photographs, court documents, experts' reports, technical manuals, product specifications, and other statistical data.

- *Calendar and track important deadlines*—such as the date by which a certain document must be filed with the court or the date by which the attorney must respond to a settlement offer.

- *Organize and maintain client files*—to keep the many documents in each client's file readily accessible.

- *Conduct legal research*—to identify, analyze, and summarize the appropriate laws, court decisions, or regulations that apply to a client's case.

- *Draft legal documents*—such as legal correspondence, interoffice memoranda, documents to be filed with the court, contracts, wills, and mortgages.

- *File legal documents with courts*—such as complaints, answers, and motions; these documents may be filed electronically.

- *Summarize witness testimony*—such as when depositions (sworn testimony) are taken of individuals out of court or when the parties have given written statements.

- *Coordinate litigation proceedings*—communicate with opposing counsel, court personnel, and other government officials; prepare all necessary documents for trial; and schedule witnesses.

Ethics Watch

PARALEGAL EXPERTISE AND LEGAL ADVICE

Paralegals often gain a great deal of knowledge in specific areas of the law. If you specialize in environmental law, for example, you will become very knowledgeable about environmental claims. In working with a client on a matter involving an environmental agency, you might therefore be tempted to advise the client on which type of action would be most favorable to him or her. Never do so. As will be discussed in detail in Chapter 4, only attorneys may give legal advice, and paralegals who give legal advice risk penalties for the unauthorized practice of law. Whatever legal advice is given to the client either must come directly from the attorney or, if from you, must reflect exactly (or nearly exactly) what the attorney said with no modification on your part and must be communicated to the client as directed by the attorney. After consulting with your supervising attorney, for example, you can say to the client that Mr. X (the attorney) "advises that you do all that you can to settle the claim as soon as possible."

The rule prohibiting the unauthorized practice of law is stated in Section 1.8 of the NFPA *Model Code of Ethics and Professional Responsibility:* "A paralegal shall comply with the applicable legal authority governing the unauthorized practice of law in the jurisdiction in which the paralegal practices." It is also required by the NALA *Code of Ethics and Professional Responsibility* Canon 4: "A paralegal must use discretion and professional judgment commensurate with knowledge and experience but must not render independent legal judgment in place of an attorney."

- *Attend legal proceedings*—such as trials, depositions, real estate closings, executions of wills, and court or administrative hearings—with an attorney.
- *Use computers and technology*—to perform many of the above tasks.

Paralegals' Duties Vary

The specific tasks that paralegals perform vary dramatically depending on the size of the office, the kind of law that the firm practices, and the amount of experience or expertise the paralegal has. If you work in a one-attorney office, for example, you may also perform certain secretarial functions. Your tasks might range from conducting legal research and investigating the facts to photocopying documents, keying data into the computer, and answering the telephone while the secretary is out to lunch. If you work in a larger law firm, you usually have more support staff (secretaries, file clerks, and others) to whom you can delegate tasks. Your work may also be more specialized, so you work on only certain types of cases. If you work in a law firm's real estate department, for example, you may deal only with legal matters relating to that area of law. (For a discussion of tasks that a paralegal might perform at a personal-injury law firm, see this chapter's *Featured Contributor* feature on the following two pages.)

Although paralegal duties vary, drafting legal documents, handling client relations, and conducting legal research are the tasks that paralegals report spending the most time performing.[3]

featured contributor

THE PARALEGAL AT WORK

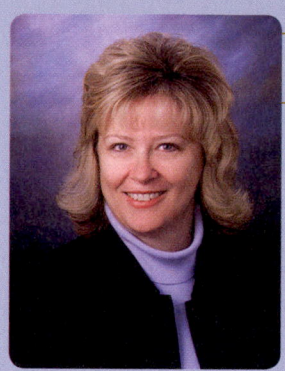

Sally B. Bisson

BIOGRAPHICAL NOTE

Sally Brown Bisson, J.D., received her bachelor of arts degree in communication and English from the University of Nebraska at Omaha in 1978 and her law degree from the University of Nebraska College of Law in 1981. She worked for a regional banking corporation and numerous nonprofit organizations before becoming a paralegal instructor in 1992. She is currently an associate professor and director of the ABA-approved paralegal studies program at the College of Saint Mary in Omaha, Nebraska, where she teaches family law, litigation, and real estate law and directs the internship program. She is also the campus pre-law adviser. In addition to her teaching responsibilities, she serves as a reviewer for several legal publishers and has been a presenter at local, state, and national paralegal conferences.

I magine that you have just graduated from a paralegal program and are starting work at your first job at the Morris and Buckley law firm. It is a personal-injury law firm that represents plaintiffs and employs seven attorneys and two paralegals. Your supervising attorney, Melanie Buckley, will be meeting with a new client, Barbara Kaiser, and has asked you to sit in on the interview.

THE FACTS

Barbara Kaiser was employed by a local plant and garden nursery when she was injured in a car accident on April 4, 2009. On the day of the accident, she was not scheduled to work, and a severe thunderstorm occurred. The greenhouse at the nursery was damaged by the storm. Another employee called Kaiser and told her that the greenhouse was flooding and its roof was damaged. Kaiser told the employee that she would help by purchasing new roofing material and a pump to remove the water.

Kaiser drove her own car as she left the house to purchase the necessary supplies. She lost control of her vehicle near a stoplight and collided with a utility company truck that was speeding on its way to repair a power outage. Kaiser was trapped in her car and suffered serious injuries, including broken bones and a back injury. She spent several weeks in the hospital recovering from the accident.

Kaiser has been unable to work and has lost her job. It has been five months since the accident. She applied for workers' compensation benefits from the state, but they were denied because the state determined she was not working when the accident occurred. The utility company's insurance company has paid her hospital expenses but has refused to pay for continuing therapy for her back pain. Kaiser wants the law firm to advise her as to whether she can sue her former employer, the state, and/or the utility company to obtain compensation for her injuries.

Paralegals and Technology

Many legal assistants have become the technology experts at law firms. Because lawyers are busy with the practice of law, paralegals are often in the best position to know the firm's needs. Increasingly, paralegals take a leading role in reviewing and recommending new specialized legal software programs and online databases.

Needless to say, computer skills and technical knowledge are highly valued. Paralegals use software packages for internal case management to organize client files, manage calendars, share research, record reference materials, and track the number of hours to be billed to clients. Attorneys and paralegals use time and billing software to manage expenses, generate bills, calculate accounts receivable, and produce financial reports. Legal databases available on the Internet or on CD-ROMs allow paralegals to perform sophisticated legal research at their desks. When

THE PARALEGAL'S ROLE—CASE MANAGEMENT

One of the first things you will do is open a case file for Barbara Kaiser. Many law firms use litigation support software for this function so that the file will be easily accessible. You will need to enter contact information for the client, her employer, the driver of the utility truck, the utility company, and the insurance companies that are involved in the case. You will also need to keep track of the time you spend on the case and include a description of the activities you perform for accurate billing.

Client Relations, Legal Research, and Investigation. Paralegals generally have a great deal of contact with clients, keeping them informed about the status of their cases and answering questions. You will be expected to provide appropriate updates to the client but must be careful to ensure you are not providing legal advice. If legal advice is requested, check with your supervising attorney, and then share the response with the client.

Attorney Buckley may ask you to help evaluate the viability of Kaiser's claim. You may be asked to research applicable statutes and case law and prepare a summary of your findings in a written memorandum. Your investigation of her claim could also include interviewing witnesses, obtaining copies of police and hospital records, and visiting the accident scene to take photographs. You may also be asked to verify the exact weather conditions that existed at the time of the accident. All of the information you gather during this phase of the case must be documented and included in the client's file.

Initiating the Lawsuit and Trial Preparation. Once the attorney has determined that there is a basis for the client's claims, you may be asked to prepare the document that initiates a lawsuit, called a *complaint*. The complaint will be taken to the courthouse and then delivered or mailed to the defendants. The filing of the complaint triggers a variety of due dates in the litigation process, so it is essential that you accurately record the applicable dates in the case management system.

The next step in the litigation process is called *discovery*. During this time, the parties to the lawsuit obtain as much information as possible from each other and from outside sources to prove their case. You may be asked to draft various discovery documents and respond to requests from the defendants.

Before scheduling a trial date, attorney Buckley is likely to try to reach an agreement with the defendant to have the defendant compensate Buckley's client without a trial. This process, called a *settlement,* is encouraged by judges to avoid unnecessary trials. You may be asked to prepare a settlement brochure that outlines your client's injuries and economic losses for presentation to the defendant's attorney.

> "Paralegals . . . are an important part of the litigation team."

Assisting at Trial. If a trial is necessary, you will be responsible for contacting the client and all of your witnesses regarding the trial date and their testimony. You may also be asked to assist with the preparation of evidence that will be used at trial and to prepare a trial notebook. It will contain all of the litigation documents and can be prepared in a written or electronic format. During the trial, you may be asked to assist the attorney in the courtroom.

As you can see, your role in the litigation process is vital to the successful representation of the client's interests. Paralegals who are organized, are proficient in the use of technology, and possess strong communication skills are an important part of the litigation team.

cases that involve many documents must be prepared for trial, litigation support software can help retrieve, categorize, and index the various materials for presentation. These technologies are discussed in the appropriate chapters throughout this book. The point here is that technology is one of the foremost areas of expanding paralegal responsibility, and those entering the profession should know that technological skills will greatly enhance their marketability.

PARALEGAL EDUCATION

The first paralegals were competent legal secretaries who learned from on-the-job training how to perform more complex legal tasks given to them by the attorneys for whom they worked. No formal paralegal education programs existed until the

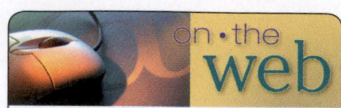

The Web site for the ABA's Standing Committee on Paralegals is **www.abanet.org**. Search on "paralegals," then go to American Bar Association Standing Committee on Paralegals.

(*Note:* No Web address ever ends in a comma, period, or semicolon. Consequently, you should ignore such punctuation when it appears at the end of Web addresses cited in this book.)

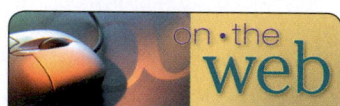

Information on paralegal education programs is available on both the NALA and NFPA Web sites at **www.nala.org** and **www.paralegals.org**.

late 1960s, when the demand for lower-cost legal services increased. Once attorneys realized that using paralegals was cost-effective and benefited both the client and the firm (as you will read in Chapter 3), the number of paralegal education programs increased dramatically. According to the ABA's Standing Committee on Paralegals (formerly known as the ABA Standing Committee on Legal Assistants), there are now more than a thousand programs operating in the United States. A great deal of variety exists, however, in the types of programs offered and the quality of the education provided.

Educational Options

The role of higher education and formal paralegal education has become increasingly important in the growth and development of the paralegal profession. Many colleges, universities, and business and private schools now offer programs. Generally, paralegal education programs fall into one of five categories:

- Two-year community college programs, leading to the award of an associate of arts degree or a paralegal certificate. Such programs usually require the completion of about 60 semester hours and include some general education requirements.

- Four-year bachelor's degree programs with a major or minor in paralegal studies. A bachelor's degree in paralegal studies usually requires about 120 semester hours, with 50 to 60 of these hours spent on general education courses. A person may select a minor field that enhances her or his desirability in the job market. Conversely, a student who majors in another field—for example, nursing—and obtains a minor in paralegal studies will also be very marketable to potential employers.

- Certificate programs offered by private institutions, usually three to eighteen months in length. Typically, these programs require a high school diploma or the equivalent for admission.

- Postgraduate certificate programs, usually three to twelve months in length, resulting in the award of a paralegal certificate. These programs require that the student already have a bachelor's degree in order to be admitted; some also require that the student have achieved a certain grade point average.

- Master's degree programs, usually two years in length, which are offered by several universities. These programs prepare students to work as paralegals, paralegal supervisors, or law office administrators. Some programs offer specific concentrations—for example, dispute resolution or intellectual property. To be admitted to a master's degree program, a student must have a bachelor's degree.

Because those seeking to become paralegals have diverse educational backgrounds, capabilities, and work experience, no one program is best for everyone. Which program is most appropriate depends on personal needs and preferences.

Curriculum—A Blend of Substantive and Procedural Law

A legal assistant's education includes the study of both substantive law and procedural law. **Substantive law** includes all laws that define, describe, regulate, and create legal rights and obligations. For example, a law prohibiting employment discrimination on the basis of age falls into the category of substantive law. **Procedural law** establishes the methods of enforcing the rights established by substantive law. Questions about what documents need to be filed to begin a lawsuit, when the documents should be filed, which court will hear the case, which witnesses will be called, and the like are all procedural law questions. In brief, substantive law defines our legal rights and obligations; procedural law specifies what methods, or procedures, must be employed to enforce those rights and obligations.

substantive law
Law that defines the rights and duties of individuals with respect to each other, as opposed to procedural law, which defines the manner in which rights and duties are enforced.

procedural law
Rules that define the manner in which the rights and duties of individuals are enforced.

The Role of the AAfPE and ABA in Paralegal Education

The American Association for Paralegal Education (AAfPE) was formed by educators in 1981 to promote high standards for paralegal education. The AAfPE and the ABA are the two major organizations responsible for developing the standards and curriculum for paralegal education programs across the nation. California was the first state to require a paralegal to meet certain minimum educational requirements.[4] Although most states do not have such requirements, many employers either require or prefer job candidates with a certain level of education. Some employers select only graduates from established programs. A searchable database of schools offering paralegal programs is available at the AAfPE Web site, at **www.aafpe.org**, in the "Find a School" menu.

In 1974, the ABA first established a set of educational standards for paralegal training programs. Since then, the ABA guidelines have been revised several times to keep pace with changes in the paralegal profession. Paralegal schools are not required to be approved by the ABA. Rather, ABA approval is a voluntary process that gives extra credibility to the schools that successfully apply for it. Programs that meet the ABA's quality standards and that are approved by the ABA are usually referred to as **ABA-approved programs**. Of the paralegal education programs in existence today, approximately 250 have chosen to seek ABA approval.

Certification

Certification refers to formal recognition by a professional group or state agency that a person has met certain standards of ability specified by that group. Generally, this means passing an examination given by the organization and meeting certain requirements with respect to education and/or experience. Note that the term *certification*, as used here, does not refer to receiving a paralegal certificate. You may obtain a paralegal certificate after completing school, but you will not be considered a *certified paralegal* unless you complete the NALA, NFPA, NALS, AAPI, or state certification process. These certification programs are discussed in the following paragraphs. Currently, no state *requires* paralegals to take a certification examination. Although most employers also do not require certification, earning a voluntary certificate from a professional society or the state can offer a competitive advantage in the labor market and lead to a higher salary (see Chapter 2).

NALA and NFPA Certification

Paralegals who meet the background standards set by NALA are eligible to take a two-day, comprehensive examination to become a **Certified Legal Assistant (CLA)** or, since 2004, a **Certified Paralegal (CP)**, for those who prefer to use the term *paralegal*. NALA also sponsors the **Advanced Paralegal Certification (APC)** program (before 2006, this was called the Certified Legal Assistant Specialty, or CLAS). The APC program provides a series of courses composed of text lessons, slides, exercises, and interactive tests via the Internet. NALA offers APC certification to those who are already CLAs or CPs and who want to demonstrate special competence in a particular field of law.[5] Appendix G provides more detailed information on NALA certification and requirements.

Paralegals who have at least two years of work experience and who have met specific educational requirements can take the Paralegal Advanced Competency Exam (PACE) through NFPA. The PACE is broken down into two tests, one on general issues and ethics and one on specialty areas. Those who pass the examination use the designation **Registered Paralegal (RP)**. Further information on the PACE program is provided in Appendix H of this book.

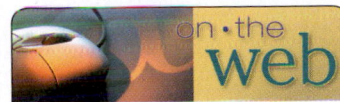

You can learn more about the APC program at the NALA Web site at **www.nala.org**.

From the "Certification" menu, select "Advanced Paralegal Certification."

For more information on NFPA's PACE program, go to **www.paralegals.org**. From the menu, select "PACE/RP."

ABA-approved program

A legal or paralegal educational program that satisfies the standards for paralegal training set forth by the American Bar Association.

certification

Formal recognition by a private group or a state agency that a person has satisfied the group's standards of ability, knowledge, and competence; ordinarily accomplished through the taking of an examination.

Certified Legal Assistant (CLA) or Certified Paralegal (CP)

A legal assistant whose legal competency has been certified by the National Association of Legal Assistants (NALA) following an examination that tests the legal assistant's knowledge and skills.

Advanced Paralegal Certification (APC)

A credential awarded by the National Association of Legal Assistants to a Certified Paralegal (CP) or Certified Legal Assistant (CLA) whose competency in a legal specialty has been certified based on an examination of the paralegal's knowledge and skills in the specialty area.

Registered Paralegal (RP)

A paralegal whose competency has been certified by the National Federation of Paralegal Associations (NFPA) after successful completion of the Paralegal Advanced Competency Exam (PACE).

Certification by Other Paralegal Organizations

NALS (the association for legal professionals)[6] offers three different certifications:

- Paralegals who have completed an accredited curriculum course or who have one year of work experience may take the basic certification exam (ALS) for legal professionals.

- Paralegals who have three years of work experience or who have earned a prior certification may take the advanced certification exam (PLS) for legal professionals.

- Paralegals who have five years of work experience may take an examination to obtain Professional Paralegal (PP) certification, which was developed by paralegals.

The American Alliance of Paralegals, Inc. (AAPI), also provides a Paralegal Certification Program for paralegals who possess at least five years of work experience and have met specific educational requirements.

State Certification

Several states, including California, Florida, Louisiana, North Carolina, Ohio, and Texas, have implemented voluntary, state-specific certification programs. Details for state programs can be found on the Internet; for example, for Texas, see **www.tbls.org**. Some state bar associations have information on certification as well. For example, for Ohio, see **www.ohiobar.org**. Other states are considering implementing such programs. Generally, paralegal organizations (such as NALA) are in favor of *voluntary* certification and oppose *mandatory* (legally required) certification or state licensing (as you will read in Chapter 4).

Continuing Legal Education

Paralegals, like attorneys, often supplement their formal education by attending **continuing legal education (CLE) programs**. CLE courses, which are offered by state bar associations and paralegal associations, are usually seminars and workshops that focus on specific topics or areas of law. Such programs are a good way to learn more about a specialized area of law or keep up to date on the latest developments in the law and in technology. Many employers encourage their paralegals to take CLE courses and often pay some or all of the costs involved.[7]

Additionally, some paralegal organizations require their members to complete a certain number of CLE hours per year as a condition of membership. Both NALA and NFPA require paralegals who are certified to take CLE courses every year in order to maintain their certification status. The NFPA requires certified paralegals to complete twelve hours of continuing education every two years. California requires a minimum number of CLE hours from *all* persons who work as paralegals. Paralegals in California are required to complete four CLE hours in legal ethics every three years and four CLE hours in either general law or a specialized area of law every two years.[8]

PARALEGAL SKILLS AND ATTRIBUTES

As noted earlier, paralegals today perform many tasks that lawyers have customarily performed. Thus, the demands on paralegals to be professional and efficient have increased. To be successful, a paralegal not only must possess specific legal knowledge but also should exhibit certain aptitudes and personality traits. For example, paralegals need to be able to think logically and to analyze complex issues of law and conflicting descriptions of fact. Being well organized is a part of this, as the *In the Office* feature discusses. Some general characteristics that paralegals should have (or try to develop) are discussed below.

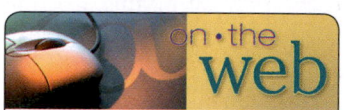

NALA provides an online campus for continuing legal education (CLE) at **www.nalacampus.com**.

For information on NFPA's online CLE offerings, go to **www.paralegals.org**.

From the menu, select "CLE."

continuing legal education (CLE) programs
Courses through which attorneys and other legal professionals extend their education beyond school.

In the **Office**

USE TIME WISELY

Paralegals often work on many cases at once. To be responsive to job requirements and to meet the needs of clients, set aside a little time each day to review the demands on your time. Think about what must be done that day as well as what must be completed over time to meet deadlines. Make a list of what you need to accomplish; the list might be built into your calendaring software. Each morning, reevaluate what you got done the day before. If work was not completed, think about why. When working on multiple cases, it is critical to understand what must be accomplished on each case so that one deadline does not "sneak up" on you while you are paying attention to another.

Analytical Skills

In any working environment, paralegals may be responsible for gathering and analyzing certain types of data. A corporate paralegal, for example, may be required to analyze new government regulations to see how they will affect the corporation. A paralegal working for the Environmental Protection Agency may be responsible for collecting and analyzing data on toxic waste disposal and drafting a memo setting forth conclusions on the matter.

Legal professionals need to be able to take complex theories and fact patterns and break them down into smaller, more easily understandable components. That is how lawyers formulate arguments and judges decide cases. The process of legal analysis is critical to the paralegal's duties, especially when the paralegal is engaged in factual investigation, trial preparation, and legal research and writing. Analytical reasoning will be discussed in greater depth in Chapters 7 and 9 of this book. For now, it is important that you focus on developing a step-by-step approach to tackling each new subject or task that you encounter. Making analytical thinking a habit will improve your proficiency as a legal assistant.

Communication Skills

Good communication skills are critical to people working in the legal area. It is sometimes said that the legal profession is a "communications profession" because effective legal representation depends to a great extent on how well a legal professional can communicate with clients, witnesses, court judges and juries, opposing attorneys, and others. Poor communication can damage a case, destroy a client relationship, and harm the legal professional's reputation. Good communication, in contrast, wins cases, clients, and sometimes promotions.

Communication skills include reading skills, speaking skills, listening skills, and writing skills. We look briefly at each of these skills here. Although we focus on communication skills in the law office setting, realize that good communication skills are essential to success in any work environment.

Reading Skills

Reading skills involve more than just being able to understand the meaning of written letters and words. Reading skills also involve understanding the *meaning* of a sentence, paragraph, section, or page. As a legal professional, you need to be able to read and comprehend many different types of written materials, including statutes and court decisions. You therefore need to be familiar with legal terminology and concepts so that you know the meaning of these legal writings. You also need to develop the ability to read documents *carefully* so that you do not miss important distinctions, such as the difference in meaning that can result from the use of *and* instead of *or*. The importance of proofreading as a reading skill is highlighted in the *Developing Paralegal Skills* feature.

Speaking Skills

Paralegals must be able to speak well. In addition to using correct grammar, legal assistants need to be precise and clear in communicating ideas or facts to others. For example, when you discuss facts learned in an investigation with your supervising attorney, your oral report must explain exactly what you found, or it could mislead the attorney. A miscommunication in this context could have serious consequences if it leads the attorney to take an action that harms the client's interests. Oral communication also has a nonverbal dimension—that is, we communicate our thoughts and feelings through gestures, facial expressions, and other "body language."

Listening Skills

Good listening skills are an important part of paralegal work. Instructions must be followed carefully. To understand instructions, you must listen to them carefully. Asking follow-up questions helps to clarify anything that you do not understand. In addition, repeating the instructions not only ensures that you understand them but also gives the attorney a chance to add anything that may have been forgotten initially. Listening skills are particularly important in the interviewing context. In Chapter 11, you will read in detail about various listening skills and techniques that will help you conduct effective interviews.

Writing Skills

Finally, it is important for paralegals to have good writing skills. Legal assistants draft letters, memoranda, and a variety of legal documents. Letters to clients, witnesses, court clerks, and others must be clear and well organized and must follow

Excellent reading skills are a plus in any profession, but they are especially important in the legal arena. As a paralegal, you must be able not only to read well but also to interpret what you are reading, whether it be a statute, a court's decision, or a contract's provision. What other important skills should every paralegal acquire?

(Courtesy of © PhotoAlto™)

Developing Paralegal Skills

PROOFREADING LEGAL DOCUMENTS

Geena Northrop, a paralegal, works for a solo practitioner (a one-attorney law firm). Among her other duties, she handles a significant part of the legal writing for the attorney who owns the firm. Geena has learned that when creating a legal document, writing the document is only half the job. The rest is proofreading—and not just once. She has learned the hard way that one proofreading is simply not enough to catch every error. Now she has adopted the motto of one of the instructors in her paralegal program: "Proof, proof, and proof again!"

Today, she has set aside some time to proofread carefully a last will and testament that her supervising attorney and she created for one of the firm's clients. Geena prints out a copy of the document for proofreading purposes, because she has learned that it is difficult to proofread a document on a computer screen. Moreover, style and formatting problems are often not as evident on even a high-resolution screen as they are on hard copy.

Her first step in proofreading the document is to make sure that the document reflects all of the relevant information from her notes. Geena reviews her notes point by point from the client interview and from her later discussion with the attorney about the will and checks the document. All looks well in this respect, so she proceeds to her second step in proofreading: checking style and format. Are all of the headings in the correct size and font? Is the spacing between headings consistent? Are all of the paragraphs properly indented? She finds a couple of problems and marks her hard copy to make the appropriate changes. She then reads through the document word for word to ensure that there are no grammatical problems, spelling errors, or typos. Finally, she revises the document on her computer, prints it out, and takes it to the attorney for his review.

CHECKLIST FOR PROOFREADING LEGAL DOCUMENTS

- When you create a legal document, do not assume that one proofreading will be sufficient to catch all problems or errors that the document may contain.
- Read through the document again to make sure that the style and formatting elements are consistent throughout.
- Print out the document, and go through the contents line by line to make sure that it includes all required or relevant information.
- Finally, read through the document word for word to ensure that it is free of grammatical errors, misspelled words, and typos.

the rules of grammar and punctuation. Legal documents must also be free of errors. Lawyers are generally very attentive to detail in their work, and they expect legal assistants to be equally so. Remember, you represent your supervising attorney when you write. You will learn more about writing skills in Chapter 9.

Computer Skills

In any workplace today, computer skills are essential. At a minimum, you will be expected to have experience with word processing (generating and revising documents using a computer) and to have some data-entry skills. Paralegals who are well versed in computer technology will increasingly have an edge in the job market over those who are not. Already, some of the best-paying paralegal positions are held by paralegal specialists who know how to use sophisticated computer equipment and software, such as database-management systems, and how to adapt new technology to their workplace needs to improve efficiency.

We cannot stress enough that to become a successful paralegal, the best thing you can do during your training is to become as knowledgeable as possible about computer technology, including online communications. Throughout this book, you will read about how technology is being applied to all areas of legal practice. You will also learn how you can use technology, particularly the Internet, to perform various paralegal tasks and to keep up to date on the law. (See this chapter's *Technology and Today's Paralegal* feature for some online resources for paralegals.) As technology continues to advance, high-tech paralegals will increasingly be in demand.

Organizational Skills

Being a well-organized person is a plus for a legal assistant. Law offices are busy places. There are phone calls to be answered and returned, witnesses to get to court and on the witness stand on time, documents to be filed, and checklists and procedures to be followed. If you are able to organize files, create procedures and checklists, and keep things running smoothly, you will be doing a great service to the legal team and to clients.

If you work in a nontraditional setting, such as for a corporation or for the government, you will similarly find that good organizational skills are the key to success. No matter where you work, you will need to organize files, data, and—most important—your time.

If organization comes naturally to you, you are ahead of the game. If not, now is the time to learn and practice organizational skills. You will find plenty of opportunities to do this as a paralegal student—by organizing your notebooks, devising an efficient tracking system for homework assignments, creating a study or work schedule and following it, and the like. Other suggestions for organizing your time and work, both as a student and as a paralegal on the job, are included in the **Introduction to the Student** placed before Chapter 1. You will also find in any library many books that offer guidelines on how to efficiently organize your work, your use of time, and your life generally.

Interpersonal Skills

The ability to communicate and interact effectively with other people is an important asset for the paralegal. Paralegals work closely with their supervising attorneys, and the capacity to develop a positive working relationship helps get tasks done more efficiently. Paralegals also work with legal secretaries and other support staff in the law office, with attorneys and paralegals from other firms, with court personnel, and with many other people. Paralegals frequently interview clients and witnesses. As you will read in Chapter 11, if you can relate well to the person whom you are interviewing, your chances of obtaining useful information are increased (see the *Developing Paralegal Skills* feature on page 16 for more on interviews).

There may be times when you will have to deal with clients who are experiencing difficulties in their lives, such as a divorce or the death of a loved one. These people will need to be handled with sensitivity, understanding, and courtesy. There will also be times when you will have to deal with people in your office who are under a great deal of stress or who for some other reason are difficult to deal with. You will need to know how to respond to these people in ways that promote positive working relationships.

The Ability to Keep Confidences

One of the requirements of being a paralegal is the ability to keep client information confidential. The word *requirement* is used here because being able to keep confidences is not just a desirable attribute in a paralegal, but a mandatory one.

Technology and Today's Paralegal

ONLINE RESOURCES FOR PARALEGALS

There are many career development resources available online. To keep your skills up to date, and stay on top of developments in the law, here are some of the best Web sites.

PARALEGAL ASSOCIATIONS AND MAGAZINES

Many paralegals belong to either the National Association of Legal Assistants (NALA) or the National Federation of Paralegal Associations (NFPA). Both organizations offer excellent gateways for paralegal resources. NALA's Web site (**www.nala.org**) collects information on many professional certification and continuing education programs. It also provides links to state and local affiliated organizations. The NFPA Web site (**www.paralegals.org**) offers a continuing education calendar, a gateway to legal research sites, and a variety of career advice. *Legal Assistant Today,* an independent magazine for paralegals, also has a Web site (**www.legalassistanttoday.com**) that collects salary data, job listings, continuing education information, and downloadable forms, and hosts a discussion listserv. (Some services are only for subscribers.)

AMERICAN BAR ASSOCIATION

The ABA is not just for lawyers! The Standing Committee on Paralegals provides career information, continuing education, directories, a gateway to "blawgs" (law blogs) by paralegals, and information on paralegal education standards. The ABA also hosts the largest legal technology conference, which provides the opportunity for paralegals to learn about the latest developments.

BRYAN GARNER'S LEGAL WRITING SITE

America's most celebrated legal writing guru and Southern Methodist University law professor Bryan Garner is best known for his books, *The Elements of Legal Style, Garner's Modern American Usage,* and *Legal Writing in Plain English,* and as the current editor of the famous *Black's Law Dictionary.* Garner's Web site, *LawProse, Inc.* (**www.lawprose.org**), offers a bibliography of articles on legal writing, the schedule of his legal writing seminars, and a way to subscribe to his e-mailed "usage tip of the day."

THE PARALEGAL GATEWAY

The Paralegal Gateway (**www.paralegalgateway.com**) focuses on job advice, examples of successful résumés and interviews, and networking tools. It also offers links to continuing education resources and legal humor.

TECHNOLOGY TIP ON LEGAL NEWS AND RESOURCES

There is a wide range of online newsletters and Web sites on specific areas of law produced by law firms around the country and the world. The greatest danger of such sites, however, is that the information they provide may not be trustworthy. The best gateway to verifiable legal information is the Cornell University Legal Information Institute (**www.law.cornell.edu**), which provides links to trustworthy online legal resources. The LawProf blog network (**www.lawprofessorblogs.com**) provides a network of subject-specific blogs (blawgs) by law professors that offer up-to-the-minute commentary on important new cases, statutes, and news from trustworthy sources.

Developing Paralegal Skills

INTERVIEWING A CLIENT

Brenda Lundquist is a paralegal in a one-attorney firm. She has many responsibilities, including interviewing prospective divorce clients. Using a standard set of forms, Brenda meets with a prospective client and obtains information about the reasons for the divorce, finances and assets, and desired custody arrangements. This information is needed to assist the supervising attorney in determining whether to take the case. The information will also help Brenda in preparing the documents to be filed with the court should the attorney decide to represent the client. Brenda enjoys the work because she likes helping people, and often people who are getting divorced need both emotional and legal support.

CHECKLIST FOR CLIENT INTERVIEWS

- Plan the interview in advance.
- Print out forms and checklists to use during the interview.
- Introduce yourself as a paralegal or legal assistant.
- Explain the purpose of the interview to the client.
- Communicate your questions precisely.
- Listen carefully and be supportive, as necessary.
- Summarize the client's major concerns.
- Give the client a "time line" for what will happen next in the legal proceedings.

As you will read in Chapter 4, attorneys are ethically and legally obligated to keep all information relating to the representation of a client strictly confidential unless the client consents to the disclosure of the information.[9] The attorney may disclose this information only to people who are also working on behalf of the client and who therefore need to know it. Paralegals share in this duty imposed on all attorneys. If a paralegal reveals confidential client information to anyone outside the group working on the client's case, the lawyer (and the paralegal) may face legal consequences (including being sued by the client) if the client suffers harm as a result.

Keeping client information confidential means that you, as a paralegal, cannot divulge such information even to your spouse, family members, or closest friends. You should not talk about a client's case in hallways, elevators, or any areas in which others may overhear your conversation. Keeping work-related information confidential is an essential part of being a responsible and reliable paralegal.

Professionalism

Paralegals should behave professionally at all times. That means you must be responsible and reliable in order to earn the respect and trust of the attorneys and clients with whom you work. It also means you must put aside any personal bias or emotion that interferes with your representation of a client or assessment of a case. Paralegals need to be honest and assertive in letting others know what things paralegals can and cannot do (for example, they cannot give legal advice). This is particularly important because not everyone is sure what legal assistants are, and some people may have misconceptions about the role paralegals play.

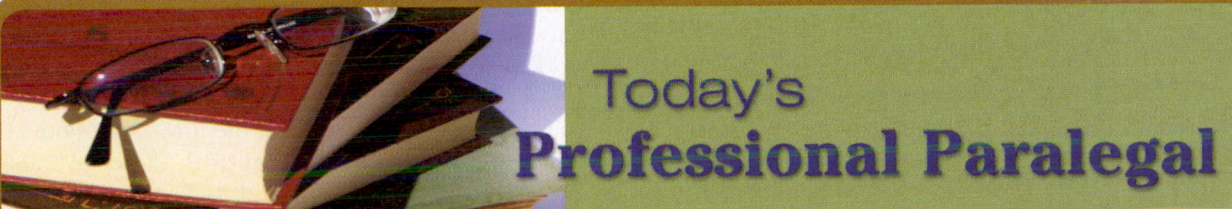

Today's **Professional Paralegal**

A WINNING COMBINATION

Susan Latham is a legal secretary for Melinda Oakwood, a real estate attorney who is a partner in the law firm of Morris, Crowther, Oakwood & Miller. The law firm is one of the largest in the state, employing over 300 attorneys, 75 paralegals, 130 secretaries, and many support staff members. Susan, who has become more of a legal assistant than a secretary to Melinda, has decided, at the age of forty, to return to a local college to obtain a paralegal degree. This way, Susan can be rewarded (in higher wages) for the work that she actually does already and can seek advancement in the firm.

Susan has worked for Melinda for eleven years. She has been given increased responsibility because she has shown Melinda that she is dependable and reliable in handling her work assignments. Her work is always turned in on time, and it is always accurate.

LEARNING ON THE JOB

Susan is lucky to work for Melinda, who had been a teacher for ten years before she went to law school. Melinda instructs Susan on how to undertake new work assignments. When Susan has a new type of document to prepare, Melinda gives her a sample document and good instructions. Now that Susan is studying to be a paralegal, Melinda has started giving her sample documents and copies of the laws that require those documents. Melinda also points out the differences between the class assignments and the sample documents and discusses with Susan why the differences matter from a legal perspective.

Additionally, Melinda encourages Susan to ask questions about school assignments and to take her time completing them so that when they are turned in, they are accurate. Susan has a strong sense of commitment, so she always sees a project through even if it seems to take forever.

USING PERSONAL ATTRIBUTES

Melinda is also lucky to have Susan as an employee. Susan has many personal attributes that help her on the job. She learns quickly and performs her work competently and efficiently. She also pays attention to detail, which is one of the reasons Melinda encouraged Susan to get a paralegal degree. Unlike Melinda's former paralegal, who would send out letters and sometimes forget to include documents that should have been enclosed, Susan is meticulous. And Melinda can always count on Susan to keep client information confidential.

Susan already had good computer and organizational skills when Melinda hired her. She did need to improve her analytical and listening skills, though. Susan's analytical skills are already getting better as a result of a course she is taking in legal research, which requires case analysis. Susan has learned to listen carefully to Melinda's instructions and to ask questions when it is unclear what Melinda wants her to do.

THE RESULT: A WINNING TEAM

Melinda and Susan have developed a solid working relationship. It took time for Susan to develop some of the skills that she needed, but Melinda was a good and patient teacher. It also took time to develop a trusting relationship, but now Melinda can confidently delegate significant assignments to Susan, knowing that she will complete them accurately. Now that Susan is in a paralegal program, Melinda can also assign more challenging work to her, and Susan will eventually be promoted to paralegal status. Melinda and Susan work productively and efficiently together. They like and rely on each other and enjoy their work. Theirs is a winning combination of talents and skills.

As a paralegal, you will find that you are judged not only by your actions and words but also by your appearance, attitude, and other factors. When deadlines approach and the pace of office work becomes somewhat frantic, it can be difficult to meet the challenge of acting professionally. For example, you may have to complete a brief (a document to support an attorney's argument) and file it with the court by noon. It is 11 A.M., and you still have a considerable portion of the brief to finish. When the pressure is on, it is important to remain calm and focus on completing your task quickly and accurately to ensure quality work. If you are interrupted by a client's call or another attorney, be aware that the way you react to that interruption is likely to affect whether others view you as professional. Try to be courteous and respectful during such interruptions. Remember that it is imperative that the paralegal be detail oriented and accurate, even when working under pressure.

THE FUTURE OF THE PROFESSION

The paralegal profession is a dynamic, changing, and expanding field within the legal arena. Legal assistants continue to assume a growing range of duties in the nation's legal offices and perform many of the same tasks as lawyers. According to the U.S. Department of Labor, the employment of paralegals should grow "much faster than the average for all occupations," and "formally trained paralegals should have the best employment opportunities."[10] It is estimated that between 2006 and 2016, 53,000 new paralegal positions will become available in the United States. This growth stems from the fact that law firms and other employers with legal staffs are hiring more paralegals to lower the cost—and increase the availability and efficiency—of legal services. Those entering the profession today will find a broader range of career options than ever before. In addition, they will have the opportunity to help chart the course the profession takes in the future. The paralegal profession has become a popular career choice for many, so competition for jobs will continue, but formally trained and highly skilled paralegals will have excellent employment potential.

KEY TERMS AND CONCEPTS

ABA-approved program *9*

Advanced Paralegal Certification (APC) *9*

American Association for Paralegal Education (AAfPE) *4*

American Bar Association (ABA) *3*

certification *9*

Certified Legal Assistant (CLA) *9*

Certified Paralegal (CP) *9*

continuing legal education (CLE) program *10*

legal assistant *3*

National Association of Legal Assistants (NALA) *3*

National Federation of Paralegal Associations (NFPA) *3*

paralegal *3*

procedural law *8*

Registered Paralegal (RP) *9*

substantive law *8*

CHAPTER SUMMARY

TODAY'S PROFESSIONAL PARALEGAL

What Is a Paralegal?

1. *Paralegal or legal assistant*—Many people use the terms *paralegal* and *legal assistant* interchangeably. Some persons trained as paralegals may use a different label, such as *legal technician* or *legal research specialist,* at their workplace. Paralegals perform many of the tasks traditionally handled by attorneys.

2. *Formal definition*—A legal assistant or paralegal is a person qualified by education, training, or work experience who is employed or retained by a lawyer, law office, corporation, governmental agency, or other entity and who performs specifically delegated substantive legal work, for which a lawyer is responsible.

What Do Paralegals Do?

1. *Typical duties*—Legal assistants typically perform many of the following tasks: interviewing and maintaining general contact with clients and witnesses, locating and interviewing witnesses, conducting legal investigations, calendaring and tracking important deadlines, organizing and maintaining client files, conducting legal research, drafting legal documents, filing legal documents with courts, summarizing witness testimony, coordinating litigation proceedings, attending legal proceedings, and using computers and technology.

2. *Duties often vary*—Paralegals perform different functions depending on where they work and on their capabilities and experience. In law firms, paralegals' duties also vary according to the size of the firm and the kind of law practiced by the firm. Although their duties vary, paralegals commonly spend the bulk of their time performing document management, client relations, and research.

3. *Paralegals and technology*—Technology is the number-one area of expanding paralegal responsibility. Paralegals who are skilled in using newly available technologies to assist them in performing their duties will excel in the profession.

Paralegal Education

Higher education and paralegal education programs have become increasingly important in the growth and development of the profession.

1. *Educational options*—Colleges, universities, and private institutions offer a wide variety of programs to train paralegals, ranging in length from three months to four years.

2. *ABA-approved programs*—Since 1974, the American Bar Association (ABA) has set educational standards for paralegal training programs. ABA-approved programs are those that meet with the ABA's approval. ABA approval is a voluntary process; paralegal programs are not required to be approved by the ABA.

3. *Certification*—The term *certification* refers to formal recognition by a professional group or state agency that an individual has met certain standards of proficiency specified by that group. Generally, this means passing an examination and meeting certain requirements with respect to education and/or experience. Paralegals may be certified by NALA, NFPA, or a state agency. Currently, no state requires paralegal certification.

4. *Continuing legal education (CLE)*—Continuing legal education courses are offered by state bar associations and paralegal associations. Such programs provide a way to learn more about a specialized area of law or keep up to date on the latest developments in law and technology.

Paralegal Skills and Attributes

Because paralegals today perform many of the tasks that lawyers used to perform, the demands on paralegals to be professional and efficient have increased. Paralegals need a variety of skills. It is especially important to have good analytical, communication, computer, organizational, and interpersonal skills and to be able to keep confidences and behave professionally.

STUDENT STUDYWARE™ CD-ROM

Interactive student CD in this book includes additional quizzing, plus video clips, case studies, and Key Terms flashcards.

ONLINE COMPANION™

For additional resources, please go to **www.paralegal.delmar.cengage.com**.

QUESTIONS FOR REVIEW

1. What is a paralegal? Is there any difference between a paralegal and a legal assistant?

2. What types of educational programs and training are available to paralegals? Must a person meet specific educational requirements to work as a paralegal?

3. What role does the American Bar Association play in paralegal education?

4. What does *certification* mean? What is a CLA or a CP? What is the APC program? What does PACE stand for?

5. List and describe the skills that are useful in paralegal practice. Do you have these skills?

ETHICAL QUESTIONS

1. Richard attends a six-month paralegal course and earns a certificate. In the West Coast city where he lives, certified paralegals—those with a CP or a CLA designation—are in great demand in the job market. Richard responds to a newspaper advertisement for a certified paralegal, indicating that he is one. Has Richard done anything unethical? What is the difference between a certificate and certification?

2. Paula Abrams works as a paralegal for a small law firm that specializes in tax law. Recently, Paula purchased some new tax-return software and was trained in how to use it. Last week, Paula used the software to prepare tax returns for the Benedetto family. Paula saved the forms on a disk. She then retrieved the Benedetto forms and used them for the Marshalls' tax return. Paula entered much of the Marshalls' tax

information into the computer. Mr. Marshall had not provided the children's Social Security numbers to Paula, though, so she decided to add the Social Security numbers later. In the meantime, Paula left the Benedetto children's Social Security numbers on the form.

In the tax-season rush, Paula inadvertently neglected to enter the children's Social Security numbers on the Marshalls' tax return. Several months later, the Marshalls received a letter from the Internal Revenue Service stating that their exemptions had been denied because their children's Social Security numbers had been claimed on someone else's tax return. How might this situation be resolved? What other kinds of ethical problems might result from using computer-generated forms?

PRACTICE QUESTIONS AND ASSIGNMENTS

1. Refer to Appendix F at the end of this book (or go to **www.findlaw.com**), and find the answers to the following questions:

   a. Is there an affiliate of the National Association of Legal Assistants or the National Federation of Paralegal Associations in your city? Where is the nearest affiliate of either of these organizations located?

   b. Are there any regional or local paralegal associations in your area? If so, what are their names, street and e-mail addresses, and phone numbers?

2. Using the material on paralegal skills presented in the chapter, identify which of the following are skills that a paralegal should have, and explain why.

   a. Reading skills.

   b. Interpersonal skills.

   c. Marketing skills.

   d. Oral communication skills.

   e. Math skills.

   f. Computer skills.

   g. Management skills.

QUESTION FOR CRITICAL ANALYSIS

1. Tom and Sandy are having coffee after their first paralegal class. The instructor discussed the ongoing debate within the profession about whether to use the term *paralegal* or *legal assistant*. Tom says he agrees with NFPA that the term *paralegal* is preferable because no one will confuse paralegals with legal secretaries. Sandy, who has been working as a legal secretary for the last few years, is offended by Tom's remarks. What label do you prefer—*legal assistant* or *paralegal*—and why? Is it an important issue, in your opinion?

PROJECT

1. Arrange an interview with an experienced paralegal, such as a graduate of your program or another paralegal whom you may know. Ask the paralegal what he or she thinks are the most important skills and characteristics that paralegals should have.

USING INTERNET RESOURCES

Browse through the materials on the Web sites of the National Association of Legal Assistants, or NALA (at **www.nala.org**), and the National Federation of Paralegal Associations, or NFPA (at **www.paralegals.org**). Then do the following:

1. Look closely at the benefits of membership listed by each of these organizations. How do they compare? Are there any significant differences?

2. Examine the information that is included on each site about the organization's certification program. For each program, summarize the requirements that a paralegal must meet to become certified.

3. Go to the Web site for Delmar Cengage Learning at **www.paralegal.delmar.cengage.com**, and select "State Specific Resources." You will find links to relevant state-specific Web sites and to sites that furnish legal forms for individual states. Click on your state's Web links, and browse through the resources available. List the Web sites you find, and briefly describe the kind of information available at each site. Can you access your state's bar association? Is there a way to view any of your state's codes (laws) or judicial opinions? Does the state attorney general or secretary of state have a Web site listed?

END NOTES

1. Heidi Lowry, "Paralegal Salaries Reach New Heights," *Legal Assistant Today,* March/April 2009, p. 34.

2. The members of NFPA voted to remove the term *legal assistant* from their definition of *paralegal* at the annual conference in May 2002. The American Association for Paralegal Education (AAfPE) took a similar position at its annual meeting in 2002.

3. This is according to a survey conducted by *Legal Assistant Today* magazine in 2004, reported in March/April 2005, p. 54.

4. California Business and Professions Code, Sections 6450–6456. Enacted in 2000.

5. California Advanced Specialist (CAS) certification is also available as a specialty exam through NALA to paralegals who possess CLA or CP certification. For more information on this state-specific NALA certification, see Appendix G.

6. Originally, *NALS* was an acronym for National Association of Legal Secretaries. The organization no longer regards the name *NALS* as an acronym and describes the association as "the association of legal professionals." For more information, go to the association's Web site at **www.nals.org**, and select "About NALS."

7. According to a 2004 survey by *Legal Assistant Today,* 77.2 percent of employers paid at least part of the cost of continuing legal education. *Legal Assistant Today,* March/April 2005, p. 57.

8. California Business and Professions Code, Sections 6450–6456. Enacted in 2000.

9. Exceptions to the confidentiality rule are made in certain circumstances, as will be discussed in Chapter 4.

10. Bureau of Labor Statistics, *Occupational Outlook Handbook, 2008–09 Edition,* p. 3. Available at **www.bls.gov/OCO**. (From the "Professional" menu, select "Legal," then "Paralegals and legal assistants.")

CAREER OPPORTUNITIES

CHAPTER OUTLINE

Introduction

Where Paralegals Work

Paralegal Specialties

Paralegal Compensation

Planning Your Career

Locating Potential Employers

Marketing Your Skills

Reevaluating Your Career

AFTER COMPLETING THIS CHAPTER, YOU WILL KNOW:

► What types of firms and organizations hire paralegals.

► Some areas of law in which paralegals specialize.

► How much paralegals can expect to earn.

► How paralegals are compensated for overtime work.

► How to prepare a career plan and pursue it.

► How to search for an employer.

► How to present yourself to prospective employers.

INTRODUCTION

Paralegals enjoy a wide range of employment opportunities in both the private and the public sectors. They are in demand in law firms because they help provide competent legal services at a lower cost to clients. Furthermore, although most legal assistants work in law offices, almost any business that uses legal services can also use the services of paralegals. Corporations, insurance companies, banks, and real estate agencies regularly employ legal assistants. In addition, the government has created positions for paralegals at many agencies. Paralegals now work in many court systems, in county offices, and in legal-services clinics across the nation.

This chapter provides you with a starting point for planning your career. In the pages that follow, you will read about where paralegals work and what compensation paralegals receive. You will also learn about the steps you will need to follow to plan your career, locate potential employers, and find a job.

For helpful information on all aspects of paralegal careers, go to the National Association of Legal Assistants' Web site at **www.nala.org** and the National Federation of Paralegal Associations' Web site at **www.paralegals.org**.

WHERE PARALEGALS WORK

Paralegal employers fall into a number of categories. This section describes the general characteristics of each of the major types of working environments. Regardless of where you work, on-the-job stress is a potential problem, as discussed in the *In the Office* feature on the following page.

Law Firms

When paralegals first established themselves in the legal community in the 1960s, they worked in law firms. Today, law firms continue to hire more paralegals than do any other organizations. Two-thirds of all paralegals work in law firms. Law firms vary in size from the small, one-attorney office to the huge "megafirm" with hundreds of attorneys. As you can see in Exhibit 2.1, most paralegals work in settings that employ fewer than twenty-five attorneys.

Working for a Small Firm

Many paralegals begin their careers working for small law practices, such as one-attorney firms or firms with just a few attorneys. To some extent, this is because small law firms (those with twenty-five or fewer attorneys) simply outnumber large ones. It may also be due to geographic location. For example, a paralegal who lives in a small community may find that his or her only option is to work for a small legal practice.

Working for a small firm offers many advantages to the beginning paralegal. If the firm is a general law practice, you will have the opportunity to gain experience in many different areas of the law. You will be able to learn whether you enjoy working

Number of Attorneys	Percentage of Paralegals	Average Salary
1	14%	$46,618
2–5	29%	$51,639
6–10	18%	$55,822
11–25	17%	$55,491
26–50	13%	$59,426
51–100	6%	$56,750
Over 100	3%	$67,374

EXHIBIT 2.1
Paralegal Employment and Salary by Size of Firm or Legal Department

The authors compiled this chart using data from a variety of sources, including NALA, *Legal Assistant Today* magazine, and the International Paralegal Management Association, or IPMA.

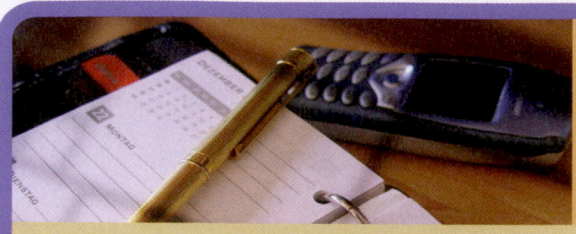

In the **Office**

STRESS PROBLEMS

Stress can cause health problems. It is also related to making mistakes at work. When that happens, even more stress is generated. Errors increase when we rush to meet deadlines and have our minds on many things at once.

How can you reduce stress problems that may result in sloppy work and missed deadlines? First, be candid about your workload when a supervisor adds new work. Second, prioritize your tasks. Determine, perhaps by consulting with your supervising attorney, which projects take priority. Third, consider asking your supervisor to assign another person in the office to help you. Finally, keep in mind that being aware of stress is a key step in learning to deal with it in a realistic way. Being organized and clear about responsibilities will increase your productivity, concentration, and performance. It will also reduce the likelihood of stress building up in the office.

in one area (such as family law) more than another area (such as personal-injury law) in the event that you later decide to specialize. Some paralegals also prefer the more personal and less formal environment that often exists in a small law office, as well as the variety of tasks and greater flexibility that characterize this setting.

Small size may also involve disadvantages, however. Paralegals who work for small firms may have less support staff to assist them. This means that if you work in a small law office, your job may involve a substantial amount of secretarial or clerical work.

Compensation is another area of potential concern. Small firms pay, on average, slightly lower salaries than larger firms do, as shown in Exhibit 2.1 on the previous page. Generally, the larger the firm, the higher the paralegal salaries. Small firms also may provide fewer employee benefits, such as pension plans and health benefits. At the same time, however, a small firm may be in a convenient location, may not insist on an expensive wardrobe, and may offer free parking.

Working for a Large Firm

In contrast to the (typically) more casual environment of the small law office, larger law firms usually are more formal. If you work for a larger firm, your responsibilities will probably be limited to specific, well-defined types of tasks. For example, you may work for a department that handles (or for an attorney who handles) only certain types of cases, such as real estate transactions. Office procedures and employment policies will also be more clearly defined and may be set forth in a written employment manual.

The advantages of the large firm often include greater opportunities for promotions and career advancement, higher salaries and often better benefits packages, more support staff for paralegals, and more sophisticated technology and greater access to research resources.

You may see certain characteristics of large law firms as either advantages or disadvantages, depending on your personality and preferences. For example, if you favor the more specialized duties and more formal working environment of the large law firm, then you will view these characteristics as advantages. If you prefer to handle a greater variety of tasks and enjoy the more personal, informal atmosphere of the small law office, then you might think the specialization and formality of the large law firm are disadvantages.

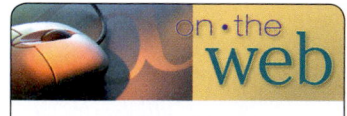

You can obtain a host of information on specific law firms by going to their Web pages. For example, go to the Web site for Wachtell, Lipton, Rosen & Katz at **www.wlrk.com**.

(To find Web sites for law firms, check one of the legal directories discussed later in this chapter.)

Paralegals who work for large law firms often need to research statutes, court cases, or regulations in the firm's law library. Notebook computers and smart phones facilitate the ease with which paralegals can do research and communicate with attorneys, clients, and others. What are the pros and cons of working for a large law firm?

(Courtesy of ©Thinkstock)

Corporations and Other Business Organizations

As we've already mentioned, many paralegals work in business environments outside of law firms. Almost any business that uses legal services may find it beneficial to hire paralegals. An increasing number of paralegals work for corporate legal departments. Most large firms hire in-house attorneys to handle corporate legal affairs. Some large corporations have hundreds of attorneys on their payrolls. Legal assistants who are employed by corporations usually work under the supervision of in-house attorneys.

Paralegals in a corporation perform a variety of functions, such as organizing corporate meetings and maintaining the necessary records, drafting employee contracts and benefit plans, and preparing financial and other reports for the corporation. Paralegals often are responsible for monitoring and reviewing government regulations to ensure that the corporation is operating within the law. When the corporation is involved in a lawsuit, paralegals may be assigned duties related to that lawsuit. (For more information on the duties of corporate paralegals, see Chapter 18.)

Nearly one-fifth of all paralegals work in corporate environments. Paralegals who are employed by corporations frequently receive higher salaries than those working for law firms. In addition, paralegals who are employed by corporations may work more regular hours and experience less stress than paralegals who work for law firms. For example, unlike paralegals in law firms, corporate paralegals typically have not been required to generate a specific number of "billable hours" per year (hours billed to clients for paralegal services performed, to be discussed in Chapter 3). Increasingly, though, corporate law departments bill clients within the corporation much as a regular law firm bills its clients.

Government

Paralegals employed by government agencies work in various settings and often specialize in one aspect of the law.

Administrative Agencies

Most paralegals who work for the government work for administrative agencies, such as the federal Environmental Protection Agency (EPA) or a state environmental resources department. Paralegals who work for government agencies may conduct legal research and analysis, investigate welfare eligibility and claims or disability claims, examine documents (such as loan applications), and engage in many other tasks. Within the federal government, the U.S. Department of Justice employs the largest number of paralegals, followed by the Social Security Administration and the Department of the Treasury. Your best source of information about employment positions in a particular administrative agency is the agency itself. You can find the names and telephone numbers of federal agencies, as well as a description of their functions, in the *United States Government Manual,* available in your library. The information is also available online.

Paralegals who work for government agencies normally work regular hours and tend to work fewer total hours per year (have more vacation time) than paralegals in other environments. Like paralegals in corporations, they may not have to worry about billable hours, although other measures of productivity are likely to be used. Additionally, paralegals who work for the government usually enjoy comprehensive employment benefits. Salaries, however, are sometimes lower than those offered by traditional law firms and other employers in the private sector.

Legislative Offices

Legislators in the U.S. Congress and in some state legislatures typically have staff members to help them with their duties. These duties often include legal research and writing, and paralegals sometimes perform such services. For example, a senator who plans to propose an amendment to a law may ask a paralegal on her or his staff to research the legislative history of that law carefully (to discern the legislature's intention when passing the law—see Chapters 5 and 7) and write up a summary of that history.

Law Enforcement Offices and Courts

Many paralegals work for government law enforcement offices and institutions. As you will read in Chapter 13, which discusses criminal law and procedures, a person accused of a crime is prosecuted by a *public prosecutor.* Public prosecutors (such as district attorneys, state attorneys general, and U.S. attorneys) are government officials who are paid by the government. Accused persons may be defended by private attorneys or, if they cannot afford to hire a lawyer, by *public defenders*—attorneys paid for by the state to ensure that criminal defendants are not deprived of their constitutional right to be represented by counsel. Both public prosecutors and public defenders rely on paralegals to handle much of their legal work.

Paralegals also find work in other government settings, such as federal or state court administrative offices. Court administrative work ranges from recording and filing court documents (such as the documents filed during a lawsuit—see Chapter 10) to working for a small claims court (a court that handles claims below a specified amount—see Chapter 6). Paralegals also work for bankruptcy courts (see page 31 for a discussion of bankruptcy law).

Legal Aid Offices

Legal aid offices provide legal services to those who find it difficult to pay for legal representation. Most legal aid is government funded, although some support comes from private legal foundations.

Many paralegals who work in this type of setting find their jobs rewarding, even though they usually receive lower salaries than they would in other areas. In part, this is because of the nature of the work—helping needy individuals. Additionally,

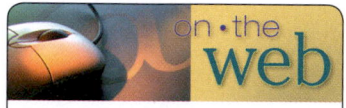

You can locate information on government agencies at numerous Web sites, including that of FindLaw at **www.findlaw.com**.

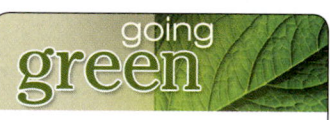

WHAT'S IN THAT OFFICE LAMP?

Soon there will be a mandatory change from incandescent bulbs, which give off 90 percent heat and only 10 percent light, to fluorescent bulbs, which are more efficient, and even to LED light, which is even more energy thrifty. You can start now by beginning to make the switch.

paralegals in legal aid offices generally assume a wider array of responsibilities than they would in a traditional law office. For example, some federal and state administrative agencies, including the Social Security Administration, allow paralegals to represent clients in agency hearings and judicial proceedings. As you will read in Chapter 4, paralegals normally are not allowed to represent clients—only attorneys can do so. Exceptions to this rule exist when a court or agency permits nonlawyers to represent others in court or in administrative agency hearings.

Freelance Paralegals

A number of experienced paralegals operate as freelancers. **Freelance paralegals** (also called *independent contractors* or *contract paralegals*) own their own businesses and perform specified types of legal work for attorneys on a contract basis. Attorneys who need temporary legal assistance sometimes contract with freelance paralegals to work on particular projects. In addition, attorneys who need legal assistance but cannot afford to hire full-time paralegals might hire freelancers to work on a part-time basis. (The suggestions offered later in this chapter on how you can find work as a paralegal apply to freelance jobs as well.)

Freelancing has both advantages and disadvantages. Because freelancers are their own bosses, they can set their own schedules. Thus, they enjoy a greater degree of flexibility in their working hours. In addition, depending on the nature of their projects, they may work at home or in attorneys' offices. With flexibility, however, comes added responsibility. A freelance paralegal's income depends on the ability to promote and maintain business. If there are no clients for the month, there will be no income. Also, freelancers do not enjoy job benefits such as employer-provided group medical insurance. A freelance paralegal needs to be self-motivated to make the business work.

Realize that freelance paralegals work under attorney supervision. Freelancers are not to be confused with **legal technicians**—often called **independent paralegals**—who do *not* work under the supervision of an attorney and who provide (sell) legal services directly to the public. These services include helping members of the public obtain and fill out forms for certain types of legal transactions, such as bankruptcy filings and divorce petitions. As you will read in Chapter 4, legal technicians run the risk of violating state statutes prohibiting the unauthorized practice of law.

freelance paralegal
A paralegal who operates his or her own business and provides services to attorneys on a contract basis. A freelance paralegal works under the supervision of an attorney, who assumes responsibility for the paralegal's work product.

legal technician or independent paralegal
A paralegal who offers services directly to the public without attorney supervision. Independent paralegals assist consumers by supplying them with forms and procedural knowledge relating to simple or routine legal procedures.

PARALEGAL SPECIALTIES

While many paralegals perform a wide range of legal services, others have found it satisfying to specialize in one area of law. The major areas of law in which paralegals report that they work are litigation (51 percent), corporate law (32 percent), contract law (29 percent), real estate law (27 percent), and personal-injury law (26 percent). Other specialty areas exist, and some are listed in Exhibit 2.2 on the next page, along with the average compensation for paralegals in each area. Here, we discuss just a few of the areas in which paralegals may specialize. This chapter's *Developing Paralegal Skills* feature on page 29 also discusses an area of specialization.

Litigation

Working a lawsuit through the court system is called **litigation**. Paralegals who specialize in assisting attorneys in the litigation process are called **litigation paralegals**. Litigation paralegals work in general law practices, small litigation firms, litigation departments of larger law firms, and corporate legal departments. Litigation paralegals often specialize in a certain type of litigation, such as personal-injury litigation (which will be discussed shortly) or product liability cases (which involve injuries caused by defective products).

litigation
The process of working a lawsuit through the court system.

litigation paralegal
A paralegal who specializes in assisting attorneys in the litigation process.

EXHIBIT 2.2
Average Compensation by Specialty

The authors compiled this chart using data from *Legal Assistant Today* magazine.

Area of Legal Specialty	Average Compensation
Administrative	$51,053
Bankruptcy	$58,371
Contracts	$58,908
Corporate	$57,308
Criminal	$48,125
Employment	$56,364
Environmental	$52,000
Family	$45,200
Insurance	$54,413
Intellectual property	$71,308
Litigation	$56,823
Medical malpractice	$49,831
Personal injury	$48,919
Probate (wills and estates)	$49,236
Real estate	$49,546
Workers' compensation	$50,641

plaintiff
A party who initiates a lawsuit.

defendant
A party against whom a lawsuit is brought.

Work performed by litigation paralegals varies with the substantive law area being litigated. It also varies according to whether it is done on behalf of **plaintiffs** (those who bring lawsuits) or on behalf of **defendants** (those against whom lawsuits are brought). Some litigation paralegals investigate cases, review documents containing evidence, interview clients and witnesses, draft documents to file with the courts, and prepare for hearings and trials. You will read in detail about litigation procedures and the important role played by paralegals in the litigation process in Chapters 10 through 13.

Corporate Law

corporate law
Law that governs the formation, financing, merger and acquisition, and termination of corporations, as well as the rights and duties of those who own and run the corporation.

Corporate law consists of the laws that govern the formation, financing, merger and acquisition, and termination of corporations, as well as the rights and duties of those who own and run corporations. You will read in detail about the meaning of these terms and the tasks that corporate paralegals typically perform in Chapter 18.

Paralegals who specialize in corporate law may work for a corporation, in its legal department, or for a law firm that specializes in corporate law. Corporate paralegals often perform such tasks as preparing and filing documents with a state agency to set up corporations and to keep them in good standing, keeping corporate records, organizing and scheduling shareholders' meetings in accordance with state law, and preparing stock certificates. As you can see in Exhibit 2.2, which lists the average compensation by specialty, paralegals who work in corporate law generally receive higher salaries than paralegals in some other specialty areas. In addition, corporate paralegals who further narrow their expertise to an area such as mergers are among the highest-paid paralegals today.

Contract Law

contract
An agreement (based on a promise or an exchange of promises) that can be enforced in court.

A number of paralegals work in contract law. As you will read in Chapter 15, a **contract** is an agreement (based on a promise or an exchange of promises) that can be enforced in court. Paralegals who specialize in this area may work for a corporation's legal department, for a large law firm, or for a government agency.

Developing
Paralegal Skills

WORKING FOR A PUBLIC DEFENDER

Michele Sanchez works as a paralegal for the public defender's office in her county. Today, she has been assigned to go to the county jail to meet with a new client, Geraldine Silverton. Silverton had been arrested for child abuse after her child's school notified the police. According to school officials, the child had bruises all over his body. The child also told his teacher that his mother frequently "beat him up" for no reason at all.

The client, Silverton, is very upset and tells Michele that "no way in the world would she harm her boy." Silverton claims that her son was hurt when he fell off the trampoline in their backyard and that he's just "making up" the abuse story to get attention.

Silverton demands to be released from jail immediately. Michele makes a note of Silverton's concerns and then explains the scheduling for the bail hearings.

TIPS FOR MEETING WITH A NEW CLIENT

- Review the police report before meeting with the client.
- During the interview with the client, ask the client for his or her side of the story.
- Listen carefully and supportively to the client, and communicate with empathy.
- Minimize note taking.
- Do not appear to judge the client.

The work of paralegals in contract law often involves preparing contracts and contract forms, and reviewing contracts to determine whether one of the parties to the contract has or has not complied with the terms of the contract. In a lawsuit for breach of contract, for example, a paralegal might be asked to look closely at the contract terms and do some factual investigation to find out whether the contract has been breached (broken). Contract specialists also may conduct research in the law governing contracts, either before a contract is formed or during litigation concerning the contract's provisions. Note that because contracts are so common in our legal environment, many paralegals—not just contract specialists—are involved with work relating to contracts.

Real Estate Law

At law, **real estate**, or *real property*, consists of land and all things permanently attached to the land, such as houses, buildings, and trees. Because of the value of real estate (for most people, a home is the most expensive purchase they will ever make), attorneys frequently assist persons or companies that buy or sell real property to make sure that nothing important is overlooked. Paralegals who specialize in real estate may find employment in a number of environments, including small law firms that specialize in real estate transactions, real estate departments in large law firms, corporations or other business firms that frequently buy or sell real property, banking institutions (which finance real estate purchases), title companies, and real estate agencies. As we will discuss in Chapter 16, paralegals working in real estate law often draft contracts for the sale of real estate, draft mortgage agreements, draft and record deeds, and schedule closings on the sale of property.

real estate
Land and things permanently attached to the land, such as houses, buildings, and trees.

Personal-Injury Law

Much litigation involves claims brought by persons who have been injured in automobile accidents or other incidents as a result of the negligence of others. *Negligence* is a **tort**, or civil wrong, that occurs when a person's carelessness causes harm to another. Someone who has been injured as a result of another's negligence is entitled under tort law to obtain compensation from the wrongdoer. (Tort law, including negligence, will be discussed in Chapter 14.)

Paralegals who specialize in personal-injury litigation often work for law firms that concentrate their efforts on this domain. Legal assistants in this area obtain and review medical and employment records to determine the client's injuries and lost wages. These items are needed to ascertain the plaintiff's damages in a personal-injury lawsuit. Personal-injury paralegals are also hired by insurance companies to investigate claims. Defendants in personal-injury cases are typically insured by automobile or other insurance, and a defendant's insurance company has a duty to defend an insured customer who is being sued.

Insurance Law

Insurance is essentially a contract by which an insurance company (the insurer) promises to pay a sum or give something of value to another (either the insured or the beneficiary of the insurance policy) to compensate the other for a specified loss. Insurance may provide compensation for the injury or death of the insured or another, for damage to the insured's property, or for other losses, such as those resulting from lawsuits. Paralegals who specialize in the area of insurance law may work for law firms that defend insurance companies in litigation brought against the companies. They may also work directly for insurance companies.

Paralegals in this area may review government insurance regulations and monitor an insurance firm's compliance with these regulations. Paralegals may also be asked to review insurance contracts, undertake factual and legal investigations relating to insurance claims, or provide litigation assistance in lawsuits involving the insurance company. Often, paralegals may be asked to help in litigation involving insurance. For example, a paralegal may be asked to provide investigative or litigation assistance for a client who is bringing a lawsuit or defending against a personal-injury, malpractice, or other litigation in which insurance is an important factor.

Employment and Labor Law

As will be discussed in Chapter 18, laws governing employment relationships are referred to collectively as *employment and labor law*. This body of law includes laws governing health and safety in the workplace, labor unions and union-management relations, employment discrimination, sexual harassment, wrongful termination, pension plans, retirement and disability income, employee privacy rights, the minimum wage, and overtime wages.

Paralegals who are experienced in these areas may work for law firms, businesses, or government agencies. Some paralegals specialize in just one area of employment law, such as workers' compensation. Under **workers' compensation statutes**, employees who are injured on the job are compensated from state funds or insurance funds (obtained from taxes or insurance premiums paid by employers). Paralegals in this area assist persons injured on the job in obtaining compensation from the state workers' compensation program. As mentioned earlier, some government agencies allow paralegals to represent clients during agency hearings, which are conducted to settle disputes, or during negotiations with the agencies. Many state workers' compensation boards allow paralegals to represent clients in such hearings.

Frequently, working in the area of employment law involves interacting with numerous administrative agencies, such as the Occupational Safety and Health

---

tort
A civil wrong not arising from a breach of contract; a violation of a legal duty that causes harm to another.

insurance
A contract by which an insurance company (the insurer) promises to pay a sum of money or give something of value to another (either the insured or the beneficiary) to compensate for a specified loss.

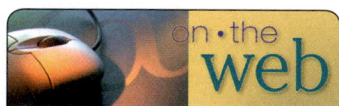

Some law firms that specialize in labor and employment issues post newsletters on the Web. One such firm is Ogletree Deakins, which you can access at **www.ogletreedeakins.com**.

workers' compensation statutes
State laws establishing an administrative procedure for compensating workers for injuries that arise in the course of their employment.

Administration and the Equal Employment Opportunity Commission. Each governmental agency has its own set of rules and legal procedures. Paralegals who work in employment or labor law must be familiar with the relevant federal and state agencies, as well as with their specific roles in resolving disputes. We will cover employment law in Chapter 18 and administrative agencies in Chapter 5.

Estate Planning and Probate Administration

Estate planning and probate administration have to do with the transfer of an owner's property, or *estate,* on the owner's death. Through **estate planning**, the owner decides, *before* death, how his or her property will be transferred to others. The owner may make a **will** to designate the persons to whom his or her property is to be transferred. If someone contests the validity of the will, it must be **probated** (proved) in a **probate court.** Depending on the size of the estate, it may take months—in some cases, over a year—for the probate court to approve the property distribution and for the property to be transferred to the rightful heirs.

Because the probate process is time consuming and expensive, many people engage in estate planning to avoid probate. For example, a person may establish a **trust** agreement, which is a legal arrangement in which the ownership of property is transferred to a third person (the *trustee*) to be used for the benefit of another (the beneficiary). Paralegals often are responsible for interviewing clients to obtain information necessary to draft wills and trust agreements, for gathering information on debts and assets, and for locating heirs if necessary (see Chapter 17). A paralegal who is sensitive and caring toward clients, yet professional and conscientious in explaining and working out procedures, is well suited for this specialty.

Bankruptcy Law

Bankruptcy law allows debtors to obtain relief from their debts. Bankruptcy law is federal law, and bankruptcy proceedings take place in federal courts (see the discussion of the federal court system in Chapter 6). The twin goals of bankruptcy law are (1) to protect a debtor by giving him or her a fresh start and (2) to ensure that creditors who are competing for a debtor's assets are treated fairly. Bankruptcy law provides for several types of relief, and both individuals and business firms may petition for bankruptcy. Both large and small firms practice bankruptcy law and hire paralegals who specialize in this area.

Bankruptcy law, discussed in Chapter 19, imposes many strict requirements, which means that paralegals working in this area may have detailed responsibilities. The paralegal might be responsible for interviewing debtors to obtain information about their income, assets, and debts; verifying the accuracy of information provided by debtors; and ensuring that debtors have completed required credit counseling. The paralegal may also review the validity of creditors' claims and prepare the documents that must be submitted to the bankruptcy court.

Intellectual Property Law

Intellectual property consists of the products of individuals' minds—products that result from creative processes. Those who create intellectual property acquire certain rights over the use of that property. Literary works, such as books, and artistic works, such as songs, are protected by *copyright law. Trademark law* protects firms' distinctive marks or logos. Inventions are protected by *patent law.* The owner of intellectual property rights may sell the rights to another, may collect royalties on the use of the property (such as a popular song) by others, and may prevent unauthorized publishers from reproducing the property (such as a novel). Chapter 15 will provide more detail about laws governing intellectual property.

Some law firms (or departments of large law firms) specialize in intellectual property law, such as patent law. Other firms provide a variety of legal services, of

estate planning

Making arrangements, during a person's lifetime, for the transfer of that person's property to others on the person's death. Estate planning often involves executing a will or establishing a trust fund to provide for others, such as a spouse or children, on a person's death.

will

A document directing how and to whom the maker's property and obligations are to be transferred on his or her death.

probate

The process of "proving" the validity of a will and ensuring that the instructions in a valid will are carried out.

probate court

A court that probates wills; usually a county court.

trust

An arrangement in which title to property is held by one person (a trustee) for the benefit of another (a beneficiary).

bankruptcy law

The body of federal law that governs bankruptcy proceedings. The twin goals of bankruptcy law are (1) to protect a debtor by giving him or her a fresh start and (2) to ensure that creditors competing for a debtor's assets are treated fairly.

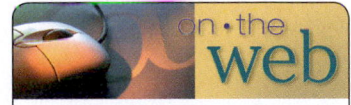

If you are interested in bankruptcy law, a good site for learning about current bankruptcy issues is that of the American Bankruptcy Institute at **www.abiworld.org**.

intellectual property

Property that results from intellectual, creative processes. Copyrights, patents, and trademarks are examples of intellectual property.

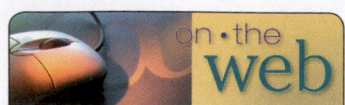

If you are interested in how cyberspace is affecting the laws governing intellectual property, a good site covering current issues is that offered by the Bureau of National Affairs at **ipcenter.bna.com**.

which intellectual property law is a part. In addition, corporate legal departments may be responsible for registering copyrights, patents, or trademarks with the federal government.

Paralegals who work in this area research existing patents and trademarks. They also assist in compiling patent applications in accordance with detailed regulations, draft documents necessary to apply for trademark and copyright protection, and assist in litigating disputes. Because of the expertise required, paralegal intellectual property specialists are paid more than average (see Exhibit 2.2 on page 28). This is an especially good practice area for paralegals with a science background. In fact, anyone, including a paralegal, with three years of undergraduate science courses can apply to the U.S. Patent and Trademark Office to become a registered patent agent, who prepares patent applications.

Environmental Law

environmental law

All state and federal laws or regulations enacted or issued to protect the environment and preserve environmental resources.

Environmental law consists of all laws that have been created to protect the environment. Environmental law involves the regulation of air and water pollution, natural resource management, endangered species protection, hazardous waste disposal and the clean-up of hazardous waste sites, pesticide control, and nuclear power regulation.

Employers of paralegal specialists in environmental law include administrative agencies (such as the federal Environmental Protection Agency, state natural resource departments, and local zoning boards), environmental law departments of large law firms, law firms that specialize in environmental law, and corporations. For example, a company may employ a paralegal as an *environmental coordinator* to help in maintaining compliance with regulations, overseeing company environmental programs, and obtaining permits to use land in certain ways. Paralegals working in law firms that handle environmental matters often assist in litigation concerning alleged violations of environmental laws. They perform tasks similar to those described previously for litigation and personal-injury paralegals.

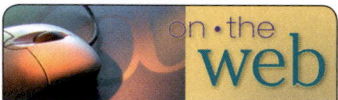

For a comprehensive and up-to-date collection of news articles, laws, and agency regulations involving environmental law issues, go to the Environmental Law Net at **lawvianet.com**.

Family Law

family law

Law relating to family matters, such as marriage, divorce, child support, and child custody.

Family law, as the term implies, deals with family matters, such as marriage, divorce, alimony, child support, and child custody. We will discuss it in detail in Chapter 17. Family law is governed mostly by state statutes, so if you specialize in this area, you will need to become familiar with your state's requirements.

As a family law specialist, you might work for a small family law practice, for a family law department in a large law firm, or with a state or local agency, such as a community services agency, that assists persons who need help with family-related problems. As a paralegal working in family law, you might research and draft documents that are filed with the court in divorce and adoption proceedings. You might also perform investigations into assets and the grounds for divorce. Paralegals in this area often have extensive contact with clients and need to be skilled at extracting information from sometimes emotionally distraught persons. Those with a background or interest in social work or counseling are particularly well suited to this specialty.

Criminal Law

civil law

Law dealing with the definition and enforcement of private rights, as opposed to criminal matters.

criminal law

Law that governs and defines those actions that are crimes and that subjects persons convicted of crimes to punishment imposed by the government (a fine or jail time).

Law is sometimes classified into the two categories of civil law and criminal law. **Civil law** is concerned with the duties that exist between persons or between citizens and their governments, excluding the duty not to commit crimes. Contract law, for example, is part of civil law. Tort law, which has to do with the infringement by one person of the legally recognized rights of another (see Chapter 14), is an area of civil law. **Criminal law**, in contrast, is concerned with wrongs committed against the public as a whole. Criminal acts are prohibited by federal, state, or local statutes (criminal law and procedures will be discussed in Chapter 13). In a criminal case, the government seeks to impose a penalty (a fine or jail time) on a person who is alleged to have committed a crime. In a civil case, one party tries to make the other party comply with a duty or pay for the damage caused by the failure to so comply.

Paralegals who specialize in criminal law may work for public prosecutors, public defenders, or criminal defense attorneys. A legal assistant working for the prosecutor's office, for example, might draft search or arrest warrants. A paralegal working for the defense attorney (public or private) might obtain police reports, conduct research, and draft documents to be filed with the court, such as a document arguing that the police violated the defendant's constitutional rights. Although criminal law and civil law are very different, the trial process is similar, and paralegals perform similar types of tasks (investigation, summarizing witness testimony, and so forth) in preparation for litigation.

Additional Specialty Areas

The above listing of specialty areas is by no means exhaustive. Other areas offer opportunities for paralegals. As the U.S. population ages, for example, more attorneys are focusing on serving the needs of older clients. **Elder law** is the term used to describe this broad specialty. Paralegals who work in this practice area may be asked to assist in a variety of tasks, including those relating to estate planning (discussed earlier), age-discrimination claims, financial arrangements for long-term care, Medicare and Medicaid, abuse suffered by elderly persons, and the visitation rights of grandparents.

Many nurses have found profitable and challenging work as paralegals. A paralegal who is also a trained nurse is well equipped to evaluate legal claims involving injuries, such as those involved in personal-injury, medical malpractice, or product liability lawsuits. A relatively new specialty area among nurses—and within the legal profession—is that of the **legal nurse consultant (LNC)**. An LNC consults with legal professionals and others on medical aspects of legal claims or issues. LNCs usually work independently (offering their services on a contract basis) and are typically well paid for contract services—up to $200 per hour. Some LNCs work for law firms, insurance companies, government offices, and risk management departments of companies as salaried employees. The American Association of Legal Nurse Consultants offers a certification program in which nurses who meet the eligibility criteria (including educational credentials and sufficient experience as a legal nurse) and pass an examination can become certified as LNCs.

Developments in technology are also opening doors to other areas of specialization. Paralegals who acquire expertise in high-tech equipment and software applications can perform valuable services for their employers and command high salaries. (For a discussion of career opportunities for paralegals with expertise in technology, see this chapter's *Technology and Today's Paralegal* feature on the following two pages.)

PARALEGAL COMPENSATION

What do paralegals earn? This is an important question for anyone contemplating a career as a paralegal. You can obtain some idea of what paralegals make, on average, from paralegal compensation surveys. Following a discussion of these surveys, we look at some other components of paralegal compensation, including job benefits and compensation for overtime work.

Compensation Surveys

Paralegal income is affected by a number of factors. We have already covered the effects of the size of the firm or legal department (see Exhibit 2.1 on page 23) and the specialty area in which the paralegal practices (see Exhibit 2.2 on page 28). Another income-determining factor is the paralegal's years of experience. Typically, as shown in Exhibit 2.3 on the next page, more experienced paralegals enjoy higher rates of

Technology and Today's Paralegal

MORE CAREER OPPORTUNITIES FOR TECH-SAVVY PARALEGALS

Paralegals who possess superior computer and technological skills are in great demand in law firms across the nation. Nearly every person entering the profession will be required to use a computer on a daily basis. Knowing the basics—word processing, database management, computerized legal research, and navigating the Internet—is essential, but this knowledge may not be enough to give you a competitive edge in the marketplace. In this feature, we explore some of the skills that paralegals can master in order to secure their future in the job market.

MASTER KEYBOARDING SKILLS

Good keyboarding skills are an invaluable asset. The faster you can accurately key in data on a computer, the more work you can complete in a shorter time—and, consequently, the more valuable you are to an employer. This is true whether you are creating documents, scheduling court dates, managing calendars, or performing legal research. Make it a point, during your education, to practice your touch-typing skills (typing without looking at the keys) every day so that keyboarding becomes second nature to you. Practice entering numbers as well as letters so that you can accurately key in court dates and deadlines in calendaring programs and figures in billing programs. Many inexpensive typing programs are available on CD-ROM or are downloadable from the Internet.

BE PROFICIENT WITH TYPICAL OFFICE SOFTWARE

Most law firms use a variety of software applications, including computerized billing programs, e-mail, calendaring software, and legal research applications. To be competitive in the job market, paralegals should be skilled at using these programs. For example, paralegals are often responsible for keeping track of the deadlines for filing court documents, along with court filing fees and requirements. Local

compensation. This is particularly noticeable when a paralegal has worked for the same employer for a long period of time.

Another major factor that affects paralegal compensation is geographical location. Exhibit 2.3, like earlier exhibits, illustrates *national* averages. Exhibit 2.4, by contrast, shows *regional* averages. As you can see, paralegals who work in the West enjoy higher levels of compensation than paralegals in other regions of the country. Remember, though, that these figures represent averages and can therefore be deceptive. For example, a paralegal working in a rural area of Washington State may not earn as much as a paralegal who works in Chicago.

Keep in mind, too, that salary statistics do not tell the whole story. Although paralegals earn more in California than in Nebraska, the cost of living is higher in

EXHIBIT 2.3
Paralegal Compensation by Years of Experience

Legal Assistant Today, March 2008, p. 4, **www.legalassistanttoday. com**.

Years of Experience on Current Job	Average Compensation
1–5	$47,531
6–10	$54,733
11–15	$53,247
16–20	$57,336
21–25	$57,497
More than 25	$64,174

court rules specify the filing dates and fees for different kinds of cases, but these rules change regularly. Failure to submit documents by the due date can result in a court's dismissing the case or the client's dismissing the firm. Moreover, missed deadlines are a leading cause of malpractice (professional negligence) lawsuits filed by clients against attorneys.

Many firms have computerized calendaring software to help ensure that attorneys do not miss important dates and to calculate required fees based on the local court rules. Such software could suit the needs of a small law firm that handles only local cases, but it might not be adequate if the firm handles cases in numerous counties or states. Rather than buying a more comprehensive and expensive calendaring program and incurring the costs of installation and training, the firm could use an online calendaring service. A paralegal who knows about the availability of online calendaring applications could suggest that the firm use these services on a pay-per-use basis, which could save the firm time and funds. The paralegal might gain the respect and appreciation of the firm and might be asked for her or his input regarding future technology decisions.

CONTINUE TO TAKE ON NEW CHALLENGES

Developing technologies provide avenues for paralegals to advance their positions and become indispensable to their firms. For example, many courts now allow documents to be filed electronically. Paralegals are often responsible for making sure that these documents are in the proper electronic format and that they include hyperlinks to relevant resources. Courts also allow electronic discovery—that is, prior to a trial, a party can obtain evidence in electronic form from the opposing party's e-mails, cell phones, computers, BlackBerry devices, and other electronic equipment. Some law firms also take video depositions (testimony from witnesses) when witnesses are unable to appear in person. Paralegals with skill in locating and obtaining electronic evidence or with the ability to film and produce videos are likely to be in demand.

TECHNOLOGY TIP

Along with technological advances come certain legal questions that are now considered by the courts. For example, how long does electronic evidence need to be retained on a computer system? Who should be required to pay for the discovery of electronic evidence? A paralegal who understands the various legal issues surrounding the use of new technologies and who knows how the courts in the area are resolving these disputes will likely become a key member of the legal team.

California than in Nebraska. This means that your real income—the amount you can purchase with your income—may, in fact, be the same in both states despite the differences in salary. Salary statistics also do not reveal another important component of compensation—job benefits.

Job Benefits

Part of your total compensation package as an employee will consist of job benefits. These benefits may include paid holidays, sick leave, group insurance coverage (life, disability, medical, dental), pension plans, and possibly others. Benefits packages vary from firm to firm. One employer may pay the entire premium for your health insurance, for example, while another employer may require you to contribute part of the

Region	Average Salary
West	$60,340
South	$49,591
Northeast	$59,692
Midwest	$51,123
National Average	$54,859

EXHIBIT 2.4
Average Paralegal Salary by Region

Legal Assistant Today, March/April 2009, pp. 46–47, **www.legalassistanttoday.com.**

cost. Usually, the larger the firm, the greater the value of the benefits package. When evaluating any job offer, you need to consider the benefits that you will receive and what these benefits are worth to you. You will read more about the importance of job benefits later in this chapter, in the context of evaluating a job offer.

Salaries versus Hourly Wages

Most paralegals are salaried employees. In other words, they receive a specified annual salary regardless of the number of hours they work. Others are paid an hourly wage rate for every hour worked. Paralegals are frequently asked to work overtime, and how they are compensated for overtime work usually depends on whether they are salaried employees or are paid hourly wages. Many firms compensate their salaried paralegals for overtime work through year-end **bonuses**, which are payments made to employees in recognition of their devotion to the firm and the high quality of their work. Paralegals often receive annual bonuses ranging from around $2,000 to around $5,000, depending on years of experience, firm size, and so forth. Some firms allow salaried employees to take compensatory time off work (for example, an hour off for every hour worked beyond usual working hours). Employees who are paid an hourly wage rate are normally paid overtime wages. In such cases, there may be no bonus or only a small one.

bonus
An end-of-the-year payment to a salaried employee in appreciation for that employee's overtime work, diligence, or dedication to the firm.

Federal Law and Overtime Pay

Compensation for overtime pay has been a major issue in the paralegal profession. Complicating the debate over this issue are the provisions of the Fair Labor Standards Act (FLSA) of 1938. This act requires employers to pay employees **overtime wages**—one and a half times their normal hourly rate—for all hours worked beyond forty hours per week. The act exempts certain types of employees from this overtime-pay requirement, however. *Exempt employees* include those who qualify under the terms of the act as holding "administrative," "executive," or "professional" positions.

overtime wages
Wages paid to workers who are paid an hourly wage rate to compensate them for overtime work (hours worked beyond forty hours per week). Under federal law, overtime wages are at least one and a half times the regular hourly wage rate.

The Professional Exemption

For a number of years, the U.S. Department of Labor (DOL), which enforces the FLSA, generally held that paralegals were not exempt as professional employees and thus should receive overtime pay for work beyond forty hours per week. Nonetheless, many employers classified their paralegal employees as professionals to avoid the overtime-pay requirements of the act. The paralegal profession was split on the issue. Some paralegals who received year-end bonuses questioned whether their bonuses sufficiently compensated them for the amount of overtime that they had worked. Other paralegals preferred year-end bonuses and their designation as professionals under the FLSA. In the early 1990s, the issue came before a federal court. A group of paralegals who worked for a law firm in Dallas, Texas, sued their employer for $40,000 in back wages for overtime hours that they had worked. The court held that paralegals *could* be classified as professional (exempt) employees because they perform important work and exercise discretion and independent judgment.[1] This decision, while significant, did not resolve the problem in jurisdictions in which that court decision did not apply, and the debate continued.

The FairPay Initiative

In 2004, to provide a clearer test for determining which employees are exempt from the overtime provisions of the FLSA, the DOL issued a regulation concerning overtime pay, known as the FairPay rule. Under this rule, any worker who is paid less than $23,660 per year, or $455 per week, must be paid overtime wages. To qualify under this rule for any of the three exemptions (executive, administrative, or professional), an employee's earnings must exceed this threshold.

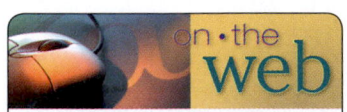

For information on the DOL's FairPay rules, go to the DOL's FairPay Web site at **www.dol.gov/esa/regs/ compliance/fairpay/main.htm**.

The rule also clarified the meaning of the term *professional.* To qualify for the professional exemption, the employee's work must require advanced knowledge in a field of science or learning, and the knowledge must normally have been acquired through a prolonged course of specialized intellectual instruction. The DOL's rule specifically addressed paralegal employees, stating as follows:

> Paralegals and legal assistants generally do not qualify as exempt learned professionals because an advanced specialized academic degree is not a standard prerequisite for entry into the field. Although many paralegals possess general four-year advanced degrees, most specialized paralegal programs are two-year associate degree programs from a community college or equivalent institution.[2]

Thus, most paralegals do not qualify for the professional exemption under the FLSA, which means they are eligible for overtime pay. Realize, though, that paralegals remain professionals in the broader sense of the term, as well as under the criteria defined by the paralegal and legal professions.

PLANNING YOUR CAREER

Career planning involves three key steps. The first step is defining your long-term goals. The second involves coming up with short-term goals and adjusting them to meet the realities of the job market. We look at these two steps in this section. (For some tips on how to succeed in your career, see this chapter's *Featured Contributor* feature beginning on the next page.) Later in this chapter, we discuss the third step: reevaluating your career after you have had some on-the-job experience as a paralegal.

Defining Your Long-Term Goals

From the beginning, you want to define, as clearly as possible, your career goals. This requires some personal reflection and self-assessment. What are you looking for in a career? Why do you want to become a paralegal? Is income the most important factor? Is job satisfaction (doing the kind of work you like) the most important factor? Is the environment in which you work the most important factor? What profession could best utilize your talents and skills? Asking yourself these and other broad questions about your personal preferences and values will help you define more clearly your overall professional goals.

Do not be surprised to find that your long-term goals change over time. As you gain experience as a paralegal and your life circumstances alter, you may decide that your long-term goals are no longer appropriate. For example, the level of career involvement that suits you as a single person may not be appropriate should you marry and have children. Similarly, later in life, when your children leave home, you may have different goals with respect to work.

Also, at the outset of your career, you cannot know what opportunities might present themselves in the future. Career planning is an ongoing challenge for everyone. Throughout your career as a paralegal, you will probably meet other paralegals who have made career changes. A high percentage of paralegals, for example, decided on the field after several years of working in another profession, such as nursing, law enforcement, business administration, or accounting. Changes within the profession, your own experiences, and new opportunities affect the career choices before you. The realities you face during your career are likely to play a significant role in modifying your long-term goals.

Short-Term Goals and Job Realities

Long-term goals are just that—goals that we hope to achieve over many years or even a lifetime. Short-term goals are the steps we take to realize our long-term goals. As an entry-level paralegal, one of your short-term goals is simply to find a job.

featured contributor

PLAN AND PURSUE YOUR DESIRED CAREER

Linda J. Wolf, ACP

BIOGRAPHICAL NOTE

Linda J. Wolf, ACP, earned her bachelor's degree in journalism and political science from Baylor University. She worked as a news editor for the Waco Tribune Herald before moving to Dallas. She began her paralegal career in 1980 with the intellectual property boutique firm of Richards, Medlock & Andrews, where she handled all aspects of intellectual property work. The firm was acquired by Sidley Austin LLP in 1996. She continues to specialize in intellectual property work at the firm, and since 2000 she has also been responsible for managing the library in the Dallas office.

Wolf earned her CLA/CP credential in 1985 and her CLAS in intellectual property in 1995. She has served NALA in many capacities, including as chair of the NALA Certifying Board and, most currently, as president. She is a charter member of the Paralegal Division of the State Bar of Texas and a founding member of the first NALA affiliate in Dallas, the North Texas Paralegal Association. She is also a member of the Society of Professional Journalists.

In tough economic times, it is good to remind ourselves that our profession was born out of the recession of the 1960s and 1970s. History teaches us that a bad economy is fertile ground for people with vision and focus. So there is no better time to be a paralegal, as long as we remember a few golden rules.

For those of us who are veteran paralegals, we need to constantly hone and develop our skill sets to help set us apart in the competitive climate that we currently find ourselves. None of us can sit back on their laurels and assume their job is safe. How do we stay on top? First, ask yourself what would make you better at your career? What would help you stand out from the crowd? For me, it was the choice to take some chemistry courses when I found myself working for a lawyer with a chemical engineering degree at an intellectual property boutique. Find courses and programs in areas of law that interest you and take them. When you do so, you prove to your employer that regardless of your accomplishments to date, you are serious about learning. Plus, those educational offerings will help you stay on top of your game.

Take control of your career. If you don't like to do e-discovery, then take courses that will enable you to migrate out of litigation

Ideally, you will find a job that provides you with a salary consistent with your training and abilities, a level of responsibility that is comfortable (or challenging) for you, and excellent job benefits. The realities of the job market are not always what we wish them to be, however. You should be prepared for the possibility that you might not find the "right" employer or the "perfect" job when you first start. You may be lucky from the outset, but it may take several attempts before you find the employer and the job that best suit your needs, skills, and talents. Remember that even if you do not find the perfect job right away, you can gain valuable skills and experience in *any* job environment—skills and experience that can help you achieve long-term goals in the future. In fact, you might want to "try on" jobs at different-sized firms and in different specialty areas to see how they "fit" with your particular needs.

and into your new area of law. But go about it the right way. Don't wake up one morning and decide you want to do bankruptcy. Allow yourself time to dream about what your ideal job would be, and then develop a plan to create that perfect career for yourself. For instance, a good friend of mine worked in litigation for many years and realized that what she really wanted to do was work for the school district. She literally created her ideal career by educating her school board on why they needed a paralegal and how she could help them.

Keep your eyes open to new opportunities. Several years ago, the National Association of Legal Assistants (NALA) offered an Institute in Social Security benefits administration during the annual educational conference. It was taught by an administrative law judge and was very successful. Because of the nature of the work, some paralegals who attended the Institute saw an opportunity to take that training and turn it into a second career for themselves after they retired. They saw an opportunity where none existed before.

Remember to market yourself within your firm or company. Don't wait for the work to come to you—go out and find it. Attorneys have to market themselves within the company or firm, so why would it be any different for paralegals? If you are looking to segue into a different practice group within your firm or company, let a trusted adviser know that you are looking for new challenges. And if you've recently acquired new skills or knowledge, make sure you let management know. We do ourselves a grave injustice when we fail to market ourselves. After all, if we don't toot our own horn, who will?

For those who are new to the profession, networking is the first key to success. If you haven't found a job yet, use all the networking tools at your fingertips to make contacts. Join the local and state associations, which all have job banks. Join NALA and participate in the conference center, where members can exchange ideas and share job hunting tips. Take advantage of all the special networking tools such as LinkedIn, Plaxo, and Classmates to connect with people who might be able to help you.

... *"networking is the first key to success."*

... *"market yourself"* ...

Once you have found a job, those connections can be a tremendous help. If you need help finding someone who can translate Russian, for example, you can reach out to your colleagues through your networking tools to see if anyone can recommend a resource for you. This is particularly helpful if you happen to work in a rural area, or in a narrow field of law.

Regardless of your experience level, there are plenty of wonderful opportunities for paralegals in the job market today. The Department of Labor still lists our profession as one of the fastest growing professions in the United States today, with over 200,000 paralegals across the country.

So keep up with trends, stay on top of your education, and stay connected with your colleagues and you'll always be in demand.

LOCATING POTENTIAL EMPLOYERS

Looking for a job is time consuming and requires attention to detail, persistence, and creativity. Your paralegal education is preparing you, among other things, to do investigative research. The investigative skills that you will use on the job as a paralegal are the ones that you should apply when looking for a job.

Where do you begin your investigation? How can you find out what paralegal jobs are available in your area or elsewhere? How do you know which law firms practice the type of law that interests you? The following suggestions will help you answer these questions.

Networking

Career opportunities often go unpublished. Many firms post notices within their own organizations before publishing online or in the "Help Wanted" section of a newspaper or periodical. This opens doors to their own employees before the general public. It also spares employers from having to wade through many applications for a vacant position. If you have connections within an organization, you may be told that a position is opening up before other candidates are aware that an opportunity exists.

> **networking**
>
> Making personal connections and cultivating relationships with people in a certain field, profession, or area of interest.

More paralegals find employment through networking than through any other means. For paralegals, **networking** is the process of making personal connections with the other paralegals, paralegal instructors, attorneys, and others who are involved in (or who know someone who is involved in) the paralegal or legal profession. Online networking, such as that provided by LinkedIn (**www.linkedin.com**), is becoming popular as well. Professional organizations and internships offer important networking opportunities.

Join a Professional Association

Students can form a network of paralegal connections through affiliation with professional associations and student clubs. You have already learned about NALA and NFPA, the two largest national associations for legal assistants. Other organizations of paralegals exist across the country. Some such organizations are listed in Appendix F at the end of this book. See if your local paralegal association allows students to be members. If it does, attend meetings and get to know other paralegals, who may know of job opportunities in your area. Persons involved with other groups—such as the International Paralegal Management Association, or IPMA (an association of individuals who manage legal assistants), and the **state bar association** (a state-level association of attorneys)—can also provide valuable inside knowledge of potential job openings.

> **state bar association**
>
> An association of attorneys within a state. In most states, an attorney must be a member of the state bar association to practice law in the state.

Network during Internships

Most paralegal education programs include an internship in which students are placed temporarily in a law firm or other work setting. The people you meet and deal with in these settings often turn out to be very beneficial to you in finding future employment. In many cases, an intern who has performed well is offered a full-time position after graduation. Even if you are not interested in working for the firm with which you do your internship, be careful not to "burn your bridges." The legal community is relatively small, and lawyers are more inclined to hire paralegals about whom their colleagues have made positive remarks. Many online social networks, such as Facebook and MySpace, are now being used by professionals to provide and obtain work-related information.

Finding Available Jobs

Your next effort should be to locate sources that list paralegal job openings. Classified ads in the newspaper were used traditionally, but not as much these days. **Trade journals** and similar publications, such as your local or state bar association's journal, newsletter, or Web site, may list openings for legal professionals. Increasingly, employers advertise job openings in online publications and turn to online databases to find prospective employees. In fact, today the best starting point when launching your search is probably the Internet.

> **trade journal**
>
> A newsletter, magazine, or other periodical that provides a certain trade or profession with information (products, trends, or developments) relating to that trade or profession.

Identifying Possible Employers

You should also identify firms and organizations for which you might like to work and submit an employment application to them. In a well-organized job search, locate and contact organizations that offer the benefits, salary, opportunities for advancement, work environment, and legal specialty of your choice. Even though

Ethics Watch

THE IMPORTANCE OF BEING HONEST

When looking for a job, be honest with others about your skills and experience. Even though you may want to impress a prospective employer, never give in to the temptation to exaggerate your qualifications. For example, suppose that you are working for a law firm during your internship and would really like to be hired by the firm in the future as a paralegal. In conversations with people in the firm, don't try to impress them by making misleading statements about your qualifications or skills. For instance, suppose you tell your supervisor that your GPA was 3.8 when in fact it was 3.4. This "little white lie" may come back to haunt you in the future. If the firm offers you a permanent job, it will likely check your credentials, including your college or professional school transcripts. Any misrepresentation, no matter how minor it may seem, could doom your chance of being hired. Professional responsibility requires, among other things, that you be honest and pay close attention to detail—not only on the job but also when you are looking for a job.

This scenario is consistent with the NFPA *Model Code of Ethics and Professional Responsibility,* Section 1.3, "A paralegal shall maintain a high standard of professional conduct," and "A paralegal shall avoid impropriety and the appearance of impropriety and shall not engage in any conduct that would adversely affect his/her fitness to practice."

these employers may not have vacancies in your field at the moment, you want your job application to be immediately available when an opening occurs. Most firms, if they are interested in your qualifications, will keep your application on file for six months or so and may contact you if a position becomes available. As the *Ethics Watch* feature discusses, be truthful about your background.

It is a good idea to begin compiling employer information for your job search while you are still completing your studies. Many of the resources you will need are available at the college you attend or through your paralegal program (and increasingly, online).

The Yellow Pages

An obvious source of information is the Yellow Pages of your local telephone directory, which is available online. Look under "Attorneys" or "Law Firms" for the names of potential contacts. If you want to work in a specialty area, such as real estate, you might look under other listings, such as "Title Companies."

Legal Directories

Legal directories provide lists of attorneys, their locations, and their areas of practice. The *Martindale-Hubbell Law Directory,* which you can find at most law libraries (and online at **www.martindale.com**), lists the names, addresses, telephone numbers, areas of legal practice, and other data for many lawyers and law firms around the country. It is an excellent resource for paralegals interested in working for law firms or corporate legal departments. *West's Legal Directory* is another valuable source of information. It is on the Internet at **lawyers.findlaw.com**. The directory contains a detailed listing of U.S. attorneys and law firms, state and federal attorneys and offices, and corporate legal departments and general counsel.

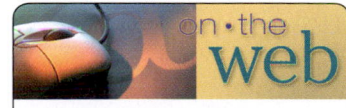

You can search the Yellow Pages online at a number of Web sites, including Yahoo's Yellow Pages at **yp.yahoo.com**.

Job-Placement Services

Throughout your job search, make full use of your school's placement service. Many colleges with paralegal programs provide job-placement services, and ABA-approved schools are required to provide ongoing placement services. Placement offices have personnel trained to assist you in finding a job, as well as in preparing job-search tools, such as your résumé and a list of potential employers.

A growing trend is to use legal staffing or placement companies (also known as *recruiters*) to locate employment. Usually, the employer pays the fees for the placement company's services, and the company recruits candidates for the paralegal position and arranges interviews. Placement services can be located through paralegal program directors, local paralegal associations, and state bar associations, as well as on the Web.

Legal staffing companies place paralegal employees in both temporary (called "contract") and full-time (called "direct-hire") positions. Temporary contract employees are often used when a regular employee needs to take leave or when a special project requires additional paralegals, such as in large-scale litigation cases. Contract jobs can last from a few days to over a year. Long-term contract opportunities can provide valuable work experience in a particular specialty. Direct-hire positions typically provide long-term employment with salary and benefits, which are not provided in most temporary employment contracts.

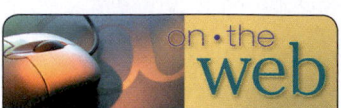

If you are looking for a job in a corporate legal department, Hoovers Online offers company and contact information for many public and private companies worldwide at **www.hoovers.com**.

MARKETING YOUR SKILLS

Once you have located potential employers, the next step is to market your skills and yourself effectively. Marketing your skills involves three stages: the application process, interviewing for jobs, and following up on job interviews.

Keep in mind throughout your job search that each personal contact you make, whether it results in employment or not, has potential for your future. A firm may not hire you today because you lack experience or because it has no opening, but it may hire you a year from now. Therefore, keep track of the contacts you make during your search, be patient, and be professional. You may be surprised how many doors will open for you—if not today, then tomorrow.

The Application Process

When looking for paralegal employment, you need to assemble and present professional application materials. The basic materials you should create are a résumé, a cover letter, a list of professional references, and a portfolio. The following discussion explains each of these and gives some practical tips on how to create them.

The Résumé

For most job applications, you must submit a personal *résumé* that summarizes your employment and educational background. Your résumé is an advertisement, and you should invest the time to make that advertisement effective. Because personnel officers in law firms, corporations, and government agencies may receive many résumés for each position they advertise, your résumé should create the best possible impression if you want to gain a competitive edge over other job seekers.

Either generate your résumé yourself, using a computer and a laser printer, or have a professional résumé-preparation service do it for you. Format each page so that the reader is able to scan it quickly and catch the highlights. You might vary the type size, but never use a type size or style that is difficult to read.

EXHIBIT 2.5
A Sample Résumé of a Person
with Paralegal Experience

ELENA LOPEZ

1131 North Shore Drive

Nita City, NI 48804

Telephone: (616) 555-0102 • Fax: (616) 555-2103 • E-mail: elopez@nitanet.net

---

EMPLOYMENT OBJECTIVE

A position as a paralegal in a private law firm that specializes in personal-injury practice.

EDUCATION

2006   Postbaccalaureate certificate
          Midwestern Professional School for Paralegals, Green Bay, WI
          Focus: Litigation Procedures, Legal Investigation, Torts, Arbitration
          and Mediation, Case Preparation, and Trial. GPA 3.8.

2003   Bachelor of Arts degree
          University of Wisconsin, Madison, WI 53706.
          Political Science major. GPA 3.1.

PARALEGAL EXPERIENCE

- Caldwell Legal Clinic , Nita City, NI
  Paralegal: June 2006 to the present.
  Responsibilities: Legal research and document review; drafting discovery
  documents, including interrogatories, deposition summaries, and requests
  for admissions; and trial preparation in personal-injury cases.

- Legal Aid Society, Green Bay, WI
  Paralegal: June 2003 to May 2006.
  Responsibilities: Part-time assistance to legal aid attorneys in their
  representation of indigent clients in matters such as divorce, abuse, child
  custody, paternity, and landlord/tenant disputes.

- University of Wisconsin, Madison, WI
  Research Assistant: Political Science Department, January 2001 to May 2003.
  Responsibilities: Research on the effectiveness of federal welfare
  programs in reducing poverty in the United States.

AFFILIATIONS

Paralegal Association of Wisconsin
National Association of Legal Assistants

What to Include in Your Résumé.   Your name, address, telephone number, e-mail address, and fax number belong in the heading of your résumé. The body of the résumé should be simple, brief, and clear. As a general rule, it should contain only information relevant to the job that you are seeking. A one-page résumé is usually sufficient, unless two pages are required to list relevant educational background and work experience. Exhibit 2.5 above shows a sample résumé of a person with paralegal experience, and Exhibit 2.6 on the next page shows one of a person without such experience. Note that you should avoid placing your name and address in the upper left-hand corner, as this area is often stapled.

Divide your résumé into logical sections with headings, such as those shown in the exhibits. Whenever you list dates, such as educational and employment dates, list them chronologically, in reverse order. In other words, list your most recent educational or work history first. When discussing your education, list the names, cities, and states of the colleges or universities that you have attended and the degrees that you have received. You may want to indicate your major and minor

EXHIBIT 2.6
A Sample Résumé of a Person without Paralegal Experience

MARCUS BOHMAN

335 W. Alder Street

Gresham, CA 90650

Home Phone: (562) 555-6868 • Mobile Phone: (562) 555-2468 • E-mail: mboh44@gresham.net

---

OBJECTIVE

To obtain a paralegal position in a firm that specializes in real estate transactions.

QUALIFICATIONS

I am a self-motivated, certified paralegal (CLA 2010) with knowledge and background in real estate and a strong academic record (3.7 GPA). In addition to the education listed below, I have completed several courses on real estate financing and possess excellent accounting skills.

EDUCATION

2010   *Baccalaureate Degree*—ABA-Approved Program
            University of LaVerne, Legal Studies Program, LaVerne, CA
            Major: Paralegal Studies; Minor: Business Management
            Emphasis on Real Property and Land-Use Planning, Legal Research and
            Writing.

EMPLOYMENT

2009–2010   *Intern, Hansen, Henault, Richmond & Shaw*
            Researched and drafted numerous real estate documents, including land
            sale contracts, commercial leases, and deeds. Scheduled meetings with
            clients. Participated in client interviews and several real estate closings.
            Filed documents with county.

2004–2009   *Office Assistant, Eastside Commercial Property*
            Maintained files and handled telephone inquiries at commercial real estate
            company. Coordinated land surveys and obtained property descriptions.

2003–2004   *Clerk, LandPro Title Company*
            Coordinated title searches and acted as a liaison among banks, mortgage
            companies, and the title company.

2001–2003   *Clerk, San Jose County Recorder's office*
            Handled inquiries from the public and provided instruction to those
            seeking to look up records via microfiche.

---

concentrations and those courses that are most related to your professional goal, such as "Major: Paralegal Studies" or "Minor: Political Science." When listing your work experience, specify your responsibilities in each position. Also include any volunteer work that you have done.

Scholarships or honors should also be indicated. If you have a high grade point average (GPA), you should include the GPA in your résumé. Under the heading "Selected Accomplishments," you might indicate your ability to speak more than one language or other special skill, such as online research skills.

What if you are an entry-level paralegal and have no work experience to list? What can you include on your résumé to fill out the page? If you are facing this situation, add more information on your educational background and experience. You can list specific courses that you took, particular skills—such as computer skills—that you acquired during your paralegal training, and student affiliations.

Do Not Include Personal Data.   Avoid including personal data (such as age, marital status, number of children, gender, or hobbies) in your résumé. Employers are prohibited by law from discriminating against employees or job candidates on the basis of race, color, gender, national origin, religion, age, or disability. You can help them fulfill this legal obligation by not including in your résumé any information that could serve as a basis for discrimination. For the same reason, you would be wise not to include a photograph of yourself with your résumé. Also, most prospective employers are not interested in such information as personal preferences, pastimes, or hobbies.

Proofread Your Results.   Carefully proofread your résumé. Use the spelling checker and grammar checker on your computer, but do not totally rely on them. Have a friend or instructor review your résumé for punctuation, syntax, grammar, spelling, and content. If you find an error, you need to fix it, even if it means having new résumés printed. A mistake on your résumé tells the potential employer that you are a careless worker, and this message may ruin your chances of landing a job.

The Cover Letter

To encourage the recruiter to review your résumé, you need to capture his or her attention with a *cover letter* that accompanies the résumé. Because the cover letter is usually your first contact with an employer, it should be written carefully. It should be brief, perhaps only two or three paragraphs in length. Exhibit 2.7 on the next page shows a sample cover letter. When possible, you should learn the name of the person in charge of hiring (by phone or e-mail, if necessary) and direct your letter to that person. If you do not know that person's name, use a generic title, such as "Human Resources Manager" or "Legal Assistant Manager."

Your cover letter should point out a few things about yourself and your qualifications for the position that might persuade a recruiter to examine your résumé. As a recently graduated paralegal, for example, you might draw attention to your academic standing at school, your eagerness to specialize in the same area of law as the employer (perhaps listing some courses relating to that specialty), and your willingness to relocate to the employer's city. Your job is to convince the recruiter that you are a close match to the mental picture that he or she has of the perfect candidate for the job. Make sure that the reader knows when and where you can be reached. Often this is best indicated in the closing paragraph of the letter, as shown in the exhibit.

As with your résumé, read through your letter several times and have someone else read it also to make sure that it is free from mistakes and easily understood. You should use the same type of paper for your cover letter as you use for your résumé.

What about e-mailing your cover letter and résumé to prospective employers? This is a difficult question. On the one hand, e-mail is much faster than regular mail or express delivery services. On the other hand, an e-mail résumé does not look as nice. While some firms are accustomed to receiving applications by e-mail, others are not, and attorneys generally prefer traditional résumés. If the job you are applying for was advertised online or if the employer provided an e-mail address for interested job candidates to use, then e-mail is probably appropriate. Generally, though, job candidates who submit applications by e-mail should also send, by regular mail, printed copies of their letters and résumés.

List of Professional References

If a firm is interested in your application, you will probably be asked for a list of references—people the firm can contact to obtain information about you and your abilities. An instructor who has worked closely with you, an internship supervisor who has knowledge of your work, or a past employer who has observed your problem-solving ability

EXHIBIT 2.7
A Sample Cover Letter

ELENA LOPEZ

1131 North Shore Drive

Nita City, NI 48804

Telephone: (616) 555-0102 • Fax: (616) 555-2103 • E-mail: elopez@nitanet.net

August 22, 2010

Allen P. Gilmore, Esq.
Jeffers, Gilmore & Dunn
553 Fifth Avenue, Suite 101
Nita City, NI 48801

Dear Mr. Gilmore:

I am responding to your advertisement in the *Vegas Law Journal* for a paralegal to assist you in personal-injury litigation. I am confident that I possess the skills and qualifications that you seek.

As you can see from the enclosed résumé, I received my paralegal certificate from Midwestern Professional School for Paralegals after obtaining a Bachelor of Arts degree from the University of Wisconsin. My paralegal courses included litigation procedures, legal research, legal investigation, and legal writing, and I graduated with a G.P.A. of 3.8.

After completing school, I obtained a position with a legal aid office, where I worked for several years and honed my legal research and writing skills. My current position with Caldwell Legal Clinic has provided me with valuable experience in preparing personal-injury cases for trial. I very much enjoy this area of law and hope to specialize in personal-injury litigation.

I am excited about the possibility of meeting with you to learn more about the position that you have available. I have enclosed my résumé, as well as a list of professional references and a brief writing sample for your perusal.

Please contact me to schedule an interview. You can contact me by phone after 3:00 P.M., Monday through Friday. I look forward to hearing from you.

Sincerely yours,

Elena Lopez

Elena Lopez

Enclosures

would all make excellent references. You should have at least three professionally relevant references, but more than five references are rarely necessary. Never include the names of family members, friends, or others who are clearly biased in your favor.

List your references on a separate sheet of paper, making sure to include your name, address, and telephone number at the top of the page, in the same format as on your résumé. For each person included on the list, include his or her current institutional affiliation or business firm, address, telephone number, fax number, and e-mail address. Make it easy for prospective employers to contact and communicate with your references.

When creating your list of references, always remember the following rule: never list a person's name as a reference unless you have that person's permission to do so. After all, it will not help you win the position you seek if one of your references is surprised by the call. Such events raise a red flag and indicate that you are not concerned with details.

Obtaining permission from legal professionals to use them as references also gives you an opportunity to discuss your plans and goals with them, and they may be able to advise you and assist you in your networking. Additionally, it gives you a chance to discuss with them the kinds of experience and skills in which a prospective employer may be interested.

Your Professional Portfolio

When a potential employer asks you for an interview, have your *professional portfolio* ready to give to the interviewer. The professional portfolio should contain another copy of your résumé, a list of references, letters of recommendation written by previous employers or instructors, samples of legal documents that you have composed, college or university transcripts, and any other relevant professional information, such as proof of professional certification or achievement. This collection of documents should be well organized and professionally presented. Depending on the size of your portfolio, a cover sheet, a table of contents, and a commercial binder may be appropriate.

The interviewer may be interested in your research and writing skills. Therefore, your professional portfolio should contain several samples of legal writing. If you are looking for your first legal position, go through your paralegal drafting assignments and pull out those that reflect your best work and that relate to the job skills you wish to demonstrate. Working with an instructor or other mentor, revise and improve those samples for inclusion in the portfolio. You might also use documents that you drafted while an intern or when working as a paralegal. These documents make excellent writing samples because they involve real-life circumstances. Be careful, however, and always remember, on any sample document, to completely blacken out (or "white out") any identifying reference to a client unless you have the client's permission to disclose his or her identity or the information is not confidential.

Always include a résumé, as well as a list of references, in your professional portfolio, even though you already sent your résumé to the prospective employer with your cover letter. Interviewers may not have the résumé at hand at the time of the interview, and providing a second copy with your professional portfolio is a thoughtful gesture on your part.

Some interviewers may examine your professional portfolio carefully. Others may keep it to examine later, after the interview. Still others may not be interested in it at all. If there is a particular item in your portfolio that you would like the interviewer to see, make sure you point it out before leaving the interview.

The Interview

After an employer has reviewed your cover letter and résumé, the employer may contact you to schedule an interview. Interviews with potential employers may be the most challenging (and stressful) part of your search for employment.

Every interview will be different. Some will go well, but you will lose out to another candidate. Nonetheless, you have made a good contact, and you may be able to use this interviewer as a resource for information about other jobs. Remember what went right about the interview, and try to use that information at the next one. Other interviews may go poorly, but good lessons can be learned from poor interviews.

You will find that some interviewers are more skilled at interviewing than others. Some have a talent for getting applicants to open up, while others are confrontational and put the already nervous candidate on the defensive. Still others may be unprepared for the interview. They may not have had time to compare applicants' qualifications with the job requirements, for example. As the person being interviewed, you have no control over who will interview you. You do, however, have control over your preparations for the interview. The following discussion will help you with these preparations.

Before the Interview

You can do many things prior to the interview to improve your chances of getting the job. First, do your "homework." Learn as much about the employer as possible. Check with your instructors or other legal professionals to find out if they are familiar with the firm or the interviewer. To see what you can learn about the firm and its members, check the employer's Web site, if there is one, and consult relevant directories, such as legal and company directories, as well as business publications. When you are called for an interview, learn the full name of the interviewer, so that you will be able to address him or her by name during the interview and properly address a follow-up letter. During the interview, use Mr. or Ms. in addressing the interviewer unless directed by the interviewer to be less formal.

Anticipate and review the questions that you might be asked during the interview. Then prepare (and possibly rehearse with a friend) your answers to these questions. For example, if you did not graduate from high school with your class but later received a general equivalency diploma (GED), you might be asked why you dropped out of school. If you have already prepared an answer for this question, it may save you the embarrassment of having to decide, on the spot, how to reduce a complicated story to a brief sentence or two.

You should also prepare yourself to be interviewed by a "team" of legal professionals, such as an attorney, a paralegal, and perhaps others from the firm. Some prospective employers invite others who will be working with a new paralegal to participate in the interviewing process.

Promptness is extremely important. Plan to arrive for the interview at least ten minutes early, and allow plenty of extra time to get there. If the firm is located in an area that is unfamiliar to you, make sure that you know how to get there, how long it will take, and, if you are driving, whether parking is available nearby.

Appearance is also important. Wear a relatively conservative suit or dress to the interview, and limit your use of jewelry or other accents. You can find further tips on how to prepare for a job interview by checking online career sites or by looking at books dealing with careers and job hunting.

At the Interview

During the interview, pay attention and listen closely. The interviewer asks questions to learn whether a candidate will fit comfortably into the firm, whether the candidate is organized and competent and will satisfactorily perform the job, and whether the candidate is reliable and will work hard to master the tasks presented. Your answers should be directly related to the questions, and you should not stray from the point. If you are unsure of what the interviewer means by a certain question, ask for clarification.

Interviewers use certain question formats to elicit certain types of responses. Four typical formats for questions are the following:

- *Closed-ended questions*—to elicit simple "Yes" or "No" answers.
- *Open-ended questions*—which invite you to discuss, in some detail, a specific topic or experience.
- *Hypothetical questions*—to learn how you might respond to situations that could arise during the course of your employment.

> **Q** **Are you married?**
>
> **A.** If you are concerned that my social life will interfere with work, I can assure you that I keep the two very separate.
>
> **Q.** **Do you have any children yet?**
>
> **A.** That question leads me to believe that you would be concerned about my ability to prioritize my job and other responsibilities. Is that something that you are worried about?
>
> **Q.** **Are you or your husband a member of the Republican Party?**
>
> **A.** That is a private matter. Please realize that my family and political life will not interfere with my ability to do excellent work for your firm.
>
> **Q.** **You're quite a bit more mature than other applicants. Will you be thinking of retiring in the next ten years?**
>
> **A.** I don't understand how my age relates to my ability to perform this job.

EXHIBIT 2.8
Objectionable or Illegal Questions and Possible Responses

- *Pressure questions*—to see how you deal with uncomfortable situations or unpleasant discussions.

You will learn more about question formats in Chapter 11, when we discuss some techniques that paralegals use when interviewing clients.

Certain questions are illegal or objectionable. These include questions about your marital status, family, religion, race, color, national origin, age, health or disability, or arrest record. You do not have to answer such questions unless you choose to do so. Exhibit 2.8 shows some examples of how you might respond to these types of questions. Note that because of record-keeping requirements imposed by the federal Equal Employment Opportunity Commission, an employer is likely to ask you to fill out a form that details your race, age, and other personal facts. This information is needed for the record but is not to be discussed in the interview process.

As odd as it may seem, one of the most difficult moments is when the interviewer turns the inquiry around by asking, "Now then, do you have any questions?" Be prepared for this. Before the interview, take time to list your concerns. Bring the list to the interview with you. Questioning the interviewer gives you an opportunity to learn more about the firm and how it uses paralegal services. Questioning the interviewer may also give the interviewer an opportunity to see how you might interview a client on behalf of the firm. Exhibit 2.9 on the next page lists some sample questions that you might ask the interviewer. You should not raise the issue of salary at the first interview unless you are offered the job. It is also not wise to ask early in the process about vacation time. The employer wants someone eager to work, not to take time off.

After the Interview

You should not expect to be hired as the result of one interview, although occasionally this does happen. Often, two and even three interviews take place before you are offered a job. After leaving the interview, jot down a few notes to provide a refresher for your memory should you be called back for a second (or third) interview. You will impress the interviewer if you are able to "pick up where you left off" from a discussion initiated several weeks earlier. Also, list the names and positions of the people you met during the interview process.

The Follow-Up/Thank-You Letter

A day or two after the interview, but not longer than a week later, you should send a *follow-up letter* to the interviewer. In this brief letter, you can mention again your availability and interest in the position, thank the interviewer for his or her time

EXHIBIT 2.9
Questioning the Interviewer

Questions that you might want to ask the interviewer include the following:

- What method does the firm use to assign duties to paralegals?
- How do paralegals function within the organization?
- What clerical support staff is available for paralegals?
- Does the job involve travel? How will travel expenses be covered?
- What computer technology is used by the firm?
- Does the firm support paralegal continuing education and training programs?
- Will client contact be direct or indirect?
- Does the firm have an in-house library and access to computerized research services that paralegals can use?
- Will the paralegal be assigned work in a given specialty, such as real estate or family law?
- When does the job begin?
- What method is used to review and evaluate paralegal performance?
- How are paralegals supervised, and by whom?
- Are paralegals classified as exempt employees by this firm?
- Is there a written job description or employee policy manual for the job that I may review?

in interviewing you, and perhaps refer to a discussion that took place during the interview.

You may have left the interview with the impression that the meeting went poorly. But the interviewer may have a different sense of what happened at the meeting. Interviewers have different styles, and what you interpreted to be a bad interview may just have been a reflection of that interviewer's style. You simply have no way of being certain, so follow through and make yourself available for the job or at least for another meeting. For an example of a follow-up letter, see Exhibit 2.10.

Job-Hunting Files

In addition to keeping your professional portfolio materials up to date, you need to construct a filing system to stay on top of your job-search activities. Create a separate file for each potential employer, and keep copies of your letters, including e-mail messages, to that employer in your file, along with any responses. You might also want to keep lists or notes for addresses, telephone numbers, e-mail addresses, dates of contacts, advantages and disadvantages of employment with the various firms that you have contacted or by which you have been interviewed, topics discussed at interviews, and the like. Then, when you are called for an interview, you will have information on the firm at your fingertips. Always keep in mind that when looking for paralegal employment, your "job" is finding work as a paralegal—and it pays to be efficient.

Your files will also provide you with an excellent resource for networking even after you have a permanent position. The files may also provide useful information for a career change in the future.

Salary Negotiations

Sometimes a firm states a salary or a salary range in its advertisement for a paralegal. During a first interview, a prospective employer may offer that information as well. In other situations, an applicant does not know what the salary for a certain position will be until he or she is offered the job.

EXHIBIT 2.10
A Sample Follow-Up Letter

ELENA LOPEZ

1131 North Shore Drive
Nita City, NI 48804
Telephone: (616) 555-0102 • Fax: (616) 555-2103 • E-mail: elopez@nitanet.net

September 3, 2010

Allen P. Gilmore, Esq.
Jeffers, Gilmore & Dunn
553 Fifth Avenue, Suite 101
Nita City, NI 48801

Dear Mr. Gilmore:

Thank you for taking time out of your busy schedule to meet with me last Thursday about your firm's paralegal position. I very much enjoyed our discussion, as well as the opportunity to meet some of your firm's employees.

I am extremely interested in the possibility of becoming a member of your legal team and look forward to the prospect of meeting with you again in the near future.

Sincerely yours,

Elena Lopez

Elena Lopez

When you are offered a job, be prepared for the prospective employer to indicate a salary figure and ask you if that figure is acceptable to you. If it is acceptable, then you have no problem. If you think it is too low, then the situation becomes more delicate. If you have no other job offer and really need a job, you may not want to foreclose this job opportunity by saying that the salary is too low. You might instead tell the prospective employer that the job interests you and that you will consider the offer seriously. Also, remember that salary is just one factor in deciding what a job is worth to you. In addition to salary, you need to consider job benefits and other factors, including those listed in Exhibit 2.11 on the next page.

Some prospective employers do not suggest a salary or a salary range but rather ask the job applicant what kind of salary he or she had in mind. You can prepare for this question by researching paralegal salaries in the area. You can find information on salaries by checking local, state, and national paralegal compensation surveys. Check first with your local paralegal association to see if it has collected data on local paralegal salaries. You might also find helpful information in your school's placement office.

Suppose that you have found in your research that paralegals in the community usually start at $36,000 but that many with your education and training start at $43,000. If you ask for $45,000, then you may be unrealistically expensive—and the job offer may be lost. If you ask for $43,000, then you are still "in the ballpark"—and you may win the job.

Negotiating salaries can be difficult. On the one hand, you want to obtain a good salary and do not want to underprice your services. On the other hand, overpricing

EXHIBIT 2.11
Salary Negotiations: What Is This Job Worth to You?

BENEFITS

What benefits are included? • Will the benefits package include medical insurance? • Life insurance? • Disability insurance? • Dental insurance? • What portion, if any, of the insurance premium will be deducted from your wages? • Is there an employee pension plan? • How many paid vacation days will you have? • Will the firm cover your paralegal association fees? • Will the firm assist you with tuition and other costs associated with continuing paralegal education? • Will the firm assist with day-care arrangements and/or costs? • Will you have access to a company car? • Does the firm help with parking expenses (important in major cities)?

CAREER OPPORTUNITIES

Does the position offer you opportunities for advancement? You may be willing to accept a lower salary now if you know that it will increase as you move up the career ladder.

COMPENSATION

Will you receive an annual salary or be paid by the hour? • If you will receive an annual salary, will you receive annual bonuses? • How are bonuses determined? • Is the salary negotiable? (In some large firms and in government agencies, it may not be.)

COMPETITION

How stiff is the competition for this job? If you really want the job and are competing with numerous other candidates for the position, you might want to accept a lower salary just to land the job.

JOB DESCRIPTION

What are the paralegal's duties within the organization? Do you have sufficient training and experience to handle these duties? • Are you underqualified or overqualified for the job? • Will your skills as a paralegal be utilized effectively? • How much overtime work will likely be required? • How stressful will the job be?

JOB FLEXIBILITY

How flexible are the working hours? • If you work eight hours overtime one week, can you take a (paid) day off the following week? • Can you take time off during periods when the workload is less?

LOCATION

Do you want to live in this community? • What is the cost of living in this area? Remember, a $40,000 salary in New York City, where housing and taxes are very expensive, may not give you as much real income as a $30,000 salary in a smaller community in the Midwest.

PERMANENCE

Is the job a permanent or a temporary position? Usually, hourly rates are higher for temporary assistance than for permanent employees.

TRAVEL

Will you be required to travel? • If so, how often or extensively? • How will travel expenses be handled? Will you pay them and then be reimbursed by the employer?

your services may extinguish an employment opportunity or eliminate the possibility of working for an otherwise suitable employer. Your best option might be to state a salary range that is acceptable to you. That way, you are not pinned down to a specific figure. Note, though, that if you indicate an acceptable salary range, you invite an offer of the lowest salary—so the low end of the salary range should be the threshold amount that you will accept.

REEVALUATING YOUR CAREER

Once you have gained several years' experience working as a paralegal, you can undertake the third step in career planning: reevaluating your career goals and reassessing your abilities based on your accumulated experience. Paralegals who want to advance in their careers normally have three options: (1) being promoted or transferring to another department or branch office of the firm; (2) moving

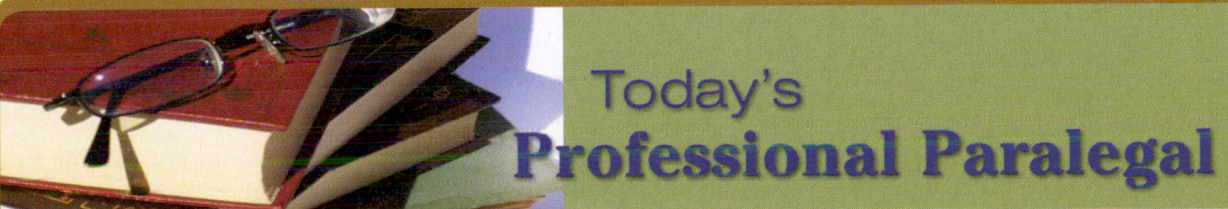

Today's Professional Paralegal

A VIEW FROM THE INSIDE: ASSISTING A CIVIL LITIGATION PARALEGAL

One of the best ways for a student to get a sense of a professional paralegal's trial responsibilities is to assist with a case being tried in court. As a project concluding their Introduction to Paralegal Studies course, paralegal students Jay Herrera and Kelly Devon spent two weeks assisting in and observing a federal court case.

The case, conducted in a U.S. district court, originated when a union member brought a federal civil rights action against the Santa Corina Police Department (SCPD) and several officers. The lawsuit was the result of an altercation between a group of police officers and several union members who were picketing outside the gate of their employer, Duhaime News Service (DNS). The plaintiff was seeking to recover damages from the officers and the SCPD for excessive use of force, false arrest, and conspiring with DNS to suppress picketing activities.

Kelly and Jay worked with the state attorney general's office, which represented the police department in the case, both before and during the trial as paralegals. The project extended over two weeks. Kelly and Jay first assisted in the final trial-preparation work and then played supporting roles on the day of the trial.

ASSISTING WITH TRIAL PREPARATIONS

Shawna Jameson, a civil paralegal specialist for the state attorney general's office, talked with Jay and Kelly about the trial process and about Shawna's role as a paralegal. Shawna described her functions during the initial interview and explained how she conducted or assisted with other interviews and investigations. Shawna showed them how her office's filing system was organized. She then described how she assisted the attorneys by researching and organizing information to be used in drafting pretrial documents and requests for information from the opposing party. She also demonstrated how she compiled and organized litigation files.

The week before the trial, with Shawna's guidance, Kelly organized all of the photographs, diagrams, and other exhibits that would be used as evidence. Kelly scanned the documents into the computer and helped Shawna set up a PowerPoint presentation. Meanwhile, Jay organized all of the documents needed for the trial notebook according to Shawna's instructions. (Detailed information on a paralegal's role in pretrial preparation is provided in Chapter 10.)

THE DAY OF THE TRIAL

Kelly and Jay arrived early on the day of the trial. Jay sat next to Shawna and right behind the attorney representing the state, keeping a copy of the trial notebook in hand and following along as the trial progressed. Kelly sat at a nearby table with her laptop computer. As soon as she arrived, Kelly opened and tested her PowerPoint presentation. Jay watched as the room gradually filled with police officers, union representatives, corporate officers from DNS, and, finally, the judge.

Kelly ran the PowerPoint presentation software to display evidence when the attorney was presenting their side of the case. Jay was responsible for retrieving the proper documents for the attorney as they were needed during the trial. To stay on track and be prepared, each needed to follow the attorney's presentation carefully.

MEETING THE PARTICIPANTS

During the lunch break, Kelly and Jay had an opportunity to meet the attorneys briefly and talk with some of the police officers. Kelly briefly spoke with the judge. Both expressed excitement after meeting some of the players.

When the trial was over, Jay and Kelly each wrote a report describing what they had learned. They had gained insights into the trial process and expanded their understanding of a paralegal's role. At the conclusion, Kelly and Jay both expressed gratitude to Shawna for this valuable window of insight into the paralegal profession. They also told Shawna how impressed they were with her ability to effectively manage all the aspects of her job.

to another firm, and perhaps another specialty; and (3) going back to school for additional education.

Career Paths

Large firms often provide career paths for their paralegal employees. Moving from the entry-level position of *legal-assistant clerk* to the position of *legal-assistant manager*, for example, may be one career track within a large law firm. A career track with a state government agency might begin at a *legal-technician* level and advance to a *legal-specialist* level.

Creating Opportunities

Smaller firms usually have no specific career path or opportunities for promotion and advancement. If you are the only paralegal in a small law firm, there will be no career path for you to follow. In this situation, you might stay with the firm and create your own position or career ladder. Moving up the ladder is often a matter of bringing in someone new to assist you with your responsibilities. Are you prevented from taking on more complicated tasks (which you are capable of performing) because of your heavy workload, much of which could be handled by a paralegal with less experience? Suggest a plan to your employer that shows how you can provide more complex legal services if you delegate many of your existing responsibilities to a new employee. One of the advantages of working for a small firm is the lack of any set, formal structure for promotions. If the firm is expanding, the paralegal may have significant input into how and to whom responsibilities will be assigned as new people are hired.

You can also create opportunities by acquiring additional education. If you are interested in a particular specialty area, course work in that area, in addition to your existing paralegal training and experience, may help land a job that can advance your career. Alternatively, you might decide to work toward an advanced degree, such as a master's in business administration (MBA), to create new career opportunities. Some paralegals opt to go to law school and become attorneys.

Other Options

There are many other alternatives. You may apply for a job with another firm that offers you a better position or more advancement opportunities. You might apply for a position that has become available in a branch office of your firm. You might volunteer to speak to paralegal classes and seminars and, in so doing, establish new contacts and contribute to paralegal professional development. Researching and writing law-related articles for your paralegal association's newsletter or trade magazine improves your professional stature in the legal community as well. Any of these activities will increase your visibility both inside and outside the firm. In a broad sense, these activities are part of networking. The people you meet may offer you employment opportunities that you did not even know existed but that are perfect for you.

KEY TERMS AND CONCEPTS

bankruptcy law *31*	defendant *28*	independent paralegal *27*
bonus *36*	elder law *33*	insurance *30*
civil law *32*	environmental law *32*	intellectual property *31*
contract *28*	estate planning *31*	legal nurse consultant (LNC) *33*
corporate law *28*	family law *32*	legal technician *27*
criminal law *32*	freelance paralegal *27*	litigation *27*

litigation paralegal   *27*

networking   *40*

overtime wages   *36*

plaintiff   *28*

probate   *31*

probate court   *31*

real estate   *29*

state bar association   *40*

tort   *30*

trade journal   *40*

trust   *31*

will   *31*

workers' compensation statutes   *30*

CHAPTER SUMMARY

CAREER OPPORTUNITIES

Where Paralegals Work

1. *Law firms*—Over two-thirds of paralegals work in law firms—most of them in firms employing fewer than twenty attorneys. Working for a small firm allows a legal assistant to gain experience in a number of areas of law and to work in a more personal and less formal environment. Paralegals in small firms often earn a little less than those in larger firms, however, and often must perform secretarial duties. Paralegals working for larger firms tend to specialize in one or more areas of law, enjoy better employee benefits, and have more support staff.

2. *Corporations and other businesses*—About one-fifth of legal assistants work in corporations. Corporate legal departments may have hundreds of attorneys and paralegals on their staffs. Paralegals working for corporations work regular hours, do not have to be concerned with billable hours (discussed in Chapter 3), and generally receive above-average salaries. They may specialize in certain aspects of corporate law. In addition, paralegals work in many other public and private institutions, such as insurance companies, banks, real estate companies, title insurance companies, law book publishers, legal-software companies, and law schools.

3. *Government*—Paralegals work in many government administrative agencies, such as the Social Security Administration. Other employment opportunities exist with legislative offices, public prosecutors' offices, public defenders' offices, and federal and state courts.

4. *Legal aid offices*—Some paralegals find it rewarding to work in legal aid offices, which provide legal services to those who find it difficult to pay for legal representation. These offices are largely funded by the government, but some support comes from private legal foundations.

5. *Freelance paralegals*—Some experienced paralegals own their businesses and work for attorneys on a contract basis. This work can have more flexible working hours and often can be done from a home office. The success (and income) of a paralegal in this area depends on the person's skill, business sense, and motivation.

Paralegal Specialties

Many paralegals specialize in one or two areas of law. The five areas in which the largest numbers of paralegals currently specialize are litigation, corporate law, contract law, real estate law, and personal-injury law. Other areas in which a legal assistant can specialize include insurance law, employment and labor law, estate planning and probate administration, bankruptcy law, intellectual property law, environmental law, family law, criminal law, elder law, and legal nurse consulting.

Continued

Paralegal Compensation

Salaries and wage rates for paralegal employees vary. Factors affecting compensation include location, firm size, years of experience, and type of employer (law firm, corporation, or government agency). The U.S. Department of Labor's FairPay rule holds that most paralegals do not qualify for the professional exemption under the Fair Labor Standards Act and so are to be paid overtime when they work more than forty hours a week. When evaluating a job, paralegals should consider not only salary or wages but also job benefits, such as insurance coverage, sick/vacation/holiday leave, and pension plans.

Planning Your Career

Career planning involves three steps: defining your long-term career goals, devising short-term goals and adjusting those goals to fit job realities, and reevaluating your career and career goals after you have had some on-the-job experience.

Locating Potential Employers

When looking for employment, paralegals should apply the investigative skills that they learned in their paralegal training.

1. *Networking*—Many jobs come through networking with other professionals. You can begin networking while you are a student. If your local paralegal association allows students to become members, join the association. Knowing others in the legal community is a great asset when looking for a job.

2. *Advertised job openings*—You can locate potential employers by reviewing published and posted information about law firms and other possible employers. Advertisements can be found in trade journals, in newspapers, on the Internet, and at your school's placement office.

3. *Legal directories*—Paralegals can also use the Yellow Pages of the phone book and attorneys' directories to identify potential employers. Most of these resources can be accessed via the Internet.

4. *Job-placement services*—

    a. **SCHOOL PLACEMENT SERVICES**—Paralegals should stay in contact with their school's placement office, which is often staffed with personnel trained to assist paralegals with job hunting.

    b. **LEGAL STAFFING OR PRIVATE PLACEMENT COMPANIES**—Paralegals may locate employment through private placement companies. Usually, the employer pays the placement company's fees, and the company recruits candidates for the position and schedules interviews. Placements may be for temporary or long-term positions. Paralegals can find out about job-placement companies through school program directors, local paralegal associations, state bar associations, or the Web.

Marketing Your Skills

1. *The application process*—Prepare a professional résumé to outline your educational and work background. Do not include personal details. The cover letter that accompanies your résumé represents you, so draft it carefully. You

should also have available a list of persons who have agreed to be professional references and a professional portfolio.

2. *The interview*—Do background research on any firm at which you interview. Think through the answers you will give to likely questions, and be prepared to ask questions that indicate your interest and knowledge. After an interview, make notes of relevant issues so you can discuss them if called back.

3. *The follow-up/thank-you letter*—After an interview, send a personalized thank-you letter expressing continued interest.

4. *Job-hunting files*—Keep your records organized as you look for work by creating a filing system for all your job-search activities.

5. *Salary negotiations*—Some employers will ask you to specify an acceptable salary. Be prepared to give a salary or a salary range, depending on the job requirements. Do research on the salaries paralegals earn in your area.

Reevaluating Your Career

Career goals change over time, as do job opportunities. Advancing in your career may mean educating your employer about your abilities so that you can take on more responsibility, looking for a job in a different department or branch office of the same firm or with another firm, or attending continuing education programs. Participation in paralegal professional organizations or in paralegal education is a way to achieve higher visibility in the profession and to learn of new professional opportunities.

STUDENT STUDYWARE™ CD-ROM

Interactive student CD in this book includes additional quizzing, plus video clips, case studies, and Key Terms flashcards.

ONLINE COMPANION™

For additional resources, please go to **www.paralegal.delmar.cengage.com**.

QUESTIONS FOR REVIEW

1. Name and describe five types of organizations that hire paralegals. Where do most paralegals work?

2. List and briefly describe each of the paralegal specialties discussed in this chapter. Which specialty area or areas interest you the most? Why?

3. What is the Department of Labor's FairPay rule of 2004? What is the professional exemption to this rule? Do most paralegals qualify for the professional exemption? Why or why not?

4. How can paralegals locate potential employers? What is networking? How might networking help paralegals find jobs?

5. Of the methods suggested in this chapter for locating potential employers, which method do you think would be the most effective? Why?

ETHICAL QUESTION

1. Dennis Walker works at a very busy law firm. On each side of his desk, there are one-foot-high stacks of work, leaving only enough room for a small work space in the center of the desk and a spot for the telephone. His floor is likewise stacked high with legal documents. Dennis constantly misses deadlines and is often in trouble for turning work in late or doing work incorrectly. Dennis has tried to get organized but feels that it is impossible to do so because he has such a heavy workload. What are Dennis's ethical obligations in this situation.

PRACTICE QUESTIONS AND ASSIGNMENTS

1. In addition to the traditional law firm, for what types of employers do paralegals work?

2. What are some advantages and disadvantages of working for a small law firm? What are some advantages and disadvantages of working for a large law firm? Which would you prefer to do? Why?

QUESTION FOR CRITICAL ANALYSIS

1. What are your long-term career goals? Do your short-term goals relate logically to the attainment of your long-term goals? Why or why not? Write one to two paragraphs explaining your long-term goals and how your short-term goals relate to them. Write these paragraphs to a potential employer.

PROJECTS

1. Locate the *Martindale-Hubbell Law Directory* or the *West Legal Directory* in your library or online. Find three law firms in your locale that practice areas of law in which you are interested. Write down the names and addresses of the firms. Also try to find the names of the hiring partners or human resources managers whom you could contact about a job in the future. Start your job file today!

2. Draft a résumé for yourself using the ones in this chapter for guidance. Think of your strong suits that should be highlighted. Also write a cover letter.

USING INTERNET RESOURCES

1. On the Internet, access LAW MATCH, an online résumé bank, at **www.lawmatch.com**. How do you use it? Would you post your résumé there? Why or why not? If you are currently looking for a position, try posting your résumé on that site.

2. Visit the Web site for *Legal Assistant Today* magazine at **www.legalassistanttoday.com**. Under the heading "Becoming a Paralegal," you will find many useful articles about the paralegal profession, education, and employment. Select an article about paralegal education, and write a three-paragraph summary of the article. Print and attach the first page of the article to submit with your summary.

END NOTES

1. *U.S. Department of Labor v. Page & Addison, P.C.,* U.S. District Court, Dallas, Texas, No. 91-2655, March 15, 1994.

2. 29 C.F.R. Section 541.301(e)(7). See Chapter 7 for a discussion of how to read citations to the *Code of Federal Regulations.*

THE INNER WORKINGS OF THE LAW OFFICE

CHAPTER

3

CHAPTER OUTLINE

Introduction

The Organizational Structure of Law Firms

Law Office Management and Personnel

Employment Policies

Filing Procedures

Financial Procedures

Communicating with Clients

Law Office Culture and Politics

AFTER COMPLETING THIS CHAPTER, YOU WILL KNOW:

► How law firms are organized and managed.

► Some typical policies and procedures governing paralegal employment.

► The importance of an efficient filing system in legal practice and some typical filing procedures.

► How clients are billed for legal services.

► How law office culture and politics affect the paralegal's working environment.

INTRODUCTION

The variety of environments in which paralegals work makes it impossible to describe in any detail how the firm where you will work will be run. Typically, though, the way in which that firm operates will relate, at least in part, to the firm's form of business organization. Because most paralegals are employed by private law firms, this chapter focuses on the organization, management, and procedures characteristic of these firms.

First, we look at how the size and structure of a law firm affect the paralegal's working environment. As you would imagine, the working environment in a firm owned and operated by one attorney is significantly different from that in a large law firm with two or three hundred attorneys or a large corporate enterprise—or even a government agency.

We then look at other aspects of the working environment of paralegals. Typically, a law firm will have specific policies and procedures relating to employment conditions, filing systems, billing and timekeeping procedures, and financial procedures. We conclude the chapter with a brief discussion of law office culture and politics.

THE ORGANIZATIONAL STRUCTURE OF LAW FIRMS

Law firms range in size from one-attorney firms to megafirms with hundreds of attorneys. Regardless of their size differences, though, in terms of business organization, law firms typically organize as sole proprietorships, partnerships, or professional corporations. Because the way in which a business is organized affects the office environment, we next look briefly at each of these three major organizational forms. These organizational forms and others will be discussed in greater detail in Chapter 18.

Sole Proprietorships

sole proprietorship
The simplest form of business organization, in which the owner is the business. Anyone who does business without creating a formal business entity has a sole proprietorship.

personal liability
An individual's personal responsibility for debts or obligations. The owners of sole proprietorships and partnerships are personally liable for the debts and obligations incurred by their businesses. If their firms go bankrupt or cannot meet debts, the owners will be personally responsible for the debts.

The **sole proprietorship** is the simplest business form and is often used by attorneys when they first set up legal practices. In a sole proprietorship, one individual—the sole proprietor—owns the business. The sole proprietor is entitled to any profits made by the firm but is also personally liable for all of the firm's debts or obligations. **Personal liability** means that the owner's personal assets (such as a home, savings or investment accounts, and other property) may have to be sacrificed to pay business obligations if the business fails.

An attorney who practices law as a sole proprietor is often called a *sole (solo) practitioner.* To save on office overhead expenses, a sole practitioner may share an office with other attorneys. A paralegal may split time among sole practitioners who share an office and staff.

Working for a sole practitioner is a good way for a paralegal to learn about law office procedures because the paralegal will typically perform a wide variety of tasks. Many sole practitioners hire one person to act as secretary, paralegal, administrator, and manager. Paralegals holding this kind of position would probably handle many tasks: receiving and date-stamping the mail, organizing and maintaining the filing system, interviewing clients and witnesses, bookkeeping (receiving payments from clients, preparing and sending bills to clients, and the like), conducting investigations and legal research, drafting legal documents, assisting the attorney in trial preparation and perhaps in the courtroom, and other jobs, including office administration.

Working for a sole practitioner is a good way to find out which area of law you most enjoy because you will learn about procedures relating to many different areas. Alternatively, if you work for a sole practitioner who specializes in one area of law, you will have an opportunity to develop expertise in that area. In sum, working in a small law firm gives you an overview of law office procedures and legal practice that will help you throughout your career.

Partnerships

Most law firms are organized as partnerships, limited liability partnerships, or professional corporations. In a **partnership**, two or more people do business jointly as **partners**. A partnership may consist of just a few attorneys or over a hundred attorneys. In a partnership, each partner owns a share of the business and shares in the firm's profits or losses.

In smaller partnerships, the partners may participate equally in managing the partnership. They will likely meet to make decisions about clients, policies, procedures, and other matters important to the firm. In larger partnerships, managerial decisions are usually made by a committee of partners, one of whom may be designated as the **managing partner**.

Partnerships (and professional corporations, which are discussed below) frequently employ other attorneys who are not partners in the firm and thus do not share in the profits. Typically, these other attorneys are called **associate attorneys**. They are usually less experienced attorneys and may be invited to become partners after working for the firm for several years. Sometimes, firms hire **staff attorneys**, who work for the firm but will never become partners. Staff attorneys differ from *contract attorneys*, who provide services for busy firms on a project basis. Many firms also hire **law clerks**—law students who work for the firm during the summer or part-time during the school year to gain practical legal experience. Law clerks who meet with the approval of the members of the firm are often offered positions as associates when they graduate and pass the bar exam.

Liability of Partners

Like sole proprietors, attorneys in a partnership are personally liable for the debts and obligations of the business if the business fails. In addition, a partner can be held personally responsible for the misconduct or debts of another partner. For example, suppose a client sues a partner in the firm for malpractice and wins a large judgment. The firm carries malpractice insurance, but it is insufficient to pay the obligation. The court will order the attorney who committed the wrongful act to pay the balance due. Once the responsible attorney's personal assets are exhausted, the assets of the other (innocent) partners can be used to pay the judgment. This unlimited personal liability of partners is a disadvantage for law firms organized as partnerships.

Limited Liability Partnership (LLP)

In recent years, a new form of partnership called the **limited liability partnership (LLP)** became available to firms in many states. The LLP normally allows professionals to avoid personal liability for the malpractice of other partners. Although LLP statutes vary from state to state, generally state law limits the liability of partners in some way. For example, Delaware law protects each innocent partner from the "debts and obligations of the partnership arising from negligence, wrongful acts, or misconduct." You will read more about LLPs in Chapter 18. Note that professionals who are not attorneys can also organize as an LLP and that this form of business may provide certain tax advantages as well as limits to the partners' liability.

Professional Corporations

A **professional corporation (P.C.)** is a corporation formed by licensed professionals, such as lawyers or physicians. Like other kinds of corporations, it is owned by **shareholders**, so called because they have purchased the corporation's stock, or

---

partnership
An association of two or more persons to carry on, as co-owners, a business for profit.

partner
A person who operates a business jointly with one or more other persons. Each partner is a co-owner of the business firm.

managing partner
The partner in a law firm who makes decisions relating to the firm's policies and procedures and who generally oversees the business operations of the firm.

associate attorney
An attorney working for a law firm who is not a partner and does not have an ownership interest in the firm. Associates are usually less experienced attorneys and may be invited to become partners after working for the firm for several years.

staff attorney
An attorney hired by a law firm as an employee. A staff attorney has no ownership rights in the firm and will not be invited to become a partner in the firm.

law clerk
A law student working as an apprentice with a law firm to gain practical experience.

limited liability partnership (LLP)
A business organizational form designed for professionals who normally do business as partners in a partnership. The LLP limits the personal liability of partners.

professional corporation (P.C.)
A corporation formed by licensed professionals, such as lawyers or physicians. The liability of shareholders is often limited to the amount of their investments.

shareholder
One who purchases corporate stock, or shares, and who thus becomes an owner of the corporation.

shares, and thus own a share of the business. The shareholders share in the profits and losses of the firm in proportion to how many shares they own. Their personal liability, unlike that of partners, may or may not be limited to the amount of their investments, depending on the circumstances and on state law. Limited personal liability is one of the key advantages of the corporate form of business.

In many respects, the professional corporation is run like a partnership, and the distinction between these two forms of business organization is often more a legal formality than an operational reality. Because of this, attorneys who organize their business as a professional corporation are nonetheless sometimes referred to as partners. For simplicity, in this chapter we will refer to anyone who has ownership rights in the firm as a partner.

LAW OFFICE MANAGEMENT AND PERSONNEL

When you take a job as a paralegal, you will want to quickly learn the relative status of the office personnel. Particularly, you will want to know who has authority over you and to whom you are accountable. You will also want to know who is accountable to you—whether you have an assistant or a secretary (or share an assistant or a secretary with another paralegal), for example. In a small firm, you will have no problem learning this information. If you work for a larger law firm, the lines of authority may be more difficult to perceive. Your supervisor will probably instruct you on the relative status of the firm's personnel. If you are not sure about who has authority over whom and what kinds of tasks are performed by various employees, you should ask your supervisor.

The lines of authority and accountability vary from firm to firm, depending on the firm's size and its management preferences. A sample organizational chart for a relatively small law partnership is shown in Exhibit 3.1. The decision makers in the firm represented by that chart are the partners. Next in authority are the associate attorneys and law clerks. The paralegals are supervised by both the attorneys (in regard to legal work) and the office manager (in regard to office procedural and paralegal staffing matters). In larger firms, there may be a **legal-assistant manager** or **paralegal manager**, who coordinates paralegal staffing and programs relating to paralegal educational and professional development.

Besides attorneys and paralegals, law firm employees include administrative personnel. In large firms, the partners may hire a **legal administrator** to run the business end of the firm. The legal administrator might delegate some authority to an office manager and other supervisory employees. In small firms, such as that represented by Exhibit 3.1, an **office manager** handles the administrative aspects of the firm. The legal administrator or office manager typically is in charge of docketing (calendaring) legal work undertaken by the attorneys; establishing and overseeing filing procedures; implementing new legal technology, such as new docketing software; ordering and monitoring supplies; and generally making sure that the office runs smoothly and that office procedures are established and followed. In a small firm, the office manager might also handle client billing procedures. The firm represented in Exhibit 3.1 has an accountant to perform this function.

The **support personnel** in a large law office may include secretaries, receptionists, bookkeepers, file clerks, messengers, and others. Depending on their functions and specific jobs, support personnel may fall under the supervision of any number of other personnel in the firm. In a very small firm, just one person—the legal secretary, for example—may perform all of the above-mentioned functions.

EMPLOYMENT POLICIES

Employees of a law firm, which include all personnel other than the partners or those who work for the firm on a contract basis, are subject to the firm's employment policies. A firm's policies governing employment may be published in an

legal-assistant manager
or **paralegal manager**
An employee in a law firm who is responsible for overseeing the paralegal staff and paralegal professional development.

legal administrator
An administrative employee of a law firm who manages day-to-day operations. In smaller law firms, legal administrators are usually called office managers.

office manager
An administrative employee who manages the day-to-day operations of a firm. In larger law firms, office managers are usually called legal administrators.

support personnel
Employees who provide clerical, secretarial, or other support to the legal, paralegal, and administrative staff of a law firm.

employment manual in larger firms. In smaller firms, these policies are often unwritten. In either case, when you take a job as a paralegal, or perhaps before you accept a position, you will want to become familiar with the firm's basic conditions of employment. There will be a policy, for example, on how much vacation time you are entitled to during the first year, second year, and so on. Other policies will govern which holidays are observed by the firm, how much sick leave you can take, when you are expected to arrive at work, and what will serve as grounds for the employer to terminate your employment.

Employment policies vary from firm to firm. A leading concern of paralegals (and employees generally) is how much they will be paid, how they will be paid (that is, whether they will receive salaries or hourly wages), and what job benefits they will receive. These issues were discussed in Chapter 2, so we will not examine them here. Rather, we look at some other areas of concern to paralegals, including performance evaluations and termination procedures.

> **employment manual**
> A firm's handbook or written statement that specifies the policies and procedures that govern the firm's employees and employer-employee relationships.

Performance Evaluations

Many law firms conduct periodic performance evaluations to determine if employees will receive raises. Usually, performance is evaluated annually, but some firms conduct evaluations every six months, and some conduct them more often for new employees.

Know What Is Expected of You

Because paralegal responsibilities vary from firm to firm, no one evaluation checklist applies to every paralegal. Some of the factors that may be considered during a performance evaluation are indicated in Exhibit 3.2 on the following page. Note, though, that performance evaluations are often much longer and more detailed than the list shown in the exhibit. For example, each major item in that list may have several subheadings and perhaps further subheadings under those. Normally, under each item is a series of options—ranging from "excellent" to "unsatisfactory" or something similar—for the supervisor or attorney to check.

When you begin work as a paralegal, you should learn at the outset exactly what your duties will be and what performance is expected of you. This way, you will be able to prepare for your first evaluation from the moment you begin working. You will not have to wait six months or a year before you learn that you were supposed to be doing something differently.

EXHIBIT 3.1
A Sample Organizational Chart for a Law Partnership

EXHIBIT 3.2
Factors That May Be Considered
in a Performance Evaluation

1. **RESPONSIBILITY**
   Making sure that all tasks are performed on time and following up on all pending matters.

2. **EFFICIENCY**
   Obtaining good results in the least amount of time possible.

3. **PRODUCTIVITY**
   Producing a sufficient quantity of work in a given time period.

4. **COMPETENCE**
   Knowledge level and skills.

5. **INITIATIVE**
   Applying intelligence and creativity to tasks and making appropriate recommendations.

6. **COOPERATION**
   Getting along well with others on the legal team.

7. **PERSONAL FACTORS**
   Appearance, grooming habits, friendliness, and poise.

8. **DEPENDABILITY**
   Arriving at work consistently on time and being available when needed.

Be Prepared

Make sure that you prepare for the evaluation and conduct yourself professionally at all times. Be your own advocate. This is especially important in larger offices, where you may not be well known to the supervisor doing your evaluation. Keep track of your accomplishments, such as the number of billable hours per week or month that you normally generate, so that you can point them out to your supervisor. If you were part of a team that worked many extra hours to win a big case for the firm, mention it during the evaluation. Make your supervisor aware of ways in which you have saved the firm money or contributed to the firm's success. If you have mastered a new software program or passed the CLA (or CP) or PACE exam, tell your supervisor.

Get the Most from Your Performance Evaluation

Both paralegals and their employers can benefit from the discussions that take place during a performance evaluation. In the busy workplace, you may not have much time to talk with your supervisor about issues that do not relate to immediate work needs. Even if you do find a moment, you may feel awkward bringing up the topic of your performance or discussing a workplace problem. Performance evaluations are designed to allow both sides to exchange views on such matters.

During reviews, you will learn how the firm rates your performance. You can gain valuable feedback from your supervisor, learn more about your strengths and weaknesses, and identify the areas in which you need to improve your skills. Do not react negatively to criticisms of your performance. Even during an evaluation you are being evaluated. Adopting a positive outlook and showing that you appreciate constructive criticism will impress your supervisor.

You can also use the evaluation to give your supervisor feedback on the workplace. This is especially useful if you believe you are capable of handling more complex tasks than you are being assigned. Attorneys sometimes underutilize paralegals because they do not know their capabilities. If you suggest ways in which your knowledge could be put to better use, sometimes that is all it takes to earn more challenging and rewarding responsibilities. Also, if you and your supervising attorney never seem to have the time to meet face-to-face for the evaluation, consider writing up your own evaluation and presenting it to him or her for review.

Employment Termination

Policy manuals almost always deal with the subject of employment termination. A policy manual will likely specify what kind of conduct can serve as a basis for firing employees. For example, the manual might specify that if an employee is absent more than twelve days a year for two consecutive years, the employer has grounds to terminate the employment relationship. The manual will also probably describe termination procedures. For example, the firm might require that it be notified one month in advance if an employee decides to leave the firm; if the employee fails to give such notice, he or she may lose accumulated vacation time or other benefits on termination.

Employment Discrimination

Traditionally, employment relationships have been governed by the common law doctrine of employment at will. Under this doctrine, employers may hire and fire employees "at will"—that is, for any reason or no reason. Today, courts have created several exceptions to this doctrine, and state and federal statutes now regulate some aspects of the employment relationship. Under federal law (and state statutes), employers may not refuse to hire job applicants, refuse to promote employees, or fire employees for discriminatory reasons—because of the employee's age, gender, or race, for example. These and other laws regulating employment relationships will be discussed in Chapter 18, but it should be mentioned here that virtually every large law firm has special policies and procedures that must be followed with respect to claims of employment discrimination.

For example, an employee who experiences sexual harassment—a form of gender-based discrimination that is prohibited by federal and state laws—may be required by the firm's harassment policy to follow formal complaint procedures to attempt to resolve the issue. If an employee fails to follow the required procedures, the firm may be able to avoid legal responsibility for the harassment. Similarly, if an employer does not have established procedures in place for dealing with discrimination, the employer may find it difficult to avoid liability for the discriminatory treatment by supervisors or others against an employee.

on the web

For information on federal laws governing employment discrimination, access the Equal Employment Opportunity Commission's Web site at **www.eeoc.gov**.

FILING PROCEDURES

Every law firm, regardless of its size or structure, has some kind of established filing procedures. Efficient procedures are vital because the paperwork generated is substantial, and important documents must be safeguarded yet be readily retrievable when needed. The need to protect client information is stressed in the *Developing Paralegal Skills* feature on the next page. If a client file is misplaced or lost, the client may suffer costly harm.

Additionally, documents must be filed in such a way as to protect client confidentiality. The duty of confidentiality is discussed in Chapter 4, but it deserves mention here because of the extent to which it frames all legal work and procedures. This is particularly true of filing procedures. All information received from or about clients, including files and documents, is considered confidential. A breach of confidentiality by a paralegal or other employee can cause the law firm to incur extensive liability.

If you work for a small firm, filing procedures may be rather informal, and you may need to assume the responsibility for organizing and developing an efficient and secure filing system. Larger firms normally have specific procedures concerning the creation, maintenance, use, and storage of office files. If you take a job with a large firm, a supervisor will probably train you in office procedures, including filing. Although the trend today, particularly in larger firms, is toward computerized filing systems, many firms create "hard copies" to ensure that files are not lost if computer systems crash.

Generally, law offices maintain several types of files. Typically, a law firm's filing system will include client files, work product files and reference materials, and forms files (as well as personnel files, which we do not discuss here).

Developing Paralegal Skills

CONFIDENTIALITY AND CLIENT INFORMATION

One of the most important professional obligations of a paralegal is to treat all of your clients' information as confidential. The obligation to treat information as confidential has been long recognized by the common law, and some jurisdictions even provide criminal sanctions for professionals who violate this duty.

As a general rule, never share *any* information about your clients—even the fact that they are clients—with anyone outside your firm. Don't share "war stories" from work with friends or relatives if doing so could reveal information about the client. Never leave *any* information about your clients where others might see it.

To protect client confidentiality, you should:

- Keep all identifiable information about clients off the cover of files.

- Never leave a file unattended for even a short time in a publicly accessible location such as a library table or courtroom.

- Make sure all client files are removed from internal workspaces where outsiders might be present, such as conference rooms, before meetings.

- Do not allow outsiders access to firm computer systems or networks.

- Use only secure networks or encrypted communications systems for transmission of confidential information. Wireless networks in airports or Internet cafés are *not* secure.

The obligation to maintain confidentiality continues even after a file is closed. Your firm should have document-retention policies that set out how long closed files are kept and how they are to be destroyed. Be sure to follow your firm's policies carefully. An excellent guide to such policies is Lee R. Nemchek, *Records Retention in the Private Legal Environment: Annotated Bibliography and Program Implementation Tools*, available at **www.abanet.org**. In the "search" box, type Lee Nemchek and it will take you to the article.

In addition to the general obligation of confidentiality, there are many laws that require particular information or documents to be kept confidential. For example, the Health Insurance Portability and Accountability Act (HIPAA) imposes stringent privacy requirements on anyone who obtains personally identifiable medical information in an insurance-related transaction. Check your state's statutes and regulations for obligations about other specific types of information.

Client Files

To illustrate client filing procedures, we present below the phases in the "life cycle" of a hypothetical client's file. The name of the client is Katherine Baranski; she has just retained (hired) one of your firm's attorneys to represent her in a lawsuit that she is bringing against Tony Peretto. Because Baranski is initiating the lawsuit, she is referred to as the *plaintiff*. Peretto, because he has to defend against Baranski's claims, is the *defendant*. The name of the case is *Baranski v. Peretto*. Assume that you will be working on the case and that your supervising attorney has just asked you to open a new case file. Assume also that you have already verified, through a "conflicts check" (to be discussed in Chapter 4), that no conflict of interest exists.

Opening a New Client File

The first step that you (or a secretary, at your request) will take in opening a new file is to assign the case a file number. For reasons of both efficiency and confidentiality, many firms identify their client files by numbers or some kind of numerical and/or alphabetical sequence instead of the clients' names. The *Baranski v. Peretto* case file might be identified by the letters BAPE—the first two letters of the plaintiff's name followed by the first two letters of the defendant's name.

Increasingly, law firms are using computerized databases to record and track case titles and files. For example, some firms use file labels containing bar codes that contain attorney codes, subject-matter codes, the client's name and file number, and so forth. The databases are also used for contract and billing information.

Typically, law firms maintain a master client list on which clients' names are entered alphabetically and cross-referenced to the clients' case numbers. If file numbers consist of numerical sequences, there is also a master list on which the file numbers are listed in numerical order and cross-referenced to the clients' names.

Adding Subfiles

As the work on the *Baranski* case progresses and more documents are generated or received, the file will expand. To ensure that documents will be easy to locate, you will create subfiles. One subfile might be created for client documents (such as a contract, will, stock certificate, or photograph) that the firm needs for reference or for evidence at trial. As correspondence relating to the *Baranski* case is generated, you will probably add a correspondence subfile. You will also want a subfile for your or the attorney's notes on the case, including research results.

As you will read in Chapters 10 through 12, litigation involves several stages. As the *Baranski* litigation progresses through these stages, subfiles for documents relating to each stage will be added to the *Baranski* file. Many firms find it useful to color-code or add tabs to subfiles so that they can be readily identified. Often, in large files, an index of each subfile's contents is created and attached to the inside cover of the subfile.

Documents are typically filed within each subfile in reverse chronological order, with the most recently dated document on the top. Usually, to safeguard the documents, they are punched at the top with a two-hole puncher so they can be secured within the file with a clip. Note, though, that an original client document should not be punched or altered in any way. It should always be left loose within the file (or paper-clipped to a copy of the document that *is* punched and secured in the file). For example, if you were holding in the file a property deed belonging to a client, you would not want to alter that document in any way.

File Use and Storage

Often, files are stored in a file room or area. Most firms have some kind of procedure for employees to follow when removing files from the storage area. A firm might require the office staff to replace a removed file with an "out card" indicating the date, the name of the file, and the name or initials of the person who removed it.

Note that documents should not be removed from a client file or subfile. Rather, the entire file or subfile should be removed for use. This ensures that important documents will not be separated from the file and possibly mislaid or lost. Many paralegals make copies of documents in the file for their use. For example, if you are working on the *Baranski* case and need to review certain documents in the file, you might remove them from the file temporarily, copy them, and immediately return the file to storage.

Closing a File

Assume that the *Baranski* case has been settled out of court and that no further legal work on Baranski's behalf needs to be done. For a time, her file will be retained in the inactive files, but when it is fairly certain that no one will need to refer to it very often, if ever, it will be closed. Closed files are often stored in a separate area of the building or even off-site. Traditionally, many larger law firms stored the contents of old files on microfilm. Today, firms can use scanning technology to scan

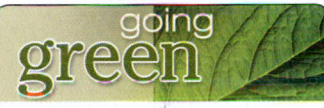

FEWER CDs

Most computer programs require purchasers to buy a license for every computer on which the programs are installed. Rather than buy programs on discs, you can generally buy them online and download them with site licenses. Registration allows you to download a program again if you change to a new computer. That helps cut down on the production of more CDs and packaging materials.

file contents for storage on CD-ROMs, DVDs, magnetic tapes, or other data-storage devices such as flash drives.

Specific procedures for closing files vary from firm to firm. Typically, when a case is closed, original documents provided by the client (for example, a deed to property) are returned to the client. Other materials, such as extra copies of documents or cover letters, are destroyed.

Destroying Old Files

Law firms do not have to retain client files forever, and at some point, the *Baranski* case file will be destroyed. Old files are normally destroyed by shredding so that confidentiality is preserved. Because shredded files can be pieced back together, many firms hire companies that have equipment guaranteed to destroy such materials so recovery is not possible. Law firms use great care when destroying client files because a court or government agency may impose a heavy fine on a law firm that destroys a file that should have been retained for a longer time. How long a particular file must be retained depends on many factors, including the nature of the client's legal matters and governing statutes, such as the statute of limitations.

statute of limitations
A statute setting the maximum time period within which certain actions can be brought to court or rights enforced. After the period of time has run, no legal action can be brought.

Statutes of limitations limit the time period during which specific types of legal actions may be brought to court. Statutes of limitations for legal-malpractice actions vary from state to state—from six months to ten years after the attorney's last contact with the client. When the statute of limitations in your state expires is an important factor in determining how long to retain a client file, because an attorney or law firm will need the information contained in the client's file to defend against a malpractice action. If the file has been destroyed, the firm will not be able to produce any documents or other evidence to refute the plaintiff's claim.

Work Product Files and Reference Materials

Many law firms keep copies of research projects, legal memoranda, and various case-related documents prepared by the firm's attorneys and paralegals so these documents can be referred to in future projects. In this way, legal personnel do not have to start all over again when working on a claim similar to one dealt with in the past.

Traditionally, hard copies of work product files, or legal-information files, were filed in the firm's law library with other reference materials and publications. Today, work product documents and research materials are often generated on computers and stored on CD-ROMs, DVDs, portable hard drives, flash drives, or other data-storage devices. Often, in large firms, these materials are kept in a central data bank that is accessible by the firm's personnel.

forms file
A reference file containing copies of the firm's commonly used legal documents and informational forms. The documents in the forms file serve as models for drafting new documents.

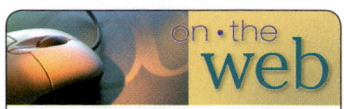

For a sampling of the types of legal forms available on the Web, check the following sites: **www.lectlaw.com** (select "Legal Forms" from the menu) and **www.legaldocs.com**.

Forms Files

Every law firm keeps on hand various forms that it commonly uses. These forms are usually stored in a **forms file**. A forms file might include forms for retainer agreements (to be discussed shortly), for filing lawsuits in specific courts, for bankruptcy petitions, for real estate matters, and for many other types of legal matters. Often, to save time, copies of documents relating to specific types of cases are kept for future reference. Then, when the attorney or paralegal works on a similar case, those documents can serve as models, or guides. (These forms may also be kept in a work product file, as just mentioned.)

Forms files are almost always computerized. Computerized forms have simplified legal practice by allowing legal personnel to generate customized documents within minutes. Forms for many standard legal transactions are available from legal-software companies on CD-ROMs and DVDs. They are also available online at Web sites, as you will read in Chapter 8.

FINANCIAL PROCEDURES

Like any other business firm, a law firm needs to at least cover its expenses, or it will fail. In the business of law, the product is legal services, which are sold to clients. A major concern of any law firm is to have a clear policy on fee arrangements and efficient procedures to ensure that each client is billed appropriately for the time and costs associated with serving that client. Efficient billing procedures require that attorneys and paralegals keep accurate records of the time that they spend working on a given client's case or other legal matter.

Fee Arrangements

A major ethical concern of the legal profession has to do with the reasonableness of attorneys' fees and the ways in which clients are billed for legal services. Among other things, state ethical codes governing attorneys require legal fees to be reasonable. For example, Rule 1.5 of the American Bar Association's Model Rules of Professional Conduct (to be discussed in Chapter 4) states, "A lawyer's fees shall be reasonable." The rule then lists the factors that should be considered in determining the reasonableness of a fee. The factors include the time and labor required to perform the legal work, the fee customarily charged in the locality for similar legal services, and the experience and ability of the lawyer performing the services.

Normally, fee arrangements are discussed and agreed on at the outset of any attorney-client relationship. Most law firms require each client to agree, in a signed writing called a **retainer agreement**, to whatever fee arrangements have been made. (Some states also require, by law, that fee arrangements be stated in writing.) The agreement specifies that the client is retaining (hiring) the attorney and/or firm to represent the client in a legal matter and states that the client agrees to the fee arrangements set forth in the agreement. Exhibit 3.3 on the following page shows a sample retainer agreement.

Basically, there are three types of fee arrangements: fixed fees, hourly fees, and contingency fees. We examine here each of these types of fees, as well as some alternative fee arrangements.

> **retainer agreement**
> A signed document stating that the attorney or the law firm has been hired by the client to provide certain legal services and that the client agrees to pay for those services.

Fixed Fees

The client may agree to pay a **fixed fee** for a specified legal service. Certain procedures, such as incorporation and simple divorce filings, are often handled on a fixed-fee basis because the attorney can reasonably estimate how much time will be involved in completing the work. Charging fixed fees is an increasingly popular method of billing. It helps attorneys avoid lawsuits and other problems that can result when clients allege that their legal fees were excessive.

> **fixed fee**
> A fee paid to the attorney by his or her client for having provided a specified legal service, such as the creation of a simple will.

Hourly Fees

With the exception of litigation work done on a contingency-fee basis (discussed below), most law firms charge clients hourly rates for legal services. Hourly rates vary widely from firm to firm. Some litigation firms charge high rates ($700 an hour or more) for their services because of their reputation for obtaining favorable settlements or court judgments for their clients. In contrast, an attorney just starting up a practice as a sole practitioner will have to charge a lower, more competitive rate (perhaps $100 per hour) to attract clients.

Law firms also bill clients for hourly rates for paralegal services. Because the hourly rate for paralegals is lower than that for attorneys, clients benefit from attorneys' use of paralegal services. Generally, the billing rate for paralegal services depends on the size and location of the firm. According to a compensation survey conducted by *Legal Assistant Today* in 2009, billing rates for paralegals begin at about $60 per hour and may exceed $155 per hour. About 40 percent of all billing for paralegal services ranged between $96 and $135 per hour.

EXHIBIT 3.3
A Sample Retainer Agreement

RETAINER AGREEMENT

I, Katherine Baranski, agree to employ Allen P. Gilmore and his law firm, Jeffers, Gilmore & Dunn, as my attorneys to prosecute all claims for damages against Tony Peretto and all other persons or entities that may be liable on account of an automobile accident that caused me to sustain serious injuries. The accident occurred on August 4, 2010, at 7:45 A.M., when Tony Peretto ran a stop sign on Thirty-eighth Street at Mattis Avenue and, as a result, his car collided with mine.

I agree to pay my lawyers a fee that will be one-third (33 percent) of any sum recovered in this case, regardless of whether the sum is received through settlement, lawsuit, arbitration, or any other way. The fee will be calculated on the sum recovered, after costs and expenses have been deducted. The fee will be paid when any money is actually received in this case. I agree that Allen P. Gilmore and his law firm have an express attorney's lien on any recovery to ensure that their fee is paid.

I agree to pay all necessary costs and expenses, such as court filing fees, court reporter fees, expert witness fees and expenses, travel expenses, long-distance telephone and facsimile costs, and photocopying charges. I understand that these costs and expenses will be billed to me by my attorney on a monthly basis and that I am responsible for paying these costs and expenses, even if no recovery is received.

I agree that this agreement does not cover matters other than those described above. This agreement does not cover an appeal from any judgment entered, any efforts necessary to collect money due because of a judgment entered by a court, or any efforts necessary to obtain other benefits, such as insurance.

I agree to pay a carrying charge amounting to the greater of five dollars ($5.00) or four percent (4%) per month on the average daily balance of bills on my account that are thirty (30) days overdue. If my account is outstanding by more than sixty (60) days, all work by the attorney shall cease until the account is paid in full or a monthly payment plan is agreed on.

This contract is governed by the law of the state of Nita.

I AGREE TO THE TERMS AND CONDITIONS STATED ABOVE:

Date: 2 / 4 / 2011   *Katherine Baranski*
                              Katherine Baranski

I agree to represent Katherine Baranski in the matter described above. I will receive no fee unless a recovery is obtained. If a recovery is obtained, I will receive a fee as described above.

I agree to notify Katherine Baranski of all developments in this matter promptly, and I will make no settlement of this matter without her consent.

I AGREE TO THE TERMS AND CONDITIONS STATED ABOVE:

Date: 2 / 4 / 2011   *Allen P. Gilmore*
                              Allen P. Gilmore
                              Jeffers, Gilmore & Dunn
                              553 Fifth Avenue
                              Suite 101
                              Nita City, NI 48801

Note that although your services might be billed to the client at a certain hourly rate—say, $100—the firm will not actually pay you $100 an hour as wages. The billable rate for paralegal services, as for attorney services, takes into account the firm's expenses for overhead (rent, utilities, employee benefits, supplies, and the like).

Contingency Fees

A common practice among litigation attorneys, especially those representing plaintiffs in certain types of cases (such as personal-injury or negligence cases) is to charge the client on a contingency-fee basis. A **contingency fee** is contingent

contingency fee
A legal fee that consists of a specified percentage (such as 30 percent) of the amount the plaintiff recovers in a civil lawsuit. The fee is paid only if the plaintiff wins the lawsuit (recovers damages).

(dependent) on the outcome of the case. If the plaintiff wins the lawsuit and recovers damages or settles out of court, the attorney is entitled to a percentage of the amount recovered (refer to Exhibit 3.3 for an example of a contingency-fee retainer agreement). If the plaintiff loses the lawsuit, the attorney gets nothing—although the client normally reimburses the attorney for the costs and expenses involved in preparing for trial (costs and expenses are discussed below, in regard to billing procedures).

Often, the attorney's contingency fee is one-fourth to one-third of the amount recovered. The agreement may provide for modification of the amount depending on how and when the dispute is settled. For example, an agreement that provides for a contingency fee of 33 percent of the amount recovered for a plaintiff may state that the amount will be reduced to a lower percentage if the case is settled out of court.

Do Contingency Fees Violate Ethics Rules?   Some people maintain that the use of contingency fees is ethically questionable because it encourages attorneys to resort to aggressive tactics to win a case. The legal profession points out, however, that contingency-fee arrangements allow clients who could not otherwise afford a lawyer to obtain representation.

Limitations on Contingency Fees.   The law restricts the use of contingency-fee agreements to certain types of cases. An attorney can request a contingency fee only in civil matters, not in criminal cases. In a civil case, the plaintiff is often seeking monetary damages from the defendant to compensate the plaintiff for injuries suffered. In criminal cases, as you will read in Chapter 13, the government is seeking to punish the defendant for a wrongful act committed against society as a whole. If the defendant is found not guilty of the charges, he or she will not receive monetary damages that the attorney could share.

Attorneys are also typically prohibited (by state law) from entering into contingency-fee agreements in divorce cases and probate cases (see Chapter 17) and in workers' compensation cases (see Chapter 18). States usually prohibit contingency fees in these civil cases because lawmakers have determined that allowing attorneys to share in the proceeds recovered would be contrary to public policy.

Alternative Fee Arrangements

Some attorneys offer alternative fee arrangements to their clients. One alternative billing practice, called "task-based billing," is similar to a fixed-fee arrangement: fixed fees are charged for specific types of tasks that are involved in a legal matter. For example, the attorney might charge a flat fee for conducting a pretrial deposition (in which a party to a lawsuit or a witness gives sworn testimony—see Chapter 10). Another alternative billing practice is sometimes referred to as "value billing." When this arrangement is used, the fees charged to the client vary depending on the results of the representation—whether a lawsuit is lost, won, or settled, for example.

Client Trust Accounts

Law firms often require new clients to pay a **retainer**—an initial advance payment to the firm to cover part of the fee and costs that will be incurred on the client's behalf (such as travel expenses, fax charges, and the like). Some businesses keep an attorney on retainer. This means that the client pays the attorney a fixed amount every month or year, and the attorney handles all necessary legal business that arises during that time. Retainer arrangements allow businesses to make legal costs predictable over time.

Funds received as retainers, as well as any funds received on behalf of a client (such as a payment to a client to settle a lawsuit), are placed in a special bank account. This account is usually referred to as a client **trust account** (or escrow account). The *Developing Paralegal Skills* feature on page 73 reviews trust account

retainer
An advance payment made by a client to a law firm to cover part of the legal fees and/or costs that will be incurred on that client's behalf.

trust account
A bank account in which one party (the trustee, such as an attorney) holds funds belonging to another person (such as a client); a bank account into which funds advanced to a law firm by a client are deposited. Also called an *escrow account*.

procedure. It is extremely important that the funds held in a trust account be used *only* for expenses relating to the costs of serving that client's needs. Software programs designed for law offices simplify holding multiple accounts.

In many states, certain trust accounts come under the requirements of Interest on Lawyers' Trust Accounts (IOLTA) programs. All states have IOLTA programs, and in all but a dozen states lawyers are required to participate. Client funds are deposited in an IOLTA account when the amount is small or is to be held for a short time. In either case, the interest that could be earned for the client is less than the cost of maintaining a separate client account. The funds are instead placed in a single, pooled, interest-bearing trust account. Banks forward the interest earned on the account to the state IOLTA program, which uses the money to fund charitable causes, mostly to support legal assistance for the poor.

Misuse of client funds constitutes a breach of the firm's duty to its client. An attorney's personal use of the funds, for example, can lead to disciplinary action and possible disbarment, as well as criminal penalties. *Commingling* (mixing together) a client's funds with the firm's funds also constitutes abuse and is one of the most common ways in which attorneys breach their professional obligations. If you handle a client's trust account, you should be especially careful to document your use of the funds to protect yourself and your firm against the serious problems that may arise if there are any problems with the account.

Billing and Timekeeping Procedures

As a general rule, a law firm bills its clients monthly. Each client's bill reflects the amount of time spent on the client's matter by the attorney or other legal personnel. Client billing serves an obvious financial function (collecting payment for services rendered). It also serves a communicative function (keeping the client informed of the work being done on a case), as discussed later in this chapter.

Generally, client bills are prepared by a legal secretary or a bookkeeper or, in larger firms, by someone in the accounting department. The bills are based on the fee arrangements made with the client and the time slips collected from the firm's attorneys and paralegals. The time slips (discussed below) indicate how many hours are to be charged to each client and at what hourly rate.

A paralegal keeps track of the time she spent in the law office library. Later, she will enter the information into her firm's computerized billing program. Why is accuracy in time tracking so important for both the paralegal and the law firm?

(Courtesy of © PhotoDisc, Inc.)

Developing Paralegal Skills

CREATING A TRUST ACCOUNT

Louise Larson has been hired to work for Don Jones. Don is just starting his own solo practice of law after years of working with a medium-sized law firm in which he had nothing to do with the firm's financial management. Louise's first assignment is to establish a client trust accounting system.

Don and Louise review the ethical rules regarding client property and funds. These rules require that client funds not be commingled with the lawyer's funds. "It's too easy to 'borrow' from a client's funds when they are in the lawyer's own bank account," explains Don. "Therefore," Don continues, "the first thing we need to do is open a checking account for client trust funds." Don and Louise then discuss what needs to be done in order to open the trust account and what other bookkeeping procedures will be involved in creating a client trust accounting system.

CHECKLIST FOR CREATING A CLIENT TRUST ACCOUNT

- Obtain and prepare the necessary forms from the bank in which the account will be maintained.
- Devise a bookkeeping method for tracking all fees and expenses for a particular case and/or client.
- Retain all deposit slips and canceled checks.
- Keep a record of payments made to clients.
- Decide who will have access to the account.

The *legal fees* billed to clients are based on the number of billable hours generated for work requiring legal expertise. **Billable hours** are the hours or fractions of hours that attorneys and paralegals spend in client-related work that requires legal expertise and that can be billed directly to clients. The *costs* billed to clients include expenses incurred by the firm (such as court fees, travel expenses, express-delivery charges, and copying costs) on the client's behalf. If an attorney is retained on a contingency-fee basis, the client is not billed monthly for legal fees. The client is normally billed monthly for any costs incurred on the client's behalf, however.

Typically, a preliminary draft of the client's bill is given to the attorney responsible for that client's account. After the attorney reviews and possibly modifies the bill, the final bill is generated and sent to the client. Exhibit 3.4 on the following page illustrates a sample client bill. Most law firms have computerized billing procedures and use time-and-billing software designed specifically for law offices. Time-and-billing software is based on traditional timekeeping and billing procedures. A familiarity with essential features of such programs, combined with a knowledge of the basic principles and procedures involved in client billing, will help you understand whatever type of time-and-billing software your employer may use.

Documenting Time and Expenses

Accurate timekeeping by attorneys and paralegals is crucial because clients cannot be billed for time spent on their behalf unless that time is documented. Traditionally, **time slips** have been used to document time spent by attorneys and paralegals working for a client. Today, time slips are incorporated into timekeeping software programs. We look here at *Timeslips*, a software program created by Sage Software. This is one of the most commonly used time-and-billing programs, according to a survey published in *Legal Assistant Today*.

billable hours

Hours or fractions of hours that attorneys and paralegals spend in work that requires legal expertise and that can be billed directly to clients.

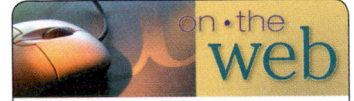

You can obtain information on selected time-and-billing software at the following Web sites: **www.pclaw.com**, **www.timeslips.com**, and **www.tussman.com**.

time slip

A record documenting, for billing purposes, the hours (or fractions of hours) that an attorney or a paralegal worked for each client, the date on which the work was done, and the type of work done.

EXHIBIT 3.4
A Sample Client Bill

Jeffers, Gilmore & Dunn
553 Fifth Avenue
Suite 101
Nita City, NI 48801

BILLING DATE: February 28, 2011

Thomas Jones, M.D.
508 Oak Avenue
Nita City, NI 48801

RE: Medical-Malpractice Action Brought against Dr. Jones,
        File No. 15789

DATE	SERVICES RENDERED	PROVIDED BY	HOURS SPENT	TOTAL
1/30/11	Initial client consultation	APG (attorney)	1.00	$200.00
1/30/11	Client interview	EML (paralegal)	1.00	74.00
1/30/11	Document preparation	EML (paralegal)	1.00	74.00
2/5/11	Interview: Susanne Mathews (nurse)	EML (paralegal)	1.50	111.00
	TOTAL FOR LEGAL SERVICES			$459.00

DATE	EXPENSES			
2/5/11	Hospital charges for a copy of the medical documents			$75.00
	TOTAL FOR EXPENSES			$75.00
	TOTAL BILL TO CLIENT			**$534.00**

In the slip entry form shown in Exhibit 3.5, the user enters his or her name, the task being billed for, the client for whom the work is being performed, the case referenced, and a description of the task. The user then either enters the time spent on the task or turns on an automated stopwatch timer—shown in Exhibit 3.6 on page 76—to track the time spent on the task. Tasks can also be recorded as recurring, and rates can be adjusted according to any special agreements. Notice that in Exhibit 3.5 the time is noted to the minute. While we refer to "hourly billing," the time recorded in client bills should also be expressed in parts of hours, not rounded to whole hours.

Costs incurred on behalf of clients have traditionally been entered on **expense slips**. Expenses are now usually entered into the billing program on a form similar to the time slip entry form shown in Exhibit 3.5. The form records a line-by-line description of each expense, along with the quantity and price of each item purchased on behalf of the client.

expense slip
A slip of paper on which any expense, or cost, that is incurred on behalf of a client (such as the payment of court fees or long-distance telephone charges) is recorded.

Billable versus Nonbillable Hours

The time recorded in timekeeping software is charged either to a client (billable hours) or to the firm (nonbillable hours). As mentioned, billable time generally includes the hours that attorneys and paralegals spend in client-related work that

EXHIBIT 3.5
Timeslips Slip Entry Form

Slip Entry						_ □ X
ID 55			WIP			
Type	⊙ Time ⚪ Expense			Value		500.00
Timekeeper	D. Brickley ▼		DavidB			
Task	Analysis/Strategy ▼		L120			
Client	Bishop ▼		03-0400			
Reference	Bishop v. Ketterer ▼		BIS-1480P			
Extra						

B *I*
U
➕ ➖
Strategizing and planning for Bishop v. Ketterer

Start date	4/6/2009	Time estimated	0:00:00		On
End date	4/6/2009	Time spent	2:30:00		Off

Billing Status and Rate Settings ▲

Billing status	Billable ▼	☐ Hold	☐ Recurring		
Rate	Timekeeper ▼	3 ▼	200.00	Hourly ▼	

Markup, Adjustment, and Do Not Bill Time ▲

Markup(+/-)	⊙ default ⚪	0.00	%		
Adjustment	⊙ default ⚪	0.00	Do Not Bill time	0:00:00	

Screen shot is reprinted with the permission of Sage Software, Inc. Timeslips is the registered trademark of Sage Software, Inc.

requires legal expertise. For example, the time you spend researching or investigating a client's claim is billable time. So is the time spent conferring with or about a client, drafting documents on behalf of a client, interviewing clients or witnesses, and traveling on a client's behalf (to and from the courthouse to file documents, for example).

Time spent on other tasks, such as administrative work, staff meetings, or performance reviews, is nonbillable time. For example, suppose that you spend thirty minutes photocopying forms for the forms file, time sheets, or a procedures manual for the office. That thirty minutes is not considered billable time. In *Timeslips*, the user designates whether the task being recorded is billable, as you can see in the "Billing status" box in Exhibit 3.5.

Generally, law firms have a legitimate reason for wanting to maximize their billable hours: the financial well-being of a law firm depends to a great extent on how many billable hours are generated by its employees. Nonbillable time ultimately cuts into the firm's profits. Therefore, the more billable hours generated by the firm's legal professionals, the more profitable the business will be.

EXHIBIT 3.6
Timeslips Timer

Screen shot is reprinted with the permission of Sage Software, Inc. Timeslips is the registered trademark of Sage Software, Inc.

The Pressure to Generate Billable Hours

Law firms normally tell their paralegals and associate attorneys how many billable hours they are expected to produce and the consequences of not being able to meet that number. The majority of law firms require between 1,750 and 2,050 billable hours per year from attorneys; and at most firms, the base salary for associate attorneys is determined by a billable-hours target that the attorneys are expected to reach. Depending on the firm, a paralegal may be expected to generate between 800 and 2,000 billable hours per year.

Attorneys and paralegals face pressure to produce billable hours for the firm. As a paralegal, you may be subject to this pressure and must learn how to handle it. For example, suppose that your employer expects you to produce 1,800 billable hours per year. Discounting vacation time and holidays (assuming a two-week vacation and ten paid holidays), this equates to 37.5 hours weekly. Assuming that you work 40 hours a week, you will have 2.5 hours a week for such nonbillable activities as interoffice meetings, performance reviews, coffee breaks, reorganizing your work area, and chatting with others in the office. As you can imagine, unless you are willing to work more than eight hours a day, you may have difficulty meeting the billable-hours requirement. Since your time is valuable, make sure your work is clearly prioritized, as discussed in the *In the Office* feature on page 78.

Ethics and Client Billing Practices

Because attorneys have a duty to charge their clients "reasonable" fees, legal professionals must be careful in their billing practices. They must not "pad" their clients' bills by including more billable hours than actually worked on behalf of those clients. They also must avoid **double billing**—billing more than one client for the same time. Accuracy in billing is only one ethical obligation, as the *Ethics Watch* feature reminds us.

double billing
Billing more than one client for the same billable time period.

Double Billing

Sometimes, situations arise in which it is difficult to determine which client should be billed for a particular segment of time. For example, suppose that you are asked to travel to another city to interview a witness in a case for Client A. You spend three hours traveling in an airplane to get to that city. On the plane, you spend two hours

Ethics Watch

BACK UP YOUR WORK

Even a person who uses computers on a routine basis can easily forget—while the computer system is working—that a power failure or other problem can occur at any time. Should this happen, you may lose all current work that has not been saved to your hard disk. Surge protectors help to protect against "computer meltdown," but you should have, in addition, back-up copies of all of your work as well as a contingency plan—such as a second computer available to use.

Backing up your work frequently on a CD-ROM, flash drive, or external hard drive is particularly important and can "save the day" if the computer system crashes or fails to the extent that data on the hard drive cannot be retrieved. If you routinely back up documents, you may save yourself the hours of valuable time that could be required to re-create a document or file. You will also save yourself and the firm from the problem of deciding who will pay—the client or the law firm—for the extra time you had to spend to complete the work. Moreover, with back-up copies available, your employer will never have to be without a crucial document when it's needed. Another important precaution you can take to prevent loss of work is to have a crash-saving program available to recover lost data.

This practice is consistent with the NFPA Model Code of Ethics and Professional Responsibility, which we will discuss in Chapter 4. Section 1.2 of the code states: "A paralegal shall maintain a high standard of professional conduct." Section 1.5 states: "A paralegal shall preserve all confidential information provided by the client or acquired from other sources before, during, and after the course of the professional relationship."

summarizing a document relating to a case for Client B. Who should pay for those two hours, Client A, Client B, or both? In this situation, you could argue—as many attorneys do in similar circumstances—that you generated five billable hours, three on Client A's work, since travel time was required for Client A, and two on Client B's case. This is an example of how double billing can occur.

Double billing also occurs when a firm bills a new client for work that was done for a previous client. For example, suppose that an attorney is working on a case for Client B that is very similar to a case handled by the firm a year ago for Client A. The firm charged Client A $2,000 for the legal services. Because much of the research, writing, and other work done on Client A's case can transfer over to Client B's case, the firm is able to complete the work for Client B in half the time. In this situation, would it be fair to bill Client B $2,000 also? After all, $1,000 of that amount represents hours spent on Client A's case (and for which Client A has already been billed). At the same time, would it be fair to Client A to bill Client B less for essentially the same services? Would it be fair not to allow the firm to profit from cost efficiencies generated by overlapping work? Could the firm split the savings created by the overlapping research ($1,000) with Client B by billing Client B $1,500 instead of $2,000?

The American Bar Association's Response to Double Billing

The American Bar Association (ABA) addressed double billing in a formal ethical opinion. In that opinion, the ABA stated that attorneys are prohibited from charging more than one client for the same hours of work. Additionally, the ABA rejected the notion that the firm, and not the client, should benefit from cost efficiencies created by the firm's work for previous clients. "The lawyer who has

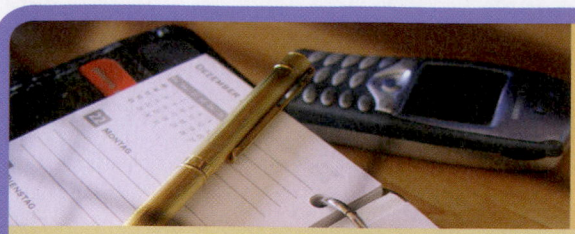

In the **Office**

GET PRIORITIES RIGHT

Staff members in a law office are frequently under pressure to meet deadlines. A paralegal can get caught between attorneys with competing demands or even between the demands of cases being handled by one supervising attorney who is under pressure. Do not let conflicts for your time build up. Discuss which tasks should be accomplished first. Identify conflicts between you and your supervisor about the best use of your limited time. Other people may forget, or may not know about, other work you have to accomplish and may unintentionally be unreasonable in their expectations. Clear communications about what is needed, when work is due, and what gets priority will help you to avoid appearing unresponsive.

agreed to bill solely on the basis of time spent is obliged to pass the benefit of these economies on to the client."

Although ABA opinions are not legally binding on attorneys unless they are adopted by the states as law, they do carry significant weight in the legal community. Courts, for example, have tended to follow the ABA's position in resolving fee disputes. Typically, a court will not award attorneys' fees that it finds to be "excessive, redundant, or otherwise unnecessary."[1] States will sanction or even disbar an attorney for double billing a client.[2]

COMMUNICATING WITH CLIENTS

To succeed as a paralegal, excellent communication skills are a must. (See this chapter's *Featured Contributor* feature on pages 80 and 81 for tips on effective communication.)

Sending monthly bills to clients is one way to keep attorney-client communication channels open. Attorneys have a duty to keep clients reasonably informed. Rule 1.4 of the ABA's Model Rules of Professional Conduct reads as follows:

> (a) A lawyer shall keep a client reasonably informed about the status of a matter and promptly comply with reasonable requests for information.
> (b) A lawyer shall explain a matter to the extent reasonably necessary to permit the client to make informed decisions regarding the representation.

As a paralegal, you need to be aware that keeping clients reasonably informed about the progress being made on their cases goes beyond courtesy—it is a legal duty of attorneys. The meaning of "reasonably informed" varies depending on the client and on the nature of the work being done by the attorney. In some cases, a phone call every week or two will suffice to keep the client informed. In other cases, the attorney may ask the paralegal to draft a letter to a client explaining the status of the client's legal matter. Some firms have regular monthly mailings to update clients on the status of their cases. Generally, you should discuss with your supervising attorney how each client should be kept informed of the status of that client's case. (See the *Technology and Today's Paralegal* feature.)

Copies of all letters and e-mails to a client should, of course, be placed in the client's file. The file should also contain a written record of each phone call made to or received from a client. That way, there is a "paper trail" in the event it is ever

Technology and Today's Paralegal

CYBERSPACE COMMUNICATIONS

E-mail is a standard communication tool for businesses, including law firms. The reason e-mail is so popular is simple: it is a quick, easy-to-use, and inexpensive way to communicate. In large law firms and corporate enterprises, as well as in government agencies, e-mail messages have largely replaced the printed interoffice memos of the past. E-mail is also a common way for attorneys and paralegals to communicate with clients, opposing counsel, witnesses, and others.

APPLY PROFESSIONAL STANDARDS TO E-MAIL COMMUNICATIONS

Because e-mail is transmitted instantly, it may be difficult to remember that it is also a *written communication.* People using e-mail tend to adopt a casual, conversational tone and to ignore the traditional rules of writing, such as sentence structure, spelling, and capitalization. E-mail is still mail, however, and it should reflect the same professional tone and quality that you use in the firm's paper correspondence. If you want to convey a message to someone (especially a client), you need to use clear and effective language.

There are several things you can do to ensure that your e-mail messages are professional and error free. First, use a spell checker. Typos, misspellings, punctuation errors, and grammatical problems detract from the message and can easily be avoided. Make sure that you also proofread your e-mail carefully. Many times, it is helpful to print out an important message, let it sit for a while, and review it later when you can see it from a fresh perspective. Also, make sure that you use the same form as you would in an ordinary letter (see Chapter 9), with perhaps a few variations—adding your e-mail address below your name in the closing and the word *confidential* at the top (when appropriate), for example.

TIPS FOR FORMATTING E-MAIL MESSAGES

Because e-mail often looks different on the recipient's computer screen than it does on your screen, keep the format as simple as possible. Use double spacing between paragraphs rather than indenting with tabs, and do not underline or boldface text (these features often do not transmit clearly from one e-mail system to another). If the message concerns a legal matter and is being sent to a client's workplace or a shared e-mail address, be careful what you identify in the subject line of the e-mail. For example, you could write "documents ready for signature" rather than "bankruptcy petition complete." Also, if your e-mail has an attachment, tell the recipient what word-processing program you used to create the attachment, and offer to resend it as a text document if the recipient cannot open it.

TECHNOLOGY TIP

Always print out a copy of your e-mail and retain it in the client's file so that a record exists. Be sure that any e-mail you send discloses your status as a paralegal (to avoid liability for the unauthorized practice of law). Request recipients to verify that important messages have been received (such as when you are notifying a person of a court date). E-mail systems often have a function that allows senders to request a "return receipt," which will confirm that the message you sent was received. You should also respond to incoming e-mail promptly so that the sender knows that you have received the e-mail. Finally, make sure that you know the policies of your firm regarding confidential e-mail. If used carefully, e-mail can be an efficient way to fulfill your duties and communicate with the firm's clients.

featured contributor

TEN TIPS FOR EFFECTIVE COMMUNICATION

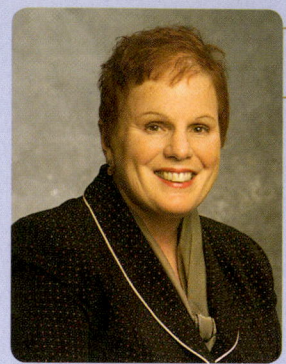

Wendy B. Edson

BIOGRAPHICAL NOTE

Wendy B. Edson received her master's degree in library science (M.L.S.) from the University of Rhode Island and served as law librarian at a Buffalo, New York, law firm. Later, she joined the Paralegal Studies faculty at Hilbert College, in Hamburg, New York, and helped to develop an ABA-approved bachelor's degree program.

As chairperson of the Paralegal Studies Department, Edson teaches paralegalism and legal ethics, legal research and writing, Internet research, and alternative dispute resolution (ADR). She also developed and coordinates the internship program. Edson reviews and publishes on the topics of paralegal education and legal research and writing. She has lectured to legal professionals on legal research, teaching skills, internships, legal ethics, and ADR. A contributor to AAfPE materials and programs, Edson also serves as a volunteer mediator for the family courts in her area.

Words! They are the building blocks of human communication. Whether words are exchanged face to face—or by e-mail, phone, fax, or letter—communication is a two-way street. But how do we become skilled at maneuvering the two-way traffic of interpersonal communication? As in driving, we need to follow the "rules of the road." The rules of the road in regard to communication traffic are embodied in the following ten tips.

1. Establish Communication Equality. Communication equality does not require that individuals hold equal status in an office or organization but requires that each party believe in *equal rights* to speak and listen. Observe someone whom you consider to be a good communicator. You will note that he or she demonstrates equality by actively listening and responding appropriately to whoever is speaking. Workplace problems often reflect communication ailments rooted in inequality. A firm belief in communication equality, despite job titles, will help to create a cooperative, productive working environment.

2. Plan for Time and Space. Effective communication requires *time.* Imagine your reaction to a request to work overtime if your supervising attorney took thirty seconds to order you to do the work versus taking two minutes to explain the reason for the request and listening to your response. In the first situation, the attorney saved one and a half minutes but scored "zero" in terms of communication skills. In today's rushed world, it is easy to overlook the importance of communication skills in morale building and creating a cooperative, efficient workforce.

Effective communicators are aware of how the physical environment in which a conversation takes place can affect the communication process. Communication is always enhanced when the parties have reasonable privacy and are not continually interrupted. Another important factor is physical comfort.

Choosing an inappropriate time and place for communication denies the importance of the matters being discussed and may send the wrong message to both the speaker and the listener.

3. Set the Agenda. Skilled communicators prepare an *agenda*—whether written or mental—of matters to be discussed in order of their priority. Frequently, both parties bring their respective agendas to a discussion, which means that priorities may need to be negotiated. A subordinate who brings up the topic of desired vacation time when the supervisor is preoccupied with a major project clearly demonstrates that his or her priorities are different from those of the supervisor.

Successful communication requires that the parties first negotiate a *common agenda*—that is, determine jointly the agenda for a particular discussion or meeting and what topics should take priority. Then, the topics can be dealt with one by one, in terms of their relative importance, to the satisfaction of both parties. *Agenda awareness* prevents parties from jumping from topic to topic without successfully resolving anything.

4. Fine-Tune Your Speaking Skills. Observe an individual whom you consider to be a good speaker, whether before a group of persons or on a one-on-one basis. What skills does that individual demonstrate? Effective speakers work hard to express thoughts clearly; sometimes, they refer to notes or lists to refresh their memories. Skilled speakers also try to communicate accurately and to talk about matters that they know will interest their listeners. They cultivate *communication empathy*—the sincere effort to put themselves in their listeners' shoes. As you speak to others, pause occasionally and ask yourself: "Would I enjoy listening to what I am saying and how I am saying it?"

5. Cultivate Listening Skills. Listening is not just refraining from speaking while another person is talking but is an *active process*—the other half of the communication partnership. An active listener does not interrupt the speaker. If you sense that the speaker is engaging in a monologue, you can use responsive behavior—including body language, attentiveness, and appropriate remarks—to steer the conversation back to a dialogue without cutting off the speaker.

An active listener realizes that listening is an investment in effective communication. By truly responding to what is being said, rather than regarding listening time as insignificant or as a time to plan his or her own remarks, the skilled listener establishes a bond of trust with the speaker. Active listeners avoid preconceived ideas about topics being discussed and assume that they do not know all the answers.

6. Watch for Body Language. Body language is nonverbal communication that reflects our emotional state. Physical positions, such as leaning forward or away from the speaker while listening, can reinforce or negate our spoken responses. Body attitudes, whether relaxed (comfortable posture, leaning forward, uncrossed arms and legs, relaxed neck and shoulders) or tense (stiff posture, backing away, crossed arms and legs, rigid neck and shoulders), vividly illustrate our responses before we utter a word. Eye contact is one of the most important tools in the body language tool kit for communication. Interviewers, social workers, and police officers have learned that steady and responsive eye contact means sincerity and credibility.

7. Put Note Taking in Perspective. Overinvolvement in note taking detracts from the communication process because

opportunities to listen actively, speak responsively, and be sensitive to body language are reduced. The speaker may ramble while the listener records the ramblings in extensive notes.

When it is necessary to take notes, it is helpful to establish some rapport with the speaker or listener before launching the note-taking process. Alternatively, follow-up notes can be a workable solution to the problem. The note taker can devote the interview time to communication and, after the interview, record his or her general impressions of the interview and identify specific issues that need to be discussed further.

> *"Eye contact is one of the most important tools in the body language tool kit for communication."*

8. Recognize the Role of Criticism. *Constructive criticism* focuses on specific actions or behaviors rather than personalities. It is objective rather than subjective. Criticism that is stated calmly and objectively ("We need to rewrite the section on holographic wills") is much more palatable for the person being criticized than is criticism in the form of a personal attack ("You did a terrible job"). By placing emphasis on actions instead of personalities, the parties can more easily work toward a satisfactory solution. If both the critic and the person being criticized can remain calm and can separate actions from personalities, then criticism will usually produce the desired result and *mutual* satisfaction.

9. Aim for Satisfactory Closure. Closure means "wrapping up" the communication. Successful communicators know that handling closure properly can leave a participant with a good feeling even if the solution was not exactly what he or she initially desired. Summarizing the discussion and checking for agreement or a need for further discussion will encourage all participants to follow the tenth tip.

10. Commit to Communicate. Excellent speakers and listeners have positive, self-confident attitudes that problems can be solved if the "rules of the road" are followed. Skilled communicators cultivate open minds, self-knowledge, and the ability to tolerate differences and empathize with others. They are committed to exercising their rights and responsibilities as speakers and listeners in the communication process.

Developing Paralegal Skills

ORGANIZING E-MAIL

Jolene Sandler works as a paralegal for a music distribution company that represents several thousand musical artists. Like most businesses today, Jolene's company relies on its computer network.

Jolene receives over a hundred e-mails per day, including many unsolicited commercial messages (*spam*) that pass through her company's spam-filtering and antivirus programs. She must keep track of and respond to a large volume of e-mail, so it is critical for her to maintain an organized e-mail system. Jolene learned how to manage her e-mails better at a workshop she attended. She now carefully follows guidelines for responding to and organizing her e-mails. In addition, she learned to deal more effectively with spam and to guard against potentially dangerous e-mail attachments. After all, the company cannot afford a disruption of its computer system as a result of a malicious program, such as a virus, sent via e-mail.

TIPS FOR MANAGING E-MAIL

- Be as specific as possible in your e-mail subject lines. This allows you (and your recipients) to find specific messages quickly when necessary.

- Save time by keeping messages and replies as concise as possible and limiting the number of people to whom you send copies or forwarded messages so as to minimize the number of follow-up e-mails.

- Create folders in your e-mail program and name them clearly. For example, you might create folders to hold messages to or from specific persons. Subfolders within the folders can identify particular topics. It may be helpful to have a folder titled "Priority" for messages that require immediate action. Print hard copies of important e-mails for the file.

- Make it a regular practice to clear messages from your Inbox after reading them. Delete messages you do not need to keep, and move others to the appropriate folders.

- If you suspect that e-mail is spam, delete it without opening it. Do not click on anything in a suspicious e-mail, as you could inadvertently install a virus, spyware, or other harmful program by doing so.

- Do not reply to spam messages. A reply confirms to spammers that they have an active e-mail address, which they can then sell to other spammers.

- Only open e-mail attachments if you know the sender or are expecting to receive a specific attachment from the sender.

necessary to provide evidence of communication with the client. (Actually, this is a good practice for all phone calls relating to a client's matter.) You will learn about the various forms of letters that attorneys send to clients in Chapter 9. Increasingly, attorneys and paralegals communicate with clients via e-mail. Because every paralegal will receive and reply to numerous e-mails, e-mail organization is critical and is the subject of the *Developing Paralegal Skills* feature above.

LAW OFFICE CULTURE AND POLITICS

As a paralegal, you will find that each law firm you work for is unique. Even though two firms may be the same size and have similar organizational structures, they will have different cultures, or "personalities." The culture of a given legal workplace is

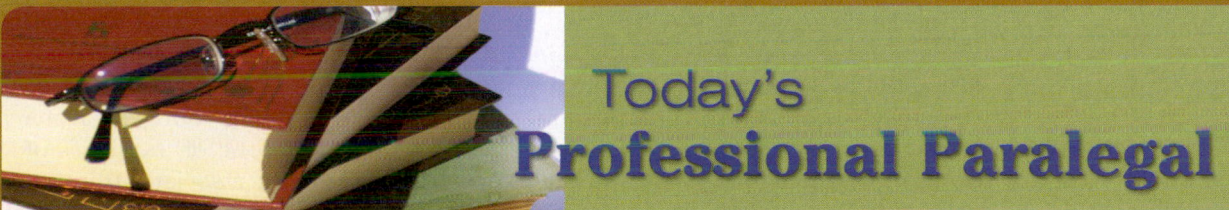

Today's
Professional Paralegal

A PARALEGAL MANAGER AT WORK

The law firm of Brooks and Chandler employs over four hundred attorneys in four cities. Andrea Giancarlo, who works in the Chicago office, has been serving as a paralegal manager since 2001. Andrea is responsible for managing over eighty people in the Chicago office. Most of the people who work under her supervision are paralegals, but she also manages accountants, purchasing agents, and patent specialists. Additionally, she oversees those who work in the litigation technology department. Her job duties focus heavily on human resource issues and a variety of administrative responsibilities.

EXIT INTERVIEW

Andrea has a full schedule for today, but she must always remain flexible and be ready to change her schedule on short notice when necessary. Her morning begins with an exit interview with Maria Tullane, an insurance paralegal who has resigned after three years at the firm. Maria tells Andrea that she has enjoyed her work and the working environment generally at Brooks and Chandler but that another firm has offered her a job with a higher salary. Andrea assures Maria that she understands Maria's concerns about the pay level. She continues by saying that Maria has been a valued member of the insurance staff and that the partners at Brooks and Chandler would like her to continue working for them. She also tells Maria that the firm is rethinking the compensation of its paralegals with an eye toward a more competitive pay structure. Maria says that she has already accepted the offer from the other firm.

COMPENSATION ANALYSIS

After the meeting with Maria, Andrea remembers that she still needs to finish preparing for a meeting with the managers of the Chicago office that is scheduled for the following day. Andrea is meeting with them to discuss the new pay structure. Andrea has read many articles about law firm pay structures, analyzed compensation plans from other organizations, and attended a seminar on the subject. She is prepared to recommend a new pay structure based on market rates and objective performance standards. Andrea's recommendation will also factor in seniority, experience, and area of specialization. She spends the next half hour putting the finishing touches on the agenda for the meeting and copying documents to be distributed to the participants.

MANAGING EMPLOYEE CONFLICT

While Andrea is finishing her preparations for the meeting, one of the paralegals from the contracts section, Andrew Kirkland, appears in her doorway. He looks upset and asks if he can talk to her. Andrea puts her meeting notes aside, invites him in, and asks him to close her office door behind him. Andrew sits down and explains that attorney David Blummer has repeatedly been flirting with some of Andrew's female co-workers while regularly demeaning Andrew and assigning him an excessive workload. Andrea spends over an hour discussing Andrew's concerns and assures him that she will look into this matter discreetly and will assess Andrew's workload. If appropriate, Andrea will also discuss with the managing attorneys possible disciplinary action against Blummer. Andrew is calmer by the time he leaves Andrea's office. Andrea immediately begins making notes to prepare for interviews she will conduct with staff about the working environment in the contracts section.

CONNECTING WITH CO-WORKERS

While she is making notes, several co-workers show up for a lunch date with Andrea. After lunch, Andrea is scheduled to attend an important meeting with other administrative managers to plan the budget for technology purchases for the coming fiscal year. Andrea makes a note on her to-do list to follow up on Andrew's concerns after the technology meeting and heads to lunch.

ultimately determined by how the firm's owners (the partners, for example) define the fundamental goals of the firm.

Each firm also has a political infrastructure that may have little to do with the lines of authority and accountability that are spelled out in the firm's employment manual or other formal policy statement. An up-and-coming younger partner in the firm, for example, may exercise more authority than one of the firm's older partners who is about to retire. There may be rivalry among associate attorneys for promotion to partnership status, and you may be caught in the middle of it. In such cases, you may find yourself tempted to take sides—which could jeopardize your own future with the firm.

Unfortunately, paralegals have little way of knowing about the culture and politics of a given firm until they have worked for the firm awhile. Of course, if you know someone who works for or who has worked for a firm and value that employee's opinion, you might gain some advance knowledge about the firm's environment. Otherwise, when you start to work for a firm, you will need to learn for yourself about interoffice politics. One way to do this is to listen carefully whenever a co-worker discusses the firm's staff and ask discreet questions to elicit information from co-workers about office politics and unwritten policies. This way, you can both prepare yourself to deal with these issues and protect your own interests. After you've worked for the firm for a time, you will be in a position to judge whether the company you have chosen is really the right firm for you.

KEY TERMS AND CONCEPTS

associate attorney 61

billable hours 73

contingency fee 70

double billing 76

employment manual 63

expense slip 74

fixed fee 69

forms file 68

law clerk 61

legal administrator 62

legal-assistant manager, or **paralegal manager** 62

limited liability partnership (LLP) 61

managing partner 61

office manager 62

partner 61

partnership 61

personal liability 60

professional corporation (P.C.) 61

retainer 71

retainer agreement 69

shareholder 61

sole proprietorship 60

staff attorney 61

statute of limitations 68

support personnel 62

time slip 73

trust account 71

CHAPTER SUMMARY

THE INNER WORKINGS OF THE LAW OFFICE

The Organizational Structure of Law Firms

Law firms can be organized in the following ways:

1. *Sole proprietorship*—In a sole proprietorship, one attorney owns the business and is entitled to all the firm's profits. That individual also bears the burden of any losses and is personally liable for the firm's debts or other obligations.

2. *Partnership*—In a partnership, two or more lawyers jointly own the firm and share in the firm's profits and losses. Attorneys who are employed by the firm but who are not partners (such as associates and staff attorneys) do not share in the profits and losses of the firm.

a. Generally, partners are subject to personal liability for all of the firm's debts or other obligations.

b. In many states, firms can organize as *limited liability partnerships,* in which partners are not held personally liable for the malpractice of other partners in the firm.

3. *Professional corporation*—In a professional corporation, two or more individuals jointly own the business as shareholders. The owner-shareholders of the corporation share the firm's profits and losses (as partners do) but are not held personally liable for the firm's debts or obligations beyond the amount they invested in the corporation.

Law Office Management and Personnel

Each law firm has a unique system of management and lines of authority. Generally, the owners of the firm (partners, for example) oversee and manage all other employees. Law firm personnel include associate attorneys; law clerks; paralegals; administrative personnel, who are supervised by the legal administrator or the office manager; and support personnel, including receptionists, secretaries, file clerks, and others.

Employment Policies

Employment policies relate to compensation and employee benefits, performance evaluations, employment termination, and other rules of the workplace, such as office hours. Frequently (particularly in larger firms), the policies of the firm are spelled out in an employment manual or other writing. Most large firms have specific policies and procedures that apply to discrimination in the workplace.

Filing Procedures

Every law firm follows certain filing procedures. In larger firms, these procedures may be written down. In smaller firms, procedures may be more casual and based on habit or tradition.

1. *Confidentiality*—Confidentiality is a major concern and a fundamental policy of every law firm. A breach of confidentiality by anyone in the law office can subject the firm to extensive legal liability. The requirement of confidentiality shapes, to a significant extent, filing procedures.

2. *Types of files*—A typical law firm has client files, work product files and reference materials, forms files, and personnel files.

3. *Objective*—Proper file maintenance is crucial to a smoothly functioning firm. An efficient filing system helps to ensure that important documents will not be misplaced and will be available when needed. Filing procedures must also maximize client confidentiality and the safekeeping of documents.

Financial Procedures

A major concern of any law firm is to have a clear policy on fee arrangements and efficient billing procedures so that each client is billed appropriately.

1. *Fee arrangements*—Types of fee arrangements include fixed fees, hourly fees, and contingency fees. Clients who pay hourly fees are billed monthly for the time spent by attorneys and other legal personnel on the clients' cases or projects, as well as all costs incurred on behalf of the clients.

Continued

2. *Client trust accounts*—Law firms are required to place all funds received from a client into a special account called a client trust account. This is to ensure that the client's money remains separate from the firm's money. It is important that the funds held in the trust account be used only for expenses relating to the costs of serving that client's needs.

3. *Billing and timekeeping*—Firms require attorneys and paralegals to document how they use their time. Because the firm's income depends on the number of billable hours produced by employees, firms usually require attorneys and paralegals to generate a certain number of billable hours per year. Double billing presents a major ethical problem for law firms.

Communicating with Clients

Attorneys have a duty to keep their clients reasonably informed. Paralegals should be aware that this is a legal duty and that they can play a significant role in meeting this duty. Sending billing statements to clients is one way to communicate; phone calls, letters, and e-mail messages are other ways to keep clients informed.

Law Office Culture and Politics

Each office has its own culture, or personality, which is largely shaped by the attitudes of the firm's owners and the qualities they look for when hiring employees. Each firm also has a political infrastructure that is not apparent to outsiders. Office culture and politics make a great difference in terms of job satisfaction and comfort. Wise paralegals learn as soon as possible from co-workers or others about these aspects of the law office.

STUDENT STUDYWARE™ CD-ROM

Interactive student CD in this book includes additional quizzing, plus video clips, case studies, and Key Terms flashcards.

ONLINE COMPANION™

For additional resources, please go to **www.paralegal.delmar.cengage.com**.

QUESTIONS FOR REVIEW

1. What are the basic organizational structures of law firms?

2. What is the difference between an associate and a partner? Who handles the administrative tasks of a law firm? Who supervises the work performed by paralegals?

3. What kinds of files do law firms maintain? What general procedures are typically followed in regard to client files?

4. How does a law firm arrange its fees with its clients? What ethical obligations do attorneys have with respect to legal fees?

5. How do lawyers and legal assistants keep track of their time? What is the difference between billable and nonbillable hours? What is a client trust account?

ETHICAL QUESTION

1. Sam Martin, an attorney, receives a settlement check for a client's case. It is made out jointly to Sam and his client. Sam signs it and instructs his paralegal to deposit it into his law firm's bank account, instead of the client's trust account, because he wants to take out his fee before he gives the client his portion of the money. Can Sam do this? Why or why not? What should Sam's paralegal do?

 ## PRACTICE QUESTIONS AND ASSIGNMENTS

1. Using the material presented in the chapter, identify the following law practices by their organizational structure:

   a. Bill James is an attorney who practices law on his own. He owns his legal practice, the building in which he works, and most of the office furniture. He leases his office equipment. Bill has one secretary and one paralegal who work for him.

   b. Roberta Wagner owns a law firm with Joe Rosen. They own equal interests in the firm, participate equally in the firm's management, and share jointly in its profits and losses. Wagner & Rosen has three associates, six secretaries, and three paralegals who work for the firm.

   c. Randall Smith and Susan Street own a law firm together as shareholders. They employ eight associate attorneys, twelve secretaries, and five legal assistants.

2. Identify the type of billing that is being used in each of the following examples:

   a. The client is billed $200 per hour for a partner's time, $150 per hour for an associate attorney's time, and $125 per hour for a paralegal's time.

   b. The attorney's fee is one-third of the amount that the attorney recovers for the client, either through a pretrial settlement or through a trial.

   c. The attorney charges $250 to change the name of a client's business firm.

3. Louise Lanham hires John J. Roberts, an attorney with the law firm of Sands, Roberts & Simpson, located at 1000 Plymouth Road, Phoenix, Arizona, to represent her in a divorce. She agrees to pay attorney Roberts a rate of $200 per hour and to pay a paralegal rate of $100 per hour. She also agrees to pay all costs and expenses, such as filing fees, expert-witness fees, court-reporter fees, and other fees incurred in the course of her representation. Using Exhibit 3.3 on page 70, *A Sample Retainer Agreement,* draft a retainer agreement between Louise Lanham and John J. Roberts.

 ## QUESTIONS FOR CRITICAL ANALYSIS

1. Do you think that performance evaluations are beneficial? What would happen if performance evaluations were not used? What types of information are included in them? What would you include to make them better?

2. Why are efficient and confidential filing systems and procedures particularly necessary in law offices, more so than in other types of businesses? What might happen without them?

3. Why is it so important for members of a legal team to meticulously keep track of their hours? Why are some hours billable and others not? What happens if accurate billing records are not kept? Why are client trust funds required? Why are these accounts so important? What can happen if client funds are misused?

4. James Johnson is a sole practitioner. His office is about an hour's drive from the federal district court in which he files many of his lawsuits. He used to talk on his cell phone to clients as he traveled the two hours to and from the courthouse. He would then bill the client on whose behalf he was going to the courthouse for two hours and the clients with whom he talked on the phone for increments of the same two hours. When the American Bar Association issued its rule prohibiting double billing, he was concerned that the rule would drive him out of business. Johnson feels that there should be different billing rules for lawyers in large firms and lawyers in small practices, such as his. What do you think?

5. Many law firms require their legal assistants to meet a quota of billable hours. Often, legal assistants can only generate the number of billable hours required per week by working more than the number of hours that they are paid to work. This can lead to the temptation to "pad the bill." Can you think of ways to meet the quota without breaching ethical standards?

PROJECTS

1. Research legal periodicals, such as *Legal Assistant Today* and the ABA's *Journal of Law Practice Management,* for articles on document/case management software. Write a one-page paper summarizing your findings. Be sure to describe how the software works and how its features and cost compare with other software on the market.

2. Search the Internet for information on law office software. You will find that many sites give a description of their software and how much it costs. Some will provide a demonstration. Write down the features of the alternatives and compare what is offered.

USING INTERNET RESOURCES

1. Find legal forms on the Internet by going to the following Web site: **www.legaldocs.com**. Make a general list of the types of forms that are available. Are they free? If not, how much do the forms cost? How can they be purchased? What methods of payment are accepted?

2. Research time-and-billing software on the Internet by going to the following Web site: **www.timeslips. com**. Under the pull-down menu for Products, select "Timeslips," then click "Product Features" to read about the latest version of Timeslips. What are some of the features of this software? Is it limited to one type of billing arrangement, or is it flexible? Can it create reports? What else can it do? Select "Online Demo" from the Products menu, if you want to try out the program for yourself.

END NOTES

1. *EEOC v. Clear Lake Dodge,* 60 F.3d 1146 (5th Cir. 1995).

2. See, for example, *Kentucky Bar Association v. Emerson,* 276 S.W.3d 823 (Ky., 2009) (attorney suspended from practice of law for failing to provide client with detailed billing).

ETHICS AND PROFESSIONAL RESPONSIBILITY

CHAPTER OUTLINE

Introduction

The Regulation of Attorneys

Attorney Ethics and Paralegal Practice

The Indirect Regulation of Paralegals

The Unauthorized Practice of Law

Should Paralegals Be Licensed?

A Final Note

AFTER COMPLETING THIS CHAPTER, YOU WILL KNOW:

▶ Why and how legal professionals are regulated.

▶ Some important ethical rules governing the conduct of attorneys.

▶ How the rules governing attorneys affect paralegal practice.

▶ The kinds of activities that paralegals are and are not legally permittted to perform.

▶ Some of the pros and cons of regulation, including the debate over paralegal licensing.

INTRODUCTION

Paralegals preparing for a career in today's legal arena have a variety of career options. Regardless of which career path you choose to follow, you should have a firm grasp of your state's ethical rules governing the legal profession. When you work under the supervision of an attorney, as most paralegals do, you and the attorney become team members. You will work together on behalf of clients and share in the ethical and legal responsibilities arising as a result of the attorney-client relationship.

In preparing for a career as a paralegal, you must know what these responsibilities are, why they exist, and how they affect you. The first part of this chapter is devoted to the regulation of attorneys because the ethical duties imposed on attorneys by state law affect paralegals as well. If a paralegal violates one of the rules governing attorneys, that violation may result in serious consequences for the client, for the attorney, and for the paralegal. As you read through the rules governing attorney conduct that are discussed in this chapter, keep in mind that these rules also govern paralegal practice, even if indirectly.

Although attorneys are subject to direct regulation by the state, paralegals are not, except in California. Other states may directly regulate paralegals in the future through licensing requirements. Paralegals are regulated indirectly both by attorney ethical codes and by state laws that prohibit nonlawyers from practicing law. As the paralegal profession develops, professional paralegal organizations, the American Bar Association, and state bar associations continue to issue guidelines that also serve to indirectly regulate paralegals.

THE REGULATION OF ATTORNEYS

According to Webster's dictionary, to regulate means "to control or direct in agreement with a rule." To a significant extent, attorneys engage in **self-regulation** because they establish the majority of the rules governing their profession. One of the hallmarks of a profession is the establishment of minimum standards and levels of competence for its members. The accounting profession, for example, has established such standards, as have physicians, engineers, and members of most other professions.

Attorneys are also regulated by the state, because the rules of behavior established by the legal profession are adopted and enforced by state authorities. The purpose of regulating attorney behavior is to protect the public interest. First, by establishing educational and licensing requirements, state authorities ensure that anyone practicing law is competent to do so. Second, by defining specific ethical requirements for attorneys, the states protect the public against unethical attorney behavior that may affect clients' welfare. We will discuss these requirements and rules shortly. Before we do, however, let's look at how these rules are created and enforced.

Who Are the Regulators?

Key participants in determining what rules should govern attorneys and the practice of law, as well as how these rules should be enforced, are bar associations, state supreme courts, state legislatures, and, in some cases, the United States Supreme Court. Procedures for regulating attorneys vary, of course, from state to state. What follows is a general discussion of some of the possible regulators.

Bar Associations

Lawyers determine the requirements for entering the legal profession and the rules of conduct they will follow. Traditionally, lawyers have joined together in professional groups, or bar associations, at the local, state, and national levels to discuss issues affecting the legal profession and to decide on standards of professional conduct.

self-regulation

The regulation of the conduct of a professional group by members of the group. Self-regulation involves establishing ethical or professional standards of behavior with which members of the group must comply.

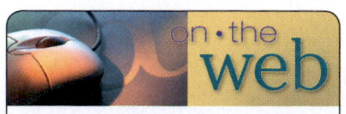

You can access information on state bar associations, legislatures, and courts, including the United States Supreme Court, at **www.findlaw.com**. The American Bar Association is online at **www.abanet.org**.

Although membership in local and national bar associations is always voluntary, membership in the state bar association is mandatory in many states. In these states, before an attorney can practice law, he or she must be admitted to the state's bar association. Approximately half of the lawyers in the United States are members of the American Bar Association (ABA), the voluntary national bar association discussed in Chapter 1. As you will read shortly, the ABA plays a key regulatory role by proposing model (uniform) codes, or rules of conduct, for adoption by the various states.

State Supreme Courts

Typically, the state's highest court, often called the state supreme court, is the ultimate regulatory authority in that state. The court's judges decide what conditions (such as licensing requirements, discussed below) must be met before an attorney can practice law within the state and under what conditions that privilege will be suspended or revoked. In many states, the state supreme court works closely with the state bar association. The association may recommend rules and requirements to the court. If the court so orders, these rules and requirements become state law. Under the authority of the courts, state bar associations often perform routine regulatory functions, including disciplinary proceedings against attorneys who fail to comply with professional requirements.

State Legislatures

State legislatures regulate the legal profession by passing laws affecting attorneys—statutes prohibiting the unauthorized practice of law, for example. In a few states, the states' highest courts delegate significant regulatory responsibilities to the state legislatures, which may include the power to bring disciplinary proceedings against attorneys.

The United States Supreme Court

Occasionally, the United States Supreme Court decides issues relating to attorney conduct. For example, until a few decades ago, state ethical codes, or rules governing attorney conduct, prohibited lawyers from advertising their services to the public. These restrictions on advertising were later determined by the United States Supreme Court to be an unconstitutional limitation on attorneys' rights to free speech.

Licensing Requirements

The **licensing** of attorneys, which gives them the right to practice law, is accomplished at the state level. Each state has different requirements that individuals must meet before they are allowed to practice law and give legal advice. Generally, however, there are three basic requirements:

1. In most states, prospective attorneys must have a bachelor's degree from a university or college and must have graduated from an accredited law school (in many states, the school must be accredited by the ABA), which requires an additional three years of study.

2. In all states, a prospective attorney must pass a state bar examination—a rigorous and thorough examination that tests the candidate's knowledge of the law and (in some states) of the state's ethical rules governing attorneys. The examination covers both state law (law applicable to the particular state in which the attorney is taking the exam and wishes to practice) and multistate law (law applicable in most states, including federal law).

3. The candidate must pass an extensive personal background investigation to verify that he or she is a responsible individual and otherwise qualifies to engage in an ethical profession. An illegal act committed by the candidate in

licensing

A government's official act of granting permission to an individual, such as an attorney, to do something that would be illegal in the absence of such permission.

the past, for example, might disqualify the individual from being permitted to practice law.

Only when these requirements have been met can an individual be admitted to the state bar and legally practice law within the state.

Licensing requirements for attorneys are part of a long history of restrictions on entry into the legal profession. Beginning in the 1850s, restrictions on who could (or could not) practice law were put in place by state statutes prohibiting the **unauthorized practice of law (UPL)**. Court decisions relating to unauthorized legal practice also date to this period. By the 1930s, almost all states had enacted legislation prohibiting anyone but licensed attorneys from practicing law. As you will see, many of the regulatory issues facing the legal profession—and particularly paralegals—are directly related to these UPL statutes.

Ethical Codes and Rules

The legal profession is also regulated through ethical codes and rules adopted by each state—in most states, by order of the state supreme court. These codes of professional conduct evolved over a long period of time. A major step toward ethical regulation was taken in 1908, when the ABA approved the Canons of Ethics, which consisted of thirty-two ethical principles. In the following decades, various states adopted these canons as law.

Today's state ethical codes are based, for the most part, on two later revisions of the ABA canons: the Model Code of Professional Responsibility (published in 1969) and the Model Rules of Professional Conduct (first published in 1983 to replace the Model Code and revised many times since then). Although most states have adopted laws based on the Model Rules, the Model Code is still in effect in some states. New York still uses the Model Code, for example, while California and Maine have developed their own rules. You should be aware of both the Model Code and the Model Rules and become familiar with the set of rules that is in effect in your state.

The Model Code of Professional Responsibility

The ABA Model Code of Professional Responsibility, often referred to simply as the Model Code, consists of nine canons (major principles). In the Model Code, each canon is followed by sections entitled "Ethical Considerations" (ECs) and "Disciplinary Rules" (DRs). The ethical considerations are "aspirational" in character—that is, they suggest ideal conduct, not necessarily behavior that is required by law. For example, Canon 6 ("A lawyer should represent a client competently") is followed by EC 6–1, which states (in part) that a lawyer "should strive to become and remain proficient in his practice." In contrast, disciplinary rules are mandatory in character—an attorney may be subject to disciplinary action for breaking one of the rules. For example, DR 6–101 (which follows Canon 6) states that a lawyer "shall not . . . neglect a legal matter entrusted to him."

The Model Rules of Professional Conduct

The 1983 revision of the ABA Model Code—referred to as the Model Rules of Professional Conduct or, more simply, as the Model Rules—represented a thorough revamping of the code. The Model Rules replaced the canons, ethical considerations, and disciplinary rules of the Model Code with a set of rules organized under eight general headings, as outlined in Exhibit 4.1. Each rule is followed by comments shedding additional light on the rule's application and how it compares with the Model Code's treatment of the same issue.

Because the 1983 Model Rules serve as models for the ethical codes of most states, we use the 1983 rules as the basis for our discussion in this text. It is important to note, however, that the ABA's ethics commission periodically updates and revises the Model

unauthorized practice of law (UPL)
The performance of actions defined by a legal authority, such as a state legislature, as constituting the "practice of law" without authorization to do so.

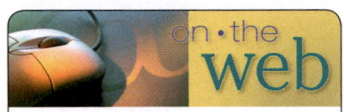

To read the ethics code adopted by your state, go to **http://www.law.cornell. edu**, go to LII topical libraries, then American Legal Ethics Library.

For a comprehensive collection of ethics articles and laws, as well as links to other ethics sources, go to **www. legalethics.com**.

You can access the entire text of the Model Rules of Professional Conduct, along with an explanation of various changes to the rules, on the ABA's Web site at **www.abanet.org**. From the "Member Resources" menu, select "Ethics/Professional Conduct." On the page that opens, select "Model Rules of Professional Conduct" from the listing of "Top Ethics Resources."

Rules as necessary in light of the realities of modern law practice. For example, the ABA's ethics commission has revised the Model Rules to address new ethical concerns raised by technological developments (for example, e-mail and client confidentiality).

Sanctions for Violations

Attorneys who violate the rules governing professional conduct are subject to disciplinary proceedings brought by the state bar association, state supreme court, or state legislature—depending on the state's regulatory scheme. In most states,

EXHIBIT 4.1
The ABA Model Rules of Professional Conduct (Headings Only)

CLIENT-LAWYER RELATIONSHIP		TRANSACTIONS WITH PERSONS OTHER THAN CLIENTS	
1.1	Competence	4.1	Truthfulness in Statements to Others
1.2	Scope of Representation and Allocation of Authority between Client and Lawyer	4.2	Communication with Person Represented by Counsel
1.3	Diligence	4.3	Dealing with Unrepresented Person
1.4	Communications	4.4	Respect for Rights of Third Persons
1.5	Fees	**LAW FIRMS AND ASSOCIATIONS**	
1.6	Confidentiality of Information	5.1	Responsibilities of a Partner or Supervisory Lawyer
1.7	Conflict of Interest: Current Clients	5.2	Responsibilities of a Subordinate Lawyer
1.8	Conflict of Interest: Current Clients: Specific Rules	5.3	Responsibilities Regarding Nonlawyer Assistant
1.9	Duties to Former Clients	5.4	Professional Independence of a Lawyer
1.10	Imputation of Conflicts of Interest: General Rule	5.5	Unauthorized Practice of Law; Multijurisdictional Practice of Law
1.11	Special Conflicts of Interest for Former and Current Government Officers and Employees	5.6	Restrictions on Right to Practice
1.12	Former Judge, Arbitrator, Mediator, or Other Third-Party Neutral	5.7	Responsibilities Regarding Law-Related Services
1.13	Organization as Client	**PUBLIC SERVICE**	
1.14	Client with Diminished Capacity	6.1	Voluntary *Pro Bono Publico* Service
1.15	Safekeeping Property	6.2	Accepting Appointments
1.16	Declining or Terminating Representation	6.3	Membership in Legal Services Organization
1.17	Sale of Law Practice	6.4	Law Reform Activities Affecting Client Interests
1.18	Duties to Prospective Client	6.5	Nonprofit and Court Annexed Limited Legal Services Programs
COUNSELOR		**INFORMATION ABOUT LEGAL SERVICES**	
2.1	Advisor	7.1	Communication Concerning a Lawyer's Services
2.2	(Deleted)	7.2	Advertising
2.3	Evaluation for Use by Third Persons	7.3	Direct Contact with Prospective Clients
2.4	Lawyer Serving as Third-Party Neutral	7.4	Communication of Fields of Practice and Specialization
ADVOCATE		7.5	Firm Names and Letterheads
3.1	Meritorious Claims and Contentions	7.6	Political Contributions to Obtain Legal Engagements or Appointments by Judges
3.2	Expediting Litigation	**MAINTAINING THE INTEGRITY OF THE PROFESSION**	
3.3	Candor toward the Tribunal	8.1	Bar Admission and Disciplinary Matters
3.4	Fairness to Opposing Party and Counsel	8.2	Judicial and Legal Officials
3.5	Impartiality and Decorum of the Tribunal	8.3	Reporting Professional Misconduct
3.6	Trial Publicity	8.4	Misconduct
3.7	Lawyer as Witness	8.5	Disciplinary Authority; Choice of Law
3.8	Special Responsibilities of a Prosecutor		
3.9	Advocate in Nonadjudicative Proceedings		

unethical attorney actions are reported (by clients, legal professionals, or others) to the ethics committee of the state bar association, which is obligated to investigate each complaint thoroughly. For serious violations, the state bar association or the court initiates disciplinary proceedings against the attorney.

Sanctions imposed for violations range from a **reprimand** (a formal "scolding" of the attorney—the mildest sanction[1]), to **suspension** (a more serious sanction by which the attorney is prohibited from practicing law in the state for a given period of time, such as one month or one year, or for an indefinite period of time), to **disbarment** (revocation of the attorney's license to practice law in the state—the most serious sanction).

In addition to these sanctions, attorneys may be subject to civil liability for negligence. As will be discussed in Chapter 14, *negligence* (called **malpractice** when committed by a professional, such as an attorney) is a tort (a wrongful act) that is committed when an individual fails to perform a legally recognized duty. Tort law allows one who is injured by another's wrongful or careless act to bring a civil lawsuit against the wrongdoer for **damages** (compensation in the form of money). A client may bring a lawsuit against an attorney only if the client has suffered harm because of the attorney's failure to perform a legal duty.

If a paralegal's breach of a professional duty causes a client to suffer substantial harm, the client may sue not only the attorney but also the paralegal. Although law firms' liability insurance policies typically cover paralegals as well as attorneys, these policies do not cover paralegals working on a contract (freelance) basis. Just one lawsuit could ruin a freelance paralegal financially—as well as destroy that paralegal's reputation in the legal community. (Hence, obtaining liability insurance is important for freelance paralegals as well as for independent paralegals.)

Attorneys and paralegals are also subject to potential criminal liability under federal and state criminal statutes prohibiting fraud, theft, and other crimes.

ATTORNEY ETHICS AND PARALEGAL PRACTICE

Because most state codes are guided by the Model Rules of Professional Conduct, the rules discussed in this section are drawn from the Model Rules. Keep in mind, though, that your own state's code of conduct is the governing authority on attorney conduct in your state.

As a paralegal, one of your foremost professional responsibilities is to carefully follow the rules in your state's ethical code. You will want to obtain a copy of your state's ethical code and become familiar with its contents. A good practice is to keep the code near at hand in your office.

Professional duties—and the possibility of violating them—are involved in almost every task you will perform as a paralegal. Even if you memorize every rule governing the legal profession, you can still quite easily violate a rule unintentionally (paralegals rarely breach professional duties intentionally). To minimize the chances that you will accidentally violate a rule, you need to know not only what the rules are but also how they apply to the day-to-day realities of your job.

The rules relating to competence, confidentiality, and conflict of interest deserve special attention here because they pose particularly difficult ethical problems for paralegals. Other important rules that affect paralegal performance—including the duty to charge reasonable fees, the duty to protect clients' property, and the duty to keep the client reasonably informed—will be discussed elsewhere in this text as they relate to special topics.

The Duty of Competence

Rule 1.1 of the Model Rules states one of the most fundamental duties of attorneys—the duty of competence. The rule reads as follows:

---

reprimand

A disciplinary sanction in which an attorney is rebuked for misbehavior. Although a reprimand is the mildest sanction for attorney misconduct, it is serious and may significantly damage the attorney's reputation in the legal community.

suspension

A serious disciplinary sanction in which an attorney who has violated an ethical rule or a law is prohibited from practicing law in the state for a specified or an indefinite period of time.

disbarment

A severe disciplinary sanction in which an attorney's license to practice law in the state is revoked because of unethical or illegal conduct.

malpractice

Professional misconduct or negligence—the failure to exercise due care—on the part of a professional, such as an attorney or a physician.

damages

Money awarded as a remedy for a civil wrong, such as a breach of contract or a tort (wrongful act).

The ABA provides links to the rules of professional conduct of every state at **www.abanet.org**. From the "Member Resources" menu, select "Ethics/Professional Conduct." Then select "State Resources" from the "Top Ethics Resources" list.

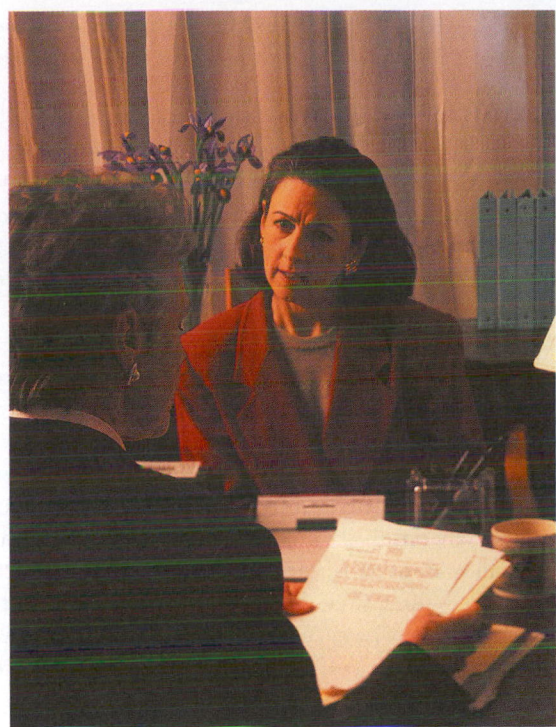

A paralegal discusses a potential conflict of interest with her supervising attorney. Attorneys and paralegals must be careful to avoid violating the ethical rules of the legal profession, because violations of the rules can have serious professional and financial consequences.

(Courtesy of © PhotoDisc®).

A lawyer shall provide competent representation to a client. Competent representation requires the legal knowledge, skill, thoroughness and preparation reasonably necessary for representation.

Competent legal representation is a basic requirement of the profession. **Breaching** (failing to perform) this duty may subject attorneys to one or more of the sanctions discussed earlier. As a paralegal, you share in this duty when you undertake work on an attorney's behalf. If your supervising attorney asks you to research a particular legal issue for a client, for example, you must make sure that your research is careful and thorough—because the attorney's reputation (and the client's welfare) may depend on your performance. Carelessly conducting research, if it results in substantial injury to the client's interests, can subject you personally to liability for negligence, not to mention the loss of a job or career opportunities.

breach

To violate a legal duty by an act or a failure to act.

How the Duty of Competence Can Be Breached

Most breaches of the duty of competence are inadvertent. Often, breaches of the duty of competence have to do with inadequate research, missed deadlines, and errors in legal documents filed with the court.

Inadequate Research. Paralegals frequently do both legal and factual research for attorneys. Depending on the situation, an attorney's first step after meeting with a new client is often to have a paralegal research the facts involved, such as who did what to whom, when, where, and how. If the paralegal fails to discover a relevant fact and the attorney then relies on the paralegal's research in advising the client, the result could be a breach of the duty of competence.

Similarly, a paralegal conducting legal research might breach the duty of competence by failing to find or report a specific court decision that controls the outcome of a client's case. For example, suppose that a paralegal performs initial research into the law surrounding a particular dispute and reports her findings to the attorney. Then, while the paralegal is working on unrelated cases over the next few months, a state court rules on a case with issues very similar to those involved in the client's dispute. If the paralegal or the attorney does not go back and confirm

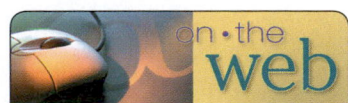

The Web sites of the two national paralegal associations, the National Association of Legal Assistants (NALA) and the National Federation of Paralegal Associations (NFPA), are good sources for information on the ethical responsibilities of paralegals, including new, technology-related ethical challenges. You can access NALA's site at **www.nala.org**. The URL for NFPA's site is **www.paralegals.org**.

that the initial research results are still accurate, a ruling that would influence the client's case could be overlooked. This would breach the attorney's duty of competence to the client.

Although attorneys are ultimately responsible for competent representation, paralegals play an important role in providing accurate information to their attorneys. If you are ever unsure of the accuracy of your research results, make sure to let the attorney know of your doubts. Also, keep good notes recording each step you took in conducting research so that you know what still needs to be done. These measures will help prevent accidental breaches of the duty of competence.

Missed Deadlines.   Paralegals often work on several cases at once. Keeping track of every deadline in every case can be challenging. Organization is the key to making sure that all deadlines are met. All dates relating to actions and events for every case or client should be entered on a calendar. Larger firms typically use computerized calendaring and "tickler" (reminder) systems. Even the smallest firm normally has calendaring procedures and tickler systems in place. Besides making sure that all deadlines are entered into the appropriate systems, you should also have your own personal calendar for tracking dates that are relevant to the cases on which you are working—and then make sure that you consistently use it. Check your calendar every morning when you get to work or at some other convenient time. Also, check frequently with your attorney about deadlines that he or she may not have mentioned to you.

Errors in Documents.   Breaches of the duty of competence can involve errors in documents. For example, incorrect information might be included (or crucial information omitted) in a legal document to be filed with the court. If the attorney fails to notice the error before signing the document, and the document is delivered to the court, a breach of the duty of competence has occurred. Depending on its effect, this breach may expose the attorney and the paralegal to liability for negligence. To prevent these kinds of violations, be especially careful in drafting and proofreading documents.

Generally, if you are ever unsure about what to include in a document, when it must be completed or filed with the court, how extensively you should research a legal issue, or any other aspect of an assignment, ask your supervising attorney for instructions. Make sure that your work is adequately overseen by an attorney to reduce the chances that it will contain costly mistakes or errors.

Attorney's Duty to Supervise

Rule 5.3 of the Model Rules defines the responsibilities of attorneys to nonlawyer assistants. This rule states, in part, that a "lawyer having direct supervisory authority over the nonlawyer shall make reasonable efforts to ensure that the person's conduct is compatible with the professional obligations of the lawyer." The rule also specifies the circumstances under which a lawyer is held responsible for conduct of a nonlawyer that violates the standards set out for attorneys. The lawyer is responsible, for example, if she orders the conduct or ratifies (approves of) it, with knowledge of the specific conduct. Lawyers who have managerial authority in a law firm or have supervisory authority over a nonlawyer can also be held responsible for the nonlawyer's unethical conduct if they knew about it and failed to take any action to prevent it.

This rule applies not only to lawyers who work in private law firms but also to lawyers in corporate legal departments, government agencies, and elsewhere. In addition, in the statements outlining attorneys' responsibilities toward nonlawyer employees in this area, the ABA commission changed the word *should* to *must*. Attorneys *must* both instruct and supervise nonlawyer employees concerning the appropriate ethical conduct and can be held personally responsible for the ethical violations of their subordinates.

Inadequate Supervision

Because attorneys are held legally responsible for their assistants' work, it may seem logical to assume that attorneys will take time to direct that work carefully. In fact, paralegals may find it difficult to ensure that their work is adequately supervised. For one thing, most paralegals are kept very busy. Making sure that all their tasks are properly overseen can be time consuming. At the same time, attorneys—especially if they know their paralegals are competent—often do not want to take the time to read every document the paralegals draft. Nonetheless, as a paralegal, you have a duty to assist your supervising attorney in fulfilling his or her ethical obligations, including the obligation to supervise your work.

If you ever feel that your attorney is not adequately supervising your work, there are several things you can do. You can try to improve communications with the attorney—generally, the more you communicate with your supervising attorney, the more likely the attorney will take an active role in directing your activities. You can also ask the attorney for feedback on your work. Sometimes, it helps to place reminders on your calendar to discuss particular issues or questions with the attorney. When the opportunity to talk arises, these issues or questions will be fresh in your mind. Another tactic is to attach a note to a document that you have prepared for the attorney, requesting him or her to review the document (or revised sections of the document) carefully before signing it. Ensuring proper supervision to protect yourself is discussed in the *Developing Paralegal Skills* feature on the next page.

Confidentiality of Information

Rule 1.6 of the Model Rules concerns attorney-client confidentiality. This rule is one of the oldest and most important rules of the legal profession. It would be very difficult for a lawyer to properly represent a client without such a rule. A client must be able to confide in the attorney so that the attorney can best represent the client's interest. Because confidentiality is one of the easiest rules to violate, a thorough understanding of the rule is essential.

The general rule of confidentiality is that all information relating to representation of a client must be kept confidential. There are exceptions to the rule, which we discuss shortly.

Note that the rule simply states that a lawyer may not reveal "information relating to representation of a client." Does this mean that if a client tells you that he is the president of a local company, you have to keep that information confidential, even when it is common knowledge? For example, could you tell your spouse, "Mr. X is the president of XYZ Corporation"? It may seem permissible, because that fact is so widely known. But in so doing, you must not indicate, by words or conduct, that Mr. X is a client of your firm. Mr. X may not want it known that he is talking to a lawyer at a law firm. People who learn that he is may think "something is up," which is likely to be true. Confidence has been breached. Consider another example. Suppose that one evening at dinner you told your spouse that you had met Mr. X that day. Your spouse might reasonably assume that your firm was handling some legal matter involving Mr. X and might repeat that to other people. Because it may be difficult to decide what information is or is not confidential, a good rule of thumb is to regard all information about a client or a client's case as confidential information.

Exceptions to the Confidentiality Rule

Rule 1.6 provides for certain exceptions, each of which we look at here.

Client Gives Informed Consent to the Disclosure. The rule indicates that an attorney can reveal confidential information if the client gives informed consent to the disclosure. The attorney must fully explain the risks and alternatives involved in the disclosure for the consent to be informed. For example, suppose that an

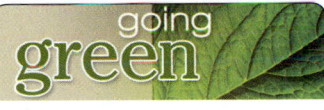

SAVING JUICE

Computer experts agree that, generally speaking, there is no reason not to turn off your computer when you leave the office for the day. Turning off the machine saves on office electricity bills and means the production of a bit less electricity. Because carbon emission goes with most electricity production, it may also mean fewer carbon emissions.

Developing
Paralegal Skills

ADEQUATE SUPERVISION

Michael Patton is a paralegal in a small general-practice law firm. His supervising attorney, Muriel Chapman, answers his question about the specific information that he should insert into the complaints (the documents filed with the court to initiate a lawsuit) for two different clients' cases. Muriel is scheduled to attend a deposition (a pretrial procedure in which testimony is given under oath) in another matter this afternoon and has asked Michael to prepare the two complaints and file them with the court today. Muriel tells Michael to use a complaint from a previous client's case as a model for creating the new complaints, replacing that client's information as necessary.

Michael has drafted complaints before, and he is fairly certain that he knows what needs to be done. He leaves Muriel's office and starts revising the model document into a complaint for each of the clients. By the time he is finished, however, it is 4:00 P.M., and Muriel is involved in the deposition in the conference room. Michael needs to file the complaints at the courthouse by 5:00 P.M., but he remembers the adequate supervision rule and does not want to file the documents before Muriel has reviewed them. What should he do? He finally decides that he must interrupt the deposition so that Muriel can look over the complaints before they are filed with the court. He flags a few passages that he is unsure about and proceeds into the conference room. When Muriel sees him, she asks the opposing counsel if the group will agree to take a short break from the proceeding. Then Muriel and Michael step out of the room so that she can review the documents that he has prepared.

TIPS FOR OBTAINING ADEQUATE SUPERVISION

- Always request your supervising attorney to review your work.
- Use notes or ticklers as reminders to ask for a review.
- Try to make the review as convenient as possible for your supervising attorney, and point out or mark anything that needs particular attention.
- Discuss any ethical concerns with the attorney.
- Be persistent.

attorney is drawing up a will for a client, and the client is making her only son the sole beneficiary under the will and leaving nothing to her daughter. The daughter calls and wants to know how her mother's will reads. The attorney cannot divulge this confidential information to the daughter because the client has not consented to such disclosure. Now suppose that the attorney explains to the client that if her daughter does not learn about the provisions of the will until after her mother's death, it is more likely that she can contest the will in court. After the attorney and client discuss the various alternatives and the risks of each, the client can give her informed consent to the attorney to disclose information to her daughter.

Impliedly Authorized Disclosures.   Rule 1.6 also states that an attorney can make "disclosures that are impliedly authorized in order to carry out the representation." This exception is clearly necessary. Legal representation of clients necessarily involves the attorney's assistants, and they must have access to the confidential information to do their jobs. If a paralegal is working on the client's case, for example, he must know what the client told the attorney about the legal matter and must have access to information in the client's file concerning the case.

Developing
Paralegal Skills

WHAT IF YOU LEARN YOUR CLIENT IS PLANNING TO COMMIT A CRIME?

Communications between a client and his or her attorney, including with the attorney's paralegal, are usually covered by the *attorney-client privilege.* Privileged statements may not be disclosed without the client's consent. When the client makes statements that suggest he or she is going to commit a crime, however, the privilege does not apply.

For example, in one criminal case, the defendant told his lawyer that he was going to attempt to bribe one or more witnesses against him and that if he was unable to do so, he would "whack" the witnesses.[a] Later the defendant also threatened the lawyer. The lawyer reported these threats to the district attorney and withdrew as the defendant's counsel. The defendant's new lawyer tried to have the first lawyer's testimony about the threats excluded, but failed. Because the defendant had threatened a criminal act (assaulting the witnesses and lawyer) that could involve serious bodily harm or death, the California appeals court held that privilege did not apply.

State rules on privilege differ, and you should make sure that you understand the range of crimes covered by your state's laws. All states exempt threats of death or serious injury, and such statements should be reported immediately. In addition, some states require reporting of certain criminal acts.

a. *People v. Dang,* 93 Cal.App.4th 1293, 113 Cal.Rptr.2d 763 (2001).

Disclosures to Prevent Harm. The Model Rules recognize that there are certain circumstances in which an attorney should be allowed to disclose confidential information when it is necessary to prevent harm to persons or property. Rule 1.6 specifically lists four exceptions to the confidentiality rule for this purpose:

1. An attorney is allowed to reveal a client's information to prevent reasonably certain death or substantial bodily harm. For example, suppose that the client confides in the attorney that he assaulted and nearly killed several people recently. The attorney is not allowed to disclose this information. If that client then tells the attorney that he is going to attack a specific person in the future, however, the attorney can disclose this information to prevent reasonably certain bodily harm to the person. This is discussed further in the *Developing Paralegal Skills* feature above.

2. In certain situations, an attorney can disclose confidential information to prevent a client from committing a crime or fraud. The crime or fraud must be reasonably certain to result in substantial injury to the financial interests or property of another. Also, the client must have used or be using the attorney's services to perpetrate the crime or fraud. If both these conditions are present, then the attorney can disclose information to the extent necessary to enable the affected person to contact the appropriate authorities.

3. If a client used the attorney to help commit a crime or fraud, and the crime or fraud will likely cause injury to the financial interests or property of another, the attorney can disclose confidential information to the extent necessary to prevent or reduce that injury.

4. An attorney can also disclose confidential information to establish a defense to a criminal charge in a controversy between the attorney and the client

based on conduct involving the client or to respond to allegations in any proceeding regarding the attorney's representation of the client.

Disclosures to Ensure Compliance with Model Rules.   If a lawyer is unsure what is required to comply with the Model Rules of Professional Conduct in a particular situation, the lawyer can seek legal advice from another lawyer without violating confidentiality. For example, suppose that an attorney who is representing a corporation becomes suspicious that the corporation is engaged in fraud. The attorney is not sure what her professional responsibilities are in that particular situation, so she can seek confidential legal advice from another lawyer to assist her in complying with the Model Rules.

Defending against a Client's Legal Action.   An attorney may also disclose confidential information if the information is necessary to establish a defense in an action brought by a client against the attorney. For example, if the client sues the attorney for malpractice, the lawyer must reveal confidential information to prove that he was not negligent. Note, though, that the attorney is permitted to disclose confidential information only to the extent that it is essential to defend against the lawsuit.

Disclosures to Comply with Court Order or Other Law.   An attorney may also reveal information relating to the representation of a client if ordered to do so by a court or other governmental entity. For example, suppose that one of the attorney's clients in a divorce case was allegedly hiding valuable assets from his wife. In that situation, a court could require the attorney to reveal any confidential information from the client related to the hidden assets. The attorney should first attempt to persuade the client to disclose the location and value of the assets. Nevertheless, the attorney can reveal as much information as he thinks reasonable to satisfy the needs of the court or other governmental entity.

Violations of the Confidentiality Rule

Paralegals, like other professionals, spend a good part of their lives engaged in their work. Naturally, they are tempted to discuss their work with family members, co-workers, and friends. As a paralegal, one of the greatest temptations you will face is the desire to discuss an interesting case with someone you know. You can deal with this temptation in two ways: you can decide never to discuss anything concerning your work, or you can limit your discussion to issues and comments that will not reveal the identity of clients. The latter approach is more realistic for most people, but it requires great care. Something you say may reveal a client's identity, even though you are not aware of it. (See the *Ethics Watch* feature.)

Conversations Overheard by Others.   Violations of the confidentiality rule can happen simply by oversight. Suppose that you and a secretary in your office are working on the same case and continue, as you walk to the elevator, a conversation that you have been having about the case. In the hall or on the elevator, your conversation could be overheard, and the confidential information revealed could have an adverse effect on your client's interests. It is important to avoid the possibility of unwittingly revealing confidential information to **third parties** in such situations. Therefore, never discuss confidential information when you are in common areas.

Electronic Communications and Confidentiality.   Whenever you talk to or about a client on the telephone, make sure that your conversation will not be overheard by a third party. You may be sitting in your private office, but if your door is open, someone may overhear the conversation. Even employees of the firm should not hear information about cases they are not working on.

third party
A person or entity not directly involved in an agreement (such as a contract), legal proceeding (such as a lawsuit), or relationship (such as an attorney-client relationship).

Ethics Watch

SOCIAL EVENTS AND CONFIDENTIALITY

Assume that you are at a party with some other paralegals. You tell a paralegal whom you know quite well of some startling news—that a client of your firm, a prominent city official, is being investigated for drug dealing. Although your friend promises to keep this information strictly confidential, she nonetheless relays it to her husband, who tells a co-worker, who in turn tells a friend, and so on. Soon, the news has reached the press, and the resulting media coverage results in irreparable harm to the official's reputation and standing in the community. Revealing the juicy gossip breached your obligation to the client. If it can be proved that the harm is the direct result of your breach of the duty of confidentiality, the official could sue both you and the attorney for whom you work for damages.

In this situation, you would have violated the NFPA Model Code of Ethics and Professional Responsibility, Section 1.5(f), which states: "A paralegal shall not engage in any indiscreet communications concerning clients." This behavior would also have violated the ABA Model Guidelines for the Utilization of Paralegal Services, Guideline 6: "A lawyer is responsible for taking reasonable measures to ensure that all client confidences are preserved by a paralegal." Finally, you would have violated the NALA Code of Ethics and Professional Responsibility, Canon 7: "A paralegal must protect the confidences of a client."

Paralegals should take special care when using cellular phones. Cell phones are not secure. Although conversations on digital cell phones are more difficult to intercept than conversations on analog phones (which can be overheard by anyone in the area with a scanner), there is still a security risk. As a precaution, you should never disclose confidential information when talking on a cell phone. Because of the widespread use of mobile phones, paralegals often, as a precaution, ask a client who is calling whether he or she is calling from a mobile unit. If the client is using a cell phone, the paralegal can caution the client not to discuss confidential information.

Even such a simple operation as sending a fax can pose ethical pitfalls. Generally, you should exercise great care to make sure that you (1) send the fax to the right person (for example, when a letter is addressed to an opposing party in a lawsuit but is supposed to be sent to the client for approval) and (2) dial the correct fax number.

You also need to be cautious when sending e-mail messages. Suppose that you are asked by your supervising attorney to send an e-mail message to a client and to attach a document containing the attorney's analysis of confidential information submitted by the client. The client's e-mail address is in your e-mail "address book," along with other addresses. You click on the client's name, type a brief message, attach the document, and click "send." Too late, you realize that you accidentally clicked on the opposing counsel's name instead of your client's. By a click of the mouse, you have disclosed important confidential information. To avoid this kind of problem, before you click "send," take a minute not only to review the message—grammar, sentence structure, and spelling—but also to verify the recipient's name and address. (For further discussions of e-mail issues, see the *In the Office* feature on page 102 and the *Technology and Today's Paralegal* feature on pages 104 and 105.)

Other Ways of Violating the Confidentiality Rule.   There are many other ways in which you can reveal confidential information without intending to do so. A

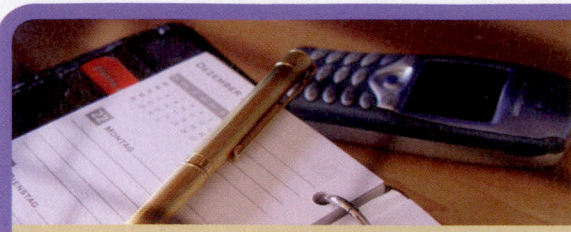

In the **Office**

AM I CLEAR?

E-mail is a common form of communication, but it can cause problems. Follow office e-mail procedures carefully. Remember, too, that e-mails are the equivalent of letters or memos. When we write a letter or a memo, we usually read it more than once and think carefully about what we're saying. Too many times, we treat e-mails as if they were oral communications—that is, we write in a chatty and imprecise manner. Before sending any e-mail to a client, print it, read it, and edit it. Remember that the matter you're discussing is important to the client, and your communication should be professional and clear.

file or document sitting on your desk, if observed by a third party, may reveal the identity of a client or enough information to suggest the client's identity. A computer screen, if visible to those passing by your desk, could convey information to someone who is not authorized to know that information. You might be speaking to an expert witness about rescheduling a meeting and accidentally let something about the case slip out. Alternatively, you might be friendly with a paralegal at the opposing attorney's office because the two attorneys have worked on many cases together. You are on the phone trying to work out a date for an important meeting. This paralegal suggests a date, and you tell her that the attorney that you work for is scheduled to be in court on a specific client's case that day. If you name the client, or indicate that the attorney will be arguing a particular type of motion in the case, you may breach the duty of confidentiality.

Confidentiality and the Attorney-Client Privilege

All information relating to a client's representation is considered confidential information. Some confidential information also qualifies as privileged information, or information subject to the **attorney-client privilege**.

The attorney-client privilege can be vitally important during the litigation process. As you will read in Chapter 10, prior to a trial each attorney is permitted to obtain information relating to the case from the opposing attorney and other persons, such as witnesses. This means that attorneys must exchange certain information relating to their clients. An attorney need not provide privileged information, however—unless the client consents to the disclosure or a court orders it. Similarly, if an attorney is called to the witness stand during a trial, the attorney may not disclose privileged information unless the court orders him or her to do so.

What Kind of Information Is Privileged?

State statutes and court cases define what constitutes privileged information. Generally, any communications concerning a client's legal rights or problems fall under the attorney-client privilege. Suppose that an attorney's client is a criminal defendant, for example. The client tells the attorney that she was actually in the vicinity of the crime site at the time of the crime, but to her knowledge, no one noticed her presence there. This is privileged information that the attorney may disclose only with the client's consent or on a court's order to do so.

Other types of information, although confidential, are not necessarily privileged. For example, information relating to a client's identity is usually not

attorney-client privilege
A rule of evidence requiring that confidential communications between a client and his or her attorney (relating to their professional relationship) be kept confidential, unless the client consents to disclosure.

privileged. Nor, as a rule, is information concerning client fees. Furthermore, information concerning the client's personal or business affairs is not privileged unless it is related to the legal claim. For example, suppose that a client who is bringing a malpractice suit against a physician mentions to the attorney that he is divorcing his wife. Unless the client's divorce is related in some way to the malpractice suit being handled by the attorney, the information about the divorce normally is not considered privileged.

Certain materials relating to an attorney's preparation of a client's case for trial are protected as privileged information under what is known as the **work product** doctrine. Usually, information concerning an attorney's legal strategy for conducting a case is classified as work product and, as such, may be subject to the attorney-client privilege. Legal strategy includes the legal theories that the attorney plans to use in support of the client's claim, how the attorney interprets the evidence relating to the claim, and the like. Certain evidence gathered by the attorney to support the client's claim, however, such as financial statements relating to the client's business firm, would probably not be classified as work product.

Because it is often difficult to tell what types of information (including work product) qualify as privileged, paralegals should consult with their supervising attorneys whenever issues arise that may require that such a distinction be made. It is important to note that like any other confidential information relating to a client's case, privileged information is subject to the exceptions to the confidentiality rule discussed above.

When the Attorney-Client Privilege Arises

The attorney-client privilege comes into existence the moment a client communicates with an attorney concerning a legal matter. People sometimes mistakenly assume that there is no duty to keep client information confidential unless an attorney agrees to represent a client and the client signs an agreement. This is not so. The privilege—and thus the duty of confidentiality—arises even if the lawyer decides not to represent the client and even when the client is not charged any fee.

Duration of the Privilege

The client is the holder, or "owner," of the privilege, and only the client can waive (set aside) the privilege. Unless waived by the client, the privilege lasts indefinitely. In other words, the privilege continues even though the attorney has completed the client's legal matter and is no longer working on the case.

Privileged information is confidential information. If such information is disclosed to others, it is no longer confidential and can no longer be considered privileged information. This is another reason why it is so important to guard against accidental violations of the confidentiality rule: if the rule is violated, information that otherwise might have been protected by the attorney-client privilege can be used in court, which may be harmful to the client's interests. Consider the e-mail example given earlier, in which the paralegal inadvertently sent a confidential document to opposing counsel instead of the client. The document, because it contained the attorney's analysis of confidential client information, might be classified as privileged information under the work product doctrine. The disclosure of the information to the opposing counsel destroyed its confidential character—and therefore any possibility that it might be protected as privileged information.

Conflict of Interest

A **conflict of interest** arises when representing one client injures the interests of another client. Model Rules 1.7, 1.8, 1.9, 1.10, and 1.11 pertain to conflict-of-interest situations. The general rule is that an attorney should not represent a client if doing so would be directly adverse to another client or if there is a significant risk that

work product
An attorney's mental impressions, conclusions, and legal theories regarding a case being prepared on behalf of a client. Work product normally is regarded as privileged information.

conflict of interest
A situation in which two or more duties or interests come into conflict, as when an attorney attempts to represent opposing parties in a legal dispute.

Technology and Today's Paralegal

ELECTRONIC COMMUNICATIONS AND CONFIDENTIALITY

Almost everyone has had the experience of sending an e-mail to the wrong recipient or accidentally sending a personal message intended for one person to a group. Similarly, some law firm employees have sent inappropriate e-mails concerning personal behavior to lists including partners and clients. (For an incident at a major law firm, see "Skadden on Thin Ice" at **www.snopes.com**. In the "Search" box, enter "Skadden.")

Such mistakes can be serious when they occur in a work environment. Confidential information could be disclosed to an opposing party. Such an incident can damage a person's employment prospects, the interests of the client, and the reputation of the firm. It is not just work-related electronic communications that pose problems. Personal Web pages or social networking site pages with inappropriate content may be discovered by employers or clients. See Tracy Mitrano, *Thoughts on Facebook,* **www.cit.cornell.edu** (in the "Search" box, enter "thoughts on facebook"), for a discussion of how social networking postings can affect employment.

There are three major issues for paralegals to consider when using electronic communications (e-mail, text messages, twitters, and the like) at work and at home:

1. Is a work-related communication confidential, or could an opposing party discover it during litigation?
2. Is a communication an appropriate use of the employer's property?
3. What sort of personal information is appropriate to share with the world through Facebook, MySpace, Twitter, and other services?

CONFIDENTIALITY

Just labeling an e-mail or text message "confidential" does not mean that it will be treated as confidential. And adding nonprivileged material to a privileged communication won't protect the nonprivileged portion. Your firm should have a policy about when it is appropriate to send confidential information electronically and when it is not. Always seek guidance from your supervising attorney if you have any doubt about the appropriateness of electronically transmitting confidential information.

---

the attorney's ability to consider, recommend, or carry out an appropriate course of action for the client would be materially (significantly) limited as a result of the attorney's other responsibilities or interests. A classic example of a conflict of interest exists when an attorney simultaneously represents two adverse parties in a legal proceeding. Clearly, in such a situation, the attorney's loyalties must be divided.

Simultaneous Representation

If an attorney reasonably believes that representing two parties in a legal proceeding will not adversely affect either party's interest, then the attorney is permitted to do so—but only if both parties give informed consent. Normally, attorneys avoid this kind of situation because what might start out as a simple, uncontested proceeding could evolve into a legal battle. Divorce proceedings, for example, may begin amicably but end up in heated disputes over child-custody arrangements or property division. If the husband and wife employ only one attorney, the attorney then faces a conflict of interest: assisting one party will necessarily be adverse to the interests of the other. Because of the potential for a conflict of interest in divorce

PERSONAL USE OF BUSINESS SYSTEMS

Many employers, including law firms, provide employees with communication devices and services, such as BlackBerries, PDAs, and laptops. Firms often allow some personal use of these devices but retain the right to monitor and audit the content of the e-mails, messages, and Web traffic on them. Be sure to check your employer's policies on appropriate use of such devices before making personal use of firm-provided hardware or services.

Employers are also under a duty to ensure that workplace systems are not used inappropriately. For example, in one case, a New Jersey court held that an employer breached its duty to exercise reasonable care to prevent employees from viewing child pornography on workplace computers.[a] Other courts have used internal e-mails as evidence in racial and gender discrimination cases. An employer has good reason to be concerned about how company communications devices and systems are used.

There are limits on employers' abilities to monitor personal communications, however. In another case, the federal Ninth Circuit Court of Appeals held that a pager text messaging service could not provide to the employer the content of employees' text messages without advance notice and unless employees were given a chance to redact personal messages.[b] The court reached this conclusion despite a clear, written policy stating that the pagers were not to be used for personal or confidential communications because the employer had informally allowed personal use in the past. The bottom line is that you need to think carefully about how you are using employer-provided communications devices and systems. Make sure your use is within your employer's policies.

TECHNOLOGY TIP ABOUT ONLINE PERSONAL INFORMATION

Remember, when you post the details of your latest date or pictures of your vacation online, your employer or clients may stumble across those postings simply by Googling your name. Even if you change a Facebook page later, caching by search engines means that an embarrassing picture or post could linger in cyberspace for years. It is not just information about you that can cause trouble: a group of employees at a law firm got into hot water when their "Skadden Insider" blog started a "Hottest Female Associate" contest. The bottom line: don't post pictures or text online that you would feel uncomfortable showing to your boss.

---

a. *Doe v. XYC Corp.*, 382 N.J.Super. 122 (App. Div. 2005).

b. *Quon v. Arch Wireless Operating Co.*, 529 F.3d 892 (2008).

---

proceedings, some courts do not permit attorneys to represent both spouses, even if the spouses consent to such an arrangement.

Similar conflicts arise when the "family attorney" is asked to handle a family matter and the family members eventually disagree on what the outcome should be. Consider a situation in which two adult children request the family lawyer to handle the procedures required to settle their deceased parent's estate. The will favors one child, and the other child decides to challenge the will's validity. The attorney cannot represent both sides without facing a conflict of interest.

Attorneys representing corporate clients may face conflicts of interest when corporate personnel become divided on an issue. For example, assume that Carl Finn, an attorney, represents ABC Corporation. Finn typically deals with the corporation's president, Julie Johnson, when giving legal assistance and advice. At times, however, Finn deals with other corporate personnel, including Seth Harrison, the corporation's accountant. Harrison and Johnson disagree on several major issues, and eventually Johnson arranges to have Harrison fired. Harrison wants attorney Finn to represent him in a lawsuit against the corporation for wrongful termination of his employment. Finn now faces a conflict of interest.

Former Clients

A conflict of interest may involve former clients. Model Rule 1.9 states that a "lawyer who has formerly represented a client in a matter shall not thereafter represent another person in the same or substantially related matter in which that person's interests are materially adverse to the interests of the former client unless the former client gives informed consent, confirmed in writing." The rule regarding former clients is closely related to the rule on preserving the confidentiality of a client. The rationale behind the rule is that an attorney, in representing a client, is entrusted with certain information that may be unknown to others. That information should not be used against the client—even after the *representation* has ended.

Assume that a year ago an attorney defended a company against a lawsuit for employment discrimination brought by one of the company's employees. At that time, the attorney learned a great deal about the company. Now, someone who was injured while using one of the company's products consults with the attorney about the possibility of bringing a product liability lawsuit against the company. The attorney normally must refuse to represent this person. Because the attorney has confidential information about the company that could harm the company's interest, a conflict of interest exists.

Job Changes and Former Clients.

The rule concerning former clients does not prohibit an individual attorney or paralegal from working at a firm or agency that represents interests contrary to those of a former client. If that were the situation, many of those who have worked for large firms would find it hard to change jobs. The rules vary depending on the specific circumstances. In some situations, when a conflict of interest results from a job change, the new employer can avoid violating the rules governing conflict of interest through the use of screening procedures. That is, the new employer can erect an **ethical wall** around the new employee so that the new employee remains ignorant about the case that would give rise to the conflict of interest.

Walling-Off Procedures.

Law offices usually have procedures for "walling off" an attorney or other legal professional from a case when a conflict of interest exists. The firm may announce in a memo to all employees that a certain attorney or paralegal should not have access to specific files, for example, and may set out procedures to be followed to ensure that access to those files is restricted. Computer documents relating to the case may be protected by passwords or in some other way. Commonly, any hard-copy files relating to the case are flagged with a sticker to indicate that access to the files is restricted.

Firms normally take great care to establish and observe such procedures because if confidential information is used in a way harmful to a former client, the client may sue the firm for damages. In defending against such a suit, the firm must show that it took reasonable precautions to protect that client's interests. How steps are taken to accomplish this are discussed in the *Developing Paralegal Skills* feature on the facing page.

Other Conflict-of-Interest Situations

Several other situations may give rise to conflicts of interest. Gifts from clients may create conflicts of interest, because they tend to bias the judgment of the attorney or paralegal. Some types of gifts are specifically prohibited. For example, the Model Rules prohibit an attorney from preparing documents (such as wills) for a client if the client gives the attorney or a member of the attorney's family a gift in the will. (An exception to this rule exists when the attorney is a relative of the client.) Note that as a paralegal, you may be offered gifts from appreciative clients at Christmas or other times. Generally, such gifts pose no ethical problems. If a client offers you a gift that has substantial value, however, you should discuss the issue with your supervising attorney.

---

ethical wall

A term that refers to the procedures used to create a screen around a legal employee to shield him or her from information about a case in which there is a conflict of interest.

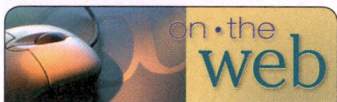

To read an article by NFPA's ethics coordinator entitled "The Ethical Wall: Its Application to Paralegals," go to **www.paralegals.org**. Select "Positions & Issues" from the menu, and then select "Ethics" to find a link to the article.

Developing
Paralegal Skills

BUILDING AN ETHICAL WALL

Lana Smith, a paralegal, has been asked by her supervising attorney to set up an ethical wall because a new attorney, Sandra Piper, has been hired from the law firm of Nunn & Bush. While employed by Nunn & Bush, Piper represented the defendant, Seski Manufacturing, in the ongoing case of *Tymes v. Seski Manufacturing Co.* Smith's firm—and Piper's new employer—represents the plaintiff, Joseph Tymes, in that case. Consequently, Piper's work for Nunn & Bush creates a conflict of interest, which Piper has acknowledged in a document signed under oath. Smith makes a list of the walling-off procedures to use to ensure that the firm does not violate the rules on conflict of interest.

CHECKLIST FOR BUILDING AN ETHICAL WALL

- Prepare a memo to the office manager regarding the conflict and the need for special arrangements to ensure that Piper will have no involvement in the *Tymes* case.

- Prepare a memo to the team representing Tymes to inform them of the conflict of interest and the special procedures to be used.

- Prepare a memo to the firm giving the case name, the nature of the conflict, the parties involved, and instructions to maintain a blanket of silence with respect to Sandra Piper.

- Arrange for Piper's office to be on a different floor from the team (if possible) to demonstrate, if necessary, that the firm took steps to separate Piper and the team and to prevent them from having access to one another's files.

- Arrange with the office manager for computer passwords to be issued to the team members so that access to computer files on the *Tymes* case is restricted to team members only.

- Place "ACCESS RESTRICTED" stickers on the files for the *Tymes* case.

- Develop a security procedure for signing out and tracking the case files in the *Tymes* case—to prevent inadvertent disclosure of the files to Piper or her staff members.

Attorneys also need to be careful about taking on a client whose case may create an "issue conflict" for the attorney. Generally, an attorney cannot represent a client on a substantive legal issue if the client's position is directly contrary to that of another client being represented by the lawyer—or the lawyer's firm. This is especially true for a case being brought within the same jurisdiction (the geographic area or subject matter over which a court has authority to decide legal disputes). The reason for this rule is that courts are obligated to follow precedents—earlier decisions on cases involving similar facts and issues (see Chapter 5). The court's ruling in one of the attorney's cases could therefore alter the outcome of the other case.

Occasionally, conflicts of interest may arise when two family members who are both attorneys or paralegals are involved in the representation of adverse parties in a legal proceeding. Because there is a risk that the family relationship will interfere with professional judgment, generally an attorney should not represent a client if the opposing party to the dispute is being represented by a member of the attorney's family (such as a spouse, parent, child, or sibling). If you, as a paralegal, are married to or living with another paralegal or an attorney, you should inform your firm of this fact if you ever suspect that a conflict of interest might result from your relationship. Similarly, if you discover that you may have a financial interest in the outcome of a lawsuit that your firm is handling, you should notify the attorney of the potential conflict.

Conflicts Checks

Whenever a potential client consults with an attorney, the attorney will want to make sure that no potential conflict of interest exists before deciding whether to represent the client. Running a **conflicts check** is a standard procedure in the law office and one that is frequently undertaken by paralegals. Before you can run a conflicts check, you need to know the name of the prospective client, the other party or parties that may be involved in the client's legal matter, and the legal issue involved. Normally, every law firm has some established procedure for conflicts checks, and in larger firms there is usually a computerized database containing the names of former clients and the other information you will need in checking for conflicts of interest.

conflicts check
A procedure for determining whether an agreement to represent a potential client will result in a conflict of interest.

THE INDIRECT REGULATION OF PARALEGALS

Paralegals are regulated *indirectly* in several ways. Clearly, the ethical codes for attorneys just discussed indirectly regulate the conduct of paralegals. Additionally, paralegal conduct is regulated indirectly by standards and guidelines created by paralegal professional groups, as well as guidelines for the utilization of paralegals developed by the American Bar Association and various states.

Paralegal Ethical Codes

Paralegals are becoming increasingly self-regulated. Recall from Chapter 1 that the two major national paralegal associations in the United States—the National Federation of Paralegal Associations, or NFPA, and the National Association of Legal Assistants, or NALA—were formed to define and represent paralegal professional interests on a national level. Shortly after they were formed, both of these associations adopted codes of ethics defining the ethical responsibilities of paralegals.

NFPA's Code of Ethics

In 1977, NFPA adopted its first code of ethics, called the Affirmation of Responsibility. The code has since been revised several times and, in 1993, was renamed the Model Code of Ethics and Professional Responsibility. In 1997, NFPA revised the code, particularly its format, and took the bold step of appending to its code a list of enforcement guidelines setting forth recommendations on how to discipline paralegals who violate ethical standards promulgated by the code. The full title of NFPA's current code is the Model Code of Ethics and Professional Responsibility and Guidelines for Enforcement.

Exhibit 4.2 presents the rules from Section 1 of the code, entitled NFPA Model Disciplinary Rules and Ethical Considerations. For reasons of space, only the rules are included in the exhibit, not the ethical considerations that follow each rule. The ethical considerations are very important to paralegals, however, because they explain what conduct the rule prohibits. The full text of NFPA's code (including the rules, ethical considerations, and guidelines for enforcement) is presented in Appendix C of this book.

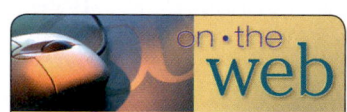

You can find NFPA's Model Code of Ethics and Professional Responsibility and Guidelines for Enforcement on the Web at **www.paralegals.org**. Select "Positions & Issues" from the menu. Then select "Model Code of Ethics."

NALA's Code of Ethics

In 1975, NALA issued its Code of Ethics and Professional Responsibility, which, like NFPA's code, has since undergone several revisions. Exhibit 4.3 on pages 110 and 111 presents NALA's code in its entirety. Note that NALA's code, like the Model Code of Professional Responsibility discussed earlier in this chapter, presents ethical precepts as a series of "canons." (Prior to the 1997 revision of its code, NFPA also listed its ethical standards as "canons.")

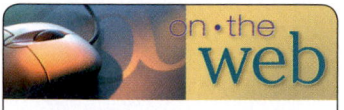

You can find NALA's Code of Ethics and Professional Responsibility online by going to **www.nala.org**. From the "About Paralegals" menu, select "NALA Code of Ethics and Professional Responsibility."

§1. NFPA MODEL DISCIPLINARY RULES AND ETHICAL CONSIDERATIONS

1.1 A PARALEGAL SHALL ACHIEVE AND MAINTAIN A HIGH LEVEL OF COMPETENCE.

1.2 A PARALEGAL SHALL MAINTAIN A HIGH LEVEL OF PERSONAL AND PROFESSIONAL INTEGRITY.

1.3 A PARALEGAL SHALL MAINTAIN A HIGH STANDARD OF PROFESSIONAL CONDUCT.

1.4 A PARALEGAL SHALL SERVE THE PUBLIC INTEREST BY CONTRIBUTING TO THE IMPROVEMENT OF THE LEGAL SYSTEM AND THE DELIVERY OF QUALITY LEGAL SERVICES, INCLUDING *PRO BONO PUBLICO* SERVICES.

1.5 A PARALEGAL SHALL PRESERVE ALL CONFIDENTIAL INFORMATION PROVIDED BY THE CLIENT OR ACQUIRED FROM OTHER SOURCES BEFORE, DURING, AND AFTER THE COURSE OF THE PROFESSIONAL RELATIONSHIP.

1.6 A PARALEGAL SHALL AVOID CONFLICTS OF INTEREST AND SHALL DISCLOSE ANY POSSIBLE CONFLICT TO THE EMPLOYER OR CLIENT, AS WELL AS TO THE PROSPECTIVE EMPLOYERS OR CLIENTS.

1.7 A PARALEGAL'S TITLE SHALL BE FULLY DISCLOSED.

1.8 A PARALEGAL SHALL NOT ENGAGE IN THE UNAUTHORIZED PRACTICE OF LAW.

Courtesy of the National Federation of Paralegal Associations, Inc.

EXHIBIT 4.2

Rules from Section 1 of NFPA's Model Code of Ethics and Professional Responsibility and Guidelines for Enforcement

Only the disciplinary rules are shown in this exhibit. The ethical considerations, which are important to a paralegal's understanding of these rules, can be read in Appendix C of this book.

Compliance with Paralegal Codes of Ethics

Paralegal codes of ethics state the ethical responsibilities of paralegals generally, but they particularly apply to members of paralegal organizations that have adopted the codes. Any paralegal who is a member of an organization that has adopted one of these codes is expected to comply with the code's requirements. Note that compliance with these codes is not legally mandatory. In other words, if a paralegal does not abide by a particular ethical standard of a paralegal association's code of ethics, the association cannot initiate state-sanctioned disciplinary proceedings against the paralegal. The association can, however, expel the paralegal from the association, which may have significant implications for the paralegal's future career opportunities. See this chapter's *Featured Contributor* article on pages 112 and 113 for a further discussion of how setting high ethical standards can enhance a paralegal's career opportunities.

Guidelines for the Utilization of Paralegals

As mentioned earlier, the reason attorneys are regulated by the state is to protect the public from the harms that could result from incompetent legal advice and representation. While licensing requirements may help to protect the public, they also give lawyers something of a monopoly over the delivery of legal services—a monopoly that, in turn, may hurt those who cannot afford to pay attorneys for their services. The increased use of paralegals stems, in part, from the legal profession's need to reduce the cost of legal services. The use of paralegals to do substantive legal work benefits clients because the hourly rate for paralegals is lower than that for attorneys.

For this reason, bar associations (and courts, when approving fees) encourage attorneys to delegate work to paralegals to lower the costs of legal services for clients—and thus provide the public with greater access to legal services. In fact, some courts, when determining awards of attorneys' fees, have refused to approve fees at the attorney's hourly rate for work that could have been performed by a paralegal at a lower rate.

NALA, the ABA, and many of the states have adopted guidelines for the utilization of paralegal services. These guidelines were created in response to questions concerning the role and function of paralegals within the legal arena that had arisen in earlier years, including the following: What are paralegals? What kinds of tasks do they perform? What are their professional responsibilities? How can attorneys best utilize paralegal services? What responsibilities should attorneys assume with respect to their assistants' work?

EXHIBIT 4.3
NALA's Code of Ethics and Professional Responsibility

Preamble: A paralegal must adhere strictly to the accepted standards of legal ethics and to the general principles of proper conduct. The performance of the duties of the paralegal shall be governed by specific canons as defined herein so justice will be served and goals of the profession attained.

The canons of ethics set forth hereafter are adopted by the National Association of Legal Assistants, Inc., as a general guide intended to aid paralegals and attorneys. The enumeration of these rules does not mean there are not others of equal importance although not specifically mentioned. Court rules, agency rules and statutes must be taken into consideration when interpreting the canons.

Definition: Legal assistants, also known as paralegals, are a distinguishable group of persons who assist attorneys in the delivery of legal services. Through formal education, training and experience, legal assistants have knowledge and expertise regarding the legal system and substantive and procedural law which qualify them to do work of a legal nature under the supervision of an attorney.

CANON 1.

A paralegal must not perform any of the duties that attorneys only may perform nor take any actions that attorneys may not take.

CANON 2.

A paralegal may perform any task which is properly delegated and supervised by an attorney, as long as the attorney is ultimately responsible to the client, maintains a direct relationship with the client, and assumes professional responsibility for the work product.

CANON 3.

A paralegal must not:

    (a) engage in, encourage, or contribute to any act which could constitute the unauthorized practice of law; and

    (b) establish attorney-client relationships, set fees, give legal opinions or advice or represent a client before a court or agency unless so authorized by that court or agency; and

    (c) engage in conduct or take any action which would assist or involve the attorney in a violation of professional ethics or give the appearance of professional impropriety.

Copyright 2007; Adopted 1975, revised 1979, 1988, 1995, 2007. Reprinted with permission of the National Association of Legal Assistants, **www.nala.org**, 1516 S. Boston, #200, Tulsa, OK 74119.

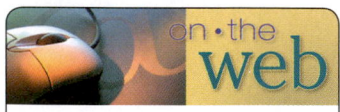

NALA's Model Standards and Guidelines are online at **www.nala.org**. From the "About Paralegals" menu, select "Model Standards and Guidelines for the Utilization of Paralegals."

NALA's Model Standards and Guidelines

NALA's Model Standards and Guidelines for the Utilization of Paralegals provides guidance on several important issues. It begins by listing the minimum qualifications that legal assistants should have and then, in a series of guidelines, indicates what paralegals may and may not do. We will examine these guidelines in more detail shortly. (See Appendix B for the complete text of the annotated version of NALA's Model Standards and Guidelines, as revised in 2007.)

The ABA's Model Guidelines

The ABA adopted its Model Guidelines for the Utilization of Legal Assistant Services in 1991. In 2003, the ABA Standing Committee on Paralegals revised these guidelines by basing them on the ABA's Model Rules of Professional Conduct. The document consists of ten guidelines, each followed by a lengthy comment on the origin, scope, and application of the guideline. The guidelines indicate, among other things, the types of tasks that a lawyer may not delegate to a paralegal and, generally, the responsibilities of attorneys with respect to paralegal performance and compensation. For further detail on what is included in the revised guidelines, now entitled "Model Guidelines for the Utilization of Paralegal Services," go to **www.abanet.org/legalservices/paralegals** and select the guideline title.

EXHIBIT 4.3
NALA's Code of Ethics and Professional Responsibility—Continued

---

CANON 4.

A paralegal must use discretion and professional judgment commensurate with knowledge and experience but must not render independent legal judgment in place of an attorney. The services of an attorney are essential in the public interest whenever such legal judgment is required.

CANON 5.

A paralegal must disclose his or her status as a legal assistant at the outset of any professional relationship with a client, attorney, a court or administrative agency or personnel thereof, or a member of the general public. A paralegal must act prudently in determining the extent to which a client may be assisted without the presence of an attorney.

CANON 6.

A paralegal must strive to maintain integrity and a high degree of competency through education and training with respect to professional responsibility, local rules and practice, and through continuing education in substantive areas of law to better assist the legal profession in fulfilling its duty to provide legal service.

CANON 7.

A paralegal must protect the confidences of a client and must not violate any rule or statute now in effect or hereafter enacted controlling the doctrine of privileged communications between a client and an attorney.

CANON 8.

A paralegal must disclose to his or her employer or prospective employer any pre-existing clients or personal relationships that may conflict with the interests of the employer or prospective employer and/or their clients.

CANON 9.

A paralegal must do all other things incidental, necessary, or expedient for the attainment of the ethics and responsibilities as defined by statute or rule of court.

CANON 10.

A paralegal's conduct is guided by bar associations' codes of professional responsibility and rules of professional conduct.

Copyright 2007; Adopted 1975, revised 1979, 1988, 1995, 2007. Reprinted with permission of the National Association of Legal Assistants, **www.nala.org**, 1516 S. Boston, #200, Tulsa, OK 74119.

State Guidelines

Most states have adopted some form of guidelines concerning the use of legal assistants by attorneys, the respective responsibilities of attorneys and legal assistants in performing legal work, the types of tasks paralegals may perform, and other ethically challenging areas of legal practice. Although the guidelines of some states reflect the influence of NALA's standards and guidelines, the state guidelines focus largely on state statutory definitions of the practice of law, state codes of ethics regulating the responsibilities of attorneys, and state court decisions. As a paralegal, you should make sure that you become familiar with your state's guidelines.

The Increasing Scope of Paralegal Responsibilities

The ethical standards and guidelines just discussed, as well as court decisions concerning paralegals, all support the goal of increasing the use of paralegals in the delivery of legal services. Today, paralegals can perform almost any legal task as long as the work is supervised by an attorney and does not constitute the unauthorized practice of law (to be discussed shortly).

Paralegals working for attorneys may interview clients and witnesses, investigate legal claims, draft legal documents for attorneys' signatures, attend will executions (in some states), appear at real estate closings (in some states), and undertake

featured contributor

TEN TIPS FOR ETHICS AND THE PARALEGAL

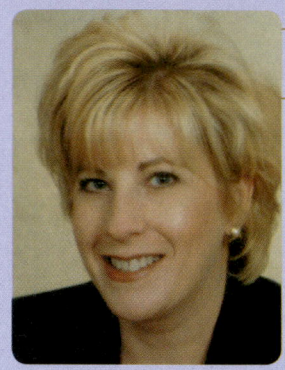

Lisa L. Newcity

BIOGRAPHICAL NOTE

Lisa L. Newcity, J.D., is a professor in the Legal Studies Department at Roger Williams University in Bristol, Rhode Island, where she serves as the program coordinator for the Legal Studies Program. She also serves as a prelaw adviser and as the faculty adviser and coach to the Roger Williams University Mock Trial Club. She is a former chair of the NFPA Ethics Board and teaches a number of courses with an ethics component.

Newcity was formerly a practicing attorney in Massachusetts concentrating in civil litigation in state and federal courts. Her areas of interest, research, and publication include the licensing and regulation of paralegals, professional ethics, and the interdisciplinary study of law at the undergraduate level.

A paralegal with a clear understanding of the rules of ethics is an invaluable asset to any law practice. Ethical behavior in the workplace increases client satisfaction, reduces the risk of liability for the employer, and, perhaps even more important, fosters a sense of respect and pride for the profession. The following tips offer some suggestions on how you can incorporate the rules of ethics and professional responsibility into your daily life as a practicing paralegal.

1. **Set a High Standard for Competence.** The best paralegals know that in order to remain current and productive, they must keep abreast of changes in the law, in law office technology, and in legal ethics. Attend CLE (continuing legal education) seminars in your area of practice, as well as in ethics. Read your local, state, and national legal newspapers and journals for updates and changes in these areas. Take advantage of the educational opportunities offered by paralegal associations and bar associations. Understand that your paralegal education and experience provide a foundation on which you are expected to build throughout your career. The codes of professional responsibility for attorneys and paralegals require us to maintain a certain level of competence. Do this at a minimum, but always strive for the highest possible standard with respect to competence and skills.

2. **Demonstrate Respect for Others and for the Profession.** In recent years, there has been much discussion regarding the "lack of civility" within the legal profession. Do your part to promote an atmosphere of mutual respect and civility in your workplace by behaving professionally at all times. All legal professionals, attorneys and paralegals alike, should understand that clients and members of the public hold us to a higher standard of ethical conduct. We are expected to comport ourselves with dignity and to show respect for the law and for each other. Indeed, the codes of professional responsibility require us to avoid even the "appearance of impropriety." To that end, you must from time to time put your sense of professionalism and dignity before your own emotions when faced with uncivil conduct on the part of others. Do this for the good of your clients and for the good of the profession.

3. **Become Active in Local and National Professional Associations.** Collaborate with, and learn from, your colleagues as a member of a paralegal professional association, such as NFPA or NALA. Both organizations have made great strides in raising awareness about the paralegal profession, and both provide excellent sources of information for their members and for the public. In addition, these organizations (as well as state and local paralegal associations) have promulgated ethical guidelines for paralegals and publish ethics opinions and cases on ethics to guide their members.

4. **Understand and Observe the Rules of Confidentiality.** The ethical rules on confidentiality create the underpinnings of the attorney-client relationship. Our ability to provide the best possible legal services for our clients hinges on the

trust and confidence that our clients place in us. Do nothing that could jeopardize this. Recognize common "danger zones" for paralegals in preserving confidentiality. Among other things, these danger zones include discussing clients and cases with family and friends, interviewing clients in your office when other clients' files and documents are in plain view, and discussing a client's case with a witness during an investigation.

5. **Demonstrate Loyalty to the Client by Recognizing Potential Conflicts of Interest.** You know from studying the ethical rules concerning conflicts of interest that any conflict is a potential danger to the client and to your employer. Be diligent in following your firm's practices for conflict checking. Also, if you believe that a conflict may arise in a case that you are handling, speak to your supervising attorney immediately. It is always better to address conflict issues at the earliest possible opportunity. Waiting until later may result in unnecessary cost and embarrassment for you and for your employer.

6. **Demonstrate Loyalty to Your Employer through Your Professionalism.** As a legal professional and an employee, you are a representative of your firm or agency. Paralegals interact with clients, witnesses, and court personnel on a regular basis. Refrain from gossip or negative remarks about your firm or employer. Attorneys and paralegals work together as integral members of a team on behalf of their clients. If difficulties or conflicts arise with your supervisor, speak to that person directly in an effort to resolve them. Your professionalism will be respected and appreciated.

7. **Practice Diligence in Completing Your Work Promptly and Efficiently.** Prioritize your work to avoid neglecting important projects. Be scrupulous in maintaining your calendar and tickler system. Understand your own limits, and speak to your supervisor if the volume of work becomes so overwhelming that you run the risk of neglecting projects or missing deadlines. It is better to ask for assistance from your paralegal co-workers or from your supervisor than to ignore the problem until it is too late.

8. **Recognize Your Role as the Client's Contact, and Promote Responsiveness to the Client's Questions and Concerns.** Paralegals are often the persons within the firm to whom clients will look when questions arise. Unfortunately, one of the most common complaints about attorneys and their professional staff members is that they are unresponsive. Make it a point to return your clients' telephone calls in a prompt and courteous manner. When a client has a question calling for legal advice, bring it to the attorney's attention quickly, and encourage the attorney to respond to the client promptly. If the attorney is busy, offer to pass along the message (being careful to avoid giving legal advice yourself).

9. **Recognize "Pitfalls for Paralegals" in the Unauthorized Practice of Law (UPL).** As you gain the confidence and trust of your firm's clients, you will, on occasion, be faced with questions calling for legal advice. Learn to develop strategies for handling these situations with tact and empathy. Remember that if a client has a pressing problem that calls for immediate attention, it is not sufficient to tell him or her that as a paralegal you are not permitted to give legal advice. Inform the client that you will find an attorney who can assist the client and that either you or the attorney will get right back to the client. Then be sure to do just that. Of course, paralegals may face other situations with serious UPL implications as well. When in doubt, consult the rules for guidance and speak with your supervising attorney.

10. **Know When to Ask for Help and Where to Get It.** Every paralegal should have a copy of the ethical rules for attorneys and paralegals. Every paralegal should also regularly review ethics opinions, disciplinary proceedings, and cases interpreting the rules of professional conduct. Also, when questions or concerns about ethics arise, you should know where to turn for help. Many firms designate a particular individual within the firm as the "contact person" for ethical inquiries. Further, many state and local attorney licensing and regulatory agencies, bar associations, and paralegal associations provide services to legal professionals who have ethical questions. Inquire about your firm's policies regarding ethical questions, and take advantage of all available resources.

> *"Ethical behavior in the workplace increases client satisfaction, reduces the risk of liability for the employer, and, perhaps even more important, fosters a sense of respect and pride for the profession."*

numerous other types of legal work, as long as the work is supervised by attorneys. When state or federal law allows it, paralegals can also represent clients before government agencies. Paralegals may perform freelance services for attorneys and, depending on state law and the type of service, perform limited independent services for the public.

Legal assistants may also give information to clients on many matters relating to a case or other legal concern. When arranging for client interviews, they let clients know what kind of information is needed and what documents to bring to the office. They inform clients about legal procedures and what clients should expect to experience during the progress of a legal proceeding. Clearly, as a legal assistant, you will be permitted to give clients all kinds of information. Nonetheless, you must make sure that you know where to draw the line between giving permissible types of advice and giving "legal advice"—advice that only attorneys are licensed to give under state laws.

The types of tasks that paralegals are legally permitted to undertake are described throughout this book; it would be impossible to list them all here. As stated in the ABA's guidelines, paralegals may not perform tasks that only attorneys can legally perform. If they do so, they risk liability for the unauthorized practice of law—an important topic to which we now turn.

THE UNAUTHORIZED PRACTICE OF LAW

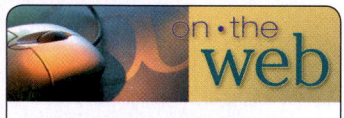

State statutes prohibit the unauthorized practice of law (UPL). Although the statutes vary, they all aim to prevent nonlawyers from providing legal counsel. These statutes do not apply only to paralegals. Rather, they apply to all persons—including real estate agents, bankers, insurance agents, and accountants—who might provide services that are typically provided by licensed attorneys. For example, an insurance agent who offers advice to a client on a personal-injury claim might be liable for UPL.

UPL statutes are not always clear about what constitutes the practice of law. Consequently, courts decide whether a person has engaged in UPL on a case-by-case basis. This may make it difficult to know exactly what activities constitute UPL. To avoid violating UPL laws, a person must be aware of the state courts' decisions on UPL. As we will see below, some states are addressing this problem.

Paralegals, of course, can also refer to the general guidelines for their profession provided by NALA. Guideline 2 in NALA's Model Standards and Guidelines prohibits a legal assistant from engaging in any of the following activities:

- Establishing attorney-client relationships.
- Setting legal fees.
- Giving legal opinions or advice.
- Representing a client before a court, unless authorized to do so by the court.
- Engaging in, encouraging, or contributing to any act that could constitute the unauthorized practice of law.

State UPL Statutes

Because of the difficulty in predicting with certainty whether a court would consider a particular action to be UPL, some states have made efforts to clarify what is meant by the "practice of law." About half of the states have a formal definition of what constitutes the practice of law, either by statute or by court ruling. For example, the Texas UPL statute provides, in part:

> the practice of law means the preparation of a pleading or other document incident to an action or special proceeding or the management of the action or proceeding on behalf

of a client before a judge in court as well as a service rendered out of court, including the giving of advice or the rendering of any service requiring the use of legal skill or knowledge, such as preparing a will, contract, or other instrument, the legal effect of which under the facts and conclusions involved must be carefully determined.[2]

The Texas statute also states that this definition is not exclusive and that the state courts have the authority to determine that other activities, which are not listed, also constitute UPL. Other states' definitions focus on various factors, such as appearing in court or drafting legal papers, pleadings, or other documents in connection with a pending or prospective court proceeding. The enforcement of UPL statutes also varies widely among the states. In some states, the attorney general prosecutes violators; in others, the local or state prosecutor enforces UPL statutes; and in some states, the state bar association is in charge of enforcement.

In the following pages, we discuss some of the activities that are considered to constitute UPL in most states. But it must be emphasized that a paralegal should know the details of the UPL statute in the state in which she or he works. Avoiding UPL problems is also discussed in the *Developing Paralegal Skills* feature on page 116.

The Prohibition against Fee Splitting

An important ethical rule related to the unauthorized practice of law is Rule 5.4 of the Model Rules of Professional Conduct. That rule states, "A lawyer or law firm shall not share legal fees with a nonlawyer." For this reason, paralegals cannot become partners in a law partnership (because the partners share the firm's income), nor can they have a fee-sharing arrangement with an attorney.

One of the reasons for this rule is that it protects the attorney's independent judgment concerning legal matters. For example, if an attorney became partners with two or three nonattorneys, the nonattorneys would have a significant voice in determining the firm's policies. In this situation, a conflict might arise between a policy of the firm and the attorney's duty to exercise independent professional judgment in regard to a client's case. The rule against fee splitting also protects against the possibility that nonlawyers would indirectly, through attorneys, be able to engage in the practice of law, which no one but an attorney can do.

Giving Legal Opinions and Advice

Giving legal advice goes to the essence of legal practice. After all, a person would not seek out a legal expert if he or she did not want legal advice on some matter. Although a paralegal can communicate an attorney's legal advice to a client, a paralegal cannot give legal advice.

The Need for Caution

You need to be careful to avoid giving legal advice even when discussing matters with friends and relatives. Although other nonlawyers often give advice affecting others' legal rights or obligations, paralegals should not do so. For example, when a person gets a speeding ticket, a friend or relative who is a nonlawyer might suggest that the person should argue the case before a judge and explain his side of the story. When a paralegal gives such advice, however, she may be accused of engaging in the unauthorized practice of law. Legal assistants are prohibited from giving even simple, common-sense advice because of the understandably greater weight given to the advice of someone who has legal training.

Similarly, you need to be cautious in the workplace. Although you may develop expertise in a certain area of law, you must refrain from advising clients with respect to their legal obligations or rights. Suppose you are a bankruptcy specialist and know that a client who wants to petition for bankruptcy has two realistic options to pursue under bankruptcy law. Should you tell the client about these options and their consequences? No. In effect, advising someone of his legal options is

Developing
Paralegal Skills

THE DANGERS OF THE UNAUTHORIZED PRACTICE OF LAW

Every state restricts the "practice of law" to licensed attorneys. State bar associations takes this restriction seriously and aggressively enforce unauthorized practice of law rules against anyone the bar suspects is infringing on attorneys' control of the practice of law.

Unfortunately, the definition of the "practice of law" is unclear, making it a trap for the unwary. The ABA defines it as "the rendition of services for others that call for the professional judgment of a lawyer." In essence, "practicing" law includes:

- Giving legal advice;
- Preparing legal documents; and
- Representing a client in court.

Of course, paralegals routinely do the first two of these. Each is perfectly legal to do as long as these activities are done under the supervision of a licensed attorney. For example, you will often have to relay legal advice from the attorney to the client. To protect yourself, you must make clear that the advice comes from the lawyer, not you. You can avoid unauthorized practice problems by:

- Being clear that everyone understands you are a paralegal in all communications and meetings by:
  —Including your title when signing letters, e-mails, and other documents and on your business cards.
  —Introducing yourself with your title in meetings.
  —Disclosing your status when communicating with a court.
- Ensuring that activities that might be construed to be the "practice of law" are supervised by a licensed attorney by:
  —Making sure that an attorney reviews and signs off on all legal documents you prepare.
  —Explicitly stating that the attorney is the source of any legal advice when relaying advice to a client by stating, "I asked Attorney Smith about that and she said . . . ."
- Informing yourself on your state's unauthorized practice rules by:
  —Researching court decisions, regulations, and state bar opinions on the topic.
  —Contacting your state paralegal associations and state bar for information and publications on the topic.

Taking care to follow such guidelines will protect the law firm you work for and will protect you, your career, and your firm's clients.

very close to advising a person of his legal rights and may therefore—in the view of many courts, at least—constitute the unauthorized practice of law. Also, even though you may qualify what you say by telling the client that he needs to check with an attorney, this does not alter the fact that you are giving advice on which the client might rely.

Be on the Safe Side

What constitutes the giving of legal advice can be difficult to pin down. Paralegals are permitted to advise clients on a number of matters, so drawing the line between permissible and impermissible advice may be difficult. To be on the safe side—and avoid potential liability for the unauthorized practice of law—never advise anyone regarding any matter if the advice may alter that person's legal position or legal rights.

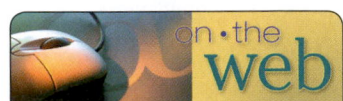

on•the
web

For some tips on how to avoid UPL, go to **www.paralegals.org**. Select "Site Search" at the upper right, and type "avoid UPL". In the search results, select the article "Professional Development— Unauthorized Practice of Law."

Whenever you are pressured to render legal advice—as you surely will be at one time or another, by your firm's clients or others—say that you cannot give legal advice because it is against the law to do so. Offer to find an attorney who can answer the client's questions. Paralegals usually find that a frank and honest approach provides the best solution to the problem.

Representing Clients in Court

The rule that only attorneys can represent others in court has a long history. There are two limited exceptions to this rule. First, in 1975 the United States Supreme Court held that people have a constitutional right to represent themselves in court.[3] Second, paralegals are allowed to represent clients before some federal and state government agencies, such as the federal Social Security Administration. Hence, as a paralegal you should know that you are not allowed to appear in court on behalf of your supervising attorney—although local courts in some states have made exceptions to this rule for limited purposes.

Disclosure of Paralegal Status

Because of the close working relationship between an attorney and a paralegal, a client may have difficulty perceiving that the paralegal is not also an attorney. For example, a client's call to an attorney may be transferred to the attorney's paralegal. The paralegal may assume that the client knows who she is and may speak freely with the client about a legal matter, advising the client that the attorney will be in touch with the client shortly. The client, however, may assume that the paralegal is an attorney and may make inferences based on the paralegal's comments that result in actions with harmful consequences—in which event the paralegal might be charged with the unauthorized practice of law. To avoid such problems, make sure that clients or potential clients know that you are a paralegal and, as such, are not permitted to give legal advice. Similarly, in correspondence with clients or others, you should indicate your nonattorney status by adding "Paralegal" or "Legal Assistant" after your name. If you have printed business cards or if your name is included in the firm's letterhead or other literature, also make sure that your non-lawyer status is clearly indicated there.

Guideline 1 of NALA's Model Standards and Guidelines emphasizes the importance of disclosing paralegal status by stating that all legal assistants have an ethical responsibility to "disclose their status as legal assistants at the outset of any professional relationship with a client, other attorneys, a court or administrative agency or personnel thereof, or members of the general public." Disciplinary Rule 1.7 of NFPA's Model Code of Ethics and Professional Responsibility also stresses the importance of disclosing paralegal status. Guideline 4 of the ABA's Model Guidelines places on attorneys the responsibility for disclosing the nonattorney status of paralegals:

> A lawyer is responsible for taking reasonable measures to ensure that clients, courts, and other lawyers are aware that a paralegal, whose services are utilized by the lawyer in performing legal services, is not licensed to practice law.

Paralegals Freelancing for Attorneys

Some paralegals work on a freelance basis, as discussed in Chapter 2. In the early 1990s, there was some concern over whether freelance paralegals were, by definition, sufficiently supervised by attorneys to avoid liability for the unauthorized practice of law. In a landmark decision in 1992, the New Jersey Supreme Court stated that it could find no reason why freelance paralegals could not be just as adequately supervised by the attorneys for whom they worked as those paralegals working in attorneys' offices. Since that decision, courts in several other states and ethical opinions issued by various state bar associations have held that freelance paralegals who are adequately supervised by attorneys are not engaging in the unauthorized practice of law.

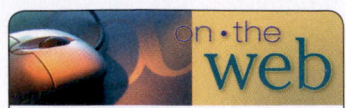

To read an article discussing the report from the New Jersey Supreme Court's Committee on Paralegal Education and Regulation, go to **http://www.nala.org**, go to Certification

In its opinion, the New Jersey Supreme Court also called for the establishment of a Committee on Paralegal Education and Regulation to study the practice of paralegals and make recommendations to the court. The committee's report, submitted to the court in 1998, recommended that paralegals in New Jersey should be subject to state licensing requirements. This recommendation caused widespread debate among legal professionals in New Jersey and elsewhere—as you will read shortly.

Legal Technicians (Independent Paralegals) and UPL

As mentioned in Chapter 2, legal technicians (also called independent paralegals) provide "self-help" legal services directly to the public. The courts have had to wrestle with questions such as the following: If an independent paralegal advises a customer on what forms are necessary to obtain a simple, uncontested divorce, how those forms should be filed with the court, how the court hearing should be scheduled, and the like, do those activities constitute the practice of law?

Generally, the mere dissemination of legal information does not constitute the unauthorized practice of law. There is a fine line, however, between disseminating legal information (by providing legal forms to a customer, for example) and giving legal advice (which may consist of merely selecting the forms that best suit the customer's needs)—and the courts do not always agree on just where this line should be drawn.

Early Cases

An early case on this issue was *The Florida Bar v. Brumbaugh*,[4] which was decided in 1978 by the Florida Supreme Court. The case was brought by the Florida Bar against Brumbaugh, who prepared legal documents for people who sought a simple, uncontested divorce. Brumbaugh prepared all the necessary court documents and told her customers how to file the documents with the court, how to schedule the court hearings, and—in a conference the day before the hearing—what would occur at the hearing.

The Florida Bar claimed that Brumbaugh was engaging in the practice of law in violation of the state's UPL statute. The Florida Supreme Court held that Brumbaugh could sell legal forms and other printed information regarding divorces and other legal procedures, that she could fill in the forms as long as the customer provided the information in writing, and that she could advertise her services. She could not, however, advise customers of their legal rights; tell them which forms should be used, how they should be filled out, and where to file them; or tell customers how to present their cases in court.

A year later, the same court decided *The Florida Bar v. Furman* case,[5] which involved a woman who performed legal services very similar to those performed by Brumbaugh. The court held that Furman had engaged in the unauthorized practice of law by failing to comply with the decision in *Brumbaugh*. The *Furman* case received substantial publicity when Furman disobeyed an *injunction* (a court order to cease engaging in the prohibited activities) and was sentenced to prison for **contempt of court** (failing to cooperate with a court order).

An Ongoing Problem

Legal technicians continue to face UPL allegations brought against them primarily by UPL committees and state bar associations. In one case, an Oregon appellate court upheld the conviction of Robin Smith for engaging in UPL. The bar association complained that Smith provided consumers with various legal forms, advised them on which forms to use, and assisted them in completing the documents. The court reasoned that by drafting and selecting documents and giving advice with regard to their legal effect, Smith was practicing law.[6]

contempt of court
The intentional obstruction or frustration of a court's attempt to administer justice. A party to a lawsuit may be held in contempt of court (punishable by a fine or jail sentence) for refusing to comply with a court's order.

Some legal technicians were facing UPL charges in California when the legislature authorized nonlawyers to provide certain types of legal services directly to the public. Under that law, a person who qualifies and registers with the county as a "legal document assistant" (LDA) may assist clients in filling out legal forms but cannot advise clients which forms to use.[7] After the LDA law passed, the case was settled.

The Controversy over Legal Software

Even publishers of self-help law books and computer software programs have come under attack for the unauthorized practice of law. For example, a Texas Court held that the legal software program *Quicken Family Lawyer* violated Texas's UPL statute.[8] The program provided a hundred different legal forms (including contracts, real estate leases, and wills), along with instructions on how to fill out these forms.

The Texas legislature then amended the UPL statute to reverse the court's ruling. The new law explicitly authorizes the sale of legal self-help software, books, forms, and similar products to the public.[9] Note, however, that the Texas law authorizes these products to be used *only* for "self-help." The law does not permit persons who are not licensed to practice law (such as legal technicians) to use these programs to give legal advice or assistance to others.

Do Paralegals Who Operate as Legal Technicians Engage in UPL?

Debate continues as to whether it is legal, at least in some situations, for legal technicians to operate without a lawyer's supervision. Generally, unless a state statute or rule specifically allows paralegals to assist the public directly without the supervision of an attorney, paralegals would be wise not to engage in such practices. Most state courts are much more likely to find that a paralegal is engaging in UPL than that a publisher of legal software is doing so. This is because of the relationship of trust that develops between the paralegal and the client and the potential for abuse. The consequences of violating state UPL statutes can be serious. Any paralegal who contemplates working as a legal technician (independent paralegal) therefore must thoroughly investigate the relevant state laws and court decisions on UPL before offering any services directly to the public and must rigorously abide by the letter of the law.

SHOULD PARALEGALS BE LICENSED?

One of the major issues facing legal professionals is whether paralegals should be subject to direct regulation by the state through licensing requirements. Unlike certification, which was discussed in Chapter 1, licensing involves direct and mandatory regulation, by the state, of an occupational or professional group. When licensing requirements are established for a professional group, such as for attorneys, a member of the group must have a license to practice his or her profession.

Movements toward regulation of paralegals have been motivated in large part by the activities of legal technicians, or independent paralegals—those who provide legal services directly to the public without attorney supervision. Many legal technicians call themselves paralegals even though they have little, if any, legal training, background, or experience. Yet at the same time, those who cannot afford to hire an attorney can benefit from the self-help services provided by legal technicians who do have training and experience.

General Licensing

A number of states—including Arizona, Florida, Hawaii, Maine, Minnesota, New Jersey, New York, Oklahoma, Rhode Island, South Dakota, Texas, Utah, and Wisconsin—have considered implementing a **general licensing** program. A general

general licensing
Licensing in which all individuals within a specific profession or group (such as paralegals) must meet licensing requirements imposed by the state in order to legally practice their profession.

licensing program would require all paralegals to meet certain educational requirements and other specified criteria before being allowed to practice their profession.

For example, after five years of study, the New Jersey Supreme Court Committee on Paralegal Education and Regulation recommended that paralegals be licensed. The committee's report proposed that paralegals be subject to state licensure based on demonstrated educational requirements and knowledge of the ethical rules governing the legal profession. The New Jersey Supreme Court, however, declined to follow the committee's recommendations. The court concluded that direct oversight of paralegals is best accomplished through attorney supervision rather than through a state-mandated licensing system.

Although other states have considered licensing for paralegals, California is the only state that currently makes it unlawful for persons to identify themselves as paralegals unless they meet certain qualifications. The California law requires paralegals to meet minimum education standards, work under lawyer supervision, and complete continuing education requirements (four hours of ethics courses every three years and four hours of either general or specialized law every two years). Individuals who are registered as legal document assistants (LDAs) cannot call themselves paralegals because they do not work under attorney supervision.[10]

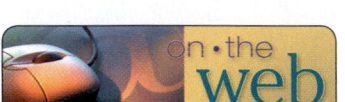

You can keep up on issues involving paralegals and the practice of law at **www.abnet.org**, search on "paralegals", then go to American Bar Association Standing Committee on Paralegals.

limited licensing

Licensing in which a limited number of individuals within a specific profession or group (such as legal technicians within the paralegal profession) must meet licensing requirements imposed by the state in order to legally practice their profession.

Limited Licensing

As an alternative to general licensing, many states are considering **limited licensing**, which would limit licensing requirements to those paralegals (legal technicians, or independent paralegals) who wish to provide specified legal services directly to the public. With limited licensing, qualified paralegals would be authorized to handle routine legal services traditionally rendered only by attorneys, such as advising clients on simple divorces, will executions, bankruptcy petitions, incorporation, real estate transactions, selected tax matters, and other specified services as designated by the state licensing body. Already, a number of states allow some form of limited nonlawyer practice, and some states would like to establish a regulatory mechanism—such as a limited licensing program—to protect the consumers of these services.

Direct Regulation—The Pros and Cons

A significant part of the debate over direct regulation has to do with the issue of who should do the regulating. Certainly, state bar associations and government authorities would want to have a say in the matter. Yet paralegal organizations and educators, such as NALA, NFPA, and the American Association for Paralegal Education (AAfPE), would also want to play a leading role in developing the education requirements, ethical standards, and disciplinary procedures required by a licensing program. The problem is, NALA, NFPA, and the AAfPE have expressed different views on these matters.

NFPA's Position

NFPA endorses the regulation of the paralegal profession on a state-by-state basis. Given that lower-cost legal services are in great demand, NFPA asserts that the regulation of paralegals would improve consumers' access to quality legal services. NFPA favors establishing minimum education requirements to protect the public and to weed out the "bad apples" in the profession—those who call themselves paralegals but who do not have the necessary education or training to perform paralegal work competently.

NFPA contends that the licensing of paralegals would benefit both the public and attorneys because only qualified paralegals would be licensed to practice. Attorneys' search costs in finding quality legal assistants would be reduced. Moreover, licensing would be a step forward in the development of the paralegal profession, enhancing recognition and encouraging employers to give paralegals greater responsibilities. Because licensing would permit paralegals to perform specified tasks, there would also be less chance of violating UPL laws.

NFPA proposes a two-tiered system of licensing: general licensing and specialty licensing. General licensing by a state board or agency would require all paralegals within the state to satisfy education, experience, and continuing education requirements; it would also subject practicing paralegals to disciplinary procedures by the licensing body. (As mentioned, NFPA has already developed a set of model enforcement guidelines—see Appendix C.) Specialty licensing would require paralegals who wish to practice in a specialized area to demonstrate, by an examination (see the discussion of the PACE examination in Chapter 1), their proficiency in that area.

NALA's Position

NALA supports voluntary certification (self-regulation) but opposes licensing requirements for paralegals. It takes the position that state licensing would only serve to control entry into the profession and would not improve the quality of the services that paralegals provide. Because a license grants a paralegal permission to work, NALA believes that licensing criteria would be kept at the lowest level of professional competency.

According to NALA, there is no need to regulate paralegals at this time. Most paralegals work under the supervision of attorneys, who are regulated by state ethical codes. NALA believes that regulation would increase the cost of paralegals to employers. This increase would be passed on to consumers, resulting in higher-cost legal services. NALA therefore considers licensing an unnecessary burden to both employers and paralegals.

NALA further contends that licensing would not encourage the growth of the paralegal profession and would not expand the functions of paralegals. Paralegals already perform a wide range of tasks and work in a variety of settings. To impose mandatory, uniform requirements on all paralegals would be harmful. Some paralegals who perform competently in one specified area (elder law, for example) might not qualify for a paralegal license (because they did not graduate from an ABA-accredited program, for example) and thus would be prohibited from employment as a paralegal.

NALA also objects to specific limited licensing proposals for legal technicians (independent paralegals). These objections, however, do not reflect opposition to the idea of limited licensing for legal technicians so much as disagreement with specific aspects of the proposed regulatory schemes.

The AAfPE's Position

The American Association for Paralegal Education (AAfPE) does not take a position on paralegal licensing. The major concern of the AAfPE is that if paralegals are regulated, certain educational standards should be required. Obviously, the AAfPE recommends that states adopt AAfPE's minimum educational standards in any regulatory plan they enact. It is the view of the AAfPE that paralegals (through associations such as NALA and NFPA) and paralegal educators should put aside their differences and present a united front in influencing licensing proposals. Otherwise, by default, the decision will not be theirs to make.

Other Considerations

While the positions taken by NFPA, NALA, and the AAfPE outline the main contours of the debate over regulation, other groups emphasize some different considerations. For example, one of the concerns of lawyers is that if legal technicians are licensed—through limited licensing programs—to deliver low-cost services directly to the public, the business (and profits) of law firms would suffer. Many lawyers are also concerned that if paralegals are subject to mandatory licensing

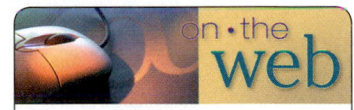

For updates on the positions taken by NFPA, NALA, and the AAfPE on regulation, as well as regulatory developments, check their Web sites: for NFPA, **www.paralegals.org**; for NALA, **www.nala.org**; for the AAfPE: **www.aafpe.org**.

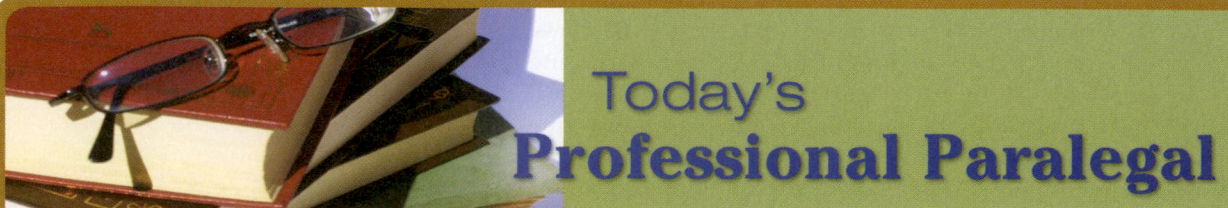

Today's Professional Paralegal

WORKING FOR THE ATTORNEY DISCIPLINE BOARD

Denise James is a legal assistant who works for the attorney discipline board in her state. She has an interesting job that entails a variety of responsibilities. One of Denise's job responsibilities is to contact attorneys to sit on the attorney discipline board's hearing panel. She consults the list of attorneys who have volunteered to sit on the panel and calls them to make arrangements for the hearing panels. She forwards to them background information and briefs on the cases that they will hear. On the day of the hearing, she meets the attorneys, escorts them to the hearing room, provides them with hearing examiners' robes, and assists them in getting the hearing started.

PREPARING "NOTICES OF DISCIPLINE"

Another of Denise's duties is to prepare the "notices of discipline" that are published every month in the state bar association journal, a monthly publication that is sent to all licensed attorneys in the state. These notices identify which attorneys have been subject to disciplinary actions, and for what reasons. To prepare this month's notices, Denise pulls out all of the "final orders of discipline" that were entered this month. Then she reads and summarizes each order.

SUMMARIZING DISCIPLINARY PROCEEDINGS

Denise reads through a final order sanctioning an attorney. The attorney, who commingled a client's funds with her own personal funds, was suspended. The funds involved consisted of a check in the settlement of a personal-injury lawsuit. The attorney deposited the check to her personal account and used the funds to pay her monthly bills. She did not issue a check to the client for the full amount until three months later. The client continually called the attorney's office and demanded the settlement check, but the attorney did not return the client's phone calls.

Denise summarized the disciplinary proceedings against the attorney as follows: "[attorney's name], P12345, Binghamton, by Attorney Discipline Board, Binghamton County, Hearing Panel #6, effective June 3, 2010. Respondent commingled client's funds by using the client's money, received in a settlement, to pay her personal bills, then paid the client three months later. The hearing panel found respondent's conduct to be in violation of Court Rule 1.15 and the state Rules of Professional Conduct. A suspension was issued and costs were assessed in the amount of $951.53."

There is never a dull moment working for the attorney discipline board. The unfortunate part is that Denise sees many cases in which clients have lost legal rights because their cases were neglected for a variety of reasons.

requirements, law firms will not be able to hire and train persons of their choice to become paralegals.

Some paralegals and paralegal associations are concerned that mandatory licensing would require all paralegals to be "generalists." As it is, a large number of paralegals specialize in particular areas, such as bankruptcy or family law, and do not need to have the broad knowledge of all areas of paralegal practice that licensing might require.

A FINAL NOTE

As a professional paralegal, you will have an opportunity to voice your opinion on whether paralegals should be regulated by state governments and, if so, what qualifications should be required. Whatever the outcome of the licensing debate, keep in mind that all of the issues discussed in this chapter are directly relevant to your paralegal career. The most important point to remember as you embark on a paralegal career is that you need to think and act in a professionally responsible manner. Although this takes time and practice, in the legal arena there is little room for learning ethics by "trial and error." Therefore, you need to be especially attentive to the ethical rules governing attorneys and paralegal practice discussed in this chapter.

The *Ethics Watch* features throughout this book offer further insights into some of the ethical problems that can arise in various areas of paralegal performance. Understanding how violations can occur will help you anticipate and guard against them as you begin your career. Once on the job, you can continue your preventive tactics by asking questions whenever you are in doubt and by making sure that your work is adequately supervised.

KEY TERMS AND CONCEPTS

attorney-client privilege *102*	disbarment *94*	reprimand *94*
breach *95*	ethical wall *106*	self-regulation *90*
conflict of interest *103*	general licensing *119*	suspension *94*
conflicts check *108*	licensing *91*	third party *100*
contempt of court *118*	limited licensing *120*	unauthorized practice of law (UPL) *92*
damages *94*	malpractice *94*	work product *103*

CHAPTER SUMMARY

ETHICS AND PROFESSIONAL RESPONSIBILITY

The Regulation of Attorneys

Attorneys are regulated by licensing requirements and by the ethical rules of their state. The purpose of attorney regulation is to protect the public against incompetent legal professionals and unethical attorney behavior.

1. *Self-regulation*—Lawyers establish the majority of rules governing their profession through state bar associations and the American Bar Association (ABA), which has established model rules and guidelines relating to professional conduct.

2. *External regulation*—Other key participants in the regulation of attorneys are state supreme courts, state legislatures, and (occasionally) the United States Supreme Court.

3. *Model Code or Model Rules*—Most states have adopted a version of either the 1969 Model Code of Professional Responsibility or the 1983 revision of the Model Code, called the Model Rules of Professional Conduct, both of which were published by the ABA. The Model Rules are often amended by the ABA to keep up to date with the realities of modern law practice. Most states have adopted laws based on the Model Rules.

4. *Sanctions for violations*—The Model Code and Model Rules spell out the ethical and professional duties governing attorneys and the practice of law. Attorneys who violate these duties may be subject to reprimand, suspension, or disbarment. Additionally, attorneys (as well as paralegals) face potential liability for malpractice or for violations of criminal statutes.

Continued

Attorney Ethics and Paralegal Practice

Some of the ethical rules governing attorney behavior pose difficult problems for paralegals, so paralegals should consult their state's ethical code to learn the specific rules for which they will be accountable. The following rules apply in most states.

1. *Duty of competence*—This duty is violated whenever a client suffers harm as a result of the attorney's (or paralegal's) incompetent action or inaction.

   a. Breaching the duty of competence may lead to a lawsuit against the attorney (and perhaps against the paralegal) for negligence.

   b. Attorneys must adequately supervise a paralegal's work to ensure that this duty is not breached.

2. *Confidentiality*—The confidentiality rule requires that all information relating to a client's representation be kept in confidence and not revealed to third parties who are not authorized to know the information.

   a. Paralegals should be careful both on and off the job not to discuss client information with third parties.

   b. Client confidences can be revealed only in certain circumstances, such as when the client gives informed consent to the disclosure, when disclosure is necessary to represent the client or to prevent harm to persons or property, or when a court orders the attorney to reveal the information.

   c. Some client information is regarded as privileged information under the rules of evidence and receives even greater protection.

3. *Conflict of interest*—An attorney is prohibited from representing a client if doing so will injure the interests of another client, including a former client. An attorney is also prohibited from representing a client if there is a significant risk that the attorney's ability to consider, recommend, or carry out an appropriate course of action for the client will be materially limited as a result of the attorney's other responsibilities or interests.

   a. An attorney may represent both sides in a legal proceeding only if the attorney believes that neither party's rights will be injured and only if both clients are aware of the conflict and have given informed consent to the representation. Paralegals also fall under this rule.

   b. When a firm is handling a case and one of the firm's attorneys or paralegals cannot work on the case because of a conflict of interest, that attorney or paralegal must be "walled off" from the case—that is, prevented from having access to files or other information relating to the case.

   c. Normally, whenever a prospective client consults with an attorney, a conflicts check is done to ensure that if the attorney or firm accepts the case, no conflict of interest will arise.

The Indirect Regulation of Paralegals

Paralegals are regulated indirectly by attorney ethical rules, by ethical codes created by NFPA and NALA, and by guidelines on the utilization of paralegals, which define the status and function of paralegals and the scope of their authorized activities. The ABA and several states have adopted guidelines on the utilization of paralegals. These codes and guidelines provide paralegals, attorneys, and the courts with guidance on the paralegal's role in the practice of law. The general rule is that paralegals can perform almost any legal task that attorneys can (other than represent a client in court) as long as they work under an attorney's supervision. (Other exceptions to this rule are noted in the following section.)

The Unauthorized Practice of Law

State laws prohibit nonlawyers from engaging in the unauthorized practice of law (UPL). Violations of these laws can have serious consequences.

1. *What constitutes UPL?*—Determining what constitutes UPL is complicated by the fact that many state laws give vague or very broad definitions. Some states have made efforts to address this problem.

2. *The need for caution*—Paralegals working for attorneys and legal technicians (independent paralegals) need to be careful not to engage in activities that the state will consider UPL.

3. *Prohibited acts*—The consensus is that paralegals should not engage in any of the following acts:

   a. Establish an attorney-client relationship.

   b. Set legal fees.

   c. Give legal advice or opinions.

   d. Represent a client in court (unless authorized to do so by the court).

   e. Encourage or contribute to any act that could constitute UPL.

Should Paralegals Be Licensed?

A major concern today for both legal professionals and the public is whether paralegals should be directly regulated by the state through licensing requirements.

1. *General licensing*—General licensing would establish minimum standards that every paralegal would have to meet in order to practice as a paralegal in the state. California has adopted such a law, and other states may do so.

2. *Limited licensing*—Limited licensing would require paralegals wishing to offer routine legal services directly to the public in certain areas, such as family law and bankruptcy law, to demonstrate their proficiency in that area.

3. *The debate over licensing*—The pros and cons of direct regulation through licensing are being debated vigorously by the leading paralegal and paralegal education associations, state bar associations, state courts, state legislatures, and public-interest groups.

STUDENT STUDYWARE™ CD-ROM

Interactive student CD in this book includes additional quizzing, plus video clips, case studies, and Key Terms flashcards.

ONLINE COMPANION™

For additional resources, please go to **www.paralegal.delmar.cengage.com**.

QUESTIONS FOR REVIEW

1. Why is the legal profession regulated? Who are the regulators? How is regulation accomplished?

2. How is the paralegal profession regulated by attorney ethical codes? How is it regulated by paralegal codes of ethics?

3. What does the duty of competence involve? How can violations of the duty of competence be avoided?

4. What is the duty of confidentiality? What is the attorney-client privilege? What is the relationship between confidentiality and the attorney-client

privilege? What are some potential consequences of violating the confidentiality rule?

5. What is the practice of law? What is the unauthorized practice of law (UPL)? How might paralegals violate

state statutes prohibiting UPL? What types of tasks can legally be performed by paralegals?

ETHICAL QUESTION

1. Norma Sollers works as a paralegal for a small law firm. She is a trusted, experienced employee who has worked for the firm for twelve years. One morning, Linda Lowenstein, one of the attorneys, calls in from her home and asks Norma to sign Linda's name to a document that must be filed with the court that day. Norma has just prepared the final draft of the document and placed it on Linda's desk for her review

and signature. Linda explains to Norma that because her child is sick, she does not want to leave home to come into the office. Norma knows that she should not sign Linda's name—only the client's attorney can sign the document. She mentions this to Linda, but Linda says, "Don't worry. No one will ever know that you signed it instead of me." How should Norma handle this situation?

PRACTICE QUESTIONS AND ASSIGNMENTS

1. Peter Smith, a paralegal, is using the Internet to find property tax records for a client. The client has come to the firm because he wants to buy a parcel of property, but he also wants to make sure that the property taxes have been paid. Peter finds a Web site for the county register of deeds. He locates the property and notes that, according to the information on the Web page, the taxes have been paid. He prints the page and writes a brief memo to the attorney. The attorney then advises the client that the taxes have been paid and that it is okay to go ahead and purchase the property. The client does so, but several weeks later he receives a notice that he owes $6,500 in back taxes. The client, who is understandably upset, complains to Peter's boss. Peter is sent to the county register of deeds to look up the records relating to the property. Peter finds that the correct information was in the county's records but was not on the Web site. He makes a copy of what he finds and returns to the office. What ethical rule has been violated here? What do these "facts" reveal about the reliability of information posted on the Internet?

2. In which of the following instances may confidential client information be disclosed?

   a. A client's daughter calls to find out whether her mother has left her certain property in her will.

   The mother does not want the daughter to know that the daughter has been disinherited until the will is read after the mother's death.

   b. The client in a divorce case threatens to hire a hit man to kill her husband because she believes that killing her husband is the only way that she can stop him from stalking her. It is clear that the client intends to do this.

   c. A former client sues her attorney for legal malpractice in the handling of a breach-of-contract case involving her cosmetics home-sale business. The attorney discloses that the client is having an affair with her next-door neighbor, a fact that is unrelated to the malpractice or breach-of-contract case.

3. According to this chapter's text, which of the following tasks can a paralegal legally perform?

   a. Draft a complaint at an attorney's request.

   b. Interview a witness to a car accident.

   c. Represent a client before an administrative agency.

   d. Investigate the facts of a car accident case.

   e. Work as a freelance paralegal for attorneys.

   f. Work as a legal technician providing legal services directly to the public.

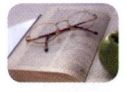

QUESTIONS FOR CRITICAL ANALYSIS

1. Why are ethical rules needed? What could happen if the legal profession were not regulated? What might happen if, for example, there were no rule governing competence in the profession?

2. The material in the chapter indicates that lawyers are largely responsible for regulating their own conduct.

What do you think of a system in which members of a profession regulate themselves? Is this a good system? Can you think of a better alternative?

3. An experienced legal secretary opened a business, Northside Secretarial Services, to provide certain legal services directly to the public. She prepared legal

documents—and provided detailed instructions for filing the documents with the court and for service of process—in divorce and adoption cases. She held briefing sessions during which she gave detailed instructions about trials and hearings, including the types of questions that the court would ask and the responses that her "clients" should give to the court. The secretary advertised her services in a newspaper, calling herself an "expert in family law." She also sold "do-it-yourself" divorce kits. She charged $50 for her services, and many of her "clients" were indigent and illiterate.

The state bar association charged her with the unauthorized practice of law. A former client testified that when he had found out that his wife was abusing the children, he had been advised he should not try to change the petition for divorce to seek custody of the minor children but should leave it to the state agency to handle abuse and custody issues.

What was the likely result of the state bar association's filing of unauthorized-practice-of-law charges against the legal secretary? How might she have responded to these charges? What would happen if she was prohibited by court order from engaging in these activities and continued to do so anyway?

4. Compare the activities that constitute the unauthorized practice of law with the activities in which paralegals can lawfully engage under the guidelines for the utilization of legal assistants. Why do you think that the activities that constitute the unauthorized practice of law are prohibited for nonlawyers? Could someone with training as a legal assistant competently handle some of these activities? If so, which ones?

5. Do you think that paralegals should be licensed? If you think that they should be licensed, what type of license should they be granted—general or limited? What impact would this have on paralegals and on the legal profession as a whole?

 ## PROJECTS

1. Access your state's rules online to find out the requirements for becoming licensed to practice law in your state. Do your state's rules differ from the requirements mentioned in the text? If so, how?

2. Go to **www.law.com** and enter "unauthorized practice" in the search box. List ten recent cases that discuss unauthorized practice of law and see what the major reasons were for such cases.

 ## USING INTERNET RESOURCES

1. Go to **www.paralegals.org**, the home page for the National Federation of Paralegal Associations (NFPA). Select "Positions & Issues," and then "Ethics," and then "Opinions." This will take you to a page that lists, among other things, NFPA's ethics opinions. Then do the following:

   a. List five issues that NFPA has addressed in these opinions.

   b. Choose one opinion and write a paragraph explaining why the issue dealt with in the opinion is important for paralegals.

   c. Choose a different opinion, read it carefully, and write a paragraph summarizing NFPA's advice on the issue being addressed in the opinion.

END NOTES

1. Even this mildest sanction can seriously damage an attorney's reputation within the legal community. In some states, state bar associations publish in their monthly journals the names of violators and details of the violations for all members of the bar to read.

2. Title 2 of the Texas Government Code, Section 81.101.

3. *Faretta v. California*, 422 U.S. 806 (1975).

4. 355 So.2d 1186 (Fla. 1978).

5. 376 So.2d 378 (Fla. 1979).

6. *Oregon State Bar v. Smith*, 942 P.2d 793 (1997).

7. This law is codified in California Business and Professions Code, Sections 6400–6416.

8. *In re Nolo Press/Folk Law, Inc.*, 991 S.W.2d 768 (1999).

9. Texas Government Code Section 81.101(c) (Vernon Supp. 2000).

10. California Business and Professions Code, Sections 6450–6456.

SOURCES OF AMERICAN LAW

CHAPTER OUTLINE

Introduction

The Framework of American Law

Case Law and the Common Law Tradition

Constitutional Law

Statutory Law

Administrative Law

National and International Law

AFTER COMPLETING THIS CHAPTER, YOU WILL KNOW:

▶ The meaning and relative importance in the American legal system of case law, constitutional law, statutory law, and administrative law.

▶ How English law influenced the development of the American legal system.

▶ What the common law tradition is and how it evolved.

▶ The difference between remedies at law and equitable remedies.

▶ Some of the terms that are commonly found in case law.

▶ How national law and international law differ and why these bodies of law sometimes guide judicial decision making in U.S. courts.

INTRODUCTION

The American legal system originated with colonists who came to America and were governed by English law. The law of England continued to be the model for American judges and legislators after the colonies declared independence from England in 1776. But although the American legal tradition grew out of English law, it was modified over time to suit conditions unique to America.

We open this chapter with a discussion of the nature of law and then examine the common law tradition and its significance in the American legal system. Next we focus on other sources of American law, including constitutional law, statutory law, and administrative law. We also explain how the law of other countries and international law affect judicial decision making in American courts. Another major part of the American legal structure—the court system—will be examined in Chapter 6.

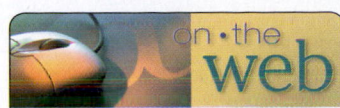

on·the web

The University of Michigan maintains a useful site with links to almost all U.S. government Web sites and many foreign government Web sites at **www.umich.edu**, search "library documents center".

THE FRAMEWORK OF AMERICAN LAW

The law means different things to different people. Before beginning your study of American law, it is useful to have an understanding of what the law is and some of the different approaches to the law that influence judges' decisions. These topics are covered in the following subsections.

What Is the Law?

How a person defines *law* frequently depends on the person's views on such matters as morality, ethics, and truth. Generally, though, **law** can be defined as a body of rules of conduct established and enforced by the controlling authority (the government) of a society. These "rules of conduct" may consist of written principles of behavior, such as those established by ancient societies. They may be set forth in a law code, such as the ones used in European nations. They may consist of written laws and court decisions created by legislative and judicial bodies, as they do in the United States. Regardless of how such rules are created, they all have one thing in common: they establish rights, duties, and privileges for the citizens they govern.

One of the important functions of law in any society is to provide stability, predictability, and continuity so that people can be sure of how to order their affairs. If a society is to survive, its citizens must be able to determine what is legally right and legally wrong. ▶ **EXAMPLE 5.1** Citizens must know what penalties will be imposed on them if they commit wrongful acts. If they suffer harm as a result of others' wrongful acts, they need to know whether and how they can receive compensation for their injuries. ◀ By setting forth the rights, obligations, and privileges of citizens, the law enables them to go about their business and personal lives with confidence and a certain degree of predictability.

law
A body of rules of conduct established and enforced by the controlling authority (the government) of a society.

Primary Sources of American Law

American law has numerous sources. **Primary sources of law**, or sources that establish the law, include the following:

1. Case law and common law doctrines.
2. The U.S. Constitution and the constitutions of the various states.
3. Statutory law—including laws passed by Congress, state legislatures, and local governing bodies.
4. Regulations created by administrative agencies, such as the U.S. Food and Drug Administration (FDA).

primary source of law
In legal research, a document that establishes the law on a particular issue, such as a case decision, legislative act, administrative rule, or presidential order.

We describe each of these important sources of law in the following pages. Note that treaties with other nations are also a primary source of law, although most legal practitioners do not deal with them. We discuss international law near the end of the chapter.

Secondary sources of law are books and articles that summarize and explain the primary sources of law. Examples include legal encyclopedias, treatises, articles in law reviews, and compilations of law, such as the *Restatements of the Law* (which will be discussed later in this chapter). Courts often refer to secondary sources of law for guidance in interpreting and applying the primary sources of law discussed here.

CASE LAW AND THE COMMON LAW TRADITION

An important source of law consists of the decisions rendered by judges in cases that come before the courts. This body of law, called **case law**, arose from the English common law tradition. As mentioned earlier, because of our colonial heritage, much of American law is based on the English legal system.

The English **common law** was a body of general rules that applied throughout the English realm. Courts developed the common law rules from the principles underlying judges' decisions in actual legal controversies. Judges attempted to be consistent. When possible, they based their decisions on the principles suggested by earlier cases. They sought to decide similar cases in a similar way. Each interpretation became part of the law on the subject and served as a legal **precedent**. Later cases that involved similar legal principles or facts could be decided with reference to that precedent. The courts were thus guided by traditions and legal doctrines that evolved over time.

The Doctrine of *Stare Decisis*

The practice of deciding new cases with reference to former decisions, or precedents, eventually became a cornerstone of the English and American judicial systems. It forms a doctrine called *stare decisis*[1] ("to stand by things decided"). Under this doctrine, judges are obligated to follow the precedents established by their own courts or by higher courts within their jurisdictions (the areas over which they have authority—see Chapter 6). These controlling precedents are referred to as binding authorities. A **binding authority** is any source of law that a court must follow when deciding a case. Binding authorities include constitutions, statutes, and regulations that govern the issue being decided, as well as court decisions that are controlling precedents within the jurisdiction. When no binding authority exists, courts will often review **persuasive precedents**, which are precedents decided in similar cases in other jurisdictions. The court may either follow or reject persuasive precedents, but these decisions are entitled to respect and careful consideration.

The doctrine of *stare decisis* performs many useful functions. It helps the courts to be more efficient because if other courts have carefully reasoned through similar cases, their legal reasoning and opinions can serve as guides. *Stare decisis* also makes the law more stable and predictable. If the law on a given subject is well settled, someone bringing a case to court can usually rely on the court to make a decision based on what the law has been.

Departures from Precedent

Sometimes a court will depart from the rule of precedent if it decides that the precedent should no longer be followed. If a court decides that a ruling precedent is wrong or that technological or social changes have made the precedent inappropriate, the court might rule contrary to the precedent. Cases that overturn precedent often receive a great deal of publicity.

▶ **EXAMPLE 5.2** In *Brown v. Board of Education of Topeka,*[2] decided in 1954, the United States Supreme Court expressly overturned precedent when it held

---

secondary source of law

In legal research, any publication that indexes, summarizes, or interprets the law, such as a legal encyclopedia, a treatise, or an article in a law review.

case law

Rules of law announced in court decisions.

common law

A body of law developed from custom or judicial decisions in English and U.S. courts and not by a legislature.

precedent

A court decision that furnishes authority for deciding later cases in which similar facts are presented.

stare decisis

The doctrine of precedent, under which a court is obligated to follow earlier decisions of that court or higher courts within the same jurisdiction. This is a major characteristic of the common law system.

binding authority

Any source of law that a court must follow when deciding a case. Binding authorities include constitutions, statutes, and regulations that govern the issue being decided, as well as court decisions that are controlling precedents within the jurisdiction.

persuasive precedent

A precedent decided in another jurisdiction that a court may either follow or reject but that is entitled to careful consideration.

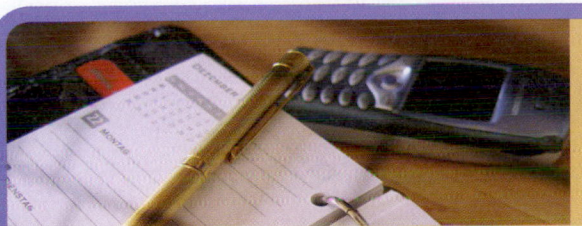

In the Office

DAILY CLEANUP

A neat office is important. For one thing, a messy desk presents a less-than-professional appearance. But beyond that, staying neat forces us to stay organized. When papers are piled up on a desk or in a file cabinet, files might be lost even though we may not realize it. The only work item that should be on a desk is what you are working on that day. At the end of every day, the desk should be cleared. As a part of that, all papers must be filed in their proper files (and copies made if copies are needed). Don't presume you will do it tomorrow. Have everything put away where it belongs so you can start fresh the next work day.

that separate schools for whites and African Americans, which had been upheld as constitutional in numerous previous cases, were unequal and in violation of the Constitution. The Supreme Court's departure from precedent in *Brown* received tremendous publicity as people began to realize the impact of this change in the law. It helped to launch the civil rights movement, which led to further lawsuits involving racial discrimination. ◀

Cases of First Impression

Sometimes, there is no precedent on which to base a decision. ▶ **EXAMPLE 5.3** In 1986, a New Jersey court had to decide whether a surrogate-parenting contract should be enforced against the wishes of the surrogate parent (the natural mother).[3] This was the first such case to reach the courts, and there was no precedent in any jurisdiction to which the court could look for guidance. ◀ Developments in technology sometimes result in cases for which there is no precedent. (See this chapter's *Technology and Today's Paralegal* feature on the following two pages for a case of this kind involving a threat made by a posting on YouTube.)

When deciding cases such as these, called **cases of first impression**, or when there are conflicting precedents, courts may consider a number of factors, including legal principles and policies underlying previous court decisions or existing statutes, fairness, social values and customs, **public policy** (a governmental policy based on widely held societal values), and data and concepts drawn from the social sciences. Which of these sources is chosen or receives the greatest emphasis will depend on the nature of the case being considered and the particular judge hearing the case.

Judges try to be free of personal bias in deciding cases. Each judge, however, has a unique personality, set of values or philosophical leanings, and intellectual attributes—all of which necessarily frame the decision-making process.

Remedies at Law versus Remedies in Equity

The early English courts could grant only limited **remedies**. If one person wronged another in some way, the court could award as compensation land, items of value, or money. The courts that awarded these things became known as **courts of law**, and the three remedies awarded by these courts became known as **remedies at law**.

This system helped to standardize the ways in which disputes were settled, but parties who wanted a remedy other than economic compensation could not be helped. Sometimes these parties petitioned the king for relief. Most petitions were decided by an adviser to the king, called a *chancellor,* who was said to be the "keeper

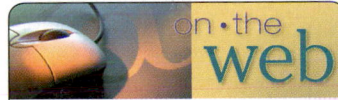

To learn how the Supreme Court justified its departure from precedent in the 1954 *Brown* decision, you can access the Court's opinion online at **www.law.cornell.edu/supct**. Under the heading "Supreme Court collection," select "search," and type in "Brown v. Board of Education" to find a link to the opinion.

case of first impression
A case presenting a legal issue that has not yet been addressed by a court in a particular jurisdiction.

public policy
A governmental policy based on widely held societal values.

remedy
The means by which a right is enforced or the violation of a right is prevented or compensated for.

court of law
A court in which the only remedies were things of value, such as money. Historically, in England, courts of law were different from courts of equity.

remedy at law
A remedy available in a court of law. Money damages and items of value are awarded as a remedy at law.

Technology and Today's Paralegal

CASES OF FIRST IMPRESSION AND THE INTERNET

The widespread use of the Internet has led to many cases of first impression. Here, we look at one such case—a Connecticut case involving a claim of a threat of physical harm. The question raised was whether a person threatened by an Internet posting could get help from a court.[a]

Because the Internet knows no boundaries, cases involving the Internet can raise jurisdictional questions. *Jurisdiction* is an important legal concept that relates to the authority of a court to hear and decide a case. (You will read more about jurisdiction in Chapter 6.) In the United States, jurisdiction over individuals and businesses located in other states is based on the requirement of minimum contacts. Essentially, this requirement means that a defendant in a lawsuit or other action must have a minimum level of contact with a resident of a particular state for that state's courts to exercise jurisdiction over the defendant. For example, suppose that a Wisconsin driver, while on vacation in California, crashes into a California resident's car. If the crash resulted from the Wisconsin driver's negligence, a *tort,* or civil wrong (see Chapter 14), will have been committed. The commission of the tort occurred in California, and that contact will be sufficient to allow a California court to exercise jurisdiction over the Wisconsin defendant. The principle of minimum contacts forms the basis for *long arm statutes*—state statues permitting courts to exercise jurisdiction over nonresidents.

DETERMINING WHETHER THE COURT HAD JURISDICTION

Stacy Rios, who lives in Connecticut, sought a restraining order (a form of court-ordered protection that will be discussed in Chapter 17) against Christopher Fergusan, a resident of North Carolina who is the father of Rios's young child. When Rios brought the action, she provided the court in Connecticut with proof that she had served Fergusan with appropriate documents (discussed in Chapter 10) informing

---

a. *Rios v. Fergusan,* 2008 WL 5511215 (Super.Ct.Conn. 2008).

---

remedy in equity
A remedy allowed by courts in situations where remedies at law are not appropriate. Remedies in equity are based on rules of fairness, justice, and honesty.

court of equity
A court that decides controversies and administers justice according to the rules, principles, and precedents of equity.

equitable principles and maxims
Propositions or general statements of rules of law that are frequently involved in equity jurisdiction.

of the king's conscience." When the chancellor thought that the claim was a fair one for which there was no adequate remedy at law, he would fashion new and unique remedies, called **remedies in equity**, to resolve the case. In this way, a new body of rules and remedies came into being and eventually led to the establishment of formal courts of chancery, or **courts of equity**.

Equity is that branch of law, founded on what might be described as notions of justice and fair dealing, that seeks to supply a remedy when there is no adequate remedy available at law. Once the courts of equity were established, plaintiffs could bring claims in either courts of law (if they sought money damages) or courts of equity (if they sought equitable remedies). Plaintiffs had to specify whether they were bringing an "action at law" or an "action in equity," and they chose their courts accordingly. Only one remedy could be granted for a particular wrong.

Equitable Principles and Maxims

Courts of equity often supplemented the common law by making decisions based on considerations of justice and fairness. Today, courts in the United States can award both legal and equitable remedies, so plaintiffs may request both equitable and legal relief in the same case. Yet judges continue to be guided by so-called **equitable principles and maxims** when deciding whether to grant equitable remedies. *Maxims* him that he should appear in court to defend himself. He did not appear, and the court took testimony from Rios.

Rios established that Fergusan had posted a video on YouTube in which he carried a gun while performing a rap song in which he said he wanted to shoot her and "put her face on the dirt until she can't breathe no more." Rios filed an application for relief from abuse in the form of a restraining order.

The court noted that this was a case of first impression. It had no Connecticut case law (precedent) to draw on that involved similar circumstances. Fergusan had never been in Connecticut. There was only the video posted on YouTube. Was that sufficient to give the court authority to issue a restraining order?

The court held for Rios. It found authority in cases in Iowa, Massachusetts, and New Jersey involving different facts but similar situations. The court held that even if personal jurisdiction could not be established, as would normally be required, there was a "status exception" in cases involving domestic abuse. Because of this, the state's long arm statute applied. The court found that Fergusan had committed a tort in Connecticut by posting a video on the Internet threatening violence. The posting was done in North Carolina, but the threat was intended to be seen by Rios in Connecticut. The court issued the restraining order against Fergusan.

RESEARCHING CASES OF FIRST IMPRESSION

Clearly, the Internet has posed many new difficulties for the courts in attempting to adapt traditional legal principles to cyberspace. Your approach to research thus needs to be flexible. First, look to see if there is any existing statutory law that the judge might determine should apply to your case (or that your supervising attorney can argue should apply). This is particularly important given that new technologies, and especially the Internet, have forced the courts to adapt many existing statutes, such as federal copyright law, to meet the needs of modern society. Second, look to see if any other court (in a different state or district, for example) has considered a similar legal issue and, if so, what that court concluded. Although cases decided in other jurisdictions are not binding precedents, courts often look at the way other courts have handled an issue when deciding matters of first impression.

TECHNOLOGY TIP

Generally, when researching cases of first impression involving Internet transactions, you will need to broaden the scope of your search of the sources of law. A wise paralegal will be creative and adopt a research strategy aimed at discovering both which laws may apply and which laws should apply given the specific facts of the case.

are propositions or general statements of rules of law that courts often use in arriving at a decision. Some of the most influential maxims of equity are the following:

- Whoever seeks equity must do equity. (Anyone who wishes to be treated fairly must treat others fairly.)
- One who seeks the aid of an equity court must come to the court with clean hands. (The plaintiff must have acted fairly and honestly.)
- Equity will not suffer a right to exist without a remedy. (Equitable relief will be awarded when there is a right to relief and there is no adequate legal remedy.)
- Equity regards substance rather than form. (Equity is more concerned with fairness and justice than with legal technicalities.)
- Equity aids the vigilant, not those who slumber on their rights. (Individuals who fail to assert their legal rights within a reasonable period of time will not be helped.)

The last maxim listed above has become known as the equitable doctrine of **laches**. The doctrine of laches encourages people to bring lawsuits while the evidence is still fresh. The idea is that if a party waits too long, the party has "slept on his rights" and lost the ability to bring a claim. What constitutes a reasonable time

laches
An equitable doctrine that bars a party's right to legal action if the party has neglected for an unreasonable length of time to act on his or her rights.

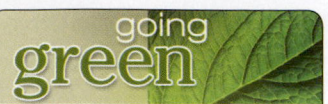

RECYCLE ELECTRONIC JUNK
Don't put old electronics equipment in the garbage bin. Send it to the electronics recycling center. Most cities have centers where you can take used equipment such as computers and printers no longer needed at the office. Some major electronics makers, such as Hewlett-Packard and Dell, are also willing to take old equipment. The U.S. Environmental Protection Agency maintains a list of recycling locations at **www.epa.gov/osw**. In the "Wastes Quick Finder" list, select "Electronics Recycling (eCycling)."

depends on the circumstances of the case. The time period for pursuing a particular claim against another party is now usually fixed by a statute of limitations (see Chapter 3). After the time allowed under the statute of limitations has expired, further action on that claim is barred. (See *Ethics Watch* on page 143.)

For various torts, or civil wrongs, the statute of limitations varies from state to state. It may be two years, three years, or even longer for certain types of wrongs. The statute of limitations for contracts involving the sale of goods is normally four years. In regard to criminal actions, the duration of the statute of limitations is often directly related to the seriousness of the offense. The statute of limitations for petty theft (the theft of an item of insignificant value), for example, may be a year while the statute of limitations for armed robbery might be twenty years. (For certain crimes, such as treason and first degree murder, there is no statute of limitations.)

Equitable Remedies

A number of equitable remedies are available. As mentioned, equitable remedies are normally granted only if the court concludes that the remedy at law (monetary damages) is inadequate. The most important equitable remedies—specific performance and injunction—are briefly discussed here.

specific performance
An equitable remedy requiring the performance that was specified in a contract; usually granted only when money damages would be an inadequate remedy and the subject matter of the contract is unique (for example, real property).

Specific Performance. A judge's decree of **specific performance** is an order to perform what was promised. This remedy was, and still is, only available when the dispute before the court concerns a contractual transaction involving something unique and money damages are inadequate. Contracts for the sale of goods that are readily available on the market rarely qualify for specific performance. Monetary damages ordinarily are adequate in such situations because substantially identical goods can be bought or sold in the market.

If the goods are unique, however, a court of equity may grant specific performance. For example, paintings, sculptures, and rare books and coins are so unique that money damages will not enable a buyer to obtain substantially identical substitutes in the market. The same principle applies to contracts relating to sales of land or interests in land, because each parcel of land is unique. Specific performance is rarely granted in cases involving personal services, but see *Developing Paralegal Skills* for a practical example of how the issue arises.

injunction
A court decree ordering a person to do or to refrain from doing a certain act.

Injunction. An **injunction** is a court order in equity directing the defendant to do or to refrain from doing a particular act. For example, an injunction may be obtained to stop a neighbor from burning trash in his yard or to prevent an estranged husband from coming near his wife. Persons who violate injunctions are typically held in *contempt of court* (see Chapter 4) and punished with a jail sentence or a fine.

The Merging of Law and Equity

During the nineteenth century, most states adopted rules of procedure that combined courts of law and equity or chancery—although some states, such as New Jersey, still retain the distinction. Today, as mentioned, a plaintiff may request both legal and equitable remedies in the same action, and the trial court judge may decide whether to grant either or both forms of relief.

Despite the merging of the courts, some procedures used when law and equity courts were separate still exist. Courts continue to distinguish between remedies at law and equitable remedies, and differences in procedure sometimes also depend on whether a civil lawsuit involves an action in equity or an action at law. For example, in actions at law, a party has the right to demand a jury trial, but actions in equity are not decided by juries. The procedural differences between an action at law and an action in equity are summarized in Exhibit 5.1, which is applicable to most states.

Procedure	Action at Law	Action in Equity
Initiation of lawsuit	By filing a complaint	By filing a petition
Decision	By judge or jury	By judge (no jury)
Result	Judgment	Decree
Remedy	Monetary damages	Injunction or decree of specific performance

EXHIBIT 5.1
Procedural Differences between an Action at Law and an Action in Equity

The Common Law Today

The common law—which consists of the rules of law announced in previous court decisions—plays a significant role in the United States today. Federal and state courts frequently must interpret and enforce constitutional provisions, statutes enacted by legislatures, and regulations created by administrative agencies. For example, if a federal court holds that a regulation issued by the Environmental Protection Agency is unconstitutional, the court's opinion becomes part of the common law. Courts looking at the same issue in other cases will then typically follow the ruling announced in the federal court.

To summarize and clarify common law rules and principles, the American Law Institute (ALI) has published a number of treatises called *Restatements of the Law*. The ALI, which was formed in the 1920s, is a group of practicing attorneys, legal scholars, and judges. *Restatements of the Law* generally summarize and explain the common law rules that are followed in most states with regard to a particular area of law, such as contracts or torts. Although the *Restatements* do not have the force of law, they are important secondary sources of legal analysis and opinion on

Developing **Paralegal Skills**

REQUIREMENTS FOR SPECIFIC PERFORMANCE

Louise Lassen, a wealthy heiress, buys a painting from an artist in New York for $75,000. The artist agrees to ship the painting to Louise's home in Chicago within two weeks. After Louise returns home, she learns from the artist that he has changed his mind—he is no longer interested in selling the painting and is returning her payment.

Louise contacts the firm of Murdoch & Larson to have the contract enforced. Kevin Murdoch, one of the firm's partners, asks paralegal Bob Humboldt to assist him in determining whether the remedy of specific performance can be sought. Bob is to research case law on specific performance and prepare a research memorandum summarizing his results. Bob lets the attorney know that he will have the memorandum on the attorney's desk by the next morning.

CHECKLIST FOR ANALYZING A LEGAL PROBLEM

* Gather the facts involved in the problem.
* Determine whether unique or rare articles are involved.
* Find out what type of remedy the client wants.
* Determine whether an adequate legal remedy, such as money damages, will compensate the client.
* Apply the law to the client's facts to reach a conclusion regarding the appropriate remedy.

which judges often rely in making their decisions. You will read more about the *Restatements of the Law* in Chapter 7, in the context of legal research.

Statutory Law and the Common Law

The common law governs all areas not covered by statutory law, which generally consists of those laws enacted by state legislatures and by the U.S. Congress. In the early years of this nation, the body of statutory law was relatively small compared with the body of common law principles and doctrines. Statutory law has expanded greatly since then, however, and continues to grow. To some extent, this expansion has resulted from the enactment of statutes that essentially codify common law doctrines—that is, statutes that are based largely on common law rules. For example, criminal law was at one time governed extensively by common law. Over time, common law doctrines were codified, expanded on, modified, and enacted in statutory form. Today, criminal law is primarily statutory law.

The expansion of statutory law has also resulted from the regulation of business. ▶ **EXAMPLE 5.4** Many federal and state statutes have been enacted in an attempt to protect consumers, employees, investors, and others from business practices that are potentially harmful to these groups. Many statutes and regulations exist to protect the environment, and a whole body of law—antitrust law—is based on statutes passed to protect the public's interest in a freely competitive society. ◀ Another reason why the body of statutory law has expanded is to address the need for uniform laws among the states, such as the laws governing commercial transactions.

Even when legislation has been substituted for common law principles, a court's interpretation and application of a statute may become a precedent that lower courts in the jurisdiction must follow. Furthermore, courts often look to the common law when determining how to interpret a statute, on the theory that the people who drafted the statute intended to codify an existing common law rule. In a sense, then, common law and statutory law are never totally separate bodies of law.

The Terminology of Case Law

Throughout this text, you will encounter various terms that have traditionally been used to describe parties to lawsuits, case titles, and the types of decisions that judges write. Although details on how to research case law will be given in Chapter 7, it is worthwhile at this point to explain some of the terminology of case law.

Case Titles

The title of a case, which is sometimes referred to as the *style* of the case or the *case name*, indicates the names of the parties to the lawsuit. Note that a case title, such as *Baranski v. Peretto*, includes only the parties' surnames, not their first names. The *v.* in the case title stands for *versus*, which means "against." In the trial court (the court in which a lawsuit is first brought and tried), Baranski is the plaintiff, so Baranski's name appears first in the case title. If the case is appealed to a higher court for review, however, the appeals court sometimes places the name of the party appealing the decision first, so that the case may be called *Peretto v. Baranski*. Because some appeals courts retain the trial court order of names, it is often impossible to distinguish the plaintiff from the defendant in the title of a reported appeals court decision. You must read the facts of the case to identify the parties. Otherwise, the discussion by the appeals court will be difficult to understand.

When attorneys or paralegals refer to a court decision, they give not only the title of the case but also the case citation. The **citation** indicates the reports or reporters in which the case can be found (reports and reporters are volumes in which cases are published, or "reported"). For example, a citation to 251 Kan. 728 following a case title indicates that the case (the court decision) is found in volume

citation
A reference that indicates where a particular constitutional provision, statute, reported case, or article can be found.

251 of the Kansas reports on page 728. You will read more about how to read case citations and locate case law in Chapter 7.

The Parties

The **parties** to a lawsuit are the plaintiff, who initiates the lawsuit, and the defendant, against whom the lawsuit is brought. Lawsuits frequently involve multiple parties—that is, more than one plaintiff or defendant. For example, a person who is injured by a defective product might sue both the manufacturer of the product and the retailer from whom the product was bought to try to get compensation for injuries caused by the product. In this situation, the manufacturer and the retailer would be *co-defendants*.

party
With respect to lawsuits, the plaintiff or the defendant. Some cases involve multiple parties (more than one plaintiff or defendant).

Judges and Justices

The terms *judge* and *justice* are usually synonymous and represent two designations given to judges in various courts. All members of the United States Supreme Court, for example, are referred to as justices. Justice is also the formal title usually given to judges of appeals courts, although this is not always the case. Different states use different terms. Justice is commonly abbreviated to J., and justices to JJ. A Supreme Court case might refer to Justice Kennedy as Kennedy, J., or to Chief Justice Roberts as Roberts, C.J.

In a trial court, a case is heard by one judge. In an appeals court, normally a panel of three or more judges (or justices) sit on the bench. Most decisions reached by appeals courts are explained in written court opinions.

on the web

To learn about the justices of the United States Supreme Court, go to the Legal Information Institute, sponsored by Cornell University, at **www.law.cornell.edu**, go to "Court opinions" then go to "US Supreme Court Opinions."

Decisions and Opinions

The **opinion** contains the court's reasons for its decision, the rules of law that apply, and the judgment. There are four types of opinions. When all judges or justices agree on an opinion, the opinion is written for the entire court and is called a *unanimous opinion*. When there is not a unanimous opinion, a *majority opinion* is written, explaining the views of the majority of the judges deciding the case. The name of the judge immediately preceding the unanimous or majority opinion indicates the author of the opinion—that is, the judge who wrote the opinion on behalf of the others.

Often, a judge who feels strongly about making or emphasizing a point that was not made or emphasized in the majority opinion writes a *concurring opinion*, which appears just following the majority opinion. In a concurring opinion, the judge agrees (concurs) with the decision given in the majority opinion but for different reasons. When an opinion is not unanimous, a *dissenting opinion* may also be written by a judge who does not agree with the majority. The dissenting opinion is important because it may form the basis of the arguments used later in overruling the majority opinion. The names of the judges authoring any concurring or dissenting opinions are also indicated at the beginning of those opinions.

opinion
A statement by the court setting forth the applicable law and the reasons for its decision in a case.

COMMON LAW AND THE PARALEGAL

As a paralegal, you will find that an understanding of the common law tradition is necessary when you research and analyze case law. The doctrine of *stare decisis* and the distinction between legal and equitable remedies are critical concepts when applied to real-life situations faced by clients.

For example, suppose that a client wants to sue another party for breaching a contract to perform computer consulting services. In this situation, the common law of contracts would apply to the case. (In contrast, as you will read in Chapter 15, contracts for the sale of *goods* are usually governed by statutory law.) To research this matter, you would search for previous cases dealing with similar issues to see how those cases were decided. You would want to know of any precedents set by a higher court in your jurisdiction—and, of course, by the

United States Supreme Court—on that issue. Even in an area governed by statutory law, such as sales contracts, you will want to find out how the courts have interpreted and applied the relevant state statute or statutory provision.

In addition to lawsuits involving contract law, the common law also applies to *tort law* (the law governing civil wrongs, such as negligence or assault and battery, as opposed to criminal wrongs). As a paralegal, you may be working on behalf of clients bringing or defending against the following types of actions, all of which involve tort law:

- *Personal-injury lawsuits*—actions brought by plaintiffs to obtain compensation for injuries allegedly caused by the wrongful acts of others, either intentionally or through negligence.

- *Malpractice lawsuits*—actions brought by plaintiffs against professionals, such as physicians and attorneys, to obtain compensation for injuries allegedly caused by professional negligence (breach of professional duties).

- *Product liability lawsuits*—actions brought by plaintiffs to obtain compensation for injuries allegedly caused by defective products.

Numerous other areas, such as property law and employment law, are also still governed to some extent by the common law. Depending on the nature of your job as a paralegal, you may be dealing with many common law issues.

The Adversarial System of Justice

adversarial system of justice

A legal system in which the parties to a lawsuit are opponents, or adversaries, and present their cases in the light most favorable to themselves. The impartial decision maker (the judge or jury) determines who wins based on an application of the law to the evidence presented.

U.S. courts, like English courts, follow the **adversarial system of justice**, in which the parties act as adversaries, or opponents. Parties to a lawsuit come before the court as contestants, both sides presenting the facts of their cases in the light most favorable to themselves, in an attempt to "win" the "battle." The parties do not come together in the courtroom with the idea of working out a compromise solution to their problems or of looking at the dispute from each other's point of view. Rather, they take sides, present their best case to the judge or jury (if it is a jury trial), and hope that this impartial decision maker rules in their favor.

The Goal Is to Win

Most people do not fully appreciate the impact that the adversarial nature of the legal system has on those who work within the system. In an adversarial system, the goal of the attorneys (and paralegals) is not so much to determine the truth as to win the case. An attorney's job is not to seek out or reveal the truth to judges (although ethical rules prohibit attorneys from presenting evidence that they know to be untrue). Rather, the role of the attorney is to discover and present the strongest legal argument on behalf of a client, regardless of the attorney's personal feelings about the client or the client's case. Because of the adversarial nature of our system, you may be asked to work on cases that you do not believe in or for clients you do not like.

Criticisms of the Adversarial System

The adversarial nature of proceedings frames the practice of law in many respects. Lawyers are under pressure to win cases. Lawyers may be pressured by the other attorneys in a law firm to win a particular client's case. Additionally, others who work in the lawyer's firm will likely be affected by the lawyer's success or failure in court.

Some people criticize our adversarial system of justice, believing that it contributes to a lack of integrity in the legal profession. After all, the idea is that a trial is supposed to lead to justice. Some attorneys actually make higher incomes by prolonging disputes and obscuring the truth. The public may even view a lawyer who has successfully defended a criminal client as unethical because the client was found not guilty due to a "technicality."

Although our system is not perfect, most Americans agree that everyone should be allowed her or his "day in court" and should be given the opportunity to have legal advice and guidance in presenting her or his case. These are the foundations of the

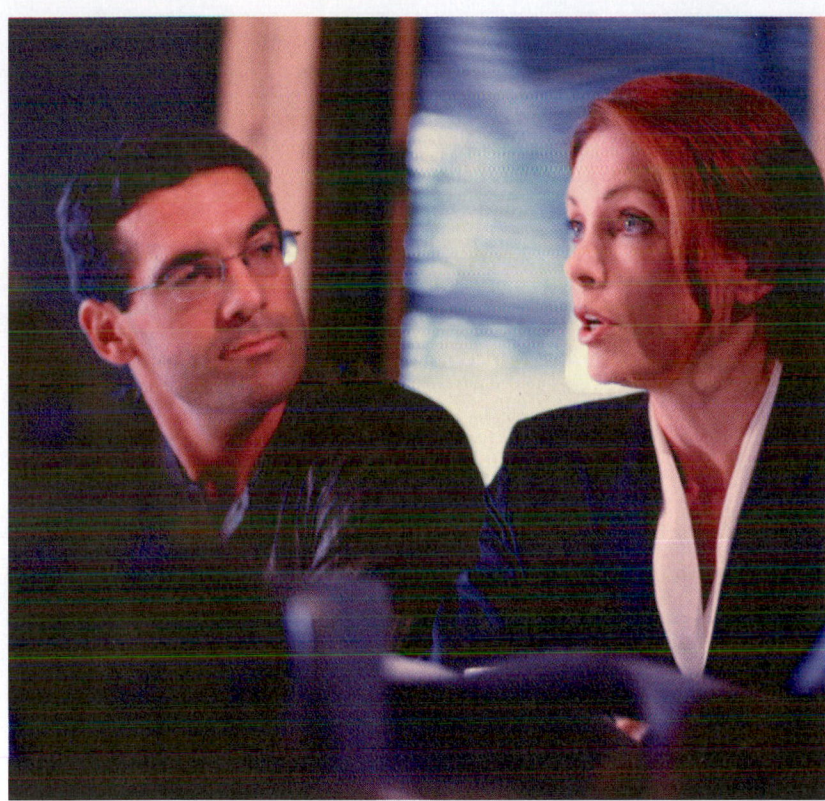

Why is the common law important even in areas that are primarily governed by statutory law?

(Courtesy of © Thinkstock)

concept of due process of law (which you will read more about in Chapter 13). The adversarial system is basic to what we consider to be justice in the United States.

CONSTITUTIONAL LAW

We turn next to another primary source of law. The federal government and the states have separate written constitutions that set forth the general organization, powers, and limits of their respective governments. **Constitutional law** is the law as expressed in these constitutions.

constitutional law
Law based on the U.S. Constitution and the constitutions of the states.

The Federal Constitution

The U.S. Constitution is often called the nation's highest law. This principle is set forth in Article VI of the Constitution, which states that the Constitution, laws, and treaties of the United States are "the supreme Law of the Land." This provision is commonly referred to as the **supremacy clause**. A law in violation of the Constitution (including its amendments), no matter what its source, will be declared unconstitutional if it is challenged. For example, if a state legislature enacts a law that conflicts with the federal Constitution, a person or business firm that is subject to that law may challenge its validity in a court action. If the court agrees with the complaining party that the law is unconstitutional, it will declare the law invalid and refuse to enforce it.

The U.S. Constitution consists of seven articles. These articles, which are listed and summarized in Exhibit 5.2 on the next page, set forth the powers of the three branches of government and the relationships among the three branches.

supremacy clause
The provision in Article VI of the U.S. Constitution that declares the Constitution, laws, and treaties of the United States "the supreme Law of the Land."

Constitutional Rights

The need for a written declaration of rights of individuals eventually caused the first Congress of the United States to submit amendments to the Constitution to the states for approval. Ten amendments, commonly known as the **Bill of Rights**,

Bill of Rights
The first ten amendments to the U.S. Constitution.

EXHIBIT 5.2
The Articles of the U.S. Constitution

Article I creates and empowers the legislature. It provides that Congress is to consist of a Senate and a House of Representatives and fixes the composition of each house and the election procedures, qualifications, and compensation for senators and representatives. Article I also establishes the procedures for enacting legislation and the areas of law in which Congress has the power to legislate.

Article II establishes the executive branch, the process for electing and removing a president from office, the qualifications to be president, and the powers of the president.

Article III creates the judicial branch and authorizes the appointment, compensation, and removal of judges. It also sets forth the jurisdiction of the courts and defines *treason.*

Article IV requires that all states respect one another's laws. It requires each state to give citizens of other states the same rights and privileges it gives its own citizens. It requires that persons accused of crimes be returned to the state in which the crime was committed.

Article V governs how constitutional amendments are formally proposed and ratified.

Article VI establishes the Constitution as the supreme law of the land. It requires that every federal and state official take an oath of office promising to support the Constitution. It specifies that religion is not a required qualification to serve in any federal office.

Article VII required the consent of nine of the original thirteen states to ratify the Constitution.

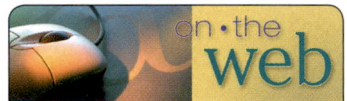

The National Constitution Center provides extensive information on the U.S. Constitution, including its history and current debates over constitutional provisions, at **www.constitutioncenter.org**.

were adopted in 1791 and provide protections for individuals—and in some cases, business entities—against various types of government interference. Summarized below are the protections guaranteed by the Bill of Rights. The full text of the Constitution, including its amendments (there are now twenty-seven), is presented in Appendix J at the end of the book.

1. The First Amendment guarantees the freedoms of religion, speech, and the press and the rights to assemble peaceably and to petition the government.

2. The Second Amendment guarantees the right to keep and bear arms.

3. The Third Amendment prohibits, in peacetime, the lodging of soldiers in any house without the owner's consent.

4. The Fourth Amendment prohibits unreasonable searches and seizures of persons or property.

5. The Fifth Amendment guarantees the rights to indictment by grand jury and to due process of law and prohibits compulsory self-incrimination and double jeopardy. (These terms and concepts will be defined in Chapter 13, which deals with criminal law and procedures.) The Fifth Amendment also prohibits the taking of private property for public use without just compensation.

6. The Sixth Amendment guarantees the accused in a criminal case the right to a speedy and public trial by an impartial jury and the right to counsel. The accused has the right to cross-examine witnesses against him or her and to solicit testimony from witnesses in his or her favor.

7. The Seventh Amendment guarantees the right to a trial by jury in a civil case involving at least twenty dollars.[4]

8. The Eighth Amendment prohibits excessive bail and fines, as well as cruel and unusual punishment.

9. The Ninth Amendment establishes that the people have rights in addition to those specified in the Constitution.

10. The Tenth Amendment establishes that those powers neither delegated to the federal government nor denied to the states are reserved for the states.

Originally, the Bill of Rights limited only the powers of the national government. Over time, however, the Supreme Court incorporated these rights into protections against state actions through the Fourteenth Amendment to the Constitution. That amendment, passed in 1868 after the Civil War, provides in part: "No State shall . . . deprive any person of life, liberty, or property, without due process of law." Starting in 1925, the Supreme Court began to define various rights and liberties guaranteed in the national Constitution as "due process of law," which was required of state governments under the Fourteenth Amendment. Today, most of the rights set forth in the Bill of Rights—such as the freedoms of speech and religion guaranteed by the First Amendment—apply to state governments as well as to the national government.

The Courts and Constitutional Law

The rights secured by the Bill of Rights are not absolute. The principles outlined in the Constitution are given form and substance by the courts. Courts often have to balance the rights and freedoms stated in the Bill of Rights against other rights, such as the right to be free from the harmful actions of others. Ultimately, it is the United States Supreme Court, as the final interpreter of the Constitution, that both gives meaning to our constitutional rights and determines their boundaries.

Courts Balance the Right to Free Speech. An example of how the courts must balance the rights and freedoms granted by the Constitution can be found by looking at our right to free speech. Even though the First Amendment guarantees the right to free speech, we are not, in fact, free to say anything we want. ▶ **EXAMPLE 5.5** In interpreting the meaning of the First Amendment, the Supreme Court has made it clear that certain speech will not be protected. Speech that harms the good reputation of another, for instance, is commonly considered to be a tort, or civil wrong. If the speaker is sued, she may be ordered by a court to pay damages to the harmed person (as you will read in Chapter 14). ◀

Free Speech and the Internet. The Internet has raised new problems for the courts in determining how to define and apply the protections conferred by the Constitution, particularly with regard to free speech. For example, the Supreme Court has ruled that obscene speech, though difficult to define, is not entitled to complete First Amendment protection. Regulating obscene speech in the online environment, however, has proved to be difficult. ▶ **EXAMPLE 5.6** Congress first attempted to prohibit *online obscenity* in the Communications Decency Act (CDA) of 1996, which made it a crime to make available to minors online any "obscene or indecent" message.[5] Civil rights groups claimed the CDA was an unconstitutional restraint on speech. The Supreme Court held that portions of the act were unconstitutional in *Reno v. American Civil Liberties Union*.[6] Congress then passed the Child Online Protection Act (COPA).[7] That law was struck down by a federal appeals court as being unconstitutional because it was too vague.[8] In 2009, the Supreme Court agreed with that ruling.[9] ◀

State Constitutions

Each state has a constitution that sets forth the general organization, powers, and limits of the state government. The Tenth Amendment to the U.S. Constitution, which defines the powers and limitations of the federal government, reserves all powers not granted to the federal government to the states. Unless they conflict

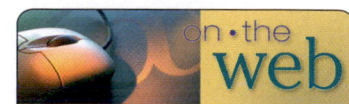

Information on the role of the United States Supreme Court in interpreting the Constitution is available at **www.supremecourt.gov**. From the "About the Supreme Court" menu, select "The Court and Constitutional Interpretation."

If you are interested in looking at state constitutions, including the one for your state, go to **lp.findlaw.com**. From the "Research the Law" menu near the bottom of the page, select "Cases and Codes."

142 PART 1 THE PARALEGAL PROFESSION

with the U.S. Constitution, state constitutions are supreme within the states' borders. State constitutions are thus important sources of law.

CONSTITUTIONAL LAW AND THE PARALEGAL

Many paralegals assist attorneys in handling cases that involve constitutional provisions or rights. For example, a corporate client might claim that a regulation issued by a state administrative agency, such as the state department of natural resources, is invalid because it conflicts with a federal law or regulation. (Administrative agencies will be discussed later in this chapter.) You may be assigned the task of finding out which regulation takes priority. Many cases arise in which the plaintiff claims that his or her First Amendment rights have been violated. Suppose that a plaintiff's religious beliefs forbid working on a certain day of the week. If he or she is required to work on that day, the plaintiff may claim that the employer's require-

ment violates the First Amendment, which guarantees the free exercise of religion.

No matter what kind of work you do, you will find a knowledge of constitutional law helpful. This is because the authority and underlying rationale for the substantive and procedural laws governing many areas of law are ultimately based on the Constitution. For example, knowledge of constitutional law is useful in the area of criminal law, because criminal procedures are essentially designed to protect the constitutional rights of accused persons—as you will read in Chapter 13. (For a further discussion of the application of constitutional law concepts to legal work in other areas, see this chapter's *Featured Contributor* article starting on page 144.)

STATUTORY LAW

statute
A written law enacted by a legislature under its constitutional lawmaking authority.

statutory law
The body of written laws enacted by the legislature.

Statutes, which are laws enacted by legislative bodies at any level of government, make up another source of law. The body of written laws created by the legislature is generally referred to as **statutory law**.

Federal Statutes

Federal statutes are laws that are enacted by the U.S. Congress. As mentioned, any law—including a federal statute—that violates the U.S. Constitution will be held unconstitutional. Examples of federal statutes include laws protecting intellectual property rights (see Chapter 15), laws regulating the purchase and sale of corporate stock (see Chapter 18), statutes prohibiting employment discrimination (see Chapter 18), many environmental regulations (see Chapter 19), and consumer protection statutes (discussed in Chapter 14).

The Federal Government's Constitutional Authority to Enact Laws

federal system
The system of government established by the Constitution, in which the national government and the state governments share sovereign powers.

In the **federal system** of government established by the Constitution, the national government (often called the federal government) and the state governments *share* sovereign power. The Constitution specifies, however, that certain powers can be exercised only by the national government. For example, the national government was authorized to regulate domestic and foreign commerce (trade). The president of the United States was declared to be the nation's chief executive and commander in chief of the armed forces. And, as already noted, the Constitution made it clear that laws made by the national government take priority over conflicting state laws. At the same time, the Constitution provided for certain states' rights, including the right to control commerce within state borders and to exercise powers to protect public health, safety, morals, and general welfare.

To prevent the possibility that the national government might use its power arbitrarily, the Constitution divided the national government's powers among three branches:

- The legislative branch, or Congress, which makes the laws.

Ethics Watch

THE STATUTE OF LIMITATIONS AND THE DUTY OF COMPETENCE

The duty of competence requires, among other things, that attorneys and paralegals be aware of the statute of limitations governing a client's legal matter. Assume, for example, that a client of your firm, a restaurant owner, wants to sue a restaurant-supply company for breaking a contract for the sale of dishes. If the attorney asks you to look into the matter, the first thing you should check is your state's statute of limitations covering contracts for the sale of goods. If the time period has already expired, then your attorney will need to advise the client accordingly. If the time period is about to expire, then you and your supervising attorney need to act quickly to make sure that the complaint (the document that initiates a lawsuit) is filed before the time period expires.

Of course, the attorney is responsible to the client, but it is normal for an attorney to rely on a paralegal to check such details. This example reflects the NFPA Model Code of Ethics and Professional Responsibility, Section 1.1(a), "A paralegal shall achieve competency through education, training, and work experience," and Section 1.1(c), "A paralegal shall perform all assignments promptly and efficiently."

- The executive branch, which enforces the laws.
- The judicial branch, which interprets the laws.

Each branch performs a separate function, and no branch may exercise the authority of another branch. Each branch, however, has some power to limit the actions of the other two branches. Congress, for example, can enact legislation relating to spending and commerce, but the president can veto that legislation. The executive branch is responsible for foreign affairs, but treaties with foreign governments require approval by the Senate. Although Congress determines the jurisdiction of the federal courts, the federal courts have the power to hold acts of the other branches of the federal government unconstitutional. With this system of **checks and balances**, no one branch of government can accumulate too much power.

The Expansion of National Powers under the Commerce Clause

Congress cannot legislate on a matter unless it has constitutional authority to act on that matter. Article I, Section 8, of the Constitution expressly permits Congress to "regulate Commerce with foreign Nations, and among the several States, and with the Indian Tribes." This clause, which is known as the **commerce clause**, was initially interpreted to mean that the federal government's regulatory powers were limited to *interstate* commerce (business across state lines) and not applicable to *intrastate* commerce (business within a state). In 1824, however, the United States Supreme Court concluded that business within a state could also be regulated by the national government as long as the commerce *substantially affected* commerce involving more than one state.[10]

As the nation grew and faced new kinds of problems, this interpretation of the commerce clause was used to expand the national government's regulatory powers. Even activities that seemed purely local came under the regulatory reach of the federal government. ▶ **EXAMPLE 5.7** In a landmark ruling in 1942, the Supreme Court held that a small amount of wheat grown by one farmer intended

checks and balances
A system in which each of the three branches of the national government—executive, legislative, and judicial—exercises a check on the actions of the other two branches.

commerce clause
The provision in Article I, Section 8, of the U.S. Constitution that gives the national government the power to regulate interstate commerce.

featured contributor

THE INTERRELATIONSHIP OF THE VARIOUS AREAS OF LAW

S. Whittington Brown

BIOGRAPHICAL NOTE

S. Whittington Brown earned a bachelor of arts degree from Rhodes College in 1981 and earned a law degree from the University of Arkansas in 1984. He is licensed to practice in the state of Arkansas, the United States District Court, and the United States Court of Appeals. He has served as an attorney and an attorney supervisor for the Arkansas Department of Human Services. He is currently the chief investigator for Developmental Disabilities Services and is a licensed polygraph examiner.

At Pulaski Technical College, Brown taught American national government, legal terminology, legal research and writing, legal environment of business, business organizations, and torts. He is also the author of *Legal Terminology,* published by Delmar Cengage Learning. Brown was recognized as an Outstanding Citizen of the State of Arkansas by then-governor Bill Clinton.

L aw is divided into many different subject areas. An attorney may specialize in personal-injury, property, employment, or contract law, for example. None of these areas, however, exists in a vacuum. One legal principle may apply to many different areas of the law, and one subject area may influence others. An important skill that a paralegal must develop is the ability to see the relationships among areas of law that may appear to be totally unrelated. Consider just one example: the application of constitutional law concepts to the areas of criminal law and employment law. At first, it would appear that criminal law and employment law have nothing in common, but there are provisions of constitutional law that apply to both areas.

Article VI, Clause 2, of the Constitution of the United States states, "This Constitution and the Laws of the United States which shall be made in pursuance thereof . . . shall be the supreme Law of the Land." In other words, the Constitution is the highest source of law in the country, and other laws are inferior to the Constitution. Because of this clause, known as the supremacy clause, provisions of the U.S. Constitution can apply to many different areas of the law.

One of the main provisions of constitutional law is the principle of due process of law. According to the Fifth and Fourteenth Amendments to the Constitution, no person shall be deprived of life, liberty, or property, without due process of law. The concept of due process has two parts, substantive due process and procedural due process. *Substantive due process* means that the law itself, that which is being enforced, must be fair. The law must be applied the same way to every person and must not discriminate against anyone. *Procedural due process* means that the method used to enforce the law must be fair; it must be applied the same way to every person. One such element of due process of law is contained in the Fourth Amendment—the prohibition against unreasonable searches and seizures.

The application of this principle to the area of criminal law is fairly obvious. A person, because of an alleged violation

for consumption on his own farm was subject to federal regulation because even a tiny amount had some impact on the interstate wheat business.[11] ◄

Today, the commerce power is presumed to authorize the national government to regulate every commercial enterprise in the United States. Many of the federal statutes that you will read about in this book rest on Congress's authority to regulate interstate commerce. Federal statutes now govern almost every major activity conducted by businesses—from hiring and firing decisions to workplace safety, competitive practices, and financing.

of the law, faces the loss of property, liberty, or even life, depending upon the seriousness of the offense. Before the state can deprive the person of any of these things, the person is entitled to due process of law. This includes such rights as the right to be represented by an attorney, the right to a trial by a jury of his or her peers, the right to know the charges against him or her, the right to confront his or her accusers, and the right to present evidence in his or her defense. Also, any evidence seized in violation of the Fourth Amendment cannot be used against the defendant. A paralegal working in the area of criminal law must not only be aware of the crimes and what makes up each element of the crime but also must be aware of the due process rights guaranteed by the U.S. Constitution to a person who is accused of a crime.

Principles of constitutional law also apply to the employment relationship. The Fourth Amendment limitations on unreasonable searches and seizures apply to the workplace in combination with the right to privacy. The right to privacy—the right to be left alone and to be free from unwarranted publicity and interference—was created by the United States Supreme Court in the case of *Griswold v. Connecticut*.[a] The Court has stated that there are zones of privacy that apply to a person regardless of the situation in which a person may find himself or herself, including the workplace.

The limitations on searches and seizures and the right to privacy apply in the workplace when an employer wants to conduct searches of employees. An employer may have several reasons for wanting to conduct employee searches: to protect itself against employee theft, to protect sensitive material, and to ensure that illegal conduct is not occurring at the work site.

> *"An important skill that a paralegal must develop is the ability to see the relationships among areas of law that may appear to be totally unrelated."*

An employee, however, is protected against unreasonable searches and seizures by the Fourth Amendment and has an expectation of privacy, even in the workplace. In order for a workplace search to take place, certain criteria must be met.

The United States Supreme Court case of *O'Connor v. Ortega*[b] helped set out the criteria for when a search of an employee can take place. First, the employee's expectation of privacy must be reduced. In order to lessen the expectation, the employer is required to implement a policy establishing when and under what circumstances a search of the workplace may take place. Also, in order to conduct a valid workplace search, the search must be reasonable and based on allegations made against the employee, the purpose of the search should be clearly established, and the search should be limited in scope. The principles established by the limitation on searches and seizures and the right to privacy have also been applied to the use of lie-detector tests, drug tests, background checks, references, and credit checks in employment situations.

These are just two examples of how one area of law may interact with other areas. A basic principle of constitutional law applies to both criminal law and employment law. Employment law not only involves elements of constitutional law but also contains elements of contract law and agency law. Product liability and environmental protection laws are based in part on tort law principles, and insurance law contains elements of contract law and tort law. A paralegal must be able to see how the different areas of the law interact with each other and realize that no area of the law exists in a vacuum.

---

a. 381 U.S. 479 (1965).

b. 480 U.S. 708 (1987).

The Federal Lawmaking Process

Each law passed by Congress begins as a *bill*, which may be introduced either in the House of Representatives or in the Senate. Often, similar bills are introduced in both chambers of Congress. In either chamber, the House or the Senate, the bill is then referred to a committee and its subcommittees for study, discussion, hearings, and rewriting. If the committee does not approve the bill, it "dies" and goes no further. If approved, it is scheduled for debate by the full House or Senate. Finally, a vote is taken, and the bill is either passed or defeated. If the two chambers pass similar bills containing somewhat different provisions, a *conference committee* is formed to write a compromise bill, which must then be approved by both chambers before it is sent to the president to sign. Once the president signs the bill, it becomes law.

During the legislative process, bills are identified by a number. A bill in the House of Representatives is identified by a number preceded by "HR" (such as HR 212), indicating that it is a House of Representatives bill. In the Senate, the bill's number is preceded by an "S" (such as S 212). When both chambers pass the bill and it is signed into law by the president, the statute is initially published in the form of a pamphlet or a single sheet, known as a *slip law*. The slip law is assigned a **public law number**, or P.L. number (such as P.L. 5030). At the end of the two-year congressional term, or session, the statute is published in the term's *session laws*, which are collections of statutes contained in volumes and arranged by year or legislative session. Ultimately, the statute is included in the *United States Code*, in which all federal laws are codified (systematized, or arranged in topical order) and published. (See Chapter 7 for further details on how federal statutes are published.)

> **public law number**
> An identification number assigned to a statute.

State Statutes

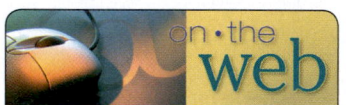

State statutes are laws enacted by state legislatures. Any state law that is found by a court to conflict with the U.S. Constitution or with the state's constitution will be deemed unconstitutional. State statutes include state laws governing real property and insurance (see Chapter 16), estates and family law (discussed in Chapter 17), the formation of corporations and other business entities (see Chapter 18), and certain crimes (see Chapter 13), along with state versions of the Uniform Commercial Code (to be discussed shortly).

> A good starting point to access state statutes online is **www.law.cornell.edu**. From the "Law by source or jurisdiction" menu, select "State law." Then select "state list."

Conflicts between Federal and State Laws

If a state statute is found to conflict with a federal statute, the state law is invalid. Because some powers are concurrent, however, it is necessary to determine which law governs in a particular circumstance. *Concurrent powers* are shared by the federal government and the states, such as the power to impose taxes or to establish courts.

Preemption occurs when Congress chooses to act exclusively in a concurrent area. In this circumstance, a valid federal law or regulation in the preempted area will take precedence over a conflicting state or local law or regulation. Often, it is not clear whether Congress, in passing a law, intended to preempt an entire area of law. In these situations, it is left to the courts to determine Congress's intention. No single factor determines whether a court will find preemption. Generally, congressional intent to preempt will be found if a federal law regulating an activity is so comprehensive or detailed that the states have little or no room to regulate in that area. Also, when a federal statute creates an agency—such as the National Labor Relations Board—to enforce the law, matters that come within the agency's jurisdiction will likely preempt state laws. Congress has held that the states may regulate some areas of business, such as insurance. In those areas, Congress generally does not preempt state law. As the *Developing Paralegal Skills* feature discusses, federal preemption of state law can be a critical issue.

> **preemption**
> A doctrine under which a federal law preempts, or takes precedence over, conflicting state and local laws.

The State Lawmaking Process

When passing laws, state legislatures follow procedures similar to those followed in Congress. All of the states except one have bicameral (two-chamber) legislatures. (Nebraska has a unicameral, or one-chamber, legislature.) Typically, bills may be introduced in either chamber, or both chambers, of the legislature. As in the U.S. Congress, if the two chambers pass similar bills that differ from one another in any respect, a conference committee works out a compromise, which must then be approved by both chambers before being sent to the state's governor to sign into law.

STATE VERSUS FEDERAL REGULATION

Stephanie Wilson works as a paralegal in the legal department of National Pipeline, Inc., whose business is transporting natural gas to local utilities, factories, and other sites around the country. Last month, one of National's pipelines, which ran under a residential street in Minneapolis, Minnesota, exploded, resulting in several injuries and one death.

The federal government has regulated pipeline safety and maintenance since 1968, under the Natural Gas Pipeline Safety Act. As a result of the explosion, the state of Minnesota wants to regulate pipeline safety as well. Stephanie's boss, the general counsel of the company, and several other executives believe that the federal act preempts this field of law, preventing the state from enacting another layer of safety legislation. Stephanie is assigned the task of researching the statute and relevant case law to determine if the federal law does in fact preempt the state's regulation.

TIPS FOR DETERMINING FEDERAL PREEMPTION

- Read through the statute to see if it expressly states that Congress intended to preempt the relevant field (in this case, pipeline safety).

- Look for indications that Congress has impliedly occupied the field: Is the federal regulatory scheme pervasive? Is federal occupation of the field necessitated by the need for national uniformity? Is there a danger of conflict between state laws and the administration of the federal program?

- Locate and read cases discussing the issue of federal preemption in this area. Brief any cases that appear to be relevant to this issue. (See Chapter 7 for instructions on how to brief a case.)

Local Ordinances

Statutory law also includes local ordinances. An **ordinance** is an order, rule, or law passed by a city or county government to govern matters not covered by federal or state law. Ordinances may not violate the U.S. Constitution, the relevant state constitution, or federal or state law. Local ordinances often have to do with land use (zoning ordinances), building and safety codes, construction and appearance of housing, and other matters affecting a local area. Persons who violate ordinances may be fined, jailed, or both.

> **ordinance**
> An order, rule, or law enacted by a municipal or county government to govern a local matter not addressed by state or federal legislation.

Uniform Laws

State laws vary from state to state. The differences were particularly notable in the 1800s, when conflicting statutes created problems for the rapidly developing trade among the states. To counter these problems, a group of legal scholars and lawyers formed the National Conference of Commissioners on Uniform State Laws (NCCUSL) in 1892 to draft uniform ("model") statutes for adoption by the states. The NCCUSL continues to issue uniform statutes, often in conjunction with the American Law Institute.

Adoption of uniform laws is a state matter, and a state may reject all or part of model laws or rewrite them as the state legislature wishes. Hence, even when a uniform law is said to have been adopted in many states, the laws may not be entirely "uniform." Once adopted by a state legislature, a uniform act becomes a part of the statutory law of that state. A good example of a uniform law that has been adopted (at least in part) by all fifty states is the Uniform Commercial Code (UCC) (discussed in Chapter 15), which provides a set of rules governing commercial transactions and sales contracts.

STATUTORY LAW AND THE PARALEGAL

As a paralegal, you are likely to deal with cases that involve violations of statutory law. If you work for a small law firm, you may become familiar with the statutory law governing a wide range of activities. If you specialize in one area, such as bankruptcy law, you will become very familiar with the law governing that area. Here are a few examples of areas in which you might work that are governed extensively by statutory law:

- *Corporate law*—governed by state statutes.
- *Patent, copyright, and trademark law*—governed by federal statutes.
- *Employment law*—governed more and more by federal statutes concerning discrimination in employment, workplace safety, labor unions, pension plans, Social Security, and other aspects of employment. Each state also has statutes governing certain areas of employment, such as safety standards and employment discrimination.

- *Antitrust law*—governed by federal statutes prohibiting specific types of anticompetitive business practices.
- *Consumer law*—governed by state and federal statutes protecting consumers against deceptive trade practices (such as misleading advertising), unsafe products, and activities that threaten consumer health and welfare.
- *Wills and probate administration* (relating to the transfer of property on the property owner's death)—governed by state statutes.

You will read about some of these areas of law in later chapters. A paralegal working on a case governed by statutory law needs to know how to locate and interpret the relevant state or federal statutes. You will learn how to find and analyze statutory law in Chapter 7.

ADMINISTRATIVE LAW

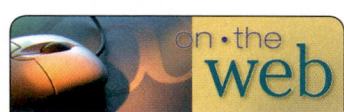

The *United States Government Manual* describes the origins, purposes, and administrators of every federal department and agency. You can access this publication online at **www.gpoaccess.gov/gmanual**.

administrative law

A body of law created by administrative agencies in the form of rules, regulations, orders, and decisions in order to carry out their duties and responsibilities.

administrative agency

A federal or state government agency established to perform a specific function. Administrative agencies are authorized by legislative acts to make and enforce rules relating to the purpose for which they were established.

Another important source of American law is **administrative law**. It consists of the rules, orders, and decisions of administrative agencies. An **administrative agency** is a federal, state, or local government agency established to perform a specific function, such as the regulation of food sold to consumers. Rules issued by administrative agencies affect most aspects of a business's operation, including the firm's financing, its hiring and firing procedures, its relations with employees and unions, and the way it manufactures and markets its products.

At the federal level, there are many administrative agencies, each of which has been established to perform specific governing tasks. ▶ **EXAMPLE 5.8** The federal Environmental Protection Agency coordinates and enforces federal environmental laws. The federal Food and Drug Administration enforces federal laws relating to the safety of foods and drugs. The Securities and Exchange Commission regulates purchases and sales of securities (corporate stocks and bonds). ◀

There are administrative agencies at the state and local levels as well. Some state agencies are created as parallels to a federal agency. State environmental agencies, for example, parallel the federal Environmental Protection Agency. Other state agencies, such as those dealing with workers' compensation, have no comparable federal agency. Just as federal statutes take precedence over conflicting state statutes, so do federal agency regulations take precedence over conflicting state regulations. Because the rules of state and local agencies vary widely, we focus here exclusively on federal administrative law. Notice that some administrative agencies allow paralegals to practice before them, as discussed in the *Developing Paralegal Skills* feature.

Agency Creation

Because Congress cannot possibly oversee the actual implementation of all the laws it enacts, it must delegate such tasks to others, particularly when the issues relate to technical areas, such as air and water pollution. Congress creates an administra-

Developing
Paralegal Skills

APPROVAL TO PRACTICE BEFORE THE IRS

Damian Forsythe has an associate's degree in accounting and is also interested in law. He has learned that some administrative agencies allow nonlawyers to practice before them. One of those agencies is the Internal Revenue Service (IRS). Damian would be allowed to represent clients before the IRS and to advise clients on tax matters without engaging in the unauthorized practice of law.

Damian contacts the Office of the Director of Practice in Washington, D.C. The administrative assistant who answers the telephone explains that the IRS allows nonlawyers and noncertified public accountants to practice before the agency. First, though, they must pass the "Enrolled Agents" exam and be admitted to practice. A person wishing to apply for admission to practice must submit Form 23 and must meet certain requirements, such as being current in one's own personal income tax payments. There are no educational requirements, but the exam is very difficult and requires a knowledge of accounting, tax laws, and regulations. It is given only once a year, usually in September.

Damian is told that Form 2587, which he can use to register for the exam, is available online at the IRS's Web site at **www.irs.gov**. He can also obtain a copy of Form 23 from the Web site. Damian uses his computer to explore the possibility of representing clients before the IRS.

TIPS FOR CONTACTING AN ADMINISTRATIVE AGENCY

- Try to identify a person at the agency who can help you obtain the information you seek.
- Consider checking online sources to see if there is an agency directory that lists employee names and departments.
- If you place a blind call, think about your question ahead of time and about which department might be able to answer it.
- Obtain the name and telephone number of the person you are trying to reach before being transferred to that person.
- Be patient and polite.

---

tive agency by passing **enabling legislation**, which specifies the name, composition, purpose, and powers of the agency being created.

► **EXAMPLE 5.9** The Federal Trade Commission (FTC) was created in 1914 by the Federal Trade Commission Act. This act prohibits unfair and deceptive trade practices. It also describes the procedures the agency must follow to charge persons or organizations with violations of the act, and it provides for judicial review (review by the courts) of agency orders. Other portions of the act grant the agency powers to "make rules and regulations for the purpose of carrying out the Act," to conduct investigations of business practices, to obtain reports from interstate corporations concerning their business practices, to investigate possible violations of the act, to publish findings of its investigations, and to recommend new legislation. The act also empowers the FTC to hold trial-like hearings and to **adjudicate** (resolve judicially) certain kinds of trade disputes that involve FTC regulations. ◄

Note that the FTC's grant of power incorporates functions associated with the legislative branch of government (rulemaking), the executive branch (investigation and enforcement), and the judicial branch (adjudication). Taken together, these functions constitute *administrative process*.

enabling legislation
A statute enacted by a legislature that authorizes the creation of an administrative agency and specifies the name, purpose, composition, and powers of the agency being created.

adjudicate
To resolve a dispute judicially.

Rulemaking

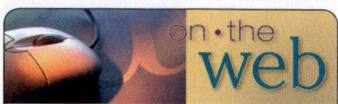

One of the major functions of an administrative agency is **rulemaking**—creating or modifying rules, or regulations. The Administrative Procedure Act of 1946 imposes strict procedural requirements that agencies must follow in their rulemaking and other functions.

The most common rulemaking procedure involves three steps. First, the agency must give public notice of the proposed rulemaking proceedings, where and when the proceedings will be held, the agency's legal authority for the proceedings, and the terms or subject matter of the proposed rule. The notice must be published in the *Federal Register,* a daily publication of the U.S. government. Second, following this notice, the agency must allow time for interested parties to comment in writing on the proposed rule. After the comments have been reviewed, the agency takes them into consideration when drafting the final version of the regulation. The third and last step is the drafting of the final rule and its publication in the *Federal Register.* (See Chapter 7 for an explanation of how to find agency regulations.)

Investigation and Enforcement

Agencies have both investigatory and prosecutorial powers. When conducting an investigation, an agency can request that individuals or organizations hand over specific papers, files, or other documents. In addition, agencies may conduct on-site inspections, although a search warrant is normally required for inspections. Sometimes, a search of a home, an office, or a factory is the only way to obtain evidence needed to prove a regulatory violation. Agencies investigate a wide range of activities, including coal mining, automobile manufacturing, and the discharge of pollutants into the environment.

After investigating a suspected rule violation, an agency may take administrative action against an individual or a business. Most actions are resolved through negotiated settlements, without the need for formal adjudication. If a settlement cannot be reached, the agency may issue a formal complaint against the suspected violator, and the case may proceed to adjudication.

Adjudication

Agency adjudication involves a trial-like hearing before an **administrative law judge (ALJ)**. The ALJ presides over the hearing and has the power to administer oaths, take testimony, rule on questions of evidence, and make determinations of fact. Although the ALJ works for the agency prosecuting the case, he or she is required by law to be an unbiased adjudicator (judge). Hearing procedures vary from agency to agency. They may be informal meetings conducted at a table in a conference room, or they may be formal hearings resembling trials. In some agencies, paralegals are allowed to represent clients at these hearings.

After the hearing, the ALJ issues a decision on the case. The ALJ may compel the charged party to pay a fine or may prohibit the party from carrying on a certain activity. Either side may appeal the ALJ's decision to the commission or board that governs the agency. If the party fails to get relief there, appeal can be made to a federal court. If no party appeals the case, or if the commission and the court decline to review the case, the ALJ's decision becomes final.

ADMINISTRATIVE LAW AND THE PARALEGAL

The functions of administrative agencies permeate almost every area of legal practice. No matter where you work, sooner or later you will be interacting with a government agency. As an example, suppose you work for a small law firm that specializes in personal-injury claims. You may be required to communicate directly with an investigator for the Occupational Safety and Health Administration when the firm handles a personal-injury claim involving an employer's violation of workplace safety standards.

Paralegals who work for law firms that have many corporate clients may be extensively involved in researching and analyzing agency regulations and their applicability to certain business activities. If you work in a corporate legal department, you may be asked to determine which agency regulations apply to the business and whether it is complying with those regulations. Of course, if you work for an administrative agency, you may be involved in drafting new rules, analyzing survey results to see if a new regulation is necessary, mediating disputes between private parties and the agency, conducting investiga-

tions to gather facts about compliance with agency rules, and numerous other agency-related tasks.

Paralegals often become familiar with the administrative process when helping clients obtain benefits from state or federal agencies. A paralegal helping homeless persons to obtain medical assistance, for example, would work closely with local agencies. As already mentioned, some administrative agencies, including the Social Security Administration and the Internal Revenue Service, allow paralegals to represent clients at agency hearings and other procedures. Finally, in any law practice, you may be asked to assist clients who are involved in disputes with administrative agencies.

NATIONAL AND INTERNATIONAL LAW

Because business and other activities are increasingly global in scope, many cases now brought before U.S. courts relate to issues involving foreign parties or governments. The laws of other nations and international doctrines or agreements may affect the outcome of these cases. Hence, those laws, doctrines, and agreements are sources of law that guide judicial decisions in U.S. courts. Many paralegals, particularly those who work for law firms with clients operating in foreign countries, may need to become familiar with the legal systems of other nations during the course of their careers. For example, if you work in a firm in Arizona, California, New Mexico, or Texas, you may assist in the representation of Mexican clients. In this situation, you will want to have some familiarity with Mexican law and any international agreements that regulate U.S.-Mexican relations, such as the North American Free Trade Agreement (NAFTA).

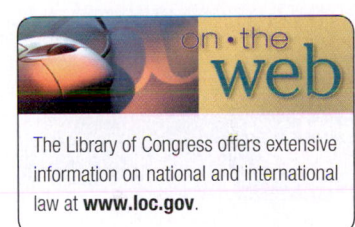

The Library of Congress offers extensive information on national and international law at **www.loc.gov**.

National Law

The law of a particular nation is referred to as **national law**. The laws of nations differ because each country's laws reflect that nation's own unique cultural, historical, economic, and political background. Broadly speaking, however, there are two types of legal systems used by the various countries of the world. We have already discussed one of these systems—the common law system of England and the United States. Generally, countries that were once colonies of Great Britain retained their English common law heritage after they achieved their independence. Today, common law systems exist in several countries, including Australia, Canada, India, Ireland, and Nigeria.

In contrast to Great Britain and the common law countries, most European nations base their legal systems on Roman *civil law*, or "code law." The term *civil law*, as used here, refers not to civil as opposed to criminal law but to *codified law*—an ordered grouping of legal principles enacted into law by a legislature or governing body. In a **civil law system**, the primary source of law is a statutory code, and case precedents are not judicially binding, as they normally are in a common law system. This is not to say that precedents are unimportant in a civil law system; judges in such systems do refer to previous decisions as sources of legal guidance. The difference is that judges in a civil law system are not obligated to follow precedent to the extent that judges in a common law system are; in other words, the doctrine of *stare decisis* does not apply.

Today, the civil law system is followed in most of the continental European countries, as well as in the Latin American, African, and Asian countries that were once colonies of the continental European nations. Japan and Thailand also have civil law systems. Ingredients of the civil law system are also found in the Islamic courts of predominantly Muslim countries. In the United States, the state of Louisiana, because of its historical ties to France, has in part a civil law system. The legal systems of Puerto Rico, Québec, and Scotland also have elements of a civil law system.

national law
Law that relates to a particular nation (as opposed to international law).

civil law system
A system of law derived from that of the Roman Empire and based on a code rather than case law; the predominant system of law in the nations of continental Europe and the nations that were once their colonies.

international law

The law that governs relations among nations. International customs and treaties are generally considered to be two of the most important sources of international law.

treaty

An agreement, or compact, formed between two independent nations.

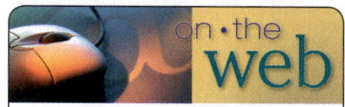

To find information on the laws governing other nations, including constitutions around the world, go to **www.confinder.richmond.edu**.

International Law

Relationships among countries are regulated to an extent by international law. **International law** can be defined as a body of written and unwritten laws observed by independent nations and governing the acts of individuals as well as governments. The key difference between national law and international law is the fact that national law can be enforced by government authorities, whereas international law is enforced primarily for reasons of courtesy or expediency. In essence, international law is the result of centuries-old attempts to reconcile the traditional need of each nation to be the final authority over its own affairs with the desire of nations to benefit economically from trade and good relations with one another. Although no independent nation can be compelled to obey a law external to itself, nations can and do voluntarily agree to be governed in certain respects by international law for the purpose of facilitating international trade and commerce and civilized discourse.

Traditional sources of international law include the customs that have been historically observed by nations in their dealings with each other. Other sources are treaties and international organizations and conferences. A **treaty** is an agreement between two or more nations that creates rights and duties binding on the parties to the treaty, just as a private contract may be used to create rights and duties binding on the parties to the contract. To give effect to a treaty, the supreme power of each nation that is a party to the treaty must ratify it. For example, the U.S. Constitution requires approval by two-thirds of the Senate before a treaty executed by the president will be binding on the U.S. government. *Bilateral agreements,* as their name implies, occur when two nations form an agreement that will govern their relations with one another. *Multilateral agreements* are formed by several nations. The European Union, for example, which regulates commercial activities among its European member nations, is the result of a multilateral trade agreement. Other multilateral agreements have led to the formation of regional trade associations, such as the North American Free Trade Agreement (NAFTA), which was formed by Canada, Mexico, and the United States.

International organizations and conferences also play an important role in the international legal arena. International organizations and conferences adopt resolutions, declarations, and other types of standards that often require a particular behavior of nations. The General Assembly of the United Nations, for example, has adopted numerous resolutions and declarations that embody principles of international law and has sponsored conferences that have led to the formation of international agreements. The United States is a member of more than one hundred multilateral and bilateral organizations, including at least twenty through the United Nations.

INTERNATIONAL LAW AND THE PARALEGAL

Communications technology, improved transportation facilities, and international organizations and treaties have all helped to form a global environment of business. What this means for attorneys and paralegals is that an increasing amount of legal work has an international dimension. As a paralegal, you may be asked to assist your supervising attorney in many tasks that involve an international aspect, including the following:

- Research the law of a foreign country on a particular issue, such as labor law, to determine whether a corporate client (or your corporate employer) with business operations overseas is complying with the laws of the host country.

- Assist a client who has a manufacturing plant overseas in forming employment policies that are consistent with the national law of the host country and (if U.S. employees work at the plant) with U.S. employment laws.

- Determine whether a client's patented product will be protected under the patent laws of a specific foreign country or whether an international treaty provides for such protection.

- Determine what special contractual provisions should be included in a client's contract for the international sale of goods to protect the client's interest.

- Send communications via mail, express delivery services, telephone, e-mail, or fax to the foreign offices of a U.S. firm or a foreign firm with which a U.S. client has business dealings.

Today's
Professional Paralegal

WORKING FOR AN ADMINISTRATIVE AGENCY

The Environmental Protection Agency (EPA) employs several paralegals. One is Mary Ulrich, who works for the Freedom of Information Act (FOIA) officer. As you will read in Chapter 11, the Freedom of Information Act of 1966 requires federal government agencies to disclose certain records to any person on request. Some records, however, are exempt from the requirement. These records include those containing classified information (information concerning national security), confidential materials dealing with trade secrets, government personnel rules, and personal medical files.

A person wishing to obtain government records must submit a written request to the FOIA officer of the federal agency holding the records. The letter should indicate which records are being sought and why (although specifying the purpose of the request is optional). If the request is denied by the federal agency because an exemption applies, the agency must cite the specific exemption. (A sample letter for requesting information under the FOIA is also shown in Chapter 11.)

Mary Ulrich's job involves responding to FOIA requests on behalf of the EPA. FOIA requests must be made in writing, but often legal assistants or attorneys from law firms or corporations call before they submit written requests.

RECEIVING AN INFORMATION REQUEST

Mary's telephone rings. It is Scott Webb, a paralegal with Sims and Howard in Chicago. He wants to talk to Mary about the EPA's file on the Black Hole landfill, a toxic waste site to which one of Sims and Howard's clients has allegedly contributed hazardous waste. Scott wants to know the size of the file on the landfill and the type of information that it contains. If the EPA's file is small enough, Scott will request copies of most of its relevant contents. He will request the copies over the phone and will also follow up on the conversation with a letter. Mary will be able to tell Scott if there are documents in the file that might have to be reviewed by an agency attorney before they can be reproduced.

Mary pulls the file and finds that it contains at least ten thousand pages of documents. She informs Scott of this. Because the agency charges for copying costs, including the time that Mary spends copying the records, Scott asks for specific types of documents. One kind of record that he wants is a list of the types and quantities of hazardous waste that other parties have allegedly contributed to the site.

DEALING WITH FOIA EXEMPTIONS

Mary looks for this information in the file. She finds it but also sees that information on several of the alleged contributors is exempt from FOIA disclosure requirements under trade secrets exemptions. Mary informs Scott of this fact. Scott also wants information on why the agency decided to include his firm's client in the list of contributors to the toxic waste site. Mary reminds Scott that interagency memos are usually privileged and that his request will have to be reviewed by agency counsel to determine if the agency could disclose this information.

Mary and Scott finish their conversation. Mary decides to wait for Scott's formal FOIA letter before starting to work on the request because so many of the documents will have to be reviewed by counsel before they can be sent out. Maybe Scott and the attorney for whom he works will rethink their strategy or make a different request now that they know they will have to wait for a decision from the agency's counsel office, especially when a good part of their request might be denied.

KEY TERMS AND CONCEPTS

adjudicate *149*

administrative agency *148*

administrative law *148*

administrative law judge (ALJ) *150*

adversarial system of justice *138*

Bill of Rights *139*

binding authority *130*

case law *130*

case of first impression *131*

checks and balances *143*

citation *136*

civil law system *151*

commerce clause *143*

common law *130*

constitutional law *139*

court of equity *132*

court of law *131*

enabling legislation *149*

equitable principles and maxims *132*

federal system *142*

injunction *134*

international law *152*

laches *133*

law *129*

national law *151*

opinion *137*

ordinance *147*

party *137*

persuasive precedent *130*

precedent *130*

preemption *146*

primary source of law *129*

public law number *146*

public policy *131*

remedy *131*

remedy at law *131*

remedy in equity *132*

rulemaking *150*

secondary source of law *130*

specific performance *134*

stare decisis *130*

statute *142*

statutory law *142*

supremacy clause *139*

treaty *152*

CHAPTER SUMMARY

SOURCES OF AMERICAN LAW

The Framework of American Law

1. *Definition of law*—The law has been defined variously over time, yet all definitions rest on the assumption that law consists of a body of rules of conduct established and enforced by the controlling authority (the government) of a society.

2. *Primary sources of American law*—There are four primary sources of American law: the common law doctrines developed in cases; the U.S. Constitution and the constitutions of various states; statutory law, including laws passed by Congress, state legislatures, and local governing bodies; and regulations created by administrative agencies.

Case Law and the Common Law Tradition

Case law consists of the decisions issued by judges in cases that come before the court. Case law evolved through the common law tradition, which originated in England and was adopted in America during the colonial era.

1. *Stare decisis*—*Stare decisis* means "to stand on things decided" and is the doctrine of precedent, which is a major characteristic of the common law system. Under this doctrine, judges are obligated to follow the earlier decisions of that court or a higher court within their jurisdiction if the same points arise again in litigation.

   a. A court will depart from precedent if the court decides that the precedent should no longer be followed, such as if the ruling was incorrect or does not apply in view of changes in the social or technological environment.

   b. If no precedent exists, the court considers the matter as a case of first impression and looks to other areas of law and public policy for guidance.

2. *Remedies at law versus remedies in equity*—In medieval England, two types of courts emerged: courts of law and courts of equity. Courts of law granted remedies at law (such as money damages). Courts of equity arose in response to the need for other types of relief. In the United States today, the same court can typically grant either legal or equitable remedies.

3. *Remedies in equity*—Remedies in equity, which are normally available only when the remedy at law (money damages) is inadequate, include the following:

   a. **SPECIFIC PERFORMANCE**—A court decree ordering a party to perform a contractual promise.

   b. **INJUNCTION**—A court order directing someone to do or refrain from doing a particular act.

4. *Statutory law and the common law*—The common law governs all areas of law not covered by statutory law. As the body of statutory law grows to meet different needs, the common law covers fewer areas. Even if an area is governed by a statutory law, however, the common law plays an important role because statutes are interpreted and applied by the courts, and court decisions may become precedents that must be followed by lower courts within the jurisdiction.

5. *Case law terminology*—

   a. **CASE TITLE AND CITATION**—A case title consists of the surnames of the parties, such as *Baranski v. Peretto.* The citation indicates the volume and page number of the reporter in which the case can be found.

   b. **PARTY**—The plaintiff or the defendant. Some cases involve multiple parties—that is, more than one plaintiff or defendant.

   c. **JUDGE AND JUSTICE**—These terms are often used synonymously. Usage of the terms varies among courts. The term *justice* is traditionally used to designate judges who sit on the bench of the United States Supreme Court.

   d. **OPINION**—A document containing the court's reasons for its decision, the rules of law that apply, and the judgment. If the opinion is not unanimous, a majority opinion—reflecting the view of the majority of judges or justices—will be written. Concurring and dissenting opinions may also be written.

6. *The adversarial system of justice*—American courts, like English courts, follow a system of justice in which the parties to a lawsuit are opponents, or adversaries, and present their cases in the light most favorable to themselves. The impartial decision maker (the judge or jury) then determines who wins and who loses based on the evidence presented.

Constitutional Law

Constitutional law is all law that is based on the provisions in the U.S. Constitution, as amended, and the various state constitutions. The U.S. Constitution creates and empowers the three branches of government, sets forth the relationship between the states and the federal government, and establishes procedures for amending the Constitution.

1. *Supremacy*—The U.S. Constitution is the supreme law of the land. A law in violation of the Constitution or one of its amendments, no matter what its source, will be declared unconstitutional and will not be enforced. A state constitution, so long as it does not conflict with the U.S. Constitution, is the supreme law within the state's borders.

Continued

2. *The Bill of Rights*—The first ten amendments to the federal constitution are known as the Bill of Rights. These amendments embody a series of protections for individuals—and in some instances, business entities—against certain government actions. The Bill of Rights originally limited only the powers of the federal government. After the Fourteenth Amendment was passed, the Supreme Court began to apply the protections of the Bill of Rights against state government actions.

3. *The courts and constitutional law*—The rights secured by the constitution are not absolute. The courts, and ultimately the Supreme Court, interpret and define the boundaries of the rights guaranteed by the Constitution.

Statutory Law

Statutory law consists of all laws enacted by the federal Congress, a state legislature, a municipality, or some other governing body. Laws passed by Congress and state legislatures are called *statutes.* Laws passed by local governing units (cities and counties) are called *ordinances.* Statutory law takes precedence over the common law.

Administrative Law

Administrative law consists of the rules, regulations, and decisions of administrative agencies at all levels of government.

1. *Agency creation*—Congress creates administrative agencies by passing enabling legislation, which specifies the name, purpose, function, and powers of the agency being created.

2. *Administrative process*—Administrative agencies exercise three basic functions:

   a. **RULEMAKING**—Agencies make rules governing activities within the areas of their authority. Typically, rulemaking procedure involves publishing notice of the proposed rulemaking, allowing a comment period, and then drafting the final rule.

   b. **INVESTIGATION AND ENFORCEMENT**—Agencies conduct investigations of regulated entities both to gather information and to monitor compliance with agency rules. When a regulated entity fails to comply with agency rules, the agency can take administrative action. Most violations are resolved through negotiated settlements.

   c. **ADJUDICATION**—If a settlement cannot be reached, the agency may issue a formal complaint, and an administrative law judge (ALJ) conducts a hearing and decides the issue. Either party can appeal the ALJ's order to the board or commission that governs the agency if dissatisfied. Most agency decisions can also then be appealed to a court.

3. *State administrative agencies*—State administrative agencies regulate state affairs. Often, a state agency is created as a parallel to a federal agency. If the actions of parallel state and federal agencies come into conflict, the federal agency will prevail, based on the supremacy clause of the U.S. Constitution.

4. *Paralegals in agency hearings*—Paralegals and other nonlawyers are permitted to represent clients before certain federal and state agencies.

National and International Law

1. *National law*—The law of a particular nation. National law differs from nation to nation because each nation's laws have evolved from that nation's unique

customs and traditions. Most countries have one of the following types of legal systems:

  a. **THE COMMON LAW SYSTEM**—Great Britain and the United States have a common law system. Generally, countries that were once colonies of Great Britain retained their English common law heritage after achieving independence. Under the common law, case precedents are judicially binding.

  b. **THE CIVIL LAW SYSTEM**—Many of the continental European countries and the nations that were formerly their colonies have civil law systems. Based on Roman codified law, civil law (or code law) is an ordered grouping of legal principles enacted into law by a governing body. The primary source of law is a statutory code. Although important, case precedents are not judicially binding.

2. *International law*—A body of laws that govern relationships among nations. International law allows nations to enjoy good relations with each other and to benefit economically from international trade. Sources of international law include international customs and traditions developed over time, treaties among nations, and international organizations and conferences.

STUDENT STUDYWARE™ CD-ROM

Interactive student CD in this book includes additional quizzing, plus video clips, case studies, and Key Terms flashcards.

ONLINE COMPANION™

For additional resources, please go to **www.paralegal.delmar.cengage.com**.

QUESTIONS FOR REVIEW

1. What does *stare decisis* mean? Why is it said that the doctrine of *stare decisis* is the cornerstone of English and American law?

2. What is the difference between courts of law and courts of equity? Why did courts of equity evolve?

3. What kinds of remedies could be granted by courts of law? Name two remedies that could be granted by courts of equity.

4. What is a statute? How is statutory law created? What is an ordinance? What happens when a state statute conflicts with a federal statute?

5. What is an administrative agency? How and why are such agencies created? What are their primary functions?

ETHICAL QUESTION

1. John Scott, an attorney, has asked his legal assistant, Nanette Lynch, to do some research. Nanette is to research the state statutes to find out how many persons are required to witness a will. Nanette looks up the relevant state statute and finds it difficult to understand because it is so poorly written. After studying the statute for a while, Nanette decides that two witnesses are required and conveys this information to John. Actually, the statute requires that a will be witnessed by three persons or it will not be valid. John, relying on Nanette's conclusion, has two persons witness a client's will the next day. Have John and Nanette violated any ethical rules? Explain.

PRACTICE QUESTIONS AND ASSIGNMENTS

1. In the following hypothetical situations, identify the type of case (criminal or civil), the remedy being sought, and whether it is a remedy at law or a remedy in equity:

   a. Beth files a petition with the court. She is seeking compensation from Travis who failed to deliver new furniture as promised.

   b. Jim sues Bob, seeking to be compensated for the cost of replacing several new trees that Bob's dog has destroyed.

   c. Laurie seeks to have a contract for the sale of an antique Mercedes automobile enforced.

   d. Sam files a petition seeking to prevent the electric company from cutting down a large tree on his property.

2. Identify the type of law (common law, constitutional law, statutory law, or administrative law) that applies in each of the following scenarios:

   a. Jean Gorman strongly disagrees with the U.S. government's decision to declare war on a foreign country. She places an antiwar sign in the window of her home. The city passes an ordinance that bans all such signs.

   b. An official of the state department of natural resources learns that the Ferris Widget Company has violated the state's Hazardous Waste Management Act. The official issues a complaint against the company for not properly handling and labeling its toxic waste.

   c. Mrs. Sams was walking down a busy street when two teenagers on in-line skates crashed into her because they weren't watching where they were going. As a result of the teenagers' conduct, Mrs. Sams broke her hip, and according to her doctor, she will never walk normally again. She sues the teenagers for damages.

   d. Joseph Barnes is arrested and charged with the crime of murder.

3. Indicate whether each of the following is an example of an administrative law case:

   a. An employment-discrimination case that is filed with the EEOC.

   b. A family law case pending in circuit court.

   c. A dispute pending before the Internal Revenue Service.

   d. An issue of securities law.

   e. A tax matter pending before the Court of Federal Claims.

QUESTIONS FOR CRITICAL ANALYSIS

1. The rights guaranteed by the U.S. Constitution would be of little significance if they were not enforced by the government. In view of this fact, is a written constitution really necessary? Would the rights and privileges enjoyed by Americans be any different if we did not have a written constitution?

2. Laws in the United States come primarily from four sources: the federal Constitution and state constitutions, statutes, administrative agencies, and the courts. Why are there so many different sources? What might happen if there were not? How could the law be changed if only courts made the law?

3. Why do legislatures delegate authority to administrative agencies? Give examples of two federal administrative agencies and the type of work that paralegals might perform with respect to the areas regulated by these agencies.

PROJECTS

1. Look at the U.S. Constitution in Appendix J of this text. Identify the amendment and quote the relevant language in the Bill of Rights that gives U.S. citizens the following rights and protections:

   a. The right to freely exercise one's religion.

   b. Protection against unreasonable searches and seizures.

   c. Protection against self-incrimination.

   d. The right to counsel in criminal prosecutions.

   e. The right to free speech.

2. Find out if your state's courts use different procedures for cases that involve equity matters than for cases that do not. Are there any trial courts in your state that cannot grant equitable remedies?

USING INTERNET RESOURCES

1. Go to FindLaw's home page at **www.lp.findlaw.com**. This site offers links to many of the federal and state sources of law that you have read about in this chapter. In this exercise, you will be examining state laws, so select "Cases and Codes" from the "Research the Law" menu near the bottom of the page. Under "State Resources," select the name of your state. Browse through the state sources of law that can be accessed online, and then answer the following questions:

   a. Were you able to access the text of your state's constitution?

   b. Did the site include your state's code (compilation of statutes) and administrative regulations?

   c. What other primary materials were included in the site?

   d. Now browse through the site for three other states. How does your state's site compare with those of other states in terms of comprehensiveness and ease of use?

2. The Web site of the United States Supreme Court, located at **www.supremecourtus.gov**, contains a description of the Court's role in interpreting the Constitution. Go to this Web site, select "About the Supreme Court," and then select "The Court and Constitutional Interpretation." What is judicial review? What role did the case *Marbury v. Madison* have in shaping the Supreme Court's power of judicial review? Can the Supreme Court give "advisory opinions"? Why or why not?

END NOTES

1. Pronounced *stahr-ee* dih-*si-ses*.

2. 347 U.S. 483, 74 S.Ct. 686, 98 L.Ed. 873 (1954).

3. *In re Baby M*, 217 N.J.Super. 313, 525 A.2d 1128 (1987).

4. Twenty dollars was forty days' pay for the average person when the Bill of Rights was written.

5. 47 U.S.C. Section 223(d)(1)(B). Specifically, the CDA prohibited any obscene or indecent message that "depicts or describes, in terms patently offensive as measured by contemporary community standards, sexual or excretory activities or organs."

6. 521 U.S. 844, 117 S.Ct. 2329, 138 L.Ed.2d 874 (1997).

7. 47 U.S.C. Section 231. COPA made it a criminal act to post "material that is harmful to minors" on the Web.

8. *American Civil Liberties Union v. Mukasey*, 534 F.3d 181 (3d Cir. 2008).

9. *Cert.* denied, 129 S.Ct. 1032 (2009).

10. *Gibbons v. Ogden*, 22 U.S. (9 Wheat.) 1, 6 L.Ed. 23 (1824).

11. *Wickard v. Filburn*, 317 U.S. 111, 63 S.Ct. 82, 87 L.Ed. 122 (1942).

THE COURT SYSTEM AND ALTERNATIVE DISPUTE RESOLUTION

CHAPTER

6

CHAPTER OUTLINE

Introduction

Basic Judicial Requirements

State Court Systems

The Federal Court System

Alternative Dispute Resolution

AFTER COMPLETING THIS CHAPTER, YOU WILL KNOW:

▶ The requirements that must be met before a lawsuit can be brought in a particular court by a particular party.

▶ The difference between jurisdiction and venue.

▶ The types of courts that make up a typical state court system and the different functions of trial courts and appellate courts.

▶ The organization of the federal court system and the relationship between state and federal jurisdiction.

▶ How cases reach the United States Supreme Court.

▶ The various ways in which disputes can be resolved outside the court system.

INTRODUCTION

As explained in Chapter 5, American law is based on many elements—the case decisions and legal principles that form the common law, the federal Constitution and state constitutions, statutes passed by federal and state legislatures, administrative law, and, in some instances, the laws of other nations and international law. But the laws would be meaningless without the courts to interpret and apply them.

Paralegals working in all areas of the law, and particularly litigation paralegals, need to understand the different types of courts that make up the American court system. There are fifty-two court systems—one for each of the fifty states, one for the District of Columbia, and a federal system. And even though similarities among these systems abound, there are differences as well.

In the first part of this chapter, we examine the structure of the American court system. Because of the costs, in time and money, and the publicity that can come from court trials, many parties are turning to alternative methods of dispute resolution to resolve disputes outside of court. In some cases, parties are required by the courts to try to resolve their disputes by one of these methods. In the latter part of this chapter, we provide an overview of these alternative methods of dispute resolution and the role that attorneys and paralegals play in facilitating out-of-court dispute settlements.

BASIC JUDICIAL REQUIREMENTS

Before a lawsuit can be brought before a court, certain requirements must be met. We examine here these important requirements and some of the basic features of the American system of justice.

Standing to Sue

To bring a lawsuit before a court, a party must have **standing to sue**, or a sufficient "stake" in a matter to justify seeking relief through the court system. In other words, a party must have a legally protected and real interest at stake in the litigation in order to have standing. The party bringing the lawsuit must have suffered a harm as a result of the action about which he or she complained. ▶ **EXAMPLE 6.1** Assume that a friend of one of your firm's clients was injured in a car accident caused by defective brakes. The client's friend would have standing to sue the automobile manufacturer for damages. The client, who feels horrible about the accident, would not have standing because the client was not injured and has no legally recognizable stake in the controversy. ◀

Note that in some cases, a person has standing to sue on behalf of another person. ▶ **EXAMPLE 6.2** Suppose that a child suffered serious injuries as a result of a defectively manufactured toy. Because the child is a minor, a lawsuit could be brought on his behalf by another person, such as the child's parent or legal guardian. ◀

Standing to sue also requires that the controversy at issue be justiciable. A **justiciable**[1] **controversy** is one that is real and substantial, as opposed to hypothetical or academic. ▶ **EXAMPLE 6.3** In the scenario discussed in Example 6.2, the child's parent could not sue the toy manufacturer merely on the ground that the toy was defective and the parent feared that the toy could cause injury. The issue would become justiciable only if the child had actually been injured due to a defect in the toy as marketed. In other words, the parent normally could not ask the court to determine what damages might be obtained *if* the child had been injured, because this would be a hypothetical question. ◀

---

standing to sue
A sufficient stake in a controversy to justify bringing a lawsuit. To have standing to sue, the plaintiff must demonstrate an injury or a threat of injury.

justiciable controversy
A controversy that is real and substantial, as opposed to hypothetical or academic.

Types of Jurisdiction

In Latin, *juris* means "law," and *diction* means "to speak." Thus, "the power to speak the law" is the literal meaning of the term **jurisdiction**. Before any court can hear a case, it must have jurisdiction over the person against whom the suit is brought or over the property involved in the suit. The court must also have jurisdiction over the subject matter.

Jurisdiction over Persons

Generally, a court can exercise personal jurisdiction (*in personam* jurisdiction) over residents of a certain geographic area. A state trial court, for example, normally has jurisdictional authority over residents within the state or within a particular area of the state, such as a county or district. A state's highest court (often called the state supreme court[2]) has jurisdictional authority over all residents within the state.

In some cases, under the authority of a **long arm statute**, a state court can exercise personal jurisdiction over certain nonresident defendants based on activities that took place within the state. Before a court can exercise jurisdiction over a nonresident under a long arm statute, though, it must be demonstrated that the nonresident had sufficient contacts *(minimum contacts)* with the state to justify the jurisdiction. ▶ **EXAMPLE 6.4** If a California citizen committed a wrong within the state of Arizona, such as causing an injury in a car accident or selling defective goods, an Arizona state court usually could exercise jurisdiction over the California citizen. Similarly, a state may exercise personal jurisdiction over a non-resident defendant who is sued for breaching a contract that was formed within the state. ◀

In regard to corporations, the minimum-contacts requirement is usually met if the corporation does business within the state. ▶ **EXAMPLE 6.5** A Maine corporation that has a branch office or warehouse in Georgia has sufficient minimum contacts with the state to allow a Georgia court to exercise jurisdiction over the Maine corporation. If the Maine corporation advertises and sells its products in Georgia, those activities are likely to be sufficient to meet the minimum-contacts requirements. ◀ A state court may also be able to exercise jurisdiction over a corporation in another country if it can be demonstrated that the alien (foreign) corporation has met the minimum-contacts test. ▶ **EXAMPLE 6.6** Suppose an Italian corporation markets its products through an American distributor. If the corporation knew that its products would be distributed to local markets throughout the United States, it could be sued in any state by a plaintiff who was injured by one of the products. ◀

Jurisdiction over Property

A court can also exercise jurisdiction over property that is located within its boundaries. This kind of jurisdiction is known as *in rem* jurisdiction, or "jurisdiction over the thing." ▶ **EXAMPLE 6.7** Suppose a dispute arises over the ownership of a boat at a dock in Fort Lauderdale, Florida. The boat is owned by an Ohio resident, over whom a Florida court normally cannot exercise personal jurisdiction. The other party to the dispute is a resident of Nebraska. In this situation, a lawsuit concerning the boat could be brought in a Florida state court on the basis of the court's *in rem* jurisdiction. ◀

Jurisdiction over Subject Matter

Jurisdiction over subject matter is a limitation on the types of cases a court can hear. In both the state and federal court systems, there are courts of *general jurisdiction* and courts of *limited jurisdiction*. The basis for the difference is the subject matter of cases heard. A **probate court**—a state court that handles only matters relating to the transfer of a person's assets and obligations on that person's death—is an example

jurisdiction
The authority of a court to hear and decide a specific case.

long arm statute
A state statute that permits a state to obtain jurisdiction over nonresidents. The nonresidents must have certain "minimum contacts" with that state for the statute to apply.

probate court
A court having jurisdiction over proceedings concerning the settlement of a person's estate.

of a court with limited subject-matter jurisdiction. One type of federal court of limited subject-matter jurisdiction is a bankruptcy court. **Bankruptcy courts** handle only bankruptcy proceedings, which are governed by bankruptcy law (a federal law that allows debtors to obtain relief from their debts when they cannot make ends meet). In contrast, a court of general jurisdiction can decide almost any type of case.

The subject-matter jurisdiction of a court is usually defined in the statute or constitution creating the court. In both the state and federal court systems, a court's subject-matter jurisdiction can be limited not only by the subject of the lawsuit but also by the amount in controversy, by whether a case is a felony (a more serious type of crime) or a misdemeanor (a less serious type of crime), or by whether the proceeding is a trial or an appeal.

Original and Appellate Jurisdiction

The distinction between courts of original jurisdiction and courts of appellate jurisdiction normally lies in whether the case is being heard for the first time. Courts having **original jurisdiction** are courts of the first instance, or **trial courts**—that is, courts in which lawsuits begin, trials take place, and evidence is presented. In the federal court system, the *district courts* are trial courts. In the state court systems, the trial courts are known by different names. The key point is that normally, any court having original jurisdiction is known as a trial court. Courts having **appellate jurisdiction** act as reviewing courts, or **appellate courts**. In general, cases can be brought before them only on appeal from an order or a judgment of a trial court or other lower court. State and federal trial and appellate courts will be discussed more fully later in this chapter.

Jurisdiction of the Federal Courts

Because the federal government is a government of limited powers, the jurisdiction of the federal courts is limited. Article III of the U.S. Constitution establishes the boundaries of federal judicial power. Section 2 of Article III states that "the judicial Power shall extend to all Cases, in Law and Equity, arising under this Constitution, the Laws of the United States, and Treaties made, or which shall be made, under their Authority."

Federal Questions

Whenever a plaintiff's cause of action is based, at least in part, on the U.S. Constitution, a treaty, or a federal law, then a **federal question** arises, and the case comes under the judicial power of the federal courts. Any lawsuit involving a federal question can originate in a federal district (trial) court. People who claim that their constitutional rights have been violated can begin their suits in a federal district court.

▶ **EXAMPLE 6.8** J-H Computers, a California company, sues Ball Computers, a Texas company, for patent infringement. J-H claims that some parts Ball used in its new laptop computers are based on J-H inventions. J-H contends that it has exclusive rights to these inventions and that Ball has used them without permission. Because patent law is federal law and the federal courts have exclusive jurisdiction over such suits, J-H must file suit against Ball in federal court. ◀

Diversity Jurisdiction

Federal district courts can also exercise original jurisdiction over cases involving **diversity of citizenship**. Such cases may arise between (1) citizens of different states, (2) a foreign country and citizens of a state or of different states, or (3) citizens of a state and citizens or subjects of a foreign country. The amount in controversy must be more than $75,000 before a federal court can take jurisdiction in such cases. For purposes of diversity-of-citizenship jurisdiction, a corporation is a citizen of the state

---

bankruptcy court
A federal court of limited jurisdiction that hears only bankruptcy proceedings.

original jurisdiction
The power of a court to take a case, try it, and decide it.

trial court
A court in which cases begin and in which questions of fact are examined.

appellate jurisdiction
The power of a court to hear and decide an appeal; the authority of a court to review cases that have already been tried in a lower court and to make decisions about them without holding a trial. This process is called *appellate review*.

appellate court
A court that reviews decisions made by lower courts, such as trial courts; a court of appeals.

federal question
A question that pertains to the U.S. Constitution, acts of Congress, or treaties. It provides a basis for jurisdiction by the federal courts. This jurisdiction is authorized by Article III, Section 2, of the Constitution.

diversity of citizenship
Under the Constitution, a basis for federal district court jurisdiction over a lawsuit between (1) citizens of different states, (2) a foreign country and citizens of a state or states, or (3) citizens of a state and citizens of a foreign country. The amount in controversy must be more than $75,000 before a federal court can exercise jurisdiction in such cases.

Developing Paralegal Skills

CHOICE OF COURTS: STATE OR FEDERAL?

Susan Radtke, a lawyer specializing in employment discrimination, and her legal assistant, Joan Dunbar, are meeting with a new client. The client wants to sue her former employer for gender discrimination. The client complained to her employer when she was passed over for a promotion. She was fired, she claims, as a result of her complaint. The client appears to have a strong case, because several of her former co-workers have agreed to testify that they heard the employer say that he would never promote a woman to a managerial position.

Because both state and federal laws prohibit gender discrimination, the case could be brought in either state or federal court. The client tells Susan that because of Susan's experience, she wants her to decide whether the case should be filed in a state or federal court. Joan will be drafting the complaint, so Susan and Joan discuss the pros and cons of filing the case in each court. Joan reviews a list of considerations with Susan.

TIPS FOR CHOOSING A COURT

- Review the jurisdiction of each court.
- Evaluate the strengths and weaknesses of the case.
- Evaluate the remedy sought.
- Evaluate the jury pool available for each court.
- Evaluate the likelihood of winning in each court.
- Evaluate the length of time it will take each court to decide the case.
- Evaluate the costs and procedural rules involved in filing in each court.

in which it is incorporated and of the state in which its principal place of business is located. A case involving diversity of citizenship can be filed in the appropriate federal district court.

▶ **EXAMPLE 6.9** Maria Ramirez, a citizen of Florida, was walking near a busy street in Tallahassee, Florida, when a crate fell off a passing truck and hit and seriously injured her. She incurred medical expenses and could not work for six months. She wants to sue the trucking firm for $500,000 in damages. The firm's headquarters are in Georgia, although the company does business in Florida. Maria could bring suit in a Florida court because she is a resident of Florida, the trucking firm does business in Florida, and that is where the accident occurred. She could also bring suit in a Georgia court, because a Georgia court could exercise jurisdiction over the trucking firm, which is headquartered in that state. Maria could also sue in a federal court because the requirements of diversity jurisdiction have been met—the lawsuit involves parties from different states, and the amount in controversy (the damages Maria is seeking) exceeds $75,000. ◀

Note that in a case based on a federal question, a federal court will apply federal law. In a case based on diversity of citizenship, however, a federal court will normally apply the law of the state in which the court sits. This is because cases based on diversity of citizenship generally do not involve activities that are regulated by the federal government. Therefore, federal laws do not apply, and state law will govern the issue.

Exclusive versus Concurrent Jurisdiction

When both federal and state courts have the power to hear a case, as is true in suits involving diversity of citizenship (such as Maria's case described in Example 6.9), **concurrent jurisdiction** exists. When cases can be tried only in federal courts or only in state courts, **exclusive jurisdiction** exists. Federal courts have exclusive jurisdiction in cases involving federal crimes, bankruptcy, patents, trademarks, and copyrights; in most class-action lawsuits;[3] in suits against the United States; and in some areas of admiralty law (law governing transportation on the seas and ocean waters). States also have exclusive jurisdiction in certain subject matters—for example, in divorce and adoptions. The concepts of concurrent and exclusive jurisdiction are illustrated in Exhibit 6.1.

When concurrent jurisdiction exists, a party has a choice of whether to bring a suit in a federal or a state court. As described in *Developing Paralegal Skills* on the facing page, the party's lawyer will consider several factors in counseling the party as to which choice is preferable. The lawyer may prefer to litigate the case in a state court, perhaps because of familiarity with the state court's procedures or a belief that the state's judge or jury would be more sympathetic to the client and the case.

Alternatively, the lawyer may advise the client to sue in federal court. Perhaps the state court's **docket** (the court's schedule listing the cases to be heard) is crowded, and the case could be brought to trial sooner in a federal court. Perhaps some feature of federal procedure could offer an advantage in the client's case. Other important considerations include the law in an available jurisdiction, how that law has been applied in the jurisdiction's courts, and what the results in similar cases have been in that jurisdiction.

Jurisdiction in Cyberspace

The Internet's capacity to bypass political and geographic boundaries undercuts traditional basic limitations on a court's authority to exercise jurisdiction. These limits include a party's contacts with a court's geographic jurisdiction. As already discussed, for a court to compel a defendant to come before it, there must be at least minimum contacts—the presence of a company's salesperson within the state, for example. Are there sufficient minimum contacts if the only connection to a jurisdiction is an ad on the Web originating from a remote location?

▶ **EXAMPLE 6.10**   Tom, who lives in Idaho, orders $20,000 worth of merchandise from Juanita's On-Line Emporium, a New Mexico company that operates on the Internet. After paying for and receiving the merchandise, Tom claims Juanita's

---

concurrent jurisdiction
Jurisdiction that exists when two different courts have the power to hear a case. For example, some cases can be heard in either a federal or a state court.

exclusive jurisdiction
Jurisdiction that exists when a case can be heard only in a particular court, such as a federal court.

docket
The list of cases entered on the court's calendar and scheduled to be heard by the court.

EXHIBIT 6.1
Exclusive and Concurrent Jurisdiction

Exclusive Federal Jurisdiction
(cases involving federal crimes, federal antitrust law, bankruptcy, patents, copyrights, trademarks, most class-action suits, suits against the United States, some areas of admiralty law, and certain other matters specified in federal statutes)

Concurrent Jurisdiction
(some cases involving federal questions, diversity-of-citizenship cases)

Exclusive State Jurisdiction
(cases involving all matters not subject to federal jurisdiction)

goods are not of the quality described on the company Web site. Tom sues Juanita's in state court in Idaho. Does the Idaho state court have jurisdiction over the matter? Yes. The company offers to sell goods around the country, and it did make a sale to Tom, so it has sufficient contacts with Idaho to give courts there jurisdiction. ◀

The "Sliding-Scale" Standard

Gradually, the courts are developing a standard—called a "sliding-scale" standard—for determining when the exercise of jurisdiction over an out-of-state party is proper. The courts have identified three types of Internet business contacts: (1) substantial business conducted over the Internet (with contracts or sales, for example), (2) some interactivity through a Web site, and (3) passive advertising. Jurisdiction is proper for the first category, is improper for the third, and may or may not be appropriate for the second.

International Jurisdictional Issues

Because the Internet is international in scope, international jurisdictional issues arise. What seems to be emerging is a standard that echoes the requirement of minimum contacts applied by the U.S. courts. Courts in many nations are indicating that minimum contacts—doing business within the jurisdiction, for example—are enough to compel a defendant to appear and that the defendant's physical presence is not required for the court to exercise jurisdiction. The effect of this standard is that a company may have to comply with the laws of any jurisdiction in which it targets customers for its products.

Venue

venue
The geographic district in which an action is tried and from which the jury is selected.

Jurisdiction has to do with whether a court has authority to hear a case involving specific persons, property, or subject matter. **Venue**[4] is concerned with the most appropriate location for a trial. For example, two state courts may have the authority to exercise jurisdiction over a case, but it may be more appropriate or convenient to hear the case in one court than in the other.

The concept of venue reflects the policy that a court trying a suit should be in the geographic area (usually the county) in which the parties involved in the lawsuit reside or in which the incident leading to the lawsuit occurred. Pretrial publicity or other factors, though, may require a change of venue to another community, especially in criminal cases in which the defendant's right to a fair and impartial jury has been impaired. ▶ **EXAMPLE 6.11** A bomb was set off at a federal building in Oklahoma City, killing 168 persons and injuring hundreds of others. Timothy McVeigh was indicted in connection with the bombing and scheduled for trial in an Oklahoma federal court. The defense attorneys argued—and the court agreed—that McVeigh could not receive a fair trial in Oklahoma because an impartial jury could not be chosen. Although the federal court in Oklahoma had jurisdiction, the court ordered a change of venue to a federal court in Denver for trial. ◀

Judicial Procedures

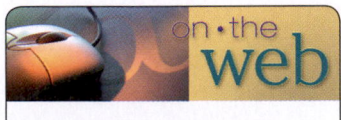

The Federal Rules of Civil Procedure are available online at **www. law.cornell.edu**. Select "Constitutions & Codes" which provides Federal Rules of Civil Procedure.

Litigation in court, from the moment a lawsuit is initiated until the final resolution of the case, must follow specifically designated procedural rules. The procedural rules for federal court cases are set forth in the Federal Rules of Civil Procedure. State rules, which are often similar to the federal rules, vary from state to state—and even from court to court within a given state. Rules of procedure also differ in criminal and civil cases. Paralegals who work for trial lawyers need to be familiar with the procedural rules of the relevant courts (this includes complying with deadlines—see the *In the Office* feature). Because judicial procedures will be examined in detail in Chapters 10 through 13, we do not discuss them here.

In the **Office**

WATCH THOSE DEADLINES!

One of the paralegal's most important responsibilities is making sure that court deadlines are met. Suppose your supervising attorney asks you to file with the court a motion to dismiss, which is a document requesting the court to dismiss a lawsuit for a specific reason. You know that the deadline for filing the motion is three days away. After you prepare the document, and have it reviewed by your attorney, you put it in the client's file. You plan to deliver the motion to the court the next day.

As soon as you get to work the next morning, you are called to help with a rush matter on another case. Busy with that, you forget about the motion to dismiss until next week. Too late! Court deadlines are hard rules. To prevent such things from happening, *always* enter every deadline on the office calendaring system, and *always* check your calendar several times a day no matter what else is happening. Missed deadlines can be the basis for malpractice suits by clients against attorneys.

BASIC JUDICIAL REQUIREMENTS AND THE PARALEGAL

Paralegals should be familiar with the concepts of jurisdiction, venue, and standing to sue because these concepts affect pretrial litigation procedures. For example, a defendant in a lawsuit may claim that the court in which the plaintiff filed the lawsuit cannot exercise jurisdiction over the matter—or over the defendant or the defendant's property. If you are working on behalf of the defendant, you may be asked to draft a motion to dismiss the case on this ground. You may also be asked to draft a legal memorandum in support of the motion, outlining the legal reasons why the court cannot exercise jurisdiction over the case. (Motions to dismiss and supporting documents are discussed in Chapter 10.) Additionally, a party to a lawsuit may request that a case filed in a state court be "removed" to a federal court (if there is a basis for federal jurisdiction) or vice versa. You may be asked to draft a document requesting a change of venue (or objecting to an opponent's request for a change of venue) or requesting that the court dismiss the case because the plaintiff lacks standing to sue.

If you work for a plaintiff's attorney, you might be asked to draft a complaint to initiate a lawsuit. Once the attorney reviews the facts with you, he or she may expect you to know whether concurrent jurisdiction exists. If it does, the attorney may expect you to be able to discuss whether the suit should be filed in a state or a federal court. If it does not, the attorney may assume that you know in which court the case will be filed and how to prepare the complaint for the appropriate court.

Recall from Chapter 1 that paralegal education and training emphasize both substantive and procedural law. A paralegal can be a valuable member of a legal team if he or she has adequate knowledge of the procedural requirements relating to litigation and to different types of legal proceedings. You will read in detail about litigation procedures in Chapters 10 through 13.

STATE COURT SYSTEMS

Each state has its own system of courts, and no two state systems are the same. As Exhibit 6.2 on the next page indicates, there may be several levels, or tiers, of courts within a state court system: (1) state trial courts of general jurisidiction and limited jurisdiction, (2) appellate courts, and (3) the state's highest court (often called the state supreme court). Judges in the state court system are usually elected by the voters for a specified term.

EXHIBIT 6.2
Levels in a State Court System

State's Highest Court
Usually called supreme court.

Intermediate Appellate Court
Three-fourths of the states have intermediate courts of appeals.

Trial Courts

- Trial courts of general jurisdiction (which may be called county, district, superior, or circuit courts) exercise jurisdiction over a variety of subjects, including both civil and criminal cases.

- Trial courts of limited jurisdiction (such as probate, domestic relations, and municipal courts) may be separate courts or may be part of a trial court of general jurisdiction.

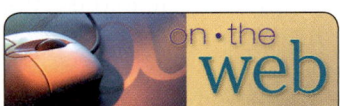

State court systems vary widely from state to state. To learn about your state's court system, go to the National Center for State Courts' Web site at **www.ncsconline.org**. Select "Information" and then "Court Web Sites."

Generally, any person who is a party to a lawsuit has the opportunity to plead the case before a trial court and then, if she loses, before at least one level of appellate court. Finally, if a federal statute or federal constitutional issue is involved in the decision of a state supreme court, that decision may be further appealed to the United States Supreme Court.

Trial Courts

Trial courts are exactly what their name implies—courts in which trials are held and testimony taken. You will read about trial procedures in Chapter 12. In that chapter, we follow a hypothetical case through the various stages of a trial. Briefly, a trial court is presided over by a judge, who issues a decision on the matter before the court. If the trial is a jury trial (many trials are held without juries), the jury will decide the outcome of factual disputes, and the judge will issue a judgment based on the jury's conclusion. During the trial, the attorney for each side introduces evidence (such as relevant documents, exhibits, and testimony of witnesses) in support of the client's position. Each attorney is given an opportunity to cross-examine witnesses for the opposing party and challenge evidence introduced by the opposing party.

State trial courts have either general or limited jurisdiction. Trial courts that have general jurisdiction as to subject matter may be called county, district, superior, or circuit courts.[5] The jurisdiction of these courts is often determined by the size of the county in which the court sits. State trial courts of general jurisdiction have jurisdiction over a wide variety of subjects, including both civil disputes (such as landlord-tenant matters or contract claims) and criminal prosecutions. In some states, trial courts of general jurisdiction may hear appeals from courts of limited jurisdiction.

Courts with limited jurisdiction as to subject matter are often called "inferior" trial courts or minor judiciary courts. Courts of limited jurisdiction include small claims courts, which hear only civil cases involving claims of less than a certain amount, such as $5,000; domestic relations courts, which handle only divorce actions, paternity suits, and child-custody and support cases; local municipal courts, which mainly handle traffic violations; and probate courts, which, as previously mentioned, handle the administration of wills, estate-settlement problems, and related matters.

Appellate, or Reviewing, Courts

After a trial, the parties have the right to file an appeal to a higher court if they are unsatisfied with the trial court's ruling. Practically speaking, parties are unlikely to file an appeal unless a reversible error was committed by the trial court that would cause the appellate court to overturn the trial court's decision. A **reversible error** is a legal error at the trial court level that is significant enough to have affected the outcome of the case. For example, the judge may have given improper instructions about the law to the jury. Usually, appellate courts do not look at questions of *fact* (such as whether a party did, in fact, commit a certain action, such as burning a flag) but at questions of *law* (such as whether the act of flag-burning is a form of speech protected by the First Amendment to the Constitution). Only a judge, not a jury, can rule on questions of law.

Appellate courts normally defer to a trial court's findings on questions of fact because the trial court judge and jury were in a better position to evaluate testimony by directly observing witnesses' gestures, demeanor, and nonverbal behavior during the trial. When a case is appealed, an appellate panel of three or more judges reviews the record (including the written transcript of the trial) of the case on appeal, and the record does not include these nonverbal elements. Generally, then, appellate courts look for errors of law rather than evaluating the trial court judge's or jury's conclusions on questions of fact.

> **reversible error**
> A legal error at the trial court level that is significant enough to have affected the outcome of the case. It is grounds for reversal of the judgment on appeal.

Intermediate Appellate Courts

About three-fourths of the states have intermediate appellate courts, or courts of appeals. The subject-matter jurisdiction of these courts is substantially limited to hearing appeals. Usually, appellate courts review the records, read appellate briefs filed by the parties, and listen to the oral arguments presented by the parties' attorneys. Then the panel of judges renders (issues) a decision. If a party is unsatisfied with the appellate court's ruling, that party can appeal to the highest state court.

Highest State Courts

The highest appellate court in a state is usually called the supreme court but may be called by some other name. For example, in both New York and Maryland, the highest state court is called the court of appeals. The decisions of each state's highest court on all questions of state law are final. Only when issues of federal law are involved can a decision made by a state's highest court be overruled by the United States Supreme Court.

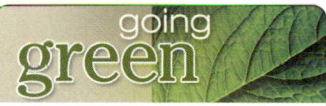

HOW DO YOU DRINK YOUR COFFEE OR TEA?

Many offices provide disposable cups for drinks. These are good for clients and guests, but you should consider supplying your own reusable mug or cup. We consume more than 14 billion disposable cups a year in the United States—enough to circle the earth fifty times! An attractive mug works fine and can add a personal touch to your desk.

STATE COURT SYSTEMS AND THE PARALEGAL

Because each state has its own unique system of courts, you will need to become familiar with the court system of your state. What is the official name of your state's highest court? How many intermediate state appellate courts are in your state, and to which of these courts should appeals from your local trial court or courts be made? What courts in your area have jurisdiction over what kinds of disputes?

In addition to knowing the names of your state's courts and their jurisdictional authority, you will also need to become familiar with the procedural requirements of specific courts. Paralegals frequently assist their attorneys in drafting legal documents to be filed in state courts, and the required procedures for filing these documents may vary from court to court. You will read more about court procedures in Chapters 10 and 12.

As indicated earlier and illustrated in Exhibit 6.1 on page 165, state courts exercise exclusive jurisdiction over all matters that are not subject to federal jurisdiction. Family law and probate law (both discussed in Chapter 17), for example, are two areas in which state courts exercise exclusive jurisdiction. If you work in an area of the law over which state courts exercise exclusive jurisdiction, you will need to be familiar with procedural requirements established by state (or local) courts relating to those areas.

Realize also that many paralegals work within the court system, in both state courts and county courts (which are part of the state court system). Some paralegals work as assistants to court clerks. In addition, many paralegals work for bankruptcy courts, which are part of the federal court system—a topic to which we now turn.

THE FEDERAL COURT SYSTEM

The federal court system is basically a three-tiered model consisting of (1) U.S. district courts (trial courts of general jurisdiction) and various courts of limited jurisdiction, (2) U.S. courts of appeals (intermediate courts of appeals), and (3) the United States Supreme Court, located in Washington, D.C. Exhibit 6.3 shows the organization of the federal court system.

According to the language of Article III of the U.S. Constitution, there is only one national Supreme Court. All other courts in the federal system are considered "inferior." Congress has the power to create inferior courts. The courts that Congress has created include those on the first and second tiers in our model—the district courts and courts of limited jurisdiction, as well as the U.S. courts of appeals.

Unlike state court judges, who are often elected, federal court judges—including the justices of the United States Supreme Court—are appointed by the president of the United States and confirmed by the U.S. Senate. Federal judges receive lifetime appointments (because under Article III they "hold their Offices during good Behavior").

The Web site for the federal courts offers information on the federal court system and links to all federal courts at **www.uscourts.gov**.

EXHIBIT 6.3
The Organization of the Federal Court System

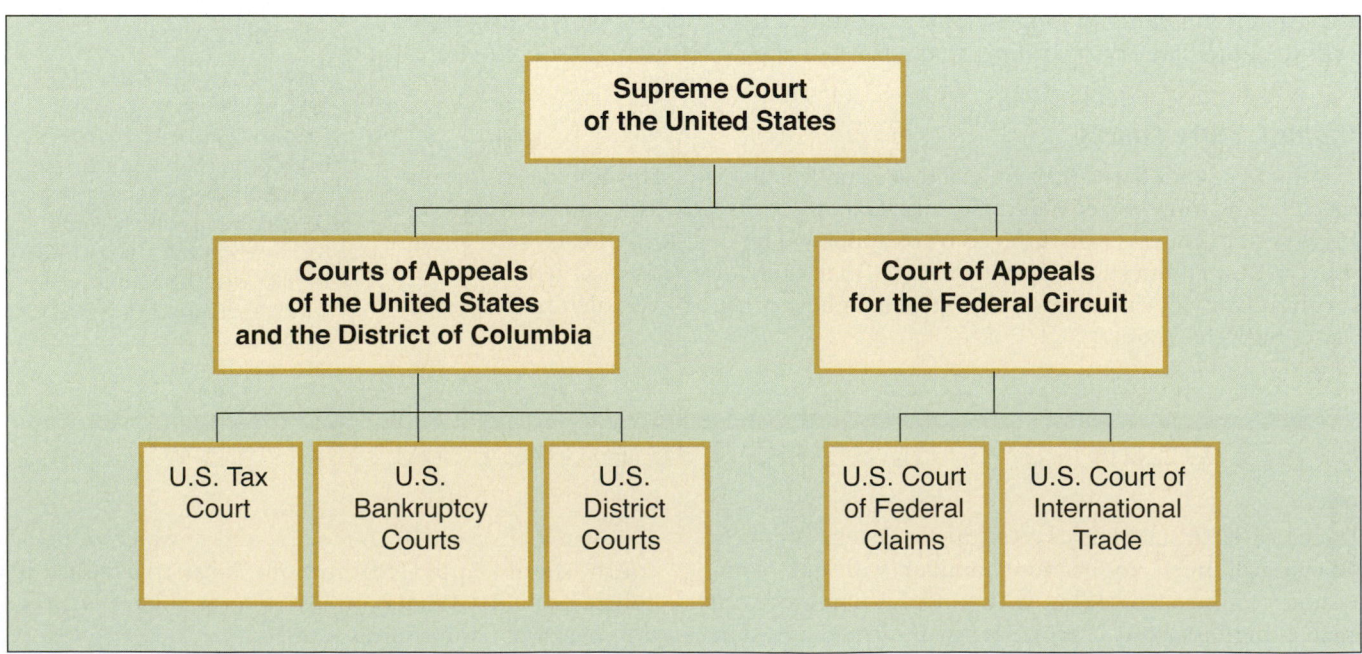

U.S. District Courts

At the federal level, the equivalent of a state trial court of general jurisdiction is the district court. There is at least one federal district court in every state. The number of judicial districts can vary over time, primarily owing to population changes and corresponding case-loads. Currently, there are ninety-four judicial districts.

U.S. district courts have original jurisdiction in matters of federal law. Federal cases typically originate in district courts. There are other trial courts with original but special (or limited) jurisdiction, such as the federal bankruptcy courts and others shown in Exhibit 6.3.

U.S. Courts of Appeals

In the federal court system, there are thirteen U.S. courts of appeals—also referred to as U.S. circuit courts of appeals. The federal courts of appeals for twelve of the circuits (including the District of Columbia Circuit) hear appeals from the federal district courts located within their respective judicial circuits. The court of appeals for the thirteenth circuit, called the Federal Circuit, has national appellate jurisdiction over certain types of cases, such as cases involving patent law and cases in which the U.S. government is a defendant.

A party who is dissatisfied with a federal district court's decision on an issue may appeal that decision to a federal circuit court of appeals. The judges on the court review decisions made by trial courts to see if any errors of law were made. The judges generally defer to a district court's findings of fact. The decisions of the circuit courts of appeals are final in most cases, but appeal to the United States Supreme Court is possible. Exhibit 6.4 shows the geographic boundaries of the U.S. circuit courts of appeals and the boundaries of the U.S. district courts within each circuit.

At the Web site of the Legal Information Institute, at **www.law.cornell.edu**, you can search the opinions of U.S. circuit courts. From the "Court opinions" menu, select "Other federal court opinions."

EXHIBIT 6.4
Boundaries of the U.S. Courts of Appeals and U.S. District Courts

Source: Administrative Office of the United States Courts.

The United States Supreme Court

The highest level of the three-tiered model of the federal court system is the United States Supreme Court. The Supreme Court consists of nine justices. Although the Supreme Court has original, or trial, jurisdiction in rare instances (set forth in Article III, Section 2, of the Constitution—see Appendix J), most of its work is as an appeals court. The Supreme Court can review any case decided by any of the federal courts of appeals, and it also has appellate authority over some cases decided in the state courts.

How Cases Reach the Supreme Court

Many people are surprised to learn that there is no absolute right of appeal to the United States Supreme Court. Thousands of cases are filed with the Supreme Court each year, yet in recent years, it has heard fewer than eighty cases each year.

To bring a case before the Supreme Court, a party requests the Court to issue a writ of *certiorari*. A **writ of** *certiorari*[6] is an order issued by the Supreme Court to a lower court requiring the lower court to send it the record of the case for review. Parties can petition the Supreme Court to issue a writ of *certiorari*, but the Court will not issue a writ unless at least four of the nine justices approve of it. This is called the **rule of four**. Most petitions for writs are denied. A denial is not a decision on the merits of a case, nor does it indicate agreement with the lower court's opinion. It simply means that the Supreme Court declines to grant the request (petition) for appeal. Furthermore, denial of the writ has no value as a precedent.

Types of Cases Reviewed by the Supreme Court

Typically, the petitions granted by the Court involve cases that raise important constitutional questions or decisions that conflict with other state or federal court decisions. Similarly, if federal appellate courts are rendering inconsistent opinions on an important issue, the Supreme Court may review a case involving that issue and generate a decision to define the law on the matter.

▶ **EXAMPLE 6.12** Suppose that an employer fires an employee who refuses to work on Saturdays, which is forbidden by the employee's religion. The fired employee applies for unemployment benefits from the state unemployment agency, and the agency, concluding that the employer had good reason to fire the employee, denies unemployment benefits. The fired employee sues the state unemployment agency on the ground that the employee's right to freely exercise her religion—a constitutional right—was violated. The case is ultimately appealed to a state supreme court, which decides the issue in a way that is contrary to several recent federal appellate courts' interpretations of freedom of religion in the employment context. If the losing party petitions the Supreme Court for a writ of *certiorari*, the Court may grant the petition and review the case. ◀

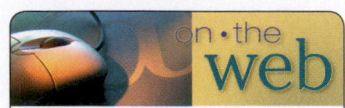

An excellent site for information on the United States Supreme Court—including its functions and procedures, biographies and photographs of the justices, and even the history of the Supreme Court building—is at **www.supremecourtus.gov**.

writ of *certiorari*

A writ from a higher court asking a lower court to send it the record of a case for review. The United States Supreme Court uses *certiorari* to review most of the cases it decides to hear.

rule of four

A rule of the United States Supreme Court under which the Court will not issue a writ of *certiorari* unless at least four justices approve of the decision to issue the writ.

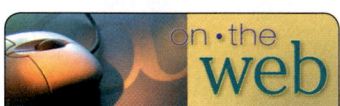

United States Supreme Court cases can be accessed online at **www. supremecourtus.gov**. From the menu, select "Opinions."

THE FEDERAL COURT SYSTEM AND THE PARALEGAL

In your work as a paralegal, you will probably deal occasionally with the federal court system. As discussed above, certain cases involving diversity of citizenship may be brought in either a state or a federal court. Some litigants who could sue in a state court will opt for a federal court in this situation. (The *Developing Paralegal Skills* feature gives an example of a diversity question.)

You may also work on behalf of plaintiffs whose claims concern a federal question. An increasing num-

ber of cases in federal courts are brought by plaintiffs who allege employment discrimination in violation of federal laws, such as Title VII of the Civil Rights Act of 1964, which prohibits employment discrimination based on race, color, national origin, gender, or religion. Other federal laws prohibit discrimination based on age or disability. Sexual harassment and pregnancy discrimination are considered by the courts to fall under the protective umbrella of Title VII's prohibition against

Developing
Paralegal Skills

FEDERAL COURT JURISDICTION

Mona, a new client, comes to the law offices of Henry, Jacobs & Miller in Detroit, Michigan. She wants to file a lawsuit against a New York hospital where she had emergency gallbladder surgery. Mona contracted an infection as a result of the surgery and nearly died. She was so sick that she missed several months of work and lost wages of $18,000. She also has medical expenses exceeding $60,000. Jane Doyle, a paralegal, is asked to review the case to determine if it can be filed in federal court.

CHECKLIST FOR DETERMINING FEDERAL COURT JURISDICTION

- Is the case based, at least in part, on the U.S. Constitution, a treaty, or other question of federal law?
- If the case does not involve a question of federal law, does it involve more than $75,000 and one of the following:
  - ✓ Citizens of different states?
  - ✓ A foreign country and citizens of a state or different states?
  - ✓ Citizens of a state and citizens or subjects of a foreign country?

If the case involves a combination of more than $75,000 and one of the citizenship requirements above, then diversity jurisdiction exists.

---

gender discrimination, and such cases frequently come before federal courts.

As indicated in Exhibit 6.1 on page 165, federal courts exercise exclusive jurisdiction over cases relating to bankruptcy, patents, copyrights, trademarks, federal crimes, and certain other claims. If you work on such cases, you will be dealing with the federal court system and the court procedures set forth in the Federal Rules of Civil Procedure. As with state courts, you should make sure that you know the specific requirements of the particular federal court in which a client's lawsuit is to be filed, because each federal court has some discretionary authority over its procedural rules. (See the *Technology and Today's Paralegal* feature on the following two pages for a discussion of how to obtain court information online.) You will read in detail about the procedural rules governing litigation proceedings in federal courts in Chapters 10 and 12.

ALTERNATIVE DISPUTE RESOLUTION

Litigation is expensive. It is adversarial. It is also time consuming. Because of the backlog of cases pending in many courts, several years may pass before a case is actually tried. For these and other reasons, more and more individuals are turning to **alternative dispute resolution (ADR)** as a means of settling their disputes.

Methods of ADR range from neighbors sitting down over a cup of coffee in an attempt to work out their differences to huge multinational corporations agreeing to resolve a dispute through a formal hearing before a panel of experts. The great advantage of ADR is its flexibility. Normally, the parties themselves can control how the dispute will be settled, what procedures will be used, and whether the decision reached (either by themselves or by a neutral third party) will be legally binding or nonbinding.

Today, about 95 percent of cases are settled before trial through some form of ADR. Indeed, over half of the states either require or encourage parties to

alternative dispute resolution (ADR)

The resolution of disputes in ways other than those involved in the traditional judicial process. Negotiation, mediation, and arbitration are forms of ADR.

Technology and Today's Paralegal

COURTS IN THE INTERNET AGE

Most courts have sites on the Web. Some courts display only the names of court personnel, office phone numbers, and general information. Others add judicial decisions, electronic forms, court rules, filing guidelines and fees, legal resources, and employment opportunities within the court system. We look here at some useful Web sites for paralegals who wish to become familiar with the various court systems and their Internet interfaces. Experience with navigating pertinent court Web sites may give you an advantage in the employment market and make you a valued member of the legal team.

FEDERAL, STATE, AND LOCAL COURT STRUCTURES

It is important for paralegals to understand the structures of federal and state court systems so they know which types of cases are tried in which courts. You will find a description of the types of federal courts and links to all federal courts at the Federal Judiciary Web site, accessible at **www.uscourts.gov**. Villanova University hosts a federal court locator at **www.law.villanova.edu**. (From the "Library" menu, select "Research & Study Guides," and then select "Federal Court Locator.") This site also includes links to federal agencies and other legal information sources.

Each state's court system is structured uniquely. The National Center for State Courts (NCSC), a nonprofit organization dedicated to improving state courts, presents flowcharts depicting the structure of each state court system at **www.ncsconline.org**. (From "NCSC Top 10 Web Pages," select "State Court Structure Charts.") At the NCSC site, you can also find links to state court Web sites, state court statistics, articles about state court trends, and job announcements. Many state judicial systems have centralized Web sites with links to circuit and trial courts' Web sites. For example, the Web site for Michigan courts offers a directory of trial courts, maps of local court jurisdictions, and local trial court

---

undertake ADR prior to trial. Several federal courts have instituted ADR programs as well. Here, we examine various forms of ADR. Keep in mind, though, that new methods of ADR—and new combinations of existing methods—are continually being devised and employed. Additionally, ADR services are now being offered via the Internet. Paralegals who develop expertise in the area of ADR can expand their career opportunities (by becoming mediators, for example). Paralegals can also help attorneys to clarify the issues for clients who must decide whether to take a case to court or choose ADR, as described in *Developing Paralegal Skills* on page 177.

Negotiation

Negotiation is one alternative means of resolving disputes. Attorneys frequently advise their clients to try to negotiate a settlement of their disputes voluntarily before they proceed to trial. During pretrial negotiation, the parties and/or their attorneys may meet one or more times to see if a mutually satisfactory agreement can be reached.

▶ **EXAMPLE 6.13** Assume that Katherine Baranski is suing Tony Peretto for damages. Peretto ran a stop sign. His van crashed into Baranski's car, causing her to suffer injuries and damages exceeding $100,000. After pretrial investigations into the matter, both plaintiff Baranski and defendant Peretto realize that Baranski has a good chance of winning the suit. At this point, Peretto's attorney may make

negotiation
A process in which parties attempt to settle their dispute voluntarily, with or without attorneys to represent them.

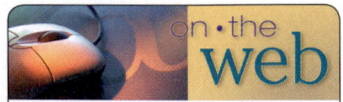

You can find publications pertaining to ADR by accessing the Federal Judicial Center at **www.fjc.gov**.

links at **courts.michigan.gov**. (From the menu at the left, select "State Court Administration." On the page that opens, select "Site Map." Then, under "Home Pages," select "Trial Courts and Maps.")

COURT DECISIONS

Paralegals are often called on to find court decisions on topics related to current or pending cases. Most state courts include judicial decisions (often referred to as opinions) on their Web sites, and the majority of state courts provide case archives dating back several years. Decisions by the United States Supreme Court are posted on the Court's official Web site at **www.supremecourtus.gov** within hours after the decisions are rendered.

Even decisions that are designated as unpublished opinions by the appellate courts are often published online. "Unpublished" decisions generally do not contain the same detailed recital of facts or comprehensive legal analysis as published opinions. Today, some courts permit unpublished decisions to be cited, although usually as persuasive rather than binding authority. You may also sometimes cite slip opinions. A slip opinion (discussed further in Chapter 7) is the second version of an opinion, and it may contain corrections not appearing in the initial opinion. As a paralegal, it is important that you specify to the attorneys you are assisting whether any court opinions you refer to are unpublished decisions or slip opinions rather than published opinions.

TECHNOLOGY TIP

Paralegals should be comfortable gathering court information through the Internet, and regular practice is the way to achieve such comfort. Use the links mentioned above to find Web sites for courts in your area, review various courts' rules, examine court dockets, and check out what forms are available online. As an example, use the NCSC Web site to locate the Web site for the California courts. (On the home page, select "Information," then "Court Web Sites.") At the California site, review some trial, pretrial, and probate rules. Then browse the dockets for the California appellate courts, including the Supreme Court. A paralegal should be comfortable finding, filling out, and submitting court forms online. Click on "Forms" from the menu at the top of the California Courts Web site, read the instructions, choose a form from the list, and fill out the form. Then search the Web site to locate the specific procedures that are required for filing the documents with the court. You will find valuable court information through such exercises and be on the road to becoming the technology expert of your legal team.

a settlement offer on behalf of Peretto. Baranski may be willing to accept a settlement offer for an amount lower than the amount of damages she claimed in her complaint simply to avoid the time, trouble, and expense involved in taking the case to trial.

To facilitate an out-of-court settlement, Baranski's attorney may ask his paralegal to draft a letter to Baranski pointing out the strengths and weaknesses of her case against Peretto, the ADR options for settling the case before trial, and the advantages and disadvantages associated with each ADR option. Additionally, the paralegal may be asked to draft a letter to Peretto's attorney indicating the strengths of Baranski's case against him and the advantages to Peretto of settling the dispute out of court. ◄

As a result of pretrial negotiations, such as those just described in Example 6.13, a settlement agreement may be reached. In a **settlement agreement**, one party gives up the right to initiate or continue litigation in return for a sum to be paid by the other party. Exhibit 6.5 on the following page shows an example of a settlement agreement.

Mediation

Another alternative to a trial is mediation. In the **mediation** process, the parties attempt to negotiate an agreement with the assistance of a neutral third party, a mediator. In mediation, the mediator talks with the parties separately as well as

settlement agreement
An out-of-court resolution to a legal dispute, which is agreed to by the parties in writing. A settlement agreement may be reached at any time prior to or during a trial.

mediation
A method of settling disputes outside of court by using the services of a neutral third party, who acts as a communicating agent between the parties; a method of dispute settlement that is less formal than arbitration.

EXHIBIT 6.5
A Sample Settlement Agreement

SETTLEMENT AGREEMENT

THIS AGREEMENT is entered into this twelfth day of May, 2011, between Katherine Baranski and Tony Peretto.

WITNESSETH

WHEREAS, there is now pending in the U.S. District Court for the District of Nita an action entitled *Baranski v. Peretto,* hereinafter referred to as "action."

WHEREAS, the parties hereto desire to record their agreement to settle all matters relating to said action without the necessity of further litigation.

NOW, THEREFORE, in consideration of the covenants and agreements contained herein, the sufficiency of which is hereby mutually acknowledged, and intending to be legally bound hereby, the parties agree as follows:

1. Katherine Baranski agrees to accept the sum of seventy-five thousand dollars ($75,000) in full satisfaction of all claims against Tony Peretto as set forth in the complaint filed in this action.

2. Tony Peretto agrees to pay Katherine Baranski the above-stated amount, in a lump-sum cash payment, on or before the first day of July, 2011.

3. Upon execution of this agreement and payment of the sum required under this agreement, the parties shall cause the action to be dismissed with prejudice.

4. When the sum required under this agreement is paid in full, Katherine Baranski will execute and deliver to Tony Peretto a release of all claims set forth in the complaint filed in the said action.

Katherine Baranski
Katherine Baranski

Tony Peretto
Tony Peretto

Sworn and subscribed before me this twelfth day of May, 2011.

Leela M. Shay
Leela M. Shay
Notary Public
State of Nita

TO SUE OR NOT TO SUE

Millie Burke, a paralegal, works for a sole practitioner. She has just been asked by the firm's owner, attorney Jim Wilcox, to draw up a checklist. It is to consist of questions that clients should consider before initiating a lawsuit. Wilcox wants to have the checklist on hand when he first interviews clients who come to him for advice on whether to bring a lawsuit or to settle a dispute by some alternative means. Millie drafts a checklist for Wilcox's review.

CHECKLIST FOR DECIDING WHETHER TO SUE

- Now that you have a rough idea of what it might cost to litigate your dispute, are you still interested in pursuing a trial? If so, you will need to pay a retainer now from which I will pay the initial filing fees and court costs. You will also need to sign an agreement that you will pay me hourly rates if the costs exceed the amount of the retainer.

- Do you have the time and patience to follow a court case through the judicial system, even if it takes several years?

- Is there a way to settle your grievance privately, without going to court? Even if the settlement is less than you think you are owed, you may be better off settling now for the smaller figure. An early settlement will save time on future expenses and prevent the time loss and frustration associated with litigation.

- Can you use some form of alternative dispute resolution (negotiation, mediation, or arbitration) to settle the dispute? Before you say no, let's review these dispute-settlement methods and discuss the pros and cons of each alternative.

---

jointly. The mediator emphasizes points of agreement, helps the parties evaluate their positions, and proposes solutions. The mediator, however, does not make a binding decision on the matter being disputed.

The parties may select a mediator on the basis of expertise in a particular field or a reputation for fairness and impartiality. The mediator need not be a lawyer. The mediator may be one person, such as a paralegal, an attorney, or a volunteer from the community, or a panel of mediators may be used. Usually, a mediator charges a fee, which can be split between the parties. Many state and federal courts now require that parties mediate their disputes before being allowed to resolve the disputes through trials. In this situation, the mediators may be appointed by the court.

A Nonadversarial Forum

Mediation is not adversarial in nature, as lawsuits are. In litigation, the parties "do battle" with each other in the courtroom, while the judge is the neutral party. Because of its nonadversarial nature, the mediation process tends to reduce the hostility between the parties and may allow them to resume their former relationship. For this reason, mediation is often the preferred form of ADR for disputes involving business partners, employers and employees, family members, or other parties involved in long-term relationships.

A paralegal mediates a dispute by emphasizing the common ground shared by the parties as she proposes possible solutions. Who are the most common parties in mediation?

(Courtesy of © Brand X Pictures)

▶ **EXAMPLE 6.14** Suppose that two business partners have a dispute over how the profits of their firm should be distributed. If the dispute is litigated, the parties will be adversaries, and their attorneys will emphasize how the parties' positions differ, not what they have in common. In contrast, if the dispute is mediated, the mediator will emphasize the common ground shared by the partners and help them work toward agreement. ◀

Paralegals as Mediators

Because a mediator need not be a lawyer, this field is open to paralegals who acquire appropriate training and expertise. If you are interested in becoming a mediator, you can check with your local paralegal association or with one of the national paralegal associations to find out how you can pursue this career goal. You can also check with a county, state, or federal court in your area to see how to qualify as a mediator for court-referred mediation (to be discussed shortly). Generally, any paralegal aspiring to work as a mediator must have excellent communication skills. This is because, as a mediator, it will be your job to listen carefully to each party's complaints and communicate possible solutions to a dispute in a way that is not offensive to either party. (See this chapter's *Featured Contributor* article on pages 180 and 181 for further details on the functions performed by mediators and the role played by paralegals in the mediation process.)

Arbitration

arbitration

A method of settling disputes in which a dispute is submitted to a disinterested third party (other than a court), who issues a decision that may or may not be legally binding.

A more formal method of ADR is **arbitration**, in which an arbitrator hears a dispute and determines the outcome. The key difference between arbitration and the forms of ADR just discussed is that in arbitration, the third party hearing the dispute makes the decision for the parties—a decision that may be legally binding. In negotiation and mediation, in contrast, the parties decide for themselves, although a third party may assist them. In a sense, the arbitrator acts as a private judge, even though the arbitrator is not required to be a lawyer. Often, a panel of experts arbitrates the dispute.

In some respects, formal arbitration resembles a trial, although the procedural rules are much less restrictive than those governing litigation. In the typical hearing format, the parties present arguments to the arbitrator and state what remedies should or should not be granted. Evidence is then presented, and witnesses may be called and examined by both sides. The arbitrator then issues a decision.

Depending on the parties' circumstances and preferences, the arbitrator's decision may be legally binding or nonbinding on the parties. In nonbinding arbitration, the parties submit their dispute to a third party but remain free to reject the third party's decision. Nonbinding arbitration is more similar to mediation than to binding arbitration. As will be discussed later in this chapter, arbitration that is mandated by the courts usually is not binding on the parties. If, after mandatory arbitration, the parties are not satisfied with the results of arbitration, they may ignore the arbitrator's decision and have the dispute litigated in court. Even if the arbitrator's decision is binding, a party can appeal the decision to a court for judicial review—as will be discussed next.

Arbitration Clauses and Statutes

Almost any commercial matter can be submitted to arbitration. When a dispute arises, parties can agree to settle their differences through arbitration rather than through the court system. Frequently, however, disputes are arbitrated because of an arbitration clause in a contract entered into before the dispute arose. An **arbitration clause** provides that any disputes arising under the contract will be resolved by arbitration. For example, an arbitration clause in a contract for the sale of goods might provide that "any controversy or claim arising under this contract will be referred to arbitration before the American Arbitration Association."[7]

Most states have statutes (often based on the Uniform Arbitration Act of 1955) under which arbitration clauses will be enforced, and some state statutes compel arbitration of certain types of disputes, such as those involving public employees. At the federal level, the Federal Arbitration Act (FAA) of 1925 enforces arbitration clauses in contracts involving maritime activity and interstate commerce. Because of the wide scope of the commerce clause in the Constitution (see Appendix J), even business activities that have only remote or minimal effects on commerce between two or more states may be regarded as interstate commerce. Thus, arbitration agreements involving transactions only slightly connected to the flow of interstate commerce may fall under the FAA.

The FAA does not establish a set arbitration procedure. The parties themselves must agree on the manner of resolving their disputes. The FAA provides only that if the parties have agreed to arbitrate disputes arising in relation to their contract, through an arbitration clause, the arbitration clause will be enforced by the courts. In other words, arbitration must take place before a party can take a dispute to the courts.

arbitration clause
A clause in a contract that provides that, in case of a dispute, the parties will determine their rights through arbitration rather than the judicial system.

The Arbitration Process

The first step in the arbitration process is the **submission agreement**, in which the parties agree to submit their dispute for arbitration. If an arbitration clause was included in a contract, the clause itself is the submission to arbitrate. Most states require that an agreement to submit a dispute to arbitration must be in writing. The submission agreement typically identifies the parties, the nature of the dispute to be resolved, the monetary amounts involved in the dispute, the place of arbitration, and the powers that the arbitrator will exercise. Frequently, the agreement includes a signed statement that the parties intend to be bound by the arbitrator's decision.

The next step in the process is the *hearing*. Normally, the parties agree prior to arbitration—in an arbitration clause or in a submission-to-arbitrate agreement, for example—on what procedural rules will govern the proceedings. This includes the method to be used to select an arbitrator or a panel of three arbitrators. In a typical hearing, the parties begin as they would at a trial by presenting opening arguments and stating what remedies should or should not be granted. After the opening

submission agreement
A written agreement to submit a legal dispute to an arbitrator or arbitrating panel for resolution.

featured contributor

MEDIATION: CAREER OPPORTUNITIES FOR PARALEGALS

Fernaundra Ferguson

BIOGRAPHICAL NOTE

Fernaundra Ferguson is an assistant dean in the College of Arts and Sciences at the University of West Florida. She earned a bachelor of arts degree in political science and history from Bennett College and a J.D. degree from Howard University School of Law. Her current focus is in the area of conflict resolution, specifically mediation; and she has published several articles on mediation. Ferguson serves the Association of Conflict Resolution as vice president, co-chair of the Diversity and Equity executive committee, and co-chair of the governance committee and is past co-chair of the Training Section. She also serves as Southern Regional chair of Conflict Resolution/ Positive Solutions for Delta Sigma Theta Sorority, Inc. She is a member of the Phi Delta Phi Legal Fraternity, the Southern Association for Pre-Law Advisors, and Societas Docta, Inc.

L itigation is costly and time consuming. For these and other reasons, the legal system in the United States is rapidly adopting alternative methods to the traditional adversarial process of litigation. Many state court systems, as well as the federal court system, now provide for one or more alternatives to litigation. Methods of alternative dispute resolution, or ADR, include negotiation, settlement conference, mediation, arbitration, mini-trial, summary jury trial, private judging, and conciliation.

Conflict resolution through mediation is often thought of as "win/win" resolution, because there is no winner or loser. Unlike litigation and some methods of alternative dispute resolution (such as arbitration), mediation is not adversarial in nature. This is because the focus of mediation is not on the parties' differences but on those points on which the parties agree.

THE MEDIATION PROCESS

Mediation is a voluntary and confidential process in which a neutral third party, the mediator, facilitates the resolution of a dispute between the parties. The mediator's role is to help the parties discuss difficult issues, propose solutions, and negotiate an agreement. The mediator does not have any decision-making power over the outcome; rather, it is up to the parties to decide which proposed solution to adopt. For the mediation process to work, the mediator must do the following:

- Gather information.
- Remain neutral and unbiased throughout the process.
- Be a good listener.
- Articulate the issues being disputed.
- Assess the interests of the parties and the realities they face.

statements have been made, evidence is presented. Witnesses may be called and examined by both sides. After all evidence has been presented, the parties give their closing arguments. Although arbitration is in some ways similar to a trial, the rules (such as those regarding what kinds of evidence may be introduced) are usually much less restrictive than those involved in formal litigation.

After each side has had an opportunity to present evidence and to argue its case, the arbitrator reaches a decision. The final decision of the arbitrator is called an **award**, even if no monetary award is conferred on a party as a result of the proceedings. Under most arbitration statutes, the arbitrator must render an award within thirty days of the close of the hearing.

A paralegal may become involved in preparations for arbitration, just as he or she would in preparing for a trial. The paralegal will assist in obtaining and organiz-

award
In the context of ADR, the decision rendered by an arbitrator.

- Obtain information from each party that will assist in resolving the dispute.
- Evaluate alternative solutions to the dispute.
- Identify the points on which the parties agree and propose solutions to the parties.
- Encourage the parties to settle their dispute.
- Formalize any agreement reached by the parties.
- Believe in the process.

ASSISTING ATTORNEYS IN THE MEDIATION PROCESS

Paralegals play a major role in assisting attorneys in the mediation of disputes, both before and during the mediation itself. Prior to the mediation, paralegals interview clients, assist in gathering any information (such as police reports, medical records, or child-care expenses) that will help the attorney when advising the client, draft documents that may be needed for the mediation, and prepare a list of mediators in the relevant geographic and specialty area. During the mediation, the paralegal may be asked to provide additional information and draft other documents (such as a settlement agreement). If the attorney serves as the mediator, the paralegal may be asked to schedule dates with the parties or their attorneys for the mediation, prepare any necessary forms, and draft a final settlement agreement.

PARALEGALS AS MEDIATORS

Paralegals with mediation training are employed in a variety of dispute-resolution settings outside the law office. For example,

> *"Paralegals play a major role in assisting attorneys in the mediation of disputes, both before and during the mediation itself."*

some paralegals with mediation training work for administrative agencies that offer dispute-resolution services. Other paralegals who are trained in mediation have supervised and trained volunteer mediators in community centers. Increasingly, mediation is being utilized to address community issues, including hostilities leading to violence in the schools. Peer mediation, for example, helps to diffuse such feelings as anger, distrust, and fear before those feelings escalate into violent acts. Paralegals may also serve as mediators in disputes between communities and the local police force or between city governments and representatives of the local citizenry.

Organizations promoting community mediation have sprung up around the country. There is now a national association of such groups—the National Association for Community Mediation (NAFCM). The NAFCM is an association of community mediation centers, their staff and volunteer mediators, and other individuals and organizations interested in the community mediation movement. Paralegals who are interested in participating in community mediation should check to see what community mediation organizations exist in their city or state.

Mediation training also provides the paralegal with opportunities in international settings. Some paralegals have exciting careers as members of a team mediating disputes between countries.

ing all evidence relating to the dispute, may interview witnesses and prepare them for the hearing, and generally will assist in other tasks commonly undertaken prior to a trial (see Chapter 10).

The Role of the Courts in Prearbitration

The role of the courts in the arbitration process is limited. One important role is played at the prearbitration stage. When a dispute arises as to whether the parties have agreed in an arbitration clause to submit a particular matter to arbitration, one party may file suit to force arbitration. The court before which the suit is brought will not decide the basic controversy but must decide whether the dispute is *arbitrable*—that is, whether the matter is one that can be resolved through arbitration. ▶ **EXAMPLE 6.15** Suppose that a dispute involves a claim of employment discrimination on the basis of age. If the issue of arbitrability reaches a court, the court will have to decide whether the Age Discrimination in Employment Act of 1967 (which protects persons forty years of age and older against employment discrimination on the basis of age) permits claims brought under this act to be arbitrated. ◀

If the court finds that the subject matter in controversy is covered by the agreement to arbitrate, then a party is likely to be compelled to arbitrate the dispute. Even when a claim involves a violation of a statute passed to protect a certain class of people, such as a statute prohibiting age discrimination against employees in the workplace, a court may determine that the parties must nonetheless abide by their agreement to arbitrate the dispute. Usually, a court will allow the claim to be arbitrated if the court, in interpreting the statute, can find no legislative intent to the contrary.

No party will be ordered to submit a dispute to arbitration unless the court believes the party has consented to do so. The courts will not compel arbitration if the arbitration rules and procedures are inherently unfair to one of the parties. ▶ **EXAMPLE 6.16** Suppose that an employer's arbitration agreement with an employee states that the employer establishes the rules for the arbitration. In this situation, the court may conclude that the rules are unfair and thus refuse to enforce the arbitration agreement. ◀ See the *Ethics Watch* feature for the paralegal's role in ensuring that arbitration clauses are proper.

The Postarbitration Role of the Courts

Courts also may play an important role at the postarbitration stage. If the arbitration has produced an award, one of the parties may appeal the award or may seek a court order compelling the other party to comply with the award. In determining whether an award should be enforced, a court conducts a review that is much more restricted in scope than an appellate court's review of a trial court decision. The general view is that because the parties were free to frame the issues and set the powers of the arbitrator at the outset, they cannot complain about the result. An arbitration award may be set aside, however, if the award resulted from the arbitrator's misconduct or "bad faith" or if the arbitrator exceeded his or her powers in arbitrating the dispute. (That does not happen very often.) An arbitrator is permitted to resolve only those issues that are covered by the agreement to submit to arbitration.

Other ADR Forms

The three forms of ADR just discussed are the oldest and traditionally the most commonly used forms. In recent years, a variety of new types of ADR have emerged. Some of them combine elements of mediation and arbitration. For example, in **binding mediation**, a neutral mediator tries to facilitate agreement between the parties, but if no agreement is reached the mediator issues a legally binding decision on the matter. In **mediation arbitration (med-arb)**, an arbitrator first attempts to help the parties reach an agreement, just as a mediator would. If no agreement is reached, then formal arbitration is undertaken, and the arbitrator issues a legally binding decision.

Other ADR forms are sometimes referred to as "assisted negotiation" because they involve a third party in what is essentially a negotiation process. For example, in **early neutral case evaluation**, the parties select a neutral third party (generally an expert in the subject matter of the dispute) to evaluate their respective positions. The parties explain their positions to the case evaluator however they wish. The case evaluator then assesses the strengths and weaknesses of the parties' positions, and this evaluation forms the basis of negotiating a settlement.

The mini-trial is a form of assisted negotiation that is often used by business parties. In a **mini-trial**, each party's attorney briefly argues the party's case before representatives of each firm who have the authority to settle the dispute. Typically, a neutral third party (usually an expert in the area being disputed) acts as an adviser. If the parties fail to reach an agreement, the adviser renders an opinion as to how a

---

binding mediation
A form of ADR in which a mediator attempts to facilitate agreement between the parties but then issues a legally binding decision if no agreement is reached.

mediation arbitration (med-arb)
A form of ADR in which an arbitrator first attempts to help the parties reach an agreement, just as a mediator would. If no agreement is reached, formal arbitration occurs, and the arbitrator issues a legally binding decision.

early neutral case evaluation
A form of ADR in which a neutral third party evaluates the strengths and weaknesses of the disputing parties' positions; the evaluator's opinion forms the basis for negotiating a settlement.

mini-trial
A private proceeding that assists disputing parties in determining whether to take their case to court. Each party's attorney briefly argues the party's case before the other party and (usually) a neutral third party, who acts as an adviser. If the parties fail to reach an agreement, the adviser issues an opinion as to how a court would likely decide the issue.

Ethics Watch

POTENTIAL ARBITRATION PROBLEMS

Many individuals and business firms prefer to arbitrate disputes rather than take them to court. For that reason, they often include arbitration clauses in their contracts. These clauses normally specify who or what organization will arbitrate the dispute and where the arbitration will take place. To safeguard a client's interests, when drafting and reviewing arbitration clauses in contracts, the careful paralegal will be alert to the possibility that those who arbitrate the dispute might not be totally neutral or that the designated place of arbitration is so geographically distant from the client's location that it may pose a great inconvenience and expense for the client should an arbitrable dispute arise. The paralegal should call any such problems to his or her supervising attorney's attention. The attorney can then discuss the problem with the client and help the client negotiate an arbitration clause that is more favorable to the client's position.

This is necessary to be consistent with the NFPA Model Code of Ethics and Professional Responsibility, Section 1.6(a): "A paralegal shall act within the bounds of the law, solely for the benefit of the client." It is also consistent with the ABA Model Guidelines for the Utilization of Paralegal Services, Guideline 2: "Provided the lawyer maintains responsibility for the work product, a lawyer may delegate to a paralegal any task normally performed by the lawyer, except those tasks proscribed to a nonlawyer by statute, court rule, administrative rule or regulation, controlling authority, the applicable rule of professional conduct of the jurisdiction in which the lawyer practices, or these guidelines."

court would likely decide the issue. The proceeding assists the parties in determining whether they should negotiate a settlement of the dispute or take it to court.

Yet Another Approach—Collaborative Law

Still another method of resolving disputes is the collaborative law approach, which is increasingly being used by spouses during separation procedures. In *collaborative law,* both parties, their attorneys, and any professionals working with the parties agree to meet to resolve all of their issues without litigation. The lawyers act as negotiators and communication moderators while advising their clients about their legal rights, entitlements, and obligations. Both parties promise to take a reasoned stand on every issue, to keep discovery cooperative and informal, and to work together to craft an agreement. Any abusive communications are identified, discussed, and eliminated. Because the attorneys agree not to take part in any litigation that may occur if an agreement is not reached, the attorneys focus only on settlement rather than on preparing documents or presentations for court. If either party seeks court intervention, both attorneys must withdraw from representation.

Court-Referred ADR

Today, most states require or encourage parties to undergo mediation or arbitration prior to trial. Generally, when a trial court refers a case for arbitration, the arbitrator's decision is not binding on the parties. If the parties do not agree with the arbitrator's decision, they can go forward with the lawsuit.

The types of court-related ADR programs in use vary widely. In some states, such as Missouri, ADR is voluntary. In other states, such as Minnesota, parties are required to undertake ADR before they can have their cases heard in court. Some states, such as Minnesota, offer a menu of options. Other states, including Florida (which has a statewide, comprehensive mediation program), offer only one alternative.

Today's courts are also experimenting with a variety of ADR alternatives to speed up justice and reduce its cost. Some federal and state courts now hold **summary jury trials (SJTs)**, in which the parties present their arguments and supporting evidence (other than witness testimony—witnesses are not called in an SJT). The jury renders a verdict, but unlike the verdict in an actual trial, the jury's verdict is not binding. The verdict does, however, act as a guide to both sides in reaching an agreement during the mandatory negotiations that immediately follow the SJT. If no settlement is reached, both sides have the right to a full trial later. Other alternatives being employed by the courts include summary procedures for commercial litigation and the appointment of special masters to assist judges in deciding complex issues.

Providers of ADR Services

ADR services are provided by both government agencies and private organizations. A major provider of ADR services is the **American Arbitration Association (AAA)**, which was founded in 1926. Most of the nation's largest law firms are members of this non-profit association. About 200,000 disputes are submitted to the AAA for resolution each year in its offices around the country and overseas. Cases brought before the AAA are heard by an expert or a panel of experts in the area relating to the dispute and are usually settled quickly. Generally, about half of the panel members are lawyers. To cover its costs, the AAA charges a fee, paid by the party filing the claim. In addition, each party to the dispute pays a specified amount for each hearing day. An additional fee is charged for cases involving personal injuries or property loss.

Hundreds of for-profit firms around the country also provide ADR services. Many firms hire retired judges to conduct arbitration hearings or assist parties in settling their disputes. Private ADR firms normally allow the parties to decide on the date of the hearing, the presiding judge, whether the judge's decision will be legally binding, and the site of the hearing—which may be a conference room, a law school office, or a leased courtroom. The judges follow procedures similar to those of the federal courts and use similar rules. Usually, each party to the dispute pays a filing fee and a designated fee for a hearing session or conference.

As mentioned, courts also have ADR programs in which disputes are resolved by court-appointed attorneys or paralegals who are qualified to act as arbitrators or mediators in certain types of disputes. Many paralegals have found that becoming a mediator or an arbitrator is an especially rewarding career option.

Online Dispute Resolution

A number of companies and organizations offer **online dispute resolution (ODR)**, which is conducted on the Internet. The disputes resolved in online forums usually involve disagreements over the right to use a certain Web site address or the quality of goods purchased over the Internet (including goods sold through Internet auction sites). Those who do business in cyberspace (and the attorneys who represent them) should be aware of this ADR option.

Most online forums do not automatically apply the law of any specific jurisdiction. Instead, results are often based on general, universal legal principles. As with traditional methods of dispute resolution, a party normally may appeal to a court at any time. Negotiation, mediation, and arbitration services are all available to disputants over the Internet.

Online Negotiation

Several Web-based firms offer online forums for negotiating monetary settlements. Typically, one party files a complaint, and the other party is notified by e-mail. Password-protected access to the online forum site is made available. Fees are gen-

summary jury trial (SJT)
A settlement method in which a trial is held but the jury's verdict is not binding. The verdict acts as a guide to both sides in reaching an agreement during mandatory negotiations that follow the trial. If a settlement is not reached, both sides have the right to a full trial later.

American Arbitration Association (AAA)
The major organization offering arbitration services in the United States.

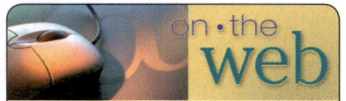

To obtain information on the services offered by the American Arbitration Association (AAA), as well as forms used to submit a case for arbitration, go to the AAA's Web site at **www.adr.org**.

online dispute resolution (ODR)
The resolution of disputes with the assistance of an organization that offers dispute-resolution services via the Internet.

Today's Professional Paralegal

ARBITRATING COMMERCIAL CONTRACTS

Julia Lorenz has worked as a legal assistant for International Airlines (IA) for ten years. She works in the legal department on the staff of the general counsel. Her job has been to work with Jim Manning, senior attorney. This attorney is responsible for all of the corporation's contracts, including major contracts with jet manufacturers for the purchase of aircraft, contracts with catering companies to supply food during flights, fuel contracts, employment and labor contracts, and many small contracts for the purchase and lease of equipment and supplies for the numerous airline offices and ticket counters.

REVIEWING PROPOSED CONTRACTS

Julia's job is to review the provisions of proposed major contracts, such as contracts to purchase jet aircraft, and to provide Jim with an article-by-article summary of the contracts' provisions. Jim then negotiates these contracts to obtain the most favorable terms possible for the airline. Once he has negotiated a contract, Julia makes the final changes and forwards it to the appropriate IA corporate official to review and sign.

ATTENDING ARBITRATION PROCEEDINGS

All of the airline's major contracts contain arbitration clauses that require all contract disputes to be resolved through binding arbitration services provided by the American Arbitration Association (AAA). On many occasions, Julia has attended arbitration proceedings with Jim. In preparing for arbitration, Julia obtains affidavits, prepares subpoenas, and arranges for witnesses to be present to testify. During the arbitration proceedings, she assists in presenting material into evidence. She and Jim have developed a good rapport with several arbitrators at the local AAA office, and they usually request these arbitrators when they have a case that must be arbitrated.

BECOMING AN ARBITRATOR

Julia's knowledge of arbitration procedures and her outstanding work in preparing for arbitration, as well as during the proceedings, have won her significant recognition from this group of arbitrators. One of the arbitrators eventually suggests that she apply for approval as an arbitrator. She says that she will consider it.

Julia later mentions the arbitrator's suggestion to Jim. He encourages her to contact the AAA to inquire about the possibility of being approved as an arbitrator. When Julia calls the AAA, she learns that arbitrators in the area of commercial arbitration are not required to be attorneys. She would need eight years of experience in her field and would have to meet certain educational requirements. When Julia realizes that she has the necessary qualifications, she submits an application. About two months later, she is approved as an arbitrator.

erally low (often 2 to 4 percent, or less, of the disputed amount). The parties can drop the negotiations at any time. The Web-based firm Smartsettle offers a unique blind-bidding system to help resolve disputes.

Online Arbitration

A number of organizations, including the American Arbitration Association, offer online arbitration services. For instance, Resolution Forum, Inc. (RFI), a nonprofit organization associated with the Center for Legal Responsibility at the South Texas

College of Law, offers arbitration services through its CAN-WIN conferencing system. Using standard browser software and an RFI password, the parties to a dispute access an online conference room. When multiple parties are involved, private communications and breakout sessions are possible through private messaging facilities. RFI also offers mediation services.

ADR AND THE PARALEGAL

The time and monetary costs associated with litigating disputes in court continue to rise, and, as a result, disputing parties are increasingly turning to ADR as a means of settling their disagreements. As a way to reduce their caseloads, state and federal courts are also increasingly requiring litigants to undergo arbitration before bringing their suits in front of the courts. Although paralegals have always assisted attorneys in work relating to the negotiation of out-of-court settlements for clients, they may play an even greater role in the future. Some paralegals are qualified mediators and directly assist parties in reaching a mutually satisfactory agreement. Some paralegals serve as arbitrators. As more and more parties utilize ADR, paralegals will have increasing opportunities in this area of legal work. (See *Today's Professional Paralegal* on the previous page for an example.)

If you are interested in becoming a mediator, you need to be thoroughly familiar with ADR law in the state in which you work. Some states do not require mediators to meet any special training requirements. For example, Florida law requires that a family mediator "shall be a person with the appropriate attributes who can demonstrate sensitivity toward the parties involved and facilitate solutions to the problem." Other states require mediators to have up to sixty hours of training in certain fields, such as family law, child development, or family dynamics.

KEY TERMS AND CONCEPTS

alternative dispute resolution (ADR)   *173*

American Arbitration Association
   (AAA)   *184*

appellate court   *163*

appellate jurisdiction   *163*

arbitration   *178*

arbitration clause   *179*

award   *180*

bankruptcy court   *163*

binding mediation   *182*

concurrent jurisdiction   *165*

diversity of citizenship   *163*

docket   *165*

early neutral case evaluation   *182*

exclusive jurisdiction   *165*

federal question   *163*

jurisdiction   *162*

justiciable controversy   *161*

long arm statute   *162*

mediation   *175*

mediation arbitration (med-arb)   *182*

mini-trial   *182*

negotiation   *174*

online dispute resolution (ODR)   *184*

original jurisdiction   *163*

probate court   *162*

reversible error   *169*

rule of four   *172*

settlement agreement   *175*

standing to sue   *161*

submission agreement   *179*

summary jury trial (SJT)   *184*

trial court   *163*

venue   *166*

writ of *certiorari*   *172*

CHAPTER SUMMARY

THE COURT SYSTEM AND ALTERNATIVE DISPUTE RESOLUTION

Basic Judicial Requirements

1. *Standing to sue*—A legally protected and real interest in a matter sufficient to justify seeking relief through the court system. The controversy at issue must also be a justiciable controversy—one that is real and substantial, not hypothetical or academic.

2. *Jurisdiction*—Before a court can hear a case, it must have jurisdiction over the person against whom the suit is brought (*in personam* jurisdiction) or the property involved in the suit (*in rem* jurisdiction), as well as jurisdiction over the subject matter.

   a. **LIMITED VERSUS GENERAL JURISDICTION**—Limited jurisdiction exists when a court is limited to a specific subject matter, such as probate or divorce. General jurisdiction exists when a court can hear any kind of case.

   b. **ORIGINAL VERSUS APPELLATE JURISDICTION**—Courts that have authority to hear a case for the first time (trial courts) have original jurisdiction. Courts of appeals, or reviewing courts, have appellate jurisdiction; generally, these courts do not have original jurisdiction.

   c. **FEDERAL JURISDICTION**—Arises (1) when a federal question is involved (when the plaintiff's cause of action is based, at least in part, on the U.S. Constitution, a treaty, or a federal law) or (2) when a case involves diversity of citizenship (as in disputes between citizens of different states, between a foreign country and citizens of a state or states, or between citizens of a state and citizens of a foreign country) and the amount in controversy exceeds $75,000.

   d. **CONCURRENT VERSUS EXCLUSIVE JURISDICTION**—Concurrent jurisdiction exists when two different courts have authority to hear the same case. Exclusive jurisdiction exists when only state courts or only federal courts have authority to hear a case.

3. *Jurisdiction in cyberspace*—Because the Internet does not have physical boundaries, traditional jurisdictional concepts have been difficult to apply. The courts are developing standards to use in determining when jurisdiction over a Web owner or operator in another state is proper.

4. *Venue*—Venue has to do with the most appropriate location for a trial, which is usually the geographic area where the event leading to the dispute took place or where the parties reside.

5. *Judicial procedures*—Rules of procedure prescribe the way in which disputes are handled in the courts. The Federal Rules of Civil Procedure govern all civil litigation in federal courts. Each state has its own procedural rules (often similar to the federal rules), and each court within a state has specific court rules that must be followed.

State Court Systems

1. *Trial courts*—Courts of original jurisdiction, in which legal actions are initiated. State trial courts have either general jurisdiction or limited jurisdiction.

2. *Intermediate appellate courts*—Many states have intermediate appellate courts that review the proceedings of the trial courts; generally, these courts do not have original jurisdiction. Appellate courts ordinarily examine questions of law and procedure while deferring to the trial court's findings of fact.

3. *Supreme (highest) courts*—Each state has a supreme court, although it may be called by some other name. Decisions of the state's highest court are final on all questions of state law. If a federal question is at issue, the case may be appealed to the United States Supreme Court.

4. *Judges and justices*—State court judges and justices are normally elected by the voters for specified terms.

Continued

The Federal Court System

1. *U.S. district courts*—The federal district court is the equivalent of the state trial court. The district court exercises general jurisdiction over claims arising under federal law or based on diversity of citizenship. Federal courts of limited jurisdiction include the U.S. Tax Court, the U.S. Bankruptcy Court, and the U.S. Court of Federal Claims.

2. *U.S. courts of appeals*—There are thirteen intermediate courts of appeals (or circuit courts of appeals) in the federal court system. Twelve of the courts hear appeals from the district courts within their circuits. The thirteenth court has national appellate jurisdiction over certain cases, such as cases involving patent law and cases in which the U.S. government is a defendant.

3. *United States Supreme Court*—The United States Supreme Court is the highest court in the land and the final arbiter of the Constitution and federal law. There is no absolute right of appeal to the Supreme Court, and the Court hears only a fraction of the cases that are filed with it each year.

   a. Although the Supreme Court has original jurisdiction in some cases, it functions primarily as an appellate court.

   b. If the Supreme Court decides to review a case, it will issue a writ of *certiorari*, an order to a lower court requiring the latter to send it the record of the case for review. As a rule, only petitions that raise the possibility of important constitutional questions are granted.

4. *Judges and justices*—Federal court judges and justices are appointed by the president of the United States and confirmed by the Senate. They receive lifetime appointments.

Alternative Dispute Resolution

The costs and time-consuming character of litigation, as well as the public nature of court proceedings, have caused many to turn to various forms of alternative dispute resolution (ADR) for settling disagreements. The methods of ADR include the following:

1. *Negotiation*—The simplest form of ADR, in which the parties come together, with or without attorneys to represent them, and try to reach a settlement without the involvement of a third party.

2. *Mediation*—A form of ADR in which the parties reach an agreement with the help of a neutral third party, called a mediator, who proposes solutions and emphasizes areas of agreement.

3. *Arbitration*—The most formal method of ADR, in which the parties submit their dispute to a neutral third party, the arbitrator (or panel of arbitrators), who issues a decision. The decision may or may not be legally binding, depending on the circumstances.

   a. Arbitration clauses that are voluntarily agreed on in contracts require the parties to resolve their disputes in arbitration (rather than in court).

   b. Arbitrators' decisions, even when binding, may be appealed to the courts for review. The court's review is much more restricted than an appellate court's review of a trial court record.

4. *Other types of ADR*—These include binding mediation, mediation arbitration (med-arb), early neutral case evaluation, mini-trials, and summary jury trials; generally, these are forms of "assisted negotiation."

5. *Collaborative law*—A form of ADR in which both parties, their attorneys, and any professionals working with the parties meet to resolve their issues without litigation. The lawyers act as negotiators and communication moderators while advising their clients about their legal rights, entitlements, and obligations. If either party seeks court intervention, both attorneys must withdraw from representation.

6. *Providers of ADR services*—The leading nonprofit provider of ADR services is the American Arbitration Association. Hundreds of for-profit firms also provide ADR services.

7. *Online dispute resolution*—A number of organizations and firms offer negotiation and arbitration services through online forums. These forums have been a practical alternative for the resolution of disputes over the right to use a certain Web site address or the quality of goods purchased over the Internet.

STUDENT STUDYWARE™ CD-ROM

Interactive student CD in this book includes additional quizzing, plus video clips, case studies, and Key Terms flashcards.

ONLINE COMPANION™

For additional resources, please go to **www.paralegal.delmar.cengage.com**.

QUESTIONS FOR REVIEW

1. Define *jurisdiction*, and explain why jurisdiction is important. What is the difference between personal jurisdiction and subject-matter jurisdiction? What is a long arm statute?

2. Over what types of cases can federal courts exercise jurisdiction?

3. What is the relationship between state and federal jurisdiction?

4. Describe the functions of a trial court. How do they differ from the functions of an appellate court?

5. How do cases reach the United States Supreme Court?

6. List and explain the various methods of alternative dispute resolution.

ETHICAL QUESTION

1. Suzanne Andersen's supervising attorney, Amy Lynch, works occasionally as a mediator for family law cases in the local courts. Amy has mediated a divorce case today involving the property settlement of a wealthy businessperson, who happens also to be a defendant in another lawsuit in which Amy represents the plaintiff. As a result of her mediation today, Amy has learned some confidential financial information about this man. She now has come to Suzanne, her paralegal, and asked her to use this information to his disadvantage in the lawsuit. How should Suzanne handle this situation?

PRACTICE QUESTIONS AND ASSIGNMENTS

1. A plaintiff and defendant are involved in an auto accident. Both are residents of the county and state in which the accident takes place. The plaintiff files an auto negligence lawsuit in the county circuit court where the trial will occur. What types of jurisdiction does the court have? (The types to be considered include *in*

personam jurisdiction, *in rem* jurisdiction, subject-matter jurisdiction, limited jurisdiction, general jurisdiction, original jurisdiction, appellate jurisdiction, concurrent jurisdiction, and exclusive jurisdiction.)

2. Marcia, who is from Toledo, Ohio, drives to Troy, Michigan, and shops at a popular mall. When leaving the parking lot, Marcia causes a car accident when she runs a stop sign. On what basis could a Michigan court obtain jurisdiction over Marcia?

3. Identify each of the following courts. If not indicated, specify whether it is a state or federal court.

   a. This state court takes testimony from witnesses and receives evidence. It may have either general or limited subject-matter jurisdiction.

   b. This court has appellate jurisdiction and is part of a court system that is divided into geographic units called *circuits.*

   c. This state court reviews the record of a case for errors of law and procedure. It does not have original jurisdiction.

   d. This court can exercise diversity-of-citizenship jurisdiction and receives testimony and other evidence.

   e. The decisions of this court are usually final. It is the highest appellate court in its geographic area.

   f. This federal court has nine justices. It has original jurisdiction over a few types of cases but functions primarily as an appellate court. There is no automatic right to appeal cases to this court.

4. Look at Exhibit 6.4 on page 171. In which federal circuit is your state located? How many federal judicial districts are located in your state? In which federal district is your community located?

5. Using the materials presented in the chapter, identify the following methods of alternative dispute resolution:

   a. The parties to a divorce meet with a neutral third party who emphasizes points of agreement and proposes solutions to resolve their dispute. After several hours, the parties come to a solution.

   b. The parties to a contract dispute submit it to a neutral third party for a legally binding resolution. The neutral third party is not a court.

   c. The plaintiff and defense attorneys in a personal-injury case propose settlement figures to one another and their clients in an effort to resolve the lawsuit voluntarily.

   d. The attorneys from the personal-injury example above are able to reach an acceptable settlement figure of $100,000. They draft an agreement whereby the plaintiff gives up her right to sue in exchange for a payment of $100,000 by the defendant.

   e. A commercial dispute involving $95,000 in damages is filed in a federal court. The judge requires the parties' attorneys to present their arguments and supporting evidence, excluding witnesses, to the jury. The jury then renders a nonbinding verdict. Once the nonbinding verdict is rendered, the parties reach a settlement.

 ## QUESTIONS FOR CRITICAL ANALYSIS

1. The federal courts have jurisdiction primarily over diversity cases and over questions of federal law. State courts have jurisdiction over matters such as wills, divorces, and property concerns. Why? What would happen if federal courts decided divorce cases, for example? What would happen if state courts decided cases between a citizen of the state and a foreign citizen?

2. Most state court judges are elected, while federal court judges are appointed. Which system, in your opinion, is fairer? Does either system affect the quality of the judiciary?

3. Do you think that it is fair that in most cases there is no right to appeal to the United States Supreme Court? Should citizens have to petition for *certiorari* to be heard by the Supreme Court? What does the requirement of a grant of *certiorari,* coupled with the limited number of cases that the Supreme Court hears, tell you about the role and purpose of the Supreme Court?

4. Some individuals have claimed that mandatory ADR infringes on a person's constitutional right to a jury trial. Do you agree with this view? Why or why not?

 ## PROJECTS

1. Review a local legal newspaper or bar association journal. Locate advertisements for firms offering ADR services. Call one of these firms and find out what services are offered and what rates are charged.

2. Visit the American Arbitration Association online at **www.adr.org**. Find out what kinds of disputes (con-

tract disputes, employment disputes, and the like) it arbitrates. Look at its procedural rules for the arbitration of disputes in one of the areas it handles. Review the rules and summarize the procedures involved.

USING INTERNET RESOURCES

1. Paralegals frequently assist in ADR proceedings and even, in some cases, serve as mediators or arbitrators. To learn more about ADR procedures, go to **www.adr.org**, the home page for the American Arbitration Association (AAA). Browse through the site's offerings and find the answers to the following questions:

   a. When was the AAA founded? What types of services does it offer?

   b. Where is the AAA regional office nearest you? Does the AAA engage in arbitration outside the United States?

   c. How many arbitration forms are available to download from this site? Is there any cost for downloading these forms? How many states provide state-specific forms on this site?

2. Several businesses offer clients the opportunity to resolve legal disputes online. To review one such Web site, go to **www.cybersettle.com**. Then answer the following questions:

   a. Select "About," then "History," and read about Cybersettle's history and methods. For what types of disputes would Cybersettle's services be most useful?

   b. Go to "Demo" and watch the demonstration of how the system works. How useful do you think Cybersettle's services are to business managers? How important is it that Cybersettle's services are conducted online? Would you feel that your information was secure and private if you used the service?

   c. Select "News & Information," then "Frequently Asked Questions (FAQs)," and then "Attorney FAQ." How does Cybersettle address concerns about security and privacy? Why might a party use Cybersettle's services instead of traditional ADR methods?

END NOTES

1. Pronounced jus-*tish*-a-bul.

2. A state's highest court is often referred to as the state supreme court, but there are exceptions. For example, in New York the supreme court is a trial court.

3. Under the Class Action Fairness Act (CAFA) of 2005, it is likely that most class-action lawsuits will not qualify for state court jurisdiction.

4. Pronounced *ven*-yoo.

5. The name in Ohio is Court of Common Pleas; the name in New York is Supreme Court; the name in Florida, Illinois, and Missouri is Circuit Court.

6. Pronounced sur-shee-uh-*rah*-ree.

7. As discussed later in the chapter, the American Arbitration Association is a leading provider of arbitration services in the United States.

LEGAL PROCEDURES AND PARALEGAL SKILLS

CHAPTER 7

Legal Research and Analysis

CHAPTER 8

Contemporary Online Legal Research

CHAPTER 9

Legal Writing: Form and Substance

CHAPTER 10

Civil Litigation: Before the Trial

CHAPTER 11

Conducting Interviews and Investigations

CHAPTER 12

Trial Procedures

CHAPTER 13

Criminal Law and Procedures

LEGAL RESEARCH AND ANALYSIS

CHAPTER OUTLINE

Introduction

Researching Case Law—The Preliminary Steps

Finding Relevant Cases

The Case Reporting System

Analyzing Case Law

Researching Constitutional and Statutory Law

Analyzing Statutory Law

Researching Administrative Law

AFTER COMPLETING THIS CHAPTER, YOU WILL KNOW:

▶ How primary and secondary sources of law differ and how to use each of these types of sources in the research process.

▶ How court decisions are published and how to read case citations.

▶ How to analyze case law and summarize, or brief, cases.

▶ How federal statutes and regulations are published and the major sources of statutory and administrative law.

▶ How to interpret statutory law and understand what kinds of resources are available for researching the legislative history of a statute.

INTRODUCTION

For many paralegals, legal research is a central and fascinating part of their jobs. They find it interesting to read the actual words of a court's opinion on a legal question or the text of a statute. Additionally, they acquire a firsthand knowledge of the law and how it applies to real people and events. The ability to conduct research thoroughly yet efficiently enhances a paralegal's value to the legal team.

As a paralegal, you may be asked to perform a variety of research tasks. Some tasks will be simple, such as locating and printing out a court case. Other tasks may take days or weeks to complete. In all but the simplest tasks, legal research overlaps with legal analysis. To find relevant case law, for example, you need to be able to analyze the cases you find to ensure that they are indeed relevant.

Many paralegals conduct research without entering a law library. Computerized legal services such as Westlaw and Lexis allow legal professionals to find the text of cases, statutes, and other documents without leaving their desks. (See Chapter 8 for a discussion of online legal research.) Regardless of how you conduct legal research, it is essential to know what sources to consult for different types of information.

RESEARCHING CASE LAW— THE PRELIMINARY STEPS

To illustrate how to research case law, we use a hypothetical case. One of your firm's clients, Trent Hoffman, is suing Better Homes Store for negligence. During the initial client interview, Hoffman explained to you and your supervising attorney that he had gone to the store to buy a large mirror. As he was leaving the store through a side entrance, carrying the mirror, he ran into a large pole just outside the door. He did not see the pole because the mirror blocked his view. When he hit the pole, the mirror broke, and a piece of glass went into his left eye, causing permanent loss of eyesight. Hoffman claims that the store was negligent in placing a pole so close to the door and is suing the store for $3 million in damages.

You have already done a preliminary investigation and obtained evidence supporting Hoffman's account of the facts. Your supervising attorney now asks you to research case law to find other cases with similar fact patterns and see what the courts decided in those cases.

Before you begin, you need to define the issue to be researched and determine your research goals. We look now at these two preliminary steps in researching case law.

Defining the Issue

In defining the legal issue that you need to research, your first task is to examine the facts of Hoffman's case to determine the nature of the legal issue involved. (An example is provided in *Developing Paralegal Skills* on the next page.) Based on his description of the circumstances (verified through your preliminary investigation) and on his allegation that Better Homes Store should not have placed a pole just outside one of the store's entrances, you know that the legal issue relates to the tort of negligence. As a starting point, you should therefore review what you know about negligence theory. If you are unfamiliar with negligence law or any other legal subject, you can start by doing background research to familiarize yourself with the topic, as described in the section on legal encyclopedias later in this chapter.

The tort of negligence is defined as the failure to exercise reasonable care. (Chapter 14 will discuss negligence in detail.) To succeed in a negligence action, a plaintiff must establish four elements:

1. The defendant had a duty of care to the plaintiff.

2. The defendant breached that duty.

3. The plaintiff suffered a legally recognizable injury.

4. The injury was caused by the defendant's breach of the duty of care.

Developing Paralegal Skills

DEFINING THE ISSUES TO BE RESEARCHED

Federal government agents observed David Berriman in his parked car talking on his cellular phone. Later, other cars were seen driving up to David's car and stopping. The drivers received brown paper bags in exchange for money. David was questioned, and his car was searched. Cocaine was found in the car. He was arrested for transporting and distributing cocaine, and the police took his car and cellular phone. David's lawyer is arguing that the government agents did not have the authority to seize David's car and cellular phone and force him to forfeit this property. Natalie Martin, a legal assistant with the U.S. attorney's office, has been assigned the task of researching the federal statutes and cases on this issue.

Natalie can begin her research project only if she first frames the issues critical to the case. To that end, she must thoroughly review the case to determine what specific issues need to be researched. Using a checklist method that she learned in school, she breaks the facts of the case down into five categories and inserts the relevant facts from her assignment. Now Natalie is ready to begin her research.

CHECKLIST FOR DEFINING RESEARCH ISSUES

- Parties: Who are the people involved in the action or lawsuit?
- Places and things: Where did the events take place, and what items are involved in the action or lawsuit?
- Basis of action or issue: What is the legal claim or issue involved in the action or lawsuit?
- Defenses: What legal justification did the police have for seizing David's car and cellular phone? Will this justification still exist if David is found not guilty of the underlying charges, or will the police be required to return the forfeited property?
- Relief sought: What is the legal remedy or penalty sought in the case?

business invitee
A person, such as a customer or client, who is invited onto business premises by the owner of those premises for business purposes.

These elements help you determine the issue that needs to be researched. There is little doubt that the third requirement has been met—Hoffman's loss of sight is a legally recognizable injury for which he can be compensated—*if* he succeeds in proving the other three elements of negligence. Proving the fourth element, causation, depends largely on proving the first two elements. In your research, you will therefore focus on the first two elements. Specifically, you need to answer the following questions:

- Did Better Homes Store owe a duty of care to its customer, Hoffman? You might phrase this question in more general terms: Do business owners owe a duty of care to **business invitees**—customers and others invited onto their premises?
- If so, what is the extent of that duty, and how is it measured? In other words, are business owners always liable when customers are injured on their premises? Or must some condition be met before store owners will be liable? For example, must a customer's injury be a *foreseeable* consequence of a condition on the premises, such as the pole outside the store's door, for the store owner to be liable for the injury?
- If the injury must be a foreseeable consequence of a condition, would a court find that Hoffman's injury in this case was a foreseeable consequence of the pole's placement just outside the store's door?

Although today most legal research is carried out using online resources, some paralegals still consult printed legal volumes when conducting legal research. When might you consult printed versions of legal resources?

(Courtesy © PhotoDisc, Inc.).

These are the issues you need to research. Notice that there is more than one issue. This is common in legal research—only rarely will you be researching a single legal issue.

Determining Your Research Goals

Once you have defined the issues to be researched, you will be in a better position to determine your research goals. Remember that you are working on behalf of a client, who is paying for your services (see the *In the Office* feature on the following page). Your overall goal is thus to find legal support for Hoffman's claim. To do so, you want to find cases on point and cases that are binding authorities. Depending on what you find, you may also need to look for persuasive authorities.

Cases on Point

One of your research goals is to find cases on point in which the court held for the plaintiff. A **case on point** is a previous case involving fact patterns and legal issues similar to those in the case you are researching. For Hoffman's negligence claim, a case on point would be one in which the plaintiff alleged that he was injured while on a store's premises because of a dangerous condition on those premises.

The ideal case on point would be one in which all four elements (the parties, the circumstances, the legal issues involved, and the remedies sought by the plaintiff) are very similar to those in your case. Such a case is called a case on "all fours." Here, a **case on "all fours"** would be a case in which the plaintiff-customer did not expect a condition (such as an obstacle in her path) to exist and was prevented from seeing the condition by some action that a customer would reasonably undertake (such as carrying a large box out of a store). The parties and the circumstances of the case would thus be very similar to those in Hoffman's case. In addition, the plaintiff would have sustained a permanent injury, as Hoffman did, and sought damages for negligence.

> **case on point**
> A case involving factual circumstances and issues that are similar to those in the case being researched.

> **case on "all fours"**
> A case in which all four elements (the parties, the circumstances, the legal issues involved, and the remedies sought) are very similar to those in the case being researched.

Binding Authorities

Another research goal is to find cases that are binding authorities. As discussed in Chapter 5, a *binding authority* is one that the court must follow in deciding the issue. A binding authority may be a statute, regulation, or constitution that governs the issue, or it may be a previously decided court case that is controlling in your jurisdiction.

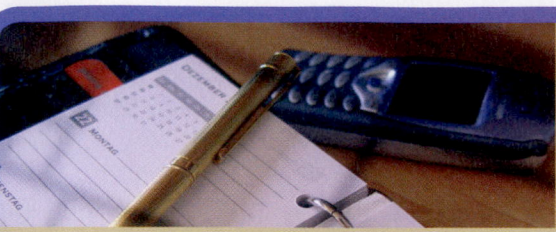

In the **Office**

EFFICIENCY IN RESEARCH

Attorneys have a duty to charge their clients reasonable fees. As a paralegal, you help fulfill this duty by working efficiently so as to minimize the number of hours you spend on work relating to the client's matter. Legal research can be extremely time consuming, as every paralegal knows. To reduce the time spent in researching an issue, start your quest with a clear idea of your research task. After all, your time is expensive not only for the client (who pays for it) but also for your supervising attorney (who may need your assistance on other cases as well). By knowing as precisely as possible what the goal of your research is, you can reach that goal more quickly and thus better serve the interests of both the client and your supervising attorney.

For a case to serve as a binding authority, it must be on point and must have been decided by a superior court. A superior court, in the sense used here, refers to the levels in a court system. Recall from Chapter 6 that both the federal and state court systems consist of several levels, or tiers, of courts. *Trial courts,* in which evidence is presented and testimony given, are on the bottom tier. Decisions from a trial court can be appealed to a higher court, which commonly is an intermediate *court of appeals,* or *appellate court.* Decisions from appellate courts may be appealed to an even higher court, such as a state supreme court or, if a federal question is involved, the United States Supreme Court.

A lower court is bound to follow the decisions set forth by a higher court in the same jurisdiction. An appellate court's decision in a case involving facts and issues similar to a case brought in a trial court in the same jurisdiction would thus be a binding authority—the trial court would be bound to follow the appellate court's decision on the issue. A higher court is never required to follow an opinion written by a lower court in the same jurisdiction. When you are performing research, look for cases on point decided by the highest court in your jurisdiction, because those cases carry the most weight.

State courts have the final say on state law, and federal courts have the final say on federal law. Thus, except in deciding an issue that involves federal law, state courts do not have to follow the decisions of federal courts. In deciding issues that involve federal law, however, state courts must abide by the decisions of the United States Supreme Court.

Persuasive Authorities

persuasive authority
Any legal authority, or source of law, that a court may look to for guidance but on which it need not rely in making its decision. Persuasive authorities include cases from other jurisdictions, discussions in legal periodicals, and so forth.

A **persuasive authority** is not binding on a court. In other words, the court is not required to follow that authority in making its decisions. Examples of persuasive authorities include:

- Persuasive precedents—previous court opinions from other jurisdictions, as discussed in Chapter 5.
- Legal periodicals, such as law reviews, in which the issue at hand is discussed by legal scholars.
- Encyclopedias summarizing legal principles or concepts relating to a particular issue.
- Legal dictionaries that describe how the law has been applied in the past.

Often, a court refers to persuasive authorities when deciding a *case of first impression,* which is a case involving an issue that has never been specifically addressed by that court before. For example, if in researching Hoffman's claim you find that no similar cases have ever reached a higher court in your jurisdiction, you will look for similar cases decided by courts in other jurisdictions. Decisions by these courts may help guide the court deciding Hoffman's case. Your supervising attorney will want to know about these persuasive authorities so that she can present them to the court for consideration.

FINDING RELEVANT CASES

When conducting legal research, you need to distinguish between two basic categories of legal sources: primary sources and secondary sources. As discussed in Chapter 5, *primary sources of law* include court decisions, statutes enacted by legislative bodies, rules and regulations created by administrative agencies, presidential orders, and generally any documents that *establish* the law. *Secondary sources of law* consist of books and articles that summarize, systematize, compile, explain, and interpret the law.

Generally, when beginning research projects, paralegals look first to secondary sources of law to help them find relevant primary sources and to educate themselves on topics of law with which they are unfamiliar. For this reason, secondary sources of law are often referred to as *finding tools.* Consider the research project involving the Hoffman claim. How can you find cases on point and binding authorities on this issue? American case law consists of millions of court decisions, to which more than forty thousand decisions are added each year. Finding relevant precedents would be a terrible task if not for secondary sources of law that classify decisions according to subject. Two important finding tools that are helpful in researching case law are legal encyclopedias and case digests, which we describe next. We also look at some other secondary sources that may be helpful.

We should note that very often the research discussed here is done online (a topic covered in Chapter 8). It is important to learn to do research "in the books," though, for two reasons. First, not all attorneys use online research. Second, to be an effective online researcher, you need to understand the structure of the original published sources on which online research is based.

Legal Encyclopedias

In researching Hoffman's claim, you might look first at a legal encyclopedia to learn more about negligence and the duty of care that business owners owe to business invitees. A popular legal encyclopedia is *American Jurisprudence,* Second Edition, commonly referred to as *American Jurisprudence 2d* or, more briefly, as Am. Jur. 2d. (An excerpt from this encyclopedia is shown in Exhibit 7.1 on the following page. It is also available online from Westlaw.) *American Jurisprudence* covers hundreds of topics in more than 140 volumes. The topics are presented alphabetically, and each topic is divided into subtopics describing rules of law that have emerged from generations of court decisions. The encyclopedia also provides cross-references to specific court cases, statutory law, and relevant secondary sources of law. Additionally, each volume includes an index, and a separate index covers the entire encyclopedia. The printed volumes are kept current through supplements called **pocket parts.** Pocket parts, so named because they slip into a pocket (sleeve) in the front or back of the volume, contain changes and additions to various topics and subtopics.

A similar encyclopedia is *Corpus Juris Secundum,* or C.J.S. Like Am. Jur. 2d, this encyclopedia provides detailed information on almost every area of the law and includes indexes for each volume as well as for the entire set. Its 164 volumes cover 433 topics, which are presented alphabetically and divided into subtopics. One of the volumes of this set is shown in Exhibit 7.2 on page 201. Like *American Jurisprudence,* this encyclopedia is available online from Westlaw.

pocket part
A pamphlet containing recent cases or changes in the law that is used to update legal encyclopedias and other legal authorities. It is called a "pocket part" because it slips into a pocket, or sleeve, in the front or back binder of the volume.

EXHIBIT 7.1
Excerpt from *American Jurisprudence 2d*

Reprinted with permission from Thomson Reuters.

PREMISES LIABILITY
by
Irwin J. Schiffres, J.D. and Sheila A. Skojec, J.D.

Scope of topic: This article discusses the principles and rules of law applicable to and governing the liability of owners or occupants of real property for negligence causing injury to persons or property by reason of defects therein or hazards created by the activities of such owners or occupants or their agents and employees. Treated in detail are the classification of persons injured as invitees, licensees, or trespassers, and the duty owed them, as well as the rules applicable in those jurisdictions where such status distinctions are no longer determinative of the duty owed the entrant; the effect of "recreational use" statutes on the duty owed persons using the property for such purposes; the greater measure of duty owed by the owner to children as compared to adult licensees and trespassers, including the attractive nuisance doctrine; and the specific duties and liabilities of owners and occupants of premises used for business or residential purposes. Also considered is the effect of the injured person's negligence on the plaintiff's right to recover under principles of contributory or comparative negligence.

Federal aspects: One injured on premises owned or operated by the United States may seek to recover under general principles of premises liability discussed in this article. Insofar as recovery is sought under the Federal Torts Claims Act, see 35 Am Jur 2d, FEDERAL TORTS CLAIMS ACT § 73.

Treated elsewhere:

Mutual obligations and liabilities of adjoining landowners with respect to injuries arising from their acts or omissions, see 1 Am Jur 2d, ADJOINING LANDOWNERS AND PROPERTIES §§ 10, 11, 28 et seq., 37 et seq.

Liability for the acts or omissions of the owners or occupants of premises abutting on a street or highway which cause injury to those using the way, see 39 Am Jur 2d, HIGHWAYS, STREETS, AND BRIDGES §§ 517 et seq.

Liability for violation of building regulations, see 13 Am Jur 2d, BUILDINGS §§ 32 et seq.

Liability of employer for injuries caused employees on the employer's premises, see 53 Am Jur 2d, MASTER AND SERVANT §§ 139 et seq.

Liability for injuries caused by defective products on the premises, see 63 Am Jur 2d, PRODUCTS LIABILITY

Respective rights and liabilities of a landlord and tenant where one is responsible for an injury suffered by the other, or by a third person, on leased premises or on premises provided for the common use of tenants, see 49 Am Jur 2d, LANDLORD AND TENANT §§ 761 et seq.

Liability of a receiver placed in charge of property for an injury sustained thereby or thereon by someone other than the persons directly interested in the estate, see 66 Am Jur 2d, RECEIVERS § 364

Duties and liabilities of occupiers of premises used for various particular types of businesses or activities, see 4 Am Jur 2d, AMUSEMENTS AND EXHIBITIONS §§ 51 et seq.; 14 Am Jur 2d, CARRIERS §§ 964 et seq.; 38 Am Jur 2d, GARAGES, AND FILLING AND PARKING STATIONS §§ 81 et seq.; 40 Am Jur 2d, HOSPITALS AND ASYLUMS § 31; 40 Am Jur 2d, HOTELS, MOTELS, AND RESTAURANTS §§ 81 et seq.; 50 Am Jur 2d, LAUNDRIES, DYERS, AND DRY CLEANERS §§ 21, 22; 54 Am Jur 2d, MOBILE HOMES, TRAILER PARKS, AND TOURIST CAMPS § 17; 57 Am Jur 2d, MUNICIPAL, COUNTY, SCHOOL, AND STATE TORT LIABILITY; AND 59 Am Jur 2d, PARKS, SQUARES, AND PLAYGROUNDS §§ 43 et seq.

Duties and liabilities with respect to injuries caused by particular agencies, such as

317

Still another encyclopedia is *Words and Phrases,* which offers definitions and interpretations of legal terms and phrases. Each term or phrase in this 132-volume set is followed by brief summary statements from federal or state court decisions in which the word or phrase has been interpreted or defined. The summary statements also indicate the names of the cases and the reporters in which they can be located. **Reporters** are publications containing the actual text of court cases, as will be discussed later.

The encyclopedias just described are published by West. When beginning your research into the Hoffman claim, you could use any of these secondary sources, or finding tools, to lead you to the primary sources (cases) that you will need to read and analyze. You could search any of the sources for such terms as *premises liability,*

reporter
A book in which court cases are published, or reported.

business invitees, duty of care, and *landowners,* for example. Remember, though, that legal encyclopedias contain only general rules of law. They do not include specific rules of law from your state, which you will need to locate.

Case Digests

In researching Hoffman's case against Better Homes Store, you might want to check a case digest as well as a legal encyclopedia for references to relevant case law. **Digests**, which are produced by various publishers, are helpful research tools because they provide indexes to case law—from the earliest recorded cases through the most current opinions. Case digests arrange topics alphabetically and provide information to help you locate referenced cases, but they do not offer the detail found in legal encyclopedias. Collected under each topic heading in a case digest are annotations. **Annotations** are comments, explanatory notes, or case summaries. In case digests, annotations consist of very short statements of relevant points of law in reported cases. The digests published by West offer the most comprehensive system for locating cases by subject matter. Exhibit 7.3 on the next page shows some excerpts from one of West's federal digests on the standard of care that is owed to an invitee.

The West Key-Number System

West's key-number system has simplified the task of researching case law. The system divides all areas of American law into specific categories, or topics, arranged in alphabetical order. The topics are further divided into many subtopics, each designated by a **key number**, which is accompanied by the West key symbol: ⌕. You can see the use of this key symbol in Exhibit 7.3 on the next page. Exhibit 7.4 on page 203 shows some of the key numbers used for other subtopics under the general topic of negligence.

The key-number system organizes millions of case summaries under specific topics and subtopics. For example, in researching the Hoffman claim, suppose that you locate a negligence case on point decided by a court in your state five years ago. Your goal is to find related—and perhaps more recent—cases that support Hoffman's claim. Here is how the key-number system can help. When you read through any case in a West's case reporter, you will find that a series of **headnotes** precedes the court's actual opinion. Each headnote summarizes one portion of the opinion. West editors create each headnote and assign it to a particular topic with a key number.

Key numbers correlate the headnotes in cases to the topics in digests and can be very useful in finding cases on a particular subject. Once you find the key number in a case that discusses the issue you are researching, you can easily find every other case in your state or region that discusses this issue. You simply go to the West case digest and locate the particular key number and topic. Beneath the key number, the digest provides case summaries, titles, and citations to cases discussing the issue in the area covered by the digest. When you find a case that seems on point, you know exactly where to find it because you have the citation.

Types of Digests

As mentioned, West offers a comprehensive system of digests. West publishes digests of both federal court opinions and state court opinions, as well as regional digests and digests that correspond with its reporters covering specialized areas, such as bankruptcy. For example, the *Lawyers' Edition of the Digest of the Supreme Court Reports* corresponds to decisions listed in the West case reporter entitled *Lawyers' Edition of the Supreme Court Reports.*

Other publishers also publish digests. For instance, Callahan's *Michigan Digest* is a digest specific to Michigan courts. Note that other publishers' digests do not use the key-number system.

EXHIBIT 7.2
Corpus Juris Secundum

Reprinted with permission from Thomson Reuters.

digest
A compilation in which brief summaries of court cases are arranged by subject and subdivided by jurisdiction and court.

annotation
A brief comment, an explanation of a legal point, or a case summary found in a case digest or other legal source.

key number
A number (accompanied by the symbol of a key) corresponding to a specific topic within West's key-number system to facilitate legal research of case law.

headnote
A note, usually a paragraph long, near the beginning of a reported case summarizing the court's ruling on an issue.

EXHIBIT 7.3
Excerpts from West's *Federal Practice Digest 4th* on Negligence

Reprinted with permission from Thomson Reuters.

77A F P D 4th—173

NEGLIGENCE ☞ 1037(4)

For references to other topics, see Descriptive-Word Index

E.D.Mich. 1998. Under Michigan law, a property owner is not an absolute insurer of the safety of invitees.

Meyers v. Wal-Mart Stores, East, Inc., 29 F.Supp.2d 780.

E.D.Mich. 1995. under Michigan law, property owner is not insurer of safety of invitees.

Bunch v. Long John Silvers, Inc., 878 F.Supp. 1044.

E.D.Mich. 1994. Under Michigan law, property owner is not insurer of safety of invitees.

Dose v. Equitable Life Assur. Soc., 864 F.Supp. 682.

E.D.N.C. 1993. Premises owner does not automatically insure safety of invitees and is not liable in absence of negligence.

Faircloth v. U.S., 837 F.Supp. 123.

E.D.Va. 1999. Under Virginia law, owner of premises is not insurer of his invitees safety; rather, owner must use ordinary care to render premises reasonably safe for invitee's visit.

Sandow-Pajewski v. Busch Entertainment Corp., 55 F.Supp.2d 422.

☞ **1037(4). Care required in general.**

C.A.7 (Ill.) 1986. Under Illinois law, landowner is liable for physical harm to his invitees caused by condition on his land: where landowner could by exercise of reasonable care have discovered condition; where landowner should realize that condition involves unreasonable risk of harm to invitees; where landowner should expect that invitees will not discover danger or will fail to protect against it; and where landowner fails to exercise reasonable care to protect invitees.

Higgins v. White Sox Baseball Club, Inc., 787 F.2d 1125.

C.A.7 (Ind.) 1994. Under Indiana law, landowner's duty to invitee while that invitee is on premises is that of reasonable care.

Salima v. Scherwood South, Inc., 38 F.3d 929.

Under indiana law, landowner is liable for harm caused to invitee by condition on land only if landowner knows of or through exercise of reasonable care would discover condition and realize that it involves unreasonable risk of harm to such invitees, should expect the invitee will fail to discover or realize danger or fail to protect against it, and fails to exercise reasonable care in protecting invitee against danger.

Salima v. Scherwood South, Inc., 38 F. 3d 929.

Under Indiana law, landowner is not liable for harm caused to invitees by conditions whose

For cited U.S.C.A. sections and legislative histo

danger is known or obvious unless landowner could anticipate harm despite obviousness.

Salima v. Scherwood South, Inc., 38 F.3d 929.

C.A.6 (Mich.) 1998. Under Michigan law, where invitor has reason to expect that, despite oper... neve... have... steps...

to e... dang... or to... tee,... tee's... will... he c... hims...

sesso... caus... sesso... care... reali... harm... they... fail t... exer... the c...

und... and... expe... hims...

of o... invit... prem... man...

ity, i... tee t... egres... keep...

NEGLIGENCE

77A F P D 4th—542

XVI. DEFENSES AND MITIGATING CIRCUMSTANCES.—Continued.

    570. _____ Professional rescuers; "firefighter's rule."

    575. Imputed contributory negligence.

XVII. PREMISES LIABILITY.

  (A) IN GENERAL.

    ☞ 1000. Nature.

    1001. Elements in general.

    1002. Constitutional, statutory and regulatory provisions.

    1003. What law governs.

    1004. Preemption.

  (B) NECESSITY AND EXISTENCE OF DUTY.

    ☞ 1010. In general.

    1011. Ownership, custody and control.

    1012. Conditions known or obvious in general.

    1013. Conditions created or known by defendant.

    1014. Foreseeability.

    1015. Duty as to children.

    1016. _____ In general.

    1017. _____ Trespassing children.

    1018. Duty to inspect or discover.

    1019. Protection against acts of third persons in general.

    1020. Duty to warn.

    1021. Duty of store and business proprietors.

    1022. _____ In general.

    1023. _____ Duty to inspect.

    1024. _____ Protection against acts of third persons.

    1025. Duty based on statute or other regulation.

  (C) STANDARD OF CARE.

    ☞ 1030. In general.

    1031. Not insurer or guarantor.

    1032. Reasonable or ordinary care in general.

    1033. Reasonably safe or unreasonably dangerous conditions.

    1034. Status of entrant.

    1035. _____ In general.

    1036. _____ Care dependent on status.

    1037. _____ Invitees.

      (1). In general.

      (2). Who are invitees.

      (3). Not insurer as to invitees.

      (4). Care required in general.

      (5). Public invitees in general.

      (6). Implied invitation.

      (7). Persons working on property.

      (8). Delivery persons and haulers.

    1040. _____ Licensees.

      (1). In general.

      (2). Who are licensees.

EXHIBIT 7.4
Subtopics and Key
Numbers in a West Digest

Reprinted with permission from
Thomson Reuters.

NEGLIGENCE

SUBJECTS INCLUDED

General civil negligence law and premises liability, including duty, standards of care, breach of duty, proximate cause, injury, defenses, and comparative fault, whether based on the common law or statute, as well as procedural aspects of such actions

General civil liabilities for gross negligence, recklessness, willful or wanton conduct, strict liability and ultrahazardous instrumentalities and activities

Negligence liabilities relating to the construction, demolition and repair of buildings and other structures, whether based on the common law or statute

General criminal negligence offenses and prosecutions

SUBJECTS EXCLUDED AND COVERED BY OTHER TOPICS

Accountants or auditors, negligence of, see ACCOUNTANTS ⌨ 8,9

Aircraft, accidents involving, see AVIATION ⌨ 141–153

Attorney's malpractice liability, see ATTORNEY AND CLIENT ⌨ 105–129.5

Banks, liabilities of, see BANKS AND BANKING ⌨ 100

Brokers, securities and real estate, liabilities of, see BROKERS

Car and highway accidents, see AUTOMOBILES

Common carriers, liabilities to passengers, see CARRIERS

Domestic animals, injuries by or to, see ANIMALS

Dram Shop liability and other liabilities for serving alcohol, see INTOXICATING LIQUORS ⌨ 282–324

* * * *

For detailed references to other topics, see Descriptive-Word Index

Analysis

- I.   IN GENERAL, ⌨ 200–205.
- II.   NECESSITY AND EXISTENCE OF DUTY, ⌨ 210–222.
- III.   STANDARD OF CARE, ⌨ 230–239.
- IV.   BREACH OF DUTY, ⌨ 250–259.
- V.   HEIGHTENED DEGREES OF NEGLIGENCE, ⌨ 272–276.
- VI.   VULNERABLE AND ENDANGERED PERSONS; RESCUES, ⌨ 281–285.
- VII.   SUDDEN EMERGENCY DOCTRINE, ⌨ 291–295.
- VIII.   DANGEROUS SITUATIONS AND STRICT LIABILITY, ⌨ 301–307.

Annotations: *American Law Reports*

The *American Law Reports (A.L.R.)* and *American Law Reports Federal (A.L.R. Federal)*, published by West, are also useful resources for legal researchers. These multivolume sets present the full text of selected cases in many areas of the law. They are helpful in finding cases from jurisdictions around the country with similar facts and legal issues.

There are five different series of *American Law Reports,* covering case law since 1919. The first and second series contain separate digests that provide references to cases and also have word indexes to assist the researcher in locating specific areas.

The remaining sets of *A.L.R.* volumes use a different approach, called a *Quick Index,* which lets the user quickly access cases and information on a particular topic. The cases presented in these reporters are followed by annotations—that is, references to articles that explain or comment on the specific issues involved in the cases. These reporters can be a good source to turn to for an overview of a specific area of law or current trend in the law.

When using any of the volumes of *A.L.R.,* you must be sure to update your results. *A.L.R.* annotations are periodically updated by the addition of relevant cases. For the first series, the annotations are updated in a set of books called the *A.L.R. Blue Book of Supplemental Decisions.* The second series is updated in the *A.L.R. Later Case Service,* and the remaining series are made current by pocket-part supplements located in the front of each volume. In addition, you can consult the annotation history table at the end of the Quick Index to see whether any new annotations supplement or change an earlier annotation.

Other Secondary Sources

A number of other secondary sources are useful in legal research. We look here at three of these sources: treatises, *Restatements of the Law,* and legal periodicals. Like other secondary sources of law, these sources do not have the force of law. Nevertheless, they are important sources of legal analysis and opinion and are often cited as persuasive authorities.

Treatises

> **treatise**
> In legal research, a work that provides a systematic, detailed, and scholarly review of a particular legal subject.

> **hornbook**
> A single-volume scholarly discussion, or treatise, on a particular legal subject.

A **treatise** is a formal scholarly work by a law professor or other legal professional that treats a particular subject systematically and in detail. Some treatises are published in multivolume sets, while others are contained in a single book. Single-volume treatises that synthesize the basic principles of a given legal area are known as **hornbooks**. Some, but not all, hornbooks are available online. These texts are useful to paralegals who want to familiarize themselves with a particular area of the law, such as torts or contracts. For example, in researching the issues in Hoffman's negligence case, you might want to locate the treatise entitled *Prosser and Keeton on the Law of Torts,* Fifth Edition, which is included in West's Hornbook Series, and read the sections on negligence. (Exhibit 7.5 shows the page of this book that opens the chapter on defenses to negligence.) In addition to providing a clear and organized discussion of the subject matter, hornbooks such as *Prosser and Keeton on the Law of Torts* present many examples of case law and references to cases that may be helpful to a researcher.

Restatements of the Law

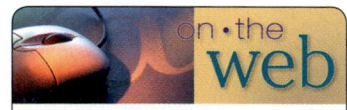

You can learn more about the American Law Institute (ALI) and its publications, including information on which *Restatements of the Law* are in the process of being revised, by accessing the ALI's Web site at **www.ali.org**.

The *Restatements of the Law* are also a helpful resource, and one on which judges often rely as a persuasive authority when making decisions. The *Restatements* are compilations of the common law that have been drafted and published by the American Law Institute. They are available online via Lexis and Westlaw. There are *Restatements* in the areas of contracts, torts, agency, trusts, property, restitution, security, judgments, and conflict of laws. Many of the *Restatements* are now in their second or third editions. Exhibit 7.6 shows a volume of the *Restatement (Third) of Torts.* Each section in the *Restatements* contains a statement of the principles of law that are generally accepted by the courts or embodied in statutes, followed by a discussion of those principles. The discussions present cases as examples and also discuss variations.

Legal Periodicals

Legal periodicals, such as law reviews and law journals, are also important secondary sources of law that can be very helpful to paralegals. If an article in a legal periodical deals with the specific area that you are researching, the article will likely

Chapter 11

NEGLIGENCE: DEFENSES

Table of Sections

Sec.
65. Contributory Negligence.
66. Last Clear Chance.
67. Comparative Negligence.
68. Assumption of Risk.

§ 65.   Contributory Negligence

The two most common defenses in a negligence action are contributory negligence and assumption of risk. Since both developed at a comparatively late date in the development of the common law,[1] and since both clearly operate to the advantage of the defendant, they are commonly regarded as defenses to a tort which would otherwise be established. All courts now hold that the burden of pleading and proof of the contributory negligence of the plaintiff is on the defendant.[2]

Contributory negligence is conduct on the part of the plaintiff, contributing as a legal cause to the harm he has suffered, which falls below the standard to which he is required to conform for his own protection.[3] Unlike assumption of risk, the defense does not rest upon the idea that the defendant is relieved of any duty toward the plaintiff. Rather, although the defendant has violated his duty, has been negligent, and would oth-

§ 65

1. The earliest contributory negligence case is Butterfield v. Forrester, 1809, 11 East 60, 103 Eng.Rep. 926. The first American case appears to have been Smith v. Smith, 1824, 19 Mass. (2 Pick.) 621. Assumption of risk first appears in a negligence case in 1799. See infra, § 68 n. 1.

2. E.g., Wilkinson v. Hartford Accident & Indemnity Co., La.1982, 411 So.2d 22; Moodie v. Santoni, 1982, 292 Md. 582, 441 A.2d 323; Addair v. Bryant, 1981, ___ W.Va. ___, 284 S.E.2d 374; Pickett v. Parks, 1981, 208 Neb. 310, 303 N.W.2d 296; Hatton v. Chem-Haulers, Inc., Ala.1980, 393 So.2d 950; Sampson v. W. F. Enterprises, Inc., Mo.App.1980, 611 S.W.2d 880; Howard v. Howard, Ky.App.1980, 607 S.W.2d 119; cf. Reuter v. United States, W.D.Pa.1982, 534 F.Supp. 731 (presumption that person killed or suffering loss of memory was acting with due care).

Illinois and certain other jurisdictions held to the contrary for some time. See West Chicago Street Railroad Co. v. Liderman, 1900, 187 Ill. 463, 58 N.E. 367; Kotler v. Lalley, 1930, 112 Conn. 86, 151 A. 433; Dreier v. McDermott, 1913, 157 Iowa 726, 141 N.W. 315. See Green, Illinois Negligence Law II, 1944, 39 Ill.L.Rev. 116, 125–130.

3. Second Restatement of Torts, § 463. See generally, Malone, The Formative Era of Contributory Negligence, 1946, 41 Ill.L.Rev. 151; James, Contributory Negligence, 1953, 62 Yale L.J. 691; Bohlen, Contributory Negligence, 1908, 21 Harv.L.Rev. 233; Lowndes, Contributory Negligence, 1934, 22 Geo.L.J. 674; Malone, Some Ruminations on Contributory Negligence, 1981, 65 Utah L.Rev. 91; Schwartz, Contributory and Comparative Negligence: A Reappraisal, 1978, 87 Yale L.J. 697; Note, 1979, 39 La.L.Rev. 637.

451

EXHIBIT 7.5
A Page from the *Hornbook on the Law of Torts*

Reprinted with permission from Thomson Reuters.

EXHIBIT 7.6
Restatement (Third) of Torts: Products Liability

Reprinted with permission from Thomson Reuters.

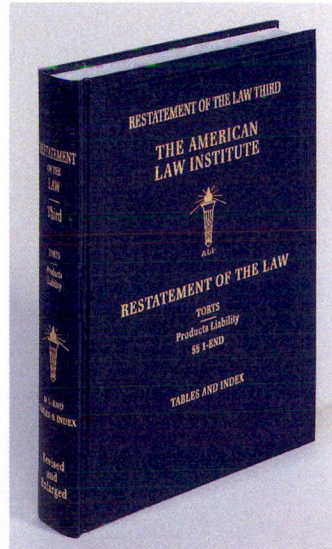

include footnotes citing cases relating to the topic. These references can save you hours of research time in finding relevant case law.

Many periodicals are available on Westlaw and Lexis. A popular nonscholarly periodical is *The National Law Journal*. It can be seen online at **www.law.com** (from the "National Legal News" menu, select "National Law Journal").

THE CASE REPORTING SYSTEM

The primary sources of case law are the cases themselves. Once you have learned what cases are relevant to the issue you are researching, you need to find the cases and examine the court opinions. (See the *Featured Contributor* article on pages 208 and 209 for tips on conducting legal research.) Assume, for example, that in researching Hoffman's case, you learn that your state's supreme court issued a decision a few years ago on a case with a similar fact pattern. In that case, the state supreme court upheld a lower court's judgment that a retail business owner had to pay damages to a customer who was injured on the store's premises. You know that the state supreme court's decision is a binding authority, and, to your knowledge, the decision has not been overruled or modified. Therefore, the case will likely provide weighty support to your attorney's arguments in support of Hoffman's claim.

Ethics Watch

USING SECONDARY SOURCES

When rushing to meet a deadline, you may be tempted to avoid a critical step in the research process—checking primary sources. For example, suppose a firm's client complains that a publisher of his novels is now publishing the novels online, as e-books. The client wants to know if the online publication constitutes copyright infringement. At issue is whether the publisher, which has the right to publish the printed texts, also has the right to publish the books online. An attorney for the firm asks Sarah, a paralegal, to research case law to see how the courts have dealt with this issue.

Sarah has just read a detailed article in a law journal about a similar case that was recently decided by the United States Supreme Court. Without taking the time to read the case itself, she relies on the author's conclusions in the article. She prepares a memo to the attorney presenting her "research" results. In the memo, she summarizes the background and facts of the case, the issue before the Court, the Court's holding, and the reasoning behind the Court's decision.

Based on Sarah's memo, the attorney advises the client that the publisher had no right to publish the client's works online. The client decides to sue the publisher. During Sarah's more extensive pretrial research, she reads the case itself. Unfortunately for Sarah (and the client and the attorney), the author of the article did not discuss an important qualification made by the Court in its ruling relating to the terms of the publishing contract. The Court's decision does not apply to the client's situation, and the case cannot be used as a binding authority after all!

While the attorney is responsible for the work product for the client, Sarah's failure to rely on primary sources may be viewed as a failure to produce competent work. Such a failure could injure the position of the client and violate the NFPA Model Disciplinary Rule 1.1, "A paralegal shall achieve and maintain a high level of competence."

At this point, however, you have only read *about* the case in secondary sources. To locate the case itself and make sure it is applicable (the *Ethics Watch* explains why this is important), you must understand the case reporting system and the legal "shorthand" employed in referencing court cases.

State Court Decisions

Most state trial court decisions are not published. Except in New York and a few other states that publish some opinions of their trial courts, decisions from state trial courts are only filed in the office of the clerk of the court, where they are available for public inspection.

State Reporters

Written decisions of the appellate courts are published chronologically in volumes called *reports* or *reporters,* which are numbered consecutively. State appellate court decisions are found in the state reporters of that particular state. The reporters may be either the "official" reporters, designated as such by the state legislature, or "unofficial" reporters, published by West. Although some states still have official reporters (and a few states, such as New York and California, have more than one official reporter), many states have eliminated their own official reporters in favor of West's National Reporter System, discussed next.

Regional Reporters

State court opinions also appear in regional units of West's National Reporter System. Many lawyers and libraries have the West reporters because they report cases more quickly and are distributed more widely than the state-published reports.

The National Reporter System divides the states into the following geographic areas: *Atlantic* (A. or A.2d), *South Eastern* (S.E. or S.E.2d), *North Eastern* (N.E. or N.E.2d), *North Western* (N.W. or N.W.2d), *Pacific* (P., P.2d, or P.3d), *South Western* (S.W., S.W.2d, or S.W.3d), and *Southern* (So. or So.2d). The *2d* and *3d* in the abbreviations refer to *Second Series* and *Third Series*. The states included in each of these regional divisions are indicated in Exhibit 7.7 on page 210, which illustrates West's National Reporter System. The names of the areas may not be the same as what we commonly think of as a geographic region. For example, the *North Western* reporter does not include the Pacific Northwest but does include states, such as Iowa, that people do not think of as being in the Northwest. Similarly, Oklahoma is in the Pacific Reporter.

Citation Format

To locate a case, you must know where to look. After a decision has been published, it is normally referred to (cited) by the name of the case, the volume number and the abbreviated name of the book in which the case is located, the page number on which the case begins, and the year. In other words, there are five parts to a standard **citation**:

Case name	Volume number	Name of book	Page number	(Year)

This basic format is used for every citation regardless of whether the case is published in an official state reporter or a regional reporter (or both). When more than one reporter is cited for the same case, each reference is called a **parallel citation** and is separated from the next citation by a comma. The first citation is to the state's official reporter (if there is one), although the text of the court's opinion will be the same (parallel) at any of the listed locations.

To illustrate how to find case law from citations, suppose you want to find the following case: *North American Expositions Co. v. Corcoran*, 452 Mass. 852, 898 N.E.2d 831 (2009). You can see that the opinion in this case can be found in Volume 452 of the official *Massachusetts Reports,* on page 852. The parallel citation is to Volume 898 of the *North Eastern Reporter, Second Series,* page 831. In some cases, additional information may appear in parentheses at the end of a citation, usually indicating the court that heard the case (if that information is not clear from the citation alone). Exhibit 7.8 on pages 211 through 213 further illustrates how to read case citations.

When conducting legal research, you should write down the citations to the cases or other legal sources that you have consulted, quoted, or want to refer to in a written summary of your research results. Several guides have been published on how to cite legal sources. Traditionally, the most widely used guide has been *The Bluebook: A Uniform System of Citation,* published by the Harvard Law Review Association. This book explains the proper format for citing cases, statutes, constitutions, regulations, and other legal sources. It is a good idea to memorize the basic format for citations to cases and statutory law because these legal sources are frequently cited in legal writing. An alternative guide is a booklet entitled *ALWD Citation Manual: A Professional System of Citation,* which is published by the Association of Legal Writing Directors. Legal practitioners should check the rules of their jurisdiction for guidelines on the proper format for citations in documents submitted to a court.

citation

In case law, a reference to a case by the name of the case, the volume number and name of the reporter in which the case can be found, the page number on which the case begins, and the year. In statutory and administrative law, a reference to the title number, name, and section of the code in which a statute or regulation can be found.

parallel citation

A second (or third) citation for a given case. When a case is published in more than one reporter, each citation is a parallel citation to the other(s).

TEN TIPS FOR EFFECTIVE LEGAL RESEARCH

E. J. Yera

BIOGRAPHICAL NOTE

In 1987, E. J. Yera graduated from the University of Miami School of Law, where he subsequently served as a research instructor until 1989.

After clerking for the U.S. District Court for the Southern District of Florida, Yera served as corporate counsel for Holmes Regional Medical Center in Melbourne, Florida, and its affiliates until 1995. He then became a member of the Health Care Task Force in the Antitrust Division of the U.S. Department of Justice in Washington, D.C.

In 1997, Yera became a member of the U.S. Attorney's Office in the Southern District of Florida. He has taught and lectured in various paralegal programs and has published several articles.

If you perform legal research frequently, you will develop a routine. The purpose of this article is not to give you ironclad rules but to set out ten guidelines that will help you find the routine that is most comfortable for you. You may come back to this article and reread it over time. Now, however, as you read it for the first time, think about how you can use the tips in your future research tasks.

1. **Before You Start, Make Sure You Know the Exact Legal Issue You Will Be Researching.** You would be surprised at how many students, paralegals, and lawyers research a question for hours only to discover they were not researching the correct legal question. Before you start your research, you should determine the legal question or issue that needs to be researched. You might learn this from reviewing information you already have available, such as a summary of a client interview. If you have an opportunity to ask questions of the attorney giving you a research assignment, do so. What counts, in the end, is coming back with the correct answers, not impressing the attorney by appearing to understand the research task completely when you first hear about it. It will take you twice as long to finish the assignment if you research the wrong issue or if you are unsure what the issue is.

2. **Understand the Language of the Issue.** Often, the researcher finds that he or she cannot find the answer because the legal terms used in defining the problem are unfamiliar to him or her. Legal terms, or "terms of art," as they are often called, are as unfamiliar to many people as a foreign language. If you are uncertain about

the meaning of any term or phrase, look it up in a law dictionary or encyclopedia to get a general idea of its meaning. Depending on how broad the term is, you may want to read a hornbook on the topic to give you a basic understanding of it. For example, assume you are researching an issue relating to securities law. If you do not have a clear understanding of what securities are, there is no way in the world that you can conduct effective research on the issue. You will need to acquire some background knowledge before you focus on the particular research topic.

3. **Be Aware of the Circular Nature of Legal Research and Use It to Your Advantage.** Students often ask whether primary or secondary sources should be researched first. The answer is that it does not matter, as long as you always research both types of sources. By researching both primary and secondary sources on a topic, you can be assured that you are almost always double-checking your own work. For example, in a case (primary source of law) on a particular issue, the judge writing the opinion will discuss any pertinent statutes on the issue. Similarly, most annotated versions of a statute (annotations are secondary sources of law) give a listing, following the text of the statute, of cases applying the statute and the context in which the statute was applied. The reason you check both sources is to make sure you have found all of the relevant materials.

4. **Until You Submit the Assignment, Always Assume There Are Additional Relevant Materials to Find.** You

need to keep on your toes until you complete your research task. Always assuming that further relevant materials must be located will help you do this. Of course, there comes a point when you *have* to assume that you *have* covered the research territory, and knowing when to stop doing research is perhaps one of the hardest things to learn. Certain legal issues can be researched for months and even years. The intent of this tip, though, is to encourage you not to cut corners when conducting research.

5. **Keep a List of What Sources You Have Found and Where They Have Led You.** You do not want to spend valuable time wondering if you have already checked certain sources. Therefore, it is important to construct a "road map" of where you have been and where you are going.

6. **Take the Time to Become Familiar with the Sources You Are Using.** It probably seems obvious that you need to become familiar with your sources, yet this requirement is sometimes overlooked. For example, a case digest (a volume summarizing cases) may indicate on its spine that the digest covers the years "1961 to Date." "To Date," however, does not mean that it is the most current digest; it only means that the digest covers cases up to the date of publication. You should take the time to read the first few pages of the digest to verify its contents. This is true generally for any source you are using—look it over carefully before assuming it contains the sources you need.

7. **Be Aware of the Jurisdiction and the Time Frame You Are Researching.** If you are researching an issue that will be resolved by a Florida state court, then your emphasis should be on Florida cases. Of course, there are times when no case law is available, and you must then find cases on point from other states to use as persuasive authorities. You must also be aware of the time frame covered by the source you are using (as mentioned in Tip 6). Be aware when researching any area of the law that very often there is either a loose-leaf service or a pamphlet or pocket part (a small booklet that slips into a pocket of the bound volume) containing newer information. Always ask yourself the following question: Where can the most up-to-date material be found? If you don't know, ask a law librarian who does.

> *"What counts, in the end, is coming back with the correct answers . . . ."*

8. **Always Refer to *Shepard's* to Make Sure the Cases You Are Using Are Up to Date.** *Shepard's Citations* is a set of volumes that helps the researcher of case law in two ways. First, it lists other cases that have cited the cases you have found. This information is helpful because if another case has cited a case you have found, that other case may also be relevant to your issue, and thus you may be able to use it. Also, cases that cite your case are more recent, and using one or more of those cases may thus be advantageous. Second, *Shepard's* tells you, among other things, whether the cases that you have found are still "good law"—that is, whether the cases have been overruled, reversed, or the like. Knowing this information is crucial—because presenting a case to your attorney that no longer represents good law could well be a short cut to the unemployment line.

9. **Use Computerized Legal Research Services to Update Your Research Results.** Computerized legal databases such as Westlaw and Lexis allow you to update your research results by using online citators. Also, these services allow you to search the available case law for words or phrases. By doing so, you can actually create your own indexing system. Additionally, the Internet is a great source for legal materials. Several state and federal courts, government agencies, law schools, and bar associations have developed Web sites containing different types of primary and secondary legal materials.

10. **Twice a Year, Take Three or Four Hours and Browse through Your Local Law Library.** You cannot use sources effectively if you do not know that they exist. You should periodically—say, twice a year—spend an afternoon in the law library browsing through the shelves. Read the first few pages of each new source; then make a note of what the source contains. Ask the librarian for new sources in your area. The time you save later will more than compensate for an afternoon's time spent in the library. You will be surprised at how quickly the new sources you discovered or were told about at the law library come to mind when you receive a research assignment, and they may figure significantly in your research.

EXHIBIT 7.7
West's National Reporter System—Regional and Federal

Regional Reporters	Coverage Beginning	Coverage
Atlantic Reporter (A. or A.2d)	1885	Connecticut, Delaware, Maine, Maryland, New Hampshire, New Jersey, Pennsylvania, Rhode Island, Vermont, and District of Columbia.
North Eastern Reporter (N.E. or N.E.2d)	1885	Illinois, Indiana, Massachusetts, New York, and Ohio.
North Western Reporter (N.W. or N.W.2d)	1879	Iowa, Michigan, Minnesota, Nebraska, North Dakota, South Dakota, and Wisconsin.
Pacific Reporter (P., P.2d, or P.3d)	1883	Alaska, Arizona, California, Colorado, Hawaii, Idaho, Kansas, Montana, Nevada, New Mexico, Oklahoma, Oregon, Utah, Washington, and Wyoming.
South Eastern Reporter (S.E. or S.E.2d)	1887	Georgia, North Carolina, South Carolina, Virginia, and West Virginia.
South Western Reporter (S.W., S.W.2d, or S.W.3d)	1886	Arkansas, Kentucky, Missouri, Tennessee, and Texas.
Southern Reporter (So. or So.2d)	1887	Alabama, Florida, Louisiana, and Mississippi.

Federal Reporters		
Federal Reporter (F., F.2d, or F.3d)	1880	U.S. Circuit Court from 1880 to 1912; U.S. Commerce Court from 1911 to 1913; U.S. District Courts from 1880 to 1932; U.S. Court of Claims (now called U.S. Court of Federal Claims) from 1929 to 1932 and since 1960; U.S. Court of Appeals since 1891; U.S. Court of Customs and Patent Appeals since 1929; and U.S. Emergency Court of Appeals since 1943.
Federal Supplement (F.Supp. or F.Supp.2d)	1932	U.S. Court of Claims from 1932 to 1960; U.S. District Courts since 1932; and U.S. Customs Court since 1956.
Federal Rules Decisions (F.R.D.)	1939	U.S. District Courts involving the Federal Rules of Civil Procedure since 1939 and Federal Rules of Criminal Procedure since 1946.
Supreme Court Reporter (S.Ct.)	1882	U.S. Supreme Court since the October term of 1882.
Bankruptcy Reporter (Bankr.)	1980	Bankruptcy decisions of U.S. Bankruptcy Courts, U.S. District Courts, U.S. Courts of Appeals, and U.S. Supreme Court.
Military Justice Reporter (M.J.)	1978	U.S. Court of Military Appeals and Courts of Military Review for the Army, Navy, Air Force, and Coast Guard.

NATIONAL REPORTER SYSTEM MAP

EXHIBIT 7.8
How to Read Citations

From *Business Law Today: Standard Edition,* 9th ed., by Roger LeRoy Miller and Gaylord A. Jentz, © 2010 South-Western, a part of Cengage Learning, Inc. Reproduced by permission. www.cengage.com/permissions

STATE COURTS

277 Neb. 756, 759 N.W.2d 484 (2009)[a]

> *N.W.* is the abbreviation for West's publication of state court decisions rendered in the *North Western Reporter* of the National Reporter System. *2d* indicates that this case was included in the *Second Series* of that reporter. The number 759 refers to the volume number of the reporter; the number 484 refers to the page in that volume on which this case begins.

> *Neb.* is an abbreviation for *Nebraska Reports,* Nebraska's official reports of the decisions of its highest court, the Nebraska Supreme Court.

171 Cal.App.4th 700, 89 Cal.Rptr.3d 890 (2009)

> *Cal.Rptr.* is the abbreviation for West's unofficial reports—titled *California Reporter*—of the decisions of California courts.

12 N.Y.3d 1, 903 N.E.2d 1146, 875 N.Y.S.2d 826 (2009)

> *N.Y.S.* is the abbreviation for West's unofficial reports—titled *New York Supplement*—of the decisions of New York courts.

> *N.Y.* is the abbreviation for *New York Reports,* New York's official reports of the decisions of its court of appeals. The New York Court of Appeals is the state's highest court, analogous to other states' supreme courts. In New York, a supreme court is a trial court.

295 Ga.App. 505, 672 S.E.2d 471 (2009)

> *Ga.App.* is the abbreviation for *Georgia Appeals Reports,* Georgia's official reports of the decisions of its court of appeals.

FEDERAL COURTS

_____ U.S. _____, 129 S.Ct. 695, 172 L.Ed.2d 496 (2009)

> *L.Ed.* is an abbreviation for *Lawyers' Edition of the Supreme Court Reports,* an unofficial edition of decisions of the United States Supreme Court.

> *S.Ct.* is the abbreviation for West's unofficial reports—titled *Supreme Court Reporter*—of decisions of the United States Supreme Court.

> *U.S.* is the abbreviation for *United States Reports,* the official edition of the decisions of the United States Supreme Court. The blank lines in this citation (or any other citation) indicate that the appropriate volume of the case reporter has not yet been published and no page number is available.

a. The case names have been deleted from these citations to emphasize the publications. It should be kept in mind, however, that the name of a case is as important as the specific page numbers in the volumes in which it is found. If a citation is incorrect, the correct citation may be found in a publication's index of case names. In addition to providing a check on errors in citations, the date of a case is important because the value of a recent case as an authority is likely to be greater than that of older cases from the same court.

Continued

EXHIBIT 7.8
How to Read Citations—Continued

FEDERAL COURTS (Continued)

551 F.3d 1099 (9th Cir. 2009)

> *9th Cir.* is an abbreviation denoting that this case was decided in the U.S. Court of Appeals for the Ninth Circuit.

533 F.Supp.2d 740 (W.D.Mich. 2008)

> *W.D.Mich.* is an abbreviation indicating that the U.S. District Court for the Western District of Michigan decided this case.

ENGLISH COURTS

9 Exch. 341, 156 Eng.Rep. 145 (1854)

> *Eng.Rep.* is an abbreviation for *English Reports, Full Reprint,* a series of reports containing selected decisions made in English courts between 1378 and 1865.

> *Exch.* is an abbreviation for *English Exchequer Reports*, which includes the original reports of cases decided in England's Court of Exchequer.

STATUTORY AND OTHER CITATIONS

18 U.S.C. Section 1961(1)(A)

> *U.S.C.* denotes *United States Code*, the codification of *United States Statutes at Large*. The number 18 refers to the statute's U.S.C. title number and 1961 to its section number within that title. The number 1 in parentheses refers to a subsection within the section, and the letter A in parentheses to a subdivision within the subsection.

UCC 2–206(1)(b)

> *UCC* is an abbreviation for *Uniform Commercial Code*. The first number 2 is a reference to an article of the UCC, and 206 to a section within that article. The number 1 in parentheses refers to a subsection within the section, and the letter b in parentheses to a subdivision within the subsection.

Restatement (Second) of Torts, Section 568

> *Restatement (Second) of Torts* refers to the second edition of the American Law Institute's *Restatement of the Law of Torts*. The number 568 refers to a specific section.

17 C.F.R. Section 230.505

> *C.F.R.* is an abbreviation for *Code of Federal Regulations*, a compilation of federal administrative regulations. The number 17 designates the regulation's title number, and 230.505 designates a specific section within that title.

EXHIBIT 7.8
How to Read Citations—Continued

WESTLAW® CITATIONS[b]

2009 WL 649691

WL is an abbreviation for Westlaw. The number 2009 is the year of the document that can be found with this citation in the Westlaw database. The number 649691 is a number assigned to a specific document. A higher number indicates that a document was added to the Westlaw database later in the year.

UNIFORM RESOURCE LOCATORS (URLs)

http://www.westlaw.com[c]

The suffix *com* is the top level domain (TLD) for this Web site. The TLD *com* is an abbreviation for "commercial," which usually means that a for-profit entity hosts (maintains or supports) this Web site.

westlaw is the host name—the part of the domain name selected by the organization that registered the name. In this case, West Group registered the name. This Internet site is the Westlaw database on the Web.

www is an abbreviation for "World Wide Web." The Web is a system of Internet servers that support documents formatted in *HTML* (hypertext markup language). HTML supports links to text, graphics, and audio and video files.

http://www.uscourts.gov

This is "The Federal Judiciary Home Page." The host is the Administrative Office of the U.S. Courts. The TLD *gov* is an abbreviation for "government." This Web site includes information and links from, and about, the federal courts.

http://www.law.cornell.edu/index.html

This part of a URL points to a Web page or file at a specific location within the host's domain. This page is a menu with links to documents within the domain and to other Internet resources.

This is the host name for a Web site that contains the Internet publications of the Legal Information Institute (LII), which is a part of Cornell Law School. The LII site includes a variety of legal materials and links to other legal resources on the Internet. The TLD *edu* is an abbreviation for "educational institution" (a school or a university).

http://www.ipl.org/div/news

This part of the Web site points to a static *news* page at this Web site, which provides links to online newspapers from around the world.

div is an abbreviation for "division," which is the way that the Internet Public Library tags the content on its Web site as relating to a specific topic.

ipl is an abbreviation for "Internet Public Library," which is an online service that provides reference resources and links to other information services on the Web. The IPL is supported chiefly by the School of Information at the University of Michigan. The TLD *org* is an abbreviation for "organization" (normally nonprofit).

b. Many court decisions that are not yet published or that are not intended for publication can be accessed through Westlaw, an online legal database.

c. The basic form for a URL is "service://hostname/path." The Internet service for all of the URLs in this text is *http* (hypertext transfer protocol). Because most Web browsers add this prefix automatically when a user enters a host name or a hostname/path, we have omitted the http:// from the URLs listed in this text.

Federal Court Decisions

Court decisions from the U.S. district courts (federal trial courts) are published in West's *Federal Supplement* (F.Supp. or F.Supp.2d), and opinions from the courts of appeals are reported in West's *Federal Reporter* (F., F.2d, or F.3d). These are both unofficial reporters (there are no official reporters for these courts). Both the *Federal Reporter* and the *Federal Supplement* incorporate decisions from specialized federal courts. West also publishes separate reporters, such as its *Bankruptcy Reporter,* that contain decisions in certain specialized fields under federal law. All of these reporters are published online.

United States Supreme Court Decisions

Opinions from the United States Supreme Court are published in several reporters, including the *United States Reports,* West's *Supreme Court Reporter,* and the *Lawyers' Edition of the Supreme Court Reports,* each of which we discuss below. A sample citation to a Supreme Court case was also included in Exhibit 7.8 on page 211.

The United States Reports

The *United States Reports* (U.S.) is the official edition of all decisions of the United States Supreme Court for which there are written opinions. Published by the federal government, the series includes reports of Supreme Court cases dating from the August term of 1791. Soon after the Supreme Court issues a decision, the official slip opinion is published by the U.S. Government Printing Office. (It is published online more quickly at the Supreme Court's Web site. Go to **www.supremecourtus. gov**, and select "Opinions," then "Latest Slip Opinions.") The **slip opinion** is the first authoritative text of the opinion and is printed as an individual pamphlet. After a number of slip opinions have been issued, the advance sheets of the official *United States Reports* appear. These are issued in pamphlet form to provide a temporary resource until the official bound volume is finally published.

The Supreme Court Reporter

Supreme Court cases are also published in West's *Supreme Court Reporter* (S.Ct.), which is an unofficial edition of Supreme Court opinions dating from the Court's term in October 1882. In this reporter, the case report—the formal court opinion—is preceded by a **syllabus** (summary of the case) and headnotes with key numbers (used throughout the West reporters and digests) prepared by West editors. This reporter, like the others, can be accessed through online legal search services, as discussed later in the chapter.

The Lawyers' Edition of the Supreme Court Reports

The *Lawyers' Edition of the Supreme Court Reports* (L.Ed. or L.Ed.2d) is an unofficial edition of the entire series of the Supreme Court reports containing many decisions not reported in early official volumes. The advantage offered to the legal researcher by the *Lawyers' Edition* is its research tools. In its second series, it precedes each case report with a summary of the case and discusses in detail selected cases of special interest to the legal profession. Also, the *Lawyers' Edition* is the only reporter of Supreme Court opinions that provides summaries of the briefs presented by counsel.

Unofficial Loose-Leaf Service

United States Law Week, published by the Bureau of National Affairs (BNA), is an unofficial loose-leaf service that publishes decisions of the federal appellate courts and the United States Supreme Court the day after a decision is announced. BNA lawyer-editors select and summarize federal, state, and administrative law cases that establish new precedents, address new statutes, or address current controversies. Like most legal research tools, *United States Law Week* is available online. (Go to

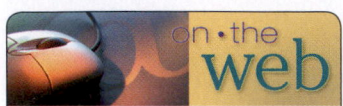

To find Supreme Court opinions and opinions issued by the federal appellate courts, as well as information on the federal court system, a good starting point is the official U.S. courts Web site at **www.uscourts.gov**.

slip opinion
A judicial opinion published shortly after the decision is made and not yet included in a case reporter or advance sheets.

syllabus
A brief summary of the holding and legal principles involved in a reported case, which is followed by the court's official opinion.

www.bna.com. Select "All Products" from the menu, and then, under "U," select "United States Law Week.")

ANALYZING CASE LAW

Attorneys often rely heavily on case law to support a position or argument. One of the difficulties all legal professionals face in analyzing case law is the length and complexity of many court opinions. While some opinions may be only two or three pages long, others can be hundreds of pages in length. Understanding the components of a case—that is, the basic format in which cases are presented—can simplify your task of reading and analyzing case law. Over time, as you acquire experience, case analysis becomes easier. This section focuses on how to read and analyze cases, as well as how to summarize, or *brief,* a case.

The Components of a Case

Reported cases contain much more than just the court's decision. Cases have different parts, and you should know why each part is there and what information it communicates. To illustrate the various components of a case, we present an annotated sample court case in Exhibit 7.9 starting on the next page. This exhibit shows an actual case that was decided by the highest court in Massachusetts in 2009.

Important sections, terms, and phrases in the case are defined or explained in the margins. You will note also that triple asterisks (* * *) and quadruple asterisks (* * * *) frequently appear in the exhibit. The triple asterisks indicate that we have deleted a few words or sentences from the opinion for the sake of readability or brevity. Quadruple asterisks mean that an entire paragraph (or more) has been omitted. Also, when the opinion cites another case or legal source, the citation to the referenced case or source has been omitted to save space and to improve readability.

We discuss below the various parts of a case. As you read through the descriptions of these parts, refer to Exhibit 7.9, which illustrates most of them. Remember, though, that the excerpt presented in Exhibit 7.9, because it has been pared down for illustration, may be much easier to read than some court opinions that you will encounter.

Case Title

The title of a case indicates the names of the parties to the lawsuit, and the *v.* in the case title stands for *versus,* or "against." In the trial court, the plaintiff's last name appears first, and the second name is the defendant's. If the case is appealed, however, the appellate court will *sometimes* place the name of the party appealing the decision first, so the parties' names may be reversed. Because some appellate courts retain the trial court order of names, it is often impossible to distinguish the plaintiff from the defendant in the title of a reported appellate court decision. One must carefully read the facts of each case to identify the parties.

Case Citation

Typically, the citation to the case is found just above or just below the case title (and often at the tops of consecutive printed or online pages). If the citation appears on Westlaw and one of the parallel citations is not yet available, the citation may include underlined spaces for the volume and page numbers to be filled in once they become available (such as "___ U.S. ___").

Docket Number

The docket number immediately follows the case title. A docket number is assigned by the court clerk when a case is initially filed. The number serves as an identifier for all papers submitted in connection with the case. A case published in a reporter

EXHIBIT 7.9
A Sample Court Case

| This section contains the case citation—the name of the case, the name of the court that heard the case, the year of the court's decision, and the reporter in which the court's decision can be found. | → | Boston Housing Authority

v.

Emmitt Bridgewaters

Supreme Judicial Court of Massachusetts, 2009

452 Mass. 833, 898 N.E.2d 848 |

| The *docket number* assigned by the Supreme Judicial Court of Massachusetts. | → | SJC-10107 |

| The *syllabus*—a brief summary of the issues and decisions in the case. Prepared by West editors. | → | **Background:** [The Boston Housing Authority (BHA)] brought summary process action against tenant in public housing complex, seeking eviction of tenant. The Housing Court Department, Suffolk County, Boston Division, Steven D. Pierce, J., 2004 WL 5031620, evicted tenant, and tenant appealed. The Appeals Court, 69 Mass.App.Ct. 757, 871 N.E.2d 1107, affirmed.

Holdings: On application for further review, the Supreme Judicial Court, Marshall, C.J., held that:

(1) housing authority had notice that tenant had mental disability;

(2) tenant made reasonable accommodation* request; and

(3) housing authority was required to consider whether causal link existed between tenant's disability and assault. |

| The Supreme Judicial Court of Massachusetts concluded that the lower court was incorrect in its interpretation of the law. | → | Judgment of Appeals Court vacated; remanded to Housing Court. |

| Names of counsel for the plaintiff (appellant) and the defendant (appellee). | → | Ann Jochnick (Richard M. W. Bauer & James M. McCreight with her) for the defendant.

Jay S. Koplove for the plaintiff. |

*[Note to readers: The rules of the BHA state: "A 'reasonable accommodation' is a modification or change the BHA can make to its procedures and rules or to the person's apartment . . . which would assist an otherwise eligible person with a disability to benefit from BHA housing, provided that the change does not pose an undue financial and administrative burden to the BHA or result in a fundamental alteration of its program." Most accommodations concern access for physical disabilities. This case concerns the obligation of the BHA to consider what arrangements might be feasible for a mental disability.]

EXHIBIT 7.9
A Sample Court Case—Continued

This line gives the name of the judge who authored the opinion of the court.	Marshall, Chief Justice

* * * *

The court divides the opinion into four major parts. The first part of the opinion summarizes the procedural background of the case.	1. *Procedural background.* On March 22, 2004, the BHA brought an eviction action against Bridgewaters by filing a **summary process complaint** in the Housing Court. The BHA claimed that Bridgewaters had caused serious physical harm to another tenant, his twin brother. Trial commenced and was concluded on April 22, 2004. On May 17, 2004, the judge issued written findings of fact and conclusions of law, and entered judgment for possession for the BHA.
A request that a tenant be evicted.	

Bridgewaters, now represented by counsel, moved for reconsideration and for relief from judgment * * *.

* * * *

The Appeals Court then affirmed the judgment and the Housing Court judge's order denying the postjudgment motions, concluding that "an individual who engages in conduct that violates a housing authority's rules" [as Bridgewaters had done] * * * is not a qualified handicapped person.

The second major section of the opinion sets out the facts determined by the Housing Court judge.	2. *Factual background.* We summarize the facts found by the judge, supplemented by undisputed facts of record and uncontested **affidavits** and exhibits considered by the judge in Bridgewaters's posttrial motions. The BHA owns and operates Holgate Apartments, a federally assisted residential complex for the elderly and
Written sworn testimony entered into evidence.	

the disabled, where Bridgewaters resides. His twin brother, Eric, also resided at Holgate, in a different apartment. In the late evening of January 9 or the early morning of January 10, 2004, Bridgewaters assaulted Eric inside Eric's apartment. As a result of the altercation, Eric, who was paralyzed on the left side of his body due to a stroke he suffered as a child, sustained severe injuries, and temporary paralysis in his right leg. After the assault, the BHA brought this action; the BHA had not previously attempted to terminate Bridgewaters's tenancy.

During the trial, Bridgewaters, who was not represented by counsel, testified that he had not initiated the assault, that he had punched his brother once, and [that he] had thrown water at him. Bridgewaters also testified that he suffers from a mental disability, which he termed manic depression or bipolar disorder. He

Continued

EXHIBIT 7.9

A Sample Court Case—Continued

stated that he had been prescribed medication, but that he was unmedicated at the time of the assault on the advice of his physician.

* * * *

In support of his posttrial motion, Bridgewaters submitted affidavits and exhibits that elaborated on his trial testimony. These materials indicate that Bridgewaters had been determined to be disabled by the Social Security Administration and unable to support himself, and that he was diagnosed with bipolar disorder and borderline personality disorder.

* * * *

> | The third major section of the opinion sets out and applies the law to the plaintiff's arguments. |

3. *Discussion.* Because the issue whether Bridgewaters made a reasonable accommodation request arises meaningfully only if the BHA is obligated to entertain his request, we first address whether Bridgewaters's misconduct foreclosed consideration of any reasonable accommodation request.

> | The first issue considered is whether Bridgewaters is a threat to other tenants. |

a. *The "direct threat" exception.* Much of this case turns on what is known as the "direct threat" exception to a public housing authority's ordinary obligation to accommodate tenants with disabilities. * * *

* * * *

> | The second issue concerns the duty of the BHA to provide help for a disabled tenant. |

b. *Reasonable accommodation request.* Because the BHA's obligation to assess individually whether Bridgewaters posed a threat to the health or safety of others turns on whether Bridgewaters requested a reasonable accommodation, we now address whether the BHA knew that Bridgewaters was disabled and whether he made a request for a reasonable accommodation, leaving for later discussion the BHA's claim that no causal link existed between Bridgewaters's disability and the assault on his brother.

* * * *

> | In the fourth major section of this opinion, the court states its decision and gives its order. |

4. *Conclusion.* Bridgewaters's twin brother has the right to be safe and secure in his home, as do all tenants of public housing. We do not minimize the severity of the attack on him. However, the law mandates that, before a public housing authority may terminate the lease of a disabled tenant such as Bridgewaters because he poses "a significant risk to the health or safety of others" that cannot

should not be cited by its docket number, but the number may serve as a valuable tool in obtaining background information on the case. Cases appearing in slip-opinion form (cases that have been decided but not yet published in a reporter) are usually identified, filed, and cited by docket number. After publication of the

EXHIBIT 7.9
A Sample Court Case—Continued

> be eliminated by a reasonable accommodation, the housing authority "must make an individualized assessment, based on reasonable judgment that relies on current medical knowledge or on the best available objective evidence to ascertain: the nature, duration, and severity of the risk; the probability that the potential injury will actually occur; and whether reasonable modifications of policies, practices, or procedures will mitigate the risk." No such individualized assessment has taken place in this case as it must. We vacate the judgment and remand the case to the Housing Court for further proceedings consistent with this opinion.

Court order. →

---

decision, the docket number may continue to serve as an identifier for appellate records and briefs (appellate briefs will be discussed in Chapter 9).

Dates Argued and Decided

An important component of a case is the date on which it was decided by the court. Usually, the date of the decision immediately follows the docket number. In addition to the date of the court's decision on the matter, the date on which the case was argued before the court (in appellate court cases) may also be included here.

Syllabus

Following the docket number is the *syllabus*—a brief synopsis of the facts of the case, the issues analyzed by the court, and the court's conclusion. In official reporters, the courts usually prepare the syllabi; in unofficial reporters, the publishers of the reporters usually prepare them. The syllabus is often a helpful research tool. It provides an overview of the case and points out legal issues discussed by the court. But keep in mind that reading the syllabus is not a substitute for reading the case if the case is relevant.

Headnotes

Often, unofficial reporters, such as those published by West, make extensive use of case *headnotes*. As discussed earlier, headnotes are short paragraphs that highlight and summarize specific rules of law mentioned in the case. In reporters published by West, they are correlated to the comprehensive West key-number system. In Exhibit 7.9, the headnotes were deleted for reasons of space.

Names of Counsel

The published report of the case usually contains the names of the lawyers (counsel) representing the parties. The attorneys' names are typically found just following the syllabus (and headnotes, if any).

Name of Judge or Justice Authoring the Opinion

The name of the judge or justice who authored the opinion in the case will also be included in the published report of the case, just before the court's opinion. In some cases, instead of the name of a judge or justice, the decision will be authored *per curiam* (Latin for "by the court"), which means that the opinion is that of the whole court and not the opinion of any one judge or justice. Sometimes the phrase is used to indicate that the chief justice or presiding judge wrote the opinion. The phrase also may be used for an announcement of a court's disposition of a case that is not accompanied by a written opinion.

Opinion

As you may have noticed, the term *opinion* is often used loosely to refer to a court case or decision. In fact, the term has a precise meaning. The opinion of the court contains the analysis and decision of the judge or judges who heard and decided the case. Most opinions contain a brief statement of the facts of the case, a summary of the legal issues raised by the facts, and the remedies sought by the parties. In appellate court cases, the court summarizes the errors of the lower court, if any, and the impact of these errors on the case's outcome. The main body of the opinion is the application of the law to the particular facts. The court often mentions case precedents, relevant statutes, and administrative rules and regulations to support its reasoning. Additionally, court opinions may contain discussions of policy and other factors that clarify the reason for the court's decision.

When all of the judges on a court of appeals agree in the legal reasoning and the decision, the opinion is called a *unanimous* opinion. When the opinion is not unanimous, a *majority* opinion is written, outlining the views of the majority of the judges deciding the case. If a judge agrees, or concurs, with the majority's decision, but for different reasons, that judge may write a *concurring opinion*. A *dissenting opinion* presents the views of one or more judges who disagree with the majority's decision. The dissenting opinion is important because it may form the basis of the arguments used years later in overruling the majority opinion.

The Court's Conclusion

In the opinion, the judges indicate their conclusion, or decision, on the issue or issues before the court. If several issues are involved, as often happens, there may be a conclusion at the end of the discussion of each issue. Often, at the end of the opinion, the conclusions presented within the opinion are briefly summarized. If no conclusions have yet been presented, they are presented in the concluding section of the opinion.

An appellate court also specifies what the *disposition* of a case should be. If the court agrees with a lower court's decision, it will *affirm* that decision, which means that the decision of the lower court remains unchanged. If the appellate court concludes that the lower court erred in its interpretation of the law, the court may *reverse* the lower court's ruling. Sometimes, if an appellate court concludes that further factual findings are necessary or that a case should be retried and a decision made that is consistent with the appellate court's conclusions of law, the appellate court will *remand* the case to the lower court for further proceedings consistent with its opinion. In the sample case presented in Exhibit 7.9 on pages 216 through 219, the Supreme Judicial Court of Massachusetts remanded the case to the Housing Court.

Analyzing Cases

When you are researching case law, your main focus should be on the opinion—the words of the court itself. Some opinions are easier to understand than others. Some judges write more clearly and logically than others do. You may need to reread a case (or a portion of a case) to understand what is being said, why it is being said at that point in the case, and what the judge's legal reasoning is. Some cases contain several pages describing facts and issues of previous cases and how those cases relate to the one being decided by the court. You might want to reread these discussions several times to distinguish between comments made in the previous case and comments that are being made about the case at bar (before the court).

Look for Guideposts in the Opinion

Often, the judge writing the opinion provides some guideposts, perhaps by indicating sections and subsections within the opinion by numbers, letters, or subtitles. Note that in Exhibit 7.9, numbers are used to divide the opinion into basic sections. Scanning through the opinion for these types of indicators can help orient you to the opinion's format.

In cases that involve dissenting or concurring opinions, make sure that you identify these opinions so that you do not mistake one of them for the majority opinion. Generally, you should scan through the case a time or two to identify its components and then read the case (or sections of the case) until you understand the facts and procedural history of the case, the issues involved, the applicable law, the legal reasoning of the court, and how the reasoning leads to the court's conclusion on the issues.

Distinguish the Court's Holding from Dicta

When analyzing cases, you should determine which statements of the court are legally binding and which are not. Only the **holding** (the legal principle to be drawn from the court's decision) is binding. Other views expressed in the opinion are referred to as *dicta* and are not binding. *Dicta* is the plural of *dictum*. As used here, *dictum* is an abbreviated form of the Latin term *obiter dictum,* which means "a remark by the way." *Dicta* are any statements made in a decision that go beyond the facts of the case or that do not directly relate to the facts or to the resolution of the issue being addressed. *Dicta* include comments used by the court to illustrate an example and statements concerning a rule of law not essential to the case. You can probably assume that statements are *dicta* if they begin with "If the facts were different" or "If the plaintiff had . . ." or some other "if/then" phrase.

holding
The binding legal principle, or precedent, that is drawn from the court's decision in a case.

dicta
A Latin term referring to nonbinding (nonprecedential) judicial statements that are not directly related to the facts or issues presented in the case and thus not essential to the holding.

Summarizing and Briefing Cases

After you have read and analyzed a case, you may decide that it is on point and that you want to include a reference to it in your research findings. If so, you will summarize in your notes the important facts and issues in the case, as well as the court's decision, or holding, and the reasoning used by the court. This is called **briefing a case**.

There is a fairly standard procedure for briefing court cases. First, read the case opinion carefully. When you feel you understand the case, begin to prepare the brief. Typically, a brief presents the essentials of the case under headings such as those listed below. Many researchers conclude their briefs with an additional section in which they note their own comments or conclusions about the case.

briefing a case
Summarizing a case. A case brief gives the full citation, the factual background and procedural history, the issue or issues raised, the court's decision, the court's holding, and the legal reasoning on which the court based its decision. It may also include conclusions or notes concerning the case made by the one briefing it.

1. **Citation.** Give the full citation for the case, including the name of the case, the date it was decided, and the court that decided it.
2. **Facts.** Briefly indicate (a) the reasons for the lawsuit (who did what to whom) and (b) the identity and arguments of the plaintiff(s) and defendant(s).
3. **Procedure.** Indicate the procedural history of the case in a sentence or two. What was the lower court's decision? What did the appellate court do (affirm, reverse, remand)? How did the matter arrive before the present court?
4. **Issue.** State, in the form of a question, the essential issue before the court. (If more than one issue is involved, you may have two—or even more—questions here.)
5. **Decision.** Indicate here—with a "yes" or "no," if possible—the court's answer to the question (or questions) that you noted in the *Issue* section.
6. **Reasoning.** Summarize as briefly as possible the reasons given by the court for its decision (or decisions) and the case or statutory law relied on by the court in arriving at its decision.
7. **Holding.** State the rule of law for which the case stands.

EXHIBIT 7.10
A Briefed Version of
the Sample Court Case

BOSTON HOUSING AUTHORITY v. BRIDGEWATERS

452 Mass. 833, 898 N.E.2d 848 (S.J.C., Mass., 2009)

FACTS   The Boston Housing Authority (BHA) owns and operates federally assisted residential complexes for the elderly and disabled. Emmitt Bridgewaters, who is mentally disabled with bipolar disorder, lives in a BHA apartment. It is not contested that one night he assaulted and injured his brother, who is physically disabled and lives in another apartment. After the assault, Bridgewaters was an inpatient in a mental health facility for three weeks, after which he was declared able to return to live safely in the community. His brother supports his return to the BHA complex.

PROCEDURE   BHA filed a motion with the Housing Court to have Bridgewaters evicted because of the assault. Bridgewaters, not represented by counsel at the hearing, was found to have committed a crime in the BHA property that "threatened the health and safety of another resident" and was ordered evicted. Bridgewaters appealed to the Massachusetts Appeals Court and was represented by counsel before the court. It affirmed the decision of the Housing Court. Bridgewaters appealed to the Supreme Judicial Court of Massachusetts.

ISSUES   (1) Did Bridgewaters's conduct eliminate the requirement that the BHA consider his request for a reasonable accommodation based on his disability? (2) Does Bridgewaters have a reasonable accommodation request that the BHA must consider?

DECISION   (1) No. (2) Yes. The Supreme Judicial Court of Massachusetts vacated the judgment of the Appeals Court and remanded the case to the Housing Court.

REASONING   Ordinarily, the BHA could be required to accommodate Bridgewaters's disability, but the Fair Housing Act provides an exception when a "direct threat" is posed by a tenant. A disabled tenant does not qualify for protection under the housing law if "he or she would pose a threat to the safety of others, unless such threat can be eliminated by reasonable accommodation." BHA evicted Bridgewaters due to the assault but did not evaluate whether, after treatment, he posed a threat. He made a reasonable accommodation request that was not properly considered in the eviction process.

HOLDING   To lawfully evict Bridgewaters, the BHA must show the failure of an accommodation instituted at the request of the tenant or show that no reasonable accommodation will acceptably control the risk the tenant poses to other tenants. The BHA knew Bridgewaters was disabled but did not fulfill its obligation to evaluate whether he posed a threat to other tenants that would not be eliminated by accommodation of his disability.

Exhibit 7.10 presents a briefed version of the sample court case presented in Exhibit 7.9 to illustrate the typical format used in briefing cases.

IRAC: A Method for Briefing Cases

Besides the example just provided, another standard format for briefing cases is called the *IRAC method,* referring to *issue, rule, application,* and *conclusion.* This method, which will be discussed more in Chapter 9, involves the following steps:

1. First, decide what legal *issues* are involved in the case. For the case presented in Exhibit 7.9, these are identified under "Issues" in the case briefing in Exhibit 7.10.

2. Next, determine the *rule of law* that applies to the issues. In Exhibit 7.10, the rule of law is discussed under "Reasoning."

3. After identifying the applicable law, determine the *application* of the law to the facts of the case. In Exhibit 7.10, the "Holding" section deals with the court's application of the law.

4. Finally, draw a *conclusion*. Exhibit 7.10 calls that the "Decision." It is the determination of the court after it has applied the law to the case.

Different lawyers and law offices have different preferences for the format to be used in briefing cases. What is most important is accuracy in explaining the key facts, the issues under consideration, the rule of law or legal reasoning used by the court, the application of the law, and the conclusion resulting from that application.

RESEARCHING CONSTITUTIONAL AND STATUTORY LAW

Up to this point, we have been discussing case law, which is sometimes called *judge-made* law because it is made by the judges in the state and federal court systems. Judge-made law is also known as the common law, as explained in Chapter 5. Another primary source of law is *statutory law*—the statutes and ordinances enacted by legislative bodies, such as the U.S. Congress, state legislatures, and town governments.

Congress draws its authority to enact federal legislation from the U.S. Constitution; a state legislature draws its authority from the state constitution. In some legal disputes, the constitutionality of a statute or government action may be an issue. In such instances, you may have to go behind the statutes to the relevant constitution, so we look at constitutional law before going into detail about statutes.

Finding Constitutional Law

The federal government and all fifty states have constitutions describing the powers, responsibilities, and limitations of the various branches of government. Constitutions, especially state constitutions, are amended over time.

The text of the U.S. Constitution can be found in a number of publications. A useful source of federal constitutional law is *The Constitution of the United States of America*, published under the authority of the U.S. Senate and available through the Library of Congress. It includes the full text of the U.S. Constitution, corresponding annotations concerning United States Supreme Court decisions interpreting the Constitution, and a discussion of each provision, including background information on its history and interpretation. Additional constitutional sources are found in the *United States Code Annotated* and the *United States Code Service*, which contain the text of the Constitution and its amendments as well as citations to cases discussing particular constitutional provisions. We discuss these publications shortly. Annotated state codes provide a similar service for state constitutions. Constitutional annotations are updated through supplementary pocket parts. State constitutions are usually included in the publications containing state statutes.

Finding Statutory Law

Some statutes supplement the common law, while other statutes replace it. State legislatures and the U.S. Congress have broad powers in establishing law, and if a common law principle conflicts with a statutory provision, the statute will normally take precedence. Additionally, a legislature may create statutes that deal with areas, such as age discrimination, that are not covered by the common law.

Statutes are published in compilations referred to as **codes**, which arrange materials by topic. Most statutory codes are updated through the issuance of supplemental pocket parts or by loose-leaf services. Paralegals conducting research on statutory law should begin by reviewing the index for the relevant statutory code.

code
A systematic and topically organized presentation of laws, rules, or regulations.

EXHIBIT 7.11
Titles in the *United States Code*

TITLES OF UNITED STATES CODE

*1. General Provisions.
2. The Congress.
*3. The President.
*4. Flag and Seal, Seat of Government, and the States.
*5. Government Organization and Employees; and Appendix.
†6. [Surety Bonds.]
7. Agriculture.
8. Aliens and Nationality.
*9. Arbitration.
*10. Armed Forces; and Appendix.
*11. Bankruptcy; and Appendix.
12. Banks and Banking.
*13. Census.
*14. Coast Guard.
15. Commerce and Trade.
16. Conservation.
*17. Copyrights.
*18. Crimes and Criminal Procedure; and Appendix.
19. Customs Duties.
20. Education.
21. Food and Drugs.
22. Foreign Relations and Intercourse.
*23. Highways.
24. Hospitals and Asylums.
25. Indians.
26. Internal Revenue Code.

27. Intoxicating Liquors.
*28. Judiciary and Judicial Procedure; and Appendix.
29. Labor.
30. Mineral Lands and Mining.
*31. Money and Finance.
*32. National Guard.
33. Navigation and Navigable Waters.
‡34. [Navy.]
*35. Patents.
36. Patriotic Societies and Observances.
*37. Pay and Allowances of the Uniformed Services.
*38. Veterans' Benefits.
*39. Postal Service.
40. Public Buildings, Property, and Works.
41. Public Contracts.
42. The Public Health and Welfare.
43. Public Lands.
*44. Public Printing and Documents.
45. Railroads.
*46. Shipping; and Appendix.
47. Telegraphs, Telephones, and Radiotelegraphs.
48. Territories and Insular Possessions.
*49. Transportation; and Appendix.
50. War and National Defense; and Appendix.

*This title has been enacted as law. However, any Appendix to this title has not been enacted as law.
†This title was enacted as law and has been repealed by the enactment of Title 31.
‡This title has been eliminated by the enactment of Title 10.

Page III

Federal Statutes

Federal statutes are contained in the *United States Code,* or U.S.C. This official compilation of federal statutes is published by the U.S. government every six years and is updated annually. The U.S.C. is divided into fifty topic classifications. As shown in Exhibit 7.11 above, each of these topics, called *titles,* carries a descriptive name and a number. For example, laws relating to commerce and trade are in Title 15. Laws concerning the courts and judicial procedures are in Title 28. Titles are divided into chapters (sections) and subchapters. A citation to the U.S.C. includes title and section numbers. Thus, a reference to "28 U.S.C. Section 1346" means that the statute can be found in Section 1346 of Title 28. "Section" may also be designated by the symbol §, and "Sections" by §§.

Statutes are listed in the U.S.C. by their official names. Many legislative bills enacted into law are commonly known by a popular name, however. Some have descriptive titles reflecting their purpose; others are named after their sponsors. Sometimes a researcher may know the popular name of a legislative act but not its official name. In this situation, the researcher can consult the U.S.C. volume entitled *Popular Name Table,* which lists statutes by their popular names. For example, suppose you have learned that the Landrum-Griffin Act governs an issue that you

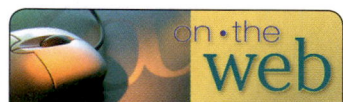

You can access and search (by title and section number) the *United States Code* online at **www.law.cornell.edu**. From the "Constitutions and Codes" menu, select "U.S. Code."

are researching. This is the popular name for the act, not the official name. You can consult the *Popular Name Table* to find the act's official title, which is the Labor-Management Reporting and Disclosure Act of 1959.

There are also two unofficial versions of the federal code, each of which contains additional information that is helpful to researchers. West's *United States Code Annotated* (U.S.C.A.) contains the full text of the U.S.C., the U.S. Constitution, the Federal Rules of Evidence, and various other rules, including the Rules of Civil Procedure and the Rules of Criminal Procedure. This useful set of approximately two hundred volumes includes historical notes relating to the text of each statute, along with any amendments to the act. Annotations offer additional assistance by listing cases that have analyzed, discussed, or interpreted the particular statute. The other unofficial version of the code is the *United States Code Service* (U.S.C.S.), also published by West. The U.S.C.S. and the U.S.C.A. provide somewhat different research tools. For example, the U.S.C.S. contains references and citations to some sources, such as legal periodicals and the legal encyclopedia *American Jurisprudence,* that are not included in the U.S.C.A. Both codes are available on Westlaw and Lexis.

State Statutes

State codes follow the U.S.C. pattern of arranging statutes by subject. Depending on the state, they may be called codes, revisions, compilations, consolidations, general statutes, or statutes. In some codes, subjects are designated by number. In others, they are designated by name. For example, "13 Pennsylvania Consolidated Statutes Section 1101" means that the statute can be found in Section 1101 of Title 13 of the Pennsylvania code. "California Commercial Code Section 1101" means that the statute can be found in Section 1101 under the heading "Commercial" in the California Code. Abbreviations may be used. For example, "13 Pennsylvania Consolidated Statutes Section 1101" may be abbreviated to "13 Pa.C.S. § 1101," and "California Commercial Code Section 1101" may be abbreviated to "Cal. Com. Code § 1101."

In many states, official codes are supplemented by annotated codes published by private publishers. Annotated codes follow the numbering scheme set forth in the official state code but provide outlines, explanations, and indexes to assist in locating information. These codes also provide references to case law, legislative history sources, and other documents in which the statute has been considered or discussed.

ANALYZING STATUTORY LAW

Because of the tremendous growth in statutory and regulatory law in the last century, the legal issues dealt with by attorneys are often governed by statutes and administrative agency regulations. Paralegals must understand how to interpret and analyze this body of law. Although we use the terms *statute* and *statutory law* in this section, the following discussion applies equally well to regulations issued by administrative agencies.

To determine how well a statute applies to the legal issues in your case, you must understand the statute. The first step in statutory analysis is therefore to read the language of the statute.

As with court cases, some statutes are more difficult to read than others. Some are extremely wordy or lengthy or difficult to understand for some other reason. By carefully reading a statute, however, you can usually determine the reasons for the statute's enactment, the date on which it became effective, the class of parties to which the statute applies, the kind of conduct regulated by the statute, and the circumstances in which that conduct is prohibited, required, or permitted. You can also learn whether the statute allows for exceptions and, if so, in what circumstances.

The second step in statutory analysis is to interpret the meaning of the statute. Generally, when trying to understand the meaning of statutes, you should do as the courts do. We therefore now look at some of the techniques used by courts when

Developing Paralegal Skills

READING STATUTORY LAW

Statutes are a major source of law at both the state and federal level. Being able to read statutes properly is a crucial skill for paralegals (and lawyers!). However, reading and understanding a statute is not the same as reading a court decision. It takes application of special techniques (called *principles of statutory interpretation*) to properly interpret a statute. Here are five of the most important principles:

- *The Plain Meaning Rule:* If the language of a statute is clear, the courts apply the language as written. While that seems obvious and easy to apply, it is not because courts and agencies often stumble over how to interpret particular words. A famous Supreme Court case involved a challenge to the Environmental Protection Agency's interpretation of the exact same words in different sections of the Clean Air Act to mean different things.[a]

- *Read a Statute as a Whole:* Provisions in different parts of a statute should be interpreted to fit together, not conflict. As a result, understanding a statute will usually require you to look at all of the statute, not just a single section. For example, the purpose of the statute will help guide your reading of later sections by telling you what the drafters of the statute intended. A good first step is to skim the statute quickly, noting the organizational structure, location of definition sections, and other key elements. Then locate the most relevant sections and read them carefully. You may need to resort to rules of grammar to unsnarl a particularly complicated section. Check back for appropriate definitions, cross-references to other sections or statutes, and exceptions.

- *Statutory Definitions Govern.* When a statute includes a specific definition, or an area of law uses a word as a term of art, that meaning will be used in interpreting the statute. Dictionary definitions are

---

a. *Chevron U.S.A., Inc. v. Natural Resources Defense Council, Inc.,* 467 U.S. 837 (1984),

faced with the task of interpreting the meaning of a given statute or statutory provision. Some practical tips for reading statutes are provided in the *Developing Paralegal Skills* feature.

Rules of Construction

Certain rules of interpretation, called **rules of construction**, may prove helpful in your analysis of a statute's language and intent. Examples of statutory rules of interpretation are the following:

- Specific provisions are given greater weight than general provisions when there is a conflict between the two.
- Recent provisions are given greater weight than earlier provisions when there is a conflict between the two.
- Masculine pronouns refer to both males and females.
- Singular nouns also include the plural forms of the nouns.

The Plain Meaning Rule

In interpreting statutory language, courts also apply the **plain meaning rule**. Under this rule, the words chosen by the legislature must be understood according to their common meanings. If the statute is clear *on its face* (in its obvious meaning), and guides when there is no statutory definition, but dictionaries differ and the meaning of words can shift over time. The Supreme Court has relied on dictionaries in more than 600 cases; dictionaries are becoming increasingly important in decisions. For example, Justice Sandra Day O'Connor relied on dictionary definitions of the word *use* in her opinion for the Supreme Court to hold that the word included "to convert to one's service" or "to employ."[b] As a result, an individual who traded a gun for drugs "used" the gun in the commission of the drug crime, even though he did not use it as a weapon. You should check to see if a particular dictionary is recognized as authoritative by the court involved and use an edition of the dictionary that was current at the time legislation was drafted. Just Googling™ a word is *NOT* an acceptable research technique!

- *Distinguish between "and" and "or":* When a list of requirements in a statute uses *and,* all of the things in the list must be satisfied. When the list in a statute uses *or,* then only one of the items in a list must be satisfied.

- *"Shall" does not mean "may" and "may" does not mean "shall":* When a statute uses the word *shall,* it will be interpreted as requiring a particular action. When a statute uses the word *may,* it will be interpreted as allowing discretion.

Like any area of the law, learning how to do statutory interpretation takes practice and effort. The most important concept to remember is that you must read statutes carefully and look at the entire statute, not just one provision. Of course, you will also always want to check for interpretations of the relevant provision as found in court decisions as well as agency guidelines, regulations, and other documents that may provide information about how a government agency interprets a statute.

FOR FURTHER STUDY

Excellent books on statutory interpretation include William N. Eskridge, Jr.'s *Dynamic Statutory Interpretation;* Abner Mikva and Eric Lane's *An Introduction to Statutory Interpretation and the Legislative Process;* Frank Cross's *The Theory and Practice of Statutory Interpretation;* and Linda Jellum's *Mastering Statutory Interpretation.* Another good resource is the *Statutory Construction Blog,* part of the Law Professor Blogs Network (**lawprofessors.typepad.com**, scroll down to "statutory").

---

b. *Smith v. United States,* 508 U.S. 223 (1993).

therefore capable of only one interpretation, that interpretation must be given to it. No additional inquiries, such as inquiries into legislative intent or history, are permitted.

The plain meaning rule, although seemingly simple, is usually not so simple to apply. For one thing, the meaning of a statute is rarely totally clear, because legal language, especially in statutes, is difficult to understand. Also, each word or phrase in a statute takes on meaning only in context—as it relates to the surrounding text. Thus, the meaning of a statutory word, phrase, or provision can be very difficult to pin down.

Furthermore, laws, by their very nature, cannot be too specific. When enacting a statute, the legislators often state a broad principle of law and then leave it up to the courts to apply this principle to specific circumstances—which vary from case to case. In interpreting a particular provision, you usually need to research case law to see how the courts have interpreted the provision or study the legislative history of the act to understand the legislators' intent in wording the statute in a particular way.

Previous Judicial Interpretation

Researching statutory law also involves researching case law to see how the courts have interpreted and applied statutory provisions. As discussed, courts are obligated to follow the precedents set by higher courts in their jurisdictions. A statutory interpretation made by a higher court therefore must be accepted as binding by lower courts in the same jurisdiction. You can find citations to court cases relating to specific statutes by referring to annotated versions of state or federal statutory codes, such as the U.S.C.A.

Legislative Intent

Another technique used in statutory interpretation is learning the intent of the legislature. A court relying on this method determines the meaning of the statute by attempting to find out why the legislators chose to word the statute as they did or, more generally, what the legislators sought to accomplish by enacting the statute. To learn the intent of the legislators who wrote a particular law, it is often necessary to investigate the legislative history of the statute. This can be done by researching such sources as committee reports and records of congressional hearings and other proceedings.

Before you can study these sources, of course, you need to know how to find them. The easiest way to locate them is to refer to the unofficial, annotated versions of the federal code, such as the U.S.C.A. and the U.S.C.S. These codes often contain information regarding the legislative history of a statute. For example, the statute's date of passage is included, as are cross-references to sources that provide more detailed information on a statute's legislative history. Each source will likely lead to other useful sources.

Committee Reports

Committee reports provide the most important source of legislative history. Congressional committees produce reports for each bill, and these reports often contain the full text of the bill, a description of its purpose, and the committee's recommendations. Several tables are also included to set out dates for certain actions. The dates can help the researcher locate floor debates and committee testimony in the *Congressional Record* and other publications. Committee reports are published according to a numerical series and are available through the U.S. Government Printing Office.

The Congressional Record

The *Congressional Record,* which is published daily while Congress is in session, contains *verbatim* (word-for-word) transcripts of congressional debates and proceedings. The transcripts include remarks made by various members of Congress, proposed amendments, votes, and occasionally the text of the bill under discussion.

Legislative hearings are another source of information. During these hearings, various interested parties give testimony before the House and Senate committees considering proposed legislation. The researcher may find some helpful testimony in transcripts of hearings, yet it is important to remember that much of it may be biased because of the interested positions of the parties presenting the information. Hearings may be informative but are not as authoritative as committee reports in determining legislative intent.

Other Sources of Legislative History

The two tools most frequently used in conducting research on legislative history are the *United States Code Congressional and Administrative News* (U.S.C.C.A.N.) and the *Congressional Information Service* (C.I.S.). The U.S.C.C.A.N., a West publication, contains reprints of statutes and sections describing the statutes' legislative history, including committee reports. Statutes in the U.S.C.A. are followed by notations directing the researcher to the corresponding legislative history in the U.S.C.C.A.N. The C.I.S., a U.S. government publication, contains information from committee

You can find the *Congressional Record* online at the Web site of the Government Printing Office. Go to **www.gpoaccess.gov**, and find the "GPO Access Resources by Branch" menu. Under "Legislative Resources," select "Congressional Record."

reports, hearing reports, documents from both houses, and special publications. Both the C.I.S. and the U.S.C.C.A.N. provide a system of indexing and abstracting that allows quick access to information.

While our focus here has been on existing statutes and related materials, there are times when we need to know what may be coming. Resources devoted to new developments are reviewed in *Technology and Today's Paralegal* on the next page.

RESEARCHING ADMINISTRATIVE LAW

Administrative rules and regulations constitute a growing source of American law. As discussed in Chapter 5, Congress frequently delegates authority to administrative agencies through enabling legislation. For example, in 1914 Congress passed the Federal Trade Commission Act, which established the Federal Trade Commission, or FTC. The act gave the FTC the authority to issue and enforce rules and regulations relating to unfair and deceptive trade practices in the United States. Other federal administrative agencies include the Occupational Safety and Health Administration, the Consumer Product Safety Commission, and the Securities and Exchange Commission. The orders, regulations, and decisions of such agencies are legally binding and, as such, are primary sources of law.

The *Code of Federal Regulations*

The *Code of Federal Regulations* (C.F.R.) is a government publication containing all federal administrative agency regulations. The regulations are compiled from the *Federal Register,* a daily government publication consisting of executive orders and administrative regulations, in which administrative regulations are first published. (See Chapter 5 for a discussion of administrative rulemaking procedure.)

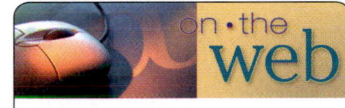

The Government Printing Office Web site at **www.gpoaccess.gov** offers helpful tips for finding information in the C.F.R. In "GPO Access Resources by Branch," under "Executive Resources," select "Code of Federal Regulations." Then select "Search Tips."

The C.F.R. uses the same titles as the *United States Code* (shown previously in Exhibit 7.11 on page 224). This subject-matter organization allows the researcher to determine the section in the C.F.R. in which a regulation will appear. Each title of the C.F.R. is divided into chapters, subchapters, parts, and sections.

The C.F.R. is revised and formally republished four times a year. Recent regulations appear in the *Federal Register* until they are incorporated into the C.F.R. The online version is updated continuously. If, as a paralegal, you are searching for administrative regulations in the C.F.R., you can begin with the index section of the *Index and Finding Aids* volume. This index will allow you to locate the relevant title and section of the C.F.R. Next, locate the regulation in the most recent volume of that title in the C.F.R. You should also review the *List of C.F.R. Sections Affected,* issued in monthly pamphlets, to determine if any changes have been made to the section since the last revision.

Finding Tools for Administrative Law

The *Congressional Information Service* (C.I.S.) also provides an index to the C.F.R. The C.I.S. index is helpful in locating C.F.R. regulations by subject matter and also in determining the geographic areas affected by the regulation. The *American Digest System,* one of West's multivolume digests, can be of additional help, because it provides coverage of court cases dealing with administrative questions. The digests, however, do not contain any agency rulings. Additionally, certain looseleaf services provide administrative decisions for particular specialty fields, such as taxation. If available, they are a useful research tool. The *Today's Professional Paralegal* feature on page 231 reviews research strategy.

Technology and
Today's Paralegal

LOOKING AHEAD

Every day, it seems, legislatures propose or pass new laws, administrative agencies propose or issue new regulations, and new cases begin to work their way through the court system. A few of these may reach the nation's highest court. As a paralegal, you can perform a valuable service for your supervising attorney by keeping up with new developments in the legal arena or in your specialty area.

WHAT NEW FEDERAL STATUTES ARE LIKELY TO BE ENACTED?

You can keep up to date on what bills are pending in Congress by subscribing to national law journals. Law journals such as the *National Law Journal* (a weekly publication) and *Lawyers USA* (issued monthly by Lawyers Weekly, Inc.) discuss new developments in the law, including legislation that is being considered by Congress. To find out more about these two publications, visit their Web sites. For the *National Law Journal,* go to **www.law.com** and select "National Law Journal" from the "National Legal News" menu. For *Lawyers USA,* go to **lawyersusaonline.com**. Both sites offer information on new statutes, cases, regulations, and other developments of interest to legal professionals, as well as information about how to subscribe. You can get an idea of the coverage of the journals by viewing the most recent issues online.

ARE ANY NEW UNIFORM LAWS BEING DEVELOPED?

To find out about new uniform laws being developed by the National Conference of Commissioners on Uniform State Laws (NCCUSL), you can visit its Web site at **www.nccusl.org**. There, you will find the full text of all uniform acts, including every draft of the final uniform act. You can also find out which states have already adopted an act and which states have adoption legislation pending. In addition, the site provides legislative reports by act or by state so that you can see the status of bills that are being considered by legislatures across the country. The site also includes the text of all in-process drafts and proposed revisions to existing uniform laws. While these drafts are just that—they are not law—they may become law in the future once approved by the NCCUSL and submitted to the states for adoption. In the meantime, provisions in these drafts may serve as persuasive authorities.

WHAT CASES ARE ON THE SUPREME COURT DOCKET?

You can find out what cases are pending before the Supreme Court from a number of online sources. For example, at **otd.oyez.org**, you will find a list of cases that the Supreme Court has heard recently or is scheduled to hear in the current term. If you are aware of a case pending before the Court, or want to search for cases on a particular issue, you can find the case name and a brief description at this site. Then you will know if it is relevant to your search. All details of cases, including briefs, can be found at **www.supremecourtus.gov**. You can also search the Supreme Court's database by docket number or case name and view case information and decisions at **www.supremecourtus.gov** (select "Docket" from the menu).

TECHNOLOGY TIP

Paralegals can readily access information online to stay current on new developments in the law. More difficult is sorting through the wealth of information available. Search for Web sites that will quickly and efficiently provide information that is pertinent to the area of law in which you are interested. After identifying a site as useful, bookmark it and check it regularly.

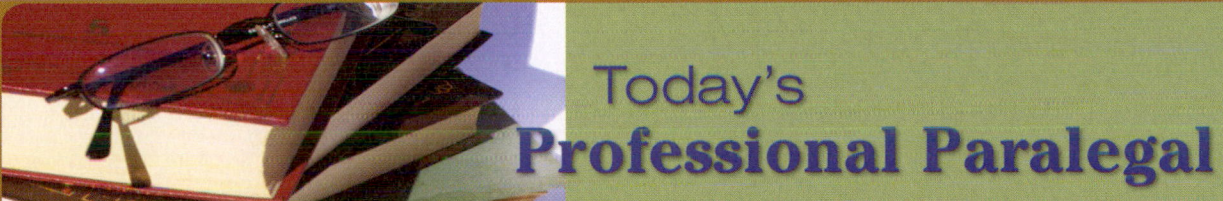

Today's
Professional Paralegal

MAPPING OUT A RESEARCH STRATEGY

Bill Cather is a paralegal in a criminal defense firm located in a major metropolitan area. Bill has been assigned a research project on a case involving one of the firm's clients, who was arrested for drug dealing. The police had seen the client making phone calls from a public telephone booth and suspected that he was engaged in drug trafficking. The police placed an electronic device in the phone booth—without a warrant—and learned that what they suspected was true. Bill is now going to map out his research strategy before he undertakes the project.

STEP ONE: IDENTIFYING THE ISSUE

Bill's first step is to analyze the facts and identify the issue involved. He knows that the police may search certain areas without a warrant. The courts determine which areas are entitled to the protection of a warrant by considering whether a person has a reasonable expectation of privacy in the area. Bill wonders whether a person has a reasonable expectation of privacy in a public phone booth. Do people customarily expect others to hear what they are saying on the phone when they are in a phone booth with the door closed? Bill will have to research the issue. If a person using a phone booth is entitled to a reasonable expectation of privacy, then probably the police would have to obtain a search warrant before using an electronic device to listen to—and record—any telephone conversation taking place in a public phone booth.

STEP TWO: IDENTIFYING SECONDARY SOURCES

Because he is not familiar with the topic that he is going to research, Bill will begin by doing some background research. He can choose from a variety of secondary sources, such as legal encyclopedias and treatises. He prefers legal encyclopedias because they are easy to understand. He especially likes the *Corpus Juris Secundum* (C.J.S.) because it provides many citations to cases. He writes "C.J.S." on his list as the first source to consult. Because Bill knows that organization is the key to research, he always tries to make his checklist complete so that he does not have to return to the same source later. He therefore writes "pocket part" on his list under C.J.S. so that he will remember to check the supplement to get the citations to the most recent cases on the issue.

STEP THREE: IDENTIFYING PRIMARY SOURCES

Next, he will consult the various primary sources of law. He will look at the Fourth Amendment to the U.S. Constitution to find the exact wording of its provisions on freedom from unreasonable searches and seizures and the warrant requirement. He can find the Constitution in the U.S.C.A. He writes "U.S.C.A.—Constitution" on his list of primary sources to check, and "pocket part" beneath it. Once he has found the most recent case annotations citing the Fourth Amendment in the pocket part, he will put a check next to that item in his list. Bill also includes a notation to check a West federal digest for other relevant cases.

   Bill will also consult state and federal statutory codes to find out whether a wiretapping statute exists and, if so, whether the police's action violated it. He therefore writes "U.S.C.A.—Wiretapping" to check for a federal statute and "State Annotated Code—Wiretapping" to check for a state statute, including the notation "pocket part" below each so that he remembers to check for updates.

STEP FOUR: UPDATING AND VERIFYING RESEARCH RESULTS

After Bill finds and reads relevant cases, he will have to verify in *Shepard's* that they are still good law. *Shepard's* will also provide an additional source of case law because it includes every subsequent case that cited the case being "Shepardized." He writes *"Shepard's"* on his list.

   As a final measure, Bill will use an online citator to verify that his research results are as up to date as possible. Bill adds "online citator" to his list. Once Bill completes his research, he will prepare a memorandum of law to inform his supervisor of his findings. In the next chapter, we look at the tools used in this step of the research.

KEY TERMS AND CONCEPTS

annotation *201*

briefing a case *221*

business invitee *196*

case on "all fours" *197*

case on point *197*

citation *207*

code *223*

dicta *221*

digest *201*

headnote *201*

holding *221*

hornbook *204*

key number *201*

parallel citation *207*

persuasive authority *198*

plain meaning rule *226*

pocket part *199*

reporter *200*

rules of construction *226*

slip opinion *214*

syllabus *214*

treatise *204*

CHAPTER SUMMARY

LEGAL RESEARCH AND ANALYSIS

Researching Case Law—The Preliminary Steps

1. *Defining the issue*—The first step in the research process is to identify the legal question, or issue, to be researched (often, more than one issue is involved).

2. *Determining your research goals*—The next step is to determine the goal of the research project. In researching case law, the researcher's goal is to find cases that are on point (ideally, cases on "all fours") and that are binding authorities.

   a. Binding authorities are all legal authorities (statutes, regulations, constitutions, and cases) that courts must follow in making their decisions.

   b. Courts are not bound to follow persuasive authorities (such as cases decided in other jurisdictions), although courts often consider such authorities, particularly when deciding cases of first impression.

Finding Relevant Cases

Primary sources of law include all documents that establish the law, including court decisions, statutes, regulations, constitutions, and presidential orders. *Secondary sources of law* are publications written about the law, such as legal encyclopedias, digests, treatises, and periodicals.

1. *Legal encyclopedias*—Legal encyclopedias provide detailed summaries of legal rules and concepts and are useful for finding background information on issues being researched. These books arrange topics alphabetically and contain citations to cases and statutes relating to the topic.

   a. Two popular legal encyclopedias are *American Jurisprudence,* Second Edition (Am. Jur. 2d), and *Corpus Juris Secundum* (C.J.S.).

   b. A third encyclopedia, *Words and Phrases,* covers legal terms and phrases and cites cases in which the terms or phrases appear.

2. *Case digests*—West's case digests are major secondary sources of law and helpful finding tools. These digests, which use the West system of topic

classification and key numbers, provide cross-references to other West publications. Digests arrange topics alphabetically with annotations to cases on each topic but are not as detailed as encyclopedias.

3. *American Law Reports*—The *American Law Reports* are multivolume sets that present leading cases, each followed by an annotation that discusses the key issues in the case and that refers the researcher to other sources on the issues.

4. *Other secondary sources*—Other secondary sources of law include the following:

   a. **TREATISES**—Treatises are scholarly publications that discuss specific areas of law. They summarize, evaluate, or interpret the law either in a single volume or in multivolume sets. Hornbooks are single-volume treatises.

   b. **RESTATEMENTS OF THE LAW**—The *Restatements* are respected scholarly compilations of the common law. They present particular cases as examples and also discuss variations.

   c. **LEGAL PERIODICALS**—Legal periodicals, such as law reviews, contain articles on specific areas of law.

The Case Reporting System

The primary sources of case law are the cases themselves. Cases are published in various case reporters.

1. *State court decisions*—

   a. Most state trial court decisions are not published in printed volumes. State appellate court opinions, including those of state supreme courts, are normally published in official state reporters. Many states have eliminated their own reporters in favor of West's National Reporter System, which reports state cases in its regional reporters.

   b. To locate a case in a reporter, you use the case citation. There are five parts to a standard case citation: the case name, the volume number, the abbreviated name of the book (volume), the page number on which the decision begins, and the year the case was decided. A parallel citation may appear after the first citation when the case is reported in more than one book.

2. *Federal court decisions*—Federal trial court opinions are published unofficially in West's *Federal Supplement,* and opinions from the federal circuit courts of appeals are published unofficially in West's *Federal Reporter.* United States Supreme Court opinions are published officially in the *United States Reports,* published by the federal government, and unofficially in West's *Supreme Court Reporter* and the *Lawyers' Edition of the Supreme Court Reports.*

Analyzing Case Law

1. *Case format*—Reported cases contain more information than just the court's decision. Typically, case formats include the following components:

   a. The title (case name, usually plaintiff versus defendant).

   b. The name of the court that decided the case.

   c. The case citation.

   d. The docket number assigned by the court.

   e. The date on which the case was decided.

   f. The syllabus (a brief summary of the facts, issues, and ruling).

Continued

g. The headnotes (short paragraphs that summarize the rules of law discussed in the case; in West's reporters, headnotes correlate with the key-number system).

h. The names of counsel.

i. The name of the judge who authored the opinion.

j. The opinion (the court's own words on the matter).

k. The conclusion (holding, ruling).

2. *Briefing cases*—Legal professionals often brief, or summarize, the cases they research. Knowing how to read, analyze, and summarize cases makes it easier to compare cases and bring together research results accurately and efficiently. Although the format of briefs varies, the following headings are typical: citation, facts, procedure, issue, decision, reasoning, and holding.

Researching Constitutional and Statutory Law

1. *Constitutional law*—Constitutions are primary sources of law. The U.S. Constitution can be found in a number of publications, including *The Constitution of the United States of America* (available through the Library of Congress). Annotated versions of state constitutions are also available.

2. *Statutory law*—Bills and ordinances passed by legislative bodies (federal, state, and local) become statutory law, a primary source of American law. Statutes are eventually published in codes, which are updated by supplemental pocket parts and loose-leaf services and are also available online.

   a. **FEDERAL STATUTES**—Federal laws are published officially in the *United States Code* (U.S.C.). The U.S.C. organizes statutes into fifty subjects, or titles, and further divides each title into chapters (sections) and subchapters. The *United States Code Annotated* (U.S.C.A.) and the *United States Code Service* (U.S.C.S.) are unofficial publications of federal statutes. They are useful because they provide annotations (comments) and citations to other resources.

   b. **STATE STATUTES**—State codes follow the U.S.C. pattern of arranging statutes by subject. They may be called codes, revisions, compilations, general statutes, or statutes. In many states, official codes are supplemented by annotated codes published by private publishers.

Analyzing Statutory Law

1. *Reading statutory law*—Analyzing statutory law is often difficult, so careful reading and rereading are often required.

2. *Interpreting statutes*—To interpret statutory law, one can turn to several helpful guidelines: the statutory rules of construction; the plain meaning rule; previous judicial interpretations of the statute, if any exist; and the legislative history of the statute.

3. *Legislative intent*—The legislative history of a statute can reveal the intent of the legislature and thus help to establish the relevance of the statute to the issue being researched. Sources include transcripts of committee reports and hearings, transcripts of congressional proceedings, and the wording of statutes as first published. Helpful resources include the *Congressional Record,* the *United States Code Congressional and Administrative News,* and the *Congressional Information Service.*

Researching Administrative Law

Regulations issued by federal administrative agencies are primary sources of law. Agency regulations are published in the *Code of Federal Regulations* (C.F.R.). The C.F.R. follows a format similar to that of the *United States Code* (U.S.C.), and the subject classifications (titles) of the C.F.R. correspond to the titles in the U.S.C. To locate recently published regulations, the researcher should refer to the *Federal Register*'s cumulative *List of C.F.R. Sections Affected,* which reflects changes made during the current month.

STUDENT STUDYWARE™ CD-ROM

Interactive student CD in this book includes additional quizzing, plus video clips, case studies, and Key Terms flashcards.

ONLINE COMPANION™

For additional resources, please go to **www.paralegal.delmar.cengage.com**.

QUESTIONS FOR REVIEW

1. What is a case on point? What is a case on "all fours"? Why is finding such a case important when researching case law? What is the difference between a binding authority and a persuasive authority?

2. What are the differences between primary and secondary sources of law? How is each of these types of sources used in legal research? What is the West key-number system, and how does it simplify the legal research process?

3. Identify the various parts of a case citation. How do case citations help you locate a case? List and briefly describe the components of a reported case. Which part should you focus on when analyzing a case?

4. How do you brief a case? What is the purpose of briefing a case? What should be included in a case brief?

5. Describe how statutes are published. What government bodies create statutes and regulations? What are some points to consider when reading and interpreting statutory law?

ETHICAL QUESTION

1. Kristine Connolly, a paralegal in a litigation firm, has finished reading a brief that the opposing side submitted to the court in support of a motion for summary judgment. In the brief, she notices a citation to a state supreme court case of which she is unaware. She is experienced in the field and keeps current with new cases as they are decided. She wants to look at the case because it gives the other side a winning edge. She checks in case digests and state encyclopedias, as well as on Westlaw. She finally calls the state supreme court clerk's office and asks about the case. The office has no record of such a case. She asks the legal assistant for the opposing counsel to give her a copy of the case. When she does not receive it, she decides that the case is probably fictional. What should Kristine do?

PRACTICE QUESTIONS AND ASSIGNMENTS

1. Identify the case name, volume number, reporter abbreviation, page number, and year of decision for each of the following case citations, including the parallel citations:

   a. *Liles v. Damon Corp.*, 345 Or. 420, 198 P.3d 926 (2008).

   b. *Musaelian v. Adams*, 45 Cal.4th 512, 87 Cal.Rptr.3d. 475, 198 P.3d 560 (2009).

   c. *Montgomery v. Nostalgia Lane, Inc.*, 383 Ill.App.3d 1098, 891 N.E.2d 994 (2008).

   d. *Miranda v. Arizona*, 384 U.S. 436, 86 S.Ct. 1602, 16 L.Ed.2d 694 (1966).

2. Identify the title number, code abbreviation, and section number for the following statutory citations:

   a. 42 U.S.C. Section 1161(a).

   b. 20 C.F.R. 404.101(a).

3. Sleeping Beauty is awakened by a kiss from Prince Charming. She can think of nothing more repulsive than to be kissed by him. Sleeping Beauty suffers from nightmares and depression as a result of this incident and contacts a law firm regarding filing a lawsuit against the prince for the damages, which include medical expenses, that she has suffered as a result of the kiss. The paralegal is assigned the task of researching Sleeping Beauty's case to determine whether she can sue. What are the issue(s) to be researched? What would the paralegal's research goals be?

4. Mr. John D. Consumer bought a new car eight months ago. The car frequently stalls. The problem began the first week after he purchased the vehicle. It stalled late at night on an expressway while he was returning home from a business trip. It has stalled at least monthly since then, often in potentially dangerous areas. Not only has he taken the car to the dealer, who has repeatedly attempted to repair the problem without success, but he has also notified the manufacturer in writing of the problem.

   Most states have a lemon law that requires manufacturers to replace vehicles that cannot be repaired, even if the warranty has expired. Does your state have a lemon law? If so, would the lemon law help Mr. Consumer?

   Research this question and try to find the answer to Mr. Consumer's problem. Begin by analyzing the facts. Then make a list of relevant legal terms to look up in an index.

   Select a legal resource—such as *American Jurisprudence* or *Corpus Juris Secundum*—to use in your research. Write down the name of the source. Consult the general index volumes.

   a. Write down the index topics under which you found relevant information. (If you have difficulty locating relevant information, try checking the topic indexes in the individual volumes.)

   b. Write down the citations to sections containing relevant information.

   c. Look up these citations in the appropriate volumes of the legal resource to find an answer to Mr. Consumer's problem. Be sure to check the pocket part for more current citations. According to the resource, what is the answer to John D. Consumer's problem?

5. After analyzing the facts of Mr. Consumer's problem and making a list of legally and factually relevant terms, as described in the preceding question, do the following:

   a. Locate the index to the annotated version of your state statutes. Using your list of terms, look in the index for citations to relevant statute sections. Write down the citations.

   b. Refer back to the preceding question. Compare how you found the citations in the index to your state statutes with how you found them in the legal resource you selected. Under what topics did you look in each situation?

   c. Now that you have found relevant citations, go to the volume of the statute containing the cited sections and read those sections. (Be sure to check the pocket part of the volume.) What answer does the statute in your state give to Mr. Consumer's problem? Is the answer given in the resource you selected the same as the answer for the preceding question? If not, how do the answers differ?

6. Using the annotated version of your state statutes, look for relevant case law on Mr. Consumer's problem. If no annotated version of your state statute exists or if no cases appear in the annotated version— or if you want to learn to use another source—locate a state digest. Find the relevant section(s) and locate case law that interprets the statute and that is as similar to Mr. Consumer's problem as possible.

   a. Write down the citations to no more than three relevant cases. Now look up those cases in the case reporters.

   b. Read through the summary and headnotes of each case. Do the cases still appear to be relevant? If not, go back to the annotated statute or digest and look for more relevant cases.

   c. What did you find? Did the courts' application of the statute change in any way your answer to the problem facing Mr. Consumer?

QUESTIONS FOR CRITICAL ANALYSIS

1. Sources of law are divided into two broad categories, primary and secondary sources. What is the difference between these two types? Why do attorneys generally cite only primary sources in documents filed with the courts?

2. What is the difference between a binding and a persuasive authority? Why is this distinction important for the courts? Which source is preferable to find when doing legal research? Why?

3. What is the difference between a case on point and a case on "all fours"? Which is it preferable to locate? How do these cases fit into the research goals? How likely is it that you might find a case on point or on "all fours"?

4. Explain the West key-number system. What is its purpose? Is its use limited to digests? How can the key-number system be of assistance to a researcher?

5. What is West's National Reporter System? What geographic units does it include? Is it widely used? Why or why not? How might the West key-number system tie into it?

6. What is the difference between case law and statutory law? Why is the difference significant? In what forms are statutes published? What is the name of the official code containing the statutes of the U.S. government?

PROJECTS

1. Using a state bar directory or other type of legal directory, find out which law libraries in your area are open to the public. Make arrangements to visit a law library. If tours of the library are offered, try to be present for a tour.

2. Make arrangements through your professor, a local bar association, or your personal contacts to visit the law library of a law firm or the legal department of a corporation or government office. If you also participated in Project 1 above, compare the materials available in the libraries of firms or government agencies with those available in law libraries. Why is it necessary for legal professionals to use law libraries other than those located in their offices?

3. Obtain a copy of *The Bluebook: A Uniform System of Citation* or the *ALWD Citation Manual* and look up the citation formats for your state court reporters and statutes.

USING INTERNET RESOURCES

1. Go to the U.S. government's official Web site at **www.usa.gov**. Browse through the page that opens, and then answer the following questions:

   a. Under "Reference and General Government," select "Laws and Regulations." What types of primary sources can you access through this site?

   b. Now select "Code of Federal Regulations—Electronic" from the list. On the page that opens, select one of the titles of the *Code of Federal Regulations* (C.F.R.) from the drop-down menu and select "Go." How are the sections and subsections of the C.F.R. title organized on this page? Is this a user-friendly site for researchers?

CONTEMPORARY ONLINE LEGAL RESEARCH

CHAPTER OUTLINE

Introduction

Going Online—An Internet Primer

Free Legal Resources on the Internet

Lexis and Westlaw

Alternative Online Programs

Conducting Online Research

AFTER COMPLETING THIS CHAPTER, YOU WILL KNOW:

▶ Some strategies for planning and conducting research on the Internet.

▶ How you can find people and investigate companies using Internet search tools and databases.

▶ How to find some of the best legal resources available on the Internet.

▶ The advantages of the major fee-based online programs.

INTRODUCTION

Computers and online databases have simplified and improved the ability of paralegals to do high-quality legal research. One of the great benefits of computer technology for legal practitioners is computer-assisted legal research. As you learned in Chapter 7, thorough and up-to-date legal research requires access to a huge volume of source materials, including state and federal court decisions and statutory law. Today, attorneys and paralegals can access most of these materials online.

An obvious advantage of online research is that you can locate, download, and print out court cases, statutory provisions, and other legal documents within minutes without leaving your desk. Another advantage is that new case decisions and changes in statutory law are entered almost immediately into certain online legal databases, especially Westlaw and Lexis. This means that you can find out quickly whether a case decided three months ago is still "good law" today.

In this chapter, we describe various forms of online research. By the time you read the chapter, some of what we say will have changed, particularly with respect to Internet resources. Some of these resources may have improved, others may have been removed, and new ones may have been added. (See this chapter's *Featured Contributor* article on the following two pages for tips on conducting research online.) The general approach to conducting research online will not have altered, however. If you master the basic principles of online research discussed in this chapter, you will be able to conduct research on the Internet no matter how much its content changes.

GOING ONLINE—AN INTERNET PRIMER

The Internet is a global communication network. Business computers, university computers, government computers, and personal computers comprise the "network of networks" that constitutes cyberspace. Here we discuss many ways in which you can use the Internet to conduct legal and fact-based research. We begin by looking at Internet tools and navigation methods. You are probably familiar with many of these tools and methods. If so, consider this section a review of the basics of Internet access, use, and terminology.

Expanded online access to legal resources has changed the nature of legal research. Today, paralegals and attorneys conduct most of their legal research online. What skills do you need to perform effective online research?

(Image copyright Kristian Sekulic, 2009. Used under license from Shutterstock.com)

featured contributor

TIPS FOR DOING ONLINE LEGAL RESEARCH

Matt Cornick

BIOGRAPHICAL NOTE

Matthew Cornick is a graduate of the State University of New York at Buffalo and the Emory University School of Law. He has been teaching legal research, family law, and introduction to law and ethics to paralegal students for over twenty years. He frequently speaks to paralegal associations and law firms on the topic of technology in the law office. Cornick has served on the Approval Commission to the American Bar Association's Standing Committee on Paralegals. He is the author of A Practical Guide to Family Law (Cengage Learning) and is currently working on another text.

Online legal research can make research easier, more efficient, and more thorough. But for some students, and some practicing legal professionals, online legal research offers the prospect of the inherent difficulties of legal research with the frustration of working with computers.

I have been in your shoes, and I can assure you that everything is going to be all right. In that spirit, here is some advice for completing your online legal research with a minimum of hassle and distress.

1. **Think before you begin the research.** Much of the frustration that students feel when researching online is due to the lack of proper preparation. Make sure you know precisely which terms you will use in your search query. Prepare a list of alternate terms. For example, if you are researching an issue relating to divorce, it might be found under "Divorce" or "Dissolution" or "Marriage, Termination of" or "Husband and Wife."

2. **There is no need to reinvent the wheel.** By searching in legal encyclopedias, law journals, treatises, and the like, you can tap into a world of useful information. This is especially true if you review the footnotes. This is where you will find specific references to cases, statutes, and administrative regulations.

Internet Tools

Two of the most widely used parts of the Internet are e-mail and the World Wide Web. Getting around on the World Wide Web requires the use of uniform resource locators (URLs).

E-Mail

One of the most common uses of the Internet is for e-mail (short for "electronic mail"). While mostly used for messages, e-mail can be a research tool as well. For example, e-mail is the basis for services associated with listservs and newsgroups, which are discussed later in this chapter.

World Wide Web

When most people think of the Internet, they think of the **World Wide Web** (the Web). To the user, the Web is a system of Web pages or Web sites. A **home page** is the main page of a Web site, which generally serves as a table of contents to other

World Wide Web
A hypertext-based system through which specially formatted documents are accessible on the Internet.

home page
The main page of a Web site. Often, the home page serves as a table of contents to other pages at the site.

3. **Both Westlaw and Lexis offer online training lessons.** Westlaw, for example, has a site called the Paralegal Proficiency Certification program. LexisNexis has a site called the LexisNexis Paralegal Community. Both offer online training and instructional aids that are great learning tools.

4. **There is more to online legal research than Westlaw, Lexis, Loislaw, and other similar services.** You can use a general-purpose search engine, such as Google, to search for information about a specific area of law. Sometimes, you can jump-start your legal research by "Googling" your query. For example, if you enter "Georgia negligence statute of limitations" in a search engine, you will find the relevant Georgia code sections.

5. **When using online legal research services, time may literally be money.** Make sure you know whether the tool you plan to use permits unlimited use or charges by the minute. While in paralegal school, you may have free access to Westlaw or Lexis. Rest assured, in the real world there is no "free access." Make sure you have permission to use Westlaw or Lexis and keep an eye on the clock. Use common sense; do not use $500 worth of time to solve a $100 problem.

> " . . . everything is going to be all right."
> "You are not going to break the Internet."

6. **Keep track of your research.** Making mistakes during legal research is unavoidable. Making the same mistakes twice (or more) is completely avoidable. Making a list of all the cases, statutes, articles, and other sources you have reviewed will save you time and aggravation.

7. **Perhaps the most valuable online legal research skill you can develop is the ability to cite check primary authorities.** Be sure you take the time in school to gain the expertise employers will value.

8. **Know when to walk away.** Once you start seeing the same cases and statutes over and over again, you have probably found everything worth finding.

9. **Don't worry.** You are not going to break the Internet. Make mistakes, but learn from them.

pages in the site. Technically, the Web is a hypertext-based information system that makes specially formatted documents available on the Internet through a browser (discussed shortly). *Hypertext* refers to a means of linking different objects (text, graphics, and the like) together. Thus, in a hypertext-based system, we can jump easily from one object to another, even if their formats are different.

Uniform Resource Locators

A uniform resource locator (URL) is an Internet "address." A paralegal might think of a URL as an electronic citation. The basic format of a URL is "service://directorypath/filename." For example, **http://www.paralegal.delmar.cengage.com** is the URL for the Paralegal Web site of Delmar Cengage Learning, a resource center for paralegal instructors, students, and professionals (shown in Exhibit 8.1 on the next page). This URL indicates that you use the *http* service to reach the directory path **www.paralegal.delmar.cengage.com**. The letters **http** stand for **hypertext transfer protocol**, which is an interface that enables computers to communicate. Several protocols are used on the Internet, but "http" is the one used most commonly on the World Wide Web—which, as noted,

hypertext transfer protocol (http)
An interface program that enables computers to communicate. Hypertext is a system by which disparate objects, such as text and graphics, can be linked. A protocol is a system of formats and rules.

EXHIBIT 8.1
The Home Page of Delmar

From Delmar, Cengage Learning
Paralegal Home Page.

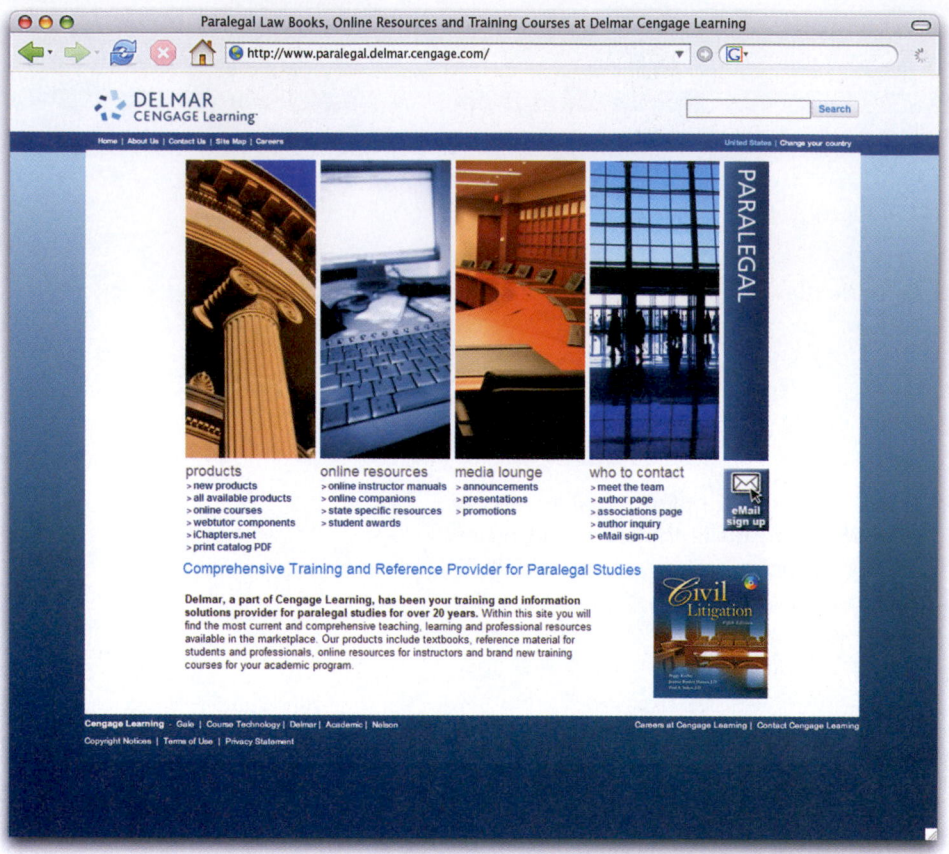

is a hypertext-based system. When you enter a URL into a browser, you normally do not need to type in "http://" or "www." The browser will enter those terms automatically.

Note also that in many cases, a specific URL may no longer function due to the quickly evolving nature of the Internet. In this situation, try renaming the URL by removing the characters following the last slash. Continue this process until you find a functional Web page on which you can look for a link to the information you are seeking. If this does not help you locate a particular Web site, use one of the search engines listed on page 244.

Navigating the Internet

Using the Internet to conduct legal research involves navigating through vast numbers of Internet resources until you find the information you are seeking. The Internet is similar to an enormous library, but there is a key difference—the Internet has no centralized, comprehensive card catalogue. In place of a card catalogue, a researcher uses browsers, guides, directories, and search engines.

Browsers

The Web is accessed through a software program called a *browser*. Popular browsers include the following:

- Microsoft Internet Explorer—**www.microsoft.com** (from the "Windows" menu, select "Windows Internet Explorer").
- Mozilla Firefox—**www.mozilla.com**.
- Google Chrome—**www.google.com/chrome**.
- Apple Safari—**www.apple.com**. Search on "Safari."
- Microsoft Bing—**www.bing.com**.

These browsers can be used with any Internet service.

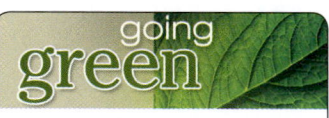

SAVE BY SNOOZING

Having computers and monitors go into the "sleep" mode during the day, after a certain number of minutes of not being used, saves electricity. You can control this by going into the power management settings for the monitor and hard drive. Similarly, using the "standby" button on a copier machine cuts the machine's energy use by as much as 70 percent.

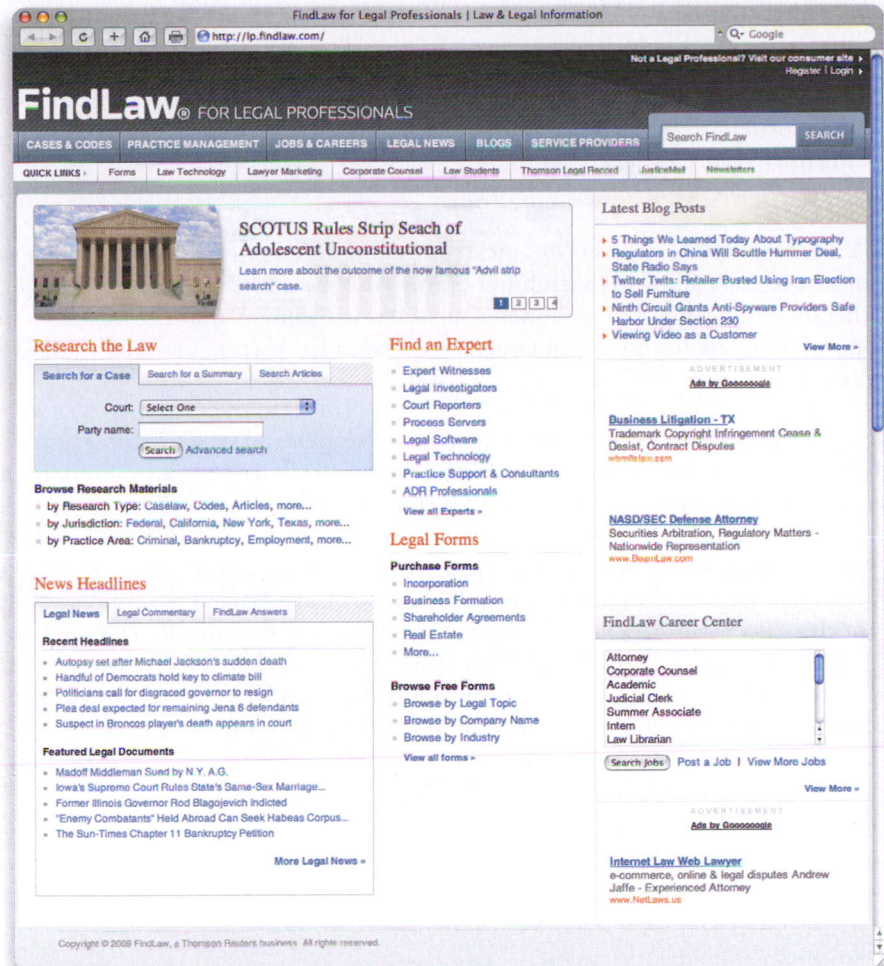

Browsers enable computers to roam the Web. They also make it possible to copy text from Web sites and paste it into a word-processing document. With a browser, you can download images, software, and documents to your computer. Finally, with a browser you can search only the document that appears in your window. This last feature is most helpful when the document is long and your time is short.

Guides and Directories

The lack of a single, comprehensive catalogue of what is available on the Internet has led to hundreds of attempts to survey and map the Web. Lists of Web sites categorized by subject are organized into guides and directories, which can be accessed at Web sites online. These sites provide menus of topics that are usually subdivided into narrower subtopics, which themselves may be subdivided, until a list of URLs is reached. If you're uncertain of which menu to use, directories allow you to run a search of the directory site. Popular examples of online directories include Google (**www.google.com**) and, for legal professionals, FindLaw (**lp.findlaw.com**). Exhibit 8.2 presents the FindLaw for Legal Professionals home page. FindLaw offers an increasingly complete array of resources. Topic areas include cases and codes, U.S. federal resources, forms, legal subjects, software and technology, reference resources, law student resources, and many others. You should familiarize yourself with FindLaw before you undertake any legal research.

Search Engines

Next to browsers, the most important tools for conducting research on the Web are search engines. A search engine scans the Web and indexes the contents of pages into a database. Whereas people compile directories, a computer generates most of the results delivered by a search engine. This means that the results are limited by the researcher's ability to phrase a query within the constraints of the search engine's capabilities. Search engines include the following:

- Google—**www.google.com**.
- Yahoo—**search.yahoo.com**.
- Microsoft Search—**www.bing.com**.

Kinds of Searches. Search engines conduct searches in two ways: by key word and by concept. A key-word search generates Web sources that use the exact terms that the researcher types in. A concept search adds sources that use related words. In general, the best results are obtained in a search for Web pages that contain very specific terms.

Search Operators. In a response to a search query, a Web search engine will likely return many irrelevant results. Sometimes, a researcher can eliminate irrelevant sites only by going to the sites and scrolling through them. The use of certain *operators* can greatly refine search results and help you to avoid this problem.

Quotation marks are one of the most useful operators available in most search engines. Placing quotation marks around words or phrases that must appear together in a specific order will effectively narrow search results. For example, a Google search using the key words "Arizona Music Educators" in quotation marks may return about three thousand results. A Google search using the same key words but without the quotation marks around the phrase may return a half-million results.

Other useful operators are the so-called logical operators of Boolean logic. As it is used in Internet search engines, **Boolean logic** is a system in which connecting words, primarily *and, or,* and *not,* are used to link key words and make search requests more precise. The effect of using each of these logical operators is shown in Exhibit 8.3. As you can see, using *and* or *not* can be an effective way to narrow a search. Many search engines automatically use *and* between key words if you do not specify the connector to be used.

Some search engines also allow proximity operators, such as *near* or *n/5* (within five words). Here, a source is included in the search results only if the key words appear close together in the source.

> **Boolean logic**
> As applied to Internet search engines, a system in which connecting words (primarily *and, or,* and *not*) are used to establish a logical relationship among key words in order to make a search more precise.

A Threshold Question: Is the Internet the Right Research Tool for Your Project?

Before using the Internet for a research project, you need to decide whether it is the right tool for your needs. The Internet is only one tool for doing research. Knowing which tool to use and when to use it is the key to obtaining quick, accurate results. Ask yourself the following questions: What sources are needed? Are they on the Internet? Are they available elsewhere? Either way, what is the cost? How much time do you have to produce results? The availability (accessibility) of a source, what it costs, and the time it would take to use it are the basic considerations. As the *Developing Paralegal Skills* feature on page 246 discusses, there are a number of things to take into account to help ensure accuracy.

If the Internet is the right tool for your research, you will have much at your disposal. The fee-based Lexis and Westlaw services are the dominant legal research resources on the Internet, and we discuss them later in the chapter. First, we consider some free services available online.

FREE LEGAL RESOURCES ON THE INTERNET

We have already noted a number of legal resources on the Internet, but now let us focus on legal research sites. Most public documents, such as statutes and cases, are available to the public. If these documents are on the Internet, they may be acces-

EXHIBIT 8.3
Examples of Boolean Searches

When you use the Boolean connector AND between key words, only pages including all of the key words will be returned. The shaded area below shows the results of a search for "Georgia AND bankruptcy AND forms."

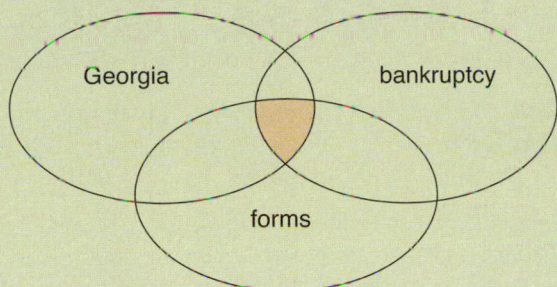

When you use the connector OR between key words, any page containing at least one of the key words will be included in the search results. The shaded area below shows the results of a search for "vehicle OR car OR automobile."

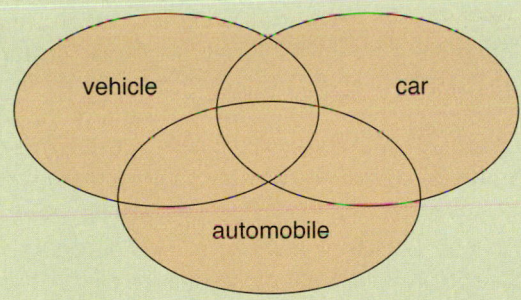

The connector NOT can be used to exclude certain key words. The shaded area below shows the results of a search for "gambling NOT online NOT Internet." These results will include only pages that contain the key word *gambling* but not either of the other two key words.

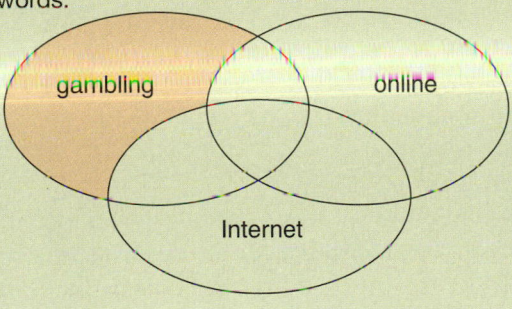

sible through various Web sites, but some sites have evolved to have lead positions in legal research. Here, we look at leading free legal information sites. Later we look at subscription-based sites.

General Legal Resources

The dominant legal information portal for those not using fee-based services is FindLaw. FindLaw has a consumer site (**www.findlaw.com**) and a site for legal professionals (**lp.findlaw.com**). You can see the home page of the version for legal professionals if you look back at Exhibit 8.2 on page 243. That is the version you will use. As you will see, FindLaw provides access to a massive amount of legal material. Because it is so large and constantly expands, the best way to learn about it, as with most Web resources, is to explore it.

Another major legal resource site is provided by the Legal Information Institute (LII) at Cornell University Law School (**www.law.cornell.edu**). Besides

Developing
Paralegal Skills

INTERNET-BASED RESEARCH

Many legal materials are available on the Internet, with both fee-based (Westlaw, Lexis, Loislaw, VersusLaw) and free (Cornell Law School's Legal Information Institute) services providing court opinions, statutes, and agency materials. Courts, legislatures, and agencies also operate their own Web sites, which are often useful resources. Interest groups maintain specialized collections of key materials as well. For example, you could look at the Web sites for the National Rifle Association and for the Brady Campaign to find important news and legal information on all sides of firearms issues. The number of law-related blogs, called "blawgs," is skyrocketing. Finally, many law firms post newsletters, analyses of recent cases, and useful tips.

With all that information at your fingertips, often the most important problem is winnowing it down to what is really useful. Here are five questions you should ask about any legal resource you find on the Internet.

- *Who created it, and why did they post it on the Internet?* Does the information come from a neutral source or an interest group? From someone with experience and credentials or a crank? Before you rely on the results of a Web search, check to make sure your results have a legitimate pedigree.

- *Is it accurate?* Joe's Legal Blog may be fun to read, but has Joe accurately reproduced a court opinion or statute? It is always best to check unofficial materials against either an official Web resource or a commercial service that certifies the accuracy of its materials.

- *Is it up to date?* Last year's brilliant Web site on employment law in Arizona might be wrong if there has been a new statute, regulation, or case since it was posted.

- *Is it easy to use?* Many court Web sites are harder to use than commercial services such as Westlaw. It may save your client a few dollars in search costs, but if it takes you twice as long to find the information, the total bill won't be any less.

- *What is the coverage?* Does the resource cover material only up to a certain date? Can you tell easily? How can you get the most up-to-date information? Your clients are paying for your expertise in research—you must be able to deliver them a comprehensive answer.

One of the most important skills you have as a paralegal is the ability to do quality legal research. Your clients and your employer deserve your best efforts—always make sure you use the best research tools to obtain the best information.

legal documents, it provides other useful information, such as a guide to legal citations. Another popular site is maintained by the Washburn University Law school at **www.washlaw.edu**. As you will see, it has a plain, no-nonsense menu that provides easy access to certain categories of legal information. A good source for foreign and international legal research is Hieros Gamos at **www.hg.org**. Similarly, LawRunner at the Internet Legal Research Group (**www.ilrg.com**) provides many links to domestic and international legal information.

Specific Legal Resources

Besides the general sites just mentioned, which offer access to a broad range of resources, many Web sites provide legal information within specific areas. We discuss just a sampling here.

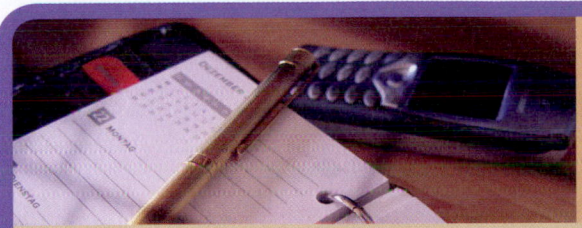

In the **Office**

CLEAN ELECTRONIC FILES

Almost all work is now stored in electronic files on computers. For security, a computer should be connected to an external hard drive in case the computer crashes. Offices should also have secure off-site backup systems so copies of files exist in case of fire. Many firms organize files by specific practice area, such as personal-injury litigation. Within the area, there may be files for clients' cases, research by topic, memoranda of law, and so forth. Besides following procedure about filing and backup, make sure your computer is well organized so your supervisor could go into it and find files. Files are a law firm's work products, not your personal property, so they should always be professionally maintained.

Secondary Sources of Law

Many secondary sources, such as legal encyclopedias and treatises, are not likely to be found on the Web for free. An increasing number of law review articles are published free on the Internet, however. FindLaw allows you to search for such articles, as do the following sites:

- American Law Sources On-line—**www.lawsource.com** (select "Law Reviews and Periodicals" from the "United States" menu).
- University of Southern California Law School—**lawweb.usc.edu** (from the "Library" menu, select "Online Resources & Research Links").

The savvy legal researcher realizes that consulting a relevant secondary source at the beginning of a research project may save time and effort, as the source should provide a good overview of the law in an area and point to leading cases and issues.

Court Opinions

More than a century's worth of Supreme Court opinions are available on FindLaw, and several decades' worth are available on LII at Cornell Law School. You can also find the Supreme Court's opinions on its Web site (**www.supremecourtus.gov**). Federal appeals courts began to place opinions on the Internet in the early 1990s. For information about federal courts and cases they post, see **www.uscourts.gov**. The Emory University Law Library has a Federal Courts Finder that offers access to posted federal court decisions and key-word searches (**www.law.emory.edu**, go to Law Library, search "federal courts"). FindLaw also provides access to federal district courts, as well as state courts and other state bodies.

Other Resources

When you are first looking into an area, you can check the Law Library Resource Xchange (LLRX) at **www.llrx.com** for discussions or research guides that relate to your topic. LLRX, which is discussed more in *Technology and Today's Paralegal* on the following page, is a Web site that provides up-to-date information on a wide range of Internet research resources for legal professionals.

Various state resources can be found online. For example, the New York State Library has a useful guide for researching legislative history at **www.nysl.nysed.gov/ leghist**. While it focuses on New York, the development of legislation is similar in

Technology and Today's Paralegal

BE PREPARED FOR DISASTER!

Legal research has come a long way in the past decade and is easier than ever, thanks to Internet-based research tools. It is tempting to think that research requires only turning on a computer and connecting to Lexis or Westlaw. But a street repair project could accidentally sever a cable, cutting off Internet access; budget considerations on a project can mean limits on use of Westlaw or Lexis; a computer hard drive might crash; a power failure could close your office unexpectedly for days. Here are five rules you can follow to be ready for disasters, budget constraints, and other problems that often make life unexpectedly difficult.

Rule 1: Never put off research to the last minute. What seems like a simple research question can turn out to be complicated, and even the most reliable Internet connection may fail at a crucial time. Start your research early to allow yourself time to be thorough and to follow up any unexpected leads you discover.

Rule 2: Be familiar with low-cost and free alternatives to commercial legal research databases. Westlaw and Lexis are useful tools, but sometimes clients cannot afford the cost of their use. LLRX.com, named one of the ten best Web sites of the decade by *Law Technology News,* provides free access to court rules and forms as well as links to useful sources of legal information on the Web. As we see numerous times throughout this text, Cornell Law School's Legal Information Institute (LII), **www.law.cornell.edu**, has free and reliable access to court opinions, statutes, and more. Both can help you get research done on the cheap.

Rule 3: Have a backup system and use it. Make sure you regularly archive your research on a server or other location. Your firm will likely have a backup system for computers. Find out how it works and what steps you need to take to keep your research files securely backed up. But don't rely on comprehensive backups that occur nightly or weekly. Make sure your work is regularly backed up during the day as well, just in case your computer picks a critical moment to die. Be equally sure you are not putting sensitive materials on a flash drive or other portable media that could be lost.

Rule 4: Download and archive. Don't rely on being able to find that crucial document on the Web again —Web sites vanish, are reorganized, and change their content. Download and store crucial information on your computer or print it out, but make sure you can find what you need quickly. Tools such as Google Desktop (**http://desktop.google.com**) and X1 (**www.x1.com**) make finding files stored on your computer quick and easy. Free-form databases, such as AskSam (**www.asksam.com**), allow you to create sets of information of varied materials for quick retrieval. Find a tool that works for you and master it.

Rule 5: Plan ahead. You can't know when a computer will crash, an Internet connection will fail, or a power failure will shut down your office for an extended period. You can be ready, however, if a problem crops up. As you plan your work on a case, think about what resources you must have to accomplish each task. What documents would you need to keep working on the project if your office was closed? Are there things that can be done off-site if necessary? Do you have all the relevant passwords and login information needed to access Web sites to continue researching from another location? Which deadlines are coming up? How will you meet them if your computer isn't working / the power is out / the office floods when a pipe breaks?

TECHNOLOGY TIP

We can never know what challenges tomorrow will bring. The best we can do is to be prepared to adapt to those challenges. As a paralegal, you will likely be working on projects where a missed deadline can mean that your client loses her case. Making sure you can respond to the challenges of everything from malfunctioning technology to natural disasters is a crucial part of your job.

all states, and the tutorial provided is very helpful. Sites like this one will help you understand more about the legislative history of a law.

Government Sites

The site of the Documents Center of the University of Michigan Library is a reference point for local, state, federal, foreign, and international law resources on the Web (**www.lib.umich.edu** and search "library documents center"). This site has one of the most comprehensive lists of links to government documents on the Web, with descriptions of what is included at each link. Here, we discuss some federal government sites, but state governments have similar resources.

Federal Law Starting Points

USA.gov (**www.usa.gov**), the official portal to U.S. government information, provides links to every branch of the federal government, including federal agencies. The U.S. Government Printing Office (**www.gpoaccess.gov**) also posts official information from each of the three branches of the federal government. Click on "A–Z Resource List" to access the *Code of Federal Regulations*, the *Congressional Record*, the *Federal Register*, all bills introduced in Congress, the *United States Code*, and other government publications. The Library of Congress's THOMAS site (**thomas.loc.gov**) provides a daily congressional digest, a link to the Law Library of Congress, and full text and summaries of bills. The U.S. Department of Justice (**www.usdoj.gov**) provides information on many areas of law, including civil rights, employment discrimination, crime, and immigration.

Federal Legislative Home Pages

The U.S. House of Representatives Web site at **www.house.gov** provides links to representatives' roll-call votes, the congressional schedule, current debates on the House floor, and Web sites of representatives. The Web site of the U.S. Senate at **www.senate.gov** hosts a Virtual Reference Desk with Senate procedures explained via Web links arranged according to topic. The Senate site also provides roll-call votes, information about recent legislative activity, and links to the Web sites of senators.

Business Information

The Web site of the U.S. Department of Commerce (**www.commerce.gov**) provides a wealth of business and economic statistical data and other information. Some of it is available only for a fee. The U.S. Patent and Trademark Office provides many educational resources regarding patents and trademarks at **www.uspto.gov**. Information on copyrights and a searchable database of copyright records is provided by the U.S. Copyright Office at **www.copyright.gov**. The Equal Employment Opportunity Commission (EEOC) posts information on employment discrimination, EEOC regulations, compliance, and enforcement at **www.eeoc.gov**. Numerous resources to help in forming, financing, and operating small businesses are offered by the U.S. Small Business Administration at **www.sbaonline.sba.gov**. The Securities and Exchange Commission maintains public companies' electronic filings at **www.sec.gov** (see the "Filings & Forms" menu).

LEXIS AND WESTLAW

Most legal researchers use Lexis and Westlaw. They are the dominant fee-based providers in the legal research business. The services are comprehensive, and once one becomes familiar with them, they are user friendly. Subscribers pay for the use

Ethics Watch

FINDING ETHICS OPINIONS ON THE WEB

Paralegals can provide a valuable service to their employers by knowing how to access online the ethical opinions issued by the American Bar Association (ABA) and state bar associations. For example, suppose that your supervising attorney is defending a client in court, and the attorney learns that the client has given testimony that the attorney knows is false. What is the attorney's ethical responsibility in this situation? Should the attorney disclose the client's perjury to the court? Would this be a violation of the attorney-client privilege? Or suppose the attorney learns that the client intends to testify falsely in court. Must the attorney inform the court of the client's intention? In these situations, the attorney may ask you to find out if the state bar association or the ABA has issued an ethical opinion on this issue. You can find this information quickly by going online and accessing **www.abanet.org**, where the ABA posts summaries of its ethical opinions. (From the "Member Resources" menu, select "Ethics/Professional Conduct," and then select "ABA Formal Ethics Opinons.") The ABA also posts ethical opinions issued by state bar associations. Go to **www.abanet.org**, and select "Ethics/Professional Conduct" from the "Member Resources" menu. Select "Lawyer Ethics and Professionalism" from the menu at the left, and then select "Other Links" from the "Additional Resources" menu.

of these services, and they are expensive. Different law firms pay different rates depending on their contracts with the providers.

We discussed FindLaw and many other online sites, in part, because the use of those services can reduce the amount of time spent on Westlaw or Lexis and thereby keep down research costs. Doing initial work on free sites, and organizing materials in advance, will enable you to be more efficient in the use of these costly resources. Your employer will set the rules for use of the fee-based research sites so you will know what is expected.

While we focus on Lexis and Westlaw, there are lower-cost competitors that are making inroads. Competitors get a share of the market by offering lower prices for similar, if less comprehensive, services. After examining Westlaw and Lexis, we discuss some of these alternatives.

Westlaw includes more than 23,000 databases of case law, federal and state statutes, administrative rules, law journals and reviews, treatises, legal encyclopedias, legal forms, public records, newspapers and magazines, and other sources. Lexis is the legal research part of LexisNexis. (Nexis is mostly for journalism research.) The Lexis databases contain most published cases in the history of the United States, unpublished cases since 1980, statutes, and other materials, including foreign jurisdiction cases. Both services are particularly popular for their *KeyCite* and *Shepard's* citatory services.

Accessing Westlaw or Lexis

A subscriber can access Westlaw and Lexis via **www.westlaw.com** and **www.lexis.com**, respectively. To use most of the legal research tools offered by these services, you must subscribe to them and obtain a password. Once you have a password,

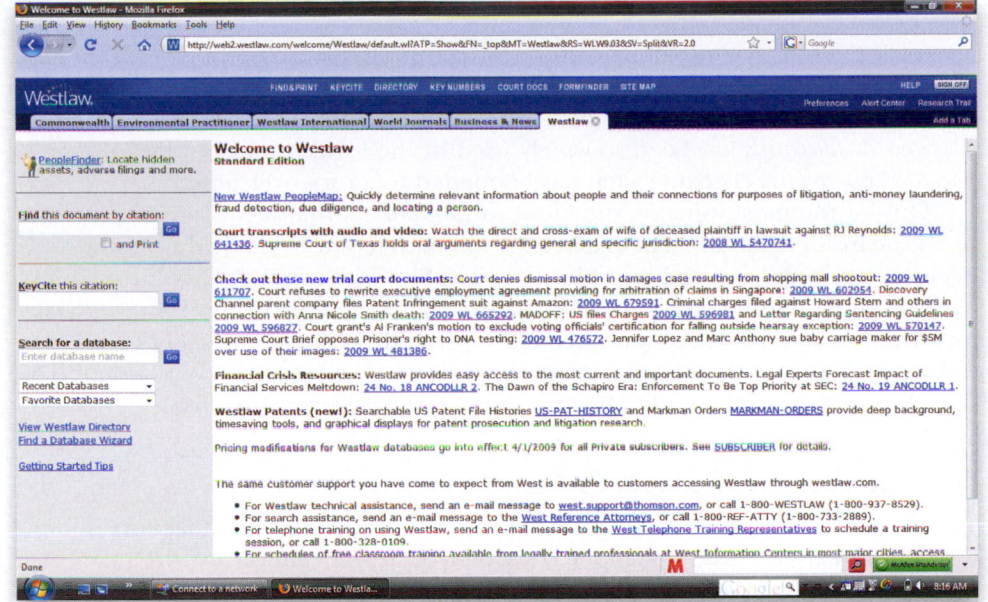

EXHIBIT 8.4
The Opening Page of Westlaw

Reprinted with permission from
Thomson Reuters.

when you sign on to the service, a welcome page is displayed. (The opening page of Westlaw is shown in Exhibit 8.4.) You can then begin your research. You can conduct a search, check citations, review documents related to a case or topic, set up alerts, and track previous research trails.

Conducting a Search

Both Westlaw and Lexis allow subscribers to locate documents using various search and browse methods. If you have the citation for a document, such as a court case or statute, you can enter the number and quickly call up the document. If you do not know the citation number, you can search according to legal topic, by case or party name, or by publication. If you do not know the best search terms to use for a particular search, both services will suggest terms to use. In both, you can search multiple sources simultaneously, and you can sort results by source type (cases, statutes and regulations, and law reviews and journals).

In addition to using the search methods just described, you can locate documents with Westlaw using two different browsing methods. Westlaw's "Table of Contents" organizes the federal, state, and municipal laws of several countries into submenus, including both primary and secondary sources of law. Westlaw also allows you to browse a directory of laws, practice areas, periodicals, public records, news, and many other topics and subtopics arranged hierarchically into menus.

Checking Citations

All paralegals should become familiar with citators. A **citator** provides a list of legal references that have cited or interpreted a case or law. A *case citator* provides, in addition, a history of the case. After all, a case decided a year ago may now be "bad law" if it has been reversed or modified on appeal. So whether you are looking at cases, regulations, or statutes, you want to know if your findings are up to date and still considered "good law."

Both Westlaw and Lexis provide online citators. In Lexis, the primary citator is *Shepard's*. Westlaw provides a similar service, called *KeyCite*. For practical purposes, you can think of *Shepard's* and *KeyCite* as performing much the same functions. We discuss these services here, starting with the classic *Shepard's Citations*.

citator

A book or online service that provides the history and interpretation of a statute, regulation, or court decision and a list of the cases, statutes, and regulations that have interpreted, applied, or modified a statute or regulation.

Shepard's Citations

Shepard's Citations has developed the most comprehensive system of case citators in the United States. *Shepard's* lists every case published in an official or unofficial reporter by its citation. Every region of the National Reporter System, and more, is covered. *Shepard's* has been so widely used in the legal profession that the term *Shepardizing* means checking what has happened to a case over time.

One of the most valuable functions of *Shepard's* is that it provides a means to verify the history of a case. For example, if you want to know whether a certain court decision has been reversed by a higher court, *Shepard's* provides that information. Note, though, that it takes some time before the printed versions of *Shepard's* citators are updated. Although we discuss the printed versions of *Shepard's* here, you will most likely use the online version to make sure your research is up to date. The structure of the printed and online versions of *Shepard's* are the same.

The Organization of Shepard's Citations

The researcher begins by finding the appropriate citator, the one that corresponds with the researched case's citation. For example, if the citation for the main case indicates that it is from the *Atlantic Reporter,* the citator to locate is *Shepard's Atlantic Citations.* Then, to locate the case in this publication, the researcher finds the pages covering the relevant volume of the *Atlantic Reporter.* The volume numbers are printed in the upper left-hand corner of each page for easy reference. Once the correct pages are found, the researcher reviews the listings to locate the page on which the case begins. Parallel citations to other reporters are listed in parentheses with the case. Following this is a listing of citations identifying any higher courts that have reviewed the case. Then comes a listing of cases that have cited the main case. Of course, if you are doing your research online, you are taken to the equivalent point right away.

Types of Information Provided by Shepard's Citations

Paralegals use *Shepard's* citators to accomplish several research objectives:

- Parallel citations—*Shepard's* provides parallel citations for the cited cases, allowing the paralegal to locate the case in other official or unofficial reporters.

- Other cases—*Shepard's* lists other cases ("citing cases") that have cited the main case ("the cited case"). For example, suppose that in researching a matter you have found a case on point. You can check *Shepard's Citations* to find out what other cases have dealt with one or more issues in your case (the cited case). Also, *Shepard's* listing of citing cases may include other cases on point that you will want to check.

- References to periodicals—If you are researching a case on point, *Shepard's* provides further research tips by referring to helpful periodical articles and annotations in the *American Law Reports.*

- Case history—As mentioned, *Shepard's* provides a history of the cited case. For example, it will tell you if the decision in your case on point has been overturned on appeal (or if any further action has been taken).

Shepard's uses an elaborate abbreviation system to provide information on how the cited case has been used in the citing case. For example, if the ruling in the cited case has been followed by a citing case, the symbol *f* (for "followed") will appear after the name of the citing case. Exhibit 8.5 explains other symbols used in *Shepard's.*

Administrative Regulations

Shepard's Code of Federal Regulations Citations provides citations to decisions of federal and state courts relating to administrative law, articles in legal periodicals discussing sections of the C.F.R., and other reference sources. The citation lists in *Shepard's*

EXHIBIT 8.5
Abbreviations Used in *Shepard's*

Reprinted by permission of LexisNexis.

ABBREVIATIONS—ANALYSIS

History of Case

a	(affirmed)	Same case affirmed on rehearing.
cc	(connected case)	Different case from case cited but arising out of same subject matter or intimately connected therewith.
m	(modified)	Same case modified on rehearing.
r	(reversed)	Same case reversed on rehearing.
s	(same case)	Same case as case cited.
S	(superseded)	Substitution for former opinion.
v	(vacated)	Same case vacated.
US	cert den	*Certiorari* denied by U.S. Supreme Court.
US	cert dis	*Certiorari* dismissed by U.S. Supreme Court.
US	reh den	Rehearing denied by U.S. Supreme Court.
US	reh dis	Rehearing dismissed by U.S. Supreme Court.

Treatment of Case

c	(criticized)	Soundness of decision or reasoning in cited case criticized for reasons given.
d	(distinguished)	Case at bar different either in law or fact from case cited for reasons given.
e	(explained)	Statement of import of decision in cited case. Not merely a restatement of the facts.
f	(followed)	Cited as controlling.
h	(harmonized)	Apparent inconsistency explained and shown not to exist.
j	(dissenting opinion)	Citation in dissenting option.
L	(limited)	Refusal to extend decision of cited case beyond precise issues involved.
o	(overruled)	Ruling in cited case expressly overruled.
p	(parallel)	Citing case substantially alike or on all fours with cited case in its law or facts.
q	(questioned)	Soundness of decision or reasoning in cited case questioned.

C.F.R. are organized by title and C.F.R. section. To acknowledge the frequent republication of the C.F.R., each citation is followed by either the date of the publication of the C.F.R. edition cited or the date of the citing reference. *Shepard's* uses a system of abbreviations, including those listed below, to indicate the impact that a court decision has had on the cited regulation.

- **C** (constitutional).
- **U** (unconstitutional).
- **Up** (unconstitutional in part).
- **V** (void).
- **Va** (valid).

Shepard's also publishes a variety of topical citators covering the regulations of federal agencies in specific areas. Examples include *Occupational Safety and Health Citations, Federal Energy Law Citations,* and *Bankruptcy Citations.*

Legal Periodicals

Shepard's Law Review Citations includes citations to several hundred legal periodicals and law reviews. Researchers can use it to locate references to law review articles mentioned in court decisions and other legal services. The researcher finds the cited source by looking for the name of the legal periodical and then locating the volume and page number. Once the article has been found, the researcher reviews the list of citing sources that referred to the article. *Shepard's* provides coverage of many local and national law reviews in each of its state citators. At the federal level, *Shepard's* publishes *Federal Law Citations in Selected Law Reviews,* which provides indexes of law-review citations to federal court cases and other statutory information.

KeyCite

Let's now consider the *KeyCite* online citator. Suppose that you want to find out whether the holding in a particular case decided by a California appellate court is still good law. If you are using Lexis, you can use *Shepard's* to find out if the decision was appealed to the California Supreme Court (or to the United States Supreme Court) and, if so, whether the holding was affirmed, overturned, or modified on appeal. You can also "Shepardize" the case to find out how courts in other jurisdictions have referred to this case. That is, has the case become precedent? Is it referred to in a positive or negative manner by later courts?

If you are using Westlaw, you can use the **KeyCite** citator service (see Exhibit 8.6). An enhancement to documents accessible through Westlaw is the *KeyCite* case status flag, which indicates when there is case history that should be investigated. As described in the *Developing Paralegal Skills* feature, a case status flag, depending on its color, will warn you that a case is not good law for at least one of its points, that the case has some negative history but its holding has not been reversed, or that the case has been overruled. *KeyCite* provides other features to make research more efficient as well. Suppose that you have found a case in the *KeyCite* database that cites the case you are researching. Stars added to the citation of the citing case show the extent to which your case is discussed in the citing case. For example, four stars indicate that the citing case contains an extended discussion of your case, usually more than a printed page of text. One star indicates the reference is brief, usually no more than as part of a list of case citations.

The tools provided by *KeyCite* and *Shepard's* allow you to access updated law within seconds. As emphasized in Chapter 7, a crucial part of legal research is making sure your findings are accurate and up to date. If your supervising attorney is preparing for trial, for example, the attorney will want to base a legal argument on current authorities. A precedential case that may have been good law last month may not remain so today.

KeyCite

An online citator on Westlaw that can trace case history, retrieve secondary sources, categorize legal citations by legal issue, and perform other functions.

EXHIBIT 8.6
KeyCite from Westlaw

Reprinted with permission from Thomson Reuters.

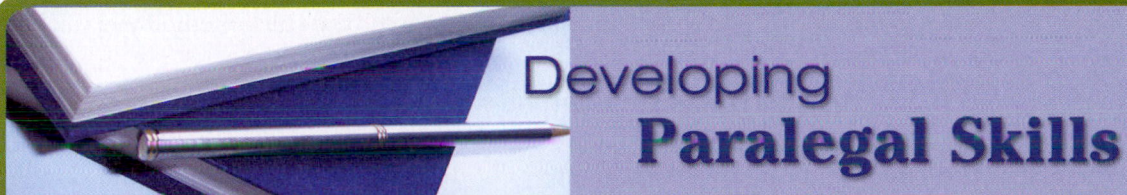

Developing Paralegal Skills

CITE CHECKING ON WESTLAW

Katie, a paralegal, needs to quickly check a citation for a case from the court of appeals to see if it is still good law. Her supervising attorney wants to use the case in a brief that must be filed within a few hours. Katie accesses Westlaw. She enters her password and client-identifying information. Once she has gained access, she clicks on the "KeyCite this citation" box and enters the case citation. The search turns up a red flag, which means that the case has been reversed or overruled and is no longer good law. Katie clicks on the red flag, which takes her to the decision in which the case was reversed or overruled. It turns out that the case was reversed on grounds that were not related to the rule of law for which her supervising attorney wants to cite the case. Katie and her supervisor can use the case in their brief after all. For their purpose, it is still good law.

TIPS FOR USING KEYCITE

- A red flag means that a case has been reversed or overruled for at least one point of law and must be reviewed.
- A yellow flag means that the case has been questioned and should be checked.
- Never cite a case without verifying that it is still good law.
- Always read a citing case to find out why your case has a red or yellow flag and to determine what issue in your case has been questioned, reversed, or overruled.

Selecting a Database

The legal research materials available through Westlaw and Lexis draw from thousands of databases, so a search by case name or legal topic can easily return an overwhelming number of documents. As a result, paralegals often need to limit their searches to specified databases. To do this, you first select a database that you want to search. If you are using Westlaw, for example, you click on the box labeled "Search for a Database" and enter a database identifier (for example, "ca-cs" to search all California cases). If you do not know the abbreviation for the database you wish to search, you can choose "Directory."

For example, suppose that your supervising attorney has asked you to research case law on the liability of tobacco products manufacturers for cancer caused by the use of those products. To do a thorough investigation, you will need to search the databases containing decisions from all state courts as well as from all federal courts. By working your way through Westlaw directories, you will be able to find the databases containing decisions from all state courts and all federal courts.

After you become familiar with the database identifiers on whatever service you are using, you can access that database more directly. For example, on the opening page of Westlaw, you can click on "Find a Database Wizard" at the bottom left of the screen. From the list provided, you select the information you wish to research, such as "Case, statute, or legal text or periodical." Next you can select the specific database you want, such as "Cases–Federal" and then "ALLFEDS."

Searching a Database

Once you have chosen a specific database, such as "ALLFEDS," a search box will open on the screen. You will enter your *search query* in this box. In addition to the "Terms and Connectors" (Boolean) method of searching, both Lexis and Westlaw allow users to draft search queries using "Natural Language" (or plain English). Before beginning your search, you should indicate in the search box which method you will use.

The Terms and Connectors Method

In a search employing terms and connectors, you use numerical and grammatical connectors to specify the relationships of the terms. For example, to find cases on the liability of tobacco products manufacturers for cancer caused by the use of those products, you could type the following terms and connectors in the query box:

> liability /p cancer /s tobacco

This would retrieve all cases in which the term *liability* is in the same paragraph ("/p") as the term *cancer,* with the term *cancer* in the same sentence ("/s") as the term *tobacco.* To restrict the scope of your search, you can add a field restriction. For example, you might want to retrieve only court opinions rendered after 2009. If you are using Westlaw, you could add the following to your query to restrict the search results to cases decided after 2009:

> & added date (after 12/31/2009)

Exhibit 8.7 illustrates the results of running a search with these terms and connectors on Westlaw.

Many other grammatical and numerical connectors can be used to efficiently search a database. These are listed in the instructions provided to Lexis and Westlaw subscribers.

Generally, when drafting queries, make sure your query is not too broad. If you entered just the term *liability*, for example, your search would be futile because so many thousands of documents contain that term. At the same time, you do not want your search to be so narrow that no cases will be retrieved.

The Natural Language Method

The natural language method allows you to type a description of an issue in plain English to retrieve the most relevant documents. In searching for cases relating to the topic in the previous example, your query might read as follows:

> Is a tobacco manufacturer liable for cancer caused by the use of its products?

This query would retrieve the documents most closely matching your description.

EXHIBIT 8.7
Search Research Results on Westlaw

Reprinted with permission from Thomson Reuters.

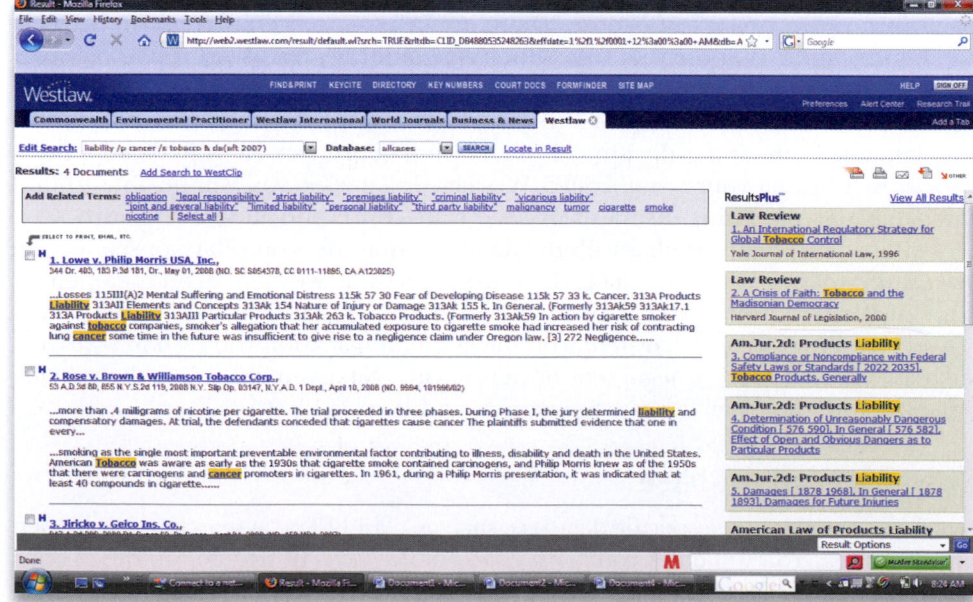

Including synonyms in the search may sometimes be necessary to produce more comprehensive results. A thesaurus feature on Westlaw (and a "Suggest Terms for My Search" function on Lexis) can suggest additional terms for your search. After entering your natural language query on Westlaw, click on "Thesaurus." Select a term from the list, and then click on "View Related Terms." If you want to add one of the terms to your description, select the term and click on "Add Term to Description." Note that Westlaw may also suggest additional terms without being asked to do so.

Searching within Results

Often, once you have retrieved your search results, you would like to quickly locate certain key information. For example, suppose that your search resulted in a list of twenty cases relevant to your topic. At this point, Westlaw's "Locate in Results" tool allows you to scan the documents in your search result for terms that were not included in your query. Assume that your original request was, in natural language, "Is a tobacco manufacturer liable for cancer caused by the use of its products?" If you want to know whether "death" is discussed in any of your search-result documents, you can use the "Locate" tool.

When browsing through your search results, remember that the time you spend using the service is costly. If you have found a case or cases that appear to be on point, you can print them out (or download them) for further study.

Is Lexis or Westlaw Better?

Because Lexis and Westlaw compete head on, they provide similar services. The formats are somewhat different, and there are differences in the specialty publications offered. Some users prefer one to the other, but that may be largely a matter of which program they have learned to use. A survey done in 2008 by the law library at Stanford University showed that most large law firms subscribe to both services, allowing research staff to choose the one they prefer. Asked which system they would pick if allowed only one service, 245 respondents said Westlaw, and 89 picked Lexis. By similar margins, however, respondents said that legal researchers could switch between the systems and use *KeyCite* or *Shepard's* to accomplish the same tasks. So while Westlaw appears to have pulled ahead of Lexis as the dominant seller of premier online services, both do the task well. Respondents to the survey also noted that it is desirable to learn about other, less costly, programs. So we now turn to some of those offerings.

ALTERNATIVE ONLINE PROGRAMS

Several fee-based online programs offer services more limited but less expensive than those of Westlaw and Lexis. All take advantage of public-access databases, such as those for federal cases. Some have extra search features, usually for higher subscription fees. None is as comprehensive as Westlaw and Lexis, but many can perform much of the research needed.

PACER

Public Access to Court Electronic Records (PACER) is an easy-to-use Internet service that allows users to obtain court cases and docket information from federal appeals, district, and bankruptcy courts. Links to all of these federal courts are provided from the PACER Web site (**pacer.psc.uscourts.gov**). PACER is run by the federal judiciary, and its prices are based on the cost of supplying the system.

Besides cases, PACER offers access to case dockets, enabling researchers to retrieve information such as:

- A listing of all parties and participants, including judges, attorneys, and trustees.

- A compilation of case-related information, such as cause of action, nature of the suit, and compensation demanded.
- A list of dates of case events entered into the case record.
- A list of new cases daily.
- Judgments or case status.
- Copies of documents filed for certain cases.

Cases in the PACER system are similar to those included in the proprietary programs we discuss next.

Fastcase

Fastcase (**www.fastcase.com**) provides access to all Supreme Court decisions, federal appeals decisions back to 1924, and federal district court decisions back to 1932. For most research, that is adequate. It also has bankruptcy court decisions, as well as decisions of state supreme courts and appeals courts back to about 1950. All federal and state statutes, constitutions, and administrative codes are included. Research features include:

- Sorting by document authority (the most-cited cases first).
- Search by date range, jurisdiction, and other fields.
- Hyperlinked case citations.
- Most relevant sections displayed in search results, which is particularly helpful in long cases.
- Search using Boolean or natural language.

Fastcase also provides Authority Check, which looks to see if a case is still good law and provides links to relevant cases. For an extra fee, a user can double-check by linking with *Shepard's* or *KeyCite*. Annual and monthly subscription fees are lower than those of Lexis and Westlaw, which has added to the system's popularity. Some state bar associations, such as those in Illinois and Ohio, have arranged for members to have access to Fastcase as part of membership, so it is becoming more widely used.

Loislaw

Loislaw (**www.loislaw.com**) is a part of Wolters Kluwer, a business and law publishing company. Like Fastcase, it has large federal and state case, statutory, and regulatory databases, but Loislaw also allows subscribers access to its specialized databases of secondary sources. Wolters Kluwer is the publisher of CCH, a major tax treatise, and owns Aspen publishers, which provides specialized treatises in various areas of law including bankruptcy, construction, employment, estates, family law, and tax. Thus, Loislaw offers more than public-access documents—as, of course, do Westlaw and Lexis. Loislaw is not as comprehensive as Lexis and Westlaw, but it is competitive among the lower-priced alternatives.

When doing topical searches, in Boolean or natural language, Loislaw uses Key Words in Context. This feature highlights the key words in your search in documents, making it easier to review the documents by pinpointing the terms. Loislaw also features GlobalCite, a research citation tool. When you click on this feature, you view the federal or state cases within the results of your search. It also retrieves rules, regulations, treatises, and other documents that have cited a case or other document of interest. LawWatch is a feature that tracks trends in areas you have identified.

Casemaker

Like Fastcase, Casemaker is working its way into more common use by lawyers through its ties to state bar associations. Its Web site (**www.casemaker.com**) lists the bar associations that allow their members to use Casemaker as a part of their bar membership.

Casemaker provides essentially the same set of federal and state case reports, statutes, and regulations as most other services. In some states, it provides state-specific documents, such as opinions of attorneys general, jury instructions, links to court forms, local federal rules, and other helpful materials. Casecheck is a citatory-type service that, when a document or case is located, provides links to cases that discuss the case or document in question. As with most legal research services, searches on Casemaker can use natural language or Boolean inquiries. Casemaker does not claim to be as comprehensive as Lexis or Westlaw but offers a reasonably priced service that covers much of the research ordinarily needed.

VersusLaw

VersusLaw (**www.versuslaw.com**) is a low-cost service that includes Supreme Court and U.S. court of appeals cases and current federal district court cases, as well as state appellate court cases and cases of some specialized courts. A higher-level subscription plan includes federal district court opinions back to about 1950, along with state statutes and regulations. The highest-level plan includes the *U.S. Code* and the *Code of Federal Regulations* and provides added search features. VersusLaw has limited access to publications that are not in the public domain and so offers primarily a reasonably priced means to access cases. At the time this text was written, it was available to paralegal students for $3.50 per month.

CONDUCTING ONLINE RESEARCH

As we have seen, the Internet offers many sources of information for paralegals doing legal research. Paralegals often research other matters as well. They may need to locate people, investigate companies, and conduct other practical, fact-based research into matters not directly related to legal issues. The numerous databases available online make it possible to perform such research quickly and efficiently.

Your goal when conducting any online research is to find accurate, up-to-date information on the topic you are researching in a minimum amount of time. As anyone who has used the Internet knows, it is possible to spend hours navigating through cyberspace to find specific information. Planning your research in advance and using various research strategies, such as those discussed in this section, can help you achieve your goal of conducting online research efficiently.

Plan Ahead—Analyze the Facts and Identify the Issues

Once you have been given a particular research project, you should plan your research steps before going online. The first step is to know what it is you are seeking. To avoid wasting time and money, outline your objectives clearly and be sure that you understand your goals. To narrow the scope of your research, you may need to know the reason for the research or how the results will be used.

Online Research Strategies

Once online, you can use many strategies to find what you are looking for. We discuss some of them here (see *Developing Paralegal Skills* for tips on medical research).

Starting Points

Sometimes, a research session begins with one of the online directories or guides discussed earlier in this chapter. For example, if the object of your search is to find a law firm that practices in a specialized area of the law, you could start with Yahoo's

Developing Paralegal Skills

MEDICAL RESEARCH ON THE INTERNET

Tom Shannon needs to locate information on bipolar disorder. Tom's supervising attorney is trying to prove that the defendant in a case has this mental disorder. Tom, who has worked as a paralegal for ten years, knows the Internet is an excellent source for medical information. Tom accesses the American Medical Association's Web site at **www.ama-assn.org**. He searches for articles describing this disorder. Tom finds several citations to articles, along with summaries of the articles, but the full text of the articles is not online. He prints out the information he has found and goes to the library at the local medical school to obtain the full text of the articles.

TIPS FOR PERFORMING MEDICAL RESEARCH ONLINE

- Become familiar with medical terminology.
- Search the appropriate medical categories on the Web site.
- Locate appropriate articles and summaries.
- If the full text of the articles is not available online, go to the nearest medical school's library to obtain them.

"Law" menu. You can find this menu by going to **dir.yahoo.com** and selecting "Law" from the "Government" menu. On this page, you will see various submenus, including one titled "Law Firms and Legal Services." Within that list is a general list of "Firms," which can be arranged alphabetically (see Exhibit 8.8).

A search engine can be used to compile a list of Web sites containing certain key words. A search engine tailored to zero in on specific topical sites may be more useful than a general search engine. Keep in mind the limitations of search engines, however. Your search may locate many irrelevant sources and may not spot every site that you would find helpful. In addition, different search engines will yield different results or order the results differently.

From the preliminary results of a general search, you can click on the links to the sites and determine which are useful. Many sites include their own links to other sources you may find helpful. Some Web sites attempt to collect links to all online resources about particular topics. These sites include directories, which were discussed earlier, as well as other sites, such as USA.gov (**www.usa.gov**), which provides links to federal offices and agencies. For more experienced researchers, there is Hieros Gamos (**www.hg.org**), an extensive guide to legal information available online. Some sites are more eclectic in what they offer (see, for example, the 'Lectric Law Library at **www.lectlaw.com**).

Discovering Available Resources

Despite your best intentions and attempts to focus your research, you may have to approach a project without a clear objective regarding what you need to find. Your initial research goal may be to discover the extent of resources available online, with your ultimate goal to obtain more precise results.

One source of information is a Web page containing links to important resources in particular topic areas. These pages often include directory-style menus

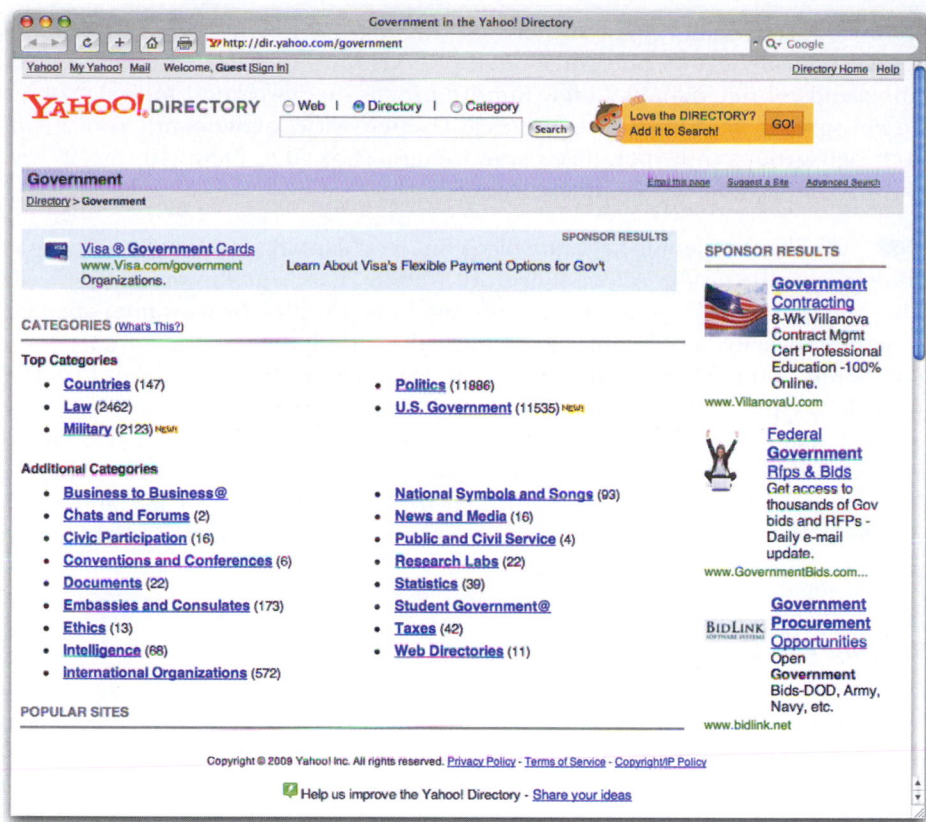

EXHIBIT 8.8
Yahoo! Government Categories

Reproduced with permission of Yahoo! Inc. © 2009 Yahoo! Inc. and the Yahoo! logo are registered trademarks of Yahoo!

and search utilities. Remember that these sources often change and may even disappear, and new ones can develop overnight.

Many libraries provide access to their catalogues online (see, for example, the New York Public Library's Web site at **catnyp.nypl.org**). You can search these catalogues on the Internet just as you would search them in the library. This can save the time that you otherwise might spend in a futile trip to the library. You can search the catalogues of your local libraries as well as those of more distant libraries. Often, you can arrange to have source material from a distant library delivered to a closer library or directly to you.

Another way to find out what resources are available is to begin with a listserv list, a newsgroup, or a blog. These can also be used to update your research.

Listservs. A **listserv list** (or mailing list) is basically a list of e-mail addresses of persons interested in a particular topic. By placing their names on the list, they agree to receive e-mail from others about the topic. A message sent to the list's address is automatically sent to everyone on the list. Anyone on the list can respond to whoever sent the message. As a researcher, you might post a message that asks for suggestions about online resources for your research. You can also add your name to the list to receive mass e-mailings. In some cases, you may be able to browse an archive of messages to see if another researcher has previously called attention to a resource that matches your search. For an example of a listserv list, go to **www.tile.net** and select "Email Newsletters and Ezines" from the menu. You can access some listservs by subscription or by invitation only.

Newsgroups. A **newsgroup** (also known as a **Usenet group**) is a forum that resembles a community bulletin board. A researcher can select a newsgroup by topic, post a question or problem (for example, "Does anyone know a good source for what I want to know?"), and check back hours or days later for others'

---

listserv list

A list of e-mail addresses of persons who have agreed to receive e-mail about a particular topic.

newsgroup (Usenet group)

An online bulletin board service. A newsgroup is a forum, or discussion group, that usually focuses on a particular topic.

responses. A researcher might also browse the newsgroup's archive, although messages are typically stored only for limited periods of time. There are perhaps tens of thousands of newsgroups (a few hundred focus on law-related topics). You can skim newsgroup directories at such sites as Usenet (**www.usenet.com**). You can also search newsgroups with specialized search engines, such as Newsville (go to **www. newsville.com** and select "complete listing").

Blogs.   Millions of people generate blogs on a regular basis, and millions more will be doing so in the future. A *blog*, short for "Weblog," is essentially an online journal. To find blogs on legal topics, try the links regularly provided by **www.inter-alia.net**.

Some blogs are well established, while others disappear as the authors tire of them. Some of the best-recognized blogs in law include the general Am Law Daily (**amlawdaily.typepad.com**) and Legal Times (**legaltimes.typepad.com**). There are also blogs that contain information and opinion about legal issues, such as **volokh. com**, which is hosted by a UCLA law professor and has several other law professors as contributors. Some blogs are dedicated to individual areas of law and will be noted in later chapters where specific topics are covered. Blogs that focus on legal topics are sometimes called "blawgs."

Browsing the Links

As you browse through the links that could be useful for your research, you will need to keep track of the Web sites you visit. Marking a site as a "Favorite" (Explorer) or adding a "Bookmark" (Firefox or Safari) for the site is an electronic substitute for keeping a book on your desk. With these, you can create an automatic link to any point on the Web and return to it at any time. For example, you might want an automatic link to the site at which you begin your research: a directory, a search engine, or a site that has many links that relate to what you need.

Narrowing Your Focus

Once you find a Web site that could be useful, you will probably need to zero in on specific data within that site. One way to do this, of course, is to use the links within the site. In addition, many sites provide internal search utilities. (See, for example, Harvard University's internal search tool at **search.harvard.edu**, which allows you to search an extensive database.)

Remember that your browser also has the ability to search a Web page that you are viewing. This can be particularly helpful when scrolling through a document for a bit of information would be tedious and time consuming. Using your browser's "find" tool, you can search, for example, the text of a specific bill before Congress at the Library of Congress's THOMAS site (**thomas.loc.gov**), which contains legislative information. You might also use your find tool to search a company's document in the Electronic Data Gathering, Analysis, and Retrieval (EDGAR) database of the Securities and Exchange Commission (SEC) (go to **www.sec.gov** and select "Filings & Forms"). EDGAR is an indexed collection of documents and forms that public companies and others are required to file with the SEC. Exhibit 8.9 presents the first page of the EDGAR online collection. Alternatively, you can access EDGAR's private-sector competitor, Edgar Online at **www.edgar-online.com**.

Evaluating What You Find

After you have found what appears to be exactly what you are looking for, you need to consider its reliability and credibility.

In evaluating a source's credibility, ask yourself whether the source of the information is a primary, a secondary, or a tertiary source. Primary sources include company Web sites, experts, and persons with firsthand knowledge. For example, the inventor of a product would be a primary source for information about his or her invention. Publicly filed documents are also primary sources. For example, the legal

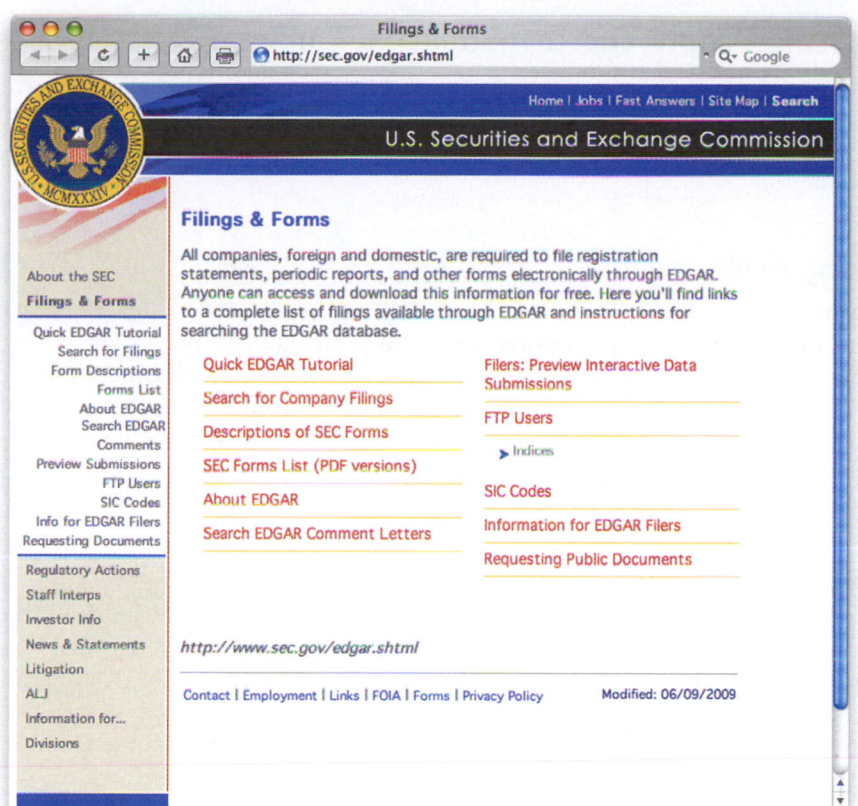

EXHIBIT 8.9
The Securities and Exchange
Commission's EDGAR Database

sec.gov/edgar.shtml

forms that some companies are required to file with the Securities and Exchange Commission are good primary sources for the information that they contain (see the discussion of company investigations later in this chapter). Secondary sources include books and periodicals (such as law journals, newspapers, and magazines) and their online equivalents that contain "secondhand" information. Tertiary sources are any other sources that might be used in research (*tertiary* means "third" or "thirdhand"). It is always a good idea to find and interpret primary sources yourself before forming conclusions based on secondary or tertiary sources.

A researcher also needs to be aware of whether a source is reputable. A reputable source might be an organization that has established itself in a particular field. A less reputable source might be a personal, self-serving home page. Was the information placed on the Web by a source that may be biased in a certain way? Some people providing information on the Internet may not even be who they represent themselves to be. Online resources are available to help you evaluate Web sites. Ohio State University's Web site includes an interactive tutorial and checklist for evaluating Web sites. You can access this tutorial by going to **liblearn.osu.edu** and selecting "net.TUTO" from the menu.

Updating Your Results

Staying current with events in the law, and in other areas that relate to your research, is important. One way to confirm whether your research results represent the most recent data available is by going online. News sites abound on the Internet. There are general sites sponsored by news organizations, as well as sources like Google's news search feature (go to **www.google.com** and select "News"). There are also sites directed at those interested only in updates on specific subjects, such as the law (for example, FindLaw offers many free legal news e-mail services at **newsletters.findlaw. com**). Corporate press releases—both current and from archives—can be reviewed at PRNewswire's site (**www.prnewswire.com**).

Locating People and Investigating Companies

As mentioned earlier, paralegals often need to locate people or find information about specific companies (see *Today's Professional Paralegal* feature on page 266 for an example), and the Internet can be especially useful in searching for this type of information.

Finding People

A paralegal may need to find particular persons to assist a lawyer in collecting debts, administering an estate, preparing a case for court, and so on. Public records are helpful in looking for people, but some of these records (including many historic records) are not on the Internet. Despite this limitation, Web searches can be useful, and they can also be cheaper and faster than going to a government office or a library. Sometimes, using a commercial locator service or database can also be less costly than a trip out of the office.

Broad Searches.   On the Web, a researcher can run a broad search with a general search engine such as Yahoo or Google. A researcher might also narrow the focus of a search to, for example, all U.S. telephone books. There are several phone book Web sites. Each has unique features. Some provide e-mail addresses (for example, Yahoo People Search at **people.yahoo.com**). Some include business listings (for example, **www.superpages.com**). Some can conduct a search with a telephone number or an e-mail address to reveal a name and a street address (for example, **www.iaf.net**).

Narrow Searches.   If you know something about the person you are searching for, you can use that information to narrow the search. Narrowed searches can be based on various characteristics, such as the person's profession or place of employment. For example, if you are looking for an attorney, you can link to the *West Legal Directory* in Westlaw, a comprehensive compilation of lawyers in the United States, or conduct a free search on **lawyers.findlaw.com**.

If you are looking for a professor at a particular university or an employee at a certain company, you can often search the staff directory of the school or business firm online. Similarly, directories in Westlaw offer searches in numerous categories, such as expert witnesses.

With the right database, a person's business license can be verified, information about a federal prison inmate can be accessed, and a military member or veteran can be found. (See, for example, **www.gisearch.com**.) Information can also be obtained about persons who contribute to federal election campaigns (see CQ MoneyLine at **moneyline.cq.com**). Adoptees and their birth parents can be located through databases such as **www.adoption.com** and **www.omnitrace.com**. For genealogy searches, there are huge databases of historical facts (see, for example, **www. ancestry.com**).

Fee-Based Searches.   Some commercial services provide access to their compilations of information for a price. For example, possible aliases, home value and property ownership, bankruptcies, tax liens, and small claims civil judgments can be searched through U.S. Search at **www.ussearch.com**. Through a service with access to states' incorporation data and other information, people can be pinpointed based on their ownership interest in business organizations. Real property records, bankruptcy filings, and documents relating to court dockets, lawsuits, and judgments can be searched through such sites as KnowX at **www.knowx.com**. Social Security numbers can also be verified (see **www. veris-ssn.com**).

Investigating Companies

Lawyers often need to know about their clients' companies and the companies of their clients' competitors. For example, if a client has suffered an injury caused by a defectively designed product, a lawyer will need to identify the defendant manufacturer, find out whether the manufacturer is the subsidiary of a larger company, and learn the defendant's address. If a client wants to acquire or invest in a particular business firm, research into the firm's background may be vital. There are many ways to find some of this information on the Web.

Finding Company Names and Addresses. A researcher can run a search with a telephone number to find a company's name and address (for example, see **www. superpages.com**). Without a telephone number, a company's name and address can be found with the help of a directory that searches by industry and state (see the Switchboard.com page at **www.switchboard.com**, for example). A search with such a directory can also help determine whether a specific firm name is in use anywhere in the United States. You can find out who owns a domain name by using the free services of Network Solutions (**www.networksolutions.com**).

Uncovering Detailed Information about Companies. In general, you can find specific company information on the Web at company Web sites, which may contain annual reports, press releases, and price lists. Some companies put their staff directories online.

Information about publicly held companies may be available through the sites of government agencies. For example, the Securities and Exchange Commission (SEC) regulates public companies and requires them to file documents and forms revealing certain information. This material can be accessed through the SEC's EDGAR database, as already mentioned. More up-to-date filings can be found at Edgar Online.

Other information about public companies can be found at numerous free sites, as well as fee-based sites. Some free sites provide data on the companies and links to the companies' home pages and other sources of information, such as news articles. The *Wall Street Journal*, at **www.wsj.com**, often includes archives of information that may span decades and may cover companies in other countries. Some of this information is free; some must be purchased. Another source of both free and for-a-fee information on public companies is **www.corporateinformation.com**. The BizTech Network maintains **www.brint.com**, which provides extensive links to U.S. and international businesses.

Data on privately held companies is more difficult to find because these firms are not subject to the SEC's disclosure requirements. Much of the information available includes only what the companies want to reveal. There are a few sites that compile some data on private companies, associations, and nonprofit organizations. For example, Hoover's Online at **www.hoovers.com** provides brief profiles of many companies, with links to other sites, including search engines. For a fee, Hoover's will provide expanded profiles.

Associations and Organizations

When gathering information about a person or a company, you may find it useful to check various professional organizations and associations. The Internet Public Library provides lists of associations by category at **www.ipl.org** (select "Special Collections" and then "Associations on the Net"). Yahoo also provides a directory of business and professional organizations at **dir.yahoo.com** (select "Business and Economy," then "Organizations," then "Professional"). Private business organizations are listed at **www.nvst.com** (select "Resources," and then select "Professional Associations" from the "Venture" menu). Access to lists of many nonprofit organizations can be found at **www.idealist.org**.

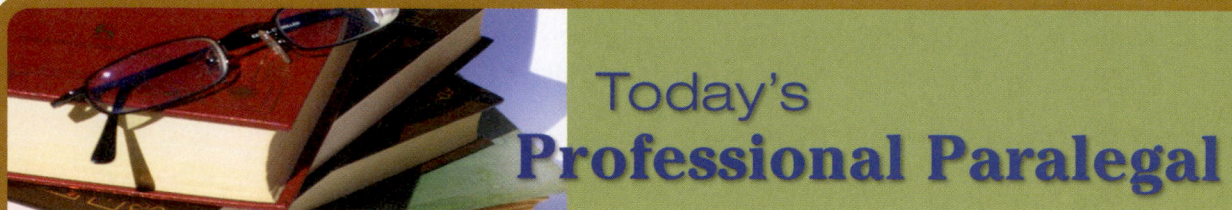

Today's
Professional Paralegal

LOCATING GUARDIANS AND WARDS

Patrick Mitchell works as a legal assistant for a sole practitioner, Anne Urso. Anne takes probate court assignments in which the court appoints her guardian *ad litem.* (A guardian *ad litem* is a special guardian appointed by a court to protect the interests of minors or incapacitated persons in legal proceedings.) This requires Anne to determine whether someone who has previously been appointed as a legal guardian for an incapacitated person needs to continue as guardian. In order to make this determination, Anne must visit the ward and meet with the guardian.

Today, Anne has received an envelope in the mail appointing her guardian *ad litem* in five cases. The paperwork that comes from the court contains the names and addresses of both the guardians and the wards. Anne knows from experience that the court's records are often out of date and that this information needs to be updated.

Anne assigns the task of locating the guardians and wards to Patrick. He will call them first to see if the information from the court is accurate and to set up a meeting between them and either Anne or himself. The forms have to be submitted to the court within two weeks of their receipt by Anne, which is a quick turnaround time, especially in light of Anne's caseload. Patrick calls the ward and the guardian on the first sheet and finds that their telephone numbers have been disconnected. He sets this sheet aside and calls the people listed on the next sheet. He succeeds in contacting the guardian and learns that the ward, an eighty-five-year-old man, Mr. Ahern, died almost a year ago. Patrick adds this to his notes for Anne. Patrick continues calling the guardians and wards listed on the sheets. He is able to contact the next three and sets up appointments with them.

Now Patrick must locate the guardian and the ward from the first sheet. He decides that the fastest way to do this is to use a people locator on the Internet. From past experience, Patrick is familiar with a number of reliable Web sites. He goes to **www.phonenumbers.com** and enters the name of the ward, Thomas Ford, and the address, 2335 Three Mile Drive, Detroit, Michigan. The computer retrieves a telephone number and an address for Mr. Ford. The telephone number is different from the one that was on the court's forms. Patrick runs another search for the guardian and turns up a new telephone number and address for him as well. Patrick then calls the guardian and the ward and schedules an appointment to meet with them.

Patrick then goes online to the Web site **www.knowx.com** (a LexisNexis service) to verify the death records of the second ward, Mr. Ahern. Using Mr. Ahern's Social Security number, he is able to access these records and print out a copy to include with his report. Patrick places a copy in the file.

Next, Patrick needs to use a mapping Web site to create maps for, and driving directions to, the five different locations to which he and Anne will need to go. Patrick accesses **www.mapquest.com**. He enters the address of the office and then the address of the first ward. A map with driving directions appears. Patrick prints out five maps with driving directions and places them in the file. Having finished this project, he then turns to his next task.

KEY TERMS AND CONCEPTS

Boolean logic 244

citator 251

home page 240

hypertext transfer protocol (http) 241

KeyCite 254

listserv list 261

newsgroup (Usenet group) 261

World Wide Web 240

CHAPTER SUMMARY

CONTEMPORARY ONLINE LEGAL RESEARCH

Going Online—An Internet Primer

Today's legal professionals can access a vast amount of information using the Internet, which is a global network of interconnected computers. Many online resources are available for free, while others charge a fee for accessing their databases.

1. *Internet tools*—Commonly used Internet tools include e-mail and the World Wide Web, a data network that is accessed through a browser.

2. *Navigating the Internet*—Getting around on the Web requires the use of uniform resource locators (URLs), which are Internet addresses. To navigate the Internet, one uses browsers (software such as Microsoft Explorer and Mozilla Firefox that allows a computer to roam the Web), guides and directories (menus of topics at various Web sites), and search engines (such as Google and Yahoo) that scan the Web for certain key words or concepts.

3. *Before going online*—Before beginning an online research session, you should first decide whether the Internet is the right tool for your research project. Ask yourself what sources you will need and whether they are available on the Internet.

Free Legal Resources on the Internet

A great deal of legal information, especially public documents such as statutes and cases, is accessible through free Internet sites.

1. *General legal resources*—Some free legal sites act as portals, giving access to a broad range of free information. The major site of this type is FindLaw. Another is the Legal Information Institute at Cornell University Law School.

2. *Specific legal resources*—Secondary sources are generally not found at free sites. However, an increasing number of law review articles are available. One can also find court opinions and various other legal resources at free sites.

3. *Government sites*—All federal government organizations have Internet sites, and many state government bodies also provide information via the Internet.

Lexis and Westlaw

For serious legal research, legal professionals often use online commercial legal research services, particularly Lexis and Westlaw. Subscribers to these fee-based services can access the services' databases via the Internet. Both Lexis and Westlaw provide their users with access to an extensive collection of legal, business, and other resources. Using these services, paralegals can access specific documents, check citations, update the law, and search hundreds of databases. For citation checking, Lexis provides *Shepard's Citations* and Westlaw provides KeyCite. Both services enable researchers to make sure their research results are still valid. Both Lexis and Westlaw allow users to search databases with queries using terms and connectors or natural language.

Continued

Alternative Online Programs

Since Westlaw and Lexis are costly to use, less expensive and less comprehensive alternatives have become more popular. Examples include PACER, Fastcase, Loislaw, Casemaker, and VersusLaw. Such services may be adequate for some projects and may also be used for preliminary research.

Conducting Online Research

1. *Plan ahead*—To avoid wasting time, define what you are seeking and determine which sources are most likely to lead you to the desired results.

2. *Research strategies*—Once online, you can use various search tools and other resources (such as listservs, newsgroups, and blogs) to locate information relevant to your topic. Often, researchers need to "browse the links" for a time before finding a site that is particularly relevant. Once you find a useful site, you can use your browser or the site's internal search tool to look for specific information within the site.

3. *Evaluating what you find*—In evaluating your research results, it is especially important to consider the reliability of any information obtained online.

4. *Updating your results*—To update results, you can access news sites online to look for articles or press releases concerning recent developments in the area you are researching.

5. *Locating people and investigating companies*—Paralegals often engage in online research to locate information about persons and to investigate companies. Sometimes, a person can be located through a broad search of the Web using a search engine such as Yahoo. Narrow searches can be conducted by accessing—for free or for a fee—specialized databases, such as compilations of physicians, lawyers, or expert witnesses. Searches for persons may also be conducted based on specific characteristics, such as place of employment. Numerous online sites contain information about both private and public companies.

STUDENT STUDYWARE™ CD-ROM

Interactive student CD in this book includes additional quizzing, plus video clips, case studies, and Key Terms flashcards.

ONLINE COMPANION™

For additional resources, please go to **www.paralegal.delmar.cengage.com**.

QUESTIONS FOR REVIEW

1. What is the difference between the Internet and the World Wide Web? What are uniform resource locators?

2. What should you do before going online to conduct a research session?

3. List five free legal resources that can be accessed via the Internet.

4. What kinds of legal resources can be accessed at various government sites?

5. How can Lexis and Westlaw be used to update the law? Describe two ways in which you can search databases on Lexis and Westlaw.

ETHICAL QUESTIONS

1. Janice, a paralegal in a firm specializing in labor law, joins a listserv. It is a discussion group about the Americans with Disabilities Act (ADA) of 1990 and related laws. Another member of the group posts a question about what companies the ADA applies to and whether his company is subject to the law. Janice knows the answer and could answer it. Should Janice answer the question? Why or why not?

2. The partners in the law firm of Dewey & Howe learn about a plane crash in the morning newspaper. They instruct their legal assistant to contact all of the families of the victims via e-mail to see if they are interested in filing a class-action lawsuit against the airline. Is this type of activity allowed under the ethical rules?

PRACTICE QUESTIONS AND ASSIGNMENTS

1. Explain the parts of the following URL:

   www.urisko.edu

2. Assume that the legal researchers in the situations described below all have access to an excellent law library, to Web resources, and to Westlaw or Lexis. Which of these three research sources or tools would you advise the legal professional to use for his or her particular research need? Why?

   a. Matthew, a paralegal, needs to find out if a case cited in a legal motion he is drafting is still good law.

   b. Cindy, an attorney, needs to locate a psychiatric expert witness.

   c. Robert, a paralegal, has been asked to locate a statutory provision; he needs to make sure that the result is up to date.

   d. Tom, a paralegal, needs to locate a witness to a car accident.

   e. Megan, a paralegal, needs to find an heir who is to inherit $500,000 under her uncle's will.

QUESTIONS FOR CRITICAL ANALYSIS

1. What benefit can Boolean logic provide regarding search engines? If you wanted to find information about copyright attorneys through a search engine, what operators could you use to narrow your search?

2. Why would a paralegal who is performing factual research on the Internet need to evaluate the credibility of the Web sites located? Would this be neces-sary for government Web sites as well? What might the results be if a researcher does not evaluate the credibility of Web sites?

3. What are some advantages of using Westlaw or Lexis when doing legal research rather than using the printed resources in a law library? Are there any disadvantages?

PROJECTS

1. Using a word-processing program, create a Web page for yourself, your employer, or your paralegal program. What information needs to be included?

2. Go to PACER, Loislaw, Casemaker, and Fastcase. Describe the strengths and weaknesses you see for doing research in each one.

USING INTERNET RESOURCES

1. The American Bar Association's Web site contains helpful information on legal research sources on the Internet. Access the Web site at

   www.abanet.org

   Answer the following questions about the research sources available online:

   a. Under "Public Resources" go to "Legal Topic Resources" and see what categories are available.

   b. At the bottom of the ABA home page, go to Topic A–Z at the bottom. In there, find "Lawlink: Legal Research Jumpstation." Survey the range of resources.

   c. In "Lawlink" (the Legal Tech Resources Center), drop down to "Legal Research Resources." In that, go to "Legal Information Institute" to see the different materials that may be accessed.

LEGAL WRITING: FORM AND SUBSTANCE

CHAPTER

9

CHAPTER OUTLINE

Introduction

Legal Writing—The Preliminaries

The Importance of Good Writing Skills

Pleadings and Discovery

General Legal Correspondence

The Legal Memorandum

AFTER COMPLETING THIS CHAPTER, YOU WILL KNOW:

▶ What factors you should consider before undertaking a legal-writing assignment.

▶ What factors you should consider when drafting a legal document.

▶ Some techniques for improving your writing skills.

▶ Some basic guidelines for structuring sentences and paragraphs.

▶ The purpose and format of the most common types of legal letters.

▶ How to prepare a legal memorandum.

INTRODUCTION

To some extent, legal research, analysis, and writing are all part of the same process. Once you locate the law that applies to an issue in dispute, you need to interpret that law and analyze how it applies to the facts of the client's case. After that, you must be able to summarize the results of your research and analysis in writing to communicate those results clearly to your supervising attorney.

Much legal writing, of course, is not directly related to the research process. As a paralegal, your day will often involve other types of writing responsibilities as well. You will be expected to know how to draft letters to clients and opposing counsel, internal memos, pleadings to be submitted to the court, and a variety of other documents.

Although a paralegal may be involved in drafting many kinds of legal documents, the same basic principles of writing apply to all. In this chapter, we provide some guidelines and suggestions for how to write effectively and describe some of the types and formats of legal documents commonly prepared by paralegals.

LEGAL WRITING—THE PRELIMINARIES

Much of your work as a paralegal will involve writing. We will look at writing skills and the kinds of legal materials that paralegals create in subsequent sections. Here, you will read about some general requirements involved in legal writing.

Whenever you receive a writing assignment, you need to understand at the outset (1) the nature of your assignment, (2) when it must be completed, and (3) what type of writing approach is appropriate to the assignment. We examine each of these basic requirements here.

Understanding the Assignment

The practice of law is often hectic, and frequently paralegals are asked to research, analyze, and report results on particular issues within a short time. When you receive a writing assignment, make sure you understand the exact nature of the request so you can execute your task as efficiently as possible. The writing style, format, and methodological approach used in legal writing vary, depending on the specific objectives of the document you are supposed to create. If you need to ask questions, do so. Do not equate asking questions with incompetence. If the assignment is not clear in your mind, you may waste time doing irrelevant work. As the old saying goes, the only "dumb question" is the one that is not asked.

Time Constraints and Flexibility

The time factor is an important consideration in legal writing. When you receive a writing assignment, you need to know when it must be completed. In some situations, you will be required to submit writings to a court by a certain date, which is inflexible. Additionally, clients usually demand quick responses to questions. And frequently, during the course of litigation or other legal activities, important new issues arise that must be addressed quickly. As a paralegal, you will need to assess such situations realistically. If little time is given for the completion of a project, use your informed judgment to decide what information is crucial to the writing and what can be omitted.

In addition to time constraints, other circumstances may influence the way a paralegal handles an assignment. For example, external events, such as newly enacted laws, may affect the legal treatment of an issue. Additionally, a client may unexpectedly demand a change in the course of action. These situations require flexibility. Whenever you undertake a writing task, be prepared for the possibility

Much of a paralegal's work involves legal writing, whether it be a research memorandum, a letter to a client, or a pleading or motion to be filed with a court. Excellent writing skills are a must for the professional paralegal. How can you become a better writer?

(Courtesy of © PhotoDisc, Inc.)

that you may have to make quick changes and go in new directions before your assignment is completed.

Writing Approaches

Another thing to determine when you receive a writing assignment is what type of writing is required. Some documents require an *objective* (unbiased) analysis, which either focuses on the facts or presents a balanced discussion of both sides of an issue. Other documents are *persuasive* and require you to advocate by presenting the facts and issues in the light most favorable to your client.

For example, assume that your supervising attorney hands you two lease agreements. You are to compare them and note whether the differences in the wording of the agreements lead to different obligations. Your concern is not to point out which agreement is better but to compare the documents objectively and point out which clauses lead to what kinds of obligations. Objective analysis may also be required when an attorney seeks assistance in providing clients with information regarding a particular legal matter. Clients often seek the advice of an attorney to determine whether they have a claim that merits filing a lawsuit. In this situation, an attorney may request the paralegal to investigate the issues and provide a memorandum containing an accurate and unbiased analysis of the issue.

If the writing assignment is intended to advocate a position, a different style of writing is required. For example, when you draft a pretrial motion asking the court to exclude certain evidence from a trial, you need to adopt a persuasive style of writing. Your goal is to convince the judge that the argument proposed is stronger than the opposing party's position. You therefore need to develop supportive legal arguments and present the matter in the light most favorable to the client.

THE IMPORTANCE OF GOOD WRITING SKILLS

The legal profession is primarily a communications profession. Effective written communications are particularly important. For paralegals, good writing skills go hand in hand with successful job performance. The better writer you are, the more likely it is that your finished products will be satisfactory to your supervising attorney. You should also keep in mind that some of your written projects, such as correspon-

Developing Paralegal Skills

CREATING A USER-FRIENDLY DOCUMENT

Lisa Barnes works as a paralegal for a large law firm. A partner of the firm asks Lisa to draft a policy on sexual harassment for a corporate client. The attorney gives Lisa several sheets of handwritten instructions and notes on what should be contained in the document. Lisa creates a draft of the policy and begins to proofread it. She realizes that although she used plain English when possible and followed the rules of good writing, the document is somewhat daunting in its appearance. She decides to add a series of headings and subheadings to break up the "fine print" and make the document more inviting to readers.

TIPS FOR CREATING A USER-FRIENDLY DOCUMENT

- Use plain English whenever it is feasible to do so, especially when writing for an audience that may have little legal training.
- Use short sentences, but do not overdo it—too many short sentences in a row can make the writing choppy and interrupt the flow of the text.
- Use the active voice unless the situation calls for a passive construction.
- Be consistent in style and word usage. For example, do not hyphenate a phrase in one place in the document and not elsewhere, and use the same line spacing between paragraphs and sections in the document.
- Format the document attractively. For example, add enough margin space to frame the text appropriately.
- Divide the document into sections preceded by headings to make the progression of thought immediately clear to the reader.
- Add subheadings to further divide visually long sections of text. If you add subheadings, always add at least two.
- Make sure that the relationship between the sections and subsections is clear. Often, this can be done in the document's introduction. Alternatively, transitional sentences at the beginning of each section or subsection can be used to clarify the progression of thought from one section or subsection to the next.

dence, represent the firm for which you work. A well-written document reflects positively on the firm and upholds its reputation for good performance. Some additional guidance is given in the *Developing Paralegal Skills* feature above.

In the following sections, we offer some guidelines you can follow as you strive to improve your writing. Paralegals seriously interested in improving their writing skills also will have close at hand a dictionary, a thesaurus, a style manual (such as Strunk and White's *The Elements of Style* or *The Chicago Manual of Style),* and perhaps a book on English grammar.

Organize and Outline Your Presentation

Once you know what it is you want to demonstrate, discuss, or prove to your reader, you need to decide how best to organize your ideas to achieve this end. Organization is essential to effective legal writing, so you should have an organizational framework in mind before you begin writing. Most people find that an outline—whether it is a simple sketch in pencil or a detailed outline created by a computer program—makes writing easier. It not only saves time but also produces a more organized result.

When creating an outline, you decide the sequence in which topics should be discussed. Often, lawyers put their strongest argument first in legal writing. Aside from that, some issues will need to be addressed before others, either for logical reasons or for purposes of clarity and readability. Similar issues should be grouped together, either in the same section or under the same topic heading. Other factors to consider when organizing your presentation are format and structural devices.

Choice of Format

An important requirement in legal writing is selecting the appropriate format. The format of a document concerns such things as the width of margins, the indentation of paragraphs, and the number of line spaces between paragraphs or other sections. Documents to be filed with a court must conform to the procedural rules of the particular jurisdiction. (Many courts post their requirements online.) Most law firms also adopt special formats for other types of documents, such as correspondence sent to clients and opposing counsel and internal legal memoranda. When writing such documents, you need to know what format your firm prefers to use.

Structural Devices

If you are writing about a complex legal research project involving many issues, you may want to divide your presentation into several sections, with a section for each issue. You can make it easier for the reader to follow the discussion by including a "road map" to the document. For example, you might begin with an introduction that highlights the points that will be discussed and the conclusion that will be reached, thus orienting the reader to the document's contents. You might also use numbered or bulleted lists as a device to let the reader know the structure of your argument or discussion. In addition, try to "walk" your reader through the analysis and discussion by including descriptive headings and subheadings in the body of the document so that the reader never gets lost.

chronologically
In a time sequence; naming or listing events in the time order in which they occurred.

Arranging events **chronologically**—that is, in a time sequence—can also serve as a structural device. A chronologically structured discussion is sometimes easier to follow. This is particularly true when you are describing the factual background leading to a lawsuit. Even if you are discussing legal issues instead of facts, you might want to use a chronological structure for at least part of your discussion. For example, if you are writing about the development of a particular rule of law over time, you will want to structure that part of the discussion chronologically.

Write to Your Audience

Paralegals prepare legal documents and correspondence for a wide range of people. When you draft legal correspondence or legal documents, keep in mind that these documents are not ends in themselves. They are created for someone (a judge, an attorney, a client, a witness, or some other person) to read. The goal of legal writing is to *communicate* information or ideas clearly to the reader. It is therefore important to tailor the writing to the intended audience. For example, a letter directed to an attorney may include legal terms and concepts that would be inappropriate in a letter to a client, who probably would not understand them. Similarly, a motion written to present to a judge should not include detailed explanations of classic cases, as the judge would be familiar with the facts of such cases.

In addition to the reader's legal knowledge, paralegals should consider how well the reader understands the subject matter. You cannot presume, especially in cases dealing with technical and scientific matters, that your reader knows as much as the attorney or yourself. Indeed, you should normally assume the contrary—that the reader has had neither the time nor the background to gain an understanding of every legal or factual matter presented. Both in consideration of your reader's needs and in the interests of effective communication, you should present your information or analysis clearly, carefully leading the reader from Point A to Point B, from Point B to Point C, and so on.

Avoid Legalese: Use Everyday English

As a paralegal, writing to your audience often requires you to minimize or eliminate legal jargon, or **legalese**. Legalese consists of terms that are used by legal professionals but that are unknown to most people outside the legal profession. Therefore, if you are writing a letter to a client, either avoid using legal terms the client may not understand or define such terms. For example, if you are advising a client of the date on which *voir dire* will take place, consider saying "jury selection"—or perhaps "*voir dire* (jury selection)"—instead. Although some legal terminology in legal writing is unavoidable, you should minimize the use of language that may confuse the reader. (See this chapter's *Technology and Today's Paralegal* feature on the next page for a discussion of online sources offering instructions on and some examples of "plain English" writing.)

Lawyers have traditionally used certain terms in legal documents—words such as *hereof*, *therein*, and *thereto*—that you should avoid whenever possible in your writing. These and similar words sound strange and excessively formal to the ordinary person. Legal documents are also often filled with redundancies, or repetiton. Consider the following phrase from an agreement to finance a business:

> If Borrower shall have made any representation or warranty herein . . . which shall be in any material respect false and/or erroneous and/or incorrect . . .

What is the difference between *false, erroneous,* and *incorrect*? Often, these terms are used synonymously, and it is hard to imagine that something could be erroneous and still be correct—so why should it be necessary to add *incorrect* to the clause?

Other commonly used legal phrases containing obvious redundancies include *all the rest, residue, and remainder; null and void; full and complete;* and *cease and desist.* In the first phrase, the words *rest, residue,* and *remainder* mean essentially the same thing. In the second phrase, the words *null* and *void* are synonymous, as are the coupled terms in the other phrases. Yet such phrases are commonplace in legal documents, largely because they have traditionally been used in the legal profession. Also, lawyers have a natural inclination to want to make sure that all aspects of a given subject are covered.

As a paralegal, you should try to minimize the use of legalese, including redundancies, in your own writing. When translating legalese into plain English, however, you need to make sure that you correctly understand the intent of the legal phrase. If you have any doubts, always ask your supervising attorney.

Be Brief and to the Point

Just as the use of legalese can hinder communication, so, too, can the use of too many words. Writing effectively requires efficiency in word usage. Unnecessary words can become stumbling blocks for readers and prevent a clear understanding of the point you wish to make. Moreover, concise statements are much more powerful and persuasive. When proofreading your document, take time to make sure that your statements are brief and to the point. Exhibit 9.1 on page 277 offers some examples of how efficient word usage can enhance clarity.

Writing Basics: Sentences

A good writer uses a high proportion of short, concrete sentences because they are easier to understand. Additionally, forceful sentences include active, dynamic verbs rather than nominalizations (verbs transformed into nouns). For example, it is

legalese
Legal language that is difficult for the general public to understand.

For a good discussion about legal writing, go to the American Bar Association Web site at **www.abanet.org** and enter "legal writing" in the search box.

Technology and Today's Paralegal

ONLINE "PLAIN ENGLISH" GUIDELINES

The ability to write clearly and effectively is a valuable asset to any paralegal, because almost every paralegal's job requires a certain amount of writing. As mentioned elsewhere, clear and effective writing means keeping legalese—legal terminology typically understood only by legal professionals—to a minimum or even eliminating it entirely. The problem is how to convert traditional legal language into clear and understandable prose. Today's paralegals can find helpful instruction in the art of writing in plain English at many online locations.

GOVERNMENT PUBLICATIONS

The U.S. government publishes some of the best online plain English guides. *A Plain English Handbook,* put out by the Securities and Exchange Commission (SEC), is available at **www.sec.gov/pdf/handbook.pdf**. Although the handbook was intended to help individuals create clearer and more informative SEC disclosure documents, the guidelines given in the booklet can apply to any written communication. For guidelines on legal writing, see the Office of the Federal Register's booklet *Drafting Legal Documents* at **www.archives.gov**. (Enter "Drafting Legal Documents" in the Search box.)

The U.S. government has an official Web site dedicated to the use of plain language (**www.plainlanguage.gov**) and publishes a guide called *Writing User-Friendly Documents.* Foreign governments also provide useful information. For example, the Australian government publishes a booklet called *Plain English at Work* that can be accessed online by doing a search for the title "Plain English at Work" and "Australia."

WORLDWIDE ORGANIZATIONS

Since the 1970s, the plain English movement, which is fighting to have public information (such as laws) written in plain English, has received worldwide attention. A British organization called the Plain English Campaign is one of the most prominent groups in this movement. The Plain English Campaign has worked to promote the use of plain English in many nations, including the United States. You can find several helpful guides at its Web site (**www.plainenglishcampaign.com**), including *How to Write in Plain English* and *The A-Z of Alternative Words.* Another campaign, called Fight the Fog, is directed at institutions in the European Union (EU). Search for "Fight the Fog Europa" to get to the EU Web site that offers a booklet called *How to Write Clearly,* as well as other news and publications in several languages.

TECHNOLOGY TIP

Paralegals interested in improving their plain English writing skills have many Internet resources to which they can turn. The guides mentioned above provide practical information and suggest alternative wording. In addition, paralegals can take online writing courses. Many universities now offer such courses that you may find worth your time to take.

simpler and more effective to say "the plaintiff decided to settle the case" than "the plaintiff made a decision to settle the case." In the first example, the verb *decide* is direct and forceful. In the second example, the conversion of *decided* into *made a decision* detracts from the forcefulness of the verb.

Writing in the active voice also makes sentences easier to understand. The active voice sets up a subject-verb-object sentence structure, whereas the passive voice uses an object-verb-subject format. For example, "The defendant stole the dia-

Do not write:
Ms. Carpenter never drives at night due to the fact that she has poor night vision.

Write instead:
Ms. Carpenter does not drive at night because she has poor night vision.

Do not write:
The new client who brought his business to our attention yesterday has a number of issues pertaining to his legal problems that he needs to discuss with us as soon as possible.

Write instead:
The client who hired us yesterday needs to discuss his legal problems immediately.

Do not write:
The defendant worked for one of the members of an organized crime ring for a period of seven years. During that seven-year period of time, the defendant witnessed crimes numbering in the hundreds.

Write instead:
During the seven years that the defendant worked for a member of an organized crime ring, he witnessed hundreds of crimes.

EXHIBIT 9.1
Using Words Efficiently

mond" uses the active voice. Contrast the simplicity and strength of this statement with its passive equivalent: "The diamond was stolen by the defendant." The use of the active voice puts people, actors, movers, and doers into your writing and thus makes your writing more lively. Sometimes, however, you may want to maintain the facelessness of the actor or doer. For example, if your firm is defending a plaintiff who has been accused of stealing a diamond, consider writing "the diamond that was stolen" instead of "the diamond that the plaintiff allegedly stole." In this situation, the passive voice effectively removes the plaintiff from the action.

Make sure you use correct grammar when writing legal documents. Grammatical and punctuation errors, such as those in the following sentences, distract your reader and may reflect poorly on your (and your firm's) professional reputation.

- *Incorrect:* The plaintiff should *of* consulted with the defendant.
- *Correct:* The plaintiff should *have* consulted with the defendant.
- *Incorrect:* The defendant could not possibly have *did* what the plaintiff alleged.
- *Correct:* The defendant could not possibly have *done* what the plaintiff alleged.
- *Incorrect:* The *plaintiffs* allegations were vague and ambiguous.
- *Correct:* The *plaintiff's* allegations were vague and ambiguous.

When proofreading documents, make sure they are free of errors involving subject-verb agreement, punctuation, spelling, the use of apostrophes, and other elements.

Writing Basics: Paragraphs and Transitions

A paragraph is a group of sentences that develops a particular idea. A paragraph should have unity and coherence. Each paragraph should begin with a *topic sentence* that indicates what the paragraph is about. Each subsequent sentence in the paragraph should contribute to the development of the topic; if it does not, consider placing the sentence elsewhere or simply deleting it. When you write, be conscious of why you begin a new paragraph—or why you do not. Keep paragraphs short, if possible. Create a new paragraph whenever you start discussing another idea. Paragraphs that are not logically constructed are often confusing.

Take your reader with you as you move from one paragraph to another. Although the connection between paragraphs may be clear to you, the writer, it may not be clear to your reader. You need to show, by including transitional sentences or phrases, how a topic discussed in one paragraph relates to the subsequent paragraph. Exhibit 9.2 lists some terms and phrases writers commonly use to effect smooth transitions.

Avoid Pronoun Confusion

It is common to use a pronoun (such as *she, it,* or *this*) to refer to a noun mentioned earlier. Confusion can arise, though, when the pronoun might refer to several different nouns. Suppose you are explaining an area of the law that is currently under review. You write: "Amendments have been proposed to the Federal Trade Commission's Telemarketing Sales Rule, commonly known for the Do Not Call Registry. This has been a point of contention because. . . ." It is not clear what *this* refers to in the second sentence. Is the point of contention, the proposed amendments, the Telemarketing Sales Rule, or the Do Not Call Registry? To make your meaning clear, you need to repeat the noun: "The Do Not Call Registry has been a point of contention because. . . ."

Be Alert for Sexist Language

The language of the law has traditionally used masculine pronouns inclusively—that is, to refer to both males and females. Jurists, legal scholars, and others in the legal profession are moving away from this tradition. Take special care to become aware

EXHIBIT 9.2
Transitional Terms and Phrases

---

1. **Words that indicate a conceptual or causal sequence or relationship. Examples:**

   The *third* element required for a cause of action under negligence theory is that the plaintiff must have suffered a legally recognizable injury.

   As a result of the fall, the plaintiff was injured.

2. **Words that indicate a chronological sequence of events. Examples:**

   After the fall, the plaintiff was taken to Nita City Hospital & Clinic.

   Before the plaintiff's accident, she was in excellent health.

3. **Words that refer back to the subject discussed in the previous paragraph. Examples:**

   Courts make exceptions to *this rule* in certain situations, however.

   The act does not apply to employers who have fewer than fifteen employees, however.

   If the *above-mentioned conditions* are not met, the injured party cannot recover damages.

   In contrast to negligence actions, actions in strict liability do not require the plaintiff to prove that the defendant breached a duty of care.

   If the *plaintiff* had not been *injured in the fall*, then she would have no cause of action against the store owner.

4. **Words that introduce summaries. Examples:**

   In short, the plaintiff has a valid claim against the defendant.

   In summary, the plaintiff met all four conditions for a negligence action against the defendant.

   To conclude, the plaintiff established the element of causation by demonstrating that she would not have been injured if it had not been for the defendant's actions.

of and avoid sexist language in your own writing. For example, if you see a word with "man" or "men" in it (such as *policeman, fireman,* or *workmen's compensation*) use a gender-neutral substitute (such as *police officer, firefighter,* or *workers' compensation*). In the past few decades, writers have devised various ways to avoid using masculine pronouns when the referent's gender is unknown, including the following:

- Use *he or she* rather than *he.*
- Alternate between the use of masculine and feminine pronouns.
- Make the noun plural so that a gender-neutral plural pronoun (*they, their,* or *them*) can be used.
- Repeat the noun rather than using a pronoun.

Proofread and Revise Your Document

A crucial part of legal writing involves proofreading and revising your document. When you receive a writing assignment, allow time to proofread and revise whatever you are writing. A writer can rarely turn out an error-free document on the first try, and as a paralegal, you will be especially concerned with accuracy. Proofreading allows you to discover and correct typographical errors, to see whether your document reflects a logical progression of thought from one topic to another, and to verify whether you have covered all of the relevant facts or issues. You should use the spell checker in your word-processing program, and perhaps the grammar checker as well, to assist you in proofreading. Don't, however, count on these tools to catch all your errors.

Writing is a process, and the best legal writing goes through many drafts before it is submitted to a court or sent to an opponent. When going over the initial drafts of a document, look for gaps in the content development or legal reasoning. Check to make sure that the argument is organized effectively and the rationale is well developed. It is often helpful to read the document out loud or have someone who is unfamiliar with the case or topic read the draft to provide constructive criticism. Another technique is to take a break and work on another project, then come back to revise the document when you can look at it from a fresh perspective. Ask yourself whether the document says what you intended it to say and what you can do to improve its effectiveness. Additional tips for good editing are offered in the *Developing Paralegal Skills* feature on page 282.

When you write your first draft, you have much to think about, and you may overlook many details. When proofreading your document, you can pay more attention to organizational coherence, transitions, paragraph construction, sentence formation, word choice, sexist language, and the like. You might find it helpful to develop a "writing checklist" to remind you of certain things you want to avoid or achieve in your writing—particularly if there is a required format for the type of document on which you are working. In short, when you are writing legal documents, realize that creating a polished document takes time, and a good portion of that time should be spent in proofreading and revising your written work product. (For some tips for making your legal writing easier, see this chapter's *Featured Contributor* article on the following two pages.)

PLEADINGS AND DISCOVERY

Many writing tasks undertaken by paralegals involve forms that must be submitted to the court or to opposing counsel before a trial begins or after the trial has commenced. These documents will be covered in detail later in this text, in Chapters 10, 12, and 13. You can see those chapters for explanations and illustrations of the forms required for pretrial procedures (pleadings, discovery procedures, and pretrial motions) and for motions made during the trial. Keep in mind that most documents submitted to the court should be written persuasively.

featured contributor

TIPS FOR MAKING LEGAL WRITING EASIER

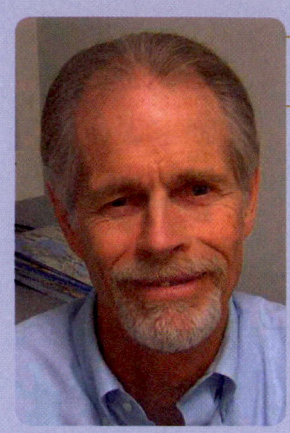

William Putman

BIOGRAPHICAL NOTE

William Putman received his Juris Doctor degree from the University of New Mexico School of Law and has been a member of the New Mexico Bar since 1975. For ten years, he was an instructor in the Paralegal Studies programs at Central New Mexico Community College in Albuquerque, New Mexico, and Santa Fe Community College in Santa Fe, New Mexico.

Putman is the author of the Pocket Guide to Legal Writing *and the* Pocket Guide to Legal Research. *He also wrote the textbooks* Legal Analysis and Writing; Legal Research, Analysis, and Writing; *and* Legal Research. *He authored the legal writing column in* Legal Assistant Today *for two years and published several articles on legal analysis and writing in the magazine.*

UNDERSTAND THE ASSIGNMENT

A legal-writing assignment may seem to be a daunting task. But all writing assignments are made easier if you answer some preliminary questions before you begin to conduct research or start writing.

Is the assignment clearly understood? An important step in the writing process is to be sure that you understand the task you have been assigned. If you have any questions concerning the general nature or specifics of the assignment, ask. Most attorneys welcome inquiries and prefer that a paralegal ask questions rather than proceed in a wrong direction. Misunderstanding the assignment can result in wasting a great deal of time performing the wrong task or addressing the wrong issue.

What type of legal writing (document) is required? Before you begin, determine what type of legal writing the assignment requires—a legal research memorandum, correspondence, the rough draft of a court brief, and so on. This is important

because each type of legal writing has a different function, requirements, and format.

Who is the audience? When assessing the requirements of an assignment, identify the intended audience. The intended reader may be a judge, an attorney, or a client. It is necessary to ensure that the writing is crafted in a manner suited to meet the needs of that reader. A legal writing designed to inform a client or other layperson of the legal analysis of an issue is drafted differently than a writing designed to convey the same information to an attorney.

What are the constraints on the assignment? Most assignments have time and length constraints. Assignments usually have a time deadline. Most assignments have a length constraint—that is, they should not exceed a certain number of pages. These constraints govern the amount of research you will conduct and require that you allocate sufficient time for both research and writing.

It is especially important that such documents contain the required information and be presented in the appropriate format. Form books and computerized forms offer guidelines, but you should always become familiar with the rules of the court in which the documents are being filed to ensure that you use the proper format.

GENERAL LEGAL CORRESPONDENCE

Paralegals often draft letters to clients, witnesses, opposing counsel, and others. Even when a message has already been conveyed orally (in person or by phone) to one of these parties, the paralegal may write a letter confirming in writing what was

What is the format for the type of document being prepared? Most law offices have rules or guidelines that govern the organization and format of most types of legal writing, such as case briefs, office memoranda, and correspondence. Courts have formal rules governing the format and style of briefs and other documents submitted for filing. Because the assignment must be drafted within the constraints of the required format, identify the format at the beginning of the process.

These preliminary questions are often overlooked or not given sufficient attention by beginning writers, resulting in headaches later. The task is made easier if you answer these questions.

SOME WRITING TIPS

Many paralegals assigned a legal-writing task find it difficult to make the transition from the research stage to the drafting stage. Here are some guidelines that help make the writing process easier.

Select the right time and place for your writing. Write during the time of day when you do your best work. For example, if you are a "morning person," write in the morning and save other tasks for later in the day. Also, make sure that the work environment is pleasant and physically comfortable. Have available and at hand all of the resources you will need—writing paper, a computer, research materials, and so on. Legal writing requires focus and concentration. Therefore, select a writing time and an environment that allow you to be as free from interruptions and distractions as possible.

Begin writing—do not procrastinate. Often, one of the most difficult steps in writing is starting to write. Do not put it off. The longer you put it off, the harder it will become to start your writing project. Start writing anything that has to do with

> *"All writing assignments are made easier if you answer some preliminary questions."*

the project. Do not expect what you start with to be great—just start. Once you begin writing, it will get easier.

Begin with a part of the assignment about which you feel confident. You do not have to write in the sequence of the outline. Write the easiest material first, especially if you are having trouble starting.

Do not try to make the first draft the final draft. The goal of the first draft should be to translate the research and analysis into organized paragraphs and sentences, not to produce a finished product. Just write the information in rough form. It is much easier to polish a rough draft than to try to make the first draft a finished product.

Do not begin to write until you are prepared. Do all the research and analysis before you begin to write. It is much easier to write a rough draft if you have completed the research and if the research is thorough.

If you become stuck, move to another part of the assignment. If you are stuck on a particular section, leave it. The mind continues to work on a problem when you are unaware of it. That is why solutions to problems often seem to appear in the morning. Let the subconscious work on the problem while you move on. The solution to the difficulty may become apparent when you return to the problem.

Establish a timetable. Break the project into logical units and allocate your time accordingly. This helps you avoid spending too much time on one section of the writing and running out of time. Do not become fanatical about the time schedule, however. You created the timetable, and you can break it. It is there as a guide to keep you on track and alert you to the overall time constraints.

discussed. Lawyers are extremely conscious of the need to document communications to avoid future problems. The existence of the written document clarifies any ambiguities that might have arisen in the oral conversation and confirms that the conversation took place.

Law firms normally have official letterhead and stationery. The letterhead contains certain information about the firm. Most letterheads include the firm's name, address, phone and fax numbers, and an e-mail address. Some firms have more descriptive letterheads that include the names of partners or the various geographic locations in which the firm has offices. You should always use your firm's letterhead when writing a letter on behalf of one of the firm's attorneys or when writing as a representative of the firm. The first page of any correspondence from

Developing Paralegal Skills

EFFECTIVE EDITING

Paralegal Dixie Guiliano is asked by her supervising attorney to draft a letter on behalf of the firm's client, Nora Ferguson, to an insurance company demanding settlement. Nora is an eighty-year-old woman who will never be able to walk again because her physician allegedly performed her hip-replacement surgery poorly. The attorney wants to settle the case out of court because of Nora's age and declining health.

Dixie creates the first draft using a settlement letter from another case as a sample. She then uses the spell-check and grammar-check features on her word-processing program to check for errors. Dixie knows, however, that using these features is only a preliminary step in proofreading the document. She also knows that careful editing will improve the quality and persuasiveness of her letter.

TIPS FOR EDITING

- Always edit from a printed copy of the document. It is much easier to proofread and revise on paper than on a computer screen.

- If you use another document as a sample, or cut and paste text from another document, double-check that you have accurately changed the names, dates, and other information.

- Allow some time to pass (preferably a day) before editing the first draft so that you can look at what you have written more critically. Review each draft in its entirety, checking for different elements.

- Edit the content first. Ensure that the document is complete and says what you intended. Look for gaps in your reasoning. Make sure you have discussed all the points (including cases or statutes) that you planned to discuss. Check the organization to ensure that the progression of ideas is logical.

- Next, look at your style. Make sure the document is aimed at the appropriate audience and that you have omitted unnecessary words. Change passive sentences into active voice, if possible.

- Make sure that you use terms, headings, and other devices (such as numbered lists) consistently throughout the document.

- Check your grammar and spelling. Confirm that the verb agrees with the subject in every sentence and that the proper verb tense is used. Check plurals and possessives.

- Finally, check your punctuation to verify that it is correct and used consistently throughout the document.

the firm should be on letterhead paper. Additional pages can be printed on numbered continuing sheets using plain, matching stationery.

In this section, you will read about some typical requirements relating to legal correspondence. Keep in mind, though, that the particular law firm, corporate legal department, or government agency for which you work will probably have its own specific procedures and requirements.

General Format for Legal Correspondence

Although there are many types of legal correspondence, the general format of a legal letter includes the components discussed below and illustrated in Exhibit 9.3.

Date

Legal correspondence must be *dated*. The date appears below the official letterhead of the firm. The date should also be part of the file name in electronic files. Make sure that the date is correctly keyed in. Be especially careful after the turn of a year.

EXHIBIT 9.3
Components of a Legal Letter

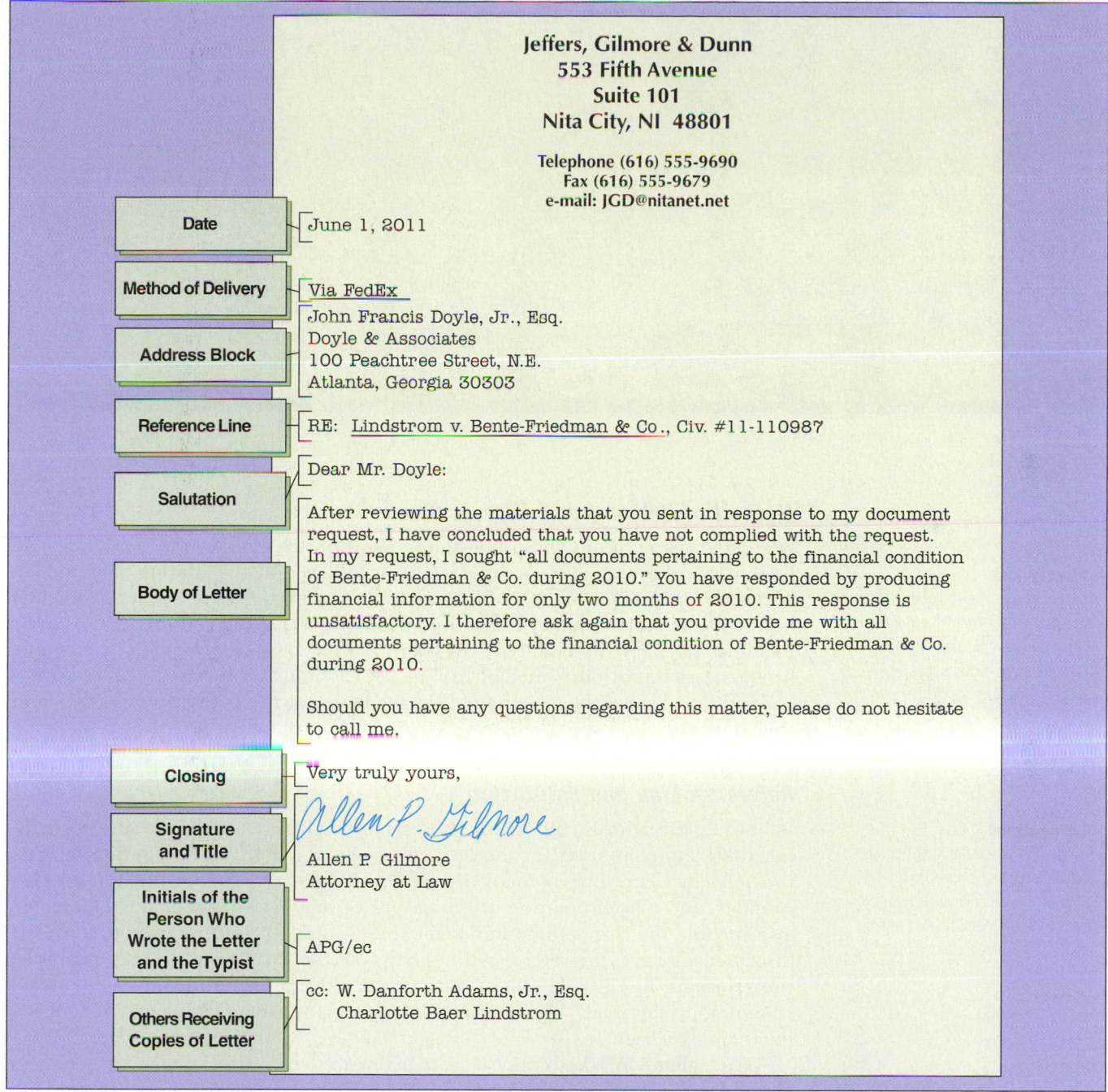

Many people continue to use the preceding year on correspondence, checks, and other documents simply out of habit. In a legal document, however, entering the wrong year could have legal consequences.

As explained earlier, dates serve an important function in legal matters. The date of a letter may be critical in matters involving legal notice of a particular event. Additionally, legal correspondence normally is filed chronologically. Without any indication of when the letter was written, accurate filing of the letter would be difficult, if not impossible. As a general rule, you should always place a date on every written item that you create, including telephone messages, memos to file, and personal reminders to yourself.

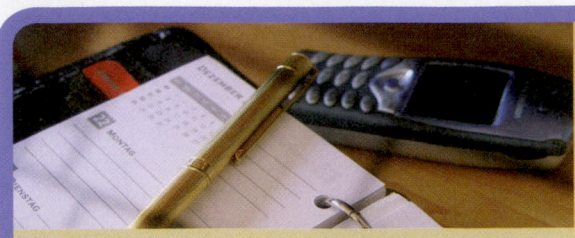

In the **Office**

TIME MANAGEMENT

Many paralegals learn the hard way—through trial and error—that the ability to manage time effectively is an essential part of doing a good job. One of the easiest things to overlook when engaging in research and writing is that good writing takes time—you may need to revise a document several times before you are satisfied with its quality. Whenever you are given a writing assignment, make sure you allow yourself enough time to revise and polish your final document. You have a duty to your supervising attorney, the firm, and the client to serve their best interests. Their interests are served by the production of clear and convincing legal documents—and by your ability to manage your time so that this goal can be achieved.

address block

The part of a letter that indicates to whom the letter is addressed. The address block is placed in the upper left-hand portion of the letter, above the salutation (or reference line, if one is included).

Method of Delivery and Address Block

Below the date is a line indicating the method of delivery, or how the letter is to be sent (if other than by U.S. mail), which is followed by the **address block**, which indicates to whom the letter is addressed. If the letter is to be sent by FedEx, the line before the recipient's name and address will read "Via FedEx." If the letter is to be hand-delivered, the line will read "By Hand Delivery." Communication by facsimile can be described by the words "By Fax" or "By Facsimile." The address block should contain the name of the person to whom the letter is written, the person's title, and the name and address of the person's firm or place of business.

Reference Line and Salutation

reference line

The portion of the letter that indicates the matter to be discussed in the letter, such as "RE: Summary of Cases Applying the Family and Medical Leave Act of 1993." The reference line is placed just below the address block and above the salutation.

Following the address block, the writer may include a **reference line** identifying the matter discussed in the letter. In a letter regarding a pending lawsuit, the reference line may contain the name of the case, its case file (or docket) number, and a brief notation of the nature of the legal dispute. Many attorneys also include the firm's file number for the case. In an informative letter (to be discussed shortly), the reference line may take the form of a title. For example, the reference line in a letter concerning the closing procedures for a financing transaction may read "RE: Closing Procedures for ABC Company's $4,000,000 Financing Package."

salutation

In a letter, the formal greeting to the addressee. The salutation is placed just below the reference line.

The **salutation**, which appears just below the reference line, is a greeting to the addressee. Because legal correspondence is a professional means of communication, the salutation, as well as the body of the letter, should be formal. There are, of course, circumstances in which a formal greeting may not be necessary. For example, if the addressee is someone you know quite well, it may be appropriate to address the person by his or her first name, rather than by "Mr." or "Ms." In these situations, you must use your discretion to determine the appropriate level of formality. Generally, when in doubt, use a formal salutation.

Body and Closing

The main part of the letter is the body of the letter. The body of the letter should be formal and should effectively communicate information to the reader. As a representative of the firm, the paralegal must carefully proofread all outgoing correspondence to ensure that the letter is accurate, clearly written, and free of grammatical or spelling errors.

Following the body of the letter are standard concluding sentences. These final sentences are usually courteous statements such as "Thank you for your time and attention to this matter" or "Should you have any questions or comments, please call me at the above-listed number." These brief concluding statements are followed by the **closing**. The closing in legal correspondence is formal—for example, "Sincerely" or "Very truly yours."

Finally, you should always include your title in any correspondence written by you on behalf of the firm. Your title ("Paralegal" or "Legal Assistant" or other title) should immediately follow your name. This, of course, is not a concern when you prepare correspondence for an attorney who will provide a signature.

closing

In a letter, an ending word or phrase placed above the signature, such as "Sincerely" or "Very truly yours."

Types of Legal Letters

There are several types of legal correspondence, and each type serves a different purpose. Types of legal letters with which you should become familiar include informative letters, confirmation letters, opinion (advisory) letters, and demand letters.

Informative Letters

A letter that conveys information to another party is an **informative letter**. As a paralegal, you will write many such letters—to clients, for example. Informative letters might be written to advise a client about current developments in a case, an upcoming meeting or procedure, the general background on a legal issue, or simply a breakdown of the firm's bill. The letters should be tailored to the client's level of legal understanding.

Informative letters are also sent to opposing counsel and other individuals. For example, law firms often send litigation-scheduling information to opposing counsel, witnesses, and other persons who may be involved in a trial. Informative letters may also be used as transmittal (cover) letters when documents or other materials are sent to a client, a court, opposing counsel, or some other person. Exhibit 9.4 on the following page shows a sample letter written to an individual who will testify during an arbitration procedure.

informative letter

A letter that conveys information to a client, a witness, an adversary's counsel, or some other person regarding some legal matter (such as the date, time, place, and purpose of a meeting) or a cover letter that accompanies other documents being sent to a person or court.

Confirmation Letters

Another type of letter frequently written by paralegals is the confirmation letter. **Confirmation letters** are similar to informative letters in that they communicate certain information to the reader. Confirmation letters put into written form the contents of an oral discussion. In addition to providing attorneys with a permanent record of earlier conversations, confirmation letters also safeguard against any misinterpretation or misunderstanding of what was communicated orally. See Exhibit 9.5 on page 287 for an example of a confirmation letter.

confirmation letter

A letter that states the substance of a previously conducted verbal discussion to provide a permanent record of the oral conversation.

Opinion Letters

The function of an **opinion letter**, or **advisory letter**, is to provide not only information but also advice. In contrast to informative letters, opinion letters actually give a legal opinion about the matter discussed. Attorneys providing opinion letters are required to provide a detailed analysis of the law and to bring the analysis to a definite conclusion, setting forth the firm's opinion on the matter.

In addition to rendering the law firm's legal opinion, opinion letters may also be used to inform a client of the legal validity of a specific action. For example, a company seeking to establish operations in a foreign country may seek a lawyer's opinion on whether a certain action it plans to undertake is legally permissible. The attorney (or a paralegal) will research the issue and then draft an advisory letter to the client. Opinion letters are commonly quite long and include detailed explanations of how

opinion (advisory) letter

A letter from an attorney to a client containing a legal opinion on an issue raised by the client's question or legal claim. The opinion is based on a detailed analysis of the law.

EXHIBIT 9.4
A Sample Informative Letter

Jeffers, Gilmore & Dunn
553 Fifth Avenue
Suite 101
Nita City, NI 48801

Telephone (616) 555-9690
Fax (616) 555-9679
e-mail: JGD@nitanet.net

June 24, 2011

Bernadette P. Williams
149 Snowflake Drive
Irving, TX 75062

RE: Kempf/Joseph Arbitration Proceedings

Dear Ms. Williams:

The arbitration will resume on Monday, August 1, 2011. Please arrive at the offices of the American Arbitration Association (the AAA) before 8:30 A.M. The offices of the AAA are located at 400 West Ferry Boulevard in Dallas. You will be called as a witness sometime before 12:00 noon.

Should you have any questions or concerns regarding your responsibilities as a witness, please do not hesitate to contact me.

Sincerely,

Elena Lopez

Elena Lopez
Paralegal

---

the law applies to the client's factual situation. Sometimes, the attorney just summarizes his or her conclusion in the opinion letter (as in the opinion letter shown in Exhibit 9.6 on page 288) and attaches a legal memorandum to the letter explaining the legal sources and reasoning used in forming that conclusion.

Opinion letters issued by a firm reflect legal expertise and advice on which a client can rely. Note that opinion letters must be signed by attorneys (see the *Ethics Watch* feature on page 291). Should doubts about the legal validity of an opinion letter surface at a later date, the client may bring a malpractice suit against the firm. The signature of an attorney represents the attorney's acceptance of responsibility for what is stated in the document and can serve as the basis for liability.

Demand Letters

demand letter
A letter in which one party explains its legal position in a dispute and requests that the recipient take some action (such as paying money owed).

Another basic type of letter is the demand letter. In a **demand letter**, one party explains its legal position in a dispute and requests that the recipient take some action (such as paying a debt owed). Typically, attorneys send a demand letter to a person or company before filing a lawsuit against that person or company. For example, your supervising attorney may ask you to draft a letter to a client's debtor demanding payment for an amount owed. Whatever the content of a demand letter, its purpose is to demand something on behalf of the client. In some situations, a demand letter is actually a prerequisite to filing suit (as is the case for suits based on certain consumer protection laws).

The demand letter should adopt a serious and persuasive tone, and the client's demand must not be frivolous. Although the letter should be insistent and adversarial, it should not come across as unreasonable or harassing. After all, demand letters seek to accomplish something rather than foreclose opportunities. A common form

EXHIBIT 9.5
A Sample Confirmation Letter

Jeffers, Gilmore & Dunn
553 Fifth Avenue
Suite 101
Nita City, NI 48801

Telephone (616) 555-9690
Fax (616) 555-9679
e-mail: JGD@nitanet.net

August 3, 2011

Pauline C. Dunbar
President
Minute-Magic Corporation
7689 Industrial Boulevard
San Francisco, CA 80021

RE: Purchase of real estate from C. C. Barnes, Inc.

Dear Ms. Dunbar:

The following information describes the current status of the negotiations between C. C. Barnes, Inc., and Minute-Magic Corporation:

Selling Price: $800,000
Financing Agreement: Citywide Bank
Interest Rate: 7.5%

This information confirms what I told you on the phone today, August 3, 2011. I look forward to seeing you next week. Should you have any questions or comments in the meantime, please give me a call.

Very truly yours,

Allen P. Gilmore
Attorney at Law

APG/ec

of demand letter in litigation firms is a letter in which an attorney requests a response from an adversarial party in a lawsuit to an offer to settle the case. Exhibit 9.7 on page 289 illustrates this type of demand letter.

THE LEGAL MEMORANDUM

The legal memorandum is prepared for internal use within a law firm, legal department, or other organization. Generally, the legal memo presents a thorough summary and analysis of a particular legal problem.

As a paralegal, you may be asked to draft a legal memorandum for your supervising attorney. The attorney may be relying on the memo for a number of reasons. For example, the attorney may be preparing a brief on behalf of a client or an opinion letter regarding a client's claim. Thus, if you draft the memo, you will want it to be extremely thorough and clearly written. Because the legal memo is directed to attorneys who are knowledgeable in the law, there is no need to avoid sophisticated legal terminology or to define basic legal theories or procedures. As with all documents, attention to detail is important as is discussed in the *Developing Paralegal Skills* feature on page 290.

The purpose of the memo is to provide an attorney with all relevant information regarding the case, so the document is written objectively. It is an explanatory memo informing the attorney of all sides of the issues presented, including both the strengths

EXHIBIT 9.6
A Sample Opinion Letter

Jeffers, Gilmore & Dunn
553 Fifth Avenue
Suite 101
Nita City, NI 48801

Telephone (616) 555-9690
Fax (616) 555-9679
e-mail: JGD@nitanet.com

December 9, 2011

J. D. Joslyn
President and Chief Executive Officer
Joslyn Footwear, Inc.
700 Kings Avenue, Suite 4000
New City, NI 48023

Dear Ms. Joslyn:

After careful consideration of your plans to expand Joslyn Footwear, Inc., into Latin American markets, I have concluded that to implement the current plans would subject you to potentially significant liability.

The most serious flaw in the current plans concerns your construction of massive shoe-producing industrial plants. Unfortunately, the plans fail to conform to the minimum legal and industrial regulations in Mexico, Uruguay, and Argentina.

The enclosed legal memorandum explains in detail how the law applies to your situation and the reasons for my conclusion. Please call me if you have any questions.

Very truly yours,

Allen P. Gilmore

Allen P. Gilmore
Attorney at Law

APG/ec

Enclosure

---

and weaknesses of the client's claim or defense. Keep in mind that your goal in drafting a legal memorandum is to inform, explain, and evaluate the client's claim or defense.

A legal memorandum is organized in a logical manner. Although there is no one way to structure the legal memo, most are divided into sections that perform distinct functions. Of course, if the law firm or the attorney for whom you are working prefers a particular format, that format should be followed. Generally, legal memos contain the following sections: a heading, a statement of the facts, the questions presented, a brief conclusion in response to the questions presented, a discussion and analysis of the facts and the applicable law, and a conclusion.

Heading

The *heading* of a legal memorandum contains four types of information:

- The date on which the memo is submitted.
- The name of the person for whom the memo was prepared.
- The name of the person submitting the memo.
- A brief description of the matter, usually in the form of a reference line.

Exhibit 9.8 illustrates a sample heading for a legal memorandum.

EXHIBIT 9.7
A Sample Demand Letter

Jeffers, Gilmore & Dunn
553 Fifth Avenue
Suite 101
Nita City, NI 48801

Telephone (616) 555-9690
Fax (616) 555-9679
e-mail: JGD@nitanet.com

June 15, 2011

Christopher P. Nelson, Esq.
Nelson, Johnson, Callan & Sietz
200 Way Bridge
Philadelphia, PA 40022

RE: *Furman v. Thompson*

Dear Mr. Nelson:

This morning, I met with my clients, Mark and Andrea Furman, the plaintiffs in the lawsuit against your client, Laura Thompson. Both Mark and Andrea expressed a desire to withdraw their complaint and settle with Ms. Thompson. The Furmans' settlement demand is $50,000, payable by certified check no later than July 7, 2011. Considering the strength of the plaintiffs' claims against Ms. Thompson and the possibility of a jury award exceeding $200,000, the Furmans and I think that you and your client will find this demand quite reasonable.

Please contact me by Friday, June 25, 2011, if you plan to take advantage of the Furmans' settlement demand. If we do not hear from you by that date, we will interpret your inaction as a rejection of the Furmans' settlement offer.

Very truly yours,

Allen P. Gilmore

Allen P. Gilmore
Attorney at Law

APG/ec

Statement of the Facts

The *statement of the facts* introduces the legal issues by describing the factual elements of the dispute. Only the relevant facts are included in this section. Thus, a key requirement of paralegals is that they learn which facts are legally significant. In other words, as a paralegal, you will need to determine which facts have a bearing on the legal issues in the case and which facts are irrelevant.

Facts presented in a legal memo must not be slanted in favor of the client. The legal memo is not an adversarial argument on the client's behalf. Rather, it is an

EXHIBIT 9.8
Legal Memorandum—Heading

MEMORANDUM

DATE: August 6, 2011

TO: Allen P. Gilmore, Partner

FROM: Elena Lopez, Paralegal

RE: Neely, Rachel: Emotional Distress—File No. 00-2146
          Neely, Rachel, and Melanie: Emotional Distress—File No. 00-2147

Developing
Paralegal Skills

REVIEWING ATTORNEY-GENERATED DOCUMENTS

Leslie Carroll works as a paralegal for Jeremy O'Connell, a sole practitioner who owns a small general law practice. Jeremy frequently creates motions and other legal documents himself, because Leslie has her hands full with other writing tasks and general legal work associated with the practice. Typically, Jeremy e-mails his documents to Leslie, instructing her to send them to the recipients (if they are letters) or file them with a court (if they are pleadings, motions, or similar documents). Usually, though, Leslie takes the time to quickly review Jeremy's documents. Even though Jeremy has practiced law for more than twenty years, Leslie occasionally finds errors in his documents, some of which could have serious consequences.

TIPS FOR REVIEWING AN ATTORNEY'S DOCUMENTS

- Check all names, addresses, and other client data in the documents to ensure that they are current and correct. The attorney may have forgotten that a client moved to a different address recently, for example, and may have mistakenly taken the client's address from an older document.

- Check any documents to be filed with the court against the applicable court rules regarding the form and style that should be used in those documents.

- If you have a file on specific judges' preferences, review the information on the relevant judge to confirm that the document complies with his or her preferences.

- Make sure that you have the court's most current rules, and see to it that the document is filed with the court before the required deadline. Court rules and deadlines change, and it's important to keep up to date on the current rules.

- Check with the attorney if you have any question about how a particular document should be delivered.

objective presentation of both the facts and the legal issues. Therefore, you should never omit facts that are unfavorable to the client's claim or defense. The attorney for whom you work needs to know all of the facts that will influence the outcome of the case.

The statement of the facts should contain a logical and concise description of the events surrounding the conflict. Presenting events chronologically often helps to clarify the factual pattern in a case. Alternatively, facts relating to the same issue can be grouped together. The latter organizational technique is especially useful when the facts are complicated and numerous legal issues are presented.

Exhibit 9.9 on page 292 indicates what kinds of information are typically included in a statement of the facts. It also shows what writing style is generally used.

Questions Presented

The *questions presented* address the legal issues arising from the factual circumstances described in the statement of the facts. The questions should be specific and straightforward. They should refer to the parties by name, succinctly set out the legal problems, and specifically indicate the important and relevant events. The questions-presented section may involve just one simple issue or a number of complex issues. Regardless of the complexity of the matter, this section helps bring the main points of the conflict into focus. See Exhibit 9.10 on page 292 for an example of how the questions presented might be phrased.

Ethics Watch

LETTERS AND THE UNAUTHORIZED PRACTICE OF LAW

As has frequently been stressed in this text, engaging in the unauthorized practice of law is one of the most serious potential ethical and legal problems facing paralegals. To avoid liability for the unauthorized practice of law, never sign opinion (advisory) letters with your own name, and when you sign other types of letters, always indicate your status as a paralegal. Even if the person to whom you are sending the letter knows you quite well and knows you are a paralegal, indicate your status on the letter itself. By doing so, you will prevent potential confusion as well as potential legal liability. Even if your name and status are included in the letterhead (as is permitted under some state laws), as a precaution, type your title below your name at the end of the letter as well.

This advice is consistent with several rules and guidelines:

- NALA Code of Ethics, Canon 3: "A paralegal must not: (a) engage in, encourage, or contribute to any act which could constitute the unauthorized practice of law."

- ABA Model Guidelines, Guideline 4: "A lawyer is responsible for taking reasonable measures to ensure that clients, courts, and other lawyers are aware that a paralegal, whose services are utilized by the lawyer in performing legal services, is not licensed to practice law."

- NFPA Model Code of Ethics, Section EC 1.7(c): "A paralegal shall not use letterhead, business cards or other promotional materials to create a fraudulent impression of his/her status or ability to practice in the jurisdiction in which the paralegal practices."

Brief Conclusion

The *brief conclusion* (or *short answer* or *brief answer*) sets forth succinct responses to the questions presented in the previous section. The responses may vary in length. For example, as indicated in Exhibit 9.11 on the next page, certain questions can be answered simply by "yes," "no," "probably so," or "probably not," followed by a brief summary of the reason for that answer. For complicated legal questions, a more detailed statement might be appropriate. Even so, each conclusion should be limited to a maximum of one paragraph. The discussion of the legal analysis, which is the main part of the memo, provides ample opportunity for supporting details.

Discussion and Analysis

The *discussion and analysis* section of the legal memorandum, as the phrase implies, contains a discussion and legal analysis of each issue to be resolved. If the facts of the dispute concern only one legal issue, the entire discussion will revolve around that issue. Legal memoranda usually address multiple issues, however. When multiple issues are involved, the paralegal should organize the discussion into separate parts so that each legal issue can be analyzed separately. For example, if the dispute involves two potential legal claims, the discussion should be divided into

EXHIBIT 9.9
Legal Memorandum—
Statement of the Facts

STATEMENT OF THE FACTS

Rachel Neely ("Neely") and Melanie Neely ("Melanie") seek advice in connection with possible emotional distress claims against Miles Thompson. The claims arose as a result of (1) Neely's distress at hearing a car crash caused by Thompson and involving her eleven-year-old daughter, Melanie, and subsequently viewing Melanie's injuries; and (2) Melanie's distress related to statements made by Thompson.

In February 2009, Neely and Melanie moved to Union City from San Francisco. Neely began working for an investment firm in downtown Union City. At that firm, she became acquainted with the defendant, Thompson, who was Neely's boss. At first, the two had a friendly, professional relationship.

The relationship between Thompson and Neely became strained approximately six months after Neely began working as a result of Thompson's expression of romantic interest in Neely.

On April 2, 2011, Thompson visited the Neely home. Melanie was not aware of the problem her mother was having with Thompson. Thompson invited Melanie for a ride in his Corvette. Melanie willingly went with him. Meanwhile, Neely, who had gone to the grocery store, returned to the house to find Melanie missing. She panicked, called the neighbors, and then the police.

Thompson, who claims that he took Melanie for a ride so that she could be informed about her mother's "bad behavior," drove around Union City with Melanie for approximately thirty minutes. During this ride, Thompson told Melanie that her mother was a "selfish woman" who did not care about Melanie. Thompson also told Melanie that her mother would leave Melanie "once the right man came along." Upon returning to the Neely home, Thompson made a left turn from Oak Street onto Maple Road, and his car was hit by an oncoming vehicle. According to the police report of the accident, Thompson's blood-alcohol level indicated that he was intoxicated.

The Neely home is located on the corner of the intersection of Maple Road and Oak Street. Neely heard the crash and ran outside. Seeing the accident and recognizing Thompson's car, she approached the site of the accident. She saw Melanie bleeding profusely from head injuries.

As a result of the accident, Melanie spent two days at Union City Hospital, where she was kept under observation for possible internal injuries. Melanie is severely depressed and emotionally unstable as a result of Thompson's comments. She has frequent nightmares. Since the time of the accident, she has been under psychiatric therapy for these problems. Neely, who fainted after viewing her daughter's injuries, spent one day in Union City Hospital for extreme anxiety and trauma.

EXHIBIT 9.10
Legal Memorandum—
Questions Presented

QUESTIONS PRESENTED

1. Does Neely have a claim for the negligent infliction of emotional distress as a result of viewing the injuries sustained by her daughter in a car accident caused by Thompson's negligence?

2. Does Melanie have a claim for the intentional infliction of emotional distress arising out of Thompson's statements to her on April 2, 2011?

EXHIBIT 9.11
Legal Memorandum—
Brief Conclusion

BRIEF CONCLUSION

1. Probably not. Neely cannot recover under the rule that is currently applied in this jurisdiction. This rule requires that the plaintiff be present at the scene when the accident occurs.

2. Most likely, yes. Thompson's conduct toward Melanie appears to have been (1) reckless, (2) outrageous and extreme, and (3) the direct cause of Melanie's severe emotional distress.

two sections with a descriptive heading for each section. The headings of the two sections might read as follows:

I. Negligent Infliction of Emotional Distress.

II. Intentional Infliction of Emotional Distress.

The legal analysis presented in the memo should answer the following questions:

- What is the likelihood that the client's claim or defense will be successful?
- What law supports the strongest position?
- Is it case law or statutory law?
- If the strongest argument is under case law, how are the relevant cases factually similar and factually distinct from the client's?
- What law (or case) goes against the client's claim or defense?
- What arguments could the other side make?
- How can the attorney respond to the other side's strongest arguments?
- Are there any other options available to the client for resolving the dispute?

The discussion is the core of the legal memo. It provides an opportunity to demonstrate good research and writing skills. After the research is completed, you must relate the legal findings to the facts of the matter. One method of legal reasoning and analysis commonly used by paralegals and other legal professionals is called the *IRAC method*. As mentioned in Chapter 7, IRAC is an acronym consisting of the first letters of the words *issue, rule, application*, and *conclusion*. To use the IRAC method, you first state the issue you are researching. Then you state the rule of law that applies to the issue. The rule of law may be a rule stated by the courts in previous decisions, a state or federal statute, or a state or federal administrative agency regulation. Next, you apply the rule of law to the set of facts involved in the client's case. Finally, you set forth your conclusion on the matter. If there are two or more issues involved in the client's case, you can analyze each issue using the IRAC method.

Points of law should be identified and supported with proper citations. Occasionally, legal sources directly address a point that applies to the case at hand. In these situations, it is effective to quote directly from the text of the case, statute, or other legal source. You should not rely too heavily on quoted material, however. Although quotations from a case or other legal authority can lend extremely helpful support, the attorney for whom you are preparing the memo wants to see your analysis, not a reiteration of a court's opinion. Exhibit 9.12 on the following page presents a portion of a discussion section in a legal memorandum. We have annotated the exhibit to illustrate the basic IRAC elements.

When discussing how other cases have addressed certain issues, you need to include citations to the cases. As mentioned in Chapter 7, there are various guides to citation formats, including *The Bluebook: A Uniform System of Citation*, which is published by the Harvard Law Review Association, and the *ALWD Citation Manual*, which is published by the Association of Legal Writing Directors.

Conclusion

The *conclusion* is the culmination of the legal memo. Many issues have been analyzed, and both the strengths and weaknesses of the client's matter have been evaluated. Now you should conclude the analysis by taking a position. The conclusion is your opinion of how the issues discussed may be resolved. Exhibit 9.13 on the next page shows an example of a conclusion to a legal memorandum.

The concluding section may acknowledge the fact that research into a particular area bore little fruit. For example, there may be no cases on point to support one of the issues. The conclusion also may instruct the attorney that more information is needed or may demonstrate that a certain issue needs to be evaluated further.

EXHIBIT 9.12
Legal Memorandum—
Discussion (Excerpt Using the
IRAC Method)

DISCUSSION (excerpt)

I. Negligent Infliction of Emotional Distress

Recovery Restriction

Issue   *Are there any restrictions on recovering for the negligent infliction of emotional distress?*

Rule   An individual's right to emotional tranquillity is recognized by the law protecting persons against the negligent infliction of emotional distress. The method for determining whether protection should be afforded for emotional distress caused by the knowledge of a third person's injury as a result of a defendant's negligent actions is clear in this jurisdiction. *The rule adopted in this jurisdiction is the "impact rule," which requires that a plaintiff alleging emotional distress must also suffer a direct, physical impact from the same force that injured the victim. Saechao v. Matskoun,* 78 Or.App. 340, 717 P.2d 165, *rev. dismissed* 302 Or. 155, 727 P.2d 126 (1986). This "bright line" rule provides the courts with a test from which they can easily determine the relationship between compensability and the defendant's breach of duty owed to the victim. *Id.* at 169.

Application   *Neely was in her house when the accident occurred. She heard the crash and ran outside. Recognizing Thompson's car, Neely approached it and found Melanie bleeding profusely from head injuries. Neely did not suffer any direct physical impact from the car accident that injured Melanie.* Thus, Neely could not recover under the impact rule because she did not suffer any direct physical impact and Thompson owed her no duty.

Conclusion   The impact rule originated a century ago in some of the first cases recognizing negligent infliction of emotional distress. Although many states used to follow this rule, most jurisdictions have now abandoned it in favor of the "relative bystander" test or the "zone of danger" test. Some strong arguments can be made against the application of the impact rule. Although the rule limits a defendant's liability and offers an easy decision-making criterion for the courts, it also lends itself to arbitrary and often unjust results.

    Our state, however, most closely follows the rule as set forth in the Oregon courts. The impact test applied by the Oregon courts allows emotional distress claims only when (1) the defendant's conduct was intentional or equivalently reckless of another's feelings in a responsible relationship or (2) the defendant's conduct infringed some legally protected interest apart from causing the claimed distress, even when only negligently. See, e.g., *Hammond v. Central Lane Communications Center,* 312 Or. 17, 24, 816 P.2d 593 (1991); *Sherwood v. Oregon Department of Transportation,* 11 P.3d 664, 170 Or.App. 66 (2000); *Chouinard v. Health Ventures,* 179 Or.App. 507, 39 P.3d 951 (2002).

Finally, this section gives you an opportunity to make strategic suggestions. Paralegals should feel comfortable—especially after a careful legal analysis—in recommending a course of action. Not only do your recommendations reflect thorough analysis, but they also indicate that you are willing to exercise initiative and make a mature judgment, which will be helpful to your supervising attorney.

EXHIBIT 9.13
Legal Memorandum—
Conclusion

CONCLUSION

    It is unlikely that Neely has a cause of action against Thompson for the emotional distress that she suffered due to Thompson's negligence.

    It is likely that Melanie has a cause of action for the intentional infliction of emotional distress based on Thompson's outrageous comments to her about her mother.

    Note that Neely might pursue, on her own behalf, a claim for the intentional infliction of emotional distress against Thompson for his reckless behavior in taking Melanie from her home and telling Melanie outrageous things. I recommend that we speak with Neely about the effect on her of Thompson's statements to Melanie. This, in my opinion, is a strong claim. I believe that we could argue successfully that Thompson intended to injure Neely through this egregious act.

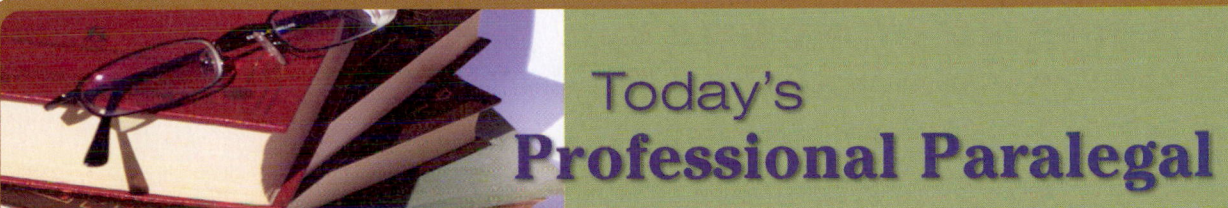

Today's
Professional Paralegal

PREPARING THE INTERNAL MEMORANDUM

Ken Lawson, a legal assistant, works for Rhonda Mulhaven. Rhonda is representing the defendant, the Gourmet House Restaurant, in a slip-and-fall case. Ken is surprised that the plaintiff filed suit, because the plaintiff admitted that she saw water on the floor but walked through it anyway. Ken knows that there are several defenses available, including assumption of risk.

RESEARCHING AND ANALYZING CASE LAW

Ken consults an online legal encyclopedia, which defines *assumption of risk* as follows:

> The plaintiff knew that the situation was dangerous and, despite her knowledge of the danger involved, voluntarily subjected herself to the danger or risk. When a plaintiff has assumed the risk of danger, then the plaintiff cannot recover from the defendant for her injuries.

Ken often uses the IRAC method to analyze legal problems. First, he states the issue. Second, he states the rule of law. Third, he applies the rule to the client's facts. And fourth, he reaches a conclusion. Ken has found this method useful because it helps him to think through all aspects of the problem and to apply the law to the facts to reach a conclusion. He decides to apply the IRAC method to the client's case.

APPLYING THE IRAC METHOD

First, Ken identifies the issue: Did the plaintiff assume the risk of falling when she walked across the wet floor? Next, Ken notes the applicable rule of law: a plaintiff who knows of a dangerous condition and voluntarily subjects himself or herself to it has assumed the risk and cannot hold a defendant liable. Ken then applies the rule of law to the facts: The plaintiff knew of the dangerous condition, because she knew that the floor was wet. She voluntarily subjected herself to the danger by walking across the wet floor. Ken then forms a conclusion: because the plaintiff knew of the dangerous condition and voluntarily subjected herself to it, she assumed the risk involved in walking across the wet floor. She normally cannot hold the defendant liable when she assumed the risk and was injured as a result.

Ken believes that the defense of assumption of risk might be appropriate in the client's case. He decides to continue researching case law and looks through a state digest. There he finds several cases that contain a definition of assumption of risk similar to the one he read in the encyclopedia. He reviews the cases and then uses KeyCite to check each case on Westlaw to make sure that it is still current law.

CREATING THE LEGAL MEMORANDUM

Ken sits down at his computer and prepares the following outline for a memorandum to Rhonda:

I.   Statement of the Facts—A chronological statement of the events that led to the injury.

II. Question Presented—Did the plaintiff assume the risk of falling when she walked across the wet floor?

III. Brief Conclusion—Yes.

IV. Discussion

    A. Did the plaintiff assume the risk of falling when she walked across the wet floor?

    B. Check the encyclopedia's definition of assumption-of-risk defense and state case law supporting this definition.

    C. Apply the rules in B above to the facts in this case.

V.   Conclusion—Based on the results of C above.

Having outlined the memo, Ken writes a first draft, edits and revises it, proofreads it carefully, and delivers it to Rhonda. Rhonda says that based on his research and the memorandum, she has been able to settle the case by convincing the plaintiff's attorney that his client has a weak case.

KEY TERMS AND CONCEPTS

address block *284*

chronologically *274*

closing *285*

confirmation letter *285*

demand letter *286*

informative letter *285*

legalese *275*

opinion (advisory) letter *285*

reference line *284*

salutation *284*

CHAPTER SUMMARY

LEGAL WRITING: FORM AND SUBSTANCE

Legal Writing—The Preliminaries

On receiving a writing assignment, paralegals should make sure that they clearly understand the nature of the assignment, when the assignment should be completed, and what type of writing approach should be used.

1. *Objective approach*—Some documents, such as legal memoranda, require an objective, or unbiased, analysis.

2. *Persuasive approach*—Other documents, such as pretrial motions, are persuasive and require the writer to advocate a particular position.

The Importance of Good Writing Skills

Good writing skills are essential for creating legal documents. The quality of your writing can improve with practice if you keep in mind the following guidelines:

1. *Organization*—The writing should be well organized and in the appropriate format. Create an outline before you begin writing. Use structural devices to help the reader follow the discussion.

2. *Audience*—Tailor your writing to the intended audience.

3. *Language*—Avoid legalese: use plain English. Be brief and to the point, omitting unnecessary words.

4. *Grammar and construction*—Present well-constructed sentences and paragraphs. Use short, concrete words and the active voice (subject-verb-object arrangement), if possible. Use effective transitions and gender-neutral pronouns.

5. *Proofread your documents*—Creating a polished document takes time, and a good portion of that time should be spent in proofreading and revising your written work product. Proofread to make sure that the document reflects a logical progression of thought from one topic to another, as well as for spelling, typographical, and other errors.

Pleadings and Discovery

Much legal writing consists of documents relating to litigation procedures, such as pleadings and discovery documents. Documents filed with the court are nearly always written persuasively. It is especially important that such documents contain all required information and be formatted correctly for the particular court.

General Legal Correspondence

Paralegals frequently are responsible for maintaining correspondence files and writing legal letters.

1. *Format*—Most firms (and other employers) have a preferred format for legal correspondence. The first page of a letter typically is printed on the firm's letterhead. Generally, letters should be formal in tone and include the following:

   a. The date.

   b. The method of delivery (mail, fax, hand delivery).

   c. The address block.

   d. The reference line (including case or file numbers when appropriate).

   e. The salutation.

   f. The body of the letter.

   g. The closing.

   h. The signature and title of the author (always include your title as a paralegal on letters you write).

   i. The initials of the person who wrote the letter and the typist.

   j. The names of any other persons who received a copy of the letter.

2. *Types of letters*—Paralegals commonly draft the following types of letters.

   a. Informative letters notify clients or others of some action or procedure or serve as transmittal documents (cover letters).

   b. Confirmation letters confirm an oral transaction, agreement, or conversation.

   c. Opinion letters convey to a client or other party a formal legal opinion or give advice on an issue. Only attorneys can sign opinion letters (not paralegals).

   d. Demand letters are letters in which one party explains its legal position in a dispute and requests the recipient to take some action (such as paying money owed).

The Legal Memorandum

The legal memorandum is a thoroughly researched and objectively written summation of the facts, issues, and applicable law relating to a particular legal claim. The purpose of the memo is to inform the attorney for whom the document is written of the strengths and weaknesses of the client's position.

1. *Format*—Generally, the legal memo is presented in a format that includes the following sections:

   a. Heading.

   b. Statement of facts.

   c. Questions presented.

   d. Brief conclusion in response to questions presented.

   e. Discussion and analysis of the facts and the applicable law.

   f. Conclusion.

2. *Legal analysis*—In addition to assessing the strengths and weaknesses of a client's case, a memorandum should analyze and present the legal arguments that the opponent can offer and explain how the attorney can respond to those arguments. Other options available to the client to resolve the dispute should also be analyzed.

STUDENT STUDYWARE™ CD-ROM

Interactive student CD in this book includes additional quizzing, plus video clips, case studies, and Key Terms flashcards.

ONLINE COMPANION™

For additional resources, please go to **www.paralegal.delmar.cengage.com**.

QUESTIONS FOR REVIEW

1. What factors should you consider before undertaking a legal-writing assignment?

2. What is the active voice? What is the passive voice? Why is it better to use the active voice in your legal writing?

3. List the component parts of a typical legal letter. What are the four types of letters discussed in this chapter? What is the function of each type?

4. How is an internal memorandum organized? List and describe its components. What must you know and understand before you begin to prepare a legal memorandum?

5. What are some questions that should be answered in the legal analysis section of a legal memorandum?

ETHICAL QUESTIONS

1. Bill Richardson, a legal assistant, has been asked by his supervising attorney to prepare an internal memorandum analyzing a client's claim. When Bill reviews the facts, he realizes that the client has a very weak case and will probably lose. But Bill thinks that the client was taken advantage of and that she should be given a chance to try to recover at least something. He knows that his supervisor will not take a losing case to court, so he writes the memo in such a way as to favor the client's position as much as possible. He is not objective in analyzing the potential pitfalls of the case. Is what Bill has done ethical? Is it professional? How should he have handled the situation?

2. Ken Hall, a legal assistant, is handling all of his supervising attorney's mail while she is out of town on business for the week. The supervising attorney only wants to be contacted if absolutely necessary. She receives a letter marked "personal and confidential." Ken does not recognize the return address on the letter. How should Ken handle the situation?

PRACTICE QUESTIONS AND ASSIGNMENTS

1. Analyze the construction of the following paragraphs. How could they be improved?

   The first is knowing of the danger. The second is voluntarily subjecting oneself to the danger. The defense of assumption of risk has two elements.

   She did not voluntarily subject herself to the danger when the stadium assigned seats to season-ticket holders. She knew that balls were often hit into the stands. The plaintiff knew of the danger involved in attending a baseball game.

2. Proofread the following paragraph, circling all of the mistakes. Then rewrite the paragraph.

   The defendent was aressted and chrge with drunk driving. Blood alcohol level of .15. He refused to take a breahalyzer test at first. After the police explained to him that he would loose his lisense if he did not take it, he concented. He also has ablood test to verify the results of the breathalyzer.

3. Review the *Practice Questions and Assignments* at the end of Chapter 7. If you did the research required by those questions, use the lemon law and the cases and statutes that you found to prepare a legal memorandum analyzing Mr. Consumer's problem and whether the lemon law in your state will help him. Be sure to include your opinion of the strength of his case.

4. Prepare an informative letter to a client using the following facts:

The client, Dr. Brown, is being sued for medical malpractice and is going to be deposed on January 15, 2011, at 1:00 P.M. The deposition will take place at the law offices of Callaghan & Young. The offices are located at 151 East Jefferson Avenue, Cincinnati, Ohio. The client needs to call your supervising attorney's office to set up an appointment, so that the attorney can prepare Dr. Brown for the deposition.

QUESTIONS FOR CRITICAL ANALYSIS

1. Why is it important to write to your audience? To what audience should legislators write when drafting legislation?

2. Analyze the following hypothetical by applying the IRAC method, and write a one-page paper reporting your results:

Mr. Damien is a teacher at the Wabash Academy, a private boarding school. He has a twenty-one-year-old son who has bipolar affective disorder, formerly called manic-depressive psychosis, a mood disorder. While visiting Mr. Damien, his son has repeatedly threatened members of the school community. On one occasion, Mr. Damien's son abducted the headmaster's sixteen-year-old daughter and attempted to have the teenager admitted to a psychiatric hospital. Mr. Damien's son also made threatening phone calls to the headmaster. In one such call, he claimed to have drained several quarts of his own blood from his body because he was not permitted to communicate with the headmaster's sixteen-year-old daughter. Mr. and Mrs. Damien refuse to prevent their son from visiting their home on the school's campus. As a result, the school has fired Mr. Damien. Mr. Damien claims that the termination of his employment violates the Americans with Disabilities Act (ADA) of 1990.

The case law interpreting the ADA does not require employment of an individual with disabilities if that individual, or that individual's disabled relative or associate, poses a direct threat to the health and safety of others.

PROJECTS

1. If possible, find a copy of a business letter. Identify its component parts. How does it differ from the sample legal letter presented in Exhibit 9.3 on page 283? How is it similar?

2. Contact the court of appeals in your state. Ask if the court gives tours, has any programs available for college students, or allows observation of oral arguments. If you can, arrange to take a tour and observe an oral argument. Obtain a copy of each side's brief and read it prior to the oral argument if possible. Check with your instructor for any special directions before contacting the court. Write a one-page paper summarizing your visit to the court of appeals. Include a comparison of trial court proceedings, as described in Chapter 6, and appellate court oral arguments.

USING INTERNET RESOURCES

1. Access the Securities and Exchange Commission's *A Plain English Handbook* at the following site:

www.sec.gov/pdf/handbook.pdf

Scroll through the handbook to find answers to the following questions:

a. Describe the "unoriginal but useful" writing tip given in the handbook's preface. Why did the writer of the preface find the tip useful?

b. How does Chapter 1 of the handbook describe a plain English document?

c. Browse through Chapter 6, titled "Writing in Plain English." Write down two "before-and-after" examples showing how the use of plain English improved the writing.

d. What is a nominalization? Write a sentence including a nominalization (not one of those listed in Chapter 6), and then rewrite the sentence to make the nominalization the main verb of the sentence.

CIVIL LITIGATION: BEFORE THE TRIAL

CHAPTER

10

CHAPTER OUTLINE

Introduction

Civil Litigation—A Bird's-Eye View

The Preliminaries

The Pleadings

Pretrial Motions

Traditional Discovery Tools

The Duty to Disclose under FRCP 26

Discovery of Electronic Evidence

AFTER COMPLETING THIS CHAPTER, YOU WILL KNOW:

▶ The basic steps involved in the civil litigation process and the types of tasks that may be required of paralegals during each step of the pretrial phase.

▶ What a litigation file is, what it contains, and how it is organized, maintained, and reviewed.

▶ How a lawsuit is initiated and what documents are filed during the pleadings stage of the civil litigation process.

▶ What a motion is and how certain pretrial motions, if granted by the court, will end the litigation before the trial begins.

▶ What discovery is and what kinds of information attorneys and their paralegals obtain from parties to the lawsuit and from witnesses when preparing for trial.

INTRODUCTION

The paralegal plays a particularly important role in helping the trial attorney prepare for and conduct a civil trial. Preparation for trial involves a variety of tasks. The law relating to the client's case must be carefully researched. Evidence must be gathered and documented. The litigation file must be created and carefully organized. Procedural requirements and deadlines for filing certain documents with the court must be met. **Witnesses**—persons asked to testify at trial—must be prepared in advance and be available to testify at the appropriate time during the trial. Any exhibits, such as charts, photographs, or digital video recordings, to be used at the trial must be properly prepared, mounted, scanned into the computer, or filmed. Arrangements must be made to have any necessary equipment, such as a DVD player and projector, available for use at the trial. The paralegal's efforts are critically important in preparing for trial, and attorneys usually rely on paralegals to ensure that nothing has been overlooked.

Attorneys may request that their paralegals assist them during the trial as well. In the courtroom, the paralegal can perform numerous tasks. For example, the paralegal can locate documents or exhibits as they are needed. The paralegal can also observe jurors' reactions to statements made by attorneys or witnesses, check to see if a witness's testimony is consistent with sworn statements made by the witness before the trial, and perhaps give witnesses some last-minute instructions outside the courtroom before they are called to testify.

The complexity of even the simplest civil trial requires that the paralegal have some familiarity with the litigation process and the applicable courtroom procedures. Much of this expertise, of course, can only be acquired through hands-on experience. Yet every paralegal should be acquainted with the basic phases of civil litigation and the forms and terminology commonly used in the process. In this chapter, you will learn about the pretrial stages of a civil lawsuit, from the initial attorney-client meeting to the time of trial. In the next chapter, you will read about conducting investigations and interviews prior to trial.

> **witness**
> A person who is asked to testify under oath at a trial.

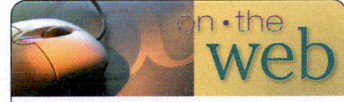

For an example of many of the online services provided by one state court system, Arizona, go to **www.supreme. state.az.us** and study the links that are available.

CIVIL LITIGATION—A BIRD'S-EYE VIEW

Although civil trials vary greatly in terms of complexity, cost, and detail, they all share similar structural characteristics. They begin with an event that gives rise to the legal action, and (provided the case is not settled by the parties at some point during the litigation process—as most cases are) they end with the issuance of a **judgment**, the court's decision on the matter. In the interim, the litigation itself may involve all sorts of twists and turns. Even though each case has its own "story line," most civil lawsuits follow some version of the course charted in Exhibit 10.1 on the following page.

> **judgment**
> The court's final decision regarding the rights and claims of the parties to a lawsuit.

Pretrial Settlements

As just mentioned, in most cases, the parties reach a *settlement*—an out-of-court resolution of the dispute—before the case goes to trial. Lawsuits are costly in both time and money, and it is usually in the interest of both parties to settle the case out of court. Throughout the pretrial stage of litigation, the attorney will therefore attempt to help the parties reach a settlement. At the same time, though, the attorney and the paralegal will operate under the assumption that the case will go to trial because if it does, all pretrial preparation must be completed prior to the trial date.

Procedural Requirements

Understanding and meeting procedural requirements is essential in the litigation process. These requirements are spelled out in the procedural rules of the court in which a lawsuit is brought. All civil trials held in federal district courts are governed

EXHIBIT 10.1
A Typical Case Flowchart

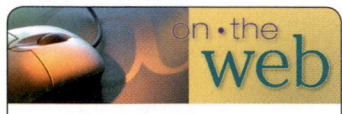

The Federal Rules of Civil Procedure are available online at the Legal Information Institute Web site at **www.law.cornell. edu**. (Select "Federal Rules of Civil Procedure" from the "Constitutions & codes" menu.)

You can also access the rules governing civil procedure in most states. Go to **www.law.cornell.edu**, search "wex" and then "all pages" to get to civil procedure and other areas of law.

by the **Federal Rules of Civil Procedure (FRCP)**. These rules specify what must be done during the various stages of the federal civil litigation process. For example, FRCP 4 (Rule 4 of the FRCP) describes the procedures that must be followed in notifying the defendant of the lawsuit. Each state also has its own rules of civil procedure (which in many states are similar to the FRCP). In addition, many courts have their own rules of procedure that supplement the federal or state rules. The attorney and the paralegal must comply with the rules of procedure that apply to the specific court in which the trial will take place.

A Hypothetical Lawsuit

To illustrate the procedures involved in litigation, consider a hypothetical civil lawsuit. The case involves an automobile accident in which a car driven by Tony Peretto collided with a car driven by Katherine Baranski. Baranski suffered injuries and incurred substantial medical and hospital costs. She also lost wages for the five months that she was unable to work. Baranski has decided to sue Peretto for damages. Because Baranski is the person bringing the lawsuit, she is the plaintiff. Peretto, because he must defend against Baranski's claims, is the defendant. The plaintiff and the defendant are referred to as the *parties* to the lawsuit, as discussed in Chapter 5. (Some cases involve several plaintiffs and/or defendants.)

The attorney for the plaintiff (Baranski) is Allen P. Gilmore. Gilmore is assisted by paralegal Elena Lopez. The attorney for the defendant (Peretto) is Elizabeth A. Cameron. Cameron is assisted by paralegal Gordon McVay. Throughout this chapter and the following two chapters, *Case at a Glance* features in the page margins will remind you of the names of the players in this lawsuit.

THE PRELIMINARIES

Katherine Baranski arranges to meet with Allen P. Gilmore, an attorney with the law firm of Jeffers, Gilmore & Dunn, to see if Gilmore will represent her in the lawsuit. Gilmore asks paralegal Elena Lopez to prepare the usual forms and information sheets, including a retainer agreement and a statement of the firm's billing procedures, and to bring them to the initial interview with Baranski. Gilmore also asks Lopez to run a conflicts check (see Chapter 4) to ensure that representing Baranski in this action will not create a conflict of interest.

The Initial Client Interview

Most often, an initial client interview is conducted by the attorney—for several reasons. First, if attorney Gilmore is interested in taking on a new client, he will want to explain to the client the value of his services and those of his firm. Second, only an attorney can agree to represent a client. Third, only an attorney can set fees, and if Gilmore takes Baranski on as a client, fee arrangements will be discussed, and possibly agreed on, during the initial client interview. Finally, only an attorney can give legal advice, and the initial client interview may involve advising Baranski of her legal rights and options. In short, what transpires during the initial client interview normally falls under the umbrella of "the practice of law," and, as you read in Chapter 4, only attorneys are permitted to practice law.

Because attorney Gilmore and paralegal Lopez will be working together on the case, however, Gilmore will ask Lopez to sit in on the interview. Gilmore will want Lopez to meet Baranski, become familiar with Baranski's claim, and perhaps make arrangements for follow-up interviews with Baranski should Gilmore take the case.

During the initial client interview, Katherine Baranski explains to attorney Gilmore and paralegal Lopez the facts of her case as she perceives them. Baranski tells them that Tony Peretto, who was driving a Dodge van, ran a stop sign and crashed into the driver's side of her Ford Fusion as she was driving through the intersection of Mattis Avenue and Thirty-eighth Street in Nita City, Nita. The accident occurred at 7:45 A.M. on August 4, 2010. Baranski has misplaced Peretto's address, but she knows that he lives in another state, the state of Zero.[1] Baranski claims that as a result of the accident, she has been unable to work for five months and has lost about $20,000 in wages. Her medical and hospital expenses total $95,000, and the damage to her car is estimated to be $15,000. Throughout the initial interview, Lopez takes notes to record the details of the case as relayed by Baranski.

Gilmore agrees to represent Baranski in the lawsuit against Peretto. He explains the fee structure to Baranski, and she signs the retainer agreement. He has Baranski sign forms authorizing Gilmore to obtain relevant medical, employment, and other records relating to the claim. (These forms, called *release forms,* will be discussed in Chapter 11.) At the end of the interview, Gilmore asks Lopez to schedule a follow-up interview with Baranski. Lopez will conduct that interview and obtain more details from Baranski about the accident and its consequences.

Preliminary Investigation

After Baranski leaves the office, attorney Gilmore asks paralegal Lopez to undertake a preliminary investigation to get as much information as possible concerning the facts of Baranski's accident. Sources of this information will include the police

---

Case at a Glance

The Plaintiff—
Plaintiff: Katherine Baranski
Attorney: Allen P. Gilmore
Paralegal: Elena Lopez

The Defendant—
Defendant: Tony Peretto
Attorney: Elizabeth A. Cameron
Paralegal: Gordon McVay

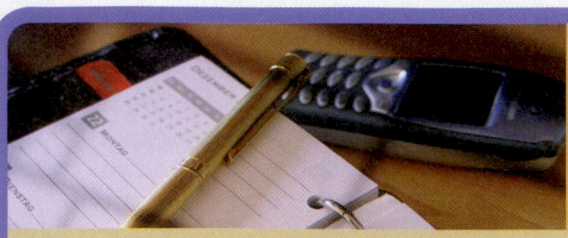

In the **Office**

HACKING LEGAL FILES

Hackers work to steal information or destroy computer files. Protecting the privacy and security of client files, and all other office files, from hackers is a major concern. Security failures can affect a law firm's cases and its reputation. Large law firms usually have a specialist assigned to computer and Internet security. Smaller firms may be less formal, but the concerns are the same: Are files safe? Is the transmission of files to courts safe from interception? Could a hacker destroy the contents of the firm's computers? Are files stored off site secure? While you are probably not a security expert, you should be aware of security for the computers you use.

report of the accident, medical records, employment data, and eyewitness accounts of the accident.

You will read in Chapter 11 about the steps in investigating the facts of a client's case, so we will not discuss investigation here. Bear in mind, though, that at this point in the pretrial process, the paralegal may engage in extensive investigation. Legal investigation is an important part of pretrial work, and facts discovered (or not discovered) by the investigator may play an important role in determining the outcome of the lawsuit.

Creating the Litigation File

Attorney Gilmore also asks paralegal Lopez to create a litigation file for the case. As the litigation progresses, Lopez will carefully maintain the file to make sure that such items as correspondence, bills, research and investigation results, and all documents and exhibits relating to the litigation are in the file and arranged in an organized manner.

Each law firm or legal department has its own organizational scheme to follow when creating and maintaining client files. Recall from Chapter 3 that there are three goals of any law office filing system: to preserve confidentiality, to safeguard legal documents, and to ensure that the contents of files can be easily and quickly retrieved when needed. Usually, it is the paralegal's responsibility to make sure that the litigation file is properly created and maintained.

As a case progresses through the litigation process, subfiles may be created for documents relating to the various stages. For example, at this point in the Baranski case, the litigation file contains notes taken during the initial client interview, the signed retainer agreement, and information and documents gathered by Lopez during her preliminary investigation of the claim. As the lawsuit progresses, Lopez will make sure that subfiles are created for documents relating to the pleadings and discovery stages (to be discussed shortly). Depending on the office filing system, the file folders for these subfiles may be color coded or numbered so that each subfile can be readily recognized and retrieved. Many firms also scan documents and create electronic copies of the files. Lopez will also prepare an index for each subfile to indicate what documents are included in it. The index will be placed at the front of the folder for easy reference.

A properly created and maintained litigation file provides a comprehensive record of the case so that others in the firm who become involved with it can quickly acquaint themselves with the progress of the proceedings. Because well-

Litigation files can easily expand into thousands of documents. Part of the paralegal's job is to file and organize these documents in such a way that they can be quickly retrieved when needed. When might you wish to scan file documents and put them onto an external hard drive?

(Courtesy of © PhotoDisc®)

organized files are critical to the success of any case, Lopez should take special care to properly maintain the file. The *Developing Paralegal Skills* feature on the next page discusses this in more depth. The *Featured Contributor* on page 307 also discusses the critical nature of case management.

THE PLEADINGS

The next step is for plaintiff Baranski's attorney, Gilmore, to file a complaint in the appropriate court. The **complaint** (called a *petition* in some courts) is a document that states the claims the plaintiff is making against the defendant. The complaint also contains a statement regarding the court's jurisdiction over the dispute and a demand for a remedy (such as money damages).

The filing of the complaint is the step that begins the formal legal action against the defendant, Peretto. The complaint is one of the **pleadings**, which inform each party of the claims of the other and specify the issues (disputed questions) involved in the case. We examine here two basic pleadings—the plaintiff's complaint and the defendant's answer.

The complaint must be filed within the period of time allowed by law for bringing legal actions. The allowable period is fixed by state statutes of limitations (discussed in Chapter 5), and this period varies for different types of lawsuits. For example, actions concerning breaches of sales contracts must usually be brought within four years. For negligence lawsuits, statutes of limitations vary from state to state. After the time allowed under a statute of limitations has expired, normally no action can be brought, no matter how strong the case was originally. For example, if the statute of limitations covering the auto-negligence lawsuit that plaintiff Baranski is bringing against defendant Peretto allows two years for bringing an action,

complaint
The pleading made by a plaintiff or a charge made by the state alleging wrongdoing on the part of the defendant.

pleadings
Statements by the plaintiff and the defendant that detail the facts, charges, and defenses involved in the litigation.

Developing
Paralegal Skills

FILE WORKUP

Once a litigation file has been created, the paralegal typically "works up" the file. In the Baranski case, after paralegal Lopez has completed her initial investigation into Baranski's claim, she will review and summarize the information that she has amassed so far, including the information that she has gathered through the initial client interview, subsequent client interviews, and any investigation that she has conducted.

Lopez will also identify areas that might require the testimony of an expert witness. For example, if Baranski claimed that as a result of the accident she had broken her hip and would always walk with a limp, Gilmore would want a medical specialist to give expert testimony to support Baranski's claim. (How to locate expert witnesses will be discussed in later chapters.) Lopez would prepare a list of potential experts for Gilmore to review.

Once Lopez has worked up the file, she will prepare a memo to Gilmore summarizing the file. This memo will provide Gilmore with factual information for deciding which legal remedy or strategy to pursue, what legal issues need to be researched, and generally how to proceed with the case.

TIPS FOR PREPARING A FILE WORKUP MEMO

- Summarize the information that has been obtained about the case.
- Suggest a plan for further investigation in the case (you will read about investigation plans in Chapter 11).
- Suggest additional information that might be obtained during discovery (discussed later in this chapter).
- Include a list of expert witnesses to contact, explaining which witnesses might be preferable, and why.

Baranski normally has to initiate the lawsuit within that two-year period or give up forever the possibility of suing Peretto for damages caused by the car accident.

Drafting the Complaint

The complaint itself may be no more than a few paragraphs long, or it may be many pages in length, depending on the complexity of the case. In the Baranski case, the complaint will probably be only a few pages long unless special circumstances justify additional details. The complaint will include the following sections, each of which we discuss below:

- Caption.
- Jurisdictional allegations.
- General allegations (the body of the complaint).
- Prayer for relief.
- Signature.
- Demand for a jury trial.

Exhibit 10.2 on pages 308 and 309 shows a sample complaint.

Baranski's case is being filed in a federal court, so the Federal Rules of Civil Procedure (FRCP) apply. If the case were being filed in a state court, paralegal Lopez might need to review the appropriate state rules of civil procedure. The rules for drafting pleadings in state courts differ from the FRCP. The rules also

featured contributor

LITIGATION PARALEGAL

Janet M. Powell

Janet M. Powell is a commercial litigation paralegal specializing in computerized litigation support, case management, and trial support in Miami, Florida. She has been working in the legal field for more than twenty years. She is an adjunct professor in the paralegal studies program at Miami-Dade College and focuses her teaching on online public records and other investigation resources. She obtained her NALA certification in 1991 and served in the Miami–Dade County guardian ad litem program. She is the case manager in the Miami office of Ogletree, Deakins, Nash, Smoak & Stewart, a national firm specializing in management consulting and labor and employment case representation.

What do you like best about your work?

"Litigation has always interested me because it is intellectually stimulating. In order to understand the documentation and the investigation stream in cases, often you have to learn quite a bit about various other kinds of businesses, industries, products, and commercial transactions. This depth of understanding is important if you are involved in the discovery process, as investigation and strategizing are generally necessary for successful handling. I am always learning something new, it makes each day different. Boredom is out of the question."

What is the greatest challenge that you face in your area of work?

"My greatest challenge specific to my profession is to keep current with emerging technologies, specifically various computer-based case management and practice management tools. In many instances, litigation paralegal roles are evolving into positions that are more technical. If you work at a firm that will invest in your continuing education, that is a huge benefit. Regardless of whether your firm offers such training, however, we all have to take responsibility for continuing to build our knowledge base and manage our own professionalism. I am a great believer in taking charge of one's own education, as it builds self-confidence and enhances future employability and prospects. Education is available today through many avenues, such as continuing legal education (CLE) seminars sponsored by associations, schools, and independent paralegal organizations."

What advice do you have for would-be paralegals in your area of work?

"My role as a paralegal is to support the needs and anticipated needs of the attorneys I work for and to tailor my output accordingly. To that end, it is helpful to have a supportive, caring disposition. Some people may need help defining what their case needs are, and being willing to go the extra mile goes a long way toward establishing professional friendships that can turn into personal ones. Generally, you should be as adaptable and as helpful as you can be. You must also think deeply about what is truly important, and keep your priorities clearly in mind. You can be a top-notch paralegal and a valued member of your firm, but if you do not have balance in your work and personal life, it will be difficult to be happy and successful."

> *"My greatest challenge . . . is to keep current with emerging technologies . . . ."*

What are some tips for success as a paralegal in your area of work?

"Learn to manage yourself, your projects, and your time well. Be reasonable in understanding your limitations, and ask for help or relief when it looks like you might be getting overwhelmed. Trying to do too much in too short a time will not let you produce your best work, and it will reflect poorly on you. Learn to communicate effectively, be appreciative for projects and work assigned to you, and take pride in your work product. Double-check your work for accuracy; proofread everything backwards. If there are few or no in-house educational opportunities, take charge of your own professional development. Set your own professional goals, and do not wait for permission to better yourself. Learn from everyone, especially your co-workers and colleagues. Attend your local association's meetings and luncheons. The more paralegals you know, the more you will learn."

Janet Powell is also featured in Lessons from the Top Paralegal Experts, *by Carole Bruno.*

EXHIBIT 10.2
The Complaint

The caption

Jurisdictional allegations

General allegations

The **court** in which the complaint is filed.

Names of the **parties**

The court will insert the **file (docket) number** here.

Name/type of document

*This is a reference to the **title and section numbers in the *United States Code,*** which is a compilation of all federal statutes. See Chapter 7 for a further discussion of how to understand citations (references) to statutory law.

UNITED STATES DISTRICT COURT
FOR THE WESTERN DISTRICT OF NITA

Katherine Baranski

      Plaintiff,

v.

Tony Peretto

      Defendant.

CASE NO: _____

COMPLAINT AND
DEMAND FOR JURY TRIAL

JURISDICTIONAL ALLEGATIONS

1. That Plaintiff, Katherine Baranski, resides in the City of Nita, County of Nita, State of Nita.

2. That Defendant, Tony Peretto, is a resident of the City of Zero, County of Zero, State of Zero.

3. That the cause of action arose in the City of Nita, County of Nita, State of Nita.

4. That the amount in controversy exceeds $75,000.00 and Plaintiff is entitled to relief based on Diversity of Citizenship under 28 U.S.C. Section 1332.*

GENERAL ALLEGATIONS

5. That on August 4, 2010, at approximately 7:45 A.M., the Plaintiff, Katherine Baranski, was exercising reasonable care in driving her car in a southbound direction on Mattis Avenue when a vehicle driven by the Defendant, Tony Peretto, collided with the Plaintiff's vehicle. The collision occurred as Defendant Peretto attempted to drive his vehicle across Mattis Avenue on Thirty-eighth Street.

6. That the Defendant, Tony Peretto, owed the Plaintiff, Katherine Baranski, the following duties of care:

    A. Duty to stop at the stop sign on Thirty-eighth Street before crossing Mattis Avenue.
    B. Duty to make reasonable observations of vehicles in plain view before crossing Mattis Avenue.
    C. Duty not to drive his motor vehicle in a reckless, careless, or heedless manner with willful and wanton disregard for the safety and rights of others, within the meaning of Section 9.2326(2) of the Nita Statutes Annotated.

7. That the Defendant, Tony Peretto, breached each of the above duties and violated the following statutes of the State of Nita:

    A. That he was guilty of reckless driving within the meaning of Section 9.2326 of the Nita Statutes Annotated.
    B. That he was guilty of careless and negligent driving within the meaning of Section 9.2326(2) of the Nita Statutes Annotated.

8. That at the time of the collision, the weather conditions were clear and it was daylight.

EXHIBIT 10.2
The Complaint—Continued

9. That at the time of the collision, the Plaintiff, Katherine Baranski, was a generally healthy female, twenty-five years of age.

10. That as a result of the collision, the Plaintiff, Katherine Baranski, suffered severe physical injuries, which prevented her from working for five months, and property damage to her vehicle. The costs that the Plaintiff, Katherine Baranski, incurred as a result of the collision included $95,000 in medical bills, $20,000 in lost wages, and $15,000 in automobile-repair costs.

11. That the injuries sustained by the Plaintiff as a result of the collision were solely caused by the negligence of the Defendant, Tony Peretto.

WHEREFORE, the Plaintiff prays for the following relief:

The prayer for relief

A. That the Plaintiff be awarded appropriate compensatory damages;

B. That the Plaintiff be awarded an amount deemed fair and just by a Jury to compensate the Plaintiff for damages sustained as presented by the evidence in this case;

C. That the Plaintiff be awarded such other further relief as the Court deems proper. Plaintiff Katherine Baranski claims judgment against the Defendant in an amount in excess of $75,000 in actual, compensatory, and exemplary damages together with attorneys' fees, court costs, and other costs as provided by law.

Date: 2/10/11

The signature of the plaintiff's attorney

Jeffers, Gilmore & Dunn

Allen P Gilmore

Allen P Gilmore
Attorney for Plaintiff
553 Fifth Avenue
Suite 101
Nita City, NI 48801

Katherine Baranski, being first duly sworn, states that she has read the foregoing Complaint by her subscribed and that she knows the contents thereof, and the same is true, except those matters therein stated to be upon information and belief, and as to those matters, she believes to be true.

Katherine Baranski

Plaintiff

Affidavit (and plaintiff's signature)

Sworn and subscribed before me this 10th day of February, 2011.

Leela M Shay

Notary Public, Nita County,
State of Nita

My Commission Expires:

March 10, 2013

DEMAND FOR A JURY TRIAL

The Plaintiff demands a trial by jury.

Demand for a jury trial

Date: 2/10/11

Jeffers, Gilmore & Dunn

Allen P Gilmore

Allen P Gilmore
Attorney for the Plaintiff
553 Fifth Avenue
Suite 101
Nita City, Nita 48801

differ from state to state and even from court to court within the same state. Lopez could obtain pleading forms, either from "form books" available in the law firm's files or library (or on CD-ROM, DVD, or online) or from pleadings drafted previously in similar cases litigated by the firm in the court in which the Baranski case will be filed.

The Caption

All documents submitted to the court or other parties during the litigation process begin with a caption. The caption is the heading, which identifies the name of the court, the title of the action, the names of the parties, the type of document, and the court's file number. Note that the court's file number may also be referred to as the case number or *docket number*, depending on the jurisdiction. (A **docket** is the list of cases entered on a court's calendar and thus scheduled to be heard.) The caption for a complaint leaves a space for the court to insert the number that it assigns to the case. Courts typically assign the case a number when the complaint is filed. Any document subsequently filed with the court in the case will list the file, case, or docket number on the front page of the document. Exhibit 10.2 on the preceding pages shows how the caption will read in the case of *Baranski v. Peretto.*

> **docket**
> The list of cases entered on a court's calendar and thus scheduled to be heard by the court.

Jurisdictional Allegations

Because attorney Gilmore is filing the lawsuit in a federal district court, he will have to include in the complaint an allegation that the federal court has jurisdiction to hear the dispute. (An **allegation** is an assertion, claim, or statement made by one party in a pleading that sets out what the party expects to prove to the court.) Recall from Chapter 6 that federal courts can exercise jurisdiction over disputes involving either a *federal question* or *diversity of citizenship*. A federal question arises whenever a claim in a civil lawsuit relates to a federal law, the U.S. Constitution, or a treaty executed by the U.S. government. Diversity of citizenship exists when the parties involved in the lawsuit are citizens of different states and the amount in controversy exceeds $75,000. Because Baranski and Peretto are citizens of different states (Nita and Zero, respectively) and because the amount in controversy exceeds $75,000, the case meets the requirements for diversity-of-citizenship jurisdiction. Gilmore thus asserts that the federal court has jurisdiction on this basis, as illustrated in Exhibit 10.2.

> **allegation**
> A party's statement, claim, or assertion made in a pleading to the court. The allegation sets forth the issue that the party expects to prove.

As explained in Chapter 6, certain matters—such as those involving patent or copyright disputes, the Internal Revenue Service, or bankruptcy—can *only* be brought in federal courts. Certain other cases, however, including those involving diversity of citizenship, may be brought in either a state court or a federal court. Thus, an attorney in Gilmore's position can advise the client that he or she has a choice. Gilmore probably considered several factors when advising Baranski on which court would be preferable for her lawsuit. An important consideration is how long it would take to get the case to trial. Many courts are overburdened by their caseloads, and sometimes it can take years before a court will be able to hear a case. If Gilmore knows that the case could be heard two years earlier in the federal court than in the state court, that will be an important factor to consider.

General Allegations (The Body of the Complaint)

The body of the complaint contains a series of allegations that set forth a claim for relief. In plaintiff Baranski's complaint, the allegations outline the factual events that gave rise to Baranski's claims.[2] The events are described in a series of chronologically arranged, numbered allegations so that the reader can understand them easily. As Exhibit 10.2 shows, the numbers of the paragraphs in the body of the complaint continue the sequence begun in the section on jurisdictional allegations.

Advocate Plaintiff's Position. When drafting the complaint, Lopez will play the role of advocate. She must present the facts forcefully and in a way that supports and strengthens the client's claim. The recitation of the facts should demonstrate that defendant Peretto engaged in conduct that entitles plaintiff Baranski to relief. Even though she will want to present the facts in a light most favorable to Baranski, Lopez must be careful not to exaggerate the facts or make false statements. Rather, she must present the facts in such a way that the reader could reasonably infer that Peretto was negligent and that his negligence caused Baranski's injuries and losses.

What if her research into the case had given Lopez reason to believe that a fact was probably true even though she could not verify it? She could still include the statement in the complaint by prefacing it with the phrase, "On information and belief." This language would indicate to the court that the plaintiff, Baranski, had good reason to believe the truth of the statement but that the evidence for it either had not yet been obtained or might not hold up under close scrutiny.

Be Clear and Concise. The most effective complaints are those that are clear and concise. Moreover, brevity and simplicity are required under FRCP 8(a). As in all legal writing, Lopez should strive for clarity. When drafting the complaint, Lopez should use clear language and favor simple and direct statements over more complex wording. This is because the court may, at the request of opposing counsel, strike (delete) from the complaint ambiguous phrases—phrases whose meaning is unclear or that could be interpreted in more than one way. Lopez should also resist the temptation to include facts that are not absolutely necessary for the complaint. By reducing the body of the complaint to the simplest possible terms, Lopez will not only achieve greater clarity but also minimize the possibility of divulging attorney Gilmore's trial strategies or hinting at a possible defense that the opponent might use to defeat the claim.

Outline the Harms Suffered and the Remedy Sought. After telling Baranski's story, Lopez will add one or more paragraphs outlining the harms suffered by the plaintiff and the remedy (in monetary damages) that the plaintiff seeks. In general, it is preferable that all allegations of damages—such as hospital costs, lost wages, and auto-repair expenses—be included in a single paragraph, as in Exhibit 10.2 Paragraph 10 toward the top of page 309. Lopez should check the relevant court rules, however, to see whether the court requires that certain types of damages (Baranski's lost wages, for example) be alleged in a separate paragraph.

Prayer for Relief

Paralegal Lopez will include at the end of the complaint a paragraph, similar to that shown in Exhibit 10.2, asking that judgment be entered for the plaintiff and appropriate relief be granted. This **prayer for relief** will indicate that plaintiff Baranski is seeking money damages to compensate her for the harms that she suffered.

Signature

In federal practice, the signature following the prayer for relief certifies that the plaintiff's attorney (or the plaintiff, if he or she is not represented by an attorney) has read the complaint and that the facts alleged are true to the best of his or her knowledge. In addition to the attorney's signature, some state courts require an affidavit signed by the plaintiff verifying that the complaint is true to the best of the plaintiff's knowledge. **Affidavits** are sworn statements attesting to the existence of certain facts. They are acknowledged by a notary public or another official authorized to administer such oaths or affirmations. Exhibit 10.2 illustrates an affidavit for the Baranski complaint.

prayer for relief
A statement at the end of the complaint requesting that the court grant relief to the plaintiff.

affidavit
A written statement of facts, confirmed by the oath or affirmation of the party making it and made before a person having the authority to administer the oath or affirmation.

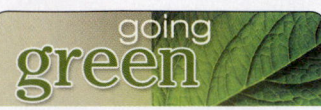
Demand for a Jury Trial

A trial can be held with or without a jury. If there is no jury, the judge determines the truth of the facts alleged in the case. The Seventh Amendment to the U.S. Constitution guarantees the right to a jury trial in federal courts in all "suits at common law" when the amount in controversy exceeds $20 (the equivalent of 40 days' salary at that time). Most states have similar guarantees in their own constitutions, although many states put a higher minimum dollar restriction on the guarantee (for example, in Maryland the minimum amount is $10,000). If this threshold requirement is met, either party may request a jury trial.

The right to a trial by jury does not have to be exercised, and many cases are tried without one. In most states and in federal courts, one of the parties must request a jury trial, or the right is presumed to be waived (that is, the court will presume that neither party wants a jury trial). The decision to exercise the right to a jury trial usually depends on what legal theory the party is using and which judge is assigned to the trial. In the Baranski case, Gilmore may advise Baranski to demand a jury trial if he believes that a jury would be sympathetic to her position. If Baranski wants a jury trial, Gilmore will ask Lopez to include a demand for a jury trial (similar to the one illustrated in Point B of Exhibit 10.2 on page 309) with the complaint. More tips for drafting a complaint are presented in the *Developing Paralegal Skills* feature. Although the feature focuses on a complaint in a federal civil case, most of the points are also valid for a state civil case.

Filing the Complaint

Once the complaint has been prepared, carefully checked for accuracy, and signed by attorney Gilmore, paralegal Lopez will file the complaint with the court in which the action is being brought. To file the complaint, Lopez will either deliver the paper document to the court—the traditional method—or file the complaint with the court electronically—for example, by e-mail or CD-ROM. Different courts have different rules in this regard.

Traditional Method of Filing

Traditionally, a person filing a complaint personally delivers the complaint to the clerk of the court, together with a specified number of copies of the complaint and a check payable to the court in the amount of the required filing fee. Usually, a summons (which will be discussed shortly) is also attached. If Lopez uses this method of filing, she can either deliver the complaint to the court clerk or have someone deliver it for her. If she is not aware of the court's procedures for filing the complaint, she will need to contact the court to verify the amount of the filing fee and how many copies of the complaint need to be filed. Typically, the original (signed) complaint is filed with at least two copies (the court keeps the original, and the plaintiff and defendant receive a copy), although additional copies may be required, particularly if there are multiple plaintiffs or defendants.

The court clerk files the complaint by stamping the date on the first page of all the documents (original and copies); assigning the case a file number, or docket number; and assigning the case to a particular judge. (In some state courts, the file number or judge may not be assigned until later.) The clerk then returns the date-stamped copies to the person who delivered the documents for service on the defendant (to be discussed shortly).

E-Filing

Instead of delivering a paper document to the court, Lopez may be able to file the complaint electronically. Indeed, electronic filing is becoming more and more common. Because of the reduced time and paperwork involved, electronic filing can result in substantial savings for attorneys, their clients, and the courts.

Developing
Paralegal Skills

A CHECKLIST FOR DRAFTING A COMPLAINT IN A FEDERAL CIVIL CASE

Civil cases begin when the complaint is filed in court. To draft a complaint you need to know the facts your client alleges and the law that supports your client's claim for relief. You will need to review any notes from client interviews and meetings with the attorneys, factual materials (e.g., police or hospital reports), and preliminary research. It is also a good idea to review complaints from similar cases handled by your firm in the past, which can give you a feel for the appropriate writing style. Form books also can provide guidance on how to draft particular claims. It is also critical to check the appropriate court's rules for local requirements.

For civil suits in federal court, Federal Rule of Civil Procedure 8 sets out the required elements. State rules have an equivalent and often similar provision. Generally, the local rules will cover the typeface, type and size of paper, and other such matters.

A well-drafted complaint contains the information needed to answer the following questions:

- Who is the plaintiff? Use the plaintiff's legal name and include a statement of the jurisdiction where the plaintiff is a legal resident. If the plaintiff is suing as the representative of someone else, identify the relationship.

- Who is the defendant? It is critical to use the defendant's correct legal name so that you sue the proper person or firm. You also need to provide the defendant's legal residence.

- Why is the suit being filed in this court? If you are filing in federal court, how does the court have jurisdiction over the case? List the specific statutes involved. For example, list 28 U.S.C. 1331 for federal question jurisdiction, 28 U.S.C. 1332 for diversity-of-citizenship jurisdiction, or 42 U.S.C. 1983 for civil rights violations. Remember, the court must have jurisdiction over both the cause of action and the persons or firms sued.

- Did any administrative prerequisites have to be satisfied prior to filing suit? If so, how were they satisfied?

- Is the claim timely filed? Is it within the relevant statute of limitations?

- What are the facts that make up the plaintiff's case? State these accurately, clearly, and briefly. Give names and dates where known.

- What are the legal claims made by the plaintiff? Draft each distinct claim in a separate "count" in the complaint.

- Are there special pleading requirements for particular claims (e.g., fraud)? How has the plaintiff satisfied them?

- What is the plaintiff asking for? Clearly describe the relief the plaintiff wants—is it monetary damages? An injunction? Declaratory relief? Attorneys' fees and costs? Prejudgment interest? Postjudgment interest? Are special damages requested (such as statutory damages or punitive damages)?

- Who is the attorney filing the suit? Include an appropriate signature block for the lawyer to sign, certifying that she has conducted a reasonable inquiry into the facts that support the claim.

- Is a jury requested? Check to see if the claim is one for which a jury is available. Find out whether the attorney overseeing the case wants to request a jury. If so, you will need to include the appropriate language demanding a jury trial.

All parts of the complaint should be written in clear, direct English. Such professionalism is appreciated by a court.

electronic filing (e-filing) system
A computer system that enables attorneys to file case documents with courts over the Internet twenty-four hours a day, seven days a week.

The Federal Courts.

The FRCP provides that federal courts may permit filing by electronic means that are consistent with any technical standards established by the Judicial Conference, which sets policy for the administration of the federal courts. The federal court system first experimented with an **electronic filing (e-filing) system** in 1996. E-filing systems are now used in almost all federal courts. Some courts require it. Exhibit 10.3 shows the home page of the federal court e-filing system. With e-filing, registered attorneys can file case documents over the Internet twenty-four hours a day, seven days a week, right up to the filing deadline, with no additional filing fees.

State and Local Courts.

State and local courts are also setting up electronic filing systems. E-filing is used statewide in the courts of Alabama, Arizona, California, Colorado, Connecticut, Delaware, New Jersey, New York, North Carolina, Ohio, Texas, and Washington. It is also used in some individual courts in states that do not have statewide systems. The move to e-filing is constantly expanding, and many courts provide online tutorials. Some states do e-filing through the LexisNexis File and Serve system.

The security of the e-filing process is important. Only registered parties may access a court's e-filing system. As with most secure electronic communications, the registered party has a user ID and a password. An attorney may give a paralegal authority to use the system on his or her behalf. Consent of the parties to use e-filing may be required. Once parties agree to e-filing, the court assigns a docket number to the case. From that point forward, all documents filed and served by consenting parties must use the system. Often, documents must be formatted as PDF (Portable Document Format) files so they cannot be altered. The parties must provide e-mail addresses for notification of service of documents.

For information about the federal judiciary's Case Management/Electronic Case Files (CM/ECF) system, go to **www.uscourts.gov**. From the list at the left, select "Electronic Access to Courts," and then select "Case Management/Electronic Case Files Project."

EXHIBIT 10.3
PACER Home Page for Federal Court E-Filing

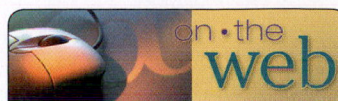

A party to an action being handled by e-filing may have the right to request hard copies of documents. When hard copies are used, they are to include a clear notice that they have been filed electronically. Special steps are taken to protect private information, such as Social Security numbers, credit-card information, a minor child's name, or trade secrets. Fees for documents filed are paid electronically. Therefore, in many cases, all paperwork and communications between the parties and the court may be electronic.

Service of Process

Before the court can exercise jurisdiction over the defendant—in effect, before the lawsuit can begin—the court must have proof that the defendant was notified of the lawsuit. Serving the summons and complaint—that is, delivering these documents to the defendant in a lawsuit—is referred to as **service of process**.

The Summons

The **summons** identifies the parties to the lawsuit, as well as the court in which the case will be heard, and directs the defendant to respond to the complaint within a specified period of time. In the Baranski case, paralegal Lopez will prepare a summons by filling out a form similar to that shown in Exhibit 10.4. Lopez will also prepare a cover sheet for the case (a preprinted form), which is required in the federal courts and in most state courts.

If the case were being brought in a state court, Lopez would deliver the summons to the court clerk at the same time she delivered the complaint. (In federal court cases, as will be discussed, the complaint may already have been filed under the FRCP provisions relating to waiver of notice.)

After the clerk files the complaint and signs, seals, and issues the summons, attorney Gilmore will be responsible for making sure that the summons and complaint are served on defendant Peretto. The service of the complaint and summons

service of process
The delivery of the summons and the complaint to a defendant.

summons
A document served on a defendant in a lawsuit informing the defendant that a legal action has been commenced against him or her and that the defendant must appear in court or respond to the plaintiff's complaint within a specified period of time.

EXHIBIT 10.4
A Summons in a Civil Action

UNITED STATES DISTRICT COURT
FOR THE WESTERN DISTRICT OF NITA

Katherine Baranski)
  Plaintiff,)
v.)   **Civil Action, File Number 11-14335-NI**
)   *Summons*
Tony Peretto)
  Defendant.)

To the above-named Defendant:

You are hereby summoned and required to serve upon A. P. Gilmore, Jeffers, Gilmore & Dunn, plaintiff's attorney, whose address is 553 Fifth Avenue, Suite 101, Nita City, NI 48801, an answer to the complaint which is herewith served upon you, within 20 days after service of this summons upon you, exclusive of the day of service. If you fail to do so, judgment by default will be taken against you for the relief demanded in the complaint.

C. H. Hynek _____   February 10, 2011 _____
CLERK   DATE

John Dolan
BY DEPUTY CLERK

must be effected within a specified time—120 days under FRCP 4(m)—after the complaint has been filed.

Serving the Complaint and Summons

How service of process occurs depends on the rules of the court or jurisdiction in which the lawsuit is brought. Under FRCP 4(c)(2), service of process in federal court cases may be effected "by any person who is not a party and who is at least 18 years of age." Paralegal Lopez, for example, could serve the summons by personally delivering it to defendant Peretto. Alternatively, she could make arrangements for someone else to do so, subject to the approval of attorney Gilmore. Many law firms contract with independent companies that provide process service in the local area. In some cases, the attorney might request that the court have a U.S. marshal or other federal official serve the summons.

Under FRCP 4(e)(1), service of process in federal court cases may also be effected "pursuant to the law of the state in which the district court is located." Some state courts require that the complaint and summons be served by a public officer, such as a sheriff.

Alternative Service Methods.   Although the most common way to serve process on a defendant is through personal service, or actual delivery, as described above, other methods are permissible at times, depending on the jurisdiction. *Substituted service* is any method of service allowed by law in place of personal service, such as service by certified mail, fax, or e-mail. Most states allow a process server to effect service by leaving a copy of the documents at the defendant's place of work, at his or her home address, or with someone else who resides in the home (such as a wife or an older child). In some circumstances, if the defendant cannot be physically located, the law may allow the process server to effect service by mailing a copy of the summons and complaint to the defendant's last known address and/or publishing a notice in the local newspaper. In other situations, delivering the documents to an authorized agent is sufficient. The paralegal and attorney thus need to know the types of service authorized by the laws of civil procedure in their own state.

Proof of Service.   Regardless of how the summons is served, attorney Gilmore will need some kind of proof that defendant Peretto actually received the summons. In federal court cases, unless service is made by a U.S. marshal or other official, proof of service is established by having the process server fill out and sign a form similar to the **return-of-service form** shown in Exhibit 10.5. This form is then submitted to the court as evidence that service has been effected.

return-of-service form
A document signed by a process server and submitted to the court to prove that a defendant received a summons.

Jurisdictions Vary.   Paralegal Lopez must be very careful to comply with the service requirements of the court in which plaintiff Baranski's suit has been filed. If service is not properly made, defendant Peretto will have a legal ground (basis) for asking the court to dismiss the case against him, thus delaying the litigation. As mentioned earlier, the court will not be able to exercise jurisdiction over Peretto until he has been properly notified of the lawsuit being brought against him.

Serving Corporate Defendants

In cases involving corporate defendants, the summons and complaint may be served on an officer or a *registered agent* (representative) of the corporation. The name of a corporation's registered agent and its business address can usually be obtained from the secretary of state's office in the state in which the company incorporated its business (and, usually, the secretary of state's office in any state in which the corporation does business).

EXHIBIT 10.5
A Return-of-Service Form

RETURN OF SERVICE

Service of the Summons and Complaint was made by me	DATE 2/11/11
NAME OF SERVER Elena Lopez	TITLE Paralegal

Check one box below to indicate appropriate method of service

☒ Served personally upon the defendant. Place where served: _Defendant Peretto's Home: 1708 Johnston Drive, Zero City, Zero 59806_

☐ Left copies thereof at the defendant's dwelling house or usual place of abode with a person of suitable age and discretion then residing therein. Name of person with whom the summons and complaint were left: _____

☐ Returned unexecuted: _____

☐ Other (specify): _____

DECLARATION OF SERVER

I declare under penalty of perjury under the laws of the United States of America that the foregoing information contained in the Return of Service and Statement of Service Fees is true and correct.

Executed on ___2/11/11___   *Elena Lopez*
                Date   *Signature of Server*

308 University Avenue, Nita City, Nita 48804
Address of Server

Finding the Defendant

Because some defendants may be difficult to locate, paralegals sometimes have to investigate and attempt to locate a defendant so that process can be served. Helpful information sources include telephone directories, banks, former business partners or fellow workers, credit bureaus, Social Security offices, insurance companies, landlords, state and county tax rolls, utility companies, automobile-registration bureaus, bureaus of vital statistics, and the post office. (Chapter 11 discusses these and other possible sources, including various online sources, that the paralegal might consult when trying to locate parties or witnesses involved in lawsuits.)

The Defendant Can Waive Service

In many instances, the defendant is already aware that a lawsuit is being filed (often the plaintiff's attorney has been in contact with the defendant and has indicated that a complaint would be filed). In such cases, a plaintiff can request the defendant to *waive* (give up) her or his right to be formally served with a summons. FRCP 4(d) sets forth the procedure by which a plaintiff's attorney can request the defendant to accept service of the documents through the mail or "other reliable means." Many states have similar rules.

The aim of FRCP 4(d) is to eliminate the costs associated with service of process and to foster cooperation among adversaries. As an incentive, defendants who agree to waive formal service of process under the federal rules receive additional time to respond to the complaint (sixty days, compared with the twenty days that a defendant normally has to respond to the complaint under FRCP 12). Some state rules of civil procedure provide other types of incentives, such as making a party who will not agree to waive service pay for reasonable expenses thereafter incurred in serving or attempting to serve the party.

The Defendant's Response

Once a defendant receives the plaintiff's complaint, the defendant must respond to the complaint within a specified time period (typically twenty days). If the defendant fails to respond within that time, the court, on the plaintiff's motion, will enter a **default judgment** against the defendant. The defendant will then be liable for the entire amount of damages that the plaintiff is claiming and will lose the opportunity to either defend against the claim in court or settle the issue with the plaintiff out of court.

In the Baranski case, assume that defendant Peretto consults with an attorney, Elizabeth A. Cameron, to decide on a course of action. Before Cameron advises Peretto on the matter, she will investigate plaintiff Baranski's claim and obtain evidence of what happened at the time of the accident. She may ask her paralegal, Gordon McVay, to call anyone who may have witnessed the accident and any police officers who were at the scene. Cameron will also ask McVay to gather relevant documents, including the traffic ticket that Peretto received at the time of the accident and any reports filed by the police. If all goes well, Cameron and McVay will complete their investigation in a few days and then meet to assess the results.

As mentioned earlier, most cases are settled out of court before they go to trial. But even if Peretto's attorney suspects that an out-of-court settlement might be financially preferable to a trial, she will draft a response to Baranski's claim. She knows that if Peretto does not respond to the complaint within the proper time period, the court will enter a default judgment against him. In deciding how best to respond to the complaint, Cameron must consider whether to file an answer or a motion to dismiss the case.

The Answer

A defendant's **answer** must respond to each allegation in the plaintiff's complaint. FRCP 8(b) permits the defendant to admit or deny the truth of each allegation. Peretto's attorney may advise him to admit to some of the allegations in Baranski's complaint, because doing so narrows the number of issues in dispute. Any allegations that are not denied by the defendant will be deemed to have been admitted.

If Peretto does not know whether a particular allegation is true or false, then, Cameron may indicate that in the answer. This puts the burden of proving the allegation on Baranski, just as if it were an outright denial. It is not necessary for Peretto's attorney to include in the answer any of the reasons for the denial of particular allegations in Baranski's complaint. These reasons may be revealed during the discovery phase of the litigation process (discussed later in this chapter).

Exhibit 10.6 on the following two pages illustrates the types of responses that Peretto might make in his answer. Like the complaint, the answer begins with a caption and ends with the attorney's signature. It may also include, following the attorney's signature, an affidavit signed by the defendant, as well as a demand for a jury trial, as in Exhibit 10.6.

Answer and Affirmative Defenses.   A defendant may assert, in the answer, a reason why he or she should not be held liable for the plaintiff's injuries even if the facts, as alleged by the plaintiff, are true. This is called raising an **affirmative defense**.

For example, Peretto might claim that someone else was driving his Dodge van when it crashed into Baranski's car. Peretto's attorney might also raise the defense of *contributory negligence*. That is, she could argue that even though Peretto's car

---

default judgment
A judgment entered by a clerk or court against a party who has failed to appear in court to answer or defend against a claim that has been brought against him or her by another party.

Case at a Glance

The Plaintiff—
Plaintiff: Katherine Baranski
Attorney: Allen P. Gilmore
Paralegal: Elena Lopez

The Defendant—
Defendant: Tony Peretto
Attorney: Elizabeth A. Cameron
Paralegal: Gordon McVay

---

answer
A defendant's response to a plaintiff's complaint.

---

affirmative defense
A response to a plaintiff's claim that does not deny the plaintiff's facts but attacks the plaintiff's legal right to bring an action.

collided with Baranski's, Baranski was also negligent because she was exceeding the speed limit when the accident occurred and was thus unable to avoid being hit. As will be discussed in Chapter 14, in a few states, if it can be shown that the plaintiff was contributorily negligent, the plaintiff will be completely barred from recovery. Most states, however, use the *comparative negligence* standard. In these states, a plaintiff whose own negligence contributed to an injury can still recover damages, but the damages are reduced by a percentage that represents the degree of the plaintiff's negligence. Although affirmative defenses are directed toward the plaintiff, the plaintiff is not required to file additional pleadings in response to these defenses.

EXHIBIT 10.6
The Answer

UNITED STATES DISTRICT COURT
FOR THE WESTERN DISTRICT OF NITA

Katherine Baranski)
        Plaintiff,)
)
v.)
)
Tony Peretto)
        Defendant.)

CASE NO. 11-14335-NI
Honorable Harley M. Larue

ANSWER AND
DEMAND FOR JURY TRIAL

<u>JURISDICTIONAL ALLEGATIONS</u>

1. Defendant lacks sufficient information to form a belief as to the truth of the allegations contained in paragraph 1 of Plaintiff's Complaint.

2. Defendant admits the allegations contained in paragraph 2 of Plaintiff's Complaint.

3. Defendant admits the allegations contained in paragraph 3 of Plaintiff's Complaint.

4. Defendant lacks sufficient information to form a belief as to the truth of the allegations contained in paragraph 4 of Plaintiff's Complaint.

<u>GENERAL ALLEGATIONS</u>

5. Defendant admits the allegations contained in paragraph 5 of Plaintiff's Complaint.

6. Defendant admits the allegations contained in paragraph 6 of Plaintiff's Complaint.

7. Defendant contends that he was operating his vehicle properly and denies the allegations contained in paragraph 7 of Plaintiff's Complaint for the reason that the allegations are untrue.

8. Defendant admits the allegation contained in paragraph 8 of Plaintiff's Complaint.

9. Defendant lacks sufficient information to form a belief as to the truth of the allegation contained in paragraph 9 of Plaintiff's Complaint.

10. Defendant lacks sufficient information on the proximate cause of Plaintiff's injuries to form a belief as to the truth of the averments contained in paragraph 10 of Plaintiff's Complaint.

11. Defendant denies the allegation of negligence contained in paragraph 11 of Plaintiff's Complaint.

Continued

EXHIBIT 10.6
The Answer—Continued

NEW MATTER AND AFFIRMATIVE DEFENSES

Although denying that the Plaintiff is entitled to the relief prayed for in the Plaintiff's Complaint, Defendant further states that the Plaintiff is barred from recovery hereunder by reason of the following:

1. That the Plaintiff's injuries were proximately caused by her own contributory negligence and want of due care under the circumstances prevailing at the time of the accident.

2. That the Plaintiff was exceeding the posted speed limit at the time and place of the accident and therefore was guilty of careless and negligent driving within the meaning of Section 9.2325(1) of the Nita Statutes Annotated.

3. That the Plaintiff failed to exercise that standard of care that a reasonably prudent person would have exercised under the same or similar conditions for her own safety and that her own negligence, contributory negligence, and/or comparative negligence caused or was a contributing factor to the incident out of which the Plaintiff's cause of action arises.

4. The Defendant reserves the right, by an appropriate Motion, to move the Court to amend the Defendant's Answer to the Plaintiff's Complaint, to allege other New Matters and Affirmative Defenses as may be revealed by discovery yet to be had and completed in this case.

WHEREFORE, the Defendant prays for a judgment of no cause of action with costs and attorneys' fees to be paid by the Plaintiff.

Cameron & Strauss, P.C.

Elizabeth A. Cameron

Date: 2/25/11

Elizabeth A. Cameron
Attorney for the Defendant

310 Lake Drive
Zero City, ZE 59802

Tony Peretto, being first duly sworn, states that he has read the foregoing Answer by him subscribed and that he knows the contents thereof, and the same is true, except those matters therein stated to be upon information and belief, and as to those matters, he believes to be true.

Tony Peretto

Defendant

Sworn and subscribed before me this 25th day of February, 2011.

Laura Curtis

Notary Public, Zero County,
State of Zero

My Commission Expires:
December 8, 2012

DEMAND FOR A JURY TRIAL

The Defendant demands a trial by jury.

Cameron & Strauss, P.C.

Elizabeth A. Cameron

Date: 2/25/11

Elizabeth A. Cameron
Attorney for the Defendant
310 Lake Drive
Zero City, Zero 59802

counterclaim
A claim made by a defendant in a civil lawsuit against the plaintiff; in effect, a counterclaiming defendant is suing the plaintiff.

Answer and Counterclaim. Peretto's attorney may follow the answers to the plaintiff's allegations with one or more counterclaims. A **counterclaim** is like a reverse lawsuit in which the defendant asserts a claim against the plaintiff for injuries that the defendant suffered from the same incident. For example, Peretto might contend that Baranski lost control of her car and skidded into Peretto's car, causing him to be injured. This allegation would be a counterclaim. The plaintiff is required to reply to any counterclaims made by the defendant.

Answer and Cross-Claim.   In cases in which a complaint names multiple defendants, the answer filed by one defendant might be followed by a **cross-claim**, in which the defendant asserts a claim against another defendant. (Note that cross-claims may also be filed by one plaintiff against another plaintiff in the same case.) For example, suppose that plaintiff Baranski had been struck by two vehicles, one belonging to defendant Peretto and one belonging to Leon Balfour. If Peretto and Balfour had been named as co-defendants in Baranski's complaint, Peretto's attorney might have filed an answer to Baranski's complaint that included a cross-claim against Balfour. The party against whom the cross-claim is brought is required to reply to (answer) the claim.

Under the federal rules, a defendant who has a claim against the plaintiff related to the same incident is normally required to file a counterclaim within the defendant's pleading. A party who fails to do so may forgo the possibility of asserting the claim at a later date. This requirement is intended to prevent multiple lawsuits between the same parties.

Motion to Dismiss

A **motion** is a procedural request submitted to the court by an attorney on behalf of his or her client. When one party files a motion with the court, that party must also send to, or serve on, the opposing party a *notice of motion*. The notice of motion informs the opposing party that the motion has been filed and indicates when the court will hear the motion. The notice gives the opposing party an opportunity to prepare for the hearing and argue before the court why the motion should not be granted.

The **motion to dismiss**, as the phrase implies, requests the court to dismiss the case for reasons provided in the motion. Defendant Peretto's attorney, for example, could file a motion to dismiss if she believed that Peretto had not been properly served, that the complaint had been filed in the wrong court, that the statute of limitations for that type of lawsuit had expired, or that the complaint did not state a claim for which relief (a remedy) could be granted. See Exhibit 10.7 on the next page for an example of a motion to dismiss.

If Peretto's attorney decides to file a motion to dismiss Baranski's claim, she may want to attach one or more **supporting affidavits**—sworn statements as to certain facts that may contradict the allegations made in the complaint. Peretto's attorney may also have her paralegal draft a **memorandum of law** (which is called a *brief* in some states) to be submitted along with the motion to dismiss and the accompanying affidavits. The memorandum of law will present the legal basis for the motion, citing any statutes and cases that support it. A supporting affidavit gives factual support to the motion to dismiss, while the memorandum of law provides the legal grounds for the dismissal of the claim.

The Scheduling Conference

After the complaint and answer have been filed, the court typically schedules a conference to consult with the attorneys for both sides. (A party who is not represented by an attorney will attend the conference himself or herself.) Following this meeting, the judge enters a *scheduling order* that sets out the time limits within which pretrial events (such as the pleadings, the discovery, and the final pretrial conference) must be completed, as well as the date of the trial. Under FRCP 16(b), the scheduling order should be entered "as soon as practicable but in any event within 90 days after the appearance of a defendant and within 120 days after the complaint has been served on a defendant." The purpose of this meeting is to enable the court to manage the case efficiently and establish time restrictions that are appropriate given the facts and circumstances of the case.

---

cross-claim

A claim asserted by a defendant in a civil lawsuit against another defendant or by a plaintiff against another plaintiff.

Case at a Glance

The Plaintiff—
   Plaintiff: Katherine Baranski
   Attorney: Allen P. Gilmore
   Paralegal: Elena Lopez

The Defendant—
   Defendant: Tony Peretto
   Attorney: Elizabeth A. Cameron
   Paralegal: Gordon McVay

motion

A procedural request or application presented by an attorney to the court on behalf of a client.

motion to dismiss

A motion filed by the defendant in which the defendant asks the court to dismiss the case for a specified reason, such as improper service, lack of personal jurisdiction, or the plaintiff's failure to state a claim for which relief can be granted.

supporting affidavit

An affidavit accompanying a motion that is filed by an attorney on behalf of his or her client. The sworn statements in the affidavit provide a factual basis for the motion.

memorandum of law

A document (known as a *brief* in some states) that delineates the legal theories, statutes, and cases on which a motion is based.

EXHIBIT 10.7
A Motion to Dismiss

UNITED STATES DISTRICT COURT
FOR THE WESTERN DISTRICT OF NITA

Katherine Baranski	)	
Plaintiff,	)	CASE NO. 11-14335-NI
	)	Honorable Harley M. Larue
v.	)	
	)	
	)	MOTION TO DISMISS
Tony Peretto	)	
Defendant.	)	

The Defendant, Tony Peretto, by his attorney, moves the court to dismiss the above-named action because the statute of limitations governing the Plaintiff's claim has expired, as demonstrated in the memorandum of law that is being submitted with this motion. The Plaintiff therefore has no cause of action against the Defendant.

Cameron & Strauss, P.C.

Elizabeth A. Cameron

Date: 2/20/11

Elizabeth A. Cameron
Attorney for the Defendant
310 Lake Drive
Zero City, ZE 59802

Amending the Pleadings

An attorney may be called on by a client to file a complaint or an answer without having much time to become familiar with the facts of the case. Because no attorney can anticipate how a case will evolve, the complaint or answer may have to be amended to account for newly discovered facts or evidence. Amendments may also be desirable when circumstances dictate that a different legal theory or defense be put forward.

PRETRIAL MOTIONS

Many motions may be made during the pretrial litigation process, including those described in Exhibit 10.8. Some pretrial motions, if granted by the court, end a case before trial. These motions include the motion to dismiss (which has already been discussed), the motion for judgment on the pleadings, and the motion for summary judgment. Here we examine the latter two motions.

Motion for Judgment on the Pleadings

Once the two attorneys in the Baranski case, Gilmore and Cameron, have finished filing their respective pleadings and amendments, either one of them may file a **motion for judgment on the pleadings**. Such a motion is often filed when the pleadings indicate that no facts are in dispute and the only question is how the law applies to a set of undisputed facts. For example, assume for a moment that in the Baranski case, Peretto admitted to all of Baranski's allegations in his answer and raised no affirmative defenses. In this situation, Baranski's attorney, Gilmore, would file a motion for judgment on the pleadings in Baranski's favor.

Motion for Summary Judgment

A **motion for summary judgment** is similar to a motion for judgment on the pleadings in that the party filing the motion is asking the court to grant a judgment in his or her favor without a trial. As with a motion for judgment on the pleadings, a

---

motion for judgment on the pleadings
A motion that may be filed by either party in which the party asks the court to enter a judgment in his or her favor based on information contained in the pleadings. A judgment on the pleadings will only be made if there are no facts in dispute and the only question is how the law applies to a set of undisputed facts.

motion for summary judgment
A motion that may be filed by either party in which the party asks the court to enter judgment in his or her favor without a trial. Unlike a motion for judgment on the pleadings, a motion for summary judgment can be supported by evidence outside the pleadings, such as witnesses' affidavits, answers to interrogatories, and other evidence obtained prior to or during discovery.

EXHIBIT 10.8
Pretrial Motions

MOTION TO DISMISS

A motion filed by the defendant in which the defendant asks the court to dismiss the case for a specified reason, such as improper service, lack of personal jurisdiction, or the plaintiff's failure to state a claim for which relief can be granted.

MOTION TO STRIKE

A motion filed by the defendant in which the defendant asks the court to strike (delete) from the complaint certain paragraphs contained in the complaint. Motions to strike help to clarify the underlying issues that form the basis for the complaint by removing paragraphs that are redundant or irrelevant to the action.

MOTION TO MAKE MORE DEFINITE AND CERTAIN

A motion filed by the defendant to compel the plaintiff to clarify the basis of the plaintiff's cause of action. The motion is filed when the defendant believes that the complaint is too vague or ambiguous for the defendant to respond to it in a meaningful way.

MOTION FOR JUDGMENT ON THE PLEADINGS

A motion that may be filed by either party in which the party asks the court to enter a judgment in his or her favor based on information contained in the pleadings. A judgment on the pleadings will only be made if there are no facts in dispute and the only question is how the law applies to a set of undisputed facts.

MOTION TO COMPEL DISCOVERY

A motion that may be filed by either party in which the party asks the court to compel the other party to comply with a discovery request. If a party refuses to allow the opponent to inspect and copy certain documents, for example, the party requesting the documents may make a motion to compel production of the documents.

MOTION FOR SUMMARY JUDGMENT

A motion that may be filed by either party in which the party asks the court to enter judgment in his or her favor without a trial. Unlike a motion for judgment on the pleadings, a motion for summary judgment can be supported by evidence outside the pleadings, such as witnesses' affidavits, answers to interrogatories, and other evidence obtained prior to or during discovery.

court will only grant a motion for summary judgment if it determines that no facts are in dispute and the only question is how the law applies to a set of facts agreed on by both parties.

When the court considers a motion for summary judgment, it can take into account *evidence outside the pleadings.* This distinguishes the motion for summary judgment from the motion to dismiss and the motion for judgment on the pleadings. To support a motion for summary judgment, one party can submit evidence obtained at any point prior to trial (including during the discovery stage of litigation—to be discussed shortly) that refutes the other party's factual claim. In the Baranski case, for example, suppose that Peretto was in another state at the time of the accident. Peretto's attorney could make a motion for summary judgment in Peretto's favor and attach to the motion a witness's sworn statement that Peretto was in the other state at the time of the accident. Unless Baranski's attorney could bring in sworn statements by other witnesses to show that Peretto was at the scene of the accident, Peretto would normally be granted his motion for summary judgment.

A motion for summary judgment would be particularly appropriate if Baranski had previously signed a release waiving her right to sue Peretto on the claim. In that situation, Peretto's attorney, Cameron, would attach a copy of the release to the motion before filing the motion with the court. Cameron would also prepare and attach a memorandum of law in support of the motion. When the motion was heard by the court, Cameron would argue that the execution of the waiver barred Baranski from pursuing her claim against Peretto.

The burden would then shift to Baranski's attorney, Gilmore, to demonstrate that the release was invalid or otherwise not binding on Baranski. If the judge believed that the release had been voluntarily signed by Baranski, then the judge might grant the motion for summary judgment in Peretto's favor. If Gilmore convinced the judge that the release signed by Baranski had been procured by coercive or fraudulent practices, however, then the judge would deny the motion for summary judgment and permit the case to go to trial.

TRADITIONAL DISCOVERY TOOLS

Before a trial begins, the parties can use a number of procedural devices to obtain information and gather evidence about the case. Baranski's attorney, for example, will want to know how fast Peretto was driving, whether he had been drinking, and whether he saw the stop sign. The process of obtaining information from the opposing party or from other witnesses is known as **discovery**.

Discovery serves several purposes. It preserves evidence from witnesses who might not be available at the time of the trial or whose memories will fade as time passes. It can pave the way for summary judgment if both parties agree on all of the facts. It can lead to an out-of-court settlement if one party decides that the opponent's case is too strong to challenge. Even if the case does go to trial, discovery prevents surprises by giving parties access to evidence that might otherwise be hidden. This allows both parties to learn as much as they can about what to expect at a trial before they reach the courtroom. It also serves to narrow the issues so that trial time is spent on the main questions in the case.

The FRCP and similar rules in the states set forth the guidelines for discovery activity. Discovery includes gaining access to witnesses, documents, records, and other types of evidence. The rules governing discovery are designed to make sure that a witness or a party is not unduly harassed, that **privileged information** (communications that ordinarily may not be disclosed in court) is safeguarded, and that only matters relevant to the case at hand are discoverable. The trend today is toward allowing more discovery and thus fewer surprises.

Traditional discovery devices include interrogatories, depositions, requests for production and physical examination, and requests for admission. Each of these tools is examined below.

Interrogatories

Interrogatories are written questions that must be answered, in writing, by the parties to the lawsuit and then signed by the parties under oath. Typically, the paralegal drafts the interrogatories for the attorney's review and approval. In the Baranski case, for example, attorney Gilmore will probably ask paralegal Lopez to draft interrogatories to be sent to defendant Peretto.

Drafting Interrogatories

All discovery documents, including interrogatories, normally begin with a caption similar to the complaint caption illustrated earlier in this chapter. Following the caption, Lopez will add the name of the party who must answer the interrogatories, instructions to be followed by the party, and definitions of certain terms that are used in the interrogatories. The body of the document consists of the interrogatories themselves—that is, the questions that the opposing party must answer. The interrogatories should end with a signature line for the attorney, followed by the attorney's name and address.

discovery
Formal investigation prior to trial. Opposing parties use various methods, such as interrogatories and depositions, to obtain information from each other and from witnesses to prepare for trial.

privileged information
Confidential communications between certain individuals, such as an attorney and his or her client, that are protected from disclosure except under court order.

interrogatories
A series of written questions for which written answers are prepared and then signed under oath by a party to a lawsuit (the plaintiff or the defendant).

Ethics Watch

KEEPING CLIENT INFORMATION CONFIDENTIAL

As it happens, attorney Gilmore's legal assistant, Lopez, is a good friend of plaintiff Baranski's sister. Lopez learns from the results of Baranski's medical examination that Baranski has a terminal illness. Lopez is sure that the sister, who quarreled with Baranski two months ago and hasn't spoken to her since, is unaware of the illness and would probably be hurt if she learned that Lopez knew of it and didn't tell her. Should Lopez tell her friend about the illness? No. This is confidential information at this point, which Lopez only became aware of by virtue of her job. Should the information be revealed publicly during the course of the trial, then Lopez would be free to disclose it to her friend if the friend still remained unaware of it. In the meantime, Lopez is ethically (and legally) obligated to protect the information from anyone who is not working on the case, including her friend.

This behavior is consistent with the NFPA Model Disciplinary Rules and Ethical Considerations, Section EC-1.5(f): "A paralegal shall not engage in any indiscreet communications concerning clients."

Before drafting the questions, Lopez will want to review carefully the contents of the case file (including the pleadings and the evidence and other information that she obtained during her preliminary investigation into Baranski's claim). She will want to consult with Gilmore on the litigation strategy he believes should be pursued as the case moves forward. For further guidance, she might consult form books containing sample interrogatories, as well as interrogatories used in similar cases previously handled by the firm.

Depending on the complexity of the case, interrogatories may be few in number, or they may run into the hundreds. Exhibit 10.9 on the next two pages illustrates the types of interrogatories that have traditionally been used in cases similar to the Baranski-Peretto case. Depending on the rules of the court in which the Baranski lawsuit is being filed, Lopez might draft similar interrogatories for Peretto to answer. Realize that many state courts limit the number of interrogatories that can be used. FRCP 33 limits the number of interrogatories in federal court cases to twenty-five (unless a greater number are allowed by stipulation of the parties or by court order). Therefore, before drafting interrogatories, the paralegal should always check the rules of the court in which an action is being filed to find out if that court limits the number of interrogatories.

Answering Interrogatories

After receiving the interrogatories, Peretto must answer them within a specified time period (thirty days under FRCP 33) in writing and under oath, as mentioned above. Depending on the rules of the court system, this can likely be handled electronically. Very likely, Peretto will have substantial guidance from his attorney and his attorney's paralegal in forming his answers. He must answer each question truthfully, of course, because he is under oath. His attorney and her paralegal will counsel him, though, on how to phrase his answers so that they are both truthful and strategically sound. For example, they will advise him on how to limit his answers to prevent disclosing more information than necessary.

EXHIBIT 10.9
Sample Interrogatories

UNITED STATES DISTRICT COURT
FOR THE WESTERN DISTRICT OF NITA

Katherine Baranski   )
           Plaintiff,   )   CASE NO. 11-14335-NI
)   Honorable Harley M. Larue
v.   )
)   PLAINTIFF'S FIRST
)   INTERROGATORIES
Tony Peretto   )   TO DEFENDANT
          Defendant.)

PLEASE TAKE NOTICE that the following Interrogatories are directed to you under the provisions of Rule 26(a)(5) and Rule 33 of the Federal Rules of Civil Procedure. You are requested to answer these Interrogatories and to furnish such information in answer to the Interrogatories as is available to you.

You are required to serve integrated Interrogatories and Answers to these Interrogatories under oath, within thirty (30) days after service of them upon you. The original answers are to be retained in your attorney's possession, and a copy of the answers is to be served upon Plaintiff's counsel.

The answers should be signed and sworn to by the person making answer to the Interrogatories.

When used in these Interrogatories the term "Defendant," or any synonym thereof, is intended to and shall embrace and include, in addition to said Defendant, all agents, servants and employees, representatives, attorneys, private investigators, or others who are in possession of or who may have obtained information for or on behalf of the Defendant.

These Interrogatories shall be deemed continuing, and supplemental answers shall be required immediately upon receipt thereof if Defendant, directly or indirectly, obtains further or different information from the time answers are served until the time of trial.

1. Were you the driver of an automobile involved in an accident with Plaintiff on August 4, 2010, at about 7:45 A.M. at the intersection of Mattis Avenue and Thirty-eighth Street, in Nita City, Nita? If so, please state:

    (a) Your name;
    (b) Every name you have used in the past;
    (c) The dates you used each name;
    (d) The date and place of your birth.

2. Please list your current residence and all residences you occupied in the five years preceding your move to your current residence, including complete addresses, dates of residence, and names of owners or managers.

3. Please indicate where you are presently employed and where you were employed during the five years preceding the beginning of your current employment. In so doing, please indicate the following:

    (a) The names, addresses, and telephone numbers of each employer or place of business, including the dates during which you worked there;
    (b) How many hours you worked, on average, per week;
    (c) The names, addresses, and telephone numbers of your supervisors (or owners of the business);
    (d) The nature of the work that you performed.

EXHIBIT 10.9

Sample Interrogatories—Continued

4. At the time of the incident, were you acting as an agent or employee for any person? If so, state:

 (a) The name, address, and telephone number of that person;
 (b) A description of your duties.

5. At the time of the incident, did you have a driver's license? If so, state:

 (a) The state or other issuing entity;
 (b) The license number and type;
 (c) The date of issuance and expiration;
 (d) Any violations, offenses, or restrictions against your license.

6. Indicate whether you have ever had your driver's license suspended, revoked, or canceled and whether you have ever been denied the issuance of a driver's license for mental or physical reasons. If you have, please indicate the date and state of such occurrence as well as the reasons for it.

7. At the time of the incident, did you or any other person have any physical, emotional, or mental disability or condition that may have contributed to the occurrence of the incident? If so, for each person state:

 (a) The name, address, and telephone number;
 (b) The nature of the disability or condition;
 (c) The name, address, and telephone number of any qualified person who treated or diagnosed the condition and the dates of such treatment;
 (d) The manner in which the disability or condition contributed to the occurrence of the incident.

8. Within twenty-four hours before the incident, did you or any person involved in the incident use or take any of the following substances: alcoholic beverage, marijuana, or other drug or medication of any kind (prescription or not)? If so, for each person state:

 (a) The name, address, and telephone number;
 (b) The nature or description of each substance;
 (c) The quantity of each substance used or taken;
 (d) The date and time of day when each substance was used or taken;
 (e) The address where each substance was used or taken;
 (f) The name, address, and telephone number of each person who was present when each substance was used or taken;
 (g) The name, address, and telephone number of any health-care provider that prescribed or furnished the substance and the condition for which it was prescribed or furnished.

9. For each time you have had your vision checked within the last five years, please indicate the following:

 (a) The date and reason for the vision examination;
 (b) The name, address, and telephone number of the examiner;
 (c) The results and/or actions taken.

10. For each time you have had your hearing checked within the last five years, please indicate the following:

 (a) The date and reason for the hearing examination;
 (b) The name, address, and telephone number of the examiner;
 (c) The results and/or actions taken.

[Additional questions would be asked relating to the accident, including questions concerning road conditions and surface, posted speed limits, shoulders and curbs on the road, general character of the neighborhood, when the defendant noticed the plaintiff's vehicle, where it was located and the speed at which the plaintiff was traveling, whether there were other vehicles between the plaintiff's and the defendant's vehicles, and so forth.]

Dated: _____

_____
Allen P. Gilmore
Attorney for Plaintiff

Depositions

deposition

A pretrial question-and-answer proceeding, usually conducted orally, in which a party or witness answers an attorney's questions. The answers are given under oath, and the session is recorded.

deponent

A party or witness who testifies under oath during a deposition.

Like interrogatories, **depositions** are given under oath. Unlike interrogatories, however, depositions are usually conducted orally (except in certain circumstances, such as when the party being deposed is at a great distance and cannot be deposed via telephone). Furthermore, they may be taken from witnesses. As indicated earlier, interrogatories can only be taken from the parties to the lawsuit.

When an attorney takes the deposition, the attorney is able to question the person being deposed (the **deponent**) *in person* and then follow up with any other questions that come to mind. The attorney is not limited in the number of questions that she or he may ask in a deposition, whereas many courts limit the number of interrogatory questions. Moreover, because the questioning is usually done in person, the deponent must answer the questions without asking an attorney or paralegal how he or she should respond. Thus, the answers to deposition questions are not filtered through counsel in the same way answers to interrogatories are.

Normally, the defendant's attorney deposes the plaintiff first, and then the plaintiff's attorney deposes the defendant. Following these depositions, the attorneys may depose witnesses and other parties to obtain information about the event leading to the lawsuit. When both the defendant and the plaintiff are located in the same jurisdiction, the site of the deposition will usually be the offices of the attorney requesting the deposition. When the parties are located in different jurisdictions, other arrangements may be made. In the Baranski case, attorney Gilmore will travel to Peretto's city, which is in another state, and depose Peretto in the office of Peretto's attorney, Cameron.

Procedure for Taking Depositions

The attorney wishing to depose a party or witness must give reasonable notice in writing to all other parties in the case. This is done by serving the opposing attorney (or attorneys) with a notice of taking deposition, which states the time and place of the deposition and the name of the person being examined (see Exhibit 10.10).

If the person scheduled to be deposed would not attend voluntarily, a paralegal may also need to prepare a subpoena for deposition and submit it to the court for signature. Generally, a **subpoena** is an order issued by the court clerk directing a party to appear and to testify at trial, as will be discussed in Chapter 12. A *subpoena for deposition* orders the person to appear at a deposition rather than in a court proceeding. A subpoena should also be prepared if the attorney wants the deponent to bring certain documents or tangible things to the deposition (this is called a *subpoena duces tecum*).

Under FRCP 30 and 31, court permission is required for depositions to be taken before the parties have made the initial disclosures required by Rule 26 (discussed later in this chapter). Also, court approval may be required if either party wants to take more than one deposition from the same person or more than a total of ten depositions in the case.

subpoena

A document commanding a person to appear at a certain time and place to give testimony concerning a certain matter.

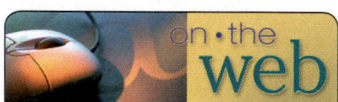

To see an example of the subpoena process, visit the Web site of the state government of Alaska at **www. state.ak.us**. Search on the term "court form," and on the "Forms, Instructions & Publications: By Number" page, select form civ-109.pdf, "How to Subpoena a Witness."

Drafting Deposition Questions

Depositions are conducted by attorneys. Although paralegals may attend depositions, they do not ask questions. Deposition questions are often drafted by paralegals, however. In the Baranski case, for example, attorney Gilmore might ask paralegal Lopez to draft questions for a deposition of defendant Peretto or someone else, such as an eyewitness to the accident. For Peretto's deposition, Lopez might draft questions similar to those presented in Exhibit 10.11 on page 330. Gilmore can then use Lopez's questions as a kind of checklist during the deposition. Note, though, that Gilmore's questions will not be limited to the questions included in the list. Other, unforeseen questions may arise as Gilmore learns new information during the deposition. Also, the deponent's answer to one question may reveal the answer to another, so that not all questions will need to be asked.

EXHIBIT 10.10
Notice of Taking Deposition

**UNITED STATES DISTRICT COURT
FOR THE WESTERN DISTRICT OF NITA**

Katherine Baranski)	
Plaintiff,)	CASE NO. 11-14335-NI
)	Honorable Harley M. Larue
v.)	
)	NOTICE OF TAKING
Tony Peretto)	DEPOSITION
Defendant.)	

TO: Elizabeth A. Cameron
      Cameron & Strauss, P.C.
      310 Lake Drive
      Zero City, ZE 59802

   PLEASE TAKE NOTICE that Katherine Baranski, by and through her attorneys, Jeffers, Gilmore & Dunn, will take the deposition of Tony Peretto on Wednesday, April 15, 2011, at 1:30 P.M., at the law offices of Cameron & Strauss, P.C., 310 Lake Drive, Zero City, ZE 59802, pursuant to the Federal Rules of Civil Procedure, before a duly authorized and qualified notary and stenographer.

Dated: March 20, 2011

                                        Jeffers, Gilmore & Dunn

                                        Allen P Gilmore
                                        Allen P Gilmore
                                        Attorney for Katherine Baranski
                                        553 Fifth Avenue, Suite 101
                                        Nita City, NI 48801

Preparing the Client for a Deposition

No attorney can predict a deponent's answers beforehand. Spontaneous and perhaps even contradictory statements can seriously damage the deponent's case. For this reason, the deposed party and his or her lawyer will want to prepare for the deposition by formulating mock answers to anticipated questions. For example, if defendant Peretto's attorney plans to depose plaintiff Baranski, attorney Gilmore and paralegal Lopez might have Baranski come into their office for a run-through of possible questions that Peretto's attorney might ask her during the deposition. This kind of preparation does not mean that the lawyer tells the deponent what to say. Instead, the lawyer offers suggestions as to how the answers to certain questions should be phrased. The answers must be truthful, but the truth can be presented in many ways.

   Gilmore would also caution Baranski to limit her responses to the questions and not to engage in speculative answers that might prejudice her claim. If Baranski was asked whether she had ever been involved in an automobile accident before, for example, Gilmore would probably caution her to use a simple (but truthful) "yes" or "no" answer. Attorney Gilmore normally would permit Baranski to volunteer additional information only in response to precisely phrased questions.

The Role of the Deponent's Attorney

The deponent's attorney will attend the deposition, but the attorney's role will be limited. Under FRCP 30, the attorney may instruct a deponent not to answer a question only when necessary to preserve a privilege, to enforce a limitation directed by the court, or to present a motion to terminate the deposition. In other words, if Baranski was being deposed by Peretto's attorney, Cameron, she would have to answer Cameron's questions even if the questions were not clearly relevant to the issues of the case—unless the court had previously limited this line of questioning. The deponent's attorney, Gilmore, could object only to questions that called for

Case at a Glance

The Plaintiff—
   Plaintiff: Katherine Baranski
   Attorney: Allen P. Gilmore
   Paralegal: Elena Lopez

The Defendant—
   Defendant: Tony Peretto
   Attorney: Elizabeth A. Cameron
   Paralegal: Gordon McVay

EXHIBIT 10.11
Sample Deposition Questions

<u>DEPOSITION QUESTIONS</u>

1. Please state your full name and address for the record.
2. Please state your age, birth date, and Social Security number.
3. What is your educational level, and what employment position do you hold?
4. Do you have a criminal record, and if so, for what?
5. Have you been involved in previous automobile accidents? What driving violations have you had? Has your driver's license ever been suspended?
6. What is your medical history? Have you ever had health problems? Are you in perfect health? Were you in perfect health at the time of the accident?
7. Do you wear glasses or contact lenses? If so, for what condition? Were you wearing your glasses or contacts at the time the accident occurred?
8. Do you take medication of any kind?
9. Do you have any similar lawsuits or any claims pending against you?
10. Who is your automobile insurer? What are your policy limits?
11. Were there any passengers in your vehicle at the time of the accident?
12. Describe your vehicle. What was the mechanical condition of your vehicle at the time of the accident? Do you do your own mechanical work? If so, what training do you have in maintaining and repairing automobiles? Had you taken your vehicle to a professional mechanic's shop prior to the accident?
13. Please state the date on which the accident occurred.
14. Where were you prior to the accident, for at least the six hours preceding the accident?
15. Where were you going when the accident occurred, and for what purpose?
16. What were you doing during the last few moments before the accident? Were you smoking, eating, drinking, or chewing gum?
17. What were you thinking about just before the accident occurred?
18. What route did you take to reach your destination, and why did you take this particular route?
19. Describe the weather conditions at the time of the accident.
20. Please recite the facts of how the accident occurred.
21. Please describe the area in which the accident occurred. Were there many cars and pedestrians on the streets? Were there traffic controls, obstructions, or the like?
22. What was your location, and in what direction were you going?
23. When did you see the plaintiff's automobile approaching?
24. How far away were you when you first saw the auto? What was your rate of speed?
25. Did your vehicle move forward or was it pushed backward by the impact?
26. When did you first apply your brakes? Were your brakes functioning properly?
27. Did you attempt to avoid the accident? If so, how?
28. Did you receive a traffic ticket as a result of the accident?
29. Do you own the vehicle that you were driving at the time of the accident?
30. Were you acting within the scope of your employment when the accident occurred?
31. What were the conditions of the parties affected by the accident just after the accident occurred?
32. Did you attempt to provide first aid to any party?
33. How did the plaintiff leave the scene, and what was the plaintiff's physical condition?
34. What was the damage to your vehicle, and has it been repaired?

privileged information to be disclosed. Under Rule 30, that attorney is also required to state objections concisely, in a nonargumentative and nonsuggestive manner.

As will be discussed shortly, deposition proceedings are recorded. If both attorneys agree to do so, however, they can go "off the record" to clarify a point or discuss a disputed issue. Depositions are stressful events, and tempers often flare. In the event that the deposition can no longer be conducted in an orderly fashion, the attorney conducting the deposition may have to terminate it.

The Deposition Transcript

deposition transcript
The official transcription of the recording taken during a deposition.

Every utterance made during a deposition is recorded. A court reporter usually records the deposition proceedings and creates an official **deposition transcript**. Methods of recording a deposition include stenographic recording (a traditional

EXHIBIT 10.12
A Deposition Transcript (Excerpt)

67	Q: Where were you at the time of the accident?
68	A: I was on the southwest corner of the intersection.
69	Q: Are you referring to the intersection where Thirty-eighth Street crosses Mattis Avenue?
70	A: Yes.
71	Q: Why were you there at the time of the accident?
72	A: Well, I was on my way to work. I usually walk down Mattis Avenue to the hospital.
73	Q: So you were walking to work down Mattis Avenue and you saw the accident?
74	A: Yes.
75	Q: What did you see?
76	A: Well, as I was about to cross the street, a dark green van passed within three feet of me and ran the
77	stop sign and crashed into another car.
78	Q: Can you remember if the driver of the van was a male or a female?
79	A: Yes. It was a man.
80	Q: I am showing you a picture. Can you identify the man in the picture?
81	A: Yes. That is the man who was driving the van.
82	Q: Do you wear glasses?
83	A: I need glasses only for reading. I have excellent distance vision.
84	Q: How long has it been since your last eye exam with a doctor?
85	A: Oh, just a month ago, with Dr. Sullivan.

page 4

method that involves the use of a shorthand machine), audio recording, video recording, or some combination of these methods. Rule 30(b)(2) of the FRCP states that unless the court orders otherwise, a deposition "may be recorded by sound, sound-and-visual, or stenographic means."

The deposition transcript may be used by either party during the trial to prove a particular point or to **impeach** (call into question) the credibility of a witness who says something during the trial that is different from what he or she stated during the deposition. For example, a witness in the Baranski case might state during the deposition that Peretto *did not* stop at the stop sign before proceeding to cross Mattis Avenue. If, at trial, the witness states that Peretto *did* stop at the stop sign before crossing Mattis Avenue, Baranski's attorney (Gilmore) could challenge the witness's credibility on the basis of the deposition transcript. Exhibit 10.12 above shows a page from a transcript of a deposition conducted by Gilmore in the Baranski case. The deponent was Julia Williams, an eyewitness to the accident. On the transcript, the letter "Q" precedes each question asked by Gilmore, and the letter "A" precedes each of Williams's answers.

impeach
To call into question the credibility of a witness by challenging the truth or accuracy of his or her trial statement.

Summarizing and Indexing the Deposition Transcript

Typically, the paralegal summarizes the deposition transcript. The summary, which along with the transcript will become part of the litigation file, allows the members of the litigation team to review quickly the information obtained from the deponent during the deposition.

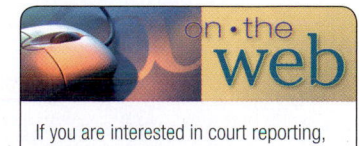

If you are interested in court reporting, visit the Web site of the National Court Reporters Association at **www.ncraonline.org**.

Developing Paralegal Skills

DEPOSITION SUMMARIES

After a deposition is taken, each attorney orders a copy of the deposition transcript. Copies may be obtained in printed form or in an electronic file. When the transcript is received, the legal assistant's job is to prepare a summary of the testimony that was given. The summary is typically only a few pages in length.

The legal assistant must be very familiar with the lawsuit and the legal theories that are being pursued so that he or she can point out inconsistencies in the testimony or between the testimony and the pleadings. The paralegal might also give special emphasis to any testimony that will help to prove the client's case in court.

After the deposition summary has been created, the paralegal places the summary in the litigation file, usually in a special discovery folder or binder within the larger file. The deposition summary will be used to prepare for future depositions, to prepare pretrial motions, and to impeach witnesses at the trial, should they give contradictory testimony.

TIPS FOR SUMMARIZING A DEPOSITION

- Find out how the deposition is to be summarized—by chronology, by legal issue, by factual issues, or otherwise.
- Read through the deposition transcript and mark important pages.
- Using a dictaphone or dictation software, dictate a summary of the information on the marked pages.
- Be sure to include a reference to the page and line that is being summarized.
- Take advantage of any software that will assist in summarizing the deposition transcript.

Case at a Glance

The Plaintiff—
 Plaintiff: Katherine Baranski
 Attorney: Allen P. Gilmore
 Paralegal: Elena Lopez

The Defendant—
 Defendant: Tony Peretto
 Attorney: Elizabeth A. Cameron
 Paralegal: Gordon McVay

In the Baranski case, assume that Lopez is asked to summarize the deposition transcript of Julia Williams. Typically, the transcript is summarized sequentially—that is, in the order in which it was given during the deposition—as shown in Exhibit 10.13. Notice that the summary includes the page and line numbers in the deposition transcript where the full text of the information can be found.

Often, in addition to summarizing the transcript, the paralegal provides an index to the document. The index consists of a list of topics (such as education, employment status, injuries, and medical costs) followed by the relevant page and line numbers of the deposition transcript. Together, the summary and the index allow anyone involved in the case to locate information quickly. Today, key-word indexes allow attorneys and paralegals to locate within seconds deposition testimony on a particular topic. Often, court reporters provide key-word indexes on request. More tips for summarizing a deposition are provided in the *Developing Paralegal Skills* feature.

Requests for Production and Physical Examination

Another traditional method of discovery is the request for the production of documents or tangible things or for permission to enter on land or other property for inspection and other purposes. FRCP 34 authorizes each party to request documents and other forms of evidence from any other party. If the item requested is very large or cannot be "produced" for some reason (Baranski's car, for example), then the party

EXHIBIT 10.13
A Deposition Summary (Excerpt)

| Case: | Baranski v. Peretto | Attorney: Allen P. Gilmore |
| | Plaintiff 15773 | Legal Assistant: Elena Lopez |

Deponent:	Julia Williams	Date: March 16, 2011
	3801 Mattis Avenue	
	Nita City, Nita 48800	

Page	Line(s)	
		* * * *
4	72–77	Williams stated that she was on the way to work at the time of the accident. She was about to cross the street when Peretto's car ("a dark green van") passed within three feet of her, ran the stop sign, and crashed into Baranski's car.
4	80–81	When shown a picture of Peretto, she identified him as the driver of the green van.
4	82–83	Williams has excellent distance vision and does not require corrective lenses. She does need reading glasses for close work.
		* * * *

can request permission to enter on the other party's land to inspect, test, sample, and photograph the item. In federal courts, the duty of disclosure under FRCP 26 (to be discussed shortly) has greatly decreased the need to file such production requests.

When the mental or physical condition of a party is in controversy, the opposing party may also request the court to order the party to submit to a physical or mental examination by a licensed examiner. For example, if Peretto claims that Baranski's injuries were the result of a preexisting medical condition, rather than the collision, defense attorney Cameron may file a request to have Baranski examined by a licensed physician. Because the existence, nature, and extent of Baranski's injuries are important in calculating the damages that she might be able to recover from Peretto, the court may order Baranski to undergo a physical examination if requested.

Requests for Admission

During discovery, a party can also request that the opposing party admit the truth of matters relating to the case. For example, Baranski's attorney can request that Peretto admit that he did not stop at the stop sign before crossing Mattis Avenue at Thirty-eighth Street. Such admissions save time at trial because the parties will not have to spend time proving facts on which they already agree. Any matter admitted under such a request is conclusively established as true for the trial. FRCP 36 permits requests for admission but stipulates that a request for admission cannot be made, without the court's permission, prior to the prediscovery meeting of the attorneys. In view of the limitations on the number of interrogatories under the FRCP (and under some state procedural rules), requests for admission are a particularly useful discovery tool.

THE DUTY TO DISCLOSE UNDER FRCP 26

Each party to a lawsuit has a duty to disclose to the other party specified types of information prior to the discovery stage of litigation. Under FRCP Rule 26(f), once a lawsuit is brought, the parties (the plaintiff and defendant and/or their attorneys, if the parties are represented by counsel) must schedule a prediscovery meeting to discuss the nature of the lawsuit, any defenses that may be raised against the claims being brought, and possibilities for promptly settling or otherwise resolving the dispute. The meeting should take place as soon as practicable but at least fourteen days before a scheduling conference is held or a scheduling order issued. Either at this meeting or within ten days after it, the parties must also make the initial disclosures described below and submit to the court a plan for discovery. As the trial date approaches, the attorneys must make subsequent disclosures relating to witnesses, documents, and other information that is relevant to the case.

These rules do not replace the traditional methods of discovery discussed in the preceding section. Rather, the rules impose a duty on attorneys to disclose specified information automatically to opposing counsel early in the litigation process so that the time and costs of traditional discovery can be reduced. Attorneys may still use the traditional discovery tools (depositions and interrogatories, for instance) to obtain information, but they cannot use these methods until the prediscovery meeting has been held and initial disclosures have been made. Also, to save the court's time, the rules give attorneys a freer hand in crafting a discovery plan that is appropriate to the nature of the claim and the parties' needs.[3]

Initial Disclosures

FRCP 26(a)(1) requires each party to disclose the following information to the other party either at an initial meeting of the parties or within ten days following the meeting:

- The name, address, and telephone number of any person who is likely to have "discoverable information" and the nature of that information.

- A copy or "description by category and location" of all documents, data, and other "things in the possession, custody, or control of the party" that are relevant to the dispute.

- A computation of the damages being claimed by the disclosing party. The party must make available to the other party, for inspection and copying, documents and other materials on which the computation of damages is based, "including materials bearing on the nature and extent of injuries suffered."

- Copies of any insurance policies that cover the injuries or harms alleged in the lawsuit and that may pay part or all of a judgment (damages, for example) resulting from the dispute.

In the Baranski case, attorney Gilmore and paralegal Lopez must work quickly to assemble all relevant information, documents, and other evidence that Lopez has gathered during client interviews and during her preliminary investigation. Lopez will prepare copies of the documents or other information—or a description of them—for Gilmore's review and signature. The copies or descriptions will then be filed with the court and delivered to Peretto's attorney.

Note that in the information disclosed to Peretto's attorney, Lopez must include even information that might be damaging to Baranski's position. Lopez need not disclose *privileged information,* however, such as confidential discussions between Baranski and Gilmore.

Failure to Disclose

A party will not be excused from disclosing relevant information simply because the party has not yet completed an investigation into the case or because the other party has not yet disclosed the required information. FRCP 37(c) makes it clear that the failure to make these initial disclosures can result in serious sanctions. If a party fails to disclose certain relevant information, that party will not be able to use the information as evidence at trial. In addition, the court may impose other sanctions, such as ordering the party to pay reasonable expenses, including attorneys' fees, created by the failure to disclose. In sum, Gilmore and Lopez need to make sure that all relevant information (that is not privileged) is disclosed, or Gilmore will not be able to use it in court (and may face other sanctions as well).

Discovery Plan

As mentioned above, at the initial meeting of the parties, the attorneys must work out a **discovery plan** and submit a report describing the plan to the court within ten days of the meeting. The type of information to be included in the discovery plan is illustrated in Exhibit 10.14, which shows Form 35, a form generated for this purpose. As indicated by the form, Rule 26(f) allows the attorneys substantial room to negotiate the details of discovery, including the time schedules to be followed.

In the Baranski case, paralegal Lopez will make sure that attorney Gilmore takes a copy of Form 35 with him to the initial prediscovery meeting of the parties

discovery plan

A plan formed by the attorneys litigating a lawsuit, on behalf of their clients, that indicates the types of information that will be disclosed by each party to the other prior to trial, the testimony and evidence that each party will or may introduce at trial, and the general schedule for pretrial disclosures and events.

EXHIBIT 10.14
Form 35—Report of Parties' Planning Meeting (Discovery Plan)

[Caption and Names of Parties]

1. Pursuant to Fed. R. Civ. P. 26(f), a meeting was held on _____(date)_____ at _____(place)_____ and was attended by:

_____(name)_____ for plaintiff(s) _____(party name)_____
_____(name)_____ for defendant(s) _____(party name)_____
_____(name)_____ for defendant(s) _____(party name)_____

2. Pre-Discovery Disclosures. The parties [have exchanged] [will exchange by _____(date)_____] the information required by [Fed. R. Civ. P. 26(a)(1)] [(local rule _____)].

3. Discovery Plan. The parties jointly propose to the court the following discovery plan: [Use separate paragraphs or subparagraphs as necessary if parties disagree.]

Discovery will be needed on the following subjects:
_____(brief description of subjects on which discovery will be needed)_____
All discovery commenced in time to be completed by _(date)_. [Discovery on _(issue for early discovery)_ to be completed by _____(date)_____.]
Maximum of ____ interrogatories by each party to any other party. [Responses due ____ days after service.]
Maximum of ____ requests for admission by each party to any other party. [Responses due ____ days after service.]
Maximum of ____ depositions by plaintiff(s) and ____ by defendant(s).
Each deposition [other than of _____] limited to maximum of ____ hours unless extended by agreement of parties.
Reports from retained experts under Rule 26(a)(2) due:
     from plaintiff(s) by _____(date)_____.
     from defendant(s) by _____(date)_____.
Supplementations under Rule 26(e) due _(time(s) or intervals(s))_.

4. Other Items. [Use separate paragraphs or subparagraphs as necessary if parties disagree.]

The parties [request] [do not request] a conference with the court before entry of the scheduling order.
The parties request a pretrial conference in_____(month and year)_____.
Plaintiff(s) should be allowed until _(date)_ to join additional parties and until _(date)_ to amend the pleadings.
Defendant(s) should be allowed until _(date)_ to join additional parties and until _(date)_ to amend the pleadings.
All potentially dispositive motions should be filed by_(date)_.
Settlement [is likely] [is unlikely] [cannot be evaluated prior to _(date)_] [may be enhanced by use of the following alternative dispute resolution procedure: _____].
Final lists of witnesses and exhibits under Rule 26(a)(3) should be due
     from plaintiff(s) by _(date)_.
     from defendant(s) by _(date)_.
Parties should have _____ days after service of final lists of witnesses and exhibits to list objections under Rule 26(a)(3).
The case should be ready for trial by _(date)_ [and at the time is expected to take approximately _(length of time)_].
[Other matters.]

Date: _____

to use as a checklist. After the attorneys decide on the details of the plan to be proposed to the court, Gilmore will probably have Lopez draft a final version of the plan for his review and signature.

Subsequent Disclosures

In addition to the initial disclosures just discussed, each party must make other disclosures prior to trial. All subsequent disclosures must also be made in writing, signed by the attorneys, and filed with the court. Subsequent disclosures include information relating to expert witnesses and other witnesses and exhibits that will or may be used at trial.

Expert Witnesses

Under FRCP 26(a)(2), each party must disclose to the other party the names of any expert witnesses who may be called to testify during the trial. Additionally, the following information about each expert witness must be disclosed in a report signed by the expert witness:

- A statement by the expert witness indicating the opinions that will be expressed, the basis for the opinions, and the data or information considered by the witness when forming the opinions.
- Any exhibits that will be used to summarize or support the opinions.
- The qualifications of the expert witness, including a list of all publications authored by the witness within the preceding ten years.
- The compensation to be paid to the expert witness.
- A list of any other cases in which the witness has testified as an expert at trial or by deposition within the preceding four years.

These disclosures must be made either at times set by the court or, if the court does not indicate any times, at least ninety days prior to the trial date.

Other Pretrial Disclosures

Under revised FRCP 26(a)(3), each party must also disclose to the other party the following information about other witnesses who will testify at trial or any exhibits that will or may be used:

- A list containing the names, addresses, and telephone numbers of other witnesses who may or will be called during the trial to give testimony. The witness list must indicate whether the witness "will be called" or "may be called."
- A list of any witnesses whose deposition testimony may be offered during the trial and a transcript of the relevant sections of the deposition testimony, if the testimony was not taken stenographically.
- A list of exhibits that indicates which exhibits will be offered and which exhibits may be offered if the need arises.

These disclosures must be made at least thirty days before trial, unless the court orders otherwise. Once the disclosures have been made, the opposing party has fourteen days within which to file with the court any objections to the use of any deposition or exhibit. If objections are not made, they are deemed to be waived (unless a party can show good cause why he or she failed to object to the disclosures within the fourteen-day time period).

An attorney's duty to disclose relevant information is ongoing throughout the pretrial stage. Any time an attorney learns about relevant supplemental information concerning statements or responses made earlier, that information must be disclosed to the other party.

DISCOVERY OF ELECTRONIC EVIDENCE

Over the past few decades, electronic evidence has significantly changed litigation and has become a major consideration in pretrial discovery. Electronic evidence, or e-evidence, consists of all computer-generated or electronically recorded information, such as e-mail, voice mail, spreadsheets, word-processing documents, and other data. E-evidence has become increasingly important because it can reveal significant facts that are not often discoverable by other means. The Federal Rules of Civil Procedure and state rules (as well as court decisions) specifically allow discovery of electronic "data compilations" (or e-evidence).

The discovery of e-evidence is fundamentally different from the discovery of paper documents and physical evidence, although traditional discovery methods, such as interrogatories and depositions, are still used in obtaining it. The following subsections describe the features of e-evidence that make it uniquely important. They are intended only as an introduction to the rapidly advancing area of electronic evidence. For a discussion of the costs of electronic discovery, see this chapter's *Technology and Today's Paralegal* feature on the following pages.

The Advantages of Electronic Evidence

E-evidence has several advantages over paper discovery. People and businesses use computers to store and communicate enormous amounts of data. Most information stored on computers is never printed on paper. In addition, whenever a person is working on a computer, information is being recorded on the hard drive without being saved by the user. This information, called **metadata**, is the hidden data kept by the computer about a file, including location, path, creator, date created, date last accessed, hidden notes, earlier versions, passwords, and formatting. It reveals information about how, when, and by whom a file was created, accessed, modified, and transmitted. This information can only be obtained from the file in its electronic format—not from printed versions.

metadata
Embedded electronic data recorded by a computer in association with a particular file, including location, path, creator, date created, date last accessed, hidden notes, earlier versions, passwords, and formatting. Metadata reveal information about how, when, and by whom a document was created, accessed, modified, and transmitted.

E-Mail Communications

Billions of e-mail messages are sent each year. Because e-mail is so widespread, it has become a fertile ground for gathering evidence in litigation. In fact, e-mail has proved to be the "smoking gun" in many cases. This is largely due to the fact that most people converse freely and informally in their e-mail communications, as if talking to a close friend or business associate. This makes e-mail believable and compelling evidence—evidence that can be very damaging if discovered by outsiders.

In addition, in its electronic form, e-mail contains information that provides links to other e-mails, e-mail attachments, erased files, and metadata. These metadata reveal the identity of any person who received copies of an e-mail message (even "blind" copies). Thus, e-evidence can be used to trace a message to its true originator, reconstruct an e-mail conversation, and establish a timeline of the events in dispute (who knew what, when). Attorneys also use it to verify clients' claims or discredit the claims of the opposition. Whether it is evidence of adultery, sexual harassment, employment discrimination, fraud, or the theft of trade secrets, e-mail often contains the most compelling evidence in a case.

Deleted Files Can Be Retrieved

Another major advantage of e-evidence is that even deleted files can often be retrieved from the "residual data" within the computer. This is because deleting a file does not actually destroy the data but simply makes the space occupied by those data available to be overwritten by new information. Until that space is actually used for new data (which may be in weeks, in months, or never), the deleted record can be retrieved with special software.

Technology and Today's Paralegal

WHO BEARS THE COSTS OF ELECTRONIC DISCOVERY?

Traditionally, the party responding to a discovery request has had to pay the expenses involved in obtaining the requested materials. If compliance would be too burdensome or too costly, however, the judge could either limit the scope of the request or shift some or all of the costs to the requesting party. How do these traditional rules governing discovery apply to requests for electronic evidence?

WHY COURTS MIGHT SHIFT THE COSTS OF ELECTRONIC DISCOVERY

Electronic discovery has dramatically increased the costs associated with complying with discovery requests. It is no longer simply a matter of photocopying paper documents. Now the responding party may need to hire computer forensics experts to make "image" copies of desktop, laptop, and server hard drives, as well as removable storage media (such as DVDs and flash drives), back-up drives and tapes, voice mail, cell phones, and any other form of digitally stored data.

In cases involving multiple parties or large corporations with many offices and employees, the electronic discovery process can easily run into hundreds of thousands—if not millions—of dollars. For example, Viacom, which owns Comedy Central and other television channels, sued YouTube, owned by Google, for more than $1 billion. Viacom claimed that YouTube had committed copyright violations by allowing clips from Viacom's television shows to be posted on YouTube without Viacom's permission.[a] Viacom hired another company, BayTSP, to watch for possible violations on YouTube. BayTSP identified more than 150,000 clips posted on YouTube, and Viacom claimed losses from each such posting.

YouTube demanded to see evidence of the violations. BayTSP estimated that it had gathered more than 1 million documents, all electronic, related to the clip postings. It protested to the court that the document request was unreasonable. BayTSP spent 2,000 hours over six months searching and

---

a. *Viacom International v. YouTube, Inc.,* Slip Copy, 2009 WL 102808 (N.D.Cal. 2009).

Most people believe that when they delete a record or e-mail and empty the recycle bin, the message is gone from their computer. This increases the probability of candid e-mail communications. As just described, however, deleted data remain on the computer until overwritten by new data (or wiped out by certain utility software). In fact, experts have even been able to retrieve data, in whole or in part, from computers that have been damaged by water, fire, or severe impact. Furthermore, all transmissions on the Internet are stored in a server somewhere. Therefore, don't assume that e-evidence is not available just because a file was deleted, a computer was damaged, or a utility program was run.

The Sources of Electronic Evidence

Key to conducting electronic discovery is developing an understanding of the kinds of information that computers can provide so that you will know where to look for particular kinds of information. Generally, computer data can be located in active files, in back-up files, or as residual data. Active files are those currently accessible on the computer (word-processing documents, e-mail, and spreadsheets, for example). Back-up files are those that have been copied to removable media such as flash drives, CDs, or DVDs or to remote servers. As mentioned, residual data are data that appear to be gone but are still recoverable from somewhere on the com-reviewing the documents. By using electronic filters, it narrowed the list to 650,000 potentially relevant documents. The court allowed YouTube's request for these documents to go forward. Given the monetary amount at stake in the litigation, YouTube was within its rights, and BayTSP had to provide those documents. The cost of document production would be borne by BayTSP or, the court noted, probably by Viacom because BayTSP worked for it. The court held, however, that when costs are burdensome, a court may order the costs to be split between defendant and plaintiff.

WHAT FACTORS DO COURTS CONSIDER IN DECIDING WHETHER TO SHIFT COSTS?

At what point should this cost-shifting occur? In *Zubulake v. UBS Warburg LLC*,[b] the court identified a three-step analysis for deciding disputes over discovery costs. First, if the data are kept in an accessible format, the usual rules of discovery apply: the responding party should pay the costs of producing the data. A court should consider cost-shifting only when electronic data are in a relatively inaccessible form, such as in deleted files.

Second, the court should determine what data may be found on the inaccessible media and whether a sampling of the data might be sufficient. Requiring the responding party to restore and produce documents from a small sample of the requested medium is a sensible approach in most cases. Third, the court should consider a series of other factors, including, for example, the availability of the information from other sources, the total cost of producing the information compared with the amount in controversy, and each party's ability to pay these costs.

TECHNOLOGY TIP

Paralegals should keep in mind not only the high costs of some electronic discovery requests but also the possibility that the court may shift some of these costs to the party requesting discovery. Suppose, for example, that you are assisting a corporate defendant in a product liability lawsuit brought by a plaintiff who was seriously harmed by one of the defendant's products. If the plaintiff requests extensive electronic evidence during discovery, the defendant corporation may be required to pay a significant portion of the costs of the discovery.

---

b. 217 F.R.D. 309 (S.D.N.Y. 2003).

---

puter system. Residual data no longer have pointers to indicate their location and can only be retrieved by special software.

Back-Up Data

Back-up files can be a source of hidden treasure for the legal team. Reviewing back-up copies of documents and e-mail provides useful information about how a particular matter progressed over several weeks or months.

Companies vary in their policies about backing up data. Most companies back up files at routine intervals (daily or weekly), but some have no formal back-up schedule. Some companies have back-up routines for word-processing documents but not for e-mail. Because the current location of the data depends on the back-up policy (or practice) in use, you need to find out what the policy is as soon as you can during discovery. See the *Developing Paralegal Skills* feature on page 340 for more tips on e-discovery.

Note that back-up files contain not only the e-mail messages and word-processing documents but also other embedded information that can be useful. For example, when computers are networked, computer logs and audit trails that keep track of network usage may be available. An audit trail will tell you who accessed the system, when it was accessed, and whether those who accessed the system copied, downloaded, modified, or deleted any files. In addition, back-up data files include certain

Developing
Paralegal Skills

ELECTRONIC DISCOVERY

Paralegals need to be prepared to deal with electronic discovery. This means not only formulating electronic discovery plans but also making sure to preserve the integrity of any electronic evidence acquired. It is important, too, to remember that e-evidence is fragile. Although—as discussed in the chapter text—it may be difficult to delete files from a computer system, it is certainly not impossible. Every time a user enters new data, loads new software, or performs routine maintenance procedures, the data on the computer are permanently altered. Just booting up a computer can change dates and times on numerous files. The following are some general guidelines to follow in conducting e-discovery.

TIPS FOR CONDUCTING E-DISCOVERY

- Write a preservation-of-evidence letter to all parties involved, including your own client, at the outset of discovery. This letter informs the parties that they have a duty to take immediate action to preserve the evidence.

- Use interrogatories to gather information about the opposing party's computer system so that you can learn as much as you can about the system with which you are dealing.

- Follow up with depositions. Once you know the names of the parties who oversee the system or have special knowledge of it, take depositions from them.

- After you have found out the details of where electronic evidence is located, draft a request for production of the evidence.

- When the e-evidence is acquired, determine how best to manage, review, and interpret the data, which may involve using the services of an outside company that specializes in this field.

nonprinting information, such as the date and time the files were created. Some word-processing software allows users to insert hidden comments or track changes while drafting and revising documents. These comments and revisions can also be accessed from the electronic version of the back-up file.

Other Sources of E-Evidence

It is important to remember that electronic evidence is not limited to the data found on computer systems. As stated, e-evidence includes *all* electronically recorded information, such as voice mail, back-up voice mail, video, electronic calendars, phone logs, BlackBerries and other personal digital assistants, laptops, cell phones, and any other devices that digitally store data. You should not overlook any possible sources of e-evidence during discovery. Use traditional discovery tactics (such as interrogatories and depositions) to find out about other sources of potential e-evidence. Consider all possible sources that might prove fruitful, but such requests must be reasonable and in good faith.

The Special Requirements of Electronic Evidence

The law has been developing to accommodate electronic evidence. While courts allow discovery of electronic evidence, judges know that electronic evidence can be manipulated. To ensure that the evidence you obtain during discovery will be admissible as evidence in court, you must do two things. First, make sure that you obtain an exact image copy of the electronic evidence. Second, make sure that you can prove that nothing has been altered or changed from the time the image copy was made.

Acquiring an Image Copy

To use any evidence in court, you must convince the court that the evidence is authentic. In the case of electronic evidence, you must show that the electronic version of the evidence that you have acquired is exactly the same as the version that was present on the target system. The way to do this is to have an image copy made.

Suppose the target system is a computer hard drive. Making an image copy would involve creating a sector-by-sector mirror image of the drive being copied. The image copy would capture all data, including residual data. This is different from the usual file-by-file back-up copying method.

Making an image copy of a computer drive is complicated and is best left to an expert in computer forensics. Computer forensics experts collect, preserve, and analyze electronic evidence and testify in court if needed. Unskilled attempts to acquire an image of a computer's drive can easily lead to disaster, wrecking the evidence and making it inadmissible at trial.

Preserving the Chain of Custody

Once you have acquired an exact copy of the electronic evidence, you must establish and maintain a chain of custody to avoid any claims that the evidence has been tampered with. The phrase **chain of custody** refers to the movement and location of evidence from the time it is obtained to the time it is presented in court. It is crucial when dealing with electronic evidence to make sure that you can track the evidence from its original source to its admission in court. This will provide the court with the assurance that nothing has been added, changed, or deleted. The original image copy should be write-protected so that it is tamperproof, labeled as the original, and kept in a secure location. Typically, a forensic specialist will make copies of the original data that are write-protected and scanned for viruses. You should always use the copies when reviewing e-evidence.

> **chain of custody**
> A series describing the movement and location of evidence from the time it is obtained to the time it is presented in court. The court requires that evidence be preserved in the condition in which it was obtained if it is to be admitted into evidence at trial.

Federal Rule of Evidence 502

The use of electronic evidence can result in a huge number of documents being made available to an opposing party. This has meant that more documents have accidentally been released that could compromise a party's position. In a number of cases, for example, a party had the right to access e-mails of the opposing party relating to a particular matter. While attempts were made to filter out nonrelevant e-mails, some e-mails that should have been protected by attorney-client confidentiality rules were accidentally among the thousands of e-mails seen by the opposing party.

To deal with such realities, Congress changed Federal Rule of Evidence 502 in late 2008. It holds that if there is an accidental release of material that should have been protected, the court may rule that protection was not waived by accidental disclosure. Dealing with such instances, the courts have listed the main factors to see if a privileged document has been lost to the opposing party or is still protected: (1) the reasonableness of precautions taken to prevent inadvertent disclosure in view of the extent of document production, (2) the number of inadvertent disclosures, (3) the extent of the disclosures, (4) the promptness of steps taken to remedy the disclosure, and (5) whether interests of justice would be served by relieving the party of its error of disclosing a protected document.

Paralegals often play a key role in organizing documents, so they must be alert to such issues. In complex cases involving a huge number of electronic documents, firms that are experts in such matters can be hired to help filter and sort documents. Because e-mails are often the center of such information releases, problems can be headed off in advance by using software that flags, sorts, and preserves e-mail.

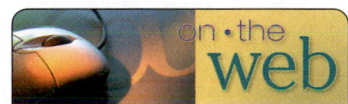

To help handle compliance, e-discovery, and archiving, many organizations use e-mail management software. A leading provider is Sherpa Software, which can be viewed at **www.sherpasoftware.com**.

Today's
Professional Paralegal

WITNESS COORDINATION

Barbara Lyons works as a paralegal for a busy litigation firm. Today she is assisting with a medical-malpractice trial. Susan Weiss, the attorney for whom Barbara works, has asked Barbara to coordinate Susan's witnesses. It is 8:30 A.M., and Barbara and Susan are waiting in the courtroom for Dr. Max Brennan, the first witness Susan will call today.

PLANNING A WITNESS'S ARRIVAL TIME

Susan tells Barbara that she expects Dr. Brennan to be on the stand testifying until at least the lunch break. Then she expects that he will be cross-examined for an hour or two after lunch. Susan wants Barbara to have the next witness, Laura Lang, at the courthouse and ready to testify by 11 A.M., though, in the event that Dr. Brennan is excused earlier than expected.

Barbara has already arranged for Lang to arrive by 11 A.M. but is concerned that she will not be on time. Barbara has met with Lang to review her testimony and prepare her for the trial, and Lang has always been late. Susan tells Barbara to call Lang. "Tell her that things are moving more quickly than planned and to be here at ten o'clock. That should make sure that she will be here by eleven."

A WITNESS IS DELAYED

It is 8:35 A.M., and Dr. Brennan has not arrived. Susan asks Barbara to go out to the hallway and call him. Barbara opens her trial notebook to the witness section. Dr. Brennan's page is first because he is the first witness scheduled to appear. She locates the number for his cell phone and leaves the courtroom. As she starts dialing Dr. Brennan walks out of the elevator. "Sorry I'm late, but I had an emergency this morning and I had to stop by the hospital before I came here," he explains.

"I'm just glad to see you!" exclaims Barbara. "You are the first witness." Barbara and Dr. Brennan enter the courtroom, and Susan and Dr. Brennan talk briefly before the judge enters. The court is called to order, and the trial resumes. Barbara sits at the counsel table while Susan questions Dr. Brennan on the stand. At 9 A.M., Barbara leaves the courtroom and calls Laura Lang.

TAKING PRECAUTIONS—ARRANGING FOR A WITNESS TO ARRIVE EARLY

Lang answers the phone. "Hello Ms. Lang. It's Barbara Lyons from Smith, White & White. Susan Weiss asked me to call you and tell you that the trial is moving faster than we anticipated. Susan would like you to be here at ten o'clock instead of eleven," advises Barbara. "Oh. Well, I suppose I can be there by then," responds Lang. "Good. I'll see you at ten o'clock," says Barbara.

At 9:55 A.M., Barbara leaves the courtroom to wait in the hallway for Lang. By 10:15 A.M., Lang has still not arrived. Barbara opens the courtroom door to listen. The testimony is going faster than anticipated, and Barbara can tell that Susan will be ready to put Lang on the stand in thirty minutes or so. Barbara closes the courtroom door. She gets out her cell phone and dials Lang's number. There is no answer.

A TIMELY ARRIVAL

Now it is 10:45 A.M., and Lang has still not arrived. Barbara dials Lang's number again. No answer. Barbara continues to wait, and a few minutes later Lang appears. Barbara breathes a sigh of relief. She opens the courtroom door, catches Susan's eye, and nods her head.

KEY TERMS AND CONCEPTS

affidavit *311*

affirmative defense *318*

allegation *310*

answer *318*

chain of custody *341*

complaint *305*

counterclaim *320*

cross-claim *321*

default judgment *318*

deponent *328*

deposition *328*

deposition transcript *330*

discovery *324*

discovery plan *335*

docket *310*

electronic filing (e-filing) system *314*

Federal Rules of Civil
  Procedure (FRCP) *302*

impeach *331*

interrogatories *324*

judgment *301*

memorandum of law *321*

metadata *337*

motion *321*

motion for judgment on the
  pleadings *322*

motion for summary judgment *322*

motion to dismiss *321*

pleadings *305*

prayer for relief *311*

privileged information *324*

return-of-service form *316*

service of process *315*

subpoena *328*

summons *315*

supporting affidavit *321*

witness *301*

CHAPTER SUMMARY

CIVIL LITIGATION—BEFORE THE TRIAL

Civil Litigation—A Bird's-Eye View

1. *Pretrial settlements*—Throughout the pretrial stage of litigation, the attorney and paralegal attempt to help the parties reach a settlement at the same time as they are preparing the case for trial.

2. *Procedural requirements*—Although civil lawsuits vary from case to case in terms of complexity, cost, and detail, all civil litigation involves similar procedural steps, as described in Exhibit 10.1 on page 302.

    a. The Federal Rules of Civil Procedure (FRCP) govern all civil cases heard in federal courts and specify what must be done during the various stages of litigation.

    b. Each state has adopted its own rules of civil procedure, which in many states are similar to the FRCP.

    c. Many courts also have (local) rules of procedure that supplement the federal or state rules.

The Preliminaries

1. *The initial client interview*—The first step in the civil litigation process occurs when the attorney initially meets with a client who wishes to bring a lawsuit against another party or parties. Before the meeting, the paralegal will conduct a conflicts check to ensure that representing the client would not create a conflict of interest. The attorney normally conducts the initial client interview, although the paralegal often attends the interview and may make arrangements with the client for subsequent interviews.

2. *Preliminary investigation*—Once the attorney agrees to represent the client in the lawsuit and the client has signed the retainer agreement, the attorney and the paralegal undertake a preliminary investigation to ascertain the facts alleged by the client and gain other factual information relating to the case.

Continued

3. *The litigation file*—A litigation file is created to hold all documents and records pertaining to the lawsuit. Each law firm or legal department has its own specific procedures for organizing and maintaining litigation files. Generally, the file will expand, as the case progresses, to include subfiles for the pleadings, discovery, and other documents and information relating to the litigation.

The Pleadings

The pleadings inform each party of the claims of the other and detail the facts, charges, and defenses involved in the litigation. Pleadings typically consist of the plaintiff's complaint, the defendant's answer, and any counterclaim or cross-claim.

1. *The complaint*—A complaint states the claim or claims that the plaintiff is making against the defendant. A lawsuit in a federal or state court normally is initiated by the filing of a complaint with the clerk of the appropriate court.

   a. The complaint includes a caption, jurisdictional allegations, general allegations (body of the complaint) detailing the cause of action, a prayer for relief, a signature, and, if appropriate, a demand for a jury trial.

   b. A complaint can be filed either by personal delivery of the papers to the court clerk or, if the court permits, by electronic filing. The procedural requirements of courts that allow electronic filing vary and should be researched prior to any electronic filing.

2. *Service of process*—Typically, the defendant is notified of a lawsuit by delivery of the complaint and a summons (which is called service of process). The summons identifies the parties to the lawsuit, identifies the court in which the case will be heard, and directs the defendant to respond to the complaint within a specified time period.

   a. Although often the complaint and summons are personally delivered to the defendant, other methods of service are allowed in some cases, depending on the jurisdiction.

   b. In federal cases and in many states, the defendant can waive, or give up, the right to be personally served with the summons and complaint (and accept service by mail, for example).

   c. Under FRCP 4, if the defendant waives service of process, the defendant receives additional time to respond to the complaint.

3. *The defendant's response*—On receiving the complaint, the defendant has several options.

   a. The defendant may submit an answer. The answer may deny wrongdoing or assert an affirmative defense against the plaintiff's claim, such as the plaintiff's contributory negligence. The answer may be followed by a counterclaim, in which the defendant asserts a claim against the plaintiff arising out of the same incident; or it may be followed by a cross-claim, in which the defendant makes claims against another defendant named in the complaint.

   b. Alternatively or at the same time, the defendant may make a motion to dismiss the case. That motion asserts that, even assuming that the facts of the complaint are true, the plaintiff has failed to state a cause of action or there are other grounds for dismissal of the suit.

Pretrial Motions

1. *Motion for judgment on the pleadings*—A pretrial motion that may be filed by either party after all pleadings and amendments have been filed. The motion asks the court to enter a judgment in favor of one party based on information contained in the pleadings alone. A judgment on the pleadings will only be made if there are no facts in dispute and the only question is how the law applies to the facts.

2. *Motion for summary judgment*—A motion that may be filed by either party during or after the discovery stage of litigation. This motion, like the motion for judgment on the pleadings, asks the court to enter judgment without a trial. Unlike a motion for judgment on the pleadings, however, a motion for summary judgment can be supported by evidence outside the pleadings (including affidavits, depositions, and interrogatories). The motion will not be granted if any facts are in dispute.

Traditional Discovery Tools

In preparing for trial, the attorney for each party undertakes a formal investigative process called discovery to obtain evidence helpful to his or her client's case.

1. *Interrogatories*—Interrogatories are written questions that the parties to the lawsuit must answer, in writing and under oath. The FRCP and some states' rules limit the number of questions that may be asked, as well as the total number of interrogatories that may be filed.

2. *Depositions*—Like interrogatories, depositions are given under oath, but unlike interrogatories, depositions may be taken from witnesses as well as from the parties to the lawsuit. Also, the attorney is able to question the deponent (the person being deposed) in person. There is no limit on the number of questions that may be asked. Usually, a court reporter records the official transcript of the deposition.

3. *Requests for production*—During discovery, the attorney for either side may request that another party produce documents or tangible things or allow the attorney access to them for inspection and other purposes.

4. *Requests for physical or mental examinations*—When the mental or physical condition of a party is in controversy, the opposing party may request the court to order the party to submit to an examination by a licensed examiner.

5. *Requests for admission*—A party can request that the opposing party admit the truth of matters relating to the case. Such admissions save time at trial because the parties do not have to spend time proving facts on which they agree.

The Duty to Disclose under FRCP 26

In federal court cases, FRCP 26 requires that the attorneys cooperate in forming a discovery plan early in the litigation process. The rule also requires attorneys to disclose relevant information *automatically*. Under FRCP 26, only after initial disclosures have been made can attorneys resort to the use of traditional discovery tools. An attorney's duty to disclose relevant information under FRCP 26 is ongoing throughout the pretrial stage.

Continued

Discovery of Electronic Evidence

Electronic evidence consists of all computer-generated or electronically recorded information, such as e-mail, voice mail, spreadsheets, and word-processing documents. The federal rules and state rules allow discovery of evidence in electronic form. E-evidence has significantly changed discovery in civil litigation because it can reveal facts not discoverable by other means.

1. *Advantages of e-evidence*—Electronic evidence often provides more information than paper discovery, because many data that are on the computer are never printed out. In addition, the computer records hidden data (called metadata) about documents and e-mail, which can be very useful. Even files that were deleted by the user can be retrieved from the residual data within the computer.

2. *Sources of e-evidence*—E-evidence may be located in computers, the back-up data copied to removable media or remote servers, or the residual data that appear to be gone from the computer. Not all e-evidence is located on computers, and you should investigate other potential sources, such as voice mail, phone logs, personal digital assistants, and so forth.

3. *Requirements of e-evidence*—To ensure that e-evidence will be admissible as evidence in the trial, you can obtain an exact image copy of the original data and preserve the chain of custody until trial, making sure to do nothing that will alter the evidence.

STUDENT STUDYWARE™ CD-ROM

Interactive student CD in this book includes additional quizzing, plus video clips, case studies, and Key Terms flashcards.

ONLINE COMPANION™

For additional resources, please go to **www.paralegal.delmar.cengage.com**.

QUESTIONS FOR REVIEW

1. What happens during the initial client interview? Who normally conducts this interview, the attorney or the paralegal? Why?

2. What documents constitute the pleadings in a civil lawsuit? What is the effect of each type of document on the litigation?

3. What is service of process? Why is it important?

4. What is discovery? When does it take place? List three discovery devices that can be used to obtain information prior to trial.

5. How has the duty to disclose under FRCP 26 changed the discovery process in federal court cases?

ETHICAL QUESTION

1. Your next-door neighbor's son was beaten up while at school. The boy's mother is facing over $3,000 in medical and dental expenses as a result of his injuries, which she cannot afford to pay. She knows that you work as a paralegal in a law firm that specializes in personal-injury litigation, so she asks you if you will

help her. She wants you to write a letter threatening legal action, which she will then sign, and she also wants to know whether she can sue the parents of the boys who beat up her son. Should you write the letter?

Should you advise her on what action she might take against the other boys' parents? What are your ethical obligations in this situation? How could you help her without violating professional ethical standards?

PRACTICE QUESTIONS AND ASSIGNMENTS

1. Assume that you work for attorney Tara Jolans of Adams & Tate, 1000 Town Center, Suite 500, White Tower, Michigan. Jolans has decided to represent Sandra Nelson in her lawsuit against David Namisch. Based on the following information, draft a complaint to be filed in the U.S. District Court for the Eastern District of Michigan.

   Sandra Nelson is a plaintiff in a lawsuit resulting from an automobile accident. Sandra was turning left at a traffic light at the intersection of Jefferson and Mack Streets, while the left-turn arrow was green, when she was hit from the side by a car driven by David Namisch, who failed to stop at the light. The accident occurred on June 3, 2011, at 11:30 P.M. David lives in New York, was visiting his family in Michigan, and just prior to the accident had been out drinking with his brothers. Several witnesses saw the accident. One of the witnesses called the police.

   Sandra was not wearing her seat belt at the time of the accident, and she was thrown against the windshield, sustaining massive head injuries. When the police and ambulance arrived, they did

not think that she would make it to the hospital alive, but she survived. She wants to claim damages of $500,000 for medical expenses, $65,000 for lost wages, and $55,000 for property damage to her Rolls Royce. The accident was reported in the local newspaper, complete with photographs.

2. Using Exhibit 10.4, *A Summons in a Civil Action,* on page 315, draft a summons to accompany the complaint against David Namisch. David's address is 1000 Main Street, Apartment 63, New York, NY 10009. The court clerk's name is David T. Brown.

3. Draft the first ten questions for a set of interrogatories to be directed to the plaintiff, Sandra Nelson, based on the facts given in Question 1 above.

4. Using Exhibit 10.10, *Notice of Taking Deposition,* on page 329, draft a notice that Sandra Nelson's attorneys will be taking the deposition of David Namisch on September 10, 2011, at 9:00 A.M., at the law offices of Adams & Tate. Mr. Namisch's attorney is Mark Simmons of Simmons & Smith, 444 Park Avenue, New York, NY 10007.

QUESTIONS FOR CRITICAL ANALYSIS

1. What is the difference between preliminary investigation and discovery? What impact does this difference have on a case? Which would you prefer to undertake to determine the facts of a case?

2. A complaint must be served on the defendant in a lawsuit. What happens if the defendant is not properly served? Is this a fair result? Why or why not?

3. If a defendant fails to respond to the plaintiff's complaint within a specified time period, what can happen? Is this a fair rule? Why?

4. What happens if a defendant fails to deny an allegation in answering a complaint? Is this fair to the defendant? What happens if a defendant is uncertain as to the truth of a matter being alleged by a plaintiff in a complaint?

5. What is the difference between interrogatories and depositions? Which is more efficient? Which is more cost-effective? Which would you prefer to use?

PROJECTS

1. Visit the county court clerk's office (or the clerk's office of a local court) and obtain the following: local court rules, summons and return-of-service forms, and a filing-fee schedule. (Check first to see if this information is available online.)

2. Find out when a local court's "motion day" is, and attend court for two to three hours on that day. Observe as many motions as possible. Write a one-page summary of what you observed. Be sure to include the name of the court you visited, the date, and the judge's name.

USING INTERNET RESOURCES

1. Several years ago, casino owner and billionaire Steve Wynn accidentally poked a hole in a painting by Pablo Picasso that he owned. He had paid $48.4 million for the painting and claimed that it was worth $139 million when he damaged it. He also claimed that the damage reduced this value by $54 million and insisted that his insurance company pay him for the loss. It refused, so he sued. Look up the filing at the Web site of The Smoking Gun, which posts public documents involving celebrities, crimes, and other matters that get a lot of public attention. Go to **www. thesmokinggun.com**, select "archive," and search with the words "Wynn Picasso" to get to the case filing. Read the complaint and answer these questions:

a. In what court was the complaint filed?

b. Who were the defendants?

c. What gave the court jurisdiction?

d. What did the plaintiff demand?

e. What was the cause of action—that is, what legal claim was asserted?

f. What evidence of loss was provided?

g. What remedies did the plaintiff request?

END NOTES

1. Nita and Zero are fictitious states invented for the purpose of this hypothetical.

2. The body of the complaint described in this section is a *fact pleading*, in which sufficient factual circumstances must be alleged to convince the court that the plaintiff has a cause of action. State courts often require fact pleadings, whereas federal courts only require *notice pleading*. FRCP 8(a) requires only that the complaint have "a short and plain statement of the claim showing that the pleader is entitled to

relief." Fact pleading and notice pleading are not totally different—that is, the same allegation of facts could be in the body of a complaint submitted to either a federal or a state court. Federal courts simply have fewer requirements in this respect, and therefore they are often more attractive to litigants.

3. Under the provisions of the FRCP, federal district courts can modify or opt not to follow the rules requiring early disclosures.

CONDUCTING INTERVIEWS AND INVESTIGATIONS

CHAPTER OUTLINE

Introduction

Planning the Interview

Interviewing Skills

Interviewing Clients

Interviewing Witnesses

Planning and Conducting Investigations

AFTER COMPLETING THIS CHAPTER, YOU WILL KNOW:

▶ How to prepare for an interview and the kinds of skills employed during the interviewing process.

▶ The common types of client interviews paralegals may conduct and the different types of witnesses paralegals may need to interview during a preliminary investigation.

▶ How to create an investigation plan.

▶ The variety of sources that you can use to locate information or witnesses.

▶ Rules governing the types of evidence that are admissible in court.

▶ How to summarize investigation results.

INTRODUCTION

Paralegals frequently interview clients. After the initial client interview (which is usually conducted by the supervising attorney), the paralegal may conduct additional interviews to obtain detailed information from the client. How the paralegal relates to the client has an important effect on the client's attitude toward the firm and the attorney or legal team handling the case.

Additionally, paralegals often conduct pretrial investigations. As part of a preliminary investigation into a client's claim, the paralegal may interview one or more witnesses to gain as much information as possible. The more factual evidence that can be gathered in support of a client's claim, the better the client's chances in court—or in any other dispute-settlement proceeding.

Learning how to conduct interviews and investigations is thus an important part of preparing for your career as a paralegal. In this chapter, you will read about the basic skills and concepts that you can apply when interviewing clients or witnesses and when conducting investigations.

PLANNING THE INTERVIEW

Planning an interview involves organizing many details. As a paralegal, you may be responsible for locating a witness, scheduling the interview, determining where the interview should take place, arranging for the use of one of the firm's conference rooms or other office space for the interview, and managing additional related details. Crucial to the success of any interview is how well you prepare for it.

Know What Information You Want

interviewee
The person who is being interviewed.

Before any interview, you should have clearly in mind the kind of information you want to obtain from the client or witness being interviewed—the **interviewee**. If possible, discuss with your supervising attorney the goal of the interview and the type of information that the attorney hopes to obtain. This will ensure that you and the attorney share an understanding of what topics need to be covered in the interview. Once you know the questions that you want to ask, prepare a checklist or outline in advance so that you can refer to it during the interview. (Similarly, you may also have to draw up questions for interrogatories. See the *Featured Contributor* article on pages 358 and 359 for tips on doing this.)

Standardized Interview Forms

Many law firms have created preprinted or computerized forms indicating the kinds of information that should be gathered during client interviews relating to particular types of claims. Firms that frequently handle personal-injury claims, for example, often use a personal-injury intake sheet such as that shown in Exhibit 11.1 on pages 352 and 353. Standardized client intake forms are also available as part of many legal software programs and from a variety of online sources and may be done electronically. Using standardized forms helps to ensure that all essential information will be obtained, especially for the beginning interviewer.

In some cases, the information needed will be clear from the legal forms or documents that may eventually be filed with the court. For example, a paralegal interviewing a client who is petitioning for bankruptcy or divorce can look at the bankruptcy or divorce court forms during the interview to make sure all required information is obtained.

Remain Flexible

Keep in mind that prepared questions and preprinted forms should only be used as guidelines during the interview. Do not simply read the questions word for word from a prepared list or stick rigidly to a planned outline of topics. If you do, you lose an opportunity to interact with the interviewee and gain the interviewee's trust, and he or she will probably not disclose any information other than what is specifically asked for.

During any interview, the interviewer should be flexible, listen carefully to the interviewee's responses, and let those responses guide the questioning. (Remember that you can always ask the interviewee to return to a certain topic later on in the interview.) By focusing too much on your own role and on what your next question will or should be, you can overlook the importance of what the client or witness is saying. Therefore, make sure that you listen to the interviewee's responses and modify your questions accordingly. Effective listening techniques are discussed later in this chapter.

Plan to Ask Follow-Up Questions

Another important point to remember is to ask for details and clarification after the interviewee has made a statement. Find out who, what, when, where, and how. If an interviewee says, for example, that he saw someone hit Jane in the face, you will need to ask for more specifics, such as:

- How far away was the interviewee at the time?
- What exactly did he see?
- How many times was Jane hit and with what (open hand, fist, weapon)?
- Who else was present?
- Was it light or dark? Inside or outside?
- From what angle did the interviewee view the incident?
- Does he know Jane or her assailant? How?
- What were Jane and the assailant doing before and after the incident?
- What was the witness doing before the incident?

Also, although you should read the case file thoroughly before the interview, try to set aside what you have read or heard about the case. Let the interviewee tell you the story from his or her own perspective and avoid preconceived notions about what the person will say. One approach is to pretend that you know nothing about the case and let the interviewee tell you her or his version of the facts. Then, as the interview unfolds, think about what the person is saying from the perspective of your opponent—why should anyone believe that story? Ask follow-up questions aimed at establishing what makes the person's story more or less believable. If a witness says a car was going fifty-five miles per hour, for example, ask how he or she could tell the speed. If it turns out the witness has been racing cars for the past fifteen years, this fact can be used to help make the witness's testimony more believable.

Recording the Interview

Some interviewers record their interviews. Before you record an interview, you should obtain permission to do so from both your supervising attorney and the person being interviewed. When you are using a digital recorder, you should state or include at the beginning of the recording the following identifying information:

- The name of the person being interviewed and any other relevant information about the interviewee.
- The name of the person conducting the interview.
- The names of other persons present at the interview, if any.
- The date, time, and place of the interview.
- On the record, the interviewee's consent to having the interview recorded.

If more than one recording file is used, you should indicate at the end of each file that the interview will be continued on the next file in the series, and each subsequent file should contain identifying information. Secure copies of the interview should be stored electronically.

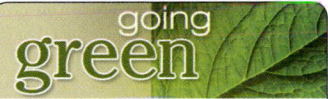

GETTING TO THE OFFICE

When the price of gas rose to $4 a gallon in 2008, more people began to carpool or to take the bus or light rail to the office. Some people realized that, at least sometimes, they could walk or bicycle to work. Regardless of the current price of gas, consider using alternative transportation to get to work. Walking or bicycling will reduce your energy consumption and your carbon "footprint"—and it's better for your health.

EXHIBIT 11.1
Personal-Injury Intake Sheet

PERSONAL-INJURY INTAKE SHEET

Prepared for Clients of
Jeffers, Gilmore & Dunn

1. Client Information:

Name: Katherine Baranski

Address: 335 Natural Blvd.

Nita City, NI   48802

Social Security No.: 206-15-9858

Marital Status: Married   Years Married: 3

Spouse's Name: Peter Baranski

Children: None

Phone Numbers: Home (616) 555-2211   Work (616) 555-4849

Employer: Nita State University

Mathematics Department

Position: Associate Professor of Mathematics

Responsibilities: Teaching

Salary: $58,000

2. Related Information:

Client at Scene: Yes

Lost Work Time: 5 months

Client's Habits: Normally drives south on Mattis Avenue on way to university each morning at about the same time.

There are several advantages to recording an interview. For one thing, having a digital audio record of the interview reduces the need to take extensive notes during the interview. You can either have the audio file transcribed for future reference or listen to the file later (when creating an interview summary, for example, as discussed later) to refresh your memory of how the interviewee responded to certain questions. You may also want to have other members of the legal team read the transcript or listen to the file. Sometimes, what seemed insignificant to you may seem significant to someone else working on the case. Also, as a case progresses, a remark made by an interviewee that did not seem important at the time of the interview may take on added significance in view of evidence gathered later.

There are also some disadvantages to recording interviews. If clients and witnesses know everything they are saying is being recorded, they may feel uncomfortable and be less willing to disclose information freely. Such reluctance is understandable in view of the fact that the interviewee does not know what exactly

EXHIBIT 11.1
Personal-Injury Intake Sheet—
Continued

3. Incident/Accident:

Date: August 4, 2010   Time: 7:45 A.M.

Place: Mattis Avenue and 38th Street, Nita City, Nita

Description: Mrs. Baranski was driving south on Mattis Avenue when a car driven by Tony Peretto, who was attempting to cross Mattis at 38th Street, collided with Mrs. Baranski's vehicle.

Witnesses: None known by Mrs. Baranski

Defendant: Tony Peretto

Police: Nita City

Action Taken: Mrs. Baranski was taken to City Hospital by ambulance (Nita City Ambulance Co.).

4. Injuries Sustained:

Nature: Multiple fractures to left hip and leg; lacerations to left eye and left side of face; multiple contusions and abrasions

Medical History: No significant medical problems prior to the accident

Treating Hospital: Nita City Hospital

Treating Physician: Dr. Swanson

Hospital Stay: August 4, 2010   to September 20, 2010

Insurance: Southwestern Insurance Co. of America

Policy No: 00631150962-B

Interview Conducted by:

Allen P. Gilmore   January 30, 2011
Attorney   Date

Elena Lopez   January 30, 2011
Paralegal/Witness   Date

---

will happen during the interview or how the digital audio file may later be used. When asking an interviewee for permission to record an interview, you should evaluate carefully how the interviewee responds to this question. Depending on the interviewee's response, you might consider taking notes instead of recording the session. Another option is to go through the questions you will ask with the interviewee once before asking permission to turn on the recorder.

INTERVIEWING SKILLS

Interviewing skills are essentially any skills—particularly interpersonal and communication skills—that help you to conduct a successful interview. In this section, you will learn how the use of interpersonal and communication skills can help you establish a comfortable relationship with the interviewee. Then, you will read about specific questioning and listening techniques that can help you control the interview and elicit various types of information.

Interpersonal Skills

In conducting an interview, your primary goal is to obtain information. Although some people communicate information readily and effectively, others may need prompting and encouragement. If such people feel comfortable in your presence and in the interviewing environment, they will generally be more willing to disclose information.

As you begin, remember that the interviewee may be nervous or uncomfortable. You should put that person at ease as quickly as possible. A minute or two spent chatting casually is time well spent. Also, saying or doing something that shows your concern for the interviewee's physical comfort helps to make the interviewee feel more relaxed. For example, you might offer a cup of coffee or other beverage.

Using language that the interviewee will understand is essential in establishing a good working relationship. If you are interviewing a client with only a grade-school education, for example, do not use the phrase "facial lacerations" when talking about "cuts on the face." If you are interviewing a witness who does not speak English very well, and you are not fluent in the witness's language, have an interpreter present. Because most clients and witnesses are not familiar with legal terminology, avoid using legal terms that will not be clearly understood. If you must use a legal term, be sure that you define the term clearly.

Questioning Skills

When questioning witnesses or clients, remain objective at all times and gather as much relevant factual information as possible. Sometimes, you may find it hard to remain objective when questioning witnesses because you sympathize with the client and may not want to hear about facts contrary to the client's position. But you need to uncover details that could weaken the client's case as well as those that support it. Indeed, your supervising attorney must know *all* of the facts, especially any that might damage the client's case in court.

In some situations, it may be difficult to remain objective not because of your sympathy *for* the client but because of your own personal biases *against* the client, the witness, or the case. Interviewers must be careful to evaluate their own feelings prior to conducting an interview. If you feel a person's conduct is morally wrong, you may convey those feelings during the interview. You may communicate your feelings verbally or nonverbally, through unspoken signals such as gestures and facial expressions. Nonverbal comunication can be especially powerful. Once the interviewee senses your disapproval, he or she is likely to limit the information disclosed. For example, suppose you are interviewing Sandra, a client who is trying to regain custody of her children. The state took Sandra's children away because she abused drugs and failed to properly care for the children. You have read through the file and strongly disapprove of Sandra's past conduct. You also have doubts about whether she has recovered from her drug problem. If you do not set aside your personal feelings before meeting with Sandra, they may affect your interaction and limit the success of the interview.

The experienced legal interviewer uses certain questioning techniques to prompt interviewees to communicate the information needed. There are several types of questions, including open-ended, closed-ended, leading, and hypothetical questions. Exhibit 11.2 provides some examples of the types of questions discussed in the following subsections.

Open-Ended Questions

open-ended question
A question phrased in such a way that it elicits a relatively unguided and lengthy narrative response.

The **open-ended question** is a broad, exploratory question that invites any number of possible responses. It can be used when you want to give the interviewee an opportunity to talk at some length about a given subject. "What happened on the

EXHIBIT 11.2
Types of Interview Questions

Type of Question	Open-Ended Question	Closed-Ended Question	Leading Question	Hypothetical Question
Definition	A broad, exploratory question that elicits a lengthy response.	A question phrased in such a way that it elicits a "yes" or "no" response.	A question phrased in such a way that it suggests the desired answer.	A question that asks the interviewee to assume a certain set of facts in forming an answer.
Typical Uses	Used mostly with friendly witnesses and clients.	Used to clarify a witness's statement or to keep her or him on track. Used with adverse or reluctant witnesses.	Used at times with adverse witnesses in interviews. Used often by attorneys to cross-examine witnesses at trial (see Chapter 12).	Used primarily with expert witnesses in interviews and during trial.
Examples	• Describe the morning of the accident. What did you do that morning? • What did you see before entering the intersection? • When did you first see the defendant's car, and where was it? • How fast was the defendant going at the time of the accident?	• Were you late for work that morning? • Was there anyone in the car with you at the time? • Were you already in the intersection at the time you first saw the plaintiff's car? • Were you exceeding the speed limit at the time the accident occurred?	• You were running late for work that morning, correct? • You saw that the light had turned red before you entered the intersection, didn't you? • Isn't it true that you were driving over the speed limit at the time of the accident? • Isn't it true that you had been out drinking at a bar until late on the night before the accident?	• If a full-sized van is going sixty miles per hour, how far before an intersection must the driver apply the brakes in order to stop the vehicle? • If a 200-pound man drank fourteen beers in six hours, how long would it take before the alcohol was out of his system so that it would not affect his ability to drive?

night of October 28—the night of the murder?" is an open-ended question. Other examples of open-ended questions are "And what happened next?" and "What did you see as you approached the intersection?" When you ask a question of this kind, be prepared for a lengthy response. If a witness has difficulty narrating the events he or she observed or if a lull develops during the explanation, you will need to encourage the witness to continue by using prompting responses (which will be discussed shortly in the context of listening skills).

Open-ended questions are useful in interviewing clients or friendly witnesses (witnesses who favor the client's position). These interviewees are usually forthcoming, and you will be able to gain information from them by indicating in broad terms what you want them to describe. Open-ended questions are also a good way for the interviewer to evaluate whether the interviewee's behavior and overall effectiveness would make him or her a good witness at trial.

Closed-Ended Questions

closed-ended question
A question phrased in such a way that it elicits a simple "yes" or "no" answer.

The **closed-ended question**, in contrast, is intended to elicit a "yes" or "no" response from the interviewee. "Did you see the murder weapon?" is an example of a closed-ended question. Although closed-ended questions tend to limit communication, they are useful in some situations. For example, if an interviewee tends to wander from the topic being discussed, using closed-ended questions can help keep him or her on track. Closed-ended questions, because they invite specific answers, also may be useful to clarify the interviewee's previous response and to relax the interviewee in preparation for more difficult questions that follow. In addition, closed-ended questions may help to draw information from adverse witnesses (those who are not favorable to the client's position), who may be reluctant to volunteer information.

Leading Questions

leading question
A question that suggests, or "leads to," a desired answer. Interviewers may use leading questions to elicit responses from witnesses who otherwise would not be forthcoming.

The **leading question** is one that suggests to the listener the answer to the question. "Isn't it true that you were only ten feet away from where the murder took place?" is a leading question. Leading questions can be very effective for drawing information out of eyewitnesses or clients, particularly when they are reluctant to disclose information. They can also be useful for interviewing adverse witnesses who are hesitant to communicate information that may be helpful to the client's position. (In fact, they are the primary method of questioning used by attorneys when cross-examining witnesses at trial, as you will read in Chapter 12.) When used with a client or friendly witnesses, however, leading questions have a major drawback. They may lead to distorted answers because the client or witness may tailor the answer to fit his or her perception of what the interviewer wants to know. For this reason, in the interviewing context, leading questions should be used cautiously and only when the interviewer is aware of the possible distortions that might result.

Hypothetical Questions

hypothetical question
A question based on hypothesis, conjecture, or fiction.

As a paralegal, you may be asked to interview an expert witness either to gather information about a case or to evaluate whether that person would be an effective expert witness at trial (expert witnesses will be discussed later in this chapter). The **hypothetical question** is frequently used with expert witnesses. Hypothetical questions allow you to obtain an answer to an important question without giving away the facts (and confidences) of a client's case. For example, you might invent a hypothetical situation involving a certain type of knee injury (the same kind of injury as that sustained by a client) and then ask an orthopedic surgeon what kind of follow-up care would ordinarily be undertaken for that type of injury.

Listening Skills

The interviewer's ability to listen is perhaps the most important communication skill used during the interviewing process. Whenever you conduct an interview, you will want to completely absorb the interviewee's verbal answers, as well as his or her nonverbal messages. Before the interview, you should make sure that the room in which it is to be held will be free of noises, phone calls, visitors, and other interruptions or distractions. During the interview, you can use several listening techniques to maximize communication and guide the interviewee toward the fullest disclosure of needed information.

Passive Listening

As mentioned earlier, the interviewer should listen attentively when the interviewee is answering questions. It is extremely important that the client or witness get the impression that the interviewer is interested in what he or she is saying. If the interviewee pauses briefly or there is a lull in the conversation, the interviewer can use **passive listening** techniques, which are verbal or nonverbal cues that encourage the speaker to continue. For example, the interviewer might say, "I'm listening; please go on" or "And what happened then?" A nonverbal cue can be any facial expression or body language that shows you are interested in what is being said. Nodding positively, for example, is an effective nonverbal way to convey your interest. Maintaining eye contact is another nonverbal cue to indicate your interest.

Active Listening

For communication to be truly an interactive process, the listener must engage in active listening. **Active listening** involves not only paying close attention to what the speaker is saying but also providing appropriate feedback to show that you understand and may have sympathy for what is being said. Because people do not always say what they mean to say—or what they think they are saying—active listening is critical to a productive interview. Active listening allows the interviewer to clarify and confirm the interviewee's statements throughout the interview.

Reflecting Back.   One very effective active listening technique is for the interviewer to "reflect back," or "mirror," what the interviewee has already said. For example, after the interviewee has expressed her or his thoughts on a particular topic, you might say, "Let me see if I understand you correctly" and then summarize your impression of what she or he has said. If your interpretation is incorrect, the interviewee now has the opportunity to make you understand what she or he meant to say. This technique is useful for clarifying the person's statement. In addition, it reinforces the idea that you are listening carefully and are interested in what the interviewee has to say.

Controlling the Flow of the Interview.   Active listening also enables the interviewer to put the person's statements into the context of the larger picture and facilitates smooth transitions between interview topics. For example, suppose you are interviewing a client who is suing her former employer. After telling you about the rude and offensive behavior of her co-workers, she says she just couldn't go back to work and starts to cry. You can restate what she has told you in a way that makes the client feel you support and identify with her: "I understand that you did not return to work because of the hostility of your co-workers toward you." You might then move into a discussion of damages by saying, "It sounds as if you've been through a lot. Did you go see a counselor or get help from anyone during that time?" The interviewer who engages in active listening can thus direct the flow of the interview according to the reactions and responses of the person being interviewed.

INTERVIEWING CLIENTS

Typically, the paralegal interviews either clients or witnesses. Here, we look at client interviews. (We discuss witness interviews shortly.) The various types of client interviews include the initial interview, subsequent interviews to obtain further information, and informational interviews, or meetings, to inform the client of the status of his or her case and to prepare the client for trial or other legal proceedings.

The Initial Client Interview

As discussed in previous chapters, when a client seeks legal advice from an attorney, the attorney normally holds an initial interview with the client. During this interview, the client explains his or her problem so that the attorney can advise the client on possible legal options and the legal fees that may be involved. Either then or at a

passive listening
The act of listening attentively to the speaker's message and responding to the speaker by providing verbal or nonverbal cues that encourage the speaker to continue; in effect, saying, "I'm listening, please go on."

active listening
The act of listening attentively to the speaker's message and responding by giving appropriate feedback to show that you understand what the speaker is saying; restating the speaker's message in your own words to confirm that you accurately interpreted what was said.

featured contributor

TEN TIPS FOR THE EFFECTIVE USE OF INTERROGATORIES

P. David Palmiere

BIOGRAPHICAL NOTE

P. David Palmiere received his bachelor's degree magna cum laude in economics from the University of Michigan in 1972 and his law degree from the University of Michigan Law School in 1975. Palmiere, currently a member of the firm of Secrest, Wardle, Lynch, Hampton, Truex & Morley in Farmington Hills, Michigan, has practiced litigation for more than twenty-five years in courts from California to New York.

For the past twenty-four years, Palmiere has also been an adjunct professor in an ABA-accredited legal assistant program at Oakland University in Rochester, Michigan, where he teaches litigation and also assisted in designing the litigation specialty curriculum. Palmiere has been a guest lecturer at Wayne State University School of Law and a featured speaker at the state convention of the Legal Assistants Association of Michigan.

I nterrogatories are written questions to an opposing party requiring written answers. Interrogatories are a mainstay of discovery, but often interrogatory effort is wasted because of poor topic selection or ineffective drafting. Here are some guidelines for the effective use of interrogatories.

1. **Interrogatories and Answers Are a Struggle between Adversaries.** Good answers start with good questions. An interrogatory (question) is wasted if the answer is not meaningful. There are sanctions for bad faith answers to good questions. Ambiguous questions, however, allow the opponent to dodge the question without incurring sanctions. The more direct, crisp, and clear your phrasing, the more a fear of sanctions will compel informative answers. Always assume that your opponent will seize any excuse to decline to answer, and minimize such opportunities. If your questions pass the clarity test, they will probably be effective.

2. **Limit Interrogatories to Appropriate Subjects.** There are five basic discovery tools: interrogatories, requests for production of documents and things, requests for admission, depositions, and physical or mental examinations of persons. Each tool has its own role in discovery. Interrogatories are best used to elicit concrete items of factual information, such as names, addresses, dates, times, and places. Interrogatories are usually ineffective in asking for narrative accounts of complex facts or for the basis for opinions— tasks that are more appropriate to a deposition. Similarly, instead of wasting interrogatories asking for specifics about documents (other than who has them), it is better practice to join the interrogatories to a request for production of the documents themselves. Limit interrogatories to their most appropriate purpose—learning hard, factual data.

3. **Use Contention Interrogatories.** One exception to the foregoing is a "contention interrogatory," which asks the opponent for all facts supporting some assertion from the opponent's pleading. If the defendant asserts that the plaintiff's claim is barred by the statute of limitations, the plaintiff's contention interrogatory says, "Please state each fact that supports your contention that the plaintiff's claim is barred by the statute of limitations." Contention interrogatories can effectively smoke out and dispose of sham issues. Note, however, that contention interrogatories have a major blind spot: they do not elicit, except indirectly, information to *refute* the opponent's contentions. Other questions are needed for that.

4. **Use Several Sets of Interrogatories at Strategic Points during the Discovery Process.** Interrogatories are primarily used early in the case to gather leads for further investigation. But interrogatories are not "just for breakfast." They are also useful to follow up on leads developed in other discovery, such as document productions or depositions. As you read every new document and deposition, list new or unanswered questions, and consider interrogatories as the tool of choice for following up on the matter.

5. **Be Aware of Court Rules Concerning Interrogatories.** The court hearing the case will have rules about interrogatories. Know those rules. For example, the Federal Rules of Civil Procedure allow interrogatories only *after* the lawyers have conferred about a discovery schedule. The federal rules also require court permission to ask more than twenty-five questions, including subparts. State courts have their own rules limiting or affecting the use of interrogatories. These limitations must be observed.

6. **Each Interrogatory Must Stand on Its Own—The "Stranger in the Street" Test.** Interrogatory questions are often flawed because they lack context. Give every question this test: If a stranger approached you in the street, and asked the question just as you have written it, without more, could you answer it? For example, a stranger approaches you and says, "What time was it?" Your natural response would be, "What time was what?" or "What are you talking about?" This question does not pass the "stranger in the street" test. Any question that fails the test will probably not bring a meaningful answer from the opponent.

7. **Use Definitions to Supply Context for Questions.** Open your interrogatories with definitions of terms to be used, such as "the incident." Be sure that your definitions are nonargumentative—for example, if a plaintiff defines "the incident" as "the collision caused by defendant's negligence," the defendant will object to every question using the term. Then, in the interrogatories, you can ask

"Limit interrogatories to their most appropriate purpose—learning hard, factual data."

what time "the incident" took place or who saw any part of "the incident" without having to repeat the entire description to supply the necessary context. Once you define a term, however, use it consistently. Remember that this word now has a special meaning and cannot be used as if it were ordinary English.

8. **Some Questions You *Always* Ask.** Questions that you should always ask include questions about eyewitnesses, about the opponent's trial witnesses, and about the opponent's expert witnesses. Ask these even if you ask nothing else.

9. **Master Standard Phrasing.** Like other legal drafting, interrogatories tend to fall into standard patterns and phrases. Master these. Many lawyers begin each interrogatory, "Please state . . . ." If you do so, each item that follows must be an item of information. (Students often submit questions reading, "Please state each car that you own." One cannot "state" a car, but only information about the car, which is not what the question asks.) When an interrogatory contains a condition, description, or qualification, place it at the beginning of the question: "For each lawsuit to which you have ever been a party, please state . . . ." This phrasing is an effective substitute for questions that would otherwise have an "if-then" structure ("If you have ever been a party to a lawsuit, then please state . . ."). Drafting will be simpler if you use singular word forms rather than plural. When using subparts, make sure each one follows grammatically from the body of the main question.

10. **Make Effective Use of the Duty to Supplement Responses.** Federal Rule 26(e) and many state rules establish a duty to supplement interrogatory responses. This duty is often overlooked. Send periodic letters to the opposition, requesting supplements of prior interrogatory answers under the applicable rule. This places your side in a strong position to object if surprises are sprung at the trial.

later time, the client and the attorney will agree on the terms of the representation, if the attorney decides to take the case.

Paralegals often attend initial client interviews. Although the attorney normally conducts this first interview, the paralegal plays an important role. Usually, you will observe the client; take notes on what the client is saying; and provide the client with forms, statements explaining the firm's fees, and other prepared information normally given to new clients. Following the interview, you and the attorney may compare your impressions of the client and of what the client said during the interview.

All of the people present at the interview should be introduced to the client, their titles given, and the reason for their presence at the interview made known. In introducing you, the paralegal, to the potential client, the attorney will probably stress that you are not a lawyer and cannot give legal advice. If your supervising attorney does not indicate your nonattorney status to the client, you should do so. If a firm decides to take a client's case, the client should be introduced to every member of the legal team who will be working on the case.

A follow-up letter, such as the one shown in Exhibit 11.3, will be sent or e-mailed to the client after the interview. The letter will state whether the attorney has decided to accept the case or, if the attorney orally agreed during the initial client interview to represent the client, will confirm the oral agreement in writing.

Subsequent Client Interviews

Paralegals are often asked to conduct additional interviews with clients whose cases have been accepted. For example, assume that a client wants to obtain a divorce. After the initial interview, your supervising attorney may ask you to arrange for an interview to get the information necessary to prepare the divorce pleadings. When scheduling the interview, you should tell the client what kinds of documents or other data he or she should bring to the interview. Then send the client a letter confirming the date and time of the interview and listing all the items you would like the client to bring. During the interview, you will fill out the form that the firm uses to record client information in divorce cases. Paralegals often assume responsibility for gathering most of the information needed to file for a divorce or to begin child-custody proceedings.

When conducting a client interview, the paralegal should disclose his or her nonlawyer status if this fact was not made clear earlier. Remember, even if you have been introduced to the client as a legal assistant, the client may not realize that a legal assistant is not an attorney. To protect yourself against potential claims that you have engaged in the unauthorized practice of law, clearly state that you are not an attorney and cannot give legal advice.

The Informational Interview

The informational interview, or meeting, is an interview in which the client is brought in to discuss upcoming legal proceedings. Most clients know very little about the procedures involved in litigation, and firms often have their paralegals explain these procedures to clients and prepare clients for the trial experience. For example, the paralegal can describe to clients what will take place during the trial, how to dress and conduct themselves appropriately for trial, where to look when they testify, and so forth. The informational interview helps the client understand why certain proceedings are taking place and his or her role in those proceedings.

Summarizing the Interview

The interviewing process does not end with the close of the interview. A final and crucial step in the process involves summarizing the results of the interview for the legal team working on the case. As a paralegal, you are likely to create an intake memorandum following each initial client interview. If the firm has a prepared intake form for particular types of cases, such as the personal-injury intake sheet referred to earlier and

EXHIBIT 11.3
A Sample Follow-Up Letter
E-Mailed to a Client

From: Allen P. Gilmore, Attorney at Law <allen.p.gilmore@jgd.com>
To: Ms. Katherine Baranski <k.baran@nitamail.net>
Cc: Ms. Elena Lopez <elena.lopez@jgd.com>
Subject: Case Involving Tony Peretto

February 2, 2011
Ms. Katherine Baranski
335 Natural Blvd.
Nita City, Nita 48802

Dear Ms. Baranksi:

It was a pleasure to meet and talk with you on January 30. Jeffers, Gilmore & Dunn will be pleased to act as your representative in your action against Tony Peretto to obtain compensation for your injuries.

Attached is a copy of a fee agreement for your review. A copy of this letter and the agreement are being sent to you by mail. The mailing will contain a self-addressed, stamped envelope for your convenience. As soon as I receive the completed agreement, we will begin investigating your case.

As I advised during our meeting, to protect your rights, please refrain from speaking with the driver of the vehicle, Mr. Peretto; his lawyer; or his insurance company. If they attempt to contact you, simply tell them that you have retained counsel and refer them to me. I will handle any questions that they may have.

If you have any questions, please do not hesitate to call me or my paralegal, Ms. Elena Lopez.

Sincerely,

Allen P. Gilmore, Attorney at Law
Jeffers, Gilmore & Dunn
553 Fifth Avenue, Suite 101
Nita City, NI 48801
Telephone: (616) 555-9690
Fax: (616) 555-9679

---

1 Attachment
Baransky Agreement.doc
194K View as HTML Download

The preceding e-mail message (including any attachments) contains information that may be confidential, be protected by the attorney-client or other applicable privileges, or constitute nonpublic information. It is intended to be conveyed only to the designated recipient(s). If you are not an intended recipient of this message, please notify the sender by replying to this message and then delete it from your system. Use, dissemination, distribution, or reproduction of this message by unintended recipients is not authorized and may be unlawful.

illustrated in Exhibit 11.1 on pages 352 and 353, the completed form might constitute the interview summary. Information obtained during any subsequent interviews with a client should be analyzed and summarized in a memo for your supervising attorney or other team members to review and for later inclusion in the client's file.

Your interview summary should be created immediately after the interview, while the session is still fresh in your mind. When summarizing the results of a client interview, carefully review your notes and, if the session was recorded, review the file. Never rely totally on your memory of the statements made during the interview. It is easy to forget the client's specific words, and it may be important later to know exactly how the client phrased a certain comment or response. Relying on memory

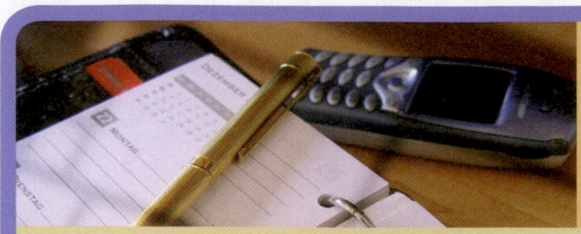

In the **Office**

HANDLING CLIENT DOCUMENTS

Clients frequently give paralegals important documents relating to their cases during interviews. A client might, for example, give you the only copy she has of her divorce agreement. States impose strict requirements on attorneys about the safekeeping of clients' funds and other property, including documents. You should never rely on memory when it comes to client documents. Instead, immediately after the conclusion of the interview, record the receipt of any documents or other items received from the client. The information may be recorded in an evidence log (discussed later in this chapter) or in some other way, depending on the procedures established by your firm to govern the receipt and storage of such property. An evidence log or its equivalent provides you with evidence—should it be necessary—of what you did (or did not) receive from a client. In addition, paper documents should be scanned into electronic case files so backup copies exist.

is also risky because, as mentioned earlier, sometimes a statement that seemed irrelevant at the time of the interview may turn out to be very important to the case. Make sure that the facts are accurately recorded and are as reliable as possible. Also note your impressions of the client and the client's nonverbal behaviors.

Depending on the nature of the legal claim being made by the client, you may want to include a visual element or two in your summary. For example, if the claim concerns an automobile accident, you might consider creating a graphic depiction of the accident to attach to the summary. (For a further discussion of the value of visual communications, see this chapter's *Technology and Today's Paralegal* feature.)

INTERVIEWING WITNESSES

Witnesses play a key role in establishing the facts of an event. As a legal investigator, your goal is to elicit as much relevant and reliable information as possible from each witness about the event that you are investigating. Interviewing witnesses is in many ways similar to interviewing clients, and many of the interviewing skills that we have already discussed apply to interviews of witnesses. A major difference between clients and witnesses, however, is that the latter may not always be friendly to the client's position. Here we describe the various types of witnesses as well as some basic skills and principles that are particularly relevant to investigative interviews.

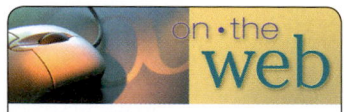

You can find databases containing the names of numerous expert witnesses at various Web sites, including **www. experts.com**, **www.hgexperts.com**, and **www.jurispro.com**.

Types of Witnesses

Witnesses include expert witnesses, lay witnesses, and eyewitnesses. Witnesses are also sometimes classified as friendly witnesses or hostile (adverse) witnesses.

Expert Witnesses

expert witness
A witness with professional training or substantial experience qualifying him or her to testify as to his or her opinion on a particular subject.

An **expert witness** is a person who has professional training, advanced knowledge, or substantial experience in a specialized area, such as medicine, computer technology, ballistics, or construction techniques. Paralegals often arrange to hire expert witnesses either to testify in court or to render an opinion on some matter relating to the client's case. Expert witnesses are often used in cases involving medical malpractice

Technology and Today's Paralegal

COMMUNICATING THROUGH GRAPHICS

If a picture is worth a thousand words, a bad picture can do as much damage as a thousand badly chosen words. Many times information is easier to convey through a chart or diagram than in narrative form. Unfortunately, it is also easy to confuse people with cluttered graphics and badly designed diagrams. Learning to communicate graphically is an important skill for paralegals, because they may be called upon to help design courtroom graphics and can use graphic skills to assist in developing the facts of a case.

DIAGRAMS AND INTERVIEWS

Diagrams can help you when you are interviewing witnesses. For example, if you are talking to a car accident victim or witness, sketching the scene can help the person you are interviewing remember crucial details. Creating an accurate diagram of the accident scene can help you uncover potential contradictions in witnesses' testimony or discover information you are missing. An accurate diagram can also give everyone working on the case a quick way to refresh themselves on the facts while they are working on the case. And, of course, diagrams may be critical to communicating information to a jury about your case. In an accident case, a diagram can show the jury where the various parties were, helping them to understand the witnesses' testimony.

GRAPHICS SOFTWARE

There are many graphics packages to help you produce diagrams and charts. *SmartDraw Legal Edition* (**www.smartdraw.com**) provides business graphics as well as templates for crime scene diagrams, accident reconstruction diagrams, patent drawings, and other legal uses. *Serif Draw Plus* (**www. freeserifsoftware.com**) is an inexpensive drawing program (one version is free; other are modestly priced) you can use to practice computer graphic skills. There are many other programs available that help produce accident or crime scene reconstructions and other useful graphics. Skills in graphics will give you an edge in the value you create for a law firm.

DESIGN PRINCIPLES

One of the best resources for visual display of information is the work of Edward Tufte, dubbed the "Minister of Information" by *New York* magazine and the "Leonardo da Vince of data" by the *New York Times*. Tufte's books (*The Visual Display of Quantitative Information, Envisioning Information, Visual Explanations,* and *Beautiful Evidence*) have been cited as influencing everything from the iPhone to the *New York Times*. Tufte regularly offers seminars on presenting information at various locations around the country (**www.edwardtufte.com**).

An example of the impact of the misleading nature of some visual presentations occurred in NASA's PowerPoint™ presentation to senior management on the damage to the Space Shuttle *Columbia*. Tufte's critique of the presentation was included in the final report of the Columbia Accident Investigation Board as part of its explanation of why NASA made bad decisions.

TECHNOLOGY TIP

To practice your graphic skills, watch director Errol Morris's award-winning documentary film *The Thin Blue Line,* which shows a crime scene repeatedly, based on different witnesses' testimony in a criminal trial. The film pioneered modern methods of crime scene reconstruction. To improve your graphic skills, make crime scene diagrams based on each witness's testimony as you listen to each one, and then use your diagrams to illustrate the inconsistencies among the testimonies.

Ethics Watch

INTERVIEWING CLIENTS AND THE UNAUTHORIZED PRACTICE OF LAW

Paralegals must be especially careful not to give legal advice when interviewing clients. Suppose that you are interviewing a client, Sue Collins. Collins was injured in a car accident and is suing the driver of the other car for negligence. Collins previously told you and your supervising attorney that the accident was all the result of the other driver's negligence. During your follow-up interview, however, Collins says to you, "What would happen, in a lawsuit such as mine, if the plaintiff was not watching the road when the accident occurred? What if the plaintiff was looking in the backseat to see why her baby was crying? Could the plaintiff still expect to win in court?" You know that under the laws of your state, contributory negligence on the part of the plaintiff (to be discussed in Chapter 14) could bar recovery of damages. Should you explain this to Collins? No. Even though the question is phrased as a hypothetical, it is possible that your answer could affect Collins's actions. Your best option is to tell Collins that you are not permitted to give legal advice but that you will relay the "hypothetical" question to your supervising attorney.

This action would be consistent with the following codes and guidelines:

- NFPA Model Code of Ethics and Professional Responsibility, Section EC-1.8: "A paralegal shall comply with the applicable legal authority governing the unauthorized practice of law in the jurisdiction in which the paralegal practices."

- ABA Model Guidelines for the Utilization of Paralegal Services, Guideline 3: "A lawyer may not delegate to a paralegal: . . . (C) Responsibility for a legal opinion rendered to a client."

- NALA Code of Ethics and Professional Responsibility, Canon 4: "A paralegal must use discretion and professional judgment commensurate with knowledge and experience but must not render independent legal judgment in place of an attorney."

and product liability to establish the duty, or standard of care, that the defendant owed to the plaintiff. For example, if a client of your firm is suing a physician for malpractice, your supervising attorney might arrange to have another physician testify as to the standard of care owed by a physician to a patient in similar circumstances.

Lay Witnesses

lay witness
A witness who can truthfully and accurately testify on a fact in question without having specialized training or knowledge; an ordinary witness.

Most witnesses in court are lay witnesses. In contrast to expert witnesses, **lay witnesses** do not possess any particular skill or expertise relating to the matter before the court. They are people who happened to observe or otherwise have factual knowledge about an event. A professional or expert in one field may be a lay witness in another field about which he or she does not have expert knowledge. A physician involved in a financial fraud case, for example, might give testimony about the fraud as a lay witness but not as an expert witness.

Eyewitnesses

eyewitness
A witness who testifies about an event that he or she observed or experienced firsthand.

Eyewitnesses are lay witnesses who may testify in court about an event they observed or experienced firsthand. The term *eyewitness* is deceiving; a better term might be "sense" witness. This is because an eyewitness's firsthand knowledge of an event need not have been derived from the sense of sight—that is, from actually seeing the event. An eyewitness may be someone who listened in on a telephone conversation between an accused murderer and his or her accomplice. A blind man may have been an eyewitness to a car crash, because he heard it.

In interviews, eyewitnesses are ordinarily asked to describe an event, in their own words and as they recall it, that relates to the client's case. Eyewitness accounts may be lengthy, and the paralegal may want to record the interview session to ensure accuracy. The experienced paralegal may also find that different eyewitnesses to the same event have contradictory views on what actually took place. People's perceptions of reality differ, as paralegals often find when comparing eyewitness reports.

Friendly Witnesses

Some witnesses to an event may be the client's family members, friends, co-workers, neighbors, or other persons who know the client and who want to be helpful in volunteering information. These witnesses are regarded as **friendly witnesses**. You may think that friendly witnesses are the best kind to interview, and they often are. They may also be biased in the client's favor, however, so the paralegal should look closely for the actual facts (and not the witness's interpretation of the facts) when interviewing friendly witnesses.

friendly witness
A witness who is biased against your client's adversary or sympathetic toward your client in a lawsuit or other legal proceeding.

Hostile Witnesses

Witnesses who may be prejudiced against your client or friendly to your client's adversary are regarded as **hostile witnesses** (or *adverse witnesses*). Interviewing hostile witnesses can be challenging. Sometimes the witness has an interest in the outcome of the case and would be in a better position if your client lost in court. For example, if the client is a tenant who refuses to pay rent until the landlord repairs the roof, then the paralegal interviewing the landlord's building manager should be prepared to deal with that person as a potentially hostile witness.

hostile witness
A witness who is biased against your client or friendly toward your client's adversary in a lawsuit or other legal proceeding; an adverse witness.

Sometimes, hostile witnesses refuse to be interviewed. On learning that the alternative might be a subpoena, however, a hostile witness may consent to at least a limited interview. If you plan to interview hostile witnesses, contact and interview them in the early stages of your investigation. The longer you wait, the greater the chance that they may be influenced by the opposing party's attorney or the opinions of persons sympathetic to the opposing party.

When interviewing hostile witnesses, be especially careful to be objective, fair, and unbiased in your approach. This does not mean that you have to ignore your client's interests. On the contrary, you will best serve those interests by doing all you can to keep from further alienating a witness whose information might ultimately help your client's case.

Questioning Witnesses

When you are asking questions as a legal investigator, you should phrase your questions so that they lead to the most complete answer possible. Investigative questions should thus be open ended. Compare, for example, the following two questions:

1. "Did you see the driver of the green van run the stop sign?"
2. "What did you see at the time of the accident?"

The first question calls for a "yes" or "no" answer. The second question, in contrast, invites the witness to explain fully what he or she actually saw. Something else that the witness saw could be important to the case—but unless you allow room for the witness's full description, you will not learn about this information.

Notice that the first question also assumes a fact—that the driver of the green van ran the stop sign. The second question, however, makes no assumptions and conveys no information to the witness that may influence his or her answer. Generally, the less the witness knows about other witnesses' descriptions, the better, because those other descriptions could influence the witness's perception of the event. You want to find out exactly what the witness observed, in his or her own words.

As part of a factual investigation into a client's legal claim, a paralegal may contact witnesses or other sources for information. Although a restaurant is not an ideal setting for discussing confidential information, sometimes it is not possible to meet a witness or other information source in an office environment. Is there a possible benefit of holding an interview in a restaurant, nonetheless?

(Courtesy of © Ingram Publishing)

Checking a Witness's Qualifications

When you are interviewing a witness during the course of an investigation, you often will not know whether the testimony of that witness will be needed in court or even whether the claim you are investigating will be litigated. Nonetheless, you should operate under the assumption that each witness is a potential court witness. Thus, you should make sure that the witness is competent to testify, reliable, and credible.

Competence

Under the Federal Rules of Evidence, any person is competent to be a lay witness as long as the individual has personal knowledge of the matter. Thus, only if a potential witness did not actually see, hear, or perceive the events in some way (because of a physical or mental disability, for example) will that person be judged incompetent to testify. Although state rules of evidence vary, most states also define competence for lay witnesses broadly. Expert witnesses are qualified only if they possess special knowledge, skill, experience, training, or education.

Credibility

Because it is easy to establish competence for most witnesses, the primary issue is generally not whether a witness can testify but whether the testimony will be credible, or believable. The parties to a lawsuit can attack the credibility of an opponent's witness and try to show that the witness is not telling the truth or is unreliable. In federal courts and most state courts, the credibility or reliability of a witness's testimony can be called into question by evidence, in the form of opinion or reputation, that points to the witness's character for truthfulness or untruthfulness. Thus, the paralegal investigating the case should inquire into any matters that tend to show whether the witness is honest. For example, does the witness abuse drugs or have a reputation in the community as a troublemaker or liar? Has the witness been convicted of a crime? If so, was it a felony, or did it involve any dishonesty or false statement? How long ago was the conviction? Under the federal rules, a witness's credibility can be attacked by evidence of a conviction for a crime punishable by incarceration for over one year or a conviction for any crime involving dishonesty or false statements that occurred within the last ten years.

Bias

The paralegal should also investigate the witness's possible bias. Does the witness have an interest in the claim being investigated that would tend to make his or her testimony prejudicial? Is the witness a relative or close friend of one of the parties involved in the claim? Does the witness hold a grudge against one of the parties? If the answer to any of these questions is yes, the witness's testimony may be discredited in court. In any event, it will probably not be as convincing as testimony given by a neutral, unbiased witness.

Winding Up the Interview

At the conclusion of an interview, the paralegal should ask the witness if there is anything else the witness would like to add to his or her statement. This gives the witness the opportunity to expand on areas not previously discussed or explain an answer previously given. The paralegal should verify the witness's complete mailing address, physical address, e-mail address, and telephone number. It is also a good idea to get the name and telephone number of a friend or relative living in the immediate area whom you can contact to locate the witness if he or she moves before the trial.

Witness Statements

Whenever you interview a witness, take thorough and accurate notes and prepare a memo to your supervising attorney. Include in the memo your evaluation of the witness's credibility and a description of any nonverbal communication that you felt was relevant (if the witness seemed uncomfortable with some aspect of the interview or became nervous when asked questions about a particular topic, for example).

You may also prepare a formal witness statement. Check with your supervising attorney before preparing such a statement, because formal witness statements may have to be given to the opposing party under applicable discovery rules (as discussed in Chapter 10). A **witness statement** is a written document setting forth what the witness said during the interview. The witness is given an opportunity to review the contents of the statement and then signs the statement to verify its contents. Exhibit 11.4 shows the type of information normally contained in a witness statement, and Exhibit 11.5 on page 368 presents excerpts from a sample witness statement.

witness statement
The written record of the statements made by a witness during an interview, signed by the witness.

EXHIBIT 11.4
Information Contained
in a Witness Statement

1. **Information about the Witness**
   —Name, address, and phone number.
   —Name, address, and phone number of the witness's employer or place of business.
   —Interest, if any, in the outcome of the claim being investigated.

2. **Information about the Interview**
   —Name of the interviewer.
   —Name of the attorney or law firm for which the claim is being investigated.
   —Date, time, and place of the interview.

3. **Identification of the Event Witnessed**
   —Nature of the action or event observed by the witness.
   —Date of the action or event.

4. **Witness's Description of the Event**

5. **Attestation Clause**
   —Provision or clause at the end of the statement affirming the truth of the witness's description as written in the statement.

[Witness's Signature]

EXHIBIT 11.5
A Sample Witness
Statement (Excerpt)

STATEMENT OF JULIA WILLIAMS

I, Julia Williams, am a thirty-five-year-old female. I reside at 3765 Mattis Avenue, Nita City, Nita 48800, and my home telephone number is (616) 555-8989. I work as a nurse at the Nita City Hospital & Clinic, 412 Hospital Way, Nita City, Nita 48802. My work telephone number is (408) 555-9898. I am making this statement in my home on the afternoon of February 8, 2011. The statement is being made to Elena Lopez, a paralegal with the law firm of Jeffers, Gilmore & Dunn.

In regard to the accident on the corner of Mattis Avenue and Thirty-eighth Street on August 4, 2010, at approximately 7:45 A.M. on that date, I was standing at the southwest corner of that intersection, waiting to cross the street, when I observed . . .

* * * *

I affirm that the information given in this statement is accurate and true to the best of my knowledge.

Julia Williams
Julia Williams

Statutes and court rules vary as to the value of witness statements as evidence. Usually, statements made by witnesses during interviews cannot be introduced as evidence in court, but they can be used for other purposes. For example, if a hostile witness's testimony in court contradicts something he or she said during your interview, the witness statement may be used to impeach the witness—that is, to call into question the witness's testimony or demonstrate that the witness is unreliable. Witness statements also can be used to refresh a witness's memory.

PLANNING AND CONDUCTING INVESTIGATIONS

Because factual evidence is crucial to the outcome of a legal problem, investigation is necessarily an important part of legal work. Attorneys often rely on paralegals to conduct investigations, and you should be prepared to accept the responsibility for making sure that an investigation is conducted thoroughly and professionally. In the following pages, you will read about the basics of legal investigation—how to plan and undertake an investigation, how the rules of evidence shape the investigative process, and how important it is to carefully document the results of your investigation.

Of course, you have already read about one aspect of investigations—interviewing witnesses. A preliminary investigation, however, can involve much more. For one thing, before witnesses can be interviewed, they must be located. Information relating to the case may also have to be obtained from a police department, weather bureau, or other source.

Where Do You Start?

Assume that you work for Allen Gilmore, the attorney representing the plaintiff in the hypothetical case discussed in Chapter 10. Recall that the plaintiff in that case, Katherine Baranski, is suing Tony Peretto for negligence. Peretto ran a stop sign at an intersection, and his car collided with Baranski's. Further assume that the case is still in its initial stages. Attorney Gilmore has just met with Katherine Baranski for the initial client interview. You sat in on the interview, listened to Baranski's description of the accident and of the damages she sustained as a result (medical expenses, lost wages, and so on), and took thorough notes.

CHECKING THE ACCIDENT SCENE

Gina Hubbard, a paralegal, works for a small law firm. She and her supervising attorney, John Calpert, have just concluded an intake interview with a new client. The client was involved in an automobile accident, and the driver of the other car, who sustained serious injuries, is suing the client for damages. The client maintains that the accident was not his fault and has asked Calpert to defend him in the lawsuit. The attorney asks Gina to first obtain a copy of the police report on the accident to verify the exact location of the accident, along with other pertinent information, such as photographs taken by police officers. Then, Gina should go to the accident site to learn what she can about the site.

Both Gina and the attorney know that this case may be settled early on, and therefore it may be too soon to hire a private investigator to investigate the accident scene. Even if the case is not settled before trial and an investigator is hired later, months may have passed, and the scene may have changed considerably. Road repairs may alter the area, new signs may be installed, the street may be widened, and the like. It is therefore important that Gina visit the site right away. She makes a list of the equipment she needs to take with her to use when checking the site.

TIPS FOR CHECKING AN ACCIDENT SCENE

- Take a digital camera with you at all times, because it will enable you to include the photos in computer documents relating to the case.
- Consider taking a digital camcorder.
- Take a digital audio recorder as well. You may want to dictate notes about your observations or record an interview with an eyewitness should you encounter someone at the site who saw the accident.
- Take a pencil and pad of paper to create sketches of the area, and be sure to include in the sketches any obstacles that could interfere with visibility.
- Include a tape measure or other measuring device in the tool kit as well. This will allow you to obtain precise measurements so that you can create a scale for your photographs and sketches.

After the interview, Gilmore asks you to do a preliminary investigation into Baranski's claim. It is now your responsibility to find the answers to a number of questions. Did the accident really occur in the way perceived by Baranski? Exactly where and when did it happen (see the *Developing Paralegal Skills* feature above)? How does the police report describe the accident? Were there any witnesses? Was Peretto insured, and if so, by what company? What other circumstances (such as weather) are relevant? Your supervising attorney will want to know the answers to such questions before advising Baranski as to what legal action should be pursued.

As in any legal investigation, your logical point of departure is the information you already have about the matter. This information consists of the statements made by Baranski during the initial client interview and summarized in your notes. Baranski described what she remembered about the accident, including the date and time it occurred. She said she thought that the police investigator had the names of some persons who had witnessed the accident. She also stated that she was employed as an associate professor in the math department at Nita State University, earning approximately $58,000 a year. Now you can map out an investigation plan based on this information.

EXHIBIT 11.6
An Investigation Plan

INVESTIGATION PLAN
File No. 15773

	Date Requested	Date Received

1. Contact Police Department
—To obtain police report
—To ask for photographs of accident scene
—To talk with investigating officer

—SOURCE: Nita City Police Dept.
—METHOD: Request in person or by mail

2. Contact Known Witnesses
—Tony Peretto, van driver
—Michael Young, police officer at accident scene
—Julia Williams, witness at accident scene
—Dwight Kelly, witness at accident scene

—SOURCE: Police report
—METHOD: Contact witnesses by initial phone
call and personal interview when possible

3. Obtain Employment Records
—To learn Baranski's employment status and income

—SOURCE: Nita State University
—METHOD: Written request by mail with
Baranski's release enclosed

4. Obtain Hospital Records
—To learn necessary information about
Baranski's medical treatment and costs

—SOURCE: Nita City Hospital
—METHOD: Written request by mail with
Baranski's release enclosed

Creating an Investigation Plan

investigation plan
A plan that lists each step involved in obtaining and verifying facts and information relevant to the legal problem being investigated.

An **investigation plan** is a step-by-step list of the tasks that you plan to do to verify or obtain factual information relating to a legal problem. In the Baranski case, the steps in your investigation plan would include those summarized in Exhibit 11.6 above and on the facing page and discussed next. The paralegal should make sure that his or her supervising attorney approves the investigation plan. Generally, throughout the investigation, it is important to keep in close touch with your supervising attorney about progress being made.

Contacting the Police Department

The initial step in your plan should be to contact the police department. You will want to look at a copy of the police report of the accident, view any photographs that were taken at the scene, get the names of persons who may have witnessed the accident, and, if possible, talk to the investigating officer.

Contacting and Interviewing Witnesses

Next, you will want to contact and interview any known witnesses and document their descriptions of what took place at the time of the accident. Known witnesses include the driver (Tony Peretto) of the vehicle that hit Katherine Baranski, the police officer at the scene, and the other witnesses noted in the police investigation report. Keep in mind that if Peretto is aware of Baranski's intention to sue him, he

EXHIBIT 11.6
An Investigation Plan—Continued

	Date Requested	Date Received
5. Contact National Weather Service —To learn what the weather conditions were on the day of the accident —SOURCE: National Weather Service or newspaper —METHOD: Phone call or written request	_____	_____
6. Obtain Title and Registration Records —To verify Peretto's ownership of the vehicle —SOURCE: Department of Motor Vehicles —METHOD: Order by mail	_____	_____
7. Contact Peretto's Insurance Company —To find out about insurance coverage —To check liability limits —SOURCE: Insurance company —METHOD: Written request by mail	_____ _____	_____ _____

8. Use a Professional Investigator
—To contact such witnesses as
  –ambulance attendants
  –doctors
  –residents in neighborhood of accident scene
—To inspect vehicle
—To take photos of accident site
—To investigate accident scene, and so on
 	
—SOURCE: Regular law firm investigator
—METHOD: In person
	_____
	
	_____
	_____
	_____
		_____
		
		_____
		_____
		_____

will probably have retained an attorney. If he has, then you are not permitted to contact him directly—you may communicate with him only through his attorney.

Obtaining Medical and Employment Records

To justify a claim for damages, you will need to determine the nature of the injuries suffered by Baranski as a result of the accident, the medical expenses that she incurred, and her annual or monthly income (to determine the amount of wages she lost as a result of the accident). To get this information, you will need copies of her medical and employment records.

The institutions holding these records will not release them to you unless Baranski authorizes them to do so. Therefore, you will also need to arrange with Baranski to sign release forms to include with your requests for copies. A sample authorization form to release medical records is shown in Exhibit 11.7 on page 372. You should make sure that Baranski signs these forms before she leaves the office after the initial interview. Otherwise, waiting for her to return the signed forms may delay your investigation. In addition to obtaining medical records, you may be asked to do some research on the type of injury sustained by Baranski and related information.

Contacting the National Weather Service

Weather conditions at the time of the accident may have an important bearing on the case. If it was raining heavily, for example, Peretto's attorney may argue that Peretto did not see the stop sign or that water on the road prevented him from

on • the
web

The National Weather Service is online at **www.nws.noaa.gov**.

EXHIBIT 11.7
Authorization to Release
Medical Records

TO: Nita City Hospital & Clinic
      Nita City, NI 48803

PATIENT: Katherine Baranski
      335 Natural Boulevard
      Nita City, NI 48802

    You are hereby authorized to furnish and release to my attorney, Allen P. Gilmore of Jeffers, Gilmore & Dunn, all information and records relating to my treatment for injuries incurred on August 4, 2010. Please do not disclose information to insurance adjusters or to other persons without written authority from me. The foregoing authority shall continue in force until revoked by me in writing, but for no longer than one year following the date given below.

Date: January 30, 2011
    Katherine Baranski
    Katherine Baranski

Please attach your invoice for any fee or photostatic costs and send it with the information requested above to my office.

Thank you,

Allen P. Gilmore

Allen P. Gilmore
Jeffers, Gilmore & Dunn
Attorneys at Law
553 Fifth Avenue
Suite 101
Nita City, NI 48801

Helena Moritz
Helena Moritz
Notary Public State of Nita
Nita County
My Commission Expires: November 12, 2012

---

stopping. You will therefore want to find out what the weather conditions were at the time of the accident by contacting the National Weather Service. When you interview eyewitnesses, ask them about weather conditions at the place and time of the accident as well.

Obtaining Vehicle Title and Registration Records

To verify that Tony Peretto owns the vehicle that he was driving at the time of the accident, you will need to obtain title and registration records. Usually, these can be acquired from the state department of motor vehicles, although in some states the secretary of state's office handles such records. The requirements for obtaining such information vary from state to state and may include the submission of special forms and fees. As the *On the Web* feature alongside indicates, you can go online to the relevant state office to obtain what you need.

Contacting the Insurance Company

If you learned the name of Peretto's insurance company from Baranski or from the police report, you will want to contact that company to find out what kind of insurance coverage Peretto has and the limits of his liability under the insurance policy.

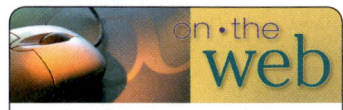

Relevant driving and vehicle registration records may be on the Web. See, for example, a list of licensed drivers for many states at **www.publicdata.com**. To find the home pages of your state's government agencies, go to **www.usa. gov** and enter the name of your state in the "Search" box.

Insurance companies usually are reluctant to give this information to anyone other than the policyholder. They sometimes cooperate with such requests, however, because they know that if they do not, the information can be obtained during discovery, should a lawsuit be initiated.

Using a Professional Investigator's Services

Depending on the circumstances, your supervising attorney may decide to use a professional investigator for certain tasks, including those just described. An experienced investigator will often have developed many useful contacts with law enforcement officers, subject-matter experts, and other sources. These contacts can speed up the investigation and may give the investigator access to information that others could not easily get. In addition, some government and private databases are restricted to government agents and licensed investigators. Attorneys also sometimes hire professional licensed investigators to obtain facts omitted from police reports, search public records, serve subpoenas, evaluate trial presentations, and conduct surveillance on parties important to the case.

You may be responsible for working with the investigator. For example, your supervising attorney may ask you to arrange for the investigator to inspect and take photographs of the accident scene. You may also work with the investigator to determine the credibility and effectiveness of certain witnesses. In addition, you may meet with the investigator to review discovery documents in order to provide additional insight or generate investigative leads.

Locating witnesses can be difficult and time consuming, and attorneys sometimes use investigators for this task. As discussed next, however, paralegals today can find people online much more easily than was once possible, potentially reducing the need to hire outside assistance.

Locating Witnesses

Perhaps one of the most challenging tasks for the legal investigator is locating a witness whose address is unknown or who has moved. Suppose, for example, that in the Baranski case the police investigation report lists the name, address, and telephone number of Edna Ball, a witness to the accident. When you call her number, a recording says that the phone has been disconnected. You go to her address, and the house appears to be vacant. What is your next step? A good starting point is to visit other homes in the neighborhood. Perhaps someone living nearby knows Edna Ball and can give you some leads as to where she is or what happened to her. Other sources are discussed below.

Telephone and City Directories

The telephone directory can be a valuable source of information. In trying to locate Edna Ball, for example, you might check to see if her name is listed in the current directory and, if so, whether it is listed jointly with someone, such as her husband. Your local telephone information service might have a new number listed for her. If the town is small enough, you could call other people with the same last name to see if Edna Bell is a relative.

City directories are also good potential sources of information. Such directories may be available in the library or on the Web through online services such as **www.infousacity.com**. A city directory generally contains more information than a phone book. For example, some city directories list places of employment and spouses' names in addition to addresses and telephone numbers. Typically, city directories provide a listing of names and phone numbers by street address. In the Baranski case, if you wanted to obtain the telephone numbers of persons who live in the area of the Baranski-Peretto accident, you could consult a city directory for addresses near the intersection where the accident occurred.

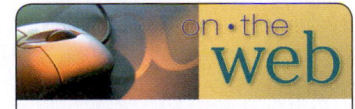

Researching family history has become popular, and many genealogy sites provide histories that can help you track down hard-to-find parties. See, for example, **www.graonline.com**, **www.genealogy.com**, and **www.family search.org**. Even **myspace.com** is becoming a useful tool for searching for people.

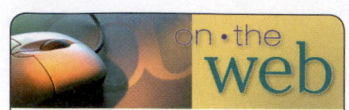

There are many online services to help find people. See, for example, **www.peoplelookup.com**, **www.peoplefinders.com**, and **www.411.com**.

Online People Finders

Today, paralegals can use one of the numerous Internet people-finding services to locate witnesses (and witnesses' assets, if needed). Some of these online services charge a small fee for each search, depending on the type of report requested (simple address record, background check, e-mail address, assets). The services check public records, telephone directories, court and criminal records, and a variety of other sources and provide results quickly and efficiently. (For an example, go to **www.whitepages.com**.) Both of the largest online legal research services (Westlaw and Lexis, discussed in Chapter 8) offer people-finding services as well.

Other Information Sources

Other sources of information include media reports (newspaper articles and television videos covering the event being investigated); court records (probate proceedings, lawsuits, and the like); deeds to property (usually located in the county courthouse); birth, marriage, and death certificates; voter-registration lists; the post office (at which the witness may have left a forwarding address); credit bureaus; the tax assessor's office; and city utilities, such as the local electric or water company.

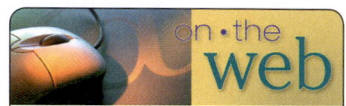

Increasingly, public records can be searched online. Many local governments provide such services, as do some private companies. See, for example, **www.onlinepublicrecordssearch.com**.

Professional organizations may be useful sources as well. For example, if you have learned from one of Edna Ball's neighbors that she is a paralegal, you can check with state and local paralegal associations to see if they have current information on her. You might also check with federal, state, or local governmental agencies or bureaus (discussed in the following section) to see if the information contained in public records will be helpful in locating Edna Ball.

Accessing Government Information

Records and files acquired and stored by government offices and agencies can be a tremendous resource for the legal investigator. Public records are available at local government buildings or offices (such as the county courthouse or post office), as mentioned above. As shown in Exhibit 11.8, you can also often find these records on the Web site of the agency that maintains them. Additionally, it is possible to obtain information from federal agencies, such as the Social Security Administration, and from state departments or agencies, such as the state revenue department or the secretary of state's office. If you wish to obtain information from any government files or records, check with the specific agency or department to see what rules apply. The *Developing Paralegal Skills* feature on page 376 provides more tips on obtaining public information.

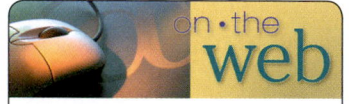

For further information on how to make an FOIA request, go to **www.nist.gov/admin**, and select "Freedom of Information Act (FOIA)." Also see **www.firstamendmentcenter.org**. In the search box, type "FOIA request."

The Freedom of Information Act (FOIA) requires the federal government to disclose certain records to any person on request. A request that complies with the FOIA procedures need only contain a reasonable description of the information sought. The FOIA exempts some types of information from the disclosure requirement, including classified information (information concerning national security), confidential material dealing with trade secrets, government personnel rules, and personal medical files. Requesting information through the FOIA is usually a slow process and should be used only when there is no other choice.

Investigation and the Rules of Evidence

Because an investigation is conducted to obtain information and verify facts that may eventually be introduced as evidence at trial, you should know what kind of evidence will be admissible in court before undertaking your investigation.

Evidence is anything that is used to prove the existence or nonexistence of a fact. Whether evidence will be admitted in court is determined by the **rules of evidence**—rules created by the courts to ensure that any evidence presented in court is fair and reliable. The Federal Rules of Evidence govern the admissibility of evidence in federal courts. For cases brought in state courts, state rules of evidence apply. (Many states have adopted evidence rules patterned on the federal rules.)

evidence
Anything that is used to prove the existence or nonexistence of a fact.

rules of evidence
Rules governing the admissibility of evidence in trial courts.

Dallas County Online Record Search Application

http://dallascounty.org/applications/english/record-search/rec-search_intro.html   Q▾ Google

WELCOME
TO THE OFFICIAL WEBSITE OF DALLAS COUNTY, TEXAS

Today is Wednesday, June 3, 2009

Dallas County
Online Record Search

Dallas County Online is pleased to offer the convenience of **Online Record Searches**. For technical assistance with the Dallas County Online Record Search, please contact the webmaster via webmaster@dallascounty.org

County Clerk Public Access Record Search

County Court Search

Probate

Criminal Background

Civil Attorney Index

Civil Court

Marriage Information

UCC/Personal Property/Deeds

Assumed Name

CONTINUE

District Clerk Public Access Record Search

District Court Search

Civil & Family Case Records

CONTINUE

Content and Liability Disclaimer
Dallas County shall not be responsible for any errors or omissions contained on this Website, and reserves the right to make changes without notice. Accordingly, any third party information is provided "AS IS." The "Official Clerks Record" is maintained by the Dallas County Clerks Office located at 133 N. Industrial Blvd., 2nd Fl Dallas, Texas 75207. Dallas County.org provides no warranty, either expressed or implied, as the accuracy, reliability, or completeness of furnished data. If you find any errors or omissions, we encourage you to report them to the contact listed in the footer of that Web page.

In no event shall Dallas County be liable for any damages whatsoever, and in particular the County Clerk shall not be liable for special, indirect, consequential, or incidental damages, or damages for lost profits, loss of revenue, or loss of use, arising out of or related to the outdated information from this website or the information contained in it, whether such damages arise in contract, negligence, tort, under statute, in equity, at law or otherwise.

Copyright © 2009 Dallas County Online. All Rights Reserved.
PRIVACY STATEMENT | HELP | CONTACT DALLAS COUNTY | ADA STATEMENT | SITE INDEX

You will not need to become an expert in evidentiary rules, but a basic knowledge of how evidence is classified and what types of evidence are admissible in court will greatly assist your investigative efforts.

Direct versus Circumstantial Evidence

Two types of evidence may be brought into court—direct evidence and circumstantial evidence. **Direct evidence** is any evidence that, if believed, establishes the truth of the fact in question. For example, bullets found in the body of a shooting victim provide direct evidence of the type of gun that fired them. **Circumstantial evidence** is indirect evidence that, even if believed, does not establish the fact in question but only the degree of likelihood of the fact. In other words, circumstantial evidence can create an inference that a fact exists.

For example, suppose that your firm's client owns the type of gun that shot the bullets found in the victim's body. This circumstantial evidence does not establish that the client shot the victim. Combined with other circumstantial evidence, however, it could help to convince a jury that the client committed the crime. For instance, if

direct evidence
Evidence directly establishing the existence of a fact.

circumstantial evidence
Indirect evidence offered to establish, by inference, the likelihood of a fact that is in question.

Developing
Paralegal Skills

ACCESSING GOVERNMENT INFORMATION

Ellen Simmons has started a new job as a paralegal for Smith & Case, a law firm that handles Superfund cases (see Chapter 19). Ellen is about to request copies of documents from the Environmental Protection Agency (EPA). Ellen calls and speaks to Christopher Peter, a paralegal with the EPA. She identifies herself as a paralegal from Smith & Chase, which is representing a client involved at the Suburban Landfill Superfund site. Ellen is greeted with silence and wonders what she might have said to offend Christopher. She asks if the EPA has the waste-in/waste-out report that gives the total volume of hazardous waste at the site and lists the potentially responsible parties.

Christopher responds, in a surprised voice, that the EPA does have the documents. "Are you new?" asks Christopher. "Is it that obvious?" jokes Ellen. Christopher responds that it's not really that obvious and explains that her predecessor always just sent in FOIA requests for everything that the EPA had in its files and that it took weeks to respond to these requests. "Believe me, your firm has quite a reputation around here," says Christopher.

Ellen knows that she is off to a good start in her new job and with an important legal assistant at the EPA. She smiles to herself as she promises to submit the FOIA request for only the waste-in/waste-out report.

TIPS FOR WORKING WITH GOVERNMENT AGENCIES

- Before you call the agency, review the file to familiarize yourself with the case, and go online to the agency Web site to search for as much background information as possible.
- Review the agency's regulations to ascertain which documents the agency prepares in specific types of cases, such as Superfund cases.
- Make a list of the various documents.
- Determine in advance (from the list) which documents you will be requesting.
- Develop a list of alternatives to use in the event that the documents that you request have not been prepared or are not available.
- Make reasonable requests from the agency.
- Cultivate good working relationships with agency staff members.

other circumstantial evidence indicates that your firm's client had a motive for harming the victim and that the client was at the scene of the crime at the time the crime was committed, a jury might conclude that the client committed the crime.

Relevance

relevant evidence
Evidence tending to prove or disprove the fact in question. Only relevant evidence is admissible in court.

Evidence will not be admitted in court unless it is relevant. **Relevant evidence** is evidence that tends to prove or disprove the fact in question. For example, evidence that the gun belonging to your firm's client was in the home of another person when the victim was shot would be relevant, because it would tend to prove that the client did not shoot the victim.

Even relevant evidence may not be admitted in court if its probative (proving) value is substantially outweighed by other important considerations. For example, even though evidence is relevant, it may not be necessary—the fact at issue may have been sufficiently proved or disproved by previous evidence. In that situation, the introduction of further evidence would be a waste of time and would cause undue delay in the trial proceedings. Relevant evidence may also be excluded if it would tend to distract the jury from the main issues of the case, mislead the jury, or cause the jury to decide the issue on an emotional basis.

Authentication of Evidence

At trial, an attorney must lay the proper foundation for the introduction of certain evidence, such as documents, exhibits, and other objects, and must demonstrate to the court that the evidence is what the attorney claims. The process by which this is accomplished is referred to as **authentication**. The authentication requirement relates to relevance, because something offered in evidence becomes relevant to the case only if it is authentic, or genuine. As a legal investigator, you need to make sure that the evidence you obtain is not only relevant but also capable of being authenticated if introduced at trial.

> **authentication**
> The process of establishing the genuineness of an item that is to be introduced as evidence in a trial.

Commonly, evidence is authenticated by the testimony of witnesses. For example, if an attorney wants to introduce an autopsy report as evidence in a case, he or she can have the report authenticated by the testimony of the medical examiner who signed it. Generally, an attorney must offer enough proof of authenticity to convince the court that the evidence is, in fact, what it is purported to be.

The rules of evidence require authentication because certain types of evidence, such as exhibits and objects, cannot be cross-examined by opposing counsel, as witnesses can, yet such evidence may have a significant effect on the jury. The authentication requirement provides a safeguard against the introduction of nonverified evidence that may strongly influence the outcome of the case.

The Federal Rules of Evidence provide for the self-authentication of specific types of evidence. In other words, certain documents or records need not be authenticated by testimony. Certified copies of public records, for example, are automatically deemed authentic. Other self-authenticating evidentiary documents include official publications (such as a report issued by the federal Environmental Protection Agency), documents containing a notary public's seal or the seal of a public official, and manufacturers' trademarks or labels.

Hearsay

When interviewing witnesses, keep in mind that the witness's testimony *in court* must be based on the witness's own knowledge and not hearsay. **Hearsay** is defined as testimony that is given in court by a witness who relates not what he or she knows personally but what another person said. Literally, it is what someone heard someone else say. Hearsay is generally not admissible in court when offered to prove the truth of the matter asserted.

> **hearsay**
> Testimony that is given in court by a witness who relates not what he or she knows personally but what another person said. Hearsay is generally not admissible as evidence.

For example, a witness in the Baranski case cannot testify in court that she heard an observer say, "That van is going ninety miles per hour"—even if the other observer was a police officer. Such testimony would be inadmissible under the hearsay rule. The witness can only testify about what she personally observed regarding the accident. Of course, during the investigation, witnesses often tell you what other people said (and you should not discourage them from doing so). If you wish to use information obtained this way as evidence in court, however, you need to find an alternative method of proving it (such as by the testimony of the people who made the original statements).

Policy Underlying the Hearsay Rule.
There are several reasons why hearsay is generally not allowed. First, the person who made the out-of-court statements (referred to as the *declarant*) was not under oath at the time of making the statements. Second, the witness who is testifying may have misunderstood what the other person said. Third, because there is no opportunity to cross-examine the person who actually made the statements, there is no way to verify that the statements were actually made, much less that the witness heard them correctly. In other words, hearsay evidence is inadmissible because it is unreliable, not because it is irrelevant.

Exceptions to the Hearsay Rule.   Exceptions to the hearsay rule are made in specific circumstances, often because the statements are made in situations that indicate a high degree of reliability. For example, a witness is usually allowed to testify about what a dying person said concerning the cause or circumstances of his or her impending death. This is because the courts have concluded that a person facing death will usually not lie about who or what caused that death. Similarly, if a person makes an excited statement at the time of a stressful or startling event (such as "Oh no! That woman has just dropped her baby out the window"), a witness can usually testify as to that statement in court. If one of the parties to a lawsuit makes an out-of-court admission (for example, if defendant Peretto in the Baranski case admits to his friends that he was driving too fast at the time of the accident), a witness's testimony about what the party said may be admissible, although the rules on out-of-court admissions vary among jurisdictions. Exhibit 11.9 describes some of the traditional exceptions to the hearsay rule.

EXHIBIT 11.9
Some Exceptions to the Hearsay Rule

Present Sense Impression—A statement describing an event or condition made at the time the declarer perceived the event or condition or immediately thereafter [FRE 803(1)].* *Example: "I smell smoke."*

Excited Utterance—A statement relating to a startling event or condition made while the declarer was under the stress or excitement caused by the startling event or condition [FRE 803(2)]. *Example: "Oh no! The brakes aren't working!"*

State of Mind—A statement of the declarer's then-existing state of mind, emotion, sensation, or physical condition (such as intent, plan, motive, design, mental feeling, pain, or bodily health). Such statements are considered trustworthy because of their spontaneity [FRE 803(3)]. *Example: "My leg is bleeding and hurts terribly."*

Recorded Recollection—A memorandum or record indicating a witness's previous statements concerning a matter that the witness cannot now remember with sufficient accuracy to testify fully about the matter. If admitted in court, the memorandum or record may be read into evidence but may not itself be received as an exhibit unless offered by an adverse party [FRE 803(5)]. *Example: An employer's memo to one of his or her employees in which the employer responds to the employee's complaint about safety violations in the workplace.*

Former Testimony—Testimony that was given at another hearing or deposition by a witness who is now unavailable, if the party against whom the testimony is now offered was a predecessor in interest and had an opportunity to examine the witness in court during the previous hearing or deposition [FRE 804(b)(1)]. *Example: An employee's testimony about his or her employer that was introduced at a trial brought by the employee's co-worker against that employer for sexual harassment. The employer is now being sued by another employee for sexual harassment, and the employee who testified in the previous trial is out of the country. The employee's testimony in the previous trial may be admissible.*

Business Records—A document or compilation of data made in the course of a regularly conducted business activity, unless the source of the information or the method or circumstances of the document's preparation indicate that it is not trustworthy as evidence. The source of information must be from a person with firsthand knowledge, although this person need not be the person who actually made the entry or created the document [FRE 803(6)]. *Example: Financial statement of a business firm.*

Dying Declarations—In a prosecution for homicide or in a civil proceeding, a statement made by a person who believes that his or her death is impending about the cause or circumstances of his or her impending death [FRE 804(b)(2)]. *Example: Derek said just before he died, "Jethro stabbed me."*

Statement against Interest—A statement that was made by someone who is now unavailable and that was, at the time of its making, so far contrary to the declarer's financial, legal, or other interests that a reasonable person in the declarer's position would not have made the statement unless he or she believed it to be true [FRE 804(b)(3)]. *Example: Sanchez says that Jackson, who is now missing, made the following statement to Sanchez just before leaving town: "I committed the perfect crime!"*

Miscellaneous Exceptions—Miscellaneous exceptions include records of vital statistics [FRE 803(9)]; records of religious organizations [FRE 803(11)]; marriage, baptismal, or similar certificates [FRE 803(12)]; family records (including charts, engravings on rings, inscriptions on family portraits, and engravings on tombstones) [FRE 803(13)]; and statements offered as evidence of a material fact that are trustworthy because of the circumstances in which they were uttered [FRE 804(b)(5) and FRE 803(24)].

---

*Federal Rules of Evidence.

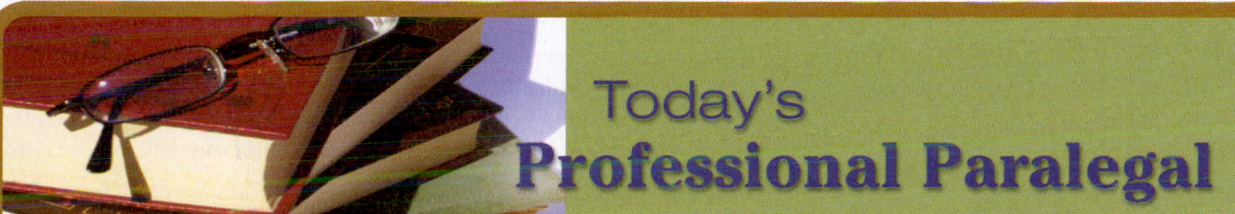

Today's Professional Paralegal

INTERVIEWING A CLIENT

Amanda Blake, a paralegal, works for John Kerrigan, a sole practitioner. A new client, Joel Sontag, calls for an appointment to make his will. The attorney has to go out of town. Because Sontag is anxious to get the will done, the attorney asks Amanda to meet with Sontag and interview him to obtain some basic information. The attorney will review the information when he returns and then advise Sontag on the will.

PREPARING FOR THE INTERVIEW

Amanda reserves the conference room. On the day of Sontag's visit, she has it set up for the interview. She has already made a copy of the will and estate-planning checklist that she will use to ensure that she gets all of the essential information from Sontag. The secretary shows Sontag into the conference room when he arrives.

MEETING THE CLIENT

Amanda introduces herself, saying, "Hello, Mr. Sontag, I'm Amanda Blake, John Kerrigan's legal assistant. I'll be meeting with you today to obtain the estate-planning information that Mr. Kerrigan needs if he is to advise you." Sontag responds, "Mr. Kerrigan told me that we would be meeting today. He also told me how capable you are." Amanda smiles and says, "Thanks. And did Mr. Kerrigan explain to you that I'm not an attorney?" Sontag responds, "Yes, he did." Amanda then removes her checklist and note pad from her file.

OBTAINING INFORMATION ABOUT THE CLIENT

"I'll be reviewing this checklist to make sure that we obtain all of the information that we need for your will," Amanda informs Joel. "First, I need you to fill out the client information form," instructs Amanda. "As you can see, it requires you to give us personal information, such as your name, legal residence, date of birth, and other data." Joel takes the form and fills it out. When he is finished, he hands it to Amanda.

"Now I need some other information. First, I need to know if you're married," states Amanda. "Yes, I am," responds Joel. "Your wife's name is?" asks Amanda. "Nicole Lynn Sontag," answers Joel. "And your wife resides with you at the address that you've given on the client information form?" asks Amanda. "Yes, she does," Joel states. "When was she born, and what's her Social Security number?" asks Amanda. "She was born on January 17, 1968, and her Social Security number is 363-46-2350," says Joel.

"Joel, do you have any children?" asks Amanda. "Yes, we have one son, Joel, Jr., aged fourteen," answers Joel. "Do you want to provide for both of them in your will?" asks Amanda. "Yes," responds Joel. "Do you have any other relatives for whom you want to provide?" asks Amanda. "Yes, I have a brother, Alfred Sontag, who lives in a home for autistic people," answers Joel. "I'll need the address for the home," responds Amanda. Joel says he will get that and that there are no other people to be included in the will.

OBTAINING INFORMATION ABOUT THE CLIENT'S PROPERTY

"Now we need to discuss property," Amanda informs Joel. "Do you own a home?" she asks. "Yes," he answers. Amanda says, "I need to know if the home is located at the address you gave on the form, when you bought it, what it cost, what its present approximate market value is, whether you own it jointly with your wife, and the balance on your mortgage." Joel gives her all of the requested information. Amanda continues questioning Joel about his property holdings until she has covered all the items on her checklist.

CONCLUDING THE INTERVIEW

"Well," says Amanda, "we've covered everything on the checklist. Now we need to set up a time for you to meet with Mr. Kerrigan to discuss your will. Because you jointly own property with your wife, Mr. Kerrigan will want to meet both of you. Would two o'clock Tuesday afternoon be a good time to come in to meet with Mr. Kerrigan?" Joel says that would be a good time. Amanda then begins to prepare a detailed summary of the interview to give to her supervising attorney on his return.

Summarizing Your Results

The final step in any investigation is summarizing the results. Generally, your investigation report should provide an overall summary of your findings, a summary of the facts and information gathered from each source that you investigated, and your general conclusions and recommendations based on the information obtained during the investigation.

Overall Summary

The overall summary of the investigation should thoroughly describe all of the facts you have gathered. This section should be written so that someone not familiar with the case could read it and become adequately informed about the case's factual background.

Source-by-Source Summaries

You should also create a list of your information sources, including witnesses, and summarize the facts gleaned from each of these sources. Each "source section" should contain all of the information gathered from that source, including direct quotes from witnesses. Each source section should also contain a subsection giving your personal comments on that particular source. You might comment on a witness's demeanor, for example, or on whether the witness's version of the facts was consistent or inconsistent with the versions of other witnesses. Your impressions of the witness's competence or reliability could be noted. If the witness provided you with further leads to be explored, this information could also be included.

General Conclusions and Recommendations

In the final section, you will present your overall conclusions about the investigation, as well as any suggestions that you have on the development of the case. Attorneys rely heavily on their investigators' impressions of witnesses and evaluations of investigative results because the investigators have firsthand knowledge of the sources. Your impression of a potentially important witness, for example, may help the attorney decide whether to arrange for a follow-up interview with the witness. Usually, the attorney will want to interview only the most promising witnesses, and your impressions and comments will serve as a screening device. Based on your findings during the investigation, you might also suggest to the attorney what further information can be obtained during discovery, if necessary, and what additional research needs to be done.

KEY TERMS AND CONCEPTS

active listening *357*

authentication *377*

circumstantial evidence *375*

closed-ended question *356*

direct evidence *375*

evidence *374*

expert witness *362*

eyewitness *364*

friendly witness *365*

hearsay *377*

hostile witness *365*

hypothetical question *356*

interviewee *350*

investigation plan *370*

lay witness *364*

leading question *356*

open-ended question *354*

passive listening *357*

relevant evidence *376*

rules of evidence *374*

witness statement *367*

CHAPTER SUMMARY

CONDUCTING INTERVIEWS AND INVESTIGATIONS

Planning the Interview

Paralegals often interview clients and witnesses. Before the interview, the paralegal should prepare the interview environment to ensure that interruptions, noises, and delays will be minimized, that the client will be comfortable, and that any necessary supplies, forms, and equipment are at hand.

1. *Planning the questions*—The interviewer should have in mind the kind of information being sought from the interviewee. Preprinted interview forms provide helpful guidelines, but the interviewer should remain flexible during the interview, tailor questions to the interviewee's responses, and ask follow-up questions.

2. *Recording the interview*—Some paralegals record their interviews for future reference. If you do, make sure to obtain permission from your supervising attorney and the person being interviewed before recording. Keep in mind that some clients and witnesses will be less willing to disclose information freely when being recorded. If the interviewee appears hesitant, consider taking notes instead.

Interviewing Skills

Interviewing skills include interpersonal skills, questioning skills, and communication skills, particularly listening skills.

1. *Interpersonal skills*—The interviewer should put the interviewee at ease, use language that the person will understand, and avoid using legal terms.

2. *Questioning skills*—Types of questions used during the interviewing process include open-ended, closed-ended, leading, and hypothetical questions. The questioning technique will depend on the person being interviewed and the type of information sought (see Exhibit 11.2 on page 355).

3. *Communication skills*—The ability to listen is perhaps the most important skill for an interviewer to develop.

   a. Passive listening involves listening attentively to the speaker and using either verbal or nonverbal cues (such as nodding) to encourage him or her to continue.

   b. Active listening involves not just listening attentively but also giving feedback that indicates to the speaker that you understand what he or she is saying.

   c. One effective active listening technique is for the interviewer to "reflect back," or restate, what the interviewee has said. This gives the speaker an opportunity to clarify or correct previous statements.

   d. Active listening enables the interviewer to control the flow of the interview. It allows the interviewer to put the interviewee's statements into the larger context and facilitates smooth transitions between topics.

Interviewing Clients

There are three types of client interviews: initial interviews (usually conducted by the attorney but often attended by the paralegal), subsequent interviews (often

Continued

conducted by the paralegal), and informational interviews (or meetings, also typically handled by the paralegal).

1. *Scheduling interviews*—In setting up an interview, the paralegal should tell the client what documents to bring to the interview and follow up with a confirmation letter giving the date and time of the interview and listing the items the client is to bring.

2. *Summarizing the interview*—As soon as possible after an interview is concluded, the paralegal should summarize in a written memorandum the information gathered in the interview. The memorandum should include the paralegal's general impressions of the client's statements and nonverbal behaviors.

Interviewing Witnesses

1. *Types of witnesses*—Types of witnesses include expert witnesses (who have specialized training that qualifies them to testify as to their opinion in a given area), lay witnesses (ordinary witnesses who have factual information about the matter being investigated), eyewitnesses (who have firsthand knowledge of an event—because they saw it happen, for example), friendly witnesses (who are favorable to the client's position), and hostile witnesses (who are biased against the client, friendly to the opponent, or resent being interviewed for other reasons).

2. *Questioning witnesses*—Investigative questions should be open ended so that they elicit the most complete answers possible. Additional questions should ascertain whether the witness is competent, credible, and reliable and whether the witness has any bias relevant to the case.

3. *Winding up the interview*—The paralegal should ask the witness at the end of the interview if the witness would like to add anything to her or his statement. This gives the witness an opportunity to explain an answer or expand on the areas discussed.

4. *Witness statements*—Following an interview of a witness, the paralegal should prepare a memo to the supervising attorney relating what the witness said during the interview and asking if the attorney wants a formal witness statement prepared. The formal witness statement identifies the witness, discloses what was discovered during the interview, and is signed by the witness.

Planning and Conducting Investigations

Factual evidence is crucial to the outcome of a legal problem, and paralegals are often asked to conduct investigations to discover any factual evidence that supports (or contradicts) a client's claims. Before starting an investigation, the paralegal should create an investigation plan—a step-by-step list of what sources will be investigated to obtain specific types of information (police reports, medical and employment records, and so forth). The paralegal should discuss the plan with his or her supervising attorney before embarking on the investigation.

1. *Locating witnesses*—Sources of factual information regarding witnesses or other persons include telephone and city directories; online people finders; media reports; court records; utility companies; professional organizations; and information recorded, compiled, or prepared by federal, state, and local government entities. Much of this information is available online. The Freedom of Information Act requires that federal agencies disclose certain records to any person on request, provided that the form of the request complies with the procedures mandated by the act.

2. *Rules of evidence*—Evidence is anything that is used to prove the existence or nonexistence of a fact. Rules of evidence established by the federal and state courts spell out what types of evidence may or may not be admitted in court.

   a. Direct evidence is any evidence that, if believed, establishes the truth of the fact in question.

   b. Circumstantial evidence is evidence that does not directly establish the fact in question but that establishes, by inference, the likelihood of the fact.

   c. Only relevant evidence, which tends to prove or disprove a fact in question, is admissible as evidence in court.

   d. For evidence to be admitted at trial, the attorney must prove to the court that the evidence is what it purports to be. This is called *authentication*.

   e. Hearsay is testimony given in court by a witness who relates not what he or she knows personally, but what someone else said. Generally, hearsay evidence is not admissible in court. Exceptions are made in circumstances that indicate a high degree of reliability—for example, a dying person's statement about who caused his or her death.

3. *Summarizing results*—When the investigation is complete, the paralegal should summarize the results. The summary should include an overall summary, a source-by-source summary, and a final section giving the paralegal's conclusions and recommendations.

STUDENT STUDYWARE™ CD-ROM

Interactive student CD in this book includes additional quizzing, plus video clips, case studies, and Key Terms flashcards.

ONLINE COMPANION™

For additional resources, please go to **www.paralegal.delmar.cengage.com**.

QUESTIONS FOR REVIEW

1. What are the types of questions that can be used in an interview? When would you use each type?

2. What types of interviews are described in the chapter? What is the purpose of each type of interview? What is the paralegal's role in each?

3. List and describe the various types of witnesses. In what kinds of situations might each of these types of witnesses be used?

4. List five sources that you would consult in attempting to locate a witness. Which would be the most useful? Which would be the least useful? Why?

5. Define and give examples of the following types of evidence: direct evidence, circumstantial evidence, relevant evidence, authenticated evidence, and hearsay.

ETHICAL QUESTIONS

1. Leah Fox, a legal assistant, has been asked by the attorney for whom she works to contact several potential witnesses to see what they know about an event.

The first witness that Leah calls says, "I don't know if I should get involved. I don't want to get in trouble. You see, I was supposed to be at work, but I called in sick. If I get involved and my employer finds out where I really was, I might get fired. You're a lawyer, what do you think?" How should Leah respond?

2. Kirsten Piels, a legal assistant, is conducting a follow-up interview with a new client, who is seeking a divorce. Kirsten is asking the client about the couple's marital property. According to the client, both spouses want to divide the property evenly on their divorce. When Kirsten asks the client about checking or savings accounts, the client says to Kirsten, "You know, Kirsten, I have this 'secret' savings account, but I don't want anybody to know about it. Please don't tell Mr. Harcourt [Kirsten's supervising attorney] what I've just told you." What should Kirsten do in this situation?

PRACTICE QUESTIONS AND ASSIGNMENTS

1. Review the Baranski-Peretto hypothetical case discussed in Chapter 10. Then write sample questions that you would ask when interviewing eyewitnesses to the accident. Phrase at least one question in each of the question formats discussed in this chapter.

2. Using the information in this chapter on questioning skills, identify the following types of questions:

   a. "Did you go on a cruise in the Bahamas with another woman, Mr. Johnson?"

   b. "Isn't it true, Mr. Johnson, that someone other than your wife accompanied you on a cruise in the Bahamas?"

   c. "Mr. Johnson, will you please describe your whereabouts between January 10 and January 17, 2011?"

3. Using the format in Exhibit 11.4 on page 367, *Information Contained in a Witness Statement,* and Exhibit 11.5 on page 368, *A Sample Witness Statement (Excerpt),* draft a witness statement based on the following facts:

   a. You work for the law firm of Thomas & Snyder. On April 1, 2011, you are interviewing a witness to a car-train accident that happened a few hours ago. The interview takes place at the police station. The witness's name is Henry Black. Henry is retired and lives at 2002 Stephens Road, Clinton Township, Pennsylvania. His telephone number is (123) 456-7890.

   b. Henry was in his Cadillac, stopped in front of the railroad tracks on Jefferson Avenue in Clinton Township, Pennsylvania, at approximately 10:00 A.M., when a red 2010 Ford Flex sped past him and across the tracks. He was very surprised that the Ford did not stop at the tracks because the train was only about thirty feet away and was blowing its whistle. There were no gates or guard rails in front of the tracks. Henry looked over at the driver of the Ford and saw that she was talking on a cellular phone as she was driving. She did not appear to hear the train. As her vehicle crossed the tracks, the train struck it on the passenger side. Fortunately, there appeared to be no one else in the vehicle.

4. Determine whether each of the following statements is a statement of fact or a statement of opinion, and explain why:

   a. "I am sure that the suspect took the money because when I saw him near the cash register, he looked around suspiciously and then tried to sneak away without being seen."

   b. "The man who took the money from the cash register was wearing a green trench coat, brown pants, and black boots and was carrying a large tan briefcase."

5. Working in groups of three, role-play the initial client interview described in Chapter 10 between Katherine Baranski and the legal team—attorney Allen Gilmore and paralegal Elena Lopez. Attorney Gilmore will need to prepare a list of questions and will ask most of the questions during the interview. Paralegal Lopez will take notes during the interview, provide the retainer agreement and release forms, and schedule the follow-up interview. Change roles if time allows.

QUESTIONS FOR CRITICAL ANALYSIS

1. Why do you think you need to obtain the client's or witness's permission to record an interview? What might happen if you did not obtain permission?

2. Leading questions tend to lead to distorted answers and are typically used only on cross-examination. Why would an attorney want to use this type of question? Is the use of leading questions ethical?

3. Several types of witnesses were described in this chapter (expert witnesses, lay witnesses, eyewitnesses, friendly witnesses, hostile witnesses). Do any of these

categories overlap—that is, could one witness fall into more than one of the categories? Explain.

4. Clients are often required to sign releases authorizing an entity (such as a hospital) to turn over information to a particular party (such as an attorney). Why is this? What might happen if releases were not required?

PROJECT

1. Watch an interview on television. Write a two-page, double-spaced paper describing the interview. Include in your description the following information:

    a. The names of the interviewer and the interviewee.

    b. The subject of the interview.

    c. The date and time of the interview and the television channel over which it was broadcast.

    d. The different types of questions (open ended, closed ended, and so forth) used by the interviewer and the types of responses elicited by the different kinds of questions.

    e. The ways in which the interviewer and interviewee communicated nonverbally.

    f. Your overall evaluation of the interviewer's skill at interviewing this particular interviewee.

USING INTERNET RESOURCES

1. KnowX.com is a public records Web site. Much of the information that can be located at this site is information that a private investigator (or a paralegal) might want to find when investigating a case. Access the site at **www.knowx.com** and select "Site Map" from the menu at the top of the screen. Based on the information contained on the site map, what can you find using KnowX.com?

    a. Click on "Ultimate People Finder" and select "Database Info." What databases does KnowX.com search to find people? Is there any cost involved? If so, how much?

    b. Return to the site map and select "The Ultimate Business Finder." What databases does KnowX.com search for business information?

    c. Return to the site map and choose "Advanced Background Check." What types of background checks does KnowX.com perform? What databases does it search? Is there any cost involved? If so, how much?

TRIAL PROCEDURES

CHAPTER

12

CHAPTER OUTLINE

Introduction

Preparing for Trial

Pretrial Conference

Jury Selection

The Trial

Posttrial Motions and Procedures

Enforcing the Judgment

AFTER COMPLETING THIS CHAPTER, YOU WILL KNOW:

▶ How attorneys prepare for trial and how paralegals assist in this task.

▶ How jurors are selected and the role of attorneys and their legal assistants in the selection process.

▶ The various phases of a trial and the kinds of trial-related tasks that paralegals often perform.

▶ The options available to the losing party after the verdict is in.

▶ How a case is appealed to a higher court for review.

INTRODUCTION

Trials are costly in both time and money. For this reason, parties to lawsuits often try to avoid going to trial. Pretrial negotiations between the parties and their attorneys often lead to an out-of-court settlement. Using the pretrial motions discussed in Chapter 10, the parties may try to end the litigation after the pleadings are filed or while discovery takes place. In many cases, parties opt for alternative dispute resolution, such as mediation or arbitration. Recall from Chapter 6 that alternative dispute resolution is not always optional—some state and federal courts *mandate* that a dispute be mediated or arbitrated before the parties are permitted to bring the dispute before a court. If the parties fail to settle their dispute through any of these means, the case will go to trial.

To illustrate how attorneys and paralegals prepare for trial, we will continue using the hypothetical scenario developed in Chapter 10, in which Katherine Baranski (the plaintiff) is suing Tony Peretto (the defendant) for negligence. In the Baranski-Peretto case, Allen P. Gilmore is the attorney for plaintiff Baranski, and Gilmore's legal assistant is Elena Lopez. Defendant Peretto's attorney is Elizabeth A. Cameron, and Cameron's legal assistant is Gordon McVay. In preparing for trial, paralegals use a wide range of skills—including visual presentation skills, as discussed in *Developing Paralegal Skills* on the following page.

Case at a Glance

The Plaintiff—
Plaintiff: Katherine Baranski
Attorney: Allen P. Gilmore
Paralegal: Elena Lopez

The Defendant—
Defendant: Tony Peretto
Attorney: Elizabeth A. Cameron
Paralegal: Gordon McVay

PREPARING FOR TRIAL

As the trial date approaches, the attorneys for the plaintiff and the defendant and their paralegals complete trial preparations. The paralegals collect and organize the documents and other evidence relating to the dispute. They may find it useful to create a trial-preparation checklist similar to the one in Exhibit 12.1 on page 389. Even though settlement negotiations may continue throughout the trial, both sides assume, for planning purposes, that the trial court will decide the issue.

At this point in the litigation process, plaintiff Baranski's attorney, Gilmore, will focus on legal strategy and how he can best use the information learned during the pleadings and discovery stages when presenting Baranski's case to the court. He will meet with his client and with his key witnesses to make last-minute preparations for trial. He might also meet with defendant Peretto's attorney to try once more to settle the dispute. Gilmore's legal assistant, Elena Lopez, will notify witnesses of the trial date and help Gilmore prepare for trial. For example, she will make sure that all exhibits to be used during the trial are ready and verify that the trial notebook (to be discussed shortly) is in order.

Contacting and Preparing Witnesses

Typically, the paralegal is responsible for ensuring that witnesses are available and in court on the day of the trial. As mentioned in previous chapters, a witness is any person asked to testify at trial. The person may be an eyewitness, an official witness (such as a police officer), an expert witness, or anyone with knowledge relevant to the lawsuit.

Several types of negligence lawsuits require expert witnesses. As discussed in Chapters 10 and 11, an expert witness is one who has specialized knowledge in a particular field. Such witnesses are often called to testify in negligence cases, because one element to be proved in a negligence case is the reasonableness of the defendant's actions. In medical-malpractice cases, for example, it takes someone with specialized knowledge in the defendant physician's area of practice to establish the reasonableness of the defendant's actions.

Contacting Witnesses and Issuing Subpoenas

In the Baranski case, attorney Gilmore and paralegal Lopez will have lined up witnesses to testify on behalf of their client. Lopez will inform the witnesses that the trial date has been set and that they will be expected to appear at the trial to

Developing
Paralegal Skills

POWERPOINT PRESENTATIONS

Joanna Newcomb, a paralegal manager, works for a large law firm. The paralegals under her supervision often assist attorneys in trial preparations, and Joanna has decided to host a series of workshops for the paralegals on trial presentation techniques. She has decided that the focus of the first workshop will be on the basics of PowerPoint presentations. She prepares a list of suggestions to hand out to the paralegals during the workshop.

TIPS FOR POWERPOINT PRESENTATIONS

- Plan your PowerPoint presentation carefully. Keep in mind that the display should clarify your presentation, not muddle it.

- Many presenters write out their presentations beforehand in a word-processing program and transfer the contents to the slides.

- Use the "four-by-four rule"—limit the text on each slide to four lines of no more than four words of text. This will keep your message simple and focused.

- The audience cannot hear your main points if you turn and talk to the screen, so be sure to talk toward the audience. Print out the slides for your reference while speaking.

- The background color should be geared to your audience. Some studies have shown that dark blue is a favorite color, so consider using that color for a background.

- The color of the text should be easy to read from afar.

- Simple fonts, such as Arial or Tahoma, are best.

- Images and graphics can enhance your presentation, but do not "paste" images into your PowerPoint file. Instead, from the "Insert" menu, select "Picture" and then "From File" to insert a graphic.

- Always rehearse your PowerPoint presentation ahead of time, *on the equipment that you will be using.* Nothing will make you look less professional than a sloppy PowerPoint presentation. Audiences understand equipment breakdowns but are not as kind when it comes to poor preparation.

- Bring copies of the slides or other handouts to distribute in case for some reason you cannot use the PowerPoint presentation that you prepared.

testify. A *subpoena* (an order issued by the court clerk directing a person to appear in court—see Chapter 10) will be served on each of the witnesses to ensure the witness's presence in court. A subpoena to appear in a federal court is shown in Exhibit 12.2 on page 390. Although not shown in the exhibit, a return-of-service form, similar to the one illustrated in Chapter 10 on page 317, will be attached to the subpoena to verify that the witness received it.

Unless she is already familiar with the court's requirements, paralegal Lopez will check with the court clerk to find out what fees and documents she needs to take to the court to obtain the subpoena. The subpoena will then be served on the witness. Most subpoenas to appear in federal court can be served by anyone who is eighteen years of age or older, including paralegals, who often serve subpoenas. Subpoenas to appear in state court are often served by the sheriff or other process server.

When contacting *friendly* witnesses (those favorable to Baranski's position), Lopez should take care to explain that all witnesses are served with subpoenas, as a

EXHIBIT 12.1
Trial-Preparation Checklist

TWO MONTHS BEFORE THE TRIAL

____ Review the status of the case and inform the attorney of any depositions, interrogatories, or other discovery procedures that need to be completed before trial.
____ Interview witnesses and prepare witness statements.
____ Review deposition transcripts/summaries, answers to interrogatories, witness statements, and other information obtained about the case. Inform the attorney of any further discovery that should be undertaken prior to trial.
____ Begin preparing the trial notebook.

ONE MONTH BEFORE THE TRIAL

____ Make a list of the witnesses who will testify at the trial for the trial notebook.
____ Prepare a subpoena for each witness, and arrange to have the subpoenas served.
____ Prepare any exhibits that will be used at trial and reserve any special equipment (such as for a PowerPoint presentation) that will be needed at the trial.
____ Draft *voir dire* (jury selection) questions and perhaps prepare a jury profile.
____ Prepare motions and memoranda.
____ Continue assembling the trial notebook.

ONE WEEK BEFORE THE TRIAL

____ Check the calendar and call the court clerk to confirm the trial date.
____ Complete the trial notebook. Keep electronic copies of everything.
____ Make sure that all subpoenas have been served.
____ Prepare the client and witnesses for trial.
____ Make the final arrangements (housing, transportation, and the like) for the client or witnesses, as necessary.
____ Check with the attorney to verify how witnesses should be paid (for lost wages, travel expenses, and the like).
____ Make final arrangements to have all equipment, documents, and other items in the courtroom on the trial date.

ONE DAY BEFORE THE TRIAL

____ Meet with others on the trial team to coordinate last-minute efforts.
____ Have a final pretrial meeting with the client.

precaution, and to tell each witness when he or she can expect to receive the subpoena. Otherwise, a friendly witness might assume that Gilmore and Lopez did not trust the witness to keep a promise to appear in court.

Preparing Witnesses for Trial

No prudent attorney ever puts a witness on the stand unless the attorney has discussed the testimony beforehand with that person. Good advance preparation can make a tremendous difference to the testimony that a witness provides. The amount of time spent preparing a witness will vary depending on the size of the case, the importance of the witness's testimony, and whether the attorney believes the witness will be able to communicate clearly and effectively in court. Additional time will be needed to prepare witnesses who are relatively inexperienced, are not very articulate, or are especially nervous about testifying.

Tell Witnesses What to Expect. Prior to trial, attorney Gilmore and paralegal Lopez will meet with each witness to prepare her or him for trial. Gilmore will discuss the types of questions that he intends to ask the witness in court and the questions that he expects the opposing attorney to ask. He will also tell the witness that during cross-examination opposing counsel will ask leading questions and may try to confuse the witness or attack his or her statements. Gilmore may recommend, for example, that the witness answer the opponent's questions in as few words

EXHIBIT 12.2
A Subpoena

AO 88 (Rev. 2/06) Subpoena in a Civil Case

Issued by the
UNITED STATES DISTRICT COURT

──────── WESTERN DISTRICT OF NITA ────────

Katherine Baranski

V.

Tony Peretto

SUBPOENA IN A CIVIL CASE

CASE NUMBER   11-14335-NI

TO: Julia Williams
3765 Mattis Avenue
Nita City, NI 48803

[X] YOU ARE COMMANDED to appear in the United States District Court at the place, date, and time specified below to testify in the above case.

PLACE OF TESTIMONY	COURT ROOM
4th and Main Nita City, NI	B
	DATE AND TIME 8/4/11 10:00 A.M.

[ ] YOU ARE COMMANDED to appear at the place, date, and time specified below to testify at the taking of a deposition in the above case.

PLACE OF DEPOSITION	DATE AND TIME

[ ] YOU ARE COMMANDED to produce and permit inspection and copying of the following documents or objects at the place, date, and time specified below (list documents or objects):

PLACE	DATE AND TIME

[ ] YOU ARE COMMANDED to permit inspection of the following premises at the date and time specified below.

PREMISES	DATE AND TIME

Any organization not a party to this suit that is subpoenaed for the taking of a deposition shall designate one or more officers, directors, or managing agents, or other persons who consent to testify on its behalf, and may set forth, for each person designated, the matters on which the person will testify. Federal Rules of Civil Procedure, 30(b)(6).

ISSUING OFFICER SIGNATURE AND TITLE (INDICATE IF ATTORNEY FOR PLAINTIFF OR DEFENDANT)	DATE
Allen P. Gilmore, Attorney for the Plaintiff	July 13, 2011

ISSUING OFFICER'S NAME, ADDRESS AND PHONE NUMBER
Allen P. Gilmore, Jeffers, Gilmore & Dunn,
553 Fifth Avenue, Suite 101, Nita City, NI 48801   (616) 555-9690

(See Rule 45, Federal Rules of Civil Procedure, Parts C & D on Reverse)
If action is pending in district other than district of issuance, state district under case number.

as possible while not appearing to be overly defensive. The attorney may not, of course, tell the witness what to say in response to questions.

Gilmore will also review with the witness any statements the witness has made about the case, particularly if the statements were given under oath (such as during a deposition). It is important that a witness understand that during the trial, he or she may be asked about any inconsistencies in statements previously given. Additionally, Gilmore may want to review the substantive legal issues involved in the case and emphasize how the witness's testimony will affect the outcome of those issues.

Role-Playing. If the witness needs additional preparation, Gilmore or Lopez may engage in some role-playing with the witness. This type of rehearsal is often valuable in helping the witness to understand more fully how the questioning will proceed and what tactics may be involved in the opposing attorney's questions. It also may alleviate some of the witness's fears. In addition, Lopez might take the witness to the courtroom in which the trial will take place to familiarize the witness with the trial setting. Testifying can be a very stressful experience. Anything that the paralegal can do to reduce a witness's discomfort will help the witness to better control his or her responses when testifying and thus will ultimately benefit the client.

Other Details. Paralegals are often responsible for handling all the details involved in preparing witnesses for court. For example, Lopez might recommend appropriate clothing and grooming or tell the witness where to look and how to remain calm and composed when speaking to the court. If the witness will be asked about any exhibits or evidence (such as photographs or documents), Lopez will show these items to the witness. Lopez will continually update the witness as to when he or she will probably be called to testify.

Exhibits and Displays

Paralegals frequently prepare exhibits or displays that will be presented at trial. Attorney Gilmore may wish to show the court a photograph of plaintiff Baranski's car taken after the accident occurred, a diagram of the intersection, an enlarged document (such as a police report), or other relevant evidence. Paralegal Lopez will be responsible for making sure that all exhibits are properly prepared and ready to introduce at trial. If any exhibits require special equipment, such as an easel, projector, or laptop computer, Lopez must also make sure that these will be available in the courtroom and properly set up when they are needed. Increasingly, attorneys are using high-tech equipment to prepare their trial presentations. For a discussion of how high-tech presentations are altering the paralegal's trial-preparation tasks, see the *Technology and Today's Paralegal* feature on the next two pages.

The Trial Notebook

To present Baranski's case effectively, Gilmore will need to have all of the relevant documents in the courtroom; he will also need to be able to locate them quickly. To accomplish these goals, Lopez will prepare a trial notebook. Traditionally, the **trial notebook** has been a three-ring binder (or several binders, depending on the complexity of the case) containing trial-related materials separated by tabbed divider sheets. Most lawyers today rely primarily on documents kept in computers, but paper copies are also still common. The discussion here applies to both.

Lopez meets with Gilmore to discuss what he wants to include in the trial notebook for Baranski's case and how the notebook should be organized. Gilmore tells Lopez that the organization of the notebook should make it possible to find quickly whatever documents they may need during the trial. Lopez should include the following materials in the notebook:

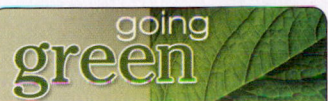

WHAT ARE YOU WEARING?

You can create a greener professional wardrobe by buying fabrics that are organic or contain recycled fibers. When an item of clothing goes out of style, recycle it through an organization that collects clothing to distribute to those in need.

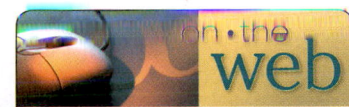

For complex cases that involve a massive number of documents, a law firm may want assistance in managing and reviewing the documents. Firms that provide this service include Providus, at **www.providusgroup.com**.

trial notebook
Traditionally, a binder that contains copies of all the documents and information that an attorney will need to have at hand during the trial.

Technology and Today's Paralegal

COURTROOM TECHNOLOGY

In the past, attorneys and paralegals involved in complex litigation had to carry boxes of papers into the courtroom and then, during trial, search through them for key documents and exhibits. Visual presentations were usually limited to enlarged photographs or text displayed on an easel. Today, advances in technology give paralegals and attorneys numerous other options.

DIGITAL RECORDS AND VIDEO

A major challenge for the paralegal in complex litigation is keeping the mountains of evidence organized, cross-referenced, and easily accessible during the trial. Suppose, for example, that a witness is making statements on the stand and the paralegal wishes to compare them with statements on the same topic made by that witness in a deposition prior to trial. Finding these earlier statements quickly can be difficult. If the documents have been scanned into a computer, however, the paralegal using litigation support software can search *all* the documents in the case in a matter of seconds. This means that counsel will not need to bring deposition transcripts, records, and reports to court. Instead, one laptop computer can access thousands of documents quickly.

Other technologies being utilized in courts today involve digital video recording and court reporting. For example, when depositions in the case are digitally recorded and loaded on a computer, that video file can be combined on a split screen with the transcript of the written words. This can be an effective way for the lawyer to demonstrate inconsistencies in a witness's statements. Rather than simply reading the deposition transcript in court (as traditionally has been done), the jurors are able to watch the deposition and see the person's face and body language.

In addition, "real-time" court reporting is available. When real-time court reporting is used, the transcript appears on the computer screen as the person is speaking. Real-time videoconferencing can

- Copies of the pleadings.
- Interrogatories.
- Deposition transcripts and summaries.
- Pretrial motions.
- A list of exhibits and a case outline indicating when they will be used.
- A witness list, the order in which the witnesses will testify, and the questions that will be asked of each witness.
- Relevant cases or statutes that Gilmore plans to cite.
- Any additional documents or information that will be important to have close at hand during the trial.

Lopez will create a general index to the notebook's contents and place this index at the front of the notebook. She may also create an index for each section of the binder and place those indexes at the beginnings of the sections. Paralegals sometimes use a notebook computer and a software retrieval system to help them quickly locate documents, especially in complicated cases involving thousands of documents. Careful, consistent organization of computer files is very important. For further discussion of litigation support software, see this chapter's *Featured Contributor* article on pages 398 and 399.

Case at a Glance

The Plaintiff—
Plaintiff: Katherine Baranski
Attorney: Allen P. Gilmore
Paralegal: Elena Lopez

The Defendant—
Defendant: Tony Peretto
Attorney: Elizabeth A. Cameron
Paralegal: Gordon McVay

also be used to bring into the courtroom the "live" testimony of experts and other witnesses who cannot be physically present. A judge's permission may be required to use these technologies in the courtroom.

TRIAL PRESENTATION SOFTWARE

Using trial presentation software can help the legal team to create a more effective, persuasive, and visually stimulating presentation of its case. Most people absorb and retain information better when it is presented visually as well as verbally. Visual information is also more engaging for jurors than long recitations of detailed facts by witnesses (and attorneys). By providing visual displays, then, the legal team's presentation can have a greater impact on juries.

For example, the legal team can create a mixed-media presentation (including video and sound) and store it on CD-ROM, DVD, or flash drive for use at trial. The order and elements of the presentation can be manipulated in a variety of ways to maximize its effectiveness. A person preparing digital images to be included in a presentation, for instance, could highlight certain portions of an image and dim others to help the jury focus on the desired part. He or she could also zoom in on part of an image, insert a box containing an enlargement of part of the image, or add arrows, labels, titles, or symbols to an image.

Presentation software also makes it easy to create diagrams of an accident scene, graphic illustrations of scientific evidence, medical models and diagrams to help explain medical procedures and injuries, and schematics of mechanical or physical evidence. Rather than simply telling the jury how a particular product or machine caused a client's injuries, for example, an attorney can show how the injury occurred. The legal team can also create flow charts to indicate the relationships between events and bulleted lists to highlight the strengths of its case or the weaknesses of the opponent's case. These exhibits can be modified easily if necessary during the trial.

TECHNOLOGY TIP

Computers and courtroom technologies can make a litigation paralegal's job easier, especially in cases that involve extensive documentation. Make sure to obtain the court's permission, if required, to use a specific technology in the courtroom. Make sure, too, that all presentations and diagrams are accurate and comply with the rules of evidence. Keep a back-up copy of all documents, cross-referenced the old-fashioned way, in the event the computer crashes. Finally, if you are working with an outside vendor to provide support or presentation services, be careful not to breach confidentiality rules.

When preparing a traditional trial notebook, remember that the notebook should contain not the original documents but copies of them. The original documents (unless they are needed as evidence at trial) should remain in the firm's files, for reasons of security (should the trial notebook be misplaced) and to ensure that paralegals or others in the office will have access to the documents while the notebook is in court.

Lopez will not wait until the last minute to prepare the trial notebook. Rather, at the outset of the lawsuit, she will make copies of the pleadings and other documents as they are generated to include in the notebook. That way, she will not have to spend time just before the trial, when there are other pressing needs, to do work that could have been done earlier.

PRETRIAL CONFERENCE

Before the trial begins, the attorneys usually meet with the trial judge in a **pretrial conference** to explore the possibility of resolving the case and, if a settlement is not possible, to at least agree on the manner in which the trial will be conducted. In particular, the parties may attempt to clarify the issues in dispute and establish ground rules to restrict such matters as the admissibility of certain types of evidence.

pretrial conference
A conference prior to trial in which the judge and the attorneys litigating the suit discuss settlement possibilities, clarify the issues in dispute, and schedule forthcoming trial-related events.

motion *in limine*
A motion requesting that certain evidence not be brought out at the trial, such as prejudicial, irrelevant, or legally inadmissible evidence.

For example, Gilmore might have Lopez draft a **motion *in limine***[1] (a motion to limit evidence) to submit to the judge at this time. The motion will request the judge to order that certain evidence not be brought out at trial.

To illustrate: Suppose that Baranski had been arrested in the past for illegal drug possession. Gilmore knows that evidence of the arrest, if introduced by the defense at trial, might prejudice the jury against Baranski. In this situation, Gilmore might submit a motion *in limine* to keep the defense from presenting the evidence. Exhibit 12.3 presents a sample motion *in limine*. Note that with the motion Gilmore would include affidavits and/or a memorandum of law (a brief)—these documents were discussed in Chapter 10—to convince the judge that the motion should be granted.

Once the pretrial conference has concluded, both parties turn their attention to the trial itself. Assuming that the trial will be heard by a jury, however, one more step is necessary before the trial begins: selecting the jurors who will hear the trial and render a verdict on the dispute.

JURY SELECTION

Before the trial gets under way, a panel of jurors must be assembled. The clerk of the court usually notifies local residents by mail that they have been selected for jury duty. The process of selecting prospective jurors varies, depending on the court, but often they are randomly selected by the court clerk from lists of registered voters or those to whom driver's licenses have been issued. The persons selected then report

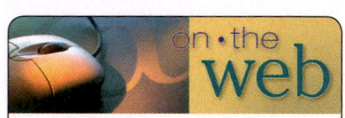

Numerous firms offer trial consulting services, including assistance in jury selection. You can access the Web site of one such firm, Jury Research Institute, at **www.jri-inc.com**.

EXHIBIT 12.3
Motion *in Limine*

A. P. Gilmore
Jeffers, Gilmore & Dunn
553 Fifth Avenue
Suite 101
Nita City, NI 48801
(616) 555-9690

Attorney for Plaintiff

UNITED STATES DISTRICT COURT
FOR THE WESTERN DISTRICT OF NITA

Katherine Baranski	)	
Plaintiff,	)	
	)	CASE NO. 11-14335-NI
v.	)	Honorable Harley M. Larue
	)	
	)	MOTION IN LIMINE
Tony Peretto	)	
Defendant.	)	

The Plaintiff respectfully moves the Court to prohibit counsel for the Defendant from directly or indirectly introducing or making any reference during the trial to the Plaintiff's arrest in 2001 for the possession of illegal drugs.

The grounds on which this motion is based are stated in the accompanying affidavits and memorandum.

Date: 6/18/11

Allen P. Gilmore
Allen P. Gilmore
Attorney for the Plaintiff

to the courthouse on the date specified in the notice. At the courthouse, they are gathered into a single pool of jurors, and the process of selecting those jurors who will actually hear the case begins. Although some types of trials require twelve-person juries, civil matters can be heard by a jury of as few as six persons in many states.

Voir Dire

Both the plaintiff's attorney and the defendant's attorney have some input into the ultimate make-up of the jury. Each attorney will question prospective jurors in a proceeding known as *voir dire.*[2] Experienced litigators know how important the *voir dire* process is—not only to picking the right jury but also as a time for attorneys to introduce themselves and their clients and make a favorable impression on the jury before the trial begins.

Legal assistants may work with their attorneys to write up the questions that will be asked of jurors during *voir dire.* Because all of the jurors will have previously filled out forms giving basic information about themselves, the questions can be tailored accordingly. The idea is to uncover any biases on the part of prospective jurors and to find persons who might identify with the plights of their respective clients.

Typically, the legal team for each side has already developed an idea of what kind of person would be most sympathetic toward or most likely to vote in favor of its client. Indeed, sometimes experts are hired to help create a juror profile (see the *Today's Professional Paralegal* feature later in this chapter on page 410). The paralegals and attorneys then formulate questions based on this notion of the ideal juror in the case.

Jury selection may last an hour or many days, depending on the complexity of the case and the rules and preferences of the particular court or judge. In some courts, the judge questions prospective jurors using questions prepared and submitted by the attorneys. In other courts, the judge has each juror answer a list of standard questions and then gives each attorney a small amount of time to ask follow-up questions. When large numbers of prospective jurors are involved, the attorneys (or the judge) may direct their questions to groups of jurors as opposed to individual jurors in order to reduce the time spent choosing a jury.

Challenges during *Voir Dire*

During *voir dire,* the attorney for each side will decide if there are any individuals he or she would like to prevent from serving as jurors in the case. The attorney may then exercise a **challenge** to exclude a particular person from the jury. There are two types of challenges available to both sides in a lawsuit: challenges for cause and peremptory challenges.

Challenges for Cause

The attorney can exercise a **challenge for cause** if the prospective juror is biased against the client or case for some reason. For example, if a juror states during *voir dire* that he or she hates immigrants and the client is foreign born, the attorney can exercise a challenge for cause. Each side's attorney can exercise an *unlimited* number of challenges for cause. Because most people are not forthcoming about their biases, the attorney must be able to prove sufficiently to the court that the person cannot be an objective juror in the case. Often, the judge will ask the challenged juror follow-up questions and then determine that the juror can be objective after all.

Peremptory Challenges

Both attorneys may exercise a *limited* number of **peremptory challenges** without giving any reason to the court as to why they object to a particular juror. In most cases, peremptory challenges are the only challenges exercised (because there is no proof that any

---

voir dire

A proceeding in which attorneys for the plaintiff and the defendant ask prospective jurors questions to determine whether any potential juror is biased or has any connection with a party to the action or with a prospective witness.

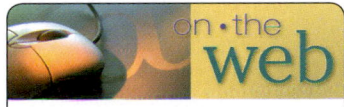

You can read the *Handbook for Trial Jurors Serving in the United States District Courts* at **www.uscourts.gov/ jury/trialhandbook.pdf**.

challenge

An attorney's objection, during *voir dire*, to the inclusion of a particular person on the jury.

challenge for cause

A *voir dire* challenge to exclude a potential juror from serving on the jury for a reason specified by an attorney in the case.

peremptory challenge

A *voir dire* challenge to exclude a potential juror from serving on the jury without any supporting reason or cause. Peremptory challenges based on racial or gender criteria are illegal.

juror is biased). A juror may thus be excused from serving on the jury for any reason, including his or her facial expressions or nonverbal behavior during the questioning. Peremptory challenges based on racial criteria or gender, however, are illegal.

Because the number of peremptory challenges is limited (a court may allow only three, for example), attorneys must exercise peremptory challenges carefully. Experienced litigators try to conserve their peremptory challenges so that they can eliminate the prospective jurors who appear the most hostile.

Procedure for Challenges

Typically, *voir dire* takes place in the courtroom, and the attorneys question the six to twelve prospective jurors who are seated in the jury box. Other prospective jurors may be seated in the audience area of the courtroom, so that as one person is excused, another person can walk up to take his or her place in the jury box. The procedure varies depending on the jurisdiction. Often, rather than making challenges orally in front of the jury, the attorneys write down on a piece of paper which juror they wish to challenge, and the paper is given to the judge. The judge thanks and dismisses the prospective juror, and the process starts over again with the next individual. When this method is used, the remaining prospective jurors do not know which side dismissed the individual and so are less likely to make guesses about the underlying reasons.

The Paralegal's Role during *Voir Dire*

As mentioned, paralegals help develop a jury profile and draft questions that will be asked during *voir dire*. In addition, a paralegal can assist an attorney by providing another pair of eyes and ears during the jury selection process. Attorneys frequently rely on the observations of other members of the legal team who are present during the questioning.

If paralegal Lopez attends *voir dire* with attorney Gilmore in the Baranski case, for example, she will watch all of the jurors as the attorneys question them. Lopez, because she is not participating in the questioning, is free to observe the prospective jurors more closely than Gilmore. She will report to Gilmore any verbal or nonverbal response she observed that Gilmore might not have noticed. For example, suppose that as Gilmore is questioning one juror, another juror is staring at plaintiff Baranski and frowning with disapproval. Gilmore might not notice this behavior, and Lopez can bring it to his attention.

Alternate Jurors

Because unforeseeable circumstances or illness may necessitate that one or more of the sitting jurors be dismissed, the court seats several *alternate jurors*. Depending on the rules of the particular jurisdiction, a court might have two or three alternate jurors present throughout the trial. If a juror has to be excused in the middle of the trial, then an alternate can take his or her place without disrupting the proceedings. Unless they replace jurors, alternate jurors do not participate in jury deliberations at the end of the trial.

THE TRIAL

Once the jury members are seated, the judge swears in the jury, and the trial begins. During the trial, the attorneys, Allen Gilmore and Elizabeth Cameron, will present their cases to the jury. Because the attorneys will be concentrating on the trial, it will fall to their paralegals to coordinate the logistical aspects of the trial and observe the trial proceedings. Because paralegal Lopez is thoroughly familiar with the case and Gilmore's legal strategy, she will be a valuable ally during the trial. She

Ethics Watch

COMMUNICATING WITH JURORS

Suppose that you are the paralegal working on the Baranski case with attorney Allen Gilmore, and one of your neighbors is a juror in the case. One evening, while you are gardening in your backyard, your neighbor approaches you and says, "You know, I didn't really understand what that witness, Williams, was saying. Did she really see the accident? Also, is it true that Mrs. Baranski will never be able to walk normally again?" You know the answers to these questions, and you would like the juror to know the truth. You also know that it would enhance Baranski's chances of winning the case if this juror were as familiar with the factual background as you are. What should you do? First, remind your neighbor that jurors are not permitted to discuss a case they are hearing with anyone. Second, inform your neighbor that as a paralegal, you have an ethical duty to abide by the professional rules of conduct governing the legal profession. One of these rules prohibits *ex parte* (private) communications with jurors about a case being tried.

These actions are consistent with NFPA's Model Code of Ethics and Professional Responsibility, Section EC-1.2(a), "A paralegal shall not engage in any *ex parte* communications involving the courts or any other adjudicatory body in an attempt to exert undue influence or to obtain advantage or the benefit of only one party," and Section EC-1.5(f), "A paralegal shall not engage in any indiscreet communications concerning clients." They are also consistent with the NALA Code of Ethics, Canon 9, "A paralegal must do all other things incidental, necessary, or expedient for the attainment of the ethics and responsibilities as defined by statute or rule of court."

will anticipate Gilmore's needs and provide appropriate reminders or documents as Gilmore needs them.

Prior to each trial day, for example, Lopez will assemble the documents and materials that will be needed in court. During the court proceedings, Lopez will make sure that attorney Gilmore has within reach any documents or exhibits that he needs for questioning parties or witnesses. At the end of the day, Lopez will organize the documents and materials, decide what will be needed for the next day, and file the documents that can remain in the office.

Lopez will also monitor each witness's testimony to ensure that it is consistent with previous statements made by the witness. Lopez will have the relevant deposition transcript (and summary) at hand when a witness takes the stand. She will follow the deposition transcript (or summary) of each witness as that witness testifies. This way, she can pass a note to Gilmore if he misses any inconsistencies in the testimony.

Lopez will also observe how the jury is responding to various witnesses and their testimony or to the attorneys' demeanor and questions. She will take notes during the trial on these observations as well as on the points being stressed and the types of evidence introduced by the opposing counsel. At the end of the day, Lopez and Gilmore may review the day's events, and Lopez's "trial journal" will provide a ready reference to what happened in the courtroom.

Opening Statements

The trial both opens and closes with attorneys' statements to the jury. In their **opening statements**, the attorneys give a brief version of the facts and the supporting evidence that they will use during the trial. Because some trials can take weeks or even months,

opening statement
An attorney's statement to the jury at the beginning of the trial. The attorney briefly outlines the evidence that will be offered during the trial and the legal theory that will be pursued.

featured contributor

LITIGATION PARALEGAL

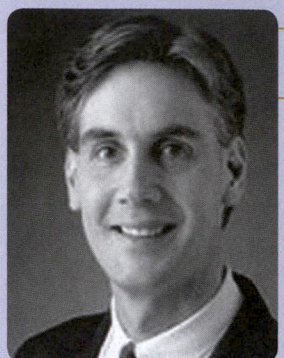

Dwayne E. Krager

BIOGRAPHICAL NOTE

Dwayne E. Krager received his bachelor of arts degree from Southern Illinois University in Carbondale, Illinois, and his paralegal certification from Roosevelt University in Chicago. In 1995, Krager received Legal Assistant Today's "Paralegal of the Year Award," and he has served as president of the Wisconsin Paralegal Association. For about two years, he wrote a column entitled "Creative Computing" for Legal Assistant Today, offering tips on how to work with technology.

By 1989, several companies were in the early stages of creating two of the most widely used litigation support programs in today's legal marketplace. One of these programs is Summation. While working in the thirty-attorney litigation department of Reinhart Boerner Van Deuren, SC, a large law firm in Milwaukee, Wisconsin, Krager was able to implement the use of Summation as the main software program used at the firm.

Reinhart, a technologically progressive law firm, allowed Krager to implement a firmwide docket system and an in-house imaging center. He also designed, built, promoted, and then ran one of the first mock courtrooms, known as the Trial Science Institute, LLC (TSI), which was one of his greatest achievements. Today, Krager teaches other paralegals how to use technological tools to help make their firms more successful. Krager is featured in the book, Lessons from the Top Paralegal Experts, *by Carole Bruno.*

What do you like best about your work?

"I enjoy my entire myriad of responsibilities. The autonomy that I have received because of my work in creating the Trial Science Institute has brought me recognition among my peers and in the legal world. In addition, the possibilities for a challenging future are constantly expanding. I am excited about continuing to operate and coordinate all activities associated with TSI as one important aspect of my job. However, I still enjoy another equally significant part of my job—mentoring and training the paralegals and attorneys in our firm on the use of litigation, imaging, and trial support programs. Because there are constant changes in the field of technology, the litigation process, and the use of litigation support, I think I will always enjoy my work."

What is the greatest challenge that you face in your area of work?

"The creation of the Trial Science Institute was one of my most exciting ventures. Utilizing the same skills as a litigation

it is helpful for jurors to hear a summary of the story that will unfold during the trial. Otherwise, they may be left wondering how a particular piece of evidence fits into the dispute.

The opening statement is a kind of "road map" that describes the destination that each attorney hopes to reach and outlines how he or she plans to reach it. Plaintiff Baranski's attorney, Gilmore, will focus on such things as his client's lack of fault and the injuries that she sustained when she was hit by defendant Peretto's car. Peretto's attorney, Cameron, will highlight the points that weaken Baranski's claim (for example, Cameron might point out that Baranski was speeding) or otherwise suggest that Peretto did not commit any wrongful act. Note that the defendant's attorney has the right to reserve her or his opening statement until after the plaintiff's case has been presented.

paralegal, I conducted extensive research to determine what the courtroom of the future would look like. In addition to conferring with architects and coordinating the bidding process for the construction of the facilities, I performed my normal paralegal duties. This required me to schedule my time and to focus specifically on the tasks that I had to complete. While this process was time consuming, one of the greatest challenges of the project was to gain approval from one of the founders of the firm, Richard Van Deuren. Before meeting with Mr. Van Deuren, I learned that he was a man who appreciated having everything presented to him in an orderly fashion. Using my litigation skills, I made sure that every supporting document was organized and indexed for Van Deuren's review. This undertaking enabled me to acquire significant knowledge about how to proceed with the project and get the task at hand done."

What advice do you have for would-be paralegals in your area of work?

"Today's litigation paralegal is faced with learning much more than procedure and how to organize a case. Because technology now offers the most efficient tools to organize the litigation process, it is imperative that litigation paralegals learn what these tools are and how to work with them. To be most effective as a litigation paralegal, paralegals must know how to use litigation support, time management, and trial presentation software; they should also have a thorough working knowledge of imaging and the electronic discovery process. Cases that have multitudinous documents require the use of a litigation support software program that will create a document database and allow for the use of imaging/OCR (optical character recognition) technology. Most importantly,

> *"Out of all the paralegal skills, organization and time management are the most critical for litigation paralegals."*

the software program must be able to handle electronic documents, seeing that most documents in today's litigation are only available in an electronic format. Paralegals who are not using a litigation support program are not working efficiently. Out of all the paralegal skills, organization and time management are the most critical for litigation paralegals."

What are some tips for success as a paralegal in your area of work?

"The first step is planning. A firm should either choose someone from its staff or use an outside trial consultant when deciding to present evidence electronically at trial. If you help present evidence electronically at trial, it is extremely important that you know as much as possible about the case (including the type of lawsuit, the number of plaintiffs and defendants, and the trial location) and the parties involved (attorneys, paralegals, and support staff). To help avoid miscommunication among team members, there must be a close working relationship among the members of the trial team who assist in accessing materials. It is important to identify vendors who can easily help with any last-minute concerns, which may arise at midnight on the day before the trial begins. If the trial is taking place outside of your normal location, it is imperative to locate nearby vendors to provide litigation support."

The Plaintiff's Case

Once the opening statements have been made, Gilmore will present the plaintiff's case first. Because he is the plaintiff's attorney, he has the burden of proving that defendant Peretto was negligent.

Direct Examination

Gilmore will call several eyewitnesses to the stand and ask them to tell the court about the sequence of events that led to the accident. This form of questioning is known as **direct examination**. For example, Gilmore will call Julia Williams, an eyewitness who saw the accident occur, and ask her questions such as those presented in Exhibit 12.4 on the next page. He will also call other witnesses, including the

direct examination
The examination of a witness by the attorney who calls the witness to the stand to testify on behalf of the attorney's client.

EXHIBIT 12.4
Direct Examination—
Sample Questions

ATTORNEY:	Mrs. Williams, please explain how you came to be at the scene of the accident.
WITNESS:	Well, I was walking north on Mattis Avenue toward Nita City Hospital, where I work as a nurse.
ATTORNEY:	Please describe for the court, in your own words, exactly what you observed when you reached the intersection of Mattis Avenue and Thirty-eighth Street.
WITNESS:	I was approaching the intersection when I saw the defendant run the stop sign on Thirty-eighth Street and crash into the plaintiff's car.
ATTORNEY:	Did you notice any change in the speed at which the defendant was driving as he approached the stop sign?
WITNESS:	No. He didn't slow down at all.
ATTORNEY:	Mrs. Williams, are you generally in good health?
WITNESS:	Yes.
ATTORNEY:	Have you ever had any problems with your vision?
WITNESS:	No. I wear reading glasses for close work, but I see well in the distance.
ATTORNEY:	And how long has it been since your last eye examination?
WITNESS:	About a month or so ago, I went to Dr. Sullivan for an examination. He told me that I needed reading glasses but that my distance vision was excellent.

police officer who was summoned to the accident scene and the ambulance driver. Gilmore will try to elicit responses from these witnesses that strengthen Baranski's case—or at least that do not visibly weaken it.

During direct examination, attorney Gilmore usually will not be permitted to ask *leading questions,* which are questions that lead the witness to a particular desired response (see Chapter 11). A leading question might be something like the following: "So, Mrs. Williams, you noticed that the defendant ran the stop sign, right?" If Mrs. Williams answers "yes," she has, in effect, been "led" to this answer by Gilmore's leading question. Leading qustions thus discourage witnesses from telling their stories in their own words.

When Gilmore is dealing with *hostile witnesses* (uncooperative witnesses or those who are testifying on behalf of the other party), however, he is normally permitted to ask leading questions. This is because hostile witnesses may be uncommunicative and unwilling to describe the events they witnessed. If Gilmore asked a hostile witness what he or she observed on the morning of August 4 at 7:45 A.M., for example, the witness might respond, "I saw two trucks driving down Mattis Avenue." That answer might be true, but it has nothing to do with the Baranski-Peretto accident. Therefore, to elicit information from this witness, Gilmore would be permitted to use leading questions, which would force the witness to respond to the question at issue.

Cross-Examination

After attorney Gilmore has finished questioning a witness on direct examination, defendant Peretto's attorney, Cameron, will begin her **cross-examination** of that witness. During her cross-examination, Cameron will be primarily concerned with reducing the witness's credibility in the eyes of the jury and the judge. Attorneys typically use leading questions during cross-examination (since the witness is hostile). Generally, experienced trial attorneys ask only questions to which they know

cross-examination
The questioning of an opposing witness during the trial.

Case at a Glance

The Plaintiff—
  Plaintiff: Katherine Baranski
  Attorney: Allen P. Gilmore
  Paralegal: Elena Lopez

The Defendant—
  Defendant: Tony Peretto
  Attorney: Elizabeth A. Cameron
  Paralegal: Gordon McVay

the answers—because otherwise a question might elicit testimony from the witness that further supports the opponent's case.

Cameron will formulate questions for Gilmore's witnesses based on the witnesses' previous answers in depositions and interrogatories. Discovery usually provides attorneys with a fairly good idea as to what areas of questioning may prove fruitful. Moreover, if a witness's testimony on the witness stand differs considerably from the answers he or she previously gave, or contradicts some other item of evidence (some physical evidence or the testimony of another witness), the attorney can use this discrepancy to attack the witness's credibility.

The defendant's attorney, Cameron, must generally confine her cross-examination to matters that were brought up during direct examination or that relate to a witness's credibility. This restriction is not followed in all states, however, and ultimately both the nature and extent of the cross-examination are subject to the discretion of the trial judge. In any event, Cameron's interrogation may not extend to matters unrelated to the case. She normally may not introduce evidence that a witness for the plaintiff is a smoker or dislikes children, for example, unless she can demonstrate that such facts are relevant to the case. In general, Cameron will try to uncover relevant physical infirmities of the plaintiff's witnesses (such as poor eyesight or hearing), as well as any evidence of bias (such as a witness's habit of playing a friendly round of golf with plaintiff Baranski every Saturday). Some questions that Cameron might ask Julia Williams, Gilmore's eyewitness, are presented in Exhibit 12.5.

Redirect and Recross

After defendant Peretto's attorney, Cameron, has finished cross-examining each witness, plaintiff Baranski's attorney, Gilmore, will try to repair any damage done to the credibility of the witness's testimony—or, indeed, to the case itself. Gilmore

EXHIBIT 12.5
Cross-Examination—
Sample Questions

ATTORNEY:	You have just testified that you were approaching the intersection when the accident occurred. Isn't it true that you stated earlier, under oath, that you were at the intersection at the time of the accident?
WITNESS:	Well, I might have, but I think I said that I was close to the intersection.
ATTORNEY:	In fact, you said that you were at the intersection. Now, you say that you were approaching it. Which is it?
WITNESS:	I was approaching it, I suppose.
ATTORNEY:	Okay. Exactly where were you when the accident occurred?
WITNESS:	I think that I was just in front of the Dairy Queen when the accident happened.
ATTORNEY:	Mrs. Williams, the Dairy Queen on Mattis Avenue is at least seventy-five yards from the intersection of Mattis Avenue and Thirty-eighth Street. Is it your testimony today that you noticed the defendant's car from seventy-five yards away as it was approaching the intersection on Mattis Avenue?
WITNESS:	Well, no, I guess not.
ATTORNEY:	Isn't it true that there were a lot of other cars driving on the road that morning?
WITNESS:	Yes.
ATTORNEY:	And you had no reason to be paying particular attention to the defendant's car, did you?
WITNESS:	Not really.
ATTORNEY:	In fact, you did not see the defendant's car until after the collision occurred, did you, Mrs. Williams?

At trial, attorneys and paralegals must have close at hand all of the documents and information that they may need to refer to during the proceedings. Typically, these materials are contained in the trial notebook, which may consist of several binders. Increasingly, for complex litigation, attorneys and paralegals retrieve necessary documents from offline or online databases using laptop computers. Why do you think that during today's trials, one sees many fewer folders on opposing counsels' tables than are shown in this photo?

(Courtesy of © PhotoDisc®)

will do this by again questioning the witness and allowing the witness to explain his or her answer. This process is known as **redirect examination**.

If Cameron's cross-examination revealed that one of Gilmore's eyewitnesses to the accident had vision problems, for example, Gilmore could ask the witness whether he or she was wearing glasses or contact lenses at the time of the accident. Gilmore might also have the witness demonstrate to the court that he or she has good vision by having the witness identify a letter or object at the far end of the courtroom. Because redirect examination is primarily used to improve the credibility of cross-examined witnesses, it is limited to matters raised during cross-examination. (If Cameron chooses not to cross-examine a particular witness, then, of course, there can be no redirect examination by Gilmore.)

Following Gilmore's redirect examination, defendant Peretto's attorney, Cameron, will be given an opportunity for **recross-examination**. When both attorneys have finished with the first witness, Gilmore will call the succeeding witnesses in plaintiff Baranski's case, each of whom will be subject to cross-examination (and redirect and recross, if necessary).

Motion for a Directed Verdict

After attorney Gilmore has presented his case for plaintiff Baranski, then Cameron, as counsel for defendant Peretto, may decide to make a **motion for a directed verdict** (now also known as a *motion for judgment as a matter of law* in federal courts). Through this motion, Cameron will be saying to the court that the plaintiff's attorney has not offered enough evidence to support a claim against Peretto. If the judge agrees to grant the motion, then a judgment will be entered for Peretto, the case will be dismissed, and the trial will be over. A sample motion for judgment as a matter of law is shown in Exhibit 12.6.

redirect examination
The questioning of a witness following the adverse party's cross-examination.

recross-examination
The questioning of an opposing witness following the adverse party's redirect examination.

motion for a directed verdict
A motion (also known as a *motion for judgment as a matter of law* in the federal courts) requesting that the court grant a judgment in favor of the party making the motion on the ground that the other party has not produced sufficient evidence to support his or her claim.

EXHIBIT 12.6
Motion for Judgment
as a Matter of Law

Elizabeth A. Cameron
Cameron & Strauss, P.C.
310 Lake Drive
Zero City, ZE 59802
(616) 955-6234

Attorney for Defendant

UNITED STATES DISTRICT COURT
FOR THE WESTERN DISTRICT OF NITA

Katherine Baranski	)	
Plaintiff,	)	CASE NO. 11-14335-NI
	)	Honorable Harley M. Larue
v.	)	
	)	
	)	MOTION FOR JUDGMENT
Tony Peretto	)	AS A MATTER OF LAW
Defendant.	)	

The Defendant, Tony Peretto, at the close of the Plaintiff's case, moves the court to withdraw the evidence from the consideration of the jury and to find the Defendant not liable.

As grounds for this motion, Defendant Peretto states that:

(1) No evidence has been offered or received during the trial of the above-entitled cause of action to sustain the allegations of negligence contained in Plaintiff Baranski's complaint.

(2) No evidence has been offered or received during the trial proving or tending to prove that Defendant Peretto was guilty of any negligence.

(3) The proximate cause of Plaintiff Baranski's injuries was not due to any negligence on the part of Defendant Peretto.

(4) By the uncontroverted evidence, Plaintiff Baranski was guilty of contributory negligence, which was the sole cause of the Plaintiff's injuries.

Date: _7/21/11_

Elizabeth A Cameron
Elizabeth A. Cameron
Attorney for the Defendant

The motion for a directed verdict (judgment as a matter of law) is seldom granted because only cases that involve genuine factual disputes are permitted to proceed to trial in the first place. If the judge had believed that Baranski's case was that weak before the trial started, then the judge would probably have granted a pretrial motion to dismiss the case, thereby avoiding the expense of a trial. Occasionally, however, the occurrence of certain events—such as the death of a key witness—might mean the plaintiff has no evidence to support his or her allegations. In that event, the court may grant the defendant's motion for a directed verdict, or judgment as a matter of law.

The Defendant's Case

Assuming that the motion for a directed verdict (motion for judgment as a matter of law) is denied by the court, the two attorneys, Gilmore and Cameron, will now reverse their roles. Attorney Cameron will begin to present evidence demonstrating the

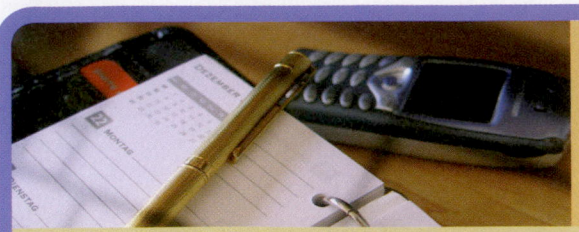

In the **Office**

PROTECTING CONFIDENTIAL INFORMATION

Some of the materials related to cases are confidential. To protect the interests of clients, help to make sure that information is not exposed to visitors to the office or to other employees who do not have a need to know information related to a particular case. Keep materials put away when you are not working on them. Because most work is done on computers, close files on your computer when you leave your desk so other people cannot read what is there. Computers using Windows can be easily locked by pressing the key with the Windows logo on it and the letter "l" key at the same time. Entering your password returns you to the same point, so you do not have to close all files or turn off the computer. Notice that many people talk on the phone as if no one around them is listening. We must be discrete when talking about legal matters. Further, cell phone calls are not difficult to intercept, so even if others are not in earshot, electronic interception can occur.

weaknesses of plaintiff Baranski's claims against defendant Peretto. She will essentially follow the same procedure used by Gilmore when he presented Baranski's side of the story. Cameron will call witnesses to the stand and question them. After Cameron's direct examination of each witness, that witness will be subject to possible cross-examination by Gilmore, redirect examination by Cameron, and recross-examination by Gilmore.

In her presentation of the defendant's case, Cameron will attempt to counter the points made by Gilmore during his presentation of Baranski's side of the story. To that end, Cameron and her paralegal, Gordon McVay, may have to prepare exhibits and assorted memoranda of law in addition to those originally prepared. The need to prepare additional exhibits and memoranda sometimes arises when the plaintiff's attorney pursues a strategy different from the one anticipated by the defense team. Depending on Cameron's preference or strategy, she may choose to begin by exposing weaknesses in the plaintiff's case (by asserting that the plaintiff was speeding, for example) or by presenting Peretto's version of the accident. Regardless of the procedure used, paralegal McVay, like paralegal Lopez, will have to keep track of the materials brought to court each day.

Once Cameron has finished presenting her case, Gilmore will be permitted to offer evidence to *rebut* (refute) evidence introduced by Cameron in Peretto's behalf. After Gilmore's rebuttal, if any, both attorneys will make their closing arguments to the jury.

Closing Arguments

closing argument

The argument made by each side's attorney after the cases for the plaintiff and defendant have been presented. Closing arguments are made prior to the jury charge.

In their **closing arguments**, the attorneys summarize their presentations and argue in their clients' favor. A closing argument should include all of the major points that support the client's case. It should also emphasize the shortcomings of the opposing party's case. Jurors will view a closing argument with some skepticism if it merely recites the central points of a party's claim or defense without also responding to the unfavorable facts or issues raised by the other side. Of course, neither attorney wants to focus too much on the other side's position, but the elements of the opposing position do need to be acknowledged and their flaws highlighted.

EXHIBIT 12.7
Jury Charge—Request
for Findings of Fact

The jury is requested to answer the following questions:

(1) Was the defendant negligent?

Answer: (yes or no) _____

(2) If your answer to question (1) is "yes," then you must answer this question: Was the defendant's negligence a proximate (direct) cause of the plaintiff's injuries?

Answer: (yes or no) _____

(3) Was the plaintiff negligent?

Answer: (yes or no) _____

(4) If your answer to question (3) is "yes," then you must answer this question: Was the plaintiff's negligence a proximate (direct) cause of the accident and injuries that she suffered?

Answer: (yes or no) _____

(5) If your answer to either question (1) or question (3) is "yes," then answer the following:

Taking 100% as the total fault causing the accident and injuries, what percentage of the total fault causing the accident and injuries do you attribute to:

_____ the defendant

_____ the plaintiff

(If you find that a party has no fault in causing the accident, then attribute 0 percentage of the fault to that party.)

(6) Regardless of how you answered the previous questions, answer this question:

Disregarding any negligence or fault on the part of the plaintiff, what sum of money would reasonably compensate the plaintiff for her claimed injury and damage?

Answer: $ _____

Both attorneys will want to organize their presentations so they can explain their arguments and show the jury how their arguments are supported by the evidence. Once both attorneys have completed their remarks, the case will be submitted to the jury, and the attorneys' role in the trial will be finished.

Jury Instructions

Before the jurors begin their deliberations, the judge gives the jury a **charge**, in which the judge sums up the case and instructs the jurors on the rules of law that apply. (In some courts, jury instructions are given prior to closing arguments and may even be given at some other point during trial proceedings.) Because the jury's role is to serve as the fact finder, the factual account contained in the charge is not binding on the jurors. Indeed, they may disregard the facts as noted in the charge. They are *not* free to ignore the statements of law, however. The charge contains a request for findings of fact, which is typically phrased in an "if, then" format. For example, in the charge presented in Exhibit 12.7 above, the jury is first asked to decide if the defendant was negligent. *If* the jury decides that the defendant was

charge
The judge's instruction to the jury setting forth the rules of law that the jury must apply in reaching its decision, or verdict.

negligent, *then* the jury must decide whether the defendant's negligence caused the plaintiff's injuries. This format helps to channel the jurors' deliberations.

Charges, which are also called jury instructions, are usually drafted by the attorneys and discussed with the judge before the trial begins, and an attorney's trial strategy will likely be linked to the charges. The paralegal may draft the instructions for the attorney's review. The judge, however, has the final decision as to what instructions will be submitted to the jury.

The Verdict

verdict
A formal decision made by a jury.

Following its receipt of the charge, the jury begins its deliberations. Once it has reached a decision, the jury issues a **verdict** in favor of one of the parties. If the verdict is in favor of the plaintiff, the jury will specify the amount of damages to be paid by the defendant. Following the announcement of the verdict, the jurors are discharged. Usually, immediately after the verdict has been announced and the jurors discharged, the party in whose favor the verdict was issued makes a motion asking the judge to issue a *judgment*—which is the court's final word on the matter—consistent with the jury's verdict. For example, if the jury in the Baranski case finds that Peretto was negligent and awards Baranski damages in the amount of $85,000, the judge will order Peretto to pay the plaintiff that amount.

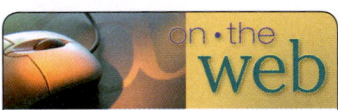

To find information on jury verdicts in assorted trials throughout the country, including the amount of damages awarded, go to **www.jvra.com**.

POSTTRIAL MOTIONS AND PROCEDURES

Every trial must have a winner and a loser. Although civil litigation is an expensive and cumbersome process, the losing party may wish to pursue the matter further after the verdict has been rendered. Assume that plaintiff Baranski wins at trial and is awarded $85,000 in damages. Cameron, as defendant Peretto's attorney, may file a posttrial motion or appeal the decision to a higher court. Note that Baranski, even though she won the case, could also appeal the judgment. For example, she might appeal the case on the ground that she should have received $130,000 in damages instead of $85,000, arguing that the latter amount inadequately compensates her for the harms that she suffered as a result of Peretto's negligence.

Case at a Glance

The Plaintiff—
 Plaintiff: Katherine Baranski
 Attorney: Allen P. Gilmore
 Paralegal: Elena Lopez

The Defendant—
 Defendant: Tony Peretto
 Attorney: Elizabeth A. Cameron
 Paralegal: Gordon McVay

Posttrial Motions

Assume that defendant Peretto's attorney, Cameron, believes that the verdict for plaintiff Baranski is not supported by the evidence. In this situation, she may file a **motion for judgment notwithstanding the verdict** (also known as a *motion for judgment as a matter of law* in the federal courts). By filing this motion, Cameron asks the judge to enter a judgment in favor of Peretto on the ground (basis) that the jury verdict in favor of Baranski was unreasonable and erroneous. Cameron may file this motion only if she previously filed a motion for a directed verdict (or judgment as a matter of law) during the trial and the motion was denied at that time. If she decides to file this motion, she must file it within ten days following the entry of judgment against Peretto. Like virtually all motions in federal court, this motion must be accompanied by a supporting affidavit or a memorandum of law, or brief (these documents were discussed in Chapter 10). The judge will then determine whether the jury's verdict was reasonable in view of the evidence presented at trial.

motion for judgment notwithstanding the verdict
A motion (also referred to as a *motion for judgment as a matter of law* in federal courts) requesting that the court grant judgment in favor of the party making the motion on the ground that the jury verdict against him or her was unreasonable or erroneous.

Rule 50 of the Federal Rules of Civil Procedure permits either party to file a **motion for a new trial**. Such a motion may be submitted along with a motion for judgment notwithstanding the verdict. A motion for a new trial is a far more drastic tactic because it asserts that the trial was so pervaded by error or so otherwise fundamentally flawed that a new trial should be held. Because such a motion reflects adversely on the way in which the judge conducted the trial, it should be filed only if the attorney truly believes that a miscarriage of justice will otherwise result.

motion for a new trial
A motion asserting that the trial was so fundamentally flawed (because of error, newly discovered evidence, prejudice, or other reason) that a new trial is needed to prevent a miscarriage of justice.

EXHIBIT 12.8
Motion for Judgment as a
Matter of Law or for a New Trial

Elizabeth A. Cameron
Cameron & Strauss, P.C.
310 Lake Drive
Zero City, ZE 59802
(616) 955-6234

Attorney for Defendant

UNITED STATES DISTRICT COURT
FOR THE WESTERN DISTRICT OF NITA

Katherine Baranski   )
    Plaintiff,   )   CASE NO. 11-14335-NI
)   Honorable Harley M. Larue
v.   )
)   MOTION FOR JUDGMENT AS
)   A MATTER OF LAW OR, IN
Tony Peretto   )   THE ALTERNATIVE,
    Defendant.   )   MOTION FOR A NEW TRIAL

    The Defendant, Tony Peretto, moves this Court, pursuant to Rule 50(b) of the Federal Rules of Civil Procedure, to set aside the verdict and judgment entered on August 15, 2011, and to enter instead a judgment for the Defendant as a matter of law. In the alternative, and in the event the Defendant's motion for judgment as a matter of law is denied, the Defendant moves the Court to order a new trial.

    The grounds for this motion are set forth in the attached memorandum.

Date: 8/16/11

Elizabeth A. Cameron
Elizabeth A. Cameron
Attorney for the Defendant

For a motion for a new trial to have a reasonable chance of being granted, the motion must allege such serious problems as jury misconduct, prejudicial jury instructions, excessive or inadequate damages, or the existence of newly discovered evidence (but not if the evidence could have been discovered earlier through the use of reasonable care). Like other posttrial motions in federal courts, the motion for a new trial must be filed within ten days following the entry of the judgment. Exhibit 12.8 above illustrates a motion for judgment as a matter of law or, in the alternative, for a new trial.

Appealing the Verdict

If attorney Cameron's posttrial motions are unsuccessful or if she decides not to file them, she may still file an **appeal**. The purpose of an appeal is to have the trial court's decision either reversed or modified by an appellate court. As discussed in Chapter 6, appellate courts, or courts of appeals, are *reviewing* courts, not trial courts. In other words, no new evidence will be presented to the appellate court, and there is no jury. The appellate court will review the trial court's proceedings to decide whether the trial court erred in applying the law to the facts of the case, in instructing the jury, or in administering the trial generally. Appellate courts rarely tamper with a trial court's findings of fact because the judge and jury were in a better position than the appellate court to evaluate the credibility of witnesses, the nature of the evidence, and the like.

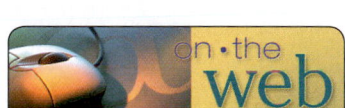

The Federal Rules of Appellate Procedure, as well as some state materials, are online at **www.law. cornell.edu**. Select "All topics" from the "Law about . . ." menu, and find the entry for "Appellate Procedure."

appeal
The process of seeking a higher court's review of a lower court's decision for the purpose of correcting or changing the lower court's judgment or decision.

As grounds for the appeal, defendant Peretto's attorney, Cameron, might argue that the trial court erred in one of the ways mentioned in the preceding paragraph. Unless she believes that a reversal of the judgment is likely, however, she will probably advise Peretto not to appeal the case, as an appeal will simply add to the costs and expenses already incurred by Peretto in defending against Baranski's claim.

Notice of Appeal

When the appeal involves a federal district court decision, as in the Baranski case, the **appellant** (the party appealing the decision) must file a notice of appeal with the district court that rendered the judgment. The clerk of the court then notifies the **appellee** (the party against whom the appeal is taken) as well as the court of appeals. The clerk also forwards to the appellate court a transcript of the trial court proceedings, along with any related pleadings and exhibits; these materials together constitute the **record on appeal**.

The Appellate Brief and Oral Arguments

When a case is appealed, the attorneys for both parties submit written *briefs* that present their positions on the issues to be reviewed by the appellate court. The briefs outline each party's view of the proper application of the law to the facts.

After the appellate court has reviewed the briefs, the court sets aside a time for both attorneys to argue their positions before the panel of judges. The attorneys will then present their arguments and answer any questions that the judges might have. Generally, the attorneys' arguments before an appellate court are limited in terms of both the time allowed for argument and the scope of the argument. Following the oral arguments, the judges decide the matter and issue a formal written opinion, which normally is published in the relevant reporter (see Chapter 7 for a discussion of how court opinions are published).

The Appellate Court's Options

Once they have reviewed the record and heard oral arguments, the judges have several options. For example, in the Baranski case, if the appellate court decided to uphold the trial court's decision, then the judgment for Baranski would be **affirmed**. If the judges decided to **reverse** the trial court's decision, however, then Peretto would no longer be obligated to pay the damages awarded to Baranski by the trial court. The court might also affirm or reverse a decision *in part*. For example, the judges might affirm the jury's finding that Peretto was negligent but **remand** the case—that is, send it back to the trial court—for further proceedings on another issue (such as the extent of Baranski's damages). An appellate court can also *modify* a lower court's decision. If, for example, the appellate court decided that the jury awarded an excessive amount in damages, the appellate court might reduce the award to a more appropriate, or fairer, amount.

The decision of the appellate court may sometimes be appealed further. A state appellate court's decision, for example, may be appealed to the state supreme court. A federal appellate court's decision may be appealed to the United States Supreme Court. It will be up to these higher courts to decide whether they will review the case. In other words, these courts normally are not *required* to review cases. Recall from Chapter 6 that although thousands of cases are submitted to the United States Supreme Court each year, it hears less than one hundred. (An action decided in a state court has a somewhat greater chance of being reviewed by the state supreme court.)

ENFORCING THE JUDGMENT

The uncertainties of the litigation process are compounded by the lack of guarantees that any judgment will be enforceable. *Developing Paralegal Skills* discusses this practical problem. It is one thing to have a court enter a judgment in your favor; it

---

appellant

The party who takes an appeal from one court to another; sometimes referred to as the *petitioner.*

appellee

The party against whom an appeal is taken—that is, the party who opposes setting aside or reversing the judgment; sometimes referred to as the *respondent.*

record on appeal

The items submitted during the trial (pleadings, motions, briefs, and exhibits) and the transcript of the trial proceedings that are forwarded to the appellate court for review when a case is appealed.

affirm

To uphold the judgment of a lower court.

reverse

To overturn the judgment of a lower court.

remand

To send a case back to a lower court for further proceedings.

Developing
Paralegal Skills

LOCATING ASSETS

Paralegal Myra Cullen works for a law firm that represented Jennifer Roth in a lawsuit brought against Best Eatery, a local restaurant. Roth won $100,000 in a lawsuit for damages she suffered when she fell and broke her leg in the restaurant's lobby on a rainy morning. Best Eatery's only insurance coverage is a small liability policy that will only pay a portion of Roth's award. Myra has been assigned the task of investigating Best Eatery's assets to determine how the judgment can be collected. Myra learned through pretrial discovery that John Dobman owns Best Eatery as a sole proprietor, which means that he is personally liable for the debts of the business. Myra now contacts the county register of deeds to research the value of the property on which Best Eatery is located and any other property owned by John Dobman. In Myra's county, the county clerk's deed records can be searched via the Internet. Myra knows, however, that after conducting an online search she will need to verify the information obtained. She therefore writes down the document numbers provided online so that she can quickly access the information at the clerk's office. Myra determines that Dobman's equity (market value minus mortgage outstanding) in the property on which Best Eatery is located is $110,000, which will cover any shortfall in the damages. Because the equity is sufficient to cover the award, Myra simply notes the record number of Dobman's other real property (his house) in the client's file.

TIPS FOR LOCATING ASSETS

- Ask what property the defendant owns during discovery, such as in interrogatories.
- Ask for the address of the property. Many times, you can do this on the Internet.
- Go to the register of deeds to learn about any liens filed against the property and the amount of any mortgage loan.
- Check with a real estate agent or an appraiser as to the market value of the property.
- Deduct the liens and the mortgage debt from the market value to determine the defendant's equity.

is another to collect the funds to which you are entitled from the opposing party. Even if the jury awarded Baranski the full amount of damages requested ($130,000), for example, she might not, in fact, "win" anything at all. Peretto's auto insurance coverage might have lapsed, in which event the company would not cover any of the damages. Alternatively, Peretto's insurance coverage might be limited to $30,000, meaning that Peretto would have to pay the remaining $100,000 personally. If Peretto did not have that amount available, then Baranski would need to go back to court and request that the court issue a **writ of execution**—an order, usually issued by the clerk of the court, directing the sheriff to seize (take temporary ownership of) and sell Peretto's assets. The proceeds of the sale would then be used to pay the damages owed to Baranski. Any excess proceeds of the sale would be returned to Peretto.

Even as a **judgment creditor** (one who has obtained a court judgment against a debtor), Baranski may not be able to obtain the full amount of the judgment from Peretto. Laws protecting debtors provide that certain property (such as a debtor's home up to a specific value and tools used by the debtor in his or her trade) is *exempt*. Exempt property cannot be seized and sold to pay debts owed to judgment creditors. Similar exemptions would apply if Peretto declared bankruptcy. Thus, even though Baranski won at trial, she, like many others who are awarded damages, might not be able to collect them. Realize, though, that judgments constitute liens (legal claims)

writ of execution
A writ that puts in force a court's decree or judgment.

judgment creditor
A creditor who is legally entitled, by a court's judgment, to collect the amount of the judgment from a debtor.

Today's
Professional Paralegal

DRAFTING *VOIR DIRE* QUESTIONS LIKE A PRO

Andrea Leed, a legal assistant, is preparing for trial. Her boss is a famous trial attorney, Mary Marshall. Mary rarely loses a case. One of the many secrets of her success is that she always draws up a jury profile and prepares carefully for *voir dire.*

Mary is defending a corporation in an environmental liability case. The case involves many complex engineering and scientific issues that the jury will need to understand in order to reach its verdict. It is a common practice in these types of cases to select a "blue ribbon" jury—a jury consisting of persons who are very well educated. Mary has suggested that Andrea locate and hire a psychologist to prepare a jury profile.

CONSULTING WITH AN EXPERT WITNESS

Andrea contacts TrialPsych, Inc., a consulting firm headed by Dr. Linda Robertson, who specializes in jury selection. Dr. Robertson would be delighted to work on the case, but her services are very expensive, and Andrea must find out whether the client is willing to pay Dr. Robertson's fee. The client agrees to pay the fee, so Andrea meets with Dr. Robertson to discuss the case. Andrea explains that the client is a corporation and that the case involves complex scientific and engineering issues. Dr. Robertson consults her files for statistical information on these types of cases. She finds that the ideal jury would be made up of white-collar professionals holding degrees in engineering or another applied science. Also, the prospective jurors would ideally be against extensive government regulation of the corporate world.

DRAFTING *VOIR DIRE* QUESTIONS

Andrea returns to the office and discusses with Mary the results of her consultation with Dr. Robertson. Mary and Andrea decide to draft questions for *voir dire* that are designed to elicit the type of information recommended by Dr. Robertson. Andrea then drafts a list of about twenty questions, including the following:

1. Please state your name and address.

2. Where are you employed, and how long have you been employed there?

3. What is the highest level of education that you have attained: high school diploma, some college but no degree, college degree, advanced degree (please specify)?

4. If you have attended college or received a college degree, what was your field of study?

5. Have you ever been fired by a corporate employer in a way that you believed was unfair?

6. Have you ever worked for a government regulatory agency, and, if so, what were your responsibilities in that position?

7. Have you, or persons or business firms with whom you are or have been associated, ever been sued for violating environmental statutes or regulations? If so, what were the violations?

8. In your opinion, what should be the government's role in regulating a company's operations?

REVIEWING THE *VOIR DIRE* QUESTIONS

Andrea e-mails the list of questions to Dr. Robertson, who reviews them and e-mails back some suggested changes, which Andrea incorporates. When the final list of questions is drawn up, Andrea presents it to Mary and places a copy of the list in the trial notebook. Mary asks Andrea to call Dr. Robertson and ask her if she is available to sit in on the actual *voir dire* process to ensure that jury selection goes smoothly.

for significant time periods. If the financial circumstances of the debtor—such as Peretto—change in the future, recovery may be possible.

The difficulty of enforcing court judgments, coupled with the high costs accompanying litigation (including attorneys' fees, court costs, and the litigants' time costs), is a major reason why most disputes are settled out of court, either before or during the trial.

KEY TERMS AND CONCEPTS

affirm *408*

appeal *407*

appellant *408*

appellee *408*

challenge *395*

challenge for cause *395*

charge *405*

closing argument *404*

cross-examination *400*

direct examination *399*

judgment creditor *409*

motion for a directed verdict *402*

motion for a new trial *406*

motion for judgment notwithstanding the verdict *406*

motion *in limine* *394*

opening statement *397*

peremptory challenge *395*

pretrial conference *393*

record on appeal *408*

recross-examination *402*

redirect examination *402*

remand *408*

reverse *408*

trial notebook *391*

verdict *406*

voir dire *395*

writ of execution *409*

CHAPTER SUMMARY

TRIAL PROCEDURES

Preparing for Trial

1. *Trial-preparation checklist*—Before the trial, attorneys for both sides and their paralegals gather and organize evidence, documents, and other materials relating to the case. It is helpful to create a checklist to ensure that nothing is overlooked during this stage.

2. *Witnesses and subpoenas*—Paralegals often assist in contacting and issuing subpoenas to witnesses, as well as in preparing witnesses for trial.

3. *Preparation of exhibits and trial notebook*—Paralegals assume responsibility for making sure that all exhibits and displays are ready by trial and that the trial notebook is complete.

Pretrial Conference

Before trial, the attorneys for both sides meet with the trial judge in a pretrial conference to decide whether a settlement is possible or, if not, to decide how the trial will be conducted and what types of evidence will be admissible.

1. *Motions in limine*—One or both of the attorneys may make a motion *in limine,* which asks the court to keep certain evidence from being offered at the trial.

Continued

Jury Selection

1. *Voir dire*—During the *voir dire* process, attorneys for both sides question potential jurors to determine whether any potential jurors should be excluded from the jury.

2. *Challenges for cause*—Attorneys for both sides can exercise an unlimited number of challenges for cause on the basis of prospective jurors' bias against the client or case.

3. *Peremptory challenges*—Both attorneys can exercise a limited number of peremptory challenges without giving any reason to the court for excluding a potential juror.

The Trial

Once the jury has been selected and seated, the trial begins. The paralegal, if he or she attends the trial, coordinates witnesses' appearances, tracks the testimony of witnesses and compares it with sworn statements that the witnesses made before the trial, and provides the attorney with appropriate reminders or documents when necessary.

1. *Opening statements*—The trial begins with opening statements in which the attorneys briefly outline their versions of the facts of the case and the evidence they will offer to support their views.

2. *Plaintiff's case*—Following the attorneys' opening statements, the plaintiff's attorney presents evidence supporting the plaintiff's claims, including the testimony of witnesses.

   a. The attorney's questioning of a witness whom he or she calls is referred to as direct examination.

   b. Following direct examination by the plaintiff's attorney, the defendant's attorney may cross-examine the witness.

   c. If the witness was cross-examined, the plaintiff's attorney may question the witness on redirect examination, after which the defendant's attorney may question the witness on recross-examination.

3. *Motion for a directed verdict*—After the plaintiff's attorney has presented his or her client's case, the defendant's attorney may make a motion for a directed verdict, also called a motion for judgment as a matter of law. This motion asserts that the plaintiff has not offered enough evidence to support the plaintiff's claim against the defendant. If the judge grants the motion, the case will be dismissed.

4. *Defendant's case*—The attorneys then reverse their roles, and the defendant's attorney presents evidence and testimony to refute the plaintiff's claims. Any witnesses called to the stand by the defendant's attorney will be subject to direct examination by that attorney, cross-examination by the plaintiff's attorney, and possible redirect examination and recross-examination.

5. *Closing arguments*—After the defendant's attorney has finished his or her presentation, both attorneys give their closing arguments. A closing argument includes all the major points that support the client's case and emphasizes shortcomings in the opposing party's case.

6. *Jury instructions*—Following the attorneys' closing arguments (or, in some courts, at some other point in the proceedings), the judge instructs the jury in a charge—a document that includes statements of the applicable law and a review of the facts as they were presented during the trial. The jury must not

disregard the judge's instructions as to what the applicable law is and how it should be applied to the facts of the case as interpreted by the jury.

7. *Verdict*—Once the jury reaches a decision, it issues a verdict in favor of one of the parties and is discharged. The court then enters a judgment consistent with the jury's verdict.

Posttrial Motions and Procedures

After the verdict has been pronounced and the trial concluded, the losing party's attorney may file a posttrial motion or an appeal.

1. *Motion for judgment notwithstanding the verdict*—A motion for judgment notwithstanding the verdict (also called a motion for judgment as a matter of law) asks the judge to enter a judgment in favor of the losing party in spite of the verdict because the verdict was not supported by the evidence or was otherwise in error.

2. *Motion for a new trial*—A motion for a new trial asserts that the trial was so flawed—by judge or juror misconduct or other pervasive errors—that a new trial should be held.

3. *Appealing the verdict*—The attorney may, depending on the client's wishes, appeal the decision to an appellate court for review. Appeals are usually filed only when the attorney believes that a reversal of the judgment is likely.

   a. If an appeal is pursued, the appellant must file a notice of appeal with the court that rendered the judgment. Then the clerk will forward the record on appeal to the appropriate reviewing court.

   b. The parties then file appellate briefs arguing their positions. Later, they are given the opportunity to present oral arguments before the appellate panel.

   c. The appellate court decides whether to affirm, reverse, remand, or modify the trial court's judgment.

   d. The appellate court's decision may sometimes be appealed further (to the state supreme court, for example).

Enforcing the Judgment

Even though a plaintiff wins a lawsuit for damages, it may be difficult to enforce the judgment against the defendant, particularly if the defendant has few assets. The paralegal is often involved in locating assets so that the attorney can request a writ of execution (court order to seize property) in an attempt to collect the amount the client is owed.

STUDENT STUDYWARE™ CD-ROM

Interactive student CD in this book includes additional quizzing, plus video clips, case studies, and Key Terms flashcards.

ONLINE COMPANION™

For additional resources, please go to **www.paralegal.delmar.cengage.com**.

QUESTIONS FOR REVIEW

1. What role does the paralegal play in preparing witnesses, exhibits, and displays for trial? How can the paralegal assist the attorney in preparing the trial notebook?

2. How are jurors selected? What is the difference between a peremptory challenge and a challenge for cause?

3. How are witnesses examined during trial? What is the difference between direct examination and cross-examination?

4. What is a jury charge? Can the jury decide matters of law?

5. Describe the procedure for filing an appeal. What factors does an attorney consider when deciding whether a case should be appealed?

ETHICAL QUESTION

1. Anthony Paletti, a paralegal, is attending a trial with his supervising attorney. Anthony leaves the courtroom to meet a witness. On his way down the hall, he runs into the defendant in the case. The defendant says to Anthony, "You work for the plaintiff's attorney, don't you? I have a question for you about that contract that your attorney offered into evidence." Should Anthony answer the defendant's question? Why or why not?

PRACTICE QUESTIONS AND ASSIGNMENTS

1. Paralegal Patricia Smith is assisting her supervising attorney, who has received a trial date for an auto accident case. The trial is set to begin in ten weeks. Discovery has been completed in the case. The depositions of the plaintiff and defendant have been taken, along with those of two eyewitnesses, a police officer, and Dr. Black, the plaintiff's physician. Additionally, the plaintiff and the defendant have answered interrogatories. Patricia's firm represents the plaintiff, and her supervising attorney plans to call not only the client but also the defendant, an eyewitness (Mr. Sams), and the police officer to testify. All of the witnesses are local. The case file contains police reports, newspaper articles about the accident, and medical records in addition to the deposition and interrogatory materials. Using the material presented in Exhibit 12.1 on page 389, *Trial-Preparation Checklist,* prepare a checklist for Patricia to complete.

2. Using Exhibit 12.2 on page 390, *A Subpoena,* draft a subpoena for a friendly witness using the following facts:

   Simon Kolstad, whose address is 100 Schoolcraft Road, Del Mar, California, is a witness to be subpoenaed in *Sumner v. Hayes,* a civil lawsuit filed in the U.S. District Court for the Eastern District of Michigan, case number 10–123492. He is being subpoenaed by the plaintiff's attorney, Marvin W. Green, whose office is located at 300 Penobscot Building, Detroit, Michigan. Kolstad is to appear in room number 6 of the courthouse, which is located at 231 Lafayette Boulevard, Detroit, Michigan, at 2:30 P.M. on January 10, 2011.

3. Identify the motion that would be filed in each of the following situations:

   a. A plaintiff's attorney loses a case, and she believes that her loss is due to prejudicial jury instructions given by the judge.

   b. The defendant's key witness was hospitalized during a trial and was unable to testify. As a result, key evidence was not presented, and the defendant was unable to prove his case.

   c. In the example given in item b above, the plaintiff's attorney made the appropriate motion, which was not granted, and ultimately lost the lawsuit. Thus, according to the plaintiff's attorney, the judgment was not supported by the evidence.

   d. The defense attorney has seen grisly photographs of an accident that the plaintiff's attorney has in her file. The defense attorney is concerned that these photographs would unfairly prejudice a jury against the defendant during the trial.

4. Indicate whether the appellate court will affirm, modify, or reverse the trial court's decision or remand the case for further proceedings:

   a. A trial court finds for the plaintiff in the amount of $150,000 in a case in which the plaintiff slipped and fell in a grocery store. The court of appeals finds that while the plaintiff is entitled to damages, the damages awarded by the jury are excessive. The appellate court sends the case back to the trial court for reevaluation of the amount of damages awarded.

b. A trial court finds that the plaintiff was slandered by the defendant. On appeal, the court of appeals finds that the trial court admitted evidence that it should not have allowed and holds that without this evidence, there was no slander.

c. A trial court finds that the defendant breached a contract and owes the plaintiff $1,000,000 in damages. The defendant appeals, claiming that the damages are not supported by the evidence. The court of appeals agrees with the trial court's decision.

 ## QUESTIONS FOR CRITICAL ANALYSIS

1. Typically, all witnesses called to appear at a trial are served with subpoenas, even friendly witnesses. Why is this? What might happen if they were not subpoenaed? How can the service of subpoenas be handled with friendly witnesses so that they are not offended?

2. Much preparation and organization go into trial work, from preparing witnesses and trial notebooks, to drafting questions, to creating exhibits and displays. Why is this done? What impact do these preparations have on the jury? What impact would (or do) disorganization and lack of preparation have on the jury?

3. Why are leading questions not allowed during direct examination? Why are leading questions allowed during cross-examination? Is the use of leading questions fair to the witness being cross-examined?

4. How is a judgment paid when there is no insurance or other cash assets available to pay the judgment? Is all of a defendant's property subject to the judgment? If not, what property is exempt? Why might these exemptions have been created?

 ## PROJECTS

1. Look up your state's court rules and find out how many challenges for cause are allowed during *voir dire*. How many peremptory challenges are permitted during *voir dire*?

2. Call your local sheriff's office and find out what happens when a writ of execution is carried out. Ask if any printed information on this procedure is available. If it is, request a copy. Share the results of your research with the class. (Discuss this assignment with your instructor prior to undertaking it.)

 ## USING INTERNET RESOURCES

1. Do a general search on the Internet for vendors of trial support services, such as imaging and coding. Pick two of the vendors, and browse through their Web sites.

   a. Write a one-page summary of the services that each company provides.

   b. Write an additional two paragraphs comparing the vendors' services and stating which of the two companies you would recommend, and why.

END NOTES

1. Pronounced in *lim*-uh-nay.

2. Pronounced vwahr *deer*. These old French verbs mean "to speak the truth." In legal language, the phrase refers to the process of questioning jurors to learn about their backgrounds, attitudes, and similar attributes.

CRIMINAL LAW AND PROCEDURES

CHAPTER OUTLINE

Introduction

What Is a Crime?

Elements of Criminal Liability

Types of Crimes

Cyber Crimes

Constitutional Safeguards

Criminal Procedures prior to Prosecution

The Prosecution Begins

The Trial

AFTER COMPLETING THIS CHAPTER, YOU WILL KNOW:

► The difference between crimes and other wrongful acts.

► The two elements that are required for criminal liability and some of the most common defenses that are raised in defending against criminal charges.

► Five broad categories of crimes and some common types of crimes.

► The constitutional rights of persons accused of crimes.

► The basic steps involved in criminal procedure from the time a crime is reported to the resolution of the case.

► How and why criminal litigation procedures differ from civil litigation procedures.

INTRODUCTION

Each year, more than 10 million people are arrested on criminal charges and enter the criminal justice system. Therefore, it is no wonder that many attorneys and paralegals work on criminal law cases. In fact, about one in every five paralegals spends most of her or his work time on criminal law.

Criminal cases are prosecuted by **public prosecutors**, who are employed by the government. The public prosecutor in federal criminal cases is called a U.S. attorney. In cases tried in state or local courts, the public prosecutor may be referred to as a *prosecuting attorney, state prosecutor, district attorney, county attorney,* or *city attorney.* Defendants in criminal cases may hire private attorneys to defend them. If a defendant cannot afford to hire an attorney, the court will appoint one for him or her. Everyone accused of a crime that may result in a jail sentence has a right to counsel, and this right is ensured by court-appointed attorneys, called **public defenders**, who are paid by the state.

Many employment opportunities exist for paralegals interested in working for public prosecutors or public defenders across the country. Private criminal defense attorneys also utilize paralegals. In addition, victims' rights organizations and police departments may employ legal assistants. Paralegals may also come into contact with criminal defendants in the course of their work in a general law practice or in a corporate legal department. A client of the firm may be arrested for driving while intoxicated or for possessing illegal drugs, for example, or a corporation might have to defend against alleged criminal violations of federal environmental laws.

In this chapter, we provide an overview of criminal law and procedure. We begin by explaining the nature of crime and the key differences between criminal law and civil law. We then discuss the elements of criminal liability and some of the many types of crime. Throughout the chapter, we emphasize the constitutional protections that come into play when a person is accused of a crime and focus on how and why criminal procedures differ from civil procedures.

public prosecutor

An individual, acting as a trial lawyer, who initiates and conducts criminal cases in the government's name and on behalf of the people.

public defender

A court-appointed attorney who is paid by the state to represent a criminal defendant who is unable to hire private counsel.

WHAT IS A CRIME?

What is a crime? To answer that question, we begin by distinguishing crimes from other wrongs, such as torts—and, hence, criminal law from tort, or civil, law. Major differences between civil law and criminal law are summarized in Exhibit 13.1. After discussing these differences, we explain how one act can qualify as both a crime and a tort. We then describe classifications of crimes and jurisdiction over criminal acts.

Issue	Under Civil Law	Under Criminal Law
Area of concern	Rights and duties between individuals and between persons and government	Offenses against society as a whole
Wrongful act	Harm to a person or to a person's property	Violation of a statute that prohibits a certain activity
Party who brings suit	Person who suffered harm	The state
Standard of proof	Preponderance of the evidence	Beyond a reasonable doubt
Remedy	Damages to compensate for the harm or a decree to achieve an equitable result	Punishment (fine, removal from public office, imprisonment, or death)

EXHIBIT 13.1
Civil Law and Criminal Law Compared

crime

A broad term for violations of law that are punishable by the state and are codified by legislatures. The objective of criminal law is to protect the public.

Key Differences between Civil Law and Criminal Law

A **crime** can be distinguished from other wrongful acts, such as torts, in that a crime is an *offense against society as a whole.* Criminal defendants are prosecuted by public officials on behalf of the state, as mentioned above, not by their victims or other private parties. In addition, those who have committed crimes are subject to penalties, including fines, imprisonment, and, in some cases, death. As will be discussed in Chapter 14, tort remedies—remedies for civil wrongs—are generally intended to compensate the injured party (by awarding money damages, for example). Criminal law, however, is concerned with punishing the wrongdoer in an attempt to deter others from similar actions.

Another factor distinguishing criminal law from tort law is that criminal law is primarily statutory law. Essentially, a crime is whatever a legislature has declared to be a crime. Although federal crimes are defined by the U.S. Congress, most crimes are defined by state legislatures.

As mentioned in Chapter 5, at one time criminal law was governed primarily by the common law. Over time, common law doctrines and principles were codified, expanded on, and enacted in statutory form. Although many crimes were originally defined by the common law, the statutory definitions of those crimes may differ significantly from the related common law definitions.

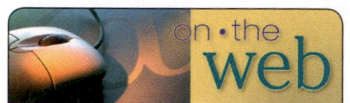

Many state criminal codes are online. To find your state's code, go to **www. findlaw.com**. Under "Browse by Jurisdictions," select "View all states."

The standards of proof required in criminal and civil cases represent another difference. Because the state has extensive resources at its disposal when prosecuting criminal cases, there are procedural safeguards to protect the rights of defendants. One of these safeguards is the higher standard of proof that applies in a criminal case. In a civil case, the plaintiff usually must prove his or her case by a *preponderance of the evidence.* Under this standard, the plaintiff must convince the court that, based on the evidence presented by both parties, it is more likely than not that the plaintiff's allegation is true.

In a criminal case, in contrast, the state must prove its case **beyond a reasonable doubt**—that is, every juror in a criminal case must be convinced, beyond a reasonable doubt, of the defendant's guilt. The higher standard of proof in criminal cases reflects a fundamental social value—a belief that it is worse to convict an innocent individual than to let a guilty person go free. We will look at other safeguards later in the chapter, in the context of criminal procedure.

beyond a reasonable doubt

The standard used to determine the guilt or innocence of a person charged with a crime. To be guilty of a crime, a suspect must be proved guilty "beyond and to the exclusion of every reasonable doubt."

Yet another factor that distinguishes criminal law from tort law is the fact that a criminal act does not necessarily involve a victim, in the sense that the act directly and physically harms another. If Marissa grows marijuana in her backyard for her personal use, she may not be physically or directly harming another's interests, but she is nonetheless committing a crime (in most states and under federal law). Why? Because she is violating a rule of society that has been enacted into law by duly elected representatives of the people.

Civil Liability for Criminal Acts

Note that those who commit crimes may be subject to both civil and criminal liability. For example, suppose Joe is walking down the street, minding his own business, when suddenly a person attacks him. In the struggle, the attacker stabs Joe several times, seriously injuring him. A police officer restrains and arrests the wrongdoer. In separate legal actions, the attacker may be subject both to criminal prosecution by the state and to a tort (civil) lawsuit brought by Joe. Exhibit 13.2 illustrates how the same act can result in both a tort action and a criminal action against the wrongdoer.

Classifications of Crimes

Crimes are generally divided into two broad classifications: felonies and misdemeanors.

EXHIBIT 13.2
Tort (Civil) Lawsuit and Criminal
Prosecution for the Same Act

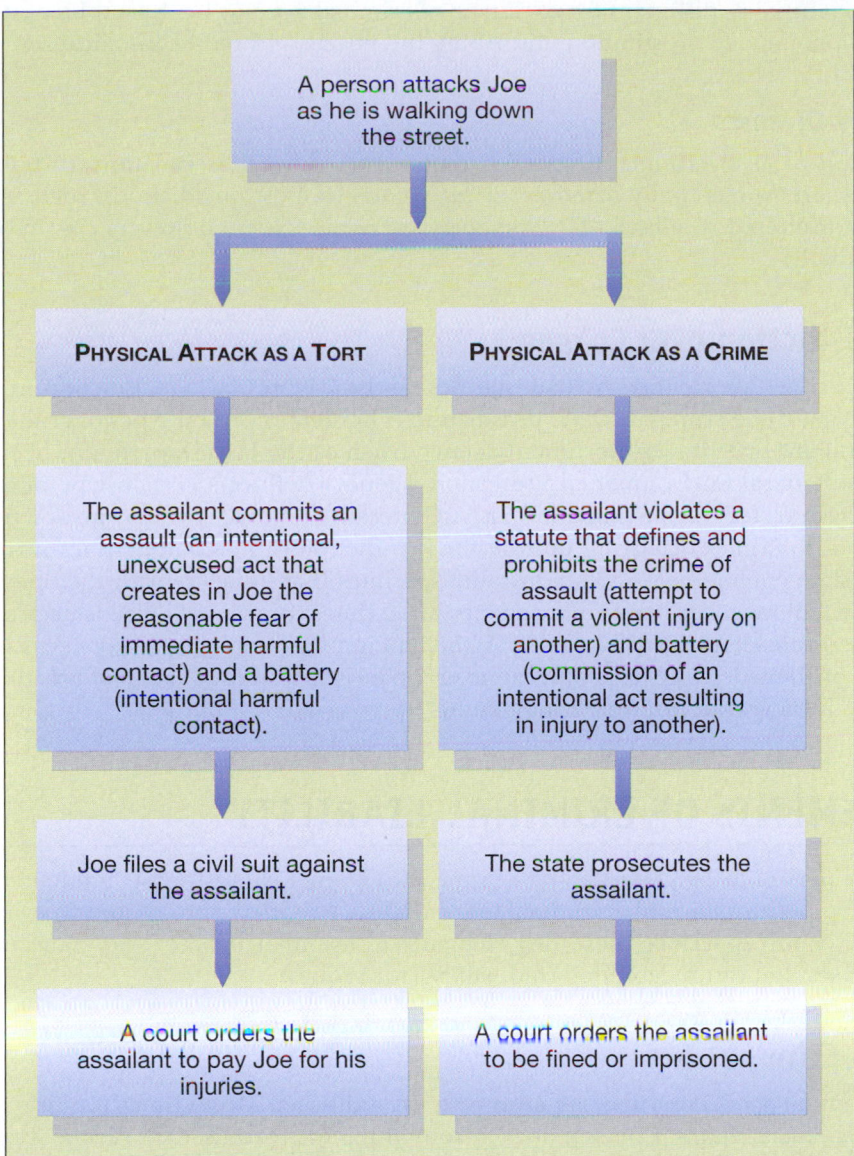

Felonies

A **felony** is a serious crime that may be punished by imprisonment for more than one year. In some states, certain felonies are punishable by death. Examples of felonies include murder, rape, robbery, arson, and grand larceny. (You will read more about these and other crimes later in the chapter.)

Felonies are commonly classified by degree. The Model Penal Code,[1] for example, provides for four degrees of felony: capital offenses, for which the maximum penalty is death; first degree felonies, punishable by a maximum penalty of life imprisonment; second degree felonies, punishable by a maximum of ten years' imprisonment; and third degree felonies, punishable by up to five years' imprisonment.

felony
A crime—such as arson, murder, assault, or robbery—that carries the most severe sanctions. Sanctions range from one year in a state or federal prison to life imprisonment or (in some states) the death penalty.

Misdemeanors

A **misdemeanor** is a crime that may be punished by incarceration for not more than one year. If incarcerated, the guilty party goes to a local jail instead of prison. A misdemeanor, by definition, is a less serious crime. Under federal law and in most states, a misdemeanor is any crime that is not defined by law as a felony. State legislatures specify what crimes are classified as felonies or misdemeanors and what

misdemeanor
A crime less serious than a felony, punishable by a fine or incarceration for up to one year in jail (not a state or federal penitentiary).

the potential punishment for each type of criminal act may be. Examples of misdemeanors include prostitution, disturbing the peace, and public intoxication.

Petty Offenses

petty offense
In criminal law, the least serious kind of wrong, such as a traffic or building-code violation.

Certain types of criminal or quasi-criminal actions, such as violations of building codes, are termed **petty offenses**, or *infractions*. In most jurisdictions, such actions are considered a subset of misdemeanors. Some states, however, classify them separately.

Jurisdiction over Crimes

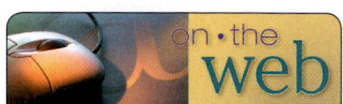

Good sources of statistical data and other information on crime are the Bureau of Justice Statistics at **www.ojp.usdoj.gov** (under "OJP Bureaus and Offices," select "Bureau of Justice Statistics") and the FBI Uniform Crime Reports at **www.fbi.gov** (select "Uniform Crime Statistics" from the "Be Crime Smart" menu).

Most crimes are defined by state statutes, and the states have jurisdiction in cases involving these crimes. Federal jurisdiction is limited to certain types of crimes. If a federal law or federal government agency (such as the U.S. Department of Justice or the federal Environmental Protection Agency) defines a certain type of action as a crime, federal jurisdiction exists. Generally, federal criminal jurisdiction is limited to crimes occurring outside the jurisdiction of any state, crimes involving interstate commerce or communications, crimes that interfere with the operation of the federal government or its agents, and crimes directed at citizens or property located outside the United States. A challenging legal issue today concerns how a state or the federal government can exercise jurisdiction over criminal acts that are committed via the Internet, which knows no geographical borders.

ELEMENTS OF CRIMINAL LIABILITY

For a person to be convicted of a crime, two elements must exist simultaneously: (1) the performance of a criminal act and (2) a specified state of mind, or intent. This section describes these two elements of criminal liability and some of the defenses that can be used to avoid liability for crimes.

The Criminal Act

actus reus
A guilty (prohibited) act. The commission of a prohibited act is one of the two essential elements required for criminal liability; the other element is the intent to commit a crime.

A criminal act is known as the ***actus reus***,[2] or guilty act. Most crimes require an act of *commission*; that is, a person must *do* something to be accused of a crime. In some cases, an act of *omission* can be a crime, but only when a person has a legal duty to perform the omitted act. Failure to file a tax return is an example of an omission that is a crime.

The guilty-act requirement is based on one of the premises of criminal law—that a person is punished for harm done to society. Thinking about killing someone or about stealing a car may be wrong, but the thoughts do no harm unless they are translated into action. Of course, a person can be punished for *attempting* murder or robbery, but normally only if substantial steps toward the criminal objective have been taken.

State of Mind

mens rea
A wrongful mental state, or intent. A wrongful mental state is a requirement for criminal liability. What constitutes a wrongful mental state varies according to the nature of the crime.

Even a completed act that harms society is not legally a crime unless the court finds that the second element—the required state of mind—was present. A wrongful mental state, or **mens rea**,[3] is as necessary as a wrongful act in establishing criminal liability. What constitutes such a mental state varies according to the wrongful action. For murder, the criminal act is the taking of a life, and the mental state is the intent to take life. For theft, the guilty act is the taking of another person's property, and the mental state involves both the knowledge that the property belongs to another and the intent to steal that property. Without the mental state required by law for a particular crime, there is no crime.

The same criminal act can result from varying mental states, and how a crime is defined and punished depends on the degree of "wrongfulness" of the defendant's state of mind. For example, taking another's life is *homicide,* a criminal act. The act can be committed coldly, after premeditation, as in *murder in the first degree,* which carries the most severe criminal penalty. The act can be committed in the heat of passion, as in *voluntary manslaughter,* which carries a less severe penalty than murder. Or the act can be committed as a result of criminal negligence (reckless driving, for example), as in *involuntary manslaughter.* In each of these situations, the law recognizes a different degree of wrongfulness, and the harshness of the punishment depends on the degree to which the act of killing another was an *intentional* act.

Corporate Criminal Liability

At one time, it was thought that a corporation could not incur criminal liability because, although a corporation is a legal person, it can act only through its agents (corporate directors, officers, and employees). Therefore, the corporate entity itself could not "intend" to commit a crime. Under modern criminal law, however, a corporation may be held liable for crimes committed by its agents and employees within the course and scope of their employment. Obviously, corporations cannot be imprisoned, but they can be fined or denied certain legal privileges.

Corporate directors and officers are personally liable for the crimes they commit, regardless of whether the crimes were committed for their personal benefit or on the corporation's behalf. Additionally, corporate directors and officers may be held liable for the actions of employees under their supervision. Under what has become known as the **responsible corporate officer doctrine**, a court may impose criminal liability on a corporate officer regardless of whether she or he participated in, directed, or even knew about a given criminal violation.

For example, in one case the chief executive officer of a national supermarket chain was held personally liable for sanitation violations in corporate warehouses, in which the food was exposed to contamination by rodents. The case was eventually heard by the United States Supreme Court, which held that the corporate officer was personally liable not because he intended the crime or even knew about it but because he was in a "responsible relationship" to the corporation and had the power to prevent the violation.[4] Courts have used similar reasoning to impose criminal liability on corporate managers whose negligence causes harm to the environment in violation of federal law, such as the Clean Water Act (discussed in Chapter 19).

Defenses to Criminal Liability

A person accused of a crime will typically offer a **defense**—a reason why he or she should not be found guilty. Asserting that a defendant lacks the required criminal intent for a specific crime is one way of defending against criminal liability. This defense and others are discussed below.

The Required Mental State Is Lacking

Proving that a defendant did or did not possess the required mental state for a given crime is difficult because a person's state of mind cannot be known. For example, assume that Jackson shot and killed Avery. Jackson is arrested and charged with the crime of murder. Jackson contends that he did not commit murder because he was too drunk to know what he was doing and thus lacked the required mental state for murder—intent to kill. Instead, Jackson claims, he committed the crime of involuntary manslaughter. There will most certainly have to be some facts in evidence tending to show that Jackson was indeed so drunk that he could not have intended to kill Avery.

Criminal defendants may assert that they lacked the required degree of criminal intent for other reasons, including *insanity* (the inability to distinguish between

responsible corporate officer doctrine

A common law doctrine under which the court may impose criminal liability on a corporate officer for actions of employees under her or his supervision regardless of whether she or he participated in, directed, or even knew about those actions.

defense

The evidence and arguments presented in the defendant's support in a criminal action or lawsuit.

right and wrong due to diminished mental capacity), *duress* (which exists when one is forced to commit a specific act), or *mistake* (for example, taking someone else's property, such as a briefcase, thinking that it is one's own).

Protection of Persons or Property

We all have the right to protect ourselves from physical attacks by others; this is the right of **self-defense**. In most states, the force we use to protect ourselves must be reasonable under the circumstances, though. The force used must be justified by the degree of threat posed in a given situation. If someone is about to take your life, the use of *deadly force* (shooting that person with a gun, for example) might be deemed reasonable. If, however, someone in a shopping mall tries to pick your pocket to steal your wallet, you normally do not have a right to shoot the thief, because there was no physical threat to your person.

Similarly, we have the right to use force in **defense of others** if they are threatened with imminent harm. If you and a friend are walking down a city street one night and someone attacks and threatens to kill your friend, you are justified in using whatever force is reasonable under the circumstances to protect your friend. As with self-defense, it must be shown that the force used was reasonable in view of the nature of the threat.

We also have the right to use reasonable force in the **defense of property**. In particular, if someone is trespassing on our property or is stealing our property, we have the right to use force to stop the trespassing or prevent the theft; again, the amount of force used must be reasonable. Because human life has a higher value than property, deadly force is normally not allowed in the protection of property unless the thief or trespasser poses a threat to human life.

Depending on the situation, the *castle doctrine* may come into play. This doctrine is based on the common law concept that you have a right to defend your home (your castle), yourself, your property, or an innocent person from the illegal acts of another. In general, if an intruder is in a home, the legal residents of the home do not have a *duty to retreat*. Rather, they have an express right to *stand their ground*. About half the states have expressed this principle in legislation, but the details of how the principle is applied vary significantly across the states.

Statutes of Limitations

With some exceptions, such as for the crime of murder, statutes of limitations apply to crimes just as they do to civil wrongs. In other words, criminal cases must be prosecuted within a certain number of years. If a criminal action is brought after the statutory time period has expired, the accused person can raise the statute of limitations as a defense.

Other Defenses

Further defenses include *mistaken identity* and other reasons why the criminal charges might not be valid. For example, a defendant may offer an *alibi* (proof that the defendant was somewhere else at the time of the crime, for example) as a defense. Still other defenses to criminal liability have to do with violations of procedural law. For example, the police officers who arrested the defendant must have had the proper authority to do so, and the court in which the action is brought must have jurisdiction over the subject matter of the case and over the person brought before the court.

Because criminal law brings the force of the state, with all its resources, to bear against the individual, law enforcement authorities must abide by the letter of procedural law when arresting and prosecuting a person accused of a crime. If they do not, the defendant may be able to use the prosecution's violations of procedural laws as a defense, depending on the nature of the right that was violated and the degree of violation.

---

self-defense

The legally recognized privilege to protect oneself or one's property against injury by another. The privilege of self-defense only protects acts that are reasonably necessary to protect oneself or one's property.

defense of others

The use of reasonable force to protect others from harm.

defense of property

The use of reasonable force to protect one's property from harm threatened by another. The use of deadly force in defending one's property is seldom justified.

TYPES OF CRIMES

The number of acts defined as criminal is nearly endless. Federal, state, and local laws provide for the classification and punishment of thousands of different criminal acts. Traditionally, though, crimes have been grouped into five broad categories, or types: violent crime (crimes against persons), property crime, public order crime, white-collar crime, and organized crime.

Violent Crime

Crimes against persons, because they cause others to suffer harm or death, are referred to as *violent crimes.* Murder is a violent crime. So is sexual assault, or rape, and assault and battery (discussed further in Chapter 14). **Robbery**—defined as the taking of money, personal property, or any other article of value from a person by means of force or fear—is another violent crime. Typically, states have more severe penalties for *aggravated robbery*—robbery with the use of a deadly weapon.

Each of these violent crimes is further classified by degree, depending on the circumstances surrounding the criminal act. These circumstances include the intent of the person committing the crime, whether a weapon was used, and the level of pain and suffering experienced by the victim. For example, at common law, killing another human being could result in one of three different offenses, depending on the defendant's intent: murder (if the killing was intentional), voluntary manslaughter (if intentional but provoked), or involuntary manslaughter (if the killing was unintentional but resulted from criminal negligence or an unlawful act, such as drunk driving).

Most states follow the common law classifications of homicide but add degrees of murder to provide penalties of different severity. For example, deliberate and premeditated killing is usually first degree murder (a *capital offense*—a crime possibly punishable by death). First degree murder may also include killings committed during certain types of felonies, such as arson, burglary, rape, or robbery. When a person is killed during other types of felonies, the charge is likely to be second degree murder, which is typically not punishable by death.

robbery
The taking of money, personal property, or any other article of value from a person by means of force or fear.

Property Crime

The most common type of criminal activity is property crime—a crime in which the goal of the offender is some form of economic gain or damage to property. Robbery is a form of property crime, as well as a violent crime, because the offender seeks to gain the property of another. Other property crimes are discussed next.

Burglary

Burglary usually involves breaking and entering onto the property of another with the intent to commit a felony. A burglary does not necessarily involve theft. The defendant may have intended to commit some other felony and still be guilty of burglary.

burglary
Breaking and entering onto the property of another with the intent to commit a felony.

Larceny

Any person who wrongfully or fraudulently takes and carries away another person's personal property is guilty of **larceny**. In other words, larceny is "stealing." To be guilty of larceny, the person must have intended to deprive the owner permanently of the property. Larceny does not involve force or fear (as in robbery) or breaking into a building (as in burglary). Taking company products and supplies home for personal use, if one is not authorized to do so, is larceny. In addition, many states have expanded the definition of larceny to include thefts of computer files, computer time, and electricity. Although the common law distinguished between grand

larceny
The wrongful or fraudulent taking and carrying away of another person's personal property with the intent to deprive the person permanently of the property.

larceny (a felony) and petit larceny (a misdemeanor) depending on the value of the property taken, many states have abolished this distinction.

Obtaining Goods by False Pretenses

It is a criminal act to obtain goods by means of false pretenses—for example, buying groceries with a check, knowing that there are insufficient funds to cover it. Statutes dealing with such illegal activities vary widely from state to state.

Receiving Stolen Goods

It is a crime to receive stolen goods. The recipient of such goods need not know the true identity of the owner or the thief. All that is necessary is that the recipient knew or *should have known* that the goods were stolen (which implies the intent to deprive the owner of those goods). In other words, if someone sells you a new laptop for ten dollars from the back of a truck full of laptops, you may be guilty of receiving stolen property.

Arson

arson
The willful and malicious burning of a building (and, in some states, personal property) owned by another; arson statutes have been extended to cover the destruction of any building, regardless of ownership, by fire or explosion.

The willful and malicious burning of a building (and, in some states, personal property) owned by another is the crime of **arson**. At common law, arson traditionally applied only to burning down another person's house. Today, arson statutes have been extended to cover the destruction of any building by fire or explosion. Every state also has a special statute that covers burning a building for the purpose of collecting insurance.

Forgery

forgery
The fraudulent making or altering of any writing in a way that changes the legal rights and liabilities of another.

The fraudulent making or altering of any writing in a way that changes the legal rights and liabilities of another is **forgery**. If, without authorization, Tyler signs Ben's name to the back of a check made out to Ben, Tyler is committing forgery. Forgery also includes changing trademarks, falsifying public records, counterfeiting, and altering a legal document.

Public Order Crime

Historically, societies have always outlawed activities considered to be contrary to public values and morals. Today, the most common public order crimes include public drunkenness, prostitution, gambling, and illegal drug use. These crimes are sometimes referred to as victimless crimes because they potentially could harm only the offender. From a broader perspective, however, they are deemed detrimental to society as a whole because they are thought to create an environment that gives rise to property and violent crimes.

White-Collar Crime

white-collar crime
A crime that typically occurs in a business context; popularly used to refer to an illegal act or series of acts committed by a person or business entity using nonviolent means.

Crimes that typically occur in the business context are commonly referred to as **white-collar crime**s. One of today's most famous white-collar criminals is Bernard Madoff, who pleaded guilty in 2009 to defrauding clients of his failed investment firm, which lost some $65 billion. Although there is no official definition of white-collar crime, the term is popularly used to mean an illegal act or series of acts committed by a person or business entity using some nonviolent means. Usually, this kind of crime is committed in the course of a legitimate occupation. Corporate crimes fall into this category.

Embezzlement

embezzlement
The fraudulent appropriation of the property or money of another by a person entrusted with that property or money.

When a person entrusted with another person's property fraudulently takes it, **embezzlement** occurs. Typically, embezzlement involves an employee who steals funds. Banks face this problem, and so do a number of businesses in which corpo-

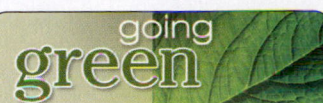

rate officers or accountants "jimmy" the books to cover up the fraudulent taking of funds for their own benefit. Embezzlement is not larceny, because the wrongdoer does not physically take the property from the possession of another, and it is not robbery, because force or fear is not used.

Mail and Wire Fraud

One of the most potent weapons against white-collar criminals is the Mail Fraud Act. Under this act, it is a federal crime (mail fraud) to use the mails to defraud the public. Illegal use of the mails must involve (1) mailing or causing someone else to mail something written, printed, or photocopied for the purpose of executing a scheme to defraud and (2) a contemplated or an organized scheme to defraud by false pretenses. If, for example, Johnson advertises by mail the sale of a cure for cancer that he knows to be fraudulent because it has no medical validity, he can be prosecuted for fraudulent use of the mails.

Federal law also makes it a crime (called *wire fraud*) to use the telephone to defraud. In addition, under the same statute, it is a crime to use almost any means of public communication, such as radio, television, or the Internet, to defraud. Violators may be fined up to $1,000, imprisoned for up to five years, or both. If the violation affects a financial institution, the violator may be fined up to $1 million, imprisoned for up to thirty years, or both.

Bribery

Basically, three types of bribery are considered crimes: bribery of public officials, commercial bribery, and bribery of foreign officials. The attempt to influence a public official to act in a way that serves a private interest is a crime. As an element of this crime, intent must be present and proved. The bribe can be anything the recipient considers to be valuable. Realize that *the crime of bribery occurs when the bribe is offered.* It does not matter whether the bribe is accepted. *Accepting a bribe* is a separate crime.

Typically, people make commercial bribes to obtain information, cover up an inferior product, or secure new business. For example, a person in one business may offer an employee in a competing business some type of payoff in exchange for trade secrets or pricing schedules. So-called *kickbacks,* or payoffs for special favors or services, are a form of commercial bribery in some situations. Bribing foreign officials to obtain favorable business contracts is also a crime.

Bankruptcy Fraud

Today, federal bankruptcy law allows individuals and businesses to be relieved of oppressive debt through bankruptcy proceedings, as will be explained in Chapter 19. Numerous white-collar crimes may be committed during the many phases of a bankruptcy proceeding. A creditor, for example, may file a false claim against the debtor, which is a crime. Also, a debtor may fraudulently transfer assets to favored parties before or after the petition for bankruptcy is filed. For example, a company-owned automobile may be "sold" at a bargain price to a trusted friend or relative. It is also a crime for the debtor to fraudulently conceal property during bankruptcy, such as by hiding gold coins.

Theft of Trade Secrets

As will be discussed in Chapter 15, trade secrets constitute a form of intellectual property that for many businesses can be extremely valuable. The Economic Espionage Act made the theft of trade secrets a federal crime. The act also made it a federal crime to buy or possess trade secrets, knowing that the trade secrets were stolen or otherwise acquired without the owner's authorization.

Violations of the act can result in steep penalties. An individual who violates the act can be imprisoned for up to fifteen years and fined up to $500,000. If a corporation or other organization violates the act, it can be fined up to $10 million. Additionally, the law provides that any property acquired as a result of the violation and any property used in the commission of the violation are subject to criminal *forfeiture*—meaning that the government can take the property. A theft of trade secrets conducted via the Internet, for example, could result in the forfeiture of every computer or other device used to commit or facilitate the violation.

Insider Trading

An individual who obtains "inside information" about the plans or financial status of a corporation with publicly traded stock can make profits by using the information to guide decisions about the purchase or sale of the stock. **Insider trading** is a violation of securities law that subjects the violator to criminal penalties. One who possesses inside information and who has a duty not to disclose it to outsiders may not profit from the purchase or sale of securities based on that information until the information is available to the public.

Organized Crime

As mentioned, white-collar crime takes place within the confines of the legitimate business world. *Organized crime,* in contrast, operates *illegitimately* by, among other things, providing illegal goods and services. For organized crime, the traditional preferred markets are gambling, prostitution, illegal narcotics, pornography, and loan sharking (lending funds at higher-than-legal interest rates), along with more recent ventures into counterfeiting and credit-card scams.

Money Laundering

The profits from illegal activities, particularly illegal drug transactions, amount to billions of dollars a year. Under federal law, banks and other financial institutions are required to report currency transactions involving more than $10,000. Consequently, those who engage in illegal activities face difficulties in depositing their cash profits from illegal transactions.

As an alternative to simply storing cash from illegal transactions in a safe-deposit box, wrongdoers and racketeers have invented ways to launder "dirty" money to make it "clean." This **money laundering** is done through legitimate businesses. For example, suppose that Matt, a successful drug dealer, becomes a partner with a restaurant owner. Little by little, the restaurant shows an increasing profit because Matt is falsely reporting income obtained through drug dealing as restaurant income. As a partner in the restaurant, Matt is able to report the "profit" as legitimate income on which he pays federal and state taxes. He can then spend that income without worrying that his lifestyle may exceed the level possible with his reported income.

The Racketeer Influenced and Corrupt Organizations Act (RICO)

To curb the entry of organized crime into the legitimate business world, Congress passed the Racketeer Influenced and Corrupt Organizations Act (RICO). The act makes it a federal crime to (1) use income obtained from racketeering activity to purchase any interest in an enterprise, (2) acquire or maintain an interest in an enterprise through racketeering activity, (3) conduct or participate in the affairs of an enterprise through racketeering activity, or (4) conspire to do any of the preceding activities. Today, RICO is used more often to attack white-collar crime than organized crime.

Racketeering activity is not a new type of crime created by RICO; rather, RICO incorporates by reference many federal crimes and state felonies and declares that

---

insider trading

Trading in the stock of a publicly listed corporation based on inside information. One who possesses inside information and has a duty not to disclose it to outsiders may not profit from the purchase or sale of securities based on that information until the information is available to the public.

money laundering

Falsely reporting income that has been obtained through criminal activity, such as illegal drug transactions, as income obtained through a legitimate business enterprise to make the "dirty" money "clean."

if a person commits *two* of these offenses, he or she is guilty of "racketeering activity." Any individual found guilty of a violation is subject to a fine of up to $25,000 per violation, imprisonment for up to twenty years, or both. Additionally, the statute provides that those who violate RICO may be required to forfeit any assets, in the form of property or cash, that were acquired as a result of the illegal activity or that were "involved in" or an "instrumentality of" the activity.

CYBER CRIMES

Many crimes are committed with computers and occur in cyberspace. These crimes fall under the broad label of **cyber crime**. Most cyber crimes are not "new" crimes. Rather, they are existing crimes in which the Internet is the instrument of wrongdoing. The challenge for law enforcement is to apply traditional laws—which were designed to protect persons from physical harm or to safeguard their physical property—to new methods of committing crime. Here, we look at several types of cyber crimes against persons and property.

cyber crime
A crime that occurs online, in the virtual community of the Internet, as opposed to the physical world.

Cyber Theft

In cyberspace, thieves are not subject to the physical limitations of the "real" world. A thief with Internet access could, in theory, steal data stored in a networked computer anywhere on the globe. Cyber theft is a growing problem.

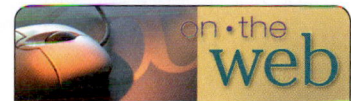

The FBI has a "cyber mission" that focuses on various aspects of cyber crime. To learn more, go to **www.fbi.gov**, and select "Cyber" from the "What We Investigate" list.

Financial Crimes

Computer networks provide opportunities for employees to commit crimes that involve serious economic losses. For example, employees of a company's accounting department can transfer funds among accounts with little effort and often with less risk than would be involved in paper transactions. The dependence of businesses on computer operations has left many companies vulnerable to sabotage, fraud, embezzlement, and the theft of proprietary data, such as trade secrets or other intellectual property.

Identity Theft

A form of cyber theft that has become particularly troublesome is **identity theft**. Identity theft occurs when the wrongdoer steals a form of identification—such as a name, date of birth, or Social Security number—and uses the information to access the victim's financial resources. This crime existed to a certain extent before the widespread use of the Internet. Thieves would "steal" calling-card numbers by watching people using public telephones, or they would rifle through garbage to find bank account or credit-card numbers. The Internet, however, turned identity theft into a fast-growing financial crime in the United States. The Internet provides not only another way to steal personal information but also a way for those who steal information to use items such as stolen credit-card numbers while protected by anonymity. Millions of Americans are victims of identity theft each year.

identity theft
The theft of a form of identification, such as a name, date of birth, or Social Security number, which is then used to access the victim's financial resources.

Cyberstalking

California passed the first antistalking law in 1990, in response to the murders of six women by stalkers. The law made it a crime to harass or follow a person while making a "credible threat" that puts the person in reasonable fear for her safety or the safety of her immediate family. Most states and the federal government followed with similar antistalking legislation.

Later, it became clear that these laws, which required a "physical act" such as following the victim, were insufficient. They could not protect persons against

cyberstalking, in which the perpetrator harasses the victim using the Internet, e-mail, or some other electronic communication. In 1998, California amended its stalking statute to include threats made through an electronic communication device. Today, the federal government and most states also have legislation that criminalizes cyberstalking.

The Threat of Cyberstalking

Cyberstalkers use various methods to harass their victims. They may send threatening e-mail messages directly to the victim or menace the victim in a chat room. Some cyberstalkers deceive other Internet users into harassing or threatening their victim by impersonating that victim while making provocative comments online.

Although no trustworthy statistics exist, most experts assume that cyberstalking is more commonplace than physical stalking. While it takes a great deal of effort to stalk someone physically, it is relatively easy to harass a victim with electronic messages. Furthermore, the possibility of personal confrontation may discourage a stalker from physically pursuing his victim. No such confrontation occurs in cyberspace. Finally, physical stalking requires that the stalker and the victim be in the same location. A cyberstalker can carry on activities from anywhere. The only requirement is an Internet or cell phone connection.

Cyberbullying

A related problem that has been on the rise is **cyberbullying**. It involves the use of communication technologies to support deliberate, repeated, and hostile behavior that harms others. The National Crime Prevention Council notes that cyberbullying may occur when the Internet and cell phones are used to send or post text or images intended to hurt or embarrass another person. The problem has been most pronounced for school-age children.

Some cyberbullying has occurred through social networks, such as Facebook and MySpace. The first case of this kind that drew national attention resulted in a trial in 2008. A woman, Lori Drew, was charged with computer fraud for creating a MySpace account for a fictitious person, a teenage boy named Josh Evans. Drew's intention was to help her daughter, Sarah, intimidate a thirteen-year-old classmate, Megan Meier. The fictitious "Josh" struck up an online friendship with Megan, but "his" communications became increasingly hostile. One day, "Josh" told Megan, via the MySpace account, that "the world would be a better place without you." Shortly afterward, Megan hanged herself. This case and others led state legislatures to begin discussing new legislation to deal directly with cyberbullying.

Hacking

Persons who use one computer to break into another are sometimes referred to as **hackers**. Hackers who break into computers without authorization often commit cyber theft. Sometimes, however, the principal aim of hackers is to cause random data errors on others' computers.

It is difficult to know how frequently hackers succeed in breaking into databases across the United States. The Federal Bureau of Investigation has estimated that only 25 percent of all corporations that suffer such security breaches report the incident to a law enforcement agency. For one thing, corporations do not want it to become publicly known that the security of their data has been breached. Admitting to a breach would be admitting to a certain degree of incompetence, which could damage their reputations.

Prosecuting Cyber Crimes

The Internet has raised new issues in the investigation of crimes and the prosecution of offenders. As discussed in Chapter 6, the issue of jurisdiction presents difficulties in cyberspace. Identifying the wrongdoers can also be difficult. Cyber criminals do not leave physical traces, such as fingerprints or DNA samples, as evidence of their crimes. Even electronic "footprints" can be hard to find and follow. For example, e-mail can be sent through a remailer, an online service that guarantees that a message cannot be traced to its source.

For these reasons, laws written to protect physical property are difficult to apply in cyberspace. Nonetheless, governments at both the state and federal levels have taken significant steps, sometimes working with foreign authorities, toward controlling cyber crime, both by applying existing criminal statutes and by enacting laws that specifically address wrongs committed in cyberspace.

The Computer Fraud and Abuse Act

Perhaps the most significant federal statute specifically addressing cyber crime is the Counterfeit Access Device and Computer Fraud and Abuse Act. This act provides, among other things, that a person who accesses or attempts to access a computer online, without authority, to obtain classified, restricted, or protected data is subject to criminal prosecution. Such data could include financial and credit records, medical records, legal files, military and national security files, and other confidential information in government or private computers. The crime has two elements: accessing a computer without authority and taking the data. This theft is a felony if it is committed for a commercial purpose or for private financial gain or if the value of the stolen data (or computer time) exceeds $5,000. Penalties include fines and imprisonment for up to twenty years. In addition, a victim of computer theft can bring a civil suit against the violator to obtain damages, an injunction, and other relief.

Other Federal Statutes

The federal wire fraud statute, the Economic Espionage Act, and RICO, which were discussed earlier, extend to crimes committed in cyberspace. Two other federal statutes that may apply are the Electronic Fund Transfer Act, which makes unauthorized access to an electronic fund transfer system a crime, and the Anticounterfeiting Consumer Protection Act, which increased penalties for stealing copyrighted or trademarked property.

CONSTITUTIONAL SAFEGUARDS

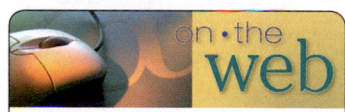

From the moment a crime is reported until the trial concludes, law enforcement officers and prosecutors must follow the specific criminal procedures that have been established to protect an accused person's constitutional rights. Before allowing a case to go to trial, the prosecutor and paralegals assigned to the case review all pretrial events closely to make sure that requirements have been properly observed. Defense attorneys and their legal assistants also investigate and review the actions of arresting and investigating police officers in an attempt to obtain grounds for a dismissal of the charges against their clients.

The U.S. Constitution provides specific procedural safeguards to protect persons accused of crimes against the potentially arbitrary or unjust use of government power. These safeguards are spelled out in the Fourth, Fifth, Sixth, and Eighth Amendments to the U.S. Constitution and are summarized below. The full text of the Constitution is presented in Appendix J.

1. The Fourth Amendment prohibits unreasonable searches and seizures and requires a showing of probable cause (which will be discussed shortly) before a search or an arrest warrant may be issued.

2. The Fifth Amendment requires that no one shall be deprived of "life, liberty, or property without due process of law." **Due process of law** means that the

> The American Civil Liberties Union (ACLU) advocates protection of civil liberties. You can learn about some of the constitutional questions raised by various criminal laws and procedures by going to the ACLU's Web site at **www. aclu.org**.

due process of law
Fair, reasonable, and standard procedures that must be used by the government in any legal action against a citizen. The Fifth Amendment to the U.S. Constitution prohibits the deprivation of "life, liberty, or property without due process of law."

government must follow a set of reasonable, fair, and standard procedures (that is, criminal procedural law) in any action against a citizen.

3. The Fifth Amendment prohibits **double jeopardy** (trying someone twice for the same criminal offense).

4. The Fifth Amendment guarantees that no person shall be "compelled in any criminal case to be a witness against himself." This is known as the privilege against compulsory **self-incrimination**.

5. The Sixth Amendment guarantees a speedy and public trial, a trial by jury, the right to confront witnesses, and the right to a lawyer at various stages in some proceedings.

6. The Eighth Amendment prohibits excessive bail and fines and cruel and unusual punishment.

double jeopardy
To place at risk (jeopardize) a person's life or liberty twice. The Fifth Amendment to the Constitution prohibits a second prosecution for the same criminal offense.

self-incrimination
The act of giving testimony that implicates oneself in criminal wrongdoing. The Fifth Amendment to the Constitution states that no person "shall be compelled in any criminal case to be a witness against himself."

exclusionary rule
In criminal procedure, a rule under which any evidence obtained in violation of the accused's constitutional rights, as well as any evidence derived from illegally obtained evidence, will not be admissible in court.

The Exclusionary Rule

Under what is known as the **exclusionary rule**, all evidence obtained in violation of the constitutional rights spelled out in the Fourth, Fifth, and Sixth Amendments normally is excluded from the trial, along with all evidence derived from the improperly obtained evidence. Evidence derived from illegally obtained evidence is known as the "fruit of the poisonous tree." For example, if during an illegal search drugs are obtained, the search is "the poisonous tree," and the drugs are the "fruit," which normally will be excluded from evidence if the case is brought to trial.

The purpose of the exclusionary rule is to deter police from conducting warrantless searches and from engaging in other misconduct. The rule is sometimes criticized because it can lead to injustice. Many a defendant has "gotten off on a technicality" because law enforcement personnel failed to observe procedural requirements. Even though a defendant may be obviously guilty, if the evidence of that guilt was obtained improperly (without a valid search warrant, for example), it normally cannot be used against the defendant in court.

Miranda rights
Certain constitutional rights of accused persons taken into custody by law enforcement officials, such as the right to remain silent and the right to counsel, as established by the United States Supreme Court's decision in *Miranda v. Arizona.*

The *Miranda* Rule

In *Miranda v. Arizona,*[5] a case decided in 1966, the United States Supreme Court established the rule that individuals who are arrested must be informed of certain constitutional rights, including their Fifth Amendment right to remain silent and their Sixth Amendment right to counsel. These rights, which have come to be called the **Miranda rights**, are listed in Exhibit 13.3. If the arresting officers fail to

EXHIBIT 13.3
The *Miranda* Rights

On taking a criminal suspect into custody and before any interrogation takes place, law enforcement officers are required to communicate the following rights and facts to the suspect:

1. **The right to remain silent.**

2. **That any statements made may be used against the person in a court of law.**

3. **The right to talk to a lawyer and have a lawyer present while being questioned.**

4. **If the person cannot afford to hire a lawyer, the right to have a lawyer provided at no cost.**

In addition to being advised of these rights, the suspect must be asked if he or she understands the rights and whether he or she wishes to exercise the rights or waive (not exercise) the rights.

inform a criminal suspect of these constitutional rights, any statements the suspect makes normally are not admissible in court. It is important to note that the police are not required to give *Miranda* warnings until the individual is placed in custody. Thus, if a person who is not in custody makes voluntary admissions to an officer, these statements are admissible.

The exact meaning of the *Miranda* rule is subject to frequent tests in the courts. Over time, as part of a continuing attempt to balance the rights of accused persons against the rights of society, the United States Supreme Court has carved out numerous exceptions to the rule. The Court has, for example, recognized a "public safety" exception. Under this exception, the need to protect the public may warrant the admission of statements made by the defendant as evidence at trial, even though the defendant was not informed of his *Miranda* rights.

The Supreme Court has also held that a confession need not be excluded even though the police failed to inform a suspect in custody that his attorney had tried to reach him by telephone. Furthermore, the Court has stated that a suspect's conviction will not be overturned solely on the ground that the suspect was coerced into making a confession by law enforcement personnel. If other, legally obtained evidence admitted at trial is strong enough to justify the conviction without the confession, then the fact that the confession was obtained illegally can, in effect, be ignored.

If you are interested in reading the Supreme Court's opinion in *Miranda v. Arizona*, go to **www.law.cornell.edu**. From the "Court opinions" menu, select "U.S. Supreme Court Opinions." Then, under "Archive of decisions," select "By party, historic," and look under the letter "M" for the case name.

CRIMINAL PROCEDURES PRIOR TO PROSECUTION

Although the Constitution guarantees due process of law to individuals accused of committing crimes, the actual steps involved in bringing a criminal action vary significantly depending on the jurisdiction and type of crime. In this section, we provide an overview of the basic procedures that take place before an individual is prosecuted for a crime. Exhibit 13.4 on the next page illustrates a general outline of criminal procedure in both federal and state cases. Because of the many procedural variations, however, a paralegal involved in a criminal case will need to research the specific procedural requirements that apply to the case. (The many roles paralegals can play in criminal cases are described in this chapter's *Featured Contributor* article on pages 438 and 439.)

Arrest and Booking

An **arrest** occurs when police officers take a person into custody and charge that person with a crime. After the arrest, the police typically search the suspect and take the suspect to a *holding facility* (usually at the police station or a jail), where booking occurs. **Booking** refers to the process of entering a suspect's name, the offense for which the suspect is being held, and the time of arrival into the police log (computer). The suspect is then fingerprinted and photographed, told the reason for the arrest, and allowed to make a phone call. If the crime is not serious, the officer may then release the suspect on personal recognizance—that is, on the suspect's promise to appear before a court at some later date. Otherwise, the suspect may be held in custody pending an initial appearance in court (which generally occurs within a few days).

Obviously, law enforcement personnel are in control of the arrest and booking of suspects. Paralegals and attorneys usually are not involved until after an arrest has been made. The defense will, however, look closely to see that the proper procedure was followed in the arrest of the client. An officer can legally arrest a person with or without a warrant, as long as the officer has probable cause to believe that the person committed a crime (discussed shortly). Before an officer questions a suspect who has been arrested, the officer must give the *Miranda* warnings discussed earlier.

arrest
To take into custody a person suspected of criminal activity.

booking
The process of entering a suspect's name, offense, and arrival time into the police log (blotter) following his or her arrest.

EXHIBIT 13.4
Major Procedural
Steps in a Criminal Case

ARREST

Police officer takes suspect into custody. Most arrests are made without a warrant. After the arrest, the officer searches the suspect, who is then taken to the police station.

⬇

BOOKING

At the police station, the suspect is searched again, photographed, fingerprinted, and allowed at least one telephone call. After the booking, charges are reviewed, and if they are not dropped, a complaint is filed and a magistrate reviews the case for probable cause.

⬇

INITIAL APPEARANCE

The suspect appears before the magistrate, who informs the suspect of the charges and of his or her rights. If the suspect requires a lawyer, one is appointed. The magistrate sets bail (conditions under which a suspect can obtain release pending disposition of the case).

⬇

GRAND JURY

A grand jury determines if there is probable cause to believe that the defendant committed the crime. The federal government and about half of the states require grand jury indictments for at least some felonies.

PRELIMINARY HEARING

In a court proceeding, a prosecutor presents evidence, and the judge determines if there is probable cause to hold the defendant over for trial.

⬇

INDICTMENT

The grand jury formally charges a criminal suspect by issuing an indictment.

INFORMATION

The prosecutor formally charges a criminal suspect by filing an information, or criminal complaint.

⬇

ARRAIGNMENT

The suspect is brought before the trial court, informed of the charges, and asked to enter a plea.

⬇

PLEA BARGAIN

The prosecutor may offer a plea bargain. A plea bargain is a prosecutor's promise to make concessions (or promise to seek concessions) in return for a suspect's guilty plea. Concessions may include a reduced charge or a lesser sentence.

⬇

GUILTY PLEA

In most jurisdictions, most cases that reach the arraignment stage do not go to trial but are resolved by a guilty plea, often as a result of a plea bargain. The judge sets the case for sentencing.

TRIAL

Generally, most felony trials are jury trials, and most misdemeanor trials are bench trials (trials before judges). If the verdict is "guilty," the judge sets the case for sentencing. Everyone convicted of a crime has the right to an appeal.

Detention Is Not an Arrest

Before we discuss probable cause, it is important to note that an arrest differs from a *stop* or *detention*, such as a traffic stop. Police officers have a right to stop and detain a person if they have a *reasonable suspicion* that the person committed, or is about to commit, a crime. Reasonable suspicion is a much lower standard than probable cause—because stopping a person is much less invasive than arresting the person. That means, for example, that an officer can stop a person who matches the description of an assailant in the neighborhood based on reasonable suspicion. The officer can even "frisk" the person being detained (pat down the person's clothes) to make sure the person is not carrying a weapon. The officer cannot legally arrest any person, however, without probable cause.

Probable Cause

The requirement of **probable cause** is a key factor that is assessed repeatedly throughout the various stages of criminal proceedings. The first stage, arrest, requires probable cause. In the context of arrest, probable cause exists if there is a substantial likelihood that both of the following events occurred:

1. A crime was committed.
2. The individual committed the crime.

Note that probable cause involves a *likelihood*—not just a possibility—that the suspect committed the crime. It is not enough that the police officer suspects that the individual has committed a crime. It must be likely. The probable cause requirement stems from the Fourth Amendment, which prohibits unreasonable searches and seizures.

If a police officer observes a crime being committed, the officer can arrest the wrongdoer on the spot without a warrant, because the probable cause requirement is met. If a victim or some other person reports a crime to the police, the police must decide whether there is enough information about the alleged wrongdoer's guilt to establish probable cause to arrest. What is and is not considered probable cause can vary depending on the case law in the particular jurisdiction. Usually, if the suspect is at home at the time of the arrest, the police will need to obtain an arrest warrant (unless the police pursued the suspect to the home or some other emergency circumstance exists).

probable cause	Reasonable grounds to believe the existence of facts warranting certain actions, such as the search or arrest of a person.

Warrants

Often, the police try to gather information to help them determine whether a suspect should be arrested. If, after investigating the matter, the police decide to arrest the suspect, they must obtain an **arrest warrant** from a judge or other public official. To obtain this warrant, the police will have to convince the official, usually through supporting affidavits, that probable cause exists. The warrant process is discussed further in the *Developing Paralegal Skills* feature on page 436.

Probable cause is also required to obtain a **search warrant**, which authorizes police officers or other criminal investigators to search specifically named persons or property for evidence and to seize the evidence if they find it (see Exhibit 13.5 on the following two pages). Probable cause requires law enforcement officials to have trustworthy evidence that would convince a reasonable person that the proposed search or seizure is more likely justified than not. Furthermore, the Fourth Amendment prohibits general warrants. It requires a particular description of that which is to be searched or seized. Once a warrant is obtained, the search cannot extend beyond what is described in the warrant. General searches through a person's belongings are impermissible.

There are exceptions to the requirement for a search warrant. For example, if an officer is arresting a person (either with an arrest warrant or sufficient probable

arrest warrant
A written order, based on probable cause and issued by a judge or public official (magistrate), commanding that the person named on the warrant be arrested by the police.

search warrant
A written order, based on probable cause and issued by a judge or public official (magistrate), commanding that police officers or criminal investigators search a specific person, place, or property to obtain evidence.

Ch. 89   SEARCH AND SEIZURE   § 7942
Rule 41

§ 7942. Search Warrant

AO 93 (Rev. 5/85) Search Warrant ⊕

United States District Court

_____ DISTRICT OF _____

In the Matter of the Search of
(Name, address or brief description of person or property to be searched)

SEARCH WARRANT

CASE NUMBER:

TO: _____ and any Authorized Officer of the United States

Affidavit(s) having been made before me by_____who has reason to
                                          Affiant

believe that ☐ on the person of or ☐ on the premises known as (name, description and/or location)

in the _____ District of _____ there is now
concealed a certain person or property, namely (describe the person or property)

I am satisfied that the affidavit(s) and any recorded testimony establish probable cause to believe that the person
or property so described is now concealed on the person or premises above-described and establish grounds for
the issuance of this warrant.

YOU ARE HEREBY COMMANDED to search on or before _____
                                                              Date

(not to exceed 10 days) the person or place named above for the person or property specified, serving this warrant
and making the search (in the daytime — 6:00 A.M. to 10:00 P.M.) (at any time in the day or night as I find
reasonable cause has been established) and if the person or property be found there to seize same, leaving a copy
of this warrant and receipt for the person or property taken, and prepare a written inventory of the person or property seized and promptly return this warrant to _____
as required by law.   U.S Judge or Magistrate

_____ at _____
Date and Time Issued   City and State

_____   _____
Name and Title of Judicial Officer   Signature of Judicial Officer   [G13950]

cause) and sees drug paraphernalia "in plain view," no search warrant is required to seize that evidence. Another exception exists when it is likely that the items sought will be removed or destroyed before a warrant can be obtained.

Investigation after the Arrest

As already mentioned, when a suspect is "caught red-handed," the police may arrest the suspect without an arrest warrant and may not have to undertake much of an investigation of the alleged offense after the arrest. In other cases, however, the police must find and interview witnesses and conduct searches (of the suspect's home or car, for example) to collect evidence. Witnesses may view the suspect in a _lineup,_ in which the suspect appears with a group of several others. In more serious cases, detectives may take charge of the investigation.

As the police review the evidence at hand, they may conclude there is not enough evidence to justify recommending the case for prosecution. If so, the

EXHIBIT 13.5
A Search Warrant—Continued

§ 7942
Rule 41   SPECIAL PROCEEDINGS   Ch. 89

AO 93 (Rev. 5/85) Search Warrant

	RETURN	
DATE WARRANT RECEIVED	DATE AND TIME WARRANT EXECUTED	COPY OF WARRANT AND RECEIPT FOR ITEMS LEFT WITH

INVENTORY MADE IN THE PRESENCE OF

INVENTORY OF PERSON OR PROPERTY TAKEN PURSUANT TO THE WARRANT

CERTIFICATION

    I swear that this inventory is a true and detailed account of the person or property taken by me on the warrant.

    _____

    Subscribed, sworn to, and returned before me this date.

    _____
         U.S. Judge or Magistrate   Date

[G13951]

suspect is released, and no charges are filed. The police can still recommend prosecution later if more evidence is obtained. Alternatively, the police may decide to change the offense with which the suspect is being charged. The police may also decide to release the suspect with a warning or a referral to a social-service agency. Unless the suspect is released, at this point in the criminal process, control over the case moves from the police to the public prosecutor.

THE PROSECUTION BEGINS

The prosecution of a criminal case begins when the police inform the public prosecutor of the alleged crime, provide the reports written by the arresting and investigating officers, and turn over evidence relating to the matter. The prosecutor may choose to investigate the case further by personally interviewing the suspect, the arresting and investigating officers, and witnesses, and gathering other evidence.

Developing
Paralegal Skills

THE PROSECUTOR'S OFFICE—WARRANT DIVISION

Kathy Perello works as a legal assistant in the warrant division of the county prosecutor's office. Officer Ryan McCarthy is at her door with a burglary report. The police have a suspect they want to arrest. Officer McCarthy presents the paperwork from the prosecutor that authorizes the arrest and requests that Kathy prepare an arrest warrant. Officer McCarthy will then take the warrant to the court, swear to the truth of its contents, and ask the judge to sign the warrant so that he can make the arrest.

CHECKLIST FOR PREPARING A WARRANT

- Obtain written authorization from a prosecutor before initiating the warrant procedure.
- Obtain a copy of the suspect's criminal history.
- Use the above to prepare the warrant.
- Verify that the criminal history matches the suspect.
- Make sure that the crime and the suspect are both specifically described.
- Review the typed warrant to ensure that it includes any other required terms.
- Call the officer to pick up the warrant and take it to a judge for a determination of probable cause.

The prosecutor's legal assistants often participate in these tasks. Based on a review of the police file or an investigation, the prosecutor decides whether to take the case to trial or drop the case and allow the suspect to be released. Major reasons for releasing the suspect include insufficient evidence and unreliable witnesses.

Prosecutors have broad discretion. If they decide to pursue a case, they also decide what charges to file. Because prosecutions are expensive and resources are limited, most prosecutors do not go forward with a case unless they think they can prove the case in court. Typically, a prosecutor who decides to file a case will allege as many criminal offenses as could possibly be proved based on the facts. If the defendant is facing numerous charges, the likelihood is greater that the prosecutor will get a conviction on at least one of them (the chances are also greater that the defendant will plead guilty to one or more of the offenses in exchange for having the others dropped).

If the decision is made to prosecute the case, then the prosecutor must undertake the necessary procedures to formally charge the person before the court. These procedures vary depending on the court and the type of case. Often, misdemeanor charges are handled somewhat differently than felony charges. Some prosecutors may file complaints involving misdemeanor charges, but a grand jury indictment (which will be discussed shortly) is required for felony charges. The way a criminal case is initiated is one area of criminal procedure that varies substantially among the states. Keep this in mind as you read the following subsections.

Complaint and Initial Appearance

The criminal litigation process may begin with the filing of a *complaint* (see Exhibit 13.6). The complaint includes a statement of the charges that are being brought against the suspect. The suspect now becomes a criminal defendant.

EXHIBIT 13.6
A Complaint

United States District Court

_____ DISTRICT OF _____

UNITED STATES OF AMERICA
V.

CRIMINAL COMPLAINT

CASE NUMBER:

(Name and Address of Defendant)

I, the undersigned complainant being duly sworn state the following is true and correct to the best of my

knowledge and belief. On or about _____ in _____ county, in the

_____ District of _____ defendant(s) did, (Track Statutory Language of Offense)

In violation of Title _____ United States Code, Section(s) _____ .

I further state that I am a(n) _____ and that this complaint is based on the following
                                          Official Title

facts:

Continued on the attached sheet and made a part hereof: ☐ Yes   ☐ No

_____
Signature of Complainant

Sworn to before me and subscribed in my presence,

_____ at _____
Date   City and State

_____   _____   [E4706]
Name & Title of Judicial Officer   Signature of Judicial Officer

---

Because the defendant is in the court system, prosecutors must show that they have legal grounds to proceed. They must show probable cause that a crime was committed and that the defendant committed the crime.

In most jurisdictions, defendants are taken before a judge or magistrate (public official) very soon after arrest. During this *initial appearance,* the judge makes sure that the person appearing is the person named in the complaint, informs the defendant of the charge or charges made in the complaint, and advises the defendant of the right to counsel and the right to remain silent. If a defendant cannot afford to hire an attorney, a public defender or member of the private bar may be appointed to represent the defendant at this time (or the defendant may be asked to fill out an application for appointed counsel).

The judge must also make a decision whether to set bail or release the defendant until the next court date. **Bail** is an amount paid by the defendant to the court as insurance that the defendant will show up for future court appearances. If the defendant shows up as promised, the court returns the funds. Courts often use

bail
The amount of money or conditions set by the court to ensure that an individual accused of a crime will appear for further criminal proceedings. If the accused person provides bail, whether in cash or by means of a bail bond, then the person is released from jail.

featured contributor

PARALEGALS AND CRIMINAL LITIGATION

Pamela Poole Weber

BIOGRAPHICAL NOTE

Pamela Poole Weber graduated from Stetson University College of Law and is licensed to practice law in Florida. In 1989, after working in both the corporate and public sectors as a litigator, she joined Seminole Community College in Central Florida. There, she developed and was the director of a two-year legal assistant program as well as serving as the executive director of the Seminole Community College Foundation. Weber has been active in various legal areas, including teaching police recruits in the area of juvenile law and lecturing to seniors on issues relating to the rights of elderly persons.

T he gavel strikes, the trial is over, and the jury is escorted to the jury room to deliberate. Your pulse begins to pound, and the gravity of the situation overwhelms you. This is the first time that you, as a paralegal, have assisted your supervising attorney in a criminal case. Now comes the most difficult time—waiting for the decision. But you take satisfaction in knowing that you have done the best job you can.

* * * *

Criminal litigation is a very fast-paced area of law that is continually changing. Many people do not understand what is involved in defending or prosecuting someone accused of a crime. First and foremost, both sides must be familiar with current laws and especially with changes or new interpretations of those laws. Attorneys do not always have the time required to keep up with these changes. A paralegal can be a valuable asset to a law office by keeping informed on current developments—by reading current court decisions, by reviewing summaries of new laws or modifications to existing laws, by being alert for emerging trends reported in the media, and by generally keeping eyes and ears open. This behind-the-scenes work is in many ways just as interesting as the spectacular trial scenes on television, and a paralegal's input with respect to current law may well determine the outcome of a case.

Both the defense and the prosecution must review every aspect of the case. This requires combining legal research with critical analysis. Attorneys and paralegals work together in planning a course of action for each case, regardless of

whether the case is simple or highly complex. This team approach is becoming more widely accepted because of the results it generates. As the old saying goes, "Two heads are better than one."

OPPORTUNITIES FOR PARALEGALS

Criminal litigation may present paralegals with a variety of opportunities, although paralegals are not utilized as extensively in criminal litigation as they are in civil litigation. Some attorneys do not use paralegals to their fullest capabilities because they do not know how to maximize paralegal services. Often, paralegals must suggest tasks that they can perform or, if appropriate, must simply go ahead and perform the tasks on their own. Remember, though, that paralegals cannot engage in any actions that only attorneys are licensed to perform.

What are some of the services that paralegals can provide? Obviously, legal research is critical to successful criminal litigation, and paralegals can perform this research for attorneys. Such research may involve a review and analysis of the law or laws that allegedly have been violated by the defendant, various defense strategies, procedural problems, and evidentiary problems—just to name a few. Sometimes, research is very detailed, requiring days and even weeks to complete. At other times, research may have to be done at the last minute.

Paralegals who want more contact with people can involve themselves in the evidentiary side of the case. Both the defense attorney and the prosecuting attorney in a criminal case have some sort of evidence—physical evidence, witnesses' testimony, or confessions, for example—with which to work. The paralegal may interview witnesses, prepare deposition questions, review police and laboratory reports, or identify photographs that may be useful at trial.

Many paralegals enjoy the challenge of critical analysis and strategic thinking. The criminal litigation paralegal is continually provided with challenges in this respect. In this area, the paralegal can assist in actually preparing the case for trial. The paralegal may be asked to draft pretrial motions, review the available research and documents, draft responses to the opposing side's motions, prepare questions for jury selection, and prepare jury instructions for the conclusion of the case.

HOW CAN I ASSIST IN THE DEFENSE OF A CRIMINAL?

This question, long asked by attorneys, is now being asked by paralegals. Many people look at this area of law and say that they could never represent such defendants as Ted Bundy and Jeffrey Dahmer (convicted serial killers). Perhaps these people believe that by representing such defendants, the attorneys are somehow condoning their criminal actions. Or perhaps they detest those defendants so much that they want them convicted and punished without the benefit of due process. But attorneys and their legal assistants must remind themselves that until the verdict is in, the defendants are only *accused* of committing the criminal acts. They are guilty of no crime until the jury decides they are guilty *beyond a reasonable doubt.* Our country's criminal justice system is founded on the principle that a person is "innocent until proven guilty." The paralegal must remember that his or her job is not to decide the guilt or innocence of an accused person. Rather, it is to ensure that justice is being served.

A paralegal working for the prosecutor will strive to ensure that the people of a particular city, county, or state, or even the United States, are having their interests protected. The prosecution does not represent the victim of a criminal act but rather the citizens of a community.

The defense paralegal will work to ensure the protection of the rights of the accused. The U.S. Constitution guarantees that all persons have certain rights, including the right to a trial

> *"The defense paralegal will work to ensure the protection of the rights of the accused."*

in which they may confront their accusers and the right to be represented by legal counsel during that trial. These rights apply to everyone—including those who actually commit the crimes with which they are charged. It is up to the defense team to make sure that the defendant has not been deprived of any of his or her constitutional rights.

The defense attorney and his or her legal assistants will examine closely all the circumstances, procedures, and evidence involving the defendant to make sure that the defendant has been allowed to exercise these rights. It may be the task of the paralegal to determine if evidence, including a confession, was properly obtained. If it was not, the paralegal may assist in drafting motions to bring this to the attention of the court. The defense team will also explore various defenses that may be available to the accused.

Paralegals who wish to work in the area of criminal justice must be prepared to be highly objective about criminal proceedings. They must be able to separate their personal and emotional responses to a particular defendant's alleged criminal acts from their professional goal of serving that defendant's best interests by doing all they can to ensure that his or her rights have been observed.

CONCLUSION

Criminal litigation offers numerous opportunities for legal assistants, but it is important to remember that in some cases it may be difficult to achieve the necessary personal and emotional distance from a case to deal with it objectively and professionally.

* * * *

The bailiff returns and announces that the jury has reached a verdict. Your heart leaps into your throat. You take a deep breath and wait. The jury returns a verdict for your side, and you realize that you have just experienced a first victory as a paralegal. After all, you say to yourself, your efforts were crucial to the success of your attorney's case. You know that not all future cases will be "won," but you experience the rewarding feeling of being an integral part of the system seeking justice for all Americans.

At a preliminary hearing, a judge or a magistrate evaluates the evidence against the defendant. If the evidence is sufficient to establish probable cause (reasonable grounds to believe that the defendant committed the crime with which he or she is charged), the prosecutor issues an *information,* and the defendant is bound over for further proceedings. Paralegals often assist either the defendant or the prosecutor in preparing for preliminary hearings. What might some of the duties of a paralegal be?

(Image copyright Junial Enterprises, 2009. Used under license from Shutterstock.com)

standard bail schedules, which set the bail for specific kinds of cases, and may deny bail for very serious crimes. The Eighth Amendment prohibits "excessive bail," and the defendant has a right to a bail hearing to reduce the amount set by the court. If the court sets bail in an amount that the defendant is unable to pay, the defendant (or the defendant's attorney or paralegal) can arrange with a *bail bondsperson* to post a bail bond on the defendant's behalf. The bail bondsperson promises to pay the bail amount to the court if the defendant fails to return for further proceedings. In return, the bail bondsperson receives a payment from the defendant, usually 10 percent of the bail amount.

Preliminary Hearing

preliminary hearing
An initial hearing in which a judge or magistrate decides if there is probable cause to believe that the defendant committed the crime with which he or she is charged.

The defendant again appears before a magistrate or judge at a **preliminary hearing**. During this hearing, the magistrate or judge determines whether the evidence presented is sufficient to establish probable cause to believe the defendant committed the crime with which he or she is charged. This may be the first adversarial proceeding in which both sides are represented by counsel. Paralegals may become involved in the process at this point by assisting in preparation for the hearing. The prosecutor may present witnesses, who may be cross-examined by defense counsel (the defense rarely presents its witnesses prior to trial). A defendant who intends to plead guilty usually waives the right to a preliminary hearing to help move things along more quickly. In many jurisdictions, however, the preliminary hearing is required in certain felony cases.

If the magistrate finds the evidence insufficient to establish probable cause, either the charge is reduced to a lesser one or charges are dropped altogether and the defendant is released. If the magistrate believes there is sufficient evidence to establish probable cause, the prosecutor issues an information. The **information** is the formal charge against the defendant and binds over the defendant for further proceedings, which usually means that the defendant is arraigned and the case proceeds to trial.

information	A formal criminal charge made by a prosecutor without a grand jury indictment.

Grand Jury Review

The federal government and about half of the states require a grand jury, and not the prosecutor, to make the decision as to whether a case should go to trial in felony cases. In other words, a grand jury's indictment is an alternative to a prosecutor's information to initiate the criminal litigation process.

A **grand jury** is a group of citizens called to decide whether there is probable cause to believe that the defendant committed the crime with which he or she is charged and therefore should go to trial. Even in cases in which grand jury review is not required, the prosecutor may call a grand jury to evaluate the evidence against a suspect, which will indicate to the prosecutor the relative strength or weakness of the case.

grand jury	A group of citizens called to decide whether probable cause exists to believe that a suspect committed the crime with which he or she has been charged and should stand trial.

The grand jury sits in closed session and hears only evidence presented by the prosecutor—the defendant cannot present evidence at this hearing. Normally, the defendant and the defendant's attorney are not even allowed to attend grand jury proceedings—although in some cases the defendant may be required to testify. The prosecutor presents to the grand jury whatever evidence the state has against the defendant, including photographs, documents, tangible objects, test results, the testimony of witnesses, and other items. If the grand jury finds that probable cause exists, it issues an **indictment**[6] against the defendant called a *true bill*. Over 97 percent of the cases that prosecutors bring to grand juries result in an indictment. The indictment is filed with the trial court and becomes the formal charge against the defendant. An example of an indictment is shown in Exhibit 13.7.

indictment	A charge or written accusation, issued by a grand jury, that probable cause exists to believe that a person has committed a crime for which he or she should stand trial.

EXHIBIT 13.7
An Indictment

[*Title of Court and Cause*]

The Grand Jury charges that:

On or about _____ , 20 __ , at _____ , _____ , in the _____ District of _____ , _____ , having been convicted of knowingly acquiring and possessing a SNAP/Food Stamp EBT card in a manner not authorized by the provisions of Chapter 51, Title 7, United States Code, and the regulations issued pursuant to said chapter, a felony conviction, in the federal district court for the _____ District of _____ , and sentenced on _____ , 20__ , did knowingly possess a firearm that had been transported in and affecting commerce, to wit: an OMC Pistol, Back Up 380 Caliber, serial number _____ ; all in violation of Section 1202(a)(1) of Title 18, United States Code, Appendix.

A True Bill

_____ ,

Foreperson.

_____ ,

United States Attorney.

Arraignment

At the **arraignment**, the defendant is informed of the charges and must respond to the charges by entering a plea. Three possible pleas can be entered: guilty, not guilty, and *nolo contendere*, which is Latin for "I will not contest it" and is often called a no-contest plea. A plea of no contest is neither an admission of guilt nor a denial of guilt—but it operates like a guilty plea in that the defendant is convicted. The primary reason for pleading no contest is so that the plea cannot later be used against the defendant in a civil trial. For example, if a defendant pleads guilty to assault, the admission of guilt can be used to impose civil liability, whereas with a no-contest plea, the plaintiff in the civil suit must prove the defendant's guilt. No-contest pleas are thus useful for the defendant who could be sued in a civil action for damages caused to a person or property.

At the arraignment, the defendant can move to have the charges dismissed, which happens in a fair number of cases for a variety of reasons. The defendant may claim, for example, that the case should be dismissed because the statute of limitations for the crime in question has lapsed. Most frequently, however, the defendant pleads guilty to the charge or to a lesser charge that has been agreed on through **plea bargaining** between the prosecutor and the defendant. If the defendant pleads guilty, no trial is necessary, and the defendant is sentenced based on the plea. If the defendant pleads not guilty, the case is set for trial.

Pretrial Motions

Defense attorneys and their paralegals will search for and be alert to any violation of the defendant's constitutional rights. Many pretrial motions are based on possible violations of the defendant's rights as provided by the Constitution and criminal procedural law. We discuss here a few of the most common motions filed in a criminal case. Note, however, that the specific requirements for pretrial motions vary depending on the jurisdiction. Not every jurisdiction allows every type of pretrial motion, and the standards used by judges to evaluate such motions may differ as well. Also keep in mind that a motion is generally accompanied by a separate pleading that sets forth the legal argument in support of the motion. A memorandum of law, a brief, affidavits, or supporting points and authorities may be filed in support of a pleading.

Motions to Suppress

One of the most common and effective motions made by defense attorneys is the **motion to suppress evidence**. A motion to suppress asserts that the evidence against the defendant was illegally obtained and should be excluded (inadmissible). Typically, this motion is filed when an officer performs a search without probable cause, seizes evidence, and then arrests the defendant based on that evidence. For example, suppose an officer stops the defendant's vehicle because his taillight is out and then searches the contents of the defendant's trunk, finding illegal narcotics. The defendant is subsequently charged with possession. A motion to suppress would be appropriate here (and probably successful) because the officer did not have probable cause to search the trunk in carrying out a traffic stop.

The defense attorney normally prepares the motion and submits a memorandum of law (legal argument) with the motion. (Often, these motions are drafted by paralegals.) Exhibit 13.8 on pages 444 and 445 shows a sample memorandum. Often, the attorney requests the court to allow oral argument on the motion, although in some jurisdictions it is automatic. The court then conducts a hearing on the motion. The attorneys for both sides may call witnesses (police officers and others who were present) to testify, and the judge makes a ruling. If the judge agrees that the evidence should be excluded and grants the motion, the defendant may be able to avoid trial. This is because frequently, without the evidence, the prosecution will not be able to prove its case against the defendant and will thus drop the charges.

Motions to Dismiss

A motion can be filed to dismiss all or some of the charges pending against the defendant. There are many grounds for filing a motion to dismiss. Motions to dismiss in criminal cases often assert that the defendant's constitutional rights—or criminal procedures stemming from the Constitution—have been violated. For example, the defense might argue that the prosecution waited too long to prosecute the case in violation of the defendant's Sixth Amendment right to a speedy and public trial (sometimes called a *speedy trial motion*). The defense will file the motion along with a supporting memorandum, which may argue that the defendant has been prejudiced by the delay, that witnesses are no longer available, and that a fair trial cannot be had. If the judge grants the motion, the case is dismissed.

Because it may eliminate charges against a client without subjecting the client to the risks of a jury trial, the motion to dismiss is one of the most useful motions for the defense to file. A paralegal who becomes skilled at writing persuasive motions to dismiss will thus be a valuable asset to the defense team.

Other Common Motions

Just as in civil cases, attorneys in criminal cases often file motions *in limine* (discussed in Chapter 12 on page 394) to keep certain evidence out of the trial. For example, a defense attorney whose client has prior criminal convictions may file a motion *in limine* requesting the court to prevent any evidence of these convictions from being offered by the prosecution. The prosecutor may also file such motions to keep possibly prejudicial evidence from being admitted (concerning a victim's reputation, for example).

Sometimes—when there is a good deal of pretrial publicity, for instance—the defense may make a **motion for a change of venue** asking the court to relocate the trial. Other times, the defense may file a **motion to recuse** asking the trial judge to remove himself or herself from the case. Such a motion usually is filed only when the judge has publicly displayed some bias or personally knows the parties or witnesses in the case. If the motion is granted, a different judge will hear the case. When a case involves more than one defendant, the defense counsel may file a **motion to sever** (separate) the cases for purposes of trial.

Various other motions—including motions to reduce the charges against the defendant, to obtain evidence during discovery, or to extend the trial date—may also be made prior to the trial. As with motions made during the civil litigation process, each motion must be accompanied by supporting affidavits and/or legal memoranda.

Discovery

In preparing for trial, public prosecutors, defense attorneys, and paralegals engage in discovery proceedings (including depositions and interrogatories), interview and subpoena witnesses, prepare exhibits and a trial notebook, examine documents and evidence, and do other tasks necessary to effectively prosecute or defend the defendant. Although similar to civil litigation in these respects, criminal discovery is generally more limited, and the time constraints are different. The *Developing Paralegal Skills* feature on page 446 gives some useful tips for discovery in criminal cases.

During discovery, defendants are generally entitled to obtain *any* evidence in the possession of the prosecutor relating to the case, including statements previously made by the defendant, objects, documents, and reports of tests and examinations. The prosecutor must hand over evidence that tends to show the defendant's innocence as well as evidence of the defendant's guilt. Defendants are given this right to offset the fact that the prosecution (the state) has more resources at its disposal than the defendant (an individual citizen).

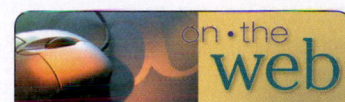

on·the web

Motions can sometimes be filed electronically. For an example involving a federal district court, go to **www.wawd.uscourts.gov**. From the menu, select "Electronic Case Filing," then "User's Manual," and then "Filing a Criminal Motion."

motion for a change of venue
A motion requesting that a trial be moved to a different location to ensure a fair and impartial proceeding, for the convenience of the parties, or for some other acceptable reason.

motion to recuse
A motion to remove a particular judge from a case.

motion to sever
A motion to try multiple defendants separately.

EXHIBIT 13.8
Memorandum in Support of Motion to Suppress

[Attorney for Defendant]

SUPERIOR COURT OF THE STATE OF NITA
FOR THE COUNTY OF NITA

THE PEOPLE OF THE STATE OF NITA,	)	Case No.: C45778
Plaintiff,	)	D.A. No.: A39996
	)	
v.	)	**MEMORANDUM OF LAW IN SUPPORT**
	)	**OF MOTION TO SUPPRESS**
	)	
	)	DATE: 10-27-11
Eduardo Jose Mendez,	)	TIME: 1:15
Defendant.	)	Estimated Time: 45 min.
	)	No. of Witnesses: 1

Defendant, Eduardo Jose Mendez, by and through his attorney the Public Defender of the County of Nita, respectfully submits the following memorandum of law in support of his motion to Suppress.

STATEMENT OF FACTS

On or about September 23, 2011, at approximately 02:15, Officer Ramirez observed Mr. Mendez riding his bicycle in the area of 1300 Elm St. and 500 C St. It was drizzling, and few people walked the streets. Officer Ramirez indicated that the area is known for narcotic activity and that he believed Mr. Mendez had been participating or was about to participate in narcotic activity.

Mr. Mendez was on his bicycle at the corner of Elm and C St. when Officer Ramirez approached him. He indicated that Mr. Mendez appeared to be nervous and was sweating profusely. He asked Mr. Mendez what he was doing, and Mr. Mendez responded that he was waiting for his girlfriend. Officer Ramirez conducted a pat-down search for weapons. He felt several hard objects inside Mr. Mendez's pants pockets and asked Mr. Mendez if he had a knife in his pocket. Mr. Mendez consented to a search of his pockets, and Officer Ramirez found only a wooden pencil.

Without asking for permission, and without notice, Officer Ramirez reached for and grabbed Mr. Mendez's baseball cap. The officer took the cap off of Mr. Mendez's head. He felt the outside of the cap and with his fingers manipulated a small soft lump in Mr. Mendez's cap. He went through the cap and moved the side material of the cap. He found a small plastic package burnt on one end. He opened the package. Officer Ramirez found a small amount of an off-white powder substance inside the package.

ARGUMENT

I. MR. MENDEZ'S FOURTH AMENDMENT RIGHT TO PRIVACY WAS VIOLATED BECAUSE THE OFFICER'S DETENTION OF MR. MENDEZ WAS NOT JUSTIFIED BY REASONABLE SUSPICION

A person has been seized within the meaning of the Fourth Amendment if, in view of all the circumstances surrounding the incident, a reasonable person would have believed that he was not free to leave. *United States v. Mendenhall*, 446 U.S. 544, 554 (1980). Here, Officer Ramirez seized Mr. Mendez when he stopped to question him. Mr. Mendez submitted to Officer Ramirez's show of authority when he responded to the questioning. Mr. Mendez's belief that he was not free to leave is evidenced by his actions during the seizure. He appeared nervous and kept looking around in all directions as if looking for someone to help him. A reasonable person such as Mr. Mendez, in view of all of the circumstances, would have believed and in fact did believe he was not free to leave. Therefore, the officer's initial stop was a seizure.

* * * *

EXHIBIT 13.8
Memorandum in Support of Motion to Suppress—Continued

Officer Ramirez did not have reasonable suspicion to stop Mr. Mendez. He fails to point to specific facts causing him to suspect criminal activity was afoot. Officer Ramirez notes in his police report that he "felt" that defendant "had been participating or was about to participate in narcotic activity." The officer also indicated that he believed the area was known for narcotic activity. However, "Persons may not be subjected to invasions of privacy merely because they are in or are passing through a high-crime area." *McCally-Bey v. Kirner,* 24 F.Supp.3d 389 (N.D. Nita 2002).

These observations taken as a whole and Officer Ramirez's explanation do not rise to the requisite level of reasonable suspicion necessary to invade the privacy of a citizen.

II. OFFICER RAMIREZ'S PAT-DOWN SEARCH EXCEEDED ITS SCOPE WHEN HE SEARCHED THE BASEBALL CAP AND MANIPULATED ITS CONTENTS

Under the *Terry* doctrine, a search is referred to as a "frisk." *Terry v. Ohio,* 392 U.S. 1 (1968). A *frisk* is justified only if the officer reasonably believes that the person is armed and dangerous. A frisk is a pat-down of a person's outer clothing. It is limited in scope to its purpose, which is to search for weapons. Even slightly lingering over a package because it feels like it contains drugs exceeds the scope of the search. *Minnesota v. Dickerson,* 508 U.S. 366 (1993). An officer cannot manipulate a package or a substance that is clearly not a weapon through an individual's clothing during a *Terry* pat-down search.

* * * *

III. OFFICER RAMIREZ DID NOT HAVE PROBABLE CAUSE TO CONDUCT A WARRANTLESS SEARCH OF MR. MENDEZ

* * * *

IV. ALL EVIDENCE OBTAINED AS A RESULT OF AN UNLAWFUL DETENTION MUST BE SUPPRESSED AS TAINTED EVIDENCE; FRUIT OF THE POISONOUS TREE

* * * *

* * * *

As discussed above, the detention of Mr. Mendez did not meet constitutionally established standards of reasonableness. Hence, all evidence obtained as a result of such unlawful detention is inadmissible. In addition, all evidence seized as a result of the arrest that followed from his unlawful detention is inadmissible as fruit of the poisonous tree.

* * * *

For the above-mentioned reasons, all evidence obtained as a result of Mr. Mendez's detention, illegal search, and subsequent arrest in this case must be suppressed.

Dated:

Respectfully submitted,

_____

Attorney for Defendant

Developing Paralegal Skills

DISCOVERY IN THE CRIMINAL CASE

The law firm of McCoy & Warner is defending Taylor Rogers in a case of attempted murder. Rogers allegedly shot a person in a drive-by shooting on the expressway. Lee Soloman, a paralegal, is working on the case. Today, as the result of a successful discovery motion that his supervising attorney received from the court, Lee has obtained copies of all of the evidence that the prosecuting attorney has in his file. Lee's job is to create the discovery file and then to work with the material in the file to prepare the case.

TIPS FOR CRIMINAL DISCOVERY

- Create a discovery file containing sections for the defendant's statements, witnesses' statements, police reports, tests, and other evidence.
- Review the evidence and prepare a memo summarizing it.
- Review the memo and/or evidence with your supervising attorney.
- If the supervising attorney agrees, contact witnesses and obtain statements.
- Interview the police officers who were involved in the arrest or who were at the crime scene.

Some state statutes allow the prosecutor access to materials that the defense intends to introduce as evidence in the trial. Also, in some jurisdictions, when the defense attorney requests discovery of case materials from the prosecutor, the defense is required to disclose similar materials to the prosecutor in return. In the absence of such statutes, courts have generally refused discovery to the prosecution. This judicial restraint is intended to protect the defendant from self-incrimination, as guaranteed by the Fifth Amendment to the U.S. Constitution (see Appendix J).

THE TRIAL

Only a small fraction of the criminal cases brought by the state actually go to trial. Some defendants are released, or the charges against them are dropped. Most defendants plead guilty to the offense or to a lesser offense prior to trial. Plea bargaining occurs at every stage of criminal proceedings, from the arraignment to the date of trial (even during a trial, defendants can accept a plea bargain). Because a trial is expensive and the outcome uncertain, both sides in criminal cases have an incentive to negotiate a plea and thus avoid the trial—just as both sides in a civil dispute are motivated to reach a settlement.

Although some criminal trials go on for weeks and are highly publicized, most criminal trials last less than one week (often only a few days). The trial itself is conducted in much the same way as a civil trial. The prosecutor and the defense attorney make their opening statements, examine and cross-examine witnesses, and summarize their positions in closing arguments. At some trials, graphics are used for illustration. These are discussed in the *Developing Paralegal Skills* feature on page 448. The jury is instructed and sent to deliberate. When the jury renders a verdict, the trial comes to an end. There are, however, a few major procedural differences between criminal trials and civil trials, including those discussed below.

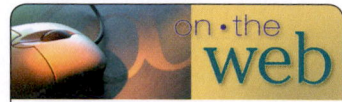

For a discussion of the steps in a criminal (or civil) trial, go to **www.abanet. org**, and search on "Steps in a Trial."

Ethics Watch

THE IMPORTANCE OF ACCURACY

In preparing exhibits for trial, especially when creating an exhibit from raw data, it is important that the paralegal ensure that the exhibit is accurate and not misleading. An attorney has a duty not to falsify evidence, and if erroneous evidence is introduced in court and challenged by opposing counsel, your supervising attorney may face serious consequences. By preparing an inaccurate exhibit (for example, by miscalculating a column of figures), the paralegal may jeopardize the attorney's professional reputation by causing the attorney to breach a professional duty.

This paralegal responsibility comes from the following codes:

- NALA Code of Ethics, Canon 10: "A paralegal's conduct is guided by bar associations' codes of professional responsibility and rules of professional conduct."

- NFPA Model Code of Ethics and Professional Responsibility, Section EC-1.3: "A paralegal shall maintain a high standard of professional conduct."

The Presumption of Innocence

In criminal trials, the defendant is innocent until proven guilty. The prosecutor bears the burden of proving the defendant guilty as charged. Defendants do not have to prove that they did not commit the offenses. In fact, they are not required to present any evidence whatsoever to counter the state's accusations (although clearly it might be in their best interests to put on a defense). Even a defendant who actually committed the crime is innocent in the eyes of the law unless the prosecutor can present sufficient evidence to convince the jury or judge of the defendant's guilt.

Not only does the state bear the burden of proving the defendant guilty, but it also is held to a very high standard of proof. Remember that in criminal cases the prosecution must prove its case *beyond a reasonable doubt*. It is not enough for the jury (or judge) to think that the defendant is probably guilty; the members of the jury must be firmly convinced of the defendant's guilt. The jurors receive instructions such as "If you think there is a real possibility that he is not guilty, you *must* give him the benefit of the doubt and find him not guilty." The presumption of innocence and the high burden of proof are designed to protect the individual from the state.

The Privilege against Self-Incrimination

As mentioned, the Fifth Amendment to the U.S. Constitution states that no person can be forced to give testimony that might be self-incriminating. Therefore, a defendant does not have to testify at trial. Witnesses may also refuse to testify on this ground. For example, if a witness, while testifying, is asked a question and answering the question would reveal her own criminal wrongdoing, the witness may "take the Fifth" and refuse to testify on the ground that the testimony may incriminate her.

The Right to a Speedy Trial

The Sixth Amendment requires a speedy and public trial for criminal prosecutions but does not specify what is meant by "speedy." Generally, criminal cases are brought to trial much more quickly than civil cases. A defendant who remains in

Developing
Paralegal Skills

PREPARING GRAPHIC PRESENTATIONS

Melanie Hofstadter, a paralegal who is about to retire from her job, is training her replacement. Melanie has worked for Johnson & Bott, a criminal law practice, for nearly twenty years and has assisted the attorneys countless times with trial preparations. Today, she is instructing the new paralegal, Kyra Mason, on how to prepare graphic presentations for the attorneys to use in the courtroom.

Melanie first explains to Kyra that trial graphics are classified into three main types: fact graphics, concept graphics, and case graphics. Fact graphics show only the facts on which both parties agree—for example, a time line indicating the order in which events occurred. Concept graphics are used to educate the judge and jury about ideas with which they may not be familiar—such as the general procedures involved in DNA fingerprinting. Case graphics, or analytical graphics, illustrate the basis of the defense or allegation—for example, a flowchart showing how certain facts are related and how they lead to a specific conclusion.

Melanie then gives Kyra a document that Melanie has prepared. The document contains a list of tips and suggestions that Kyra should keep in mind when preparing trial graphics.

TIPS FOR PREPARING A GRAPHIC PRESENTATION

- Remember that less is often more. A good graphic presentation should be simple and straightforward. Trim excess words and punctuation from charts, lists, and diagrams; using incomplete sentences and simple phrases is acceptable in graphic presentations.

- Use boldfaced text and easy-to-read fonts.

- Keep plenty of "white space" in the graphic displays.

- Know what you want the reader to focus on, and eliminate all distractions.

- Remember that it is your job to make it easy for the jury to see, read, and understand your points. Don't overburden the graphic displays with too much information or detail.

- Keep in mind that the main purpose of trial graphics is to focus attention on the points that you want to emphasize or highlight, not to focus attention on the actual presentation or display.

---

custody prior to trial, for example, is often tried within thirty to forty-five days from the date of arraignment. If the defendant (or the defendant's attorney) needs more time to prepare a defense, the defendant may give up the right to be tried within a certain number of days but will still go to trial within a relatively short period of time (a few months, typically). As noted in Chapter 5, the Sixth Amendment also guarantees accused persons the right to confront and cross-examine witnesses against them.

The Requirement for a Unanimous Verdict

Of the criminal cases that go to trial, the majority are tried by a jury. In most jurisdictions, jury verdicts in criminal cases must be *unanimous* for **acquittal** or conviction. In other words, all twelve jurors (or all six jurors, if the state allows six-person juries) must agree that the defendant is either guilty or not guilty. If the jury cannot reach unanimous agreement on whether to acquit or convict the defendant, the result is a **hung jury**. When the jury is hung, the defendant may be tried again

acquittal
A certification or declaration following a trial that the individual accused of a crime is innocent, or free from guilt, in the eyes of the law and is thus absolved of the charges.

hung jury
A jury whose members are so irreconcilably divided in their opinions that they cannot reach a verdict. The judge in this situation may order a new trial.

(although often the case is not retried). The requirement for unanimity is important because if even one juror is not convinced of the defendant's guilt, the defendant will not be convicted. Thus, the prosecuting attorney must make as strong a case as possible, while the defense attorney can aim at persuading one or more jurors to have doubts. Throughout the trial, the attorneys and their paralegals must take steps to maintain the security of information. For a discussion of this issue, see the *Technology and Today's Paralegal* feature on page 450.

Sentencing

When a defendant is found guilty by a trial court (or pleads guilty to an offense without a trial), the judge will pronounce a **sentence**, which is the penalty imposed on anyone convicted of a crime. Often, the sentence is pronounced in a separate proceeding.

> **sentence**
> The punishment, or penalty, ordered by the court to be inflicted on a person convicted of a crime.

Unless the prosecutor is seeking the death penalty, the jury normally is not involved in the sentencing of the defendant. Jurors are dismissed after they return a verdict, and the judge either sentences the defendant on the spot or schedules a future court appearance for sentencing. At the sentencing hearing, the judge usually listens to arguments from both attorneys concerning the factors in "aggravation and mitigation" (which involve why the defendant's punishment should be harsh or lenient).

Most criminal statutes set forth a maximum and minimum penalty that should be imposed for a violation. Thus, judges often have a range of options and a great deal of discretion in sentencing individual defendants. The judge typically sentences the offender to one or more of the following:

- Incarceration in a jail or a prison.
- Probation (formal or informal).
- Fines or other financial penalties.
- Public work service (for less serious offenses).
- Classes (for certain types of offenses, such as domestic violence and alcohol- or drug-related crimes).
- Death (in some states).

Incarceration

Defendants sentenced to incarceration will go to a county jail for less serious offenses (involving sentences of less than one year) or a state prison for serious crimes (involving sentences of more than one year). In some cases, the judge may consider alternatives to jail time. Defendants may be placed on house arrest (and in many jurisdictions wear an electronic device that will notify the authorities if they leave a designated area). Defendants who have alcohol or drug problems may sometimes be allowed to satisfy the incarceration portion of a sentence in an inpatient rehabilitation program. In some states, defendants may be allowed to satisfy short periods of custody time (ten to thirty days) by checking into the jail on weekends only or by participating in a supervised release program, which enables them to stay employed.

Probation

A part of many sentences (in both felony and misdemeanor cases) is probation. Typically, defendants are sentenced to substantially less than the maximum penalty and placed on probation with certain conditions for at least two or three years (depending on the maximum allowed by statute). In such cases, the sentence imposed is said to be *suspended*. If the person fails to meet the conditions of probation, probation may be revoked, and the person may be sentenced to custody time up to the maximum for the offense.

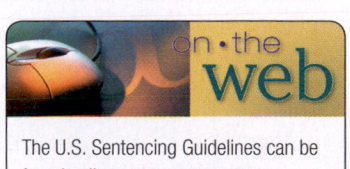

The U.S. Sentencing Guidelines can be found online at **www.ussc.gov**.

Technology and Today's Paralegal

EVOLVING TECHNOLOGY, SECURITY, AND EVIDENCE

The many technologies used in law offices change frequently, making it difficult to keep up with every development. It is, however, useful to be aware of current developments that affect the functioning of a law office and can destroy the security of information sent to other parties. Changes in technology can affect many aspects of a law office's functioning, from posing threats to the security of information to offering new opportunities in the collection and evaluation of evidence.

PROTECTING SECURITY

In one case, a lack of awareness of technological capabilities meant that a document believed to be secure was not. Members of the media were able to read parts of a confidential settlement that had been redacted (blacked out) in a settlement of a lawsuit involving Facebook and ConnectU in 2009. The computer codes that supposedly hid some information from public view were bypassed in electronic copies of documents released to the press, allowing reporters to see the supposedly private information. The lawyers for ConnectU claimed that they had received $65 million from Facebook in the settlement, but the press could see the amount was actually $31 million. ConnectU fired the law firm that made the mistake and asked the judge to throw out the settlement, but that did not happen.

KNOWING WHERE PEOPLE ARE OR WERE

Global positioning system (GPS) devices are now built into many vehicles. The digital information collected by these devices may allow investigators to determine the location of a vehicle at a certain point in time, which can help in criminal investigations. Where a suspect was at a particular time may be revealed by GPS data, for example.

As of 2012, new federal rules require cell phones to support GPS-type information so that 911 emergency calls can be pinpointed by location. This could become important in some criminal investigations, because it would enable an investigator to find out the location of persons and their cell phones, even if they did not call 911.

USING DIGITAL FORENSIC EXPERTS

The use of digital forensic experts in litigation is increasing. Qualified professionals can assist in the evaluation of digital material and identify when it has been compromised and is no longer trustworthy. Just as the use of DNA evidence has helped to convict some people accused of crimes, and free others falsely accused, digital evidence is playing an increasing role in helping establish guilt or innocence.

TECHNOLOGY TIP

The rapid evolution of technology means that law firms must watch for possibilities not envisioned before. Web sites such as eLawExchange (**www.elawexchange.com**) provide a lot of information about innovations affecting law and about how to find experts when needed. Paralegals should use such resources to keep up to date with evolving technologies.

For example, if convicted of driving while under the influence, a defendant might be sentenced to two days in custody, three years of informal probation, a fine of $3,000, ten days of public work service (picking up roadside trash), and a first-offenders program (meeting twice a week for six to eight weeks and costing several thousand dollars). If the defendant does not do all of these things, the court can revoke probation and sentence the person to spend up to a year in jail.

In the **Office**

THE BENEFITS OF GOOD RECORD KEEPING

One of your jobs as a paralegal is to make sure that witnesses are in court at the proper time. This job relates to the attorney's duty of competence, which, if breached, could expose the attorney to potential liability for malpractice. For all your efforts, however, a key witness fails to appear in court. Your supervising attorney is understandably upset about this and asks you how it could have happened. You show the attorney the memorandum of your interview with the client, in which you noted that the witness was willing to testify; the receipt from the certified letter that you sent to the witness, which contained the subpoena, indicating that the witness had received it; and a telephone memo of a call that you made to the witness a week prior to the trial in which the witness agreed to be in court on the date of the trial. Although your documentation is not a cure for the problem presented by the missing witness, it does provide evidence—should it be necessary—that neither you nor the attorney was negligent.

Probation can be either formal or informal. In formal probation, which is typical in felony cases, the defendant is required to meet regularly with a probation officer. The defendant may be required to submit to drug and alcohol testing, to possess no firearms, and to avoid socializing with those who might be engaging in criminal activity, for example. Defendants on informal probation do not have a probation officer, but they may be required to comply with certain conditions, such as paying a fine, performing public work service, participating in specified programs (such as attending Alcoholics Anonymous meetings or anger management classes), and not violating the law.

Diversion

In many states, **diversion programs** are available to defendants charged with certain offenses specified by statute. Diversion is an alternative to prosecution. Generally, these programs suspend criminal prosecution for a certain period of time and require that the defendant complete specified conditions—such as attending special classes and not having contact with the police—during that time. If the person fulfills *all* of the requirements of diversion, the case will be dismissed. If the defendant fails to complete the diversion satisfactorily, the criminal prosecution springs back to life, and the defendant is prosecuted for the crime. The objective is to deter the defendant from further wrongdoing by offering an incentive—namely, a way to avoid any record of conviction.

A defendant who is charged with a first offense of driving under the influence, for example, may qualify for diversion on the charge (eligibility requirements vary among states). The defendant might be required to (1) attend an eight-month-long course educating him or her on the dangers of drunk driving, (2) pay for that course, (3) pay a certain sum to a victims' restitution fund, and (4) not have any contact with the police for a period of two years. If the defendant complies with all of the conditions, then after two years, the case will be dismissed.

Diversion is a good option for defendants who are guilty of the crimes alleged and want to avoid having criminal convictions on their records. Most defendants who are eligible for diversion choose that option at the arraignment or soon after and thus do not proceed to trial. On occasion, however, judges may allow a person to divert even after a trial.

diversion program
In some jurisdictions, an alternative to prosecution that is offered to certain felony suspects to deter them from future unlawful acts.

Today's Professional Paralegal

WORKING FOR THE DISTRICT COURT

Amanda Bowin is a legal assistant who is assigned to work for six of the twelve judges who serve on the district court. Today is "criminal call," and she is in the courtroom observing an arraignment. She has in front of her a docket sheet for the defendant. She listens while the judge explains the criminal charges. The defendant pleads not guilty, and the date for the pretrial hearing is set. (If the defendant had pleaded guilty, then a sentencing date and probation interview would have been scheduled.) Amanda notes the plea and the pretrial hearing date on the docket sheet. She then observes five more arraignments and notes the defendants' pleas on their docket sheets.

"SHOW CAUSE" MOTIONS

Several attorneys enter the courtroom. They are present for "show cause" motions. A "show cause" motion is made when a defendant has violated the terms of his or her probation or sentence. The first motion is made by an assistant prosecutor against a defendant who was stopped on the highway for speeding and was found to be carrying a handgun. The judge evaluates the evidence and gives the defendant the option of either pleading guilty to the violation of probation or going to trial on the issue. The defendant chooses to plead guilty and is sentenced by the judge. Amanda notes all of the information on her docket sheet for this case. She listens to the remaining "show cause" motions and makes notes on the pleas and sentences.

SENTENCING HEARINGS

Next, the sentencing hearings begin. Amanda listens and notes the sentences on the relevant docket sheets. The last item up this morning is the sentencing of a woman who has been convicted for criminal neglect—she abandoned her two-year-old child at a gas station. The child has been placed in a foster home. The defense attorney is allowed to call a witness to testify as to the defendant's character and how well she cared for her daughter. This is an attempt to convince the judge to impose the lightest possible sentence allowable for this crime.

The attorney calls a social worker to the stand. The social worker testifies that the defendant-mother had previously had a drug problem for which she had sought treatment. There had been no place for her to go for treatment where she could take her baby, and she had no one with whom she could leave her baby. For those reasons, she had opted for an outpatient program, a less effective form of treatment. She had tried hard to fight her addiction to cocaine and had been doing well, but sometimes it takes more than one attempt at treatment to succeed. The social worker continues by telling the court that unfortunately, the defendant-mother had strayed from her treatment and was under the influence of cocaine at the time that a friend talked her into abandoning her child.

The mother is very sorry and regrets her actions. She loves her daughter and does not want to lose custody of her permanently. If the judge gives her a long jail sentence, she is afraid that she will lose custody. After this testimony, the social worker steps down from the stand.

The judge considers the testimony. He knows that if he puts the defendant-mother in jail, she will not receive the treatment that she needs. This will not help either the defendant or her daughter. He sentences her to one year of drug rehabilitation in a live-in facility. Her child will remain in foster care for that time. The decision regarding her daughter's custody after that time will be left up to the agency that placed the daughter in the foster home. If the mother's treatment is successful, the agency might consider returning the child to the mother. The defendant is to appear before the court every three months and give a progress report.

CRIMINAL CALL ENDS

Amanda notes this sentence on her docket sheet. She leaves the courtroom now that the criminal call is over. She takes the files containing the docket sheets and her notes for the cases to the Records Department. There the information will be entered into the county's computer system to update the status of these cases.

Appeal

Persons convicted of crimes have a right of appeal. Most felony convictions are appealed to an intermediate court of appeal. In some states, however, there is no intermediate court of appeal, so the appeal goes directly to the state's highest appellate court, usually called the supreme court of the state. Most convictions that result in supervised release or fines are not appealed, but a high percentage of the convictions that result in prison sentences are appealed. About 10 percent of such convictions are reversed on appeal. The most common reason for reversal is that the trial court admitted improper evidence, such as evidence obtained by a search that did not meet constitutional requirements.

If a conviction is overturned on appeal, the defendant may or may not be tried again, depending on the reason for the reversal and on whether the case was reversed with or without prejudice. A decision reversed "with prejudice" means that no further action can be taken on the claim or cause. A decision reversed "without prejudice" may be tried again.

on the web

Third parties may become involved in appeals. When conservative talk-show host Rush Limbaugh appealed a conviction on drug charges, the American Civil Liberties Union filed a motion to intervene in Limbaugh's behalf. You can read the motion at **www. thesmokinggun.com**. Select "archive," and then enter the search terms "Rush Limbaugh ACLU motion."

KEY TERMS AND CONCEPTS

acquittal   448

actus reus   420

arraignment   442

arrest   431

arrest warrant   433

arson   424

bail   437

beyond a reasonable doubt   418

booking   431

burglary   423

crime   418

cyberbullying   428

cyber crime   427

cyberstalking   428

defense   421

defense of others   422

defense of property   422

diversion program   451

double jeopardy   430

due process of law   429

embezzlement   424

exclusionary rule   430

felony   419

forgery   424

grand jury   441

hacker   428

hung jury   448

identity theft   427

indictment   441

information   441

insider trading   426

larceny   423

mens rea   420

Miranda rights   430

misdemeanor   419

money laundering   426

motion for a change of venue   443

motion to recuse   443

motion to sever   443

motion to suppress evidence   442

nolo contendere   442

petty offense   420

plea bargaining   442

preliminary hearing   440

probable cause   433

public defender   417

public prosecutor   417

responsible corporate officer doctrine   421

robbery   423

search warrant   433

self-defense   422

self-incrimination   430

sentence   449

white-collar crime   424

CHAPTER SUMMARY

CRIMINAL LAW AND PROCEDURES

What Is a Crime?

1. *Key differences between civil and criminal law*—Crimes are distinguished from other types of wrongs, such as torts, in several ways:

   a. Crimes are deemed to be offenses against society as a whole.

   b. Whereas tort (civil) litigation involves lawsuits between private parties, criminal litigation involves the state's prosecution of a wrongdoer.

Continued

c. Crimes are defined as such by state legislatures or the federal government.

   d. The burden of proof in criminal cases is higher than that for civil cases. The state must prove the defendant's guilt beyond a reasonable doubt. In civil cases, the plaintiff need only prove his or her case by a preponderance of the evidence.

   e. A criminal act need not involve a victim.

2. *Civil liability for criminal acts*—Those who commit crimes may be subject to both criminal and civil liability, as when a person commits an assault.

3. *Classification of crimes*—Crimes fall into two basic classifications: felonies and misdemeanors.

   a. Felonies are more serious crimes (such as murder, rape, and robbery) for which penalties may range from imprisonment for a year or longer to (in some states) death.

   b. Misdemeanors are less serious crimes (such as prostitution, disturbing the peace, and public intoxication) for which penalties may include imprisonment for up to a year. Petty offenses, or infractions, such as violations of building codes, are usually a subset of misdemeanors.

Elements of Criminal Liability

Four elements are required for criminal liability to exist: a wrongful act (*actus reus*) and a specified state of mind (*mens rea*).

1. *Actus reus*—Most crimes require that the defendant commit an act, although sometimes a person may commit a crime by failing to do something that is required, such as filing a tax return.

2. *Mens rea*—Even a wrongful act that harms society will not be punished unless the defendant had the required state of mind, or intent. What constitutes the required intent varies according to the action.

3. *Corporate criminal liability*—Under modern law, corporations may be held liable for crimes, and corporate officers and directors may sometimes be held personally liable for the crimes of the corporation.

4. *Defenses to criminal liability*—Criminal liability may be avoided if the state of mind required for the crime was lacking or some other defense against liability can be raised. Defenses include self-defense, defense of others, defense of property, and the running of a statute of limitations.

Types of Crimes

The number of acts defined as criminal by federal, state, and local laws is nearly endless. The five traditional categories of crimes are as follows:

1. *Violent crime*—Crimes that cause another person to suffer harm or death are violent crimes, such as murder, rape, robbery, and assault and battery.

2. *Property crime*—The most common criminal activities are those in which the offender either takes or damages the property of another. Property crimes include burglary, larceny (stealing), obtaining goods by false pretenses, receiving stolen goods, arson, and forgery.

3. *Public order crimes*—Crimes that do not cause direct harm to others but involve behavior that society has deemed inappropriate or immoral, such as public drunkenness and illegal drug use, are public order crimes.

4. *White-collar crime*—Illegal acts committed by individuals or business entities in the course of legitimate business—for example, embezzlement, mail

or wire fraud, bribery, theft of trade secrets, and insider trading—are white-collar crimes.

5. *Organized crime*—The criminal enterprises that make up organized crime are operated illegitimately, usually providing illegal goods and services. Preferred markets have traditionally included gambling, prostitution, and illegal narcotics.

Cyber Crimes

Cyber crimes are crimes that are committed with computers and occur in cyber-space. They are not new crimes but existing crimes in which the Internet is the instrument of wrongdoing. Cyber crimes include theft of money or data, identity theft, cyberstalking, cyberbullying, and hacking. Prosecuting cyber crimes presents special challenges.

Constitutional Safeguards

Specific procedures must be followed in arresting and prosecuting a criminal suspect to safeguard the suspect's constitutional rights. The U.S. Constitution guarantees that every person accused of a crime has certain rights and protections, including protection against unreasonable searches and seizures, the right to due process of law, protection against double jeopardy, protection against self-incrimination (the right to remain silent), the right to a speedy and public trial, the right to confront witnesses and be represented by an attorney, and protection against excessive bail and cruel and unusual punishment.

1. *Exclusionary rule*—All evidence obtained in violation of the defendant's constitutional rights normally must be excluded from the trial, along with evidence derived from illegally obtained evidence.

2. *Miranda rule*—At the time a criminal suspect is taken into custody, the arresting officers must inform the suspect of his or her rights by reading the *Miranda* warnings. Any evidence or confession obtained in violation of the suspect's rights will normally not be admissible in court. The Supreme Court has made numerous exceptions to the *Miranda* rule, such as when public safety is at stake.

Criminal Procedures prior to Prosecution and at the Beginning of Prosecution

The initial procedures undertaken by the police after a crime is reported include arrest, booking, and investigation after arrest. Criminal litigation against a suspect begins when the prosecutor decides to prosecute the case and files a complaint.

1. *Pretrial motions*—The defendant's attorney may file pretrial motions based on possible violations of the defendant's rights. For example, defense attorneys often file a motion to suppress evidence if probable cause for the search is questionable. Motions to dismiss may be filed for any number of reasons, including a violation of the defendant's right to a speedy trial.

2. *Discovery*—In criminal cases, the defendant is entitled to obtain any evidence relating to the case possessed by the prosecution, including documents, statements previously made by the defendant, objects, reports of tests or examinations, and other evidence. In some cases, the prosecutor is entitled to obtain certain evidence related to the case possessed by the defense as well.

Continued

The Trial

Most criminal cases are settled before they get to trial through plea bargaining or other means. Most criminal trials last less than one week and are similar to civil trials, except in a few major ways.

1. *The presumption of innocence*—The defendant is innocent until the prosecutor proves the defendant's guilt to the jury (or judge) beyond a reasonable doubt. The defendant is not required to present any evidence at the trial.

2. *Self-incrimination*—The defendant and witnesses cannot be forced to testify if such testimony would be incriminating.

3. *Speedy trial*—Criminal defendants have a right to a speedy and public trial. Even if they waive that right, criminal cases usually go to trial more quickly than civil cases.

4. *Unanimous jury*—Most criminal cases are tried by juries. Generally, all of the jurors must reach agreement in order to acquit or convict the defendant (whereas civil trials typically do not require unanimous agreement).

5. *Sentencing*—The judge sentences a defendant who has been found guilty (or who pleads guilty or no contest), often at a separate proceeding. Most criminal statutes set forth a range of penalties that can be imposed, and judges are free to select the appropriate penalty within that range. Typically, sentences involve fines, imprisonment, and probation (including conditions of probation). In some cases (in some states), the death penalty may be imposed.

6. *Diversion*—Alternatively, the defendant may be sentenced to a diversion program, which will result in a dismissal of the case provided that the defendant complies with all the requirements of diversion (which vary by state).

7. *Appeal*—If the defendant loses at trial, he or she may appeal the case to a higher court. A small percentage of criminal cases are reversed on appeal.

STUDENT STUDYWARE™ CD-ROM

Interactive student CD in this book includes additional quizzing, plus video clips, case studies, and Key Terms flashcards.

ONLINE COMPANION™

For additional resources, please go to **www.paralegal.delmar.cengage.com**.

QUESTIONS FOR REVIEW

1. What two elements are required for criminal liability? What defenses can be raised against criminal liability?

2. What are the constitutional rights of a person accused of a crime? Which constitutional amendments provide these rights?

3. What are the basic steps involved in criminal procedure from the time a crime is reported to the resolution of the case?

4. How is probable cause defined? Who determines whether probable cause exists?

5. What different pleas may a defendant enter during an arraignment? What is plea bargaining, and when does it typically occur?

ETHICAL QUESTIONS

1. Linda Lore is an experienced paralegal who works for a criminal defense firm. The lawyers trust her implicitly and feel that she is as knowledgeable as they are. One Monday morning, John Dodds, an attorney with the firm, is scheduled to be in court for a motion and, at the same time, at a deposition. John calls Linda into his office and asks her to take the deposition. Should Linda take it? Why or why not?

2. Larry Dow works as a paralegal for the criminal defense firm of Rice & Rowen. He and his boss have just met with Joe Dollan, an attorney from another well-known law firm. Joe has been arrested for embezzling funds from an estate he was managing for a client and needs a criminal defense attorney to handle the case. Embezzlement is a felony, and if convicted, Joe will lose his license to practice law. Larry knows that a good friend of his recently retained Joe to handle the estate of her uncle. Should Larry tell his friend that Joe has been charged with embezzlement? Is there anything that Larry can do to help his friend?

PRACTICE QUESTIONS AND ASSIGNMENTS

1. Identify each of the following crimes by its classification:

   a. Jerry refuses to mow his lawn, and it grows to a height of seven inches. The local police department receives complaints from his neighbors and gives Jerry a citation for violating the local lawn-height ordinance.

   b. Nancy is arrested for being drunk in public. She faces a possible jail sentence of six months.

   c. Susan is arrested for arson. The penalty includes confinement for over one year in prison on conviction.

2. Rafael stops Laura on a busy street and offers to sell her an expensive wristwatch for a fraction of its value. After some questioning by Laura, Rafael admits that the watch is stolen property, although he says he was not the thief. Laura pays for and receives the wristwatch. Has Laura committed any crime? Has Rafael? Explain.

3. Using the material presented in the chapter on state of mind, identify the type of homicide committed in each of the following situations:

   a. David, while driving in an intoxicated state, crashes into another car and kills its occupants.

   b. David, after pulling up next to his wife at a stoplight and observing her passionately kissing another man, smashes into her car and kills her.

   c. David, who is angry with his boss for firing him, plans to kill his boss by smashing his car into his boss's car, killing his boss and making it look like a car accident. David carries out his plan, kills his boss, and survives the accident.

4. Identify the following criminal procedures:

   a. Tom is charged with the crime of arson. He pleads not guilty and is bound over for trial in the district court.

   b. Ned is taken to the police station, searched, photographed, fingerprinted, and allowed to make one telephone call.

   c. A jury of Barbara's peers reviews the evidence against her and determines whether probable cause exists and whether the prosecutor should proceed to trial for manslaughter.

   d. Police officers stop Larry on the street because his description matches that of a reported gas-station robber. He is three blocks from the gas station when they stop him. They question him, search him, and find that he has a pocketful of $20 and $50 bills—the same denominations that were reported by the gas-station attendant as having been stolen. The police read Larry his rights and take him to the police station.

   e. Larry is taken before a magistrate, where the charges against him are read and counsel is appointed. His request to be set free on bail is denied.

   f. In exchange for a guilty plea to manslaughter, the prosecutor agrees to drop the more serious murder charges against Mary.

QUESTIONS FOR CRITICAL ANALYSIS

1. Crimes are classified into two major categories: felonies and misdemeanors (including petty offenses). What is the difference between these classifications? What does the difference indicate about the reasons for the classifications?

2. When is a crime a federal crime? Why is there a difference between state and federal crimes? Should there be?

3. A guilty act is typically required in order for a crime to be committed. Is it ever possible for a crime to be

committed without a guilty act? If so, how? Give an example of such a crime.

4. Should cyber crimes include the elements of traditional crimes (*actus reas* and *mens rea*)? Why or why not? Do you think the punishment for crimes committed in cyberspace should be more severe than the punishment for traditional crimes? Why or why not?

5. The statute of limitations is a defense to some crimes. Should it be allowed as a defense to all crimes? What about the crime of murder?

6. How is *probable cause* defined? What might be the historical reasons for this requirement?

 ## PROJECTS

1. Contact your local police department, and ask if it gives tours to students. If so, arrange to take a tour of the department and learn, to the extent possible, what procedures are followed in booking and investigation.

2. Review your state's court rules to see how the rules for criminal cases differ from those for civil cases. List and describe the major differences.

 ## USING INTERNET RESOURCES

1. Go to **www.thinkquest.org**. This site, which has become well known for its "Anatomy of a Murder," also provides a list of "Landmark Supreme Court Cases" in criminal law. To view this list, select "Library," then search on "Anatomy of a Murder." On that page, select "Rockin' Supreme Court Cases." Choose one of the cases, scan through it, and then answer the following questions:

a. Who was the defendant, and with what crime or crimes was he or she charged?

b. What defenses were raised by the defendant?

c. What constitutional issue was involved?

d. What was the Supreme Court's decision?

END NOTES

1. The American Law Institute (mentioned in Chapter 5) issued the Official Draft of the Model Penal Code in 1962. The Model Penal Code was designed to assist state legislatures in reexamining and recodifying state criminal laws. Uniformity among the states is not as important in criminal law as in other areas of the law. Crime varies with local circumstances, and it is appropriate that punishments vary accordingly.

2. Pronounced *ak*-tus *ray*-us.

3. Pronounced menz *ray*-uh.

4. *United States v. Park,* 421 U.S. 658, 95 S.Ct. 1903, 44 L.Ed.2d 489 (1975).

5. 384 U.S. 436, 86 S.Ct. 1602, 16 L.Ed.2d 694 (1966).

6. Pronounced in-`dīt-ment.

KEY ELEMENTS OF THE LAW

PART 3

CHAPTER 14

Tort Law, Product Liability, and Consumer Law

CHAPTER 15

Contracts and Intellectual Property Law

CHAPTER 16

Real Property and Insurance Law

CHAPTER 17

Family Law and Estates

CHAPTER 18

Business Organizations and Employment Law

CHAPTER 19

Bankruptcy and Environmental Law

TORT LAW, PRODUCT LIABILITY, AND CONSUMER LAW

CHAPTER

14

CHAPTER OUTLINE

Introduction

The Basis of Tort Law

Intentional Torts

Negligence

Cyber Torts: Defamation Online

Strict Liability

Product Liability

Consumer Law

AFTER COMPLETING THIS CHAPTER, YOU WILL KNOW:

▶ What a tort is, the purpose of tort law, and the basic categories of torts.

▶ The four elements of negligence.

▶ What is meant by strict liability and the underlying policy for imposing strict product liability.

▶ What defenses can be raised in product liability actions.

▶ Some of the ways in which the government protects consumers against unfair business practices and harmful products.

INTRODUCTION

Torts are wrongful actions. In fact, the word *tort* is French for "wrong." Through tort law, society compensates those who have suffered injuries as a result of the wrongful conduct of others. Although some torts, such as trespass, originated in the English common law, the field of tort law continues to expand. As new ways to commit wrongs—such as the use of the Internet to commit wrongful acts—are recognized, the courts extend tort law to cover these wrongs. Torts committed via the Internet are sometimes referred to as **cyber torts**.

Here, we discuss some of the primary concepts of tort law and how they are being applied today. We also consider *product liability,* which is the area of tort law under which sellers can be held liable for defective products. In the final pages of the chapter, we look at a growing body of law designed to protect the health and safety of *consumers*—those who purchase goods and services from businesses.

> **tort**
> A civil wrong not arising from a breach of contract; a breach of a legal duty that causes harm or injury to another.

> **cyber tort**
> A tort committed by use of the Internet.

THE BASIS OF TORT LAW

Two notions serve as the basis of all torts: wrongs and compensation. Tort law recognizes that some acts are wrong because they cause injuries to others. In a tort action, one person or group brings a personal-injury suit against another person or group to obtain compensation (money damages) or other relief for the harm suffered. Because tort suits involve "private" wrongs, they are distinguishable from criminal actions, which involve "public" wrongs. The state prosecutor brings criminal actions against individuals who commit acts that are considered to be wrongs against society as a whole (crimes are usually defined by statute, as discussed in Chapter 13). Sometimes an act may result in both a tort lawsuit and a criminal prosecution.

Generally, the purpose of tort law is to provide remedies for the invasion of personal interests or rights—such as people's interests in their physical safety and security, privacy, freedom of movement, and reputation—that society seeks to protect. In this chapter, we first discuss two broad categories of torts: *intentional torts* and *negligence.* The classification of a particular tort depends largely on how the tort occurs (intentionally or unintentionally) and the surrounding circumstances. We then examine the concept of *strict liability,* a tort doctrine under which a defendant may be held liable for harm or injury to another regardless of intention or fault, and look at the application of this doctrine in the area of product liability.

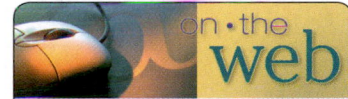

on the web

You can find cases and articles on torts in the tort law library at the Internet Law Library's Web site. Go to **www.lawguru.com**.

INTENTIONAL TORTS

An **intentional tort**, as the term implies, requires *intent*. In tort law, intent does not necessarily mean that the actor (who is sometimes called the **tortfeasor**) intended to harm someone. Rather, it means that the actor intended the consequences of the act or knew or should have known that certain consequences would result from the act. The law generally assumes that individuals intend the *normal* consequences of their actions. Thus, forcefully pushing another—even if done in fun and without any evil motive—is an intentional tort (if injury results), because the person being shoved can be expected to go flying.

Intentional torts fall into two categories: intentional torts against persons and intentional torts against property. Next, we look at both of these categories.

> **intentional tort**
> A wrongful act knowingly committed.

> **tortfeasor**
> One who commits a tort.

Intentional Torts against Persons

Intentional torts against persons include assault and battery, false imprisonment, intentional infliction of emotional distress, defamation, invasion of the right to privacy, appropriation, misrepresentation, and wrongful interference.

Assault and Battery

assault

Any word or action intended to make another person apprehensive or fearful of immediate physical harm; a reasonably believable threat.

An **assault** is any communication or action intended to make another person apprehensive or fearful of immediate physical harm. In other words, an assault is a threat that a reasonable person would believe. Note that apprehension is not the same as fear. If a contact is such that a reasonable person would want to avoid it, and if there is a reasonable basis for believing that the contact will occur, then the plaintiff suffers apprehension regardless of whether he or she is afraid. The interest protected by tort law concerning assault is the freedom from having to expect harmful or offensive contact. The occurrence of apprehension is enough to justify compensation.

battery

The intentional and offensive touching of another without lawful justification.

The *completion* of the threat, if it results in harm to the plaintiff, is a **battery**, which is defined as harmful or offensive physical contact *intentionally* performed. ▶ **EXAMPLE 14.1** Suppose that Ivan threatens Jean with a gun, then shoots her. The pointing of the gun at Jean is an assault; the firing of the gun (if the bullet hits Jean) is a battery. ◀ The interest protected by tort law concerning battery is the right to personal security and safety. The contact can be harmful, or it can be merely offensive (such as an unwelcome kiss). Physical injury need not occur. The contact can involve any part of the body or anything attached to it—for example, a hat or other item of clothing, a purse, or a chair or an automobile in which one is sitting. Whether the contact is offensive or not is determined by the *reasonable person standard* (which is discussed later in the chapter). The contact can be made by the defendant or by some force the defendant sets in motion—for example, a rock thrown, food poisoned, or a stick swung.

Compensation.   If the plaintiff shows that there was offensive contact, or fear of such contact, and the jury agrees, the plaintiff has a right to compensation. There is no need to show that the defendant acted out of malice; the person could have just been joking or playing around. The underlying motive does not matter, only the intent to bring about the harmful or offensive contact to the plaintiff. In fact, proving a motive is not necessary (but is often relevant). A plaintiff may be compensated for the emotional harm resulting from a battery, as well as for physical harm.

Defenses to Assault and Battery.   A number of legally recognized defenses, or reasons why plaintiffs should not obtain what they are seeking, can be raised by a defendant in a tort action. Later in the chapter, we review defenses that can be raised in many tort cases. The following defenses may be used by a defendant who is sued for assault, battery, or both:

- *Consent.* When a person consents to the act that damages her or him, there is generally no liability (legal responsibility) for the damage done. For instance, if Sue consents to being kissed, Bryan can raise this as a defense if she sues for battery.

- *Self-defense.* An individual who is defending her life or physical well-being can claim self-defense. In situations of both *real* and *apparent* danger, a person may use whatever force is *reasonably* necessary to prevent harmful contact. Thus, if Simon is assaulting Linda, she can claim this defense if Simon sues her for hitting him with a baseball bat.

- *Defense of others.* A person can act in a reasonable manner to protect others who are in real or apparent danger. If Fred offensively grabs Rafic's wife and Rafic hits Fred, Rafic can raise this as a defense if Fred tries to sue him for battery.

- *Defense of property.* People can use reasonable force in attempting to remove intruders from their homes, although force that is likely to cause death or great bodily injury should not be used just to protect property. For instance, if you catch someone in the act of breaking into your garage, you can use nondeadly force to stop that person without being liable for battery.

Developing Paralegal Skills

A CLAIM OF FALSE IMPRISONMENT

Julie Waterman works for a small law firm. She has just been asked to interview a new client. The client detained a customer in his video store for suspected shoplifting, and now he is facing a lawsuit brought by the customer for false imprisonment. Julie will conduct the initial interview with the client, gather as much information as she can about the incident, and summarize what she learns in a memorandum for the attorney to review later. Before the interview, Julie checks the relevant state law governing false imprisonment. During the interview, Julie makes sure that she covers the topics on her checklist for determining false imprisonment.

CHECKLIST FOR DETERMINING FALSE IMPRISONMENT

- Did the client have probable cause to believe that the customer was shoplifting? What specific behavior made the client suspect that the customer took merchandise without paying for it?
- Did the customer resist the detention?
- How long did the client detain the customer? Fifteen minutes? A half hour? An hour? Longer than an hour? Was the duration of the detention reasonable?
- Was the customer placed in a reasonably comfortable environment during the detention?
- Was the customer subjected to abusive or accusatory words or to any indignity while being confined?
- Were all procedures used to detain the client reasonable?

False Imprisonment

False imprisonment is defined as the intentional confinement or restraint of another person's activities without justification. False imprisonment interferes with the freedom to move without restraint. The confinement can be accomplished through the use of physical barriers, physical restraint, or threats of physical force. It is essential that the person being restrained not comply with the restraint willingly.

Stores are often sued for false imprisonment after they have attempted to confine a suspected shoplifter for questioning. (An example is provided in the *Developing Paralegal Skills* feature above.) Under the "privilege to detain" granted to merchants in some states, a merchant can use the defense of *probable cause* to justify delaying a suspected shoplifter. Probable cause exists when the evidence to support the belief that a person is guilty outweighs the evidence against that belief. Although laws governing false imprisonment vary from state to state, generally they require that any detention be conducted in a *reasonable* manner and for only a *reasonable* length of time.

false imprisonment
The intentional confinement or restraint of a person against his or her will.

Intentional Infliction of Emotional Distress

The tort of **intentional infliction of emotional distress** can be defined as an intentional act that amounts to extreme and outrageous conduct resulting in severe emotional distress to another. ▶ **EXAMPLE 14.2** Suppose a prankster calls Erica and says that her husband has just been in a horrible accident. As a result, Erica suffers intense mental pain or anxiety. The caller's behavior is deemed to be extreme and outrageous conduct that exceeds the bounds of decency accepted by society and is therefore **actionable** (capable of serving as the basis for a lawsuit). ◀ Courts in

intentional infliction of emotional distress
Intentional, extreme, and outrageous conduct resulting in severe emotional distress to another.

actionable
Capable of serving as the basis of a lawsuit. An actionable claim can be pursued in a lawsuit or other court action.

some jurisdictions require that the emotional distress be evidenced by some physical symptom or illness or some emotional disturbance that can be documented by a psychiatric consultant or other medical professional.

Defamation

Wrongfully hurting a person's good reputation constitutes the tort of **defamation**. The law imposes a general duty on all persons to refrain from making false, damaging statements about others. Breaching this duty orally involves the tort of **slander**; breaching it in writing involves the tort of **libel**. The tort of defamation also arises when a false statement is made about a person's product, business, or title to property.

The common law defines four types of false utterances that are considered defamation *per se* (meaning that no proof of injury or harm is required for these false statements to be actionable):

- A statement that another has a loathsome communicable disease.
- A statement that another has committed improprieties while engaging in a profession or trade.
- A statement that another has committed or has been imprisoned for a serious crime.
- A statement that an unmarried woman is unchaste.

The Publication Requirement.   The basis of the tort of defamation is the publication of a statement or statements that hold an individual up to contempt, ridicule, or hatred. Publication here means simply that the defamatory statements are communicated to persons other than the defamed party. ▶ **EXAMPLE 14.3** If Crystal writes Andrew a private letter accusing him of embezzling funds, the action does not constitute libel. If John calls Rita dishonest and incompetent when no one else is around, the action does not constitute slander. In neither case was the message communicated to a third party. ◀

The courts have generally held that even dictating a letter to a secretary constitutes publication, although the publication may be privileged (the meaning of privileged communications in defamation law will be discussed shortly). Moreover, if a third party overhears defamatory statements by chance, the courts usually hold that this also constitutes publication. Defamatory statements made via the Internet are actionable as well. Note further that anyone who republishes or repeats defamatory statements is liable even if that person reveals the source of the statements.

Defenses against Defamation.   Truth is normally an absolute defense against a defamation charge. In other words, if the defendant in a defamation suit can prove that his allegedly defamatory statements were true, the defendant will not be liable.

Another defense that is sometimes raised is that the statements were **privileged** communications and thus the defendant is immune from liability. Privileged communications are of two types: absolute and qualified. Only in judicial proceedings and certain legislative proceedings is an *absolute* privilege granted. For example, statements made in the courtroom by attorneys and judges during a trial are absolutely privileged, as are statements made by legislators during debate in a legislature. A *qualified,* or *conditional,* privilege applies when a statement is related to a matter of public interest or when the statement is necessary to protect a person's private interest and is made to another person with an interest in the same subject matter.

In general, false and defamatory statements that are made about *public figures* (public officials and any persons in the public limelight) and that are published in the press are privileged if they are made without **actual malice**. To be made with actual malice, a statement must be made *with either knowledge of falsity or a reckless*

---

defamation
Anything published or publicly spoken that causes injury to another's good name, reputation, or character.

slander
Defamation in oral form.

libel
Defamation in writing or other published form (such as videotape).

privilege
In tort law, the ability to act contrary to another person's right without that person's having legal redress for such acts. Privilege may be raised as a defense to defamation.

actual malice
Real and demonstrated evil intent. In a defamation suit, a statement made about a public figure normally must be made with actual malice (with either knowledge of its falsity or a reckless disregard of the truth) for liability to be incurred.

disregard of the truth. Statements made about public figures, especially when they are made through the media, are usually related to matters of general public interest. Furthermore, public figures generally have access to the media to respond to defamatory statements. Hence, public figures have a greater burden of proof in defamation cases (they must prove actual malice) than do private individuals.

Invasion of the Right to Privacy

A person has a right to solitude and freedom from prying public eyes—in other words, to privacy. The United States Supreme Court has held that a fundamental right to privacy is implied by various amendments to the U.S. Constitution. Some state constitutions explicitly provide for privacy rights. In addition, a number of federal and state statutes protect individual rights in specific areas. Tort law also safeguards these rights through the tort of *invasion of privacy.* Four acts qualify as an invasion of privacy:

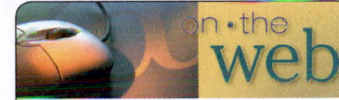

- *The use of a person's name, picture, or other likeness for commercial purposes without permission.* This tort, which is usually referred to as the tort of *appropriation,* will be examined shortly.

- *Intrusion into a person's affairs or seclusion.* For example, invading someone's home or illegally searching someone's briefcase is an invasion of privacy. The tort has been held to extend to eavesdropping by wiretap, hacking into a computer, the unauthorized scanning of a bank account, compulsory blood testing, and window peeping.

- *Publication of information that places a person in a false light.* This could be a story attributing to the person ideas not held or actions not taken by the person. (Publishing such a story could involve the tort of defamation as well.)

- *Public disclosure of private facts about an individual that an ordinary person would find objectionable.* A newspaper account of a private citizen's sex life or financial affairs could be an actionable invasion of privacy.

Appropriation

The use by one person of another person's name, likeness, or other identifying characteristic, without permission and for the benefit of the user, constitutes the tort of **appropriation**. Under the law, an individual's right to privacy normally includes the right to the exclusive use of her or his identity.

▶ **EXAMPLE 14.4** A good example of appropriation can be found in the case brought by Vanna White, the hostess of the popular television game show *Wheel of Fortune,* against Samsung Electronics America, Inc. Without White's permission, Samsung included in an advertisement for its videocassette recorders a depiction of a robot dressed in a wig, gown, and jewelry, posed in a scene that resembled the *Wheel of Fortune* set, in a stance for which White is famous. The court held in White's favor, holding that the tort of appropriation does not require the use of a celebrity's name or likeness. The court stated that Samsung's robot ad left "little doubt" as to the identity of the celebrity whom the ad was meant to depict. ◀

appropriation

In tort law, the use by one person of another person's name, likeness, or other identifying characteristic without permission and for the benefit of the user.

Misrepresentation (Fraud)

A misrepresentation leads another to believe in a condition that is different from the condition that actually exists. This is often accomplished through a false or an incorrect statement. The tort of **fraudulent misrepresentation**, or fraud, involves intentional deceit for personal gain—not misrepresentations innocently made by someone who is unaware of the facts.

fraudulent misrepresentation

Any misrepresentation, either by misstatement or omission of a material fact, knowingly made with the intention of deceiving another and on which a reasonable person would and does rely to his or her detriment.

Elements of Fraud. The tort of fraudulent misrepresentation includes several elements:

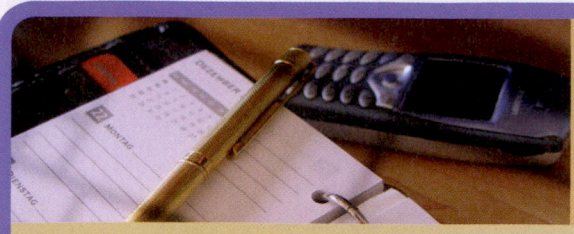

In the **Office**

ONLINE PRIVACY

A pressing issue in today's online world has to do with the privacy rights of Internet users, especially in the employment context. Law firms routinely provide their paralegals and other employees with e-mail access. What if a paralegal uses e-mail to spread rumors or to make sexually explicit or unprofessional comments about other employees? Can a paralegal claim a right to privacy in the personal e-mail sent from his or her office computer? Most courts that have considered the question have concluded that employees have no reasonable expectation of privacy in e-mails sent from their office computers. This is true even when employees were not informed that their e-mails could be read by the employer. After all, the employer has both a legal and an ethical obligation to prevent harassment and discrimination in the workplace. Although employers who provide Internet access to employees can usually monitor or access their employees' e-mail messages without liability for invasion of privacy, they would not be allowed by most courts to publicly disclose the contents of an employee's personal e-mail.

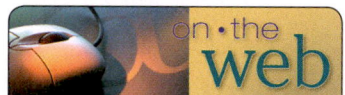

The 'Lectric Law Library's Legal Lexicon includes an informative discussion of the elements of fraud as well as different types of fraud. To access this page, go to **www.lectlaw.com**. Search on "Fraud," and select "Fraud, to Defraud" from the search results.

- Misrepresentation of facts or conditions with knowledge that they are false or with reckless disregard for the truth.
- Intent to induce another to rely on the misrepresentation.
- Justifiable reliance by the deceived party.
- Damages suffered as a result of the reliance.
- Causal connection between the misrepresentation and the injury suffered.

Fraud exists only when a person represents as a fact something he knows is untrue. It is fraud to claim that a building does not leak when one knows it does. Facts can be objectively determined, unlike *seller's talk*. ▶ **EXAMPLE 14.5** If Harry says, "I am the best accountant in town," that is seller's talk, not fraud. The speaker is not trying to represent something as fact, because the term *best* is subjective (open to interpretation) and because a "reasonable person" would not rely on Harry's statement. ◀

Fact versus Opinion. Normally, the tort of misrepresentation or fraud occurs only when there is reliance on a *statement of fact*. Sometimes, however, reliance on a *statement of opinion* may involve the tort of misrepresentation if the person making the statement of opinion has a superior knowledge of the subject matter. ▶ **EXAMPLE 14.6** When a lawyer makes a statement of opinion about the law in a state in which the lawyer is licensed to practice, a court would hold reliance on such a statement to be equivalent to reliance on a statement of fact. ◀

Wrongful Interference

Today, many lawsuits involve situations in which a person or business is accused of wrongfully interfering with the business of another. These **business torts** are generally divided into two categories: wrongful interference with a contractual relationship (contract law will be discussed in Chapter 15) and wrongful interference with a business relationship.

business tort
Wrongful interference with another's business rights.

Wrongful Interference with a Contractual Relationship. The area of tort law relating to intentional interference with a contractual relationship has expanded in recent years. Three elements are necessary to establish the tort of wrongful interference with a contractual relationship:

- A valid, enforceable contract exists between two parties.
- A third party knows that this contract exists.
- The third party *intentionally* causes either of the two parties to breach the contract.

The contract may be between a firm and its employees or a firm and its customers. Sometimes, for example, a competitor of a firm draws away one of the firm's key employees. If the original employer can show (1) that the competitor induced the employee to leave (a breach of the contract) and (2) that the employee would not otherwise have broken the contract, then the employer may be entitled to compensation from the competitor.

Wrongful Interference with a Business Relationship. Wrongful interference with a business relationship occurs when a party unreasonably interferes with another's business in an attempt to gain a larger share of the market. There is a difference between competitive methods that do not give rise to tort liability and **predatory behavior**—actions undertaken with the intention of unlawfully driving competitors completely out of the market. The distinction usually depends on whether a business is attempting to attract customers in general or to solicit only those customers who have shown an interest in a similar product or service of a specific competitor. ▶ **EXAMPLE 14.7** If a shopping center contains two shoe stores, an employee of Store A cannot be sent to the entrance of Store B to divert customers to Store A. This type of activity constitutes the tort of wrongful interference with a business relationship, which is commonly considered to be an unfair trade practice. ◀

> **predatory behavior**
> Business behavior that is undertaken with the intention of unlawfully driving competitors out of the market.

Defenses to Wrongful Interference. A person will not be liable for the tort of wrongful interference with a contractual or business relationship if it can be shown that the interference was justified, or permissible. Good faith competitive behavior is a permissible interference even if it results in the breaking of a contract. ▶ **EXAMPLE 14.8** If Antonio's Meats advertises so effectively that it induces Beverly's Restaurant Chain to break its contract with Otis Meat Company, Otis Meat will be unable to recover against Antonio's Meats on a wrongful interference theory. Public policy favors free competition through honest advertising. ◀

Intentional Torts against Property

Intentional torts against property include trespass to land, trespass to personal property, and conversion. These torts are wrongful actions that interfere with individuals' legally recognized rights to their land or personal property. The law distinguishes real property from personal property (see Chapter 16). *Real property* is land and things "permanently" attached to the land. *Personal property* consists of movable items. Thus, a house is real property, whereas the furniture inside the house is personal property. Money and stocks and bonds are also personal property. (See this chapter's *Technology and Today's Paralegal* feature on pages 468 and 469 for a discussion of how spam can constitute the tort of interference with personal property.)

Trespass to Land

A **trespass to land** occurs whenever a person, without permission, enters onto land that is owned by another, causes anything to enter onto the land, remains on the land, or permits anything to remain on it. Actual harm to the land is not an essential element of this tort because the tort is designed to protect the right of owners to exclusively possess their property. Common trespasses include walking or driving on the land, shooting a gun over the land, throwing rocks at a building that belongs

> **trespass to land**
> The entry onto, above, or below the surface of land owned by another without the owner's permission.

Technology and Today's Paralegal

IDENTITY THEFT, SPAM, AND RELATED LEGAL ISSUES

The Internet offers a wide range of valuable services, from shopping to filing legal documents. As you know, its popularity means that deceptive and destructive practices constantly evolve and cause problems. These problems can have legal dimensions. As a paralegal, you should be aware of problems, efforts to control them, and resources that can provide assistance.

IDENTITY THEFT AND PHISHING

Identity theft causes much grief and at least $50 billion in financial losses annually. We often hear individual horror stories about the millions of people each year who suffer identity theft. Most of the losses, however, fall on businesses that are victimized by the use of stolen credit-card information and other valuable data.

One common type of identity theft involves *phishing.* A perpetrator "fishes" for financial data and passwords by posing as a legitimate bank, eBay, the IRS, a credit-card company, or other reputable source. The *phisher* sends official looking e-mails asking the recipient to "update" or "confirm" vital information. Once those data are received, the phisher moves quickly to drain accounts. This data collection is also done by telephone, often by VoIP (Voice over Internet Protocol)—known as *vishing.* The thief claims to be calling from a reputable company, and the caller ID may show that to appear to be the case.

Various government agencies provide information about identify theft and advice about preventing it or dealing with its effects:

- The Federal Trade Commission offers information at **www.ftc.gov**. On the "Consumer Protection" tab, select "Consumer Information." Under "Consumer Categories," select "ID Theft, Privacy & Security" and then "Identity Theft."

- At the Department of Justice Web site, **www.usdoj.gov**, enter "identify theft" in the "Search" box and select "Identity Theft and Fraud" from the results.

- The Social Security Administration offers advice about stolen Social Security numbers at **www.ssa. gov/pubs/idtheft.htm**.

Private sources include the Identity Theft Resources Center at **www.idtheftcenter.org** and the Privacy Rights Clearinghouse at **www.privacyrights.org**.

---

to someone else, causing water to back up on someone else's land, and placing part of one's building on an adjoining landowner's property.

Trespass Criteria, Rights, and Duties. The owner of the real property must show that a person is a trespasser. For example, a person who ignores "private property" signs and enters, uninvited, onto the property is clearly a trespasser. A guest in your home is legally an invitee, not a trespasser—unless she has been asked to leave but refuses. Any person who enters onto your property to commit an illegal act (such as a thief) is a trespasser, without posted signs. Normally, a trespasser must pay for any damage caused to the property and can be removed from the premises through the use of reasonable force without the owner's being liable for assault and battery. Further, a property owner owes no duty of care to a trespasser. If a trespasser sneaks across your backyard and breaks a leg when he steps in a hole in your lawn, he cannot sue you for having a hole in the lawn.

THE FEDERAL CAN-SPAM ACT

Bulk, unsolicited e-mail, or *spam,* imposes a burden on an Internet service provider's equipment as well as on e-mail recipients. As you are no doubt aware, spam accounts for a high percentage of all e-mail. When dealing with clients who market goods or services through commercial e-mails, paralegals need to understand laws regulating spam. An important federal law in this area is the Controlling the Assault of Non-Solicited Pornography and Marketing (CAN-SPAM) Act. You can find information about it at the Federal Trade Commission's Web site. Go to **www.ftc.gov**, and select "Business Information" on the "Consumer Protection" tab. Under "Business Categories," select "E-Commerce."

CAN-SPAM applies to any "commercial electronic mail messages" sent to promote a commercial product or service. Generally, the act permits the use of unsolicited commercial e-mail but prohibits certain spamming activities, including the use of a false return address and the inclusion of false, misleading, or deceptive information. The statute also prohibits the use of "dictionary attacks"—sending messages to randomly generated e-mail addresses—and the "harvesting" of e-mail addresses from Web sites through the use of specialized software. The law requires senders of commercial e-mail to do the following:

- Include a return address on the e-mail.

- Include a clear notification that the message is an ad and provide a valid physical postal address.

- Provide a mechanism that allows recipients to "opt out" of further e-mail ads from the same source.

- Take action on a recipient "opt-out" request within ten days.

- Label any sexually oriented materials as such.

SPAMMING AS A TORT

Spamming may also constitute a tort if it interferes with a computer system's functioning. A number of plaintiffs have successfully sued, under tort law, when spam overloaded a business's computer system or impaired a business's computer equipment. In these cases, spamming was held to constitute unauthorized interference with the use of the personal property of another, which is a trespass to personal property. Because a great deal of spam comes from other countries, however, tort actions are limited in their effectiveness.

TECHNOLOGY TIP

Consumers continue to face identity theft, and spam continues to increase. Paralegals in consumer law need to keep up to date on these issues. Paralegals should also be familiar with the resources available to those with complaints of identity theft, which include the FTC and other agencies. Finally, paralegals need to be familiar with laws regulating spam, such as the CAN-SPAM Act.

Defenses against Trespass to Land. The most common defense to trespass is that the trespass was justified. For example, when a trespasser enters to assist someone in danger, a defense exists. Another defense exists when the trespasser can show that he had permission to come onto the land for a specified purpose, such as to read an electric meter. Note that the property owner can revoke such permission. If the property owner asks a meter reader to leave and the meter reader refuses, the meter reader at that point becomes a trespasser.

Trespass to Personal Property

Whenever any individual unlawfully harms the personal property of another or otherwise interferes with the owner's right to exclusively possess that personal property, **trespass to personal property** occurs. ▶ **EXAMPLE 14.9** Suppose a student takes another student's paralegal book as a practical joke and hides it so that the

trespass to personal property
The unlawful taking or harming of another's personal property; interference with another's right to the exclusive possession of his or her personal property.

owner is unable to find it for several days before a final examination. In this situation, the student has engaged in a trespass to personal property. ◄

If it can be shown that trespass to personal property was warranted, then a complete defense exists. Most states, for example, allow automobile repair shops to hold a customer's car (under what is called an *artisan's lien*) when the customer refuses to pay for repairs already completed.

Conversion

conversion
The act of wrongfully taking or retaining a person's personal property and placing it in the service of another.

Whenever personal property is wrongfully taken from its owner, the act of **conversion** occurs. Conversion is any act depriving an owner of personal property without that owner's permission and without just cause. When conversion occurs, the lesser offense of trespass to personal property usually occurs as well. If the initial taking of the property was unlawful, there is trespass; keeping the property is conversion. Even if the owner permitted the initial taking of the property, failure to return it may still be conversion. Conversion is the civil side of crimes related to theft. A store clerk who steals merchandise from the store commits a crime and engages in the tort of conversion at the same time.

Even if a person mistakenly believed that she was entitled to the goods, a tort of conversion may occur. ► **EXAMPLE 14.10** Someone who buys stolen goods may be guilty of conversion even if she did not know that the goods were stolen. If the true owner brings a tort action against the buyer, the buyer must either return the property to the owner or pay the owner the full value of the property (despite having already paid the thief). If the person accused of conversion can show that the purported owner did not in fact own the property, however, a defense exists. ◄

INTENTIONAL TORTS AND THE PARALEGAL

The common law of torts is an area of particular importance for paralegals. Tort lawsuits are frequent occurrences in the American legal arena, and many attorneys and paralegals devote a substantial amount of their time to serving clients who want to either bring or defend against tort lawsuits. The paralegal's tasks relating to a lawsuit for an intentional tort are similar to the tasks necessary for any litigation, including assisting with (or conducting) interviews with the client, investigating the client's claim, interviewing any witnesses to the alleged tort action, preparing documents to file with the court, assisting at trial if the dispute is not settled out of court, and the like. Although many tort lawsuits are brought for intentional torts, even more common are lawsuits for torts of negligence, a topic to which we now turn.

NEGLIGENCE

negligence
The failure to exercise the standard of care that a reasonable person would exercise in similar circumstances.

The tort of **negligence** occurs when someone suffers injury because of another's failure to live up to a required *duty of care*. In contrast to intentional torts, in torts involving negligence, the one committing the tort did not wish to commit the initial act or to bring about the consequences of the act. Rather, the actor's conduct creates a *risk* of such consequences. If no risk is created, there is no negligence. The risk must also be foreseeable—that is, it must be such that a reasonable person engaging in the same activity would anticipate the risk and guard against it.

Many of the actions discussed in the section on intentional torts constitute negligence if the element of intent is missing. ► **EXAMPLE 14.11** If Juan intentionally shoves Naomi, who falls and breaks an arm as a result, Juan will have committed the intentional tort of battery. If Juan carelessly runs into Naomi on the stairway, and she falls and breaks an arm as a result, Juan's action will constitute negligence. In either situation, Juan has committed a tort. ◄

To succeed in a negligence action, the plaintiff must prove the following:

- That the defendant owed a duty of care to the plaintiff.
- That the defendant breached that duty.
- That the plaintiff suffered a legally recognizable injury.
- That the defendant's breach caused the plaintiff's injury.

We discuss here each of these four elements of negligence.

The Duty of Care and Its Breach

Central to the tort of negligence is the concept of a **duty of care**. This concept arises from the belief that if we are to live in society with other people, some actions can be tolerated and some cannot; some actions are right and some are wrong; and some actions are reasonable and some are not. The basic principle underlying the duty of care is that people are free to act as they please so long as their actions do not infringe on the interests of others.

The law of torts defines and measures the duty of care by the **reasonable person standard**. In determining whether a duty of care has been breached, the courts ask how a reasonable person would have acted in the same circumstances. The reasonable person standard is not necessarily how a particular person would act. It is society's judgment of how an ordinarily sensible person should act under certain circumstances. That individuals are required to exercise a reasonable standard of care in their activities is a pervasive concept in the law, and many of the issues dealt with in subsequent chapters of this text have to do with this duty.

In negligence cases, the degree of care to be exercised varies depending on the defendant's occupation or profession, relationship with the plaintiff, and other factors. Generally, whether an action constitutes a breach of the duty of care is determined on a case-by-case basis. The outcome depends on how the trial court judge (or jury, if it is a jury trial) decides a reasonable person in the position of the defendant would have acted in the circumstances of the case. In the following subsections, we examine the degree of care typically expected of property owners and professionals.

The Duty of Property Owners

Property owners are expected to exercise reasonable care to protect persons coming onto their property from harm. Owners who rent or lease property to tenants are expected to exercise reasonable care to ensure that the tenants and their guests are not harmed in common areas, such as stairways and laundry rooms, by keeping them in safe condition.

Duty to Business Invitees.   Retailers and other firms that invite persons to come onto their premises are charged with a duty to exercise reasonable care to protect those persons, who are considered **business invitees**. ▶ **EXAMPLE 14.12** If you entered a supermarket, slipped on a wet floor from a spilled product, and suffered injuries, the owner of the supermarket would be liable for damages if, when you slipped, there was no sign warning that the floor was wet. A court would hold that the business owner was negligent because the owner failed to exercise a reasonable degree of care in protecting the store's customers against foreseeable risks about which the owner knew or *should have known*. That a patron might slip on the wet floor and be injured as a result was a foreseeable risk, and the owner should have taken care to avoid this risk or to warn the customer of it. ◀ The owner also has a duty to discover and remove any hidden dangers that might injure a customer or other invitee.

Open and Obvious Risks.   Some risks, of course, are so obvious that the owner need not warn of them. For instance, a business owner does not need to warn customers to

---

duty of care

The duty of all persons, as established by tort law, to exercise reasonable care in dealings with others. Failure to exercise due care, which is normally determined by the reasonable person standard, is the tort of negligence.

reasonable person standard

The standard of behavior expected of a hypothetical "reasonable person"; the standard against which negligence is measured and that must be observed to avoid liability for negligence.

business invitee

A person, such as a customer or a client, who is invited onto business premises by the owner of those premises for business purposes.

open a door before attempting to walk through it. Other risks, however, even though they may seem obvious to a business owner, may not be so in the eyes of another, such as a child. ▶ **EXAMPLE 14.13**   A hardware store owner may not think it is necessary to warn customers that a stepladder leaning against the back wall of the store could fall down and harm them. It is possible, though, that a child could tip the ladder over or climb on it and be hurt as a result. In that case, the store could be held liable. ◀

The Duty of Professionals

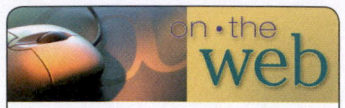

If a person has special knowledge or skill, the person's conduct must be consistent with that status. Professionals—including physicians, psychiatrists, architects, engineers, accountants, contractors, lawyers, and others—are required to have a standard minimum level of special knowledge and ability. In determining what is reasonable care in the case of professionals, their training and expertise are taken into account. In other words, an accountant cannot defend against a lawsuit for negligence by stating, "But I was not familiar with that principle of accounting." Furthermore, a business is held to the standard of care expected of knowledgeable people in that line of work. Thus, an auto repair shop cannot deny knowledge of the proper procedures for an oil change.

If a professional violates her or his duty of care toward a client, the professional may be sued for malpractice. For example, a patient might sue a physician for *medical malpractice*. A client might sue an attorney for *legal malpractice* (discussed in Chapter 4).

The Injury Requirement and Damages

To recover damages (receive compensation), the plaintiff in a tort lawsuit must prove that she or he suffered a *legally recognizable* injury—some loss, harm, wrong, or invasion of a legally protected interest. This is generally true in lawsuits for intentional torts as well as lawsuits for negligence. The facts of the case must clearly establish a basis for recovery.

Essentially, the purpose of tort law is to compensate for legally recognized injuries resulting from wrongful acts. If no harm or injury results from a given negligent action, there is nothing to compensate. ▶ **EXAMPLE 14.14**   If you carelessly bump into a passerby, who stumbles and falls as a result, you may be liable in tort if the passerby is injured in the fall. If the person is unharmed, however, there normally could be no suit for damages, because no injury was suffered. Although the passerby might be angry and might even claim emotional distress, few courts recognize negligently inflicted emotional distress as a tort unless it results in some physical disturbance. ◀

The purpose of tort law is to compensate injured parties for damages suffered, not to punish people for the torts that they commit. **Compensatory damages** are intended to compensate, or reimburse, a plaintiff for actual losses—to make the plaintiff "whole." Occasionally, however, punitive damages are also awarded in tort lawsuits. **Punitive damages** are intended to punish the wrongdoer and deter others from similar wrongdoing. Punitive damages are rarely awarded in lawsuits for ordinary negligence. They usually are given only in cases involving intentional torts. They may be awarded, however, if the defendant's negligent conduct was particularly reckless or willful.

compensatory damages
A money award equivalent to the actual value of injuries or damages sustained by the aggrieved party.

punitive damages
Money damages awarded to a plaintiff to punish the defendant and deter future similar conduct.

Causation

Another element necessary to a tort is *causation*. If a person fails in a duty of care and someone suffers injury, the wrongful activity must have caused the harm for a tort to have been committed. In deciding whether there is causation, the court must address two questions:

- *Is there causation in fact?* Did the injury occur because of the defendant's act, or would it have occurred anyway? If an injury would not have occurred with-

Paralegals who work in the area of tort law often assist in litigation involving automobile accidents. Investigating the facts of the accident and preparing sketches are often an important aspect of the paralegal's job. What is the relationship between fact investigation and preparation of sketches for trial?

(Courtesy of © Digital Vision Ltd.)

out the defendant's act, then there is causation in fact. **Causation in fact** can usually be determined by the use of the *but for* test: "but for" the wrongful act, the injury would not have occurred. For example, Arnie runs a red light and hits another car. The accident would not have occurred but for Arnie's running the red light.

- *Was the act the proximate cause of the injury?* **Proximate cause**, or legal cause, exists when the connection between an act and an injury is strong enough to justify imposing liability. ▶ **EXAMPLE 14.15** Arnie runs a red light and hits Nicki's car. Her car has a bomb in the trunk, and it explodes when the car is hit. The explosion hurts bystanders. The injured bystanders cannot sue Arnie. His negligence was the cause in fact of the accident, but it was not the proximate cause of the bystanders' injuries. ◀

Both questions must be answered in the affirmative for liability in tort to arise. If a defendant's action constitutes causation in fact but a court decides that the action is not the proximate cause of the plaintiff's injury, the causation requirement has not been met—and the defendant normally will not be liable to the plaintiff.

Defenses to Negligence

Defendants often defend against negligence claims by asserting that the plaintiffs have failed to prove the existence of one or more of the required elements for negligence. Additionally, there are three basic *affirmative* defenses in negligence cases (defenses that defendants can use to avoid liability even if the facts are as the plaintiffs state): (1) assumption of risk, (2) superseding cause, and (3) contributory or comparative negligence.

Assumption of Risk

A plaintiff who voluntarily enters into a risky situation, knowing the risk involved, will not be allowed to recover. This is the defense of **assumption of risk**. The requirements of this defense are (1) knowledge of the risk and (2) voluntary assumption of the risk.

The risk can be assumed by express agreement, or the assumption of risk can be implied by the plaintiff's knowledge of the risk and subsequent conduct. For

causation in fact
Causation brought about by an act or omission without which an event would not have occurred.

proximate cause
Legal cause; exists when the connection between an act and an injury is strong enough to justify imposing liability.

assumption of risk
Voluntarily taking on a known risk; a defense against negligence that can be used when the plaintiff has knowledge of and appreciates a danger and voluntarily exposes himself or herself to the danger.

instance, a driver entering a race knows that there is a risk of being killed or injured in a crash. Of course, the plaintiff does not assume a risk different from or greater than the risk normally carried by the activity. In the scenario just mentioned, the race driver does not assume the risk that the banking in the curves of the racetrack will give way during the race because of a construction defect.

In emergency situations, risks are not considered assumed. Neither are they assumed when a statute protects a class of people from harm and a member of the class is injured by the harm. ▶ **EXAMPLE 14.16** Employees are protected by statute from harmful working conditions and therefore do not assume the risks associated with the workplace. An employee who is injured will generally be compensated regardless of fault under state workers' compensation statutes (to be discussed in Chapter 18). ◀

Superseding Cause

An unforeseeable intervening event may break the connection between a wrongful act and an injury to another. If so, it acts as a *superseding cause*—that is, it relieves a defendant of liability for injuries caused by the intervening event. ▶ **EXAMPLE 14.17** Suppose that Derrick keeps a can of gasoline in the trunk of his car. The presence of the gasoline creates a foreseeable risk and is thus a negligent act. If Derrick's car skids and crashes into a tree, causing the gasoline can to explode, Derrick will be liable for injuries sustained by passing pedestrians because of his negligence. If lightning striking the car causes the explosion, however, the lightning supersedes Derrick's original negligence as a cause of the damage, because the lightning was not foreseeable. ◀

Contributory and Comparative Negligence

contributory negligence
A theory in tort law under which a complaining party's own negligence contributed to his or her injuries. Contributory negligence is an absolute bar to recovery in some jurisdictions.

All individuals are expected to exercise a reasonable degree of care in looking out for themselves. In a few jurisdictions, recovery for injury resulting from negligence is prevented if the plaintiff was also negligent. This is the defense of **contributory negligence**. Under the common law doctrine of contributory negligence, no matter how insignificant the plaintiff's negligence is relative to the defendant's negligence, the plaintiff will not recover any damages.

comparative negligence
A theory in tort law under which the liability for injuries resulting from negligent acts is shared by all persons who were guilty of negligence (including the injured party) on the basis of each person's proportionate carelessness.

Most states allow recovery based on the doctrine of **comparative negligence**. Here, the plaintiff's negligence and the defendant's negligence are computed and the liability for damages distributed accordingly. Some jurisdictions have adopted a "pure" form of comparative negligence that allows the plaintiff to recover, even if the extent of his or her fault is greater than that of the defendant. For example, if the plaintiff was 80 percent at fault and the defendant 20 percent at fault, the plaintiff may recover 20 percent of her damages. Many states' comparative negligence statutes, however, contain a "50 percent" rule by which the plaintiff recovers nothing if he was more than 50 percent at fault.

Special Negligence Doctrines and Statutes

There are a number of special doctrines and statutes relating to negligence. We examine only a few of them here.

Negligence Per Se

negligence *per se*
An action or failure to act in violation of a statutory requirement.

Certain conduct, whether it consists of an action or a failure to act, may be treated as **negligence *per se*** (*per se* means "in or of itself"). Negligence *per se* may occur if an individual violates a statute or an ordinance providing for a criminal penalty and that violation causes another to be injured. The injured person must prove (1) that the statute clearly sets out what standard of conduct is expected, when and where it is expected, and of whom it is expected; (2) that he or she is in the class intended to be protected by the statute; and (3) that the statute was designed to prevent the type of injury that he or she suffered. The standard of conduct required by the statute is the duty that the defendant owes to the plaintiff, and a violation of the statute is the breach of that duty.

▶ **EXAMPLE 14.18** A statute may require a property owner to keep a building in safe condition and may also subject the owner to a criminal penalty, such as a fine, if the building is not kept safe. The statute is meant to protect those who are rightfully in the building. Thus, if the owner, without a sufficient excuse, violates the statute and a tenant is injured, then a majority of courts will hold that the owner's unexcused violation of the statute conclusively establishes a breach of a duty of care—that is, that the owner's violation is negligence *per se*. ◀

Special Negligence Statutes

A number of states have enacted statutes prescribing duties and responsibilities in certain circumstances. For example, most states now have what are called **Good Samaritan statutes**. Under these statutes, persons who receive voluntary aid from others cannot turn around and sue the "Good Samaritans" for negligence. These laws were passed largely to protect physicians and medical personnel who volunteer their services in emergency situations to those in need, such as individuals hurt in car accidents.

Many states have also passed **dram shop acts**, under which a bar owner or bartender may be held liable for injuries caused by a person who became intoxicated while drinking at the bar or who was already intoxicated when served by the bartender. In some states, statutes impose liability on *social hosts* (persons hosting parties) for injuries caused by guests who became intoxicated at the hosts' homes. Under these statutes, it is unnecessary to prove that the bar owner, bartender, or social host was negligent.

> **Good Samaritan statute**
> A state statute stipulating that persons who provide emergency services to others in peril—unless they do so recklessly, thus causing further harm—cannot be sued for negligence.

> **dram shop act**
> A state statute that imposes liability on the owners of bars, as well as those who serve alcoholic drinks to the public, for injuries resulting from accidents caused by intoxicated persons when the sellers or servers of alcoholic drinks contributed to the intoxication.

NEGLIGENCE LAW AND THE PARALEGAL

Many paralegals become involved in tasks relating to lawsuits for negligence. If you work for a litigation firm, chances are that you will handle numerous assignments involving claims of negligence. Many law firms specialize in personal-injury litigation and represent plaintiffs who have been injured in car accidents or other incidents resulting from the defendant's alleged negligence.

If you work for a law firm that specializes in personal-injury litigation, you might be responsible for some of the following tasks:

- Interview a client (plaintiff) to obtain details about the accident and the injuries sustained in the accident.

- Locate and interview witnesses to gather additional information about the accident.

- Obtain medical reports from physicians and hospitals describing the plaintiff's injuries.

- Attend depositions, and summarize the testimony of witnesses, parties, and experts in the case.

- Obtain employment data to verify the amount of lost wages that should be claimed as damages if the client's current or future employment is affected by the injury.

- Obtain a copy of the police report, and, if necessary, consult with police officers and investigators who worked on the case.

- Prepare documents to initiate a lawsuit, respond to the other party's documents, and file documents and responses with the court.

- Prepare exhibits for trial, create a trial notebook for the attorney to refer to during the trial, and prepare the client and witnesses for trial.

- Generally, provide litigation assistance (as discussed in Chapters 10 through 12).

Many law firms or departments of law firms specialize in areas of tort litigation other than personal-injury liability. This chapter's *Featured Contributor* article on pages 476 and 477 focuses on medical malpractice and offers some examples of paralegal duties in this area.

featured contributor

IS THERE A PLACE FOR PARALEGALS IN THE FIELD OF MEDICAL MALPRACTICE?

Beth Walston-Dunham

BIOGRAPHICAL NOTE

Beth Walston-Dunham has been publishing legal texts since 1990. She earned a bachelor of science degree in psychology and business from Central Missouri State University in 1981 and a J.D. degree from the Saint Louis University School of Law in 1984. She has been licensed in the states of Illinois, Missouri, Nebraska, and Texas, where her practice included plaintiffs' medical malpractice litigation. She has also held the position of administrative partner in a private medical practice and has worked as a consultant on risk management issues for health-care professionals. She served as the first director of paralegal studies, legal administration, and prelaw programs at the College of Saint Mary in Omaha, Nebraska.

The role of the paralegal in the justice system, and specifically the field of tort law, is filled with opportunities for development and advancement. Civil litigation has grown exponentially in recent years. As a result, a wide variety of doors have opened for the paralegal both within and outside the traditional law office setting. One particularly large area of growth has been that of medical malpractice law. Medical malpractice is nothing new. It has been a part of civil litigation in this country for nearly two hundred years. But today, variables such as rapidly developing technology, new health-care professions, scientific advances, the concept of insurance, and even the baby boom following World War II have contributed to a virtual explosion in the number of patients and treatments. These developments have resulted in a corresponding increase in the possibility of professional malfeasance and legal claims by those allegedly injured.

Without question, the paralegal has become an invaluable part of the legal team in the field of medical malpractice. Because of the high percentage of settled claims, a great deal of the work required to successfully litigate or defend a

CYBER TORTS: DEFAMATION ONLINE

Who should be held liable for *cyber torts,* or torts committed in cyberspace? For example, who should be held liable when someone posts a defamatory message online? Should an Internet service provider (ISP)—a company, such as America Online (AOL), that provides access to the Internet through a local phone line, cable, or DSL connection—be liable for the remark if the ISP was unaware that it was being made?

Cyber torts (like cyber crimes, discussed in Chapter 13) are not new torts as much as they are new ways of committing torts that present special issues of proof. How, for example, can it be proved that an online defamatory remark was "published" (which requires that a third party see or hear it)? How can the identity of the person who made the remark be discovered? We explore some of these questions in this section. Generally, determining what tort duties apply in cyberspace and at what point one of those duties is breached is not an easy task for the courts.

malpractice case comes in the pretrial stages. Of course, the qualified paralegal in the law firm can be a valuable asset in nearly every element of trial and pretrial preparation, with the exception of giving legal advice and advocacy. Common duties include, but are not limited to, the following:

- Gathering information about the incident that allegedly caused injury.
- Interviewing potential witnesses.
- Preparing and responding to discovery materials such as interrogatories and requests for production, inspection, and physical examination.
- Securing expert witnesses.
- Preparing for depositions (both witness preparation and preparation of questions to be asked).
- Conducting legal research.
- Drafting pleadings, motions, discovery materials, and memoranda.
- Assembling evidence and preparing trial exhibits.

In addition to working in a law firm setting, paralegals have many opportunities within the health-care industry to participate in areas related to medical malpractice. A primary example is

"Clearly, the doors open to paralegals in tort law, and specifically medical malpractice, are boundless. The key is to have a thorough understanding of the legal system, and particularly the process of litigation."

the field of risk management. In recent years, this relatively new profession has become deeply embedded in the field of health care. Whether risk management is conducted by an independent risk assessment company that works on a contract basis with providers, by an in-house risk management department for a health-care provider, or by a corporate legal department for providers of insurance, health care, or related products, the goal is the same: to identify vulnerable areas and to react accordingly. The response may range from changing policies and procedures, to providing education and training to employees, to collecting information about an incident that has already occurred. All of these are areas in which a paralegal can effectively function to meet the needs of the employer.

Clearly, the doors open to paralegals in tort law, and specifically medical malpractice, are boundless. The key is to have a thorough understanding of the legal system, and particularly the process of litigation.

Additionally, a paralegal should have the ability to examine the broad aspects of a case, think "outside the box," and use organizational skills to address issues related to litigation involving professional malfeasance.

Liability of Internet Service Providers

Online forums allow anyone—customers, employees, or crackpots—to complain about a business firm's personnel, policies, practices, or products. Regardless of whether the complaint is justified or whether it is true, it might have an impact on the business. One question that created problems for the courts was whether providers of such forums could be held liable for defamatory statements. Congress responded with the Communications Decency Act, which states that Internet service providers, or "interactive computer service providers," are not liable for such material.[1]

Piercing the Veil of Anonymity

A problem for anyone who seeks to sue for online defamation is discovering the identity of the person who posted the defamatory message. ISPs can disclose personal information about their customers only when ordered to do so by a court. Because of this, businesses and individuals have resorted to lawsuits against unidentified "John

Does." Then, using the authority of the courts, they can obtain from the ISPs the identities of the persons responsible for the messages.

▶ **EXAMPLE 14.19**   In one case, Eric Hvide, a former chief executive of a company called Hvide Marine, sued a number of "John Does" who had posted allegedly defamatory statements about his company on various online message boards. Hvide, who eventually lost his job, sued the John Does for libel in a Florida court. The court ruled that Yahoo! and AOL had to reveal the identities of the defendant Does. ◀

In some cases, the rights of plaintiffs in such situations have been balanced against the defendants' rights to free speech. For example, some courts have concluded that more than a bare allegation of defamation is required to outweigh an individual's right to anonymity in the exercise of free speech.

STRICT LIABILITY

strict liability

Liability regardless of fault. In tort law, strict liability may be imposed on a merchant who introduces into commerce a good that is so defective as to be unreasonably dangerous.

Intentional torts and torts of negligence involve acts that depart from a reasonable standard of care and cause injuries. Under the doctrine of **strict liability**, liability for injury is imposed for reasons other than fault. Strict liability for damages proximately caused by an abnormally dangerous or exceptional activity is one application of this doctrine.

Abnormally Dangerous Activities

Abnormally dangerous activities have three characteristics:

- The activity involves potential harm, of a serious nature, to persons or property.
- The activity involves a high degree of risk that cannot be completely guarded against by the exercise of reasonable care.
- The activity is not commonly performed in the community or area.

Clearly, the primary basis of liability is the creation of an extraordinary risk. Even if blasting with dynamite in construction is performed with all reasonable care, for instance, there is still a risk of injury. Balancing that risk against the potential for harm, it seems reasonable to ask the person engaged in the activity to pay for any injury it causes. Although there is no fault, there is still responsibility because of the dangerous nature of the undertaking.

Other Applications of Strict Liability

Strict liability may also apply to harm caused by animals. Persons who keep wild animals are strictly liable for any harm inflicted by the animals. The basis for applying strict liability is that wild animals, should they escape, pose a serious risk of harm to persons in the vicinity. An owner of domestic animals (such as dogs, cats, or horses) may be strictly liable for harm caused by those animals if the owner knew, or should have known, that the animals were dangerous or had a propensity to harm others.

A significant application of strict liability is in the area of *product liability*—liability of manufacturers and sellers for harmful or defective products. Because of the importance of product liability in tort litigation, we discuss this type of liability at length in the following section.

PRODUCT LIABILITY

product liability

The legal liability of manufacturers, sellers, and lessors of goods to consumers, users, and bystanders for injuries or damages that are caused by the goods.

Those who manufacture, sell, or lease goods can be held liable for injuries and damages caused by defective goods under the law of **product liability**. Liability here is a matter of social policy. It is based on the notion that manufacturers are better able to bear the cost of injury than innocent victims. In addition, requiring producers to pay for injuries caused by their products encourages them to make safer products.

Theories of Product Liability

A party who is injured by a defective product can bring a suit against the product's seller or manufacturer under several theories. These theories include negligence, misrepresentation, and strict product liability.

Product Liability Based on Negligence

If a manufacturer fails to exercise due care to make a product safe, *any person* who is injured by the product can sue the manufacturer for negligence. The plaintiff does not have to be the person who bought the product. The manufacturer must use due care in designing the product, selecting the materials, producing and assembling the product, testing and inspecting the product for safety, and placing adequate warnings on the label to inform users of dangers.

Product Liability Based on Misrepresentation

When a manufacturer or seller misrepresents the quality, nature, or appropriate use of a product, and the user is injured as a result, the basis of liability may be the tort of fraud. Generally, the misrepresentation must have been made knowingly or with reckless disregard for the facts, and the party must have intended the user to rely on the statement. An example would be intentionally hiding a product's defects.

Strict Product Liability

Under the doctrine of strict liability, a manufacturer that has exercised reasonable care can still be held liable if a product is defective and injures someone. Strict product liability reflects the general principle that the law should protect consumers from unsafe and dangerous products. The rule of strict liability is also applicable to the suppliers of component parts that are used in the final product.

Strict liability will be imposed if the plaintiff can establish the following six requirements:

- The product must be in a defective condition when the defendant sells it.
- The defendant must normally be engaged in the business of selling the product.
- The product must be unreasonably dangerous to the user or consumer because of its defective condition (in most states).
- The plaintiff must incur physical harm to self or property by use or consumption of the product.
- The defective condition must be the proximate cause of the injury or damage.
- The goods must not have been substantially changed from the time the product was sold to the time the injury was sustained.[2]

Note that the plaintiff is not required to show why or how the product became defective. The plaintiff must only prove that the product was so defective as to be "unreasonably dangerous"; that the product caused the injury; and that the condition of the product was essentially the same as when it was sold. A court will find the product to be an **unreasonably dangerous product** if either (1) the product is dangerous beyond the expectation of the ordinary consumer or (2) a less dangerous alternative was *economically* feasible for the manufacturer, but the manufacturer failed to produce it. A product may be unreasonably dangerous due to a flaw in the manufacturing process, a design defect, or an inadequate warning.

unreasonably dangerous product
A product that is defective to the point of threatening a consumer's health and safety. A product will be considered unreasonably dangerous if it is dangerous beyond the expectation of the ordinary consumer or if a less dangerous alternative was economically feasible for the manufacturer, but the manufacturer failed to produce it.

Ethics Watch

CONFIDENTIALITY AND PRODUCT LIABILITY

Paralegals who work in the area of product liability may find themselves in a sticky situation. For example, suppose your firm represents a particular toy manufacturer. The toy firm has produced and distributed a toy that is very popular for children two through four years of age. The toy, however, is apparently defective and has caused serious injuries to some children. The product has not yet been recalled, and no information about the problems with the toy has appeared in the press. Everything you know about this toy you have learned from the work you have done on the case.

Now suppose that you are the parent of a child who is three years old, and many of your friends and family members have children around that age. Clearly, you would decide not to purchase that toy for your child, but what about telling others? Can you warn your friends and family about the defective toy? Can you tell your day-care provider? If you tell one person, even if it is a family member, you have technically violated the ethical rule of confidentiality. Yet what if you don't warn someone, and that person's child is injured as a result? This is just one example of ethical dilemmas that may arise for paralegals who work in the area of product liability. In circumstances such as these, it is advisable to consult your supervising attorney for direction.

The issue discussed here is related to the NALA Code of Ethics and Professional Responsibility, Canon 4: "A paralegal must use discretion and professional judgment commensurate with knowledge and experience but must not render independent legal judgment in place of an attorney." It is also related to the NFPA Model Code of Ethics, Section EC 1.5: "A paralegal shall preserve all confidential information provided by the client or acquired from other sources before, during, and after the course of the professional relationship."

Manufacturing Defects.   A product that departs from its intended design, even though all possible care was exercised in the preparation and marketing of the product, has a manufacturing defect. Liability is imposed on the manufacturer (and on the wholesaler and retailer) regardless of whether the manufacturer acted "reasonably."

Design Defects.   A product has a design defect if the foreseeable risks of harm posed by the product could have been reduced or avoided by adopting a reasonable alternative design.

Warning Defects.   A product may also be deemed to be defective because of inadequate instructions or warnings in situations in which the risk of harm was foreseeable and could have been avoided if a proper warning had been given. In evaluating the adequacy of warnings, courts consider the risks of the product and whether the content of the warning was understandable to the expected user.[3] For example, children would likely respond readily to bright, bold, simple warning labels, whereas educated adults might want more detailed information.

Note that there is no duty to warn about risks that are obvious or commonly known. Gas stations do not have to warn consumers to avoid drinking gasoline. Warnings about *obvious risks* do not add to the safety of a product and could even detract from it by making other warnings seem less significant. Also, a seller must warn those who purchase its product of the harm that can result from the *foreseeable misuse* of the product. The key is the foreseeability of the misuse; sellers are not required to take precautions against every possible unusual use of their products.

Defenses to Product Liability

To avoid liability under any theory of product liability, the defendant can show that there is no basis for the plaintiff's claim or that the plaintiff has not met the requirements for liability. For example, if the suit alleges negligence and the defendant proves that the product did not cause the plaintiff's injury, the defendant will not be liable. Additionally, if the defendant in a strict product liability suit can establish that the goods were subsequently altered, normally the defendant will not be held liable. Defendants may also assert the affirmative defenses discussed next.

Assumption of Risk

The obviousness of a risk and a user's decision to proceed in the face of that risk may sometimes be a defense in a product liability suit. For example, if a buyer failed to heed a product recall by the seller, a court might conclude that the buyer had assumed the risk. To establish this defense, the defendant must show that (1) the plaintiff knew and appreciated the risk created by the product defect and (2) the plaintiff voluntarily assumed the risk, even though it was unreasonable to do so.

Product Misuse

Defendants can also claim that the plaintiff misused the product. This defense is similar to claiming that the plaintiff has assumed the risk. Here, however, the injured party *did not know that the product was dangerous for a particular use,* but the use was not the one for which the product was designed. The courts have limited this defense. Even if the injured party does not know about the inherent danger of using the product in a wrong way, if the misuse is reasonably foreseeable, the seller must take measures to guard against it.

Comparative Negligence

Developments in the area of comparative negligence (discussed earlier in this chapter) have affected the doctrine of strict liability—the most extreme theory of product liability. Previously, the plaintiff's conduct was not a defense to strict liability. Today, many jurisdictions consider the negligent or intentional actions of both the plaintiff and the defendant when apportioning liability and damages. Even if the plaintiff misused the product, though, she or he may be able to recover at least some damages for injuries caused by a defective product.

Commonly Known Dangers

As mentioned, the dangers associated with certain products (such as sharp knives and guns) are so commonly known that manufacturers need not warn users of those dangers. If a defendant shows that a plaintiff's injury resulted from a *commonly known danger,* the defendant normally will not be liable. A related defense is the *knowledgeable user* defense. If a particular danger (such as electrical shock) is or should be known by particular users of the product (such as electricians), the manufacturer need not warn these users of the danger.

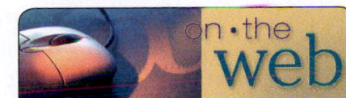

For information on product liability litigation against tobacco companies, including defenses raised by tobacco manufacturers in trial-related documents, go to the State Tobacco Information Center's Web site at **stic.neu.edu**.

PRODUCT LIABILITY AND THE PARALEGAL

As a paralegal, you may be intensively involved in product liability litigation. If you work for a law firm, you may be part of a legal team that is suing a manufacturer or seller in a product liability action, or you may be part of the legal team defending the manufacturer or seller. If you work for a corporation, you may play a role in defending against product liability claims brought by users of a product made by the corporation. The *Developing Paralegal Skills* feature on page 483 discusses that situation in greater detail.

Depending on the nature of the lawsuit, there may be thousands of documents to manage in a product liability case. For example, some such cases are brought as *class-action lawsuits*. In a class-action case, a plaintiff brings the suit on behalf of users of a product (such as tobacco) who claim that they were injured by the product. Cases of this kind can go on for years and typically involve mountains of documents that must be categorized, labeled, and catalogued so that they can be easily retrieved when needed. Often, paralegals involved in cases such as these must be experts in technology in order to manage the files and document presentations at trial.

Other product liability cases involve a single plaintiff. A plaintiff may claim that a design or manufacturing

defect in a product, such as an automobile, was responsible for the plaintiff's injury or that a manufacturer's inadequate warning was responsible for an injury.

Whether product liability litigation involves a single plaintiff or a class action, it will require extensive investigation into whether the product that allegedly caused the injury was in fact defective in any way or whether the defect, if there was one, actually caused the injury. Many of the specific tasks that paralegals perform in product liability litigation are similar to those described earlier for cases involving negligence.

CONSUMER LAW

consumer

A person who buys products and services for personal or household use.

consumer law

Statutes, agency rules, and judicial decisions protecting consumers of goods and services.

deceptive advertising

Advertising that misleads consumers, either by unjustified claims concerning a product's performance or by failure to disclose relevant information concerning the product's composition or performance.

Since the 1960s, many laws have been passed to protect the health and safety of consumers. A **consumer** is a person who purchases, for private use, goods or services from business firms. Sources of consumer protection exist at all levels of government. Exhibit 14.1 indicates some of the areas of consumer law that are regulated by statutes. Federal administrative agencies, such as the Federal Trade Commission, also provide an important source of consumer protection. Nearly every agency and department of the federal government has an office of consumer affairs, and most states have one or more offices, including the offices of state attorneys general, to assist consumers.

All statutes, agency rules, and common law judicial decisions that serve to protect the interests of consumers are classified as **consumer law**. Because of the wide variation among state consumer protection laws, our primary focus here is on federal legislation—specifically, on legislation governing deceptive advertising, labeling and packaging, sales, health protection, product safety, and credit protection. Realize, though, that state laws often provide broader protection for consumers than do federal laws.

Deceptive Advertising

Over the past several decades, consumers have received increased protection against **deceptive advertising**. This protection has come more from statutes and agency rules than from the common law. Under the common law, if a seller misrep-

EXHIBIT 14.1
Selected Areas of Consumer Law Regulated by Statutes

Developing
Paralegal Skills

PRODUCT LIABILITY PARALEGALS

Sylvia is a paralegal in the legal department of an automobile company. The company is frequently the defendant in product liability lawsuits. During the discovery phase of the litigation, attorneys for the plaintiffs normally request information about the design and manufacturing process used by the company in producing its vehicles.

Sylvia's job is to work with the corporate attorneys to gather this information and provide it to the plaintiffs' attorneys, as allowed or required by court rules. Frequently, Sylvia meets with the company's engineers to discuss information requests and to obtain the necessary information. Sylvia then reviews with her supervising attorney the material to be sent out.

TIPS FOR OBTAINING INFORMATION

- Set up a meeting with the engineers.
- Provide the engineers with copies of the discovery request.
- Discuss with the engineers the scope of the discovery request.
- Review engineering files.
- Determine if a database will be needed to index the documents.
- Analyze the documents, looking for privileged or work-product documents (see Chapter 10) that should not be included in the response to the discovery request.
- Prepare a response to the discovery request.

resented the quality, price, or availability of a certain product, the consumer's only recourse was to sue the seller for fraud. Fraud requires proof of *intent* to misrepresent the product's usefulness to the buyer. Frequently, the burden of having to prove intent was too great, and consumers were left with little or no legal recourse against deceptive practices.

Today, various agencies, both federal and state, are empowered to protect consumers from deceptive advertising. At the federal level, the most important agency regulating advertising is the Federal Trade Commission (FTC). The Federal Trade Commission Act of 1914 authorizes the FTC to determine what constitutes a deceptive practice.

Deceptive advertising comes in many forms. Deception may arise from a false statement or claim about a company's own products or a competitor's products. Some advertisements contain "half-truths," meaning that the information presented is true but incomplete, leading consumers to a false conclusion. ▶ **EXAMPLE 14.20** The makers of Campbell's soups advertised that most Campbell's soups were low in fat and cholesterol and thus were helpful in fighting heart disease. What the ad did not say was that Campbell's soups are high in sodium and that high-sodium diets may increase the risk of heart disease. The FTC ruled that Campbell's claims were thus deceptive. ◀ Generally, the test for whether an ad is deceptive is *whether a reasonable consumer would be deceived by the ad.*

The FTC has the power to investigate deceptive practices and take action. If, after its investigation, the FTC believes that an advertisement is deceptive, it drafts a formal complaint and sends it to the alleged offender. The company may agree to settle the complaint without further proceedings. If the company does not agree

A good source for information on the FTC, its regulations protecting consumers, and other government sites dealing with consumer issues is the FTC home page at **www.ftc.gov**.

to a settlement, the FTC can conduct a hearing, at which the company can present its defense. If the FTC succeeds in proving that an advertisement is deceptive, it usually issues a **cease-and-desist order** requiring that the challenged advertising be stopped. It might also impose a sanction known as **counteradvertising** by requiring the company to supply new advertising—in print, on radio, and on television—to inform the public about the earlier misinformation.

Labeling and Packaging Laws

A number of federal and state laws deal specifically with the information on labels and packages. In general, labels must be accurate, and they must use words that are easily understood by the ordinary consumer. For instance, a box of cereal cannot be labeled "giant" if that would exaggerate the amount of cereal in the box. In some instances, labels must specify the raw materials used in the product, such as the percentage of cotton or other fiber used in clothing. In other instances, the product must carry a warning. Cigarette packages must include one of several warnings about the health hazards of smoking, for example.

The Fair Packaging and Labeling Act of 1966 requires that products carry labels that identify the product; the net quantity of the contents, as well as the quantity of each serving, if the number of servings is stated; the manufacturer; and the packager or distributor. The act also establishes requirements concerning words used to describe packages, disclosure of ingredients of nonfood products, and the partial filling of packages.

Food products must bear labels detailing nutritional content, including how much fat the food contains and what kind of fat it is. The federal Food and Drug Administration (FDA) has guidelines to standardize nutritional information on packaged foods, and the FTC plays a key role in enforcing the restrictions. The Nutrition Labeling and Education Act of 1990 requires standard nutrition facts (including fat content) on food labels; regulates the use of such terms as *fresh*, *low fat*, and *organic*; and, subject to FDA approval, authorizes certain health claims.

Sales Transactions

Many of the laws that protect consumers concern the disclosure of terms in sales transactions and provide rules governing certain sales, such as door-to-door sales, mail-order sales, and the unsolicited receipt of merchandise. The FTC provides most of the federal regulation of sales. One FTC regulation requires sellers to give consumers three days to cancel any door-to-door sale. In addition, the FTC rule requires that consumers be notified in Spanish of this right if the oral negotiations for the sale were in Spanish. The FTC also has rules requiring sellers of some goods and services (such as used cars and funeral services) to disclose certain information to consumers.

Most states have enacted laws governing consumer sales transactions. Moreover, the Uniform Commercial Code (UCC), which will be discussed in Chapter 15 and has been adopted by every state, contains numerous provisions that protect consumers from unfair or deceptive trade practices.

Consumer Health and Safety

Regulating the labeling and packaging of products helps to promote consumer health and safety. But there is a difference between regulating information about a product and regulating the content of the product. ▶ **EXAMPLE 14.21** Tobacco products have not been altered by regulation or banned despite their obvious hazards. What has been regulated are the warnings that producers are required to give consumers about the hazards of tobacco. ◀ We now look at several laws that regulate the actual products made available to consumers.

In 1906, Congress passed the Pure Food and Drug Act, which was the first step toward protecting consumers against impure and misbranded food and drug prod-

---

cease-and-desist order

An administrative or judicial order prohibiting a person or business firm from conducting activities that an agency or court has deemed illegal.

counteradvertising

New advertising undertaken under a Federal Trade Commission order for the purpose of correcting earlier false claims that were made about a product.

ucts. In 1938, the Federal Food, Drug and Cosmetic Act was passed to strengthen the 1906 legislation. These acts and later amendments established standards for foods, specified safe levels of food additives, and regulated some aspects of food advertising. They also required that drugs must be proved effective as well as safe before they could receive permission to be sold. Also in 1906, Congress authorized the Department of Agriculture to set inspection requirements for meat and poultry. Most of the statutes involving food and drugs are enforced by the Food and Drug Administration.

Still other statutes, categorized as product-safety acts, regulate the distribution of hazardous or defective products. One example is the Flammable Fabrics Act of 1953, which prohibits the sale of highly flammable fabrics and clothing. Another is the Consumer Product Safety Act of 1972, enacted to protect consumers from dangerous products. The Consumer Product Safety Commission, which was created by the act, conducts research on the safety of products and maintains a clearinghouse on the risks associated with various products. The commission sets standards for consumer products and bans the sale of products it deems hazardous to consumers. Products banned by the commission include unsafe fireworks, cribs, and toys, as well as many products containing asbestos, lead, or vinyl chloride.

Consumer Credit Protection

Because of the extensive use of credit by American consumers, credit protection has become an important area regulated by consumer protection legislation. One of the most significant statutes regulating the credit and credit-card industry is the Truth-in-Lending Act (TILA), the name commonly given to Title 1 of the Consumer Credit Protection Act, which was passed by Congress in 1968.

The Truth-in-Lending Act

The TILA is basically a *disclosure law*. It is administered by the Federal Reserve Board and requires sellers and lenders to disclose credit terms or loan terms so that borrowers can shop around for the best financing arrangements. TILA requirements apply only to persons and entities that, in the ordinary course of business, lend money, sell on credit, or arrange for the extension of credit. Sales or loans made between two consumers do not come under the act. Additionally, the act only protects persons (not businesses). Under the provisions of the TILA, all of the terms of a credit instrument must be clearly and conspicuously (obviously) disclosed. The TILA provides that a consumer can cancel a contract if a creditor fails to follow exactly the required procedures.

In 1974, Congress enacted the Equal Credit Opportunity Act (ECOA) as an amendment to the TILA. The ECOA prohibits the denial of credit solely on the basis of race, religion, national origin, color, gender, marital status, or age. The act also prohibits discrimination on the basis of whether an individual receives certain forms of income, such as public-assistance benefits. Creditors may not collect information about any of these characteristics from an applicant and may not require the signature of an applicant's spouse, other than as a joint applicant.

The TILA also contains provisions regarding credit cards. One provision limits the liability of a cardholder to $50 per card for unauthorized charges made before the creditor is notified that the card has been lost. Another provision prohibits a credit-card company from billing a consumer for any unauthorized charges on a credit card that was improperly issued by the company. ▶ **EXAMPLE 14.22** Suppose that a consumer receives an unsolicited credit card in the mail, and the card is later stolen and used by the thief to make purchases. In this situation, the consumer who received the card is not liable for the unauthorized charges. ◀ Further provisions of the act concern billing disputes related to credit-card purchases. The act outlines specific procedures and time deadlines for both the consumer and the credit-card company to follow in settling a dispute.

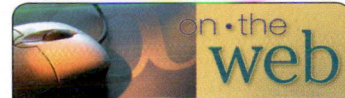

The Consumer Product Safety Commission Web site at **www.cpsc.gov** provides information about product-safety standards and product recalls. The Food and Drug Administration lists product recalls and safety alerts at **www.fda.gov**. Select "P" from the "A-Z Index" and scroll down to "Product Alerts and Warnings."

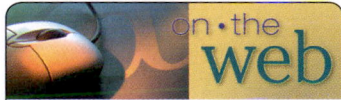

For detailed information about FTC credit regulation and enforcement activities, go to **www.ftc.gov**, and select the "Consumer Protection" tab.

Fair Credit Reporting

To protect consumers against inaccurate credit reporting, Congress enacted the Fair Credit Reporting Act in 1970. The act provides that consumer credit reporting agencies—such as Equifax, TransUnion, and Experian—may issue credit reports to users only for specified purposes. Authorized purposes include the extension of credit, the issuance of insurance policies, and compliance with a court order. A report may also be issued in response to a consumer's request for a copy of his or her own credit report. The act further provides that any time a consumer is denied credit or insurance on the basis of the credit report (or is charged more than others ordinarily would be), the consumer must be notified of that fact and of the name and address of the credit reporting agency that issued the credit report.

Under the act, consumers may request the source of any information being given out by a credit agency, as well as the identity of anyone who has received an agency's report. Consumers also have access to the information contained about them in a credit reporting agency's files. If a consumer discovers that these files contain inaccurate information, the agency, on the consumer's written request, must investigate. If the investigation reveals that the information is unverifiable or inaccurate, the agency must delete it within a reasonable period of time.

Fair and Accurate Credit Transactions Act

In an effort to combat identity theft, Congress passed the Fair and Accurate Credit Transactions (FACT) Act of 2003. The act established a national fraud alert system so that consumers who suspect that they have been or may be victimized by identity theft can place an alert on their credit files. The act also requires the major credit reporting agencies to provide consumers with free copies of their own credit reports every twelve months. Another provision requires account numbers on credit-card receipts to be shortened so that merchants, employees, and others who may have access to the receipts do not have access to the consumers' names and full credit-card numbers. Since 2008, the act has required that financial institutions work with the Federal Trade Commission to identify "red flag" indicators of identity theft and to develop rules on how to dispose of sensitive credit information.

The FACT Act gives consumers who have been victimized by identity theft some assistance in rebuilding their credit reputations. For example, credit reporting agencies must stop reporting allegedly fraudulent account information once the consumer establishes that identify theft has occurred. Business owners and creditors are required to provide consumers with copies of any records that can help the consumer prove that a particular account or transaction is fraudulent (a forged signature, for example). In addition, the act allows consumers to report the accounts affected by identity theft directly to creditors in order to help prevent the spread of erroneous credit information.

Fair Debt-Collection Practices

In 1977, Congress passed the Fair Debt Collection Practices Act in an attempt to curb perceived abuses by collection agencies. The act applies only to debt-collection agencies that, usually for a percentage of the amount owed, regularly attempt to collect debts on behalf of someone else. Creditors who attempt to collect debts are not covered unless, by misrepresenting themselves to the debtor, they cause the debtor to believe they are collection agencies.

The act prohibits such debt-collection practices as contacting consumers at their place of employment if the employers object, contacting consumers at inconvenient or unusual times, and contacting consumers if they are represented by attorneys. The act also prohibits debt-collection agencies from contacting third parties (other than parents, spouses, or financial advisers) about the payment of

For information about debt-collection practices and links to many information sources, visit the Privacy Rights Clearinghouse at **www.privacyrights. org**. Select "Fact Sheets," and open item 27, "Debt Collection Practices: When Hardball Goes Too Far."

a debt unless authorized to do so by a court, using harassment and intimidation (such as abusive language), using false or misleading information (such as posing as a police officer), and communicating with the consumer after receipt of a notice that the consumer is refusing to pay the debt (except to advise the consumer of further action to be taken by the collection agency).

Garnishment Proceedings

Creditors have numerous remedies available to them when consumers fail to pay their debts. Among these remedies is garnishment. **Garnishment** occurs when a creditor, after complying with procedures mandated by state law, legally seizes a portion of a debtor's property (such as wages) in the possession of a third party (such as an employer). The creditor must first obtain an *order of garnishment* from the court, which allows the creditor to have access to the debtor's wages while they are still in the control of the employer. State laws governing garnishment vary from state to state, and some states (for example, Texas) do not permit garnishment of wages by private parties except under a child-support order.

Garnishment can create a hardship for the consumer-debtor if he or she is relying on wages for support. To protect consumers, both federal and state laws limit the amount of income that can be taken from a debtor's weekly take-home pay. The federal Consumer Credit Protection Act provides that a debtor can keep either 75 percent of the net earnings per week or a sum equivalent to the pay for thirty hours of work at federal minimum wage rates, whichever is greater. State laws also provide dollar exemptions, and these amounts are often larger than those provided by federal law. State and federal statutes can be applied together to create a pool of funds to enable a debtor to continue to provide for family needs while reducing the amount of the debt in a reasonable way.

Understandably, employers dislike garnishment proceedings. After all, such proceedings impose time costs on employers (appearance at court hearings, record-keeping costs, and the like). To protect the job security of employees whose wages are subject to garnishment, federal law provides that garnishment of an employee's wages for any one indebtedness cannot be grounds for that employee's dismissal. The *Developing Paralegal Skills* feature on the following page discusses this issue further with respect to the role that may involve a paralegal.

garnishment
A proceeding in which a creditor legally seizes a portion of a debtor's property (such as wages) that is in the possession of a third party (such as an employer).

The U.S. Department of Labor provides details about wage garnishment procedures at **www.dol.gov**. Under "Find It," select "Topics," and then select "Wages" and "Garnishment."

CONSUMER LAW AND THE PARALEGAL

Because consumer laws protect all individuals, as a paralegal you may well encounter a client with a claim that falls under a federal or state consumer protection law. You might even find yourself working for a consumer group. In the area of consumer law, paralegals may be asked to perform the following types of tasks:

- Investigate a client's complaint alleging deceptive advertising.
- Assist in work relating to a business client who has been charged with violating Federal Trade Commission rules governing deceptive trade practices.

- Develop acceptable standards for a food producer to ensure compliance with the labeling laws implemented by the Food and Drug Administration.
- Investigate a client's use of hazardous products to ensure compliance with Consumer Product Safety Commission standards.
- Draft a letter to a credit reporting agency to rectify an error on a client's credit report.
- Assist a client in collecting a debt through garnishment proceedings.
- Maintain and keep current the law firm's consumer law library.

Developing Paralegal Skills

DISCHARGED FOR GARNISHMENT

Eva White works as a paralegal for a firm that specializes in labor law. A business client has called Eva's supervising attorney to ask for advice concerning garnishment. Basically, the client wants to know if he can fire an employee so that he can avoid having to comply with garnishment proceedings that have been initiated against the employee. The attorney has asked Eva to research recent case law on the question of whether an employer may fire an employee for this reason.

Eva goes online to research garnishment and locates a case in which an employee was fired two days after his employer received notice of the garnishment. The case turned on whether the employer had notice that the garnishment proceedings had already been initiated against the employee. She reads through the case and finds a citation to the statute. Eva's next step is to check the statute itself to ensure that she has up-to-date knowledge of how the statute is being applied.

CHECKLIST FOR LEGAL RESEARCH

- Locate case law.
- Locate statutes.
- Update your case law findings by checking a citator (see Chapter 8) to make sure that the holding in the case is still good law.
- Update the statute by using a citator to see if the statute has been amended or repealed.

KEY TERMS AND CONCEPTS

actionable   *463*

actual malice   *464*

appropriation   *465*

assault   *462*

assumption of risk   *473*

battery   *462*

business invitee   *471*

business tort   *466*

causation in fact   *473*

cease-and-desist order   *484*

comparative negligence   *474*

compensatory damages   *472*

consumer   *482*

consumer law   *482*

contributory negligence   *474*

conversion   *470*

counteradvertising   *484*

cyber tort   *461*

deceptive advertising   *482*

defamation   *464*

dram shop act   *475*

duty of care   *471*

false imprisonment   *463*

fraudulent misrepresentation   *465*

garnishment   *487*

Good Samaritan statute   *475*

intentional infliction of emotional
   distress   *463*

intentional tort   *461*

libel   *464*

negligence   *470*

negligence *per se*   *474*

predatory behavior   *467*

privilege   *464*

product liability   *478*

proximate cause   *473*

punitive damages   *472*

reasonable person standard   *471*

slander   *464*

strict liability   *478*

tort   *461*

tortfeasor   *461*

trespass to land   *467*

trespass to personal property   *469*

unreasonably dangerous product   *479*

Today's
Professional Paralegal

DEVELOPING A LIFE-CARE PLAN

Attorney Long asks her paralegal, Jessica, to assist in developing a life-care plan for one of the firm's clients, Ashley. Ashley, a sixteen-year-old girl, passed out at school one day and was taken to Dr. Shafley, who diagnosed her as having the flu and sent her home. Less than a week later, Ashley's legs had to be amputated because of Dr. Shafley's failure to diagnose the symptoms of bacterial spinal meningitis. Dr. Shafley wishes to settle out of court. Attorney Long therefore needs to establish the amount of damages to be requested.

THE LIFE-CARE PLAN

Following a serious injury, health-care costs can accumulate into millions of dollars. An attorney who represents an injured plaintiff often must develop a plan that identifies and establishes the cost of the health care that the client will need for the rest of his or her life. The life-care plan is basically a tool used to quantify the health-care needs of a client and establish the amount of damages that the client will seek in any settlement or trial of the case. Typically, developing a life-care plan involves hiring an expert qualified to assess the plaintiff's limitations and care needs and assigning a paralegal to coordinate and assist.

MEETING WITH THE CLIENT

Jessica talks with the attorney, and they go together to meet Ashley and her parents at the hospital in which Ashley has been a patient for several months. Attorney Long tells Ashley that an expert will be coming to evaluate her condition and that Jessica will always be available to answer any questions she might have. After meeting Ashley, Jessica vows to do whatever she can to help Ashley receive the best possible care in the future. Jessica then contacts the expert whom the attorney has hired.

KEY COMPONENTS OF A LIFE-CARE PLAN

Jessica learns that there are several main components of any life-care plan. The first is what type of care is needed and where it will be provided. The options available include facility care, home care, and community care. The expert tells Jessica that as long as someone can be home with Ashley at all times and the house can be modified to accommodate her disabilities, home care is a good choice for Ashley.

The expert then tells Jessica that they need to assess the types of equipment, supplies, and medications that Ashley currently requires and what she will need in the future. For example, Ashley will be confined to a wheelchair until the proper prosthetics (artificial limbs) can be obtained. Her parents' house will need to have wheelchair ramps installed and other modifications made in order to accommodate Ashley's needs. The prosthetic devices, which are very expensive, will need to be replaced during Ashley's lifetime. Other supplies and medications will be required. The cost of all of these items must be estimated for the future.

Jessica also learns that the life-care plan must take into account long-term therapy and additional medical services. Ashley will need physical therapy on a regular basis to enable her to function with her limitations and to learn how to use the prosthetics. She will also need some psychological counseling and recreational therapy, given the extent of her injuries. Additionally, persons who have had their limbs amputated have an increased risk of infections, bedsores, and other problems, and the cost of treating these foreseeable medical problems must be included.

HOW A PARALEGAL CAN ASSIST

Paralegals can play a significant role by serving as a liaison among the expert and the client, the family, physicians, and educators. Injured plaintiffs benefit from knowing that someone can always be reached if they need assistance. Paralegals also can keep track of health-care bills, set up necessary appointments, research costs, and order equipment and supplies. If the case goes to trial, the paralegal can assist in formulating the questions to ask the expert and can create useful exhibits for the jury. Moreover, helping clients who have been seriously injured to regain a degree of independence and plan their futures can be very rewarding work.

CHAPTER SUMMARY

TORT LAW, PRODUCT LIABILITY, AND CONSUMER LAW

The Basis of Tort Law

Two notions serve as the basis of all torts: wrongs and compensation. Tort law recognizes that some acts are wrong because they cause injuries to others.

1. *Definition*—A *tort* is a civil wrong. In a tort action, one person or group brings a personal-injury suit against another person or group to obtain compensation (money damages) or other relief for the harm suffered.

2. *Objective of tort law*—Generally, the purpose of tort law is to provide remedies for the invasion of various interests, such as physical security, privacy, freedom of movement, and reputation.

3. *Classification of torts*—Torts fall into two broad classifications: *intentional torts* and *negligence.* In addition, in certain circumstances, defendants may be held liable for harm caused to others under the tort doctrine of *strict liability.*

Intentional Torts

1. *Intentional torts against persons*—

   a. **ASSAULT AND BATTERY**—An assault is an intentional act that causes another person to be apprehensive or fearful of immediate harm. A battery is an assault that results in physical contact.

   b. **FALSE IMPRISONMENT**—The intentional confinement or restraint of another person's movement without justification.

   c. **INTENTIONAL INFLICTION OF EMOTIONAL DISTRESS**—An intentional act that amounts to extreme and outrageous conduct resulting in severe emotional distress to another.

   d. **DEFAMATION (LIBEL OR SLANDER)**—A false statement of fact, not made under privilege, that is communicated to a third person and that causes damage to a person's reputation. For public figures, the plaintiff must also prove actual malice.

   e. **INVASION OF THE RIGHT TO PRIVACY**—The use of a person's name or likeness for commercial purposes without permission, wrongful intrusion into a person's private activities, publication of information that places a person in a false light, or disclosure of private facts that an ordinary person would find objectionable.

   f. **APPROPRIATION**—The use of another person's name, likeness, or other identifying characteristic without permission and for the benefit of the user.

   g. **MISREPRESENTATION (FRAUD)**—A false representation made by one party, through misstatement of facts or through conduct, with the intention of deceiving another and on which the other reasonably relies to his or her detriment.

   h. **WRONGFUL INTERFERENCE**—Knowing, intentional interference by a third party with an enforceable contractual relationship or an established business relationship between other parties for the purpose of advancing the economic interests of the third party.

2. *Intentional torts against property*—

   a. **TRESPASS TO LAND**—The invasion of another's real property without consent or privilege. Specific rights and duties apply once a person is expressly or impliedly established as a trespasser.

   b. **TRESPASS TO PERSONAL PROPERTY**—Unlawfully damaging or interfering with the owner's right to use, possess, or enjoy his or her personal property.

   c. **CONVERSION**—A wrongful act in which personal property is taken from its rightful owner.

Negligence

1. *Negligence*—The careless performance of a legally required duty or the failure to perform a legally required act. Elements that must be proved are that a legal duty of care exists, that the defendant breached that duty, and that the breach caused damage or injury to another.

2. *Defenses to negligence*—The basic affirmative defenses in negligence cases are assumption of risk, superseding cause, and contributory negligence.

3. *Special negligence doctrines and statutes*—

   a. **NEGLIGENCE *PER SE***—A type of negligence that may occur if a person violates a statute or an ordinance providing for a criminal penalty and the violation causes another to be injured.

   b. **SPECIAL NEGLIGENCE STATUTES**—State statutes, such as dram shop acts and Good Samaritan laws, that prescribe duties and responsibilities in certain circumstances. The violation of such statutes will impose civil liability.

Cyber Torts: Defamation Online

General tort principles are being extended to cover cyber torts, or torts that occur in cyberspace, such as online defamation. Cyber torts often present special issues of proof. Federal and state statutes may also apply to certain forms of cyber torts.

Strict Liability

Under the doctrine of strict liability, a person or company may be held liable, regardless of the degree of care exercised, for damages or injuries caused by a product or activity. Strict liability includes liability for harms caused by abnormally dangerous activities, by dangerous animals, and by defective products (product liability).

Product Liability

1. *Theories of product liability*—

   a. **PRODUCT LIABILITY BASED ON NEGLIGENCE**—Due care must be used by the manufacturer in designing the product; selecting materials; producing, assembling, and testing the product; and placing adequate warnings on the label or product.

   b. **PRODUCT LIABILITY BASED ON MISREPRESENTATION**—When the seller misrepresents the quality, nature, or appropriate use of the product, and the user is injured as a result, the basis of liability may be the tort of fraud. The plaintiff does not have to show that the product was defective in such cases.

Continued

c. **STRICT PRODUCT LIABILITY**—A manufacturer that has exercised a reasonable degree of care can still be held liable if a product is defective and injures someone. This reflects the general principle that the law should protect consumers from unsafe and dangerous products. Liability extends to suppliers of component parts.

2. *Defenses to product liability*—

a. **ASSUMPTION OF RISK**—The user or consumer knew of the risk of harm and voluntarily assumed it.

b. **PRODUCT MISUSE**—The user or consumer misused the product in a way unforeseeable by the manufacturer.

c. **COMPARATIVE NEGLIGENCE**—Liability may be distributed between the plaintiff and the defendant under the doctrine of comparative negligence if the plaintiff's misuse of the product contributed to the risk of injury.

d. **COMMONLY KNOWN DANGERS**—If a defendant succeeds in convincing the court that a plaintiff's injury resulted from a commonly known danger, such as the danger associated with using a sharp knife, the defendant will not be liable.

Consumer Law

All statutes, agency rules, and common law judicial decisions that serve to protect the interests of consumers are classified as consumer law. Today, there are many federal consumer protection statutes, in addition to a wide variety of state consumer protection statutes. Some state statutes provide more protection than that afforded by the federal laws discussed below.

1. *Deceptive advertising*—Advertising that misleads consumers or that is based on false claims is prohibited by the Federal Trade Commission (FTC). Generally, the test for whether an ad is deceptive is whether a reasonable consumer would be deceived by the ad.

a. **CEASE-AND-DESIST ORDERS**—The FTC can require the advertiser to stop the challenged advertising.

b. **COUNTERADVERTISING**—The FTC may also require the advertiser to advertise to correct the earlier misinformation.

2. *Labeling and packaging*—Manufacturers must comply with labeling or packaging requirements for their specific products. In general, labels must be accurate and not misleading. Food products must bear labels detailing their nutritional content, and standards must be met before a product can use terms like *fresh* and *organic* on the label.

3. *Sales transactions*—Many federal and state laws regulate the disclosure of terms to consumers in sales transactions, particularly in door-to-door and mail-order sales. The FTC conducts most of the federal regulation of sales. Numerous provisions of the Uniform Commercial Code also protect consumers from unfair trade practices at the state level.

4. *Consumer health and safety*—Laws protecting the health and safety of consumers regulate the content of a food, drug, or other item, as opposed to regulating what appears on the label.

a. The Federal Food, Drug and Cosmetic Act protects consumers against impure and misbranded foods and drugs. The act establishes food standards, specifies safe levels of food additives, and regulates some aspects of food advertising.

b. The Consumer Product Safety Act seeks to protect consumers from risk of injury from hazardous products. The Consumer Product Safety Commission has the power to remove products that are deemed hazardous from the market and to ban the manufacture and sale of hazardous products.

5. *Consumer credit protection*—Credit protection has become an important area regulated by consumer protection legislation.

  a. **TRUTH-IN-LENDING ACT (TILA)**—A disclosure law requiring sellers and lenders to disclose credit terms or loan terms so that individuals can shop around to compare terms. Also provides for the following:

    1. Equal credit opportunity—Prohibits creditors from discriminating on the basis of race, religion, national origin, color, gender, marital status, or age.

    2. Credit-card protection—Limits the liability of cardholders for unauthorized charges made on unsolicited credit cards.

    3. Credit-card rules—Allows credit-card users to withhold payment for faulty products purchased by credit card and to withhold payment for charges billed in error until disputes are resolved.

  b. **FAIR CREDIT REPORTING ACT**—Protects consumers against inaccurate credit reporting and provides that credit reports can only be issued for certain purposes. Consumers are entitled to receive a copy of their credit report on request and to be notified any time they are denied credit or insurance based on the report. The reporting agency must conduct an investigation if the consumer contests any information on the credit report.

  c. **FAIR AND ACCURATE CREDIT TRANSACTIONS ACT**—Helps protect against identity theft by establishing a national fraud alert system for credit users, by requiring major credit reporting agencies to provide consumers with free copies of their credit reports every twelve months, by requiring that account numbers on credit-card receipts be shortened, and by assisting victims of identity theft in reestablishing their credit reputations.

  d. **FAIR DEBT COLLECTION PRACTICES ACT**—Prohibits debt collectors from using unfair debt-collection practices, such as contacting debtors at their place of employment if their employers object, contacting debtors at unreasonable times, contacting third parties about the debt unless authorized to do so by a court, and harassing debtors.

  e. **GARNISHMENT**—Allows a creditor to seize a portion of the debtor's property (such as wages) in the possession of a third party (such as an employer) to satisfy a debt. The creditor must comply with specific procedures mandated by state law.

STUDENT STUDYWARE™ CD-ROM

Interactive student CD in this book includes additional quizzing, plus video clips, case studies, and Key Terms flashcards.

ONLINE COMPANION™

For additional resources, please go to **www.paralegal.delmar.cengage.com**.

QUESTIONS FOR REVIEW

1. What is a tort? What is the underlying purpose of tort law? What are the main categories of torts, and how do they differ?

2. What are the four elements of negligence? Why is the duty of care for professionals different from the duty of an ordinary person?

3. What are the affirmative defenses to a negligence action? What is contributory negligence, and how is it different from comparative negligence?

4. What is meant by strict liability? In what circumstances is strict liability applied?

5. What is deceptive advertising? What agency of the federal government can take action against businesses that engage in such advertising?

ETHICAL QUESTIONS

1. Monica is a legal assistant in a law firm that specializes in representing business defendants in tort cases. Monica's supervising attorney has just been asked to defend a firm against a toxic tort claim. The attorney asks Monica to do some legal research on toxic torts—an area with which she is not familiar. It takes Monica twelve hours to complete the research assignment, which is twice as long as the attorney told her to spend on the project. Monica is uncomfortable in billing the client for twelve hours of research time, and she is contemplating billing another client for six of the twelve hours. Should she? Why or why not?

2. Claire is a new legal assistant interviewing a client who wants to sue the manufacturer of an allegedly defective treadmill. The client claims that while walking on the treadmill, he received an electrical shock that caused him to fall off and seriously injure his hip. Near the end of the interview, the client asks Claire whether she thinks he has a good case. Claire responds, "Well, as you know, I'm a paralegal, and I cannot give legal advice. Personally, though, I think that you do have a good case." Has Claire violated her ethical duties? How would you have handled the situation?

PRACTICE QUESTIONS AND ASSIGNMENTS

1. Shirley, an elderly woman, was taking a walk down the street in Santa Monica. Two teenaged boys confronted her, and one of the boys demanded that she hand over her purse. Shirley refused and began scolding the boys, telling them that their mothers would be ashamed of them. One of the boys then grabbed at the straps of her purse but was unable to dislodge it from her shoulder. When the boys realized they were not going to get the purse, they ran away. Does Shirley have a tort claim against the boys? Which tort or torts have been committed?

2. Sarah and David are divorced. While they were married, David continually accused Sarah in private of being "unfaithful" to him and sexually promiscuous. Now that the divorce is final, Sarah learns that David is sending e-mails to all their mutual friends claiming that she is promiscuous. Can Sarah sue David for defamation? Could she have brought a defamation action prior to the divorce? What would happen to Sarah's claim if David could prove that Sarah was, in fact, promiscuous?

3. In which of the following situations will the acting party be liable for the tort of negligence? Explain fully.

a. Mary goes to the golf course on Sunday morning, eager to try out a new set of golf clubs she has just purchased. As she tees off on the first hole, the head of her club flies off and injures a nearby golfer.

b. Mary's doctor gives her some pain medication and tells her not to drive after she takes it, as the medication induces drowsiness. In spite of the doctor's warning, Mary decides to drive to the store while on the medication. Owing to her lack of alertness, she fails to stop at a traffic light and crashes into another vehicle, injuring a passenger.

4. Carmen buys a television set manufactured by AKI Electronics. She is going on vacation, so she takes the set to her mother's house for her mother to use. Because the set is defective, it explodes, causing considerable damage to her mother's house. Carmen's mother sues AKI for the damage to her house. Discuss the product liability theories under which Carmen's mother can recover from AKI.

5. Using the material on consumer law presented in this chapter, identify the law that would apply to each of the following situations, and explain how it would resolve the problem:

a. Mary purchases a new computer system for $1,000 and pays for it with a credit card. The first week that Mary has her new computer, she has serious difficulty operating many of the programs, the computer constantly freezes up, and she loses work that she has prepared on the word processor. Mary complains to the company from which she purchased the computer. When the problem is not resolved, she withholds payment to her credit-card company and notifies it of the reason.

b. Dick has a credit card with an $8,000 balance. He loses his job and stops paying the credit-card company. A collection agency begins to harass him at all hours of the day and even calls his former employer to verify that Dick was fired.

QUESTIONS FOR CRITICAL ANALYSIS

1. The tort of intentional infliction of emotional distress imposes liability on a person who engages in extreme and outrageous conduct that causes another to suffer severe emotional distress. How can these types of "injuries" be measured? How can they be compensated for? Should this tort be allowed?

2. Negligence law imposes a duty on every member of society to act like a "reasonable person." How did the concept of a duty of care arise? What societal judgment does the reasonable person standard reflect?

3. A plaintiff in a negligence case must prove proximate cause, also known as legal cause, to succeed in the action. Foreseeability is one commonly used test of proximate cause. What impact does foreseeability have on the issue of causation? What might happen without such a test?

4. Even if the elements of duty, breach of duty, and causation are met, there can be no recovery in a negligence action if the injury requirement is not met. Why not? Is this principle of tort law fair?

5. Strict liability imposes liability for injuries suffered by defendants without considering fault. Is this fair in any situation? If so, in which situations? What is the underlying rationale behind imposing strict product liability on defendants?

PROJECTS

1. Find an article online or in a print newspaper on a serious-injury accident. Read the article carefully, and write a two-page memo evaluating the potential negligence claim and indicating what you think is needed to "work up" the case. For example, you might make a list of any witnesses who need to be interviewed and any reports that should be obtained. Make sure to attach the article, or a copy of it, to the memo you prepare.

2. Contact a credit reporting agency and obtain a credit report on yourself, if one exists. Does the report contain any inaccurate information about your credit transactions? If so, and if a denial of credit, employment, or insurance might have been based on the report, you can and should have it corrected, as permitted under the Fair Credit Reporting Act.

USING INTERNET RESOURCES

1. Go to FindLaw's Injury and Tort Law Web Guide at **www.findlaw.com/01topics.** Under "Practice Areas," go to "Injury & Tort Law" to find answers to the following questions:

a. Under "Web Guide by Resource Type," select "Databases and Statistics." What kind of information generally is available at this location? How might you use this information in a tort lawsuit? Can you access any data or reports from governmental agencies? Which agencies?

b. Under the heading "Publications—Journals, Newsletters and Articles," you can find many articles on tort law. Read an article that interests you and write a one-page summary.

c. Now select "Web Sites" and browse through the listings. Note how many of the listings are dedicated to providing information about defective products and product liability actions. Explore one of the Web sites provided, and write a short synopsis of what you found at that site.

END NOTES

1. 47 U.S.C. Section 230.

2. *Restatement (Second) of Torts*, Section 402A.

3. *Restatement (Third) of Torts: Products Liability*, Section 2, Comment h.

CONTRACTS AND INTELLECTUAL PROPERTY LAW

CHAPTER OUTLINE

Introduction

Requirements to Form a Valid Contract

Defenses to Contract Enforceability

Sales Contracts and Warranties

Contract Performance and Remedies

Electronic Contracting and Electronic Signatures

Intellectual Property Law

AFTER COMPLETING THIS CHAPTER, YOU WILL KNOW:

▶ The requirements for forming a valid contract and the kinds of circumstances under which contracts are not enforceable.

▶ The remedies available to the innocent party when a contract is breached, or broken.

▶ The nature of an electronic signature and the legal validity of such signatures.

▶ The nature of intellectual property and some forms of intellectual property.

▶ What conduct gives rise to a copyright infringement action.

INTRODUCTION

The law governs virtually every transaction or activity that individuals engage in across the nation. Simple, everyday transactions—such as buying a jug of milk at a convenience store or installing a new software program on your computer—are subject to laws that define the rights and duties of the parties involved. In this chapter, you will learn about two of the most important areas of law—contracts and sales. Paralegals routinely help attorneys deal with disputes involving contract and sales law. Because such disputes often deal with complicated issues, paralegals need a thorough understanding of the basic principles of these substantive law areas.

Another area of law that has become increasingly important involves intellectual property, such as patents, trademarks, and copyrights. As you will learn later in the chapter, the value of intellectual property has become very important because of the flow of ideas throughout the world. Attorneys and their paralegals are frequently called on to help their clients register and protect some form of intellectual property.

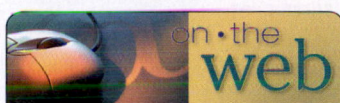

The 'Lectric Law Library provides information on many legal topics, including contracts. Go to **www. lectlaw.com**, and search on "Laypeople's Law Lounge" for a list of topics. For a more formal discussion, visit the Legal Information Institute at **www.law.cornell.edu**. From the "Law about . . ." menu, select "All topics," and scroll down to "Contracts."

REQUIREMENTS TO FORM A VALID CONTRACT

Contract law deals with, among other things, the keeping of promises. A **promise** is an assurance that one will or will not do something in the future. As mentioned in Chapter 2, a *contract* is any agreement (based on a promise or an exchange of promises) that can be enforced in court. (Today, forms for many contracts are available online—see the *Technology and Today's Paralegal* feature on page 499 for information on Web sites offering contract forms.)

promise
An assurance that one will or will not do something in the future.

Two basic terms used in discussing types of contracts are *bilateral* and *unilateral.* Most contracts are bilateral. People make a bilateral contract when they exchange a promise for a promise: Yvonne offers to sell Sean her car for $10,000, and he accepts, saying he will have the money tomorrow. When people make a unilateral contract, they exchange a promise for an act: Yvonne tells Devon she will pay him $50 if he will wax her car. He says nothing but later he waxes the car. Because he completed the requested act, he is owed $50. Both types of contracts are valid, although they may be referred to by different names. Some states do not use the term *unilateral contract.*

If a client alleges that a party has breached (failed to perform) a contract, the first issue that you and your supervising attorney need to examine is whether a *valid contract* (a contract that will be enforced by a court) was ever formed. To form a valid contract, four basic requirements must be met:

- *Agreement.* An agreement includes an offer and an acceptance. One party must offer to enter into a legal agreement, and another party must accept the terms of the offer.

- *Consideration.* Any promises made by parties must be supported by legally sufficient and bargained-for consideration (which is something of value that is received or promised to convince a person to make a deal, as you will read shortly).

- *Contractual capacity.* Both parties entering into the contract must have the contractual capacity to do so; the law must recognize them as possessing characteristics that qualify them as competent parties.

- *Legality.* The contract's purpose must be to accomplish some goal that is legal and not against public policy.

If any of these four elements is lacking, no contract will have been formed. We look more closely at these requirements in the following subsections. It is important that you understand as you read these discussions that each requirement is separate and independent.

Agreement

agreement

A meeting of the minds, and a requirement for a valid contract. Agreement involves two distinct events: an offer to form a contract and the acceptance of that offer by the offeree.

A contract is, in essence, an **agreement** between two or more parties. Therefore, if the parties fail to reach an agreement on the terms of the contract, no contract exists. Ordinarily, agreement is evidenced by two events: an *offer* and an *acceptance*. One party offers a certain bargain to another party, who then accepts that bargain.

Offer

offer

A promise or commitment to do or refrain from doing some specified thing in the future.

An **offer** is a promise or commitment to do or refrain from doing some specified thing in the future. Three elements are necessary for an offer to be effective:

offeror

The party making the offer.

- The **offeror** (the party making the offer) must have the *intent to be bound* by the offer.

- The terms of the offer must be *reasonably certain, or definite,* so that the parties and the court can determine the terms of the contract. (Note that in contracts for the sale of goods, discussed later in this chapter, the requirement of definiteness is relaxed somewhat so that a contract can exist even if certain terms are left "open," or unspecified.)

offeree

The party to whom the offer is made.

- The offer must be communicated to the **offeree** (the party to whom the offer is made).

Offers made in jest, in undue excitement, or in obvious anger do not meet the intent requirement. ▶ **EXAMPLE 15.1** Al and Sue ride to work together each day in Sue's car, which she bought for $18,000 six months ago. One cold morning, Al and Sue get into the car, but Sue cannot get it started. She yells in anger, "I'll sell you this stupid car for $600!" Al writes Sue a check for $600. Has a contract to sell the car been formed? If Al consulted with your supervising attorney, claiming that Sue had breached a contract because she had refused to give him the car, what would the attorney say? The attorney would tell Al that a reasonable person would have recognized under the circumstances that Sue's offer was not serious—she did not intend to be bound but was simply frustrated. Therefore, no valid contract was formed. ◀

Similarly, an offer will not be effective if it is too ambiguous in its terms. ▶ **EXAMPLE 15.2** Kim wants to sell her set of legal encyclopedias but has not mentioned a price. James says to Kim, "I'll buy your encyclopedias and pay you some money for them next week." In this situation, no contract will result, because "some money" is not a definite term. ◀

A real estate paralegal reviews the terms of a purchase offer with a potential home buyer to ensure that all of the contract's terms are clear. How can a paralegal help her or his supervising attorney conduct real estate transactions?

(Courtesy of ©PhotoDisc)

Technology and Today's Paralegal

CONTRACT FORMS

Before the printing press was invented, every contract form had to be handwritten. Since the advent of printing, most standard contract forms have been readily available at low cost. The introduction of computers into legal practice made preprinted forms unnecessary and allowed attorneys and paralegals to customize contract forms for each situation. This procedure has been both simplified and expanded by the inclusion of contract forms on simple-to-use CD-ROMs and DVDs.

ONLINE CONTRACT FORMS

Now the Internet has made available an even larger variety of contract forms, as well as other legal and business forms. For example, at **forms.lp.findlaw.com**, you can access over 25,000 legal forms for lawyers, businesses, and the public. The contracts range from basic sales contracts to sample software licensing agreements. Many are available free of charge. The Internet Legal Research Group also offers a number of free contract forms and links to other online resources at **www.ilrg.com**.

Yet another source for contract forms is 'Lectric Law Library's collection of forms at **www.lectlaw.com**. (Select "Legal Forms," and then select "Business & General Legal Forms.") This site includes forms for the assignment of a contract, a contract for the sale of a business, and many others (some free, some for purchase). In addition, if you become a member of the 'Lectric Law Library, you can access document assembly software that uses the forms to build a final contract to suit your needs.

There are many other sources for contract forms on the Internet. For example, **www.uslegalforms.com** has numerous forms available in many areas of practice. Not only can you search for contracts by topic (such as corporate or construction contracts), but you can also look up state-specific forms (separation agreements, for example). Most of the forms are available for a nominal fee and can be obtained in printed form (mailed to you) or downloaded in the electronic format of your choice. Similar types of services are available at many other sites, including **www.legal-forms-now.com**, **www.findforms.com**, and **www.allaboutforms.com**.

TECHNOLOGY TIP

Online contract forms are a tremendous resource for paralegals. Thousands of forms can be easily accessed and customized for use in particular transactions. Keep in mind, though, that the contracts you find online will not necessarily be valid or upheld in your state or situation. You must always research the contract requirements in your state to verify that you are using the appropriate form.

Termination of the Offer

Once an offer has been communicated, the party to whom the offer was made can accept the offer, reject the offer, or make a counteroffer. If a party accepts the offer, a contract is formed (provided all the other requirements to form a contract are met). If the party rejects the offer, the offer is terminated. In other words, the offer no longer stands (and the offeree cannot take the offeror up on the offer). The offeree also has the option of rejecting the offer and simultaneously making another offer—called a counteroffer.

In a counteroffer, the offeree becomes the offeror—offering to form a contract with different terms. ▶ **EXAMPLE 15.3** Dillon offers to perform work for Wayne for $50,000 a year. Wayne responds, "Your price is too high. I'll hire you for $40,000." Wayne's response is a counteroffer, because it terminates Dillon's offer and creates a new offer by Wayne. ◀

Both a rejection of the offer and the making of a counteroffer terminate the original offer. The original offer can also be terminated if the party making the offer withdraws the offer before it has been accepted (which is called *revoking* the offer). If the offer has already been accepted, however, then both parties are bound in contract. An offer also terminates automatically in some circumstances, such as when the specific subject matter of the offer is destroyed, one of the parties dies or becomes incompetent, or a new law is passed that makes the contract illegal. Additionally, an offer terminates if a period of time is specified in the offer and the offer is not accepted within that period. If no time for acceptance is specified in the offer, the offer expires when a *reasonable* period of time has passed. What constitutes a reasonable period of time in the eyes of the court varies, depending on the circumstances.

Acceptance

acceptance

In contract law, the offeree's indication to the offeror that the offeree agrees to be bound by the terms of the offeror's offer, or proposal to form a contract.

As mentioned, a party's **acceptance** of the offer results in a legally binding contract if all of the other elements of a valid contract are present. The acceptance must be *unequivocal*—that is, the terms of the offer must be accepted exactly as stated by the offeror. This principle of contract law is known as the **mirror image rule**—the terms of the acceptance must be the same as ("mirror") the terms of the offer. If the acceptance is subject to new conditions or if the terms of the acceptance materially change the original offer, the acceptance may be deemed a counteroffer that implicitly rejects the original offer.

mirror image rule

A common law rule that requires that the terms of the offeree's acceptance adhere exactly to the terms of the offeror's offer for a valid contract to be formed.

Another requirement, for most types of contracts, is that the acceptance be communicated to the offeror. A significant problem in contract formation has to do with the timeliness of acceptances. The general rule is that acceptance of an offer is timely if it is made before the offer is terminated. Problems arise, however, when the parties involved are not dealing face-to-face. In such cases, acceptance takes effect at the time the acceptance is communicated via the mode expressly or impliedly authorized by the offeror. This is the **mailbox rule**. Under this rule, if the offer states that it must be accepted by mail, the acceptance becomes valid the moment it is deposited in the mail (even if it is never received by the offeror).

mailbox rule

A rule providing that an acceptance of an offer takes effect at the time it is communicated via the mode expressly or impliedly authorized by the offeror, rather than at the time it is actually received by the offeror. If acceptance is to be by mail, for example, it becomes effective the moment it is placed in the mailbox.

Most of the time, the party making the offer does not indicate the preferred method of acceptance. In those cases, acceptance of an offer may be made in any manner that is *reasonable under the circumstances*. Several factors determine whether the acceptance is reasonable: the nature of the circumstances at the time the offer was made, the means used to transmit the offer, and the reliability of the offer's delivery. ▶ **EXAMPLE 15.4** An offer is sent by FedEx overnight delivery because an acceptance is urgently required. In this situation, the offeree's acceptance by fax or e-mail will be deemed reasonable. ◀ In contracts formed on the Internet, the issues of timeliness and method of acceptance usually do not arise. This is because persons often accept online offers simply by clicking on a box stating "I agree" or "I accept." Such **click-on agreements** are widely used in the formation of contracts online (as discussed later in this chapter).

click-on agreement

An agreement that arises when a buyer, engaging in a transaction on a computer, indicates his or her assent to be bound by the terms of an offer by clicking on a button that says, for example, "I agree"; sometimes referred to as a *click-on license* or a *click-wrap agreement*.

Consideration

consideration

Something of value, such as money or the performance of an action not otherwise required, that motivates the formation of a contract. Each party must give consideration for the contract to be binding.

Another requirement for a valid contract is consideration. **Consideration** is usually defined as something of value—such as money or the performance of an action not otherwise required—that is given in exchange for a promise. No promise is enforceable without consideration. ▶ **EXAMPLE 15.5** You give your friend $1,000 in exchange for her promise to take care of your house and garden for six months. This promise normally will be enforceable, because consideration has been given. Your consideration is $1,000; your friend's consideration is the assumption of an obligation (taking care of the house and garden) that she otherwise would not assume. ◀ Note that both parties to the contract must give consideration for the contract to be enforced.

Often, consideration is broken down into two parts: (1) something of *legal value* must be given in exchange for the promise, and (2) there must be a *bargained-for* exchange. The "something of legal value" may consist of a return promise that is bargained for. It may also consist of performance, which may be an act, a forbearance, or the creation, modification, or destruction of a legal relationship. Forbearance involves not doing something one has a legal right to do. ▶ **EXAMPLE 15.6** When you are twenty-one, your grandfather promises to pay you $10,000 if you agree not to smoke any cigarettes before the age of twenty-five. Your consideration in this situation is not smoking cigarettes. ◀

Once a contract has been formed, the general common law rule is that the terms of the contract cannot be modified without further consideration. For instance, after making the deal in the example just given, your grandfather cannot modify the terms by requiring you not to drink alcohol for the same $10,000—you would have to get additional consideration for this new agreement.

Legal Sufficiency of Consideration

For a binding contract to be created, consideration must be *legally sufficient*. To be legally sufficient, consideration for a promise must be either *legally detrimental to the promisee or legally beneficial to the promisor*. A party can incur legal detriment either by promising to give legal value (such as the payment of money) or by a forbearance or a promise of forbearance.

The requirement of consideration is what distinguishes contracts from gifts. ▶ **EXAMPLE 15.7** You promise to give your friend $1,000 as a gift, and she promises to accept your gift. In this situation, no contract results, because your friend has given no legally sufficient consideration. ◀

Adequacy of Consideration

Adequacy of consideration refers to the fairness of the bargain. In general, a court will not question the adequacy of consideration if the consideration is legally sufficient. Parties are normally free to bargain as they wish. If people could sue merely because they had entered into a bad bargain, the courts would be overloaded with frivolous suits. In other words, Alonzo is free to sell his 2009 Mercedes Benz, which is in perfect condition, to Herb for $1,000, even if the car is worth more (the court normally will not invalidate the contract).

In extreme cases, a court may consider the adequacy of consideration in terms of its amount or worth because inadequate consideration may indicate fraud, duress, undue influence, or a lack of bargained-for exchange. It may also reflect a party's incompetence (for example, an individual might have been too intoxicated or simply too young to make a contract).

Promissory Estoppel

In some circumstances, contracts will be enforced even though consideration is lacking. Under the doctrine of **promissory estoppel**, a person who has reasonably and substantially relied on the promise of another may be able to obtain some measure of recovery. The following elements are required:

- There must be a clear and definite promise.
- The promisee must justifiably rely on the promise.
- The reliance normally must be of a substantial and definite character.
- Justice will be better served by enforcement of the promise.

If these requirements are met, a promise may be enforced even though it is not supported by consideration. In essence, the promisor will be *estopped* (prevented) from asserting the lack of consideration as a defense. ▶ **EXAMPLE 15.8** Your uncle tells you, "I'll pay you $500 a week so you won't have to work anymore." In

promissory estoppel
A doctrine under which a promise is binding if the promise is clear and definite, the promisee justifiably relies on the promise, the reliance is reasonable and substantial, and justice will be better served by enforcement of the promise.

reliance on your uncle's promise, you quit your job, but your uncle refuses to pay you. Under the doctrine of promissory estoppel, you may be able to enforce such a promise. ◄

Contractual Capacity

For a contract to be deemed valid, the parties to the contract must have **contractual capacity**—the legal ability or competence to enter into a contractual relationship. Courts generally presume the existence of contractual capacity, but there are some situations in which capacity is lacking or questionable. In many situations, a party may have the capacity to enter into a valid contract but also have the right to avoid liability under it.

Minors usually are not legally bound by contracts. Subject to certain exceptions, the contracts entered into by a minor are *voidable* (they can be canceled, or avoided) at the option of that minor. The minor has the option of *disaffirming* (renouncing) the contract and setting aside the contract and all legal obligations arising from it. An adult who enters into a contract with a minor, however, cannot avoid his or her contractual duties on the ground that the minor can do so. Unless the minor exercises the option to set aside the contract, the adult party is bound by it.

Intoxication is a condition in which a person's normal capacity to act or think is inhibited by alcohol or some other drug. Under the common law rule, if the person was sufficiently intoxicated to lack mental capacity, the transaction is voidable at the option of the intoxicated person even if the intoxication was purely voluntary. In spite of the common law rule, most courts today rarely permit contracts to be avoided because of a party's intoxication.

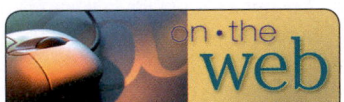

For a series of briefed contract cases that cover many issues, see **www. lectlaw.com**. Search on "Notable Court Cases Concerning Contracts."

If a person has been adjudged mentally incompetent by a court of law and a guardian has been appointed, any contract made by the mentally incompetent person is *void*—no contract exists. Only the guardian can enter into binding legal duties on the incompetent person's behalf. Even if the court has not previously ruled that the person is mentally incompetent, the contract may be avoided if incompetence is proved. ► **EXAMPLE 15.9** Rita, who suffers from Alzheimer's disease, signs a contract to buy ten new vacuums. If the contract is challenged and it can be proved that Rita did not understand what she was doing at the time she signed the contract, the contract will not be valid. ◄ The issue of contractual capacity is discussed further in the *Developing Paralegal Skills* feature.

Legality

A contract to do something that is prohibited by federal or state statutory law is illegal and, as such, void from the outset and unenforceable. For example, a contract to buy a kidney from another person is void because it is illegal. No court would enforce the contract if a lawsuit were brought for breach of contract. Any contract to commit an illegal act is unenforceable.

In some instances, the subject matter of the contract is not illegal, but one of the parties is not legally authorized to perform the contract. Consider an illustration. All states require that members of certain occupations—including physicians, lawyers, real estate brokers, architects, electricians, contractors, and stockbrokers—obtain licenses allowing them to practice. When a person enters into a contract with an unlicensed individual, the contract may still be enforceable, depending on the nature of the licensing statute. Some states expressly provide that the lack of a license in certain occupations bars the enforcement of work-related contracts. If there is no express provision, one must look to the underlying purpose of the licensing requirements for a particular occupation. If the purpose is to protect the public from unauthorized practitioners, a contract involving an unlicensed individual normally is illegal and unenforceable. If the underlying purpose of the statute is to raise government revenues, however, a contract entered into with an unlicensed practitioner generally is enforceable—although the unlicensed person is usually fined.

Developing
Paralegal Skills

ASSESSING CONTRACTUAL CAPACITY

Suppose you are a legal assistant for Jeffrey Barlow. Barlow asks you to draft a contract for Margaret Klaus, a seventy-six-year-old widow. In the contract, Margaret will convey all of her shares in NAPO Corporation to her nephew Jeremy. In return, Jeremy will take care of Margaret for the rest of her life. The attorney is leaving on vacation and asks you to have the document completed and to arrange a meeting with the client and her nephew to sign the contract when he returns in two weeks.

While drafting the agreement, you learn that the stock being conveyed is worth a great deal of money. Also, you begin to have doubts about Margaret's mental status. She has called you at least once a day for the past week. During the conversations, she often calls you by different names, repeats herself, and does not remember what you just told her. Although you know that Jeremy has been living with Margaret for the past six months (and is unemployed), whenever Margaret calls, she is alone and seems to be frightened. Now that you have finished the contract, you wonder if Margaret is capable of consenting to it and whether Jeremy has exerted too much influence over her. What should you do?

TIPS FOR DEALING WITH SUSPICIONS OF INCOMPETENCE

- Document everything. Keep a record of all the conversations you had with the client that led you to suspect a lack of contractual capacity, as well as any other facts that contributed to your suspicions (if you discovered the person was taking medication for mental illness, for example).

- Do not discuss your suspicions with anyone except your supervising attorney (particularly not with the client or the client's family). Making such statements about a person can be very damaging to his or her reputation, and you may even be held liable for defamation.

- Remember that it is the attorney's job to evaluate the client's contractual capacity, not yours. You just want to make the attorney aware of the situation in an effort to protect the client's best interests.

Additionally, some contracts are not enforced because the court deems them to be contrary to public policy. For example, contracts that restrain trade (anticompetitive contracts) and contracts that are so oppressive to innocent parties that they are deemed *unconscionable* (unconscionable contracts will be discussed shortly) are not enforceable owing to the negative impact they would have on society.

DEFENSES TO CONTRACT ENFORCEABILITY

Two competent parties have entered into a contract for a legal purpose. The agreement is supported by consideration. The contract thus meets the four requirements for a valid contract. Nonetheless, the contract may be unenforceable if the parties have not genuinely assented (agreed) to its terms, if the contract is so oppressive to one of the parties that a court will refuse to enforce it, or if the contract is not in the proper form—such as in writing, if the law requires it to be in writing.

Genuineness of Assent

Lack of **genuineness of assent** can be used as a defense to the contract's enforceability. Genuineness of assent may be lacking because of a mistake, fraudulent misrepresentation, undue influence, or duress.

genuineness of assent
Knowing and voluntary assent to the contract terms. If a contract is formed as a result of mistake, misrepresentation, undue influence, or duress, genuineness of assent is lacking, and the contract will be voidable.

Mistake

It is important to distinguish between *mistakes of fact* and *mistakes of value or quality*. If a mistake concerns the future market value or quality of the object of the contract, the mistake is one of *value,* and either party normally can enforce the contract. Each party is considered to have assumed the risk that the value would change or prove to be different from what he or she thought. Without this rule, almost any party who did not receive what he or she considered a fair bargain could argue mistake.

Only a mistake of fact allows a contract to be avoided. Mistakes of fact occur in two forms—*unilateral* and *mutual (bilateral)*. A **unilateral mistake** occurs when one party to the contract makes a mistake as to some **material fact**—that is, a fact important to the subject matter of the contract. The general rule is that a unilateral mistake does not give the mistaken party any right to relief from the contract. There are some exceptions to this rule, however. ▶ **EXAMPLE 15.10** A contractor's bid was significantly low because he made a mistake in addition when totaling the estimated costs. In this situation, any contract resulting from the bid normally can be rescinded. (**Rescission** is the act of canceling, or nullifying, a contract.) ◀

When *both* of the parties are mistaken about the same material fact, a **mutual mistake** has occurred, and either party can cancel the contract. ▶ **EXAMPLE 15.11** At Perez's art gallery, Diana buys a painting of a landscape. Both Diana and Perez believe that the painting is by the famous artist Vincent van Gogh. Later, Diana discovers that the painting is a very clever fake. Because neither Perez nor Diana was aware of this material fact when they made their deal, Diana can rescind (cancel) the contract and recover the purchase price of the painting. ◀

Fraudulent Misrepresentation

When an innocent party is fraudulently induced to enter into a contract, the contract usually can be avoided because that party has not *voluntarily* consented to its terms. Normally, the innocent party can either rescind (cancel) the contract and be restored to his or her original position or enforce the contract and seek damages for any injuries resulting from the fraud.

You read about the tort of fraud in Chapter 14. In the context of contract law, fraudulent misrepresentation occurs when one party to a contract misrepresents a material fact to the other party, with the intention of deceiving the other party, and the other party justifiably relies on the misrepresentation. To collect damages, a party must also have been injured. A party may still be able to avoid the contract in some states without proving that he or she was injured by the fraud, however.

Note that the misrepresentation may be based on conduct as well as oral or written statements. ▶ **EXAMPLE 15.12** Gene is contracting to buy Rachelle's horse for racing. While showing Gene the horse, Rachelle skillfully keeps the horse's head turned away so that Gene does not see that the horse is blind in one eye. Rachelle's conduct constitutes fraud. ◀

Undue Influence

Undue influence arises from special kinds of relationships in which one party can greatly influence another party, thus overcoming that party's free will. As illustrated in *Developing Paralegal Skills* on the previous page, elderly people may be unduly influenced by their caretakers. In addition, clients may be unduly influenced by their attorneys, and children may be unduly influenced by their parents. The essential feature of undue influence is that the party being taken advantage of does not, in reality, exercise free will in entering into a contract. A contract entered into under excessive or undue influence lacks genuine assent and is therefore voidable.

Duress

Assent to the terms of a contract is not genuine if one of the parties is *forced* into the agreement. Forcing a party to do something, including entering into a contract, through fear created by threats is legally defined as *duress*. In addition, blackmail or

---

unilateral mistake

Mistake as to a material fact on the part of only one party to a contract. In this situation, the contract is normally enforceable against the mistaken party, with some exceptions.

material fact

A fact that is important to the subject matter of the contract.

rescission

A remedy in which the contract is canceled and the parties are returned to the positions they occupied before the contract was made.

mutual mistake

Mistake as to the same material fact on the part of both parties to a contract. In this situation, either party can cancel the contract.

Ethics Watch

POTENTIAL CONFLICTS OF INTEREST

Many times in a law office, two parties come in together and want the attorney (and paralegal) to write a contract that represents their agreement. This raises an obvious conflict-of-interest issue. Can the attorney represent both parties in a contract? Conflict rules prevent an attorney from simultaneously representing adverse parties in a legal proceeding. On the one hand, drafting a contract is not really a legal proceeding, because the parties could write up a legally binding contract without an attorney. On the other hand, should a dispute arise over the contract, assisting one party will necessarily be adverse to the other. In this situation, the attorney and paralegal need to carefully research the rules on waiving conflicts in their state. If the state has adopted the 2002 Revision of the Model Rules (discussed in Chapter 4), then the attorney must obtain the informed consent of each party, and the consent must be confirmed in writing. This means the attorney must explain the risks of having one attorney draw up a contract for two people and also must discuss the alternatives. Then the attorney must have the two parties sign a consent form or, if the parties give consent orally, must promptly draft a written document evidencing the consent.

Paralegals often have a role to play in these interactions, such as conducting an initial interview with the parties. The position of a paralegal in such circumstances is covered by the NALA Code of Ethics and Professional Responsibility, Canon 2: "A paralegal may perform any task which is properly designated and supervised by an attorney, as long as the attorney is ultimately responsible to the client, maintains a direct relationship with the client, and assumes professional responsibility for the work product."

extortion to induce consent to a contract constitutes duress. Duress is both a defense to the enforcement of a contract and a ground for the rescission of a contract.

Unconscionable Contracts or Clauses

Ordinarily, a court does not look at the fairness or equity of a contract; for example, a court normally will not inquire into the adequacy of consideration. Persons are assumed to be reasonably intelligent, and the court does not come to their aid just because they have made unwise or foolish bargains.

In certain circumstances, however, a bargain is so oppressive to one of the parties that the court will refuse to enforce the contract. Such a bargain is called an **unconscionable contract** (or **unconscionable clause**). Contracts entered into because of one party's vastly superior bargaining power may be deemed unconscionable. These situations usually involve an **adhesion contract**, which is a contract drafted by the dominant party and then presented to the other—the adhering party—on a "take-it-or-leave-it" basis.

> **unconscionable contract or unconscionable clause**
> A contract or clause that is so oppressive to one of the parties that the court will refuse to enforce the contract.

> **adhesion contract**
> A contract drafted by the dominant party and then presented to the other—the adhering party—on a "take-it-or-leave-it" basis.

The Statute of Frauds

An otherwise valid contract may be unenforceable if it is not in the proper form. To ensure that there is reliable proof of the agreement, certain types of contracts are required to be in writing. If a contract is required by law to be in writing and there is no written evidence of the contract, it may not be enforceable.

Every state has a statute (or more than one statute) that specifies what types of contracts must be in writing (or be evidenced by a written document). This statute

Statute of Frauds
A state statute that requires certain types of contracts to be in writing to be enforceable.

is commonly referred to as the **Statute of Frauds**. Although the state statutes vary slightly, the following types of contracts are normally required to be in writing:

- Contracts involving interests in land or anything attached to land, such as buildings, plants, minerals, or timber.
- Contracts that cannot by their terms be performed within one year from the day after the date of formation.
- Collateral, or secondary, contracts, such as promises to answer for the debt or duty of another.
- Promises made in consideration of marriage, such as prenuptial agreements (which will be discussed in Chapter 17).
- Contracts for the sale of goods priced at $500 or more. (This is a rule under the Uniform Commercial Code, not the common law.)

Note that the test for determining whether an oral contract is enforceable under the "one-year rule" stated in the second item above is not whether an agreement is *likely* to be performed within one year but whether performance is *possible* within one year. Also, the one-year period begins to run the day *after* the contract is formed. Exhibit 15.1 illustrates the one-year rule.

In some states, an oral contract that would otherwise be unenforceable under the Statute of Frauds may be enforced under the doctrine of promissory estoppel, based on detrimental reliance. Recall that if one party makes a promise on which the other party justifiably relies to his or her detriment, a court may prevent the party who made the promise from denying that a contract exists. In these circumstances, an oral promise may be enforceable if the reliance was foreseeable and if injustice can be avoided only by enforcing the promise.

Uniform Commercial Code (UCC)
A uniform code of laws governing commercial transactions that has been adopted, in whole or in part, by all of the states. Article 2 of the UCC governs contracts for the sale of goods.

SALES CONTRACTS AND WARRANTIES

The principles we have been discussing come from the common law of contracts. Recall from Chapter 5 that legislatures can pass laws that replace common law principles. That is what happened in the case of the **Uniform Commercial Code**

EXHIBIT 15.1
The One-Year Rule

Under the Statute of Frauds, contracts that by their terms are impossible to perform within one year from the day after the date of contract formation must be in writing to be enforceable. Put another way, if it is at all possible to perform an oral contract within one year from the day after the contract is made, the contract will fall outside the Statute of Frauds and be enforceable.

(UCC). **Sales contracts**—or, more specifically, contracts for the sale of goods—are governed by state statutes based on Article 2 of the UCC. The UCC is one of the many—and one of the most significant—uniform laws created by the American Law Institute and the National Conference of Commissioners on Uniform State Laws. The UCC was first issued in 1952 and has since been revised to reflect the changing customs and needs of business and society. The UCC has been adopted, in whole or in part, by all of the states. State statutory codes are not necessarily called the Uniform Commercial Code, however. In Ohio, for example, UCC provisions are incorporated into the Ohio Commercial Code.

The Scope of UCC Article 2

In regard to Article 2 of the UCC, two things should be kept in mind. First, Article 2 deals with the sale of *goods,* not real property (real estate), services, or intangible property. Second, the rules may vary quite a bit, depending on whether the buyer or seller is a merchant. You should always note the subject matter of a dispute and the people (merchants or consumers) involved when you are dealing with cases involving contractual disputes. If the subject is goods, then the UCC will likely govern. If it is real estate or services, then the common law principles discussed earlier will apply.

As under the common law, the parties to sales contracts are free to fashion the terms of their contracts as they wish. The UCC normally comes into play only when a dispute arises over ambiguous or missing terms. Note also that the UCC does not replace the common law of contracts. A contract for the sale of goods is also subject to the common law requirements of agreement, consideration, contractual capacity, and legality. Similarly, the common law defenses against contract formation or enforceability also apply to sales contracts. If the UCC has not modified a common law principle, then the common law governs. In other words, the general rule is that when the UCC addresses a particular matter, the UCC governs; when the UCC is silent, then the common law of contracts applies.

Warranties under the UCC

The UCC provides that a ~~warranty~~ of title arises in any sale of goods—that is, a seller automatically warrants (promises) to a buyer that the seller has good title to (legitimate ownership rights in) the goods being sold and can transfer that good title to the buyer. If the goods turn out to be stolen, for example, and the buyer has to return the goods to the real owner, the seller will be liable to the buyer for the value of the goods.

The UCC also contains provisions on express and implied warranties as to the quality or nature of the goods being sold. An *express warranty* is an oral or written promise made by a seller concerning the nature of the goods being sold. ▶ **EXAMPLE 15.13** The statement, "This is a new Black & Decker lawn mower" is an express warranty, or promise, that the lawn mower is indeed a Black & Decker lawn mower and that it is new. If you purchase the lawn mower and learn that it is not new but used, the seller has breached an express warranty. ◀

Under the UCC, implied warranties arise in all sales transactions. Every merchant makes an *implied warranty of merchantability* when goods are sold. The goods must be merchantable—that is, they must be "reasonably fit for the ordinary purposes for which such goods are used." Some examples of unmerchantable goods are a lightbulb that explodes when switched on, hamburger meat that contains fragments of glass, and a new boat that leaks. Goods sold by merchants must also be fit for the particular purpose for which they are sold. For this *implied warranty of fitness for a particular purpose* to arise, the buyer must rely on the seller's skill or judgment in selecting suitable goods.

The UCC permits express and implied warranties to be disclaimed, provided that the buyer is made aware of the disclaimers at the time the sales contract is formed. To disclaim an implied warranty of fitness for a particular purpose, the

---

sales contract
A contract for the sale of goods, as opposed to a contract for the sale of services, real property, or intangible property. Sales contracts are governed by Article 2 of the Uniform Commercial Code.

You can access the Uniform Commercial Code (UCC), including Article 2, at the Web site of the Legal Information Institute. Go to **www.law. cornell.edu**, select "Constitutions & Codes" from the menu, and then select "Uniform Commercial Code."

warranty
An express or implied promise by a seller that specific goods to be sold meet certain criteria, or standards of performance, on which the buyer may rely.

Developing
Paralegal Skills

CONTRACT REVIEW

Samantha Thompson works as a paralegal for a corporation. One of her jobs is to review contracts between the corporation and outside vendors. She is reviewing a contract for the corporation's purchase of fifty new personal computers from an outside vendor. The contract, which is a preprinted form contract, was submitted by the vendor and consists of thirty paragraphs of "fine print." The blanks in the form, for such terms as price and quantity, have been filled in by the vendor. As Samantha reads through the contract, she comes across a warranty disclaimer provision. Samantha realizes that this contract provision means that there will be no warranty of merchantability or fitness for a particular purpose for the new computers. She makes a note to tell her supervising attorney about this important provision. The attorney will want to inform management of this limitation on warranties.

TIPS FOR REVIEWING A CONTRACT

- Find out which contract provisions are acceptable to the client.
- Obtain the original copy of the contract.
- Read each provision carefully.
- Be certain you understand the meaning of each provision. If you are uncertain, find out what a provision means; do not rely on the formulaic language in standard contract forms.
- Prepare a memo explaining the client's rights and liabilities under the contract.
- In the memo, mention any contract terms and provisions that the client might find objectionable.

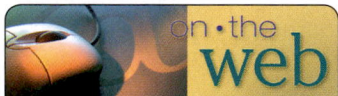

For a discussion of commercial sales and international commercial law, go to **www.hg.org**, and select "Commercial Law" from the "Law & Practice Center" listing.

disclaimer must be in writing and be conspicuous (printed in larger or contrasting type or in a different color, for example). A merchantability disclaimer must mention the word *merchantability,* but it need not be in writing. If it is made in writing, the writing must be conspicuous. Generally speaking, unless circumstances indicate otherwise, the implied warranties are disclaimed by the expression "as is," "with all faults," or similar language that is commonly understood by both parties as meaning that there are no implied warranties. An example of the application of these issues in the practice of contract law is presented in the *Developing Paralegal Skills* feature above.

CONTRACT PERFORMANCE AND REMEDIES

performance
In contract law, the fulfillment of duties arising under a contract; the normal way of discharging contractual obligations.

A party's contractual duties can be terminated in several ways. The most common way to terminate contractual duties, however, is by the **performance** of those duties. Failure to perform contractual duties as promised results in a breach of contract. When one party **breaches a contract**, the other party (the nonbreaching party) can seek remedies.

breach of contract
The failure, without legal excuse, of a contractual party to perform the obligations assumed in a contract.

Contract Performance

Conditions expressly stated in a contract must be fully satisfied for complete performance to take place. A party who in good faith performs substantially all of the terms of a contract, however, can usually enforce the contract against the other party under the doctrine of *substantial performance*. Generally, performance that

In the **Office**

LISTEN UP

Hearing is not the same as listening. Many people are not good listeners. We often hear what we want to hear as we filter information through our own experiences and interests. When clients talk, focus carefully on what they say, as they may reveal information you had not anticipated. Observing their body language is also important. Showing empathy and interest encourages clients to share more information, which may prove useful in handling the legal issues. Taking an active interest in what others say, whether clients or co-workers, can increase your productivity and gain you recognition as a person who helps solve problems.

provides a party with the important and essential benefits of a contract, in spite of any omission or deviation from the terms, is substantial performance. Because substantial performance is not perfect, the other party is entitled to damages to compensate for the failure to comply with the contract.

After a contract has been made, performance may become impossible in an objective sense ("it can't be done," rather than "I can't do it"). For example, the subject matter of the contract may be destroyed, one of the parties to a personal contract may die or become incapacitated prior to performance, or performance may become illegal because of a change in the law. In these situations, the law excuses parties from their contractual performance duties under what is known as *impossibility of performance.*

Under the doctrine of *commercial impracticability,* courts may excuse parties from their performance obligations when the performance becomes much more difficult or expensive than contemplated at the time the contract was formed. For someone to invoke this doctrine successfully, however, the anticipated performance must become *extremely* difficult or costly. ▶ **EXAMPLE 15.14** Delbert's Trucking agreed to carry a load of freight each day for a year from Molly's Factory to a train station four miles away. Delbert's and Molly's agreed that the price would be $40 per day. Two months later, the road Delbert used was torn out by highway crews which began reconstruction work expected to take six months. As a result, Delbert's must travel thirty miles to get to the train station. Molly's cannot expect Delbert's to fulfill the contract at the original price. Cost conditions have greatly changed, making fulfillment of the contract impracticable. ◀

Contract Remedies

A *remedy* is the relief provided for an innocent party when the other party has breached the contract. It is the means employed to enforce a right or to redress an injury. The most common remedies available to a nonbreaching party include damages, rescission, restitution, reformation, and specific performance.

Damages

A breach of contract entitles the nonbreaching party to sue for money damages (see Chapter 4). Damages are designed to compensate a party for the loss of the bargain. Generally, innocent parties are to be placed in the position they would have occupied had the contract been fully performed.

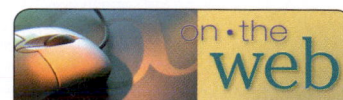

on the **web**

Information on breach of contract is available from the 'Lectric Law Library. Go to **www.lectlaw.com**, and enter the search term "nonperformance and breach of contract."

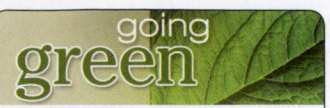

RECYCLE IN AND OUT

Office supplies, such as paper and print cartridges for printers and copier machines, can be recycled. Most printer companies encourage recycling of the cartridge itself. One thing to remember is that legal documents should be shredded before recycling the paper.

Compensatory Damages.   Damages compensating the nonbreaching party for the loss of the bargain are known as *compensatory damages*. These damages compensate the injured party only for damages actually sustained and proved to have arisen directly from the loss of the bargain caused by the breach of contract. They simply replace what was lost because of the breach.

The amount of compensatory damages is the difference between the value of the breaching party's promised performance and the value of his or her actual performance. This amount is reduced by any loss that the injured party has avoided. In addition, the injured party may be able to recover *incidental damages*—expenses resulting directly from the breach of contract, such as those incurred to obtain performance from another source. ▶ **EXAMPLE 15.15** You are hired to perform certain services during August for $3,000, but the employer breaches the contract, and you find another job that pays only $500. You can recover $2,500 as compensatory damages. In addition, as incidental damages, you can recover any expenses you incurred in finding the other job. ◀

Consequential Damages.   *Consequential damages,* or *special damages,* are a type of compensatory damages. Consequential damages are caused by special circumstances beyond the contract itself. They flow from the consequences, or results, of a breach. For consequential damages to be awarded, the breaching party must have known (or have had reason to know) that special circumstances would cause the nonbreaching party to suffer an additional loss. ▶ **EXAMPLE 15.16** Glenda contracts with Eric to ship an item that she needs to repair her printing press. The contract clearly states that Glenda must receive the item by Monday or she will not be able to print her paper and will lose $1,000. If Eric is late in shipping the item, Glenda normally can recover the consequential damages caused by the delay (that is, the $1,000 in losses). ◀

Liquidated Damages.   When writing a contract, the parties may specify an amount to be paid in the event of a future breach of the contract. This amount, called *liquidated damages,* must be reasonably related to the damages that may be suffered if the contract is not fulfilled. Liquidated damages are a form of compensatory damages. ▶ **EXAMPLE 15.17** Shondra is planning to open a new store on June 1 in a shopping center. The owner of the center assures her the store space will be ready. But what if it is not? Shondra will be stuck with inventory she will have to put in storage, employees who cannot work, and so forth. The parties may agree that if the store space is not ready when promised, the shopping center will pay Shondra $500 a day in liquidated damages to compensate her for her expenses. ◀

Punitive Damages.   *Punitive damages* are not awarded in an action for breach of contract. Punitive damages are intended to punish guilty parties, and contract law is not concerned with establishing or punishing guilt. Its intention is to compensate a party for the loss of a bargain, no more and no less. In some situations, if a tort such as fraud or negligence is involved, punitive damages may be appropriate. In such situations, a tort claim may be added.

Rescission, Restitution, and Reformation

As already discussed, *rescission* is essentially an action to undo, or terminate, a contract—to return the contracting parties to the positions they occupied prior to the transaction. When fraud, a mistake, duress, undue influence, misrepresentation, or lack of contractual capacity is present, rescission is available. The failure of one party to perform entitles the other party to rescind the contract.

Generally, to rescind a contract, the parties must make **restitution** to each other by returning goods, property, or funds previously conveyed. If physical property or goods can be returned, they must be. If the property or goods have been consumed, the restitution must be made in an equivalent dollar amount.

restitution
An equitable remedy under which a person is restored to his or her original position prior to loss or injury, or placed in the position that he or she would have been in had the breach not occurred.

When the parties have imperfectly expressed their agreement in writing, the equitable remedy of **reformation** may also be available. In cases involving breach of contract, this remedy occurs when the court revises a contract to reflect the true intention of the parties—if a mutual mistake occurred, for example.

Specific Performance

The equitable remedy of **specific performance** calls for the performance of the act promised in the contract. Normally, specific performance is not granted unless the party's legal remedy (money damages) is inadequate. For this reason, contracts for the sale of goods rarely qualify for specific performance—substantially identical goods can be bought or sold in the market. If the contract involves unique goods, however, such as a painting or a rare book, a court will grant specific performance.

Generally, courts refuse to grant specific performance of contracts for personal services—contracts that require one party to work personally for another party. This is because public policy strongly discourages involuntary servitude, and ordering one party to perform personal services against his or her will amounts to a type of servitude. Moreover, the courts do not want to monitor personal-service contracts. ▶ **EXAMPLE 15.18** If you contract with a brain surgeon to perform brain surgery on you and the surgeon refuses to perform, the court will not compel (and you certainly would not want) the surgeon to perform under these circumstances. The court cannot assure meaningful performance in such a situation. ◀

Remedies for Breach of Sales Contracts

Remedies for breach of a contract for the sale of goods are designed to put the aggrieved party in as good a position as if the other party had fully performed. The seller's remedies for breach include the right to stop or withhold delivery of the goods and the right to recover damages or the purchase price of the goods from the buyer. The buyer's remedies include (1) the right to reject *nonconforming goods* (goods that do not conform to those specifically agreed on in the contract) or improperly delivered goods; (2) the right to *cover* (buy goods elsewhere and recover from the seller the extra cost of obtaining the substitute goods); (3) the right to recover damages; and (4) in certain circumstances, the right to obtain specific performance of the sales contract.

ELECTRONIC CONTRACTING AND ELECTRONIC SIGNATURES

Today, many contracts are formed over the Internet. How the courts apply the traditional principles of contract law in cyberspace is an increasingly important issue. Most disputes concerning contracts formed online tend to center on the specific terms of the contract and whether the parties voluntarily agreed to those terms.

Online Offers and Acceptances

Generally, the terms of an online offer should be just as comprehensive as the terms in an offer made in a written (paper) document. All possible contingencies should be anticipated and provided for in the offer. Because jurisdictional issues often arise with online transactions, dispute-settlement provisions, such as arbitration clauses, are frequently used in electronic contracts. The offer should be displayed on the screen in such a way as to be easily readable and clear. An online offer should also include some mechanism, such as providing an "I agree" or "I accept" box, by which the customer can accept the offer.

---

reformation
An equitable remedy granted by a court to correct, or "reform," a written contract so that it reflects the true intentions of the parties.

specific performance
An equitable remedy requiring exactly the performance that was specified in a contract; usually granted only when money damages would be an inadequate remedy and the subject matter of the contract is unique (for example, real property).

Click-On Agreements

As described earlier, a click-on agreement (also sometimes called a *click-on license, click-through agreement,* or *click-wrap agreement*) arises when a buyer, completing a transaction on a computer, indicates assent to be bound by the terms of an offer by clicking on a button that says "I agree" or "I accept." The terms may be contained on a Web site through which the buyer is obtaining goods or services, or they may appear on a computer screen when software is loaded. The courts have normally enforced click-on agreements.

▶ **EXAMPLE 15.19**   Aaron is downloading a new software program from the Internet. A message pops up on the screen with a small window through which Aaron can read the terms of the *licensing agreement*. (Note that a contract involving software usually grants a *license* by which a party is given the right to use the software but does not own the software.) Even if Aaron clicks on the "I agree" box below the window without reading the terms, he will be bound by the terms of that agreement. ◀

Shrink-Wrap Agreements

shrink-wrap agreement
An agreement whose terms are expressed in a document located inside the box in which the goods (usually software) are packaged.

A **shrink-wrap agreement** is an agreement whose terms are expressed inside the box in which the goods are packaged. (The term *shrink-wrap* refers to the plastic that covers the box.) Usually, the party who opens the box is told that she or he agrees to the terms by keeping whatever is in the box. ▶ **EXAMPLE 15.20**   Abdul orders a new computer program. When he receives the program, he find that the box also contains an agreement setting forth the terms of the sale, including what remedies are available. The document also states that Abdul's use of the program for longer than thirty days will be construed as an acceptance of the terms. ◀

In most cases, a shrink-wrap agreement is an agreement between the manufacturer of the hardware or software and the ultimate buyer-user of the product (not between a retailer and a buyer). Thus, the terms typically concern warranties, remedies, and other issues associated with the use of the product.

Generally, the courts have enforced the terms of shrink-wrap agreements the same as the terms of other contracts, with one exception: If a court finds that the buyer learned of the shrink-wrap terms *after* the parties entered into a contract, the court may conclude that those terms were proposals for additional terms and were not part of the contract unless the buyer expressly agreed to them. ▶ **EXAMPLE 15.21**   When Abdul, in Example 15.20, entered into the contract to purchase the program, he was not informed that any dispute regarding his purchase had to be arbitrated. He installed the program when it arrived, and it ruined his computer. He then discovered that the shrink-wrap agreement included an arbitration clause. In that situation, a court may conclude that the arbitration clause—which Abdul did not know about or consent to—was a proposal rather than part of the agreement. ◀

E-Signatures

In some instances, a contract cannot be enforced unless it is signed by the party against whom enforcement is sought. A significant issue in the context of Internet transactions has to do with how electronic signatures, or **e-signatures**, can be created and verified on e-contracts.

e-signature
An electronic sound, symbol, or process attached to or logically associated with a record and executed or adopted by a person with the intent to sign the record, according to the Uniform Electronic Transactions Act.

In the days when many people could not write, documents were often signed with an "X." Then handwritten signatures become common, followed by typed signatures, printed signatures, and, most recently, digital signatures, which are transmitted electronically. Throughout the evolution of signature technology, the question of what constitutes a valid signature has arisen again and again, and with good reason—without some consensus on what constitutes a valid signature, little business or legal work could be accomplished.

Today, several technologies allow electronic documents to be signed. Because paralegals are frequently responsible for obtaining the necessary signatures on legal documents, some knowledge of digital signatures and alternative technologies is useful.

Digital Signatures

The most common e-signature technology uses two differently encoded "keys." With this system, a person attaches a digital signature to a document using a private key, or code. The key has a publicly available counterpart. Anyone with the appropriate software can use the public key to verify that the digital signature was made using the private key. A **cybernotary**, or legally recognized certification authority, issues the key pair, identifies the owner of the keys, and certifies the validity of the public key. The cybernotary also serves as a repository for public keys.

> **cybernotary**
> A legally recognized authority that can certify the validity of digital signatures.

Signature Dynamics

With another type of signature technology, known as *signature dynamics,* a sender's signature is captured using a stylus (a tracing pen) and an electronic digitizer pad. You often use this technology in stores when you pay with a credit card. A computer program takes the signature's measurements and records the sender's identity, the time and date of the signature, and the identity of the hardware. This information is then "encrypted" and attached to the document being transmitted. When this type of e-signature is used, it is not necessary to have a third party (cybernotary) verify the signature.

State Laws Governing E-Signatures

Most states have laws governing e-signatures. In an attempt to create uniformity among these laws, the National Conference of Commissioners on Uniform State Laws and the American Law Institute issued the Uniform Electronic Transactions Act (UETA) in 1999. To date, the UETA has been adopted, at least in part, by forty-six states. Among other things, the UETA states that a signature or a contract may not be denied legal effect or enforceability solely because it is in electronic form.

Under the UETA, an *e-signature* is broadly defined as "an electronic sound, symbol, or process attached to or logically associated with a record and executed or adopted by a person with the intent to sign the record." In other words, the signature does not have to be created by any specific technology and can be simply a person's name typed at the end of an e-mail message. The parties do have to agree to conduct their business electronically for the UETA provisions to apply, however. Also, the UETA states that it does not apply to (or change) the provisions of the Uniform Commercial Code (discussed earlier in this chapter) and does not apply to wills and trusts (see Chapter 17).

Federal Law on E-Signatures and E-Documents

In 2000, Congress enacted the Electronic Signatures in Global and National Commerce Act (E-SIGN Act) to provide that no contract, record, or signature may be "denied legal effect" solely because it is in an electronic form. In other words, under this law, an electronic signature is as valid as a signature on paper, and an electronic document can be as enforceable as a paper one. For an electronic signature to be enforceable, the contracting parties must have agreed to use electronic signatures. For an electronic document to be valid, it must be in a form that can be retained and accurately reproduced.

The E-SIGN Act does not apply to all types of documents. Contracts and documents that are exempt include court papers, divorce decrees, evictions, foreclosures, health-insurance terminations, prenuptial agreements, and wills. Also, only certain agreements governed by the Uniform Commercial Code fall under this law.

The E-SIGN Act has significantly expanded the possibilities for contracting online. From a remote location, a person can now open an account with a financial institution, obtain a mortgage or other loan, buy insurance, retain an attorney, and purchase real estate over the Internet. Payments and transfers of funds can be done entirely online. By using e-contracts, a person can thus avoid the time and costs associated with producing, delivering, signing, and returning paper documents.

CONTRACT LAW AND THE PARALEGAL

As a legal professional, it is vital that you have some knowledge of contract law. Regardless of where you work, you may be asked to handle matters that require an understanding of the basic principles of contract law, because contracts are so common.

Here are just a few of the tasks you might perform, in any workplace and in any capacity, that involve contracts:

- Interview a client or other person to obtain information about a contract to be drafted or a claim for breach of contract.

- Review a contract to determine a client's rights and obligations as stated in the contract.

- Research previous cases decided by courts in your jurisdiction to determine whether a defense raised against a claim for breach of contract will likely succeed or to determine how the courts have interpreted a certain type of contract provision.

- Gather evidence to determine the amount of damages sustained as a result of a breach of contract.

- Assist in litigating a breach of contract.

- Draft a settlement letter to settle a contract dispute.

- Assist in arbitration or other proceedings held for the purpose of settling a contract dispute.

- Contact representatives of business firms (perhaps in foreign countries) for the purpose of contract negotiations or the settlement of contract disputes.

In addition to these tasks, you may be involved in legal work that arises only in relation to sales contracts. You may need to determine, for example, whether one of the parties to a contract qualifies as a "merchant" as defined by Article 2 of the UCC. If so, different rules may apply to the contract. You may be asked to investigate a claim for breach of warranty to determine whether a seller warranted the goods being sold and whether the seller's actions (or failure to act) constituted a breach of warranty.

INTELLECTUAL PROPERTY LAW

intellectual property
Property resulting from intellectual, creative processes.

The contract law just discussed had its origins hundreds of years ago. Much of it is based on concepts developed in England. Now we move on to an area of law that, although it has existed for some time, has become a major concern in recent years. It has to do with the wealth created by people's minds. Most people think of wealth in terms of houses, land, cars, stocks, and bonds. Wealth, however, also includes **intellectual property**, which consists of the products that result from intellectual, creative processes. Although it is an abstract term for an abstract concept, intellectual property is nonetheless wholly familiar to virtually everyone. *Trademarks, service marks, copyrights,* and *patents* are all forms of intellectual property. The book you are reading is copyrighted. Undoubtedly, the computer you use at home is trademarked. The software you use, the movies you see, and the music you listen to are all forms of intellectual property.

The need to protect creative works was voiced by the framers of the U.S. Constitution more than two hundred years ago: Article I, Section 8, of the Constitution authorized Congress "[t]o promote the Progress of Science and useful Arts, by securing for limited Times to Authors and Inventors the exclusive Right to their respective Writings and Discoveries." Laws protecting patents, trademarks, and copyrights are designed to protect and reward inventive and artistic creativity. Exhibit 15.2 summarizes the forms of intellectual property, how they are acquired, and what remedies are available for *infringement,* or unauthorized use.

The study of intellectual property law is important because intellectual property has taken on increasing significance, not only in the United States but globally as well. In today's information age, it should come as no surprise that the value

EXHIBIT 15.2
Forms of Intellectual Property

	Definition	How Acquired	Duration	Remedy for Infringement
Patent	A grant from the government that gives an inventor exclusive rights to an invention.	By filing a patent application with the U.S. Patent and Trademark Office and receiving its approval.	For inventions, 20 years from the date of application; for design patents, 14 years from the date of application.	Money damages, including royalties and lost profits, *plus* attorneys' fees. Damages may be tripled for intentional infringements.
Copyright	The right of an author or a creator of a literary or artistic work or other production (such as a computer program) to have the exclusive use of that work for a given period of time.	Automatic (once the work or creation is put in tangible form). Only the *expression* of an idea (and not the idea itself) can be protected by copyright.	For authors: the life of the author plus 70 years. For publishers: 95 years after the date of publication or 120 years after creation.	Actual damages plus profits received by the party who infringed or statutory damages under the Copyright Act, *plus* costs and attorneys' fees in either situation.
Trademark	A distinctive word, name, symbol, or device that an entity uses to distinguish its goods or services from those of others. The owner has the exclusive right to use that mark.	1. At common law, created by use of the mark. 2. Registration with the U.S. Patent and Trademark Office; mark must already be in use or be placed in use within the next six months.	Unlimited, as long as the mark is in use. To continue notice by registration, holder must renew between the fifth and sixth years and, thereafter, every ten years.	1. Injunction prohibiting future use of mark. 2. Actual damages plus profits received by the party who infringed. 3. Destruction of articles that infringed. 4. *Plus* costs and attorneys' fees.
Trade Secret	A business secret that makes a company or product unique and that would be of value to a competitor. Trade secrets include customer lists, plans, and research and development.	Through the development of the information and processes that constitute the business secret.	Unlimited, so long as not revealed to others (once a trade secret is revealed to others, it is no longer secret).	Money damages for misappropriation (the Uniform Trade Secrets Act also permits punitive damages if willful), *plus* costs and attorneys' fees.

of the world's intellectual property exceeds the value of physical property, such as machines and houses. Ownership rights in intangible intellectual property are more important to the prosperity of U.S. companies than are their tangible assets. Because of the importance of obtaining and protecting intellectual property rights, attorneys and paralegals with specialized knowledge in this area are in great demand in law firms and in corporations. (See this chapter's *Featured Contributor* article on pages 518 and 519 for information on how to protect intellectual property.)

Patents

patent

A government grant that gives an inventor the exclusive right or privilege to make, use, or sell an invention for a limited time period.

A **patent** is a grant from the government that gives an inventor the exclusive right to make, use, and sell an invention for a period of twenty years from the date of filing the application for a patent. Patents for designs, as opposed to inventions, are given for a fourteen-year period. To secure a patent, the applicant must demonstrate to the satisfaction of the U.S. Patent and Trademark Office that the invention, discovery, process, or design is genuine, novel, useful, and not obvious in light of current technology. A patent holder gives notice to all that an article or design is patented by placing on it the word *Patent* or *Pat.* and the patent number. Unlike patent law in other countries, U.S. patent law gives protection to the first person to invent a product or process, even though someone else may have been the first to file for a patent on that product or process.

If a firm makes, uses, or sells another's patented design, product, or process without the patent owner's permission, it commits the tort of patent infringement. Patent infringement may exist even though the patent owner has not put the patented product in commerce. Patent infringement may also occur even though not all features or parts of an invention are copied. (With respect to a patented process, however, all steps or their equivalent must be copied for infringement to exist.)

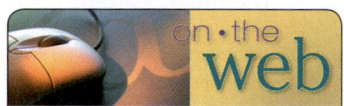

A good source for information on patents is the U.S. Patent and Trademark Office at **www.uspto.gov**. Another source is **www.patents.com**, a free patent search site.

Copyrights

copyright

The exclusive right of an author (or other creator) to publish, print, or sell an intellectual production for a statutory period of time.

Literary or artistic productions (including computer software) are protected under copyright law. A **copyright** gives the creator of a work the right to the exclusive use of that work for a given period of time. Copyrights are governed by the Copyright Act of 1976, as amended. Works created after January 1, 1978, are automatically given statutory copyright protection for the life of the author plus 70 years. For copyrights owned by publishing houses, the copyright expires 95 years from the date of publication or 120 years from the date of creation, whichever is first. For works by more than one author, the copyright expires 70 years after the death of the last surviving author.

Copyrights can be registered with the U.S. Copyright Office in Washington, D.C. (but registration is not required). A copyright owner also no longer needs to place a © or *Copyright* on the work to have the work protected against infringement. Chances are that if somebody created it, somebody owns it.

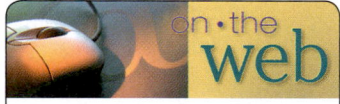

For information on copyrights, go to the U.S. Copyright Office at **www.copyright.gov**.

What Can Be Copyrighted?

Note that it is not possible to copyright an *idea.* Others may freely use the underlying ideas embodied in a work. What is copyrightable is the way in which an idea is *expressed.* Whenever an idea and an expression are inseparable, the expression cannot be copyrighted. Generally, anything that is not an original expression of an idea does not qualify for copyright protection. Facts widely known to the public are not copyrightable. Page numbers normally are not copyrightable because they follow a sequence known to everyone. Mathematical calculations are not copyrightable. The key requirement to obtain copyright protection is originality.

Copyright Infringement

Whenever the form or expression of an idea is copied, an infringement of copyright occurs. The reproduction does not have to be exactly the same as the original, nor does it have to reproduce the original in its entirety.

Penalties or remedies can be imposed on those who infringe copyrights. These range from actual damages (damages based on the actual harm caused to the copyright holder by the infringement) or statutory damages (damages provided for under the Copyright Act, not to exceed $150,000) to criminal proceedings for willful violations (which may result in fines and/or imprisonment).

An exception to liability for copyright infringement is made under the "fair use" doctrine. Under the Copyright Act, a person or organization can in certain situations reproduce copyrighted material without paying royalties (fees paid to the copyright holder for the privilege of reproducing the copyrighted material). Generally, the courts determine whether a particular use is fair on a case-by-case basis.

Trademarks and Related Property

A **trademark** is a distinctive mark, motto, device, or emblem that a manufacturer stamps, prints, or otherwise affixes to the goods it produces so that those goods can be distinguished from the goods of other manufacturers and merchants. Examples of trademarks are brand-name labels on jeans, luggage, and other products. Generally, to be protected under trademark law, a mark must be distinctive. A distinctive mark might consist of an uncommon word (such as *Kodak, Xerox,* or *Google*) or words used in an uncommon or fanciful way (such as *English Leather* for an aftershave lotion instead of for leather processed in England).

Trademarks apply to *products*. The term **trade name** is used to indicate part or all of a business's name, such as McDonald's. Unless the trade name is also used as a trademark (as with Kodak, Xerox, and Coca-Cola, for example), the name is not protected under federal trademark law. Trade names are protected under the common law, however. Holiday Inns, Inc., for example, could sue a motel owner who used that name or a portion of it (such as "Holiday Motels") without permission. As with trademarks, words must be unusual or fanciful if they are to be protected as trade names. The word *Safeway*, for example, was considered by a court to be sufficiently fanciful to obtain protection as a trade name for a chain of food stores.

At common law, the person who used a symbol or mark to identify a business or product was protected in the use of that trademark. Today, trademarks may be registered with the state or with the federal government. Federal registration dominates because it extends over all the states and provides stronger protections for trademark owners. Under current law, a mark can be registered federally (1) if it is already in commerce or (2) if the applicant intends to put the mark into commerce within six months.

Trademark Infringement

Registration of a trademark with the U.S. Patent and Trademark Office gives notice on a nationwide basis that the trademark belongs exclusively to the registrant. The registrant is also allowed to use the symbol ® to indicate that the mark has been registered. Whenever that trademark is copied to a substantial degree or used in its entirety by another (intentionally or unintentionally), the trademark has been infringed, and the owner can sue. A person need not have registered a trademark in order to sue for trademark infringement, but registration does furnish proof of the date the owner began using the trademark. Only those trademarks that are deemed sufficiently distinctive from all competing trademarks will be protected.

Trademark Dilution

Historically, federal trademark law prohibited the unauthorized use of the same mark on competing or "related" goods or services only when such use would be likely to confuse consumers. The federal Trademark Dilution Act extends that protection.

Trademark *dilution* occurs when a trademark is used, without authorization, in a way that diminishes the distinctive quality of the mark. Unlike trademark infringement,

trademark
A distinctive mark, motto, device, or emblem that a manufacturer stamps, prints, or otherwise affixes to the goods it produces so that they can be identified on the market and their origins made known. Once a trademark is established (under the common law or through registration), the owner is entitled to its exclusive use.

trade name
A term that is used to indicate part or all of a business's name and that is directly related to the business's reputation and goodwill. Trade names are protected under the common law (and under trademark law, if the business's name is the same as its trademark).

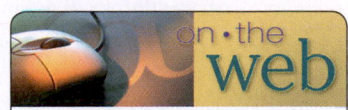

For a good discussion of trademark dilution, visit the Web site of Bitlaw. Go to **www.bitlaw.com**, and select "Dilution" from the "Trademark" menu.

featured contributor

STRATEGIES FOR PROTECTING INTELLECTUAL PROPERTY: THE INTELLECTUAL PROPERTY AUDIT

Deborah E. Bouchoux

BIOGRAPHICAL NOTE

Deborah E. Bouchoux is an attorney licensed to practice in the District of Columbia and the state of California (inactive). She has been involved in paralegal education for more than twenty years. Bouchoux currently teaches in the paralegal studies program at Georgetown University in Washington, D.C., and serves as a member of the advisory board for the paralegal studies program.

Prior to teaching at Georgetown University, Bouchoux was an instructor in the paralegal program at the University of San Diego. Bouchoux is a frequent lecturer for the National Capital Paralegal Association and is the author of Intellectual Property: The Law of Trademarks, Copyrights, Patents, and Trade Secrets, *as well as* Protecting Your Company's Intellectual Property: A Practical Guide to Trademarks, Copyrights, Patents, and Trade Secrets.

Because clients are often unaware of the value of their intangible assets or intellectual property, many law firms conduct intellectual property audits for their clients. The audit will identify the intellectual property owned by the client, and the legal team and the client will then develop a strategy to protect that property.

Audits are also conducted when a company sells its assets or merges with another entity. The buyer will want to know what type of intellectual property assets the company possesses so that it will know what assets it is acquiring and to ensure that it will not be inheriting infringement lawsuits. This type of audit is often referred to as a *due-diligence review*.

THE NEED FOR INTELLECTUAL PROPERTY AUDITS

Clients may not understand the value of their intellectual property portfolios and the need to protect their rights. They may be using unique marketing materials that should be copyrighted, slogans that should be trademarked, and confidential information that should be protected as trade secrets. Without protection, valuable rights may be lost. For example, the disclosure of confidential information will lead to a loss of trade secret rights and result in declining profits. Moreover, once companies realize what intellectual property they own, they can use that intellectual property to create revenue. Trademarks, copyrights, patents, and trade secrets

can all be licensed to others for fees to generate a continuing revenue stream for the company.

STRATEGIES FOR CONDUCTING AN INTELLECTUAL PROPERTY AUDIT

There are several steps in conducting a successful intellectual property audit. These steps are explored in the following subsections.

Designating the Team. The law firm should designate an attorney and paralegal to serve as representatives of the firm, and the company should select an individual who will serve as the company's team leader. Together, these individuals will be primarily responsible for conducting the audit and can answer any questions that may arise in the course of the audit. The team should have a preliminary meeting to discuss the scope and nature of the audit. For example, the client will need to determine whether only U.S. materials will be reviewed or whether consideration will be given to seeking protection in foreign countries for certain trademarks and patents. The involvement of legal counsel ensures that any matters discussed are subject to the attorney-client privilege and remain confidential.

Preparing the Audit Questionnaire. The legal team should prepare a worksheet or questionnaire for the client that is designed to elicit information from the client about its intellectual property assets. Paralegals play a significant role in drafting the audit questionnaire. The audit questionnaire will typically ask the following:

- Does the client use any specific names, logos, or slogans in advertising its products and services?

- Are any written materials used in marketing (such as brochures, newspaper advertisements, and slides and written materials used for presentations)?

- Has the client developed any products, software, or processes?

- Does the client use any software or products owned by another entity?

- Does the client use any confidential methods or processes in developing and marketing its products and services, including financial forecasts, marketing plans, and customer lists?

- Has the company ever been sued for or accused of infringing another party's intellectual property rights?

- How does the company control access to its valuable and proprietary materials?

The questionnaire should be tailored to the needs of the client. For example, companies engaged in telecommunications services or software development will need detailed sections designed to obtain information on software products and proprietary information. In contrast, companies engaged in consulting will likely have no "products" that need protection but will have a wealth of written materials that should be protected as trade secrets or registered as copyrights.

Conducting the Audit. On receiving the questionnaire, the client should begin gathering the materials that are responsive to the questionnaire. The legal team will then review the materials that the client has assembled to determine which materials can be protected under intellectual property law. If the client has a Web site, it should be carefully reviewed to ensure not only that the site is protected under copyright law but also that it does not infringe on the rights of another party. Paralegals often coordinate the time and manner of the audit

by scheduling the audit date, arranging for a conference room, and ensuring that a photocopy machine is available to copy documents that are responsive to the questionnaire. Generally, the audit is conducted at the client's office because this is where the pertinent materials and documents are located.

Writing the Audit Report. After conducting the audit, the legal team prepares a written report for the client summarizing the results of the audit. The report identifies all of the intellectual property owned by the client and makes recommendations for its continued protection and maintenance. For example, the audit may disclose that the client uses a distinctive slogan in its advertising materials. The legal team will then recommend that the slogan be registered as a trademark.

> "Paralegals play a significant role in drafting the audit questionnaire."

POSTAUDIT ACTIVITY

After the audit is complete, the legal team, and particularly the paralegal, will begin preparing applications to register trademarks, copyrights, and patents and will develop written policies to protect the client's trade secrets. Contracts will need to be drafted for the client to use when it hires independent contractors to develop certain products, such as software. Such contracts will clarify that the company will own all rights to any work products produced by those independent contractors. License agreements may need to be drafted so that the company can license its intellectual property to others to use. An Internet use policy may be needed so that all employees are aware of the confidential nature of the company's electronic communications.

The company will be advised to review materials used by its competitors to ensure that its competitors do not infringe on the company's valuable intellectual property rights—by using a trademark that is confusingly similar to one owned by the company, for example. Finally, the paralegal will create a docketing system to ensure that the client's intellectual property rights are maintained. For example, the paralegal should calendar the dates for maintenance and renewal of company trademarks. The paralegal should also schedule the date of the next intellectual property audit.

a dilution cause of action does not require proof that consumers are likely to be confused by a connection between the unauthorized use and the mark. For this reason, the products (or services) involved do not have to be similar. In addition, a famous mark may be diluted not only by the use of an *identical* mark but also by the use of a *similar* mark.

Trade Secrets

trade secret
Information or processes that give a business an advantage over competitors who do not know the information or processes.

Some business processes and information that are not (or cannot be) patented, copyrighted, or trademarked are nevertheless protected against appropriation by a competitor as trade secrets. **Trade secrets** consist of customer lists, plans, research and development, pricing information, marketing techniques, production techniques, and generally anything that makes an individual company unique and that would have value to a competitor. Trade secrets are often protected by confidentiality agreements, as illustrated in *Today's Professional Paralegal.*

What Is Protected?

Unlike copyright and trademark protection, protection of trade secrets extends both to ideas and to their expression. (For this reason, and because a trade secret involves no registration or filing requirements, trade secret protection may be well suited for software.) Of course, the secret formula, method, or other information must be disclosed to some persons, particularly to key employees. Businesses generally attempt to protect their trade secrets by having all employees who use the process or information agree in their contracts, or in confidentiality agreements, never to divulge it.

Misappropriation of Trade Secrets

One who discloses or uses another's trade secret, without a privilege to do so, is liable to the other if (1) he or she discovered the secret by improper means or (2) the disclosure or use constitutes a breach of confidence. The theft of confidential business data through industrial espionage, such as when a business taps into a competitor's computer, is a theft of trade secrets and is actionable.

At one time, virtually all law with respect to trade secrets was common law. In an effort to reduce the unpredictability of the law in this area, a model act, the Uniform Trade Secrets Act (UTSA), was proposed. Today, it has been adopted in more than forty-five states. Under the UTSA, a plaintiff can also recover punitive damages for willful misappropriation of business secrets.

A federal statute, the Economic Espionage Act, also addresses trade secret theft. While its focus is on the theft of trade secrets that are sold to foreign powers, it also applies to domestic theft. Violations of the statute can result in a prison term and significant fines.

INTELLECTUAL PROPERTY AND THE PARALEGAL

Many lawsuits involve the alleged infringement of intellectual property rights. If you work for a general law practice, one of the firm's clients may seek legal assistance when the client discovers that someone has used, without permission, something that the client created—such as a software program, the words or music to a song, a novel, a patented invention, or a trademark.

Many law firms specialize in such areas as patent law or have special departments dealing with these areas.

Paralegals who work in such firms or departments may face the challenge of managing voluminous materials and paperwork for just one case. A lawsuit for the alleged infringement of patent rights in a sophisticated product, such as a genetically engineered drug for treating leukemia, can result in thousands of exhibits and other documents that must be organized, safeguarded, and retrievable at the right moment. A paralegal who can meet this challenge successfully will be a great asset.

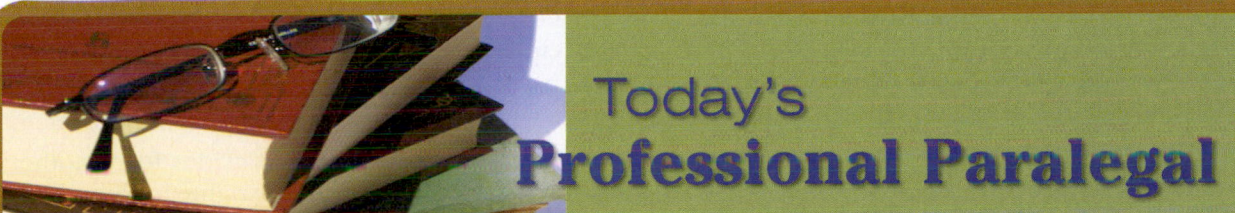

Today's
Professional Paralegal

CONFIDENTIALITY AGREEMENTS

Angela Dunn, a paralegal with the law firm of Carter, Plant, and Darrow, is training a paralegal whom the firm has just hired to assist Angela in the firm's intellectual property department. Angela is showing the new paralegal, Cory Amundson, how to draft a confidentiality agreement. As a first step, Angela reviews with Cory the legal background for such agreements.

WHY DO FIRMS CREATE CONFIDENTIALITY AGREEMENTS?

Angela explains that most successful businesses have trade secrets. The law protects trade secrets indefinitely, provided that the information is not generally known, is kept secret, and has commercial value. Sometimes, of course, a business needs to disclose secret information to a party in the course of conducting business. For example, a company may need to hire a consultant to revamp a computer system, an engineer to design a manufacturing system, or a marketing firm to implement a sales program. All of these parties may need access to some of the company's trade secrets. One way to protect against the unauthorized disclosure of such information is through confidentiality agreements. Angela then proceeds to explain to Cory what a confidentiality agreement is and the necessity of defining the scope of the agreement.

WHAT IS A CONFIDENTIALITY AGREEMENT?

In a confidentiality agreement, one party promises not to divulge information about the other party to anyone else or to use the other party's confidential information for his or her own benefit. Confidentiality agreements are often included in licensing and employment contracts, but they can also be separate contracts. The key is to make sure that the agreement adequately protects the trade secrets and applies to any related transactions between the parties. For instance, assume that a business executes a separate confidentiality agreement with a marketing firm. In this situation, it is important to make sure that the agreement refers to any other contracts that the business has already formed with the marketing firm. Also, subsequent contracts with the marketing firm should either refer back to the confidentiality agreement or include a new confidentiality provision.

DEFINING THE SCOPE OF A CONFIDENTIALITY AGREEMENT

Confidentiality agreements must be reasonable. When drafting one, you must be clear about what information needs to be protected, and for how long. Also, make certain that the client defines what is meant by *confidential information* and that this definition is included in the agreement. Does the client want to protect just a customer list or all financial, technical, and other business information? The confidentiality agreement must specify clearly what secrets are to be protected.

The duration of the agreement usually depends on the nature of the information. Very important secret information should remain confidential for a longer time than less important secrets. Sometimes, as with a marketing campaign, the time period for confidentiality may be self-evident (if the campaign ends in six months, for example). The agreement should be tailored to the client's needs as much as possible. If the party to whom the client is disclosing information will no longer need the information after a certain date—such as when the project is completed—include a provision requiring the return of confidential information after that date. This will reduce concerns that the client's confidential trade secrets might later fall into the hands of a stranger.

DRAFTING THE AGREEMENT

Angela then shows Cory where to find some forms for, and examples of, confidentiality agreements. Angela suggests which form would be the most appropriate to the client's situation and also advises Cory to look at a confidentiality agreement that Angela previously drafted for another client. Cory thanks Angela for her practical guidance.

Many paralegals work in the corporate environment. Today's corporations invest heavily in the development of new products. A major concern of these companies—and their legal departments—is to protect their investment in research and development by obtaining patents, trademarks, or copyrights. If you work for a corporation, you might be involved in researching and litigating cases concerning the infringement of intellectual property rights.

Here are some specific types of tasks that you might undertake in the area of intellectual property law:

- Interview a client (or a manager of a corporation for which you work) to obtain information regarding intellectual property to be registered.
- Contact the U.S. Patent and Trademark Office to find out if someone has applied for patent or trademark protection for a certain type of product that your firm's client (or your corporate employer) wants to develop and register.
- Draft the documents that are necessary to apply for patent, trademark, or copyright protection.
- Draft contracts that provide for another's authorized use of a copyrighted, patented, or trademarked product in return for royalties (a percentage of the proceeds received as a result of the authorized use of the intellectual property).
- Review marketing data and sales statements to verify royalties due for another's authorized use of your employer's trademarked, patented, or copyrighted product.
- Assist in litigation resulting from the infringement of rights in intellectual property.

KEY TERMS AND CONCEPTS

acceptance   *500*

adhesion contract   *505*

agreement   *498*

breach of contract   *508*

click-on agreement   *500*

consideration   *500*

contractual capacity   *502*

copyright   *516*

cybernotary   *513*

e-signature   *512*

genuineness of assent   *503*

intellectual property   *514*

mailbox rule   *500*

material fact   *504*

mirror image rule   *500*

mutual mistake   *504*

offer   *498*

offeree   *498*

offeror   *498*

patent   *516*

performance   *508*

promise   *497*

promissory estoppel   *501*

reformation   *511*

rescission   *504*

restitution   *510*

sales contract   *507*

shrink-wrap agreement   *512*

specific performance   *511*

Statute of Frauds   *506*

trade name   *517*

trade secret   *520*

trademark   *517*

unconscionable clause   *505*

unconscionable contract   *505*

Uniform Commercial Code (UCC)   *506*

unilateral mistake   *504*

warranty   *507*

CHAPTER SUMMARY

CONTRACTS AND INTELLECTUAL PROPERTY LAW

Requirements to Form a Valid Contract

A contract is any agreement (based on a promise or an exchange of promises) that can be enforced in court. To form a valid contract, four basic requirements must be met.

1. *Agreement*—An agreement includes an offer and an acceptance. One party must offer to enter into a legal agreement, and another party must accept the terms of the offer.

   a. An offer is a promise to do or to refrain from doing some specified thing in the future.

b. The offeror must have the intent to be bound, the terms must be reasonably certain or definite, and the offer must be communicated to the offeree.

  c. Both a rejection of the offer and the making of a counteroffer terminate the original offer. The offer is also terminated if the party making the offer withdraws the offer before it has been accepted. Otherwise, the offer expires after a reasonable period of time has passed.

  d. An offer may automatically terminate by law if the subject matter is destroyed, one party dies or becomes incompetent, or the contract becomes illegal.

  e. The terms of the acceptance must be the same as ("mirror") the terms of the offer.

  f. Acceptance of an offer is timely if it is made before the offer is terminated. Acceptance takes effect at the time the acceptance is communicated via the mode expressly or impliedly authorized by the offeror. This is called the *mailbox rule.*

  g. If the contract does not specify the method of acceptance, an offer may be accepted by any means that is reasonable under the circumstances.

2. *Consideration*—Consideration is usually defined as "something of value"—such as money or the performance of an action—given in exchange for a promise.

  a. To be legally sufficient, consideration must involve a legal detriment to the promisee, a legal benefit to the promisor, or both.

  b. In general, a court will not question the adequacy of consideration (fairness of the bargain). Courts will inquire into the adequacy of consideration only when fraud, undue influence, duress, or incompetence is involved.

  c. Some contracts may be enforced (or partially enforced) under the doctrine of promissory estoppel even though consideration is lacking.

3. *Contractual capacity*—The parties to the contract must have the legal ability to enter into a contractual relationship. Courts generally presume contractual capacity unless one party is a minor, intoxicated, or mentally incompetent.

4. *Legality*—A contract to do something that is prohibited by federal or state statutory law is illegal and, as such, void from the outset and thus unenforceable.

  a. Contracts entered into by persons who do not have a license, when one is required by statute, may not be enforceable.

  b. Some contracts are not enforced because the court deems them to be contrary to public policy.

Defenses to Contract Enforceability

A contract that meets all the above requirements may not be enforceable if (1) the parties have not genuinely assented (agreed) to its terms, (2) the contract is so oppressive to one of the parties that a court will refuse to enforce it, or (3) the contract is not in the proper form.

1. *Mistake*—Generally, a contract can be avoided on the basis of mistake only if the mistake was one of material fact (not value) and only when both parties are mistaken (mutual mistake). An exception to this rule exists if one party made a mathematical error (unilateral mistake) in formulating a bid or estimating costs.

2. *Fraudulent misrepresentation*—When fraud occurs, usually the innocent party can enforce or avoid the contract.

Continued

3. *Undue influence*—Undue influence arises from special relationships in which one party's free will has been overcome by the undue influence exerted by the other party. Usually, the contract is voidable.

4. *Duress*—If one party forces the other to enter a contract under fear of a threat, the forced party can avoid the contract.

5. *Unconscionable contract*—When a contract is so oppressive to one of the parties that a court will refuse to enforce it, the oppressed party will be excused from performance. These situations usually involve an adhesion contract, which is a contract drafted by the dominant party and presented on a "take-it-or-leave-it" basis.

6. *Statute of Frauds*—Every state has a Statute of Frauds, which is a statute that specifies what types of contracts must be in writing (or be evidenced by a written document). The following types of contracts are normally required to be in writing:

   a. Contracts involving interests in land.

   b. Contracts that cannot by their terms be performed within one year from the day after the date of formation.

   c. Collateral, or secondary, contracts, such as promises to answer for the debt or duty of another.

   d. Promises made in consideration of marriage.

   e. Contracts for the sale of goods priced at $500 or more.

Sales Contracts and Warranties

State statutes that are based on Article 2 of the Uniform Commercial Code (UCC) govern contracts for the sale of goods (as opposed to real property or services). The UCC primarily comes into play when disputes arise over ambiguous or missing terms and when the buyer or seller is a merchant. The UCC also contains provisions on express and implied warranties that arise when goods are sold. For example, under the UCC, every merchant warrants that the goods are reasonably fit for the ordinary purpose for which such goods are used.

Contract Performance and Remedies

The most common way to terminate contractual duties is by the performance of those duties. Failure to perform contractual duties as promised results in a breach of the contract.

1. *Substantial performance*—Performance that provides a party with the important and essential benefits of a contract, in spite of any omission or deviation from the terms, is substantial performance. Because substantial performance is not perfect, the other party is entitled to damages to compensate for the failure to comply with the contract.

2. *Performance impossible or commercially impracticable*—If, after a contract has been made, performance becomes objectively impossible (the subject matter is destroyed, for example), then performance is excused. Also, if performance becomes extremely difficult or expensive due to some event, a court may excuse performance.

3. *Remedies for breach of contract*—

   a. Money damages are a legal remedy designed to compensate a party for the loss of the bargain.

      1. Compensatory damages compensate the injured party only for damages actually sustained.

2. Incidental damages are for expenses caused directly by a breach of contract, such as the cost of obtaining performance from another source.

3. Consequential damages flow from the party's breach and were foreseeable at the time the contract was formed.

4. Liquidated damages are damages of a specified amount included in the contract.

b. The following equitable remedies are available only in limited circumstances:

1. Rescission is an action to undo or cancel the contract. When a contract is rescinded, restitution must be made.

2. Reformation is an action in which the court rewrites the contract to reflect the parties' true agreement.

3. Specific performance, which requires a party to perform the contract, is available only when money damages are inadequate and the contract is not for personal services.

c. In sales contracts, the UCC may provide additional remedies to buyers and sellers (such as the buyer's right to reject nonconforming goods).

Electronic Contracting and Electronic Signatures

Many contracts are formed over the Internet. How the courts apply the traditional rules of contract law is an increasingly important issue. Generally, the terms of the offer should be just as comprehensive as in written documents. The method of acceptance should also be specified.

1. *Click-on agreement*—An agreement that arises when the buyer, completing a transaction on a computer, is required to indicate assent to be bound by the terms of an offer by clicking on a button that says, for example, "I agree." The courts have enforced click-on agreements

2. *Shrink-wrap agreement*—An agreement whose terms are expressed inside the box in which the goods are packaged. The party who opens the box (the buyer) is informed that, by keeping the goods, she or he agrees to the terms. Courts enforce such agreements unless the buyer learned of the terms after entering the contract.

3. *Electronic signature technologies*—Signatures verify the identity of parties to a contract. A party's signature can be electronically encoded onto a key or card that is verified by a third party or can be digitally captured and attached to the electronic document.

4. *State laws on e-signatures*—The Uniform Electronic Transactions Act (UETA), which governs e-signatures, has been adopted, at least in part, by forty-six states.

5. *Federal law on e-signatures and e-documents*—The Electronic Signatures in Global and National Commerce Act (E-SIGN Act) gave validity to e-signatures by providing that no contract, record, or signature may be "denied legal effect" solely because it is in electronic form.

Intellectual Property Law

Intellectual property—the products that result from intellectual, creative processes—is becoming increasingly valuable. The following are the four basic types of intellectual property rights. If a party infringes on these rights, the owner of the property can file suit and possibly obtain damages.

1. *Patent*—A grant from the government that gives an inventor the exclusive right to make, use, and sell an invention.

Continued

2. *Copyright*—The right of an author or a creator of a literary or artistic work or other production (such as a computer program) to have the exclusive use of that work for a given period of time.

3. *Trademark*—A distinctive mark or motto that a manufacturer stamps, prints, or affixes to goods so that its products are distinguishable from those of others. Trademarks apply to products, whereas trade names apply to business names.

4. *Trade secret*—A business secret that makes a particular company or product unique and that would be of value to a competitor (such as customer lists, plans, and research and development).

STUDENT STUDYWARE™ CD-ROM

Interactive student CD in this book includes additional quizzing, plus video clips, case studies, and Key Terms flashcards.

ONLINE COMPANION™

For additional resources, please go to **www.paralegal.delmar.cengage.com**.

QUESTIONS FOR REVIEW

1. Name and describe the four basic requirements to form a valid contract. Are there any circumstances in which the court will enforce the parties' agreement even though it lacks consideration?

2. What is the Uniform Commercial Code (UCC), and to what types of contracts does it apply? How does the UCC affect the common law of contracts?

3. What remedies are available to the innocent party when a contract is breached, or broken? What is specific performance, and in what kinds of circumstances is it available?

4. What constitutes an electronic signature, and what is the legal validity of such signatures?

5. What is intellectual property, and why is it an important topic in the law today? Name four major forms of intellectual property.

ETHICAL QUESTION

1. Douglas Coleman works as a paralegal for an oil company. The attorney he works for is responsible for negotiating franchise contracts with people who want to purchase gas-station franchises. Most of those applying for franchises have lawyers who negotiate for them. Bob Little is applying for a franchise without a lawyer to represent him. It is apparent from talking to Little that he does not have much education, and he has indicated that he has never owned a gas station before. He has, however, recently inherited some money, and he wants to achieve his lifelong dream of owning his own gas station.

He has been sent a copy of the standard-form franchise agreement. The standard-form contract is very one sided and unfair to the franchisee (the person purchasing the franchise). Little calls and says that he is ready to negotiate his franchise agreement with the oil company and asks Douglas to set up a telephone conference for that purpose. Douglas would like to tell Little that he really should have a lawyer represent his interests during the negotiations. Can he recommend to Little that he retain a lawyer? Should he give Little any tips about how to negotiate a franchising arrangement with the oil company? What might happen if Douglas does either of these things? What might happen if he does nothing?

PRACTICE QUESTIONS AND ASSIGNMENTS

1. Using the material on contract law presented in this chapter, identify which defenses the defendants in the following hypothetical cases might use to defend against an action for breach of contract:

   a. Mrs. Martinez, a Spanish-speaking immigrant, buys a washing machine and signs a financing agreement that allows her to pay for it in monthly installments. The agreement contains a clause that allows the store to repossess the appliance if she misses a payment. Mrs. Martinez misses the next-to-the-last payment. The store notifies Mrs. Martinez that she has breached their contract and that it intends to repossess the washing machine. How might Mrs. Martinez defend against the store's action?

   b. Sally orally agrees to purchase a farm from her lifelong friend Fred. She promises to pay Fred $120,000 for the farm. She trusts Fred, so she does not put the deal in writing. A few days later, Fred sells the same property to Nell for $140,000. Fred and Nell put their agreement in writing. When Sally learns of Fred's contract with Nell, she sues Fred for breach of contract. What is Fred's defense?

   c. Rob enters into a contract with Tom to sell Tom fifty sweaters in Christmas colors and featuring Christmas designs. The first shipment of sweaters is due on October 1, 2011. When the sweaters are not delivered, Tom calls Rob and learns that the factory where the sweaters were produced has burned down. Tom, who is upset because he needed the sweaters for his Christmas catalogue sales, sues Rob for breach of contract. What is Rob's defense?

2. Bernie, the sole owner of a small business, has a large piece of used farm equipment for sale. He offers to sell the equipment to Hank for $10,000. Discuss what happens to the offer in the following situations:

   a. Bernie dies prior to Hank's acceptance; at the time he accepts, Hank is unaware of Bernie's death.

   b. The night before Hank accepts, a fire destroys the equipment.

3. Jerome is an elderly man who lives with his nephew, Philip. Jerome is totally dependent on Philip's support. Philip tells Jerome that unless Jerome transfers a tract of land he owns to Philip for a price 30 percent below market value, Philip will no longer support and take care of him. Jerome enters into the contract. What defense can Jerome raise to set aside this contract?

4. Based on the material on intellectual property law presented in the chapter, in which of the following situations would a court likely hold Maruta liable for copyright or trademark infringement?

   a. At the library, Maruta photocopies ten pages from a scholarly journal relating to a topic on which she is writing a term paper.

   b. Maruta makes leather handbags and sells them in her small leather shop. She advertises her handbags as "Vutton handbags," hoping that customers might mistakenly assume that they were made by Vuitton, the well-known maker of high-quality luggage and handbags.

   c. Maruta owns a video store. She purchases one copy of all the latest DVDs from various DVD manufacturers. Then, using blank discs, she makes copies to rent or sell to her customers.

 QUESTIONS FOR CRITICAL ANALYSIS

1. Consideration, a requirement for a valid contract, is defined as *something of value*. What items, other than money, meet this definition? How does consideration distinguish a contract from a gift?

2. Why are minors allowed to avoid contractual obligations by canceling or disaffirming contracts?

3. Generally, courts hold that gambling contracts are illegal and thus void. Do you think that the advent of legalized forms of gambling, such as state-operated lotteries, is consistent with a continued public policy against the enforcement of gambling contracts? Why or why not?

4. Many of our day-to-day transactions, such as buying a can of cola from a vending machine or purchasing groceries with a debit card, involve contracts. Explain how these contracts meet the requirements of a valid contract. Do they meet the requirements of the Statute of Frauds? Would a court enforce these contracts?

5. Why are patents, trademarks, and copyrights known as intellectual property? What type of property is protected by a patent, a trademark, and a copyright, respectively? How is a trade secret protected?

PROJECTS

1. Using the requirements for an offer that are stated in the chapter, draft a simple offer to purchase a laptop computer (used, including software) from a fellow paralegal student. Make sure that the offer is definite and certain. Then write an explanation (in one or two paragraphs) of how you would communicate the offer to the person, how long the offer would remain open, and what method of acceptance you would prefer.

2. Interview a paralegal who works in an intellectual property firm. Find out what his or her day-to-day work entails. Draft an outline covering the topics you discussed, and then give an oral presentation to the class.

USING INTERNET RESOURCES

1. Go to an article in the FindLaw for Legal Professionals Library, which is located at **library.findlaw.com**. Search on "Contracts Law Radcliffe" to get to the link for these questions in part a.

   a. Scroll down to the heading "Consideration," and read the summary provided. How many examples are given? Then read the next section titled "Typical Contract Provisions." How many different types of clauses are discussed? Write down the types of clauses identified.

   b. Go to FindLaw's site on business contracts, at **contracts.corporate.findlaw.com**. There, you can access contracts listed by industry, by type, or by company name, or you can browse through the most recent contracts added to the site. Using any of the methods available, select a contract to view. Note the name of the contract and its general purpose. Does the contract use all of the clauses you noted in Part a of this question (typical contract provisions)? Does it use any? If so, which of the typical clauses are used?

REAL PROPERTY AND INSURANCE LAW

CHAPTER OUTLINE

Introduction

Real Property

Insurance Law

AFTER COMPLETING THIS CHAPTER, YOU WILL KNOW:

▶ The difference between real property and personal property.

▶ How one acquires, holds, and transfers ownership rights in property and what procedures are involved in the sale of real estate.

▶ The terminology used in insurance contracts and the various classifications of insurance.

▶ What an insurable interest is and the difference between an insurance agent and an insurance broker.

▶ The types of provisions that are typically included in an insurance contract and the rights and duties of the parties under insurance contracts.

INTRODUCTION

As you study the major areas of substantive law, keep in mind that although the topics are covered individually, as if they existed in isolation from one another, there is in fact a great deal of overlap among them. For example, in tort and product liability cases, which you read about in Chapter 14, the defendant's insurance coverage—or lack of it—is often an important factor in how litigation proceeds. Similarly, property owners worry about torts or crimes that could occur on their property and buy insurance to protect themselves from possible claims.

The first part of this chapter investigates property law. About a quarter of all paralegals specialize in this area. After that, we look at insurance law, an area of specialization for about 20 percent of all paralegals. While these are distinct areas of law, in practice they are connected. Most property owners insure their property against possible losses due to fires, accidents, or other perils. Further, mortgage companies that make loans to finance property purchases require that insurance be carried.

REAL PROPERTY

real property

Immovable property consisting of land and the buildings and plant life thereon.

personal property

Any property that is not real property. Generally, any property that is movable or intangible is classified as personal property.

From an early period, the law has divided property into two classifications: real property and personal property. **Real property**, or *real estate*, is land and all things attached to the land, such as trees and buildings, as well as the minerals below the surface of the land and the air above the land. **Personal property** is all other property. Personal property can be either tangible or intangible. *Tangible* personal property, such as a television or a car, has physical substance. *Intangible* personal property represents a set of rights and interests but has no real physical existence. Stocks, bonds, and intellectual property rights (discussed in Chapter 15) are examples of intangible personal property.

Ownership Rights in Property

fee simple

Ownership rights entitling the holder to use, possess, or dispose of the property however he or she chooses during his or her lifetime.

Property ownership is often viewed as a "bundle of rights." One who owns the entire bundle—ownership rights to the greatest degree possible—is said to own the property in **fee simple**. An owner in fee simple is entitled to use, possess, or dispose of the real or personal property (by sale, gift, or other means) however he or she chooses during his or her lifetime. On the owner's death, the interests in the property descend to the owner's heirs.

eminent domain

The power of a government to take land for public use from private citizens for just compensation.

Of course, those who own real property even in fee simple may be subject to certain restrictions on their right to use the property absolutely as they choose. For example, zoning laws may prohibit an owner of property in a given area from conducting certain activities (such as running a business) on the property. Also, under its power of **eminent domain**, the government has a right to take private property for public use (for a highway, for example), as long as the government compensates the owner for the value of the land taken.

easement

The right of a person to make limited use of another person's real property without taking anything from the property.

Property owned in fee simple may also be subject to an **easement**, which is the right of another to use the owner's land for a limited purpose. Easements are said to "run with the land." That is, they usually pass with title to real property as its ownership changes over time. There are many kinds of easements:

- An easement may allow utility companies to maintain gas pipelines and electricity cables that cross the property.

- A right-of-way easement may allow people to cross the property to get to other property.

- A solar easement may be granted to a neighbor to guarantee that trees will not be allowed to grow so as to block sunlight from hitting solar panels on the neighbor's roof.

- A historic preservation easement may promise that the appearance of a house will not be changed.

Concurrent Ownership

Persons who share the bundle of ownership rights to either real or personal property are said to be concurrent owners. There are two principal types of concurrent ownership: tenancy in common and joint tenancy.

A **tenancy in common** is a form of co-ownership in which two or more persons own undivided interests in certain property. The interest is undivided because each tenant has rights in the whole property. Although the ownership is in common, tenants may have equal or unequal shares. ▶ **EXAMPLE 16.1** Rosa and Chad own a rare stamp collection together as tenants in common. This does not mean that Rosa owns certain stamps and Chad others. Rather, it means that each of them has rights in the *entire* collection. (If Rosa owned some of the stamps and Chad owned others, then the interest would be *divided*.) ◀ If a tenant in common dies, the tenant's ownership rights pass to his or her heirs.

A **joint tenancy** is also a form of co-ownership in which two or more persons own undivided interests in property. The key feature of a joint tenancy is the "right of survivorship." When a joint tenant dies, that tenant's interest passes to the surviving joint tenant or tenants and not to the deceased tenant's heirs, as it would with a tenancy in common. ▶ **EXAMPLE 16.2** Suppose that Rosa and Chad from the previous example held their stamp collection in a joint tenancy. If Rosa died before Chad, the entire collection would become the property of Chad. Rosa's heirs would receive no interest in the collection. ◀ If a joint tenant transfers his or her interest in the property, the transfer terminates the joint tenancy. The new co-owner (the one to whom the rights were transferred) and the other tenant or tenants become tenants in common.

Two other types of concurrent ownership are tenancy by the entirety and community property. A *tenancy by the entirety* is a form of co-ownership by husbands and wives that is similar to a joint tenancy, except that the spouses cannot separately transfer their interests in the property during their lifetimes. In ten states, husbands and wives can hold property as community property. In those states, *community property* is all property acquired during the marriage; each spouse technically owns an undivided one-half interest in the property.

> **tenancy in common**
> A form of co-ownership of property in which each party owns an undivided interest that passes to his or her heirs at death.

> **joint tenancy**
> The joint ownership of property by two or more co-owners in which each co-owner owns an undivided portion of the property. On the death of one of the joint tenants, his or her interest automatically passes to the surviving joint tenant or tenants.

Life Estates

A *life estate* is an interest in real property that is transferred to another for the life of that individual. A conveyance "to Allison for her life" creates a life estate. In a life estate, the life tenant cannot do anything to the property that would reduce its value for the owner of the future interest in it. The person with a life interest in property does not have to occupy the property; it may be used for rental income.

Future Interests

When someone who owns real property in fee simple conveys the property to another conditionally or for a limited time (such as with a life estate), the original owner still retains an interest in the land. This interest is called a *future interest* because it will only arise in the future. The holder of a future interest may transfer it to another during his or her lifetime. If the interest is not transferred, it will pass to the owner's heirs on his or her death.

The Transfer and Sale of Real Property

The ownership of property, or the right to use it, can be transferred in numerous ways. Property can be given to another as a gift or transferred to another by inheritance, leased to another, or sold. Most commonly, property is transferred

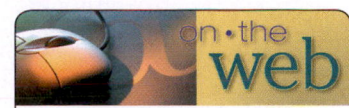

From an overview of law about real property and real estate transactions, go to **www.law.cornell.edu**, select "All topics" from the "Law about . . ." menu, and then select "Real property" from the topics list.

by sale. The sale of tangible personal property (goods) is covered by the common law of contracts, as modified by Article 2 of the Uniform Commercial Code, which we discussed in Chapter 15. Rights in certain types of intangible property (such as checks, money orders, and other documents) are covered by other articles of the UCC. The sale of real property is governed by the common law of contracts as well as state (and, to a limited extent, federal) statutory law.

Here we look at some of the basic steps and procedures involved in the sale of real estate. These steps and procedures are summarized in Exhibit 16.1.

Contract Formation—Offer and Acceptance

The common law contractual requirements discussed in Chapter 15 all apply to real estate contracts. Because the Statute of Frauds applies to contracts for the sale of real property, they must be in writing.

When a buyer wishes to purchase real estate, he submits an offer to the seller. The offer specifies all of the terms of the proposed contract—a description of the property, the price, and any other conditions that the buyer wishes to include. Often, a buyer conditions the offer on the buyer's ability to obtain financing. The offer might also specify which party will bear the cost of any repairs that need to be made. Typical provisions included in a real estate sales agreement are illustrated in Exhibit 16.2 on the following page. When signed by the buyer and the seller, the offer constitutes a contract for the sale of land that is binding on the parties.

The buyer normally puts up a sum of money, called *earnest money,* along with the offer to buy the property. By paying earnest money, the buyer indicates that he is making a serious offer. Normally, the offer provides that if the seller accepts the offer (and forms a contract with the buyer), the buyer will forfeit this money if

EXHIBIT 16.1
Steps Involved in the Sale of Real Estate

BUYER'S PURCHASE OFFER

Buyer offers to purchase seller's property. The offer may be conditioned on buyer's ability to obtain financing, on satisfactory inspections of the premises, and so on. Included with the offer is earnest money.

TITLE EXAMINATION AND INSURANCE

Title examiner investigates and verifies seller's rights in the property and discloses any claims or interests held by others. Buyer (and/or seller) may purchase title insurance to protect against a defect in title.

SELLER'S RESPONSE

If seller accepts buyer's offer, then a contract is formed. Seller can also reject the offer or make a counteroffer that modifies buyer's terms. Buyer may accept or reject seller's counteroffer or make a counteroffer that modifies seller's terms.

CLOSING

After financing is obtained and all inspections have been completed, the closing takes place. The escrow agent (such as a title company or a bank) transfers the deed to buyer and the proceeds of the sale to seller. The proceeds are the purchase price less any amount already paid by buyer and any closing costs to be paid by seller. Included in the closing costs are fees charged for services performed by the lender, escrow agent, and title examiner. The purchase and sale of the property is complete.

PURCHASE AND SALE AGREEMENT

Once an offer or a counteroffer is accepted, a purchase and sale agreement is formed.

- Names of parties and/or real estate agents.
- Date of agreement and how long seller has to accept agreement.
- Legal description of the property's location and size.
- Amount of the purchase offer.
- Amount of cash to be paid at the time of sale.
- Amount of earnest money deposit.
- Type of loan or financing the buyer plans to use.
- Whether the sale is contingent on the buyer's obtaining financing.
- Condition of the title and debt that buyer will assume.
- Warranties of title (restrictions, rights, or limitations).
- Condition of property and zoning or use rights.
- Prorations of taxes, insurance, or other obligations.
- Description of any fixtures, appliances, and furnishings that will be included in sale and any warranty as to the condition of such items.
- Inspection rights given to buyer (for example, water, well, mechanical, structural, electrical, termite), who will pay the costs of inspections, and whether the sale is contingent on inspector's approval.
- Statement of who will bear the cost for such items as transfer fees, abstracts of title, and closing costs.
- Conditions under which the offer may be canceled.

EXHIBIT 16.2
Typical Provisions in Real Estate Sales Agreements

he breaches the contract. Other damages for breach might also be specified in the agreement. If the deal goes through, the earnest money is usually applied to the purchase price of the real estate.

Once the offer is submitted to the seller, the seller has three options: accept the offer, reject it, or modify its terms—thus creating a counteroffer. The buyer, in turn, can then accept, reject, or modify the terms of the counteroffer—thus creating yet another counteroffer for the seller to consider. In real estate transactions, bargaining over price and other conditions of the sale frequently involves the exchange of one or more counteroffers. Once one of the parties accepts an offer or counteroffer, a contract is formed by which both parties normally must abide. As the *Ethics Watch* on page 534 discusses, paralegals must be sure real estate paperwork is accurate.

The Role of the Escrow Agent

The sale of real property normally involves three parties: the seller, the buyer, and the escrow agent. Frequently, both the buyer and the seller are assisted by real estate agents, attorneys, and paralegals. The *escrow agent*, which may be a title company, bank, or special escrow company, acts as a neutral party in the transaction and facilitates the sale by allowing the buyer and the seller to complete the transaction without having to exchange documents and funds directly with each other.

To understand the vital role played by the escrow agent, consider the problems that might otherwise arise. Essentially, in the sale of property, the buyer gives the seller funds, and the seller conveys (transfers) to the buyer a deed, representing ownership rights in the property (deeds will be discussed shortly). Neither the buyer nor the seller wishes to part with the funds or the deed until all conditions of the sale and purchase have been met.

ACCURATE PAPERWORK AND REAL ESTATE TRANSACTIONS

Art Guthrie, a paralegal, was drafting a real estate offer for one of the firm's clients. Instead of entering $90,000 as the amount being offered for a piece of land, he accidentally entered $900,000. The document was sent to the seller, who recognized the obvious mistake and returned the paperwork unsigned. Before the paperwork could be redone, another buyer offered the seller $100,000, and that offer was accepted. The client then bought another piece of property for $105,000 and sued Guthrie's supervising attorney for $15,000 in damages. The chance to buy property for $90,000 had been missed due to the mistake. As with all legal documents, a paralegal must be sure that real estate transaction documents are accurate, since the law firm could be liable for errors.

The duty to use care in preparing work products arises from the NALA Code of Ethics, Canon 2: "A paralegal may perform any task which is properly delegated and supervised by an attorney, as long as the attorney is ultimately responsible to the client . . . . and assumes professional responsibility for the work product."

The solution is the use of an escrow agent. The escrow agent holds the deed until the buyer pays the seller for the property at the *closing* (the final step in the sale of real estate). The escrow agent also holds any funds paid by the buyer, including the earnest money mentioned above, until the sale is completed. At the closing, the escrow agent receives funds from the buyer, the buyer is given the deed, and the seller is given the money. The triangular relationship among the buyer, the seller, and the escrow agent is depicted in Exhibit 16.3.

Financing

Because few buyers want to, or can, pay cash for real property, buyers generally need to secure financing. Commonly, a buyer of real property finances the purchase by obtaining a loan (called a **mortgage**) from a bank, a mortgage company,

---

mortgage

A written instrument giving a creditor an interest in the debtor's property as security for a debt.

EXHIBIT 16.3
The Concept of Escrow

This exhibit illustrates the triangular relationship among the escrow agent, the seller, and the buyer in a transfer of real estate. The seller gives the escrow agent the deed, the buyer gives the escrow agent the funds, and at the time of the closing, the escrow agent gives the seller the funds and the buyer the deed—simultaneously.

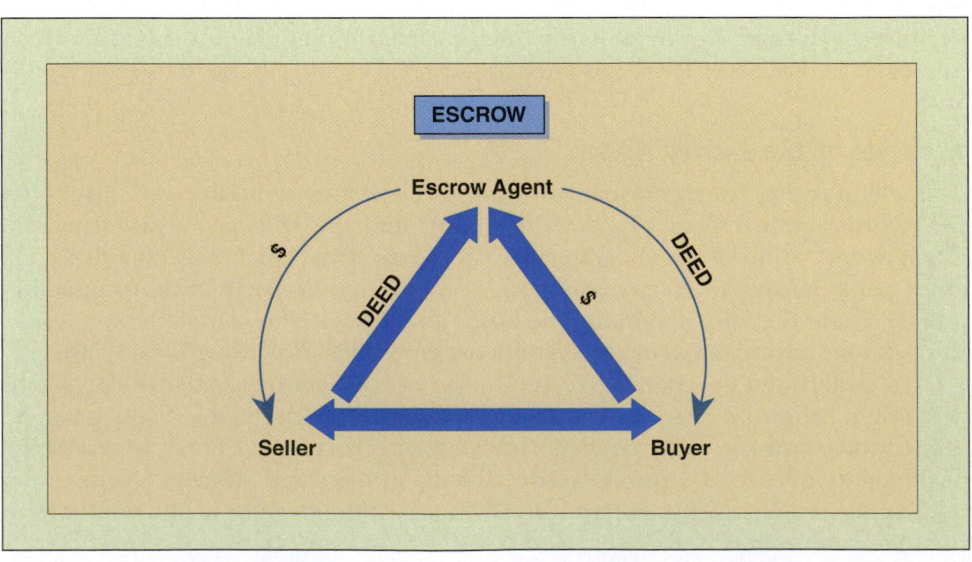

or some other party. When a buyer obtains a mortgage, the bank or mortgage company takes a security interest in the property—that is, the bank or mortgage company secures the right to claim ownership of the property if the buyer fails to make the scheduled payments.

Inspection of the Premises

In addition to obtaining financing, buyers may have the premises inspected to see if there are any major electrical or plumbing problems, structural defects, termite or insect infestations, or other concerns. Often, the contract of sale is conditioned on the outcome of these inspections. If problems surface during the inspections, the buyer and seller may negotiate (or may have included in the contract) arrangements specifying which party will pay what portion of the costs of any necessary repairs.

Title Examination and Insurance

Whenever title to property is transferred from one party to another, that transfer is recorded by the county recording office. A *title examination* involves checking these records carefully to make sure that the seller is actually the owner of the property described in the purchase offer and to determine whether claims (such as a tax lien for overdue taxes) on the property exist that were not disclosed by the seller. The title examination is an important task to be accomplished prior to the purchase of real estate. The title examination may be undertaken by the buyer or the buyer's attorney (paralegals frequently assume this responsibility) or by the lending institution, a title insurance company, or another party.

Normally, the history of past ownership and transfers of the property is already summarized in a document called an abstract, which may be in the possession of the seller (or the holder of the seller's mortgage or other company or institution). After examining the abstract, the title examiner gives an opinion as to the validity of the title. Title examinations are not foolproof, though, and buyers of real property often buy title insurance to protect their interests in the event that some defect in the title was not discovered during the examination.

The Closing

One of the terms specified in the contract is when the closing will take place. The closing—also called the settlement or the closing of escrow—is coordinated by the escrow agent. At the closing, several events happen at once: the buyer signs the mortgage note (if the purchase was financed by a mortgage), title insurance is obtained, the seller receives the proceeds of the sale (the purchase price less the amount previously paid by the buyer and less closing costs), and the deed to the property is delivered to the buyer.

A **deed** is the instrument of conveyance (transfer) of real property. As indicated on the sample deed in Exhibit 16.4 on the following page, a deed gives the names of the seller (*grantor*) and buyer (*grantee*), describes the property being transferred, evidences the seller's intent to convey (for example, "I hereby bargain, sell, grant, or give") the property, and contains the seller's signature.

Closing costs comprise fees for services, including those performed by the lender, escrow agent, and title company. These costs can range from several hundred to several thousand dollars, depending on the amount of the mortgage loan and other conditions of the sale, and must be paid, in cash, at the closing. Usually, the buyer and seller can learn in advance what the closing costs will be by checking (or having their attorneys or real estate agents check) with the escrow agent handling the closing. Also, under the federal Real Estate Settlement Procedures Act, lending institutions must notify—within a specified time period—each applicant for a mortgage loan of the precise costs that must be paid at the closing. Paralegals are often involved in this process, as illustrated in the *Developing Paralegal Skills* feature on page 537.

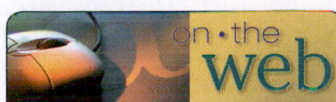

For links to many resources related to property and real estate, go to **www. hg.org**, select "Law & Practice," from the menu at the top of the page, and then select "Real Estate" from the "Main Practice Areas" list.

deed
A document by which title to property is transferred from one party to another.

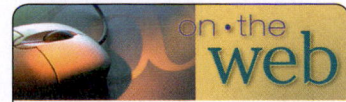

If you are interested in learning why the Real Estate Settlement Procedures Act was passed and what it requires of lending institutions, go to **www.hud. gov**, and select "RESPA" from the "A to Z" index. You can find the full act online at **www.fdic.gov**. From the menu at the top of the page, select "Regulations & Examinations." Then select "FDIC Law, Regulations & Related Acts," and find the act in the index.

EXHIBIT 16.4
A Sample Deed

Date: May 31, 2011

Grantor: RAYMOND A. GRANT AND WIFE, JOANN H. GRANT

Grantor's Mailing Address (including county):
      4106 North Loop Drive
      Austin, Travis County, Texas

Grantee: DAVID F. HOGAN AND WIFE, RUTH E. HOGAN, AS
      JOINT TENANTS WITH RIGHT OF SURVIVORSHIP

Grantee's Mailing Address (including county):
      5929 Fuller Drive
      Austin, Travis County, Texas

Consideration:
For and in consideration of the sum of Ten and No/100 Dollars ($10.00) and other
valuable consideration to the undersigned paid by the grantees herein named, the receipt
of which is hereby acknowledged, and for which no lien is retained, either express or
implied.

Property (including any improvements):
Lot 23, Block "A", Northwest Hills, Green Acres Addition, Phase 4, Travis County, Texas,
according to the map or plat of record in volume 22, pages 331-336, of the Plat Records
of Travis County, Texas.

Reservations from and Exceptions to Conveyance and Warranty:

This conveyance with its warranty is expressly made subject to the following:
Easements and restrictions of record in volume 7863, page 53, volume 8430, page 35,
volume 8133, page 152, of the Real Property Records of Travis County, Texas; and to
any other restrictions and easements affecting said property which are of record in
Travis County, Texas.

     Grantor, for the consideration and subject to the reservations from and exceptions to conveyance and
warranty, grants, sells, and conveys to Grantee the property, together with all and singular the rights and
appurtenances thereto in any wise belonging, to have and hold it to Grantee, Grantee's heirs, executors,
administrators, successors, or assigns forever. Grantor binds Grantor and Grantor's heirs, executors,
administrators, and successors to warrant and forever defend all and singular the property to Grantee and
Grantee's heirs, executors, administrators, successors, and assigns against every person whomsoever
lawfully claiming or to claim the same or any part thereof, except as to the reservations from and exceptions
to conveyance and warranty.

When the context requires, singular nouns and pronouns include the plural.

BY: _Raymond A Grant_
      Raymond A. Grant

BY: _JoAnn H. Grant_
      JoAnn H. Grant

STATE OF TEXAS
COUNTY OF TRAVIS
     This instrument was acknowledged before me on the   31st   day of   May 2011
by   Raymond A. and JoAnn H. Grant

Rosemary Potter
Notary Public, State of Texas
Notary's name (printed): ROSEMARY POTTER

Notary Seal

Notary's commission expires: 1/31/2013

Leases

An owner of either personal or real property can lease, or rent, the property to
another person or a business firm. A **lease** is a contractual agreement under which a
property owner (the *lessor*) agrees to rent his or her property to another (the *lessee*)
for a specified period of time. Leases of personal property (cars or equipment) are
covered by the Uniform Commercial Code, which spells out the rights and duties
of lessors and lessees.

     Leases of real property are governed in part by the common law of contracts
and in part (and to an increasing extent) by state statutory law. Although under

lease
In real property law, a contract by which
the owner of real property (the landlord)
grants to a person (the tenant) an
exclusive right to use and possess the
property, usually for a specified period of
time, in return for rent or some other form
of payment.

Developing Paralegal Skills

REVIEWING THE CLOSING PACKAGE

Andy Casmis, a paralegal, is reviewing a closing package for his supervising attorney, a sole practitioner. Andy's job is to request the closing package from the lender and review it before the closing takes place. The closing package consists of the purchaser's requirements, closing statement, settlement statement, deed, bill of sale, mortgage documents, and title insurance policy. Andy needs to make sure that there are no mistakes in the closing documents.

CHECKLIST FOR REVIEWING A CLOSING PACKAGE

- Order the closing package as far in advance as possible.
- Set aside uninterrupted time for reviewing the closing package.
- Review the address and legal description of the property in the mortgage note and the deed for accuracy.
- Using a calculator, review the purchaser's requirements sheet, the closing statement, the bill of sale, and the mortgage documents to make sure that there are no numerical errors.
- Review each document to make sure that the parties' names are listed and spelled correctly.
- Review the deed to ensure that the ownership rights are accurately listed and that the names are correct.
- Contact the client and remind him or her of the items that must be brought to the closing.

the common law, an oral lease is valid, a party who seeks to enforce an oral lease may have difficulty proving its existence. In most states, statutes mandate that leases exceeding one year's duration must be in writing. When real property is leased, the lessor (landlord) retains ownership rights to the property, but the lessee (tenant) obtains the right to the exclusive possession of the property. Most leases, however, give the landlord the right to come onto the property for certain purposes—to make repairs, for example.

Paralegals frequently draft or review lease agreements for clients (or for corporate employers), and you should be familiar with the types of terms that are typically included in a lease agreement, or contract. Normally, a lease contract will specify the names of the lessor and lessee, the location of the premises being leased, the amount of rent to be paid by the lessee, the duration of the lease, and the respective rights and duties of the parties in regard to the use and maintenance of the leased premises. Exhibit 16.5 on the following page illustrates the kinds of provisions that are commonly included in lease agreements.

Commercial Leases

Leases for commercial or business property are usually much more detailed than residential leases, so special expertise is needed to work with them. The terminology describing the building generally follows industry practices and terms used by the Building Owners and Managers Association. In a residential lease, the house or apartment is usually identified by address; but in a commercial lease, terms such as *gross leasable* or *net leasable square footage* are used. Specific discussion of common

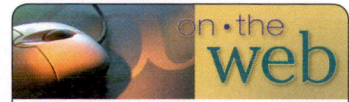

For coverage of many commercial property issues, visit the Building Owners and Managers Association International Web site at **www.boma.org**.

EXHIBIT 16.5
Typical Lease Terms

Term of lease: Indicates the duration of the lease, including the beginning and ending dates.

Rental: Indicates the amount of the rent payments and the intervals (monthly or yearly, for example) at which rent will be paid.

Maintenance and use of leased premises: Describes which areas will be repaired and maintained by the landlord and which by the tenant.

Utilities: Stipulates which utilities (electricity, water, and so forth) will be paid by the landlord and which by the tenant.

Alterations: Normally states that no structural alterations to the property will be made by the tenant without the landlord's consent.

Assignment: States whether the tenant's rights in the lease can be assigned (transferred) by the tenant to a third party.

Insurance: Indicates whether the landlord or the tenant will insure the premises against damage. (Normally, the landlord secures insurance coverage for the building, and the tenant obtains a "renter's policy" for his or her own personal property—furniture and other possessions—that will be housed in the building.)

Taxes: Designates which party will be liable for taxes or special assessments on the property. (Normally, the landlord assumes this responsibility, but in some commercial leases, the tenant agrees to take on this obligation.)

Destruction: States what will happen in the event that the premises are totally destroyed by fire or other casualty.

Quiet enjoyment: A covenant (promise) by the landlord that the tenant shall possess and enjoy the premises without interference by any third party.

Termination: Usually specifies that the tenant's right to possession of the premises ends when the lease expires.

Renewal: Indicates that the tenant has an option to renew the lease if the landlord is notified of the intent to renew within a certain period of time (such as one month or three months) before the lease expires.

areas and responsibilities for them is included. Such leases also often discuss inspection rights, what signage will be allowed, liability waivers, damage provisions, how alterations are to be handled, responsibility for repairs, and other issues usually peculiar to commercial property.

PROPERTY LAW AND THE PARALEGAL

Paralegals frequently perform tasks that require an understanding of the law governing real property. If you work for a small legal practice, some of your work may involve assisting your supervising attorney in handling real estate transactions. If you work for a law firm (or a department within a law firm) that specializes in real estate transactions, you will have extensive contact with buyers and sellers of real property, as well as with real estate agents, title companies, banking institutions that finance real estate purchases, and the attorneys and paralegals who work on behalf of the other parties in real estate sales.

If a real estate agent is involved, the agent will assist the seller or the buyer in drawing up a purchase contract, in arranging for inspections, in having the title examined and title insurance obtained, and in preparing the closing papers. In this situation, your job will be to assist the attorney in verifying, on behalf of your client, that all of the documents needed have been prepared and that they contain the correct purchase price, mortgage amount, property description, and other terms. Generally, you will be responsible for making sure that the documents are in order and that the client's interests are fully protected. (See this chapter's *Featured Contributor* article on the following two pages for a discussion of the role of a legal due-diligence team in purchases of real estate.)

Here are just some of the types of tasks that you might perform as a real estate paralegal working for a law firm:

- Interview a client who wants to buy or sell property.
- Assist the client with the preliminary negotiations (offers and counteroffers) leading up to the purchase contract.
- Draft the offers and counteroffers, as well as other documents necessary to the sale.

- Conduct a title examination by going to the county courthouse and examining previous property transfers.
- Obtain or create a title abstract.
- Contact the title company to arrange for the closing.
- Handle the escrow account.
- Attend the closing. (In some states, paralegals are allowed to represent clients at closings.)

Corporations also purchase and sell property, and some larger corporations have real estate groups within their legal departments. If you work for a corporation that buys and sells a significant amount of property, your employer will be the "client," and you will perform similar tasks on the corporation's behalf.

The law governing real property also comes into play in contexts other than real estate purchases or sales. If you work in the area of probate administration (the settling of a deceased's estate), for example, you will need to have an understanding of how ownership rights in property are acquired and transferred.

INSURANCE LAW

As mentioned in Chapter 2, *insurance* is a contract in which the insurance company (the *insurer*), in return for consideration, promises to pay a sum of money to another (either the *insured* or the *beneficiary*) if the insured suffers harm or loss from a particular, stated peril. Basically, insurance is an arrangement for *transferring and allocating risk*. In many instances, **risk** can be described as a prediction concerning potential loss based on known and unknown factors. **Risk management** normally involves the transfer of certain risks from the insured party to the insurance company by a contractual agreement. The insurance contract and its provisions will be examined shortly. First, however, we look at the different types of insurance that can be obtained, insurance terminology, and the concept of insurable interest.

risk
A prediction concerning potential loss based on known and unknown factors.

risk management
Planning that is undertaken to reduce the risk of loss from known and unknown events. In the context of insurance, risk management involves transferring certain risks from the insured to the insurance company.

Classifications of Insurance

Insurance is classified according to the nature of the risk involved. For instance, fire insurance, automobile insurance, and life insurance apply to different types of risk and protect against different types of loss. Exhibit 16.6 on page 542 lists and describes a number of insurance classifications.

Insurance Terminology

An insurance contract is called a **policy**, the consideration paid to the insurer is called a **premium**, and the insurance company is sometimes called an **underwriter**. The parties to an insurance policy are the insurer (the insurance company) and the insured (the person covered by its provisions or the holder of the policy).

Insurance contracts are usually obtained through an *agent,* who ordinarily works for the insurance company, or through a *broker,* who is ordinarily an *independent contractor.* When a broker deals with an applicant for insurance, the broker may be the applicant's agent and not an agent of the insurance company. In contrast, an insurance agent is an agent of the insurance company, not of the applicant. As a

policy
In insurance law, a contract for insurance coverage. The policy spells out the precise terms and conditions as to what will and will not be covered under the contract.

premium
In insurance law, the price paid by the insured for insurance protection for a specified period of time.

underwriter
In insurance law, the insurer, or the one assuming a risk in return for the payment of a premium.

featured contributor

PROTECTING THE REAL ESTATE PURCHASER: THE LEGAL DUE-DILIGENCE TEAM

Daniel F. Hinkel

BIOGRAPHICAL NOTE

Daniel F. Hinkel earned a J.D. from the University of Illinois School of Law and a B.S. from Eastern Illinois University. He is vice president and corporate counsel for ING Investment Management, LLC, in Atlanta, Georgia.

Hinkel has taught in paralegal programs for a number of years. He is also the author of a number of books, including Practical Real Estate Law *and* Essentials of Practical Real Estate Law, *both published by Delmar Cengage Learning.*

Home ownership is important for many families, and commercial real estate is a preferred asset for many investors. Whether the purchaser is acquiring a home for a residence or purchasing a shopping center as an investment, the transaction will be governed by the common law doctrine of *caveat emptor,* "let the buyer beware." This doctrine provides that a seller, absent an express warranty, is not liable to a buyer for any existing defects regarding the title to the land or any physical defects in the improvements located on the land. Even misrepresentations made by a seller concerning the property are generally not recoverable in an action for fraud if the purchaser could have discovered the truth from proper due diligence, such as a thorough inspection of the home or a title examination.

THE LEGAL DUE-DILIGENCE TEAM

A legal due-diligence team can save a real estate purchaser money and future headaches. Paralegals are important members of the legal due-diligence team. The extent of the team's work will depend on the nature of the property being purchased. A home may require only a title and survey review.

An investment property may require a review of title, survey, government regulations, leases, and other contracts that affect the use of the property.

TITLE DUE DILIGENCE

One of the main responsibilities of the legal due-diligence team is to determine that when the sale has been completed, the purchaser will have good title of ownership to the real property. The legal due-diligence team should require that the public real property title records be examined and the examination carefully reviewed to determine the title's marketability. It is common in many communities for a title insurance company to examine the public records and provide the legal due-diligence team with a title report or commitment to issue title insurance and copies of all the recorded documents listed in the title report. The team paralegal will review this report and, in consultation with the team attorney, determine if the title matters affect the marketability and the purchaser's proposed use of the property. The legal due-diligence team will also arrange for a title insurance policy insuring the purchaser's ownership to be issued at the time of purchase.

SURVEY DUE DILIGENCE

The legal due-diligence team should require a survey of the property. Most surveys are "as built," meaning the survey locates all physical improvements on the land in relation to the boundary lines of the land. The surveyor will locate all fences, walls, driveways, pavements, building structures, and natural features, such as streams and ponds. The survey will also indicate if the property is in a flood hazard area, which may require flood insurance.

The team paralegal may review the survey. A survey is usually reviewed in conjunction with the title commitment. This review will determine that all matters that would have a physical presence on the property, such as easements or building setback lines, are shown on the survey. The review will confirm that the description of the real property matches the description owned by the seller and that the description can be insured by the title insurance company. If there are differences between the description shown on the survey and in the title report, the legal due-diligence team will investigate the matter and determine why the differences exist and how they can be resolved.

In addition, the survey reviewer will note the location of improvements on the property and look for encroachments either onto or from the property or encroachments of buildings over easements. The reviewer will also determine if there is proper access to the property from a public street and if the necessary utilities, such as electricity, gas, and water, are available.

GOVERNMENT REGULATION DUE DILIGENCE

For an investment property, the legal due-diligence team will inquire into government regulations that affect the property. The team will obtain confirmation of the property's zoning status and determine if the purchaser's use or intended use

> *"One of the main responsibilities of the legal due-diligence team is to determine that when the sale has been completed, the purchaser will have good title of ownership to the real property."*

of the property will comply with the uses permitted by the zoning.

LEASE REVIEW

The legal due-diligence team may review leases in connection with an investment property. The leases provide income to the purchaser, and the price of the property may be based on assumptions regarding the rental income contained in the leases. The team paralegal may review the leases and prepare an abstract, or summary, of the leases. The summary review will verify the terms of the lease, such as rental terms, the duration of the lease, and the various obligations and responsibilities of both the landlord and the tenant. A lease will also be reviewed to determine if the tenant has an option to purchase the property. If the lease contains an option to purchase, the team attorney will carefully discuss the option with the purchaser to verify that it is acceptable.

The legal due-diligence team may prepare and require each tenant to sign an estoppel certificate. An estoppel certificate signed by the tenant generally confirms the basic facts regarding the lease, such as rental terms and duration and payment of security deposits. Also, it will state that there is no default under the lease and that the tenant has no defenses, setoffs, recoupments, claims, or counterclaims of any nature against the landlord.

THE LEGAL DUE-DILIGENCE TEAM PROVIDES VALUE

A legal due-diligence team made up of attorneys and paralegals performs an important role in protecting a purchaser from the harsh effects of the *caveat emptor rule.* A legal team's thorough investigation and competent review and analysis of supporting documents provide good value for the real property purchaser-client.

EXHIBIT 16.6
Selected Insurance Classifications

Type of Insurance	Coverage
Automobile	May cover damage to automobiles resulting from specified hazards or occurrences (such as fire, vandalism, theft, or collision); normally provides protection against liability for personal injuries and property damage resulting from the operation of the vehicle.
Casualty	Protects against losses incurred by the insured as a result of being held liable due to negligence for personal injuries or property damage sustained by others.
Fidelity or Guaranty	Provides indemnity against losses in trade or losses caused by the dishonesty of employees, the insolvency of debtors, or breaches of contract. May also be called a *surety bond*.
Fire	Covers losses incurred by the insured as a result of fire.
Group	Provides individual life, medical, or disability insurance coverage but is obtainable through a group of persons, usually employees; the policy premium is paid either entirely by the employer or partially by the employer and partially by the employee.
Health	Covers expenses incurred by the insured as a result of physical injury or illness and other expenses relating to health and life maintenance.
Homeowners'	Protects homeowners against some or all risks of loss to their residences and the residences' contents or liability arising from the use of the property.
Key-Person	Protects a business in the event of the death or disability of a key employee.
Liability	Protects against liability imposed on the insured as a result of injuries to the person or property of another. May also cover product liability actions.
Life	Covers the death of the policyholder. On the death of the insured, an amount specified in the policy is paid by the insurer to the insured's beneficiary.
Malpractice	Protects professionals (physicians, lawyers, and others) against malpractice claims brought against them by their patients or clients; a form of liability insurance.
Mortgage	Covers a mortgage loan; the insurer pays the balance of the mortgage to the creditor on the death or disability of the debtor.
Title	Protects against any defects in title to real property and any losses incurred as a result of existing claims against or liens on the property at the time of purchase.

general rule, the insurance company is bound by the acts of its insurance agents when they act within the agency relationship (agency relationships will be discussed in Chapter 18). In most situations, state law determines the status of all parties writing or obtaining insurance.

Insurable Interest

insurable interest
An interest either in a person's life or well-being or in property that is sufficiently substantial to justify insuring against injury to or death of the person or damage to the property.

People can insure anything in which they have an **insurable interest**. Without an insurable interest, there can be no enforceable contract. For real and personal property, an insurable interest exists when the insured derives a pecuniary (monetary) benefit from the continued existence of the property, such as a car, a home, business premises, or computer data. Put another way, a person has an insurable interest in property when she would sustain a financial loss from its damage or destruction. In regard to life insurance, a person must have a reasonable expectation of benefit from the continued life of another in order to have an insurable interest in that person's life.

The Insurance Contract

An insurance contract is governed by the general principles of contract law, although the insurance industry is regulated by each state. In this section, we consider several aspects of the insurance contract, including the application for insurance, the date when the contract takes effect, and some of the important provisions typically found in insurance contracts. In addition, we discuss the cancellation of an insurance policy and defenses that insurance companies can raise against payment on a policy.

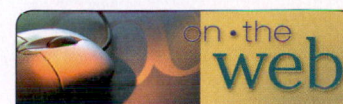

Application

The filled-in application form for insurance is usually attached to the policy and made a part of the insurance contract. Thus, an insurance applicant is bound by any false statements that appear in the application (subject to certain exceptions). Because the insurance company evaluates the risk factors based on the information included in the insurance application, misstatements or misrepresentations can void a policy, especially if the insurance company can show that it would not have extended insurance if it had known the true facts.

Effective Date

The effective date of an insurance contract—that is, the date on which the insurance coverage begins—is important. In some instances, the insurance applicant is not protected until a formal written policy is issued. In other situations, the applicant is protected between the time the application is received and the time the insurance company either accepts or rejects it. The following facts should be kept in mind:

- A broker is usually the agent of an applicant. Therefore, until the broker obtains a policy from the insurer, the applicant normally is not insured.

- A person who seeks insurance from an insurance company's agent will usually be protected from the moment the application is made, provided that some form of premium has been paid. Between the time the application is received and either rejected or accepted, the applicant is covered (possibly subject to a medical examination for life insurance). Usually, the agent will

Executives of a newly formed corporation consult with an attorney concerning the types of insurance they should purchase for the business. Many paralegals work in the area of insurance law and assist with tasks relating to insurance claims. What types of such claims arise in an insurance context?

(Image copyright Phil Date, 2009. Used under license from Shutterstock.com)

binder
A written, temporary insurance policy.

write a memorandum, or **binder**, indicating that a policy is pending and stating its essential terms.

- If the parties agree that the policy will be issued and delivered at a later time, the contract is not effective until the policy is issued and delivered or sent to the applicant, depending on the agreement. Thus, any loss sustained between the time of application and the delivery of the policy is not covered.

- The parties may agree that a life insurance policy will be binding at the time the insured pays the first premium, or the policy may be expressly contingent on the applicant's passing a physical examination. If the applicant pays the premium and passes the examination, the policy coverage is continuously in effect. If the applicant pays the premium but dies before having the physical examination, then in order to collect, the applicant's estate must show that the applicant *would have passed* the examination had he or she not died.

Coinsurance Clauses

Often, when taking out fire insurance policies, property owners insure their property for less than full value because most fires do not result in a total loss. To encourage owners to insure their property for an amount close to full value, fire insurance policies commonly include a coinsurance clause. Typically, a *coinsurance clause* provides that if owners insure the property up to a specified percentage of its replacement value—usually 80 percent—they will be fully reimbursed for any loss. If the insurance is for less than the required percentage, the owners are responsible for a proportionate share of the loss.

▶ **EXAMPLE 16.3** Assume that a property is valued at $100,000 and the owner insures this property for $80,000, satisfying the insurer's 80 percent coinsurance requirement. When the property suffers $50,000 in fire damages, the owner recovers the full $50,000. If the owner had insured the same property for only $40,000—half of the usual 80 percent ($80,000) coinsurance requirement—then the owner would have recovered only half of the $50,000 in fire damages, or $25,000. ◀

Indemnity Clauses

The term *indemnity* refers to a duty to make good on any loss, damage, or liability claims incurred by another. The term is used frequently in insurance law and insurance contracts because it involves the duty to compensate for loss. Under the principle of indemnity, indemnified parties are restored to the financial position that they were in before the loss or accident.

Indemnity clauses are frequently found in rental contracts. ▶ **EXAMPLE 16.4** Martinez is seeking to lease a building that is suitable for operating a dry-cleaning business. Commercial Property, Inc., a rental agency, has such a building for rent in the area in which Martinez wishes to locate. Martinez signs a lease agreement with Commercial that contains an indemnity clause. Under the indemnity clause, if an employee is injured while using the dry-cleaning equipment, he or she cannot sue Commercial Property. In effect, Martinez has agreed to hold the rental agency harmless for any damages caused by use of the equipment. ◀ Because indemnity clauses protect specified parties from suffering financial loss due to lawsuits, they are sometimes referred to as *hold-harmless clauses.*

Corporations often indemnify their directors and officers for any legal costs and fees that they might incur if they become involved in lawsuits by virtue of their positions. (Corporate directors and officers will be discussed in Chapter 18.) ▶ **EXAMPLE 16.5** Patricia Harding files a product liability lawsuit against Repp, Inc., and its chief executive officer, James Kerr. If Kerr's employment contract includes an indemnity clause, Repp will assume responsibility for any costs that Kerr incurs in defending himself against this lawsuit. ◀

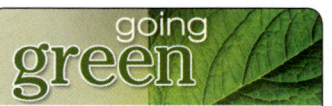

WHAT AM I BREATHING?

Although we think about outdoor air quality, most of us spend 90 to 95 percent of our time indoors. What is the air quality there? Many people have allergies to the strong chemicals used to clean carpets and for other purposes. Check to see what kind of cleaning supplies are used in your offices. There are usually green alternatives that can do the job but are not as potent and are less likely to cause breathing problems for some employees.

In the **Office**

CLARIFYING INSTRUCTIONS

Attorneys and paralegals are usually busy. Often, attorneys give instructions to paralegals quickly and briefly, assuming that the instructions are understood as intended. Problems arise, however, if the instructions are not clear to the paralegal. In such a situation, you must make sure that the instructions are made clear. For example, suppose that your supervising attorney asks you to draft a letter to an insurance company, using as a model a letter recently sent to another insurance company on behalf of a client named Janine Lattimore. The name doesn't ring a bell with you, but you assume that you can find that letter quickly in the files. The attorney then leaves the office for the rest of the day, and you spend a miserable hour searching in vain through the files and the master client list for "Janine Lattimore."

The next morning, you explain the problem to the attorney and learn that Janine Lattimore is, in fact, the married name of a client whose files are under her maiden name, Janine Calvin. You are upset, the attorney is displeased, and the sending of the letter is delayed—all of which could have been avoided if you had asked "Who is Janine Lattimore?" when the attorney was giving you instructions.

Subrogation Clauses

In simple terms, *subrogation* is the right to pursue another party's claim. In insurance, subrogation deals with the right of the insurer to be put in the position of the insured to pursue recovery from a third party who is legally responsible to the insured for a loss paid by the insurer to the insured. If the insurance company has compensated the insured for a loss sustained, and then later receives recovery from a third party in the name of the insured, the company can ask a court to order reimbursement from the proceeds. ▶ **EXAMPLE 16.6** Ryan owns a building that he leases out to several businesses. A third party negligently causes a fire on the premises, which burns down the building. Ryan can sue the third party for damages. If Ryan does not file a claim against the party who caused the fire, a subrogation clause allows the insurance company to step into Ryan's shoes and file a negligence claim against the third party on Ryan's behalf. If the fire insurance company has fully compensated Ryan for the damages, and if the lawsuit is successful, the insurance company is entitled to be reimbursed from the proceeds in the amount that it paid to Ryan to cover his loss. ◀

Most insurance contracts contain explicit subrogation clauses, which often require the insured party to cooperate with the insurance company by providing documents, records, and whatever else is necessary for the company to pursue claims on behalf of the insured. Even if the contract does not contain a subrogation clause or does not use the word *subrogation*, however, courts often hold that insurance companies have a right to subrogation unless this right is explicitly waived (given up).

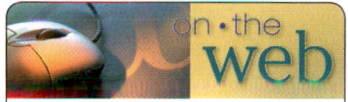

For links to many resources about insurance law and the insurance industry, go to **www.findlaw.com**. In the search box, enter "insurance law."

Other Provisions and Clauses

Some other important provisions and clauses in insurance contracts are defined in Exhibit 16.7 on the following page. Paralegals are often responsible for analyzing the various insurance clauses and summarizing the contract terms for their employers or clients. The courts are aware that most people do not have the special

EXHIBIT 16.7
Insurance Contract Provisions and Clauses

Incontestability Clause	An incontestability clause provides that after a policy has been in force for a specified length of time—usually two or three years—the insurer cannot contest statements made in the application.
Appraisal Clause	Insurance policies frequently provide that if the parties cannot agree on the amount of a loss covered under the policy or the value of the property lost, an appraisal, or estimate, by an impartial and qualified third party can be demanded.
Arbitration Clause	Many insurance policies include clauses that call for arbitration of disputes that may arise between the insurer and the insured concerning the settlement of claims.
Antilapse Clause	An antilapse clause provides that the policy will not automatically lapse if no payment is made on the date due. Ordinarily, under such a provision, the insured has a *grace period* of thirty or thirty-one days within which to pay an overdue premium before the policy is canceled.
Multiple Insurance	Many insurance policies include a clause providing that if the insured has multiple insurance policies that cover the same property and the amount of coverage exceeds the loss, the loss will be shared proportionately by the insurance companies.

training necessary to understand the intricate terminology used in insurance policies. Thus, the words used in an insurance contract have their ordinary meanings, not a technical meaning specific only to insurance. They are interpreted by the courts in light of the nature of the coverage involved. (For some online sources relating to policy interpretation and analysis, as well as sources relating to other aspects of insurance-related legal work, see this chapter's *Technology and Today's Paralegal* feature on the facing page.)

When there is an ambiguity in the policy, the provision generally is interpreted against the insurance company. Also, when it is unclear whether an insurance contract actually exists because the written policy has not been delivered, the uncertainty normally is resolved against the insurance company. The court presumes that the policy is in effect unless the company can show otherwise. Similarly, an insurer must notify the insured of any change in coverage under an existing policy.

Cancellation

The insured can cancel a policy at any time, and the insurer can cancel under certain circumstances. When an insurance company can cancel its insurance contract, the policy or a state statute usually requires that the insurer give advance written notice of the cancellation to the insured. The same requirement applies when only part of a policy is canceled. Any premium paid in advance may be refundable on the policy's cancellation. The insured may also be entitled to a life insurance policy's cash surrender value.

The insurer can cancel an insurance policy for various reasons, depending on the type of insurance. ▶ **EXAMPLE 16.7** Automobile insurance can be canceled for nonpayment of premiums or suspension of the insured's driver's license. Property insurance can be canceled for nonpayment of premiums or for other reasons, including the insured's fraud or misrepresentation, conviction for a crime that increases the hazard insured against, or gross negligence that increases the hazard insured against. Life and health policies can be canceled because of false statements made by the insured in the application, but cancellation can only take

Technology and Today's Paralegal

ONLINE RESOURCES CONCERNING INSURANCE CLAIMS

When a dispute arises between an insurance company and a policyholder regarding an insurance claim, attorneys are typically consulted to represent the parties. In these situations, paralegals fulfill many functions for both sides, including analyzing insurance policies, researching the facts involved in the policyholder's claim, and locating experts. Here, we provide some practical Internet resources to assist with these functions.

ANALYZING CLAUSES IN INSURANCE POLICIES

It is beneficial for paralegals who deal with insurance law to understand how to read and analyze an insurance policy. FindLaw offers "a step by step method that insurance professionals and attorneys use to analyze a policy" at **library.findlaw.com**; search for "Primer on Insurance Law." Insurance policies are sometimes written in terms that laypersons don't understand. A glossary of insurance terms is offered by the Insurance Information Institute (III) at **www.iii.org**.

INSURANCE COMPLAINTS AND INSURANCE FRAUD

A paralegal assisting a client with an insurance claim will sometimes need to research related complaints against the client's insurance company. The Web site of the National Association of Insurance Commissioners (NAIC) offers a good starting point for such research. NAIC's home page, at **www.naic.org**, furnishes an online fraud reporting system and links to state insurance department Web sites. Search under the "Industry" and the "Consumer" tabs for useful sources.

Paralegals sometimes assist clients who are dissatisfied with the claim payments offered by their insurance companies. A paralegal working with such a client may find helpful the many resources provided by the Fight Bad-Faith Insurance Companies (FBIC) Web site, at **www.badfaithinsurance.org**. FBIC posts a ranked list of the fifty worst bad faith insurers and the fifty best good faith insurers.

To assist in the prevention and discovery of fraudulent insurance claims, the Coalition Against Insurance Fraud (CAIF) presents many resources at **www.insurancefraud.org**. Through CAIF's Web site, you can access state regulations related to insurance fraud and links to many antifraud associations, state fraud bureaus, and investigation tools. CAIF also posts many statistical reports and research articles related to insurance fraud offenses.

LOCATING ADJUSTERS AND APPRAISERS

When a loss occurs and a policyholder files a claim, the policyholder's insurance company will often employ the services of an insurance adjuster. An insurance adjuster inspects the damaged property, analyzes the insurance policy, and estimates the amount of loss. Paralegals sometimes assist attorneys in locating adjusters. The National Association of Independent Insurance Adjusters (NAIIA) is an association of independently owned property and casualty claims adjusting companies that have been approved by insurance carriers. Through the NAIIA's Web site, **www.naiia.com**, a claim can be assigned to an NAIIA adjuster in your area. This Web site also offers many industry links. Another resource is the National Association of Public Insurance Adjusters (NAPIA), **www.napia. com**. This organization accredits public insurance adjusters, who are hired to assist consumers. The NAPIA Web site offers a search engine to locate local public insurance adjusters.

In the case of an automobile insurance claim, it may be beneficial to use the online appraiser locator available through the Independent Automotive Damage Appraisers (IADA) Web site at **www.iada.org**. IADA is an association of automotive appraisers organized to protect insurance consumers from overpaying for auto body repairs.

TECHNOLOGY TIP

As a paralegal, make a habit of browsing the additional links listed on the Web pages you use as resources. In doing so, you may find sources of information more suitable to your individual research needs.

place before the effective date of an incontestability clause. ◄ An insurer cannot cancel—or refuse to renew—a policy for discriminatory reasons or other reasons that violate public policy or because the insured has appeared as a witness in a case against the company.

Good Faith Obligations

Both parties to an insurance contract are responsible for the obligations that they assume under the contract. In addition, both the insured and the insurer have an implied duty to act in good faith. Good faith requires the party who is applying for insurance to reveal everything necessary for the insurer to evaluate the risk. In other words, the applicant must disclose all material facts, including all facts that an insurer would consider in determining whether to charge a higher premium or to refuse to issue a policy altogether. Once the insurer has accepted the risk, and some event occurs that gives rise to a claim, the insurer has a duty to investigate to determine the facts.

When a policy provides insurance against third party claims, the insurer is obligated to make reasonable efforts to settle such a claim. If a settlement cannot be reached, then regardless of the claim's merit, the insurer must defend any suit against the insured. Usually, a policy provides that in this situation the insured must cooperate. A policy provision may expressly require the insured to attend hearings and trials, to help in obtaining evidence and witnesses, and to assist in reaching a settlement.

Defenses against Payment

If an insurance company can show that a policy was obtained by fraud, it may have a valid defense for not paying on a claim. A defense also exists if the insurer can show that the insured lacked an insurable interest—thus rendering the policy void from the beginning. Improper actions, such as those that are against public policy or are otherwise illegal, can also give the insurance company a defense against the payment of a claim or allow it to rescind the contract.

An insurance company can be prevented from asserting some defenses that are normally available, however. ► **EXAMPLE 16.8** Suppose that a company tells an insured that information requested on a form is optional, and the insured provides it anyway. The company cannot use the information to avoid its contractual obligation under the insurance contract. Similarly, an insurance company normally cannot escape payment on the death of an insured on the ground that the person's age was stated incorrectly on the application. ◄

INSURANCE LAW AND THE PARALEGAL

Insurance is a pervasive aspect of American life. Nearly all citizens and businesses have insurance, often of several types. Naturally, it follows that many paralegals work with matters related to insurance law at least some of the time. If you work for a general law practice, you may assist in bringing a client's claim against an insurance company if the company refuses to pay the claim. Paralegal work relating to insurance may involve representing people who have been involved in auto accidents; those who have lost homes or property to fire, floods, hurricanes, or theft; people who receive medical disability coverage; or people who have recently lost loved ones.

A paralegal working for an insurance company may be asked to analyze current legislation, assist in drafting insurance policies or amendments to those policies, and investigate the facts behind claims filed by policyholders. A paralegal working for a real estate investment firm may analyze insurance policies related to commercial property investments. Additionally, a paralegal might work for a state insurance regulatory agency. In this context, a paralegal may assist in drafting administrative procedures, investigating insurance fraud and licensing issues, and responding to consumers' insurance claims and questions—such as claims for workers' compensation (to be discussed in Chapter 18).

Developing
Paralegal Skills

MEDICAL RECORDS

Derek Busset is a legal assistant for the small personal-injury firm of McNair and Iverson. Ralph McNair is handling a case in which Blanche Rosenthal's car was struck by an automobile driven by Daniel Gomez, who is insured by Reliable Insurance. The police report indicates that at the time of the accident, Gomez was speeding through a yellow light at the intersection when his car collided with Rosenthal's 2010 Cadillac, which had just entered the intersection on a green light. The insurance company has already compensated Rosenthal for the damage to her vehicle but disputes the amount she is claiming for medical bills. The insurance company believes that Rosenthal's back injury was a preexisting condition, not caused by the accident. After speaking with a representative from the insurance company, attorney McNair asks Derek to contact Rosenthal and acquire the medical records to support her claims. McNair also wants Derek to write up a summary of what the records show.

TIPS FOR OBTAINING AND EVALUATING MEDICAL RECORDS

- Find out from the client the names of all of the physicians who treated the client and the names of hospitals or other facilities in which the client received medical care.

- Prepare—and have the client sign—medical release forms, which authorize the treating physicians to provide the patient's medical records directly to the law firm.

- Keep a log of the records as they are received.

- If a claim involves the possibility of a preexisting condition, make certain to request the client's complete medical history (from before the injury as well as after it). You will need these records to determine whether a preexisting condition might have caused or contributed to the plaintiff's injury.

- Obtain a medical dictionary or reference book so that you can decipher the terminology and abbreviations frequently used by medical personnel in charts and records.

Paralegals who assist in insurance-related litigation involving torts will likely be involved in many of the same types of work that are required in the area of tort law (discussed in Chapter 14). Here is just a brief sampling of tasks related to insurance law that paralegals commonly manage:

- Research insurance clauses in relation to specific claims.

- Interact with experts, witnesses, and clients to obtain factual information about events giving rise to insurance claims.

- Work with representatives of an insurance company in defending an insured against a lawsuit brought against the insured.

- Obtain medical records concerning a client who needs assistance in obtaining payment from the insurer. (This involves issues covered in the *Developing Paralegal Skills* feature above.)

- Create, review, or prepare insurance application forms or insurance policies.

- Schedule medical appointments for health-insurance claimants.

KEY TERMS AND CONCEPTS

binder 544	eminent domain 530	joint tenancy 531
deed 535	fee simple 530	lease 536
easement 530	insurable interest 542	mortgage 534

Today's
Professional Paralegal

HANDLING AND AVOIDING MALPRACTICE CLAIMS

Delia Harmon works as a paralegal for the managing partner of Duke & Cruthers, LLP, a midsized law firm. The managing partner, Jeremy Wheaton, tells Delia that the partners are switching insurance companies for their malpractice insurance policy. The former company significantly increased its premium for malpractice coverage, and the partners decided that the firm could obtain similar coverage from another company at a much lower cost.

Jeremy hands the new policy to Delia and asks her to carefully review and then summarize in a memorandum the policy's major terms and conditions. Jeremy also hands Delia a handwritten list of ideas on how malpractice claims should be handled in the future and asks her to transform his notes into clear instructions to be included in the memorandum. Finally, Jeremy points out to Delia that the best way to handle malpractice claims is to avoid them to begin with. Jeremy asks Delia to draft a series of tips on this topic to include in the memorandum. "Can you finish this by tomorrow morning?" asks Jeremy. "I'd like to review it and have a final draft ready to circulate to the partners before I leave town tomorrow afternoon." "Well," responds Delia, "I could finish it by then if I could postpone the work on the research memorandum that I'm preparing for you on the *AlphaCom* case." Jeremy says that she can put off the *AlphaCom* case until the next day, so Delia clears her desk and starts reviewing the new malpractice policy.

DRAFTING THE MEMORANDUM

Once she has read the policy carefully, Delia begins to draft the memorandum to the partners. She summarizes the policy's terms and conditions in clear, concise language. Delia has had years of experience in reviewing and summarizing legal documents, so this part of the task comes easily for her. More difficult is trying to decipher Jeremy's handwritten notes on how the partners should handle malpractice claims. After she is certain that she understands Jeremy's thoughts on the matter, she creates a new subheading in the memorandum titled "How to Handle Malpractice Claims." Under the heading, she includes the following bulleted list:

personal property *530*

policy *539*

premium *539*

real property *530*

risk *539*

risk management *539*

tenancy in common *531*

underwriter *539*

CHAPTER SUMMARY

REAL PROPERTY AND INSURANCE LAW

Real Property

Real property (also called real estate or realty) includes land and all things attached to the land (such as buildings and plants), as well as subsurface and air rights. All other types of property, both tangible and intangible, are personal property.

- If a client brings a malpractice action, review the client's file immediately.

- Create a concise summary of the client's file so that you and the other partners can quickly review the nature of the client's case and the alleged basis for the client's claim of malpractice.

- Determine how the partners and the firm can best respond to the claim. At a minimum, check the statute of limitations for malpractice claims to see if the client's delay in bringing the claim could bar the action from the outset.

- If the claim is justified, determine whether the firm should offer to settle the claim out of court. If so, decide on the amount the firm should offer to the client in settlement.

- Promptly report the claim to the malpractice insurance carrier, to prevent the insurance company from later using any delay in reporting the claim as a defense against payment under the policy.

TIPS ON HOW TO AVOID MALPRACTICE CLAIMS

Delia then turns to what, for her, is the most difficult aspect of her task—thinking of suggestions for how the partners can avoid malpractice claims. Finally, she comes up with the following tips:

- Cultivate a good relationship with clients by being sensitive to their needs and dealing with those needs courteously and promptly. A satisfied client will not likely wish to bring a malpractice action.

- If you are too busy to communicate with clients on the progress of their cases, ask the paralegal who works with you to do this and help keep the communication channels open.

- Make sure that all significant communications with clients are in writing. This includes keeping a record of telephone conversations with clients. If questions arise later over what you did or did not say to a particular client on a specific matter, you can refer to your written notes.

- Before billing clients for overdue payments, try to wait until the statute of limitations on malpractice actions has passed. Then, if a client responds to the letter with a malpractice claim, it will have no legal effect.[a]

Delia can think of nothing more to say, so she prints out the draft of the memorandum and places it on Jeremy's desk for him to review the next morning.

---

a. The suggestions in this feature are based in part on a discussion of this topic in Abigail J. Gardner and Marcy L. Jankovich, "Avoiding Malpractice Claims," *Facts & Findings,* Vol. 32. No. 2 (August 2005), pp. 44–45.

1. *Ownership rights in property—*

   a. **FEE SIMPLE**—The most complete form of ownership, entitling the holder to use, possess, or dispose of the property however he or she chooses during his or her lifetime.

   b. **TENANCY IN COMMON**—Co-ownership in which each party owns an undivided interest in the property that passes to his or her heirs at death.

   c. **JOINT TENANCY**—Co-ownership in which each party owns an undivided interest in the property that automatically passes to the surviving joint tenant or tenants on his or her death.

   d. **LIFE ESTATE**—An interest in property that entitles a specified individual to possess, use, and benefit from the property for the duration of the person's life.

   e. **FUTURE INTEREST**—An interest in property that will arise in the future.

2. *The transfer and sale of real property—*Real property can be transferred as a gift, by inheritance, by lease, or by sale. Most of the time, real property is transferred by sale, which typically involves the following steps.

Continued

a. The buyer makes a purchase offer, often conditioned on obtaining financing, and pays an earnest money deposit.

b. If the seller accepts the offer, a contract is formed. Real estate agents may assist both the buyer and the seller in negotiating the terms.

c. An escrow agent acts as a neutral party in the transaction, holding the deed and any money paid by the buyer until the sale is completed.

d. Most buyers obtain a mortgage loan to finance the purchase. The holder of the mortgage then has a security interest in the property.

e. Often, the sale is contingent on certain inspections of the property.

f. A title examination is performed to ensure that the seller is actually the owner of the property and that no liens exist of which the buyer was not aware.

g. At the closing, the buyer signs the mortgage note (if the sale is financed), title insurance is obtained, the seller is paid the purchase price (less any closing costs), and the buyer is given the deed to the property.

3. *Leases*—The owner of real property (the lessor) may agree (contract) to rent the property out to another (the lessee) for a specified period of time. The lessee has the exclusive right to use the property. Leases are governed by contract law and by state statutes. Leases are usually in writing and must be written if the lease period exceeds one year. Commercial leases are usually more detailed than residential leases and contain more specialized terminology.

Insurance Law

1. *Classifications*—See Exhibit 16.6 on page 542.

2. *Terminology*—

   a. **POLICY**—The insurance contract.

   b. **PREMIUM**—The consideration paid to the insurer for the policy.

   c. **UNDERWRITER**—The insurance company.

   d. **INSURER**—The insurance company.

   e. **INSURED**—The person or property covered by the insurance.

   f. **INSURANCE AGENT**—A representative of the insurance company.

   g. **INSURANCE BROKER**—Ordinarily, an independent contractor.

   h. **BENEFICIARY**—A person to receive payment under the policy.

3. *Insurable interest*—An insurable interest exists whenever an individual or entity benefits from the preservation of the property to be insured or the continued health or life of the person to be insured.

4. *The insurance contract*—

   a. **LAWS GOVERNING**—The general principles of contract law are applied; the insurance industry is also regulated by the states.

   b. **APPLICATION**—An insurance applicant is bound by any false statements that appear in the application (subject to certain exceptions), which is part of the insurance contract. Misstatements or misrepresentations may be grounds for voiding the policy.

   c. **EFFECTIVE DATE**—Coverage on an insurance policy can begin when a binder (a written memorandum indicating that a formal policy is pending and stating its essential terms) is written; when the policy is issued; at the time of contract formation; or, depending on the terms of the contract, when certain conditions are met.

d. **PROVISIONS AND CLAUSES**—See Exhibit 16.7 on page 546. Words are given their ordinary meanings. Any ambiguity in the policy will be interpreted against the insurance company. When the written policy has not been delivered and it is unclear whether an insurance contract actually exists, the uncertainty will be resolved against the insurance company. The court will presume that the policy is in effect unless the company can show otherwise.

e. **DEFENSES AGAINST PAYMENT TO THE INSURED**—Defenses include fraud, lack of an insurable interest, and improper actions on the part of the insured.

STUDENT STUDYWARE™ CD-ROM

Interactive student CD in this book includes additional quizzing, plus video clips, case studies, and Key Terms flashcards.

ONLINE COMPANION™

For additional resources, please go to **www.paralegal.delmar.cengage.com**.

QUESTIONS FOR REVIEW

1. What is the difference between real property and personal property? What is a fee simple? What are some other ways in which ownership rights in property can be held?

2. What law governs the sale of real property? Describe the basic steps involved in the sale of real estate.

3. What are some classifications of insurance? What is an insurable interest? What is required for someone to have an insurable interest in property? In another's life?

4. What is the difference between an insurance agent and an insurance broker? Why is this difference significant for people seeking insurance coverage?

ETHICAL QUESTION

1. Joanne Dorman, a paralegal, works in the claims department of an automobile insurance company. One day, she is asked to review a claim brought by Derek Farmer, her nephew. Joanne's sister (Derek's mother) mentioned to Joanne that Derek broke his windshield recently when he accidentally ran into a mailbox beside the road leading to their rural home. In the claim that she is reviewing, however, Derek states that a rock hit his windshield. Joanne understands immediately what Derek is trying to do. Derek's policy states that his collision coverage (which would apply to the mailbox accident) has a $500 deductible. His comprehensive coverage (which would apply if a rock had hit his windshield) has a deductible of only $50. Derek is obviously trying to avoid having to pay the full $500 deductible. Joanne knows that Derek is a struggling college student with few financial resources. In contrast, the insurance company is a national entity that could easily absorb the extra cost. What should Joanne do in this situation?

PRACTICE QUESTIONS AND ASSIGNMENTS

1. Review the diagram in Exhibit 16.3 on page 534. Explain the triangular relationship among the parties to an escrow agreement, and explain each party's responsibility.

2. Using the material presented in Exhibit 16.4 on page 536, "A Sample Deed," and the following facts, draft a deed to real property.

- At a closing on January 22, 2011, Robert Smith and Sally Smith, husband and wife, of 987 Packard Street, Austin, Texas, transfer their summer cottage to John and William Jones, brothers, for consideration of $250,000.00 cash. John Jones lives at 10101 Summit Place, New City, Texas. William Jones's address is 99901 Hill Street, Casper, Texas. The Jones brothers will own the cottage as tenants in common.

- The legal description of the property is Lot 91 of Whiteacre Subdivision, Amarillo County, Texas, according to the plat map contained in volume 89, pages 123–129, of the Plat Records of Amarillo County, Texas.

- The conveyance with a warranty is expressly made subject to the Easements and Restrictions of Record in volume 7877, page 456, and volume 9988, page 431, of the Real Property Records of Amarillo County, Texas, and to any other restrictions and easements affecting the property that are of record in Amarillo County, Texas.

- The notary public who will acknowledge the deed is Rosemary Potter, and her commission expires January 31, 2013.

3. Identify the types of ownership rights described in the following statements.

a. John and Linda, a brother and a sister, jointly own a cottage that they inherited from their mother. They have rights of survivorship.

b. Jeannette conveys her beachfront property to her mother for as long as her mother lives. On her mother's death, the property is to go to Jeannette's daughter.

c. Louise Winter owns her home, and she can use, possess, or dispose of it as she pleases. On Louise's death, the property will descend to her heirs.

d. John Tully and Sam Marsh jointly own a large farm in Iowa. If either of them dies, the heirs of the deceased owner will inherit that owner's share of the farm.

4. Identify the following steps in a real estate sales transaction:

a. An offer or counteroffer is accepted.

b. Title to the property is reviewed to determine the seller's ownership interest and to determine if any liens against the property exist.

c. The escrow agent transfers the deed to the buyer and the proceeds of the sale to the seller to complete the sale.

d. The buyer tenders a sum of money, along with the offer.

QUESTIONS FOR CRITICAL ANALYSIS

1. Why is property ownership described as a "bundle of rights"? What is one called who owns the entire bundle? Is it ever possible to own less than the entire bundle? How? Give an example. Is it possible to share the bundle of rights? How? Give examples.

2. Assume that John submits an offer to Lisa to purchase Lisa's home for $300,000. Lisa responds to John's offer with a counteroffer: she will sell John her home for $325,000. John then offers to purchase the home for $325,000, and Lisa accepts the offer. In each of these transactions, who is the offeror, and who is the offeree? At what point is a contract for the sale of the home formed?

3. "When people obtain insurance to protect them against certain risks, they become more careless with respect to protecting against those risks themselves." Do you agree with this statement? Why or why not?

4. Statistics show that the extent of risk assumed by insurance companies varies depending on the gender of the insured. Many people contend that laws prohibiting gender-based insurance rates are thus fundamentally unfair. Do you agree with this contention? Explain your reasoning.

PROJECT

1. Locate a homeowners' or renters' insurance policy. Find the effective date, and determine whether a binder was initially issued. Also, try to locate coinsurance, cancellation, appraisal, antilapse, and multiple insurance clauses. Note that not all policies have the same coverage, so it is possible that not all of these clauses will be present in the insurance policy. Write a one-page description of the clauses that are included in the policy, including the effective date.

USING INTERNET RESOURCES

1. Go to the Web site of the Insurance Information Institute at **www.iii.org**. Follow the links to auto, home, and business insurance. Browse through the information given for each of these areas and then answer the following questions:

   a. What six types of coverage may be included in a basic auto policy?

   b. What is comprehensive coverage? What types of losses does this coverage protect against? What is uninsured or underinsured motorist coverage, and when does it come into play?

   c. What is covered by a standard homeowners' insurance policy? In the context of homeowners' insurance, what does liability coverage protect against?

   d. What two types of renters' insurance policies can be purchased? What is the difference between these two types of policies with respect to coverage? What is a floater policy?

   e. What does a business owner's insurance policy cover? What is business interruption insurance?

   f. What types of disasters typically are not covered by business (property) insurance?

FAMILY LAW
AND ESTATES

CHAPTER OUTLINE

Introduction

Family Law

Wills, Trusts, and Estates

AFTER COMPLETING THIS CHAPTER, YOU WILL KNOW:

▶ The legal rights and obligations of parents and children.

▶ How marital property and debts are divided when a marriage is dissolved.

▶ What estate planning is and why it is important.

▶ The various devices that are used in estate planning.

▶ The requirements for a valid will and the laws that govern property distribution when a person dies without a valid will.

INTRODUCTION

Most marriages are happy events, but about 40 percent of first marriages end in divorce. An even higher percentage of subsequent marriages end in divorce, so that about half of all marriages are terminated. When divorce happens, the parties fall under what is referred to as *family law,* the subject of the first part of this chapter. There is property to be distributed at the end of a marriage. Matters can be complicated by issues regarding child custody, child support, and alimony. Such complications can lead to ongoing conflicts that involve legal support.

Whether property is distributed before or during a marriage, or when one ends, property must be transferred when a person dies. For that reason, the laws governing the succession of property are a necessary extension to the laws concerning the ownership of property. In the latter part of the chapter, we examine various legal devices (procedures or techniques), including wills and trusts, that are often used to transfer a person's real and personal property, or *estate,* after death.

FAMILY LAW

Marriage, divorce, adoption, child support and custody, child and spousal abuse, and parental rights and duties are all areas of family law. Much of the legal work relating to family law has to do with marriage dissolution. Marriage is a status conferred by state law. Thus, when marriage ends, the state, through the court system, must become involved. Because of the high divorce rate in this country, many attorneys and paralegals deal with divorce cases. Such cases may include child-support and child-custody issues. In addition, the property owned by a divorcing couple must be divided between the spouses. In this section, you will read about some important legal concepts and doctrines governing family matters, including the matters surrounding marriage dissolution. (For a discussion of the important role that paralegals can play in the area of family law, see this chapter's *Featured Contributor* article on the following page.)

Marriage Requirements

Despite the fact that many couples today live together (cohabit) without marrying, most Americans do marry at least once during their lifetimes. Marriage confers certain legal and practical advantages. The marriage establishes the rights and duties of the spouses, as well as of any children born during the marriage. Married couples may also have an easier time obtaining insurance and credit and adopting children. Additionally, many companies offer health insurance to spouses but not to unmarried partners.

States place some limitations on who can marry. The betrothed must be man and woman (except in a few states, as you will read shortly), currently unmarried, not closely related by blood, and over a certain age—usually eighteen years. State laws vary, and some states prohibit marriage between those who are closely related even if the relation is only by marriage. Persons who are under the required age can marry with parental consent or if they are emancipated from their parents. **Emancipation** normally occurs when a child leaves home to support himself or herself. Below a certain age, such as fourteen or sixteen, marriage may be absolutely prohibited by state law except with court approval.

Procedural Requirements

Certain procedures are generally required for a legally recognized marriage to take place. The parties must first obtain a *marriage license* from the state government, usually through the county clerk's office. About half of the states also require a *blood test* to check for certain diseases. Some states require couples to go through a short *waiting period* before getting the license or between the time of acquiring the license and getting married.

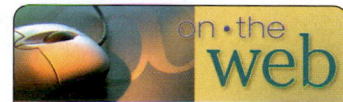

Links to many family law resources, as well as good coverage of several issues, can be found at **www.familylaw.org** and **www.abanet.org** (in the "Search" box, select "Topics A–Z," and then select "Family Law, Section of").

emancipation

The legal relinquishment by a child's parents or guardian of the legal right to exercise control over the child. Usually, a child who moves out of the parents' home and supports himself or herself is considered emancipated.

featured contributor

PARALEGALS IN FAMILY LAW PRACTICE

Nancy R. Gallo

BIOGRAPHICAL NOTE

Nancy R. Gallo is a professor and the coordinator of legal studies programs at Sussex County Community College in Newton, New Jersey. She is also the author of the textbook Introduction to Family Law *(2004) and a frequent public speaker. A* cum laude *graduate of William Paterson University, Gallo was formerly a paralegal. She received her J.D. from Nova Southeastern University and is now licensed to practice law in both Florida and New Jersey. She has volunteered as an early-settlement panel member for the Sussex County Superior Court, and her practice has included family mediation. Gallo is a member of the Family Law Syllabus Task Force (2003) of the American Association for Paralegal Education, the Family Law Section of the American Bar Association, and the Elder Law Section of the New Jersey Bar.*

An interesting development of late-twentieth-century legal practice was the creation of the *boutique* law firm. Boutique legal practices left behind the concept of a lone general practitioner handling the A to Z of a client's legal issues and instead moved toward the goal of having individual attorneys and their paralegals become specialists in one or two areas of practice. Family law is a good example of an area of the law that has flourished under specialist experts. Paralegals in this area are integral team members working with their employers toward a common goal of building and maintaining a respected and lucrative legal practice. Indeed, a new client's first contact with a law firm may be with one of the firm's paralegals. This is a very important first step in client relations, because there is a lot of truth in the maxim, "There's no second chance to make a good first impression."

The most typical comment about a family law practice is that there seldom is a typical day. Indeed, paralegals working with family law practitioners will find themselves dealing with cases reflecting a wide range of human experiences. Such a practice very often delves into a client's most personal issues. For example, a family law practice may involve the seemingly convoluted machinations

> *"The most typical comment about a family law practice is that there seldom is a typical day."*

of divorce and separation or the necessity of filing a restraining order. The drafting of prenuptial agreements, settlement agreements, and adoption paperwork may all occur in a typical day.

The statistical truth is that today, in the United States, about half of all marriages end in divorce. The high divorce rate may be good for business, but attorneys and paralegals practicing family law, more than those in most other areas of the law, must balance the client's legal needs with sensitivity to the client's emotional state. A well-trained paralegal can have a vital and important role in assisting the attorney with this dual responsibility. In fact, a paralegal may often be a client's closest link to a law firm during a very emotional time. The special emotional needs of family law clients will often inspire a paralegal to call on previously unknown reserves of patience and sensitivity.

One thing that is absolutely true is that law firms handling matters involving family law will heavily depend on paralegals to soothe often agitated clients and to keep a virtual mountain of paperwork moving efficiently. Paralegal work in a family law practice is seldom dull, usually involves very personal relationships with clients, and can result in life-changing benefits to clients. One cannot say that about too many areas of the law.

In most states, some form of *marriage ceremony* is also required. The parties must present the license to someone authorized by the state to perform marriages, such as a justice of the peace, a judge, or a member of the clergy. The marriage ceremony must involve a public statement of the agreement to marry. After the ceremony, the *marriage license must be recorded.*

Same-Sex Couples

One of the most controversial family law topics today involves the ability of gay or lesbian couples to marry. Many states expressly prohibit such marriages. In 2004, Massachusetts became the first state in which the law allowed same-sex marriages. Connecticut followed in 2008, as did Vermont, Maine, and New Hampshire in 2009.

In addition, some states have passed laws allowing same-sex couples to form "civil unions" or "domestic partnerships." For example, New Jersey has allowed civil unions since 2007 and Oregon has allowed domestic partnerships since 2008. Like a marriage, these include the right to inherit a partner's property, to divorce, to be granted child custody, to receive alimony or child support, and to decide on medical treatment for an incapacitated partner.

Common Law Marriages

A **common law marriage** is one in which the parties become married solely by mutual consent and without a license or ceremony. At one time, common law marriages were frequent. Today, in the United States, only fifteen states and the District of Columbia recognize common law marriage.

There are four general requirements for a common law marriage. The parties (1) must be eligible to marry, (2) must have a present and continuing intention and agreement to be husband and wife, (3) must live together as husband and wife, and (4) must hold themselves out to the public as husband and wife. Note that cohabitation alone does not normally produce a common law marriage. The parties must additionally *hold themselves out to others as husband and wife.*

Once a couple is legally regarded as married, they have all of the rights and obligations of a traditionally married couple—including the obligation to support each other and their children. Furthermore, while most states do not recognize common law marriages, they acknowledge the validity of a common law marriage that was formed in one of the states that do permit common law marriages. Once a couple is regarded as married by common law, they must obtain a court decree to dissolve the marriage.

> **common law marriage**
> A marriage that is formed solely by mutual consent and without a marriage license or ceremony. The couple must be eligible to marry, must have a present and continuing agreement to be husband and wife, must live together as husband and wife, and must hold themselves out to the public as husband and wife. Only fifteen states recognize common law marriages.

Marital Duties

In the old days, marriages were arranged between families through private contracts. Part of the contractual arrangement was that the husband would support and provide for his wife and children. The wife, in turn, had certain duties in the home. Although we still hear the term *marriage contract,* in fact, marriage represents a special type of contract that is governed not by contract law but by the state. In the United States, each state has laws that govern marriage and divorce and establish the spousal obligations of married partners.

Financial Support

Generally, spouses are allowed to arrange their own affairs however they see fit. Nonetheless, the law still holds that one spouse has a duty to support the other spouse and children financially by providing such basics as food, shelter, and medical care—insofar as the spouse is able to do so. In many states, this duty lasts throughout the marriage, even if the spouses are living apart. Failure to provide support for a child may be a criminal violation. Additional duties may be created by a separate agreement between the spouses.

Spousal Abuse

Each state creates its own definition of domestic violence through legislation and court decisions. In all states, however, it is a criminal act to batter a spouse. Unlawful abuse has been extended to include extreme cases of harassment (such as stalking) and threats of physical beating or confinement. In some cases, an emergency restraining order may be necessary. A **restraining order** is a court order that requires one person (such as an abusing spouse) to stay away from another (such as the victim of spousal abuse). Shelters are available to assist abused spouses.

Parental Rights and Obligations

Legally, a child is defined as an unmarried minor (under the age of eighteen) who is not emancipated. Prior to a child's emancipation, parents have certain rights of control over the child. Parents can direct the upbringing of their children and control where they live, what school they attend, and even what religion they practice. Parents also generally control the medical care to be given, although a parent's refusal to provide for such care in life-threatening situations (usually for religious reasons) can be a crime. Parents have broad legal authority to control the behavior of their children and even physically punish them—so long as the punishment does not constitute child abuse (to be discussed shortly).

Parents also have obligations toward their children. Parents must provide food, shelter, clothing, medical care, and other necessities. Parents must also ensure that their children attend school (normally until the age of sixteen or eighteen). If a couple is married, the law presumes that any newborn child was fathered by the husband, and the husband must support the child unless he can prove that he is not the biological father. (Some states do not allow the husband an opportunity to prove his lack of paternity, however.) Although parental duties to a child generally end when the child reaches the age of eighteen, these duties may continue for a longer period if the child is seriously disabled.

Liability for Children's Wrongful Acts

Generally, parents are not liable for the wrongful actions of their children, *unless the actions result from the parents' negligence.* ▶ **EXAMPLE 17.1** Vanessa Purdy permits her fourteen-year-old son, Jeremy, to drive the family car to the grocery store by himself, without supervision, although he has no driver's license. En route to the store, Jeremy causes an accident in which Thomas Boone, a passenger in the other car, is seriously injured. Boone would probably succeed in a negligence suit against Vanessa Purdy in this situation. ◀

Child Abuse and Neglect

All states allow parents to physically punish their children within reason. A parent, for example, may slap or spank a child without violating the laws prohibiting child abuse. Some states allow corporal (physical) punishment in the schools (under the doctrine of *in loco parentis,* or "in the place of the parents"). In all states, however, laws prohibit sexual molestation and extreme punishment of children by anyone. For punishment to constitute physical child abuse, the punishment normally must result in injuries—such as broken skin or bones, excessive bruising, or swelling.

Child neglect is also a form of child abuse. Child neglect occurs when parents or legal guardians fail to provide for a child's basic needs, such as food, shelter, clothing, and medical treatment. Child abuse may even extend to emotional abuse, as when a person publicly humiliates a child in an extreme way.

Children Born out of Wedlock

A large number of children are born to unmarried parents, and the law provides rights and protections for these children. One important right is the right of the child to be supported by the biological father. The biological father has a legal obligation to provide support for the child that is identical to that of a married father. The obligation usually lasts until the child is no longer a minor. The mother's subsequent marriage to another man does not necessarily extinguish the obligation of the biological father to support the child. In most states, the eventual marriage of the parents of a child born out of wedlock "legitimizes" the child.

Paternity Suits.　An unmarried mother may file a **paternity suit** to establish that a certain person is the biological father of her child. If the unwed mother is on public-welfare assistance, the government may file a paternity suit on the mother's behalf to obtain reimbursement for welfare payments given to the mother. Fathers may also file paternity actions in order to obtain visitation rights or custody of the child. The paternity of a child can be proved scientifically. DNA testing or comparable procedures that check for genetic factors can determine, with almost 100 percent accuracy, whether a person parented a particular child.

Inheritance Rights.　Under the common law, a child born out of wedlock (an illegitimate child) had no right to inherit. Today, inheritance laws governing illegitimate children vary from state to state. Generally, an illegitimate child is treated as the child of the mother and can inherit from her and her relatives. The child is usually not regarded as the legal child of the father unless paternity is established through some legal proceeding. Many state statutes permit the illegitimate child to inherit from the father if paternity has been established prior to the father's death. Even if paternity has been established, however, the illegitimate child will not necessarily have inheritance rights identical to those of legitimate children. Generally, the courts have upheld state probate statutes that discriminate between legitimate and illegitimate children for valid state purposes.

Adoption

In contrast to children born out of wedlock, adopted children normally have the same legal rights as the biological children of a married couple, including the right to inherit property from their adoptive parents on the parents' death. **Adoption** is a procedure in which persons become the legal parents of a child who is not their biological child. Once an adoption is formally completed, the adoptive parents have all the responsibilities of biological parents. Should they divorce, each adoptive parent has all the child-support obligations of a biological parent. Note that adoption is not the same as **foster care**, which is a temporary arrangement in which a family is paid by the state to care for a child for a limited period of time, often pending adoption.

Requirements for Adoptions

Adoptions are governed by state laws, and these laws vary substantially from state to state. Generally, however, there are three minimum requirements for an adoption to be legal. First, the child's biological parents must give up their legal rights (either by consent, by death, or by order of the court). The adopting parents must then follow all procedures required by the state in which the adoption occurs. Finally, the adoption must be formally approved by a judge. There may be additional requirements in specific circumstances. For example, adopting a child above a certain age generally requires the child's official consent.

All states permit single persons to adopt children, but married couples are generally preferred. Although some courts have approved adoptions by same-sex couples, generally such couples find it difficult to adopt children. Several states have enacted laws that explicitly prohibit same-sex couples from adopting children.

Agency Adoptions

Adoption is often carried out through social-service agencies that are licensed by the state to place children for adoption. The biological parents terminate their parental rights, essentially giving up these rights to the agency and authorizing

paternity suit

A lawsuit brought by an unmarried mother to establish that a certain person is the biological father of her child. DNA testing or a comparable procedure is often used to determine paternity.

adoption

A procedure in which persons become the legal parents of a child who is not their biological child.

foster care

A temporary arrangement in which a family is paid by the state to care for a child for a limited period of time, often pending adoption.

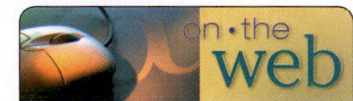

Information on adoption laws and links to state statutes can be found at **www. law.cornell.edu**. Select "All topics" from the "Law about . . ." menu, and then select "Adoption." A discussion of international adoption can be found at **adoption.state.gov**.

the agency to find legal parents for their child. Traditionally, in agency adoptions, the identities of the biological and the adoptive parents were kept confidential. Increasingly, though, state laws are allowing for the disclosure of this information in certain circumstances. In some states, for instance, if an adopted child wants to meet with his or her birth parent or vice versa, the court will contact the child or parent to see if he or she will agree to such a meeting.

Independent Adoptions

Prospective adoptive parents may also pursue independent adoption. An **independent adoption** is one that is arranged privately, as when a physician, lawyer, or other person puts a couple seeking to adopt a child in contact with a pregnant woman who has decided to give up her child for adoption. These parties make their own private arrangements. Usually, the adopting parents pay for the legal and medical expenses associated with the childbirth and adoption. The intermediary may also receive a fee. Because this method of adoption has the potential for abuse, it is prohibited by most states.

Stepparent Adoptions

Many adoptions today are stepparent adoptions, which occur when a married partner adopts his or her spouse's children from a former marriage. Usually, in such adoptions, the parental rights of the children's other biological parent are terminated either by consent or through a court proceeding.

Court Approval and Probation

All adoptions must be approved in court. The primary standard for approving an adoption is the "best interests of the child." Because this standard is so vague, the courts have a great deal of leeway in deciding whether to place children with prospective adoptive parents. The court considers the financial resources of the adopting parents, their family stability and home environment, their ages, their religious and racial compatibility, and other factors relevant to the child's future health and welfare.

After the adoption, many states place the new parents on "probation" for a time—usually from six months to one year. The agency or court appoints an individual to monitor developments in the home to ensure that the adoptive parents are caring appropriately for the child's well-being. If not, the child may be removed and returned to an agency for placement in another home.

Marriage Termination

A marriage can only be terminated by the state. In other words, even though partners want to end their marriage, and even though they separate and live apart, they will continue to have the legal rights and obligations of spouses until their marriage is legally terminated. There are two ways in which a marriage can be terminated: by annulment or by divorce.

Annulment

An **annulment** is a court decree that invalidates (nullifies) a marriage. This means that the marriage was never effective in the first place. Today, annulments are not common. Many seeking annulments do so because their religion does not condone divorce. In such situations, an annulment allows a subsequent marriage to be recognized as valid in the eyes of the church.

An annulment may be granted on various grounds. For example, lack of genuine consent, fraud, and bigamy may be grounds for annulment. **Bigamy** is the act of marrying one person while already legally married to another.

Even though the marriage is deemed invalid, children born during the marriage are considered legitimate in the eyes of the law. Also, as in a divorce, when a

independent adoption
A privately arranged adoption, as when a doctor, lawyer, or other person puts a couple seeking to adopt a child in contact with a pregnant woman who has decided to give up her child for adoption.

annulment
A court decree that invalidates (nullifies) a marriage. Although the marriage itself is deemed nonexistent, children of a marriage that is annulled are deemed legitimate.

bigamy
The act of entering into marriage with one person while still legally married to another.

marriage is annulled, issues involving child support, spousal support, child custody, and property settlement must be decided by the couple or by the court.

Divorce

The most common way to end a marriage is divorce. A **divorce** is a formal court proceeding that legally dissolves a marriage. Divorce laws vary among the states, with some states having simpler divorce procedures than others.

> **divorce**
> A formal court proceeding that legally dissolves a marriage.

Fault-Based versus No-Fault Divorces. Until the 1960s, to obtain a divorce a petitioning party had to allege reasons for the divorce—such as adultery, desertion, cruelty, or abuse—that were acceptable grounds for divorce under state law. This is called *fault-based divorce*. Unless the petitioning party could prove that his or her partner was "at fault" for the breakdown of the marriage in one of these ways, a divorce would not be granted. Eventually, changing economic and social conditions in America led to new attitudes toward divorce, which resulted in less stringent requirements for divorce. Thus arose the **no-fault divorce**—a divorce in which neither party is deemed to be at fault for the breakdown of the marriage.

> **no-fault divorce**
> A divorce in which neither party is deemed to be at fault for the breakdown of the marriage.

Today, all states allow no-fault divorces. Generally, a no-fault divorce may be based on one of three grounds:

- Irreconcilable differences (the most common ground).
- Living separately for a period of time specified by state statute (ranging from six months to three years).
- Incompatibility.

No-fault divorces effectively make it impossible for one spouse to prevent a divorce desired by the other. Even in no-fault divorces, however, fault may be taken into consideration by the court in determining a couple's property settlement or spousal support arrangements.

The majority of the states permit *both* fault-based and no-fault divorces. Sometimes, a party may seek a fault-based divorce in an attempt to gain a more favorable property settlement (to be discussed shortly) than he or she could get in a no-fault divorce.

Divorce Procedures. The first step in obtaining a divorce is to file a **petition for divorce** with the appropriate state court. Although the form and content of the petition vary, generally the petition includes:

> **petition for divorce**
> The document filed with the court to initiate divorce proceedings. The requirements governing the form and content of a divorce petition vary from state to state.

- The names and addresses of both spouses.
- The date and place of their marriage.
- The names and addresses of any minor children and whether the wife is currently pregnant.
- The reasons for the divorce.
- A summary of any arrangements made by the divorcing couple as to support, custody, or visitation.
- The relief sought.

The petition is served on the other spouse, who must file an answer to the petition within the number of days specified by state law. If the couple cannot agree on certain matters while the divorce is pending—such as who obtains custody of the children or who pays the mortgage—the court will hold a hearing to decide which partner should assume what responsibilities temporarily. Unless the case is settled through mediation or negotiation, a trial will be conducted, and the judge will decide the terms of the parties' final divorce decree.

Negotiation and Mediation. Very few divorces actually go to trial. Usually, the parties settle their differences prior to trial—though often only after lengthy negotiations,

A divorcing couple meet with a mediator in an attempt to resolve their dispute over child-custody arrangements. Couples are often required to mediate their disputes before being allowed to litigate them in court. What are the benefits of such mediation?

(Courtesy of © image 100 ltd.)

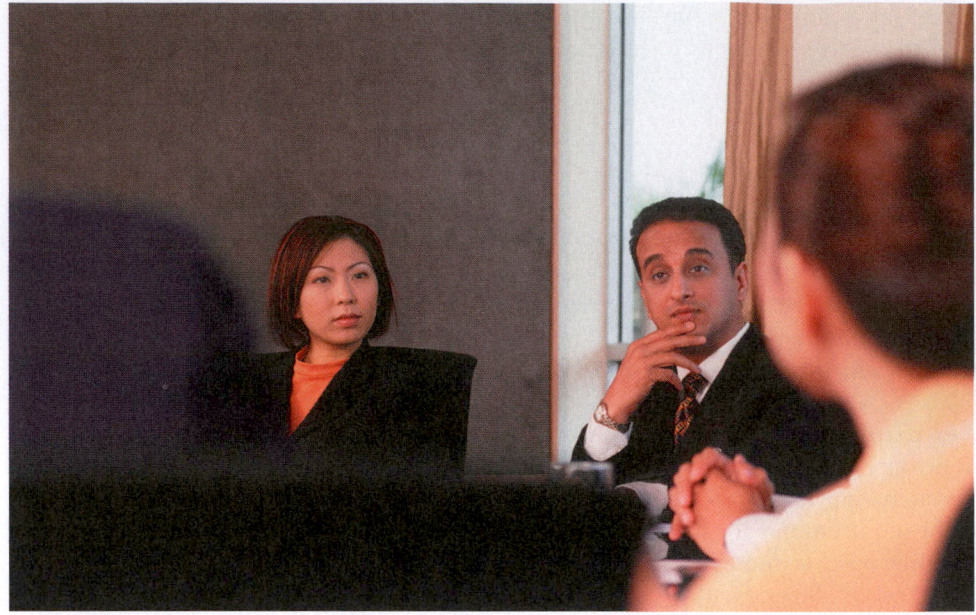

which are facilitated by their attorneys. If the parties agree to a settlement concerning contested issues, the agreement will be put in writing and presented to the court for its approval.

Divorcing spouses increasingly use mediation to settle disagreements, and in many states, mediation is mandatory in divorce cases. The mediator typically meets with the parties in the absence of lawyers and tries to guide the parties into agreeing on a mutually satisfactory settlement. As we noted in Chapter 6, some paralegals are trained mediators and conduct mediation proceedings.

Child Custody

In many divorces, the issue of child custody—the right to live with and to care for the children on an everyday basis—is the most contentious issue to be resolved. In some cases, a court may appoint a guardian *ad litem* for the child. A **guardian *ad litem*** is a person appointed by the court (often an attorney) to represent the interests of a child or a mentally incompetent person before the court.

guardian *ad litem*
A person appointed by the court to represent the interests of a child or a mentally incompetent person before the court.

Factors Considered in Determining Child Custody

Traditionally, the mother almost always received child custody. Mothers still usually receive primary custody, but courts now explicitly consider a number of factors when awarding custody. These factors include the following:

- The nature of the relationship and emotional ties with each parent.
- The ability of each parent to provide for the child's needs and education and each parent's interest in doing so.
- The ability of each parent to provide a stable environment for the child.
- The mental and physical health of each parent.
- The wishes of the child—especially older children.

In determining custody, courts may also consider other relevant factors, such as whether one parent is a smoker. Custodial arrangements are not permanent and may be changed by a court in view of the parents' changing circumstances.

Types of Custodial Arrangements

The parent who has **legal custody** of a child has the right to make major decisions about the child's life without consulting the other parent. Often, the parent who has legal custody also has physical custody.

legal custody
Custody of a child that confers on the parent the right to make major decisions about the child's life without consulting the other parent.

Many states now provide for **joint custody**—shared custody—of the children of divorcing parents. Joint *legal* custody means that both parents together make major decisions about the child. Some procedure, such as mediation, is usually available in the event of disagreement. In some states, including California, mediation is mandatory in child-custody disputes. Joint legal custody may also involve joint *physical* custody, in which both parents maintain a home for the child and have physical custody of the child for roughly comparable time periods. Joint physical custody usually works best if both parents live in the same school district or if the child attends a private school to which both parents have access.

Grandparents can petition the court to obtain custody of their grandchildren as well. In some situations, such as when a parent is disabled or when parents are not taking proper care of their children, a court may decide that grandparents should be granted custody.

> **joint custody**
> Custody of a child that is shared by the parents following the termination of a marriage.

Visitation Rights

Typically, the noncustodial parent receives **visitation rights**—the right to have contact with the child. The parent may get to spend weekends, holidays, or other time periods with the child. The times and duration of the noncustodial parent's visits are often stated in the divorce settlement, and state statutes may set standards. In some situations, the court may order supervised visitation to ensure the child's safety. This means that the noncustodial parent's visits will take place in the presence of a third party. Only in extreme situations—such as when child abuse is involved—will a court completely deny visitation rights to the noncustodial parent.

In most states, courts can grant visitation rights to grandparents, although these laws vary from state to state. Many such laws require the visitation to be in the best interest of the child, and many require the grandparent to have an established relationship with the child. If the state's requirements are met, a court may set a schedule specifying the time that grandchildren are to spend with their grandparents.

> **visitation rights**
> The right of a noncustodial parent to have contact with his or her child. Grandparents and stepparents may also be given visitation rights.

Child Support

Regardless of the custody arrangements, a court must make some provision for **child support**—the financial support necessary to provide for the child's needs. States now have official, standardized guidelines determining child-support duties. These guidelines are often percentage formulas based on parental income. Judges must follow the guidelines, unless special circumstances justify a departure or the parents agree to a different arrangement. A child with a disability, for example, may require more support than provided for under the guidelines. Child-support orders may be revised and adjusted according to the changing needs of the child and incomes of the parents.

> **child support**
> The financial support necessary to provide for a child's needs. Commonly, when a marriage is terminated, the non-custodial spouse agrees or is required by the court to make child-support payments to the custodial spouse.

Withholding Payment

It is a common misconception that if one former spouse fails to meet his or her obligations under a divorce settlement or other court order (such as by withholding visitation rights), the other party can withhold payment of child support. Child support is a court order—it cannot be withheld because a former spouse does something that the other former spouse does not like. (Similarly, a parent cannot withhold visitation rights because the other parent did not pay support.)

Interstate Enforcement of Child Support Decrees

We discussed uniform laws in Chapter 5. One such law, the Uniform Interstate Family Support Act, has been adopted by every state to help deal with the problem of nonpayment of child support by a parent who has moved to another state. Every state agrees to respect and enforce child-support orders entered by the court of the child's home state. Only the law of the state in which the child and the parent have been living will govern issues regarding child support, so a parent cannot escape

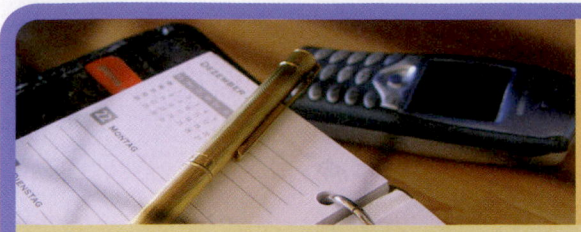

In the **Office**

PROTECTING CLIENT INFORMATION AND CLIENT INTERESTS

Paralegals who specialize in divorce law normally have frequent contact with divorcing clients. If you are a specialist in this area, you will probably come to know some of your clients quite well. You will also probably learn all kinds of information from them—about their lives, their spouses, and other things. What do you do with this information? Do you make a note of everything that a client tells you? Do you only record what you think is relevant to the case? How do you decide what is or is not relevant?

Many paralegals have solved this problem by taking thorough notes during interviews and writing notes after casual conversations with clients. Some paralegals even tape-record interviews. What seems irrelevant now may, in light of later developments, be very relevant. If you keep good notes on a case and review the notes as the case progresses, you can help to ensure that your supervising attorney will know the desires of the client.

that obligation by moving to a state with more lenient rules. The act also allows the parent who is supposed to receive the child-support payments to get the employer of the other parent to withhold payments from the other parent's paycheck for the benefit of the child.

Spousal Support

In some situations, a divorce decree may also require that one spouse provide for the other spouse's support. **Alimony** (sometimes called *maintenance*) is financial support paid to a former spouse. Historically, the husband was the wage earner and was expected to pay alimony to his former wife so that she could maintain her standard of living. Today, the law governing alimony has changed significantly, largely because so many couples are both income earners.

Alimony may be permanent or temporary. If a court orders one spouse to pay *permanent alimony* to the other, the alimony must be paid until the former spouse receiving the alimony remarries or dies (unless the court modifies the order for some reason). A more common form of alimony is temporary. This *rehabilitative alimony* is designed to provide ex-spouses with the education, training, or job experience necessary to support themselves. In deciding whether rehabilitative alimony is appropriate, a court usually considers the recipient's prospects of developing a new career. If the recipient is relatively advanced in age, for example, the court may grant permanent rather than rehabilitative alimony.

The amount of alimony awarded usually depends on the specific circumstances of the parties—their age, education, and incomes, for example. In about half the states, courts may also consider the reason for the divorce. If one party was more responsible than the other for the breakdown of the marriage, the alimony paid by that spouse might be higher than it would otherwise have been. Courts will also consider whether one spouse supported the other through college or graduate school in determining alimony awards. In some states, even if two people who have been living together never married, one of the partners may be awarded support payments, sometimes called *palimony,* after the couple breaks up.

alimony

Financial support paid to a former spouse after a marriage has been terminated. The alimony may be permanent or temporary (rehabilitative).

Developing Paralegal Skills

PREPARING FOR PROPERTY-SETTLEMENT NEGOTIATIONS

Lea, a paralegal, works for a small law firm that specializes in family law matters. One of the firm's clients, Mrs. Clark, is seeking a divorce. Tomorrow, her husband and his attorney will meet with Mrs. Clark and Lea's supervising attorney to negotiate a property settlement. Lea is preparing a settlement-agreement checklist for the attorney to take to the settlement meeting.

Lea makes a list of all of the property owned by the Clarks, along with the value of each item and outstanding liens (legal claims—to satisfy debts, for example) on the property. She also leaves blanks after "H" for husband and "W" for wife. After the parties agree to how they will divide the property, the attorney can fill in the appropriate amounts. Lea also includes a list of the debts owed by the Clarks. Again, she leaves blanks so that the attorney can write in how much of each debt will be paid by each spouse.

Property	Value	Amount Owed	Disposition	
Home	$500,000	$200,000	H ___	W ___
Cottage	$193,000	–	H ___	W ___
BMW	$52,000	$27,500	H ___	W ___
Savings Account	$9,500	–	H ___	W ___
Retirement (H)	$2,000,000	–	H ___	W ___
IRA (H)	$800,000	–	H ___	W ___
Life Insurance (H)	$1,000,000	–	H ___	W ___

Debts	Amount	Disposition	
Visa	$7,300	H ___	W ___
MasterCard	$2,500	H ___	W ___
Current Taxes (Due)	$9,456	H ___	W ___
Next Year's Taxes (Estimated)	$13,180	H ___	W ___

Lea goes over the checklist carefully to make sure that all of the Clarks' property and debts are included and that the amounts are accurate. Once she is satisfied that the checklist is accurate and complete, she takes it to her supervising attorney for review.

Property Division

When a marriage is terminated, the property owned by the couple (including their debts) must be divided. **Property settlement**—the division of property on divorce— is often a main area of disagreement. Although most divorcing couples eventually settle their financial disputes, the settlement reached is colored by the requirements of state law. As the *Developing Paralegal Skills* feature above indicates, there is often significant detail work in property-settlement cases.

The way in which any court divides a couple's property depends largely on whether the property is considered marital property or separate property. **Marital property** is all property acquired during the course of a marriage (apart from inheritances and gifts received by one of the spouses). **Separate property** is property that a spouse owned before the marriage, plus inheritances and gifts acquired during the marriage. This property belongs to the spouse personally and not to the marital unit. On dissolution of the marriage, separate property is not divided but is retained by the owner.

property settlement
The division of property between spouses on the termination of a marriage.

marital property
All property acquired during the course of a marriage, apart from inheritances and gifts made to one or the other of the spouses.

separate property
Property that a spouse owned before the marriage, plus inheritances and gifts acquired by the spouse during the marriage.

The ownership right in separate property may be lost, however, if it is combined with marital property. ▶ **EXAMPLE 17.2**   Hannah Olin owns a lot in Bangor, Maine. Hannah marries Mustafa Shamir, and they build a house together after their marriage. By building the house on the lot (thus creating marital property), Hannah has lost her separate property rights in the land. ◀ Merely renovating separately held property (sprucing up a vacation home, for instance) may transform the separate property into joint property. Placing separate property (money) into a jointly held bank account may also transform the money into joint property.

Community Property

community property

In certain states, all property acquired during a marriage, except for inheritances or gifts received during the marriage by either marital partner. Each spouse has a one-half ownership interest in community property.

As discussed in Chapter 16, in some states, mostly in the West, husbands and wives hold property as community property. In those states, **community property** is all property acquired during the marriage (not including inheritances or gifts received by either party during the marriage). Even if only one party supplied all of the income and assets during the marriage, both spouses share equally (half and half) in the ownership of that property. Property owned by either partner before the marriage—and inheritances or gifts that partner received during the marriage—remain the property of that individual, or separate property, however.

Equitable Distribution

All of the other states provide for the *equitable distribution* (fair distribution) of property to the divorcing spouses—that is, the marital property is divided according to the equities of the case (not necessarily split evenly). In some of these states, only the marital property is subject to distribution. In other states, all of the property owned by the couple, including separate property, may be factored into the property distribution. While in most settlements, separate property remains with the owner, the courts exercise substantial discretion in deciding which person should receive what property. In deciding how to divide property between divorcing spouses, the courts consider a number of factors, including the following:

- The duration of the marriage.
- The health of the parties.
- The individuals' occupations and vocational skills.
- The individuals' relative wealth and income.
- The standard of living during the marriage.
- The relative contributions to the marriage (both financial and homemaker contributions).
- The needs and concerns of any children.
- Tax and inheritance considerations.

A typical property controversy in divorce cases concerns rights to the marital residence. If there are minor children, the house is usually given to the parent with custody of the children. It may be difficult to balance the grant of the house with other property (many families have few substantial assets other than their homes). Once the children are grown, the court may order the house to be sold and the proceeds divided to ensure that the property distribution is equitable.

Prenuptial Agreements

prenuptial agreement

A contract formed between two persons who are contemplating marriage to provide for the disposition of property in the event of a divorce or the death of one of the spouses after they have married.

Increasingly, couples are using prenuptial agreements to avoid problems over property division that may arise in the future. A **prenuptial agreement** (also known as an *antenuptial agreement*) is a contract between the parties that is entered into before marriage and that provides for the disposition of property in the event of a divorce or the death of one of the spouses. Prenuptial agreements must be in writing to be enforceable.

Most states uphold prenuptial agreements, even if the agreements eliminate financial support in the event of divorce. About half of the states have adopted the Uniform Premarital Agreement Act. This act helps to standardize the legal framework governing prenuptial agreements around the country, so there is less confusion when parties are from different states. Courts do look closely at prenuptial agreements for evidence of unfairness. Courts may find a prenuptial agreement unfair if the parties did not retain independent counsel prior to signing the agreement. To enforce a prenuptial agreement, a party must also show that the agreement was made voluntarily and without threats or unfair pressure.

FAMILY LAW AND THE PARALEGAL

The opportunities for paralegals in the area of family law are extensive and probably will continue to be so. The United States has the highest divorce rate in the world (statistically, one out of every two couples who marry end up getting a divorce), and there is no indication that this high rate will decline in the future. Many paralegals work for law practices that specialize in handling divorces and legal work related to divorces, such as child-custody arrangements and property settlements.

Divorce is just one specialty within the broad area of family law, and paralegals often work in other types of family law, such as adoptions. Paralegals may work for state welfare departments, publicly sponsored legal aid foundations, or groups that assist persons of low income with family-related legal problems. Paralegals working in the area of probate and estate administration also deal with questions relating to inheritance by children. Finally, paralegals who work for general law practices will likely be involved in family law matters, such as prenuptial agreements, adoptions, and divorce cases.

Because the area of family law involves many special legal areas, paralegals working in family law perform many different types of work. Here are some examples of the kinds of tasks you might perform if you work in this area of the law:

- Interview a client who is seeking a divorce to obtain information about the married couple, their property and debts, the reasons for the marriage breakdown, and their children, if any.

- Draft a petition for divorce and file divorce-related documents with the court.

- Assist in pretrial divorce proceedings, negotiations, and mediation.

- Assist in preparing a divorcing client for trial and in other trial-preparation matters.

- Draft a settlement agreement or prenuptial agreement.

- Assist in making arrangements for a private adoption.

- Research state laws governing marriage requirements, divorce procedures, child-custody arrangements, property settlements, and other matters.

- Help battered spouses obtain protection from their abusing spouses.

WILLS, TRUSTS, AND ESTATES

As mentioned in the chapter introduction, a person's real and personal property will be transferred to others when the person dies. People usually undertake *estate planning* to control how their property will be transferred. *Wills* and *trusts* are two basic devices used in the estate-planning process. We look at these devices, as well as others, in this section. We also discuss the process of *estate administration,* which involves collecting and transferring a decedent's (deceased person's) property.

Wills

As we noted in Chapter 2, a *will* is the final declaration of how a person wishes to have his or her property disposed of after death. The maker of a will is also called a **testator** (from the Latin *testari,* "to make a will"). A will is referred to as a *testamentary disposition* of property, and one who dies after having made a valid will is said to have died **testate**. If no valid will has been executed, a decedent is said to have died **intestate**. When a person dies intestate, state **intestacy laws** govern the distribution of the property among heirs or next of kin.

testator
One who makes a valid will.

testate
The condition of having died with a valid will.

intestate
The state of having died without a valid will.

intestacy laws
State statutes that specify how property will be distributed when a person dies intestate.

Ethics Watch

WILLS AND PARALEGAL SUPERVISION

It goes without saying that wills must accurately reflect the testator's wishes and that special care must be exercised in preparing a client's will. After all, unless the will is modified or revoked, it is indeed the "final word" on how the testator intends his or her property to be distributed. You will rest easier if you make sure that your supervising attorney reviews carefully any will that you draft, any subsequent modifications that are made, and particularly the document in its final form. Attorneys have a duty to supervise paralegal work. In regard to wills, as a paralegal you should remind your supervising attorney of this duty, if necessary.

Proper supervision by an attorney is required by the NALA Code of Ethics, Canon 2: "A paralegal may perform any task which is properly delegated and supervised by an attorney, as long as the attorney is ultimately responsible to the client, maintains a direct relationship with the client, and assumes professional responsibility for the work product." It is also required by the ABA Model Guidelines for the Utilization of Paralegal Services, Guideline 2: "Provided the lawyer maintains responsibility for the work product, a lawyer may delegate to a paralegal any task normally performed by the lawyer except those tasks proscribed to a nonlawyer by statute, court rule, administrative rule or regulation, controlling authority, the applicable rule of professional conduct of the jurisdiction in which the lawyer practices, or these guidelines."

executor

A person appointed by a testator to serve as a personal representative on the testator's death.

administrator

A person appointed by a court to serve as a personal representative for a person who died intestate, who made a will but failed to name an executor, or whose executor cannot serve.

probate

To prove and validate a will; the process of proving and validating a will and settling matters pertaining to the administration of a decedent's estate, guardianship of a decedent's children, and similar matters.

A will can serve other purposes besides the distribution of property. The will can appoint a guardian for minor children or incapacitated adults. It can also appoint a *personal representative* to settle the affairs of the deceased. An **executor** is a personal representative named in a will. An **administrator** is a personal representative appointed by the court for a decedent who died without a will, who made a will but failed to name an executor for the estate, or whose executor is unable to serve.

When a person dies intestate, the value of having paid a lawyer to prepare a will becomes clear. Because there is no will, the court appoints the administrator, who may not be the person the deceased individual would have chosen. The process is usually more costly than had a will existed, and the property of the estate may not be distributed the way the decedent would have preferred. Over half of all people die without a will, leaving an additional burden on their families.

Laws Governing Wills

The laws governing wills come into play when a will is probated. To **probate** (prove) a will means to establish its validity and carry the administration of the estate through a process supervised by a *probate court*. When drafting wills for clients, attorneys and paralegals must make sure that the wills meet the specific requirements imposed by state statute.

Probate laws vary from state to state. In 1969, however, the American Bar Association and the National Conference of Commissioners on Uniform State Laws approved the Uniform Probate Code (UPC). The UPC, which has since been significantly revised, codifies general principles and procedures for the resolution of conflicts in settling estates and relaxes some of the requirements for a valid will contained in earlier state laws. About one-third of the states have adopted the UPC. Other states have incorporated some part of the UPC into their own probate codes. Nonetheless, probate laws vary widely among states, and paralegals should always check the particular laws of the state involved.

Requirements for a Valid Will

A will must comply with state statutory requirements and formalities. If it does not, it will be declared void, and the decedent's property will be distributed according to state intestacy laws. Generally, most states uphold the following basic requirements for executing a will:

- *The testator must have testamentary capacity.* In other words, the testator must be of legal age (usually eighteen) and sound mind *at the time the will is made.*

- *Generally, a will must be in writing.* A will can be handwritten (called a *holographic will*). In a few states, *nuncupative* wills (oral "deathbed" wills made before witnesses) that dispose of personal property are permitted.

- *A will must be signed by the testator, generally at the end of the document.*

- *A will must be witnessed.* The number of witnesses (often two, sometimes three), their qualifications, and the manner in which the witnessing must be done are generally determined by state law.

- *In some states, a will must be published.* A will is "published" by an oral declaration by the maker to the witnesses that the document they are about to sign is the maker's "last will and testament."

Paralegals can often help in ensuring that wills comply with relevant requirements, as illustrated in the *Developing Paralegal Skills* feature on the next page.

The Probate Process

Probate procedures may vary depending on the size of the decedent's estate. For smaller estates, most state statutes provide for the distribution of assets without formal probate proceedings. Faster and less expensive methods are then used. ▶ **EXAMPLE 17.3** The intent to transfer property to an heir may be established by *affidavit,* which is a statement of facts written down and sworn to voluntarily in the presence of an official authorized to affirm it. In addition, some state statutes provide that title to cars, savings and checking accounts, and certain other property can be passed merely by filling out forms. ◀

A majority of states also provide for *family settlement agreements,* which are private agreements among the beneficiaries. Once a will is admitted to probate, the family members can agree to settle among themselves the distribution of the decedent's assets. Although a family settlement agreement speeds the settlement process, a court order is still needed to protect the estate from future creditors and to clear title to the assets involved. The use of these and other types of summary procedures in estate administration can save time and money.

For larger estates, formal probate proceedings are normally undertaken, and the probate court supervises the settlement of the decedent's estate. Additionally, in some situations—such as when a guardian for minor children or for an incompetent person must be appointed and a trust has been created to protect the minor or the incompetent person—more formal probate procedures cannot be avoided. Formal probate proceedings may take several months to complete. As a result, a sizable portion of the decedent's assets (up to perhaps 10 percent) may go toward payment of fees charged by attorneys and personal representatives, as well as court costs.

Trusts

Trusts are important estate-planning devices that are being increasingly utilized to avoid the costs associated with probating a will. A **trust** involves any arrangement by which legal title to property is transferred from one person (the *settlor,* or *grantor*) to be administered by another (the *trustee*) for the benefit of still another party (the *beneficiary*). ▶ **EXAMPLE 17.4** If Mendel conveys (transfers) his farm to Western Bank to be held for the benefit of his daughters, Mendel has created a trust. Mendel is the *settlor,* or *grantor;* Western Bank is the *trustee;* and Mendel's daughters are the *beneficiaries* (Exhibit 17.1 on page 573 illustrates this trust arrangement). ◀

trust

An arrangement in which property is transferred by one person (the grantor, or settlor) to another (the trustee) for the benefit of a third party (the beneficiary).

Developing
Paralegal Skills

DRAFTING A CLIENT'S WILL

Mr. Perkins has come to the law firm of Smith & Hardy to have his will prepared. He has previously met with attorney Jennifer Hardy, who has been assisting him in estate planning. Today, Perkins meets with Hardy's paralegal, James Reese, who will review the information needed to prepare the will.

   After the meeting, James returns to his office and begins drafting Perkins's will. Later in the week, after going over the will with Hardy, James will meet with Perkins again so that Perkins can review and sign the will.

CHECKLIST FOR DRAFTING A WILL

- Start with a computerized standard will form.
- Review each provision, or clause, in the standard form.
- Input the client's name, address, and other information.
- Modify the clauses as necessary to fit the client's needs.
- Specifically describe the assets the client wishes to leave to specific heirs.
- Number each page and clause of the will.
- Print out the document and carefully proofread it.
- Make any necessary corrections and print out the final copy to be reviewed by your supervising attorney.

There are numerous kinds of trusts, each with its own special characteristics. We look here at some of the most common types of trusts.

Living Trusts

inter vivos trust

A trust created by the grantor (settlor) and effective during the grantor's lifetime—that is, a trust not established by a will.

A living trust—or **inter vivos trust** (*inter vivos* is Latin for "between or among the living")—is a trust executed by a grantor during his or her lifetime. A living trust may be an attractive estate-planning option because living trusts are not included in the property of a decedent's estate that is probated.

   Living trusts can be irrevocable or revocable. The distinction between these two types of living trusts is an important one for estate planners. In an *irrevocable* living trust, the grantor permanently gives up control over the property. In a *revocable* living trust, in contrast, the grantor retains control over the trust property during his or her lifetime.

   To establish an irrevocable living trust, the grantor executes a trust deed, and legal title to the trust property passes to the named trustee. The trustee has a duty to administer the property as directed by the grantor for the benefit and in the interest of the beneficiaries. The trustee must preserve the trust property; make it productive; and, if required by the terms of the trust agreement, pay income to the beneficiaries, all in accordance with the terms of the trust. Once an irrevocable *inter vivos* trust has been created, the grantor has, in effect, given over the property for the benefit of the beneficiaries.

   To establish a revocable living trust, the grantor deeds the property to the trust but retains the power to amend, alter, or revoke the trust during his or her lifetime. The grantor may also arrange to receive income earned by the trust assets

EXHIBIT 17.1

A Trust Arrangement

In a trust, there is a separation of interests in the trust property. The trustee takes *legal* title, which appears to be complete ownership and possession but does not include the right to receive any benefits from the property. The beneficiary takes *equitable* title, which is the right to receive all benefits from the property.

during his or her lifetime. Unless the trust is revoked, the principal of the trust is transferred to the trust beneficiary on the grantor's death.

Testamentary Trusts

A trust created by will to come into existence on the settlor's death is called a **testamentary trust**. Although a testamentary trust has a trustee who maintains legal title to the trust property, actions of the trustee are subject to judicial approval. This trustee can be named in the will or appointed by the court. Thus, a testamentary trust does not fail because a trustee has not been named in the will. The legal responsibilities of the trustee are the same as in an *inter vivos* trust.

If a will that establishes a testamentary trust is invalid, then the trust will also be invalid. The property that was supposed to be in the trust will then pass according to intestacy laws, not according to the terms of the trust.

testamentary trust

A trust that is created by will and that does not take effect until the death of the testator.

Special Types of Trusts

There are many kinds of special trusts. So long as a trust does not violate state law, the creator of the trust can construct any arrangement that meets his or her needs. One special kind of trust is the *life insurance trust*. In this, the trust owns a life insurance policy, which usually covers the life of the grantor of the trust. When the insured party dies, the life insurance proceeds go into the trust and are used in the manner provided by the instructions of the grantor.

A trust designed for the benefit of a segment of the public or the public in general is called a *charitable trust*. It differs from other types of trusts in that the identities of the beneficiaries are uncertain. Usually, to be deemed a charitable trust, a trust must be created for charitable, educational, religious, or scientific purposes.

In a *spendthrift trust*, the beneficiary is permitted to draw only a certain portion of the total amount to which he or she is entitled at any one time. This type of trust is used to protect the beneficiary from spending all that is in the trust. The trustee who oversees the trust may have authority to decide how much money goes to the beneficiary at any given time. Most states allow spendthrift trust provisions to prohibit creditors from attaching such trusts. A divorced spouse or a minor child of the beneficiary may be permitted to obtain alimony or child-support payments, however.

Developing Paralegal Skills

ESTATE PLANNING

Sara Bloom is an experienced paralegal who has worked for the same small law firm for several years. One of the firm's clients, Arnold Thompson, has an appointment today with David Miller, Sara's supervising attorney, to discuss estate-planning options. Thompson, a widower, is particularly interested in how, on his death, his assets can be transferred outside the probate process to his three children. David asks Sara to sit in on this initial client interview and to take thorough notes. He also asks her to draw up a checklist of points to discuss with the client during the interview.

CHECKLIST FOR AVOIDING PROBATE AND REDUCING TAX LIABILITY

- *Life insurance*—If Thompson has a life insurance policy listing the children as beneficiaries, the proceeds will be distributed to the children immediately on his death (as soon as the insurance company has completed its investigation of the claim) and will not be subject to probate. The client should be informed, though, that life insurance proceeds normally are a part of the taxable estate.

- *Joint ownership of property*—Thompson can arrange to have his children become co-owners of his personal property (such as automobiles) and real property (such as his home). If property is held in joint tenancy with rights of survivorship, the property will pass to the children outside the probate process.

- *Trusts*—Assets can also be placed in a living trust for the children, allowing the assets to pass to the children outside the probate process.

- *Minimizing estate taxes*—Thompson can minimize estate and inheritance taxes by making tax-free gifts to his children each year, within the limits set by federal law.

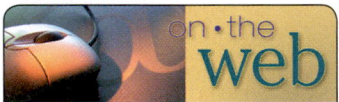

You can find a broad array of useful information about estate planning at the Web site of the National Association of Financial and Estate Planning at **www.nafep.com**.

Other Estate-Planning Devices

Commonly, beneficiaries under a will must wait until the probate process is complete—which can take several months if formal probate proceedings are undertaken—to have access to funds or other assets received under the will. For this and other reasons, some persons arrange to have property transferred in ways other than by will and outside the probate process. (For information on finding estate-planning options online, see this chapter's *Technology and Today's Paralegal* feature on the facing page.)

One method of accomplishing this is by establishing a living trust, as has already been discussed. A person can also arrange to hold title to certain real or personal property as a joint tenant with a spouse or other person. Remember from Chapter 16 that in a joint tenancy, when one joint tenant dies, the other joint tenant or tenants automatically inherit the deceased tenant's share of the property. (This is true even if the deceased tenant has provided otherwise in a will.) Yet another way of transferring property outside the probate process is by making gifts to children or others while one is still living. Finally, to make sure that a spouse, child, or some other dependent is provided for, many people take out life insurance policies. On the death of the policyholder, the proceeds of the policy go directly to the beneficiary and are not involved in the probate process. Because of the cost and time involved, parties generally wish to avoid probate. The role that a paralegal might play in this process is illustrated in the *Developing Paralegal Skills* feature above.

Technology and Today's Paralegal

ONLINE HELP FOR ESTATE PLANNING

The Internet offers an abundance of estate-planning Web sites. Many of them, however, are aimed at consumers and laypersons. The trick for paralegals and attorneys who specialize in estate planning is to find sites that are useful to professionals. A number of Web sites can help estate planners perform research on tax and probate laws and stay current with legislation and developments in the field. These sites may also provide sample forms or estate plans and estate-tax calculators.

WHERE TO BEGIN

A good place to start your research is at **www.estateplanninglinks.com**. This site offers a comprehensive collection of articles and links to Web sites pertaining to estate planning, probate, trusts, charitable trusts, IRAs (individual retirement accounts), tax law, and elder law. Created and maintained by lawyers, the site is geared toward professionals. Another good starting place is Cornell University's Legal Information Institute, from which you can access relevant federal and state statutes and agency regulations. You can also read recent estate-planning cases decided by the United States Supreme Court, the federal circuit courts, and many state appellate courts at this site. Go to **www.law.cornell. edu**, and select "All topics" from the "Law about . . ." menu. Then select "Estate planning."

OTHER WEB SITES

Paralegals and attorneys can find practical information at **www.texasprobate.com**. This site has a state focus but presents articles, forms, and links that can be utilized by all. Many organizations also have useful Web sites, including the American College of Trust and Estate Counsel at **www.actec.org**.

SOFTWARE TOOLS

Information about software programs that assist estate planning (and many other areas of practice) can be found at the Market Center of FindLaw (**marketcenter.findlaw.com**). Under the "Market Center" heading, select "Legal Software" from the pull-down menu, and enter "estate planning" (or other terms) in the "Search" field. After performing the search, you can browse the products offered.

TECHNOLOGY TIP

Paralegals will find many good estate-planning resources and tools on the Web. Only a few are mentioned here. Once you find the sites that are most helpful to your practice, you can bookmark them for later reference.

Estate Administration

Estate administration is the process of collecting a decedent's assets, settling his or her debts, and distributing all remaining assets. These tasks are undertaken by the decedent's personal representative. In some states, however, a special court, usually called a probate court, oversees the administration of decedents' estates. The rights of both creditors and beneficiaries must be protected during the estate-administration proceedings.

If a will exists, it probably names a personal representative (executor) to administer the estate. If there is no will, if the will fails to name a personal representative, or if the personal representative named in the will cannot serve, then the court must appoint one (an administrator). The personal representative must inventory

estate administration
The process in which a decedent's personal representative settles the affairs of the decedent's estate (collects assets, pays debts and taxes, and distributes the remaining assets to heirs); the process is usually overseen by a probate court.

and collect the assets of the decedent and, if necessary, have them appraised to determine their value. In addition, the personal representative is responsible for managing the assets of the estate during the administration period and for preventing them from being wasted or unnecessarily depleted.

The personal representative pays debts owed by the decedent and also arranges for the estate to pay taxes. For larger estates, a federal tax is levied on the total value of the estate after debts and expenses for administration have been deducted and after various exemptions have been allowed. The tax is on the estate itself rather than on the beneficiaries. In some states, a state inheritance tax is imposed on the recipient of a decedent's property rather than on the estate. Some states also have a state estate tax similar to the federal estate tax. In general, inheritance tax rates are graduated according to the type of relationship between the beneficiary and the decedent. The lowest rates and largest exemptions are applied to a surviving spouse and the children of the decedent.

When the ultimate distribution of assets to the beneficiaries is determined, the personal representative is responsible for distributing the estate pursuant to the court order. Once the assets have been distributed, an accounting is rendered to the court, the estate is closed, and the personal representative is relieved of any further responsibility or liability for the estate.

WILLS, TRUSTS, AND ESTATES AND THE PARALEGAL

Paralegals are often involved in legal work relating to wills, trusts, other estate-planning devices, and estate administration. If you work for a general law practice, you may be required to assist in handling tasks relating to all of these areas at one time or another. If you specialize in estate planning and administration, you may be employed by a law firm or a probate court and work extensively with probate proceedings. Among other things, you might be responsible for coordinating the efforts of the personal representative with those of the probate court. An increasing number of paralegals today are specializing in trust law and finding career opportunities in trust departments of banking institutions.

Here is a sampling of the tasks paralegals perform in the areas of wills, trusts, and estates:

- Interview clients to obtain information about their assets and liabilities for estate-planning purposes.

- Draft a will for a client.
- Create the necessary documents to establish a trust for a client.
- Monitor a trust fund's investments to ensure that the funds are not unnecessarily depleted.
- Locate beneficiaries named in a will or the next of kin of a person who died intestate.
- File a will with the probate court to initiate probate procedures.
- Research laws governing estate and inheritance taxes to determine how they apply to a decedent's estate.
- Research state laws governing wills and probate procedures.
- Perform asset appraisals.

KEY TERMS AND CONCEPTS

administrator *570*

adoption *561*

alimony *566*

annulment *562*

bigamy *562*

child support *565*

common law marriage *559*

community property *568*

divorce *563*

emancipation *557*

estate administration *575*

executor *570*

foster care *561*

guardian *ad litem* *564*

independent adoption *562*

inter vivos trust *572*

intestacy laws *569*

intestate *569*

joint custody *565*

legal custody *564*

marital property *567*

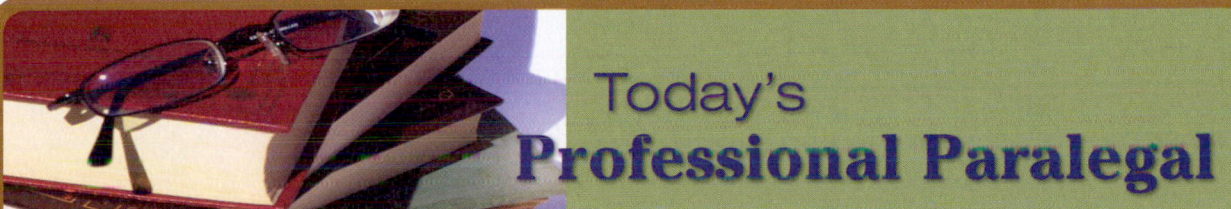

Today's Professional Paralegal

MEETING WITH THE PERSONAL REPRESENTATIVE

Jocelyn Furnow is a paralegal with a small law partnership, West & West. Terrence West, one of the two partners, told Jocelyn yesterday that a friend of his, Bob Milham, would be dropping by today. Bob's brother, Ralph Milham, died a few days ago in a car accident, and Bob, as Ralph's personal representative, wants to know what needs to be done to settle the estate.

JOCELYN'S ASSIGNMENT

Terrence tells Jocelyn that he will be out of the office all afternoon and that when Bob comes by, she should let him know what kinds of documents and information he needs to gather immediately. "Tell Bob," Terrence says, "to collect these items as quickly as possible and then come in and see me. In fact, see if you can set up an appointment for this Thursday, and tell him he should try to have the necessary information by that time."

MEETING WITH THE CLIENT

That afternoon, Bob Milham enters the office, and Jocelyn greets him. She introduces herself as Terrence West's paralegal and explains that the attorney has authorized her to indicate the kinds of information that Bob should obtain right away. Jocelyn first asks Bob if he has brought his brother's will with him. Bob hands Jocelyn the will, which Jocelyn quickly scans. She notes that Bob's name is listed as Ralph's personal representative. She then hands Bob a prepared form—a worksheet that Bob can use to inventory his brother's assets and debts.

GOING OVER THE WORKSHEET

"Basically," explains Jocelyn, "you first need to list your brother's possessions, as the worksheet indicates. Do you know if he owned any real estate, such as a home or land?" Bob states that his brother owned a house and had a car and an airplane. He is fairly sure that Ralph also had some investment securities.

"Well," Jocelyn responds, "look through his personal papers. Try to find the deed to the house, the titles to the car and the airplane, and the certificates or other evidence of the securities he owned. These papers may be in a safe-deposit box, so you need to check with his bank to find out if he had one. Also locate his checkbook and any paperwork indicating whether he had a savings account or owned any certificates of deposit.

"The next step is to find out whether Ralph had any debts outstanding. When you look through his papers, find out how much, if anything, he still owed on the house and on his car and airplane. See if you can find evidence of any other loans that must be paid off."

Jocelyn continues to go over the items listed on the worksheet. Once she is sure that Bob understands what must be done, she schedules an appointment for the coming Thursday. At that time, Terrence can further advise Bob on the probate process and on Bob's duties as personal representative.

no-fault divorce *563*

paternity suit *561*

petition for divorce *563*

prenuptial agreement *568*

probate *570*

property settlement *567*

restraining order *560*

separate property *567*

testamentary trust *573*

testate *569*

testator *569*

trust *571*

visitation rights *565*

CHAPTER SUMMARY

FAMILY LAW AND ESTATES

Family Law

1. *Marriage requirements*—Marriage is a status conferred by state law that establishes the rights and duties of spouses to one another and to any children born. Typically, the couple must be a man and a woman, currently unmarried, not closely related by blood, and at least eighteen (unless they have parental consent or are emancipated).

   a. Certain procedures may be required by the state in order for a marriage to be legally recognized. These procedures may involve a marriage license, a blood test, a waiting period, and a marriage ceremony, after which the license must be recorded.

   b. In a few states, the law allows marriages between two people of the same sex. Some other states have passed laws allowing same-sex partners to form "civil unions" or "domestic partnerships."

2. *Common law marriage*—A minority of states allow parties to be married solely by mutual consent and without a ceremony or license.

3. *Marital duties*—Spouses have the duty to support the other spouse and children financially by providing basic necessities. Abusing one's spouse is illegal in all states.

4. *Parental rights and obligations*—Parents have the legal right to control the upbringing of their minor children and to punish them within reason. They also must provide for the children's necessities and ensure that the children attend school (until a certain age).

   a. Generally, parents are not liable for the wrongful actions of their children unless the actions result from the parents' negligence.

   b. Child abuse and neglect are prohibited in all states.

   c. The biological father of a child born out of wedlock is obligated to support the child once paternity is established.

   d. An illegitimate child can usually inherit from the mother but not from the father unless paternity has been established. Even when paternity has been established, an illegitimate child may not have the same inheritance rights as legitimate children.

5. *Adoption*—Adoption is a procedure by which persons become the legal parents of a child who is not their biological child. An adopted child normally has the same legal rights as the biological children of a married couple, including inheritance rights. State law governs adoption, and procedures vary. The court must approve all adoptions.

   a. Agency adoptions are done through state-licensed social-service agencies.

   b. Independent adoptions are arranged privately, often through lawyers or doctors.

   c. Stepparent adoptions are those in which a married partner adopts his or her spouse's children from a prior marriage.

6. *Marriage termination*—A marriage can only be terminated by the state, through annulment or divorce.

a. Annulment is a court order invalidating a marriage; it is no longer common.

    b. Divorce is the most common way to end a marriage. Divorce laws vary across states and may provide for fault-based or no-fault divorces. In a fault-based divorce, the petitioner must prove certain grounds for the divorce, such as adultery, cruelty, or abuse. A party may seek a fault-based divorce in the hope of gaining a more favorable property settlement. No-fault divorces are based on the grounds that the partners have irreconcilable differences, have been living separately for the length of time required by state statute, or are incompatible.

    c. The first step in obtaining a divorce is to file a petition for divorce with the appropriate state court. The petition is served on the other spouse. If the parties cannot agree on certain matters (child custody, finances) in the interim, the court may hold a hearing to assign temporary responsibility for those matters. Many states require parties to attend mediation before trial.

7. *Child custody*—Which parent the child lives with is often contested in a divorce. The court sometimes appoints a guardian *ad litem* to protect the interests of the child. The court considers a number of factors when deciding custody.

    a. Parents granted joint legal custody make major decisions about the child together. Parents with joint physical custody have physical custody of the child for roughly comparable time periods. Many states now provide for joint custodial arrangements.

    b. Usually, one parent is awarded legal custody of the child and can make major decisions without consulting the other parent. The noncustodial parent receives visitation rights.

8. *Child support*—The noncustodial parent will likely be required to pay a certain sum monthly (often set according to guidelines) as support for the child.

9. *Spousal support*—In some situations, one of the spouses is ordered to pay support (alimony) to the other. Alimony can be temporary (rehabilitative) or permanent.

10. *Property division*—

    a. Marital property is property acquired during the marriage. It will be divided on divorce. Separate property is anything that a spouse owned prior to the marriage, plus inheritances and gifts received during the marriage. Separate property is usually not divided.

    b. In some states, all property acquired during the marriage is considered community property, even if only one party supplied all of the income and assets during the marriage. Each spouse has a one-half ownership interest in community property.

    c. All other states divide the divorcing couple's property by equitable (fair) distribution. The court decides how much of the marital property each spouse should receive given the circumstances of the parties and does not necessarily divide the property equally. In some states, only the marital property is divided; in others, separate property may also be included.

11. *Prenuptial agreements*—Agreements (contracts) made before marriage to provide for division of property in the event of divorce or death. Prenuptial agreements must be in writing. Most states enforce such agreements unless they are clearly unfair.

Continued

Wills, Trusts, and Estates

1. *Wills*—A will is the final declaration of how a person desires to have his or her property disposed of after death.

2. *Terminology*—A person who dies without leaving a will is said to have died intestate, and the decedent's property is distributed under state intestacy statutes. A person who makes a will is called a testator. The personal representative named in a will to settle the affairs of the decedent is called an executor. If the court appoints the personal representative, she or he is called an administrator.

3. *Requirements of a valid will*—A will must comply with state statutory requirements, which usually involve the following:

   a. The testator must have testamentary capacity (be of sound mind at the time the will is made).

   b. The will generally must be in writing.

   c. The testator must sign the will.

   d. The will must be witnessed by a specified number of persons (usually two or three).

   e. In some states, the will must be published.

4. *Probate procedures*—To probate a will means to establish its validity and administer the estate through a court process. Probate laws vary from state to state. Procedures may be formal or informal, depending on the size of the estate and other factors, such as whether a guardian for minor children must be appointed.

5. *Trusts*—A trust is any arrangement by which property is transferred from one person (the grantor, or settlor) to be administered by another (the trustee) for the benefit of a third party (the beneficiary).

   a. A living *(inter vivos)* trust is executed by the grantor during his or her lifetime and can be revocable or irrevocable.

   b. A testamentary trust is created by will and comes into existence on the grantor's death.

   c. Special types of trusts include life insurance trusts, charitable trusts, and spendthrift trusts.

6. *Other estate-planning devices*—Several other strategies may be used to transfer property. These include owning property as joint tenants, giving gifts to children or others while one is still alive, and purchasing life insurance policies.

STUDENT STUDYWARE™ CD-ROM

Interactive student CD in this book includes additional quizzing, plus video clips, case studies, and Key Terms flashcards.

ONLINE COMPANION™

For additional resources, please go to **www.paralegal.delmar.cengage.com**.

QUESTIONS FOR REVIEW

1. What are the rights and duties of parents with respect to their children? Can parents be held liable for their children's wrongful acts? What are the legal obligations of parents to children born out of wedlock and adopted children?

2. On the termination of a marriage, how is a couple's property divided? What is separate property? What is community property?

3. What are the requirements of a valid will? Why is it important to check the law of your specific state when determining the requirements of a will? What laws govern the distribution of the estate of a person who dies without a valid will?

4. Why and how are wills probated? What are the duties of a personal representative?

5. What is a trust? Name and describe two basic types of trusts.

ETHICAL QUESTIONS

1. During the course of their twenty-five-year marriage, Mr. and Mrs. Jones have had their family attorney, Mr. Shapiro, prepare their wills, handle their real estate purchases, and assist them with other legal matters. On Monday, Mrs. Jones calls Mr. Shapiro and makes an appointment. She explains that she wants to file a divorce action against Mr. Jones. On Wednesday, Mr. Jones calls Mr. Shapiro. He wants to make an appointment to discuss filing a divorce action against Mrs. Jones. May the attorney, Mr. Shapiro, represent both Mr. Jones and Mrs. Jones in the divorce action?

2. Cynthia Warner works as a legal assistant for a sole practitioner, Samuel Weingarten. Weingarten's practice consists mainly of estate planning and probate. Today, Weingarten has received a check for $100,000 from the sale of real property that was in an estate that he is probating. Weingarten instructs Cynthia to deposit the check into the firm's bank account, not the client trust account, because he has some bills to pay. What should Cynthia do? How might she handle this situation?

PRACTICE QUESTIONS AND ASSIGNMENTS

1. Identify which of the following factors will generally *not* be considered by the courts when determining child custody:

   a. The nature of the relationship and emotional ties between the child and each parent.

   b. The ability of each parent to provide for the child's needs and education.

   c. The ability of the parents of each spouse to support and care for the child if the spouse has a full-time job.

   d. The ability of each parent to provide a stable environment for the child.

2. Identify each of the following types of trusts:

   a. Barbara inserts a trust provision in her will requiring that all of her property be held in trust for her children until they reach the age of thirty.

   b. Steve, who is seventy years old, transfers his home into a trust for the benefit of his children and their spouses.

   c. Kathy creates a trust in her will for cancer research.

3. Identify which of the following types of estate-planning devices allow property to be transferred outside the probate process:

   a. Living trusts.

   b. Life insurance.

   c. Testamentary trusts.

   d. Holding property as joint tenants with rights of survivorship.

   e. Gifts to children.

QUESTIONS FOR CRITICAL ANALYSIS

1. Until the 1960s, to obtain a divorce, a person had to allege grounds for divorce, such as adultery, desertion, cruelty, or abuse. Today, all states allow no-fault divorces. Since the 1960s, the divorce rate has continually risen. It has now reached 50 percent—in other words, today, one out of every two marriages ends in divorce. Explain how no-fault divorce laws might have affected the divorce rate. What other social changes in the past three decades might have contributed to the increase in the divorce rate?

2. A woman agrees that in exchange for $10,000, she will be artificially inseminated, conceive a child, carry the child to term, and after delivery of the baby surrender it to the father and his wife. The mother will terminate her parental rights, and the father's wife will adopt the child. Is this a valid contract? What are the arguments in favor of its being upheld as valid? What are the arguments favoring its invalidation?

3. Suppose that a wealthy testator has a son who suffers from a severe disability that requires costly medical monitoring and treatment. Because the son can earn no income and has no independent wealth, the state assumes the costs of his treatment. If the testator's will provides that all of his wealth and property should go to charity, can the son successfully contest the will? Can the state intervene to obtain compensation for the costs associated with the son's medical care? Why or why not?

PROJECTS

1. Go to FindLaw, the Legal Information Institute at Cornell Law School, or other useful Web sites to find the answers to the following questions. Write down your answers:

   a. What are the requirements for divorce in your state?

   b. What procedural requirements are usually involved?

   c. How long must a person live in your state before a court would have jurisdiction over a family law matter such as divorce or child custody?

   d. Must a person use an attorney to file for divorce?

   e. If a person does not have the resources to pay for an attorney to help with family law matters, such as child custody, is there a state program to help?

2. A paralegal who works in the area of probate law may need to locate the heirs of a person who died without a will (intestate). Given the many online research sources, it may be possible to track down heirs without having to hire an outside search firm. On the Internet, determine what resources are available. One firm is International Genealogical Search at **www.heirsearch.com**. Look at the case studies posted on that Web site or on others, and write one paragraph summarizing the services offered.

USING INTERNET RESOURCES

1. To learn more about intestacy laws, access the Uniform Probate Code (UPC) at the Web site of the Legal Information Institute at **www.law.cornell. edu**. From the "Constitutions & codes" menu, select "Other Uniform Laws." Then, in the "Uniform Laws Locator" list, select "Probate." Using the information you find, answer the following questions:

   a. How many states have adopted the UPC in its entirety?

   b. How many states have adopted it in part or with modifications?

BUSINESS ORGANIZATIONS AND EMPLOYMENT LAW

CHAPTER OUTLINE

Introduction

Forms of Business Organization

Agency Law

Employment Law

AFTER COMPLETING THIS CHAPTER, YOU WILL KNOW:

► The most common forms of business organizations and how each type of business organizational form is created and operated.

► How profits, losses, risks, and liabilities are distributed in each business organizational form.

► What agency relationships are and the significance of agency law for business relationships.

► How the government regulates employer-employee relationships.

INTRODUCTION

Paralegals commonly work with people in the business environment, as well as being employees of business entities themselves. Knowledge of the various legal forms that businesses can take is helpful in understanding legal issues that arise in this environment. In this chapter, we begin by reviewing how a range of business organizations are formed and some of the key features of the different legal structures. Then we turn to agency law, a part of the common law that is present in almost all business relationships. Agency is related directly to employment law, which we discuss in the final part of the chapter. Because litigation in the employment relationship is common, it is a subject worth investigation.

FORMS OF BUSINESS ORGANIZATION

Traditionally, there were three basic forms of business organization: the sole proprietorship, the partnership, and the corporation. These forms continue to be used. In addition, today's business owners and professionals are turning to newer, alternative business organizational forms known as limited liability companies, limited liability partnerships, and professional corporations.

Each business form involves different relationships, rights, obligations, and regulatory schemes. In your work as a paralegal, you will want to have some idea of what rights and duties accompany each of these business forms when you work on behalf of clients.

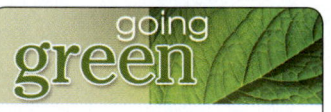

Sole Proprietorships

Remember from Chapter 3 that the simplest form of business is the *sole proprietorship,* in which one person—the sole proprietor—owns the business. The sole proprietor is entitled to all of the business's profits and bears personal responsibility for all of the business's debts and other obligations. Sole proprietors can own and manage any type of business, from an informal, home-office undertaking to a large restaurant or construction firm. There are more than 20 million sole proprietorships in the United States. In fact, they constitute over two-thirds of all American businesses. They are also usually small enterprises—only about 1 percent of the sole proprietorships in the United States earn more than $1 million per year.

Formation of a Sole Proprietorship

The sole proprietorship is easier and less costly to start than any other kind of business, as few legal forms are involved. No partnership agreement need be devised, because there are no partners. No papers need be filed with the state to establish the business. At most, minor paperwork will be required, depending on the law of the city in which the business is located. In the majority of states, if retail sales are involved, the proprietor will also need a tax number to report and remit sales taxes.

Because it is the simplest business form to create, persons first starting up businesses often choose to operate as sole proprietors. An attorney or a freelance paralegal might begin doing business as a sole proprietor.

Advantages of Sole Proprietorships

A major advantage of the sole proprietorship is that the sole proprietor is entitled to all the profits made by the firm (because he takes all the risk). The sole proprietor is also free to make all decisions concerning the business—whom to hire, when to take a vacation, what kind of business to pursue, and the like. Additionally, sole proprietors are allowed to establish tax-exempt retirement accounts. (Law offices are usually not involved in establishing retirement accounts for small businesses.)

Disadvantages of Sole Proprietorships

A major disadvantage of the sole proprietorship is that the proprietor alone, as the firm's sole owner, is personally liable for any losses, debts, and obligations incurred by the business enterprise. As discussed in Chapter 3, *personal liability* means that the personal assets of the business owner (such as a home, car, savings account, or other tangible or intangible property) may be subject to creditors' claims if the business fails.

As a paralegal, if you are asked to do a preliminary investigation of a client's claim against a business entity, one of the first things you should check is the form of the business. ▶ **EXAMPLE 18.1** Your firm's client wants to sue a business firm for damages. If you learn that the firm is a sole proprietorship, then you will know that if the firm itself has insufficient assets to pay damages to the client (should the client win in court), the firm's owner will personally be liable for the damages. Depending on what you learn about the firm's financial condition, you may want to investigate the owner's personal financial position as well. ◀

Another disadvantage of the sole proprietorship is that it may be difficult to obtain capital for expansion. The sole proprietor is dependent on loans made by lending institutions and others. For this reason, sole proprietors sometimes decide to take on partners, who will contribute capital to the business, or to incorporate and sell shares in the business to raise funds.

Taxation and Sole Proprietorships

A sole proprietor must pay income taxes on business profits, but she does not have to file a separate tax return in the name of the business. Rather, the profits are reported on the sole proprietor's personal tax return and taxed as personal income.

Termination of the Sole Proprietorship

In a sole proprietorship, the owner is the business. For that reason, when the owner dies, so does the business—it is automatically dissolved. If the business is transferred to family members or other heirs, a new proprietorship is created. Similarly, if the proprietor sells the business, whoever buys it must establish either a new sole proprietorship or some other business form, such as a partnership or a corporation.

Partnerships

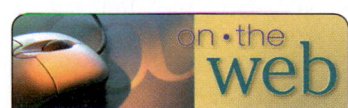

As discussed in Chapter 3, some law firms organize their business in the form of a *partnership,* which arises when two or more individuals undertake to do business together as *partners*. Each partner owns a portion of the business and shares jointly in the firm's profits or losses. Partners are personally liable for the debts and obligations of the business if the business fails, just as sole proprietors are.

The Uniform Partnership Act (UPA) governs the operation of partnerships *unless the partners have expressly agreed otherwise.* Like the Uniform Commercial Code, the UPA is a model that becomes law when adopted by a state legislature. The UPA was issued in 1994 and amended in 1997. Most states have adopted the 1997 version.

Partnership Formation

Under the UPA, a partnership is defined as "an association of two or more persons to carry on as co-owners a business for profit." To create a partnership, two or more persons interested in establishing a profit-making business simply agree to do so, as partners. The partnership agreement can be expressed orally or in writing, or it can be implied by conduct. If the partnership is to continue for over a year, then the agreement must be in writing to satisfy the Statute of Frauds, a state statute that specifies what types of contracts must be in writing to be enforceable (discussed in Chapter 15).

The Internal Revenue Service explains tax issues for sole proprietors at **www.irs.gov**. Frrom the menu bar, select "Businesses," and then select "Small Business/Self-Employed."

You can review the text of the Uniform Partnership Act, summaries of the amendments, and legislative facts about the bill by clicking on the various links at **www.nccusl.org**.

The sole proprietor on the right has so much business she has decided to form a partnership with her friend on the left. Will the new partner face the same liabilities that were faced by the sole proprietor?

(Image copyright Stephen Coburn, 2009. Used under license from Shutterstock.com).

Rights and Duties of Partners

When two or more persons agree to do business as partners, legally they enter into a special relationship with one another. A partnership is based on a voluntary contract between two or more competent persons who agree to place some or all of their money or other assets, labor, and skill in a business, with the understanding that profits and losses will be proportionately shared.

The rights of partners are often written into the partnership agreement. If the agreement does not specify these rights, then the UPA comes into play (the state's version of the UPA, as adopted). Some of the important rights of partners are listed in Exhibit 18.1.

Liability of Partners

Historically, a partnership could not be sued or bring a lawsuit or own property in its own name. This traditional rule treated all partnerships as aggregates of individuals. Under this rule, which is still followed in some states, only the individual partners—not the partnership—can be sued. Because this approach is so cumbersome, most states today recognize the partnership as a legal entity that can sue or be sued and collect judgments in the partnership's name.

EXHIBIT 18.1
Rights of Partners

PARTNERS HAVE THE RIGHT:

- To hold an ownership interest in the firm and to receive a share of the profits.

- To inspect partnership books and records.

- To an accounting of partnership assets and profits (for example, to determine the value of each partner's share in the partnership). An accounting can be performed voluntarily or can be compelled by a court order. Formal accounting occurs by right in connection with partnership dissolution proceedings.

- To participate in the management of the business operation unless the partnership agreement specifies otherwise.

A distinguishing feature of the partnership, and one that is often regarded as a disadvantage, is the potentially extensive personal liability faced by partners for partnership obligations and for the actions of the other partners. Partners have **joint liability**, or shared liability. In other words, partners may be held personally liable not only for their own actions and those of the partnership as an entity but also for the actions of other partners.

Partners may also be subject to **joint and several liability**—*several* liability means *individual* liability. Joint and several liability means that a third party may sue all of the partners (jointly) or one or more of the partners separately (severally). This is true even if one of the partners sued did not participate in, ratify, or know about whatever gave rise to the cause of action.

▶ EXAMPLE 18.2 Suppose that a plaintiff wants to recover for damages allegedly caused by a physician's negligence (medical malpractice). The physician is one of four partners in a medical practice partnership. Because partners are jointly and severally liable, the plaintiff could sue the physician who allegedly caused the harm, the partnership, one of the other physicians (even if that physician had nothing to do with the plaintiff's treatment), or all of the physicians to recover damages. ◀ The liability faced by partners is a major reason for the rapid growth of a new form of partnership, the limited liability partnership, which will be discussed later.

Taxation of Partnerships

The partnership itself, as an entity, does not pay federal income taxes. The partnership as an entity files an information return with the Internal Revenue Service on which the income received by the partnership is reported. The partners declare their shares of the partnership's profits on their personal income tax returns and pay taxes accordingly.

Partnership Termination

The partnership agreement may specify the duration of the partnership by indicating that the partnership will end on a certain date or on the occurrence of a certain event. It would be a breach of the partnership agreement for one partner to withdraw from the partnership before the specified date arrived or the specified event occurred. The withdrawing partner would be liable to the remaining partners for any related losses.

When an agreement does not specify the duration of the partnership, a partner is free to withdraw at any time without incurring liability to the remaining partners. Under the 1994 version of the UPA, withdrawal by a partner results in the **dissolution** (the formal disbanding) of the partnership (although a new partnership may arise among those who stay with the enterprise). Under the revised UPA, however, the withdrawal of a partner causes a partnership to be dissolved only if the withdrawal results in the breakup of the partnership itself and the business cannot continue. The occurrence of certain events also results in partnership termination. The death or bankruptcy of a partner, for example, terminates the partnership.

Partnership termination is a two-step process. Dissolution is the first step in the process. The second step is the **winding up** of partnership affairs. Once the firm is dissolved, it continues to exist legally until the process of winding up all business affairs (collecting and distributing the firm's assets) is complete.

Limited Partnerships

Ordinary partnerships, such as those just discussed, are often referred to as *general partnerships*. The **limited partnership**, in contrast, is a special form of partnership involving two different types of partners—general partners and limited partners. The **general partners** manage the business and have the rights and liabilities of partners in a general partnership. The **limited partners** are, for the most part, simply

---

joint liability

Shared liability. In partnership law, partners incur joint liability for partnership obligations and debts.

joint and several liability

Shared and individual liability. In partnership law, joint and several liability means that a third party may sue all of the partners (jointly) or one or more of the partners separately (severally). This is true even if one of the partners sued did not participate in, ratify, or know about whatever gave rise to the cause of action.

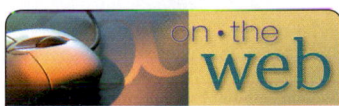
on the web

The Legal Information Institute provides a discussion of partnership law at **www.law.cornell.edu**. From the "Law about . . ." menu, select "All topics," and then select "Partnership" from the topics list.

dissolution

The formal disbanding of a partnership or a corporation.

winding up

The process of winding up all business affairs (collecting and distributing the firm's assets) after a partnership or corporation has been dissolved.

limited partnership

A partnership consisting of one or more general partners and one or more limited partners.

general partner

A partner who participates in managing the business of a partnership and has all the rights and liabilities that arise under traditional partnership law.

limited partner

One who invests in a limited partnership but does not play an active role in managing the operation of the business. Unlike general partners, limited partners are only liable for partnership debts up to the amounts that they have invested.

investors in the business. A limited partnership may be formed, for example, to purchase and develop real estate. The limited partners play a passive role. Their funds help to finance the venture, and they receive a share of the profits in return.

The limited partner does not participate in the management of the partnership and, in return, enjoys limited liability status. Unlike general partners, who are personally liable for partnership obligations, limited partners are liable only up to the amounts that they have invested. In other words, if the partnership goes bankrupt, they will lose their investments but cannot be held liable for partnership debts beyond that amount.

In contrast to the informal, private, and voluntary agreement that usually suffices to create a general partnership, the formation of a limited partnership is a public and formal proceeding that must follow state statutory requirements. The partners must sign a *certificate of limited partnership,* which requires information similar to that found in a corporate charter. The certificate must be filed with the designated state official (usually, the secretary of state). In this respect, the limited partnership resembles the corporation—another creature of statute.

Corporations

Paralegals frequently work on behalf of corporate clients or on legal matters involving corporations. (For more about what paralegals do in the corporate context, see the *Featured Contributor* essay on pages 590 and 591.) An increasing number of paralegals are also working for corporate employers. As a paralegal, you should thus have a basic knowledge of how corporations are formed and operated. You should also be familiar with the basic rights and responsibilities of corporate participants. These include the **shareholders** (the owners of the business, called shareholders because they purchase corporate **shares**, or stock), the **directors** (persons elected by the shareholders to direct corporate affairs), and the **officers** (persons hired by the directors to manage the day-to-day operations of the corporation). Corporate officers include the corporate president, vice president, secretary, treasurer, and possibly others, such as a chief financial officer and chief executive officer. Corporate officers are employees of the corporation and subject to employment contracts.

Although it is owned by individuals, the corporation is a separate legal entity, which is created and recognized by state law. In the eyes of the law, a corporation is a legal "person" that enjoys many of the rights and privileges that U.S. citizens enjoy, such as the right of access to the courts as an entity that can sue or be sued. It also has, among other rights, the right to due process of law and the right to freedom from unreasonable searches and seizures.

The Model Business Corporation Act (MBCA) is a codification of modern corporation law that has been influential in the codification of corporation statutes. Today, most state statutes are guided by the revised version of the MBCA, known as the Revised Model Business Corporation Act (RMBCA). There is, however, considerable variation among the statutes of the states that have based their statutes on the MBCA or the RMBCA, and several states do not follow either act. Because of this, as a paralegal you will need to rely on individual state corporation laws rather than the MBCA or RMBCA.

Corporate Formation

Generally, forming a corporation involves two steps. The first step consists of preliminary organizational and promotional undertakings—particularly, obtaining capital for the future corporation. Before a corporation becomes a reality, people invest in the proposed corporation as subscribers. The subscribers become the shareholder-owners of the corporation when the corporation becomes a legal entity.

For large corporations, *promoters* may be hired to help sell shares on behalf of the corporation. Promoters are those who, for themselves or others, take the preliminary steps in organizing a corporation. One of the tasks of the promoter is to

shareholder
One who has an ownership interest in a corporation through the purchase of corporate shares, or stock.

share
A unit of stock; a measure of ownership interest in a corporation.

director
A person elected by the shareholders to direct corporate affairs.

officer
A person hired by corporate directors to assist in the management of the day-to-day operations of the corporation.

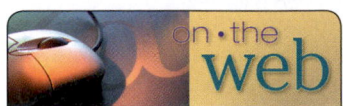

Enter "Model Business Corporation Act, Annotated" in the "Search" box at **www.abanet.org**. Other corporate law materials can be found at **www.law.cornell.edu**. Select "All topics" from the "Law about . . . " menu, and then select "Corporations" from the list.

EXHIBIT 18.2
Articles of Incorporation

Filed with Secretary of State
_____, 20_____

SHORT FORM
ARTICLES OF INCORPORATION
OF
Hiram, Inc.

ARTICLE I

The name of this corporation _____ Hiram, Inc. _____

ARTICLE II

The purpose of this corporation is to engage in any lawful act or activity for which a corporation may be organized under the General Corporation Law of New Pacum other than the banking business, the trust company business, or the practice of a profession permitted to be incorporated by the New Pacum Corporation Code.

ARTICLE III

The name and address in the State of New Pacum of this corporation's initial agent for service of process is: _____ Hiram Galliard, _____
8934 Rathburn Avenue, North Bend, New Pacum 98754

ARTICLE IV

The corporation is authorized to issue only one class of shares of stock; and the total number of shares that this corporation is authorized to issue is _____ 10,000 _____ .

ARTICLE V

The corporation is a close corporation. All the corporation's issued shares of stock shall be held of record by not more than ten (10) persons.

DATED: _____ June 3, 2011 _____

_____Hiram Galliard_____ _____Martha Bonnell_____

_____ _____
[Signature(s) of Incorporator/Directors(s)]
I (we) hereby declare that I (we) am (are) the person(s) who executed the foregoing Articles of Incorporation, which execution is my (our) act and deed.

_____Hiram Galliard_____ _____Martha Bonnell_____

---

issue a prospectus. A **prospectus** is a document that describes the corporation and its operations so that those who wish to purchase stock (invest) in the corporation have a basis for making an informed decision. (No prospectus is required for a close corporation, as we discuss shortly.)

The second step in forming a corporation is the process of incorporation. Exact procedures for incorporation differ among states, but the basic requirements are similar. The primary document needed to begin the incorporation process is called the **articles of incorporation** (see Exhibit 18.2 above for sample articles of incorporation for a small corporation). The articles include basic information about the corporation and serve as a primary source of authority for its future organization and business functions. Once they have been filed in the appropriate state office, the articles of incorporation become a public record.

Paralegals frequently assist their supervising attorneys in preparing incorporation papers and filing them with the appropriate state office. (See the *Developing Paralegal Skills* feature on page 593 for an illustration of how paralegals can help

prospectus
A document that discloses relevant facts about a company and its operations so that those who wish to purchase stock (invest) in the corporation have a basis for making an informed decision.

articles of incorporation
The document filed with the appropriate state official, usually the secretary of state, when a business is incorporated. State statutes usually prescribe what kind of information must be contained in the articles of incorporation.

featured contributor

GOING CORPORATE

Angela Schneeman

BIOGRAPHICAL NOTE

Angela Schneeman is a freelance paralegal and author who specializes in corporate law. She has been a paralegal since 1984, when she received her legal assistant certificate from the University of Minnesota, where she also earned her Bachelor of Science degree in Business and Legal Studies. Angela has worked as a paralegal for law firms, the legal departments of publicly held corporations, and a major accounting firm. She currently offers her services to attorneys in Minneapolis and St. Paul, Minnesota. Angela is the author of several textbooks for paralegals, including The Pocket Guide to Legal Ethics *and* The Law of Corporations and Other Business Organizations, *5th edition.*

If you are contemplating a new career as a paralegal, or perhaps a new focus on your current paralegal employment, you may want to explore a career as a corporate paralegal. Corporate paralegals may work in-house in a corporation's legal department, or they may work for a law firm and specialize in corporate law.

LAW FIRM VERSUS IN-HOUSE

Roughly 20 percent of all paralegals work in-house for corporations. Generally, the paralegals who work in corporate legal departments have relatively high job satisfaction. They are often paid better-than-average salaries, offered more benefits, required to work less overtime, and not subject to the billing requirements imposed on their counterparts in law firms.

Many paralegals who work for law firms, however, will tell you they wouldn't consider trading the fast-paced atmosphere of the law firm for an in-house position. Most corporate para-

legals who work in law firms assist one or more attorneys who represent a number of corporate clients. These paralegals are usually required to work at least forty hours per week and meet established billing requirements.

Most corporate paralegals have regular contact with the firm's corporate clients and may meet with them either at the law firm or at the client's office. Many corporate paralegals who work in law firms report that they enjoy the variety of their work and that they like working for a variety of corporate clients.

WHAT YOU'LL NEED TO KNOW

Corporate paralegals must be familiar with the business corporation act of the state in which they work and with federal law concerning corporations. In addition, paralegals must be familiar with the procedures of the state office, such as the secretary of state's office, that creates and regulates corporations.

certificate of incorporation (corporate charter)
The document issued by a state official, usually the secretary of state, granting a corporation legal existence and the right to function.

with incorporation tasks and the *Technology and Today's Paralegal* feature on pages 594 and 595 for a discussion of online incorporation.) Also, as a paralegal, you may need to obtain information about a corporation—for example, when you are conducting an investigation. For both of these reasons, you should know what information is generally included in the articles of incorporation. Exhibit 18.3 on page 592 lists and describes this information.

After the articles of incorporation have been prepared, signed, and authenticated by the incorporators, they are sent to the appropriate state official, usually the secretary of state, along with the appropriate filing fee. In many states, the secretary of state then issues a **certificate of incorporation** representing the state's authorization for the corporation to conduct business. (This may be called the **corporate**

WHAT YOU'LL BE DOING

The work of corporate paralegals is very diverse, and it's difficult to generalize about their duties. Paralegals who work in law firms are often responsible for maintaining the corporate minute books of all corporate clients and reviewing those books periodically to make sure annual minutes are prepared and that all documents are kept up to date. In-house paralegals may assist the corporate secretary in keeping the corporate record books up to date for the corporation and any subsidiaries. Corporate paralegals may also perform the following types of duties:

- Draft contracts and corporate documents of all types.
- Assist with incorporation and dissolution of corporations.
- Research state and federal corporate and securities law.
- Assist with mergers and acquisitions.
- Assist with completing and filing periodic reports with the Securities and Exchange Commission and stock exchanges.

CORPORATE SPECIALTIES

Because of the complexities of modern corporate law and transactions, most corporate attorneys and paralegals specialize. One popular corporate paralegal specialty is the area of mergers and acquisitions. Paralegals are essential members of most merger and acquisition teams and are often responsible for much of the related due-diligence work. Due-diligence work involves investigating the financial risks of a merger or acquisition. Large transactions can include on-site inspections of facilities and inventory, as well as the review of

> *"Because of the complexities of modern corporate law and transactions, most corporate attorneys and paralegals specialize."*

hundreds of documents. Paralegals collect, catalogue, and review the documents the other party is required to produce to close the transaction. They may also be responsible for preparing and producing documentation for the other party's review. Merger and acquisition work can require traveling and, at times, working long hours under pressure, but most paralegals who work in this area find it interesting and rewarding.

The area of mergers and acquisitions is just one example of a specialty for corporate paralegals. Some other areas corporate paralegals may specialize in include:

- Securities.
- International law.
- Contracts.
- Intellectual property.
- Labor.
- Business litigation.

In-house paralegals may specialize in one or more of the following areas:

- Corporate governance.
- Litigation.
- Contracts.
- Subsidiary maintenance.
- Shareholder relations.

The opportunities for corporate paralegals are vast and varied. If you are interested in beginning a career as a corporate paralegal, the chances are there is a position with the right specialty, working conditions, and challenges to suit you.

charter.) The certificate and a copy of the articles are returned to the incorporators, who then hold the initial organizational meeting that completes the details of incorporation. At this first organizational meeting, the corporation adopts a set of rules to govern the management of the corporation, called the **bylaws**. These bylaws grant or restrict the powers of the corporation.

bylaws
A set of governing rules adopted by a corporation or other association.

Classifications of Corporations

How a corporation is classified depends on its purpose, ownership characteristics, and location. A *private corporation* is, as the term indicates, a corporation that is privately owned. A *public corporation* is formed by the government for a political or

EXHIBIT 18.3
Information Generally Included in the Articles of Incorporation

THE NAME OF THE CORPORATION

- The choice of a corporate name is subject to state approval to ensure against duplication or deception. State statutes usually require that the secretary of state run a check on the proposed name in the state of incorporation. Once cleared, a name can be reserved for a short time, for a fee, pending the completion of the articles of incorporation.

THE NATURE AND PURPOSE OF THE CORPORATION

- The intended business activities of the corporation must be specified in the articles, and, naturally, they must be lawful. Stating a general corporate purpose (for example, "to engage in the production and sale of agricultural products") is usually sufficient to give rise to all of the powers necessary or convenient to the purpose of the organization.

THE DURATION OF THE CORPORATION

- A corporation can have perpetual existence under most state corporation statutes. A few states, however, prescribe a maximum duration, after which the corporation must formally renew its existence.

THE CAPITAL STRUCTURE OF THE CORPORATION

- The capital structure of the corporation may be set forth in the articles. A few state statutes require a relatively small capital investment (for example, $1,000) for ordinary business corporations but a greater capital investment for those engaged in insurance or banking. The number of shares of stock authorized for issuance, their valuation, the various types or classes of stock authorized for issuance, and other relevant information concerning equity, capital, and credit must be outlined in the articles.

THE INTERNAL ORGANIZATION OF THE CORPORATION

- Whatever the internal management structure of the corporation, it should be described in the articles, although it can be included in bylaws adopted after the corporation is formed.

THE REGISTERED OFFICE AND AGENT OF THE CORPORATION

- The corporation must indicate the location and address of its registered office within the state. Usually, the registered office is also the principal office of the corporation. The corporation must give the name and address of a specific person who has been designated as an agent and who can receive legal documents (including service of process) on behalf of the corporation.

THE NAMES AND ADDRESSES OF THE INCORPORATORS

- Each incorporator must be listed by name and must indicate an address. An incorporator is a person—often the corporate promoter—who applies to the state on behalf of the corporation to obtain its corporate charter. States vary on the required minimum number of incorporators; it can be as few as one or as many as three. Incorporators are required to sign the articles of incorporation when they are submitted to the state; often, this is their only duty. In some states, they participate at the first organizational meeting of the corporation.

Developing Paralegal Skills

RESERVING A CORPORATE NAME

Jon Thomas is a paralegal at a law firm. A local building contractor, Thiess Brown, comes to the law firm for assistance. He believes that his firm is going to grow and that he should incorporate. In a discussion with Jon and his supervising attorney, Brown asks about calling his new corporation Thiess Construction. The attorney says that the availability of the name will be investigated as part of the incorporation process. Jon is assigned to look into the naming issue.

Jon knows that, as in most states, he must contact the secretary of state's office to check on the availability of names for corporations. In Jon's state, the secretary of state's Department of Business Services maintains the database of registered corporate names in the state. A search of the department's Web site reveals that the names Thiess Construction and Thiess Corporation are not in use. Either name could be reserved for Brown's firm. Jon also checks a list of available domain names at the Web site of Network Solutions to find out whether Brown can purchase the domain name **thiessconstruction.com** should he want to establish a Web site. Then Jon goes to the Web site of the U.S. Patent and Trademark Office to check the availability of names for possible trademark use.

TIPS FOR CLAIMING A CORPORATE NAME, DOMAIN NAME, AND TRADEMARK

- Determine if the preferred name and several possible alternatives are available.
- Check on the possibility of registering the company name, or a part of it, as a trademark or service mark. This is especially valuable should the company grow larger.
- Check on the availability of domain names for the client to use today or in the future for a Web site. Buying a Web site (URL) before a firm becomes well known is good strategy.
- Provide the lists of possibilities to your supervising attorney for the client's consideration.
- Once the client has decided what should be done, file the appropriate forms.

---

governmental purpose, as when a town incorporates. Note that a public corporation is not the same as a publicly held corporation. A **publicly held corporation** is any corporation whose shares are or could be publicly traded in securities markets, such as the New York Stock Exchange.

Corporations may also be classified as either *for-profit corporations* or *not-for-profit* (or *nonprofit*) *corporations*. A not-for-profit corporation may be formed by a group—such as a charitable association, a hospital, or a religious organization—to conduct its business without exposing the individual owners to personal liability.

Corporations owned by a small group of shareholders, such as family members, are called **close corporations**, or *closely held corporations*. Unlike publicly held corporations, close corporations cannot sell their shares on public securities markets and usually place restrictions on the transfer of corporate shares—to keep the business in the family, for example, or for some other reason. State laws may provide more flexibility for close corporations, in terms of statutory formalities that must be observed, than for other corporations. Also, certain close corporations are permitted to elect a special corporate tax status under Subchapter S of the Internal Revenue Code. These corporations are called *S corporations*.

Lawyers, physicians, accountants, architects, engineers, and other professionals sometimes incorporate as *professional corporations*. We discuss these organizations later in this chapter.

publicly held corporation
A corporation whose shares are eligible to be publicly traded in securities markets, such as the New York Stock Exchange.

close corporation
A corporation owned by a small group of shareholders, often family members; also called a *closely held corporation*. Shares in close corporations cannot be publicly traded on the stock market, and often other restrictions on stock transfer apply. Some close corporations qualify for special tax status as *S corporations*.

Technology and Today's Paralegal

ONLINE INCORPORATION

Today, it is easy to form a corporation for any lawful purpose in any state. The requirements, however, differ from state to state. As a paralegal, your supervising attorney may ask you to assist a client who wishes to incorporate a business. The client may wish to incorporate in the state in which she already does business, in another state, or even in another country. As a paralegal, you may not advise clients on where to form a corporation. You can, however, assist in the process by using the Internet to find out the formal requirements and cost of incorporation in various states. In addition, you can find numerous online providers of company formation and registered agent services. (The *registered agent* acts as the original incorporator, files the articles of incorporation, and may remain the registered agent for the life of the corporation.)

RESEARCHING STATE REQUIREMENTS

Nearly every state has a Web site at which you can find out the state's requirements for incorporation. Typically, incorporation is handled by the secretary of state's office. You can locate the state's site by performing a general search using the state's name, or you can go to a directory such as that offered by the Library of Congress at **www.loc.gov**, open "Resources for Researchers" and enter "stategov," or by State and Local Government on the Net at **www.statelocalgov.net**. Most state sites post guidelines or instructions on forming corporations (and other business entities), fee schedules, and frequently asked

---

dividend
A distribution of profits to corporate shareholders, disbursed in proportion to the number of shares held.

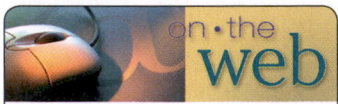

For a site that offers online incorporation services, go to **www.bizfilings.com**. For a government Web site with links to various sources of information on incorporation, go to **www.business. gov**. From the "Register, Licenses & Permits" menu, select "Incorporate a business."

Directors and Officers

The articles of incorporation name the initial board of directors, which is appointed by the incorporators. Thereafter, the board of directors is elected by a majority vote of the shareholders. The board holds formal meetings and records the minutes (formal notes of what transpired at the meetings). Each director has one vote, and generally the majority rules. The directors' rights include the right to participate in board meetings and the right to inspect corporate books and records. The directors' responsibilities to the corporation and its shareholders include declaring and paying **dividends** (payments to shareholders representing their share of corporate profits), appointing and removing officers, and making significant policy decisions.

The board of directors appoints the corporate officers, who manage the day-to-day operations of the firm. As previously mentioned, the officers are employees of the corporation and are subject to employment contracts. Officers are also agents of the corporation. (We discuss agency later in this chapter.)

Directors and officers have fiduciary duties (discussed in detail on page 599) to the corporation and its shareholder-owners, including the duty of loyalty and the duty to exercise reasonable care when conducting corporate business. The duty of loyalty is breached when an officer or director uses corporate funds or confidences for personal gain, as when an officer discloses company secrets (such as a proposed merger) to an outsider. The duty of care is breached when a director's or officer's negligence—failure to make informed and reasonable decisions—results in harmful consequences for the corporate entity. Corporate directors and officers can face criminal penalties, including imprisonment, for their actions or for the actions of employees under their supervision. In addition, a corporation may be held financially liable for any criminal acts or torts committed by its agents or officers within the course and scope of their employment.

questions (FAQs). Many also provide downloadable corporate forms. Most states also have searchable databases of corporate names and registered agents.

ONLINE INCORPORATION SERVICES

Many companies provide incorporation services online that will assist you with incorporation. Although many sites are aimed at persons seeking to incorporate, some target law firms as clients and provide additional beneficial services. For example, if your client is interested in forming a corporation in Delaware (the most popular state for incorporation), Harvard Business Services (**www.delawareinc. com**) offers a fast and efficient way to incorporate. In addition, it provides free downloadable forms and will act as the corporation's registered agent for a fixed annual fee of fifty dollars. Other companies, such as Intuit, offer such services as well (go to **mycorporatiion.intuit.com**).

Another Web site of use to corporate attorneys and paralegals is that of the Corporation Service Company (CSC) at **www.incspot.com**. CSC offers a range of services, including corporate formation and registered agent services. In addition, the company will scan and upload all the documents related to a transaction or litigation into an online database, providing centralized access to important documents for authorized users anywhere in the world and allowing multiple parties to track ongoing negotiations. Useful news and substantive law updates (federal and state) are provided at this site as well. CSC also sponsors the Paralegal Leadership Institute, which provides educational seminars (and CLE credits) to paralegals at locations across the country.

TECHNOLOGY TIP

The Web can assist paralegals with the incorporation process in many ways. It provides an efficient means of finding out state requirements, obtaining the proper forms, and keeping abreast of current developments affecting corporations. The usefulness of a particular site will depend on the paralegal's level of experience and the individual needs of the client or firm.

The Sarbanes-Oxley Act imposes numerous disclosure requirements on corporate directors and officers of publicly held companies. Chief corporate executives—and the lawyers and accountants who work for them—must take legal responsibility for the accuracy of their financial statements and reports or risk steep penalties for violating the act.

Shareholders

Any person who purchases a share in a corporation becomes an owner of the corporation. Through shareholders' meetings, the shareholders play an important role in the corporate entity—they elect the directors who control the corporation, and they have a right to vote (one vote per share) on decisions that significantly affect the corporation. They also have a right to share in corporate profits proportionate to the number of shares they hold. Shareholders do not manage the daily affairs of the corporation, nor are they liable for corporate debts or other obligations beyond the amounts of their investments. Corporate owners, or shareholders, thus have *limited liability*—a key advantage of the corporate form of business.

Corporate Taxation

The corporation as an entity pays income taxes on corporate profits. Then, when the profits are distributed to the shareholders in the form of dividends, the shareholders pay personal income taxes on the income they receive. This double-taxation feature of the corporate form of business is one of its major disadvantages.

Some small (close) corporations are permitted to avoid the double taxation of corporate profits by electing S corporation status under Subchapter S of the Internal Revenue Code. An S corporation, like a partnership, is a "pass-through"

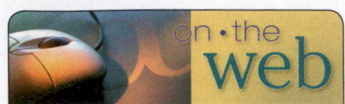

Hoover's Online has an extensive collection of data on U.S. corporations at **www.hoovers.com**.

liquidation
In regard to corporations, the process by which corporate assets are converted into cash and distributed among creditors and shareholders according to specific rules of preference.

entity for tax purposes. This means that the corporation itself does not pay income taxes. Instead, it files an information return only, as a partnership does, indicating the corporation's net profits. The S corporation shareholders declare their proportionate shares of the corporation's net income on their personal tax returns and pay taxes on that income accordingly.

Corporate Termination

Like partnership termination, corporate termination involves two steps. The first step, dissolution, extinguishes the legal existence of the corporation. The second step, **liquidation**, involves the winding up of the corporation's business affairs. After creditors have been paid, all remaining assets are distributed to the shareholders. The secretary of state is notified that the corporation no longer exists.

Corporations can be terminated at a time specified in the articles of incorporation or by the agreement of the shareholders and the board of directors. In certain circumstances, a court may dissolve a corporation. For example, if the directors are deadlocked and cannot agree on the management of the corporation, a court may grant a shareholder's petition to dissolve the corporation. A corporation may also be terminated by law if it fails to meet certain statutory requirements, such as the payment of taxes or annual fees.

Limited Liability Organizations

Recall that one of the major tax advantages of a partnership is that the partnership's income passes through to the partners as personal income. Consequently, partners avoid the double-taxation feature of the corporate form of business. But there is a price to pay for this tax advantage: partners face unlimited personal liability. The partners normally can avoid unlimited personal liability by incorporating their business, because corporate owners (shareholders) have limited liability. But again, there is a price to pay: the double taxation of profits characteristic of the corporate form of business.

As mentioned, one way to achieve both goals—limited liability and single taxation of profits—is to elect S corporation status. Certain requirements must be met, however, before a corporation can qualify for S corporation status. One requirement is that the corporation have one hundred or fewer shareholders, thus excluding large firms. Another requirement is that an S corporation may have only one class of stock (meaning that there is little flexibility in how corporate profits are distributed). Additionally, certain entities (such as partnerships and, with some exceptions, corporations) cannot be shareholders in an S corporation.

Several forms of organization have developed to address these problems. They include the limited liability company, the limited liability partnership, and the professional corporation. The use of these business forms has spread quickly because of the advantages they offer to businesspersons.

Limited Liability Companies

limited liability company (LLC)
A hybrid form of business organization authorized by a state in which the owners of the business have limited liability and taxes on profits are passed through the business entity to the owners.

The **limited liability company (LLC)** is a hybrid form of business enterprise that combines the pass-through tax benefits of S corporations and partnerships with the limited liability of limited partners and corporate shareholders. Like the limited partnership and the corporation, an LLC must be formed and operated in compliance with state law. To form an LLC, *articles of organization* must be filed with a central state agency, such as the secretary of state's office. The business's name must include the words "Limited Liability Company" or the initials "L.L.C."

A major advantage of the LLC is that, as indicated, it does not pay taxes as an entity. Rather, profits are "passed through" the LLC and paid personally by the owners of the company, who are called *members* instead of shareholders. Another key advantage is that the liability of members is limited to the amounts of their investments. In an LLC, members are also allowed to participate in management activities, and under some state statutes, the firm's managers need not even be members of the LLC. Yet another advantage is that corporations and partnerships, as well as foreign investors, can be LLC members. Additionally, in contrast to S corporations, there is no limit on the number of members of the LLC. Finally, part of the LLC's attractiveness to businesspersons is the flexibility it offers. The members can themselves decide how to operate the various aspects of the business through a simple operating agreement.

The disadvantages of the LLC are relatively few, so this form of organization has become very popular for smaller, privately held companies. Generally, the major disadvantage has been the lack of uniformity among state statutes with respect to LLCs. The differences among the states are disappearing, however.

Limited Liability Partnerships

The **limited liability partnership (LLP)** is similar to the LLC. The difference is that the LLP is designed more for professionals, such as attorneys, who normally do business as partners in a partnership. Like LLCs, LLPs must be formed and operated in compliance with state statutes. The appropriate form must be filed with a central state agency, usually the secretary of state's office, and the business's name must include either "Limited Liability Partnership" or the initials "L.L.P."

The major advantage of the LLP is that it allows a partnership to function as a pass-through entity for tax purposes but limits the personal liability of the partners for partnership tort liability. Although LLP statutes vary from state to state, generally each state statute limits in some way the liability of partners. In most states, it is relatively easy to convert a traditional partnership into an LLP because the firm's basic organizational structure remains the same. Additionally, all of the laws governing partnerships still apply (apart from those modified by the LLP statute). Normally, an LLP statute is simply an amendment to a state's already existing partnership law.

A few states provide for a specific type of limited partnership called a *limited liability limited partnership* (LLLP). In an LLLP, the liability of all partners is limited to the amounts of their investments in the firm.

> **limited liability partnership (LLP)**
> A hybrid form of business organization authorized by a state that allows professionals to enjoy the tax benefits of a partnership while limiting in some way the normal joint and several liability of partners.

Professional Corporations

Professionals in practice together, such as a group of physicians or lawyers, traditionally formed partnerships or limited partnerships. An alternative to those forms of organization that is used in many states is the **professional corporation (PC)**. While the rules vary from state to state, in general a PC may only be formed by licensed professionals, such as a group of dentists.

A practicing professional can be held personally liable for malpractice, but the existence of the professional corporation limits the liability of the other members. For example, suppose a group of physicians owns a PC through which they offer medical services. If one physician in the group is found liable for monetary damages due to medical malpractice, the other physicians in the professional corporation are not likely to be personally liable for that judgment. The physician who lost the malpractice suit would be personally liable, but other members of the medical practice would be protected.

In general, only the professionals involved in the PC can be owners. In other words, there cannot be outside investors; only members of the practice can be shareholders in the firm, and all members of the firm must be licensed members of the same profession. So that people who deal with the firm are aware of its legal status, state law requires that the name must be followed by the letters "P.C."

> **professional corporation (PC)**
> A corporation formed by professionals, such as attorneys or accountants. Each member of the firm is liable for his or her own malpractice, but generally protected by limited liability as in the corporate form.

BUSINESS ORGANIZATIONS AND THE PARALEGAL

We have already mentioned many of the ways in which paralegals benefit from a knowledge of business organizations. Because so much legal work has to do with business clients, it is impossible to summarize the many tasks involving business organizations that paralegals carry out. The following list, however, will give you an idea of some of the types of work that paralegals frequently perform in this area:

- Reserve a corporate name for an incorporator.

- Draft a partnership agreement and the documents necessary to form a limited partnership or limited liability company; file the required papers with the appropriate state office.

- Prepare articles of incorporation and file them with the appropriate state office.

- Prepare minutes of corporate meetings and maintain a minutes binder.

- Review or prepare documents relating to the sale of corporate securities (stocks and bonds); assist a supervising attorney in making sure that federal and state requirements relating to the sale of corporate securities are met.

- Assist in the dissolution of a partnership or corporation.

- Assist in litigation relating to a corporation or other form of business.

- Research state laws governing partnerships, corporations, and limited liability organizations.

AGENCY LAW

agency
A relationship between two persons in which one person (the agent) represents or acts in the place of the other (the principal).

The common law of agency involves concepts and principles with which all paralegals should be familiar. Agency is a pervasive concept in our society because little work could get done without agents. An **agency** relationship exists when one party, called the **agent**, agrees to represent or act for another party, called the **principal**. If you are working as a paralegal employee, in essence you are an agent of your employer. Attorneys, because they represent and act for their clients, are agents of those clients. All forms of business organizations involve agents. Indeed, a business world without agents is hard to imagine. Imagine the founder of Microsoft Corporation, Bill Gates, having had to design, produce, and sell all of his company's software. Obviously, other people had to be appointed to fill in—act as agents—for the owners of Microsoft—the principal.

agent
A person who is authorized to act for or in the place of another person (the principal).

principal
In agency law, a person who, by agreement or otherwise, authorizes another person (the agent) to act on the principal's behalf in such a way that the acts of the agent become binding on the principal.

Employees and Independent Contractors

Normally, all employees who deal with third parties are deemed to be agents. ▶ **EXAMPLE 18.3** A salesperson in a department store is an agent of the store's owner (the principal) and acts on the owner's behalf. Any sale of goods made by the salesperson to a customer is binding on the principal. Similarly, most representations of fact made by the salesperson with respect to the goods sold are binding on the principal. ◀

Agency relationships can also arise between employers and independent contractors (such as real estate agents) who are hired to perform special tasks or services (such as the sale of property). An **independent contractor** is a person who is hired to perform a specific undertaking but who is free to choose how and when to perform the work. ▶ **EXAMPLE 18.4** Building contractors and subcontractors are independent contractors because the property owner does not control the acts of either of these professionals. Truck drivers who own their equipment and hire themselves out on a per-job basis are independent contractors, but truck drivers who drive company trucks on a regular basis are usually classified as employees. ◀ Generally, courts look at the degree of control and supervision the employer exercised over the work performed to determine if the individual was an employee or an independent contractor. *An independent contractor may or may not be an agent.*

independent contractor
A person who is hired to perform a specific undertaking but who is free to choose how and when to perform the work. An independent contractor may or may not be an agent.

Agency Formation

Normally, agency relationships come about voluntarily by agreement of the parties. Although the parties often sign a contract (such as an agreement to list a house for sale with a real estate agent), the agreement need not be in writing. ▶ **EXAMPLE 18.5** If Deborah asks Ling, a gardener, to contract with others to landscape her yard, and Ling agrees, an agency relationship is created. If Ling then enters into a contract with a landscape architect to design Deborah's yard, Deborah, as the principal, is legally bound by that contract. ◀

An agency agreement can also be implied by conduct. ▶ **EXAMPLE 18.6** Suppose that a hotel allows Dwight to park cars to earn tips, even though Dwight does not have an employment contract there. The hotel's manager tells Dwight when to work, as well as where and how to park the cars. The hotel's conduct implies that Dwight has authority to act as a parking valet, and Dwight will be considered the hotel's agent for that purpose. ◀

An agency relationship can also arise if the *principal* causes a third person to reasonably believe that another person is his or her agent, thus creating the *appearance* of an agency that does not in fact exist. ▶ **EXAMPLE 18.7** Carmen, a sales representative, brings her friend with her to solicit orders from a customer and repeatedly refers to her friend as her assistant. The customer reasonably believes that the friend works with Carmen and proceeds to place orders with the friend. Carmen will not be allowed to deny that the friend is her agent. ◀ Similarly, if a principal approves or affirms a contract after the fact—by filling orders placed with a person who was not truly an agent, for example—an agency relationship is created.

Fiduciary Duties

An important concept in agency law is that an agency is a **fiduciary relationship**—one involving a high degree of trust and confidence. Because of this, certain fiduciary duties arise whenever an agency relationship comes into existence. Basically, this means that each party owes the other the duty to act honestly and to pursue faithfully the objective of the agency.

The principal is obligated to cooperate with the agent, provide safe working conditions for the agent, and reimburse the agent for work performed and for any expenses incurred while working on the principal's behalf. The agent, in turn, must perform his tasks competently and must obey and be loyal to the principal. The duty of loyalty means that the agent's actions must be strictly for the benefit of the principal and must not result in any secret profit for the agent. In addition, the agent cannot represent two principals in the same transaction unless both know of the dual capacity and consent to it. The agent also has a duty to notify the principal of all matters that come to her or his attention concerning the subject matter of the agency and to render an accounting to the principal of all property and funds received and paid out on behalf of the principal.

Duties also imply rights. In general, the agent has a right corresponding to every duty owed by the principal, and vice versa. Consider that when an attorney serves as an agent for a client (the principal), the attorney has a duty of loyalty to the client. The client, therefore, has a right to the attorney's loyalty. If you read through your state's ethical rules governing attorneys, you will find that many of the rules governing attorney-client relationships are rooted in these agency concepts.

> **fiduciary relationship**
> A relationship involving a high degree of trust and confidence.

Agency Relationships and Third Parties

Agency law also comes into play when disputes arise over who should be liable—the principal, the agent, or both—when an agent either forms a contract with a third party or causes injury to a third party. Generally, a principal is liable only for the authorized actions of her agent. Because the principal is frequently an employer

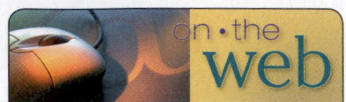

respondeat superior

A doctrine in agency law under which a principal-employer may be held liable for the wrongful acts committed by agents or employees acting within the scope of their agency or employment.

vicarious liability

Legal responsibility placed on one person for the acts of another.

or company that has greater resources with which to pay damages (has "deeper pockets") than the employee, the injured party usually seeks to hold the principal liable for the loss or damage caused by an agent.

Contract Liability

If an agent is not authorized to enter into a contract on behalf of the principal, then normally the principal will not be bound by the contract unless he or she voluntarily accepts (ratifies) it. An agent may be clearly authorized, either orally or in writing, to form certain contracts. The agent's authority may also be implied by custom—that is, an agent normally has the authority to do whatever is customary or necessary to fulfill the purpose of the agency. A paralegal office manager, for example, has the implied authority to enter into a contract to purchase office supplies on behalf of the firm because the authority to purchase supplies is necessary to the duties of office manager.

Tort Liability

Obviously, any person, including an agent, is liable for her or his own torts. Whether a principal can also be held liable for an agent's torts depends largely on whether the agent was an employee and whether the agent was acting within the scope of his or her employment at the time of committing the tort.

Under the doctrine of **respondeat superior**,[1] the principal-employer is liable for harm caused to a third party by an agent-employee *acting within the scope of employment*. The doctrine imposes **vicarious liability** on the employer—that is, liability without regard to the personal fault of the employer—for torts committed by an employee in the course or scope of employment. The theory of *respondeat superior* is similar in this respect to the theory of strict liability covered in Chapter 14.

Today's courts consider a number of factors in determining whether a particular act occurred within the course and scope of employment. If the employer authorized the act or had reason to know that the employee would do the act in question, if the injury occurred during work hours, or if the employer furnished the means or tools (for example, a truck or a machine) that caused the injury, that fact would point toward employer liability. In contrast, if the injury occurred after work hours or while the employee was on a "frolic" of his or her own, having substantially abandoned the employer's business, the employer might not be held responsible. These factors are illustrated in the *Developing Paralegal Skills* feature.

Liability for Independent Contractors' Torts

Generally, the principal is not liable for physical harm caused to a third person by the negligent act of an independent contractor in the performance of the contract. This is because the employer does not have the right to control the details of an independent contractor's performance. Exceptions to this rule are made in certain situations, however, as when exceptionally hazardous activities are involved or when the employer does in fact exercise a significant degree of control over the contractor's performance.

AGENCY LAW AND THE PARALEGAL

A knowledge of agency law is important for the paralegal for several reasons. As a paralegal employee, you will be directly involved in an agency relationship, and it is to your advantage to know what kinds of rights and duties are involved in that relationship. A knowledge of agency law also helps you understand the ethical rules of the legal profession, many of which are derived from the common law of agency.

Furthermore, in your work as a paralegal, you will often be dealing with agents and issues of agency. For instance, each partner in a partnership is considered an agent of every other partner in the firm and thus has fiduciary duties to the other partners. Corporate officers (such as corporate presidents and vice presidents) are agents of the corporation and, as such, assume the fiduciary duties that arise in agency relationships. Paralegals

Developing
Paralegal Skills

A CASE OF *RESPONDEAT SUPERIOR*

Rosie Ball, a single parent, and her son Steven were driving home from the grocery store one winter evening in their Kia. They were slowly making their way down an icy street. As they approached an intersection with a stop sign for oncoming traffic, their car was hit by a Mercedes. The Mercedes was speeding, and the driver went through the stop sign at forty-five miles per hour. In the accident, Steven sustained a severe head injury that resulted in irreparable brain damage. The occupants of the Mercedes, a married couple, had gone out for dinner, had several drinks, and then stopped to buy Christmas cards for clients of the husband's employer, a multimillion-dollar business.

Seeking representation, Rosie contacted the office of attorney Jared Mills. Jared is the supervising attorney for paralegal Tom Mintin. After meeting with Rosie, the attorney asks Tom to research the issue of whether the multimillion-dollar business can be held liable for the car accident under a theory of *respondeat superior*. Tom researches the issue and learns that an employer is liable under *respondeat superior* for the negligent acts of an employee if the acts are committed in the scope of his or her employment. The employer may also be liable for an employee's acts if the acts occur while the employee is on a brief "detour" from the employer's work—such as when a paralegal employee stops by the dry cleaner's for personal reasons while on the way to the courthouse for her employer. The employer is not liable, however, if the employee is on a "frolic" of his own and is not pursuing work that he was hired to perform.

CHECKLIST FOR DETERMINING LIABILITY
UNDER THE DOCTRINE OF *RESPONDEAT SUPERIOR*

- Did the employee's act constitute a tort?
- Did the employee commit the act within the course and scope of his employment?
- Was the act committed during work hours or after work hours?
- Did the employer authorize the act or have reason to know that the employee would do the act?
- Did the employer furnish the means by which the injury was inflicted (the car, for example)?
- Was the act committed during a brief detour from the employee's course of employment, or was the employee on a "frolic" of his own when the act occurred?

who work on behalf of corporate clients or who specialize in the area of corporate law will find that agency law permeates the corporate environment.

For paralegals working in the employment context, the doctrine of *respondeat superior* is particularly important because the outcome of many employment cases is influenced by this legal concept. For example, when an employee sues an employer for a supervisor's harassment, the employer may have to pay damages to the employee even though the employer was unaware of the supervisor's actions.

EMPLOYMENT LAW

Whenever a business organization hires an employee, an employment relationship is established. In the United States, employment relationships traditionally have been governed primarily by the common law. Today, though, federal and state statutes regulate the workplace extensively and provide employees with many rights and protections. Common law doctrines apply to areas *not* covered by statutory law.

Because attorneys and paralegals are frequently involved in legal work relating to employment relationships, you should have a basic understanding of employment law. In this section, we look at the common law doctrine governing employment relationships and at some of the ways in which the government regulates today's workplace.

Employment at Will

employment at will
A common law doctrine under which employment is considered to be "at will"—that is, either party may terminate the employment relationship at any time and for any reason, unless a contract or statute specifies otherwise.

Traditionally, employment relationships have been governed by the common law doctrine of employment at will, as well as by the common law rules governing contracts, torts, and agency. Under the doctrine of **employment at will**, either party may terminate an employment relationship at any time and for any reason, unless a contract or statute specifically provides otherwise. Today, most American workers have the legal status of "employees at will."

Nonetheless, there are many situations in which the doctrine is not applied. Sometimes, an employment contract specifies the circumstances under which an employee can be fired. Even in the absence of an express employment contract, some courts have held that an *implied* contract exists—for example, when an employee manual states that, as a matter of policy, workers will be dismissed only for "good cause." (For this reason, it is often important for a paralegal to read the employee manual when researching an employee's termination.) Also, as mentioned, federal and state statutes governing employment relationships prevent the at-will doctrine from being applied in a number of circumstances. Today's employer is not permitted to fire an employee if to do so would violate a federal or state employment statute, such as one prohibiting employment termination for discriminatory reasons (to be discussed shortly).

Wrongful Discharge

wrongful discharge
An employer's termination of an employee's employment in violation of the law.

Whenever an employer discharges an employee in violation of an employment contract or a statutory law protecting employees, the employee may bring an action for **wrongful discharge**. For example, most states have a statute prohibiting employers from discharging an employee because the employee has filed a workers' compensation claim, reported for jury duty, performed some other public duty, or refused to commit an illegal act. ▶ **EXAMPLE 18.8** An employee of a construction company is hit by a falling brick and suffers a serious injury. The employee files a claim for workers' compensation (discussed shortly). The employer then fires the employee. The employee can sue for wrongful discharge. ◀

Most wrongful discharge suits arise because an employer has violated a statutory right or duty of an employee, as just discussed. Wrongful discharge can also arise from the violation of a common law principle. ▶ **EXAMPLE 18.9** Cool Company hired Yvonne to be its representative in Detroit. She was to be paid a 20 percent commission for all business generated. After a year, Cool fired Yvonne and did not pay her a commission on business that she generated in the last three months she worked for Cool. Yvonne can sue for breach of contract and also for wrongful discharge. ◀

constructive discharge
A termination of employment that occurs when the employer causes the employee's working conditions to be so intolerable that a reasonable person in the employee's position would feel compelled to quit.

Sometimes, employees claim that they were "constructively discharged" from their jobs. **Constructive discharge** occurs when the employer causes the employee's working conditions to be so intolerable that a reasonable person in the employee's position would feel compelled to quit. This issue arises, for example, in some sexual-harassment cases, as we will soon review.

Labor Laws

In the early decades of the twentieth century, employees began to organize to protect their interests. They formed associations called *labor unions* and elected union representatives to bargain with employers for improved wages and working conditions. The ultimate weapon of the labor union was, of course, the *strike*. By their

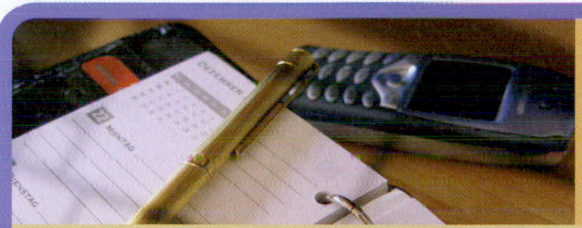

In the **Office**

PRODUCTIVE MEETINGS

When working on a case, you may attend team meetings that involve several attorneys and paralegals. Of course, you will want to prepare questions to ask at the meeting to help gather information you need to guide your work. But you will not want to be pulled into lengthy discussions about unrelated matters or about cases that are not related to your work. Once your part of the meeting is finished, you can excuse yourself to get back to work unless it is clear you are expected to stay. Most supervisors respect employees who are dedicated to the task at hand.

organized refusal to work, employees could bring their employer's operations to a halt—to the financial detriment of the employer.

In 1932, Congress established the legal right of employees to organize labor unions with the passage of the Norris-LaGuardia Act. The act protected peaceful strikes, picketing, and boycotts and restricted the power of the federal courts to enjoin (stop or prohibit) labor unions from engaging in peaceful strikes.

The Norris-LaGuardia Act was strengthened by the enactment of the National Labor Relations Act (NLRA) of 1935. The twin goals of the NLRA were to protect workers' efforts to organize into unions and to promote **collective bargaining** (bargaining between union representatives and employers) as a peaceful method of dispute resolution. The NLRA sought to curb activities that would discourage or prevent collective bargaining efforts conducted on behalf of the workers. The NLRA also created the National Labor Relations Board (NLRB) to oversee the enforcement of the statute. Congress gave the NLRB the power to investigate alleged NLRA violations and to prevent continued violations by particular employers.

Another law to protect workers was the Fair Labor Standards Act (FLSA) of 1938. Among other things, the act prohibited the oppression or exploitation of children by regulating the employment of minors. For example, under the act, children below the age of sixteen cannot be employed on a full-time basis except in very limited circumstances. The FLSA also established guidelines regulating overtime pay and minimum hourly wages. The act provided that if in any week an employee works more than forty hours, the hours in excess of the first forty must be compensated at one and a half times the employee's regular hourly rate. As for the minimum hourly wage, it represents the absolute minimum amount that an employer can pay an employee per hour. The minimum wage rate, which is set by Congress, is changed periodically.

collective bargaining
The process by which labor and management negotiate the terms and conditions of employment, including wages, benefits, working conditions, and other matters.

Several law firms that specialize in labor law publish online newsletters that discuss current issues relating to labor and employment law. For examples of the information available, go to **www.arentfox.com** or **www.wilmerhale.com**, select "Publications," and browse through the offerings.

Family and Medical Leave

In 1993, Congress passed the Family and Medical Leave Act (FMLA) to protect employees who need time off work for family or medical reasons. The FMLA requires employers who have fifty or more employees to provide employees with up to twelve weeks of family or medical leave during any twelve-month period. During the employee's leave, the employer must continue the worker's health-care coverage and guarantee employment in the same position or a comparable position when the employee returns to work. An important exception to the FMLA allows the employer to avoid reinstatement of a *key employee*—defined as an employee

Ethics Watch

DISPENSING LEGAL ADVICE

Lara, a paralegal, was interviewing a client who was considering petitioning for bankruptcy. The client's right arm was in a sling. After Lara asked him about the injury, he described how it had happened. He also said that he had been unable to work at his job as a mechanic for two weeks and that he was worried because his employer was threatening to fire him if he couldn't return to work within another week or two. When Lara looked puzzled at this news, the client asked her what was wrong. She said, "Well, I'm wondering how you could be fired, because employers are required by law to give their employees medical leave for up to twelve weeks during any one-year period." Lara said that she would check with her supervising attorney about that matter, and then she continued the interview. The client, relying on Lara's statement, later confronted his employer and demanded a twelve-week leave. The employer fired him on the spot. The employer had only a few employees and was not subject to the leave requirements of the Family and Medical Leave Act.

Lara could be considered to have engaged in the unauthorized practice of law by giving legal advice to a client. That would be a violation of the NFPA Model Code of Ethics and Professional Responsibility, Section EC-1.8: "A paralegal shall comply with the applicable legal authority governing the unauthorized practice of law in the jurisdiction in which the paralegal practices." It would also violate the NALA Code of Ethics, Canon 4: "A paralegal must use discretion and professional judgment commensurate with knowledge and experience but must not render independent legal judgment in place of an attorney."

whose pay falls within the top 10 percent of the firm's workforce. Additionally, the act does not apply to employees who have worked less than one year or less than twenty-five hours a week during the previous twelve months.

Generally, an employee may take family leave when he or she wishes to care for a newborn baby, a newly adopted child, or a foster child just placed in the employee's care. An employee may take medical leave when the employee or the employee's spouse, child, or parent has a "serious health condition" requiring care. For most absences, the employee must demonstrate that the health condition requires continued treatment by a health-care provider and includes a period of incapacity of more than three days. Employees suffering from certain chronic health conditions, such as asthma and diabetes, as well as employees who are pregnant, may take FMLA leave for their own incapacities that require absences of less than three days.

Remedies for violations of the FMLA include (1) damages for unpaid wages (or salary), lost benefits, denied compensation, and actual monetary losses (such as the cost of providing for care) up to an amount equivalent to the employee's wages for twelve weeks; (2) job reinstatement; and (3) promotion. The successful plaintiff is entitled to court costs, attorneys' fees, and—in cases involving bad faith on the part of the employer—double damages. Supervisors may also be subject to personal liability, as employers, for violations of the act.

workers' compensation laws
State statutes that establish an administrative procedure for compensating workers for injuries that arise out of or in the course of their employment, regardless of fault.

State Workers' Compensation Laws

State **workers' compensation laws** establish an administrative procedure for compensating workers injured on the job. Instead of suing, an injured worker files a claim with the administrative agency or board that administers the local workers' compensation claims. State workers' compensation statutes normally allow employers to purchase insurance from a private insurer or a state fund to pay workers' compensation benefits in the event of a claim. Most states also allow employers to be *self-insured*—that is, employers who show an ability to pay claims do not need to buy insurance.

In general, the right to recover benefits is based wholly on the existence of an employment relationship and the fact that the injury was *accidental* and *occurred on the job or in the course of employment,* regardless of fault. Intentionally inflicted self-injury, in contrast, would not be accidental and hence would not be covered. If an injury occurred while an employee was commuting to or from work, it usually would not be considered to have occurred on the job or in the course of employment and hence would not be covered.

The employee must notify the employer of the injury promptly (usually within thirty days of the injury's occurrence). Generally, the employee also must file a workers' compensation claim with the appropriate state agency or board within a certain period (sixty days to two years) from the time the injury is first noticed, rather than from the time of the accident.

The existence of workers' compensation benefits bars the employee from suing for injuries caused by the employer's negligence. ▶ **EXAMPLE 18.10** Jim was hit by a falling brick while working at a construction site. He contacts an attorney who advises him that in his state, workers' compensation benefits will likely total about $200,000, given the nature of the injury. Jim wants to reject those benefits and sue his employer, the construction site operator, for more. That is not an option; workers' compensation benefits are his exclusive remedy. ◀ By barring lawsuits for negligence, workers' compensation laws also bar employers from raising common law defenses to negligence, such as contributory negligence. For example, an employer can no longer raise such defenses as contributory negligence or assumption of risk (see Chapter 14) to avoid liability for negligence. A worker may sue an employer who *intentionally* injures the worker, but such cases are not common. The *Developing Paralegal Skills* feature on the following page reviews some procedures for workers' compensation claims.

Employment Discrimination

Federal laws prohibiting employment discrimination have done much to further employees' rights to fair treatment in the workplace. State laws also protect employees from discriminatory treatment, sometimes to a greater extent than federal laws do. The major federal laws prohibiting employment discrimination are the following:

- Title VII of the Civil Rights Act of 1964 (prohibits discrimination based on race, color, national origin, religion, and gender).

- The Age Discrimination in Employment Act of 1967 (prohibits discrimination based on age).

- The Americans with Disabilities Act of 1990 (prohibits discrimination based on disability).

Title VII of the Civil Rights Act of 1964

The most significant federal law prohibiting discrimination is the Civil Rights Act of 1964. The law was enacted to protect certain groups from the discriminatory practices of business owners, educational institutions, employers, and other groups. One section of the act, known as Title VII, pertains to employment practices. Title VII prohibits employers with fifteen or more full-time employees from discriminating against employees or potential employees on the basis of race, color, national origin, religion, or gender. The Pregnancy Discrimination Act of 1978 amended Title VII to expand the definition of gender-based discrimination to include discrimination based on pregnancy.

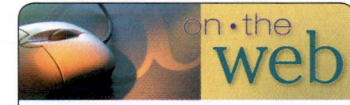

For an excellent discussion of many employment litigation issues, see the Web site of the Civil Rights Division of the Department of Justice. Go to **www. usdoj.gov**, and select "Uphold Civil Rights & Liberties" from the "What We Do" list. Select the "Civil Rights Division" link in the text, and then select "Frequently Asked Questions."

Developing Paralegal Skills

ASSISTING WITH A WORKERS' COMPENSATION CLAIM

David Calloway, an employee of GearHead Outlet, was on a ladder arranging boxes of tools when a box fell and knocked him to the floor. His wrist was broken in three places. Calloway submitted a workers' compensation claim to GearHead's personnel department two days after the incident. When the cast was removed, Calloway's wrist had swollen significantly. His physician prescribed physical therapy to alleviate the pain he experienced and to restore function to the wrist. GearHead's workers' compensation insurance provider, Delacroix Mutual, refused to authorize the therapy treatment and sent Calloway to another physician, who prescribed pain medication and declared the physical therapy unnecessary. Calloway's wrist continued to swell, and the pain increased.

Two weeks later, Calloway contacted the law firm of Shapiro and Masters, which specializes in workers' compensation litigation, to assist with his claim. Attorney Melanie Shapiro conducted an initial interview with Calloway and accepted Calloway's case. After the interview, Shapiro asked her legal assistant, Geena Tulane, to gather evidence and prepare for a hearing before a workers' compensation judge.

CHECKLIST FOR A WORKERS' COMPENSATION CLAIM

- Review the employer's workers' compensation insurance policy with the attorney to clarify coverage terms.
- Collect all medical records and compensation claim forms from the client or employer.
- Assemble evidence regarding the medical condition the client has as a result of the work-related injury or illness. If possible, photograph the scene where the injury occurred, as well as any visible injuries that may assist in proving the claim. Gather statements from any witnesses.
- Check with state insurance regulators for a record of prior complaints against the insurer.
- Compile an estimate of all medical costs. Call the offices of the physicians to whom the client has been referred for treatment of the injury or illness to inquire about their fees for specific treatments.
- Keep a log of all communications with the insurer, including e-mails and recorded phone messages. Document when the claim was submitted to the insurer, how and when the insurer responded, what the insurer asked for, and what was provided.
- Draft a request for a workers' compensation hearing with the state commission or court responsible for settling workers' compensation claims.
- Before submitting claim information for the hearing, compile the information in a coherent, organized presentation. A well-documented claim is more likely to be paid.

Title VII has been interpreted by the courts to prohibit both intentional and unintentional discrimination. The latter occurs when certain employer practices or procedures have a discriminatory effect, even though they were not intended to be discriminatory. ▶ **EXAMPLE 18.11** A city requires all of its firefighters to be at least six feet tall. In effect, that job requirement discriminates against women, because few women are that tall. The effect of the rule is discriminatory, even though the intent in adopting the rule might have been to ensure an able-bodied firefighting crew. ◀ Job qualifications should focus on ability to perform job duties, not measures that can be discriminatory.

Sexual Harassment. The courts have also extended Title VII protection to those who are subject to **sexual harassment** in the workplace. There are two types of

sexual harassment
In the employment context, (1) the hiring or granting of job promotions or other benefits in return for sexual favors (*quid pro quo* harassment) or (2) language or conduct that is so sexually offensive that it creates a hostile working environment (hostile-environment harassment).

sexual harassment. *Quid pro quo harassment* occurs when a superior doles out awards (promotions, raises, benefits, or other advantages) to a subordinate in exchange for sexual favors. (*Quid pro quo*, a Latin term, means "this for that" or "something for something.") In contrast, *hostile-environment harassment* occurs when an employee is subjected to offensive sexual comments, jokes, or physical contact in the workplace that make it difficult or impossible for the employee to perform a job satisfactorily.

Generally, under the doctrine of *respondeat superior* (discussed earlier in this chapter), an employer may be held responsible (liable) for the conduct of certain employees, such as managers and supervisors. In a sexual-harassment case, if an employee in a supervisory position did the harassing, the employer will usually be held liable *automatically* for the behavior. If the person who did the harassing was not a supervisor but a co-worker, the employer will be held liable only if the employer knew, or should have known, about the harassment and failed to take immediate corrective action. ▶ **EXAMPLE 18.12** Elena was sexually harassed by a co-worker and complained to her supervisor several times, but nothing was done. If Elena later sued her employer for a Title VII violation, the employer could be held liable because the supervisor did not take steps to deal properly with the complaint. ◀ An employer may even be held liable at times for the actions of nonemployees (customers or clients, for example) if the employer knew about the harassment and let it continue.

Note that Title VII prohibits not only sexual harassment but also the harassment of any employee on the basis of race, color, national origin, religion, age, or disability. In other words, racial or ethnic slurs against an employee may give rise to a hostile work environment claim under Title VII, just as sexually offensive comments would.

The Equal Employment Opportunity Commission. The Equal Employment Opportunity Commission (EEOC) is a federal agency that administers and enforces Title VII and the laws prohibiting employment discrimination based on disability or age (to be discussed shortly), as well as some other federal antidiscrimination laws. Claims of Title VII violations must first be filed with the EEOC or the equivalent state agency. The EEOC will either investigate and take action on the claim on behalf of the employee or allow the employee to file a civil suit against the employer. The EEOC also has established guidelines that are often used by the courts to determine if the actions complained of constitute harassment under the law.

Employers' Liability under Title VII. An employer's liability under Title VII can be extensive. In general, the court can order injunctive relief against the employer (a judicial order to prevent future discrimination), retroactive promotions that were wrongfully withheld from the employee, and past wages to compensate the employee for any time he or she was wrongfully unemployed. Damages are also available in cases involving *intentional* discrimination.

You can find the complete text of Title VII, the ADEA, and the ADA (and other federal antidiscrimination laws), as well as information about the activities of the EEOC, at the EEOC's Web site at **www.eeoc.gov**.

Discrimination Based on Age

The Age Discrimination in Employment Act (ADEA) of 1967 prevents employers from discriminating against workers who are forty years of age or older on the basis of their age. The act was passed, in part, in response to an increasing tendency on the part of employers to reduce costs by excluding older workers from their workforces and hiring younger workers (at lower salaries) instead. For the ADEA to apply, an employer must have twenty or more employees. Procedurally, discrimination suits brought under the act are very similar to suits brought under Title VII.

Discrimination Based on Disability

Congress enacted the Americans with Disabilities Act (ADA) in 1990 to strengthen existing laws prohibiting discrimination in the workplace against individuals with disabilities. Employers with fifteen or more employees are obligated to satisfy the requirements of the ADA.

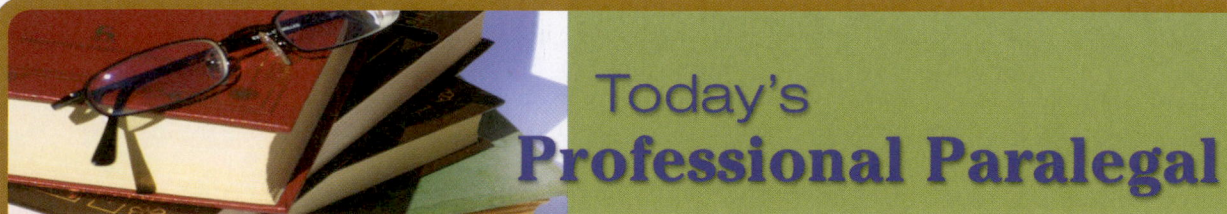

DEVELOPING A POLICY ON SEXUAL HARASSMENT

Erika Delong, a legal assistant, works in the office of the general counsel at ABC Manufacturing Corporation. She works closely with the personnel department. Today, she is attending a meeting with her supervisor, Gene Tompkins, who is the general counsel, to discuss the company's policy on sexual harassment with the vice president of human resources, the president of the corporation, and the vice presidents of several of the corporation's divisions. Erika has been asked to attend the meeting because her supervisor will be responsible for preparing the policy and he wants her to draft it. Erika has already obtained copies of other companies' policies to use as samples in the meeting.

The meeting is held in a large conference room. The president opens the meeting by explaining its purpose—to develop a policy on sexual harassment. "We want to discourage it and to have a written policy that includes reporting and investigation procedures. Erika and Gene have several samples that we can review," says the president.

SETTING POLICY GOALS AND DEFINING SEXUAL HARASSMENT

Erika passes out the sample policies. The group then reviews the various policies, with Gene explaining the legal ramifications of each one. The president remarks that he thinks the policy should begin with a statement that the corporation wants to promote an atmosphere in which authority and power are not abused and in which sexual harassment is not condoned. He points out some language that he likes in one of the samples. Erika highlights it so she will have an idea of how to draft the introduction.

Gene then states, "After an introduction and general statement of the corporation's policy, we should give the legal definition of what constitutes sexual harassment. The definition in sample three is very good from both a legal and a practical point of view because it also gives examples." Erika highlights the definition paragraph in sample three and puts a number 2 next to it, so she knows that it should come second. She flips back to the sample the president referred to and puts a number 1 next to it.

DEVELOPING PROCEDURES

As the discussion continues, the vice president of human resources comments on the procedure for filing a complaint, the investigation that will take place, and the disciplinary measures that will be imposed for sexual harassment. The vice president does not like any of the samples, and the group spends quite a bit of time working through specific language to pin down what he wants. When the meeting is over, the group goes to lunch. After lunch, Gene informs the others that Erika will prepare a draft of the policy and will circulate it among them for review and comment. Once all of their comments have been collected, the group will meet again to decide on the final provisions. Erika will then prepare and circulate a final draft of the policy. Erika returns to her office to begin working on the initial draft.

As defined by the 1990 statute, disabilities include heart disease, cancer, blindness, paralysis, acquired immune deficiency syndrome (AIDS), serious emotional illnesses, and learning disabilities. Under the ADA, an employer is not permitted to discriminate against a person with a disability if *reasonable accommodations* can be provided to assist the worker in satisfactorily performing the job. An employer is not required to accommodate a worker with a disability if the accommodation would constitute an undue hardship for the employer, however. For example, if the cost of accommodating the employee is extremely high, that high cost might constitute an undue hardship. Although enforcement of the ADA falls within the jurisdiction of the EEOC, the worker alleging discrimination in violation of the ADA may also file a civil lawsuit against the employer for violation of the act.

EMPLOYMENT LAW AND THE PARALEGAL

Employment law necessarily affects the paralegal. As an employee, you will be subject to the laws governing employment relationships. As a legal professional, you may be extensively involved in tasks relating to labor and employment laws. You may work in the corporate counsel's office of a large corporate enterprise, for example. If the corporation's employees belong to a labor union, the corporate counsel's office will handle matters governed by labor laws, such as collective bargaining agreements and labor-management disputes. As a paralegal in a law firm or a government agency, you might assist in work relating to claims of employment discrimination, which might require you to interact with the EEOC or a relevant state agency. Here are a few tasks that paralegals commonly undertake in the area of labor and employment law:

- Draft employment contracts for an employer.
- Assist with contract negotiations between labor and management.
- Prepare for arbitration proceedings before the NLRB.
- Respond to inquiries from the NLRB regarding a client's alleged unfair labor practices.

- Prepare for and attend administrative hearings before the EEOC.
- Gather factual information to counter or support a claim of employment discrimination.
- Prepare reports and furnish documentation in response to an EEOC investigation into an employee's claim of employment discrimination.
- Draft a policy manual for a business client concerning what actions constitute discriminatory employment practices.
- Research the EEOC's guidelines on sexual harassment and relevant case law to determine what types of policies and procedures will help a client avoid liability for sexual harassment.
- Prepare notices regarding a firm's employment policies, important changes in employment laws, and the like.
- Assist in litigation involving multiple plaintiffs who are suing the same employer.

KEY TERMS AND CONCEPTS

agency *598*

agent *598*

articles of incorporation *589*

bylaws *591*

certificate of incorporation *590*

close corporation *593*

collective bargaining *603*

constructive discharge *602*

corporate charter *590*

director *588*

dissolution *587*

dividend *594*

employment at will *602*

fiduciary relationship *599*

general partner *587*

independent contractor *598*

joint and several liability *587*

joint liability *587*

limited liability company (LLC) *596*

limited liability partnership (LLP) *597*

limited partner *587*

limited partnership *587*

liquidation *596*

officer *588*

principal *598*

professional corporation (PC) *597*

prospectus *589*

publicly held corporation *593*

respondeat superior *600*

sexual harassment *606*

share *588*

shareholder *588*

vicarious liability *600*

winding up *587*

workers' compensation laws *604*

wrongful discharge *602*

CHAPTER SUMMARY

BUSINESS ORGANIZATIONS AND EMPLOYMENT LAW

Forms of Business Organization

1. *Sole proprietorships*—The simplest form of business organization; used by anyone who does business without creating a separate business entity. The owner is the business, even though he or she may hire employees to run the business.

   a. The owner is personally liable for all business debts and obligations.

   b. The owner pays personal income taxes on all profits.

   c. The proprietorship terminates on the death of the sole proprietor or the sale or transfer of the business.

2. *Partnerships*—Created by the written or oral agreement of the parties to do business jointly as partners. All partners share equally in management, unless otherwise provided for in the partnership agreement. The partners may hire employees to assist them in running the business.

   a. Partners are personally liable for partnership debts and obligations.

   b. The partnership as an entity does not pay income taxes but files an informational tax return with the Internal Revenue Service each year. Each partner pays personal income tax on his or her share of the profits of the partnership.

   c. A partnership may be terminated by the agreement of the partners or by the occurrence of certain events, such as the death or bankruptcy of a partner.

   d. The creation of a limited partnership is a formal proceeding that must comply with state statutory requirements. Only the general partners may participate in management in a limited partnership, and only the general partners have unlimited personal liability; the liability of limited partners is limited to the amount of their investments.

3. *Corporations*—

   a. A corporation is created by a state-issued charter. The shareholders elect directors, who set policy and appoint officers to manage day-to-day corporate affairs.

   b. Shareholders have limited liability and are not personally liable for the debts of the corporation (beyond the amount of their investments).

   c. The corporation pays income tax on net profits; shareholders again pay income tax on profits distributed as dividends.

   d. A corporation may be terminated at the time specified in the articles of incorporation, by agreement of the shareholders and the board of directors, or by court decree.

4. *Limited liability organizations*—Other forms of business organization are the limited liability partnership (LLP), the limited liability company (LLC), and the professional corporation (PC). Generally, these organizations allow business owners to combine the tax advantages of the partnership with the limited liability of limited partners or corporate shareholders.

Agency Law

An agency relationship arises when one person (called the *agent*) agrees to act for or in the place of another person (called the *principal*).

1. *Employees versus independent contractors*—Employees who deal with third parties are normally considered to be agents of their employers. An independent contractor differs from an employee in that the employer does not control the details of the independent contractor's job performance. The independent contractor may or may not be an agent.

2. *Agency formation*—An agency relationship may be formed by express agreement (oral or written) or implied by conduct. It can also arise if the principal causes a third party to believe the agency existed.

3. *Duties of the principal*—The principal must cooperate with the agent, provide safe working conditions for the agent, and reimburse the agent for work performed and for any expenses incurred on the principal's behalf.

4. *Duties of the agent*—The agent must perform his or her tasks competently, obey and be loyal to the principal, notify the principal of matters concerning the agency, and render an accounting to the principal of how and for what purpose the principal's funds were used.

5. *Liability for an agent's contracts*—The principal normally is bound by any contract formed by the agent on behalf of the principal, as long as the action was authorized. If the action was not authorized, the principal will not be liable unless he or she voluntarily agrees to be bound by (ratifies) the contract.

6. *Liability for an agent's torts*—Agents are personally liable for the torts that they commit. If an agent commits a tort within the scope of his or her employment as an agent, the principal may also be held liable under the doctrine of *respondeat superior.*

7. *Liability for independent contractor's torts*—A principal is not liable for harm caused by an independent contractor's negligence, unless hazardous activities are involved (in which situation the principal is strictly liable for any resulting harm) or other exceptions apply.

Employment Law

1. *Employment at will*—Traditionally, the employment relationship has been governed by the doctrine of "employment at will"—that is, the relationship can be terminated at any time for any reason by either the employer or the employee—as well as by common law rules relating to contracts, torts, and agency. Most Americans have the legal status of "employees at will," but federal and state statutes prevent the doctrine from being applied in some circumstances.

2. *Wrongful discharge*—Wrongful discharge occurs whenever an employer discharges an employee in violation of the law or of an employment contract.

3. *Labor laws*—The Norris-LaGuardia Act of 1932 gave employees the legal right to organize into unions and to engage in peaceful strikes. The National Labor Relations Act of 1935 strengthened it by protecting workers' efforts to organize into unions and by promoting collective bargaining. The act also created the National Labor Relations Board to oversee enforcement of the statute.

4. *Family and medical leave*—The Family and Medical Leave Act of 1993 requires employers with fifty or more employees to provide their employees

Continued

(except for key employees) with up to twelve weeks of unpaid family or medical leave during any twelve-month period for the following reasons:

a. Family leave may be taken to care for a newborn baby, a newly adopted child, or a foster child just placed in the employee's care.

b. Medical leave may be taken when the employee or the employee's spouse, child, or parent has a serious health condition requiring care.

5. *State workers' compensation laws*—Every state has an administrative procedure for compensating workers injured on the job.

6. *Employment discrimination*—Both federal and state laws prohibit discrimination against employees in the workplace. State laws sometimes afford greater protection. The major federal laws are:

a. Title VII of the Civil Rights Act (1964), which prohibits employment discrimination against job applicants and employees on the basis of race, color, national origin, gender, or religion. The courts have interpreted Title VII to prohibit both intentional and unintentional discrimination, as well as pregnancy discrimination and sexual harassment.

b. The Age Discrimination in Employment Act (ADEA) of 1967, which prohibits employment discrimination against employees who are forty years of age or older.

c. The Americans with Disabilities Act (ADA) of 1990, which prohibits discrimination on the basis of disability against individuals qualified for a given job. Employers must reasonably accommodate the needs of persons with disabilities.

STUDENT STUDYWARE™ CD-ROM

Interactive student CD in this book includes additional quizzing, plus video clips, case studies, and Key Terms flashcards.

ONLINE COMPANION™

For additional resources, please go to **www.paralegal.delmar.cengage.com**.

QUESTIONS FOR REVIEW

1. What are the three most common traditional forms of business organization? How is each form created and terminated?

2. What is a limited liability company? What advantages does this business organizational form offer to businesspersons?

3. When is a principal liable for the contracts formed by an agent? Under what common law doctrine may a principal be held liable for the torts of the agent?

4. What federal statutes prohibit employment discrimination? What kinds of discrimination are prohibited under these statutes? What federal agency handles claims of employment discrimination?

5. What benefits are provided by workers' compensation programs? Do the programs encourage employees to sue their employers?

ETHICAL QUESTIONS

1. Peter works as a legal assistant for a law firm. The firm's client is suing her former employer for wrongful termination of the employment relationship. The employee-plaintiff has financial records that prove that her supervisor authorized nondisclosure of income to the Internal Revenue Service. Disclosing these records would seriously affect her supervisor's credibility and would strengthen the employee-plaintiff's case. Peter contacts the client to obtain the records. She refuses, fearing the effect it might have on her ability to find another job. Peter's supervising attorney is adamant about the need to obtain these records. The attorney is concerned that the firm might be guilty of malpractice if it failed to introduce this evidence. To whom is Peter obligated, the client or the firm? Why? How should Peter resolve this conflict?

2. Amy Mehall is a paralegal in the legal department of a large corporation. One day, her good friend Sarah, who works in the company's purchasing department, asks Amy for help. Sarah is being sexually harassed by her boss. Amy tells Sarah that she cannot give her any legal advice. Sarah asks Amy to make an appointment for her with Amy's supervising attorney, so that she can get the legal advice that she needs. May employees of a corporate legal department represent other employees of the corporation? Why or why not?

 ## PRACTICE QUESTIONS AND ASSIGNMENTS

1. Identify whether each of the business firms described below is a sole proprietorship, a partnership, or a corporation, and explain why:

   a. Terrence and Lars have owned a business together for three months. Terrence contributed 60 percent of the capital needed to start the business, and Lars contributed the other 40 percent. Each owner is responsible for a proportionate share of the profits and losses of the business, and each owner participates in managing the business.

   b. Four wealthy individuals create a business for the purpose of funding the construction of a new commerce center to revitalize the downtown business district in their city. Each individual contributes 25 percent of the funds necessary for the project, and each individual is liable for only 25 percent of the firm's losses. They all sign an agreement.

   c. Anne Hall, Joe Richie, and Mike Werner are all certified public accountants. They decide to do business together. By the end of its first year, the firm has become very profitable. As a result, the firm has to pay a substantial amount in income taxes on its profits.

   d. Dr. Menendez practices medicine on his own; he has not incorporated his business.

   e. The Pear Co. is a for-profit business that has a charter issued by the state. The charter provides for the limited liability of the company's owners.

2. Explain why the principal is (or is not) liable for the actions of the agent in each of the following situations:

   a. Attorney Tom Moran tells his paralegal, Jane Davis, to purchase litigation software.

   b. Attorney Jane Smith leaves a written memo to her paralegal, David Hayes, instructing David to solicit bids for a computer network for the law firm from three computer consulting firms. David not only obtains three bids but also hires one of the firms to set up the network at a cost of $10,000.

   c. Paralegal Megan Meldrum works for a sole practitioner and has office management duties in addition to her paralegal responsibilities. When the photocopier no longer functions, she enters into a lease for a new machine without discussing it with her supervising attorney. The cost of the new machine is the same as the cost of the old machine. Would it make any difference if the cost of the new machine were significantly greater than the cost of the old one?

3. Identify what type of employment discrimination, if any, is being practiced in each of the following hypothetical situations:

   a. Lana Ronsky, a legal assistant in an all-male law firm, is the object of frequent sexual jokes and comments and occasional uninvited touching—all of which are offensive to her and make it difficult for her to do her job.

   b. Monica Pierson, a partner in a large law firm, interviews seven potential legal assistants, including an Asian American. Although the Asian American is the best qualified for the job, Monica does not hire him because he speaks English with an accent, which might offend some of the firm's clients.

   c. Diana Bekins, the manager of an insurance agency, makes it clear to Jack McBride, a new sales representative, that she will promote him only if he provides sexual favors in return.

d. A post office has a rule that all mail carriers must be able to bench-press two hundred pounds, because the mailbags are so heavy. As a result, only 3 out of 150 mail carriers are women.

QUESTIONS FOR CRITICAL ANALYSIS

1. What are limited liability companies and limited liability partnerships? What are the advantages of these forms of business organization? Give an example of a situation in which each type of entity would be used.

2. Attorneys are agents of their clients and thus are governed by the principles of agency law discussed in this chapter. Do you see any similarities between the duties of agents to their principals and the ethical rules governing attorneys (discussed in Chapter 4)? If so, what are the similarities? In other words, which duties of agents, if any, correspond to the specific ethical rules discussed in Chapter 4?

3. Employers typically want their employees to be bright young people who are dedicated to their work. Some employers do not want to hire people who need to take family or maternity leaves, who are old, or whose racial or ethnic background is dissimilar to theirs. Should employers be allowed to hire only the people they want to hire? Should they be able to limit their employees to certain age groups or ethnic backgrounds? Should they be able to refuse to hire job candidates with disabilities? Why or why not? What laws protect people in these groups from employment discrimination?

PROJECTS

1. Find out if your state's corporation statute is based on the Model Business Corporation Act or the Revised Model Business Corporation Act.

2. Locate your state employment agency online. From the Web site or a resource such as FindLaw, determine whether your state adheres to the employment-at-will doctrine. Also find out if, and in what circumstances, exceptions to this doctrine are made.

USING INTERNET RESOURCES

1. Go to the Cornell Law Library Web site at **www.law. cornell.edu**, and find your state's corporation statute. Write a paragraph summarizing your state's requirements for corporate formation.

END NOTE

1. Pronounced ree-*spahn*-dee-uht soo-*peer*-ee-your.

BANKRUPTCY AND ENVIRONMENTAL LAW

CHAPTER OUTLINE

Introduction

The Bankruptcy Code

Liquidation Proceedings

Individual Repayment Plans

Reorganizations

Environmental Law

AFTER COMPLETING THIS CHAPTER, YOU WILL KNOW:

▶ The various types of relief available for debtors under federal bankruptcy law.

▶ The basic procedures involved in an ordinary, or straight, bankruptcy proceeding.

▶ How bankruptcy law provides relief for corporate debtors and what basic procedures are involved in corporate reorganizations.

▶ The major laws regulating environmental pollution.

▶ The basic purpose and provisions of Superfund.

INTRODUCTION

Historically, debtors had few rights. At one time, debtors who could not pay their debts as they came due faced harsh consequences, including imprisonment and involuntary servitude. Today, in contrast, debtors have numerous rights. One of these rights is the right to petition for bankruptcy relief under federal law.

The number of petitions for bankruptcy filed each year in the United States rose dramatically from 1980 until passage of the 2005 Bankruptcy Reform Act, which significantly reduced individual bankruptcy filings. Filings jumped again in the economic downturn of 2008 through 2010. For paralegals, this means that bankruptcy law is an area in which they will continue to be in demand.

In this chapter, you will read about the different types of relief offered under federal bankruptcy law and about the basic bankruptcy procedures required for specific types of relief. You will also learn in this chapter about the major laws regulating environmental pollution. Although bankruptcy and environmental law are quite distinct areas of law, both are based largely on federal legislation, and both are areas in which many paralegals specialize.

THE BANKRUPTCY CODE

Bankruptcy relief is provided under federal law. Although state laws may play a role in bankruptcy proceedings, particularly state laws governing property, the governing law is based on federal legislation.

Congressional authority to provide bankruptcy relief for debtors is based on Article I, Section 8, of the U.S. Constitution, which gives Congress the power to establish "uniform laws on the subject of bankruptcies throughout the United States." Federal bankruptcy legislation was first enacted in 1898 and since then has undergone several modifications.

Bankruptcy law prior to 2005 was based on the Bankruptcy Reform Act of 1978, as amended—hereinafter called the Bankruptcy Code, or more simply, the Code. In 2005, Congress enacted the Bankruptcy Reform Act, which significantly overhauled certain provisions of the Bankruptcy Code.

Goals of Bankruptcy Law

Modern bankruptcy law is designed to accomplish two main goals. The first is to provide relief and protection to debtors who have "gotten in over their heads." The second is to provide a fair means of distributing a debtor's assets among all creditors. Thus, the law attempts to balance the rights of the debtor and the creditor.

Although the twin goals of bankruptcy remain the same, the balance between them has shifted somewhat. There was growing criticism after the 1978 act that too many debtors were able to avoid paying their debts. Thus, one of the major goals of the 2005 reform legislation was to require more consumers to pay as many of their debts as they possibly could instead of having those debts fully extinguished in bankruptcy.

Bankruptcy Courts

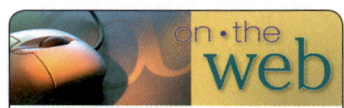

For an overview of the bankruptcy courts and procedures, go to **www. uscourts.gov**, and select "U.S. Bankruptcy Courts" from the menu.

Bankruptcy proceedings are held in federal bankruptcy courts, which are under the authority of U.S. district courts, and rulings from bankruptcy courts can be appealed to the district courts. Essentially, a bankruptcy court fulfills the role of an administrative court for the federal district court concerning matters in bankruptcy. The bankruptcy court holds the proceedings required to administer the estate of the debtor in bankruptcy. Bankruptcy court judges are appointed for terms of fourteen years. A bankruptcy court can conduct a jury trial if the appropriate district court has authorized it and the parties to the bankruptcy consent.

Bankruptcy courts follow the Federal Rules of Bankruptcy Procedure rather than the Federal Rules of Civil Procedure (see Chapter 10).

Types of Bankruptcy Relief

The Bankruptcy Code is contained in Title 11 of the *United States Code* (U.S.C.) and has eight chapters.[1] Chapters 1, 3, and 5 of the Code include general definitional provisions and provisions governing case administration, creditors, the debtor, and the estate. These three chapters apply generally to all kinds of bankruptcies. Three chapters of the Code set forth the most important types of relief that debtors can seek:

- Chapter 7 provides for **liquidation** proceedings (the selling of all nonexempt assets and the distribution of the proceeds to the debtor's creditors).
- Chapter 11 governs reorganizations.
- Chapter 13 provides for the adjustment of debts by persons with regular incomes.

In the following pages, we look at the specific type of bankruptcy relief provided under Chapters 7, 11, and 13 of the Code. To inform a **consumer-debtor** (defined as an individual whose debts are primarily consumer debts) of the types of relief available, the Code requires that the clerk of the court give all consumer-debtors written notice of the general purpose, benefits, and costs of each chapter under which they might proceed. In addition, the clerk must provide consumer-debtors with information on the types of services available from credit counseling agencies. In practice, most of these steps are handled by an attorney, not by court clerks.

LIQUIDATION PROCEEDINGS

Liquidation under Chapter 7 of the Bankruptcy Code is probably the most familiar type of bankruptcy proceeding and is often referred to as *ordinary*, or *straight*, bankruptcy. Put simply, a debtor in a liquidation bankruptcy states his or her debts and turns all assets over to a *bankruptcy trustee*. The trustee sells the nonexempt assets and distributes the proceeds to creditors (the trustee's role will be discussed in more detail later in this chapter). With certain exceptions, the remaining debts are then **discharged** (extinguished), and the debtor is relieved of the obligation to pay the debts.

Any "person"—defined as including individuals, partnerships, and corporations—may be a debtor in a liquidation proceeding. A husband and wife may file jointly under a single petition. Insurance companies, banks, savings and loan associations, investment companies licensed by the Small Business Administration, and credit unions *cannot* be debtors in a liquidation bankruptcy, however. Rather, other chapters of the Bankruptcy Code or federal or state statutes apply to them.

A straight bankruptcy can be commenced by the filing of either a voluntary or an involuntary **petition in bankruptcy**—the document that is filed with a bankruptcy court to initiate bankruptcy proceedings. If a debtor files the petition, it is a *voluntary bankruptcy*. If one or more creditors file a petition to force the debtor into bankruptcy, it is an *involuntary bankruptcy*. We discuss both voluntary and involuntary bankruptcy proceedings under Chapter 7 in the following subsections.

Voluntary Bankruptcy

To bring a voluntary petition in bankruptcy, a debtor files official forms designated for that purpose in the bankruptcy court. The Bankruptcy Reform Act of 2005 specifies that before debtors can file a petition, they must receive credit counseling from an approved nonprofit agency within the 180-day period preceding the date of filing. Debtors filing a Chapter 7 petition must include a certificate proving that

liquidation
A proceeding under Chapter 7 of the Bankruptcy Code (often referred to as *ordinary*, or *straight*, bankruptcy) in which a debtor states his or her debts and turns all assets over to a trustee, who sells the nonexempt assets and distributes the proceeds to creditors. With certain exceptions, the remaining debts are then discharged, and the debtor is relieved of the obligation to pay the debts.

consumer-debtor
A debtor whose debts are primarily consumer debts—that is, debts for purchases that are primarily for household or personal use.

discharge
The termination of an obligation. A discharge in bankruptcy terminates the debtor's obligation to pay the debts discharged by the court.

petition in bankruptcy
An application to a bankruptcy court for relief in bankruptcy; a filing for bankruptcy. The official forms required for a petition in bankruptcy must be completed accurately, sworn to under oath, and signed by the debtor.

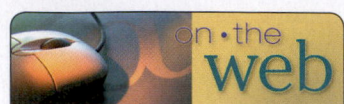

Before debtors can begin bankruptcy proceedings, they must receive credit counseling. For a list of approved programs, visit the Web site of the U.S. Trustee Program at **www.usdoj.gov/ ust**. Under the heading "Bankruptcy Reform," select "Credit Counseling & Debtor Education."

secured creditor
A lender, seller, or any other person in whose favor there is a security interest.

U.S. trustee
A government official who performs administrative tasks that a bankruptcy judge would otherwise have to perform.

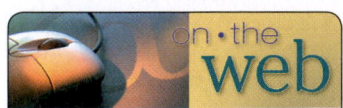

You will find the home page of the U.S. Trustee Program at **www.usdoj. gov/ust**.

they have received individual or group counseling from an approved agency within the last 180 days. One of your tasks as a paralegal may be to assist a debtor in locating and completing the required credit counseling course.

The Code requires consumer-debtors who have opted for liquidation bankruptcy proceedings to confirm the accuracy of the petition in bankruptcy that they have filed. They must also state in the petition, at the time of filing, that they understand the relief available under other chapters of the Code and have chosen to proceed under Chapter 7. Attorneys representing consumer-debtors must file an affidavit stating that they have informed the debtors of the relief available under each chapter of the Bankruptcy Code. In addition, the 2005 act requires attorneys to reasonably attempt to verify the accuracy of consumer-debtors' petitions and schedules (described below).

Chapter 7 Schedules

The voluntary petition must contain the following schedules:

1. A list of both secured and unsecured creditors, their addresses, and the amount of debt owed to each. A **secured creditor** is one who has a security interest in the collateral that secures the debt. For example, a lending institution that finances the purchase of an automobile normally takes a security interest in the automobile—the collateral for the loan.

2. A statement of the financial affairs of the debtor.

3. A list of all property owned by the debtor, including property that the debtor claims is exempt.

4. A listing of current income and expenses.

5. A certificate from an approved credit counseling agency (as discussed previously).

6. Proof of payments received from employers within sixty days prior to the filing of the petition.

7. A statement of the amount of monthly income, itemized to show how the amount is calculated.

8. A copy of the debtor's federal income tax return (or a transcript of the return) for the year ending immediately before the filing of the petition.

The official forms must be completed accurately, sworn to under oath, and signed by the debtor. To conceal assets or knowingly supply false information on these schedules is a crime under the bankruptcy laws.

In addition, at the request of the court, or of the **U.S. trustee** (a government official who performs administrative tasks that a bankruptcy judge would otherwise have to perform), or of any party in interest (a party, such as a creditor, who has a valid interest in the outcome of the proceedings), the debtor must file a tax return at the end of each tax year while the case is pending and provide a copy to the court. This requirement also applies to Chapter 11 and 13 bankruptcies (discussed later in this chapter).

Means Test

Under the 2005 Bankruptcy Reform Act, a major focus is on the *means test*. The purpose of the test is to keep upper-income people from abusing the bankruptcy process by filing for Chapter 7 as was thought to have happened in the past. The test forces more people to file for Chapter 13 bankruptcy (discussed below), rather than allow liquidation of debts. Exhibit 19.1 outlines the essentials of the means test, but there are exceptions that apply in a small percentage of cases.

Debtors wishing to file for bankruptcy must complete the means test to determine whether they qualify for Chapter 7. The debtor's average monthly income in recent months is compared with the median income in the geographical area in which the

A paralegal meets with a couple filing for Chapter 7 (liquidation) bankruptcy to obtain information about their financial situation. Under the Bankruptcy Reform Act of 2005, debtors must meet stricter requirements to be eligible for Chapter 7 bankruptcy. Why would Congress make it more difficult for individuals to declare bankruptcy?

(Courtesy of © Brand X Pictures)

person lives. (The U.S. Trustee Program provides these data at its Web site.) If the debtor's income is below the median income (of the area in which the debtor lives), the debtor is usually allowed to file for Chapter 7 bankruptcy, as there is no presumption of bankruptcy abuse.

If the debtor's income is above the median income, then further calculations must be made to project the debtor's income and expenses into the future. Recent monthly income is presumed to continue for the next sixty months. From that the

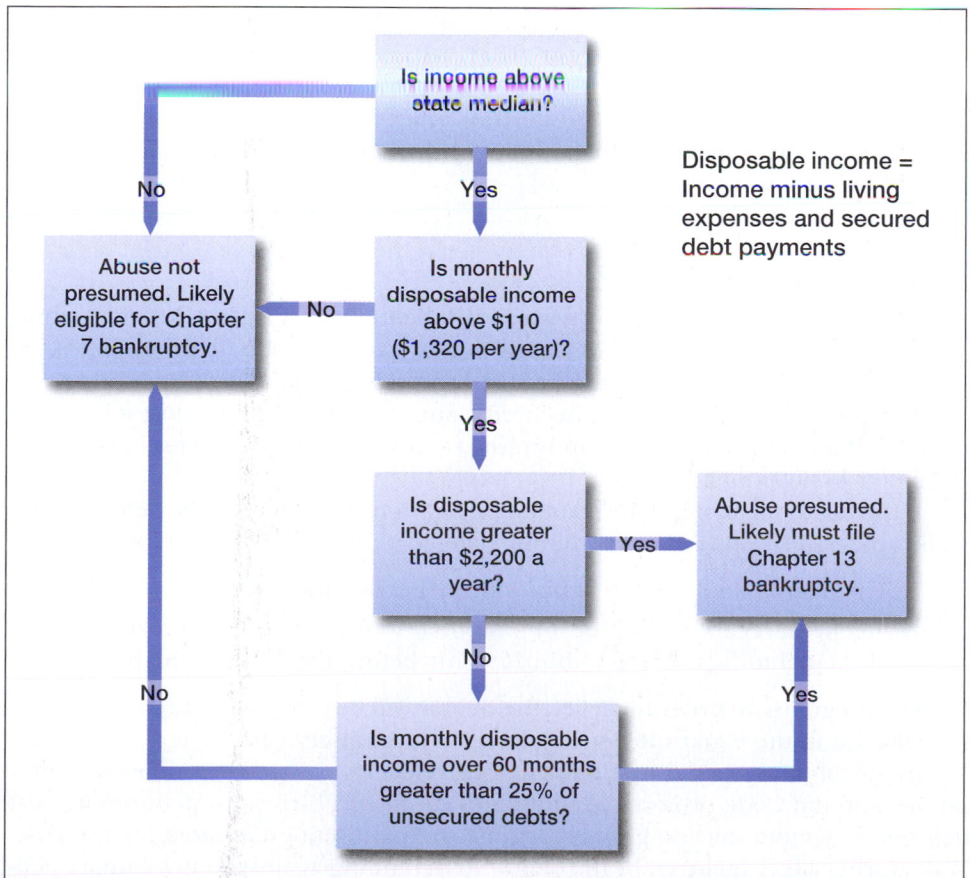

EXHIBIT 19.1

Means Test to Determine Chapter 7 Eligibility

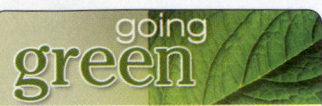

WHAT ARE YOU SITTING ON?

When furniture and other supplies are ordered for the office, look to see if recycled options are available, including furniture that is recyclable at the time of disposal. Many large office furniture makers offer environmentally friendly alternatives.

debtor subtracts the living expenses allowed by Internal Revenue Service (IRS) formulas. (The U.S. Trustee Program Web site also provides these numbers.) The IRS formula includes allowances for food, clothing, housing, transportation (including car payment), health care, and other necessary expenses. The allowances are modest and exclude such things as cell phones and cable television service. Also subtracted from income are payments on secured debts, such as mortgage payments. The amount of income left after allowed expenses have been subtracted is called disposable income. If the debtor has disposable income above $110 per month ($1,320 per year), as Exhibit 19.1 indicates, then there is income that could be applied to unsecured debts, and Chapter 13 may be required.

If the debtor's estimated future disposable income is more than $2,200 per year (these numbers are adjusted annually), then debt abuse is presumed, and Chapter 13 is required except in unusual cases. If disposable income is between $1,320 and $2,200 per year, then if that income is greater than 25 percent of unsecured debts owed, over sixty months, then abuse is presumed, and Chapter 13 is required. If it is less than 25 percent of unsecured debts owed, then Chapter 7 is allowed.

Additional Grounds for Dismissal

A debtor's petition for Chapter 7 relief may be dismissed for abuse or for failing to provide the necessary documents (such as schedules and tax returns) within the specified time. In addition, a motion to dismiss a Chapter 7 filing may be granted in two other situations under the Bankruptcy Reform Act of 2005. First, if the debtor has been convicted of a violent crime, the victim can file a motion to dismiss the voluntary petition. Second, if after filing a petition the debtor fails to pay domestic-support obligations (which include child and spousal support), the court may dismiss the petition.

Order for Relief

order for relief

A court's grant of assistance to a complainant.

If the voluntary petition for bankruptcy is found to be proper, the filing of the petition will itself constitute an **order for relief**. (An order for relief is a court's grant of assistance to a bankruptcy petitioner.) Once a consumer-debtor's voluntary petition has been filed, the clerk of the court or other appointee must give the trustee and creditors notice of the order for relief by mail not more than twenty days after entry of the order.

Involuntary Bankruptcy

An involuntary bankruptcy occurs when the debtor's creditors force the debtor into bankruptcy proceedings. For an involuntary action to be filed, the following requirements must be met: If the debtor has twelve or more creditors, three or more of these creditors having unsecured claims totaling $14,000 must join in the petition. If a debtor has fewer than twelve creditors, one or more creditors having a claim of $14,000 may file.

If the debtor challenges the involuntary petition, a hearing will be held, and the bankruptcy court will enter an order for relief if it finds either of the following:

1. The debtor is not paying debts as they become due.
2. A general receiver, assignee, or custodian took possession of substantially all of the debtor's property within 120 days before the filing of the petition.

If the court grants an order for relief, the debtor will be required to supply the same information in the bankruptcy schedules as in a voluntary bankruptcy.

An involuntary petition should not be used as an everyday debt-collection device, and the Code provides penalties for the filing of frivolous petitions against debtors. Judgment may be granted against the petitioning creditors for the costs and attorneys' fees incurred by the debtor in defending against an involuntary peti-

In the **Office**

DRESS FOR SUCCESS

Fair or not, our appearance can affect how others perceive us. Law offices have a professional air about them, and employees must dress accordingly. Appearance is especially important when interviewing for a job. A number of books and Web sites discuss professional dress, but here are some basic guidelines. Wearing a fresh-looking navy or black suit with a light-colored blouse or shirt to an interview is safe. Women should wear conservative jewelry, if any, and cover tattoos. Men should remove earrings, and women should remove jewelry from piercings other than ear piercings. On the job itself, you will observe what is expected so that you can dress to show respect for the office and for your position.

tion that is dismissed by the court. If the petition is filed in bad faith, damages can be awarded for injury to the debtor's reputation.

Automatic Stay

The moment a petition in bankruptcy—either voluntary or involuntary—is filed, there exists an **automatic stay**, or suspension, of nearly all litigation and other action by creditors against the debtor or the debtor's property. In other words, once a petition has been filed, creditors cannot contact the debtor by phone or mail or start any legal proceedings to recover debts or to repossess property. In some circumstances, a creditor may petition the bankruptcy court for relief from the automatic stay, however.

The Code provides that if a creditor *knowingly* violates the automatic stay (a willful violation), any party injured, including the debtor, is entitled to recover actual damages, costs, and attorneys' fees and may be entitled to recover punitive damages as well.

> **automatic stay**
> A suspension of all judicial proceedings upon the occurrence of an independent event. Under the Bankruptcy Code, the moment a petition to initiate bankruptcy proceedings is filed, all litigation or other legal action by creditors against a debtor and the debtor's property is suspended.

Exceptions to the Automatic Stay

The 2005 Bankruptcy Reform Act provides several exceptions to the automatic stay. An exception is created for domestic-support obligations, which include any obligation owed to a spouse, a former spouse, a child of the debtor, the child's parent or guardian, or a governmental unit. In addition, proceedings against the debtor related to divorce, child custody or visitation, domestic violence, and support enforcement are not stayed. Also excepted are investigations by a securities regulatory agency, proceedings to establish certain claims against real property (including property taxes), eviction actions on judgments obtained prior to the filing of the petition, and withholding from the debtor's wages for repayment of a retirement account loan.

Bankruptcy Estate

At the beginning of a liquidation proceeding under Chapter 7, a **bankruptcy estate** (sometimes called an *estate in property*) is created. The estate consists of all the debtor's interests in property currently held, wherever located. Interests in certain property—such as gifts, inheritances, property settlements (divorce), and

> **bankruptcy estate**
> In bankruptcy proceedings, all of the debtor's interests in property currently held and wherever located, as well as interests in certain property to which the debtor becomes entitled within 180 days after filing for bankruptcy.

life insurance death proceeds—to which the debtor becomes entitled *within 180 days after filing* may also become part of the estate. In contrast, contributions that the debtor has already made to an employee benefit plan are excluded from the estate. Generally, though, the filing of a bankruptcy petition fixes a dividing line: property acquired prior to the filing of the petition becomes property of the estate, and property acquired after the filing remains the debtor's.

Creditors' Meeting

Within a reasonable time after the order for relief has been granted, the U.S. trustee must call a meeting of the creditors listed in the schedules filed by the debtor. The bankruptcy judge does not attend this meeting. The debtor is required to attend the meeting (unless excused by the court) and to submit to examination under oath by the creditors and the trustee. Failing to appear when required or making false statements under oath may result in the debtor's being denied a discharge in bankruptcy. The trustee ensures that the debtor is aware of the potential consequences of bankruptcy and of the ability to file for bankruptcy under a different chapter of the Bankruptcy Code.

Creditors' Claims

To be entitled to receive a portion of the debtor's estate, each creditor normally files a **proof of claim** with the bankruptcy court clerk within ninety days of the creditors' meeting. The proof of claim lists the creditor's name and address, as well as the amount that the creditor asserts is owed to the creditor by the debtor. A creditor need not file a proof of claim if the debtor's schedules list the creditor's claim as liquidated (exactly determined) and the creditor does not dispute the amount of the claim. A proof of claim is necessary if there is any dispute concerning the claim.

> **proof of claim**
>
> A document filed with a bankruptcy court by a creditor to inform the court of a claim against a debtor's property. The proof of claim lists the creditor's name and address, as well as the amount that the creditor asserts is owed to the creditor by the debtor.

Exemptions

As mentioned, the bankruptcy trustee takes control over the debtor's property in a Chapter 7 bankruptcy, but an individual debtor is entitled to exempt (exclude) certain property from the bankruptcy. The Bankruptcy Code exempts (among other things) the following property:

1. Up to $20,200 in equity in the debtor's residence (the *homestead exemption,* which will be discussed shortly).
2. Interest in a motor vehicle up to $3,225.
3. Interest, up to $475 for a particular item, in household goods and furnishings, wearing apparel, appliances, books, animals, crops, and musical instruments (the aggregate total of all items is limited to $9,850).
4. Interest in jewelry up to $1,225.
5. Interest in any other property up to $975, plus any unused part of the $20,200 debtor's residence exemption up to about $10,000.
6. Any tools of the debtor's trade up to $1,850.
7. Any unmatured life insurance contract owned by the debtor.
8. Employee contributions to a qualified pension plan.
9. The right to receive Social Security and certain public assistance benefits, alimony and support, certain retirement funds and pensions, and education savings accounts held for specific periods of time.
10. The right to receive certain personal-injury and other awards up to $18,450.

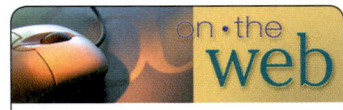

A number of Web sites provide information on state exemptions of property in bankruptcy, including **bankruptcy.lawyers.com**. Select a state from the "By State" list, and follow the links to find details of that state's bankruptcy laws.

Individual states have the power to pass legislation precluding debtors from using the federal exemptions within the state; most states have done this. In those states, debtors may use only state, not federal, exemptions. In the rest of the states, an individual debtor (or a husband and wife filing jointly) may choose either the exemptions provided under state law or the federal exemptions.

The Homestead Exemption

The 2005 Bankruptcy Reform Act significantly changed the law for debtors seeking to use state **homestead exemption** statutes. In some states, among them Florida and Texas, state homestead exemptions allow debtors petitioning for bankruptcy to shield unlimited amounts of equity in their homes from creditors. The Bankruptcy Code now requires that the debtor must have lived in the state for two years prior to filing the petition to be able to use the state homestead exemption. In addition, if the homestead was acquired within three and a half years before the date of filing, the maximum equity exempted is $125,000, even if the state law would permit a higher amount.

> **homestead exemption**
>
> A law permitting the debtor to retain the family home, either in its entirety or up to a specified dollar amount, free from the claims of unsecured creditors or trustees in bankruptcy.

The Bankruptcy Trustee

Promptly after the order for relief in the liquidation proceeding has been entered, an interim, or provisional, **bankruptcy trustee** is appointed by the U.S. trustee. The bankruptcy trustee may be a bankruptcy attorney who is not involved in the case. The basic duty of the bankruptcy trustee is to collect and reduce to cash the property in the bankruptcy estate that is not exempt. The trustee is held accountable for administering the debtor's estate in the interests of *both* the debtor and the creditors.

> **bankruptcy trustee**
>
> A person appointed by the bankruptcy court to administer the debtor's estate in the interests of both the debtor and the creditors. The basic duty of the bankruptcy trustee is to collect and reduce to cash the estate in property and to close up the estate as speedily as is compatible with the best interests of the parties.

Duties for Means Testing

The Bankruptcy Reform Act imposed new duties on trustees with regard to means testing for debtors who file Chapter 7 petitions. The trustee is required to review promptly all materials filed by the debtor. After the first meeting of the creditors, the trustee must file a statement as to whether the case is presumed to be an abuse under the means test. The trustee must provide a copy of this statement to all creditors within five days. Not later than forty days after the first creditors' meeting, the trustee must either file a motion to dismiss the petition (or convert it to a Chapter 13 case) or file a statement setting forth the reasons why the motion would not be appropriate.

Trustee's Powers

The trustee has the power to require persons holding the debtor's property at the time the petition is filed to deliver the property to the trustee. To enable the trustee to implement this power, the Code provides that the trustee occupies a position equivalent in rights to that of certain other parties, such as some types of creditors.

In addition, the trustee has specific *powers of avoidance*—that is, the trustee can set aside (avoid) a sale or other transfer of the debtor's property, taking it back as a part of the debtor's estate. These powers include voidable rights available to the debtor, preferences, and fraudulent transfers by the debtor. Each is discussed in more detail below. Additionally, certain statutory liens (creditors' claims against the debtor's property) may be avoided by the trustee.

The debtor shares most of the trustee's avoidance powers. Thus, if the trustee does not take action to enforce one of the rights just mentioned, the debtor in a liquidation bankruptcy can enforce that right.

Voidable Rights. A trustee steps into the shoes of the debtor. Thus, any reason that a debtor can use to obtain the return of property can be used by the trustee as well. These grounds include fraud, duress, incapacity, and mutual mistake (discussed in Chapter 15).

Preferences.   A debtor is not permitted to transfer property or to make a payment that favors—or gives a **preference** to—one creditor over others. The trustee is allowed to recover payments made by the debtor to one creditor in preference over another.

To have made a preferential payment that can be recovered, a debtor generally must have transferred property, for a preexisting debt, within *ninety days* of the filing of the petition in bankruptcy. The transfer must give the creditor more than the creditor would have received as a result of the bankruptcy proceedings.

If a preferred creditor (one who has received a preference) has sold the transferred property to an innocent third party, the trustee cannot recover the property from the innocent party. The creditor, however, generally can be held accountable for the value of the property sold.

Fraudulent Transfers.   The trustee can avoid fraudulent transfers or obligations if they were made within two years of the filing of the petition or if they were made with actual intent to hinder, delay, or defraud a creditor. For example, suppose that a debtor who is thinking about petitioning for bankruptcy sells his stamp collection, worth several thousand dollars, to a friend for $500. The friend agrees that in the future he will "sell" the collection back to the debtor for the same amount of money. This is a fraudulent transfer that the trustee can undo.

Distribution of Property

In the distribution of the debtor's estate in bankruptcy, secured creditors take priority over unsecured creditors. The Code provides that a consumer-debtor, within thirty days of filing a liquidation petition or before the date of the first meeting of the creditors (whichever is first), must file with the clerk a statement of intention with respect to the secured collateral. The statement must indicate whether the debtor will retain the collateral or surrender the collateral to the secured party. Also, if applicable, the debtor must specify whether the collateral will be claimed as exempt property and whether the debtor intends to redeem the property or reaffirm the debt secured by the collateral. The trustee is obligated to enforce the debtor's statement within forty-five days after it is filed. (This chapter's *Featured Contributor* article on pages 626 and 627 discusses the statement of intention and other bankruptcy terms.)

Distribution to Secured Creditors

If the collateral is surrendered to the secured party, the secured creditor can enforce the security interest either by accepting the property in full satisfaction of the debt or by selling the collateral and using the proceeds to pay off the debt. Thus, the secured party has priority over unsecured parties as to the proceeds from the disposition of the collateral. Should the collateral be insufficient to cover the secured debt owed, the secured creditor becomes an unsecured creditor for the difference.

Distribution to Unsecured Creditors

Bankruptcy law establishes an order of priority for classes of debts owed to unsecured creditors, and they are paid in the order of their priority. Each class of unsecured creditors must be fully paid before the next class is entitled to any of the remaining proceeds. If there are insufficient proceeds to pay fully all the creditors in a class, the proceeds are distributed proportionately to the creditors in the class, and classes lower in priority receive nothing. There are almost never sufficient funds

---

preference
In bankruptcy proceedings, the debtor's favoring of one creditor over others by making payments or transferring property to that creditor at the expense of the rights of other creditors. The bankruptcy trustee is allowed to recover payments made to one creditor in preference over another.

to pay all creditors. The order of priority among classes of unsecured creditors is as follows (some of these classes involve claims against bankrupt businesses):

1. Claims for domestic-support obligations, such as child support and alimony.
2. Administrative expenses—including court costs, trustee fees, and attorneys' fees.
3. In an involuntary bankruptcy, expenses incurred by the debtor in the ordinary course of business.
4. Unpaid wages, salaries, and commissions earned within ninety days of the filing of the petition; the amount is capped for each claimant.
5. Unsecured claims for contributions to be made to employee benefit plans; the amount is capped for each claimant.
6. Consumer deposits given to the debtor before the petition was filed; the amount is capped for each claimant.
7. Certain taxes and penalties due to government units, such as income and property taxes.
8. Claims for death or personal injury resulting from the unlawful operation of a motor vehicle.
9. Claims of general creditors.

If any amount remains after the priority classes of creditors have been satisfied, it is turned over to the debtor.

Discharge

From the debtor's point of view, the primary purpose of liquidation is to obtain a fresh start through a discharge of debts. Certain debts, however, are not dischargeable in bankruptcy. Also, certain debtors may not qualify to have all debts discharged in bankruptcy. These situations are discussed below.

Exceptions to Discharge

Discharge of a debt may be denied because of the nature of the claim or the conduct of the debtor. Claims that are not dischargeable in a liquidation bankruptcy include the following:

1. Claims for back taxes accruing within two years prior to bankruptcy.
2. Claims for amounts borrowed by the debtor to pay federal taxes or any nondischargeable taxes.
3. Claims against property or funds obtained by the debtor under false pretenses or by false representations.
4. Claims by creditors who were not notified of the bankruptcy; these claims did not appear on the schedules the debtor was required to file.
5. Claims based on fraud or misuse of funds by the debtor while acting in a fiduciary capacity or claims involving the debtor's embezzlement or larceny.
6. Domestic-support obligations and property settlements as provided for in a separation agreement or divorce decree.
7. Claims for amounts due on a retirement account loan.
8. Claims based on willful or malicious conduct by the debtor toward another or the property of another.
9. Certain government fines and penalties.
10. Certain student loans or obligations to repay funds received as an educational benefit, scholarship, or stipend—unless payment of the loans imposes an undue hardship on the debtor and the debtor's dependents.

featured contributor

A PRIMER ON KEY TERMS IN THE CHAPTER 7 BANKRUPTCY PROCESS

Jo-Christy Brown

BIOGRAPHICAL NOTE

Jo-Christy Brown is a graduate of Texas Tech University (1973). After graduating, she worked for several years in the computer industry, as a sales representative. While she enjoyed sales and the challenges it provided, she felt that as a long-term career, it did not provide her family with the financial stability that was best for her children. So, after being out of school for several years, she decided to attend law school. She chose to attend the University of Texas School of Law. As a single mother with primary custody of her two children, she and her children made sacrifices so that she could pursue a law degree. She graduated with a law degree, from the UT School of Law, in December of 1987. Brown passed the bar in 1988 and began her practice in Austin as an associate with the largest local firm in town.

While at that firm, she practiced in the areas of commercial litigation and environmental law. Bankruptcy is a topic that often factors into both of these areas of law. After becoming a partner with that firm, Brown decided to form her own firm which she anticipated would focus on the strengths of women lawyers and would provide a positive work environment for lawyers with family responsibilities. That firm, Brown Carls & Mitchell, a LLP specializing in commercial litigation, employment law, bankruptcy, and representation of local governmental entities, eventually grew to include twelve lawyers, both men and women, practicing in a variety of fields.

Brown continues to own and operate her own law firm. She has enjoyed an interesting career in law and believes she made the correct career decision.

Bankruptcy has some terms that are peculiar to this area of law. Your text focuses on some of the basic details of procedure under the Bankruptcy Code; I think it would be useful to review some terminology that paralegals hear when involved in bankruptcy work. The focus here is on Chapter 7 bankruptcy, but many of the terms are also relevant for Chapter 13 and other types of bankruptcy.

BEGINNING STEPS IN THE BANKRUPTCY PROCESS

A *debtor* is the party, whether a person or a business, liable for debts and the subject of the bankruptcy proceedings. The person who is owed the debt is a *creditor.* When a debtor owes money or other legal obligations to creditors, such as a bank or credit-card company that made loans, and the debt far exceeds

11. Consumer debts of more than $500 for luxury goods or services owed to a single creditor incurred within ninety days of the order for relief.

12. Cash advances totaling more than $750 that are extensions of open-end consumer credit obtained by the debtor within seventy days of the order for relief.

13. Judgments against a debtor as a result of the debtor's operation of a motor vehicle while intoxicated.

14. Fees or assessments arising from property in a homeowners' association, as long as the debtor retained an interest in the property.

15. Failure of the debtor to provide required or requested tax documents.

the debtor's ability to repay the amounts owed, a debtor may decide it is wise to file for bankruptcy under *Chapter 7*. This is the most common form of bankruptcy. It requires the debtor to liquidate its nonexempt property and to give the proceeds to its creditors. To be eligible, the debtor must satisfy the *means test* that compares income to debt. A debtor is usually seeking relief from the pressure of a debt that the debtor cannot repay. Before proceeding with bankruptcy, the debtor must complete *credit counseling*. This is a course on personal financial management that must be completed before actually filing bankruptcy.

The party declaring bankruptcy, through an attorney, files a *statement of intention*. This is a declaration made by a debtor concerning plans for dealing with consumer debts that are secured by property of the debtor. *Secured debt* is debt that is "backed" by a mortgage, a pledge of collateral, or another lien. Such debt gives the creditor, called a *secured creditor,* the right to attempt to get control of the property, such as a house, a car, or other property that the debtor originally offered to the lender to obtain a loan. All of the debtor's property in a bankruptcy proceeding is called an *estate*. The estate is all of the legal property of the debtor as of the time the bankruptcy proceeding begins. Details that will be important to the bankruptcy process are provided by the debtor in a *statement of financial affairs*. In this statement, the debtor answers questions on an official form, about income, property, and other matters relevant to the proceeding. This statement is part of the debtor's *schedule* of assets, liabilities, and other financial information.

> In most bankruptcy cases . . . the debtor is said to be given a fresh start.

WHO GETS WHAT?

The Bankruptcy Code details the rules about what property the debtor gets to keep (called *exempt assets*) and what obligations the debtor may *avoid* (eliminate or reduce) for certain debts, as well as what assets must be liquidated to meet the debtor's obligations to creditors (called *nonexempt assets*). An *automatic stay* is an injunction that prohibits collections against the debtor because of the bankruptcy. Many times, a bankrupt person will file an automatic stay to "freeze" or protect the estate until the details of a bankruptcy can be finalized. The Code also determines the *priority* of creditors beyond the secured creditors; that is, the ranking of unsecured claims. If a debtor made a payment to a creditor in the ninety-day period before filing for bankruptcy, this may be held to be a *preferential debt payment* that the creditor must return to the estate. In some cases such payments will be held to be *fraudulent transfers* where the debtor is attempting to evade responsibilities.

The estate of the bankrupt is represented by the *trustee* who is appointed by the court overseeing the bankruptcy to review the debtor's condition and to exercise statutory powers for the benefit of the creditors in sorting out everyone's claims against the bankrupt estate. Some property will be declared to be *exempt* from the estate and will not be available to pay down the claims of the creditors. Certain obligations are considered to be *nondischargeable debts* that are not eliminated in bankruptcy, such as educational loans and child support.

WRAPPING IT UP

The bankruptcy proceedings decide what debt obligations will be *discharged*—legally eliminated. In some bankruptcies, the court orders a plan for repayment of debts by the debtor, called the *confirmation*. In most bankruptcy cases, the work is done by lawyers representing the parties, and the debtor never appears in court. At the end, the debtor is said to be given a *fresh start*.

Objections to Discharge

In addition to the exceptions to discharge just listed, a bankruptcy court may also deny the discharge based on the debtor's conduct. In such a situation, the assets of the debtor are still distributed to the creditors, but the debtor remains liable for the unpaid portion of all claims. Some grounds for the denial of discharge based on the debtor's conduct follow:

1. The debtor's concealment or destruction of property with the intent to defraud a creditor.

2. The debtor's fraudulent concealment or destruction of financial records.

Ethics Watch

THE PERILS OF INDEPENDENT PRACTICE

As you read in Chapter 2, independent paralegals provide services directly to the public (without attorney supervision). Some independent paralegals assist debtors by selling them "do-it-yourself" bankruptcy kits, preparing bankruptcy forms, and the like.

Although the Bankruptcy Code allows paralegals to act as bankruptcy petition preparers without attorney supervision, it contains strict requirements that must be followed. The law prohibits petition preparers from advising bankruptcy debtors about numerous issues and from offering legal advice. For example, petition preparers may not tell a debtor whether he or she will be able to retain certain property, such as a house or car, after filing for bankruptcy. They may not say whether a particular debt will or can be discharged. They may not tell debtors how to characterize an interest in property when filling out the forms, whether to reaffirm a particular debt, or what tax consequences might be involved.

Violators may be subject to a fine; may be required to forfeit the fees they received from, or pay damages to, the debtor; and may even be ordered not to prepare bankruptcy petitions in the future. Because of the dangers involved, paralegals who prepare bankruptcy petitions without attorney supervision must be exceedingly careful to avoid pitfalls and potential lawsuits.

Such care is consistent with the NALA Code of Ethics, Canon 4: "A paralegal must use discretion and professional judgment commensurate with knowledge and experience but must not render independent legal judgment in place of an attorney."

3. The granting of a discharge to the debtor within eight years prior to the petition filing.
4. Failure of the debtor to complete the required credit counseling course.
5. Proceedings in which the debtor could be found guilty of a felony.

Effect of Discharge

The primary effect of a discharge is to void, or set aside, any judgment on a discharged debt and prohibit any action to collect a discharged debt. A discharge does not affect the liability of a co-debtor.

INDIVIDUAL REPAYMENT PLANS

As noted earlier, some debtors who file for bankruptcy may prefer liquidation under Chapter 7 but, due to the means test, may be required to file under Chapter 13. Chapter 13 of the Bankruptcy Code provides for "Adjustment of Debts of an Individual with Regular Income." Individuals (not partnerships or corporations) with regular income who owe fixed unsecured debts of less than $340,000 or fixed secured debts of less than $1 million may take advantage of bankruptcy repayment plans. Among those eligible are salaried employees and sole proprietors. Many small-business debtors have a choice of filing a plan for reorganization (discussed later in this chapter) or for repayment. There are several advantages to repayment

Developing Paralegal Skills

PREPARING A PROOF OF CLAIM

Lee Smith works as a paralegal for a bankruptcy attorney. Today, Lee has been assigned the task of preparing a proof-of-claim form to be filed with the bankruptcy court for a client. The client is Bill Peaslee, a farmer who supplies a number of local restaurants with organic produce. One of Peaslee's customers, Fred Burke (the sole owner of Greenleaf Restaurant and Grill) owes Peaslee nearly $10,000 for orders that were placed in the previous nine months. Three weeks ago, when attempting to collect the past-due balance from Burke, Peaslee learned that Burke had filed for relief under Chapter 13 of the Bankruptcy Code. Peaslee, as a creditor of an individual debtor filing for bankruptcy protection, must file a proof of claim with the bankruptcy court to establish the amount of his claim against Burke. After Lee's supervising attorney provides the necessary information, Lee turns to his computer.

CHECKLIST FOR PREPARING A PROOF-OF-CLAIM FORM

- Retrieve the proof-of-claim form from the firm's forms database.
- Key in the client-creditor's name and address.
- Insert the amount that the debtor owes to the client.
- Enter the date, the debtor's name, and other required data.
- Print out the completed form and proofread it carefully.
- Give the completed form to the supervising attorney to review.
- After the attorney has reviewed the form, make copies of it to send to the court for filing.

---

plans. One is that they are less expensive and less complicated than reorganization proceedings or liquidation proceedings.

Filing the Petition

A repayment-plan case can be initiated only by the filing of a voluntary petition by the debtor. In addition, certain liquidation and reorganization cases may be converted to repayment-plan cases with the consent of the debtor.

Upon the filing of a repayment-plan petition, a trustee, who will make payments under the plan, must be appointed. The automatic stay previously discussed also takes effect. Although the stay applies to all or part of a consumer debt, it does not apply to any business debt incurred by the debtor. When creditors learn of the bankruptcy, they may seek assistance in filing claims, as detailed in the *Developing Paralegal Skills* feature above.

Filing the Plan

Only the debtor may file a repayment plan. This plan may provide either for payment of all obligations in full or for payment of a lesser amount. The duration of the payment plan (three or five years) is determined by the debtor's median family income. If the debtor's income is greater than the state median income under the means test (previously discussed), the proposed time for repayment must be five years. The term may not exceed five years.

The Code requires the debtor to make "timely" payments from the debtor's disposable income, and the trustee is required to ensure that the debtor commences these payments. The debtor must begin making payments under the proposed plan within thirty days after the plan has been filed with the court. If the plan has not been confirmed, the trustee is instructed to hold the payments until the plan is confirmed and then distribute them accordingly. If the plan is denied, the trustee will return the payments to the debtor less any costs. Failure of the debtor to make timely payments or to begin payments within the thirty-day period will allow the court to convert the case to a liquidation bankruptcy or to dismiss the petition.

Confirmation of the Plan

After the plan is filed, the court holds a confirmation hearing, at which interested parties may object to the plan. The hearing must be held at least twenty days, but no more than forty-five days, after the meeting of the creditors. Confirmation of the plan is dependent on the debtor's certification that postpetition domestic-support obligations have been paid in full and all prepetition tax returns have been filed. The court will confirm a plan with respect to each claim of a secured creditor under any of the following circumstances:

1. If the secured creditors have accepted the plan.
2. If the plan provides that secured creditors retain their claims against the debtor's property until payment is made in full or until the debtor receives a discharge.
3. If the debtor surrenders the property securing the claim to the creditors.

Objections to the Plan

Unsecured creditors do not have a vote to confirm a repayment plan, but they can object to it. The court can approve a plan over the objection of the trustee or any unsecured creditor only in either of the following situations:

1. When the value of the property to be distributed under the plan is at least equal to the amount of the claims.
2. When all the debtor's projected disposable income to be received during the plan period will be applied to making payments. Disposable income is all income received *less* amounts needed to pay domestic-support obligations and/or amounts needed to meet ordinary expenses to continue the operation of a business.

Modification of the Plan

Prior to completion of payments, the plan may be modified at the request of the debtor, the trustee, or an unsecured creditor. If any interested party objects to the modification, the court must hold a hearing to determine approval or disapproval of the modified plan.

Discharge

After the completion of all payments, the court grants a discharge of the debts provided for by the repayment plan. Not all debts are dischargeable, however. Nondischargeable debts in a Chapter 13 bankruptcy include allowed claims not provided for by the plan; certain long-term debts provided for by the plan; claims for domestic-support obligations; payments on retirement accounts; and debts for trust fund taxes, taxes for which returns were never filed or filed late (within two years of the bankruptcy filing), student loans, and injury or property damage from driving under the influence of alcohol or drugs. Also excluded are debts arising from fraudulent tax obligations, criminal fines and restitution, fraud by a person acting in a fiduciary capacity, and restitution for willfully and maliciously causing personal injury or death.

If the debtor does not complete the plan, a hardship discharge may be granted if failure to complete the plan was due to circumstances beyond the debtor's control and if the value of the property distributed under the plan was greater than creditors would have received in a liquidation proceeding. A discharge can be revoked within one year if it was obtained by fraud.

REORGANIZATIONS

The type of bankruptcy proceedings used most commonly by a corporate debtor is the Chapter 11 *reorganization*. In a reorganization, the creditors and the debtor formulate a plan under which the debtor pays a portion of his or her debts and is discharged of the remainder. The debtor is allowed to continue in business. Although this type of bankruptcy is commonly a corporate reorganization, any debtor (except a stockbroker or a commodities broker) who is eligible for Chapter 7 relief is eligible for relief under Chapter 11. Railroads are also eligible. In 1994, Congress established a "fast-track" Chapter 11 procedure for small-business debtors whose liabilities do not exceed $2 million and who do not own or manage real estate. This procedure does not require the appointment of committees and can save time and costs.

The same principles that govern the filing of a liquidation (Chapter 7) petition apply to reorganization proceedings. The case may be brought either voluntarily or involuntarily. The same principles govern the entry of the order for relief. The automatic-stay provision is also applicable in reorganizations. An exception from the automatic stay is triggered in the event that the debtor files for bankruptcy again within two years, and new grounds for dismissal (such as substantial abuse) or conversion of the case are established.

Workouts

In some instances, to avoid bankruptcy proceedings, creditors may prefer private, negotiated adjustments or creditor-debtor relations, also known as **workouts**. Often these out-of-court workouts are much more flexible and more conducive to a speedy settlement. Speed is critical, because delay is one of the most costly elements in any bankruptcy proceeding. Another advantage of workouts is that they avoid the administrative costs of bankruptcy proceedings.

> **workout**
> An out-of-court negotiation in which a debtor enters into an agreement with a creditor or creditors for a payment or plan to discharge the debtor's debt.

Must Be in the Best Interests of the Creditors

After a petition for Chapter 11 bankruptcy has been filed, a bankruptcy court, after notice and a hearing, may dismiss or suspend all proceedings at any time if that would better serve the interests of the creditors. The Code also allows a court, after notice and a hearing, to dismiss a case under reorganization "for cause." Cause includes the absence of a reasonable likelihood of rehabilitation, the inability to effect a plan, and an unreasonable delay by the debtor that may harm the interests of creditors.

Debtor in Possession

On entry of the order for relief, the debtor generally continues to operate the business as a **debtor in possession (DIP)**. The court, however, may appoint a trustee (often referred to as a *receiver*) to operate the debtor's business if mismanagement

> **debtor in possession (DIP)**
> In Chapter 11 bankruptcy proceedings, a debtor who is allowed, for the benefit of all concerned, to maintain possession of the estate in bankruptcy (the business) and to continue business operations.

of the business is shown or if appointing a trustee is in the best interests of the estate.

The DIP's role is similar to that of a trustee in a liquidation. The DIP is entitled to avoid preferential payments made to creditors and fraudulent transfers of assets that occurred prior to the filing of the Chapter 11 petition. The DIP has the power to decide whether to cancel or assume obligations under executory contracts (contracts that have not yet been performed) that were made prior to the filing.

Creditors' Committees

As soon as practicable after the entry of the order for relief, a creditors' committee of unsecured creditors is appointed. This committee often is composed of the biggest suppliers to the business. The committee may consult with the trustee or the DIP concerning the administration of the case or the formulation of the reorganization plan. Additional creditors' committees may be appointed to represent special interest creditors. Generally, no orders affecting the estate will be entered without either the consent of the committee or a hearing in which the judge hears the position of the committee.

The Reorganization Plan

A reorganization plan to rehabilitate the debtor is a plan to conserve and administer the debtor's assets in the hope of a return to successful operation and solvency. The plan must be fair and equitable and must do the following:

1. Designate classes of claims and interests.
2. Specify the treatment to be afforded the classes. (The plan must provide the same treatment for each claim in a particular class.)
3. Provide an adequate means for execution.
4. Provide for payment of tax claims over a five-year period.

Filing the Plan

Only the debtor may file a plan within the first 120 days after the date of the order for relief. This period may be extended, but not beyond eighteen months from the date of the order for relief. If the debtor does not meet the 120-day deadline or obtain an extension, and if the debtor fails to obtain the required creditor consent within 180 days, any party may propose a plan. The plan need not provide for full repayment to unsecured creditors. Instead, creditors receive a percentage of each dollar owed to them by the debtor. If a small-business debtor chooses to avoid creditors' committees, the time for the debtor's filing is 180 days.

Acceptance and Confirmation of the Plan

Once the plan has been developed, it is submitted to each class of creditors for acceptance. For the plan to be adopted, each class that is adversely affected by the plan must accept it. A class has accepted the plan when a majority of the creditors, representing two-thirds of the amount of the total claim, vote to approve it. Confirmation is conditioned on the debtor's certifying that all postpetition domestic-support obligations have been paid in full.

Even when all classes of creditors accept the plan, the court may refuse to confirm it if it is not "in the best interests of the creditors." The plan can also be modified at the request of the debtor, the trustee, the U.S. trustee, or a holder of an unsecured claim. If an unsecured creditor objects to the plan, specific rules apply to the value of property to be distributed under the plan. Tax claims must be paid over a five-year period.

Even if only one class of creditors has accepted the plan, the court may still confirm the plan under the Code's so-called **cram-down provision**. In other words, the court may confirm the plan over the objections of a class of creditors. Before the court can exercise this right of cram-down confirmation, it must be demonstrated that the plan "does not discriminate unfairly" against any creditors and that the plan is "fair and equitable."

Discharge

The plan is binding on confirmation. The Bankruptcy Reform Act of 2005, however, provides that confirmation of a plan does not discharge an individual debtor. For individual debtors, execution of the plan must be completed before discharge will be granted, unless the court orders otherwise. For all other debtors, the court may order discharge at any time after the plan is confirmed. The debtor at this time is given a reorganization discharge from all claims not protected under the plan. This discharge does not apply to any claims that would be denied discharge under liquidation.

> **cram-down provision**
> A provision of the Bankruptcy Code that allows a court to confirm a debtor's Chapter 11 reorganization plan even though only one class of creditors has accepted it. To exercise the court's right under this provision, the court must demonstrate that the plan does not discriminate unfairly against any creditors and is fair and equitable.

BANKRUPTCY LAW AND THE PARALEGAL

Today, roughly one in every five paralegals spends about half of his or her work time on bankruptcy law. Opportunities have expanded in recent years for independent paralegals who specialize in bankruptcy. Indeed, much of the work previously handled by attorneys can now be done by paralegals with expertise in this area. For example, a debtor-client who wants to petition for bankruptcy relief must provide the court with numerous forms stating in detail the debtor's assets and liabilities. These forms must be filled out accurately and thoroughly.

Paralegals familiar with the requirements imposed by bankruptcy law know what information must be included with the petition for bankruptcy and can assist attorneys in collecting this information from clients. Paralegals may be involved in evaluating and verifying the debtor's financial statements, researching the law governing certain types of claims, and locating and perhaps appraising certain property belonging to the debtor. In addition, paralegals often help draft bankruptcy petitions and schedules and file them with the court.

As a paralegal, you may be dealing with bankruptcy cases periodically as part of your work for a general law practice. If you work for a firm that specializes in bankruptcy law, you may be working on behalf of either debtors or creditors who are involved in bankruptcy proceedings. Bankruptcy trustees also require paralegal assistance. In assisting a bankruptcy trustee, you would be working in the interests of both debtors and creditors during the administration of the debtor's estate in property. In any of these situations, a paralegal well trained in the substantive and procedural laws governing bankruptcy can provide invaluable assistance.

The specific types of work handled by bankruptcy paralegals vary, of course, depending on whether they work on behalf of the debtor, a creditor, or the bankruptcy trustee. Here are a few examples of paralegal tasks that you might be asked to perform if you were assisting a debtor-client (which could be an individual or a corporate representative) in petitioning for bankruptcy relief:

- Conduct an intake interview—and follow-up interviews as necessary—to obtain information concerning the debtor's income, debts, and assets.
- Verify the accuracy of the debtor's financial statements.
- Make arrangements for the debtor to receive credit counseling from an approved agency.
- Draft the bankruptcy petition based on the information obtained from the client.
- Verify the validity of creditors' claims that have been submitted to the bankruptcy court.
- Prepare the client for bankruptcy proceedings, such as creditors' meetings.
- Assist in work on the debtor's behalf in any legal actions relating to the bankruptcy proceedings.
- Research the Bankruptcy Code to verify that certain provisions are still effective and keep up to date on bankruptcy law.
- Research state statutes governing property exemptions.
- Research case law to see how the courts have applied a certain provision of the Bankruptcy Code or a state law applicable to the bankruptcy proceedings.

ENVIRONMENTAL LAW

We now turn to a discussion of the various ways in which businesses are regulated by the government in the interest of protecting the environment. Remember from Chapter 2 that *environmental law* is defined as all law pertaining to environmental protection.

Environmental law is not new. Indeed, the federal government began to regulate some activities, such as those involving the pollution of navigable waterways, in the late 1800s. In the last few decades, however, the body of environmental law has expanded substantially as the government has attempted to control industrial waste and to protect dwindling natural resources and endangered species. Today, businesses face the task of complying with many environmental regulations. Because of the complexity of many of these regulations, businesses often need legal assistance to make sure that they meet environmental requirements imposed by law. For this reason, many attorneys and paralegals specialize in environmental law. (This chapter's *Technology and Today's Paralegal* feature on page 636 discusses a number of helpful online resources that paralegals can turn to for detailed information on environmental laws and compliance requirements.) In this section, we look at some of the most significant statutes and regulations that have been created to protect the environment.

Federal Regulation of the Environment

Congress has passed a number of statutes to control the impact of human activities on the environment. Some of these statutes were passed in an attempt to improve the quality of air and water. Some of them specifically regulate toxic chemicals and hazardous wastes. Exhibit 19.2 lists the major federal statutes that apply to various areas of the environment. Because regulations change frequently, a paralegal who works in the area will want to keep on top of the changes as the *Developing Paralegal Skills* feature discusses on page 637.

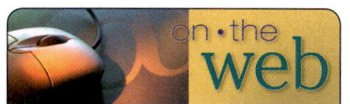

For information on the standards, guidelines, and regulations of the Environmental Protection Agency, go to **www.epa.gov**.

Environmental Regulatory Agencies

Much of the body of federal law governing business activities consists of the regulations issued and enforced by administrative agencies. The most well known of the agencies regulating environmental law is, of course, the Environmental Protection Agency (EPA), which was created in 1970 to coordinate federal environmental responsibilities. Not only the EPA, but other agencies of the federal government, must take environmental factors into consideration when making significant decisions. Most federal environmental laws also provide that citizens can sue to enforce environmental regulations if government agencies fail to do so—or to limit enforcement if agencies go too far in their enforcement actions. Finally, note that although we do not discuss state regulation here, each state has an environmental agency that parallels the EPA.

environmental impact statement (EIS)

A statement required by the National Environmental Policy Act for any major federal action that will significantly affect the quality of the environment. The statement must analyze the action's impact on the environment and explore alternative actions that might be taken.

Environmental Impact Statements

The National Environmental Policy Act (NEPA) of 1969 requires that for every major federal action that significantly affects the quality of the environment, an **environmental impact statement (EIS)** must be prepared. Construction by a private developer of a ski resort on federal land, for example, may require an EIS. Building or operating a nuclear power plant, which requires a federal permit, or constructing a dam as part of a federal project would require an EIS. An EIS must analyze (1) the impact on the environment that the action will have, (2) any adverse effects on the environment and alternative actions that might be taken, and (3) irreversible effects the action might generate. EISs have become instruments used by private citizens, consumer interest groups, businesses, and others to challenge federal agency actions on the basis that the actions improperly threaten the environment.

EXHIBIT 19.2
Federal Regulation of Environmental Pollution

From MEINERS/RINGLEB/EDWARDS. The Legal Environment of Business, 10E. © 2009 South-Western, a part of Cengage Learning, Inc. Reproduced by permission. **www.cengage.com/permissions**

Air Pollution
Clean Air Act

Environmental quality outside a plant is controlled by the EPA.

Environmental quality inside a plant is controlled by the Occupational Safety and Health Administration.

Land Pollution
Resource Conservation and
    Recovery Act (RCRA)
Comprehensive Environmental
    Response, Compensation, and
    Liability Act (Superfund)
Endangered Species Act

Environmental Quality Regulation of Products
Noise Pollution Control Act
Clean Air Act (Motor Vehicles)
Federal Insecticide, Fungicide, and
    Rodenticide Act (FIFRA)
Toxic Substances Control Act (TOSCA)
Pollution Prevention Act

Water Pollution
Clean Water Act
Rivers and Harbors Act
Safe Drinking Water Act
Marine Mammal Protection Act

Air Pollution

Federal involvement with air pollution goes back to the 1950s, when Congress authorized funds for air-pollution research. In 1963, the federal government passed the Clean Air Act, which focused on multistate air pollution and provided assistance to states. Later amendments to the act, especially in 1970, strengthened the government's authority to regulate air quality. These laws provide the basis for issuing regulations to control air pollution. The EPA attempts to update pollution-control standards when new scientific information becomes available.

Mobile and Stationary Sources of Pollution

The Clean Air Act covers both mobile and stationary sources of pollution. Mobile sources include automobiles and other moving sources. The Clean Air Act of 1970 and its amendments require automobile manufacturers to cut new automobiles' exhaust emissions by a certain percentage by a given date. Every few years, the EPA reviews the standards and usually makes them tougher, so fewer emissions are allowed.

Stationary sources include manufacturing plants, electric utilities, and other nonmoving sources of pollution. The Clean Air Act authorizes the EPA to establish air-quality standards for these sources. The EPA sets the maximum levels of certain pollutants that may be emitted by stationary sources, and the states formulate plans to achieve those standards. Different standards apply to sources of pollution in clean areas and sources in polluted areas. Different standards also apply to existing sources of pollution and major new sources. Performance standards for major sources require the use of "maximum achievable control technology" to reduce

Technology and Today's Paralegal

ENVIRONMENTAL COMPLIANCE

One of the challenges for lawyers and paralegals today is keeping abreast of environmental laws and regulations. As a paralegal, you may need to know what those laws are, how to monitor them, and what requirements they impose on businesses. With today's easy access to Internet resources, paralegals can quickly find an abundance of information not only on environmental laws but also on what businesses must do to comply with these laws. Here, we look at just a few online resources that paralegals can use to obtain such information.

ENVIRONMENTAL LAWS AND REGULATIONS

A primary source for environmental laws and regulations is, of course, the U.S. Environmental Protection Agency (EPA), which coordinates and enforces many of these laws and regulations. You can visit a page on the EPA's Web site titled "Laws, Regulations, Guidance, and Dockets" by going to **ww.epa.gov** and selecting "Laws & Regulations" from the menu bar. This Web page contains links to a number of information sources, including the major environmental laws and regulations, new regulations and proposed rules, proposed environmental legislation in Congress, and an explanation of how the EPA writes regulations.

Another helpful Web site can be found at **enviro.blr.com**, which is hosted by Business & Legal Reports, Inc. Here, you can find information on environmental laws and regulatory activity, as well as the full text of federal and state environmental regulations. You can also find various tools (such as special forms and checklists) for monitoring and implementing a firm's compliance with regulatory requirements.

COMPLIANCE ASSISTANCE

There are a number of online environmental compliance resources. You can directly access the EPA's National Environmental Compliance Assistance Clearinghouse by going to **cfpub.epa.gov/ clearinghouse**. This site includes an interactive online guide to environmental compliance requirements.

The Environmental Compliance Assistance Platform, at **www.envcap.org**, is designed to help businesses comply with environmental regulations. This site includes links to compliance assistance for various industries and groups (for example, for the construction, health-care, and automotive recycling industries). Through this site, you can also access state regulations and other information. The Small Business Environmental home page will also take you to numerous compliance resources. (Go to **www. smallbiz-enviroweb.org**, and select "Environmental Compliance" from the menu.)

ENVIRONMENTAL SOFTWARE

A growing number of firms offer special software designed to help businesses monitor and comply with environmental regulations. One software company, Prism Systems, Inc., at **www.prismsystems.com**, offers environmental management solutions and tools. At this site, you can download a free demonstration program illustrating the features of the software. Another software company, Environmental Software Providers (**www. esp-net.com**), has software products designed to manage environmental performance and risk. ESS provides software related to environment compliance and performance at **www.ess-home.com**. (Select "Environmental Compliance" from the "Solutions" menu.) Firms that want to make sure they comply with standards in Europe or China can check **www.synapsistech.com**.

TECHNOLOGY TIP

Creating a list of URLs for helpful Web resources is a must for most paralegals. To minimize the time you spend finding specific Web sites in your list, make sure that the list is well organized. For example, including subject headings in your list and sorting the headings alphabetically will help you locate Web sites more easily. Also, when you are searching for government resources and do not have a URL at hand, remember that **firstgov.gov** is a gateway to *all* federal agencies and institutions.

Developing Paralegal Skills

MONITORING THE *FEDERAL REGISTER*

Robin Hayes is a legal assistant for CARCO, Inc., a large company that manufactures automobile parts. She works in the environmental law practice group within the corporation's legal department. One of her responsibilities is to monitor the *Federal Register* on a daily basis for newly proposed environmental regulations and for changes to existing rules. Today, Robin notices a change to the hazardous waste manifest, a form that CARCO is required to use when shipping hazardous waste to a disposal facility. The change requires the company to certify its efforts in reducing the amount of hazardous waste that it generates. Robin prepares a memo to the attorneys in the group, because they will need to inform management of the change.

CHECKLIST FOR MONITORING THE *FEDERAL REGISTER*

- Review the *Federal Register* weekly without fail.
- Next, review the topics and subtopics to determine if notices, rules, or proposed rules have been issued on topics affecting your client.
- Skim through any notices, rules, and proposed rules that may apply to your client.
- Read in detail the relevant notices, rules, and proposed rules that may apply to your client.
- Print out relevant notices, rules, and proposed rules for circulation to the attorneys and others who should be advised of this information.
- Notify the attorneys and others of upcoming deadlines for comments on proposed rules and changes.

---

emissions from the combustion of fossil fuels (coal and oil). The EPA issues guidelines as to what equipment meets this requirement.

Penalties for Violating the Clean Air Act

The EPA can assess civil penalties of up to $25,000 per day for violations of emission limits under the Clean Air Act. Additional fines of up to $5,000 per day can be assessed for other violations, such as failing to maintain required records. To penalize those for whom it is more cost-effective to violate the act than to comply with it, the EPA is authorized to obtain a penalty equal to the violator's economic benefits from noncompliance. Persons who provide information about violators may be paid up to $10,000. Private citizens can also sue violators. Those who knowingly violate the act may be subject to criminal penalties, including fines of up to $1 million and imprisonment for up to two years (for false statements or failures to report violations). Corporate officers are among those who may be subject to these penalties. The threat of penalties is not an empty one, as most years there are more than a hundred criminal indictments.

Water Pollution

Federal regulations governing water pollution can be traced back to the Rivers and Harbors Appropriation Act of 1899. These regulations prohibited ships and manufacturers from discharging or depositing refuse in navigable waterways.

Navigable Waters

Navigable waters include coastal waters, freshwater wetlands, and lakes and streams used by interstate travelers and industry. In practice, essentially every body of water and every stream is considered navigable and subject to regulation. In 1948, Congress passed the Federal Water Pollution Control Act (FWPCA), but its regulatory system and enforcement proved inadequate. In 1972, amendments to the FWPCA—known as the Clean Water Act—were enacted to (1) make waters safe for swimming, (2) protect fish and wildlife, and (3) eliminate the discharge of pollutants into the water. The amendments required that polluters apply for permits before discharging wastes into navigable waters.

Focus on Point-Source Emissions

In practice, the Clean Water Act focuses on pollutants that are emitted from *point sources*. These are sources occupying small areas and heavily concentrated outputs. The act, as amended over time, has five main elements:

1. National effluent (pollution) standards set by the EPA for each industry.
2. Water quality standards set by the states under EPA supervision.
3. A *discharge permit* program that sets water quality standards to limit pollution.
4. Special provisions for toxic chemicals and for oil spills.
5. Construction grants and loans from the federal government for *publicly owned treatment works (POTWs),* primarily sewage treatment plants.

The Clean Water Act makes it illegal for any person, business, or government to dump pollutants into navigable waters without a discharge permit. These permits are issued under the National Pollution Discharge Elimination System. Any point source emitting pollutants into water must have a permit. Non-point source pollution, such as runoff from farms, is not subject to much regulation.

As Exhibit 19.3 shows, there are two major categories of point-source discharges into the nation's waters. The first are POTWs, most of which are local government sewage treatment plants. They must use the *best conventional technology* for treating waste in order to receive a permit to discharge. The EPA sets that technology standard. Subject to more strict controls are emissions from point sources such as factories. They must use the *best available technology* to treat their waste water before returning the water to a waterway. When a firm shows that it is in compliance with the technology standard, then it can obtain a discharge permit.

Penalties for Violating the Clean Water Act

Because point-source water pollution control is based on a permit system, the permits are the key to enforcement. States have primary responsibility for enforcing the permit system, subject to EPA monitoring.

Discharging emissions into navigable waters without a permit, or in violation of pollution limits under a permit, violates the Clean Water Act. Firms that have discharge permits must monitor their own performance and file *discharge monitoring reports*. These reports are available for public inspection. Violators must report their violations and are subject to fines. Lying about a violation is more serious than admitting the truth about improper discharges. Serious violations can result in criminal prosecutions, and every year people are sent to prison for dumping toxic pollutants. As with the Clean Air Act, citizens have the right to bring suits for pollutant violations that the EPA or a state environmental agency has not addressed properly.

EXHIBIT 19.3
Primary Sources of Water Effluents

From MEINERS/RINGLEB/EDWARDS. The Legal Environment of Business, 10E. © 2009 South-Western, a part of Cengage Learning, Inc.
Reproduced by permission. **www.cengage.com/permissions**

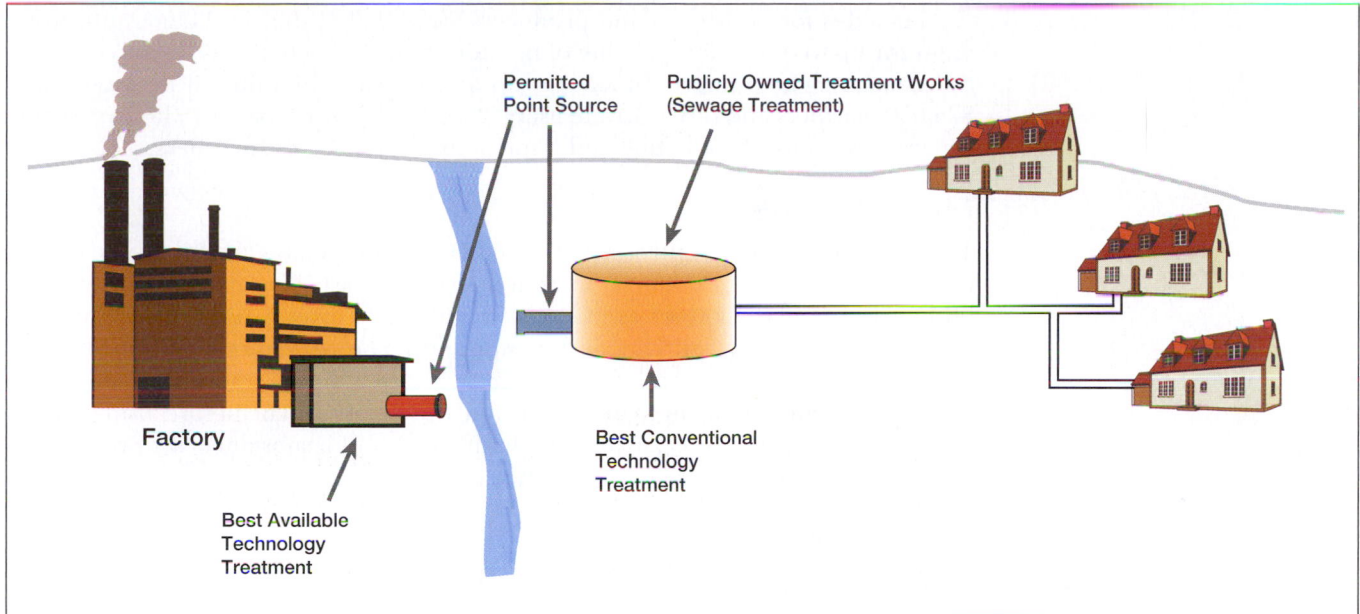

Wetlands

Years ago, wetlands were seen as nuisances to be drained and filled with dirt. The Clean Water Act recognizes the ecological value of wetlands and protects them. *Wetlands* are any lands, such as swamps and bogs, that support vegetation adapted to saturated soil conditions. They are protected no matter how large or small they are.

Under the Clean Water Act, anyone wanting to change a wetland, usually for construction purposes, must obtain a permit from the U.S. Army Corps of Engineers. Each year, the Corps of Engineers issues more than 10,000 permits that involve significant wetland impact. The Corps reviews proposals for dredging or filling, and it often limits the work or requires work to be done elsewhere in exchange for the wetland lost to construction. The Corps issues another 75,000 permits annually for activities found to have "minimal adverse environmental effects" to wetlands. The decisions of the Corps are reviewed by the EPA. Violators are subject to fines that can be in the millions of dollars.

Toxic Chemicals

Originally, most environmental clean-up efforts were directed toward reducing smog and making water safe for fishing and swimming. Over time, however, control of toxic chemicals became an important part of environmental law.

Pesticides and Herbicides

The first toxic chemical problem to receive widespread public attention was that posed by pesticides and herbicides. Using these chemicals to kill insects and weeds has increased agricultural productivity, but their residue remains in the environment. In rare instances, accumulations of this residue have killed animals, and scientists have identified potential long-term effects that are detrimental to humans. Under the Federal Insecticide, Fungicide, and Rodenticide Act of 1947 (FIFRA), pesticides and herbicides must be registered before they can be sold, used only for approved applications, and used in limited quantities when applied to food crops. If a substance is identified as harmful, the EPA can cancel its registration.

Under 1996 amendments to the act, for a pesticide to remain on the market, there must be a "reasonable certainty of no harm" to people from exposure to the pesticide. This means that there must be no more than a one-in-a-million risk to people of developing cancer from exposure in any way, including eating food that contains residues from the pesticide.

Penalties for registrants and producers for violating the act include imprisonment for up to one year and a fine of no more than $50,000. Penalties for commercial dealers include imprisonment for up to one year and a fine of no more than $25,000. Farmers and other private users of pesticides or herbicides who violate the act are subject to a $1,000 fine and imprisonment for up to thirty days.

Toxic Substances

The Toxic Substances Control Act of 1976 (TOSCA) regulates chemicals and chemical compounds that are known to be toxic (such as asbestos and polychlorinated biphenyls, popularly known as PCBs) and authorizes investigation of any possible harmful effects from new chemical compounds. The regulations permit the EPA to require that manufacturers, processors, and other organizations determine the effects of chemicals on human health and the environment before using them. The EPA may require special labeling, limit the use of a substance, set production quotas, or prohibit the use of a substance altogether.

Hazardous Wastes

Some industrial, agricultural, and household wastes pose more serious threats than others. If not properly disposed of, these toxic chemicals may present a substantial danger to human health and the environment. If released into the environment, they may contaminate public drinking water resources.

Resource Conservation and Recovery Act.   In 1976, Congress passed the Resource Conservation and Recovery Act (RCRA) in reaction to concern about the effects of hazardous waste materials on the environment. RCRA required the EPA to establish regulations to monitor and control hazardous waste disposal and to determine which forms of solid waste should be considered hazardous and thus subject to regulation. The act authorized the EPA to promulgate various technical requirements for some types of facilities for storage and treatment of hazardous waste. The act also requires all producers of hazardous waste materials to label and package properly any hazardous waste that is to be transported.

In practice, RCRA imposes a "cradle-to-grave" system of controls on hazardous substances. As Exhibit 19.4 indicates, chemicals, besides being subject to TOSCA or FIFRA standards at the point of production and sale, are subject to the use of manifests under RCRA. The hazardous substance producer must attach a *manifest*, or data sheet, to all products that will become hazardous waste. The sellers of those substances must have an EPA permit. The manifests must accompany the substances down the chain of use so parties can be held responsible for use and disposal of the products. Firms that operate *treatment, storage, and disposal (TSD) sites* must meet all regulations regarding the proper handling, use, and destruction of hazardous materials.

Under RCRA, a company may be assessed a civil penalty based on the seriousness of the violation, the probability of harm, and the extent to which the violation deviates from RCRA requirements. The assessment may be up to $25,000 for each violation. Criminal penalties include fines up to $50,000 for each day of violation, imprisonment for up to two years (in most instances), or both. Criminal fines and the time of imprisonment can be doubled for certain repeat offenders.

Superfund.   In 1980, Congress passed the Comprehensive Environmental Response, Compensation, and Liability Act (CERCLA), commonly known as Superfund. The basic purpose of Superfund, which was amended in 1986, is to regulate the clean-up of disposal sites in which hazardous waste is leaking into the environment. A special federal fund was created for this purpose.

EXHIBIT 19.4
Regulation of Hazardous Substances

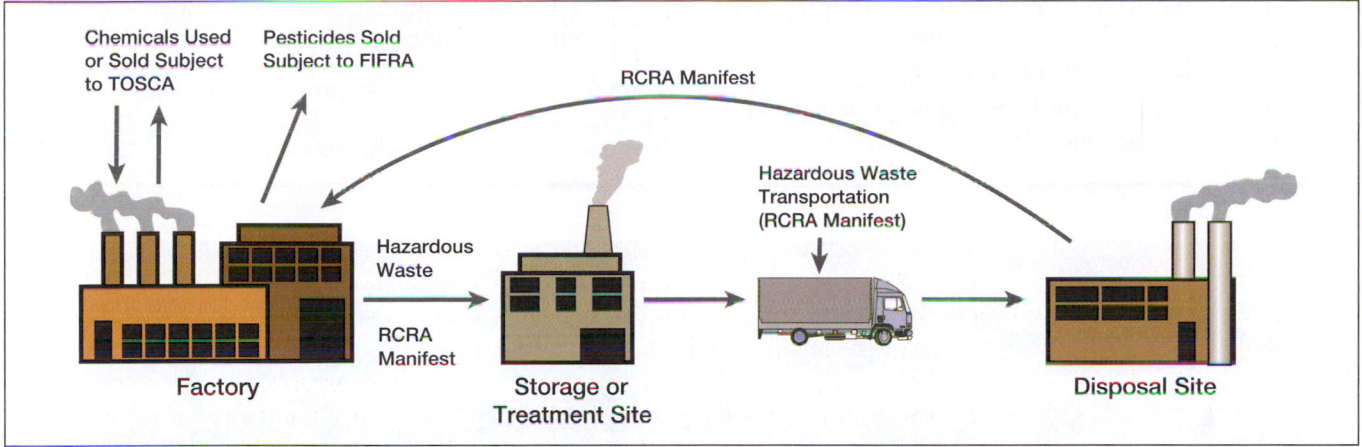

Superfund provides that when a release or a threatened release of hazardous chemicals from a site occurs, the following persons are responsible for cleaning up the site: (1) the person who generated the wastes disposed of at the site, (2) the person who transported the wastes to the site, (3) the person who owned or operated the site at the time of the disposal, and (4) the current owner or operator. A person falling within one of these categories is referred to as a **potentially responsible party (PRP)**. If the PRPs do not clean up the site, Superfund authorizes the EPA to clean up the site and recover clean-up costs from the PRPs.

Superfund imposes strict liability on PRPs. Also, liability under Superfund is usually joint and several—that is, a PRP who generated only a fraction of the hazardous waste disposed of at the site may nevertheless be liable for all of the clean-up costs. CERCLA authorizes a party who has incurred clean-up costs to bring a "contribution action" against any other person who is liable or potentially liable for a percentage of the costs.

potentially responsible party (PRP)

A party who may be liable under the Comprehensive Environmental Response, Compensation, and Liability Act, or Superfund. Any person who generated hazardous waste, transported hazardous waste, owned or operated a waste site at the time of disposal, or currently owns or operates a site may be responsible for some or all of the clean-up costs involved in removing the hazardous chemicals.

ENVIRONMENTAL LAW AND THE PARALEGAL

Paralegals who specialize in environmental law find employment in a number of settings. A paralegal specialist in this area may work for a federal or state environmental agency, a local government agency concerned with natural resources, a law firm's environmental department, or a corporate legal department.

If you work for an environmental agency, you may be involved in the research and writing necessary to create new rules or revise existing ones. You may be asked to assist in monitoring compliance with a particular regulation. You may draft documents relating to legal actions brought against violators. In a corporate environment, you may be asked to help draft the firm's environmental procedures or to obtain and fill out forms the firm is required to submit to an environmental agency.

Some paralegals working in the area of environmental law may be involved in litigation concerning environmental claims. For example, a government agency may bring an action against a business that has failed to comply with a particular law or regulation. One company may sue another company that refuses to contribute to the cost of cleaning up a hazardous site to which it furnished materials. An individual or group of individuals may sue a company for health injuries suffered because of the company's polluting activities. Often, such litigation involves massive amounts of paperwork and exhibits, and case management becomes a challenge. A paralegal who can meet this challenge will be a valuable asset to his or her employer.

Here are some of the many types of tasks that you might perform as a paralegal working in the area of environmental law:

- Draft and file permits with federal, state, or local environmental agencies to use property in certain ways (such as clearing trees or filling wetlands).

- Draft and file the documents necessary to include another polluting company as a defendant in an action brought by a government agency.

- Monitor the *Federal Register* on a routine basis to determine if new environmental regulations have been proposed by the EPA.

- Research the scope and applicability of a particular regulation to find out whether a client's planned action may violate that rule, whether a permit is required, and the like.

- Prepare for and perhaps attend hearings before environmental agencies.

- Assist in negotiations between an environmental agency and a business firm to settle a dispute over a claimed violation of an environmental regulation.

- Coordinate a corporate client's environmental policies and monitor corporate activities to ensure compliance with environmental laws.

Today's Professional Paralegal

GATHERING INFORMATION FOR A BANKRUPTCY PETITION

Jeff Jones, a paralegal, works for Amanda Peters, an attorney who specializes in bankruptcy cases. Today, Jeff is meeting with Mike Hammersmith, a client who wants to file a voluntary petition for bankruptcy under Chapter 7 of the Bankruptcy Code. Mike owns the Corner Liquor Store, a retail liquor and convenience store, and is facing serious financial difficulties. Mike owns the store as a sole proprietor.

The receptionist announces Mike's arrival, and Jeff meets him in the lobby. They walk to the conference room, which Jeff previously reserved, and sit down at the conference table. Jeff removes a checklist from a file folder that he brought with him into the conference room. The same checklist was given to Mike last week, at the end of the initial client interview. Jeff attended that interview with his supervising attorney, so he is already familiar with Mike's case.

REVIEWING THE LIST OF CREDITORS

"First, I'll need a list of your creditors, with their addresses and the amount that you owe to each," says Jeff. Mike hands Jeff a handwritten list, which is somewhat difficult to read. Jeff reviews the list and asks Mike if he owes $25,000 or $28,000 to the National Bank. "It's hard to tell which it is," says Jeff. Mike clarifies that the amount of the debt is $25,000.

REVIEWING THE LIST OF ASSETS

The next item that Jeff needs is a list of all of the assets—both personal and real property—that Mike owns. Mike hands Jeff another handwritten list, and the first thing Jeff notices is that the list is incomplete: it does not include Mike's home or his car. Jeff asks, "Didn't you tell Ms. Peters and me last week that you owned a home and a car?" "That's correct," answers Mike. "But I thought that property would be exempt." "We need to list those items here," Jeff says. "We have to disclose all of your property, including exempt property." Mike then gives Jeff the necessary information about the home and the car, and Jeff adds the information to the list.

REVIEWING THE LIST OF INCOME AND EXPENSES

"The last item that I need is the list of your income and expenses," states Jeff. Mike hands his list to Jeff. Jeff reviews it and does not find anything that is inconsistent with what Mike said in the initial client interview.

CONCLUDING THE INTERVIEW

"That's all I need for today. I'll give this information to Ms. Peters. After she reviews it, she'll want to discuss with you how the Bankruptcy Code's provisions may affect your case. Depending on your income level, you may not be able to file under Chapter 7. Can you come by tomorrow—say, at two o'clock?" Jeff asks. "Yes, I think so," Mike responds.

"Thanks for your help," says Mike, as he shakes Jeff's hand. "Come with me and I'll show you out," says Jeff.

KEY TERMS AND CONCEPTS

automatic stay   *621*

bankruptcy estate   *621*

bankruptcy trustee   *623*

consumer-debtor   *617*

cram-down provision   *633*

debtor in possession (DIP)   *631*

discharge   *617*

environmental impact statement (EIS)   *634*

homestead exemption   *623*

liquidation   *617*

order for relief   *620*

petition in bankruptcy   *617*

potentially responsible party (PRP)   *641*

preference   *624*

proof of claim   *622*

secured creditor   *618*

U.S. trustee   *618*

workout   *631*

CHAPTER SUMMARY

BANKRUPTCY AND ENVIRONMENTAL LAW

Forms of Bankruptcy Relief Compared

Purpose	Chapter 7	Chapter 11	Chapter 13
	Liquidation.	Reorganization.	Individual repayment plan.
Who Can Petition	Debtor (voluntary) or creditors (involuntary).	Debtor (voluntary) or creditors (involuntary).	Debtor (voluntary) only.
Who Can Be a Debtor	Any "person" (including partnerships and corporations) except insurance companies, banks, savings and loan institutions, investment companies licensed by the Small Business Administration, and credit unions. Farmers and charitable institutions cannot be involuntarily petitioned. If the court finds the petition to be a substantial abuse of the use of Chapter 7, the debtor may be required to convert to a Chapter 13 repayment plan.	Any debtor (except a stockbroker or a commodities broker) eligible for Chapter 7 relief; railroads are also eligible.	Any individual (not partnerships or corporations) with regular income who owes fixed unsecured debts of less than $340,000 or fixed secured debts of less than $1 million.
Procedure Leading to Discharge	Nonexempt property is sold with proceeds to be distributed (in order) to priority groups. Dischargeable debts are terminated.	Plan is submitted; if it is approved and followed, debts are discharged.	Plan is submitted (must be approved if debtor turns over disposable income for a three-year or five-year period); if it is approved and followed, debts are discharged.
Advantages	On liquidation and distribution, most debts are discharged, and the debtor has the opportunity for a fresh start.	Debtor continues in business. Creditors can accept the plan, or it can be "crammed down" on them. Plan allows for reorganization and liquidation of debts over the plan period.	Debtor continues in business or possession of assets. If plan is approved, most debts are discharged after the plan period.

Continued

Environmental Law

1. *Federal regulation of the environment—*

   a. The federal Environmental Protection Agency (EPA) was created in 1970 to coordinate federal environmental programs. The EPA administers most federal environmental policies and statutes.

   b. The National Environmental Policy Act of 1969 imposes environmental responsibilities on all federal agencies and requires the preparation of an environmental impact statement (EIS) for every major federal action. An EIS must analyze the action's impact on the environment.

2. *Important areas regulated by federal law—*

   a. **AIR POLLUTION**—Regulated primarily by the Clean Air Act of 1970 as amended. The EPA sets allowable emission standards for various pollutants emitted from mobile sources (vehicles) and stationary sources (power plants, factories). Polluters must meet specific technological control standards.

   b. **WATER POLLUTION**—Regulated primarily under the Clean Water Act of 1972 as amended. Polluters who dump waste into navigable waters must meet technical standards set by the EPA and enforced primarily by the states. The focus is on point sources such as sewer treatment plants and industrial sites, which must have discharge permits. The act also protects wetlands. Changing a wetland requires a permit from the Army Corps of Engineers.

   c. **TOXIC CHEMICALS AND HAZARDOUS WASTE**—The Federal Insecticide, Fungicide, and Rodenticide Act controls pesticides and herbicides. The Toxic Substances Control Act regulates other chemicals. These substances are subject to the Resource Conservation and Recovery Act, which requires sellers, transporters, users, and disposers to use manifests to track the history of the substances from production to destruction. The act also requires clean-up of polluted dump sites.

STUDENT STUDYWARE™ CD-ROM

Interactive student CD in this book includes additional quizzing, plus video clips, case studies, and Key Terms flashcards.

ONLINE COMPANION™

For additional resources, please go to **www.paralegal.delmar.cengage.com**.

QUESTIONS FOR REVIEW

1. How is a liquidation proceeding under Chapter 7 initiated? What is the difference between a voluntary bankruptcy and an involuntary bankruptcy? What is "means testing"?

2. What effect does the filing of a bankruptcy petition have on creditors? What is an automatic stay?

3. How does Chapter 7 bankruptcy differ from Chapter 13 bankruptcy? What happens if a company files for reorganization under Chapter 11?

4. What is an environmental impact statement (EIS), and when is one required? What factors does an EIS evaluate?

5. What is Superfund? What parties are responsible for the clean-up of hazardous waste sites?

ETHICAL QUESTION

1. Marla, an independent paralegal, provides a variety of services for the public. Among other things, she provides debtors with bankruptcy forms and petitions. Mr. Ford has sought Marla's services in filing for bankruptcy. He takes home a set of Chapter 7 forms, reads through them, and begins to provide the information needed. He is not certain that he qualifies for Chapter 7 liquidation. He calls Marla and asks her if he has any other options. How should Marla answer Mr. Ford's questions?

PRACTICE QUESTIONS AND ASSIGNMENTS

1. Douglas Worth earns a salary of $30,000 a year as a sales representative. In addition to his salary, he is entitled to a 10 percent commission on what he sells. Over the past five years, Douglas earned annual commissions of $80,000 to $100,000. Because the economy was booming and Douglas was making such large commissions, he purchased a $50,000 Cadillac and a $25,000 boat and incurred credit-card debts totaling $35,000. This year, the economy has slowed down, and Douglas has made only $10,000 in commissions in the last six months. He still owes $40,000 on the Cadillac and $20,000 on the boat. In all, he owes $95,000 to creditors. Douglas cannot pay his debts as they become due, and it does not appear that his financial situation will improve over the next two years. As a result, he is thinking about filing for bankruptcy. If the median income in Douglas's state is $35,000 a year, would he be able to obtain a Chapter 7 liquidation? Explain your answer.

2. Identify the environmental law that applies to each of the following situations and explain how it would resolve the problem:

a. The foreman at a manufacturing plant disposes of a fifty-five-gallon drum of spent solvents, a toxic waste, every week by pouring it on the ground "out back."

b. An investigation reveals that the local gas utility company has PCBs in its pipeline in excess of those allowed.

c. An oil company releases hundreds of gallons of oil into a local river, contaminating the river, which is a major source of drinking water for the area.

d. A manufacturing plant that produces metallic paint for use on motor vehicles releases more pollutants into the air than the allowable emissions limits for its vicinity.

e. Years ago, five large manufacturing companies disposed of hazardous waste by burying the waste on the property of a farmer forty miles away from the city and its inhabitants. The rural farm is now part of a suburb. The suburb's groundwater and drinking water are found to be contaminated by the waste buried on the site of the former farm. The citizens demand that the site be cleaned up.

QUESTIONS FOR CRITICAL ANALYSIS

1. Do your think that people should be able to avoid paying their debts by filing for bankruptcy? Does a person have a moral responsibility to pay his or her debts, even if it takes years and years to pay them off entirely?

2. Do you think that our bankruptcy laws are too lenient or too harsh for debtors? Do bankruptcy laws adequately balance the needs of debtors "who have gotten in over their heads" and creditors?

3. The Clean Air Act, the Clean Water Act, and the Toxic Substances Control Act, among others, regulate the amount of pollution allowed into the air, water, and other aspects of the environment. Should any pollution be allowed into the environment? Who should determine how "clean" air or water should be? What might happen if no pollution at all were allowed?

PROJECTS

1. If there is a federal bankruptcy court located near you, attend a bankruptcy proceeding for a day or part of a day. Write a one-page summary of your experience.

2. Review your state's bankruptcy laws to determine what property is exempt from the debtor's estate in property. Does your state prohibit debtors from using the federal exemptions within the state, or is a debtor allowed to choose between state and federal exemptions? Write a one-page summary of your findings.

USING INTERNET RESOURCES

1. Go to www.abiworld.org, the Web site of the American Bankruptcy Institute. Select "Online Resources" at the top of the page, and then select "Bankruptcy Statistics" from the drop-down "Online Resources" menu. Browse through the bankruptcy statistics and charts included on this page, and then answer the following questions:

   a. According to this page, which state had the most personal (nonbusiness) bankruptcy filings during the most recent year mentioned? Which state had the fewest?

   b. How many bankruptcy filings occurred in the most recent quarter? Are most of these filings business filings or nonbusiness filings?

END NOTE

1. There are no Chapters 2, 4, 6, 8, or 10 in Title 11. Such "gaps" are not uncommon in the U.S.C. This is because chapter numbers (or other subdivisional unit numbers) are sometimes reserved for future use when a statute is enacted. A gap may also appear if a law has been repealed.

NALA'S CODE
OF ETHICS AND
PROFESSIONAL
RESPONSIBILITY

A paralegal must adhere strictly to the accepted standards of legal ethics and to the general principles of proper conduct. The performance of the duties of the paralegal shall be governed by specific canons as defined herein so that justice will be served and goals of the profession attained. (See Model Standards and Guidelines for Utilization of Legal Assistants, Section II.)

The canons of ethics set forth hereafter are adopted by the National Association of Legal Assistants, Inc., as a general guide intended to aid paralegals and attorneys. The enumeration of these rules does not mean there are not others of equal importance although not specifically mentioned. Court rules, agency rules, and statutes must be taken into consideration when interpreting the canons.

CANONS OF ETHICS

Definition

Legal assistants, also known as paralegals, are a distinguishable group of persons who assist attorneys in the delivery of legal services. Through formal education, training and experience, legal assistants have knowledge and expertise regarding the legal system and substantive and procedural law which qualify them to do work of a legal nature under the supervision of an attorney.

Canon 1

A paralegal must not perform any of the duties that attorneys only may perform nor take any actions that attorneys may not take.

Canon 2

A paralegal may perform any task which is properly delegated and supervised by an attorney, as long as the attorney is ultimately responsible to the client, maintains a direct relationship with the client, and assumes professional responsibility for the work product.

Canon 3

A paralegal must not: (a) engage in, encourage, or contribute to any act which could constitute the unauthorized practice of law; and (b) establish attorney-client relationships, set fees, give legal opinions or advice, or represent a client before a court or agency unless so authorized by that court or agency; and (c) engage in conduct or take any action which would assist or involve the attorney in a violation of professional ethics or give the appearance of professional impropriety.

Canon 4

A paralegal must use discretion and professional judgment commensurate with knowledge and experience but must not render independent legal judgment in place of an attorney. The services of an attorney are essential in the public interest whenever such legal judgment is required.

Canon 5

A paralegal must disclose his or her status as a paralegal at the outset of any professional relationship with a client, attorney, a court or administrative agency or personnel thereof, or a member of the general public. A paralegal must act prudently in determining the extent to which a client may be assisted without the presence of an attorney.

Canon 6

A paralegal must strive to maintain integrity and a high degree of competency through education and training with respect to professional responsibility, local rules and practice, and through continuing education in substantive areas of law to better assist the legal profession in fulfilling its duty to provide legal service.

Canon 7

A paralegal must protect the confidences of a client and must not violate any rule or statute now in effect or hereafter enacted controlling the doctrine of privileged communications between a client and an attorney.

Canon 8

A paralegal must disclose to his or her employer or prospective employer any pre-existing client or personal relationship that may conflict with the interests of the employer or prospective employer and/or their clients.

Canon 9

A paralegal must do all other things incidental, necessary, or expedient for the attainment of the ethics and responsibilities as defined by statute or rule of court.

Canon 10

A paralegal's conduct is guided by bar associations' codes of professional responsibility and rules of professional conduct.

NALA'S MODEL STANDARDS AND GUIDELINES FOR UTILIZATION OF PARALEGALS

NALA's study of the professional responsibility and ethical considerations of paralegals is ongoing. This research led to the development of the NALA Model Standards and Guidelines for Utilization of Paralegals. This guide summarizes case law, guidelines, and ethical opinions of the various states affecting paralegals. It provides an outline of minimum qualifications and standards necessary for paralegal professionals to assure the public and the legal profession that they are, indeed, qualified. The following is a listing of the standards and guidelines.

The annotated version of the Model Standards and Guidelines was last revised in 2005. It is online at **www.nala.org** (select "Model Standards and Guidelines for Utilization of Paralegals" from the "About Paralegals" menu) and may be ordered through NALA headquarters.

PREAMBLE

Proper utilization of the services of legal assistants contributes to the delivery of cost-effective, high-quality legal services. Legal assistants and the legal profession should be assured that measures exist for identifying legal assistants and their role in assisting attorneys in the delivery of legal services. Therefore, the National Association of Legal Assistants, Inc., hereby adopts these Standards and Guidelines as an educational document for the benefit of legal assistants and the legal profession.

HISTORY

The National Association of Legal Assistants adopted this Model in 1984. At the same time the following definition of a legal assistant was adopted:

Legal assistants, also known as paralegals, are a distinguishable group of persons who assist attorneys in the delivery of legal services. Through formal education, training, and experience, legal assistants have knowledge and expertise regarding the legal system and substantive and procedural law which qualify them to do work of a legal nature under the supervision of an attorney.

Historically, there have been similar definitions adopted by various legal professional organizations. Recognizing the need for one clear definition the NALA membership approved a resolution in July 2001 to adopt the legal assistant definition of the American Bar Association (ABA). This definition continues to be utilized today.

DEFINITION

A legal assistant or paralegal is a person qualified by education, training, or work experience who is employed or retained by a lawyer, law office, corporation, governmental agency, or other entity who performs specifically delegated substantive legal work for which a lawyer is responsible. (Adopted by the ABA in 1997 and by NALA in 2001.)

STANDARDS

A legal assistant should meet certain minimum qualifications. The following standards may be used to determine an individual's qualifications as legal assistant:

Successful completion of the Certified Legal Assistant (CLA)/Certified Paralegal (CP) certifying examination of the National Association of Legal Assistants, Inc.;

1. Graduation from an ABA-approved program of study for legal assistants;

2. Graduation from a course of study for legal assistants which is institutionally accredited but not ABA approved, and which requires not less than the equivalent of 60 semester hours of classroom study;

3. Graduation from a course of study for legal assistants, other than those set forth in (1) and (2) above, plus not less than six months of in-house training as a legal assistant;

4. A baccalaureate degree in any field, plus not less than six months of in-house training as a legal assistant;

5. A minimum of three years of law-related experience under the supervision of an attorney, including at least six months of in-house training as a legal assistant; or

6. Two years of in-house training as a legal assistant.

For purposes of these Standards, "in-house training as a legal assistant" means attorney education of the employee concerning legal assistant duties and these Guidelines. In addition to review and analysis of assignments, the legal assistant should receive a reasonable amount of instruction directly related to the duties and obligations of the legal assistant.

GUIDELINES

These Guidelines relating to standards of performance and professional responsibility are intended to aid legal assistants and attorneys. The ultimate responsibility rests with an attorney who employs legal assistants to educate them with respect to the duties they are assigned and to supervise the manner in which such duties are accomplished.

Guideline 1

Legal assistants should:

- Disclose their status as legal assistants at the outset of any professional relationship with a client, other attorneys, a court or administrative agency or personnel thereof, or members of the general public;

- Preserve the confidences and secrets of all clients; and

- Understand the attorney's Rules of Professional Responsibility and these Guidelines in order to avoid any action which would involve the attorney in a violation of the Rules, or give the appearance of professional impropriety.

Guideline 2

Legal assistants should not:

Establish attorney-client relationships; set legal fees, give legal opinions or advice; or represent a client before a court, unless authorized to do so by said court; nor engage in, encourage, or contribute to any act which could constitute the unauthorized practice of law.

Guideline 3

Legal assistants may perform services for an attorney in the representation of a client, provided:

- The services performed by the legal assistant do not require the exercise of independent professional legal judgment;

- The attorney maintains a direct relationship with the client and maintains control of all client matters;

- The attorney supervises the legal assistant;

- The attorney remains professionally responsible for all work on behalf of the client, including any actions taken or not taken by the legal assistant in connection therewith; and

- The services performed supplement, merge with, and become the attorney's work product.

Guideline 4

In the supervision of a legal assistant, consideration should be given to:

- Designating work assignments that correspond to the legal assistant's abilities, knowledge, training, and experience;

- Educating and training the legal assistant with respect to professional responsibility, local rules and practices, and firm policies;

- Monitoring the work and professional conduct of the legal assistant to ensure that the work is substantively correct and timely performed;

- Providing continuing education for the legal assistant in substantive matters through courses, institutes, workshops, seminars, and in-house training; and

- Encouraging and supporting membership and active participation in professional organizations.

Guideline 5

Except as otherwise provided by statute, court rule or decision, administrative rule or regulation, or the attorney's rules of professional responsibility, and within the preceding parameters and proscriptions, a legal assistant may perform any function delegated by an attorney, including but not limited to the following:

- Conduct client interviews and maintain general contact with the client after the establishment of the attorney-client relationship, so long as the client is aware of the status and function of the legal assistant, and the client contact is under the supervision of the attorney.

- Locate and interview witnesses, so long as the witnesses are aware of the status and function of the legal assistant.

- Conduct investigations and statistical and documentary research for review by the attorney.

- Conduct legal research for review by the attorney.

- Draft legal documents for review by the attorney.

- Draft correspondence and pleadings for review by and signature of the attorney.

- Summarize depositions, interrogatories, and testimony for review by the attorney.

- Attend executions of wills, real estate closings, depositions, court or administrative hearings, and trials with the attorney.

- Author and sign letters providing the legal assistant's status is clearly indicated and the correspondence does not contain independent legal opinions or legal advice.

CONCLUSION

These Standards and Guidelines were developed from generally accepted practices. Each supervising attorney must be aware of the specific rules, decisions, and statutes applicable to legal assistants within his/her jurisdiction.

*"Copyright 1984; adopted 1984; revised 1994, 1997, 2005. Reprinted with permission of the NALA, The Association of Legal Assistants-Paralegals, **www.nala.org**, 1516 S. Boston, #200, Tulsa, OK 74119, **www.nala.org**."*

NFPA'S MODEL CODE OF ETHICS AND PROFESSIONAL RESPONSIBILITY AND GUIDELINES FOR ENFORCEMENT

   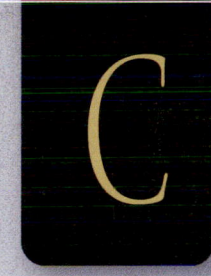

PREAMBLE

The National Federation of Paralegal Associations, Inc. ("NFPA®"), is a professional organization comprised of paralegal associations and individual paralegals through-out the United States and Canada. Members of NFPA® have varying backgrounds, experiences, education, and job responsibilities that reflect the diversity of the paralegal profession. NFPA® promotes the growth, development, and recognition of the paralegal profession as an integral partner in the delivery of legal services.

In May 1993 NFPA® adopted its Model Code of Ethics and Professional Responsibility ("Model Code") to delineate the principles for ethics and conduct to which every paralegal should aspire.

Many paralegal associations throughout the United States have endorsed the concept and content of NFPA®'s Model Code through the adoption of their own ethical codes. In doing so, paralegals have confirmed the profession's commitment to increase the quality and efficiency of legal services, as well as recognized its responsibilities to the public, the legal community, and colleagues.

Paralegals have recognized, and will continue to recognize, that the profession must continue to evolve to enhance their roles in the delivery of legal services. With increased levels of responsibility comes the need to define and enforce mandatory rules of professional conduct. Enforcement of codes of paralegal conduct is a logi-cal and necessary step to enhance and ensure the confidence of the legal commu-nity and the public in the integrity and professional responsibility of paralegals.

In April 1997 NFPA® adopted the Model Disciplinary Rules ("Model Rules") to make possible the enforcement of the Canons and Ethical Considerations contained in the NFPA® Model Code. A concurrent determination was made that the Model Code of Ethics and Professional Responsibility, formerly aspirational in nature, should be recognized as setting forth the enforceable obligations of all paralegals.

The Model Code and Model Rules offer a framework for professional discipline, either voluntarily or through formal regulatory programs.

§1. NFPA® MODEL DISCIPLINARY RULES AND ETHICAL CONSIDERATIONS

1.1 A Paralegal Shall Achieve and Maintain a High Level of Competence.

Ethical Considerations

EC–1.1(a) A paralegal shall achieve competency through education, training, and work experience.

EC–1.1(b) A paralegal shall aspire to participate in a minimum of twelve (12) hours of continuing legal education, to include at least one (1) hour of ethics education, every two (2) years in order to remain current on developments in the law.

EC–1.1(c) A paralegal shall perform all assignments promptly and efficiently.

1.2 A Paralegal Shall Maintain a High Level of Personal and Professional Integrity.

Ethical Considerations

EC–1.2(a) A paralegal shall not engage in any *ex parte* communications involving the courts or any other adjudicatory body in an attempt to exert undue influence or to obtain advantage or the benefit of only one party.

EC–1.2(b) A paralegal shall not communicate, or cause another to communicate, with a party the paralegal knows to be represented by a lawyer in a pending matter without the prior consent of the lawyer representing such other party.

EC–1.2(c) A paralegal shall ensure that all timekeeping and billing records prepared by the paralegal are thorough, accurate, honest, and complete.

EC–1.2(d) A paralegal shall not knowingly engage in fraudulent billing practices. Such practices may include, but are not limited to: inflation of hours billed to a client or employer; misrepresentation of the nature of tasks performed; and/or submission of fraudulent expense and disbursement documentation.

EC–1.2(e) A paralegal shall be scrupulous, thorough, and honest in the identification and maintenance of all funds, securities, and other assets of a client and shall provide accurate accounting as appropriate.

EC–1.2(f) A paralegal shall advise the proper authority of nonconfidential knowledge of any dishonest or fraudulent acts by any person pertaining to the handling of the funds, securities, or other assets of a client. The authority to whom the report is made shall depend on the nature and circumstances of the possible misconduct (for example, ethics committees of law firms, corporations and/or paralegal associations, local or state bar associations, local prosecutors, administrative agencies, etc.). Failure to report such knowledge is in itself misconduct and shall be treated as such under these rules.

1.3 A Paralegal Shall Maintain a High Standard of Professional Conduct.

Ethical Considerations

EC–1.3(a) A paralegal shall refrain from engaging in any conduct that offends the dignity and decorum of proceedings before a court or other adjudicatory body and shall be respectful of all rules and procedures.

EC–1.3(b) A paralegal shall avoid impropriety and the appearance of impropriety and shall not engage in any conduct that would adversely affect his/her fitness to practice. Such conduct may include, but is not limited to: violence, dishonesty, interference with the administration of justice, and/or abuse of a professional position or public office.

EC–1.3(c) Should a paralegal's fitness to practice be compromised by physical or mental illness, causing that paralegal to commit an act that is in direct violation of the Model Code/Model Rules and/or the rules and/or laws governing the jurisdiction in which the paralegal practices, that paralegal may be protected from sanction upon review of the nature and circumstances of that illness.

EC–1.3(d) A paralegal shall advise the proper authority of nonconfidential knowledge of any action of another legal professional that clearly demonstrates fraud, deceit, dishonesty, or misrepresentation. The authority to whom the report is made shall depend on the nature and circumstances of the possible misconduct (for example, ethics committees of law firms, corporations and/or paralegal associations, local or state bar associations, local prosecutors, administrative agencies, etc.). Failure to report such knowledge is in itself misconduct and shall be treated as such under these rules.

EC–1.3(e) A paralegal shall not knowingly assist any individual with the commission of an act that is in direct violation of the Model Code/Model Rules and/or the rules and/or laws governing the jurisdiction in which the paralegal practices.

EC–1.3(f) If a paralegal possesses knowledge of future criminal activity, that knowledge must be reported to the appropriate authority immediately.

1.4 A Paralegal Shall Serve the Public Interest by Contributing to the Improvement of the Legal System and Delivery of Quality Legal Services, Including *Pro Bono Publico* Services.

Ethical Considerations

EC–1.4(a) A paralegal shall be sensitive to the legal needs of the public and shall promote the development and implementation of programs that address those needs.

EC–1.4(b) A paralegal shall support efforts to improve the legal system and access thereto and shall assist in making changes.

EC–1.4(c) A paralegal shall support and participate in the delivery of *Pro Bono Publico* services directed toward implementing and improving access to justice, the law, the legal system, or the paralegal and legal professions.

EC–1.4(d) A paralegal should aspire annually to contribute twenty-four (24) hours of *Pro Bono Publico* services under the supervision of an attorney or as authorized by administrative, statutory, or court authority to:

1. persons of limited means; or
2. charitable, religious, civic, community, governmental, and educational organizations in matters that are designed primarily to address the legal needs of persons with limited means; or
3. individuals, groups, or organizations seeking to secure or protect civil rights, civil liberties, or public rights.

The twenty-four (24) hours of *Pro Bono Publico* services contributed annually by a paralegal may consist of such services as detailed in this EC-1.4(d), and/or administrative matters designed to develop and implement the attainment of this aspiration as detailed above in EC-1.4(a) B (c), or any combination of the two.

1.5 A Paralegal Shall Preserve All Confidential Information Provided by the Client or Acquired from Other Sources before, during, and after the Course of the Professional Relationship.

Ethical Considerations

EC–1.5(a) A paralegal shall be aware of and abide by all legal authority governing confidential information in the jurisdiction in which the paralegal practices.

EC–1.5(b) A paralegal shall not use confidential information to the disadvantage of the client.

EC–1.5(c) A paralegal shall not use confidential information to the advantage of the paralegal or of a third person.

EC–1.5(d) A paralegal may reveal confidential information only after full disclosure and with the client's written consent; or, when required by law or court order; or, when necessary to prevent the client from committing an act that could result in death or serious bodily harm.

EC–1.5(e) A paralegal shall keep those individuals responsible for the legal representation of a client fully informed of any confidential information the paralegal may have pertaining to that client.

EC–1.5(f) A paralegal shall not engage in any indiscreet communications concerning clients.

1.6 A Paralegal Shall Avoid Conflicts of Interest and Shall Disclose Any Possible Conflict to the Employer or Client, as Well as to the Prospective Employers or Clients.

Ethical Considerations

EC–1.6(a) A paralegal shall act within the bounds of the law, solely for the benefit of the client, and shall be free of compromising influences and loyalties. Neither the paralegal's personal or business interest, nor those of other clients or third persons, should compromise the paralegal's professional judgment and loyalty to the client.

EC–1.6(b) A paralegal shall avoid conflicts of interest that may arise from previous assignments, whether for a present or past employer or client.

EC–1.6(c) A paralegal shall avoid conflicts of interest that may arise from family relationships and from personal and business interests.

EC–1.6(d) In order to be able to determine whether an actual or potential conflict of interest exists a paralegal shall create and maintain an effective record-keeping system that identifies clients, matters, and parties with which the paralegal has worked.

EC–1.6(e) A paralegal shall reveal sufficient nonconfidential information about a client or former client to reasonably ascertain if an actual or potential conflict of interest exists.

EC–1.6(f) A paralegal shall not participate in or conduct work on any matter where a conflict of interest has been identified.

EC–1.6(g) In matters where a conflict of interest has been identified and the client consents to continued representation, a paralegal shall comply fully with the implementation and maintenance of an Ethical Wall.

1.7 A Paralegal's Title Shall Be Fully Disclosed.

Ethical Considerations

EC–1.7(a) A paralegal's title shall clearly indicate the individual's status and shall be disclosed in all business and professional communications to avoid misunderstandings and misconceptions about the paralegal's role and responsibilities.

EC–1.7(b) A paralegal's title shall be included if the paralegal's name appears on business cards, letterhead, brochures, directories, and advertisements.

EC–1.7(c) A paralegal shall not use letterhead, business cards, or other promotional materials to create a fraudulent impression of his/her status or ability to practice in the jurisdiction in which the paralegal practices.

EC–1.7(d) A paralegal shall not practice under color of any record, diploma, or certificate that has been illegally or fraudulently obtained or issued or which is misrepresentative in any way.

EC–1.7(e) A paralegal shall not participate in the creation, issuance, or dissemination of fraudulent records, diplomas, or certificates.

1.8 A Paralegal Shall Not Engage in the Unauthorized Practice of Law.

Ethical Considerations

EC–1.8(a) A paralegal shall comply with the applicable legal authority governing the unauthorized practice of law in the jurisdiction in which the paralegal practices.

§2. NFPA GUIDELINES FOR THE ENFORCEMENT OF THE MODEL CODE OF ETHICS AND PROFESSIONAL RESPONSIBILITY

2.1 Basis for Discipline

2.1(a) Disciplinary investigations and proceedings brought under authority of the Rules shall be conducted in accord with obligations imposed on the paralegal professional by the Model Code of Ethics and Professional Responsibility.

2.2 Structure of Disciplinary Committee

2.2(a) The Disciplinary Committee ("Committee") shall be made up of nine (9) members including the Chair.

2.2(b) Each member of the Committee, including any temporary replacement members, shall have demonstrated working knowledge of ethics/professional responsibility–related issues and activities.

2.2(c) The Committee shall represent a cross section of practice areas and work experience. The following recommendations are made regarding the members of the Committee.

1. At least one paralegal with one to three years of law-related work experience.
2. At least one paralegal with five to seven years of law-related work experience.
3. At least one paralegal with over ten years of law-related work experience.
4. One paralegal educator with five to seven years of work experience, preferably in the area of ethics/professional responsibility.
5. One paralegal manager.

6. One lawyer with five to seven years of law-related work experience.

7. One lay member.

2.2(d) The Chair of the Committee shall be appointed within thirty (30) days of its members' induction. The Chair shall have no fewer than ten (10) years of law-related work experience.

2.2(e) The terms of all members of the Committee shall be staggered. Of those members initially appointed, a simple majority plus one shall be appointed to a term of one year, and the remaining members shall be appointed to a term of two years. Thereafter, all members of the Committee shall be appointed to terms of two years.

2.2(f) If for any reason the terms of a majority of the Committee will expire at the same time, members may be appointed to terms of one year to maintain continuity of the Committee.

2.2(g) The Committee shall organize from its members a three-tiered structure to investigate, prosecute, and/or adjudicate charges of misconduct. The members shall be rotated among the tiers.

2.3 Operation of Committee

2.3(a) The Committee shall meet on an as-needed basis to discuss, investigate, and/or adjudicate alleged violations of the Model Code/Model Rules.

2.3(b) A majority of the members of the Committee present at a meeting shall constitute a quorum.

2.3(c) A Recording Secretary shall be designated to maintain complete and accurate minutes of all Committee meetings. All such minutes shall be kept confidential until a decision has been made that the matter will be set for hearing as set forth in Section 6.1 below.

2.3(d) If any member of the Committee has a conflict of interest with the Charging Party, the Responding Party, or the allegations of misconduct, that member shall not take part in any hearing or deliberations concerning those allegations. If the absence of that member creates a lack of a quorum for the Committee, then a temporary replacement for the member shall be appointed.

2.3(e) Either the Charging Party or the Responding Party may request that, for good cause shown, any member of the Committee not participate in a hearing or deliberation. All such requests shall be honored. If the absence of a Committee member under those circumstances creates a lack of a quorum for the Committee, then a temporary replacement for that member shall be appointed.

2.3(f) All discussions and correspondence of the Committee shall be kept confidential until a decision has been made that the matter will be set for hearing as set forth in Section 6.1 below.

2.3(g) All correspondence from the Committee to the Responding Party regarding any charge of misconduct and any decisions made regarding the charge shall be mailed certified mail, return receipt requested, to the Responding Party's last known address and shall be clearly marked with a "Confidential" designation.

2.4 Procedure for the Reporting of Alleged Violations of the Model Code/Disciplinary Rules

2.4(a) An individual or entity in possession of nonconfidential knowledge or information concerning possible instances of misconduct shall make a confidential written report to the Committee within thirty (30) days of obtaining same. This report shall include all details of the alleged misconduct.

2.4(b) The Committee so notified shall inform the Responding Party of the allegation(s) of misconduct no later than ten (10) business days after receiving the confidential written report from the Charging Party.

2.4(c) Notification to the Responding Party shall include the identity of the Charging Party, unless, for good cause shown, the Charging Party requests anonymity.

2.4(d) The Responding Party shall reply to the allegations within ten (10) business days of notification.

2.5 Procedure for the Investigation of a Charge of Misconduct

2.5(a) Upon receipt of a Charge of Misconduct ("Charge"), or on its own initiative, the Committee shall initiate an investigation.

2.5(b) If, upon initial or preliminary review, the Committee makes a determination that the charges are either without basis in fact or, if proven, would not constitute professional misconduct, the Committee shall dismiss the allegations of misconduct. If such determination of dismissal cannot be made, a formal investigation shall be initiated.

2.5(c) Upon the decision to conduct a formal investigation, the Committee shall:

1. mail to the Charging and Responding Parties within three (3) business days of that decision notice of the commencement of a formal investigation. That notification shall be in writing and shall contain a complete explanation of all Charge(s), as well as the reasons for a formal investigation, and shall cite the applicable codes and rules;

2. allow the Responding Party thirty (30) days to prepare and submit a confidential response to the Committee, which response shall address each charge specifically and shall be in writing; and

3. upon receipt of the response to the notification, have thirty (30) days to investigate the Charge(s). If an extension of time is deemed necessary, that extension shall not exceed ninety (90) days.

2.5(d) Upon conclusion of the investigation, the Committee may:

1. dismiss the Charge upon the finding that it has no basis in fact;

2. dismiss the Charge upon the finding that, if proven, the Charge would not constitute Misconduct;

3. refer the matter for hearing by the Tribunal; or

4. in the case of criminal activity, refer the Charge(s) and all investigation results to the appropriate authority.

2.6 Procedure for a Misconduct Hearing before a Tribunal

2.6(a) Upon the decision by the Committee that a matter should be heard, all parties shall be notified and a hearing date shall be set. The hearing shall take place no more than thirty (30) days from the conclusion of the formal investigation.

2.6(b) The Responding Party shall have the right to counsel. The parties and the Tribunal shall have the right to call any witnesses and introduce any documentation that they believe will lead to the fair and reasonable resolution of the matter.

2.6(c) Upon completion of the hearing, the Tribunal shall deliberate and present a written decision to the parties in accordance with procedures as set forth by the Tribunal.

2.6(d) Notice of the decision of the Tribunal shall be appropriately published.

2.7 Sanctions

2.7(a) Upon a finding of the Tribunal that misconduct has occurred, any of the following sanctions, or others as may be deemed appropriate, may be imposed upon the Responding Party, either singularly or in combination:

1. Letter of reprimand to the Responding Party; counseling;

2. Attendance at an ethics course approved by the Tribunal; probation;

3. Suspension of license/authority to practice; revocation of license/authority to practice;

4. Imposition of a fine; assessment of costs; or

5. In the instance of criminal activity, referral to the appropriate authority.

2.7(b) Upon the expiration of any period of probation, suspension, or revocation, the Responding Party may make application for reinstatement. With the application for reinstatement, the Responding Party must show proof of having complied with all aspects of the sanctions imposed by the Tribunal.

2.8 Appellate Procedures

2.8(a) The parties shall have the right to appeal the decision of the Tribunal in accordance with the procedure as set forth by the Tribunal.

DEFINITIONS

APPELLATE BODY   means a body established to adjudicate an appeal to any decision made by a Tribunal or other decision-making body with respect to formally heard Charges of Misconduct.

CHARGE OF MISCONDUCT   means a written submission by any individual or entity to an ethics committee, paralegal association, bar association, law enforcement agency, judicial body, government agency, or other appropriate body or entity, that sets forth non-confidential information regarding any instance of alleged misconduct by an individual paralegal or paralegal entity.

CHARGING PARTY   means any individual or entity who submits a Charge of Misconduct against an individual paralegal or paralegal entity.

COMPETENCY   means the demonstration of: diligence, education, skill, and mental, emotional, and physical fitness reasonably necessary for the performance of paralegal services.

CONFIDENTIAL INFORMATION   means information relating to a client, whatever its source, that is not public knowledge nor available to the public. ("Non-Confidential Information" would generally include the name of the client and the identity of the matter for which the paralegal provided services.)

DISCIPLINARY COMMITTEE   means any committee that has been established by an entity such as a paralegal association, bar association, judicial body, or government agency to: (a) identify, define, and investigate general ethical considerations and concerns with respect to paralegal practice; (b) administer and enforce the Model Code and Model Rules and; (c) discipline any individual paralegal or paralegal entity found to be in violation of same.

DISCIPLINARY HEARING means the confidential proceeding conducted by a committee or other designated body or entity concerning any instance of alleged misconduct by an individual paralegal or paralegal entity.

DISCLOSE means communication of information reasonably sufficient to permit identification of the significance of the matter in question.

ETHICAL WALL means the screening method implemented in order to protect a client from a conflict of interest. An Ethical Wall generally includes, but is not limited to, the following elements: (1) prohibit the paralegal from having any connection with the matter; (2) ban discussions with or the transfer of documents to or from the paralegal; (3) restrict access to files; and (4) educate all members of the firm, corporation, or entity as to the separation of the paralegal (both organizationally and physically) from the pending matter. For more information regarding the Ethical Wall, see the NFPA publication entitled "The Ethical Wall—Its Application to Paralegals."

EX PARTE means actions or communications conducted at the instance and for the benefit of one party only, and without notice to, or contestation by, any person adversely interested.

INVESTIGATION means the investigation of any charge(s) of misconduct filed against an individual paralegal or paralegal entity by a Committee.

LETTER OF REPRIMAND means a written notice of formal censure or severe reproof administered to an individual paralegal or paralegal entity for unethical or improper conduct.

MISCONDUCT means the knowing or unknowing commission of an act that is in direct violation of those Canons and Ethical Considerations of any and all applicable codes and/or rules of conduct.

PARALEGAL is synonymous with "Legal Assistant" and is defined as a person qualified through education, training, or work experience to perform substantive legal work that requires knowledge of legal concepts and is customarily but not exclusively performed by a lawyer. This person may be retained or employed by a lawyer, law office, governmental agency, or other entity or may be authorized by administrative, statutory, or court authority to perform this work.

PRO BONO PUBLICO means providing or assisting to provide quality legal services in order to enhance access to justice for persons of limited means; charitable, religious, civic, community, governmental, and educational organizations in matters that are designed primarily to address the legal needs of persons with limited means; or individuals, groups, or organizations seeking to secure or protect civil rights, civil liberties, or public rights.

PROPER AUTHORITY means the local paralegal association, the local or state bar association, committee(s) of the local paralegal or bar association(s), local prosecutor, administrative agency, or other tribunal empowered to investigate or act upon an instance of alleged misconduct.

RESPONDING PARTY means an individual paralegal or paralegal entity against whom a Charge of Misconduct has been submitted.

REVOCATION   means the rescission of the license, certificate, or other authority to practice of an individual paralegal or paralegal entity found in violation of those Canons and Ethical Considerations of any and all applicable codes and/or rules of conduct.

SUSPENSION   means the suspension of the license, certificate, or other authority to practice of an individual paralegal or paralegal entity found in violation of those Canons and Ethical Considerations of any and all applicable codes and/or rules of conduct.

TRIBUNAL   means the body designated to adjudicate allegations of misconduct.

Courtesy of the National Federation of Paralegal Associations, Inc. Reprinted with permission.

NALS CODE OF ETHICS AND PROFESSIONAL RESPONSIBILITY

   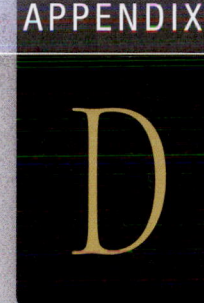

Members of NALS are bound by the objectives of this association and the standards of conduct required of the legal profession.

Every member shall:

- Encourage respect for the law and the administration of justice;
- Observe rules governing privileged communications and confidential information;
- Promote and exemplify high standards of loyalty, cooperation, and courtesy;
- Perform all duties of the profession with integrity and competence; and
- Pursue a high order of professional attainment.

Integrity and high standards of conduct are fundamental to the success of our professional association. This Code is promulgated by the NALS and accepted by its members to accomplish these ends.

CANON 1

Members of this association shall maintain a high degree of competency and integrity through continuing education to better assist the legal profession in fulfilling its duty to provide quality legal services to the public.

CANON 2

Members of this association shall maintain a high standard of ethical conduct and shall contribute to the integrity of the association and the legal profession.

CANON 3

Members of this association shall avoid a conflict of interest pertaining to a client matter.

CANON 4

Members of this association shall preserve and protect the confidences and privileged communications of a client.

CANON 5

Members of this association shall exercise care in using independent professional judgment and in determining the extent to which a client may be assisted without the presence of a lawyer and shall not act in matters involving professional legal judgment.

CANON 6

Members of this association shall not solicit legal business on behalf of a lawyer.

CANON 7

Members of this association, unless permitted by law, shall not perform paralegal functions except under the direct supervision of a lawyer and shall not advertise or contract with members of the general public for the performance of paralegal functions.

CANON 8

Members of this association, unless permitted by law, shall not perform any of the duties restricted to lawyers or do things which lawyers themselves may not do and shall assist in preventing the unauthorized practice of law.

CANON 9

Members of this association not licensed to practice law shall not engage in the practice of law as defined by statutes or court decisions.

CANON 10

Members of this association shall do all other things incidental, necessary, or expedient to enhance professional responsibility and participation in the administration of justice and public service in cooperation with the legal profession.

Courtesy of NALS . . . the association for legal professionals. Reprinted with permission.

PARALEGAL ETHICS AND REGULATION: HOW TO FIND STATE-SPECIFIC INFORMATION

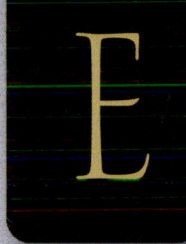

NALA NET FILES

Current information about the legal assistant profession helps you do your job better. Introduced in 1992, NALA Net is the first online information service for the legal assistant profession. NALA Net captures relevant information concerning such issues as ethics, bar guidelines, case law updates, legislative activities, bar activities, and significant research articles about the utilization of legal assistants. [Note: One must be a member of NALA to access this service. See **www.nala.org**.]

Categories of Information

Information on NALA Net is organized into several categories, as follows:

- **Legislative Activities.** Bills considered by state legislatures concerning the legal assistant profession, such as fee award statutes and UPL [unauthorized practice of law] regulations.
- **Ethics.** Ethical opinions from among the fifty states concerning legal assistants and lay personnel in the delivery of legal services.
- **Cases.** Summaries of court decisions concerning the legal assistant profession, including awards for their time in attorney fee awards, supervision, and the unauthorized practice of law.
- **Guidelines.** Several state bar associations have adopted guidelines for the utilization of legal assistants in the delivery of legal services. State supreme courts and court decisions also serve to establish guidelines.

- **Membership.** Several state and county bar associations offer associate membership to paralegals. This area includes summaries of the membership requirements.
- **Articles.** Significant articles and discussions concerning our profession.
- **Other.** General information and announcements of paralegal activities among the states.

In many instances, we have kept older documents on file for historical background and to show trends in the development of the profession. This is particularly useful in the areas of legislation and ethics.

Courtesy of the ©National Association of Legal Assistants, Inc. Reprinted with permission.

This information is current as of the publication date. For updates, please check the NALA web site (**www.nala.org**), or inquire of NALA Headquarters, 1516 S. Boston, #200, Tulsa, OK 74119.

PARALEGAL ASSOCIATIONS

   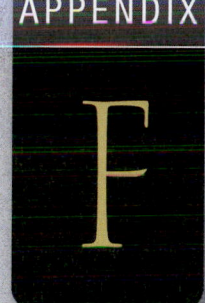

This list is current as of the publication date. For updates, please check the NALA web site (**www.nala.org**), or inquire of NALA Headquarters, 1516 S. Boston, #200, Tulsa, OK 74119.

NFPA ASSOCIATIONS

Region I

Alaska Association of Paralegals
www.alaskaparalegals.org

Hawaii Paralegal Association
www.hawaiiparalegal.org

Oregon Paralegal Association
www.oregonparalegals.org

**Paralegal Association of
  Southern Nevada**
paralegals.org/

Sacramento Valley Paralegal Association
www.svpa.org

San Francisco Paralegal Association
www.sfpa.com

Washington State Paralegal Association
www.wspaonline.org

Region II

Arkansas Paralegal Association
www.arkansasparalegal.org

Dallas Area Paralegal Association
www.dallasparalegals.org

Illinois Paralegal Association
www.ipaonline.org

Kansas Paralegal Association
www.ksparalegals.org

Minnesota Paralegal Association
www.mnparalegals.org

New Orleans Paralegal Association
www.neworleansparalegals.org

Rocky Mountain Paralegal Association
www.rockymtnparalegal.org
(CO, NE, SD, UT, WY)

Springfield Paralegal Association (MO)
paralegals.org/

Region III

Cleveland Association of Paralegals
www.capohio.org

Georgia Association of Paralegals
www.gaparalegal.org

Greater Lexington Paralegal Association
www.lexingtonparalegals.org

Indiana Paralegal Association
www.indianaparalegals.org

Memphis Paralegal Association
www.memphisparalegalassociation.org

**The Michiana Paralegal Association
  (IN, MI)**
www.michianaparalegals.org

Middle Tennessee Paralegal Association
www.mtpaonline.com

Northeast Indiana Paralegal Association
www.neindianaparalegal.org

Palmetto Paralegal Association
www.ppasc.org

Paralegal Association of Central Ohio
www.pacoparalegals.org

South Florida Paralegal Association
www.sfpa.info

Tampa Bay Paralegal Association
www.tbpa.org

Region IV

Central Pennsylvania Paralegal
   Association
www.cppamicuslex.org

Lycoming County Paralegal
   Association (PA)
www.lycolaw.org/lcpa/main.htm

Maryland Association of Paralegals
www.mdparalegals.org

Montgomery County Paralegal
   Association (PA)
www.montcoparalegals.org

National Capital Area Paralegal
   Association
www.ncapa.com

Navy Legalman Association
navyln.wordpress.com/

Paralegal Association of Northern
   Virginia
www.panv.org

The Philadelphia Association
   of Paralegals
www.philaparalegals.com

Pittsburgh Paralegal Association
www.pghparalegals.org

South Jersey Paralegal Association
www.sjpaparalegals.org

Region V

Capital District Paralegal
   Association (NY)
www.cdpa.info

Central Connecticut Paralegal
   Association
paralegals.org/

Central Massachusetts Paralegal
   Association
paralegals.org/

Connecticut Association of Paralegals
paralegals.org/

Long Island Paralegal Association
www.liparalegals.org

Massachusetts Paralegal Association
www.massparalegal.org

New Haven County Association
   of Paralegals
www.nhcp.org

Paralegal Association of
   New Hampshire
www.panh.org

Paralegal Association of Rochester
www.rochesterparalegal.org

Rhode Island Paralegals Association
paralegals.org/

Vermont Paralegal Organization
vtparalegal.googlepages.com

Western Massachusetts Paralegal
   Association
www.wmassparalegal.org

Western New York Paralegal Association
www.wnyparalegals.org

NALA STATE AND LOCAL AFFILIATES

Alabama

Alabama Association of Paralegals
www.alabamaparalegals.org

Alaska

Fairbanks Association of
   Legal Assistants
www.fairbanksparalegal.org

Arizona

Arizona Paralegal Association
www.azparalegal.org

Legal Assistants of Metropolitan
   Phoenix
www.geocities.com/azlamp

Tucson Association of Legal Assistants
www.tucsonparalegals.org

Arkansas

Arkansas Paralegal Alliance
www.arkansasparalegalalliance.org

California

Fresno Paralegal Association
www.fresnoparalegal.org

Inland Counties Association
   of Paralegals
www.icaponline.org

Los Angeles Paralegal Association
www.lapa.org

Orange County Paralegal Association
www.ocparalegal.org

Paralegal Association of
   Santa Clara County
www.sccparalegal.org

San Diego Paralegal Association
www.sdparalegals.org

Santa Barbara Paralegal Association
www.sbparalegals.org

Ventura County Paralegal Association
www.vcparalegal.org

Colorado

Pikes Peak Paralegals
www.pikespeakparalegals.org

Legal Assistants of the Western Slope

Florida

Central Florida Paralegal Association
www.cfpainc.com

Gulf Coast Paralegal Association
www.gcpa.info

Northeast Florida Paralegal Association
www.nefpa.org

Northwest Florida Paralegal Association
www.nwfpa.com

Paralegal Association of Florida
www.pafinc.org

South Florida Paralegal Association
www.sfpa.info

Southwest Florida Paralegal Association
www.swfloridaparalegals.com

Volusia Association of Paralegals
www.volusiaparalegals.org

Georgia

Southeastern Association of
   Legal Assistants
www.seala.org

Illinois

Central Illinois Paralegal Association
www.ciparalegal.org

Iowa

Iowa Association of Legal Assistants
www.ialanet.org

Kansas

Heartland Association of Legal Assistants
www.kansas.gov/hala

Kansas Association of Legal Assistants
www.accesskansas.org/kala

Kentucky

Western Kentucky Paralegals
www.kypa.org

Louisiana

Louisiana State Paralegal Association
www.la-paralegals.org

Northwest Louisiana Paralegal
  Association

Mississippi

Mississippi Paralegal Association
www.msparalegals.org

Missouri

St. Louis Association of Legal Assistants
www.slala.org

Montana

Montana Association of Legal Assistants

Nebraska

Nebraska Paralegal Association
www.nebraskaparalegal.org

Nevada

Nevada Paralegal Association
www.nevadaparalegal.org

Sierra Nevada Association of Paralegals
www.snapreno.com

New Jersey

Paralegal Association of New Jersey
www.laanj.org

North Carolina

Metrolina Paralegal Association
www.charlotteareaparalegals.com

North Carolina Paralegal Association
www.ncparalegal.org

North Dakota

Red River Valley Paralegal Association
www.rrvpa.org

Western Dakota Association
  of Legal Assistants
www.wdala.org

Ohio

Paralegal Association of Northwest Ohio
www.panonet.org

Oklahoma

Central Oklahoma Association
  of Legal Assistants
www.coala.cc

Oklahoma Paralegal Association
www.okparalegal.org

TCC Student Association of Legal
  Assistants

Tulsa Area Paralegal Association
www.tulsaparalegals.org

Oregon

Pacific Northwest Paralegal Association
www.pnpa.org

Pennsylvania

Lancaster Area Paralegal Association
www.lapaparalegals.com

South Carolina

Charleston Association
  of Legal Assistants
www.charlestonlegalassistants.org

South Carolina Upstate
  Paralegal Association
www.scupa.org

South Dakota

South Dakota Paralegal Association
www.sdparalegals.com

Tennessee

Greater Memphis Paralegal Alliance
www.memphisparalegals.org

Smoky Mountain Paralegal Association
www.smparalegal.org

Tennessee Paralegal Association
www.tnparalegal.org

Texas

Capital Area Paralegal Association
www.capatx.org

El Paso Paralegal Association
www.elppa.org

Houston Association of Bankruptcy
  Paralegals

Houston Corporate
  Paralegal Association
www.hcpa.cc

Houston Paralegal Assocation
www.hpatx.org

Paralegal Association of
  the Permian Basin
www.paralegalspb.org

North Texas Paralegal Association
www.ntparalegals.org

Northeast Texas Association
  of Paralegals
www.ntaparalegals.com

South Texas Organization of Paralegals
stopweb.org

Southeast Texas Association
  of Paralegals
www.setala.org

Texas Panhandle Paralegal Association

Tyler Area Association of
  Legal Professionals
taalp.com

West Texas Paralegal Association
www.wtparalegals.org

Utah

Legal Assistants Association of Utah
www.laau.info

Virgin Islands

Virgin Islands Association
    of Legal Assistants

Virginia

Richmond Paralegal Association
www.richmondparalegals.org

Roanoke Valley Paralegal Association
www.rvpa.org

Tidewater Paralegal Association
www.tidewaterparalegals.org

Virginia Peninsula Paralegal Association
www.vappa.org

West Virginia

Association of West Virginia Paralegals
www.awvp.org

Legal Assistants/Paralegals of
    Southern West Virginia
www.apswv.org

Wisconsin

Madison Area Paralegal Association
www.madisonparalegal.org

Wyoming

Legal Assistants of Wyoming
www.lawyo.com

NALS STATE AND CHAPTER ASSOCIATIONS

NALS . . . the association for legal professionals is a multilevel association with state and chapter associations. Following is a list of NALS state and chapter associations. If you would like contact information for a specific state or chapter association, please check with the NALS Resource Center at

NALS Resource Center
8159 East 41st Street
Tulsa, OK 74145
(918) 582-5188
www.nals.org

Alabama

Baldwin County Association of
    Legal Professionals
BLSA (Birmingham)
Dallas County Legal Secretaries
    Association
Mobile Legal Secretaries Association
Montgomery Legal Secretaries
    Association
Tuscaloosa County Legal Professionals
    Association
NALS of Shelby County

Alaska

NALS of Anchorage

Arizona

NALS of Arizona
NALS of Phoenix
NALS of Tucson and Southern Arizona
NALS of Yavapai County

Arkansas

Garland County Legal Support
    Professional
Greater Little Rock Legal Support
    Professionals
Jefferson County Association of Legal
    Support Professionals
Northeast Arkansas Legal Support
    Professionals
Saline County Legal Support
    Professionals
White County Association of Legal
    Support Professionals

California

NALS of California
NALS of Orange County
Port Stockton LSA

Colorado

NALS of Colorado

District of Columbia

District of Columbia Legal Secretaries
    Association

Florida

NALS of Central Florida

Georgia

NALS of Georgia, the association for
    legal professionals
NALS of Atlanta, the association for
    legal professionals
Cobb County Legal Secretaries
    Association

Hawaii

Hawaii Legal Support Professionals

Idaho

BLSA (Boise)
LLSA (Lewiston)
North Idaho Legal Secretaries
    Association

Illinois

NALA of Illinois

Maine

NALS of Maine
NALS of Southern Maine
NALS of Midcoast Maine
NALS of Central Maine
NALS of Northeast Maine

Michigan

NALS of Michigan
Berrien Cass LSP
NALS of Calhoun County

NALS of Detroit
Genessee Association of Legal Support
    Professionals
Grand Traverse County
NALS of Greater Kalamazoo
Jackson County Legal Support
    Professionals
NALS of Lansing
Livingston County Legal Secretaries
    Association
Mid Michigan Association of Legal
    Support Professionals
NALS of Northern Michigan
NALS of West Michigan
NALS of Washtenaw County

Minnesota

NALS of Greater Minnesota
NALS Twin Cities

Mississippi

Mississippi Division of NALS, Inc.
Columbus Legal Professionals
    Association
Greenwood Legal Professionals
    Association
Gulf Coast Association for Legal
    Support Professionals
Jackson Legal Professionals Association
Metro Legal Professionals Association
Pinebelt Legal Professionals
Tri-County Legal Support Professionals
    Association

Missouri

NALS of Missouri
Central Ozarks Legal Secretaries
    Association
Franklin County ALSP
Heart of America Legal Professionals
    Association
Kansas City Legal Secretaries
    Association
Lakes Area Legal Support Association
NALS of Greater St. Louis
Springfield Area Legal Support
    Professionals
Tri-County ALP

Montana

NALS of Montana

Nevada

NALS of Nevada
Douglas-Carson Legal Professionals

NALS of Las Vegas, a professional legal
    association
NALS of Washoe County

New Jersey

NJALS . . . the association for legal
    professionals
Union Essex Legal Professional
    Association
Hunterdon County Legal Secretaries
    Association
Monmouth Legal Secretaries Association
Morris County Legal Secretaries
    Association
Somerset County Legal Secretaries
    Association
UCLSA . . . the association for legal
    professionals

New Mexico

Albuquerque Association of Legal
    Professionals

New York

NALS of New York
NALS of Nassau County
NALS of New York City
CNY Chapter of NALS
NALS of Suffolk County
Westchester County Legal Secretaries
    Association d/b/a Lower Hudson
    Valley Legal Support Staff

North Carolina

NALS of Charlotte

North Dakota

NALS of Fargo-Moorhead
Minot Legal Secretaries Association

Ohio

NALS of Ohio
NALS of Central Ohio
MCLSA (Mahoning)
Medina County Association for Legal
    Professionals
Stark County Association for Legal
    Professionals
Summit County Legal Professionals, an
    Ohio chapter of NALS
TCLSA (Trumbull)

Oklahoma

NALS of Oklahoma

Oregon

NALS of Oregon
Central Oregon Legal Professionals
NALS of Lane County
Legal Professionals of Douglas County
NALS of Mid-Willamette Valley
Mt. Hood Legal Professionals
NALS of Portland
NALS of Southern Oregon Coast

Pennsylvania

NALS of Pennsylvania
Capital Area Association of Legal
    Professionals
Lehigh-Northhampton Counties Legal
    Secretaries Association
Philadelphia Legal Secretaries
    Association
Pittsburgh Legal Secretaries Association
Schuylkill County

South Carolina

Legal Staff Professionals of South
    Carolina
Legal Staff Professionals of the Low
    Country
Legal Staff Professionals of the
    Midlands
Legal Staff Professionals of Greenville
Hilton Head Legal Staff Professionals
Legal Staff Professionals of Orangeburg
Spartanburg County Legal Staff
    Professionals

South Dakota

Black Hills Legal Professionals
    Association

Tennessee

TALS . . . Legal Professionals of
    Tennessee
Chattanooga Legal Professionals
MLSA—Legal Professionals of Memphis
NALS of Nashville
Knoxville Association of Legal
    Professionals
Rutherford/Canon County LP
Williamson County LP

Texas

Texas Association of Legal
    Professionals
NALS of Amarillo
Arlington Legal Secretaries Association
Austin Legal Secretaries Association

Rio Grande Valley Legal Support
 Professionals
Dallam-Hartley-Moore Counties Legal
 Secretaries Association
Dallas Association of Legal Secretaries
El Paso County Legal Support
 Professionals
Fort Worth ALP
Greater Dallas Association of Legal
 Professionals
Houston Association of Legal
 Professionals
Lubbock Legal Professionals
 Association
Corpus Christi Association of Legal
 Professionals
San Antonio Legal Secretaries
 Association
Waco Legal Professionals Association
Wichita County Legal Secretaries
 Association
East Texas Area Legal Professionals
 Association
Beaumont Legal Secretaries Association
Midland Legal Secretaries Association
NALS of TSTC Harlingen
 Student Chapter

Utah

Utah Legal Professionals Association

Virginia

VALS—the Association for
 Legal Professionals
Charlottesville-Albemarle Legal
 Secretaries Association
Fredericksburg Area Legal Secretaries
 Association
New River Valley Legal Secretaries
 Association
Norfolk-Portsmouth Area Legal
 Secretaries Association
Northern Virginia Legal Secretaries
 Association
Peninsula Association of
 Legal Support Staff
Prince William County Association for
 Legal Professionals
RLSA . . . the association for legal
 professionals
Roanoke Valley Legal Secretaries
 Association
Virginia Beach Legal Staff Association

Washington

NALS of Washington
NALS of Greater Wenatchee
East King County Legal Support
 Professionals
NALS of Greater Seattle

NALS of Kitsap County
NALS of Snohomish County
NALS of Pierce County
NALS of Thurston County
NALS of Spokane
NALS of Yakima County

Wisconsin

Wisconsin Association for
 Legal Professionals
Brown County Association for
 Legal Professionals
Fox Valley Association for
 Legal Professionals
Greater Milwaukee Association of
 Legal Professionals
Lakeshore Area Association for
 Legal Professionals
Legal Professionals Association—
 East Central
Racine-Kenosha Legal Professionals
St. Croix Valley Legal Professionals
Legal Personnel of
 South Central Wisconsin
North Central Association of
 Legal Professionals

Courtesy of NFPA, NALA, and NALS. Reprinted with permission.

INFORMATION ON NALA'S CLA/CP PROGRAM

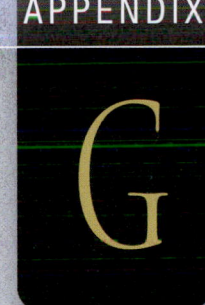

CERTIFICATION

In the working environment, professional certification is a time honored process respected by both employers and those within the career field. The following is a definition used by many to describe professional certification:

> Professional certification is a voluntary process by which a nongovernmental entity grants a time-limited recognition to an individual after verifying that the individual has met predetermined, standardized criteria. (Source: Rops, Mickie S., CAE, *Understanding the Language of Credentialing*, American Society of Association Executives, May 2002.)

The definition hits the high points. Certification is voluntary, not imposed by government. It is time limited, which means that those with the certification must fulfill ongoing educational requirements to keep the certification current, and the criteria for certification [are] recognized in the community. Keep these aspects in mind as you read more about the CP program.

Administration

The NALA Certifying Board for Legal Assistants is responsible for content, standards and administration of the Certified Legal Assistant Program. It is composed of legal assistants who have received an Advanced Paralegal Certification designation, attorneys and legal assistant educators.

In the technical areas of statistical analyses, examination construction, reliability and validity tests, the Board contracts with a professional consulting firm offering expertise in these areas as well as in occupational research. Technical analyses of the CLA/CP examination are conducted on an ongoing basis to ensure the integrity of the examination. Content analyses of the test design, accuracy of questions, and topic/subject mix for each exam section are ongoing processes of the Certifying Board. The Board also utilizes the occupational data available through surveys of legal assistants and other means, including review of textbooks and research within the field of legal assistant education. Through these analyses and procedures, the Board is assured that the examination reflects and responds to work-place realities and demands.

Background and Numbers

Established in 1976, the CLA (Certified Legal Assistant) program has enabled the profession to develop a strong and responsive self-regulatory program offering a nationwide credential for legal assistants. The CLA/CP program establishes and serves as a:

- National professional standard for legal assistants.
- Means of identifying those who have reached this standard.
- Credentialing program responsive to the needs of legal assistants and responsive to the fact that this form of self-regulation is necessary to strengthen and expand development of this career field.
- Positive, ongoing, voluntary program to encourage the growth of the legal assistant profession, attesting to and encouraging a high level of achievement.

[There are more than 15,000 CLA/CPs and more than 1,750 Advanced Certified Paralegals] in the United States. Over 25,000 legal assistants have participated in this program. [Go to **www.nala.org**, select "Certification," and find the appropriate links under "Background and Numbers"] to see the distribution of CLAs across the United States [and] the distribution of Advanced Certified Paralegals. The growth of these programs is impressive.

The Certified Paralegal Credential

Use of the CLA/CP credential signifies that a legal assistant is capable of providing superior services to firms and corporations. National surveys consistently show Certified Legal Assistants/Certified Paralegals are better utilized in a field where attorneys are looking for a credible, dependable way to measure ability. The credential has been recognized by the American Bar Association as a designation which marks a high level of professional achievement. The CLA/CP credential has also been recognized by over 47 legal assistant organizations and numerous bar associations.

For information concerning standards of professional credentialing programs, you may want to see the article: "The Certified Legal Assistant Program and the United States Supreme Court Decision in *Peel v. Attorney Registration and Disciplinary Committee of Illinois.*" In this case, the United States Supreme Court addressed the issue concerning the utilization of professional credentials awarded by private organizations. In *Peel v. Attorney Registration and Disciplinary Committee of Illinois,* 110 S.Ct. 2281 (1990), the Court suggested that a claim of certification is truthful and not misleading if it meets certain standards. This article details those standards in terms of the standards of the NALA Certified Legal Assistant Program.

Is It CLA or CP?

The terms "legal assistant" and "paralegal" are synonymous terms. This is not a choice or opinion of NALA, but a fact. The terms are defined as such throughout the United States in state supreme court rules, statutes, ethical opinions, bar association guidelines and other similar documents. These are the same documents which provide recognition of the paralegal profession and encourage the use of paralegals in the delivery of legal services.

NALA has become increasingly aware that while the terms are the same as "lawyer" and "attorney," a preference in terms is emerging. Different geographic areas use one term more than another. For this reason, we filed for a certification mark "CP" with the U.S. Patent and Trademark Office. The certification mark was successfully registered on July 20, 2004.

Those who are admitted to the Certified Paralegal program, and successfully complete the examination may use either the CLA or CP credential.

CLA is a certification mark duly registered with the U.S. Patent and Trademark Office (No. 113199). CP® is a certification duly registered with the U.S. Patent and Trademark Office (No. 78213275). Any unauthorized use of these credentials is strictly forbidden.

Am I a Certified Paralegal?

Occasionally, paralegals call themselves "certified" by virtue of completing a paralegal training course, or another type of preparatory education. Although a school may award a certificate of completion, this is not the same as earning professional certification by an entity such as NALA. In this instance the school's certificate is designation of completion of a training program.

CP EXAMINATION DESCRIPTION

The CLA examination is divided into five sections. A minimum passing score of 70% is required on all five sections in order to earn the Certified Paralegal credential.

Examinees are asked to demonstrate knowledge by responding to true/false, multiple choice and matching questions requiring knowledge of the subject and reading comprehension skills. Analytical skills and writing abilities are further tested by essay questions. The sections of the examination are as follows:

Communications

- Word usage and vocabulary
- Grammar/punctuation
- Writing skills
- Nonverbal communications
- General communications related to interviewing and client communications
- General communications related to interoffice office situations

This section contains a writing exercise.

The Elements of Style, Strunk & White, has been adopted by the NALA Certifying Board as the authority for the Communications section.

Ethics

- Ethical responsibilities centering on performance of delegated work including confidentiality, unauthorized practice of law, legal advice, conflict of interest, billing and client communications
- Client/public contact including identification as a non-lawyer, advertising and initial client contact
- Professional integrity/competence including knowledge of legal assistant codes of ethics
- Relationships with co-workers and support staff
- Attorney codes/discipline
- Knowledge of the American Bar Association's *Rules of Professional Conduct* and the NALA Code of Ethics and Professional Responsibility is required by this examination.

Legal Research

- Sources of law including primary authority, secondary authority; understanding how law is recorded
- Research skills including citing the law; shepardizing, updating decisions; procedural rules of citations
- Analysis of research problem including identification of relevant facts and legal issues

A Uniform System of Citation, Harvard Law Review Association, has been adopted by the NALA Certifying Board as the authority for the Legal Research section.

Judgment and Analytical Ability

- Comprehension of data—identifying and understanding a problem
- Application of knowledge—ability to link facts or legal issues from other cases to the problem at hand, recognizing similarities and differences by analogy
- Evaluating and categorizing data
- Organizing data and findings in a written document

This section contains an essay question which requires analysis of a research request, finding applicable law, and writing a responsive memo.

Examinees will be graded on the ability to:

- Identify which facts are relevant and state them concisely and accurately;
- Identify the threshold or main issue and any secondary issue(s);
- Identify the relevant legal authority and apply it to the facts; and
- Draw persuasive logical conclusions.

Substantive Law

The substantive law section of the examination is composed of five sub-sections. The first section, Substantive Law–General, covers concepts of the American legal system. **All examinees are required to take this section.** Subjects covered within this section include:

- Court system[s] including their structure and jurisdiction
- Branches of government, agencies, and concepts such as separation of powers
- Legal concepts and principles including sources of law, judicial decision making, appellate process
- Sources and classifications of law including the constitution, statutes, common law, civil law, statutory law and equity law

The other four sub-sections are selected by the applicants from a list of nine substantive areas of the law. These tests cover general knowledge of the following practice areas:

- Administrative Law
- Bankruptcy
- Business Organizations
- Civil Litigation
- Contracts
- Criminal Law and Procedure

- Estate Planning and Probate
- Family Law
- Real Estate

The skills required by these tests involve recall of facts and principles that form the basis of the specialty practice area. Examinees must also demonstrate an understanding of the structure of the law and procedures to be followed in each specialty practice area.

EXAMINEE INFORMATION

If you have made the decision to seek the Certified Paralegal credential, this is your place for administrative details, and information about taking the examination.

Applying for the Certified Paralegal Examination

To be eligible for the CP examination, a paralegal must meet one of the following alternate requirements:

1. Graduation from a paralegal program that is:
   - (a) Approved by the American Bar Association; or
   - (b) An associate degree program; or
   - (c) A post-baccalaureate certificate program in legal assistant studies; or
   - (d) A bachelor's degree program in legal assistant studies; or
   - (e) A legal assistant program which consists of a minimum of 60 semester hours (900 clock hours or 90 quarter hours) of which at least 15 semester hours (225 clock hours or 22.5 quarter hours) are substantive legal courses.

   NOTE: Under Category 1(e), an applicant may combine college hours from more than one institution. The applicant must have graduated from a legal assistant program consisting of a minimum of 15 semester hours (or 225 clock hours or 22.5 quarter hours.) Evidence of the minimum hours required under Category 1(e) must be provided with the application form.

2. A bachelor's degree in any field plus one year's experience as a paralegal. Successful completion of at least 15 semester hours (or 22.5 quarter hours or 225 clock hours) of substantive paralegal courses will be considered equivalent to one year's experience as a paralegal.

3. A high school diploma or equivalent plus seven (7) years' experience as a paralegal under the supervision of a member of the Bar, plus evidence of a minimum of twenty (20) hours of continuing legal education credit to have been completed within a two (2) year period prior to the examination date.

**Additional forms will be required of all candidates if filing applications prior to meeting the eligibility requirements. Contact NALA Headquarters for further information.

Dates, Deadlines & Fees

The CLA/CP examination is offered three times a year: March/April (depending on the holiday schedule); July and December. Application forms and the requisite fees must be received by the published filing dates.

Filing deadline dates are strictly enforced.

Many schools, universities and community colleges serve as testing centers through an arrangement with NALA. In addition, NALA will establish testing centers in cities where 10 or more paralegals apply. All testing center locations are subject to minimum registration.

Fees

The fee for the CLA/CP examination is $250 for NALA members and $275 for non-members of NALA. Retake fees are $60 per section.

CP STUDY MATERIALS

Preparing for the Certified Paralegal exam can be a daunting task. NALA publishes several books that are helpful, on-line programs are available, and NALA affiliated associations offer local study groups. Below is a summary of these programs.

Publications

The following publications, published by NALA through Cengage Publishers, are helpful for exam review:

- *NALA Manual for Paralegals, Fifth Edition (out in 2009),* authored by NALA members.
- *CLA Study Guide and Mock Exam, Fourth Edition,* authored by NALA members and material contributed.
- *CLA Review Manual, Second Edition,* authored by Virginia Koerselman

[Go to **www.nala.org**, select "CP Study Materials" from the "Certification" menu, and click on the live link] for a description of these books and ordering information.

Please Note: *The Elements of Style,* Strunk & White, has been adopted by the NALA Certifying Board as the authority for the Communications section of the examination. *A Uniform System of Citation,* Harvard Law Review Association, has been adopted by the NALA Certifying Board as the authority for the Legal Research section.

On-line Programs

Your source for on-line programs is NALA Campus [**www.nalacampus.com**]. NALA Campus offers continuing legal education programs in two forms:

Self Study Programs

Most of the subjects in the NALA Campus self study programs are included in the line up of these 24/7 programs. This includes:

- American Legal System
- Civil Litigation
- Contracts
- Ethics
- Judgment and Legal Analysis
- Legal Research
- Real Estate
- Written Communications

The on-line programs consist of written text and slides, with audio recordings of the text. In addition, tests of the instructional material are featured. Participation in these programs is fun—and a convenient way to update your skills and review for the exam.

Live Web Based Programs

Generally, these programs are 1½ to 2 hours in length. They consist of a web based slide presentation, and telephone conference call. NALA Campus LIVE! courses are offered from February–May and August–November. Each session consists of about 30 courses. Subjects for review for the CLA examination are offered on a regular basis. The subjects include:

- American Legal System
- Basic Business Organizations
- Civil Litigation
- Ethics
- Legal Research
- Written Communications

The subjects/topics for each NALA Campus LIVE! session change. Check the schedule on **www.nalacampus.com** for details. Also, several NALA Campus courses are recorded and available for sale in MP3 format. Those are also listed on the NALA Campus web site.

Live Programs

From NALA

Several live study programs are available to those preparing for the CLA/CP examination. This includes:

CLA/CP Short Course

The CLA/CP Short Course is a mainstay of the continuing education programs offered by NALA. The 2½ day intensive program is generally offered each fall, late October or early November. Details of the program may be found under the Continuing Education area of [**www.nala.org**].

Essential Skills

During the NALA annual convention, an Essential Skills track is often part of the educational program. This is a four day (mornings) program and specifically designed for exam preparation. The sessions are Written Communications, Judgment and Legal Analysis, the American Legal System, and Legal Research. These are the essential exam review courses.

From NALA Affiliated Associations

NALA affiliated associations are located throughout the United States. These state and local paralegal organizations are tremendous resources for paralegal activities in a specific region. Affiliated associations in 22 states offer exam review programs. [Go to **www.nala.org**, select "CP Study Materials" from the "Certification" menu, and click on the live link] for the list and web addresses—there just may be one in your area.

Another source of review programs for the CLA/CP examination are classes offered through local community colleges. These are particularly helpful if you need to review a specific subject. Remember, though, the Certified Paralegal Exam is a nationwide exam; no state laws or procedures are tested.

FOR CERTIFIED PARALEGALS

Certified Paralegals are required to meet certain continuing legal education requirements to maintain the certification. This page describes the CLE requirements, and provides links to important forms and information related to the ongoing requirements.

Use of the CLA or CP Credential

The terms "legal assistant" and "paralegal" are synonymous terms. This is not a choice or opinion of NALA, but a fact. The terms are defined as such throughout the United States in state supreme court rules, statutes, ethical opinions, bar association guidelines and other similar documents. These are the same documents which provide recognition of the legal assistant/paralegal profession and encourage the use of paralegals in the delivery of legal services.

NALA has become increasingly aware that a preference in terms is emerging; different geographic areas use one term more than another. For this reason, we filed for a certification mark "CP" with the U.S. Patent and Trademark Office. The certification mark **CP®** was successfully registered on July 20, 2004. Those who are admitted to the program and successfully complete the certification examination may use either credential, but not both. Using both credentials could imply two different certifications.

[Go to **www.nala.org**, select "For Certified Paralegals" from the "Certification" menu, and click on the appropriate link] to read the instructions on using the CP and CLA certification marks.

Continuing Education Requirements

The Certified Paralegal credential is awarded for a period of five years. To maintain Certified Paralegal status, paralegals must submit proof of participation in a minimum of 50 hours of continuing legal education programs or individual study programs, which must include five hours on the subject of legal ethics. Credit is also awarded for significant achievement in the area of continuing paralegal education such as successful completion of a state certification test, completion of an Advanced Paralegal Certification program, or teaching in a legal assistant program.

[Go to **www.nala.org**, select "For Certified Paralegals" from the "Certification" menu, and click on the appropriate link] to review the CLE requirements.

Many have questions about the CLE requirements, such as if a particular program qualifies, or when the five year period begins and ends. General questions and answers have been compiled. If you have a question, it may already be addressed in this document. [Go to **www.nala.org**, select "For Certified Paralegals" from the "Certification" menu, and click on the appropriate link to see "Frequently Asked Questions About CLE Requirements."]

Filing Requests for Continuing Education Credits

Certified Paralegals may file requests for continuing education credits as programs are attended. When credits are recorded in the file, a confirmation form from NALA Headquarters is provided. Fifty hours (50) of continuing legal education credit is required every five years; 50 minutes is equal to one hour of instruction. This is helpful in seeking credit for a luncheon seminar or shorter educational session.

ADVANCED PARALEGAL CERTIFICATION

Commitment to continued growth and life-long learning is the hallmark of a professional. Once a Certified Paralegal's career is launched, there will be a need for advanced CLE programs as one changes areas of practice, or is met with more challenging assignments. The Advanced Paralegal Certification program is designed to recognize this effort.

The APC program has its own website. Below is a summary of the program. [You can go directly to the APC site at **www.nala-apc.org**.]

Background

The CLA/CP certification program offers professional certification for paralegals immediately upon completion of their training. In 1982, NALA instituted the CLA Specialty program, to recognize a Certified Paralegal's specialized knowledge in a specialty area of practice.

In 2002, a special task force was appointed to look at the CLA Specialty Certification program and see if changes were needed. The Task Force determined it was time to redesign and restructure the program. The result is the Advanced Paralegal Certification program.

APC Program—Curriculum-Based Certification

The curriculum-based certification is an accepted model of certification and professional development programs throughout the United States and across numerous occupations. This is certification based on specific course material.

An assessment component is part of the curriculum-based program. Participants are required to demonstrate mastery of the course material throughout the process. Both the educational and assessment components are on-line.

A curriculum-based model assumes that participants will discuss course material and consult outside sources, including colleagues, reference books, and specialty practice area experts. The focus is on education and learning specific subject matter rather than testing, which has already been done by the CLA/CP Examination to ensure that candidates have the requisite analytical, research, and writing skills.

Over three years in development, this program increases access to advanced certification for paralegals working in specific practice areas.

Courses

APC courses are developed by the APC board and experienced technical writers. The courses are about 20 hours in length. The length of time spent on the courses will vary based on one's understanding of the material. Also, the courses include additional reading material and cases.

Advanced Paralegal Certification programs are now offered in the following areas. [Go to **www.nala.org**, select "Advanced Paralegal Certification" from the "Certification" menu, and click on the appropriate links for details on these APC courses.]

- Contracts Management/Contracts Administration
- Discovery
- Social Security Disability
- Trial Practice
- Alternative Dispute Resolution
- Business Organizations: Incorporated Entities
- Trademarks

Programs scheduled to begin shortly include:

- Personal Injury
- Land Use

APC Board

The Advanced Paralegal Certification program of NALA is administered by a board composed of experienced paralegals, attorneys, paralegal educators, and paralegal managers. The Chair of the APC board is also a member of the NALA Board of Directors. All paralegals on the APC board have received the advanced certification credential. The board relies heavily on the expertise of technical writers and professional testing consultants.

For Certified Paralegals

Paralegals who have a valid CLA/CP certification credential from NALA and successfully complete an APC Course are awarded use of the ACP credential to signify this outstanding achievement. In addition, Certified Paralegals may also receive 20 hours of continuing legal education credit for completion of an advanced program.

Paralegals who do not have the CLA/CP certification are welcome to participate in these advanced programs. The credential will not be awarded, however.

The Marks

CLA®, CLAS®, and CP® are certification marks duly registered with the U.S. Patent and Trademark Office (No. 113199, No. 1751731, and No. 78213275, respectively). Unauthorized use of these credentials is strictly forbidden.

Courtesy of the ©National Association of Legal Assistants, Inc. Reprinted with permission.
Note: This material, and additional material on the CLA/CP Program, is available at the NALA Web site at **www.nala.org**.

This information is current as of the publication date. For updates, please check the NALA web site (**www.nala.org**), or inquire of NALA Headquarters, 1516 S. Boston, #200, Tulsa, OK 74119.

INFORMATION ON NFPA'S PACE™ EXAMINATION

   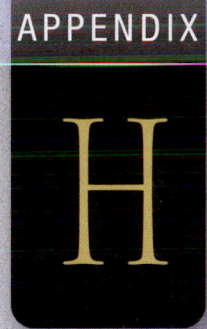

INTRODUCTION

The legal service industry is facing great change. It is trying to respond to changes in technology and increased demands from consumers for a higher level of client service.

As an active and vital part of the legal service industry, the paralegal profession is facing possible regulation through certification, licensing, or other means. The National Federation of Paralegal Associations, Inc., gathered this information to describe the step it is undertaking that may change the profession.

ABOUT PACE™

. . . .

Key Points of PACE™

The Paralegal Advanced Competency Exam (PACE™) is offered by the National Federation of Paralegal Associations, Inc.® (NFPA) to test the competency level of experienced paralegals.

Exam for Experienced Paralegals

PACE™ is offered to paralegals who have a minimum of two years' experience and meet specific educational requirements. PACE™ is designed for professional paralegals who want to pioneer the expansion of paralegal roles for the future of the profession, not to restrict entry into the profession.

Two-tier Exam

Each tier addresses different areas. Tier I addresses general legal issues and ethics. As the need arises, a section for state-specific laws may also be developed. Tier II addresses specialty sections.

Fair and Independent

PACE™ has been developed by a professional testing firm, assisted by an independent task force including paralegals, lawyers, paralegal educators and content specialists from the general public who are legal advocates. Ongoing administration will be handled by PES.

Voluntary

Paralegals will have the option to sit for the exam at more than 200 Sylvan Technology Centers. As activities and proposals for regulation of the profession increase, all paralegals will be encouraged to take the exam.

Credential Maintenance

To maintain the PACE™ RP® credential, paralegals are required to obtain 12 hours of continuing legal education, including at least one hour in ethics, every two years.

HISTORY OF PACE™

A grass-roots organization, NFPA® is directed by its membership; each member association has one vote in the future of the national organization and the profession. During NFPA's 1994 Mid-Year Meeting, the membership voted overwhelmingly to develop an exam to test the competency level of experienced paralegals.

The overwhelmingly positive vote to develop this exam is a conscientious effort by these paralegals to direct the future of the paralegal profession and acknowledges the vital role of paralegals within the legal service industry. It is also a direct response to states that are considering regulation of the paralegal profession and are seeking a method to measure job competency. While NFPA® believes in the criteria the members established to take this exam, it recognizes any state may adopt the exam and modify the criteria.

PACE™ = Paralegal Advanced Competency Exam

Offering experienced paralegals an option to:
- validate your experience and job skills;
- establish credentials; and
- increase your value to your organizations and clients.

The only exam of its kind, PACE™
- developed by a professional testing firm;
- administered by an independent test administration company;
- tests concepts across practice areas;
- offers the profession a national standard of evaluation; and
- offered at multiple locations on numerous dates and at various times.

PACE™ = Personal Advancement for the Experienced Paralegal

WHY TAKE PACE™?

Paralegals receive two major benefits by taking PACE™. The exam

- provides a fair evaluation of the competencies of paralegals across practice areas; and

- creates a professional level of expertise by which all paralegals can be evaluated.

PACE™ presents a bold opportunity to all paralegals to advance the profession. This exam provides hard facts about the competency of experienced paralegals. While PACE™ does not address all the issues of regulation, including certification and licensing, it does provide the legal service industry with an option to evaluate the competency level of experienced paralegals.

As members of a self-directed profession, all paralegals should consider the vital role the profession performs within the legal service industry. PACE™ is independently monitored and well-structured. PACE™ provides test results across practice areas and, possibly, state-specific laws. While the test is offered on a voluntary basis, all experienced paralegals are encouraged to sit for the exam.

NFPA® is committed to ensuring the paralegal profession responds to the changing needs of the public and legal service industry. In voting to develop PACE™, NFPA's membership took a bold step toward addressing the future issues facing the profession.

Lexis-Nexis has sponsored a twenty minute presentation on paralegals which highlights PACE™ and can be ordered from the PACE™ Merchandise page. [Go to **www.paralegals.org**, and select "PACE™ Merchandise" from the PACE/RP menu.]

ELIGIBILITY TO SIT FOR PACE™

Requirements for a paralegal to take either tier of PACE™ include work experience and education. The paralegal cannot have been convicted of a felony nor be under suspension, termination, or revocation of a certificate, registration, or license by any entity. PACE™ has generated a great deal of interest since the resolution to develop it was passed. Based on this interest, and the number of paralegals who may apply to take the exam (a number reported by the U.S. Department of Labor to exceed 113,000), a need exists for [such certification].

Requirements are:

- An associates degree in paralegal studies obtained from an institutionally accredited school, and/or ABA approved paralegal education program; and six (6) years substantive paralegal experience; OR

- A bachelor's degree in any course of study obtained from an institutionally accredited school and three (3) years of substantive paralegal experience; OR

- A bachelor's degree and completion of a paralegal program with an institutionally accredited school, said paralegal program may be embodied in a bachelor's degree; and two (2) years substantive paralegal experience; OR

- Four (4) years substantive paralegal experience on or before December 31, 2000.

PACE™ CREDENTIALING

Those who pass PACE™ and maintain the continuing education requirement may use the designation "PACE - Registered Paralegal®" or "RP®."

To maintain the RP® credential, 12 hours of continuing legal or specialty education is required every two years, with at least one hour in legal ethics.

Registered Paralegals should review the Facts Every RP Should Know to be aware of the ways the PACE™ credential can be used and information on registration of CLE credits. [To read this material, go to **www.paralegals.org**, select "PACE™ Credentialing" from the PACE/RP menu, and click on the appropriate link.] Also included in the fact sheet is information on non-renewal status, inactive status, suspension and revocation of the use of the RP® credential and the appeals process. . . .

Courtesy of the National Federation of Paralegal Associations, Inc. Reprinted with permission.
Note: This material, and additional material on PACE™, is available at the NFPA Web site at **www.paralegals.org**.

INFORMATION ON NALS CERTIFICATION

NALS offers members and nonmembers the opportunity to sit for three unique certifications dedicated to the legal services profession. The exams are of varying levels and are developed by professionals in the industry. ALS . . . the basic certification for legal professionals and PLS . . . the advanced certification for legal professionals are two certifications dedicated to legal professionals of all types. The third certification is dedicated to those professionals performing paralegal duties. The Professional Paralegal (PP) certification was developed by paralegals for paralegals. Each of the three certifications is developed by NALS and takes advantage of the more than seventy-five years of experience and dedication to the legal services industry only NALS has to offer.

ACCREDITED LEGAL SECRETARY CERTIFICATION

ALS . . . The Basic Certification for Legal Professionals—A Career Goal

One way to demonstrate your preparedness for the demanding field of law is by becoming an ALS. This designation is awarded after passing a four-hour, three-part examination. Attaining this goal demonstrates your commitment and aptitude for succeeding in the ever-changing legal environment.

The ALS Examination:

- demonstrates ability to perform business communication tasks;
- gauges ability to maintain office records and calendars, and prioritize multiple tasks when given real-life scenarios;

- measures understanding of office equipment and related procedures;
- denotes aptitude for understanding legal terminology, legal complexities, and supporting documents;
- assesses recognition of accounting terms to solve accounting problems; and
- appraises knowledge of law office protocol as prescribed by ethical codes.

ALS Examination Eligibility

To sit for the examination, you must have completed one of the following:

- an accredited business/legal course,
- the NALS Legal Training Course, or
- one year of general office experience.

Membership in NALS is not a requirement.

The Exam Covers

The examination covers the following parts:

- PART 1: Written Communications
- PART 2: Office Procedures and Legal Knowledge
- PART 3: Ethics, Human Relations, and Judgment

Examination Guidelines

All three parts of the examination must be taken on the first attempt. If you do not pass the entire examination on the first attempt, you may retake the examination parts you did not pass. All failed parts must be retaken at the same time. You will be charged the full exam fee each time you sit.

Those passing the exam will receive a certificate that is valid for five years.

Certification may be extended through continuing education, based on NALS guidelines, for one year.

Examination Dates and Application Deadlines

- March: First Saturday (Postmarked by January 1)
- June: First Saturday* (Postmarked by April 15)
- September: Last Saturday (Postmarked by August 1)
- December: First Saturday* (Postmarked by October 15)

  June and December testing are for those who have completed the Basic or Advanced NALS Legal Training Course.

Examination Fees

- Student/LTC Participant (minimum of 9 credit hours)—$50
- NALS member (not a full-time student)—$75
- Nonmember (not a full-time student)—$100

. . . .

PROFESSIONAL LEGAL SECRETARY CERTIFICATION

PLS . . . The Advanced Certification for Legal Professionals—A Career Goal

How do your skills compare with the hallmark of a professional? PLS® is the designation for lawyer's assistants who want to be identified as exceptional. Certification is received after passing a one-day, four-part examination which demonstrates not only dedication to professionalism but acceptance of the challenge to be exceptional. Personal motivation is necessary to attain such a goal.

The purpose of the examination is to certify a lawyer's assistant as a person who possesses:

- a mastery of office skills;
- the ability to interact on a professional level with attorneys, clients, and other support staff;
- the discipline to assume responsibility and exercise initiative and judgment; and
- a working knowledge of procedural law, the law library, and how to prepare legal documents.

PLS Examination Eligibility

Any person who has had three years' experience in the legal field may take the examination. Membership in NALS is not a requirement. A partial waiver of the three-year legal experience requirement may be granted for postsecondary degrees, successful completion of the ALS exam, or other certifications. The maximum waiver is one year.

The PLS Certification Exam Covers

- PART 1: Written Communications
- PART 2: Office Procedures and Technology
- PART 3: Ethics and Judgment
- PART 4: Legal Knowledge and Skills

Examination Guidelines

All four parts of the examination must be taken on the first attempt. If you do not pass the entire examination on the first attempt, but do pass one or more parts, you may retake the part (or parts) you failed. All failed parts must be retaken at the same time. Those passing the exam will receive a certificate that is valid for five years. Recertification is required every five years and may be achieved through the accumulation of continuing legal education hours and activities.

Examination Dates Each Year and Application Deadlines

- March: First Saturday in March (Postmarked by January 1)
- September: Last Saturday in September (Postmarked by August 1)

Examination Fees

- For the initial examination: Members—$150; Nonmembers—$200
- For part retakes: Members—$40 per part; Nonmembers—$50 per part
. . . .

PROFESSIONAL PARALEGAL (PP)

Are you looking for a way to establish your credentials nationwide as a Professional Paralegal? Established in 2004 at our members' request, the Certified PP designation is an attainable goal for paralegals who wish to be identified as exceptional in all areas of law. The certificate is received after passing a one-day, four-part examination.

Successful completion of the PP examination demonstrates:

- A mastery of procedural skills and communication skills.
- An advanced knowledge of procedural law, the law library, and the preparation of legal documents.

- A working knowledge of substantive law and the ability to perform specifically delegated substantive legal work under an attorney's supervision.
- The ability to interact on a professional level with attorneys, clients, and other staff.
- The discipline to assume responsibility and exercise initiative and judgment while adhering to legal ethical standards at all times.

Working under the supervision of a practicing lawyer or a judge, the Certified PP is expected to possess:

- The same high standard of ethical conduct imposed upon members of the Bar.
- Excellent written and verbal communication skills.
- Knowledge and understanding of legal terminology and procedures, as well as procedural and substantive law.
- The ability to assume responsibility, exercise initiative and judgment, and prepare substantive legal documents within the scope of assigned authority.
- Attaining this goal demonstrates dedication to professionalism and acceptance of the challenge to be exceptional. Personal motivation is necessary to attain such a goal.

PP Examination Eligibility

Any person who has five years' experience performing paralegal/legal assistant duties (a candidate may receive a partial waiver of one year if he or she has a postsecondary degree, other certification, or a paralegal certificate; a candidate with a paralegal degree may receive a two-year partial waiver).

The Exam Covers

- PART 1: Written Communications
- PART 2: Legal Knowledge and Skills
- PART 3: Ethics and Judgment Skills
- PART 4: Substantive Law

Examination Guidelines

All four parts of the examination must be taken on the first attempt with the exception of current PLSs, for which only Part 4 in Substantive Law is needed. If you do not pass the entire examination on the first attempt, but do pass one or more parts, you may retake the part (or parts) you failed. All failed parts must be retaken at the same time.

Those passing the exam will receive a certificate that is valid for five years. Recertification is required every five years and may be achieved through the accumulation of continuing legal education hours and activities.

Examination Dates and Application Deadlines

- March: First Saturday (Postmarked by January 1)
- September: Last Saturday (Postmarked by August 1)

Examination Fees

- For current PLSs
  Members: $150
  Nonmembers: $200
- For non-PLSs
  Members: $200
  Nonmembers: $250

- Retake fees:
  Members: $50 per part
  Nonmembers: $60 per part

Courtesy of NALS . . . the association for legal professionals. Reprinted with permission.
Note: This material, and additional material on NALS certification, is available at the NALS Web site at **www.nals.org**.

THE CONSTITUTION OF THE UNITED STATES

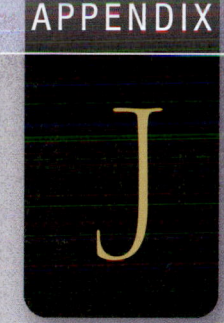

PREAMBLE

We the People of the United States, in Order to form a more perfect Union, establish Justice, insure domestic Tranquility, provide for the common defence, promote the general Welfare, and secure the Blessings of Liberty to ourselves and our Posterity, do ordain and establish this Constitution for the United States of America.

Article I

Section 1. All legislative Powers herein granted shall be vested in a Congress of the United States, which shall consist of a Senate and House of Representatives.

Section 2. The House of Representatives shall be composed of Members chosen every second Year by the People of the several States, and the Electors in each State shall have the Qualifications requisite for Electors of the most numerous Branch of the State Legislature.

No Person shall be a Representative who shall not have attained to the Age of twenty five Years, and been seven Years a Citizen of the United States, and who shall not, when elected, be an Inhabitant of that State in which he shall be chosen.

Representatives and direct Taxes shall be apportioned among the several States which may be included within this Union, according to their respective Numbers, which shall be determined by adding to the whole Number of free Persons, including those bound to Service for a Term of Years, and excluding Indians not taxed, three fifths of all other Persons. The actual Enumeration shall be made within three Years after the first Meeting of the Congress of the United States, and within every subsequent Term of ten Years, in such Manner as they shall by Law direct.

The Number of Representatives shall not exceed one for every thirty Thousand, but each State shall have at Least one Representative; and until such enumeration shall be made, the State of New Hampshire shall be entitled to chuse three, Massachusetts eight, Rhode Island and Providence Plantations one, Connecticut five, New York six, New Jersey four, Pennsylvania eight, Delaware one, Maryland six, Virginia ten, North Carolina five, South Carolina five, and Georgia three.

When vacancies happen in the Representation from any State, the Executive Authority thereof shall issue Writs of Election to fill such Vacancies.

The House of Representatives shall chuse their Speaker and other Officers; and shall have the sole Power of Impeachment.

Section 3.   The Senate of the United States shall be composed of two Senators from each State, chosen by the Legislature thereof, for six Years; and each Senator shall have one Vote.

Immediately after they shall be assembled in Consequence of the first Election, they shall be divided as equally as may be into three Classes. The Seats of the Senators of the first Class shall be vacated at the Expiration of the second Year, of the second Class at the Expiration of the fourth Year, and of the third Class at the Expiration of the sixth Year, so that one third may be chosen every second Year; and if Vacancies happen by Resignation, or otherwise, during the Recess of the Legislature of any State, the Executive thereof may make temporary Appointments until the next Meeting of the Legislature, which shall then fill such Vacancies.

No Person shall be a Senator who shall not have attained to the Age of thirty Years, and been nine Years a Citizen of the United States, and who shall not, when elected, be an Inhabitant of that State for which he shall be chosen.

The Vice President of the United States shall be President of the Senate, but shall have no Vote, unless they be equally divided.

The Senate shall chuse their other Officers, and also a President pro tempore, in the Absence of the Vice President, or when he shall exercise the Office of President of the United States.

The Senate shall have the sole Power to try all Impeachments. When sitting for that Purpose, they shall be on Oath or Affirmation. When the President of the United States is tried, the Chief Justice shall preside: And no Person shall be convicted without the Concurrence of two thirds of the Members present.

Judgment in Cases of Impeachment shall not extend further than to removal from Office, and disqualification to hold and enjoy any Office of honor, Trust, or Profit under the United States: but the Party convicted shall nevertheless be liable and subject to Indictment, Trial, Judgment, and Punishment, according to Law.

Section 4.   The Times, Places and Manner of holding Elections for Senators and Representatives, shall be prescribed in each State by the Legislature thereof; but the Congress may at any time by Law make or alter such Regulations, except as to the Places of chusing Senators.

The Congress shall assemble at least once in every Year, and such Meeting shall be on the first Monday in December, unless they shall by Law appoint a different Day.

Section 5.   Each House shall be the Judge of the Elections, Returns, and Qualifications of its own Members, and a Majority of each shall constitute a Quorum to do Business; but a smaller Number may adjourn from day to day, and may be authorized to compel the Attendance of absent Members, in such Manner, and under such Penalties as each House may provide.

Each House may determine the Rules of its Proceedings, punish its Members for disorderly Behavior, and, with the Concurrence of two thirds, expel a Member.

Each House shall keep a Journal of its Proceedings, and from time to time publish the same, excepting such Parts as may in their Judgment require Secrecy; and the Yeas and Nays of the Members of either House on any question shall, at the Desire of one fifth of those Present, be entered on the Journal.

Neither House, during the Session of Congress, shall, without the Consent of the other, adjourn for more than three days, nor to any other Place than that in which the two Houses shall be sitting.

Section 6. The Senators and Representatives shall receive a Compensation for their Services, to be ascertained by Law, and paid out of the Treasury of the United States. They shall in all Cases, except Treason, Felony and Breach of the Peace, be privileged from Arrest during their Attendance at the Session of their respective Houses, and in going to and returning from the same; and for any Speech or Debate in either House, they shall not be questioned in any other Place.

No Senator or Representative shall, during the Time for which he was elected, be appointed to any civil Office under the Authority of the United States, which shall have been created, or the Emoluments whereof shall have been increased during such time; and no Person holding any Office under the United States, shall be a Member of either House during his Continuance in Office.

Section 7. All Bills for raising Revenue shall originate in the House of Representatives; but the Senate may propose or concur with Amendments as on other Bills.

Every Bill which shall have passed the House of Representatives and the Senate, shall, before it become a Law, be presented to the President of the United States; If he approve he shall sign it, but if not he shall return it, with his Objections to the House in which it shall have originated, who shall enter the Objections at large on their Journal, and proceed to reconsider it. If after such Reconsideration two thirds of that House shall agree to pass the Bill, it shall be sent together with the Objections, to the other House, by which it shall likewise be reconsidered, and if approved by two thirds of that House, it shall become a Law. But in all such Cases the Votes of both Houses shall be determined by Yeas and Nays, and the Names of the Persons voting for and against the Bill shall be entered on the Journal of each House respectively. If any Bill shall not be returned by the President within ten Days (Sundays excepted) after it shall have been presented to him, the Same shall be a Law, in like Manner as if he had signed it, unless the Congress by their Adjournment prevent its Return in which Case it shall not be a Law.

Every Order, Resolution, or Vote, to which the Concurrence of the Senate and House of Representatives may be necessary (except on a question of Adjournment) shall be presented to the President of the United States; and before the Same shall take Effect, shall be approved by him, or being disapproved by him, shall be repassed by two thirds of the Senate and House of Representatives, according to the Rules and Limitations prescribed in the Case of a Bill.

Section 8. The Congress shall have Power To lay and collect Taxes, Duties, Imposts and Excises, to pay the Debts and provide for the common Defence and general Welfare of the United States; but all Duties, Imposts and Excises shall be uniform throughout the United States;

To borrow Money on the credit of the United States;

To regulate Commerce with foreign Nations, and among the several States, and with the Indian Tribes;

To establish an uniform Rule of Naturalization, and uniform Laws on the subject of Bankruptcies throughout the United States;

To coin Money, regulate the Value thereof, and of foreign Coin, and fix the Standard of Weights and Measures;

To provide for the Punishment of counterfeiting the Securities and current Coin of the United States;

To establish Post Offices and post Roads;

To promote the Progress of Science and useful Arts, by securing for limited Times to Authors and Inventors the exclusive Right to their respective Writings and Discoveries;

To constitute Tribunals inferior to the supreme Court;

To define and punish Piracies and Felonies committed on the high Seas, and Offenses against the Law of Nations;

To declare War, grant Letters of Marque and Reprisal, and make Rules concerning Captures on Land and Water;

To raise and support Armies, but no Appropriation of Money to that Use shall be for a longer Term than two Years;

To provide and maintain a Navy;

To make Rules for the Government and Regulation of the land and naval Forces;

To provide for calling forth the Militia to execute the Laws of the Union, suppress Insurrections and repel Invasions;

To provide for organizing, arming, and disciplining, the Militia, and for governing such Part of them as may be employed in the Service of the United States, reserving to the States respectively, the Appointment of the Officers, and the Authority of training the Militia according to the discipline prescribed by Congress;

To exercise exclusive Legislation in all Cases whatsoever, over such District (not exceeding ten Miles square) as may, by Cession of particular States, and the Acceptance of Congress, become the Seat of the Government of the United States, and to exercise like Authority over all Places purchased by the Consent of the Legislature of the State in which the Same shall be, for the Erection of Forts, Magazines, Arsenals, dock-Yards, and other needful Buildings;—And

To make all Laws which shall be necessary and proper for carrying into Execution the foregoing Powers, and all other Powers vested by this Constitution in the Government of the United States, or in any Department or Officer thereof.

Section 9.   The Migration or Importation of such Persons as any of the States now existing shall think proper to admit, shall not be prohibited by the Congress prior to the Year one thousand eight hundred and eight, but a Tax or duty may be imposed on such Importation, not exceeding ten dollars for each Person.

The privilege of the Writ of Habeas Corpus shall not be suspended, unless when in Cases of Rebellion or Invasion the public Safety may require it.

No Bill of Attainder or ex post facto Law shall be passed.

No Capitation, or other direct, Tax shall be laid, unless in Proportion to the Census or Enumeration herein before directed to be taken.

No Tax or Duty shall be laid on Articles exported from any State.

No Preference shall be given by any Regulation of Commerce or Revenue to the Ports of one State over those of another: nor shall Vessels bound to, or from, one State be obliged to enter, clear, or pay Duties in another.

No Money shall be drawn from the Treasury, but in Consequence of Appropriations made by Law; and a regular Statement and Account of the Receipts and Expenditures of all public Money shall be published from time to time.

No Title of Nobility shall be granted by the United States: And no Person holding any Office of Profit or Trust under them, shall, without the Consent of the Congress, accept of any present, Emolument, Office, or Title, of any kind whatever, from any King, Prince, or foreign State.

Section 10.   No State shall enter into any Treaty, Alliance, or Confederation; grant Letters of Marque and Reprisal; coin Money; emit Bills of Credit; make any Thing but gold and silver Coin a Tender in Payment of Debts; pass any Bill of Attainder, ex post facto Law, or Law impairing the Obligation of Contracts, or grant any Title of Nobility.

No State shall, without the Consent of the Congress, lay any Imposts or Duties on Imports or Exports, except what may be absolutely necessary for executing its inspection Laws: and the net Produce of all Duties and Imposts, laid by any State on

Imports or Exports, shall be for the Use of the Treasury of the United States; and all such Laws shall be subject to the Revision and Controul of the Congress.

No State shall, without the Consent of Congress, lay any Duty of Tonnage, keep Troops, or Ships of War in time of Peace, enter into any Agreement or Compact with another State, or with a foreign Power, or engage in War, unless actually invaded, or in such imminent Danger as will not admit of delay.

Article II

Section 1.   The executive Power shall be vested in a President of the United States of America. He shall hold his Office during the Term of four Years, and, together with the Vice President, chosen for the same Term, be elected, as follows:

Each State shall appoint, in such Manner as the Legislature thereof may direct, a Number of Electors, equal to the whole Number of Senators and Representatives to which the State may be entitled in the Congress; but no Senator or Representative, or Person holding an Office of Trust or Profit under the United States, shall be appointed an Elector.

The Electors shall meet in their respective States, and vote by Ballot for two Persons, of whom one at least shall not be an Inhabitant of the same State with themselves. And they shall make a List of all the Persons voted for, and of the Number of Votes for each; which List they shall sign and certify, and transmit sealed to the Seat of the Government of the United States, directed to the President of the Senate. The President of the Senate shall, in the Presence of the Senate and House of Representatives, open all the Certificates, and the Votes shall then be counted. The Person having the greatest Number of Votes shall be the President, if such Number be a Majority of the whole Number of Electors appointed; and if there be more than one who have such Majority, and have an equal Number of Votes, then the House of Representatives shall immediately chuse by Ballot one of them for President; and if no Person have a Majority, then from the five highest on the List the said House shall in like Manner chuse the President. But in chusing the President, the Votes shall be taken by States, the Representation from each State having one Vote; A quorum for this Purpose shall consist of a Member or Members from two thirds of the States, and a Majority of all the States shall be necessary to a Choice. In every Case, after the Choice of the President, the Person having the greater Number of Votes of the Electors shall be the Vice President. But if there should remain two or more who have equal Votes, the Senate shall chuse from them by Ballot the Vice President.

The Congress may determine the Time of chusing the Electors, and the Day on which they shall give their Votes; which Day shall be the same throughout the United States.

No person except a natural born Citizen, or a Citizen of the United States, at the time of the Adoption of this Constitution, shall be eligible to the Office of President; neither shall any Person be eligible to that Office who shall not have attained to the Age of thirty five Years, and been fourteen Years a Resident within the United States.

In Case of the Removal of the President from Office, or of his Death, Resignation or Inability to discharge the Powers and Duties of the said Office, the same shall devolve on the Vice President, and the Congress may by Law provide for the Case of Removal, Death, Resignation or Inability, both of the President and Vice President, declaring what Officer shall then act as President, and such Officer shall act accordingly, until the Disability be removed, or a President shall be elected.

The President shall, at stated Times, receive for his Services, a Compensation, which shall neither be increased nor diminished during the Period for which he shall have been elected, and he shall not receive within that Period any other Emolument from the United States, or any of them.

Before he enter on the Execution of his Office, he shall take the following Oath or Affirmation: "I do solemnly swear (or affirm) that I will faithfully execute the Office of President of the United States, and will to the best of my Ability, preserve, protect and defend the Constitution of the United States."

Section 2.   The President shall be Commander in Chief of the Army and Navy of the United States, and of the Militia of the several States, when called into the actual Service of the United States; he may require the Opinion, in writing, of the principal Officer in each of the executive Departments, upon any Subject relating to the Duties of their respective Offices, and he shall have Power to grant Reprieves and Pardons for Offenses against the United States, except in Cases of Impeachment.

He shall have Power, by and with the Advice and Consent of the Senate to make Treaties, provided two thirds of the Senators present concur; and he shall nominate, and by and with the Advice and Consent of the Senate, shall appoint Ambassadors, other public Ministers and Consuls, Judges of the supreme Court, and all other Officers of the United States, whose Appointments are not herein otherwise provided for, and which shall be established by Law; but the Congress may by Law vest the Appointment of such inferior Officers, as they think proper, in the President alone, in the Courts of Law, or in the Heads of Departments.

The President shall have Power to fill up all Vacancies that may happen during the Recess of the Senate, by granting Commissions which shall expire at the End of their next Session.

Section 3.   He shall from time to time give to the Congress Information of the State of the Union, and recommend to their Consideration such Measures as he shall judge necessary and expedient; he may, on extraordinary Occasions, convene both Houses, or either of them, and in Case of Disagreement between them, with Respect to the Time of Adjournment, he may adjourn them to such Time as he shall think proper; he shall receive Ambassadors and other public Ministers; he shall take Care that the Laws be faithfully executed, and shall Commission all the Officers of the United States.

Section 4.   The President, Vice President and all civil Officers of the United States, shall be removed from Office on Impeachment for, and Conviction of, Treason, Bribery, or other high Crimes and Misdemeanors.

Article III

Section 1.   The judicial Power of the United States, shall be vested in one supreme Court, and in such inferior Courts as the Congress may from time to time ordain and establish. The Judges, both of the supreme and inferior Courts, shall hold their Offices during good Behaviour, and shall, at stated Times, receive for their Services a Compensation, which shall not be diminished during their Continuance in Office.

Section 2.   The judicial Power shall extend to all Cases, in Law and Equity, arising under this Constitution, the Laws of the United States, and Treaties made, or which shall be made, under their Authority;—to all Cases affecting Ambassadors, other public Ministers and Consuls;—to all Cases of admiralty and maritime Jurisdiction;—to Controversies to which the United States shall be a Party;—to Controversies between two or more States;—between a State and Citizens of another State;—between Citizens of different States;—between Citizens of the same State claiming Lands under Grants of different States, and between a State, or the Citizens thereof, and foreign States, Citizens or Subjects.

In all Cases affecting Ambassadors, other public Ministers and Consuls, and those in which a State shall be a Party, the supreme Court shall have original

Jurisdiction. In all the other Cases before mentioned, the supreme Court shall have appellate Jurisdiction, both as to Law and Fact, with such Exceptions, and under such Regulations as the Congress shall make.

The Trial of all Crimes, except in Cases of Impeachment, shall be by Jury; and such Trial shall be held in the State where the said Crimes shall have been committed; but when not committed within any State, the Trial shall be at such Place or Places as the Congress may by Law have directed.

Section 3.   Treason against the United States, shall consist only in levying War against them, or, in adhering to their Enemies, giving them Aid and Comfort. No Person shall be convicted of Treason unless on the Testimony of two Witnesses to the same overt Act, or on Confession in open Court.

The Congress shall have Power to declare the Punishment of Treason, but no Attainder of Treason shall work Corruption of Blood, or Forfeiture except during the Life of the Person attainted.

Article IV

Section 1.   Full Faith and Credit shall be given in each State to the public Acts, Records, and judicial Proceedings of every other State. And the Congress may by general Laws prescribe the Manner in which such Acts, Records and Proceedings shall be proved, and the Effect thereof.

Section 2.   The Citizens of each State shall be entitled to all Privileges and Immunities of Citizens in the several States.

A Person charged in any State with Treason, Felony, or other Crime, who shall flee from Justice, and be found in another State, shall on Demand of the executive Authority of the State from which he fled, be delivered up, to be removed to the State having Jurisdiction of the Crime.

No Person held to Service or Labour in one State, under the Laws thereof, escaping into another, shall, in Consequence of any Law or Regulation therein, be discharged from such Service or Labour, but shall be delivered up on Claim of the Party to whom such Service or Labour may be due.

Section 3.   New States may be admitted by the Congress into this Union; but no new State shall be formed or erected within the Jurisdiction of any other State; nor any State be formed by the Junction of two or more States, or Parts of States, without the Consent of the Legislatures of the States concerned as well as of the Congress.

The Congress shall have Power to dispose of and make all needful Rules and Regulations respecting the Territory or other Property belonging to the United States; and nothing in this Constitution shall be so construed as to Prejudice any Claims of the United States, or of any particular State.

Section 4.   The United States shall guarantee to every State in this Union a Republican Form of Government, and shall protect each of them against Invasion; and on Application of the Legislature, or of the Executive (when the Legislature cannot be convened) against domestic Violence.

Article V

The Congress, whenever two thirds of both Houses shall deem it necessary, shall propose Amendments to this Constitution, or, on the Application of the Legislatures of two thirds of the several States, shall call a Convention for proposing Amendments, which, in either Case, shall be valid to all Intents and Purposes, as part of this Constitution, when ratified by the Legislatures of three fourths of the several States, or by Conventions in three fourths thereof, as the one or the other Mode of Ratification may be proposed by the Congress; Provided that no Amendment which may be made prior to the Year One thousand eight hundred and eight shall in any Manner affect the first and fourth Clauses in the Ninth Section of the first Article; and that no State, without its Consent, shall be deprived of its equal Suffrage in the Senate.

Article VI

All Debts contracted and Engagements entered into, before the Adoption of this Constitution shall be as valid against the United States under this Constitution, as under the Confederation.

This Constitution, and the Laws of the United States which shall be made in Pursuance thereof; and all Treaties made, or which shall be made, under the Authority of the United States, shall be the supreme Law of the Land; and the Judges in every State shall be bound thereby, any Thing in the Constitution or Laws of any State to the Contrary notwithstanding.

The Senators and Representatives before mentioned, and the Members of the several State Legislatures, and all executive and judicial Officers, both of the United States and of the several States, shall be bound by Oath or Affirmation, to support this Constitution; but no religious Test shall ever be required as a Qualification to any Office or public Trust under the United States.

Article VII

The Ratification of the Conventions of nine States shall be sufficient for the Establishment of this Constitution between the States so ratifying the Same.

Amendment I [1791]

Congress shall make no law respecting an establishment of religion, or prohibiting the free exercise thereof; or abridging the freedom of speech, or of the press; or the right of the people peaceably to assemble, and to petition the Government for a redress of grievances.

Amendment II [1791]

A well regulated Militia, being necessary to the security of a free State, the right of the people to keep and bear Arms, shall not be infringed.

Amendment III [1791]

No Soldier shall, in time of peace be quartered in any house, without the consent of the Owner, nor in time of war, but in a manner to be prescribed by law.

Amendment IV [1791]

The right of the people to be secure in their persons, houses, papers, and effects, against unreasonable searches and seizures, shall not be violated, and no Warrants shall issue, but upon probable cause, supported by Oath or affirmation, and particularly describing the place to be searched, and the persons or things to be seized.

Amendment V [1791]

No person shall be held to answer for a capital, or otherwise infamous crime, unless on a presentment or indictment of a Grand Jury, except in cases arising in the land or naval forces, or in the Militia, when in actual service in time of War or public danger; nor shall any person be subject for the same offence to be twice put in jeopardy of life or limb; nor shall be compelled in any criminal case to be a witness against himself, nor be deprived of life, liberty, or property, without due process of law; nor shall private property be taken for public use, without just compensation.

Amendment VI [1791]

In all criminal prosecutions, the accused shall enjoy the right to a speedy and public trial, by an impartial jury of the State and district wherein the crime shall have been committed, which district shall have been previously ascertained by law, and to be informed of the nature and cause of the accusation; to be confronted with the witnesses against him; to have compulsory process for obtaining witnesses in his favor, and to have the Assistance of Counsel for his defence.

Amendment VII [1791]

In Suits at common law, where the value in controversy shall exceed twenty dollars, the right of trial by jury shall be preserved, and no fact tried by jury, shall be otherwise reexamined in any Court of the United States, than according to the rules of the common law.

Amendment VIII [1791]

Excessive bail shall not be required, nor excessive fines imposed, nor cruel and unusual punishments inflicted.

Amendment IX [1791]

The enumeration in the Constitution, of certain rights, shall not be construed to deny or disparage others retained by the people.

Amendment X [1791]

The powers not delegated to the United States by the Constitution, nor prohibited by it to the States, are reserved to the States respectively, or to the people.

Amendment XI [1798]

The Judicial power of the United States shall not be construed to extend to any suit in law or equity, commenced or prosecuted against one of the United States by Citizens of another State, or by Citizens or Subjects of any Foreign State.

Amendment XII [1804]

The Electors shall meet in their respective states, and vote by ballot for President and Vice-President, one of whom, at least, shall not be an inhabitant of the same state with themselves; they shall name in their ballots the person voted for as President, and in distinct ballots the person voted for as Vice-President, and they shall make distinct lists of all persons voted for as President, and of all persons voted for as Vice-President, and of the number of votes for each, which lists they shall sign and certify, and transmit sealed to the seat of the government of the United States, directed to the President of the Senate;—The President of the Senate shall, in the presence of the Senate and House of Representatives, open all the certificates and the votes shall then be counted;—The person having the greatest number of votes for President, shall be the President, if such number be a majority of the whole number of Electors appointed; and if no person have such majority, then from the persons having the highest numbers not exceeding three on the list of those voted for as President, the House of Representatives shall choose immediately, by ballot, the President. But in choosing the President, the votes shall be taken by states, the representation from each state having one vote; a quorum for this purpose shall consist of a member or members from two-thirds of the states, and a majority of all states shall be necessary to a choice. And if the House of Representatives shall not choose a President whenever the right of choice shall devolve upon them, before the fourth day of March next following, then the Vice-President shall act as President, as in the case of the death or other constitutional disability of the President.—The person having the greatest number of votes as Vice-President, shall be the Vice-President, if such number be a majority of the whole number of Electors appointed, and if no person have a majority, then from the two highest numbers on the list, the Senate shall choose the Vice-President; a quorum for the purpose shall consist of two-thirds of the whole number of Senators, and a majority of the whole number shall be necessary to a choice. But no person constitutionally ineligible to the office of President shall be eligible to that of Vice-President of the United States.

Amendment XIII [1865]

Section 1.   Neither slavery nor involuntary servitude, except as a punishment for crime whereof the party shall have been duly convicted, shall exist within the United States, or any place subject to their jurisdiction.

Section 2.   Congress shall have power to enforce this article by appropriate legislation.

Amendment XIV [1868]

Section 1.   All persons born or naturalized in the United States, and subject to the jurisdiction thereof, are citizens of the United States and of the State wherein they reside. No State shall make or enforce any law which shall abridge the privileges or immunities of citizens of the United States; nor shall any State deprive any person of life, liberty, or property, without due process of law; nor deny to any person within its jurisdiction the equal protection of the laws.

Section 2.   Representatives shall be apportioned among the several States according to their respective numbers, counting the whole number of persons in each State, excluding Indians not taxed. But when the right to vote at any election for the choice of electors for President and Vice President of the United States, Representatives in Congress, the Executive and Judicial officers of a State, or the members of the Legislature thereof, is denied to any of the male inhabitants of such State, being twenty-one years of age, and citizens of the United States, or in any way abridged, except for participation in rebellion, or other crime, the basis of representation therein shall be reduced in the proportion which the number of such male citizens shall bear to the whole number of male citizens twenty-one years of age in such State.

Section 3.   No person shall be a Senator or Representative in Congress, or elector of President and Vice President, or hold any office, civil or military, under the United States, or under any State, who having previously taken an oath, as a member of Congress, or as an officer of the United States, or as a member of any State legislature, or as an executive or judicial officer of any State, to support the Constitution of the United States, shall have engaged in insurrection or rebellion against the same, or given aid or comfort to the enemies thereof. But Congress may by a vote of two-thirds of each House, remove such disability.

Section 4.   The validity of the public debt of the United States, authorized by law, including debts incurred for payment of pensions and bounties for services in suppressing insurrection or rebellion, shall not be questioned. But neither the United States nor any State shall assume or pay any debt or obligation incurred in aid of insurrection or rebellion against the United States, or any claim for the loss or emancipation of any slave; but all such debts, obligations and claims shall be held illegal and void.

Section 5.   The Congress shall have power to enforce, by appropriate legislation, the provisions of this article.

Amendment XV [1870]

Section 1.   The right of citizens of the United States to vote shall not be denied or abridged by the United States or by any State on account of race, color, or previous condition of servitude.

Section 2.   The Congress shall have power to enforce this article by appropriate legislation.

Amendment XVI [1913]

The Congress shall have power to lay and collect taxes on incomes, from whatever source derived, without apportionment among the several States, and without regard to any census or enumeration.

Amendment XVII [1913]

Section 1.   The Senate of the United States shall be composed of two Senators from each State, elected by the people thereof, for six years; and each Senator shall have one vote. The electors in each State shall have the qualifications requisite for electors of the most numerous branch of the State legislatures.

Section 2.   When vacancies happen in the representation of any State in the Senate, the executive authority of such State shall issue writs of election to fill such vacancies: Provided, That the legislature of any State may empower the executive thereof to make temporary appointments until the people fill the vacancies by election as the legislature may direct.

Section 3.   This amendment shall not be so construed as to affect the election or term of any Senator chosen before it becomes valid as part of the Constitution.

Amendment XVIII [1919]

Section 1.   After one year from the ratification of this article the manufacture, sale, or transportation of intoxicating liquors within, the importation thereof into, or the exportation thereof from the United States and all territory subject to the jurisdiction thereof for beverage purposes is hereby prohibited.

Section 2.   The Congress and the several States shall have concurrent power to enforce this article by appropriate legislation.

Section 3.   This article shall be inoperative unless it shall have been ratified as an amendment to the Constitution by the legislatures of the several States, as provided in the Constitution, within seven years from the date of the submission hereof to the States by the Congress.

Amendment XIX [1920]

Section 1.   The right of citizens of the United States to vote shall not be denied or abridged by the United States or by any State on account of sex.

Section 2.   Congress shall have power to enforce this article by appropriate legislation.

Amendment XX [1933]

Section 1.   The terms of the President and Vice President shall end at noon on the 20th day of January, and the terms of Senators and Representatives at noon on the 3d day of January, of the years in which such terms would have ended if this article had not been ratified; and the terms of their successors shall then begin.

Section 2.   The Congress shall assemble at least once in every year, and such meeting shall begin at noon on the 3d day of January, unless they shall by law appoint a different day.

Section 3.   If, at the time fixed for the beginning of the term of the President, the President elect shall have died, the Vice President elect shall become President. If the President shall not have been chosen before the time fixed for the beginning of his term, or if the President elect shall have failed to qualify, then the Vice President elect shall act as President until a President shall have qualified; and the Congress may by law provide for the case wherein neither a President elect nor a Vice President elect shall have qualified, declaring who shall then act as President, or the manner in which one who is to act shall be selected, and such person shall act accordingly until a President or Vice President shall have qualified.

Section 4.   The Congress may by law provide for the case of the death of any of the persons from whom the House of Representatives may choose a President whenever the right of choice shall have devolved upon them, and for the case of the death of any of the persons from whom the Senate may choose a Vice President whenever the right of choice shall have devolved upon them.

Section 5.   Sections 1 and 2 shall take effect on the 15th day of October following the ratification of this article.

Section 6.   This article shall be inoperative unless it shall have been ratified as an amendment to the Constitution by the legislatures of three-fourths of the several States within seven years from the date of its submission.

Amendment XXI [1933]

Section 1.   The eighteenth article of amendment to the Constitution of the United States is hereby repealed.

Section 2.   The transportation or importation into any State, Territory, or possession of the United States for delivery or use therein of intoxicating liquors, in violation of the laws thereof, is hereby prohibited.

Section 3.   This article shall be inoperative unless it shall have been ratified as an amendment to the Constitution by conventions in the several States, as provided in the Constitution, within seven years from the date of the submission hereof to the States by the Congress.

Amendment XXII [1951]

Section 1. No person shall be elected to the office of the President more than twice, and no person who has held the office of President, or acted as President, for more than two years of a term to which some other person was elected President shall be elected to the office of President more than once. But this Article shall not apply to any person holding the office of President when this Article was proposed by the Congress, and shall not prevent any person who may be holding the office of President, or acting as President, during the term within which this Article becomes operative from holding the office of President or acting as President during the remainder of such term.

Section 2. This article shall be inoperative unless it shall have been ratified as an amendment to the Constitution by the legislatures of three-fourths of the several States within seven years from the date of its submission to the States by the Congress.

Amendment XXIII [1961]

Section 1. The District constituting the seat of Government of the United States shall appoint in such manner as the Congress may direct:

A number of electors of President and Vice President equal to the whole number of Senators and Representatives in Congress to which the District would be entitled if it were a State, but in no event more than the least populous state; they shall be in addition to those appointed by the states, but they shall be considered, for the purposes of the election of President and Vice President, to be electors appointed by a state; and they shall meet in the District and perform such duties as provided by the twelfth article of amendment.

Section 2. The Congress shall have power to enforce this article by appropriate legislation.

Amendment XXIV [1964]

Section 1. The right of citizens of the United States to vote in any primary or other election for President or Vice President, for electors for President or Vice President, or for Senator or Representative in Congress, shall not be denied or abridged by the United States, or any State by reason of failure to pay any poll tax or other tax.

Section 2. The Congress shall have power to enforce this article by appropriate legislation.

Amendment XXV [1967]

Section 1. In case of the removal of the President from office or of his death or resignation, the Vice President shall become President.

Section 2. Whenever there is a vacancy in the office of the Vice President, the President shall nominate a Vice President who shall take office upon confirmation by a majority vote of both Houses of Congress.

Section 3. Whenever the President transmits to the President pro tempore of the Senate and the Speaker of the House of Representatives his written declaration that he is unable to discharge the powers and duties of his office, and until he transmits to them a written declaration to the contrary, such powers and duties shall be discharged by the Vice President as Acting President.

Section 4.   Whenever the Vice President and a majority of either the principal officers of the executive departments or of such other body as Congress may by law provide, transmit to the President pro tempore of the Senate and the Speaker of the House of Representatives their written declaration that the President is unable to discharge the powers and duties of his office, the Vice President shall immediately assume the powers and duties of the office as Acting President.

Thereafter, when the President transmits to the President pro tempore of the Senate and the Speaker of the House of Representatives his written declaration that no inability exists, he shall resume the powers and duties of his office unless the Vice President and a majority of either the principal officers of the executive department or of such other body as Congress may by law provide, transmit within four days to the President pro tempore of the Senate and the Speaker of the House of Representatives their written declaration that the President is unable to discharge the powers and duties of his office. Thereupon Congress shall decide the issue, assembling within forty-eight hours for that purpose if not in session. If the Congress, within twenty-one days after receipt of the latter written declaration, or, if Congress is not in session, within twenty-one days after Congress is required to assemble, determines by two-thirds vote of both Houses that the President is unable to discharge the powers and duties of his office, the Vice President shall continue to discharge the same as Acting President; otherwise, the President shall resume the powers and duties of his office.

Amendment XXVI [1971]

Section 1.   The right of citizens of the United States, who are eighteen years of age or older, to vote shall not be denied or abridged by the United States or by any State on account of age.

Section 2.   The Congress shall have power to enforce this article by appropriate legislation.

Amendment XXVII [1992]

No law, varying the compensation for the services of the Senators and Representatives, shall take effect, until an election of Representatives shall have intervened.

SPANISH EQUIVALENTS FOR IMPORTANT LEGAL TERMS IN ENGLISH

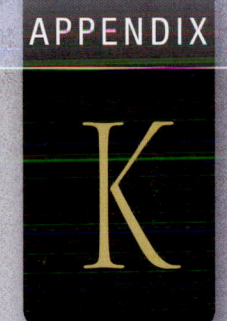

Abandoned property: bienes abandonados

Acceptance: aceptación; consentimiento; acuerdo

Acceptor: aceptante

Accession: toma de posesión; aumento; accesión

Accommodation indorser: avalista de favor

Accommodation party: firmante de favor

Accord: acuerdo; convenio; arregio

Accord and satisfaction: transacción ejecutada

Act of state doctrine: doctrina de acto de gobierno

Administrative law: derecho administrativo

Administrative process: procedimiento o metódo administrativo

Administrator: administrador (-a)

Adverse possession: posesión de hecho susceptible de proscripción adquisitiva

Affirmative action: acción afirmativa

Affirmative defense: defensa afirmativa

After-acquired property: bienes adquiridos con posterioridad a un hecho dado

Agency: mandato; agencia

Agent: mandatorio; agente; representante

Agreement: convenio; acuerdo; contrato

Alien corporation: empresa extranjera

Allonge: hojas adicionales de endosos

Answer: contestación de la demande; alegato

Anticipatory repudiation: anuncio previo de las partes de su imposibilidad de cumplir con el contrato

Appeal: apelación; recurso de apelación

Appellate jurisdiction: jurisdicción de apelaciones

Appraisal right: derecho de valuación

Arbitration: arbitraje

Arson: incendio intencional

Articles of partnership: contrato social

Artisan's lien: derecho de retención que ejerce al artesano

Assault: asalto; ataque; agresión

Assignment of rights: transmisión; transferencia; cesión

Assumption of risk: no resarcimiento por exposición voluntaria al peligro

Attachment: auto judicial que autoriza el embargo; embargo

Bailee: depositario

Bailment: depósito; constitución en depósito

Bailor: depositante

Bankruptcy trustee: síndico de la quiebra

Battery: agresión; física

Bearer: portador; tenedor

Bearer instrument: documento al portador

Bequest or legacy: legado (de bienes muebles)

Bilateral contract: contrato bilateral

Bill of lading: conocimiento de embarque; carta de porte

Bill of Rights: declaración de derechos

Binder: póliza de seguro provisoria; recibo de pago a cuenta del precio

Blank indorsement: endoso en blanco

Blue sky laws: leyes reguladoras del comercio bursátil

Bond: título de crédito; garantía; caución

Bond indenture: contrato de emisión de bonos; contrato del empréstito

Breach of contract: incumplimiento de contrato

Brief: escrito; resumen; informe

Burglary: violación de domicilio

Business judgment rule: regla de juicio comercial

Business tort: agravio comercial

Case law: ley de casos; derecho casuístico

Cashier's check: cheque de caja

Causation in fact: causalidad en realidad

Cease-and-desist order: orden para cesar y desistir

Certificate of deposit: certificado de depósito

Certified check: cheque certificado

Charitable trust: fideicomiso para fines benéficos

Chattel: bien mueble

Check: cheque

Chose in action: derecho inmaterial; derecho de acción

Civil law: derecho civil

Close corporation: sociedad de un solo accionista o de un grupo restringido de accionistas

Closed shop: taller agremiado (emplea solamente a miembros de un gremio)

Closing argument: argumento al final

Codicil: codicilo

Collateral: garantía; bien objeto de la garantía real

Comity: cortesía; cortesía entre naciones

Commercial paper: instrumentos negociables; documentos a valores commerciales

Common law: derecho consuetudinario; derecho común; ley común

Common stock: acción ordinaria

Comparative negligence: negligencia comparada

Compensatory damages: daños y perjuicios reales o compensatorios

Concurrent conditions: condiciones concurrentes

Concurrent jurisdiction: competencia concurrente de varios tribunales para entender en una misma causa

Concurring opinion: opinión concurrente

Condition: condición

Condition precedent: condición suspensiva

Condition subsequent: condición resolutoria

Confiscation: confiscación

Confusion: confusión; fusión

Conglomerate merger: fusión de firmas que operan en distintos mercados

Consent decree: acuerdo entre las partes aprobado por un tribunal

Consequential damages: daños y perjuicios indirectos

Consideration: consideración; motivo; contraprestación

Consolidation: consolidación

Constructive delivery: entrega simbólica

Constructive trust: fideicomiso creado por aplicación de la ley

Consumer protection law: ley para proteger el consumidor

Contract: contrato

Contract under seal: contrato formal o sellado

Contributory negligence: negligencia de la parte actora

Conversion: usurpación; conversión de valores

Copyright: derecho de autor

Corporation: sociedad anómina; corporación; persona juridica

Co-sureties: cogarantes

Counterclaim: reconvención; contrademanda

Counteroffer: contraoferta

Course of dealing: curso de transacciones

Course of performance: curso de cumplimiento

Covenant: pacto; garantía; contrato

Covenant not to sue: pacto or contrato a no demandar

Covenant of quiet enjoyment: garantía del uso y goce pacífico del inmueble

Creditors' composition agreement: concordato preventivo

Crime: crimen; delito; contravención

Criminal law: derecho penal

Cross-examination: contrainterrogatorio

Cure: cura; cuidado; derecho de remediar un vicio contractual

Customs receipts: recibos de derechos aduaneros

Damages: daños; indemnización por daños y perjuicios

Debit card: tarjeta de dé bito

Debtor: deudor

Debt securities: seguridades de deuda

Deceptive advertising: publicidad engañosa

Deed: escritura; título; acta translativa de domino

Defamation: difamación

Delegation of duties: delegación de obligaciones

Demand deposit: depósito a la vista

Depositions: declaración de un testigo fuera del tribunal

Devise: legado; deposición testamentaria (bienes inmuebles)

Direct examination: interrogatorio directo; primer interrogatorio

Directed verdict: veredicto según orden del juez y sin participación activa del jurado

Disaffirmance: repudiación; renuncia; anulación

Discharge: descargo; liberación; cumplimiento

Disclosed principal: mandante revelado

Discovery: descubrimiento; producción de la prueba

Dissenting opinion: opinión disidente

Dissolution: disolución; terminación

Diversity of citizenship: competencia de los tribunales federales para entender en causas cuyas partes intervinientes son cuidadanos de distintos estados

Divestiture: extinción premature de derechos reales
Dividend: dividendo
Docket: orden del día; lista de causas pendientes
Domestic corporation: sociedad local
Draft: orden de pago; letrade cambio
Drawee: girado; beneficiario
Drawer: librador
Duress: coacción; violencia

Easement: servidumbre
Embezzlement: desfalco; malversación
Eminent domain: poder de expropiación
Employment discrimination: discriminación en el empleo
Entrepreneur: empresario
Environmental law: ley ambiental
Equal dignity rule: regla de dignidad egual
Equity security: tipo de participación en una sociedad
Estate: propiedad; patrimonio; derecho
Estop: impedir; prevenir
Ethical issue: cuestión ética
Exclusive jurisdiction: competencia exclusiva
Exculpatory clause: cláusula eximente
Executed contract: contrato ejecutado
Execution: ejecución; cumplimiento
Executor: albacea
Executory contract: contrato aún no completamente consumado
Executory interest: derecho futuro
Express contract: contrato expreso
Expropriation: expropriación

Federal question: caso federal
Fee simple: pleno dominio; dominio absoluto
Fee simple absolute: dominio absoluto
Fee simple defeasible: dominio sujeta a una condición resolutoria
Felony: crimen; delito grave
Fictitious payee: beneficiario ficticio
Fiduciary: fiduciaro
Firm offer: oferta en firme
Fixture: inmueble por destino, incorporación a anexación
Floating lien: gravamen continuado

Foreign corporation: sociedad extranjera; U.S. sociedad constituída en otro estado
Forgery: falso; falsificación
Formal contract: contrato formal
Franchise: privilegio; franquicia; concesión
Franchisee: persona que recibe una concesión
Franchisor: persona que vende una concesión
Fraud: fraude; dolo; engaño
Future interest: bien futuro

Garnishment: embargo de derechos
General partner: socio comanditario
General warranty deed: escritura translativa de domino con garantía de título
Gift: donación
Gift *causa mortis:* donación por causa de muerte
Gift *inter vivos:* donación entre vivos
Good faith: buena fe
Good faith purchaser: comprador de buena fe

Holder: tenedor por contraprestación
Holder in due course: tenedor legítimo
Holographic will: testamento olográfico
Homestead exemption laws: leyes que exceptúan las casas de familia de ejecución por duedas generales
Horizontal merger: fusión horizontal

Identification: identificación
Implied-in-fact contract: contrato implícito en realidad
Implied warranty: guarantía implícita
Implied warranty of merchantability: garantía implícita de vendibilidad
Impossibility of performance: imposibilidad de cumplir un contrato
Imposter: imposter
Incidental beneficiary: beneficiario incidental; beneficiario secundario
Incidental damages: daños incidentales
Indictment: auto de acusación; acusación
Indorsee: endorsatario

Indorsement: endoso
Indorser: endosante
Informal contract: contrato no formal; contrato verbal
Information: acusación hecha por el ministerio público
Injunction: mandamiento; orden de no innovar
Innkeeper's lien: derecho de retención que ejerce el posadero
Installment contract: contrato de pago en cuotas
Insurable interest: interés asegurable
Intended beneficiary: beneficiario destinado
Intentional tort: agravio; cuasidelito intenciónal
International law: derecho internaciónal
Interrogatories: preguntas escritas sometidas por una parte a la otra o a un testigo
Inter vivos trust: fideicomiso entre vivos
Intestacy laws: leyes de la condición de morir intestado
Intestate: intestado
Investment company: compañia de inversiones
Issue: emisión

Joint tenancy: derechos conjuntos en un bien inmueble en favor del beneficiario sobreviviente
Judgment *n.o.v.:* juicio no obstante veredicto
Judgment rate of interest: interés de juicio
Judicial process: acto de procedimiento; proceso jurídico
Judicial review: revisión judicial
Jurisdiction: jurisdicción

Larceny: robo; hurto
Law: derecho; ley; jurisprudencia
Lease: contrato de locación; contrato de alquiler
Leasehold estate: bienes forales
Legal rate of interest: interés legal
Legatee: legatario
Letter of credit: carta de crédito
Levy: embargo; comiso
Libel: libelo; difamación escrita
Life estate: usufructo
Limited partner: comanditario

Limited partnership: sociedad en comandita
Liquidation: liquidación; realización
Lost property: objetos perdidos

Majority opinion: opinión de la mayoría
Maker: persona que realiza u ordena; librador
Mechanic's lien: gravamen de constructor
Mediation: mediación; intervención
Merger: fusión
Mirror image rule: fallo de reflejo
Misdemeanor: infracción; contravención
Mislaid property: bienes extraviados
Mitigation of damages: reducción de daños
Mortgage: hypoteca
Motion to dismiss: excepción parentoria
Mutual fund: fondo mutual

Negotiable instrument: instrumento negociable
Negotiation: negociación
Nominal damages: daños y perjuicios nominales
Novation: novación
Nuncupative will: testamento nuncupativo

Objective theory of contracts: teoria objetiva de contratos
Offer: oferta
Offeree: persona que recibe una oferta
Offeror: oferente
Order instrument: instrumento o documento a la orden
Original jurisdiction: jurisdicción de primera instancia
Output contract: contrato de producción

Parol evidence rule: regla relativa a la prueba oral
Partially disclosed principal: mandante revelado en parte
Partnership: sociedad colectiva; asociación; asociación de participación
Past consideration: causa o contraprestación anterior

Patent: patente; privilegio
Pattern or practice: muestra o práctica
Payee: beneficiario de un pago
Penalty: pena; penalidad
Per capita: por cabeza
Per stirpes: por estirpe
Perfection: perfeción
Performance: cumplimiento; ejecución
Personal defenses: excepciones personales
Personal property: bienes muebles
Plea bargaining: regateo por un alegato
Pleadings: alegatos
Pledge: prenda
Police powers: poders de policia y de prevención del crimen
Policy: póliza
Positive law: derecho positivo; ley positiva
Possibility of reverter: posibilidad de reversión
Precedent: precedente
Preemptive right: derecho de prelación
Preferred stock: acciones preferidas
Premium: recompensa; prima
Presentment warranty: garantía de presentación
Price discrimination: discriminación en los precios
Principal: mandante; principal
Privity: nexo jurídico
Privity of contract: relación contractual
Probable cause: causa probable
Probate: verificación; verificación del testamento
Probate court: tribunal de sucesiones y tutelas
Proceeds: resultados; ingresos
Profit: beneficio; utilidad; lucro
Promise: promesa
Promisee: beneficiario de una promesa
Promisor: promtente
Promissory estoppel: impedimento promisorio
Promissory note: pagaré; nota de pago
Promoter: promotor; fundador
Proximate cause: causa inmediata o próxima

Proxy: apoderado; poder
Punitive, or exemplary, damages: daños y perjuicios punitivos o ejemplares

Qualified indorsement: endoso con reservas
Quasi contract: contrato tácito o implícito
Quitclaim deed: acto de transferencia de una propiedad por finiquito, pero sin ninguna garantía sobre la validez del título transferido

Ratification: ratificación
Real property: bienes inmuebles
Reasonable doubt: duda razonable
Rebuttal: refutación
Recognizance: promesa; compromiso; reconocimiento
Recording statutes: leyes estatales sobre registros oficiales
Redress: reporacíon
Reformation: rectificación; reforma; corrección
Rejoinder: dúplica; contrarréplica
Release: liberación; renuncia a un derecho
Remainder: substitución; reversión
Remedy: recurso; remedio; reparación
Replevin: acción reivindicatoria; reivindicación
Reply: réplica
Requirements contract: contrato de suministro
Res judicata: cosa juzgada; res judicata
Rescission: rescisión
Respondeat superior: responsabilidad del mandante o del maestro
Restitution: restitución
Restrictive indorsement: endoso restrictivo
Resulting trust: fideicomiso implícito
Reversion: reversión; sustitución
Revocation: revocación; derogación
Right of contribution: derecho de contribución
Right of reimbursement: derecho de reembolso
Right of subrogation: derecho de subrogación
Right-to-work law: ley de libertad de trabajo

Robbery: robo
Rule 10b-5: Regla 10b-5

Sale: venta; contrato de compreventa
Sale on approval: venta a ensayo; venta sujeta a la aprobación del comprador
Sale or return: venta con derecho de devolución
Sales contract: contrato de compraventa; boleto de compraventa
Satisfaction: satisfacción; pago
Scienter: a sabiendas
S corporation: S corporación
Secured party: acreedor garantizado
Secured transaction: transacción garantizada
Securities: volares; titulos; seguridades
Security agreement: convenio de seguridad
Security interest: interés en un bien dado en garantía que permite a quien lo detenta venderlo en caso de incumplimiento
Service mark: marca de identificación de servicios
Shareholder's derivative suit: acción judicial entablada por un accionista en nombre de la sociedad
Signature: firma; rúbrica
Slander: difamación oral; calumnia
Sovereign immunity: immunidad soberana
Special indorsement: endoso especial; endoso a la orden de una person en particular
Specific performance: ejecución precisa, según los términos del contrato
Spendthrift trust: fideicomiso para pródigos
Stale check: cheque vencido
Stare decisis: acatar las decisiones, observar los precedentes
Statutory law: derecho estatutario; derecho legislado; derecho escrito
Stock: acciones

Stock warrant: certificado para la compra de acciones
Stop-payment order: orden de suspensión del pago de un cheque dada por el librador del mismo
Strict liability: responsabilidad unconditional
Summary judgment: fallo sumario

Tangible property: bienes corpóreos
Tenancy at will: inquilino por tiempo indeterminado (según la voluntad del propietario)
Tenancy by sufferance: posesión por tolerancia
Tenancy by the entirety: locación conyugal conjunta
Tenancy for years: inquilino por un término fijo
Tenancy in common: specie de copropiedad indivisa
Tender: oferta de pago; oferta de ejecución
Testamentary trust: fideicomiso testamentario
Testator: testador (-a)
Third party beneficiary contract: contrato para el beneficio del tercero-beneficiario
Tort: agravio; cuasidelito
Totten trust: fideicomiso creado por un depósito bancario
Trade acceptance: letra de cambio aceptada
Trade name: nombre comercial; razón social
Trademark: marca registrada
Traveler's check: cheque del viajero
Trespass to land: ingreso no authorizado a las tierras de otro
Trespass to personal property: violación de los derechos posesorios de un tercero con respecto a bienes muebles
Trust: fideicomiso; trust

Ultra vires: ultra vires; fuera de la facultad (de una sociedad anónima)

Unanimous opinion: opinión unámine
Unconscionable contract or clause: contrato leonino; cláusula leonino
Underwriter: subscriptor; asegurador
Unenforceable contract: contrato que no se puede hacer cumplir
Unilateral contract: contrato unilateral
Union shop: taller agremiado; empresa en la que todos los empleados son miembros del gremio o sindicato
Universal defenses: defensas legitimas o legales
Usage of trade: uso comercial
Usury: usura

Valid contract: contrato válido
Venue: lugar; sede del proceso
Vertical merger: fusión vertical de empresas
Void contract: contrato nulo; contrato inválido, sin fuerza legal
Voidable contract: contrato anulable
Voir dire: examen preliminar de un testigo a jurado por el tribunal para determinar su competencia
Voting trust: fideicomiso para ejercer el derecho de voto

Waiver: renuncia; abandono
Warranty of habitability: garantía de habitabilidad
Watered stock: acciones diluídos; capital inflado
White-collar crime: crimen administrativo
Writ of attachment: mandamiento de ejecución; mandamiento de embargo
Writ of *certiorari:* auto de avocación; auto de certiorari
Writ of execution: auto ejecutivo; mandamiento de ejecutión
Writ of mandamus: auto de mandamus; mandamiento; orden judicial

GLOSSARY

ABA-approved program A legal or paralegal educational program that satisfies the standards for paralegal training set forth by the American Bar Association.

acceptance In contract law, the offeree's indication to the offeror that the offeree agrees to be bound by the terms of the offeror's offer, or proposal to form a contract.

acquittal A certification or declaration following a trial that the individual accused of a crime is innocent, or free from guilt, in the eyes of the law and is thus absolved of the charges.

actionable Capable of serving as the basis of a lawsuit. An actionable claim can be pursued in a lawsuit or other court action.

active listening The act of listening attentively to the speaker's message and responding by giving appropriate feedback to show that you understand what the speaker is saying; restating the speaker's message in your own words to confirm that you accurately interpreted what was said.

actual malice Real and demonstrated evil intent. In a defamation suit, a statement made about a public figure normally must be made with actual malice (with either knowledge of its falsity or a reckless disregard of the truth) for liability to be incurred.

actus reus A guilty (prohibited) act. The commission of a prohibited act is one of the two essential elements required for criminal liability; the other element is the intent to commit a crime.

address block That part of a letter that indicates to whom the letter is addressed. The address block is placed in the upper left-hand portion of the letter, above the salutation (or reference line, if one is included).

adhesion contract A contract drafted by the dominant party and then presented to the other—adhering—party on a "take-it-or-leave-it" basis.

adjudication The act of resolving a controversy and rendering an order or decision based on a review of the evidence presented.

administrative agency A federal or state government agency established to perform a specific function. Administrative agencies are authorized by legislative acts to make and enforce rules relating to the purpose for which they were established.

administrative law A body of law created by administrative agencies in the form of rules, regulations, orders, and decisions to help carry out responsibilities.

administrative law judge (ALJ) One who presides over an administrative agency hearing and who has the power to administer oaths, take testimony, rule on questions of evidence, and make determinations otherwise authorized by law.

administrative process The procedure used by administrative agencies in the administration of law.

administrator A person appointed by a court to serve as a personal representative for a person who died intestate (without a valid will) or if the executor named in the will cannot serve.

adoption A procedure in which persons become the legal parents of a child who is not their biological child.

Advanced Paralegal Certification (APC) A credential awarded by the National Association of Legal Assistants to a Certified Paralegal (CP) or Certified Legal Assistant (CLA) whose competency in a legal specialty has been certified by examination of the paralegal's knowledge and skills in the specialty area.

adversarial system of justice A legal system in which the parties to a lawsuit are opponents, or adversaries, and present their cases in the light most favorable to themselves. The impartial decision maker (the judge or jury) determines who wins based on an application of the law to the evidence presented.

711

affidavit A written statement of facts, confirmed by the oath or affirmation of the party making it and made before a person having the authority to administer the oath or affirmation.

affirm To uphold the judgment of a lower court.

affirmative defense A response to a plaintiff's claim that does not deny the plaintiff's facts but attacks the plaintiff's legal right to bring an action.

agency A relationship between two persons in which one person (the agent) represents or acts in the place of another (the principal).

agent A person who is authorized to act for or in the place of another person (the principal).

agreement A meeting of the minds, and a requirement for a valid contract. Agreement involves two distinct events: an offer to form a contract and the acceptance of that offer by the offeree.

alimony Money paid to support a former spouse after a marriage has been terminated. The alimony may be permanent or temporary (rehabilitative).

allegation A party's statement, claim, or assertion made in a pleading to the court. The allegation sets forth the issue that the party expects to prove.

alternative dispute resolution (ADR) The resolution of disputes in ways other than those involved in the traditional judicial process. Negotiation, mediation, and arbitration are forms of ADR.

American Arbitration Association (AAA) The major organization offering arbitration services in the United States.

American Association for Paralegal Education (AAfPE) A national organization of paralegal educators; the AAfPE was established in 1981 to promote high standards for paralegal education.

American Bar Association (ABA) A voluntary national association of attorneys. The ABA plays an active role in developing educational and ethical standards for attorneys and in pursuing improvements in the administration of justice.

annotation A brief comment, an explanation of a legal point, or a case summary found in a case digest or other legal source.

annulment A court decree that invalidates (nullifies) a marriage. Although the marriage itself is deemed nonexistent, children of a marriage that is annulled are deemed legitimate.

answer A defendant's response to a plaintiff's complaint.

appeal The process of seeking a higher court's review of a lower court's decision for the purpose of correcting or changing the lower court's judgment or decision.'

appellant The party who takes an appeal from one court to another; sometimes referred to as the *petitioner*.

appellate court A court that reviews decisions made by lower courts, such as trial courts; a court of appeals.

appellate jurisdiction The power of a court to hear and decide an appeal; the authority of a court to review cases that already have been tried in a lower court and the power to make decisions about them without holding a trial. This process is called appellate review.

appellee The party against whom an appeal is taken—that is, the party who opposes setting aside or reversing the judgment; sometimes referred to as the *respondent*.

appropriation In tort law, the use by one person of another person's name, likeness, or other identifying characteristic without permission and for the benefit of the user.

arbitration A method of settling disputes in which a dispute is submitted to a disinterested third party (other than a court), who issues a decision that may or may not be legally binding.

arbitration clause A clause in a contract that provides that, in case of a dispute, the parties will determine their rights by arbitration rather than through the judicial system.

arraignment A court proceeding in which the suspect is formally charged with the criminal offense stated in the indictment. The suspect then enters a plea (guilty, not guilty, or *nolo contendere*) in response.

arrest To take into custody a person suspected of criminal activity.

arrest warrant A written order, based on probable cause and issued by a judge or public official (magistrate), commanding that the person named on the warrant be arrested by the police.

arson The willful and malicious burning of a building (and, in some states, personal property) owned by another; arson statutes have been extended to cover the destruction of any building, regardless of ownership, by fire or explosion.

articles of incorporation The document filed with the appropriate state official, usually the secretary of state, when a business is incorporated. State statutes usually prescribe what kind of information must be contained in the articles of incorporation.

assault Any word or action intended to make another person fearful of immediate physical harm; a reasonably believable threat.

associate attorney An attorney working for a law firm who is not a partner and does not have an ownership interest in the firm. Associates are usually less experienced attorneys and may be invited to become partners after working for the firm for several years.

assumption of risk Voluntarily taking on a known risk. A defense against negligence that can be used when the plaintiff has knowledge of and appreciates a danger and voluntarily exposes himself or herself to the danger.

attorney-client privilege A rule of evidence requiring that confidential communications between a client and his or her attorney (relating to their professional relationship) be kept confidential, unless the client consents to disclosure.

authentication The process of establishing the genuineness of an item that is to be introduced as evidence in a trial.

automatic stay A suspension of all judicial proceedings on the occurrence of an independent event. Under the Bankruptcy Code, the moment a petition to initiate bankruptcy proceedings is filed, all litigation or other legal action by creditors against a debtor and the debtor's property is suspended.

award In the context of ADR, the decision rendered by an arbitrator.

bail The amount of money or conditions set by the court to assure that an individual accused of a crime will appear for further criminal proceedings. If the accused person provides bail, whether in cash or by means of a bail bond, then the person is released from jail.

bankruptcy court A federal court of limited jurisdiction that hears only bankruptcy proceedings.

bankruptcy estate In bankruptcy proceedings, all of the debtor's interests in property presently held and wherever located, as well as interests in certain property to which the debtor becomes entitled within 180 days after filing for bankruptcy.

bankruptcy law The body of federal law that governs bankruptcy proceedings. The twin goals of bankruptcy law are (1) to protect a debtor by giving him or her a fresh start and (2) to ensure that creditors competing for a debtor's assets are treated fairly.

bankruptcy trustee A person appointed by the bankruptcy court to administer the debtor's estate in the interests of both the debtor and the creditors. The basic duty of the bankruptcy trustee is to collect and reduce to money the estate in property and to close up the estate as speedily as is compatible with the best interests of the parties.

battery The intentional and offensive touching of another without lawful justification.

beyond a reasonable doubt The standard used to determine the guilt or innocence of a person charged with a crime. To be guilty of a crime, a suspect must be proved guilty "beyond and to the exclusion of every reasonable doubt."

bigamy The act of entering into marriage with one person while still legally married to another.

Bill of Rights The first ten amendments to the U.S. Constitution.

billable hours Hours or fractions of hours that attorneys and paralegals spend in work that requires legal expertise and that can be billed directly to clients.

binder A written, temporary insurance policy.

binding authority Any source of law that a court must follow when deciding a case. Binding authorities include constitutions, statutes, and regulations that govern the issue being decided, as well as precedents within the jurisdiction.

binding mediation A form of ADR in which a mediator attempts to facilitate agreement between the parties but then issues a legally binding decision if no agreement is reached.

bonus An end-of-the-year payment to a salaried employee in appreciation for that employee's overtime work, diligence, or dedication to the firm.

booking The process of entering a suspect's name, offense, and arrival time into the police log (blotter) following his or her arrest.

Boolean logic As applied to Internet search engines, a system in which connecting words (primarily *and*, *or*, and *not*) are used to establish a logical relationship among search terms in order to make a search more precise.

breach To violate a legal duty by an act or a failure to act.

breach of contract The failure, without legal excuse, of a contractual party to perform the obligations assumed in a contract.

briefing a case Summarizing a case. A case brief gives the full citation, the factual background and procedural history, the issue or issues raised, the court's decision, the court's holding, and the legal reasoning on which the court based its decision. The brief may also include conclusions or notes concerning the case made by the one briefing it.

burglary Breaking and entering onto the property of another with the intent to commit a felony.

business invitee A person, such as a customer or client, who is invited onto business premises by the owner of those premises for business purposes.

business tort Wrongful interference with another's business rights.

bylaws A set of governing rules adopted by a corporation or other association.

case law Rules of law announced in court decisions.

case of first impression A case presenting a legal issue that has not yet been addressed by a court in a particular jurisdiction.

case on "all fours" A case in which all four elements of a case (the parties, the circumstances, the legal issues involved, and the remedies sought) are very similar to those in the case being researched.

case on point A case involving factual circumstances and issues that are similar to those in the case being researched.

causation in fact Causation brought about by an act or omission without which an event would not have occurred.

cease-and-desist order An administrative or judicial order prohibiting a person or business firm from conducting activities that an agency or court has deemed illegal.

certificate of incorporation (corporate charter) The document issued by a state official (usually the secretary of state) granting a corporation legal existence and the right to function.

certification Formal recognition by a private group or a state agency that an individual has satisfied the group's standards of proficiency, knowledge, and competence; ordinarily accomplished through the taking of an examination.

Certified Legal Assistant (CLA) or Certified Paralegal (CP) A legal assistant or paralegal whose legal competency has been certified by the National Association of Legal Assistants (NALA) following an examination that tests the legal assistant's knowledge and skills.

chain of custody A series describing the movement and location of evidence from the time it is obtained to the time it is presented in court. The court requires that evidence be preserved in the condition in which it was obtained if it is to be admitted into evidence at trial.

challenge An attorney's objection, during *voir dire*, to the inclusion of a particular person on the jury.

challenge for cause A *voir dire* challenge for which an attorney states the reason why a prospective juror should not be included in the jury.

charge The judge's instruction to the jury, following the attorneys' closing arguments, setting forth the rules of law that the jury must apply in reaching its decision, or verdict.

checks and balances A system in which each of the three branches of the national government—executive, legislative, and judicial—exercises a check on the actions of the other two branches.

child support The financial support necessary to provide for a child's needs. Commonly, when a marriage is terminated, the noncustodial spouse agrees or is required by the court to make child-support payments to the custodial spouse.

chronologically In a time sequence; naming or listing events in the time order in which they occurred.

circumstantial evidence Indirect evidence that is offered to establish, by inference, the likelihood of a fact that is in question.

citation In case law, a reference to the volume number, name, and page number of the reporter in which a case can be found. In statutory and administrative law, a reference to the title number, name, and section of the code in which a statute or regulation can be found. In criminal procedure, an order for a defendant to appear in court or indicating that a person has violated a legal rule.

citator A book or online service that provides the history and interpretation of a statute, regulation, or court decision and a list of the cases, statutes, and regulations that have interpreted, applied, or modified a statute or regulation.

civil law Law dealing with the definition and enforcement of private or public rights, as opposed to criminal matters.

civil law system A system of law derived from that of the Roman Empire and based on a code rather than case law; the predominant system of law in the nations of continental Europe and the nations that were once their colonies.

click-on agreement An agreement that arises when a buyer, engaging in a transaction on a computer, indicates his or her assent to be bound by the terms of an offer by clicking on a button that says, for example, "I agree"; sometimes referred to as a *click-on license* or a *click-wrap agreement.*

close corporation A corporation owned by a small group of shareholders, often family members; also called a *closely held corporation.* Shares in close corporations cannot be publicly traded on the stock market, and often other restrictions on stock transfer apply. Some close corporations qualify for special tax status as *S corporations.*

closed-ended question A question phrased in such a way that it calls for a simple "yes" or "no" answer or requires a specific answer.

closing A final phrase in a letter that is placed above the signature, such as "Sincerely" or "Very truly yours."

closing argument An argument made by each side's attorney after the cases for the plaintiff and defendant have been presented. Closing arguments are made prior to the jury charge.

code A systematic and topically organized presentation of laws, rules, or regulations.

collective bargaining The process by which labor and management negotiate the terms and conditions of employment, including wages, benefits, working conditions, and other matters.

commerce clause The provision in Article 1, Section 8, of the U.S. Constitution that gives the national government the power to regulate interstate commerce.

common law A body of law developed from custom or judicial decisions in English and U.S. courts and not by a legislature.

common law marriage A marriage that is formed solely by mutual consent and without a marriage license or ceremony. The couple must be eligible to marry, must have a present and continuing agreement to be husband and wife, must live together as husband and wife, and must hold themselves out to the public as husband and wife. Only fifteen states recognize common law marriages.

community property In certain states all property acquired during the marriage, except for inheritances or gifts received during the marriage by either marital partner. Each spouse has a one-half ownership interest in community property.

comparative negligence A theory in tort law under which the liability for injuries resulting from negligent acts is shared by all persons who were guilty of negligence (including the injured party) on the basis of each person's proportionate carelessness.

compensatory damages A money award equivalent to the actual value of injuries or damages sustained by the aggrieved party.

complaint The pleading made by a plaintiff or a charge made by the state alleging wrongdoing on the part of the defendant.

concurrent jurisdiction Jurisdiction that exists when two different courts have the power to hear a case. For example, some cases can be heard in either a federal or a state court.

confirmation letter A letter that states the substance of a previously conducted verbal discussion to provide a permanent record of the oral conversation.

conflict of interest A situation in which two or more duties or interests come into conflict, as when an attorney attempts to represent opposing parties in a legal dispute.

conflicts check A procedure for determining whether an agreement to represent a potential client will result in a conflict of interest.

consideration Something of value, such as money or the performance of an action not otherwise required, that motivates the formation of a contract. Each party must give consideration for the contract to be binding.

constitutional law Law based on the U.S. Constitution and the constitutions of the states.

constructive discharge A termination of employment that occurs when the employer causes the employee's working conditions to be so intolerable that a reasonable person in the employee's position would feel compelled to quit.

consumer A person who buys products and services for personal or household use.

consumer-debtor A debtor whose debts are primarily consumer debts—that is, debts for purchases that are primarily for household or personal use.

consumer law Statutes, agency rules, and judicial decisions protecting consumers of goods and services.

contempt of court The intentional obstruction or frustration of the court's attempt to administer justice. A party to a lawsuit may be held in contempt of court (punishable by a fine or jail sentence) for refusing to comply with a court's order.

contingency fee A legal fee that consists of a specified percentage (such as 30 percent) of the amount the plaintiff recovers in a civil lawsuit. The fee must be paid only if the plaintiff prevails in the lawsuit (recovers damages).

contract An agreement or bargain struck between parties in which each party assumes a legal duty to the other party. The requirements for a valid contract are agreement, consideration, contractual capacity, and legality.

contractual capacity The threshold mental capacity required by law for a party who enters into a contract to be bound by that contract.

continuing legal education (CLE) program Courses through which attorneys and other legal professionals extend their education beyond school.

contributory negligence A theory in tort law under which a complaining party's own negligence contributed to his or her injuries. Contributory negligence is an absolute bar to recovery in some jurisdictions.

conversion The act of wrongfully taking or retaining of a person's personal property and placing it in the service of another.

copyright The exclusive right of an author (or other creator) to publish, print, or sell an intellectual production for a statutory period of time.

corporate law Law that governs the formation, financing, merger and acquisition, and termination of corporations, as well as the rights and duties of those who own and run the corporation.

counteradvertising New advertising undertaken pursuant to a Federal Trade Commission order for the purpose of correcting earlier false claims that were made about a product.

counterclaim A claim made by a defendant in a civil lawsuit against the plaintiff; in effect, a counterclaiming defendant is suing the plaintiff.

court of equity A court that decides controversies and administers justice according to the rules, principles, and precedents of equity.

court of law A court in which the only remedies granted were things of value, such as money. Historically, in England, courts of law were distinct from courts of equity.

cram-down provision A provision of the Bankruptcy Code that allows a court to confirm a debtor's Chapter 11 reorganization plan even though only one class of creditors has accepted it. To exercise the court's right under this provision, the court must demonstrate that the plan does not discriminate unfairly against any creditors and is fair and equitable.

crime A broad term for violations of law that are punishable by the state and are codified by legislatures. The objective of criminal law is to protect the public.

criminal law Law that governs and defines those actions that are crimes and that subjects persons convicted of crimes to punishment imposed by the government (a fine or jail time).

cross-claim A claim asserted by a defendant in a civil lawsuit against another defendant or by a plaintiff against another plaintiff.

cross-examination The questioning of an opposing witness during the trial.

cyber crime A crime that occurs online, in the virtual community of the Internet, as opposed to the physical world.

cyber tort A tort committed by use of the Internet.

cyberbullying The use of communication technology to inflict harm on others by deliberate, repeated, hostile behavior.

cybernotary A legally recognized authority that can certify the validity of digital signatures.

cyberstalker A person who commits the crime of stalking in cyberspace. The cyber stalker usually finds a victim through Internet chat rooms, newsgroups, bulletin boards, or e-mail and proceeds to harass that person or put the person in reasonable fear for his or her safety or the safety of his or her immediate family.

damages Money awarded as a remedy for a civil wrong, such as a breach of contract or a tortious act.

debtor in possession (DIP) In Chapter 11 bankruptcy proceedings, a debtor who is allowed, for the benefit of all concerned, to maintain possession of the estate in bankruptcy (the business) and to continue business operations.

deceptive advertising Advertising that misleads consumers, either by unjustified claims concerning a product's performance or by the failure to disclose relevant information concerning the product's composition or performance.

deed A document by which title to property is transferred from one party to another.

defamation Anything published or publicly spoken that causes injury to another's good name, reputation, or character.

default judgment A judgment entered by a clerk or court against a party who has failed to appear in court to answer or defend against a claim that has been brought against him or her by another party.

defendant A party against whom a lawsuit is brought.

defense The reasons that a defendant offers and alleges why the plaintiff should not recover or establish what she or he seeks in a lawsuit.

defense of others The use of reasonable force to protect others from harm.

defense of property The use of reasonable force to protect one's property from the harm threatened by another. The use of deadly force in defending one's property is seldom justified.

demand letter A letter in which one party explains its legal position in a dispute and requests that the recipient take some action (such as paying money owed).

deponent A party or witness who testifies under oath during a deposition.

deposition A pretrial question-and-answer proceeding, usually conducted orally, in which a party or witness answers an attorney's questions. The answers are given under oath, and the session is recorded.

deposition transcript The official transcription of the recording taken during a deposition.

dicta A Latin term referring to nonbinding (nonprecedential) judicial statements that are not directly related to the facts or issues presented in the case and thus not essential to the holding.

digest A compilation in which brief summaries of court cases are arranged by subject and subdivided by jurisdiction and court.

direct evidence Evidence establishing the existence of a fact that is in question without relying on inferences.

direct examination The examination of a witness by the attorney who calls the witness to the stand to testify on behalf of the attorney's client.

director A person elected by the shareholders to direct corporate affairs.

disbarment A severe disciplinary sanction in which an attorney's license to practice law in the state is revoked because of unethical or illegal conduct.

discharge The termination of an obligation. A discharge in bankruptcy terminates the debtor's obligation to pay the debts discharged by the court.

discovery Formal investigation prior to trial. Opposing parties use various methods, such as interrogatories and depositions, to obtain information from each other and from witnesses to prepare for trial.

discovery plan A plan formed by the attorneys litigating a lawsuit, on behalf of their clients, that indicates the types of information that will be disclosed by each party to the other prior to trial, the testimony and evidence that each party will or may introduce at trial, and the general schedule for pretrial disclosures and events.

dissolution The formal disbanding of a partnership or a corporation.

diversion program In some jurisdictions, an alternative to prosecution that is offered to certain felony suspects to deter them from future unlawful acts.

diversity of citizenship Under the Constitution, a basis for federal district court jurisdiction over a lawsuit between (1) citizens of different states, (2) a foreign country and citizens of a state or different states, or (3) citizens of a state and citizens of a foreign country. The amount in controversy must be more than $75,000 before a federal court can take jurisdiction in such cases.

dividend A distribution of profits to corporate shareholders, disbursed in proportion to the number of shares held.

divorce A formal court proceeding that legally dissolves a marriage.

docket The list of cases entered on a court's calendar and scheduled to be heard by the court.

double billing Billing more than one client for the same billable time period.

double jeopardy To place at risk (jeopardize) a person's life or liberty twice. The Fifth Amendment to the Constitution prohibits a second prosecution for the same criminal offense.

dram shop act A state statute that imposes liability on the owners of bars, as well as those who serve alcoholic drinks to the public, for injuries resulting from accidents caused by intoxicated persons when the sellers or servers of alcoholic drinks contributed to the intoxication.

due process of law Fair, reasonable, and standard procedures that must be used by the government in any legal action against a citizen. The Fifth Amendment to the U.S. Constitution prohibits the deprivation of "life, liberty, or property without due process of law."

duty of care The duty of all persons, as established by tort law, to exercise reasonable care in dealings with others. Failure to exercise due care, which is normally determined by the reasonable person standard, is the tort of negligence.

early neutral case evaluation A form of ADR in which a neutral third party evaluates the strengths and weaknesses of the disputing parties' positions; the evaluator's opinion forms the basis for negotiating a settlement.

easement The right of a person to make limited use of another person's real property without taking anything from the property.

elder law A relatively new legal specialty that involves servicing the needs of older clients, such as estate planning and making arrangements for long-term care.

electronic filing (e-filing) system A computer system that enables attorneys to file case documents with courts over the Internet twenty-four hours a day, seven days a week.

emancipation The legal relinquishment by a child's parents or guardian of the legal right to exercise control over the child. Usually, a child who moves out of the parents' home and supports himself or herself is considered emancipated.

embezzlement The fraudulent appropriation of the property or money of another by a person entrusted with that property or money.

eminent domain The power of government to take land for public use from private citizens for just compensation.

employment at will A common law doctrine under which employment is considered to be "at will"—that is, either party may terminate the employment relationship at any time and for any reason, unless a contract specifies otherwise.

employment manual A firm's handbook or written statement that specifies the policies and procedures that govern the firm's employees and employer-employee relationships.

enabling legislation A statute enacted by a legislature that authorizes the creation of an administrative agency and specifies the name, purpose, composition, and powers of the agency being created.

environmental impact statement (EIS) A statement required by the National Environmental Policy Act for any major federal action that will significantly affect the quality of the environment. The statement must analyze the action's impact on the environment and explore alternative actions that might be taken.

environmental law All state and federal laws or regulations enacted or issued to protect the environment and preserve environmental resources.

equitable principles and maxims Propositions or general statements of rules of law that are frequently involved in equity jurisdiction.

e-signature An electronic sound, symbol, or process attached to or logically associated with a record and executed or adopted by a person with the intent to sign the record, according to the Uniform Electronic Transactions Act.

estate administration The process in which a decedent's personal representative settles the affairs of the decedent's estate (collects assets, pays debts and taxes, and distributes the remaining assets to heirs); the process is usually overseen by a probate court.

estate planning Making arrangements, during a person's lifetime, for the transfer of property to others on the person's death. Estate planning often involves executing a will or establishing a trust fund to provide for others, such as a spouse or children, on one's death.

ethical wall A term that refers to the procedures used to create a screen around a legal employee to shield him or her from information about a case in which there is a conflict of interest.

evidence Anything that is used to prove the existence or nonexistence of a fact.

exclusionary rule In criminal procedure, a rule under which any evidence that is obtained in violation of the accused's constitutional rights, as well as any evidence derived from illegally obtained evidence, will not be admissible in court.

exclusive jurisdiction Jurisdiction that exists when a case can be heard only in a particular court, such as a federal court.

executor A person appointed by a testator to serve as a personal representative on the testator's death.

expense slip A slip of paper on which any expense, or cost, that is incurred on behalf of a client (such as the payment of court fees or long-distance telephone charges) is recorded.

expert witness A witness with professional training or substantial experience qualifying him or her to testify as to his or her opinion on a particular subject.

eyewitness A witness who testifies about an event that he or she observed or has experienced firsthand.

false imprisonment The intentional confinement or restraint of a person against his or her will.

family law Law relating to family matters, such as marriage, divorce, child support, and child custody.

federal question A question that pertains to the U.S. Constitution, acts of Congress, or treaties. A federal question provides a basis for jurisdiction by the federal courts. This jurisdiction is authorized by Article III, Section 2, of the Constitution.

Federal Rules of Civil Procedure (FRCP) The rules controlling all procedural matters in civil trials brought before the federal district courts.

federal system The system of government established by the Constitution, in which the national government and the state governments share sovereign powers.

fee simple Ownership rights entitling the holder to use, possess, or dispose of the property however he or she chooses during his or her lifetime.

felony A crime—such as arson, murder, assault, or robbery—that carries the most severe sanctions. Sanctions range from one year in a state or federal prison to life imprisonment or (in some states) the death penalty.

fiduciary relationship A relationship involving a high degree of trust and confidence.

fixed fee A fee paid to the attorney by his or her client for having provided a specified legal service, such as the creation of a simple will.

forgery The fraudulent making or altering of any writing in a way that changes the legal rights and liabilities of another.

forms file A reference file containing copies of the firm's commonly used legal documents and informational forms. The documents in the forms file serve as a model for drafting new documents.

foster care A temporary arrangement in which a family is paid by the state to care for a child for a limited period of time, often pending adoption.

fraudulent misrepresentation Any misrepresentation, either by misstatement or by omission of a material fact, knowingly made with the intention of deceiving another and on which a reasonable person would and does rely to his or her detriment.

freelance paralegal A paralegal who operates his or her own business and provides services to attorneys on a contractual basis. A freelance paralegal works under the supervision of an attorney, who assumes responsibility for the paralegal's work product.

friendly witness A witness who is biased against your client's adversary or sympathetic toward your client in a lawsuit or other legal proceeding.

garnishment A proceeding in which a creditor legally seizes a portion of a debtor's property (such as wages) that is in the possession of a third party (such as an employer).

general licensing A type of licensing in which all individuals within a specific profession or group (such as paralegals) must meet licensing requirements imposed by the state before they may legally practice their profession.

general partner A partner who participates in managing the business of a partnership and has all the rights and liabilities that arise under traditional partnership law.

genuineness of assent Knowing and voluntary assent to the contract terms. If a contract is formed as a result of mistake, misrepresentation, undue influence, or duress, genuineness of assent is lacking, and the contract will be voidable.

Good Samaritan statute A state statute stipulating that persons who provide emergency services to, or rescue, others in peril—unless they do so recklessly, thus causing further harm—cannot be sued for negligence.

grand jury The group of citizens called to decide whether probable cause exists to believe that a suspect committed the crime with which he or she has been charged and should stand trial.

guardian *ad litem* A person appointed by the court to represent the interests of a child or a mentally incompetent person before the court.

hacker A person who uses one computer to break into another.

headnote A note, usually a paragraph long, near the beginning of a reported case summarizing the court's ruling on an issue.

hearsay Testimony that is given in court by a witness who relates not what he or she knows personally but what another person said. Hearsay is generally not admissible as evidence.

holding The binding legal principle, or precedent, that is drawn from the court's decision in a case.

home page The main page of a Web site. Often, the home page serves as a table of contents to other pages at the site.

homestead exemption A law permitting the debtor to retain the family home, either in its entirety or up to a specified dollar amount, free from the claims of unsecured creditors or trustees in bankruptcy.

hornbook A single-volume scholarly discussion, or treatise, on a particular legal subject (such as property law).

hostile witness A witness who is biased against your client or friendly toward your client's adversary in a lawsuit or other legal proceeding; an adverse witness.

hung jury A jury whose members are so irreconcilably divided in their opinions that they cannot reach a verdict. The judge in this situation may order a new trial.

hypertext transfer protocol (http) An interface program that enables computers to communicate. Hypertext is a database system by which distinct objects, such as text and graphics, can be linked. A protocol is a system of formats and rules.

hypothetical question A question based on hypothesis, conjecture, or fiction.

identity theft The theft of a form of identification, such as a name, date of birth, or Social Security number, which is then used to access the victim's financial resources.

impeach To call into question the credibility of a witness by challenging the truth or accuracy of his or her trial statement.

independent adoption A privately arranged adoption, as when a doctor, lawyer, or other individual puts a couple seeking to adopt a child in contact with a pregnant woman who has decided to give up her child for adoption.

independent contractor A person who is hired to perform a specific undertaking but who is free to choose how and when to perform the work. An independent contractor may or may not be an agent.

independent paralegal (or legal technician) A paralegal who offers services directly to the public, normally for a fee, without attorney supervision. Independent paralegals assist consumers by supplying them with forms and procedural knowledge relating to simple or routine legal procedures.

indictment A charge or written accusation, issued by a grand jury, that probable cause exists to believe that a named person has committed a crime for which he or she should stand trial.

information A formal criminal charge made by a prosecutor without a grand jury indictment.

informative letter A letter that conveys certain information to a client, a witness, an adversary's counsel, or other person regarding some legal matter (such as the date, time, place, and purpose of a meeting) or a cover letter that accompanies other documents being sent to a person or court.

injunction A court decree ordering a person to do or to refrain from doing a certain act or activity.

insider trading Trading in the stock of a publicly listed corporation based on inside information about the corporation that is not available to the public. One who possesses inside information and has a duty not to disclose it to outsiders may not profit from the purchase or sale of securities based on that information until that information is available to the public.

insurable interest An interest either in a person's life or well-being or in property that is sufficiently substantial to justify insuring against injury to or death of the person or damage to the property.

insurance A contract by which an insurance company (the insurer) promises to pay a sum of money or give something of value to another (either the insured or the beneficiary) to compensate for a specified loss.

intellectual property Property that results from intellectual, creative processes. Copyrights, patents, and trademarks are examples of intellectual property.

intentional infliction of emotional distress Intentional extreme or outrageous conduct that inflicts mental injury on another.

intentional tort A wrongful act knowingly committed.

international law The law that governs relations among nations. International customs and treaties are generally considered to be two of the most important sources of international law.

interrogatories A series of written questions for which written answers are prepared and then signed under oath by a party to a lawsuit (the plaintiff or the defendant).

interviewee The person who is being interviewed.

inter vivos **trust** A trust created by the grantor (settlor) and effective during the grantor's lifetime—that is, a trust not established by a will.

intestacy laws State statutes that specify how property will be distributed when a person dies intestate (without a valid will).

intestate The state of having died without a valid will.

investigation plan A plan that lists each step involved in obtaining and verifying the facts and information that are relevant to the legal problem being investigated.

joint and several liability Shared and individual liability. In partnership law, joint and several liability means that a third party may sue one or more of the partners separately or all of them together. This is true even if one of the partners sued did not participate in or know about whatever gave rise to the cause of action.

joint custody Custody of a child following the termination of a marriage that is shared by the parents.

joint liability Shared liability. In partnership law, partners incur joint liability for partnership obligations and debts.

joint tenancy The joint ownership of property by two or more co-owners in which each co-owner owns an undivided portion of the property. On the death of one of the joint tenants, his or her interest automatically passes to the surviving joint tenant or tenants.

judgment The court's final decision regarding the rights and claims of the parties to a lawsuit.

judgment creditor A creditor who is legally entitled, by a court's judgment, to collect the amount of the judgment from a debtor.

jurisdiction The authority of a court to hear and decide a specific case.

justiciable controversy A controversy that is real and substantial, as opposed to hypothetical or academic.

KeyCite An aid to legal research developed by the editors of Westlaw. On Westlaw, KeyCite can trace case history, retrieve secondary sources, categorize legal citations by legal issue, and perform other functions.

key number A number (accompanied by the symbol of a key) corresponding to a specific topic within West's key-number system to facilitate legal research of case law.

laches A defense raised in a case in equity claiming that the plaintiff failed to bring suit in a timely manner.

larceny The wrongful or fraudulent taking and carrying away of another person's personal property with the intent to deprive the person permanently of the property.

law A body of rules of conduct established and enforced by the controlling authority (the government) of a society.

law clerk A law student working as an apprentice with a law firm, during the summer or part-time during the school year, to gain practical experience. Some law firms refer to law clerks as *summer associates*.

lay witness A witness who can truthfully and accurately testify on a fact in question without having specialized training or knowledge; an ordinary witness.

leading question A question that suggests, or "leads to," a desired answer. Interviewers may use leading questions to get responses from witnesses who otherwise would not be forthcoming. Generally, in court leading questions may be asked only of hostile witnesses.

lease In real property law, a contract by which the owner of real property (the landlord) grants to a person (the tenant) an exclusive right to use and possess the property, usually for a specified period of time, in return for rent or some other form of payment.

legal administrator An administrative employee of a law firm who manages day-to-day operations. In smaller law firms, legal administrators are usually called office managers.

legal assistant (or paralegal) A person qualified by education, training, or work experience who is employed or retained by a lawyer, law office, corporation, governmental agency or other entity who performs specifically delegated substantive legal work, for which a lawyer is responsible.

legal-assistant (or paralegal) manager An employee in a law firm who is responsible for overseeing the paralegal staff and paralegal professional development.

legal custody Custody of a child that confers on the parent the right to make major decisions about the child's life without consulting the other parent.

legal nurse consultant (LNC) A nurse who consults with legal professionals and others about medical aspects of legal claims or issues. Legal nurse consultants normally must have at least a bachelor's degree in nursing and significant nursing experience.

legal technician (or independent paralegal) A paralegal who offers services directly to the public without attorney supervision. Independent paralegals assist consumers by supplying them with forms and procedural knowledge relating to simple or routine legal procedures.

legalese Legal writing that is difficult for the lay reader to understand; legal discussion not comprehensible to the general public.

libel Defamation in writing or other published form (such as videotape).

licensing A government's official act of granting permission to an individual, such as an attorney, to do something that would be illegal in the absence of such permission.

limited liability company (LLC) A hybrid form of business organization authorized by a state in which the owners of the business have limited liability and taxes on profits are passed through the business entity to the owners.

limited liability partnership (LLP) A business organizational form designed for professionals who normally do business as partners in a partnership. The LLP is a pass-through entity for tax purposes, like the general partnership, but limits the personal liability of partners.

limited licensing Licensing in which a limited number of individuals within a specific profession (such as legal technicians within the paralegal profession) must meet licensing requirements imposed by the state to legally practice their profession.

limited partner One who invests in a limited partnership but does not play an active role in managing the operation of the business. Unlike general partners, limited partners are only liable for partnership debts up to the amount that they have invested.

limited partnership A partnership consisting of one or more general partners and one or more limited partners.

liquidation In regard to corporations, the process by which corporate assets are converted into cash and distributed among creditors and shareholders according to specific rules of preference. In regard to bankruptcy, a proceeding under Chapter 7 of the Bankruptcy Code (often referred to as *ordinary*, or *straight*, bankruptcy), in which a debtor states his or her debts and turns all assets over to a trustee, who sells the nonexempt assets and distributes the proceeds to creditors. With certain exceptions, the remaining debts are then discharged, and the debtor is relieved of the obligation to pay the debts.

listserv list A list of e-mail addresses of persons who have agreed to receive e-mail about a particular topic.

litigation The process of working a lawsuit through the court system.

litigation paralegal A paralegal who specializes in assisting attorneys in the litigation process.

long arm statute A state statute that permits a state to obtain jurisdiction over nonresidents. Individuals or corporations, however, must have certain "minimum contacts" with that state for the statute to apply.

magistrate A public civil officer or official with limited judicial authority, such as the authority to issue an arrest warrant.

mailbox rule A rule providing that an acceptance of an offer takes effect at the time it is communicated via the mode expressly or impliedly authorized by the offeror, rather than at the time it is actually received by the offeror. If acceptance is to be by mail, for example, it becomes effective the moment it is placed in the mailbox.

malpractice Professional misconduct or negligence—the failure to exercise due care—on the part of a professional, such as an attorney or a physician.

managing partner The partner in a law firm who makes decisions relating to the firm's policies and procedures and who generally oversees the business operations of the firm.

marital property All property acquired during the course of a marriage, apart from inheritances and gifts made to one or the other of the spouses.

material fact A fact that is important to the subject matter of the contract.

mediation A method of settling disputes outside of court by using the services of a neutral third party, who acts as a communicating agent between the parties; a method of dispute settlement that is less formal than arbitration.

mediation arbitration (Med-Arb) A form of ADR in which an arbitrator first attempts to help the parties reach an agreement, just as a mediator would. If no agreement is reached, formal arbitration occurs, and the arbitrator issues a legally binding decision.

memorandum of law A document (known as a brief in some states) that delineates the legal theories, statutes, and cases on which a motion is based.

mens rea A wrongful mental state, or intent. A wrongful mental state is a requirement for criminal liability. What constitutes a wrongful mental state varies according to the nature of the crime.

metadata Embedded electronic data recorded by a computer in association with a particular file, including the file's location, path, creator, date created, date last accessed, hidden notes, earlier versions, passwords, and formatting. Metadata reveal information about how, when, and by whom a document was created, accessed, modified, and transmitted.

mini-trial A private proceeding that assists disputing parties in determining whether to take their case to court. Each party's attorney briefly argues the party's case before the other party and (usually) a neutral third party, who acts as an adviser. If the parties fail to reach an agreement, the adviser issues an opinion as to how a court would likely decide the case.

***Miranda* rights** Certain constitutional rights of accused persons taken into custody by law enforcement officials, such as the right to remain silent and the right to counsel, as established by the United States Supreme Court's decision in *Miranda v. Arizona.*

mirror image rule A common law rule that requires that the terms of the offeree's acceptance adhere exactly to the terms of the offeror's offer for a valid contract to be formed.

misdemeanor A less serious crime than a felony, punishable by a fine or incarceration for up to one year in jail (not a state or federal penitentiary).

money laundering Falsely reporting income that has been obtained through criminal activity, such as illegal drug transactions, as income obtained through a legitimate business enterprise to make the "dirty" money "clean."

mortgage A written instrument giving a creditor an interest in the debtor's property as security for a debt.

motion A procedural request or application presented by an attorney to the court on behalf of a client.

motion for a change of venue A motion requesting that a trial be moved to a different location to ensure a fair and impartial proceeding, for the convenience of the parties, or for some other acceptable reason.

motion for a directed verdict (motion for judgment as a matter of law) A motion requesting that the court grant a judgment in favor of the party making the motion on the ground that the other party has not produced sufficient evidence to support his or her claim.

motion for a new trial A motion asserting that the trial was so fundamentally flawed (because of error, newly discovered evidence, prejudice, or other reason) that a new trial is needed to prevent a miscarriage of justice.

motion for judgment notwithstanding the verdict A motion (also referred to as a motion for judgment as a matter of law in federal courts) requesting that the court grant judgment in favor of the party making the motion on the ground that the jury verdict against him or her was unreasonable or erroneous.

motion for judgment on the pleadings A motion that may be filed by either party in which the party asks the court to enter a judgment in his or her favor based on information in the pleadings. A judgment on the pleadings will only be made if there are no facts in dispute and the only question is how the law applies to a set of undisputed facts.

motion for summary judgment A motion that may be filed by either party in which the party asks the court to enter a judgment in his or her favor without a trial. Unlike a motion for judgment on the pleadings, a motion for summary judgment can be supported by evidence outside the pleadings, such as witnesses' affidavits, answers to interrogatories, and other evidence obtained prior to or during discovery.

motion *in limine* A motion requesting that certain evidence not be brought out at the trial, such as prejudicial, irrelevant, or legally inadmissible evidence.

motion to dismiss A motion filed by the defendant in which the defendant asks the court to dismiss the case for a specified reason, such as improper service, lack of personal jurisdiction, or the plaintiff's failure to state a claim for which relief can be granted.

motion to recuse A motion to remove a particular judge from a case.

motion to sever A motion to try multiple defendants separately.

motion to suppress evidence A motion requesting that certain evidence be excluded from consideration during the trial.

mutual mistake Mistake as to the same material fact on the part of both parties to a contract. In this situation, either party can cancel the contract.

National Association of Legal Assistants (NALA) One of the two largest national paralegal associations in the United States; formed in 1975. NALA is actively involved in paralegal professional development.

National Federation of Paralegal Associations (NFPA) One of the two largest national paralegal associations in the United States; formed in 1974. NFPA is actively involved in paralegal professional development.

national law Law that relates to a particular nation (as opposed to international law).

negligence The failure to exercise the standard of care that a reasonable person would exercise in similar circumstances.

negligence *per se* An action or failure to act in violation of a statutory requirement.

negotiation In dispute settlement, a process in which parties attempt to settle their dispute informally, with or without attorneys to represent them.

networking Making personal connections and cultivating relationships with people in a certain field, profession, or area of interest.

newsgroup (Usenet group) An online bulletin board service. A newsgroup is a forum, or discussion group, that usually focuses on a particular topic.

no-fault divorce A divorce in which neither party is deemed to be at fault for the breakdown of the marriage.

nolo contendere Latin for "I will not contest it." A criminal defendant's plea in which he or she chooses not to challenge, or contest, the charges brought by the government. Although the defendant will still be convicted and sentenced, the plea neither admits nor denies guilt.

offer A promise or commitment to do or refrain from doing some specified thing in the future.

offeree The party to whom the offer is made.

offeror The party making the offer.

office manager An administrative employee who manages the day-to-day operations of a business firm. In larger law firms, office managers are usually called legal administrators.

officer A person hired by corporate directors to assist in the management of the day-to-day operations of the corporation. Corporate officers include the corporate president, vice president, secretary, treasurer, and possibly others, such as a chief financial officer and chief executive officer. Corporate officers are employees of the corporation and subject to employment contracts.

online dispute resolution (ODR) The resolution of disputes with the assistance of an organization that offers dispute-resolution services via the Internet.

open-ended question A question phrased in such a way that it elicits a relatively unguided and lengthy narrative response.

opening statement An attorney's statement to the jury at the beginning of the trial. The attorney briefly outlines the evidence that will be offered during the trial and the legal theory that will be pursued.

opinion A statement by the court setting forth the applicable law and the reasons for its decision in a case.

opinion (advisory) letter A letter from an attorney to a client containing a legal opinion on an issue raised by the client's question or legal claim. The opinion is based on a detailed analysis of the law.

order for relief A court's grant of assistance to a complainant.

ordinance An order, rule, or law enacted by a municipal or county government to govern a local matter unaddressed by state or federal legislation.

original jurisdiction The power of a court to take a case, try it, and decide it.

overtime wages Wages paid to workers who are paid an hourly wage rate to compensate them for overtime work (hours worked beyond forty hours per week). Under federal law, overtime wages are at least one and a half times the regular hourly wage rate.

paralegal (or legal assistant) A person qualified by education, training, or work experience who is employed by a lawyer, law office, corporation, governmental agency, or other entity to perform specifically delegated substantive legal work, for which a lawyer is responsible.

parallel citation A second (or third) citation for a given case. When a case is published in more than one reporter, each citation is a parallel citation to the other(s).

partner A person who operates a business jointly with one or more other persons. Each partner is a co-owner of the business firm.

partnership An association of two or more persons to carry on, as co-owners, a business for profit.

party With respect to lawsuits, the plaintiff or the defendant. Some cases involve multiple parties (more than one plaintiff or defendant).

passive listening The act of listening attentively to the speaker's message and responding to the speaker by providing verbal or nonverbal cues that encourage the speaker to continue; in effect, saying, "I'm listening, please go on."

patent A government grant that gives an inventor the exclusive right or privilege to make, use, or sell his or her invention for a limited time period.

paternity suit A lawsuit brought by an unmarried mother to establish that a certain person is the biological father of her child. DNA testing or a comparable procedure is often use to determine paternity.

peremptory challenge A *voir dire* challenge to exclude a potential juror from serving on the jury without any supporting reason or cause. Peremptory challenges based on racial or gender criteria are illegal.

performance In contract law, the fulfillment of one's duties arising under a contract with another; the normal way of discharging one's contractual obligations.

personal liability An individual's personal responsibility for debts or obligations. The owners of sole proprietorships and partnerships are personally liable for the debts and obligations incurred by their businesses. If their firms go bankrupt or cannot meet debts, the owners will be personally responsible for the debts.

personal property Any property that is not real property. Generally, any property that is movable or intangible is classified as personal property.

persuasive authority Any legal authority, or source of law, that a court may look to for guidance but on which it need not rely in making its decision. Persuasive authorities include cases from other jurisdictions and secondary sources of law, such as scholarly treatises.

persuasive precedent A precedent decided in another jurisdiction that a court may either follow or reject but that is entitled to careful consideration.

petition for divorce The document filed with the court to initiate divorce proceedings. The requirements governing the form and content of a divorce petition vary from state to state.

petition in bankruptcy An application to a bankruptcy court for relief in bankruptcy; a filing for bankruptcy. The official forms required for a petition in bankruptcy must be completed accurately, sworn to under oath, and signed by the debtor.

petty offense In criminal law, the least serious kind of wrong, such as a traffic or building-code violation.

plain meaning rule A rule of statutory interpretation. If the meaning of a statute is clear on its face, then that is the interpretation the court will give to it; inquiry into the legislative history of the statute will not be needed.

plaintiff A party who initiates a lawsuit.

plea bargaining The process by which the accused and the prosecutor in a criminal case work out a mutually satisfactory disposition of the case, subject to court approval. Usually, plea bargaining involves the defendant's pleading guilty to a lesser offense in return for a lighter sentence.

pleadings Statements by the plaintiff and the defendant that detail the facts, charges, and defenses involved in the litigation.

pocket part A separate pamphlet containing recent cases or changes in the law that is used to update legal encyclopedias and other legal authorities. It is called a "pocket part" because it slips into a pocket in the front or back binder of the volume.

policy In insurance law, a contract for insurance coverage. The policy spells out the precise terms and conditions as to what will and will not be covered under the contract.

potentially responsible party (PRP) A party who may be liable under the Comprehensive Environmental Response, Compensation, and Liability Act, or Superfund. Any person who generated hazardous waste, transported hazardous waste, owned or operated a waste site at the time of disposal, or currently owns or operates a site may be responsible for some or all of the clean-up costs involved in removing the hazardous chemicals.

prayer for relief A statement at the end of the complaint requesting that the court grant relief to the plaintiff.

precedent A court decision that furnishes an example or authority for deciding later cases in which similar facts are presented.

predatory behavior Business behavior that is undertaken with the intention of unlawfully driving competitors out of the market.

preemption A doctrine under which a federal law preempts, or takes precedence over, conflicting state and local laws.

preference In bankruptcy proceedings, the debtor's favoring of one creditor over others by making payments or transferring property to that creditor at the expense of the rights of other creditors. The bankruptcy trustee is allowed to recover payments made to one creditor in preference over another.

preliminary hearing An initial hearing in which a magistrate decides if there is probable cause to believe that the defendant committed the crime for which he or she is charged.

premium In insurance law, the price paid by the insured for insurance protection for a specified period of time.

prenuptial agreement A contract formed between two persons who are contemplating marriage to provide for the disposition of property in the event of a divorce or the death of one of the spouses after they have married.

pretrial conference A conference prior to trial in which the judge and the attorneys litigating the suit discuss settlement possibilities, clarify the issues in dispute, and schedule forthcoming trial-related events.

primary source of law In legal research, a document that establishes the law on a particular issue, such as a case decision, legislative act, administrative rule, or presidential order.

principal In agency law, a person who, by agreement or otherwise, authorizes another person (the agent) to act on the principal's behalf in such a way that the acts of the agent become binding on the principal.

privilege In tort law, the ability to act contrary to another person's right without that person's having legal redress for such acts. Privilege may be raised as a defense to defamation.

privileged information Confidential communications between certain individuals, such as an attorney and his or her client, that are protected from disclosure except under court order.

probable cause Reasonable grounds to believe the existence of facts warranting certain actions, such as the search or arrest of a person.

probate The process of "proving" the validity of a will and ensuring that the instructions in a valid will are carried out, including settling matters pertaining to the administration of a decedent's estate and guardianship of a decedent's minor children.

probate court A court that handles proceedings relating to wills and the settlement of deceased persons' estates; usually a county court.

procedural law Rules that define the manner in which the rights and duties of individuals may be enforced.

product liability The legal liability of manufacturers and sellers of goods to consumers, users, and bystanders for injuries or damages that are caused by the goods.

professional corporation (P.C.) A firm owned by shareholders, who purchase the corporation's stock, or shares. The liability of shareholders is often limited to the amount of their investments.

promise An assurance that one will or will not do something in the future.

promissory estoppel A doctrine under which a promise is binding if the promise is clear and definite, the promisee justifiably relies on the promise, the reliance is reasonable and substantial, and justice will be better served by enforcement of the promise.

proof of claim A document filed with the bankruptcy court by a creditor to inform a court of a claim against a debtor's property. The proof of claim lists the creditor's name and address, as well as the amount that the creditor asserts is owed to the creditor by the debtor.

property settlement The division of property between spouses on the termination of a marriage.

prospectus A document that discloses relevant facts about a company and its operations so that those who wish to purchase stock (invest) in the corporation have the basis for making an informed decision.

proximate cause Legal cause; exists when the connection between an act and an injury is strong enough to justify imposing liability.

public defender A court-appointed attorney who is paid by the state to represent a criminal defendant who is unable to hire private counsel.

public law number An identification number assigned to a statute.

public policy A governmental policy based on widely held societal values.

public prosecutor An individual, acting as a trial lawyer, who initiates and conducts criminal cases in the government's name and on behalf of the people.

publicly held corporation A corporation whose shares are eligible to be publicly traded in securities markets, such as the New York Stock Exchange.

punitive damages Money damages that may be awarded to a plaintiff to punish the defendant and deter future similar conduct.

real estate Land and things permanently attached to the land, such as houses, buildings, and trees.

real property Immovable property consisting of land and the buildings and plant life thereon.

reasonable person standard The standard of behavior expected of a hypothetical "reasonable person"; the standard against which negligence is measured and that must be observed to avoid liability for negligence.

record on appeal The items submitted during the trial (pleadings, motions, briefs, and exhibits) and the transcript of the trial proceedings that are forwarded to the appellate court for review when a case is appealed.

recross-examination The questioning of an opposing witness following the adverse party's redirect examination.

redirect examination The questioning of a witness following the adverse party's cross-examination.

reference line The portion of the letter that indicates the matter to be discussed in the letter, such as "RE: Summary of Cases Applying the Family and Medical Leave Act of 1993." The reference line is placed just below the address block and above the salutation.

reformation An equitable remedy granted by a court to correct, or "reform," a written contract so that it reflects the true intentions of the parties.

Registered Paralegal (RP) A paralegal whose competency has been certified by the National Federation of Paralegal Associations (NFPA) after the paralegal's successful completion of the Paralegal Advanced Competency Exam (PACE).

relevant evidence Evidence tending to prove or disprove the fact in question. Only relevant evidence is admissible in court.

remand To send a case back to a lower court for further proceedings.

remedy The means by which a right is enforced or the violation of a right is prevented or compensated for.

remedy at law A remedy available in a court of law. Money damages and items of value are awarded as a remedy at law.

remedy in equity A remedy allowed by courts in situations where remedies at law are not appropriate. Remedies in equity are based on rules of fairness, justice, and honesty.

reporter A book in which court cases are published, or reported.

reprimand A disciplinary sanction in which an attorney is rebuked for misbehavior. Although a reprimand is the mildest sanction for attorney misconduct, it is serious and may significantly damage the attorney's reputation in the legal community.

rescission A remedy in which the contract is canceled and the parties are returned to the positions they occupied before the contract was made.

respondeat superior A doctrine in agency law under which a principal-employer may be held liable for the wrongful acts committed by agents or employees while acting within the scope of their agency or employment.

responsible corporate officer doctrine A common law doctrine under which the court may impose criminal liability on a corporate officer for actions of employees under her or his supervision regardless of whether she or he participated in, directed, or even knew about those actions.

restitution An equitable remedy under which a person is restored to his or her original position prior to loss or injury, or placed in the position that he or she would have been in had the breach not occurred.

restraining order A court order that requires one person (such as an abusing spouse) to stay away from another (such as an abused spouse).

retainer An advance payment made by a client to a law firm to cover part of the legal fees and/or costs that will need to be incurred on that client's behalf.

retainer agreement A signed document stating that the attorney or the law firm has been hired by the client to provide certain legal services and that the client agrees to pay for those services in accordance with the terms in the retainer agreement.

return-of-service form A document signed by a process server and submitted to the court to prove that a defendant received a summons.

reverse To overturn the judgment of a lower court.

reversible error A mistake of law that damaged a party's substantive rights and is grounds for reversal of the judgment on appeal.

risk A prediction concerning potential loss based on known and unknown factors.

risk management Planning that is undertaken to reduce the risk of loss from known and unknown events. In the context of insurance, risk management involves transferring certain risks from the insured to the insurance company.

robbery The taking of money, personal property, or any other article of value from a person by means of force or fear.

rule of four A rule of the United States Supreme Court under which the Court will not issue a writ of *certiorari* unless at least four justices approve of the decision to issue the writ.

rulemaking The actions undertaken by administrative agencies when formally adopting new regulations or amending old ones.

rules of construction The rules that control the judicial interpretation of statutes.

rules of evidence Rules governing the admissibility of evidence in trial courts.

sales contract A contract for the sale of goods, as opposed to a contract for the sale of services, real property, or intangible property. Sales contracts are governed by Article 2 of the Uniform Commercial Code.

salutation The formal greeting to the addressee of the letter. The salutation is placed just below the reference line.

search warrant A written order, based on probable cause and issued by a judge or public official (magistrate), commanding that police officers or criminal investigators search a specific person, place, or property to obtain evidence.

secondary source In legal research, any publication that indexes, summarizes, or interprets the law, such as a legal encyclopedia, a treatise, or an article in a law review.

secured creditor A lender, seller, or any other person in whose favor there is a security interest.

self-defense The legally recognized privilege to protect oneself or one's property against injury by another. The privilege of self-defense only protects acts that are reasonably necessary to protect oneself or one's property.

self-incrimination The act of giving testimony that implicates oneself in criminal wrongdoing. The Fifth Amendment to the Constitution states that no person

"shall be compelled in any criminal case to be a witness against himself."

self-regulation The regulation of the conduct of a professional group by members of the group. Self-regulation involves establishing ethical or professional standards of behavior with which members of the group must comply.

sentence The punishment, or penalty, ordered by the court to be inflicted on a person convicted of a crime.

separate property Property that a spouse owned before the marriage, plus inheritances and gifts acquired by the spouse during the marriage.

service of process The delivery of the summons and the complaint to a defendant.

settlement agreement An out-of-court resolution to a legal dispute, which is agreed to by the parties in writing. A settlement agreement may be reached at any time prior to or during a trial.

sexual harassment In the employment context, (1) the hiring or granting of job promotions or other benefits in return for sexual favors (*quid pro quo* harassment) or (2) language or conduct that is so sexually offensive that it creates a hostile working environment (hostile-environment harassment).

share A unit of stock; a measure of ownership interest in a corporation.

shareholder One who purchases corporate stock, or shares, and who thus becomes an owner of the corporation.

shrink-wrap agreement An agreement whose terms are expressed in a document located inside the box in which the goods (usually software) are packaged.

slander Defamation in oral form.

slip opinion A judicial opinion published shortly after the decision is made and not yet included in a case reporter or advance sheets.

sole proprietorship The simplest form of business organization, in which the owner is the business. Anyone who does business without creating a formal business entity has a sole proprietorship.

specific performance An equitable remedy requiring exactly the performance that was specified in a contract; usually granted only when money damages would be an inadequate remedy and the subject matter of the contract is unique (for example, real property).

staff attorney An attorney hired by a law firm as an employee. A staff attorney has no ownership rights in the firm and will not be invited to become a partner in the firm.

standing to sue A sufficient stake in a controversy to justify bringing a lawsuit. To have standing, the plaintiff must demonstrate an injury or threatened injury.

stare decisis The doctrine of precedent, under which a court is obligated to follow the earlier decisions of that court or a higher court within the jurisdiction if the same points arise again in litigation. This is a major characteristic of the common law system.

state bar association An association of attorneys within a state. In most states, an attorney must be a member of the state bar association to practice law in the state.

statute A written law enacted by a legislature under its constitutional lawmaking authority.

Statute of Frauds A state statute that requires certain types of contracts to be in writing to be enforceable.

statute of limitations A statute setting the maximum time period within which certain actions can be brought or rights enforced. After the period of time has run, no legal action can be brought.

statutory law The body of written laws enacted by the legislature.

strict liability Liability regardless of fault. In tort law, strict liability may be imposed on a producer who sells a good that is so defective as to be unreasonably dangerous.

submission agreement A written agreement to submit a legal dispute to an arbitrator or arbitrating panel for resolution.

subpoena A document commanding a person to appear at a certain time and place to give testimony concerning a certain matter.

substantive law Law that defines the rights and duties of individuals with respect to each other, as opposed to procedural law, which defines the manner in which these rights and duties may be enforced.

summary jury trial (SJT) A method of settling disputes in which a trial is held but the jury's verdict is not binding. The verdict acts as a guide to both sides in reaching an agreement during mandatory negotiations that follow the trial. If a settlement is not reached, both sides have the right to a full trial later.

summons A document served on a defendant in a lawsuit informing the defendant that a legal action has been commenced against him or her and that the defendant must appear in court or respond to the plaintiff's complaint within a specified period of time.

support personnel Employees who provide clerical, secretarial, or other support to the legal, paralegal, and administrative staff of a law firm.

supporting affidavit An affidavit accompanying a motion that is filed by an attorney on behalf of his or her client. The sworn statements in the affidavit provide a factual basis for the motion.

supremacy clause The provision in Article VI of the U.S. Constitution that declares the Constitution, laws, and treaties of the United States to be "the supreme Law of the Land."

suspension A serious disciplinary sanction in which an attorney who has violated an ethical rule or a law is prohibited from practicing law in the state for a specified or an indefinite period of time.

syllabus A brief summary of the holding and legal principles involved in a reported case, which is followed by the court's official opinion.

tenancy in common A form of co-ownership of property in which each party owns an undivided interest that passes to his or her heirs at death.

testamentary trust A trust that is created by will and that does not take effect until the death of the testator.

testate The condition of having died with a valid will.

testator One who makes a valid will.

third party A person or entity not directly involved in an agreement (such as a contract), legal proceeding (such as a lawsuit), or relationship (such as an attorney-client relationship).

time slip A record documenting, for billing purposes, the hours (or fractions of hours) that an attorney or a paralegal worked for each client, the date on which the work was done, and the type of work done.

tort A civil wrong not arising from a breach of contract; a breach of a legal duty that causes harm or injury to another.

tortfeasor One who commits a tort.

toxic tort A wrongful act (tort) that occurs when a person or business fails to properly use or clean up toxic chemicals that cause harm to a person or to society; also used to refer to an action brought against a toxic polluter.

trade journal A newsletter, magazine, or other periodical that provides a certain trade or profession with information (products, trends, or developments) relating to that trade or profession.

trade name A term that is used to indicate part or all of a business's name and that is directly related to the business's reputation and goodwill. Trade names are protected under the common law (and under trademark law, if the business's name is the same as its trademark).

trade secret Information or processes that give a business an advantage over competitors who do not know the information or processes.

trademark A distinctive mark, motto, device, or emblem that a manufacturer stamps, prints, or otherwise affixes to the goods it produces so that they can be identified on the market and their origins made known. Once a trademark is established (under the common law or through registration), the owner is entitled to its exclusive use.

treatise In legal research, a work that provides a systematic, detailed, and scholarly review of a particular legal subject.

treaty An agreement, or compact, formed between two independent nations.

trespass to land The entry onto, above, or below the surface of land owned by another without the owner's permission.

trespass to personal property The unlawful taking or harming of another's personal property; interference with another's right to the exclusive possession of personal property.

trial court A court in which cases begin and in which questions of fact are examined.

trial notebook A binder that contains copies of all of the documents and information that an attorney will need to have at hand during the trial.

trust An arrangement in which title to property is held by one person (a trustee) for the benefit of another (a beneficiary).

trust account A bank or escrow account in which one party (the trustee, such as an attorney) holds funds belonging to another person (such as a client); a bank account into which funds advanced to a law firm by a client are deposited.

unathorized practice of law (UPL) The act of engaging in actions defined by a legal authority, such as a state legislature, as constituting the "practice of law" without authorization to do so.

unconscionable contract or unconscionable clause A contract or clause that is so oppressive to one of the parties that the court will refuse to enforce the contract.

underwriter In insurance law, the insurer, or the one assuming a risk in return for the payment of a premium.

Uniform Commercial Code (UCC) A uniform code of laws governing commercial transactions that has been adopted in part or in its entirety by all of the states. Article 2 of the UCC governs contracts for the sale of goods.

unilateral mistake Mistake as to a material fact on the part of only one party to a contract. In this situation, the contract is normally enforceable against the mistaken party, with some exceptions.

unreasonably dangerous product A product that is defective to the point of threatening a consumer's health and safety. A product will be considered unreasonably dangerous if it is dangerous beyond the expectation of the ordinary consumer or if a less dangerous alternative was economically feasible for the manufacturer, but the manufacturer failed to produce it.

U.S. trustee A government official who performs administrative tasks that a bankruptcy judge would otherwise have to perform.

venue The geographical district in which an action is tried and from which the jury is selected.

verdict A formal decision made by a jury.

vicarious liability Legal responsibility placed on one person for the acts of another.

visitation rights The right of a noncustodial parent to have contact with his or her child. Grandparents and stepparents may also be given visitation rights.

voir dire A proceeding in which attorneys for the plaintiff and the defendant, or the judge, ask prospective jurors questions to determine whether any potential juror is biased or has any connection with a party to the action or with a prospective witness.

warranty An express or implied promise by a seller that specific goods to be sold meet certain criteria, or standards of performance, on which the buyer may rely.

white-collar crime A crime that typically occurs in a business context; popularly used to refer to an illegal act or series of acts committed by a person or business entity using nonviolent means.

will A document directing how and to whom the maker's property and obligations are to be transferred on his or her death.

winding up The process of winding up all business affairs (collecting and distributing the firm's assets) after a partnership or corporation has been dissolved.

witness A person who is asked to testify under oath at a trial.

witness statement The written record of the statements made by a witness during an interview, signed by the witness.

work product An attorney's mental impressions, conclusions, and legal theories regarding a case being prepared on behalf of a client. Work product normally is regarded as privileged information.

workers' compensation statutes State laws establishing an administrative procedure for compensating workers for injuries that arise in the course of their employment, regardless of fault.

workout An out-of-court negotiation in which a debtor enters into an agreement with a creditor or creditors for a payment or plan to discharge the debtor's debt.

World Wide Web A hypertext-based system through which specially formatted documents are accessible on the Internet.

writ of *certiorari* A writ from a higher court asking the lower court to send it the record of a case for review. The United States Supreme Court uses *certiorari* to review most of the cases it decides to hear.

writ of execution A writ that puts in force a court's decree or judgment.

wrongful discharge An employer's termination of an employee's employment in violation of the law.

INDEX

A

AAA (American Arbitration Association), 184, 185
AAfPE. *See* American Association for Paralegal Education
AAPI (American Alliance of Paralegals, Inc.), 10
ABA. *See* American Bar Association
ABA-approved programs, 9
Abnormally dangerous activities, 478
Absolute privilege, 464
Abstract, 535
Acceptance(s)
  of bribe, 425
  contractual, 497, 498, 500
  online, 511–512
Accident scene, checking, 360
Acquittal, 448
Act(s)
  of commission, 420
  criminal *(actus reus)*, 420
  guilty *(actus reus)*, 420
  of omission, 420
  same, tort lawsuit and criminal prosecution for, illustrated, 419
Actionable behavior, 463–464
Active listening, 357
Activities, abnormally dangerous, 478
Actual malice, 464–465
Actus reus (guilty act), 420
Address block, 284
ADEA (Age Discrimination in Employment Act) (1967), 182, 605, 607
Adhesion contract, 505
Adjudication, 149, 150
Administrative agency(ies), 129. *See also* Administrative law
  adjudication by, 149, 150
  administrative process and, 149
  creation of, 148–149
  defined, 148
  as employer, 26, 153
  enabling legislation and, 149, 229
  enforcement by, 150

information from, accessing, 374, 376
  investigation by, 150
  paralegals' representation of clients before, 27, 117, 151
  rulemaking by, 150
  working with, tips for, 376
Administrative law, 148–151. *See also* Administrative agency(ies)
  defined, 148
  finding tools for, 229
  and the paralegal, 150–151
  researching, 229
  Shepard's Code of Federal Regulations Citations and, 252–253
Administrative law judge (ALJ), 150
Administrative Procedure Act (1946), 150
Administrative process, 149
Administrator, in intestacy law, 570
Admission, request for, 333
Adoption, 561–562
ADR. *See* Alternative dispute resolution
Advanced Paralegal Certification (APC), 9
Adversarial system of justice, 138–139
Adverse (hostile) witnesses, 365, 400
Advertising, deceptive, 482–484
Advisory (opinion) letter, 285–286
  sample, illustrated, 288
Affidavit, 618
  defined, 311, 571
  supporting, 321
Affirmation of judgment, 220, 408
Affirmative defense, 318–319, 473
Age, discrimination on basis of, 65, 172, 182, 605, 607
Age Discrimination in Employment Act (ADEA) (1967), 182, 605, 607
Agency(ies)
  administrative. *See* Administrative agency(ies)
  adoption through, 561–562
  collection, 486–487
  credit reporting, 486
Agency law, 598–601
  the paralegal and, 600–601

Agency relationship(s), 598–601
  appearance of, 599
  defined, 598
  formation of, 599
  third parties and, 599–600
Agent(s). *See also* Agency relationship(s)
  defined, 598
  duties of, 599
  escrow, 533–534, 535
  insurance, 539, 542
  real estate, 598, 599
  torts of, 600
Aggravated robbery, 423
Agreement(s). *See also* Contract(s)
  antenuptial, 568. *See also* Agreement(s), prenuptial
  bilateral, 152
  click-on, 500, 512
  click-through, 512
  click-wrap, 512
  confidentiality, 521
  contractual, 497, 498–500
  defined, 498
  licensing, 512
  multilateral, 152
  prenuptial, 506, 513, 568–569
  real estate sales, typical provisions in, 533
  retainer. *See* Retainer agreement
  settlement. *See* Settlement agreement
  shrink-wrap, 512
Air pollution, 635, 637
ALI (American Law Institute), 135, 507, 513
Alibi, 422
Alimony, 566
ALJ (administrative law judge), 150
Allegation(s)
  defined, 310
  general, 310–311
  jurisdictional, 310
A.L.R. *Blue Book of Supplemental Decisions,* 204
A.L.R. *Later Case Service,* 204
Alternate jurors, 396

Alternative dispute resolution (ADR), 173–186
 arbitration as. *See* Arbitration
 court-referred, 183–184
 defined, 173
 mediation as. *See* Mediation
 mini-trial as, 182–183
 negotiation as. *See* Negotiation(s)
 online dispute resolution (ODR) as, 184–186
 the paralegal and, 186
 providers of services in, 184
 summary jury trial (SJT) as, 184
ALWD Citation Manual: A Professional System of Citation, 207, 293
America Online, Inc. (AOL), 476, 478
American Alliance of Paralegals, Inc. (AAPI), 10
American Arbitration Association (AAA), 184, 185
American Association for Paralegal Education (AAfPE)
 defined, 4
 formation of, 9
 paralegal defined by, 4
 regulation of paralegals and, 120, 121
 role of, in paralegal education, 9
 Web site of, 9
American Association of Legal Nurse Consultants, 33
American Bar Association (ABA)
 approved paralegal education programs and, 9
 Canons of Ethics of, 92. *See also* Model Code; Model Rules
 defined, 3
 ethics opinions issued by, 250
 law schools accredited by, 91
 membership in, 91
 Model Code of Professional Responsibility of, 92
 Model Guidelines for the Utilization of Legal Assistant Services of, 101, 109, 110, 183, 570
  disclosure of paralegal status and, 117, 291
  giving legal opinions to client and, 364
 Model Rules of Professional Conduct of. *See* Model Rules
 paralegal defined by, 3
 role of, in paralegal education, 9
 Standing Committee of, on Paralegals
  online resources provided by, 15
  paralegal programs approved by, 8
 Uniform Probate Code (UPC) approved by, 570
American College of Trust and Estate Counsel, 575

American Digest System (West), 229
American Jurisprudence, Second Edition (*Am.Jur.2d.*)(West), 199, 225
 excerpt from, illustrated, 200
American law
 framework of, 129–130
 sources of, 128–159
  primary and secondary, 129–130, 199–205, 206, 247
American Law Institute (ALI), 135, 507, 513
American Law Reports (A.L.R.) (West), 203–204, 252
American Law Reports Federal (A.L.R. Federal) (West), 203
Americans with Disabilities Act (ADA) (1990), 605, 607–609
Analysis
 of case law, 215–223
 of cases, 220–221
 IRAC method of, 293
  illustrated, 294
 in legal memorandum, 291, 293
  illustrated, 294
 of statutory law, 225–229
Analytical skills, 11
Animals, wild, 478
Annotation(s)
 in *American Law Reports,* 203–204
 defined, 201
Annulment, 562–563
Answer, 318–321
 affirmative defenses and, 318–319
 counterclaim and, 320–321
 cross-claim and, 321
 defined, 318
 illustrated, 319–320
Antenuptial agreements, 568. *See also* Prenuptial agreement
Anticounterfeiting Consumer Protection Act, 429
Antitrust law, 148
AOL (America Online, Inc.), 476, 478
APC (Advanced Paralegal Certification), 9
Appeal(s)
 criminal, 453
 defined, 407
 notice of, 408
 record on, 408
 of verdict, 407–408
Appellant, 408
Appellate brief, 408
Appellate court(s), 198, 407
 decisions of, reporting of. *See* Case reporting system
 federal. *See* Federal court system, appellate courts of
 options of, 220, 408
 oral arguments before, 408
 previous interpretation of statute by, 227–228

 state. *See* State court system(s), appellate courts of
Appellate jurisdiction, 163, 171, 172
Appellee, 408
Apple Safari, 242
Appropriation, 465
Arbitration, 178–182
 clause requiring, 179
 of commercial contracts, 185
 court-mandated, 387
 defined, 178
 as form of alternative dispute resolution (ADR), 178–182
 mediation (med-arb), 182
 online, 185–186
 postarbitration and, 182
 potential problems with, ethics and, 183
 prearbitration and, 181–182
 process of, 179–182
  courts' role in, 181–182
Arbitration clause, 179
Arbitration hearing, 179–180
Arbitrator, 179–180
 becoming, 185
Arraignment, 442
Arrest
 booking and, 431
 defined, 431
 detention versus, 433
 investigation after, 434–435
Arrest warrant, 429, 433–434, 436
Arson, 424
Articles
 of incorporation, 589–591
  defined, 589
  illustrated, 589
  information generally included in, 592
 of organization, 596
Assault, 462
Assets, locating, 409
"Assisted negotiation," 182
Association of Legal Writing Directors, 207, 293
Assumption of risk, 473–474, 481
Attorney(s)
 associate, 61
 attorney-client privilege and. *See* Attorney-client privilege
 city, 417
 contract, 61
 county, 417
 deponent's, role of, 329–330
 disbarment of, 94
 discipline board and, 122
 district, 417
 documents generated by, reviewing, 290
 duty(ies) of
  breach of, 447
  of competence, 94–97, 143

loyalty, 599
to supervise, 96–97, 98, 570
ethics of
codes and rules governing, 92–93.
See also Model Code; Model
Rules
violations of, sanctions for,
93–94
paralegal practice and, 94–108
confidentiality of information
and. *See* Confidentiality of
information
conflict of interest and, 103–
108. *See also* Conflict(s) of
interest
duty of competence and, 94–97,
143
fees and. *See* Fee(s)
instructions from, clarifying, 545
licensing of, 91–92. *See also*
Licensing
malpractice and, 94, 100, 167, 472,
597. *See also* Malpractice
one, drawing up contract for two
people, ethics and, 505
personal liability of, 60
prosecuting, 417, 436
regulation of, 90–94
licensing requirements and, 91–
92. *See also* Licensing
participants in, 90–91
self-, 90
reprimand of, 94
right to, 140, 430
as sole (solo) practitioner, 60–61
staff, 61
suspension of, 94
work product and, 103. *See also* Work
product
Attorney-client privilege
arising of, 103
confidentiality and, 66, 97, 102–103.
See also Confidentiality of
information
defined, 102
duration of, 103
nature of information subject to,
102–103
waiver of, 103
Australia
booklet, *Plain English at Work*,
published by government of,
276
common law system in, 151
Authentication of evidence, 377
Authority
binding, 130, 175, 197–198
persuasive, 175, 198–199
Automatic stay, 621, 627, 629
Avoidance, powers of, 623–624
Award, arbitration, 180
The A-Z of Alternative Words, 276

B

Bachelor's degree programs, 8
Backing up work, 77
Back-up data, 339–340
Bail
defined, 437, 440
excessive, constitutional prohibition
of, 140, 430, 440
Bail bondsperson, 440
Bankruptcy
automatic stay in, 621, 627, 629
cram-down position and, 633
creditors' committees and, 632
debtor in possession (DIP) and,
631–632
discharge in, 625–628, 630–631, 633
estate in property of, 621–622
distribution of, 624–625
exemptions in, 622–623, 627
involuntary, 617, 620–621, 625
means test in, 618–620, 623
order for relief in, 620
ordinary, 617
preferences in, 624
straight, 617
trustee in, 617, 623–624, 626, 632,
633
voluntary, 617–620
workouts and, 631
Bankruptcy Abuse Prevention and
Consumer Protection Act
(Bankruptcy Reform Act) (2005),
616, 617–619, 620, 621, 623, 633
Bankruptcy Code (Bankruptcy Reform
Act of 1978), 616–633. *See also*
Bankruptcy
Chapter 7 of (liquidation
proceedings), 617–628, 631,
642
Chapter 11 of (reorganization), 617,
618, 631–633
Chapter 13 of (adjustment of debts
by individuals), 617, 618, 620,
623, 626, 628–631
types of relief under, 617
Bankruptcy court, 26, 31, 163, 616–617
Bankruptcy fraud, 425
Bankruptcy law. *See also* Bankruptcy;
Bankruptcy Code
defined, 31
goals of, 616
the paralegal and, 31, 633
Bankruptcy Reform Act
of 1978. *See* Bankruptcy Code
of 2005 (Bankruptcy Abuse
Prevention and Consumer
Protection Act), 616, 617–619,
620, 621, 623, 633
Bankruptcy Reporter (West), 214
Bar associations
attorney regulation and, 90–91

state. *See* State bar association(s)
Bargained-for exchange, 501
Bargaining
collective, 603
plea, 442
Battery, 462
Behavior
actionable, 463–464
predatory, 467
Beneficiary
insurance, 539
of trust, 571
Benefits, job, 35–36
Best available technology, 638
Best conventional technology,
638
Beyond a reasonable doubt, 418, 447
Bias
of judge, 443
of prospective juror, 395, 396
of witness, 367
Bigamy, 562
Bilateral agreements, 152
Bilateral contract, 497
Bilateral mistake, 504
Bill, 145
Bill of Rights, 139–141. *See also*
individual amendments
defined, 139
safeguards under, to protect persons
accused of crimes, 429–431. *See
also individual protections*
summarized, 140–141
Billable hours
defined, 73
nonbillable hours versus, 74–75
pressure to generate, 76
Billing procedures, 72–76
Binder, 544
Binding authority, 130, 175, 197–198
Binding mediation, 182
Bisson, Sally Brown, 6–7
Blogs ("Weblogs"), 262
Blood test, 557
*The Bluebook: A Uniform System of
Citation* (Harvard Law Review
Association), 207, 293
BNA (Bureau of National Affairs),
214–215
Bonus, 36
Booking, 431
Boolean logic
defined, 244
examples of searches using,
illustrated, 245
Bouchoux, Deborah E., 518–519
Breach
of contract. *See* Contract(s), breach
of
defined, 95
of duty
of care, 471–472

of competence, 95–96
  by professional, 447
Bribery, 425
Brief, 321. *See also* Legal memorandum
  appellate, 408
Briefing a case, 215, 221–223
  briefed version of sample case and, 222
  defined, 221
  IRAC method for, 222–223
Broker, insurance, 539
Brown, Jo-Christy, 626–627
Brown, S. Whittington, 144–145
Brown v. Board of Education of Topeka, 130–131
Browsers, 242–243
Building Owners and Managers Association, 537
Bureau of National Affairs (BNA), 214–215
Business, wrongful interference with, 467
Business & Legal Reports, Inc., 636
Business invitee, 196, 471
Business organization(s)
  corporation as. *See* Corporation(s)
  as employer, 25
  forms of, 584–601
  limited liability company (LLC) as, 596–597
  limited liability limited partnership (LLLP) as, 597
  limited liability partnership (LLP) as, 597
  limited partnership as, 587–588
  the paralegal and, 598
  partnership as. *See* Partnership(s)
  sole proprietorship as, 584–595
Business tort, 466–467
Bylaws, 591

C

CAIF (Coalition Against Insurance Fraud), 547
Callahan's *Michigan Digest,* 201
Campbell's soups, 483
Canada
  common law system in, 151
  NAFTA and, 152
Cancellation of insurance policy, 546, 548
CAN-SPAM (Controlling the Assault of Non-Solicited Pornography and Marketing) Act, 469
CAN-WIN conferencing system, 186
Capacity
  contractual, 497, 502, 503
  testamentary, 571
Capital offense, 423
Caption, 310
Care, duty of, 470
  breach of, 471–472

corporate officers' and directors', 594
defined, 471
professionals', 472
Career(s), 22–58
  creating opportunities in, 54
  paths of, 54
  planning, 37–39
  reevaluating, 52, 54
Case(s). *See also* Lawsuit(s); Litigation
  on "all fours," 197
  analyzing, 220–221
  as binding authority, 197–198
  briefing, 215, 221–223
  citation of, 136–137
  components of, 215, 218–219
  criminal, major procedural steps in, summarized, 432
  defendant's, during trial, 403–404
  disposition of, 220, 408
  early neutral evaluation of, 182
  of first impression, 131, 132–133, 199
  management of, 7
  parties in, 137, 302
  as persuasive authority, 198–199
  plaintiff's, during trial, 399–402
  on point, 197
  relevant, finding, 199–205
  remandment of, 220, 408
  reporting of. *See* Case reporting system
  sample, 216–219
    briefed version of, 222
  severing of, 443
  summarizing, 221–222
  titles of, 136–137
Case citator. *See* Citator(s)
Case digests, 201–203
Case law(s)
  analyzing, 215–223, 295
  common law tradition and, 130–139
  defined, 130
  primary source of. *See* Case reporting system
  as a primary source of law, 129, 199
  researching, 195–223, 295
    case reporting system and, 205–215. *See also* Case reporting system
    defining the issue and, 195–197
      checklist for, 196
    finding relevant cases and, 199–205
    goals of, determining, 197–199
  terminology of, 136–137
Case reporting system, 205–215
  federal court decisions in, 214–215
    citations to, 211–212
  state court decisions in, 206–207
    citations to, 211
    regional reporters and, 207
    state reporters and, 206–207

United States Supreme Court decisions in, 214–215
West's National Reporter System and, 207, 210
Casemaker, 258–259
Castle doctrine, 422
Causation in fact, 472–473
Cause
  challenge for, 395
  probable, 429, 431, 433–434, 436, 440–441, 463
  proximate, 473
  superseding, 474
CDA (Communications Decency Act) (1996), 141, 477
Cease-and-desist order, 484
Center for Legal Responsibility, 185–186
CERCLA (Comprehensive Environmental Response, Compensation, and Liability Act) (Superfund) (1980), 640–641
Certificate(s)
  of incorporation (corporate charter), 590–591
  of limited partnership, 588
Certificate programs, 8
Certification, 9–10
  by American Association of Legal Nurse Consultants, 33
  defined, 9
  mandatory, 10
  by NALA, 9
  by NFPA, 9
  state, 9, 10
  voluntary, 10
Certified Legal Assistant (CLA), 9. *See also* Certification
Certified Legal Assistant Specialty (CLAS), 9
Certified Paralegal (CP), 9. *See also* Certification
Chain of custody, 341
Challenge(s)
  for cause, 395
  defined, 395
  peremptory, 395–396
  during *voir dire,* 395–396
Chancellor, 131–132
Charge, 405–406
  defined, 405
  illustrated, 405
Charitable trust, 573
Checks and balances, 143
The Chicago Manual of Style, 273
Child, children
  abuse of, 560
  adoption of, 561–562
  born out of wedlock, 560–561
  custody and, 564–565
  emancipation of, 557
  foster care and, 561

neglect of, 560
    support of, 565–566
    visitation rights and, 565
    wrongful acts of, parents' liability
        for, 560
Child abuse, 560
Child custody, 564–565
Child neglect, 560
Child Online Protection Act (COPA),
    141
Child support, 565–566
Chronological arrangement, 274
Circumstantial evidence
    defined, 375
    direct evidence versus, 375–376
C.I.S. *(Congressional Information Service),*
    228–229
Citation(s)
    case, 215
    checking, 251–255
    defined, 136, 207
    format of, 207
    how to read, 211–213
    parallel, 207, 215, 252
Citator(s)
    defined, 251
    use of, 251–255
City attorney, 417
City directories, 373
Civil law
    codified law and, 151
    criminal law versus, 32–33, 417–418
    defined, 32
Civil law system, 151
Civil liability for criminal acts, 418
Civil litigation
    a bird's-eye view of, 301–303
    disclosure(s) required in, 333–336
        failure to disclose and, 334–335
        initial, 334
        subsequent, 336
    file of. *See* Litigation file
    hypothetical, 302–303
    jury selection and, 394–396
    pleadings and. *See* Pleadings
    posttrial motions and, 406–407
    posttrial procedures and, 406–408
    preliminaries of, 303–305
    pretrial conference and, 393–394
    pretrial motions and, 322–324
        summarized, 323
    procedural requirements and,
        301–302
    steps in, illustrated, 302
    before the trial, 300–348
    trial notebook and, 391–393
    trial procedures and, 386–415. *See*
        also Trial(s)
Civil Rights Act (1964), Title VII of,
    172–173, 605–607
    employer's liability under, 607
Civil trial. *See* Trial(s)

Civil unions, 559
CLA (Certified Legal Assistant), 9. *See*
    also Certification
Claim(s)
    creditors', 622, 629
    proof of. *See* Proof of claim
CLAS (Certified Legal Assistant
    Specialty), 9
CLE (Continuing Legal Education)
    programs, 10
Clean Air Act (1970), 635, 637
Clean Water Act (1972), 421, 638, 639
Click-on agreement, 500, 512
Click-on license, 512
Click-through agreement, 512
Click-wrap agreement, 512
Client(s)
    attorney-client privilege and. *See*
        Attorney-client privilege
    billing of, 73, 74
    communicating with, 78–82
    conflict of interest and, 103–108,
        505. *See also* Conflict(s) of
        interest
    consent of
        to disclose confidential
            information, 97–98
        required for electronic filing, 314
    deposition of, preparing for, 329
    disclosure of paralegal status to, 117,
        291
    documents from, handling of, 362
    former, 106
    gifts from, 106
    information about, obtaining, 379
    information from, confidentiality
        of. *See* Confidentiality of
        information
    intent of, to commit harmful or
        illegal act, 99–100
    interview of. *See* Client interview(s)
    legal action brought by, for
        malpractice, 100, 167
        avoiding, 550
    maintaining contact with, 4, 5, 7
    meeting, 379, 577
    paralegals' representation of, before
        some administrative agencies,
        27, 117, 151
    property of, obtaining information
        about, 379
    relations with, 7
    simultaneous representation and,
        104–105, 505
    trust accounts and, 71–72
    unauthorized practice of law
        by paralegals and. *See*
        Unauthorized practice of law
Client file(s), 66–68. *See also* Filing
    adding subfiles to, 67
    closing, 67–68
    confidentiality and, 66

    maintaining, 4, 78
    new, opening, 66–67
    old, destroying, 68
    organizing, 4
Client interview(s), 4, 357, 360–362,
    379, 642. *See also* Interview(s)
    checklist for, 16
    concluding, 379
    follow-up, 303
    informational, 360
    initial, 303, 357, 360, 505
    preparing for, 379
    results of, summarizing, 360–362
    subsequent, 360
    unauthorized practice of law, ethics
        and, 364
Close corporation, 593
Closed-ended questions, 356
Closely held corporation, 593
Closing
    of escrow, 534, 535
    of letter, 285
Closing arguments, 404–405
Closing costs, 535
Closing package, reviewing, 537
Coalition Against Insurance Fraud
    (CAIF), 547
Coca-Cola, 517
Code(s)
    defined, 223
    federal, 224–225
    state. *See* State statute(s)
Code of Federal Regulations (C.F.R.), 259
    citation to, 212
    online links to, 249
    Shepard's Code of Federal Regulations
        Citations and, 252–253
    titles in, 229
Codified law, 151
Coinsurance clause, 544
Collaborative law, 183
Collateral contracts, 506
Collection agency, 486–487
Collective bargaining, 603
Color, discrimination on basis of, 172,
    485, 605, 607
Commerce clause, 143–144, 179
Commercial impracticability, 509
Commercial leases, 537–548
Commercial property, lease of, 537–548
Commission, act of, 420
Common law
    defined, 130
    in England, 129, 130, 151
    the paralegal and, 137–138
    precedent and. *See* Precedent(s)
    as a primary source of law, 129
    statutory law and, 136
    today, 135–136
    tradition of, case law and, 130–139
Common law marriage, 559
Commonly known dangers, 481

Communication(s)
  with clients, 78–82
  diagrams used in, 363
  electronic, confidentiality and,
      100–101, 104–105
  ex parte, 397
  skills in. *See* Communication skill(s)
  using graphics in, 363
Communication skill(s), 11–13
  client communication and, 80–81
  listening and, 12, 81, 356–357
  reading and, 11–12
  speaking and, 12, 81
  writing and, 12–13, 15
Communications Decency Act (CDA)
      (1996), 141, 477
Community college programs, 8
Community property, 531, 568
Comparative negligence, 474, 481
Compensation
  of paralegal. *See* Paralegal
      compensation
  for plaintiff, for assault or battery,
      462
Compensatory damages, 472, 510
Competence
  attorney's duty of. *See* Duty(ies) of
      Competence
  of witness, 366
Complaint (in civil litigation)
  allegations in, 310–311
  body of, 310–311
      sample, illustrated, 308–309
  defined, 305
  drafting, 306, 310–312
      checklist for, 313
  filing, 312, 314–315. *See also*
      Document(s), court, filing
  prayer for relief in, 311
  sample, illustrated, 308–309
  serving, 316–318
  signature on, 311
Complaint (criminal)
  filing, 436
  illustrated, 437
  initial appearance and, 436–437, 440
Comprehensive Environmental
      Response, Compensation,
      and Liability Act (CERCLA)
      (Superfund) (1980), 640–641
Computer(s)
  keyboarding skills and, 34
  paralegal use of, 5, 13–14
  skills with, 13–14
Computer forensics, 341, 450
Concurrent jurisdiction, 165
Concurrent ownership, 531
Concurrent powers, 146
Concurring opinion, 137, 220
Conference committee, 146
Confidentiality agreements, 521
Confidentiality of information, 97–102

attorney-client privilege and, 66, 97,
      102–103. *See also* Attorney-client
      privilege
  electronic communications and,
      100–101, 104–105
  ethics and, 325
      product liability and, 480
      social events and, 101
  exceptions to confidentiality rule
      and, 97–100
  filing procedures and, 66
  paralegal's ability and, 14, 16
  protecting, 404, 450, 521, 566
  rule governing, 97
      exceptions to, 97–100
      violations of, 100–102
  violations of confidentiality rule and,
      100–102
Confirmation letter, 285
  sample, illustrated, 287
Conflict(s)
  of interest, 103–108
      conflicts check and, 108
      defined, 103
      former clients and, 106
      potential, ethics and, 505
      simultaneous representation and,
          104–105
      walling-off procedures and, 106,
          107
  in the workplace, managing, 83
Conflicts check, 108
Congressional Information Service (C.I.S.),
      228–229
Congressional Record, 228
  online links to, 249
Consequential (special) damages, 510
Consideration. *See* Contract(s),
      consideration in
Constitution(s)
  federal. *See* United States
      Constitution
  state, 129, 141–142, 146
  United States. *See* United States
      Constitution
*The Constitution of the United States of
      America,* 223
Constitutional law, 139–142. *See also*
      United States Constitution
  courts and, 141
  defined, 139
  finding, 223
  the paralegal and, 142
  researching, 223–225
Constitutional rights, 139–141. *See also*
      Bill of Rights
Constructive discharge, 602
Consumer(s)
  as debtor. *See* Consumer-debtor(s)
  defined, 482
  health of, consumer law and, 484–
      485

laws protecting. *See* Consumer law(s)
  safety of, consumer law and, 484–485
Consumer Credit Protection Act
      (1968), 485
Consumer law(s), 482–488
  consumer credit protection and,
      485–487
  consumer health and safety and,
      484–485
  defined, 482
  paralegal and, 487
  selected areas of, regulated by
      statutes, 482
  statutes governing, 148
Consumer Product Safety Act (1972),
      485
Consumer Product Safety Commission,
      229, 485
Consumer-debtor(s)
  defined, 617
  special Bankruptcy Code treatment
      for, 617, 620
Contempt of court, 118, 134
Contingency fee, 70–71
Continuing Legal Education (CLE)
      programs, 10
Contract(s). *See also* Agreement(s)
  acceptance in, 497, 498, 500
      defined, 500
      unequivocal, 500
  adhesion, 505
  agreement in, 497, 498–500
  arbitration clause in, 179
  assent in, genuineness of, 503–505
  bilateral, 497
  breach of
      defined, 508
      remedy(ies) for, 509–511
          damages as, 509–510. *See also*
              Damages
          reformation as, 511
          rescission as, 510
          restitution as, 510
          specific performance as,
              511. *See also* Specific
              performance
  capacity in, 497, 502, 503
  collateral, 506
  commercial, arbitrating, 185
  consideration in, 497, 500–502
      adequacy of, 501
      legal sufficiency of, 501
  defined, 28
  e-, 511–514
  employment, 602
  enforcement of, defenses to, 503–
      506
  forms for, 499
  implied, 602
  legality of, 497, 502–503
  marriage, 559
  mirror image rule and, 500

offer in, 497, 498–500
   counteroffer and, 499–500, 533
   defined, 498
   termination of, 499–500
   terms of, definiteness of, 498
paralegals and, 27
performance of, 508–511
principal's liability and, 600
ratification of, 600
rescission of, 504, 510
review of, 508
unconscionable, 503, 505
unilateral, 497
valid, requirements of, 497–503
voidable, 502
wrongful interference with, 466–467
Contract attorneys, 61
Contract law. *See also* Contract(s)
   the paralegal and, 514
   as paralegal specialty, 28–29
Contract paralegals, 27
Contractual capacity, 497, 502, 503
Contributory negligence, 474
Controlling the Assault of Non-
   Solicited Pornography and
   Marketing (CAN-SPAM) Act, 469
Conversations overheard by others,
   100, 101
Conversion, 470
COPA (Child Online Protection Act),
   141
Copyright, 429, 497, 514, 516–517
Copyright Act (1976), 516, 517
Copyright law, 31–32
   statutory law and, 148
Cornell University, Legal Information
   Institute of. *See* Legal Information
   Institute
Cornick, Matthew, 240–241
Corporate charter, 590–591
Corporate law
   defined, 28
   as paralegal specialty, 28, 590–591
   statutory law and, 148
Corporation(s), 588–596
   bylaws of, 591
   classifications of, 591, 593
   close, 593
   closely held, 593
   criminal liability and, 421
   as defendant, serving, 316
   director of. *See* Director(s)
   dissolution of, 596
   dividend and, 594
   formation of, 588–591
   for-profit, 593
   jurisdiction over, 162
   as a legal person, 588
   limited personal liability and, 62
   liquidation of, 596
   minimum-contacts requirement and,
      162

name of, reserving, 593
nonprofit, 593
not-for-profit, 593
officer of. *See* Officer(s)
private, 591
professional (P.C.), 61–62, 593
promoters and, 588–589
public, 591, 593
publicly held, 593
responsible corporate officer
   doctrine and, 421
S, 593, 595–596
shareholder of. *See* Shareholder(s)
taxation and, 595–596
termination of, 596
working for, 25
Corporation Service Company (CSC),
   595
Corpus Juris Secundum (C.J.S.)(West), 199
   illustrated, 201
Costs, billed to clients, 73
Counteradvertising, 484
Counterclaim, 320–321
Counterfeit Access Device and
   Computer Fraud and Abuse Act,
   429
Counteroffer, 499–500, 533
County attorney, 417
Court(s), 161–173
   adoptions and, 562
   alternative dispute resolution (ADR)
      referred by, 183–184
   of appeals. *See* Appellate court(s)
   appellate. *See* Appellate court(s)
   bankruptcy, 26, 31, 163, 616–617
   basic judicial requirements to bring
      lawsuit before, 161–167
      the paralegal and, 167
   choice of, 164
   constitutional law and, 141
   contempt of, 118, 134
   decisions of, 137. *See also* Opinion(s)
      appellate court's modification of,
         408
      reporting of. *See* Case reporting
         system
   docket of, 165, 310
   employment with, 26, 452
   of equity, 132
   filing of documents with. *See*
      Document(s), court, filing
   on freedom of speech, 141
   holding of, 221
   in Internet age, 174–175
   Islamic, civil law system and, 151
   jurisdiction of. *See* Jurisdiction
   of law, 131
   opinion of. *See* Opinion(s)
   order of, disclosures to comply with,
      100
   probate, 31, 162–163, 570
   procedures in, 166

reviewing. *See* Appellate court(s)
role of, in arbitration process,
   181–182
small claims, 26
supreme
   state (highest), 167, 169, 453
      attorney regulation and, 91,
         93–94
   United States. *See* United States
      Supreme Court
   trial. *See* Trial court(s)
   trial presentation technology in,
      392–393
   venue and, 166
   Web sites of, 174–175
Cover, 511
Cover letter, 45
   sample, illustrated, 46
CP (Certified Paralegal), 9. *See also*
   Certification
Cram-down position, 633
Credibility of witness, 366, 401
Credit, protection of, consumer laws
   regarding, 485–487, 488
Credit cards, consumer protection and,
   485–487
Credit discrimination, 485
Creditor(s)
   best interests of, 631
   claims of, 622, 629
   committee of, 632
   defined, 626
   judgment, 409
   meetings of, 622
   preferred, 624
   secured. *See* Secured creditor(s)
   unsecured, bankruptcy property
      distribution and, 624–625
Crime(s)
   civil liability for, 418
   classifications of, 418–420
   criminal act and, 420
   cyber. *See* Cyber crime(s)
   defined, 417–420
   financial, 427
   jurisdiction over, 420
   liability for. *See* Criminal liability
   organized, 426–427
   persons accused of. *See* Criminal
      defendant(s)
   property, 423–424
   prosecution for, tort lawsuit for same
      act versus, illustrated, 419
   public order, 424
   types of, 423–427
   violent, 423
   white-collar, 424–426
Criminal act *(actus reus)*, 420
Criminal defendant(s)
   constitutional safeguards protecting,
      429–431. *See also individual*
      protections

initial appearance of, 436–437, 440
innocence of, presumption of, 447
Criminal law, 416–458
  civil law versus, 32–33, 417–418
  defined, 32
  as paralegal specialty, 32–33
  procedures in. *See* Criminal
    procedures
  as statutory law, 136, 418
Criminal liability
  corporate, 421
  of corporate officers and directors, 421
  defenses to, 421–422
  elements of, 420–422
Criminal litigation, paralegals and,
  438–439
Criminal negligence, 421
Criminal procedures
  discovery and, 443, 446
  major steps in processing a criminal
    case and, summarized, 432
  pretrial motions and, 442
  prior to prosecution, 431–435
  trial and. *See* Criminal trial(s)
Criminal trial(s)
  during, 446–451
  appeal following, 453
  beginning of prosecution and,
    435–437, 440–446
  criminal procedures prior to,
    435–437, 440–446
  pretrial motions and, 442
  procedures and. *See* Criminal
    procedures
  sentencing and, 449–451, 452
  standard of proof in, 418, 447
Cross-claim, 321
Cross-examination, 400–401
  defined, 400
  sample questions for, 401
  of witnesses, accused person's right
    to, 140, 430, 448
CSC (Corporation Service Company),
  595
Cyber crime(s), 427–429
  defined, 427
  prosecution of, 428–429
Cyber theft, 427
Cyber tort(s)
  defamation online and, 476–479
  defined, 461
Cyberbullying, 428
Cybernotary, 513
Cyberspace. *See* Internet; World Wide
  Web
Cyberstalking, 427–428

D

Daily cleanup, 131
Damages, 418
  awarded in judgment, enforcement
    and, 409

compensatory, 472, 510
consequential (special), 510
defined, 94
fraudulent misrepresentation and,
  466, 504
incidental, 510
injury requirement and, 466, 472,
  504
liquidated, 510
punitive, 472, 510
special (consequential), 510
Danger(s)
  abnormally dangerous activities and,
    478
  commonly known, 481
  unreasonably dangerous products
    and, 479
  wild animals and, 478
Deadlines, 11, 24, 78, 143
  important, putting on calendar and
    tracking, 4, 62, 167
  missed, 96
Deadly force, 422
Debt(s)
  collection of, consumer laws
    regarding, 486–487
  preexisting, 624
Debtor(s)
  bankruptcy creditors' meeting and,
    622
  consumer as. *See* Consumer-
    debtor(s)
  defined, 626
  in possession (DIP), 631–632
Deceptive advertising, 482–484
Decision(s), 137. *See also* Opinion(s)
  posted on Web sites, 175
Declarant, 377
Deed(s)
  defined, 535
  sample, illustrated, 536
Defamation, 464–465
  defenses against, 464–465
  defined, 464
  online, 476–479
  per se, 464
Default judgment, 318
Defendant(s)
  answer of. *See* Answer
  case of, during trial, 403–404
  co-, 137
  corporate, serving, 316
  criminal. *See* Criminal defendant(s)
  defined, 28, 66, 137, 302
  finding, 317
  in hypothetical civil lawsuit, 302
  response of, 318–321
  waiver of service by, 317–318
Defense(s)
  affirmative, 318–319, 473
  to assault and battery, 462
  to criminal liability, 421–422

against defamation, 464–465
defined, 421
to enforcement of contract,
  503–506
knowledgeable user, 481
to negligence, 473–474
of others, 422, 462
against payment under insurance
  contract, 548
to product liability, 481
of property, 422, 462
self-, 422, 462
against trespass to land, 469
to wrongful interference, 467
Demand letter, 286–287
  sample, illustrated, 289
Deponent
  attorney of, role of, 329–330
  defined, 328
Deposition(s), 328–332
  of client, preparing for, 329
  defined, 328
  questions for
    drafting, 328
    sample, illustrated, 330
  subpoena for, 329
  taking, notice of, 328
    illustrated, 329
  transcript of. *See* Deposition
    transcript
Deposition transcript, 330–332
  defined, 330
  excerpt from, illustrated, 331
  indexing, 331–332
  summarizing, 331–332
    excerpt from, illustrated, 333
    tips for, 332
Design defects, 480
Detention, arrest versus, 433
Diagrams, value of, in communicating,
  363
Dicta, 221
Digest(s)
  case, 201–203
  defined, 201
  types of, 201
Digital forensic experts, 341, 450
Digital records, 392–393
Digital signatures, 513
Dilution, trademark, 517, 520
DIP (debtor in possession), 631–632
Direct evidence
  circumstantial evidence versus,
    375–376
  defined, 375
Direct examination, 399–400
  defined, 399
  sample questions for, 400
Directed verdict, 402–403
Director(s)
  criminal liability of, 421
  defined, 588

duties of, 594–595
functions of, 594–595
Directories, 41, 243, 264, 373
Disability, discrimination on basis of, 172, 605, 607–609
Disaffirmance, 502
Disbarment, 94
Discharge
  in bankruptcy, 625–626, 630–631, 633
  constructive, 602
  of employee. *See* Employee(s), discharge of
  wrongful, 602
Disclaimer of warranty, 507–508
Disclosure(s)
  exceptions to confidentiality rule and, 97–100
  of paralegal status, 117, 291
  public, of private facts, 465
  required in civil litigation. *See* Civil litigation, disclosure(s) required in
Disclosure law, 485
Discovery
  in criminal case, 443, 446
  defined, 324
  discovery plan and, 335–336
  electronic. *See* Electronic discovery
  of electronic evidence. *See* Electronic discovery
  prediscovery meeting and, 333–334
  traditional tools of, 324–333
  writing in, 279–280
Discovery plan, 335–336
Discrimination
  on basis of
    age, 65, 172, 182, 485, 605, 607
    color, 172, 485, 605, 607
    disability, 172, 605, 607–609
    gender, 65, 172, 173, 485, 605
    marital status, 485
    national origin, 172, 485, 605, 607
    race, 65, 172, 485, 605, 607
    religion, 172, 485, 605, 607
  credit, 485
  employment. *See* Employment discrimination
Displays for trial, preparation of, 391, 392–393
Dissenting opinion, 137, 220
Dissolution
  of corporation, 596
  of partnership, 587
District attorney, 417
Diversion programs, 451
Diversity jurisdiction, 163–164, 173, 310
Diversity of citizenship, 163–164, 173, 310
Dividend, 594
Divorce, 563–564
  defined, 563
  fault-based, 563

  no-fault, 563
Docket, 165, 310
Docket number, 215, 218–219, 310
Docketing software, 62
Document(s)
  assisting consumers with, 119
  from client, handling, 362
  court
    caption on, 310
    filing, 4
      electronic, 312, 314–315
      traditional method of, 312
  drafting of, 4, 5
  e-, 513–514
  errors in, 96
  filing. *See* Filing
  generated by attorney, reviewing, 290
  proofreading, 13, 45, 279
  requests for production of, 332–333
  revising, 279
  security of, evolving technology and, 450
  user-friendly, creating, 273, 276
DOL. *See* United States Department of Labor
Domestic partnerships, 559
Domestic violence, 559–560
Double billing, 76–78
  ABA's response to, 77–78
  defined, 76
Double jeopardy, constitutional prohibition of, 140, 430
Double taxation, 595–596
Drafting Legal Documents (Office of the Federal Register), 276
Dram shop acts, 475
Drew, Lori, 428
Drew, Sarah, 428
Due process of law, 140, 141, 144, 145, 429–430
Duress
  as defense to criminal liability, 422
  genuineness of assent and, 504–505
Duty(ies)
  of care. *See* Care, duty of
  of competence, 94–97
    breach of, 95–96
    ethics and
      deadlines and, 143
      statute of limitations and, 143
  of confidentiality. *See* Confidentiality of information
  fiduciary, 594, 599. *See also* Fiduciary relationship
  marital, 559
  of property owners, 471–472
  to retreat, 422
  trespass and, 468–470

E

Early neutral case evaluation, 182
Earnest money, 532–533, 534

Easement, 530–531
ECOA (Equal Credit Opportunity Act) (1974), 485
Economic Espionage Act, 425–426, 429, 520
E-contracts, 511–514
Editing, 282
E-documents, 513–514
Edson, Wendy B., 80–81
EEOC. *See* Equal Employment Opportunity Commission
Eighth Amendment, 140, 429, 430, 440
EIS (environmental impact statements), 634
eLawExchange, 450
Elder law, 33
Electronic communications, confidentiality and, 100–101
Electronic discovery, 337–341
  conducting, tips for, 340
  cost of, party who bears and, 338–339
Electronic evidence (e-evidence), 337–341
  advantages of, 337–338
  back-up data and, 339–340
  chain of custody and, 341
  discovery of. *See* Electronic discovery
  Federal Rule of Evidence 502 and, 341
  FRCP on, 337
  image copy of, 341
  metadata and, 337
  sources of, 338–340
  special requirements of, 340–341
Electronic file(s)
  back-up data and, 339–340
  deleted, retrieval of, 337–338
  hacking, 304, 428
  professional maintenance of, 247
Electronic filing (e-filing) system, 314
Electronic signature. *See* E-signature(s)
Electronic Signatures in Global and National Commerce Act (E-SIGN Act) (2000), 513–514
Elements of Style (Strunk and White), 273
E-mail
  clarity of, 102
  confidentiality and, 104–105
  as electronic evidence, 337
  follow-up letter to client sent by, illustrated, 361
  formatting, tips for, 79
  managing, tips for, 82
  organizing, 82
  privacy and, 466
  professional standards applied to, 79
  uses of, 240
Emancipation, 557
Embezzlement, 424–425
Eminent domain, 530
Emotional distress, intentional infliction of, 463–464

Employee(s)
  agency relationships and, 598
  co-, connecting with, 83
  conflicts among, managing, 83
  with disability, reasonable
      accommodations and, 608–609
  discharge of
    constructive, 602
    for garnishment, 487, 488
    wrongful, 602
  exempt, 36–37
  key, 603–604
  privacy rights of, 466
  termination of, 64–65
  wrongful discharge and, 602
Employer(s)
  attorney discipline board as, 122
  business organizations as, 25
  corporations as, 25
  freelance paralegals and, 27,
      117–118
  government as, 25–26
  independent paralegals and. See
      Legal technician(s)
  law firms as. See Law firm(s)
  legal aid office as, 26–27
  legal technicians and. See Legal
      technician(s)
  liability of, under Title VII, 607
  potential, locating. See Job search
  public defender as, 26, 29
  types of, 23–27
Employment
  acting within scope of, 600
  discrimination in. See Employment
      discrimination
  records of, obtaining, 371
  at will, 602
Employment contract, 602
Employment discrimination, 30, 605–609
  on basis of
    age, 65, 172, 182, 605, 607
    color, 172, 605, 607
    disability, 172, 605, 607–609
    gender, 65, 172, 173, 605. See also
        Sexual harassment
    national origin, 172, 605, 607
    pregnancy, 172–173, 605
    race, 65, 172, 605, 607
    religion, 172, 605, 607
  sexual harassment and. See Sexual
      harassment
Employment law, 601–609
  the paralegal and, 30–31, 609
  as paralegal specialty, 30–31
  statutory law and, 148
Employment manual, 63
Employment records, obtaining, 371
Employment termination, 64–65
Enabling legislation, 149, 229
Encyclopedias, legal, 130, 198, 199–201,
    247

Enforcement
  by administrative agencies, 150
  of judgment, 408–409, 411
England, common law in, 129, 130, 151
English Leather, 517
Environmental Compliance Assistance
    Platform, 636
Environmental coordinator, 32
Environmental impact statements
    (EIS), 634
Environmental law(s), 634–642
  compliance with, 636
  defined, 32, 634
  federal, 634–635
  the paralegal and, 32, 641–642
Environmental Protection Agency
    (EPA), 11, 26, 32, 135, 148, 153,
    420, 635, 637, 638, 639, 640, 641,
    642
  creation of, 634
  National Environmental Compliance
      Assistance Clearinghouse of, 636
  obtaining information from, 376
  Web site of, 636
Environmental Software Providers, 636
EPA. See Environmental Protection
    Agency
Equal Credit Opportunity Act (ECOA)
    (1974), 485
Equal Employment Opportunity
    Commission (EEOC), 31
  functions of, 601
  paralegal's interaction with, 609
  record-keeping requirements of, 49
  Web site of, 249
Equifax, 486
Equitable distribution, 568
Equitable principles and maxims,
    132–134
Equity
  action in, procedural differences
      between action at law and, 135
  courts of, 132
  merging of law and, 134–135
  remedies in. See Remedy(ies) in
      equity
Error(s). See also Mistake(s)
  in document, 96
  reversible, 169
Escrow, closing, 534, 535
Escrow account, 71. See also Trust
    account(s)
Escrow agent, 533–534, 535
E-SIGN Act (Electronic Signatures in
    Global and National Commerce
    Act) (2000), 513–514
E-signature(s), 512–514
  defined, 512
  laws governing, 513–514
Estate(s)
  in bankruptcy. See Bankruptcy, estate
      in property of

defined, 31
  life, 531
Estate administration, 569, 575–576
Estate planning, 569
  defined, 31
  online help for, 575
  as paralegal specialty, 31, 576
Estate taxes, 574
Estoppel
  defined, 501
  promissory, 501–502, 506
Ethical wall, 106, 107
Ethics
  accurate paperwork and real estate
      transactions and, 534
  attorney's duty to supervise
      paralegals and, 570
  backing up work and, 77
  clarifying instructions to paralegal
      and, 545
  clients and, billing practices and,
      76–78
  codes and rules pertaining to, 92–94
  confidentiality and, 325
    product liability and, 480
    at social events and, 101
  contingency fees and, 71
  deadlines and, 96
  duty of competence and
    deadlines and, 143
    statute of limitations and, 143
  ex parte communication with jurors
      and, 397
  finding ethics opinions on the Web
      and, 250
  giving legal advice and, 5, 604, 628
  importance of being honest and, 41
  interviewing clients and
      unauthorized practice of law
      and, 364
  the paralegal and, 89–127
    ethical codes and, 108–109
    ten tips regarding, 112–113
  potential conflicts of interest and,
      505
  potential problems with arbitration
      and, 183
  preparing exhibits for trial and, 447
  professional responsibility and,
      89–127
  stress-related mistakes and, 24
  unauthorized practice of law (UPL)
      and, 5, 604
    letters and, 291
  using secondary sources and, 206
  will drafting, paralegal supervision,
      and, 570
European Union (EU), Fight the Fog
    campaign and, 276
Evidence
  authentication of, 377
  chain of custody and, 341

circumstantial. *See* Circumstantial evidence
defined, 374
direct. *See* Direct evidence
e-. *See* Electronic evidence
electronic. *See* Electronic evidence
evolving technology and, 450
hearsay and. *See* Hearsay
illegally obtained, 430
motion to suppress. *See* Motion(s) to suppress evidence
outside the pleadings, 323
preponderance of, 418
rebuttal and, 404
relevant, 376–377
requests for production of, 332–333
rules of
    defined, 374
    Federal. *See* Federal Rules of Evidence
    investigation and, 374–378
Ex parte communications, 397
Examination
    cross-. *See* Cross-examination
    direct. *See* Direct examination
    physical, request for, 332–333
    recross-, 401–402
    redirect, 402
    of witness. *See* Witness(es), examination of
Exclusionary rule, 430
Exclusive jurisdiction, 165, 173
Execution, writ of, 409
Executor, 570, 575–576
Exempt employees, 36–37
Exempt property, 109
Exemption(s)
    in bankruptcy, 622–623, 627
    homestead, 622, 623
Exhibits
    pretrial disclosures related to, 336
    for trial, preparation of, 391, 392–393
        ethics and, 447
Exit interview, 83
Expense slip, 74
Expenses, documenting, 73–76
Experian, 486
Expert witness(es), 362, 364
    consulting with, 410
    defined, 362
    required disclosures related to, 336
Express warranty, 507
Eyewitnesses, 364–365

F

FAA (Federal Arbitration Act) (1925), 179
Facebook, 428
Fact(s)
    causation in, 472–473
    material, mistake of, 504
    mistake of, 504
    private, public disclosure of, 465
    questions of, 169
    statement of, 466
FACT (Fair and Accurate Credit Transactions Act) (2003), 486
Fair and Accurate Credit Transactions Act (FACT) (2003), 486
Fair Credit Reporting Act (1970), 486
Fair Debt Collection Practices Act (1977), 486
Fair Labor Standards Act (FLSA) (1938), 36–37, 603
Fair Packaging and Labeling Act (1966), 484
FairPay rule, 36–37
False imprisonment, 463
False pretenses, obtaining goods by, 424
Family and Medical Leave Act (FMLA) (1993), 603–604
Family law, 557–569
    defined, 32, 557
    as paralegal specialty, 32, 558, 569
Family settlement agreements, 571
Fastcase, 258
Fault-based divorce, 563
FBIC (Fight Bad-Faith Insurance Companies), 547
FDA. *See* Food and Drug Administration
Federal Arbitration Act (FAA) (1925), 179
Federal Bureau of Investigation, 428
Federal court system, 170–173
    appellate courts of, 170, 171. *See also* United States Supreme Court
        decisions of, 214–215. *See also* Case reporting system
            citations to, 211–212
            reporting of, 214
    constitutional provisions regarding, 163, 170
    electronic filing in, 314
    judges of, lifetime appointments of, 170
    jurisdiction of, 163–165, 172, 173, 420
    organization of, illustrated, 170
    the paralegal and, 172–173
    state court or, choice of, 164
    trial courts (district courts) of, 163, 170, 171, 616
    United States courts of appeals of, 170, 171
    United States district court(s) of, 163, 170, 171, 616
    Web site of, 174
Federal Food, Drug and Cosmetic Act (1938), 485
Federal government
    checks and balances system and, 143
    constitutional authority of, to enact laws, 142–143
    courts of. *See* Federal court system
    lawmaking process of, 145–146
    powers of, under commerce clause, 143–144, 179
    preemption by, 146
        determining, tips for, 147
    statutes of. *See* Federal statute(s)
Federal Insecticide, Fungicide, and Rodenticide Act (FIFRA) (1947), 639–640
Federal Law Citations in Selected Law Reviews (Shepard's), 254
Federal questions, 163, 173, 310
Federal Register, 150, 229
    monitoring, 637, 642
    online links to, 249
Federal Reporter (F., F.2d, or F.3d) (West), 214
Federal Reserve Board, 485
Federal Rules of Bankruptcy Procedure, 617
Federal Rules of Civil Procedure (FRCP), 166, 306, 617
    defined, 302
    duty to disclose under, 333–336
    on electronic evidence, 337
    full text of, in U.S.C.A., 225
    waiver of service under, 317–318
Federal Rules of Criminal Procedure, full text of, in U.S.C.A., 225
Federal Rules of Evidence, 366
    authentication of evidence under, 377
    full text of, in U.S.C.A., 225
    investigation and, 374
    Rule 502 of, 341
Federal statute(s), 142–146
    finding, 224–225
    governing e-signatures and e-documents, 513–514
    lawmaking process and, 145–146
    new, likely to be enacted, 230
    state statutes and, conflicts between, 146
Federal Supplement (F.Supp. or F.Supp.2d) (West), 214
Federal system, 142
Federal Trade Commission (FTC)
    consumer protection and, 482, 483–484, 486
    consumer sales transactions and, 484
    creation of, 149, 229
    deceptive advertising and, 483–484
    functions of, 149, 229
    identity theft and, 486
    labeling and packaging laws and, 484
    Web site of, 468, 469
Federal Trade Commission Act (1914), 149, 229, 483
Federal Water Pollution Control Act (FWPCA) (1948), 638
FedEx, 500

Fee(s), 69–78
    alternative arrangements regarding, 71
    contingency, 70–71
    fixed, 69
    hourly, 69–70
    legal, billed to clients, 73
    reasonableness requirement and, 69, 198
    retainer agreement and, 69, 70
    splitting of, prohibition against, 115
Fee simple, 530
Felony, 419, 424
Ferguson, Fernaundra, 180–181
Fiduciary duty, 594, 599
Fiduciary relationship
    agency relationship as, 599
    corporate directors and officers, corporation and, 594
    defined, 599
FIFRA (Federal Insecticide, Fungicide, and Rodenticide Act) (1947), 639–640
Fifth Amendment, 140, 144, 429, 430, 446, 447
Fight Bad-Faith Insurance Companies (FBIC), 547
Fight the Fog, 276
File(s). *See also* Record(s)
    computer. *See* Electronic file(s)
    electronic. *See* Electronic file(s)
    forms, 68
    hacking, 304, 428
    litigation. *See* Litigation file
    of reference materials, 68
    work product, 68
Filing. *See also* File(s)
    adding subfiles and, 67
    closing a file and, 67–68
    destroying old files and, 68
    file use and, 67
    forms file and, 68
    opening a file and, 66–67
    procedures regarding, 65–68
    of reference materials, 68
    storage and, 67
    of work product, 68
Financial crimes, 427
Finding tools
    for administrative law, 229
    defined, 199
FindLaw
    analyzing clauses in insurance policies with, 547
    court opinions available at, 247
    as general legal resource, 245
    home page for, illustrated, 243
    Market Center of, 575
First Amendment, 140, 141
Fixed fee, 69
Flammable Fabrics Act (1953), 485
The Florida Bar v. Brumbaugh, 118

The Florida Bar v. Furman, 118
FLSA (Fair Labor Standards Act) (1938), 36–37, 603
FMLA (Family and Medical Leave Act) (1993), 603–604
FOIA. *See* Freedom of Information Act
Follow-up letter
    to client, illustrated, 361
    to prospective employer, 49–50, 51
Follow-up questions, 351
Food and Drug Administration (FDA), 129, 148
    consumer health and safety and, 485
    labeling and packaging laws and, 484
Forensics, computer, 341, 450
Foreseeability of product misuse, 480
Forfeiture, 426, 427
Forgery, 424
Form(s)
    contract, 499
    interview, standardized, 350–351
        sample, illustrated, 352–353
    release, 303
    return-of-service, 316, 388
        illustrated, 317
Forms file, 68
Foster care, 561
Fourteenth Amendment, 141, 144
Fourth Amendment, 140, 144, 145, 429, 430, 433
Four-year bachelor's degree programs, 8
France, civil law system in, 151
Fraud, 465–466
    bankruptcy, 425
    elements of, 465–466
    genuineness of assent and, 504
    insurance, 547
    mail, 425
    wire, 425
Fraudulent misrepresentation, 465–466. *See also* Fraud
Fraudulent transfers, 624
FRCP. *See* Federal Rules of Civil Procedure
Freedom of Information Act (FOIA) (1966), 153
    accessing government information using form for, 374
    information exempted from, 374
    seeking information from EPA using, 376
Freedom of religion and speech, 140, 141
Freelance paralegals, 27, 117–118
Friendly witnesses
    defined, 365
    issuing subpoenas for, 388–389
FTC. *See* Federal Trade Commission
Future interests, 531
FWPCA (Federal Water Pollution Control Act) (1948), 638

G

Gallo, Nancy R., 558
Garner, Bryan, legal writing Web site of, 15
Garnishment, 487, 488
Gates, Bill, 598
Gender
    discrimination on basis of, 65, 172, 173, 485, 605
    peremptory challenges based upon, 396
    same, couples of, 559
General jurisdiction, 162, 163, 168–169
General licensing, 119–120
General partner, 587, 588
General partnership, 587. *See also* Partnership(s)
General warrants, constitutional prohibition of, 433
Genuineness of assent, 503–505
Gift from client, 106
Goals
    long-term, defining, 37
    short-term, job realities and, 37–38
Good Samaritan statutes, 475
Goods. *See also* Product(s)
    nonconforming, 511
    obtaining, by false pretenses, 424
    sale of, 507. *See also* Sales contract(s); Uniform Commercial Code
    stolen, receiving, 424
Google, 517
Google Chrome, 242
Government(s)
    as employer, 25–26
    federal. *See* Federal government
    federal system of, 142
    information from, accessing, 374, 375, 376
    regulation by. *See* Regulation(s)
    state. *See* State(s)
    taking of private property by, for public use, 530
Grand jury, 441
Grantee, 535
Grantor, 535, 571
Graphics
    communicating with, 363
    trial, 448
Griswold v. Connecticut, 145
Guardian *ad litem*, 564
Guardians, locating, 266
Guides, 243
Guilty act *(actus reus)*, 420

H

Hacker, 304, 428
Handwritten will, 571
Harvard Business Services, 595
Harvard Law Review Association, 207, 293

Hazardous wastes, 640–641
Headnotes, 201, 219
Health Insurance Portability and
        Accountability Act (HIPAA), 66
Hearing
    arbitration, 179–180
    preliminary, 440–441
    sentencing, 452
Hearsay
    defined, 377
    rule regarding
        exceptions to, 378
        policy underlying, 377
Herbicides, 639–640
Hieros Gamos, 246, 260
Hinkel, Daniel F., 540–541
HIPAA (Health Insurance Portability
        and Accountability Act), 66
Hold-harmless clause, 544
Holding, 221
Holding facility, 431
Holiday Inns, Inc., 517
Holographic will, 571
Home page, 240–241
Homestead exemption, 622, 623
Homicide, 421
Honesty, importance of, 41
Hoover's Online, 265
Hornbook, 204, 205
Hostile witnesses, 365, 400
Hostile-environment harassment, 607
Hourly fees, 69–70
How to Write Clearly, 276
How to Write in Plain English, 276
http (hypertext transfer protocol),
        241–242
Hung jury, 448–449
Hvide, Eric, 478
Hvide Marine, 478
Hypertext, 241
Hypertext transfer protocol (http),
        241–242
Hypothetical civil lawsuit, 302–303
Hypothetical questions, 356

I

IADA (Independent Automotive
        Damage Appraisers), 547
Idea, copyrightability and, 516
Identity, mistaken, 422
Identity theft, 427, 468–469, 486
Identity Theft Resources Center, 468
III (Insurance Information Institute),
        547
Image copy, 341
Impeaching a witness, 331
Implied contract, 602
Implied warranty(ies)
    of fitness for a particular purpose,
        507
    of merchantability, 507, 508
Impossibility of performance, 509

In loco parentis, 560
In personam jurisdiction, 162
In rem jurisdiction, 162
Incarceration, 449
Incidental damages, 510
Incorporation
    articles of. *See* Articles of
        incorporation
    certificate of (corporate charter),
        590–591
    online, 594–595
Indemnity, 544
Indemnity clause, 544
Independent adoption, 562
Independent Automotive Damage
        Appraisers (IADA), 547
Independent contractor(s)
    agency relationships and, 598
    defined, 598
    freelance paralegals as, 27, 117–118
    insurance broker as, 539
    torts of, 600
Independent paralegal. *See* Legal
        technician(s)
India, common law system in, 151
Indictment, 441
Information
    confidentiality of. *See* Confidentiality
        of information
    in criminal law, 441
    government, accessing, 374, 375, 376
    inside, 426
    placing person in false light,
        publication of, 465
    privileged, 102–103, 324, 334, 341
    sought from interview, 350
Informational interview, 360
Informative letter, 285
    sample, illustrated, 286
Infractions, 420
Infringement
    copyright, 516–517
    defined, 514
    patent, 516
    trademark, 517–518
Inheritance rights, 561
Injunction
    defined, 118, 134
    as equitable remedy, 134
Injury(ies)
    to innocent party, 466
    job-related, 604–605
    legally recognizable, 472
    as requirement for damages, 466,
        472, 504
Insanity. *See* Mental incompetence
Inside information, 426
Insider trading, 426
Inspection of premises, 535
Insurable interest, 542
Insurance, 539–549
    classifications of, 539

    listed, 542
    complaints regarding, 547
    defined, 30, 539
    insurable interest and, 542
    life, 573, 574
    malpractice, 550
    the paralegal and, 30, 548–549
    policy for. *See* Insurance contract
    self-, 605
    terminology of, 539, 542
    title, 535
Insurance adjusters, 547
Insurance agent, 539, 542
Insurance appraisers, 547
Insurance broker, 539
Insurance company, contacting,
        372–373
Insurance contract, 543–546, 548
    application for, 543
    cancellation of, 546, 548
    claims under, online resources
        concerning, 547
    defined, 539
    effective date of, 543–544
    good faith obligations and, 548
    payment under, defenses against, 548
    provisions and clauses in, 544–546,
        547
Insurance fraud, 547
Insurance Information Institute (III),
        547
Insurance paralegal, 30, 548–549
Insured, 539
Insurer, 539
Intangible personal property, 530
Intellectual property, 497, 514–522.
        *See also specific forms of intellectual
        property*
    defined, 31, 514
    forms of, summarized, 515
    intellectual property audit and,
        518–519
    the paralegal and, 31–32, 520, 522
Intellectual property audit, 518–519
Intent, intention
    as an element of fraud, 466, 483, 504
    intentional torts and. *See* Intentional
        tort(s)
    legislative, 228–229
    as requirement for offer, 498
    statement of, 627
Intentional infliction of emotional
        distress, 463–464
Intentional tort(s), 461–470
    defined, 461
    the paralegal and, 470
    against persons, 461–467
    against property, 467–470
Inter vivos (living) trust, 572–573, 574
Interest(s)
    conflict of. *See* Conflict(s) of interest
    future, 531

insurable, 542
Interest on Lawyers' Trust Accounts
(IOLTA) programs, 72
Internal memorandum, preparing, 295.
See also Legal memorandum
Internal Revenue Code, Subchapter S
of, 593, 595
Internal Revenue Service (IRS)
bankruptcy means test and, 620
paralegals' representation of clients
before, 151
partnership's information return
filed with, 587
International law, 151
defined, 152
national law versus, 152
the paralegal and, 152
International Paralegal Management
Association (IPMA), 40
Internet. *See also* Web site(s); World
Wide Web
browsers and, 242–243
cases of first impression and, 132–
133
contract forms on, 499
contracts formed via, 511–514
courts on, 174–175
estate planning help on, 575
evaluation of, 244
finding associations and
organizations on, 265
finding people on, 264, 266, 374
freedom of speech and, 141
guides and directories and, 243
hacking and, 304, 428
incorporation via, 594–595
insurance claim resources on, 547
investigating companies on, 264, 265
jurisdiction and, 165–166
legal problems with, 468–469
legal research using. *See* Online
research
locating guardians and wards on, 266
medical research using, 260
navigating, 242–244
obscenity on, 141
paralegal resources on, 15
"plain English" guidelines on, 276
search engines and. *See* Search
engine(s)
tools for use on, 240–242
Internet Legal Research Group, 246, 499
Internet Public Library, 265
Internet service provider (ISP), liability
of, 476, 477
Internship, networking during, 40
Interpersonal skills, 14, 354
Interrogatories, 324–327
answering, 325
defined, 324
drafting, 324–325
sample, illustrated, 326–327

use of, effective, ten tips for, 358–359
Interstate commerce, 143
Interview(s)
of client. *See* Client interview(s)
conducting, skills in, 353–357
diagrams used in, 363
exit, 83
flow of, controlling, 357
information sought in, 350
informational, 360
job. *See* Job interview
listening skills and, 356–357
planning, 350–353
questions during
closed-ended, 356
follow-up, 351
hypothetical, 356
leading, 356
open-ended, 354–355
questioning skills and, 354–356
types of, summarized, 355
recording, 351–353, 566
reflecting back and, 357
remaining flexible in, 350–351
results of, summarizing, 360–362
using forms in, 350–351, 352–353
of witnesses. *See* Witness interview(s)
Interviewee, 350
Intestacy laws, 569
Intestate death, 569
Intrastate commerce, 143
Intrusion on individual's affairs or
seclusion, 465
Invasion of privacy, 465
Investigation(s)
by administrative agencies, 150
after arrest, 434–435
conclusions of, 380
investigation plan and. *See*
Investigation plan
legal, 4, 7
planning and conducting, 368–378,
380
preliminary, 303–304
pretrial, 350
by professional investigator, 373
recommendations based on, 380
results of, summarizing, 380
rules of evidence and, 374–378
starting, 368–369
Investigation plan
creating, 370–373
defined, 370
illustrated, 370–371
Invitee, business, 196, 471
Involuntary bankruptcy, 617, 620–621,
625
Involuntary manslaughter, 421
IOLTA (Interest on Lawyers' Trust
Accounts) programs, 72
IPMA (International Paralegal
Management Association), 40

IRAC (issue, rule, application, and
conclusion) method, 222–223,
293, 294, 295
IRAC method for briefing cases,
222–223
Ireland, common law system in, 151
Irrevocable living trust, 572
IRS. *See* Internal Revenue Service
Islamic courts, civil law system and, 151
Issue, rule, application, and conclusion
(IRAC) method, 222–223, 293,
294, 295

J

Japan, civil law system in, 151
Job(s)
change in, former clients and, 106,
107
interviewing for. *See* Job interview
looking for. *See* Job search
Job interview, 47–50
follow-up/thank-you letter after,
49–50, 51
how to dress for, 621
questions during, 48–49, 50
Job search, 39–42
application process of, 42–47
cover letter and, 45, 46
finding available jobs and, 40
identifying possible employers and,
40–41
interview and. *See* Job interview
job-placement services and, 42
maintaining files on, 50
marketing your skills and, 42–52
networking and, 40
professional portfolio and, 47
references and, 45–47
résumé and. *See* Résumé
salary negotiations and, 50–52
Job-placement services, 42
Joint and several liability, 587
Joint custody, 565
Joint legal custody, 565
Joint liability, 587
Joint physical custody, 565
Joint tenancy, 531, 574
Judge(s)
administrative law (ALJ), 150
damages awarded by, 409
federal, lifetime appointments of,
170
justice versus, 137
law made by. *See* Case law(s)
motion to recuse and, 443
scheduling order entered by, 321
Judge-made law. *See* Case law(s)
Judgment(s)
affirmation of, 220, 408
default, 318
defined, 301
enforcing, 408–409, 411

as a matter of law, 402–403, 406, 407
on the pleadings, 322
reversal of, 220, 408, 453
summary, 322–324
Judgment creditor, 409
Judicial Conference, 314
Judicial procedures, 166
Jurisdiction, 162–166
  allegations of, in complaint, 310
  appellate, 163, 171, 172
  concurrent, 165
  defined, 162
  diversity, 163–164, 173, 310
  exclusive, 165, 173
  of federal courts, 163–165, 172, 173, 420
  general, 162, 163, 168–169
  international issues and, 166
  Internet and, 165–166
  limited, 162–163, 169
  minimum contacts and, 132, 162, 166
  original, 163, 171, 172
  over corporation, 162
  over crimes, 420
  over persons, 162
  over property, 162
  over subject matter, 162–163
  in personam, 162
  in rem, 162
  service of process requirements of, 316
  "sliding-scale" standard and, 166
  types of, 162–163
  of United States Supreme Court, 172
Juror(s). See also Jury
  alternate, 396
  charge to, 405–406
  ex parte communication with, ethics and, 397
  instructions to, 405–406
  prospective
    challenges to. See Challenge(s)
    questions asked, 395, 410
  selection of, 394–396
Jury. See also Juror(s)
  charge to, 405–406
  grand, 441
  hung, 448–449
  instructions to, 405–406
  selection of, 394–396
  trial by
    demand for, 312
    right to, 140, 312, 430
  verdict of. See Verdict
Justice(s)
  adversarial system of, 138–139
  judge versus, 137
Justiciable controversy, 161
Justifiable reliance, 466, 504

K

Key employee, 603–604
Key number(s)
  defined, 201
  illustrated, 203
Keyboarding skills, 34
KeyCite, 250, 251, 254–255, 257, 258
  defined, 254
  tips for using, 255
  from Westlaw®, illustrated, 254
Kickbacks, 425
Knowledgeable user defense, 481
KnowX, 264
Kodak, 517
Krager, Dwayne E., 398–399

L

Labeling and packaging laws, 484
Labor laws, 602–603. See also Employment law
Labor unions, 602–603
Labor-Management Reporting and Disclosure Act (Landrum-Griffin Act) (1959), 224–225
Laches, 133–134
Land. See also Real property
  interests in, contracts involving, Statute of Frauds and, 506
  trespass to, 467–469
Landowners, duty of, 471–472
Landrum-Griffin Act (Labor-Management Reporting and Disclosure Act) (1959), 224–225
Larceny, 423–424
Law(s). See also Statute(s)
  action at, procedural differences between action in equity and, 135
  administrative. See Administrative law
  agency. See Agency law; Agency relationship(s)
  American. See American law
  antitrust, 148
  bankruptcy. See Bankruptcy law
  case. See Case law(s)
  civil. See Civil law
  codified, 151
  collaborative, 183
  common. See Common law
  consumer. See Consumer law(s)
  contract. See Contract law
  copyright, 31–32
  corporate. See Corporate law
  courts of, 131
  criminal. See Criminal law
  defined, 129
  disclosure, 485
  disclosures to comply with, 100
  due process of, 140, 141, 144, 145, 429–430
  elder, 33
  employment. See Employment law
  environmental. See Environmental law(s)
  family. See Family law
  governing wills, 570
  insurance, 30, 539–549. See also Insurance
  intellectual property. See Intellectual property
  intestacy, 569
  judge-made. See Case law(s)
  judgment as a matter of, 402–403, 406, 407
  labeling and packaging, 484
  labor, 602–603. See also Employment law
  memorandum of. See Legal memorandum
  merging of equity and, 134–135
  packaging and labeling, 484
  patent, 31–32
  personal-injury, 30
  practice of, unauthorized. See Unauthorized practice of law
  procedural, 8
  questions of, 169
  real estate, 29
  remedies at. See Remedy(ies) at law
  sales transactions and, 484
  session, 146
  slip, 146
  statutory. See Statutory law
  substantive, 8
  tort, 138. See also Tort(s)
  trademark, 31–32
  unauthorized practice of. See Unauthorized practice of law
  uniform, 147–148
Law clerk, 61
Law enforcement offices, employment with, 26
Law firm(s), 23–25
  culture of, 82, 84
  employment policies of, 62–65
  fees and. See Fee(s)
  funds of, commingling trust account funds with, 72
  inner workings of, 59–88
  large, working for, 24–25
  management of, 62
  organization of
    as professional corporation (P.C.), 61–62
    as sole proprietorship, 60–61
    structure of, 60–62
  organization of, as partnership, 61
    organizational chart of, illustrated, 63
  personnel of, 62
  politics in, 82, 84
  procedures of
    billing, 72–76

filing, 65–68. *See also* Filing
financial, 69–78. *See also* Fee(s)
timekeeping, 72–76
small
sample organizational chart for, 63
working for, 23–24
Law Library Resource Xchange
(LLRX), 247
Law office. *See* Law firm(s)
Law schools, 91
LawProf blog network, 15
LawRunner, 246
Lawsuit(s). *See also* Case(s); Litigation
basic judicial requirements for,
161–167
the paralegal and, 167
bringing, standing and, 161
hypothetical, 302–303
initiating, 7
malpractice, 138, 167
avoiding, 550
parties to, 137, 302
paternity, 561
personal-injury, 138
intake sheet and, 352–353
product liability, 138
tort, criminal prosecution for same
act versus, illustrated, 419
*Lawyers' Edition of the Supreme Court
Reports* (L.Ed. or L.Ed.2d), 214
citation to, 211
Lawyers USA, 230
Lawyers Weekly, Inc., 230
lawyers.findlaw.com, 41
Lay witnesses, 364
LDA (legal document assistant), 119
Leading questions, 356, 389, 400
Lease(s), 536–538
commercial, 537–548
defined, 536
review of, 541
typical terms in, summarized, 538
'Lectric Law Library, 260, 499
Legal administrator, 62
Legal aid office, as employer, 26–27
Legal assistant. *See* Paralegal(s)
Legal Assistant Today, 15
survey in, 69, 73
Legal custody, 564
Legal directories, 41, 264
Legal document assistant (LDA), 119
Legal documents. *See* Document(s)
Legal encyclopedias, 130, 198, 199–201,
247
Legal Information Institute (LII), 15
court opinions available at, 247
estate planning help and, 575
as general legal resource, 245–246
URL of, 213
Legal letter(s)
address block in, 284
body of, 284–285

closing of, 285
components of, illustrated, 283
confirmation, 285
sample, illustrated, 287
date in, 282–283
demand, 286–287
sample, illustrated, 289
editing, 282
general format for, 282–285
generated by attorney, reviewing, 290
informative, 285
sample, illustrated, 286
method of delivery of, 284
opinion (advisory), 285–286
sample, illustrated, 288
reference line in, 284
salutation in, 284
types of, 285–287
Legal malpractice, 94, 100, 167, 472, 597
Legal memorandum, 287–295
analysis in, 291, 293
illustrated, 294
conclusion of, 293–294
brief, 291
illustrated, 292
creating, 295
defined, 321
discussion in, 291, 293
illustrated, 294
heading of, 288
illustrated, 289
questions presented in, 290
illustrated, 292
statement of the facts in, 289–290
illustrated, 292
Legal nurse consultant (LNC), 33
Legal periodicals
as secondary sources of law, 130, 247
Shepard's Law Review Citations and,
253–254
Legal proceedings, attending, 5
Legal research. *See* Research
Legal research specialist. *See*
Paralegal(s)
Legal technician(s) (independent
paralegal), 3. *See also* Paralegal(s)
defined, 27
licensing of, 120
unauthorized practice of law (UPL)
and, 27, 118–119, 628
Legal value, 501
Legal writing, 270–299
approaches to, 272
arranging events chronologically in,
274
avoiding legalese in, 275
avoiding pronoun confusion in, 278
being brief and to the point in, 275
creating user-friendly document and,
273, 276
in discovery, 279–280
editing and, 282

flexibility and, 271–272
format and, 274
of general legal correspondence,
280–287. *See also* Legal letter(s)
general format for, 282–285
of legal memorandum. *See* Legal
memorandum
making easier, tips for, 280–281
organizing and outlining
presentation and, 273–274
paragraphs in, 277–278
of pleadings, 279–280
preliminaries of, 271–272
proofreading and revision of, 279
sentences in, 275–277
sexist language and, 278–279
skills in, 15
good, importance of, 272–279
structural devices in, 274
time constraints and, 271–272
transitions in, 277–278
understanding the assignment in,
271
using everyday English in, 275, 276
using words efficiently in, 277
to your audience, 274–275
Legal-assistant manager, 62
Legalese, avoiding, 275
Legality of contract, 497, 502–503
Legally recognizable injury, 472
Legislative history, 228–229
Legislative intent, 228–229
Legislative offices, employment with, 26
Lessee, 536
Lessor, 536
Letter(s)
confirmation, 285
sample, illustrated, 287
cover, 45
sample, illustrated, 46
demand, 286–287
sample, illustrated, 289
editing, 282
follow-up
to client, illustrated, 361
to prospective employer, 49–50, 51
generated by attorney, reviewing, 290
informative, 285
sample, illustrated, 286
legal. *See* Legal letter(s)
opinion (advisory), 285–286
sample, illustrated, 288
Lexis®, 195, 225, 239
accessing, 250–251
checking citations on, 251–254
conducting a search on, 251
people-finding services on, 374
quality of, quality of Westlaw® versus,
257
searching database on, 255–257
natural language method and,
256–257

searching within results of, 257
terms and connectors method and, 256
selecting database on, 255
Shepard's Citations and, 250, 251, 252–254. *See also Shepard's Citations*
use of, 249–257
LexisNexis, 250
Liability(ies)
contract, 600
criminal. *See* Criminal liability
of employer, under Title VII, 607
Internet service providers (ISPs) and, 476, 477
joint, 587
joint and several, 587
of parents, 560
personal, 60, 61, 62, 585
of principal, 600
product. *See* Product liability
of shareholders, 595
of social hosts, 475
of sole proprietors, 585
strict. *See* Strict liability
vicarious, 600
Libel, 464. *See also* Defamation
Library of Congress
The Constitution of the United States of America available through, 223
THOMAS site of, 262
online links to, 249
License, licensing
of attorneys, 91–92
click-on, 512
defined, 91, 512
general, 119–120
of legal technicians, 120
limited, 120
marriage, 557–558
of paralegals, 10, 119–122
software, 512
Licensing agreement, 512
Lien
judgment as, 409
tax, 535
Life estates, 531
Life insurance, 573, 574
Life insurance trust, 573
LII. *See* Legal Information Institute
Limited jurisdiction, 162–163, 169
Limited liability company (LLC), 596–597
Limited liability limited partnership (LLLP), 597
Limited liability partnership (LLP), 61
Limited licensing, 120
Limited partner, 587–588
Limited partnership, 587–588
Lineup, 434
Liquidated damages, 510
Liquidation

Chapter 7, in bankruptcy, 617–628, 631, 642
of corporation, 596
defined, 617
Listening
active, 357
passive, 356–357
skills in, 12, 81, 356–357
Listserv list, 261
Litigation. *See also* Case(s); Lawsuit(s)
civil. *See* Civil litigation
criminal, paralegals and, 438–439
defined, 27
proceedings in, coordination of, 4, 7
Litigation file
creation of, 304–305
working up, 306
Litigation paralegals, 27–28, 53, 307–308, 398–399, 476–477
Living (*inter vivos*) trust, 572–573, 574
LLC (limited liability company), 596–597
LLLP (limited liability limited partnership), 597
LLP (limited liability partnership), 61
LLRX (Law Library Resource Xchange), 247
LNC (legal nurse consultant), 33
Loan, mortgage, 534–535
Loislaw, 258
Long arm statute, 162
Loose-leaf services, unofficial, 214–215
Loyalty, duty of
agent's, 599
attorney's, 599
corporate officers' and directors', 594

M

Madoff, Bernard, 424
Mail fraud, 425
Mail Fraud Act, 425
Mailbox rule, 500
Maintenance, spousal, 566
Majority opinion, 137, 220
Malice, actual, 464–465
Malpractice. *See also* Negligence
defense against, 100, 597
defined, 94
insurance for, 550
lawsuits involving, 138, 167
avoiding, 550
legal, 94, 100, 167, 472, 597
medical, 472, 476–477, 597
Management
case, 7
of conflicts in the workplace, 83
law-office, 62
risk, 539
Managing partner, 61
Mandate, 387
Mandatory certification, 10

Manslaughter, 421
Manufacturing defects, 480
Marital property, 567
Marriage(s)
children born without benefit of, 560–561
common law, 559
duties of, 559
financial support and, 559
promises made in consideration of, 506
requirements to enter into, 557–559
status regarding, credit discrimination on basis of, 485
termination of, 562–569
child custody and, 564–565
child support and, 565–566
prenuptial agreement and, 568–569
property division and, 567–568
spousal support and, 566
Marriage ceremony, 558
Marriage contract, 559
Marriage license, 557–558
Martindale-Hubbell Law Directory, 41
Master's degree programs, 8
Material facts, mistake of, 504
Maxims, 132–133
"Maximum achievable control technology," 635, 637
MBCA (Model Business Corporation Act), 588
McDonald's, 517
Means test, 618–620, 623
Med-arb (mediation arbitration), 182
Mediation
binding, 182
court-mandated, 387
defined, 175
divorce and, 563–564
as form of alternative dispute resolution (ADR), 175, 177–178, 180–181
the paralegal and, 178, 180–181
Mediation arbitration (med-arb), 182
Mediator, paralegal as, 178, 181
Medicaid, 33
Medical malpractice, 472, 476–477, 597
Medical records
evaluating, 549
obtaining, 371, 549
authorization to release form for, 371
illustrated, 372
Medical research online, 260
Medicare, 33
Meetings
creditors', 622
productive, 603
Meier, Megan, 428
Members of limited liability company (LLC), 597

Memorandum
file workup, tips for preparing, 306
internal, preparing, 295. *See also*
Legal memorandum
of law. *See* Legal memorandum
in support of motion to suppress
evidence, illustrated, 444–445
Mens rea (wrongful mental state),
420–421
Mental incompetence
as defense to criminal liability, 421–422
guardian *ad litem* and, 564
suspicions of, 503
Mental state
required, lack of, as defense to
criminal liability, 421–422
wrongful *(mens rea),* 420–421
Merchantability, implied warranty of,
507, 508
Metadata, 337
Mexico, NAFTA and, 152
Michigan Digest (Callahan), 201
Microsoft Bing, 242
Microsoft Corporation, 598
Microsoft Internet Explorer, 242
Minimum contacts, 132, 162, 166
Minimum wage, 603
Mini-trial, 182–183
Miranda v. Arizona, 430
Miranda rights, 430–431
Miranda rule, 430–431
Mirror image rule, 500
Misdemeanor, 419–420, 424
Misrepresentation, 465–466. *See also*
Fraud
fraudulent, 465–466
genuineness of assent and, 504
product liability based on, 479
Mistake(s). *See also* Error(s)
bilateral, 504
as defense to criminal liability, 422
of fact, 504
genuineness of assent and, 504
mutual, 504
of quality, 504
stress-related, 24
unilateral, 504
of value, 504
Mistaken identity, 422
Mitrano, Tracy, 104
Model Business Corporation Act
(MBCA), 588
Model Rules (ABA's Model Rules of
Professional Conduct)
client communication and, 78
on confidentiality of information, 97
on conflicts of interest, 103, 106, 505
defined, 92–93
disclosures to ensure compliance
with, 100
double billing and, 77–78
on duty of competence, 94–95

fee splitting and, 115
headings of, listed, 93
reasonableness of fees and, 69
Money laundering, 426
Morris, Errol, 363
Mortgage, 534–535
Motion(s)
for change of venue, 443
defined, 321
for directed verdict, 402–403
to dismiss, 443
defined, 321
illustrated, 322
for judgment
as a matter of law, 402–403, 406
illustrated, 403, 407
notwithstanding the verdict, 406
on the pleadings, 322
in limine, 443
defined, 394
illustrated, 394
for new trial, 406–407
defined, 406
illustrated, 407
notice of, 321
posttrial, 406–407
pretrial, 322–324, 442
summarized, 323
to recuse, 443
to sever, 443
"show cause," 452
speedy trial, 443
for summary judgment, 322–324
to suppress evidence
defined, 442
memorandum in support of,
illustrated, 444–445
Mozilla Firefox, 242
Multilateral agreements, 152
Mutual mistake, 504
MySpace, 428

N

NAFCM (National Association for
Community Mediation), 181
NAFTA (North American Free Trade
Agreement), 151, 152
NAIC (National Association of
Insurance Commissioners), 547
NAIIA (National Association of
Independent Insurance
Adjusters), 547
NALA. *See* National Association of
Legal Assistants
NALS (the association for legal
professionals), 10
NAPIA (National Association of Public
Insurance Adjusters), 547
National Association for Community
Mediation (NAFCM), 181
National Association of Independent
Insurance Adjusters (NAIIA), 547

National Association of Insurance
Commissioners (NAIC), 547
National Association of Legal Assistants
(NALA)
certification of paralegals by, 9
Code of Ethics and Professional
Responsibility of
compliance with, 5, 109, 397, 447,
480, 505, 534, 570
illustrated, 110–111
indirect regulation of paralegals
and, 108
rendering independent legal
judgment in place of attorney
and, 364
violation of, 101, 604, 628
continuing legal education (CLE)
requirements of, 10
defined, 3
disclosure of paralegal status and,
117, 291
Institute in Social Security benefits
administration offered by, 39
joining, 40
Model Standards and Guidelines
for the Utilization of Legal
Assistants of, 109, 110
paralegal defined by, 3
regulation of paralegals and, 120, 121
Web site of, 15
National Association of Public
Insurance Adjusters (NAPIA), 547
National Center for State Courts
(NCSC), 174–175
National Conference of Commissioners
on Uniform State Laws
(NCCUSL), 147, 507, 513, 570
Web site of, 230
National Crime Prevention Council, 428
National Environmental Compliance
Assistance Clearinghouse, 636
National Environmental Policy Act
(NEPA)(1969), 634
National Federation of Paralegal
Associations (NFPA)
certification of paralegals by, 9
continuing legal education (CLE)
requirements of, 10
defined, 3
joining, 40
Model Code of Ethics and
Professional Responsibility and
Guidelines for Enforcement of
backing up work and, 77
compliance with, 5, 109, 143, 183,
206, 397, 480
disclosure of paralegal status and,
117, 291
excerpts from, listed, 109
high standard of professional
conduct and, 447
honesty and, 41

indirect regulation of paralegals and, 108
indiscreet communications and, 101, 325
unauthorized practice of law and, 364, 604
Paralegal Advanced Competency Exam (PACE) of, 9
paralegal defined by, 3
regulation of paralegals and, 120–121
use of term paralegal versus legal assistant and, 3
Web site of, 15
National Labor Relations Act (NLRA) (1935), 603
National Labor Relations Board (NLRB), 146, 603
paralegal's interaction with, 609
National law
defined, 151
international law versus, 152
National Law Journal, 147, 205, 230
National origin, discrimination on basis of, 172, 485, 605, 607
National Pollution Discharge Elimination, 638
National weather service, contacting, 371–372
Navigable waters, 634, 638
NCSC (National Center for State Courts), 174–175
Negligence, 461. *See also* Malpractice
of attorney, 94
comparative, 474, 481
contributory, 474
criminal, 421
defenses to, 473–474
defined, 30
duty of care and, 471–472. *See also* Care, duty of
per se, 474–475
product liability based on, 479
special doctrines and statutes regarding, 474–475
Negligence law, the paralegal and, 475
Negotiation(s)
"assisted," 182
defined, 174
divorce and, 563–564
as form of alternative dispute resolution (ADR), 174–175
online, 184–185
property-settlement, preparing for, 567
Nemchek, Lee R., 66
NEPA (National Environmental Policy Act) (1969), 634
Networking, 40
New York Public Library Web site, 261
Newcity, Lisa L., 112–113
Newsgroup (Usenet group), 261–262

NFPA. *See* National Federation of Paralegal Associations
Nigeria, common law system in, 151
Ninth Amendment, 141
NLRA (National Labor Relations Act) (1935), 603
NLRB. *See* National Labor Relations Board
No-fault divorce, 563
Nolo contendere, 442
Nonconforming goods, 511
Norris-LaGuardia Act (1932), 603
North American Free Trade Agreement (NAFTA), 151, 152
Notary public, 311
Notice(s)
of appeal, 408
of motion, 321
of taking deposition, 328
illustrated, 329
Nuncupative will, 571
Nutrition Labeling and Education Act (1990), 484

O

Objections, failure to make, consequences of, 336
Obscenity, online, 141
Obvious risks, 471–472, 480
Occupational Safety and Health Administration (OSHA), 30–31, 150–151, 229
O'Connor v. Ortega, 145
ODR (online dispute resolution), 184–186
Offer(s)
of bribe, 425
contractual. *See* Contract(s), offer in
online, 511–512
Offeree, 498
Offeror, 498
Office manager, 62
Office of the Federal Register, 276
Officer(s)
criminal liability of, 421
defined, 588
duties of, 594–595
functions of, 594–595
responsible corporate officer doctrine and, 421
service of process upon, 316
Omission, act of, 420
One-year rule, 506
Online acceptances, 511–512
Online dispute resolution (ODR), 184–186
Online obscenity, 141
Online offers, 511–512
Online research, 238–269
an Internet primer and, 239–244
conducting, 259–266
browsing the links and, 262

narrowing your focus and, 262
planning ahead for, 259
resources available for, discovering, 260–262
results of
evaluating, 262–263
updating, 263
starting points for, 259–260
strategies for, 259–262
disasters to be prepared for and, 248
evaluation of Internet in, 244
Internet tools for, 240–242
legal resources for
available, discovering, 260–262
fee-based, 249–259. *See also* Lexis®; Westlaw®
free, 244–247, 249
government, 249
questions you should ask about, 246
specific, 246–247, 249
medical, 260
navigating the Internet and, 242–244
tips for doing, 240–241
Open-ended questions, 354–355
Opening statements, 397–398
Opinion(s). *See also* Decision(s)
available online, 247
concurring, 137, 220
defined, 137
dicta in, 221
dissenting, 137, 220
guideposts in, looking for, 221
holding and, 221
majority, 137, 220
per curiam, 220
slip, 175, 214
statement of, 466
types of, 137
unanimous, 137, 220
unpublished, 175
Opinion (advisory) letter, 285–286
sample, illustrated, 288
Oral arguments, 408
Order(s)
cease-and-desist, 484
of garnishment, 487
for relief, 620
restraining, 560
Ordinance, 147
Ordinary bankruptcy, 617
Organizational skills, 14, 131
Organized crime, 426–427
Original jurisdiction, 163, 171, 172
Others, defense of, 422, 462
Overtime wages, 36–37

P

PACE (Paralegal Advanced Competency Exam), 9
PACER (Public Access to Court Electronic Records), 257–258

Home Page for Federal Court
 E-Filing, illustrated, 314
Packaging and labeling laws, 484
Palimony, 566
Palmiere, P. David, 358–359
Paralegal(s)
 administrative law and, 150–151
 agency law and, 600–601
 alternative dispute resolution (ADR)
  and, 186
 bankruptcy law and, 31, 633
 basic judicial requirements and, 167
 business organizations and, 598
 certification of. *See* Certification
 clarifying instructions to, ethics and,
  545
 common law and, 137–138
 compensation of. *See* Paralegal
  compensation
 confidentiality of information
  and. *See* Confidentiality of
  information
 constitutional law and, 142
 consumer law and, 487
 contract, 27
 contract law and, 514
 corporate, 28, 590–591
 criminal litigation and, 438–439
 defined, 3–4
 education of. *See* Paralegal education
 employers of. *See* Employer(s)
 employment law and, 30–31, 609
 environmental law and, 32, 641–642
 ethics and, 89–127. *See also* Ethics
  ethical codes and, 108–109
  ten tips regarding, 112–113
 family law and, 32, 558, 569
 federal court system and, 172–173
 freelance, 27, 117–118
 functions of, 4–7
  increasing scope of, 111, 114
  variations in, 5
 how to dress and, 621
 independent. *See* Legal technician(s)
 as independent contractor, 27
 insurance, 30, 548–549
 intellectual property and, 31–32,
  520, 522
 intentional torts and, 470
 international law and, 152
 job hunting by. *See* Job search
 legal nurse consultant (LNC) and, 33
 licensing of, 10, 119–122. *See also*
  Licensing
 litigation, 27–28, 53, 307–308, 398–
  399, 476–477
 manager of, 62, 83
 mediation and, 178, 180–181
 as mediators, 178, 181
 negligence law and, 475
 opportunities for, 54
 performance evaluations and, 63–64

personal attributes of, 10–14, 16, 17,
 18
practice by, attorney ethics and. *See*
 Attorney(s), ethics of, paralegal
 practice and
product liability and, 481–482, 483
professionalism and, 16, 18
property law and, 538–539
Registered (RP), 9
regulation of
 direct, 120–122
 indirect, 108–111, 114
  guidelines for utilization of
   paralegals and, 109–111
  increasing scope of paralegal
   responsibilities and, 111,
   114
reviewing documents generated by
 attorney and, 290
salary of. *See* Paralegal compensation
skills of. *See* Paralegal skill(s)
specialties of. *See* Paralegal
 specialty(ies)
state court systems and, 169–170
status as, disclosure of, to clients,
 117, 291
statutory law and, 148
supervision of
 attorney's duty and, 96–97, 98, 570
 clarifying instructions, ethics and,
  545
technology and, 5, 6–7, 34–35
termination of, 64–65
trusts and, 31, 576
utilization of, guidelines for, 109–111
 during *voir dire*, 396
wills and, 31, 576
Paralegal Advanced Competency Exam
 (PACE), 9
Paralegal compensation, 33–37
 average, by specialty, 28
 bonuses and, 36
 compensation analysis and, 83
 employment policies and, 63–64
 as government employee, 26
 higher, certification and, 9
 job benefits and, 35–36
 negotiating, 50–52
 overtime pay, federal law and, 36–37
 performance evaluations and, 63–64
 salaries versus hourly wages and, 36
 by specialty, 28
 survey(s) of, 3, 33–35
  billing rate for paralegals and, 69
  by law firm size, 23
  by region, 35
  by years of experience, 34
Paralegal education, 7–10
 AAfPE's role in, 9
 ABA-approved programs and, 9
 ABA's role in, 9
 certificate programs and, 8

continuing (CLE), 10
curriculum and, 8
four-year bachelor's degree
 programs and, 8
options available and, 8
postgraduate certificate programs
 and, 8
two-year community college
 programs and, 8
types of programs offered in, 8
Paralegal Gateway, 15
Paralegal manager, 62, 83
Paralegal profession
 future of, 18, 39
 personal attributes of the paralegal
  and, 10–14, 16, 17, 18
Paralegal skill(s), 10–14, 16, 18
 analytical, 11
 communication. *See* Communication
  skill(s)
 computer, 13–14. *See also*
  Computer(s)
 editing, 282
 interpersonal, 14, 354
 interviewing, 353–357
 keyboarding, 34
 listening, 12, 81, 356–357
 marketing of, 42–52
 organizational, 14, 131
 questioning, 354–356
 reading, 11–12
 speaking, 12, 81
 writing, 12–13, 15
Paralegal specialty(ies), 27–33
 average compensation by, 28
 bankruptcy law as, 31, 633
 contract law as, 28–29
 corporate law as, 28, 590–591
 criminal law as, 32–33
 elder law as, 33
 employment law as, 30–31
 environmental law as, 32,
  641–642
 estate planning as, 31, 576
 family law as, 32, 558, 569
 insurance law as, 30, 548–549
 intellectual property law as, 31–32
 legal nurse consultant (LNC) and, 33
 litigation assistance as, 27–28, 53,
  307–308, 398–399, 476–477
 personal-injury law as, 30
 probate administration as, 31
 real estate law as, 29
 trusts and, 31, 576
Parallel citation, 207, 215, 252
Parent(s)
 abuse or neglect of child by, 560
 child custody and, 564–565
 child's emancipation from, 557
 liability of, 560
 rights and obligations of, 560
 unmarried, children born to, 560–561

Partner(s), 585
  defined, 61
  general, 587, 588
  liability of, 61, 586–587
  limited, 587–588
  managing, 61
  rights and duties of, 586
Partnership(s), 585–588
  defined, 61
  dissolution of, 587
  domestic, 559
  formation of, 585
  general, 587
  law firm organized as, 61
    organizational chart of, illustrated, 63
  limited liability (LLP), 597
  limited liability limited (LLLP), 597
  taxation of, 587
  termination of, 587
  winding up of, 587
Party(ies)
  defined, 137
  to lawsuit, 137, 302
    hypothetical, 302
  potentially responsible (PRP), 641
  third. See Third parties
Passive listening, 356–357
Patent law, 31–32
  statutory law and, 148
Patents, 497, 514, 516
Paternity suit, 561
Pay. See Paralegal compensation
Payment(s)
  of child support, withholding, 565
  under insurance contract, defenses against, 548
P.C. (professional corporation), 61–62, 593
People finders, online, 264, 266, 374
Per curiam opinion, 220
Per se, 474
Peremptory challenge, 395–396
Performance
  of contract, 508–511
  defined, 508
  impossibility of, 509
  specific. See Specific performance
  substantial, 508–509
Performance evaluations, 63–64
Periodicals, legal, 204–205
Permanent alimony, 566
Person(s)
  accused of crime. See Criminal defendant(s)
  intentional torts against, 461–467
  jurisdiction over, 162
  legal, corporation as, 588
  protection of, 422
  unreasonable search or seizure of, constitutional prohibition of, 140, 144, 145, 429, 430, 433

Personal liability, 60, 61, 62, 585
Personal property
  conversion and, 470
  defined, 467, 530
  intangible, 530
  leases of, 536
  tangible, 530
  trespass to, 469–470
Personal representative
  defined, 570
  estate administration and, 575–576
  meeting with, 577
Personal-injury law, 30
Personal-injury lawsuits, 138
  intake sheet and, 352–353
Persuasive authority, 175, 198–199
Persuasive precedent, 130
Pesticides, 639–640
Petition, 305. See also Complaint
  in bankruptcy, 617–618, 620, 629
    gathering information for, 642
  for divorce, 563
Petty offenses, 420
Phishing, 468
Physical examination, request for, 332–333
Piercing the veil of anonymity, 477–478
P.L. number (public law number), 146
Plain English at Work (Australian government), 276
Plain English Campaign, 276
A Plain English Handbook, 276
"Plain English" writing, 276
Plain meaning rule, 226–227
Plaintiff
  case of, during trial, 399–402
  compensation for, for assault or battery, 462
  complaint of. See Complaint
  defined, 28, 66, 137, 302
  in hypothetical civil lawsuit, 302
Plea, 442
Plea bargaining, 442
Pleadings, 305–306, 308–322
  amending, 322
  answer as. See Answer
  complaint as. See Complaint
  defined, 305
  evidence outside of, 323
  judgment on, 322
  writing, 279–280
Pocket part, 199
Point-source emissions, 638
Police department, contacting, 370
Policy, insurance. See Insurance contract
Politics, law office, 82, 84
Pollution
  air, 635, 637
  toxic chemicals and, 639–641
  water, 634, 637–639
Possession, debtor in (DIP), 631–632

Postarbitration, 182
Postgraduate certificate programs, 8
Posttrial motions, 406–407
Potentially responsible party (PRP), 641
Powell, Janet M., 307–308
PowerPoint presentations, 388
Powers of avoidance, 623–624
Practice of law, unauthorized. See Unauthorized practice of law
Prayer for relief, 311
Prearbitration, 181–182
Precedent(s)
  defined, 130
  departures from, 130–131
  persuasive, 130
Predatory behavior, 467
Prediscovery meeting, 333–334
Preemption
  defined, 146
  determining, tips for, 147
Preexisting debt, 624
Preferences in bankruptcy, 624
Pregnancy, employment discrimination on basis of, 172–173, 605
Pregnancy Discrimination Act (1978), 605
Preliminary hearing, 440–441
Preliminary investigation, 303–304
Premium, 539
Prenuptial agreement, 506, 513, 568–569
Preponderance of the evidence, 418
Pretrial conference, 393–394
Pretrial investigation(s), 350
Pretrial motions, 322–324, 442
  summarized, 323
Pretrial settlements, 301
Primary sources of law, 129–130, 199
Principal, 599. See also Agency relationship(s)
  defined, 598
  liability of, 600
Priorities, getting right, 78
PrismSystems, Inc., 636
Privacy right(s)
  Constitution and, 465
  of employees, 466
  invasion of, 465
  online, 466
Privacy Rights Clearinghouse, 468
Private corporation, 591
Private facts, public disclosure of, 465
Privilege
  absolute, 464
  attorney-client. See Attorney-client privilege
  defined, 464
  qualified (conditional), 464
  against self-incrimination, 140, 430, 446, 447
  "to detain," 463
Privileged information, 102–104, 324, 334, 341

Probable cause, 429, 431, 433–434, 436, 440–441, 463
Probate administration, 31
  statutes governing, 148
Probate court, 31, 162–163, 570
Probate of will, 31, 570
  avoiding, checklist for, 574
Probation
  adoptions and, 562
  in criminal law, 449–451
Procedural law, 8
Proceedings, legal, attending, 5, 7
Product(s). *See also* Goods
  defects in, 480
  misuse of, 480, 481
  trademarks and, 517
  unreasonably dangerous, 479
Product liability, 461, 478–482
  confidentiality, ethics and, 480
  defenses to, 481
  defined, 478
  lawsuits involving, 138
  the paralegal and, 481–482, 483
  strict, 479–480
    requirements for, 479
  theories of, 479–480
Product liability paralegal, 481–482, 483
Product misuse, 480, 481
Production, request for, 332–333
Professional association, joining, 40
Professional corporation (P.C.), 61–62, 593
Professional exemption, 36–37
Professional investigator, 373
Professional portfolio, 47
Professional references, list of, 45–47
Professional responsibility, ethics and, 89–127
Professionalism, paralegals and, 16, 18
Professionals, duty of care of, 472
Promise(s)
  defined, 497
  made in consideration of marriage, 506
Promissory estoppel, 501–502, 506
Promoters, 588–589
Proof
  of claim
    defined, 622
    preparing, 629
  standard of. *See* Standard of proof
Proofreading, 13, 45, 279
Property
  of client, obtaining information about, 379
  community, 531, 568
  crimes involving, 423–424
  defense of, 422, 462
  division of, upon marriage termination, 567–568
  equitable distribution of, 568

exempt, 409
  intellectual. *See* Intellectual property
  intentional torts against, 467–470
  jurisdiction over, 162
  marital, 567
  ownership rights in, 530–531
  personal. *See* Personal property
  property settlement and, 567
  real. *See* Real property
  separate, 567
  testamentary disposition of, 569. *See also* Will(s)
  unreasonable search or seizure of, constitutional prohibition of, 140, 144, 145, 429, 430, 433
Property crime, 423–424
Property law, the paralegal and, 538–539
Property settlement, 567
Prosecuting attorney, 417, 436
Prosecution
  beginning of, 435–437, 440–446
  for crime, tort lawsuit for same act versus, illustrated, 419
  criminal procedures prior to, 431–435
  of cyber crimes, 428–429
Prospectus, 589
Prosser and Keeton on the Law of Torts, Fifth Edition, 204, 205
  page from, illustrated, 205
Protection of persons or property, 422
Proximate cause, 473
PRP (potentially responsible party), 641
Public Access to Court Electronic Records. *See* PACER
Public corporation, 591, 593
Public defender
  defined, 417
  employment with, 26, 29
Public figures, defamation and, 464–465
Public law number (P.L. number), 146
Public order crime, 424
Public policy, 131
Public prosecutor
  defined, 417
  employment with, 26, 436
Publication
  defamation and, 464
  of information placing person in false light, 465
Publicly held corporation, 593
Puerto Rico, civil law system in, 151
Punishment, cruel and unusual, constitutional prohibition of, 140, 430
Punitive damages, 472, 510
Pure Food and Drug Act (1906), 484–485
Purpose, particular, Implied warranty of fitness for, 507
Putman, William, 280–281

Q
Qualified (conditional) privilege, 464
Quality, mistake of, 504
Québec, civil law system in, 151
Question(s)
  asked during *voir dire,* 395, 410
  closed-ended, 356
  for cross-examination, 401
  deposition, 328, 330
  for direct examination, 400
  of fact, 169
  federal, 163, 173, 310
  follow-up, 351
  hypothetical, 356
  of law, 169
  leading, 356, 389, 400
  open-ended, 354–355
  presented in legal memorandum, 290
    illustrated, 292
  types of, summarized, 355
  of witnesses, 365–366
Questioning skills, 354–356
Quick Index, 204
Quicken Family Lawyer, 119
Quid pro quo harassment, 607

R
Race
  discrimination on basis of, 65, 172, 485, 605, 607
  peremptory challenges based upon, 396
Racketeer Influenced and Corrupt Organizations Act (RICO), 426–427, 429
Ratification of contract, 600
RCRA (Resource Conversation and Recovery Act) (1976), 640
Reading skills, 11–12
Real estate, 29. *See also* Land; Real property
Real estate agent, 598, 599
Real Estate Settlement Procedures Act, 535
Real property, 29, 530–539. *See also* Land
  defined, 467, 530
  lease of, 536–538
  owners of, duty of, 471–472
  ownership rights in, 530–531
  private, taking by government for public use, 530
  survey of, 541
  transfer and sale of, 531–536
    agreement governing, typical provisions in, 533
    closing of, 534, 535
    contract formation and, 532–533
    escrow agent and, 533–534, 535

financing and, 534–535
inspection of premises and, 535
paperwork involved in, ethics and, 534
protecting purchaser and, 540–541
steps involved in, summarized, 532
survey of property and, 541
title examination and, 535
title insurance and, 535
Reasonable accommodations, 608–609
Reasonable manner, 463, 500
Reasonable person standard, 462, 471, 483
Reasonable suspicion, 433
Reasonable time, 463, 500
Rebuttal, 404
Receiver, 631–632
Record(s). *See also* File(s)
on appeal, 408
digital, 392–393
employment, obtaining, 371
good, keeping, benefits of, 451
medical. *See* Medical records
vehicle title and registration, obtaining, 372
Recording
of interview, 351–353, 566
of marriage license, 558
Recross- examination, 401–402
Recruiters, 42
Recusal, 443
Redirect examination, 402
Reference line, 284
Reference materials, filing of, 68
References, professional, list of, 45–47
Reflecting back, 357
Reformation, 511
Regional reporters, 207
Registered agent, 316
Registered Paralegal (RP), 9
Regulation(s). *See also* Administrative law
of attorneys. *See* Attorney(s), regulation of
federal
of environment, 634–635
state regulation versus, 147
of paralegals. *See* Paralegal(s), regulation of
as primary source of law, 129
self-, 90
state, federal regulation versus, 147
Rehabilitative alimony, 566
Release forms, 303
Relevant evidence, 376–377
Reliance, justifiable, 466, 504
Religion
discrimination on basis of, 172, 485, 605, 607
freedom of, 140, 141
Remandment of case, 220, 408
Remedy(ies)

for breach of contract. *See* Contract(s), breach of,
defined, 131, 509
in equity
defined, 132
examples of, 134
remedies at law versus, 131–135
at law
defined, 131
remedies in equity versus, 131–135
Reno v. American Civil Liberties Union, 141
Reorganization, Chapter 11, 617, 618, 631–633
Reporter(s) (reports)
defined, 200
regional, 207
state, 206–207
West's National Reporter System and, 207, 210
Reprimand, 94
Request(s)
for admission, 333
for physical examination, 332–333
for production, 332–333
Rescission
of contract, 504, 510
restitution and, 510
Research, 195–269
of administrative law, 229
of case law. *See* Case law(s), researching
cases of first impression and, 133, 199
conducting, 4, 5, 7
of constitutional law, 223–225
effective, ten tips for, 208–209
efficiency in, 198
inadequate, 95–96
online. *See* Online research
of statutory law, 223–225
strategy for, mapping out, 231
technology and, 230
Resolution Forum, Inc. (RFI), 185–186
Resource Conversation and Recovery Act (RCRA) (1976), 640
Respondeat superior, 600, 601
Responsible corporate officer doctrine, 421
Restatements of the Law, 130, 135–136, 204
citation to, 212
illustrated, 205
Restitution, 511
Restraining order, 560
Résumé, 42–45
cover letter and, 45, 46
personal data and, 45
proofreading, 45
sample, illustrated, 43, 44

what not to include in, 45
what to include in, 43–44
Retainer, 71
Retainer agreement
defined, 69
sample, illustrated, 70
Return-of-service form, 316, 388
illustrated, 317
Reversal of judgment, 220, 408, 453
Reversible error, 169
Reviewing courts. *See* Appellate court(s)
Revised Model Business Corporation Act (RMBCA), 588
Revocable living trust, 572–573
RFI (Resolution Forum, Inc.), 185–186
RICO (Racketeer Influenced and Corrupt Organizations Act), 426–427, 429
Right(s)
inheritance, 561
to jury trial, 140, 312, 430
parental, 560
to speedy and public trial, 140, 430, 443, 447–448
to stand your ground, 422
of subrogation, 545
of survivorship, 531, 574
trespass and, 468–470
voidable, 623
Risk(s)
assumption of, 473–474, 481
defined, 539
management of, 539
open and obvious, 471–472, 480
transferring and allocating, 539
Rivers and Harbors Appropriation Act (1899), 637
RMBCA (Revised Model Business Corporation Act), 588
Robbery, 423
Role-playing, 391
Rome, civil law ("code law") of, 151
RP (Registered Paralegal), 9
Rule(s). *See also entries beginning with Federal Rules*
of civil procedure
federal. *See* Federal Rules of Civil Procedure
state, 306, 310, 318
of construction, 226
of evidence
defined, 374
Federal. *See* Federal Rules of Evidence
investigation and, 374–378
of four, 172
plain meaning, 226–227
Rulemaking, 150

S

S corporation, 593, 595–596
Safeway, 517

Sage Software, Inc., 73
Salary. *See* Paralegal compensation
Sale(s)
　consumer laws and, 484
　of real estate. *See* Real property,
　　transfer and sale of
Sales contract(s), 506–508. *See also*
　　Uniform Commercial Code
　breach of, remedies for, 511
　consumer laws and, 484
　defined, 507
Salutation, 284
Same-gender couples, 559
Sample court case, 216–219
　briefed version of, 222
Samsung Electronics America, Inc., 465
Sarbanes-Oxley Act, 595
Scheduling conference, 321, 334
Scheduling order, 321
Schneeman, Angela, 590–591
Scotland, civil law system in, 151
Search(es)
　and seizures, unreasonable,
　　constitutional prohibition of,
　　140, 144, 145, 429, 430, 433
　using search engine. *See* Search
　　engine(s)
Search engine(s), 243–244
　search operators and, 244
　searches with, kinds of, 244
Search operators, 244
Search warrant, 429, 430, 433–434
　defined, 433
　illustrated, 434–435
Second Amendment, 140
Secondary sources of law, 130, 199–205,
　206
　available online, 247
Secured creditor(s)
　bankruptcy property distribution
　　and, 624
　defined, 618
Securities and Exchange Commission
　　(SEC), 148, 229
　EDGAR (Electronic Data Gathering,
　　Analysis, and Retrieval)
　　database of, 262, 265
　　page from, illustrated, 263
　A Plain English Handbook of, 276
　Web site of, 249
Security, evolving technology and, 450
Seizures and searches, unreasonable,
　　prohibited by Constitution, 140,
　　144, 145, 429, 430, 433
Self-defense, 422, 462
Self-incrimination, compulsory,
　　constitutional prohibition of, 140,
　　430, 446, 447
Self-insurance, 605
Self-regulation, 90
Seller's talk, 466
Sentences, writing, 275–277

Sentencing, 449–451, 452
Separate property, 567
Serif Draw Plus, 363
Service marks, 514
Service of process, 315–318, 388
　alternative methods of, 316
　defined, 315
　proof of, 316
　substituted, 316
　waiver of, 317–318
Session laws, 146
Settlement(s)
　defined, 301
　pretrial, 301
　property, 567
Settlement agreement
　defined, 175
　family, 571
　illustrated, 176
Settlor, 571
Seventh Amendment, 140, 312
Severing of cases, 443
Sexist language, avoidance of, 278–279
Sexual harassment, 30, 65, 172–173,
　606–607
　defined, 606
　developing policy on, 608
Shareholder(s), 61–62
　defined, 588
　liability of, 595
Shepard's Citations, 250, 251, 252–254,
　257, 258. *See also entries beginning
　with Shepard's*
　abbreviations used in, illustrated, 253
　organization of, 252
　types of information provided by,
　　252–254
*Shepard's Code of Federal Regulations
　Citations,* 252–253
Shepard's Law Review Citations, 253–254
Shrink-wrap agreement, 512
Signature(s)
　on complaint, 311
　digital, 513
　e-. *See* E-signature(s)
　electronic. *See* E-signature(s)
　of testator, 571
Signature dynamics, 513
Sixth Amendment, 140, 429, 430, 443,
　447–448
SJT (summary jury trial), 184
Slander, 464. *See also* Defamation
"Sliding-scale" standard, 166
Slip law, 146
Slip opinion, 175, 214
Small Business Environmental,
　636
SmartDraw Legal Edition, 363
Smartsettle, 185
Smith, Robin, 118
Social events, confidentiality of
　information and, 101

Social hosts, liability of, 475
Social Security, benefits administration
　and, 39
Social Security Administration
　as employer, 26
　paralegals' representation of clients
　　before, 27, 117, 151
　Web site of, 468
Software
　docketing, 62
　environmental, 636
　graphics, 363
　legal, controversy over, 119
　litigation support, 392–393
　office, proficiency with, 34–35
　time-and-billing, 73
　trial presentation, 393
Software license, 512
Sole (solo) practitioner, 60–61
Sole proprietorship(s), 60–61
South Texas College of Law, Center for
　　Legal Responsibility at, 185–186
Spam (bulk, unsolicited e-mail), 469
Speaking skills, 12, 81
Special (consequential) damages, 510
Specific performance
　defined, 134, 511
　as equitable remedy, 134
　requirements for, 135
Speech, freedom of, 140, 141
Speedy trial motion, 443
Spendthrift trust, 573
Spousal abuse, 559–560
Spousal support, 566
Staff attorney, 61
Stand your ground, 422
Standard of proof
　in civil trial, 418
　in criminal trial, 418, 447
Standing to sue, 161
Stare decisis, 130–131, 137, 151
State(s)
　bar association of. *See* State bar
　　association(s)
　certification by, 9, 10
　constitutions of, 129, 141–142, 146
　courts of. *See* State court system(s)
　guidelines of, regarding paralegals,
　　111
　Interest on Lawyers' Trust Accounts
　　(IOLTA) programs and, 72
　lawmaking process and, 146
　legislatures of, attorney regulation
　　and, 91
　attorney violation of rules of,
　　sanctions for, 93–94
　of mind, 420–421
　rules of civil procedure of, 306, 310
　statutes of. *See* State statute(s)
State bar association(s)
　attorney violation of rules of,
　　sanctions for, 93–94

defined, 40
membership in, 90–91
State court system(s), 167–170
    appellate courts of, 167, 169
        decisions of, 206–207. *See also* Case
            reporting system
            citations to, 211
        federal court or, choice of, 164
        highest (supreme), 167, 169, 453
            attorney regulation and, 91,
                93–94
        levels in, illustrated, 168
        the paralegal and, 169–170
        trial courts of, 163, 167, 168–169
    electronic filing in, 314–315
State prosecutor, 417
State reporters, 206–207
State statute(s), 146
    federal statutes and, conflicts
            between, 146
    finding, 225
    governing e-signatures, 513
    lawmaking process and, 146
    of limitations, 68
Statement(s)
    environmental impact (EIS), 634
    of facts, 289–290, 466
        illustrated, 292
    of financial affairs, 627
    of intention, 627
    opening, 397–398
    of opinion, 466
    witness. *See* Witness statement
Statute(s). *See also* Law(s); Statutory law
    arbitration, 179
    defined, 142
    dram shop, 475
    federal. *See* Federal statute(s)
    of Frauds, 505–506, 585
    Good Samaritan, 475
    of limitations. *See* Statute of limitations
    long arm, 162
    state. *See* State statute(s)
    unauthorized practice of law,
            114–115. *See also* Unauthorized
            practice of law
    workers' compensation, 30,
            604–605, 606
Statute of limitations, 134
    as defense to criminal liability, 422
    defined, 68
    duty of competence, ethics and, 143
Statutory law, 142–148. *See also*
        Statute(s)
    analyzing, 225–229
    common law and, 136
    criminal law as, 136, 418
    defined, 142
    finding, 223–225
    the paralegal and, 148
    previous interpretation of, 227–228
    as primary source of law, 129

reading, 226–227
    researching, 223–225
Stepparent adoptions, 562
Stolen goods, receiving, 424
Stop, police officer's right to, 433
Straight bankruptcy, 617
Stress, mistakes and, 24
Strict liability, 461
    defined, 478
    product liability and, 478. *See also*
        Product liability
Strike, 602–603
Subchapter S of Internal Revenue
        Code, 593, 595
Subfiles, 67
Subject matter, jurisdiction over,
        162–163
Submission agreement, 179
Subpoena
    defined, 329, 388
    for deposition, 329
    duces tecum, 329
    for friendly witness, 388–389
    illustrated, 390
    issuing, 387–389
    for trial, 387–389
Subrogation clause, 545
Substantial performance, 508–509
Substantive law, 8
Substituted service, 316
Summary judgment, 322–324
Summary jury trial (SJT), 184
Summons, 315–318
    defined, 315
    illustrated, 315
    serving, 316–318
    waiver of service and, 317–318
Superfund (Comprehensive
        Environmental Response,
        Compensation, and Liability Act)
        (CERCLA) (1980), 640–641
superpages.com, 264, 265
Superseding cause, 474
Supervision
    adequate, 98
    attorney's duty to provide, 96–97,
            98, 570
    inadequate, 97
Support personnel, 62
Supporting affidavit, 321
Supremacy clause, 139
Supreme Court Reporter (S.Ct.) (West),
        214
Survey of property, 541
Suspended sentence, 449
Suspension, 94
Switchboard.com, 265
Syllabus, 214, 219

T

Tangible personal property, 530
Tax lien, 535

Taxation
    corporations and, 595–596
    double, 595–596
    estate, 574
    limited liability company (LLC) and,
            596–597
    limited liability partnership (LLP)
            and, 597
    of partnerships, 587
    sole proprietorships and, 585
Technology. *See also* Computer(s)
    best available, 638
    best conventional, 638
    career opportunities and, 34–35
    communicating through graphics
            and, 363
    confidentiality of e-mail and, 104–
            105
    contract forms on, 499
    cost of electronic evidence and,
            338–339
    evolving, security, evidence and, 450
    identity theft and, 468–469
    legal research and, 230
    looking ahead and, 230
    "maximum achievable control," 635,
            637
    online help for estate planning and,
            575
    online incorporation and, 594–595
    online "plain English" guidelines
            and, 276
    paralegal use of, 5, 6–7, 34–35
    spam and, 469
    trial presentation in courtroom and,
            392–393
Telephone directories, 373
Tenancy
    in common, 531
    joint, 531, 574
Tenth Amendment, 141
Terms, definiteness of, 498
Testamentary capacity, 571
Testamentary disposition of property,
        569. *See also* Will(s)
Testamentary trust, 573
Testate death, 569
Testator
    defined, 569
    signature of, 571
    testamentary capacity and, 571
Testimony, witness, summarizing, 4
Thailand, civil law system in, 151
Theft
    cyber, 427
    identity, 427, 468–469, 486
    of trade secrets, 425–426, 520
The Thin Blue Line (film), 363
Third Amendment, 140
Third parties
    agency relationships and,
            599–600

conversations overheard by, 100, 101
defined, 100
Time
documenting, 73–76
effective date of insurance contract and, 543–544
one-year rule and, 506
reasonable, 463, 500
using wisely, 11
Time slip
defined, 73
illustrated, 75
Timekeeping procedures, 72–76
Timeslips, 73
Title(s)
case, 215
examination of, 535
warranty of, 507
Title examination, 535
Title insurance, 535
Tort(s)
of agent, 600
business, 466–467
cyber. *See* Cyber tort(s)
defined, 30, 461
of independent contractor, 600
intentional. *See* Intentional tort(s)
law of, 138
basis of, 461
lawsuit based on, criminal prosecution for same act versus, illustrated, 419
liability for, 600
spamming as, 469
Tortfeasor, 461
TOSCA (Toxic Substances Control Act) (1976), 640
Toxic chemicals, 639–641
Toxic substances, 640
Toxic Substances Control Act (TOSCA) (1976), 640
Trade journals, job listings in, 40
Trade secrets, 425–426, 520, 521
Trademark, 429, 497, 517, 520, 593
Trademark dilution, 517, 520
Trademark Dilution Act, 517
Trademark law, 31–32
statutory law and, 148
Trademarks, 514
TransUnion, 486
Treatises, 204, 205, 247
Treaty, 152
Trespass
to land, 467–469
to personal property, 469–470
Trial(s)
appealing verdict and, 453
civil litigation and. *See* Civil litigation
closing arguments and, 404–405
criminal. *See* Criminal trial(s)
events during, 396–406
exhibits and displays for, 391, 392–393

graphics and, 448
by jury
demand for, 312
jury selection and, 394–396
right to, 140, 312, 430
mini-, 182–183
new, motion for, 406–407
notebook for, 391–393
opening statement and, 397–398
posttrial motions and, 406–407
preparing for, 7, 387–393
checklist for, illustrated, 389
presentation technology and, 392–393
pretrial conference and, 393–394
procedures after, 406–408
procedures regarding, 386–415
speedy and public, right to, 140, 430, 443, 447–448
standard of proof in, 418, 447
summary jury (SJT), 184
Trial court(s), 198
defined, 163
federal (district courts), 163, 170, 171, 616
state, 163, 167, 168–169
Trial notebook, 391–393
True bill, 441
Trust(s), 569, 571–573
arrangement established by, illustrated, 573
beneficiary of, 571
charitable, 573
defined, 31, 571
estate planning and, 574
life insurance, 573
living (*inter vivos*), 572–573, 574
paralegals and, 31, 576
spendthrift, 573
testamentary, 573
Trust account(s), 71–72
commingling with firm's funds and, 72
creating, 73
defined, 71
Trustee(s)
bankruptcy, 617, 623–624, 626, 632, 633
of trust, 31, 571
United States, 616, 623, 632
Truth-in-Lending Act (TILA) (1968), 485
Tufte, Edward, 363
Two-year community college programs, 8

U

UCC. *See* Uniform Commercial Code
UETA (Uniform Electronic Transactions Act), 513
Unanimous opinion, 137, 220
Unanimous verdict, 448–449

Unauthorized practice of law (UPL), 114–119
dangers of, 116
defined, 92
disclosure of paralegal status and, 117, 291
ethics and, 5, 604
letters and, 291
fee splitting and, 115
giving legal opinions and advice and, 115–117, 364, 604, 628
interviewing clients, ethics and, 364
legal technicians (independent paralegals) and, 27, 118–119, 628
paralegals freelancing for attorneys and, 117–118
representing clients in court and, 116, 117
Unconscionable contract or clause, 503, 505
Underwriter, 539
Undue influence, genuineness of assent and, 504
Unequivocal acceptance, 500
Uniform Arbitration Act, 179
Uniform Commercial Code (UCC), 146, 484, 506–507, 585
adoption of, 147–148, 507
Article 2 (Sales Contracts) of, 514, 532. *See also* Sales contract(s)
scope of, 507
citation to, 212
defined, 506
E-SIGN Act and, 513
leases of personal property under, 536
UETA and, 513
warranties under, 507–508
Uniform Electronic Transactions Act (UETA), 513
Uniform Interstate Family Support Act, 565–566
Uniform laws, 147–148
new, being developed, 230
Uniform Partnership Act (UPA), 585
Uniform Premarital Agreement Act, 569
Uniform Probate Code (UPC), 570
Uniform Resource Locators (URLs), 213, 240, 241–242
Uniform Trade Secrets Act (USTA), 520
Unilateral contract, 497
Unilateral mistake, 504
Unions, labor, 602–603
United Nations, 152
United States
common law system in, 151
NAFTA and, 152
United States Army Corps of Engineers, 639

United States Code (U.S.C.), 146, 259
citation to, 212
online links to, 249
Popular Name Table of, 224–225
titles in, 224
illustrated, 224
United States Code Annotated (U.S.C.A.)
(West)
constitutional law sources found in, 223
legislative history of statutes in, 228
United States Code Congressional and Administrative News (U.S.C.C.A.N.)
(West), 228–229
United States Code Service (U.S.C.S.)
(West), 228
constitutional law sources found in, 223
legislative history of statutes in, 228
United States Constitution, 139–141
amendments to. *See* Bill of Rights; *individual amendments*
Articles of, summarized, 140
bankruptcy laws and, 616
commerce clause of, 143–144, 179
federal government's authority to enact laws under, 142–143
intellectual property protection and, 514
jury trials guaranteed by, 140, 312, 430
as primary source of law, 129, 139
privacy rights and, 465
safeguards under, to protect persons accused of crimes, 429–431. *See also individual protections*
supremacy clause of, 139
treaty ratification under, 152
United States Copyright Office, 516
United States Department of Agriculture, 485
United States Department of Commerce, Web site of, 249
United States Department of Justice, 420
as employer, 26
online access to, 249
Web site of, 468
United States Department of Labor (DOL)
on employment of paralegals, 18, 39
FairPay rule of, 36–37
FLSA enforced by, 36–37
United States Department of the Treasury, 26
United States Government Manual, 26
United States Government Printing Office, 214, 228
Web site of, 249
United States House of Representatives, Web site of, 249

United States Law Week (BNA), 214–215
United States Patent and Trademark Office (USPTO), 32, 516, 517, 522, 593
Web site of, 249
United States Reports (U.S.), 214
United States Senate, Web site of, 249
United States Small Business Administration, 617
Web site of, 249
United States Supreme Court
attorney regulation and, 91
cases pending before, 230
decisions of
citations to, 211
reporting of, 214–215
exceptions to *Miranda* rule and, 431
on freedom of speech, 141
how cases reach, 172
justices of, 137
lifetime appointment of, 170
on people representing themselves in court, 117
types of cases reviewed by, 172
Web site of, 175, 214, 247
United States Trustee, 616, 623, 632
United States Trustee Program Web site, 619, 621
Unpublished opinion, 175
Unreasonably dangerous products, 479
Unsecured creditors, bankruptcy property distribution and, 624–625
UPA (Uniform Partnership Act), 585
UPC (Uniform Probate Code), 570
UPL. *See* Unauthorized practice of law
URLs (Uniform Resource Locators), 213, 240, 241–242
U.S. Search, 264
USA.gov, 249, 260
U.S.C.C.A.N. *(United States Code Congressional and Administrative News)*(West), 228–229
Usenet group (newsgroup), 261–262
USPTO. *See* United States Patent and Trademark Office
USTA (Uniform Trade Secrets Act), 520

V

Value(s)
legal, 501
mistake of, 504
Vehicle title and registration records, obtaining, 372
Venue
defined, 166
motion for change of, 443
Verdict
acquittal and, 448

appealing, 407–408
defined, 406
directed, 402–403
judgment notwithstanding, motion for, 406
unanimous, 448–449
VersusLaw, 259
Vicarious liability, 600
Videos in courtroom, 392–393
Violent crime, 423
Vishing, 468
Visitation rights, 565
Voice over Internet Protocol (VoIP), 468
Voidable rights, 623
VoIP (Voice over Internet Protocol), 468
Voir dire, 395–396
challenges during, 395–396
defined, 395
paralegal's role during, 396
questions asked during, 395, 410
volokh.com, 262
Voluntary bankruptcy, 617–620
Voluntary certification, 10
Voluntary manslaughter, 421

W

Wage(s)
garnishment of, 487, 488
minimum, 603
overtime, 36–37
Waiting period, 557
Waiver
defined, 317
of objections, 336
of service by defendant, 317–318
Wall Street Journal, 265
Walston-Dunham, Beth, 476–477
Wards, locating, 266
Warnings, defects in, 480
Warrant(s)
arrest, 429, 433–434, 436
general, constitutional prohibition of, 433
preparing, checklist for, 436
search. *See* Search warrant
Warranty(ies)
defined, 507
disclaimer of, 507–508
express, 507
implied. *See* Implied warranty(ies)
of title, 507
under UCC, 507–508
Water(s)
navigable, 634, 638
pollution of, 634, 637–639
Web site(s). *See also individual Web sites*
business and economic, 249
estate planning, 575
firstgov.gov, 636
New York Public Library, 261

online incorporation service, 595
United States Trustee Program Web, 619, 621
the Web. *See* World Wide Web
Weber, Pamela Poole, 438–439
West
  headnotes of, 201, 219
  key-number system of, 201
  publications of, 199, 200, 201, 202, 203–204, 206–207, 210, 214, 224, 225, 228–229. *See also entries beginning with West*
West Legal Directory, 264
Westlaw®, 195, 199, 225, 239
  accessing, 250–251
  checking citations on, 251–255
  citation to, 213
  conducting a search on, 251
  KeyCite citator service and, 250, 251, 254–255. *See also* KeyCite
  opening page of, illustrated, 251
  people-finding services on, 264, 374
  quality of, quality of Lexis® versus, 257
  searching database on, 255–257
    natural language method and, 256–257
    results of
      illustrated, 256
      searching within, 257
    terms and connectors method and, 256
  selecting database on, 255
  use of, 249–257
West's Digest
  excerpts from, illustrated, 202
  subtopics and key numbers in, illustrated, 203
West's Hornbook Series, 204, 205
West's Legal Directory, 41
West's National Reporter System, 207, 210
Wetlands, 639
Wheel of Fortune, 465
White, Vanna, 465
White-collar crime, 424–426
Wild animals, 478
Will(s), 569–571
  defined, 31, 569
  drafting
    checklist for, 572
    paralegal supervision, ethics and, 570
  employment at, 602

handwritten, 571
holographic, 571
laws governing, 570
nuncupative, 571
the paralegal and, 31, 576
probate of, 31, 570
  avoiding, checklist for, 574
statutes governing, 148
valid, requirements for, 571
Winding up, 587
Wire fraud, 425
Witness(es)
  accused person's right to confront and cross-examine, 140, 430, 448
  adverse (hostile), 365, 400
  bias of, 367
  competence of, 366
  contacting, 370–371, 387–389
  coordination of, 342
  credibility of, 366, 401
  defined, 301
  examination of
    cross-, 400–401
    direct, 399–400
    recross-, 401–402
    redirect, 402
  expert. *See* Expert witness(es)
  eyewitnesses and, 364–365
  friendly. *See* Friendly witnesses
  hostile, 365, 400
  impeaching, 331
  interviewing. *See* Witness interview(s)
  issuing subpoenas for, 387–389, 390
  lay, 364
  lineup viewed by, 434
  locating, 4, 373–374
  preparing for trial, 389, 391
  pretrial disclosures related to, 336
  qualifications of, checking, 366–367
  questioning, 365–366
  role-playing with, 391
  to signing of will, 571
  statement of. *See* Witness statement
  testimony of, summarizing, 4
  types of, 362, 364–365
Witness interview(s), 4, 362, 364–368
  checking witness's qualifications in, 366–367
  diagrams used in, 363
  as part of investigation plan, 370–371
  questioning in, 365–366
  statement of what witness said during. *See* Witness statement

winding up, 367
Witness statement, 367–368
  defined, 367
  information contained in, illustrated, 367
  sample excerpt from, illustrated, 368
Wolf, Linda J., 38–39
Wolters Kluwer, 258
Words and Phrases (West), 200
Work product
  defined, 103
  files of, 68
Workers' compensation statutes, 30, 604–605, 606
Workouts, 631
Workplace
  conflicts in, managing, 83
  privacy in, 145
World Wide Web (the Web), 240–241. *See also* Internet; Web site(s)
  browsers and, 242–243
  defined, 240
  finding ethics opinions on, 250
  guides and directories and, 243
  search engines and. *See* Search engine(s)
Writ(s)
  of *certiorari,* 172
  of execution, 409
Writing
  legal. *See* Legal writing
  skills in, 12–13, 15
    good, importance, 272–279
Writing requirement
  Statute of Frauds and, 505–506, 585
  will and, 571
Writing User-Friendly Documents, 276
Wrongful discharge, 602
Wrongful interference, 466–467
www.whitepages.com, 374

X

Xerox, 517

Y

Yahoo!, 478
  finding business and professional organizations at, 265
  "Law" menu of, 259–260
    government categories from, illustrated, 261
  People Search of, 264
Yellow pages, 41
Yera, E. J., 208–209

760

PROTECTION AND SECURITY

The End User shall use its best efforts and take all reasonable steps to safeguard its copy of the Licensed Content to ensure that no unauthorized reproduction, publication, disclosure, modification, or distribution of the Licensed Content, in whole or in part, is made. To the extent that the End User becomes aware of any such unauthorized use of the Licensed Content, the End User shall immediately notify Cengage Learning. Notification of such violations may be made by sending an e-mail to infringement@cengage.com.

MISUSE OF THE LICENSED PRODUCT

In the event that the End User uses the Licensed Content in violation of this Agreement, Cengage Learning shall have the option of electing liquidated damages, which shall include all profits generated by the End User's use of the Licensed Content plus interest computed at the maximum rate permitted by law and all legal fees and other expenses incurred by Cengage Learning in enforcing its rights, plus penalties.

FEDERAL GOVERNMENT CLIENTS

Except as expressly authorized by Cengage Learning, Federal Government clients obtain only the rights specified in this Agreement and no other rights. The Government acknowledges that (i) all software and related documentation incorporated in the Licensed Content is existing commercial computer software within the meaning of FAR 27.405(b)(2); and (2) all other data delivered in whatever form, is limited rights data within the meaning of FAR 27.401. The restrictions in this section are acceptable as consistent with the Government's need for software and other data under this Agreement.

DISCLAIMER OF WARRANTIES AND LIABILITIES

Although Cengage Learning believes the Licensed Content to be reliable, Cengage Learning does not guarantee or warrant (i) any information or materials contained in or produced by the Licensed Content, (ii) the accuracy, completeness or reliability of the Licensed Content, or (iii) that the Licensed Content is free from errors or other material defects. THE LICENSED PRODUCT IS PROVIDED "AS IS," WITHOUT ANY WARRANTY OF ANY KIND AND CENGAGE LEARNING DISCLAIMS ANY AND ALL WARRANTIES, EXPRESSED OR IMPLIED, INCLUDING, WITHOUT LIMITATION, WARRANTIES OF MERCHANTABILITY OR FITNESS FOR A PARTICULAR PURPOSE. IN NO EVENT SHALL CENGAGE LEARNING BE LIABLE FOR: INDIRECT, SPECIAL, PUNITIVE OR CONSE-QUENTIAL DAMAGES INCLUDING FOR LOST PROFITS, LOST DATA, OR OTHERWISE. IN NO EVENT SHALL CENGAGE LEARNING'S AGGREGATE LIABILITY HEREUNDER, WHETHER ARISING IN CONTRACT, TORT, STRICT LIABILITY OR OTHERWISE, EXCEED THE AMOUNT OF FEES PAID BY THE END USER HEREUNDER FOR THE LICENSE OF THE LICENSED CONTENT.

GENERAL

Entire Agreement. This Agreement shall constitute the entire Agreement between the Parties and supercedes all prior Agreements and understandings oral or written relating to the subject matter hereof.

Enhancements/Modifications of Licensed Content. From time to time, and in Cengage Learning's sole discretion, Cengage Learning may advise the End User of updates, upgrades, enhancements and/or improvements to the Licensed Content, and may permit the End User to access and use, subject to the terms and conditions of this Agreement, such modifications, upon payment of prices as may be established by Cengage Learning.

No Export. The End User shall use the Licensed Content solely in the United States and shall not transfer or export, directly or indirectly, the Licensed Content outside the United States.

Severability. If any provision of this Agreement is invalid, illegal, or unenforceable under any applicable statute or rule of law, the provision shall be deemed omitted to the extent that it is invalid, illegal, or unenforceable. In such a case, the remainder of the Agreement shall be construed in a manner as to give greatest effect to the original intention of the parties hereto.

Waiver. The waiver of any right or failure of either party to exercise in any respect any right provided in this Agreement in any instance shall not be deemed to be a waiver of such right in the future or a waiver of any other right under this Agreement.

Choice of Law/Venue. This Agreement shall be interpreted, construed, and governed by and in accordance with the laws of the State of New York, applicable to contracts executed and to be wholly preformed therein, without regard to its principles governing conflicts of law. Each party agrees that any proceeding arising out of or relating to this Agreement or the breach or threatened breach of this Agreement may be commenced and prosecuted in a court in the State and County of New York. Each party consents and submits to the nonexclusive personal jurisdiction of any court in the State and County of New York in respect of any such proceeding.

<u>Acknowledgment</u>. By opening this package and/or by accessing the Licensed Content on this Web site, THE END USER ACKNOWLEDGES THAT IT HAS READ THIS AGREEMENT, UNDERSTANDS IT, AND AGREES TO BE BOUND BY ITS TERMS AND CONDITIONS. IF YOU DO NOT ACCEPT THESE TERMS AND CONDITIONS, YOU MUST NOT ACCESS THE LICENSED CONTENT AND RETURN THE LICENSED PRODUCT TO CENGAGE LEARNING (WITHIN 30 CALENDAR DAYS OF THE END USER'S PURCHASE) WITH PROOF OF PAYMENT ACCEPTABLE TO CENGAGE LEARNING, FOR A CREDIT OR A REFUND. Should the End User have any questions/comments regarding this Agreement, please contact Cengage Learning at Delmar.help@cengage.com.

STUDYWARE™ to accompany Paralegal Today: The Legal Team at Work 5E

Minimum System Requirements

Operating systems: Microsoft Windows XP w/SP 2, Windows Vista w/SP 1
Processor: Minimum required by Operating System
Memory: Minimum required by Operating System
Hard Drive Space: [something]
Screen resolution: 800 x 600 pixels
CD-ROM drive
Sound card & listening device required for audio features
Flash Player 9. The Adobe Flash Player is free, and can be downloaded from **http://www.adobe.com/products/flashplayer/**
[Other software requirements]

Setup Instructions

1. Insert disc into CD-ROM drive. The StudyWare™ installation program should start automatically. If it does not, go to step 2.
2. From My Computer, double-click the icon for the CD drive.
3. Double-click the *setup.exe* file to start the program.

Technical Support

Telephone: 1-800-648-7450
8:30 A.M.–6:30 P.M. Eastern Time
E-mail: delmar.help@cengage.com

StudyWare™ is a trademark used herein under license.

Microsoft® and Windows® are registered trademarks of the Microsoft Corporation.

Pentium® is a registered trademark of the Intel Corporation.